ANXIETY AND STRESS DISORDERS

ANXIETY AND STRESS DISORDERS
Cognitive-Behavioral Assessment and Treatment

Edited by
LARRY MICHELSON
University of Pittsburgh School of Medicine

L. MICHAEL ASCHER
Temple University Health Sciences Center

THE GUILFORD PRESS
New York   London

© 1987 The Guilford Press
A Division of Guilford Publications, Inc.
200 Park Avenue South, New York, N.Y. 10003

Printed in the United States of America

Last digit is print number: 9 8 7 6 5 4 3 2 1

LIBRARY OF CONGRESS CATALOGING-IN-PUBLICATION DATA
Anxiety and stress disorders.
  Includes bibliographies and index.
  1. Anxiety. 2. Stress (Psychology) 3. Cognitive
therapy. 4. Behavior therapy. 5. Behavioral
assessment. I. Michelson, Larry, 1952–
II. Ascher, L. Michael. [DNLM: 1. Anxiety Disorders—
diagnosis. 2. Anxiety Disorders—therapy. 3. Behavior
Therapy. 4. Cognition. 5. Stress Disorders,
Post-Traumatic—therapy.   WM 172 A6362]
RC531.A576 1987   616.85′223   86-29585
ISBN 0-89862-693-5

Contributors

BARBARA L. ANDERSEN, PhD, Department of Psychology, University of Iowa, Iowa City, Iowa

FRANK ANDRASIK, PhD, Pain Therapy Centers, Greenville General Hospital, Greenville, South Carolina

L. MICHAEL ASCHER, PhD, Department of Psychiatry, Temple University Medical School, Philadelphia, Pennsylvania

ROBERT E. BECKER, PhD, Department of Psychiatry, Medical College of Pennsylvania at EPPI, Philadelphia, Pennsylvania

JOHN T. CACIOPPO, PhD, Department of Psychology, University of Iowa, Iowa City, Iowa

EDWARD M. CARROLL, PhD, Psychology Service, West Los Angeles VA Medical Center, Brentwood Division, and UCLA Medical School, Los Angeles, California

LESLIE CHERNEN, MA, MS, Department of Psychology, University of Massachusetts at Amherst, Amherst, Massachusetts

JERRY L. DEFFENBACHER, PhD, Department of Psychology, Colorado State University, Fort Collins, Colorado

CAROL I. DIENER, PhD, Department of Psychology, University of Illinois, Urbana, Illinois

ROBERT A. DiTOMASSO, PhD, West Jersey Health System Family Practice Residency Program, Tatem-Brown Family Practice Center, Voorhees, New Jersey

CYNTHIA S. DODGE, Center for Stress and Anxiety Disorders, Department of Psychology, State University of New York at Albany, Albany, New York

CLYDE P. DONAHOE, JR., PhD, Psychology Service, West Los Angeles VA Medical Center, Brentwood Division, and UCLA Medical School, Los Angeles, California

GARY EMERY, PhD, Los Angeles Center for Cognitive Therapy, Los Angeles, California

PAUL M. G. EMMELKAMP, PhD, Academic Hospital, Department of Clinical Psychology, Groningen, The Netherlands

DAVID W. FOY, PhD, Psychology Service, West Los Angeles VA Medical Center, Brentwood Division, and UCLA Medical School, Los Angeles, California

JERRY M. FRIEDMAN, PhD, private practice, Stony Brook, New York

JOHANNA GALLERS, PhD, Psychology Service, West Los Angeles VA Medical Center, Brentwood Division, Los Angeles, California

THOMAS R. GILES, PsyD, Eating Disorders Program, Rose Medical Center, Denver, Colorado

MICHAEL A. GREENWALD, PhD, Department of Psychology in Education, University of Pittsburgh, Pittsburgh, Pennsylvania

FRANCIS C. HARRIS, PhD, Department of Psychiatry, Western Psychiatric Institute and Clinic, University of Pittsburgh School of Medicine, Pittsburgh, Pennsylvania

RICHARD G. HEIMBERG, PhD, Center for Stress and Anxiety Disorders, Department of Psychology, State University of New York at Albany, Albany, New York

RICK INGRAM, PhD, Department of Psychology, San Diego State University, San Diego, California

LARS JANSSON, PhD (deceased), Psychiatric Research Center, University of Uppsala, Ulleråker Hospital, Uppsala, Sweden

ROBERT KASTENBAUM, PhD, Adult Development and Aging Program, Arizona State University, Tempe, Arizona

PHILIP C. KENDALL, PhD, Department of Psychology, Temple University, Philadelphia, Pennsylvania

THOMAS R. KRATOCHWILL, PhD, School Psychology Program, Department of Educational Psychology, The University of Wisconsin—Madison, Madison, Wisconsin

CYNTHIA G. LAST, PhD, Department of Psychiatry, University of Pittsburgh School of Medicine, Pittsburgh, Pennsylvania

RONALD LEY, PhD, Department of Educational Psychology and Statistics and Department of Psychology, State University of New York at Albany, Albany, New York

MARIAN L. MacDONALD, PhD, Department of Psychology, University of Massachusetts at Amherst, Amherst, Massachusetts

JEFFREY S. MARTZKE, PhD, Department of Psychology, University of Iowa, Iowa City, Iowa

MEREDITH STEELE McCARRAN, PhD, Department of Psychology, State University of New York at Albany, Albany, New York

RICHARD J. McNALLY, PhD, Department of Psychology, University of Health Sciences/The Chicago Medical School, North Chicago, Illinois

LARRY MICHELSON, PhD, University of Pittsburgh School of Medicine, Department of Psychiatry, Western Psychiatric Institute and Clinic, Pittsburgh, Pennsylvania

RICHARD J. MORRIS, PhD, School Psychology Program, Department of Educational Psychology, The University of Arizona, Tucson, Arizona

LARS-GÖRAN ÖST, PhD, Dr Med Sci, Psychiatric Research Center, University of Uppsala, Ulleråker Hospital, Uppsala, Sweden

CAROLYN F. PHELPS, MS, Department of Psychology, University of Pittsburgh, Pittsburgh, Pennsylvania

SYLVIA Z. RAMIREZ, MS, School Psychology Program, Department of Educational Psychology, The University of Wisconsin—Madison, Madison, Wisconsin

WILLIAM H. REDD, PhD, Departments of Neurology and Pediatrics, Memorial Sloan-Kettering Cancer Center, New York, New York

ROCHELLE RENO, PhD, Psychology Service, West Los Angeles VA Medical Center, Brentwood Division, and UCLA Medical School, Los Angeles, California

RANDI E. SCHNUR, Department of Psychology, University of Massachusetts at Amherst, Amherst, Massachusetts

RICHARD M. SUINN, PhD, Department of Psychology, Colorado State University, Fort Collins, Colorado

ANDREW A. SWEET, PsyD, Behavior Therapy Institute of Colorado, Denver, Colorado

NATHAN L. TRACY, MS, MFCC, Los Angeles County Office of Education, Division of Special Education, Downey, California

RENÉE R. YOUNG, Denver University School of Professional Psychology, Denver, Colorado

Preface

This book represents the culmination of state-of-the art developments in theory, assessment, methodology, research, and clinical application of cognitive-behavioral strategies for anxiety and stress-related disorders. The book was designed to provide a comprehensive and integrated review of conceptual, methodological, and applied issues relevant to cognitive-behavioral interventions. Although cognitive-behavioral assessment and treatment are currently enjoying increased popularity in both clinical and research settings, there are no primary sources that address all of the aforementioned issues specifically for anxiety disorders.

This book is particularly timely for several reasons. First, the expanding interest in anxiety is, in part, a reflection of increased awareness that anxiety disorders represent the most prevalent psychiatric conditions. Moreover, the "thermodynamic law of research"—that for every research question posed and answered, two more spring up to take its place—has resulted in a proliferation of papers and scientific presentations, with only a limited integration of the crucial conceptual and applied issues relevant for lucid understanding of these phenomena. This book represents a unique and unified source for contemporary theory, research, and clinical issues in cognitive-behavior therapy for anxiety disorders and related syndromes.

The book was written for a broad audience including professionals, clinicians, researchers, and graduate students. Moreover, because of its comprehensive scope, we hope that it will serve as an important reference source in the future. The volume is divided into two parts. Part I, "Theory, Assessment, and Methodology," deals with important theoretical, conceptual, and methodological issues and with contemporary assessment strategies and clinical issues, as well as future directions. Part II, "Clinical Applications," provides in-depth, scholarly, and clinically salient reviews for cognitive-behavioral interventions of each of the anxiety disorders, as well as related stress states. The various chapter authors, all nationally recognized authorities in their respective fields of expertise, have met the challenge of integrating the diverse literatures within cognitive-behavior therapy. The authors have provided a cogent, critical, and clinically relevant review of the literature while also integrating and synthesizing findings from their own programmatic research.

In addition to addressing each of the anxiety disorders, the book includes chapters on a number of related syndromes or conditions for which these cognitive-behavioral interventions might be appropriate, including hypertension, migraine headaches, sexual dysfunction, reactions to noxious medical procedures, thanatology, eating disorders, and mental retardation. Clearly, the book goes far beyond simple clinical prototypes to address a broad array of psychological, psychiatric, and medical dysfunctions.

We want to express our respect and gratitude to the many talented colleagues whose contributions to the field have made this book a reality. We would also like to thank all the clients who served so courageously as our teachers in helping us illuminate the path to scientific discovery. Special appreciation to Jack Rachman and Tim Beck, who serve as both highly valued colleagues, advisors, and exemplars in our research, and who have made substantive and scholarly contributions to the field of anxiety disorders. We would also like to acknowledge the scholarly contributions of Karen Marchione and Alan Kazdin. We would like to thank our editor, Seymour Weingarten; administrative secretary, Sharon O'Toole; and our research associates, Sandra Testa, Norman Marchione, Rita Stewart, and Margaretta McNelis for their invaluable aid during the production of the volume. Finally, our gratitude is extended to the National Institute of Mental Health whose support (MH36299) made this book possible. We hope the reader finds the book as innovative, informative, and stimulating as we have.

Larry Michelson
Pittsburgh, Pennsylvania

L. Michael Ascher
Philadelphia, Pennsylvania

Contents

PART I

THEORY, ASSESSMENT, AND METHODOLOGY

1

Theoretical Issues in the Cognitive-Behavioral Treatment of Anxiety Disorders

GARY EMERY AND NATHAN L. TRACY

This chapter addresses four major theoretical issues in the cognitive-behavioral treatment of anxiety: (1) organization of knowledge; (2) development of emotional processes; (3) nature of fear and anxiety; and (4) key elements in alleviating anxiety. The chapter also outlines a comprehensive theory of anxiety by the first author.

The Organization of Knowledge

Definition of Cognitive-Behavioral Therapy

As elaborated by Beck and Emery (1985), cognitive-behavioral therapy is a series of strategies that relieve psychological suffering by correcting distorted and maladaptive thinking. The therapy is based on a theory of psychopathology that recognizes the reciprocal interrelationship among the cognitive, behavioral, somatic, and emotional systems.

The core of the theory holds that a person's private meanings determine his or her unique emotional responses. Individuals' meanings are revealed in their conscious verbal and imagery reports. Their articulated (automatic) thoughts, feelings, and wishes are used in therapy to understand and modify their emotions and behaviors.

AUTOMATIC THOUGHTS

According to Beck (1976), automatic thoughts are specific and distinct; they occur instantly (rapidly), as if by reflex. They are autonomous and unsolicited by the person experiencing them. In the case of someone experiencing significant anxiety, these thoughts are difficult to stop or shut off. Anxious people regard their automatic thoughts as plausible and worthy of belief. Automatic thoughts are thematic and are usually shared by people with the same emotional disorder (that is, with specific phobias or anxiety disorders).

Gary Emery. Los Angeles Center for Cognitive Therapy, Los Angeles, California.
Nathan L. Tracy. Los Angeles County Office of Education, Division of Special Education, Downey, California.

Automatic thoughts are contrary to objective appraisal; those that assert the most influence on behavior usually have the greatest idiosyncrasy. The thoughts precede emotional and physiological arousal and demonstrate greater distortion in reality than other forms of thinking.

DOMAIN

People attach special importance to the circumstances surrounding their personal domain (Bedrosian & Beck, 1980). The general character of a person's emotional responding is contingent on whether he or she perceives events as adding, subtracting, endangering, or impinging on his or her domain. Eliciting a person's private meaning of an event allows you to predict his or her emotional reaction to it (Beck, 1976). Depression is devaluation of domain; hypomania, inflation of domain; anxiety, danger to domain; phobia, danger connected with specific avoidable situations; and paranoid state, unjustified intrusion on domain.

Theoretical Concerns

Wilson (1984) has voiced three major concerns about the cognitive-behavioral treatment of anxiety:

1. The assumption that cognitions have a large influence on the affective or emotional system
2. The assumption that one can identify automatic (anxiety-producing) thoughts prior to emotional arousal
3. The assumption that automatic thoughts trigger arousal

Wilson cites Rachman's (1981) conclusion that clinical data fail to identify patterns of automatic thoughts that correlate with emotional arousal or anxiety.

Similarly, Eelen (1982) says that cognitive therapists have given too much emphasis to their clients' conscious or semiconscious private "self-talks." He believes this self-talk represents epiphenomena, or surface structures, that might or might not be congruent with some deeper knowledge of their world.

In defense of the cognitive position, Beck (1976) points out that other (noncognitive) theories of emotional disorders have denied or discounted self-reports of conscious thoughts. For example, Beck points out that both the behavioral model and the psychoanalytical model minimize the importance of readily available meanings. The behaviorists reject meaning totally and the psychoanalysts emphasize unconscious meanings.

Mahoney (1980), though supporting the cognitive therapies' premise that human maladjustment is often a reflection of underlying cognitive processes, has focused on conceptual adequacies. He is particularly concerned with the theoretical underpinnings of cognitive approaches. According to Mahoney, cognitive therapies neglect and often attack the potential importance of unconscious process. Because cognitive therapies are poorly integrated with current theories of cognition, they place too much emphasis on the isomorphism between words and beliefs and on the role of rationality in adaptation. Moreover, they view feelings too narrowly, as phenomenal artifacts that are to be controlled rather than experienced.

Mahoney in general believes that cognitive therapies place too much emphasis on surface structure meaning (content) while disregarding deeper structural meaning (themes).

Structural View of Cognition

Recently, other authors (Leventhal, 1979, 1980, 1982; 1984; Lang, 1977, 1979a, 1079b, 1984; Guidano & Liotti, 1983) have discussed the link between cognitive and emotional processes. They touch on the often expressed concern, discussed earlier, that the emotional system is largely inaccessible to conscious influences (for example, cognitive-behavioral therapy).

Leventhal (1979) proposes a perceptual–motor processing model of emotion. He believes emotion is constructed in a three-level system: (1) a perceptual-motor mechanism, (2) a primary or schematic memory, and (3) an abstract conceptual processing mechanism. Similarly, but with some distinct differences, Lang (1979a) has offered his bioinformational theory of emotional imagery. According to him, a mental image is a conceptual network that controls specific somatovisceral patterns and constitutes a prototype for overt behavioral expression.

Guidano and Liotti (1983) have proposed a structural approach to understanding psychopathology and psychotherapy. Their approach is similar to Epstein's (1979) "ecological theory of personality," which postulates that everyone develops an implicit personal theory of reality that includes both a self theory and a world theory. Guidano and Liotti note a large discrepancy between the practice of behavioral therapy and the limited theory justifying its use. They reject psychoanalytical psychology because of its inadequate experimental base, length of treatment, questionable efficacy, and imprecise theoretical tenets.

Psychoanalytical and behavioral therapies, according to Guidano and Liotti, are flawed by their acceptance of the epistemological principle of associationism, a passive acquisition of knowledge. In contrast, their structural approach takes a nonassociationistic and nonreductionistic view of human behavior and psychotherapy. The organism, they say, is active. The main aspect is not forming and breaking up associations but, rather, actively processing expectations, hypotheses, and theories. The person progressively constructs knowledge over time (see also Popper & Eccles, 1977; Lang, 1979b; Mahoney, 1980; Arnkoff, 1980).

Structures of Knowledge

Guidano and Liotti propose that the structures making up an individual's organization of personal knowledge are analogous to Lakatos's (1974) research program. Each person's "research program" (self-knowledge or life program) is elaborated through three primary structures:

1. The *metaphysical hard core*, which contains deep structures of tacit self-knowledge. For example, a person might have implicit feelings of being vulnerable. This core includes rules that determine the invarient aspects of the person's

mental processing ("I have to always be careful"). These rules enable the person tacitly and directly to sustain the images of himself and of the world through self-fulfilling prophecy.

2. The *protective belt* or "testing bench," which defines and maintains personal identity ("I'm a weak person"). This includes self-identity and self-esteem.
3. *Research plans* with rules for assimilation of experiences ("Believe every danger or warning") and solving problems ("Get others to help you").

A person's continuous stream of life-experiences can effect deep self-knowledge only via his or her personal identity structure(s) (the protective belt). At the same time, tacit and irrefutable suppositions and inferences of self-knowledge enter into the research plans solely by passing through the personal identity structure (the protective belt). The self-identity and self-esteem structure controls the total program and thereby affects attitudes toward self as well as toward reality.

Functional Aspects of Knowledge and Organization

Guidano and Liotti highlight three characteristics of self-knowledge. First, only a limited amount of what is known or stored is contained within the conscious stream at any one time. Instead, knowledge is constructed anew each time in an information-processing event that depends on the person's needs at the moment.

Second, a person's inner representation of reality is the product of a reciprocal relationship between the perception of an ongoing event and information derived from remembered past experiences. Borrowing from Weimer (1977), Guidano and Liotti conceptualize memory as an active, ongoing modulation of information. This is contrary to the popular conception of memory as a simple (iconic) retrieval of stored data.

Third, tacit, deep-structural data (in contrast to surface-structural information) are processed through two interrelated avenues: the analogical and analytical codes.

Tacit Knowledge and Deep Structure

Polanyi (1966, 1968), as described by Arnkoff (1980) and Guidano and Liotti (1983), has distinguished two aspects of knowledge: *tacit* or unaware knowledge and *explicit* knowledge that can be verbalized. In the words of Arnkoff (1980, p. 344), tacit knowledge is "the truly abstract, *structural nature of our classification system*" (emphasis added). Deep structure is composed of abstract units of meaning—propositions (Lang, 1977) such as "Others are responsible for my feelings"—from which surface structure is produced ("He made me mad").

The deep-structure rules determine the meaning of surface structure. Meaning is deep-structural, but one can have only surface-structure evidence of it. A key element is that the surface structure is not necessarily identical to, or even closely related to, the understanding of deep structure (Franks, 1974). Additionally, the same deep-structure belief may be manifest by more than one surface structure. For example, a behavior is a surface structure: and a person can run or freeze in face of danger. Conversely, the same surface structure may represent more than one deep-structural belief.

Guidano and Liotti (1983) consider the person's imaginal stream (for example, seeing him- or herself as a helpless child) as one of the distinctive means by which tacit, deep-structural self-knowledge is revealed by the "research program." This is then elaborated on ("I have to please others") to become part of explicit self-knowledge ("I'm a weak person").

Tacit knowledge is mediated primarily by the right hemisphere of the brain and attains "consciousness" via transmission to the left hemisphere, which houses the linguistic areas. In the developmental sequence, tacit knowledge occurs first. The gradual emergence of explicit knowledge corresponds to a person's systematic acquisition of language. By adolescence the person has the mental ability to use concepts independent from the context in which they have occurred. At this level explicit self-knowledge assumes conscious control of the cognitive organization. However, tacit knowledge supplies a continuous frame of reference.

Guidano and Liotti propose two interrelated ways in which deep structures are processed: the analogical code and the analytical code. These are analogous to Leventhal's (1979) "schematic processing of emotion" and "abstract conceptual processing."

The Analogical Code

The analogical code, as described by Guidano and Liotti (1983), processes images (tacit knowledge). Lang (1979a), citing Pylyshyn (1973), conceives of images as "finite propositional structures." This is in contrast to the more phenomenological view of images as pictorial memories of otherwise iconic experience.

According to Lang, images are not directly stored in the sense of being recorded. Rather, what is stored are the corresponding units of meaning (Guidano & Liotti, 1983) or propositions (Lang, 1979a). The image is reconstructed by the retrieval of these meanings. Each reconstruction contains the specific data that characterize it as well as collateral data; these are then linked to further constructional or relational (imaginal) possibilities.

Lang (1979b) describes the image as a perceptual–motor set, or a specific response complex. The image is activated by the perceptual processing of the specific contents. The image includes a motor program that is a prototype of overt behavior (Lang, 1979a).

The Analytical Code

The analytical code is an abstract conceptual system that processes lexical units (Leventhal, 1979; Guidano & Liotti, 1983). Others have called it inner language (Myklebust, 1964); central language (Swartz & Tracy, 1970); and inner dialogue (Meichenbaum, 1977). The code is the basis for volitional, temporal, and sequential processing of information and verbal reasoning (Leventhal, 1979; Swartz & Tracy, 1970).

This higher-order system makes possible abstraction and inference about concrete and tacit experience. The code is a flexible (retrieval) system that develops explicit (descriptive) knowledge by creating concepts that—in comparison to images—are lasting (Guidano & Liotti, 1983). Once formed, the concepts can be detached from the original concrete (tacit) experience and become knowledge units themselves. Within the analytical code, thoughts can range from structured and intentional reasoning to automatic thoughts (Beck, 1976).

Emotional Processing

Imaginal Process

Why is emotional coloring a major characteristic of imagery? According to Leventhal (1979), imagination is the primary mediator in the retrieval of the schematic emotional memory. Experiences are, in a sense, color-coded in the memory (that is, organized into networks and linked to other conceptual networks) through feeling units, structures, or schemata. Although Leventhal sees the emotional memory as a concrete iconic affair, he believes the memory contains key perceptual features of emotion-eliciting situations. The image is representative of the primary, expressive motor reactions that accompany these episodes. The memory is an associated set of autonomic reactions—in other words, a code of subjective feelings and corresponding coping responses.

Similar to Leventhal's emotional memory mechanism is Lang's (1977, 1979a) emotional memory image. Lang sees the image as a finite structure made up of a complex network of semantic, perceptual, and imaginal information. The network contains propositions about imagery content and behavior responses. The image is a prototype for overt behavior and activates the cognitive, physiological, and behavioral systems; this in turn creates the conscious experience of emotion.

Lang believes the emotional image is an active process; the image is constructed over time, proposition by proposition, according to image script. This is in contrast to the phenomenological view of an image—an analog representation recalled from storage (memory) to which one responds. Lang's image includes prototypes of verbal and overt behavioral expression, patterns of somatovisceral arousal, and propositions that define the affective character of the emotion.

Construction of Emotions

To explain the construction of emotions, Leventhal (1979) proposes a perceptual-motor processing model. Because emotions are constructed over time, they can be described as occurring in stages. In the first, *perceptual–motor* stage, the experience of emotion is created. In the second, *planning–action* stage, both emotional and nonemotional infor-mation is used for planning and constructing overt action.

Emotion is generated within the perceptual–motor stage and is the product of adding an expressive motor reaction (body reaction) to the perception of the eliciting stimulus. Thus the emotional experience is due to the pairing of a nonperceptual response with perception or cognition.

According to Leventhal, three distinct systems within the perceptual–motor stage create emotions: (1) a facial-motor mechanism, (2) a schematic emotional memory (analogue code), and (3) a conceptual system of roles and beliefs that govern emotional experience (analytic code).

Because emotions are created by a preattentive integration of the eliciting stimulus (for example, a person sees a big dog) within the expressive motor process (the person has a facial response of fear), individuals experience emotion as tacit, intuited, and directly known. Emotions do not emerge as a conscious (cognitive) inference of feelings based on conscious appraisal of stimulus events.

Leventhal says the eliciting event and the person's expressive reaction must remain in peripheral awareness (a preattentive state) to create an emotional experience. A person who voluntarily tries to react with fear to the dog will destroy the emotion.

The schematic (emotional) memory is central to the integration of stimulus and expressive motor events in the generation of subjective (conscious) emotional feeling. The action within the facial-motor mechanism is responsible for the primary emotions of fear, anger, sadness, and happiness. This motor or physical reaction is in a sense classically conditioned to specific memories in the analogue code.

Central to the facial-motor function is an outflow or feed-forward mechanism. Emotions are created when expressive motor activity (facial movements) is spontaneous rather than voluntary. Emotions arise when the spontaneous motor system discharges or feeds forward into the voluntary motor system. In other words, spontaneous expressive motor impulses that feed forward into the voluntary (motor) system are felt as emotion when the person is not prepared to perform these expressive acts voluntarily.

Lazarus and Folkman (1984) caution against the emerging trend in cognitive psychology (as evidenced, for example, in Leventhal's linear model) to see emotions as occurring at the end of a cognitive-emotional process. Rather, in real life, cognitions and emotions are conjoined. Although cognitive appraisal is a necessary and sufficient condition for emotions, the cause is bidirectional. These authors say: "The full experience of emotion includes three fused components—thought, action impulses, and somatic disturbances—which, when separated, leaves us with something other than what we mean by an emotional state" (p. 275). Cognitive appraisal, by definition, is integral to the generation of emotions.

Consistent with their constructionistic view, Lazarus and Folkman believe that cognitive appraisal appears early in the information-processing sequence; this generates an intermixing of appraisal and emotion, often so rapidly that meaning and emotion appear to occur simultaneously with perception.

Lazarus and Folkman doubt the need for cognitive appraisal with certain phylogenetic triggers of fear—instinctual reactions to certain animals and to strangeness. They see these so-called releasers as being subordinated to higher cortical functions as they emerge or develop ontologically.

The Primacy Issue

In contrast to Lazarus (1982, 1984) and Lazarus and Folkman (1984), Zajonc (1980, 1984) believes that affect and cognition are separate and independent subsystems. He believes the systems influence each other in different ways and that they are independent sources of effects in information processing. He argues that emotions can be experienced without prior perceptual or cognitive appraisal and that they can occur with greater rapidity and conviction than cognitions.

Zajonc's argument gives support to Lang's (1968) three-systems model of fear.

According to Lang, fear is not a singular entity or response system, but a set of interrelated components—a behavioral system that includes subjective (cognitive) ideation, physiological arousal, and avoidance behavior (see also Beck & Emery, 1985).

In Lang's view (expanded by Rachman & Hodgson, 1974; Rachman, 1978), therapeutic intervention via one system (either behavioral, cognitive, or physiological) will not necessarily generate results across other systems. The three systems can co-vary or vary at different rates in response to therapeutic intervention.

Greenberg and Safran (1984) are quick to say that Rachman (1978, 1980, 1981) and Zajonc's (1980) are correct in challenging the linear causal model of emotion. However, they believe their view introduces conceptual confusion by failing to differentiate between conscious (explicit, analytical) thought and automatic preattentive (tacit, analogical) thought. Greenberg and Safran suggest this has created a false dichotomy between the (partial) independence and primacy of one system (cognitive) over another (emotional).

Greenberg and Safran agree with Lazarus (1982) that thoughts, feelings, and actions are fused in nature; they believe, however, that emotions are created by specific information-processing events that occur at automatic, preattentive (tacit or analogical) levels—as described, for example, in Leventhal's (1979) perceptual–motor model.

Nature of Fear and Anxiety

Beck's Cognitive Model

Beck (Beck & Emery, 1985; Beck, 1976) describes the subjective feeling of anxiety as one aspect of an archaic survival mechanism. Ontologically, anxiety had protective value for early humans. Today anxiety is largely counterproductive because people react to psychosocial threats in primitive and maladaptive ways that go against social values.

This archaic survival mechanism (normal as well as clinical anxiety) consists of an interplay of the cognitive, behavioral, physiological, and affective systems. The cognitive content focuses on threat to one's domain—specifically, to social attachments and sense of freedom and individuality. The person's emergency response to the threat, real or perceived, is psychological and biological. Once the emergency response has begun, the person's awareness is cleared to make room for information about the danger and possible coping mechanisms. The individual selectively enhances what is relevant to the perceived danger and suppresses what is incongruent with it.

The emergency response's cognitive appraisal activates the autonomic nervous system. This includes the automatic, primal response strategies—fight, flight, freeze, and faint—as well as the subjective anxiety to trigger coping strategies (see Figure 1.1).

Two behavioral systems are activated (separately or simultaneously): the energic, tonic sympathetic nervous system and the anergic, atonic parasympathetic nervous system. The energic system's active strategies (fight, flight, and so on) mobilize when the person feels threatened, whereas the anergic system demobilizes (for example, by fainting) when the person feels helpless. Both are complete psychobiological reactions of the cognitive, motor, somatic, and affective systems. The energic and anergic reactions are part of a larger psychophysiological reaction that activates the subjective feeling of anxiety and causes the increase or decrease in muscle tone.

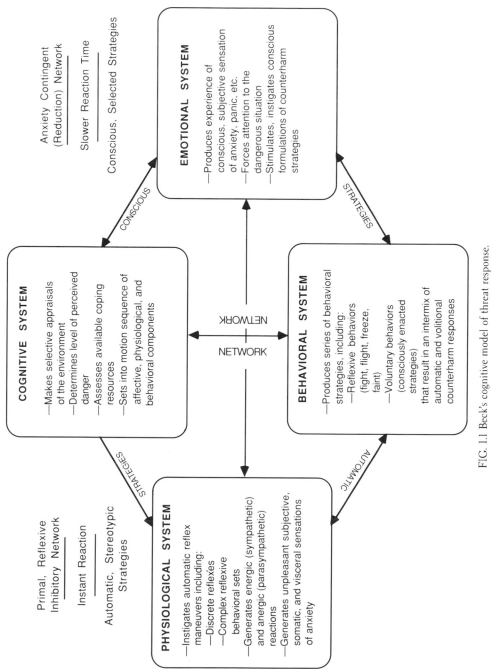

FIG. 1.1 Beck's cognitive model of threat response.

11

Beck describes two self-protective mechanisms: (1) the primal, reflective inhibitory network, which reacts instantly with automatic, stereotypic strategies, and (2) the voluntary anxiety-contingent network that is slower and uses more complete information processing and strategy selection.

Both mechanisms are activated congruently. The slower contingent system follows the reflective autonomic strategies. The reflexive system has a limited repertoire of stereotypic behavior responses, whereas the contingent system focuses attention on ways to reduce the danger.

According to Beck, anxiety is primarily the person's preoccupation with and response to danger. The person has a pervasive sense of vulnerability or sensitization (see Weekes, 1972) and sees himself or herself as subject to internal or external harm over which he or she has little or no control. This general theme varies depending on how the anxiety is manifested.

Prepotency and Preparedness

Marks (1981) discusses phyletic considerations in the origin and nature of anxiety. Because of human evolutionary history, people react with fear to evolutionary danger. Marks believes the limited and stereotyped anxiety behaviors can be explained by prepotency (Marks, 1969) and preparedness, as detailed by Seligman (1971) and Seligman and Hager (1972).

Because of prepotency, people selectively attend to *unencountered* stimuli rather than to what they have previously experienced. Preparedness is the selective facility to use certain stimulus–response connections rather than others. The concepts are supported in that phobics have selected fears rather than a random assortment of fears. They fear a few events that appear to be prepotent targets for phobias. Marks cites hereditary evidence for timidity and other phobic and obsessive symptoms.

Klein (1981) talks about two kinds of (archaic) phobic behavior: appeal behavior and avoidant behavior. People suffering from panic attacks typically "appeal" for help during the panic episode but stop when the panic subsides. However, they continue to try to avoid future anxiety attacks.

Klein says that with a crying baby, appeal is a natural reaction to an emergency; this reaction antedates the ontogenesis of fight, flight, freeze, or faint. He cites Bowlby's (1969, 1973) speculation that a child's bonding to the mother (primary caretaker) is due more to an innate biological mechanism than to learning. The child's separation anxiety, in other words, is not due to learning that the mother's absence is distressful; rather, it is an inborn protective mechanism that is automatically evoked at moments of vulnerability to help retrieve the mother.

Separation from the mother activates a three-stage sequence—protest, despair, and detachment. The protest stage—pleading, clinging, and demanding—is reminiscent of anxiety attacks, whereas the despair stage serves a conservation function and parallels depression.

Klein hypothesizes that the protest–despair mechanisms evolved to deal with the contingency of the lost child. Perhaps depressive episodes are due to a pathologically lowered threshold for distress. In short, if the threshold is lowered in the part of the on-task despair mechanism that controls protest, then anxiety occurs; if the lowered threshold occurs in the part that regulates despair, then depression occurs.

There is some support for this formulation. Klein found that 50% of severely agoraphobic inpatients had separation anxiety. In many of the cases a significant personal loss preceded the initial panic attack. Klein (Shader, Goodman, & Gever, 1982) believes antidepressants raise the threshold of this hypothetical mechanism. Specifically, antidepressants block the protest phase, whereas sedative–hypnotic drugs do not. Additionally, animal studies show morphine, clonidine, and imipramine to reduce separation anxiety. This suggests a specific pharmacological responsiveness to the separation anxiety mechanism in animals. Reinforcing the link with human panic attacks are the reports that children with severe separation anxiety and school phobia are responsive to imipramine therapy.

Biological Roots

Klein (1980, 1981) differentiates between chronic anticipatory anxiety and spontaneous panic attacks. *Panic disorder* is defined as recurrent panic attacks in the absence of any apparent precipitating stimulus (American Psychiatric Association, 1980). Infusion of sodium lactate typically precipitates anxiety attacks in persons susceptible to panics but rarely in those with no history of panic (Reiman, Raichle, Butler, Herscovitch, & Robins, 1984; Liebowitz, Fryer, Gorman, Dillion, Applby, Levy, Anderson, Levitt, Palij, Davies, & Klein, 1984). Liebowitz says that infused lactate interacts in some undefined way to trigger actual attacks in vulnerable persons. Lactate-induced panic and spontaneous panic attacks are symptomatically similar. Both respond to tricyclic antidepressant therapy as well as to monoamine oxidase (MAO) inhibitors.

Carr (Fishman & Sheehan, 1984) has found that inhaling modest amounts of carbon dioxide will similarly induce spontaneous attacks. Carr hypothesizes that the sodium lactate and carbon dioxide act on sensors—called *chemoceptors*—much as smoke acts on a smoke detector. He says this suggests a neurobiological basis for panic disorder. Carr speculates that faulty or oversensitive chemoceptors trigger panic attacks either spontaneously or in relation to minimal stress. Such a mechanism is helpful to a person who is suffocating but is otherwise maladaptive.

Other researchers (Reiman et. al., 1984) have used positron emission tomography (PET) scans to measure cerebral blood flow (CBF) in patients with panic disorder. Analysis of CBF in the area of the parahippocampal gyrus (a region thought to regulate symptoms of panic, anxiety, and vigilance) revealed abnormal discrete asymmetry of CBF between left and right sides. This important study demonstrates a focal brain abnormality in patients vulnerable to panic attacks but not with a panic state itself. Reiman and his associates believe the CBF abnormality suggests an exaggeration of normal hemisphere specialization in expressing emotions.

Redmond (1979) describes a brain norepinephrine system in anxiety. Redmond studied the locus ceruleus, an area of the brain rich in the neurotransmitter norepinephrine; he concluded that anxiety, fear, and panic may be determined by changes in norepinephrine metabolism in this part of the brain. More specifically, abnormally high reactivity of the brain noradrenergic system may relate to clinical anxiety (Charney, Heniger, & Breier, 1984).

Along the same lines, Charney, Heniger, and Breier (1984) conducted a Yohimbine challenge procedure between "healthy subjects" and patients with agoraphobia and panic disorder. Yohimbine (an A_2-adrenergic receptor antagonist that increases noradrenergic function) produced significantly greater anxiety, higher blood pressure, more autonomic symptoms, and higher plasma norepinephrine metabolite 3-methoxy-4-hydroxyphenylglycol (MHPG) levels in the patient group than in the healthy group. Results of this study support the hypothesis that increased sensitivity to augmented noradrenergic function in anxiety states is associated with panic, and provides evidence that increased brain noradrenergic activity—specifically, presynaptic noradrenergic neuronal regulation—is of causal and therapeutic significance in panic disorders.

Certain drugs with antipanic effects, including the MAO inhibitors and the tricyclic antidepressants, are thought to act on norepinephrine—perhaps by depressing activity in locus ceruleus neurons (Fishman & Sheehan, 1985). Fishman and Sheehan, however, point out that it is unknown how the drugs' antidepressant characteristics relate to their antipanic action. Interestingly, patients with histories of panic attacks experience less fear if they receive antipanic medication prior to undergoing lactate provocation.

Insel and his co-workers (Insel, Ninan, Aloi, Jimerson, Skolnick, & Paul, 1984) offer a benzodiazepine receptor–mediated model of anxiety. They cite the discovery in 1977 by two independent research groups of "high-affinity stereospecific receptors" for benzodiazepines in the mammalian brain; and they offer evidence supporting the notion that the pharmacological actions of the benzodiazepines are mediated through this specific receptor. Additionally, they note the development of high-affinity benzodiazepine receptor ligands (for example, β-CCE) that act as benzodiazepine receptor antagonists.

Their animal experiments with administration of β-CCE resulted in marked behavioral arousal, with increases in blood pressure, heart rate, and endocrine effects. However, they were able to block all behavioral and physiological effects by pretreatment with another benzodiazepine receptor antagonist, RO 15-1788. This led to their observation that there were two different kinds of antagonists, like RO 15-1788, that compete for benzodiazepine receptors but cause no activity and that "activate" antagonists, such as β-CCE, which demonstrate activating and possibly "anxiogenic" properties.

In their research with chair-adapted rhesus monkeys, diazepam, a benzodiazepine, successfully blocked β-CCE–induced effects without lowering blood pressure, heart rate, or plasma cortisol level. The implication here is that the benzodiazepine receptor may mediate anxiety and play a role in its generation by mediating anxiogenic effect.

Comparing their work with that of Redmond et. al. (1979) and with that of Charney, Heniger, and Breier (1984), Insel and his associates point out that the noradrenergic and benzodiazepine receptor models represent two different phenomena: noradrenergic activation originates in the pons, within the locus ceruleus, and represents alarm, whereas the benzodiazepine system corresponds more specifically to fear or conflict.

Based on their integration of information from provoked anxiety studies (such as the lactate challenge and carbon dioxide inhalation studies discussed earlier), Carr and Sheehan (1984a, 1984b) have formulated a provisional model of panic anxiety. They conceptualize panic attacks as operationally occurring within the "redox" regulating apparatus of the brain stem. Their model posits a neural redox dysregulation in the ventral medulla or within an adjacent efferent zone. In this model an elevation in the lactate-pyruvate ratio with a simultaneous fall in chemoceptor intraneuronal pH evokes anxiety in susceptible persons. Thus panic disorder is hypothesized to occur from pathological oversensitivity to carbon dioxide at a central chemoceptor level or a lability in the first steps of the ventilation–arousal cascade that these chemoceptors activate.

A dysfunction of a minor ion channel could account for the pattern of inheritance of panic disorder within families. Within the context of their redox theory, Carr and Sheehan do not see noradrenergic innervation to the cerebral cortex as either central or specific to the generation of panic attacks. They believe the noradrenergic system mediates some but not all features of anxiety and may or may not be mobilized in the case of panic anxiety.

Temperament

The role of temperament (see Chess & Thomas, 1984, 1986; Thomas, Chess, & Birch, 1968) in the development of anxiety and phobias is relatively unexplored. For example, what antecedent temperamental characteristics (activity level, rhythmicity, adaptability, approach–withdrawal inclination, intensity, mood, distractibility level, persistence, and the like) would lead to one's being at increased risk for the development of specific phobias or anxiety? What is the effect of different parental styles on different temperaments in the development of anxiety?

Interpersonal Factors

Interpersonal factors appear to play a role in the development and maintenance of anxiety disorders. Guidano and Liotti (1983) describe abnormal patterns of attachment (bonding) (see Bowlby, 1969, 1973) in agoraphobia and other multiple phobias. Agoraphobics have a history of attachment characterized by detachment blockage. This hampering of normal exploratory behavior is usually done in an indirect and inconspicuous manner by the parents.

Hyperprotective parents excessively warn their child of the dangers in the world and the difficulties in dealing with these dangers. Their insistence on the child's presumed physical and emotional weakness makes the child feel particularly exposed to the world's dangers. The parents, fearing loneliness, model agoraphobia by keeping the child with them. Parental threats of desertion and family scenes also contribute to the child's feelings of insecurity outside the home.

The anxious attachment patterns produce in the child a conflicted self-image. On the one hand, the excessive attention and caring the child receives lead to a lovable and valuable self-image. On the other hand, limited opportunities for exploration lead to a self-image of weakness in a hostile and dangerous world.

Such people develop inflexible attitudes toward themselves while consciously trying to control their perceived weakness. They have to integrate their needs for freedom and independence with needs for protection. The only way they can reach an equilibrium is by focusing their efforts on achievement or control and maintaining this sense of control in interpersonal endeavors.

Personality Traits and Maladaptive Thinking

The predominant (deep-structural) personality variables and cognitive (thinking) patterns are relevant to treating anxiety because both help to maintain the person's anxiety. As potential obstacles to recovery, they often warrant specific cognitive-behavioral restructuring or reeducation, for example, self-reliance training (Emery, 1981, 1982).

Zane and Milt (1984) describe five personality traits associated with panic attacks and multiple phobias. First, such people are imaginative (creative), but discount this and generally underestimate their abilities and sense of self-worth. Second, they are perfectionists, who typically set high goals and worry about failure. They are overly conscientious about personal responsibilities and obligations and place excessive demands on themselves. Basically, they reject themselves and others and try to errect a "pseudopersonality" (see Angyal, 1965) that matches their idea of perfectionism (Hardy, 1982). Third, they have a strong desire to please others. They are overly sensitive to public opinion and therefore avoid conflict and disapproval. Fourth, because they are fearful of appearing foolish and letting others see their flaws, they avoid discomfiting situations. Fifth, they focus on predictability, permanence, and regularity: they must watch their every step in a dangerous and hostile world.

THINKING ERRORS

Hardy (1982) reports that phobics think in extreme (all-or-nothing) terms. They jump to subjective conclusions without objective evidence or substantiation. Although they can see similarities and easily make generalizations (particularly with phobogenic themes like uncertainty and safety), they are unable to discern differences.

Finally, Beck (Beck & Emery, 1985) describes the phobic's "catastrophizing" (see Ellis & Harper, 1975). With any perceived discomfort or stress, phobics automatically focus on the worst. They selectively abstract data from the past and present to support the worst possible outcome. Though now dysfunctional, focusing on the worst may have initially served an evolutionary function.

Classification of Anxiety

Unlike the second edition of the *Diagnostic and Statistical Manual of Mental Disorders* (DSM-II) (American Psychiatric Association, 1968), which classified "anxiety neuroses" along the lines of psychoanalytic theory (for example, anxiety as a manifestation of unconscious impulses, intrapsychic conflict, and ego defenses), the third edition (DSM-III) (American Psychiatric Association, 1980) is a descriptive classification based on empirically derived categories. The classification provides a solid base for research into the phenomenology, natural history, prognosis, and treatment of anxiety (Barlow & Beck, 1984).

Barlow and Beck point out that the descriptive categories are problematic and have yet to be validated by research. For example, different anxiety disorders are characterized by variations on the same autonomic stress response (for example, autonomic arousal is apparent in phobic disorders as well as in anxiety states and in posttraumatic stress disorder).

In the same vein, Klein (1981) suggests that panic attacks are central to the genesis of agoraphobics. Hallam (1978) believes agoraphobia may be a variant of generalized anxiety disorder. And Mavissakalian (1982) believes that generalized anxiety disorder and panic disorder should be subsumed hierarchically under agoraphobia.

Many researchers consider anxiety dimensional rather than categorical (Barlow & Beck, 1984). Anxiety may take different forms depending on stress levels, environment, and interpersonal variables. Different anxiety disorders may just be variations on the same theme, with the form of expression (such as obsessions or panic) shifting over time. Clinically, this seems to be the case.

Sheehan (1982; Sheehan & Sheehan, 1982a, 1982b) believes the DSM-III classification for the anxiety, hysterical, and hypochondriacal disorders is complex, clinically confusing, and lacking in heuristic merit. An anxious patient can be placed in any of 25 different diagnostic categories. Indeed, because some of these overlap, 138 diagnostic combinations are possible. According to Sheehan, the categories and their combinations are manifestations of the same condition in both clinical description and natural course over time. They each describe aspects of the same phenomenon while claiming important differences in symptomatology. As distinct entities, however, they do not reflect a natural order. They fail the test of any good classification system—that of providing categories that are inherently mutually exclusive. Sheehan believes a reconceptualization is necessary if classification categories are to be useful clinically and empirically.

Going along with Klein's (1981) pharmacologically derived distinction between chronic anticipatory anxiety and spontaneous panic attacks, Sheehan proposes a new, singular classification for the anxiety states, hysterias, phobic states, psychosomatic states, hypochondriasis, and panic disorder. The system is based on the distinction between spontaneous anxiety attacks (*endogenous* anxiety) as the primary biological core of these disorders and externally triggered anxiety (*exogenous* anxiety). Subtypes are determined by chronicity and severity (Sheehan & Sheehan, 1982b):

1. Endogenous anxiety:
   a. Minor endogenous anxiety
   b. Major endogenous anxiety
   c. Minor endogenous phobic anxiety
   d. Major endogenous phobic anxiety
   e. Secondary endogenous anxiety
2. Exogenous anxiety:
   a. Acute exogenous anxiety
   b. Exogenous phobic anxiety
   c. Chronic exogenous anxiety
   d. Tonic anxiety

Endogenous anxiety has spiking and phasic symptoms that appear to have a life of their own. Exogenous anxiety is an atonic reactive response to stress that is triggered by immediate environmental stimuli.

Sheehan believes panic attacks are the central feature of endogenous anxiety. Phobias, anticipatory anxiety, derealization, depersonalization experiences, and other related anxiety symptoms are complications that occur later—depending on the severity and chronicity of the spontaneous panic attacks. The site of the attack determines the type of phobia. Sheehan outlines the following mechanisms involved in the evolution or induction of an anxiety disorder (Shader, Goodman, & Gever, 1982):

1. Activation of the metabolic core
2. Classical conditioning by the spontaneous attack
3. Phobic acquisition by stimulus generalization
4. Symptom acquisition by interoceptive conditioning
5. Symptom reinforcement by operative conditioning

Thus, Sheehan says, endogenous anxiety begins the disorder, and its activity conditions, reinforces, and maintains the subsequent conditioned symptoms and behaviors. When spontaneous anxiety episodes are recurrent in the context of a specific psychosocial event, the anxiety conditions this event to become a stimulus for anxiety independent of the original endogenous anxiety. The development of phobias is a consequence of the frequency and intensity of the panic attacks and the place where they occur.

The conceptualization of endogenous and exogenous anxiety has implications for treatment. Sheehan's suggestions for differential chemotherapeutic and psychotherapeutic treatment have relevance to Lang's (1968) three-systems model of fear (discussed earlier), specifically as related to the use of drugs with somatovisceral symptoms.

Cognitive-Behavioral Classification

One can classify anxiety according to common beliefs, automatic thoughts and avoidance behavior. For example, Beck (Beck & Emery, 1985), though roughly paralleling DSM-III, divides anxiety into five categories: (1) generalized anxiety (acute and chronic), (2) panic disorders, (3) simple phobias (singular and multiple), (4) agoraphobia, and (5) evaluation anxieties.

Acute anxiety is due to trauma (actual or perceived) or threat of trauma. In acute anxiety, the person continually labels the event as dangerous and creates a state of total mobilization.

Anticipatory anxiety is the central feature in chronic anxiety. People anticipate a social loss (being rejected or abandoned) or an individual loss (being dominated or devalued). With individuality, people think about being or appearing incompetent; with sociality they think about losing emotional or interpersonal support. People's primary childhood fears play a major role in the childhood development of anxiety and social phobias.

In generalized anxiety, people worry about losing self-confidence and personal security. In contrast, in social phobias they focus on their inadequate social skills. Unlike phobias, the fears of victims of generalized anxiety are pansituational: they occur outside the anxiety-provoking situation.

Beck (Beck, Laude, & Bohnert, 1974; Hibbert, 1984) says that in generalized anxiety (without panic) people's fears are interpersonal—being depreciated, ridiculed, or rejected. In contrast, people with panic attacks fear physical or mental disaster—having a heart attack or a psychotic break.

Although many believe panic attacks occur without cognitions, Beck believes people can be trained to identify preceding (automatic) thoughts or images. For example, panic attacks symbolically signifiy helplessness and terror in the face of acute danger. The attack creates an involuntary emergency response that differs markedly from the feeling in generalized anxiety. Beck believes panic is *designed* to produce the conviction that one is endangered by uncontrollable internal disturbances. People believe they will progress to an ultimate disaster unless they receive help from a caretaker.

Citing current factor-analytic research (Beck & Emery, 1985), Beck says that simple phobias have three main themes: (1) social rejection (public performance, personal attractiveness, criticism); (2) agoraphobic content (traveling alone, heights, crowds); and (3) exposure to blood. His study suggests that fears have two common denominators (physical or psychological). With multiple phobias, this is a conceptual continuity—the fear spreads by type of danger rather than by superficial attributes.

Agoraphobics, for example, believe an overwhelming physical or emotional disorder is imminent. Their thinking focuses on the need for safety (see also Rachman, 1984). They believe that if they have access to help or home—a place of safety—they will be safe. They avoid crowds and lines because these block the routes to safety.

Socially anxious people on the other hand, fear negative evaluation. They are afraid of doing something that will make them the center of attention. They believe exposure of their weakness (less than perfect performance) will result in social ruination and permanent banishment.

Treatment

The Cognitive Perspective

Wilson (1980) believes that cognitive approaches are helpful in explaining anxiety, but behavioral or performance-based therapy is a more effective treatment. If one equates cognitive therapy with "cognitive restructuring," his observation has merit, but this is an oversimplified view of cognitive therapy. In this view, "faulty" thinking causes faulty feelings and behavior, so changing the faulty surface thoughts will directly and automatically change the bad feelings.

This oversimplification ignores many of the emerging trends in cognitive therapy: the tenacity of deep structure (such as the metaphysical hard core) and its construction (development) over one's life span. Cognitive therapy (Beck, 1984; Beck & Emery, 1985) takes into account imagery structure, emotional processing, evolutionary factors (physiological prepotency and preparedness), and the automatic and volitional behavioral systems.

Deep-Structural Shifts

Arnkoff (1980) says the implicit goal of psychotherapy is the modification of people's deep-structure beliefs about themselves and the world. This includes modifications of their beliefs about stable as well as changing patterns in their lives. Arnkoff believes behavioral therapy limits itself by focusing solely on observable behaviors (surface structure), and that psychoanalysis is flawed by ignoring the importance of surface structure, since it assumes deep structure must be dealt with through the layers of the past. The analyst's map from surface structure to deep structure is faulty because deep structure includes the present even though it arose out of the past.

Arnkoff suspects that different types of psychotherapy can be successful because they have the same effect on deep structure, even though they approach surface structure differently.

The Therapeutic Underground

Goldfried (1980) believes therapists from many different orientations, discontent with the efficacy of their approach, are borrowing procedures from other orientations. He cites evidence showing more similarities in therapy among experienced clinicians than among the less experienced. In other words, the amount of clinical experience is more important than the orientation. Goldfried believes this shows the existence of a therapeutic underground that has gone neglected in the literature.

The underground is made up of an implicit array of clinical observations about what does and does not work in therapy. In considering the commonality of experienced clinicians, Goldfried suggests that a meaningful consensus can be found in clinical strategies—those rules of thumb, lying somewhere between theory and technique, that implicitly guide therapy. As an example, Goldfried offers two universal strategies among humanistic, behavioral, and psychoanalytic therapists: (1) providing clients with corrective experiences and (2) offering clients direct feedback.

Behavioral Aspects

Historically, cognitive-behavioral therapy has been only implicitly concerned with modifying deep-structure beliefs; however, it has explicitly recognized the importance of behavioral techniques (corrective experience, homework, positive practice, exposure, and the like) in achieving structural change (therapeutic change itself).

In discussing how people change, Goldfried (1980) quotes Wheelis (1973, p. 101): "Personality change follows change in behavior. Since we are what we do, if we want to change what we are we must begin by changing what we do, must undertake a new mode of action." This is echoed by Wolpe (1982, p. 116): "Emotional change does not follow understanding, but requires outward behavior on the basis of that understanding."

The general consensus is that therapeutic (emotional) change requires some degree of synchrony (Lang, 1968; Rachman & Hodgson, 1974; Rachman, 1978; Hugdahl, 1981) within the cognitive, behavioral, and somatic systems.

Research Trends

Barlow and Beck (1984) point out that research is beginning to show which treatment is best for a specific anxiety disorder. With agoraphobia, for example, they note that exposure is the treatment of choice. Early research suggested that prolonged intensive *in vivo* exposure was best; dropout and relapse studies, however, indicate that a graduated, self-initiated, extended exposure program using a cooperative partner is better. An advantage of this type of treatment package is that it can be used effectively in a phobia center.

A positive adjunct to the graduated-exposure program is the use of antidepressants, monoamine oxidase (MAO) inhibitors, and tricyclics, all of which appear to alleviate the severity of panic attacks. Sheehan (1982) describes the effectiveness of alprazolam (Xanax), which has similarly been found to have anti-panic-attack properties, a characteristic unique to benzodiazepines.

Barlow and Beck (1984) talk about how cognitive therapy has been confused with cognitive restructuring. Citing Emmelkamp, Kuipers, and Eggeraat (1978); Biran and Wilson (1981); Emmelkamp and Mersch (1982); and Williams and Rappaport (1983), they point to the lack of empirical support for using cognitive restructuring in isolation or added to an exposure-based treatment program.

Actually, research subjects said that incorporating cognitive procedures into their treatment (exposure) program was helpful and attributed progress to them. More specifically, Williams and Rappaport (1983), in comparing *in vivo* practice plus cognitive restructuring, found that cognitive strategies succeed in the goal of having subjects think more adaptively when confronting feared situations, but that their adaptive thoughts failed to help them feel or act more adaptively.

Williams and Rappaport concluded that the evidence supported cognitive *theory* but not cognitive *therapy*. They explained this using Bandura's (1977) theory of self-efficacy. Bandura sees fear as being codified or encased in thoughts (cognitions), but believes the best way to change the thought is to change the behavior, thereby generating evidence or confidence in one's ability.

In defense of cognitive strategies, Mavissakalian, Michelson, Greenwald, Kornblith, and Greenwald (1983) point out that in Williams and Rappaport's study neither treatment produced significant behavioral change. With the other cited studies (Emmelkamp, Kuipers, & Eggeraat, 1978; Emmelkamp, 1982; Williams & Rappaport, 1983), they say the limited amount of treatment restricted opportunities for patients to integrate their new coping skills in a natural environment. In other words, patients' limited practice in cognitive restructuring resulted in only slight modification of surface structure and no modification in deeper structure.

Although lacking controlled research data, Coleman (1981) has developed a promising cognitive-behavioral treatment package. His package includes strategies for modifying the agoraphobic's tacit beliefs or schemata about being weak, dependent, and ineffective in a dangerous world. The nucleus of treatment consists of graduated *in vivo* exposure in natural settings. The cognitive component focuses on correcting irrational beliefs about accepting anxiety in real-life situations. Coleman emphasized Weekes's (1972) concept of acceptance of anxiety; acceptance refutes the person's primary belief that anxiety is intolerable. Restructuring strategies focus on the images and memories (evoked *in vivo*) that maintain the core, deep-structure, agoraphobic belief system.

Cognitive therapy shows promise for the nonphobic anxiety disorders such as panic disorder and generalized anxiety disorder (Barlow & Beck, 1984). For example, Hollon (1981) describes the successful use of cognitive therapy with two males suffering from drug-induced pansituational panic states. The program included self-monitoring, cognitive hypothesis testing, and graduated exposure. The focus was on empirically discovering and testing the clients' erroneous beliefs and misattributions about their anxiety.

Waddell, Barlow, and O'Brian (1984) explored the use of self-statement training followed by relaxation procedures paired with the cognitive training. The three subjects demonstrated decrease in frequency and duration of panic-level anxiety. Two of the subjects, however, had little change in background or generalized anxiety. Their treatment, interestingly, focuses on both the cognitive and the physiological (somatic) systems.

Little empirical research exists about the effective treatment of generalized anxiety disorders (Barlow & Beck, 1984). Cognitive therapy, however, has promise (Beck, Laude & Bohnert, 1974; Beck & Emery, 1979, 1985). The therapy is aimed at correcting the catastrophic and negative thinking that leads to a sense of threat and vulnerability; this in turn lowers the levels of arousal, vigilance, and apprehension associated with chronic anxiety.

With somatic treatment, the benzodiazepine and beta blockers, including propranolol, which reduces heart palpitations, are the drugs of choice (Barlow & Beck, 1984; Glenberg, 1983). Biofeedback is another possible somatic treatment.

Many studies of college students with problems such as test anxiety, interpersonal or heterosocial anxiety, and fears of public speaking have found cognitive therapy to be effective (Wise & Haynes, 1983; Goldfried, Linehan, & Smith, 1978; Meichenbaum, 1972). The studies typically use a cognitive and behavioral structured learning model (see Rathjen, Rathjen, & Hiniker, 1978).

Barlow and Beck (1984) report finding only four treatment studies of homogeneous clinical social phobics (e.g., Marzillier, Lambert, & Kellett, 1976; Trower, Yardley, Bryant, & Shaw, 1978; Shaw, 1979; Ost, Jerremalm, & Johansson, 1981). These four studies have focused on systematic desensitization and social skills training. The treatment groups typically improved their social functioning but failed to reduce their anxiety significantly.

Ost, Jerremalm, and Johansson (1981) used social skills training and relaxation with social anxiety. They classified their subjects as behavioral reactors or physiological reactors. They found social skills training worked best for the behavioral reactors, whereas relaxation was better with physiological reactors.

In general the studies show that cognitive-behavioral strategies are effective with social anxiety; the results, however, fail to point out the best cognitive method or to indicate when cognitive therapy is better than exposure (Barlow & Beck, 1984) or self-efficacy (Bandura, 1977).

Effective Mechanisms

Cognitive-behavioral therapies have only occasionally mentioned the importance of synchrony in the treatment of anxiety and phobic disorders; historically, however, they have used an intermix of cognitive and behavioral strategies on both deep and surface structure.

Clare Weekes (1972, 1978a, 1978b, 1983), an early cognitive-behavioral therapy proponent, is a good example. She says that recovery from anxiety requires obtaining "a special voice deep within oneself [within deep structure] . . . that speaks with authority" (Weekes, 1983). On the behavioral component of therapy, Weekes says:

> It is a voice that must be earned by the sufferer himself . . . and . . . must make the symptoms and experience of anxiety no longer matter. . . . Recovery lies on the other side of panic—in the places and experiences one fears. Recovery to be recovery must be earned and it can be earned only in such places and experiences.

To effect deep-structural shifts ("earn the right kind of inner voice"), Weekes gives her classic four-step program for dealing with anxiety:

1. Face the anxiety.
2. Accept the anxiety.
3. Float with the anxiety.
4. Let time pass.

In this same vein, Zane (1978) has developed contextual therapy—a cognitive-behavioral treatment of phobic disorders. His approach grows out of analysis of phobic behavior as it occurs in natural environments. Zane focuses on changes of disturbed (anxious) behavior in context rather than on historical origins or implicit symbolic meaning. A person's history may predict how anxious or phobic he or she may react; however, personal history is of little value in understanding the behavioral fluctuation that is related to what an individual is thinking at the moment.

Zane describes a phobogenic process that is capable of creating spiraling disorganization and panic. Contextual therapy teaches people how to halt the growth of this spiral by shifting their attention away from the thoughts and images that make up the phobic process (experience). People can break the spell by reestablishing contact with known objects, rational ideas, and familiar activities while in the midst of a phobic reaction. The therapist guides and reinforces patients through the experience. Eventually patients develop an intuited understanding of how they create and maintain their phobic experiences.

Zane has a six-step program similar to Weekes's program:

1. Expect and allow fear to arise.
2. When fear appears, wait and let it be.
3. Label fear on a scale from 0 to 10 and watch it go up and down.
4. Focus on and perform manageable activities in the present and natural environments.
5. Function with a level of fear while appreciating achievements.
6. Expect and allow fear to reappear.

Conflict Model of Emotions

Emery has developed a conflict model of emotions (Emery & Campbell, 1985) in which there are six stages or steps in the creation of emotions.

1. The sequence starts with a mismatch between people's perception of reality and their expectations. This gap sets the stage for emotions.

2. People then attempt to fill in the gap by activating memories associated with the present contextual cues. In the case of anxiety, people activate frightening memories.

3. Using their memories as building materials, people create an image to fill in the gap—an image that is usually an exaggeration of the current situation. This image building occurs in the right hemisphere.

4. The image is then transmitted to the left hemisphere, where it activates individuals' beliefs and thoughts (analytic code) that react to the incoming images.

5. The image and thoughts clash, stopping the accepting or processing of incoming information and creating a psychological response that people experience subjectively as a feeling.

6. The feeling is a kinetic self-signal for people to take some action. Once they take this action, the self-signal stops. Because the feeling often is experienced as an unknown, this sets the stage for spiraling of emotions.

As an example, with anxiety, socially anxious people experience the following steps:

1. They encounter an unknown situation. They may have to go to a social gathering.
2. The situation cues in past frightening memories.
3. They then create a frightening image, such as being awkward and looking foolish.
4. This activates their belief and self-statements that they have to have others think well of them.
5. They stop processing current reality and focus instead on the danger; the clash creates the experience of anxiety.
6. This then becomes a self-signal to escape the social situation or to tense up while there. This behavior increases the unknown aspect, reinforces the belief that there is something to fear, and adds to the memory pool of frightening events.

Because each stage is necessary to produce and maintain the emotion, intervention at any stage can disrupt the emotion. Each stage will be discussed and the clinical implications for each stage outlined.

Stage One: Facing an Unknown

Anxiety = Unknown × Importance. The greater the unknown and the greater the importance, the greater the anxiety. Hebb (1946) suggested that fear is the result of perceptual mismatch. The cue to start the production of anxiety is a mismatch between the person's expectations and his or her perceptions. Biologically, humans appear to be wired to respond with fear when reality fails to match their expectations. Hayward (1984 p. 199) says, "The fear reaction is aroused whenever the organism has a perception which does not match its anticipation of what it should perceive in a particular situation." In evolutionary terms, it is more efficient to wire the nervous system to respond to the unknown than to the many possible dangers. Because people live in a world of unknowns—they are surrounded by a circle of fear—the fear is triggered when a person steps out or is pushed out of his or her familiar domain and confronts an unknown situation.

For this reason, people seek familiar people and places—situations where their sense of control, approval, and competence is assured. People's domains are made up of what is known to them. Behavioral intervention works because it allows people to know what was previously unknown. Knowing destroys fear, whereas avoiding what one fears increases the unknown and so increases fears.

CLINICAL IMPLICATIONS

Any procedure that helps people become familiar with what they fear will be beneficial. Self-efficacy training (Bandura, 1977), for example, works by having clients approach and master what they fear. The more one knows about something, the more confident one feels. Similarly, choosing to experience and know one's anxiety (Weekes, 1978a; Zane, 1982) reduces it.

Stage Two: Activating Emotional Memories

When people confront novel situations, they rapidly and unconsciously search their memory for similarities from the past. Their initial panic is due to failure to find any similarities. The specific memories activated depend on the person's mood and contextual features of the current situation.

Gordon Bower (1981) has developed an associative network theory to show how emotional memory units are associated with current events. Activation of this emotional memory unit aids retrieval of events associated with it and primes emotional themes for use in fantasies and perceptual categorization. The emotion memory is in the right hemisphere—the analogue code. The person's perceptions of the world are colored and twisted by past emotional experiences.

In the case of anxiety, memories of vulnerability are activated. These memories are the result of the person's early learning history and center around three general concerns: approval, competence, and control. Each concern is directly related to self-esteem (Beck & Emery, 1985). A threat to any one of the concerns is a threat to self-esteem or self-respect.

The specific memories that are activated play a significant role in which emotion is created. Because of the power of the memories that are activated, clients appear to have multiple personalities. For example, the client's subpersonality when he or she is depressed is markedly different from his or her anxious subpersonality.

CLINICAL IMPLICATIONS

The emotional memories that are elicited are associated with specific body reactions. A person who acts fearful is more likely to activate fearful memories. This is why a useful intervention is to have the client engage in a behavior associated with mastery. I (Emery) often conduct therapy with anxious patients while both the client and I are riding stationary exercise bikes, because riding the bike activates positive memories.

The use of teaching stories and metaphors is a way to modify deep-structural memories (Deikman, 1982). This appears to be one of the goals of Milton Erickson's work (Rosen, 1982).

Akhter Ahsen's eidetic technique (1977) is another way the therapist can work directly with the patient's memories. This theory holds that the eidetic image is an activated experiential point in the mind that reveals past interactive facts, particularly with one's parents. The images with the mother are related to one's close relationships, the images with the father related to dealing with the world. When these images are purposely elicited, the mind scans various layers of meaning, detecting, deciphering, revealing, and expulsing the negative experience. The awareness and experience of these eidetic images expands the image and frees the person from its effect.

By rearranging the reworking old images, a person can recreate the past. One effective procedure is to rework old memories into more happy and satisfying outcomes. Similarly, mastery experiences allow clients to build up more useful memories. A helpful strategy is to have anxious patients attend to and encode their success experiences on a daily basis (Emery & Campbell, 1985).

Stage Three: Creating Images

Rather than seeing reality, people create and see their image of reality (Lang, 1977). The unknown plus the memories set the stage for people to start "what if'ing" ("What if I go crazy?" "What if I die?"). People tend to believe their self-created images. Tversky and Kahneman's (1973) "availability heuristic" helps to explain this: whatever springs to mind most easily is judged to be most probable and most believable.

Because of the tendency to believe what one imagines, "what if" becomes "as if." Anxious people, for example, believe and act "as if" their frightening self-created imagery is true. They treat "what if" ideas (a high level of abstraction) "as if" they are real and concrete (a low level of abstraction). If such people know they are pretending, they experience mild anxiety; if they forget they are pretending, they experience panic.

Fear arises when people respond to the unknown by pretending something bad will happen. Leventhal (1979) cites evidence confirming a common clinical observation: the anxious person functions well with real problems but becomes immobilized when confronted with unknowns. In unknown situations anxious people create pseudoproblems by pretending or imagining the worst. The anxious person's fantasy is consistently worse than reality. One of the goals of therapy is to have the person *see* more and *imagine* less.

A state of anxiety has a trancelike quality and has several characteristics similar to a hypnotic trance (Shor, 1965): (1) construction of awareness (tunnel vision), (2) "as if" thinking or role taking, and (3) regression to an earlier state.

This trancelike state is due partly to a direct relationship between imagination and belief: what one imagines one believes, and what one believes, one imagines. The person who is unable to imagine being in a car accident will believe the chances of an accident are remote and may act on this belief and reinforce it by not wearing a seat belt. However, the person who can imagine a car crash will believe one is likely and, in the case of a phobia, will reinforce this by avoiding driving.

CLINICAL IMPLICATIONS

The less aware people are of their frightening images, the more effect these images have. Teaching clients how to monitor their images and detach themselves from them is an effective intervention. The therapist can use different techniques to help clients modify frightening images and create self-enhancing ones (Lazarus, 1978; Beck & Emery, 1985).

Stage Four: Activating Belief System

The images cross over to the left hemisphere where they activate the relevant analytic code. The emotional memories in the analogue code have a corresponding belief in the analytic code—a belief developed in response to the original experience. For example, a person who has painful memories of being abandoned as a child may have the corresponding belief "I can't be left alone." Both the original memories and the corresponding beliefs are deep-structured and deal with unacceptable life situations. Memories of early experiences that were never fully processed or accepted remain and form the person's belief system.

The beliefs are overcompensation for the tacit painful images. For example, a person's emotional memory of being inferior to others may have a corresponding belief such as "I have to be loved at all times" or "I have to be the best at whatever I do." Paradoxically, the overcompensating beliefs often create precisely the experiences the person is trying to avoid.

The person's conflict is between images of current events that are filtered and colored by past memories (analogue code) and automatic thoughts derived from early beliefs about the world (analytic code). The conflict is created by labeling events in an unacceptable way ("I'll die"), by exaggerating the situation ("It's awful"), by direct self-instruction ("I have to get out"), or by minimizing ability to deal with the new information ("I can't stand it").

This stage consists of reactive thinking. The person's conscious thoughts react to incoming images ("I can't stand it," "This is awful," "This should not be"). Reactive thinking, rather than stopping the intrusion of frightening images, escalates the flow of these images. Reactive thinking is based on the premise that *others are responsible for one's thoughts, feelings, and actions and one is responsible for others' thoughts, feelings, and actions.*

The role of reactive thinking (Emery & Campbell, 1985) is crucial in understanding and treating anxiety. This form of thinking is characteristic of early development, where people cement outside events to their feelings. People make the conceptual connection that other people or outside events are causing their feelings. This parallels concepts derived from the physical world, where sticks and stones can actually hurt someone. Such people project the cause of their experiences onto others and the cause of these others' experiences onto themselves. For example, socially anxious people believe they are responsible for what others think of them while also believing others are responsible for their anxiety.

People are biologically, developmentally, and socially prone to reactive thinking. Developmentally, the brain when confronted with emotional trauma is unable to respond differently until a child is around 11 years old. Reactive thinking is necessary for socialization. Helpless children need a manipulative system to get others to help them survive. Reactive thinking helped evolution. Cues lead to automatic feelings and responses that lead to survival. Further, remembering bad experiences is more economical because fewer bad events happen to remember. This parataxic type of thinking is in operation when children do their early learning—each child believes he or she is the center of the universe. Because of the primary effect, what the person learns first is what stays.

Children lack reversibility—the ability to uncouple events from strong feelings. Their early deep-structure beliefs are based on a reactive premise. The relevant beliefs in the analytic code are reactive beliefs.

Children use the physical world as a frame of reference and confuse this with the psychological world. But the physical world is a world of change and control; the psychological world is one of selection and choice.

Although we have discussed the concepts of *change* and *control* in this chapter, they are not helpful terms because they are best used to describe the physical world. People and things change physically; this involves a transfer of energy. Psychologically, however, people create different experiences by making both *aware* and *unaware* choices. People's efforts to change themselves usually lead to resistance and frustration. The people think of change and control because that is what they see happening around them. They also want to change and control things because this implies permanency and safety from anxiety.

Contrary to Guidano and Liotti's position (1983), in their early learning people appear to acquire much knowledge of the world through passive association. The advertising industry is based on the power of associative learning. Through associative or reactive learning, people weld feelings and events together. Much of people's thinking is unscientific and is based on correlational reasoning rather than experimentation.

People maintain reactive thinking largely because they are unable to see how they create their own negative feelings. Because people do not want them, cannot see how they create them, and cannot get rid of them, they assume something else must be causing these feelings. Projection plays a part: because others seem to be creating one's experiences, one must also be creating theirs. Any event, internal or external, that can be coupled with a specific feeling that triggers the creation of emotions appears to be the cause. Because some internal or external event always precedes an emotion, that event is assumed to be the cause.

People look at the most important cues and ignore the context, thereby reinforcing the idea that events are caused by feelings. Reactive thinking is unverifiable: one cannot logically prove that others do *not* cause one's feelings.

The brain does not give notice that there is a different way to think. Many people lack the learning opportunity to think in different ways. Others have difficulty moving away from reactive thinking. After the person has practiced reactive thinking on thousands of occasions, he overlearns this way of thinking. Traumatic events can lock the person into believing the events cause the feeling. Some type of neurological pathway between stimulus and response may also develop because of overlearning.

People learn through modeling that outside events cause feelings. Cultural distortions support reactive thinking. Mass culture (television, music, newspapers) reinforces the idea that others are responsible for people's feelings.

Reactive thinking is used for social control. Organizations, institutions, and parents all use this system to control and manipulate those under their control. Further, everyday language reinforces reactive thinking by encouraging people to assign psychological properties to properties that are actually one's own (e.g., "The picture is beautiful").

Social demand characteristics also come into play. One tends to respond as others are responding. Sensitivity to others' facial and other nonverbal expressions often triggers reactive thinking. People are socialized to rank others above or below themselves, and these social roles contribute to reactive thinking. Because people cannot see themselves directly, they use others' reactions as mirrors, which reinforces reactive thinking.

Psychological defenses maintain reactive thinking. A person who cannot tolerate being wrong, when confronted with old stimuli such as seeing his or her family, responds in a conditioned way. People who have not become skilled at utilizing thinking based on *choice* revert to reactive thinking when under pressure. Their insecurities lead them to hold onto old ways of thinking. Through rationalization and selective attention, people see what they believe to be true.

CLINICAL IMPLICATIONS

Therapists can help anxious clients deal with issues of approval, control, and competence by adopting more adaptive beliefs. People can, for example, learn to substitute the concept of *choice* for that of *control*. Similarly, people can learn to adopt and use more self-enhancing beliefs.

Therapists can use a variety of strategies to help clients start using thinking that is based on choices, not reactions (Emery & Campbell, 1985). Most clients can learn to move into the choice system relatively easily. However, patients can just as easily move out of it and back into the reactive system. The more they practice, the easier and more automatic this flexibility becomes. People who appear to have changed may in fact have simply reinforced a new deep-structural belief system that allows them to make this shift more easily and more often.

Stage Five: Blocking of Acceptance and Creating Subjective Feelings

The clash between people's images and their reactive thinking stops them from processing information and creates instead the experience of the feeling. An example is the shudder response: the person has a frightening image and then makes an evaluation of it ("It's terrible"), and the resulting clash creates a sudden vibration through the body. But when people imagine something bad happening and accept this image without fighting it, there is no corresponding emotion.

The model suggests that people process or take in information about the world in a normal flow through their acceptors—a hypothetical construct. People assimilate an uninterrupted stream of consciousness about internal and external events. They absorb (remember) useful information and eliminate the rest.

In summary, salient information about an event is first filtered through a person's emotional memory system (analogue code) in the right hemisphere out of the person's awareness. Past anxious memories color the event and help create the images (Lang, 1977). The information in the form of rapid images then goes to the left hemisphere, or conscious awareness, and is checked against the belief system (analytic code).

Normally the information is then processed from the left hemisphere back to the long-term memory in the right hemisphere. The person assimilates (remembers) useful information and eliminates (or ignores) the rest.

WORKING IT THROUGH

When people accept reality, they feel "in the flow." Like the workings of the digestive system, the process goes unnoticed unless it is malfunctioning. However, when people reject their images of reality, they feel "stuck," "blocked," "conflicted." Acceptance means taking in information about the world. When this process is working, people say they are "taking it [the information] easy" or "taking it in stride"; when the process is blocked, they report, "I'm taking it poorly" or "I can't take it."

Information flows unimpeded through the acceptor unless the person has a conflict with the incoming information. Such a conflict stops the acceptance process, and the person goes into a spiraling state of resistance or emotional distress. Anxious people, for example, have trouble "taking" their anxiety.

An accumulation of big and small setbacks can block a person's acceptor, and a person who is in a state of resistance has trouble accepting anything. A person who does accept information he or she has been fighting often experiences a physical change, feeling clearer, lighter, and more energetic.

Different writers have discussed emotional processing (Wilson, 1986). They describe how failure to process emotion-laden information shuts down the flow of consciousness. Rachman (1980), for example, says the main sign of faulty emotional processing is the persistence of some emotional activity, such as a phobia, an obsession, nightmares, overtalkativeness, or inappropriate expressions of emotions. According to Rachman, some indirect signs of faulty processing are excessive restlessness, irritability, and inability to concentrate.

The conflict that shuts down acceptance occurs in the left or verbal hemisphere when the analogue code clashes with the abstract code. This process is characterized by rapid automatic thoughts and a narrowing of perspective. When a person's acceptor closes down, his or her awareness becomes constricted as he or she overfocuses on the danger or problem in the environment.

Colin Wilson (1986) says: "The 'worm's eye view' of the left brain is negative by nature. The 'bird's eye view' of the right brain is positive by nature, revealing vistas of meaning and interconnectedness that are invisible to the worm." Narrow focus and racing thoughts make a person further distort reality (have a less clear picture), and anxiety builds. The information about the anxiety itself goes unprocessed.

Joanna Field (1981) contrasts *wide* and *narrow* attention. Narrow attention focuses on what serves its immediate interests and ignores the rest. Patricia Carrington (1984, p. 75) describes how this shutting down of awareness leads to tunnel vision: "Still others find their monitors regularly closing down whenever they have to meet a deadline, speak in public, face a job interview, deal with inlaws, handle children's disobedience, be alone, or under any number of other situations." Here, the person experiences the worm's eye view of the problem.

Although the concept is metaphorical, something physiologically akin to an acceptor may exist. As mentioned earlier, Reiman and his colleagues (1984) found a cerebral blood flow imbalance in people with lactate-induced panic attacks. Patients without panic attacks did not have this imbalance. The anxiety subjects had a discrete asymmetry of blood flow between the left and right sides of the brain at the parahippocampal gyrus, the part of the brain that regulates feelings. Researchers are now studying the hemispheric imbalance in blood–brain barrier and oxygen use, the link between blood flow and nerve cell activity.

Because the brain does not store oxygen, the activity of nerve cells is closely tied to brain blood flow. Any changes in the blood flow affect nerve cell activity on the two sides of the brain. Perhaps the blood flow of those with anxiety is activating a stream of frightening images that the person is actively resisting.

The clash of the image and belief systems, in addition to blocking informational processing, creates subjective feelings. This is a reactive process: the person reacts to the images, and the clash between images and thoughts creates the subjective feelings. The brain signals the person to react to an unacceptable situation, and the person receives this signal somatically as a feeling. The feeling is a reverberatory self-signal to take some corrective action in the environment. This reverberation is analogous to the striking of a tuning fork. Melges (1982, p. 221) writes:

> The long lasting, reverberatory nature of emotions is mediating by limbic–frontal circuits in the brain, whose circular structures are ideally suited for engendering amplifications of feedback and feedforward loops (Sommerhoff, 1974). The reverberatory nature of emotions make them conducive to initiating deviation-amplifications (spirals) that form the basis of virtuous as well as vicious cycles.

People experience these reverberations in different ways.

CLINICAL IMPLICATIONS

Because anxiety is caused by a self-conflict, people need to learn how to let go or accept current reality. They also, however, need to know the difference between surrendering internally and giving up to external events. Many people confuse accepting the reality of the moment with resigning themselves to circumstances.

Many different acceptance strategies can be used (Emery & Campbell, 1985). One strategy involves working the information through the acceptor by simply reviewing it systematically. Victor Raimy (1975) notes that nearly all schools of therapy have procedures by which the patient reviews emotion-laden information. These range from the analytic working-through process to behavioral flooding procedures, which would qualify as one of Goldfried's underground heuristics. Raimy describes a straightforward method of having the client repeatedly review emotionally painful material.

This can be seen as a deliberate way of getting processing the information through the acceptor. People suffering from emotional disorders appear to be trying to do this involuntarily. People may, for example, have an overpush to discuss the material or have painful intruding daydreams or recurrent nightmares. One woman repeatedly told herself, "My father is dead" until she accepted this fact.

Because anxious people take a worm's eye view, efforts can be made to get them to take a wider perspective—a bird's eye view. Therapists can use many techniques to help such people engage and expand their observing selves (Deikman, 1982). Showing anxious clients how to take a more reflective and balanced view of the situation by answering their automatic thoughts (Beck & Emery, 1985) stops the conflict and the manufacture of anxiety.

One of the first clinical steps involves helping people stop the spiraling effects of anxiety. Acceptance strategies such as the five-step AWARE strategy, developed by Emery (Beck & Emery, 1985). The goal of the AWARE program is to accept and know one's anxiety by remaining in present context while:

1. Welcoming anxiety; deciding to be with the experience.
2. Watching anxiety as an observer, separate from oneself.
3. Acting with the anxiety; normalizing the situation by acting *as if* one is not anxious.
4. Repeating acceptance; watching and acting with the anxiety until it disappears.
5. Expecting the best and accepting future anxiety by giving up the hope that the anxiety will never recur and replacing that with trust in one's ability to handle anxiety.

Another strategy to short-circuit anxiety is to have people experience or receive the brain's self-signal; they feel the anxiety for 45 to 60 seconds without trying to fight or change it and without feeding the anxiety any frightening thoughts or images.

Stage Six: Motivation

People's subjective feelings motivate them to take some action—with anger, to attack; with depression, to shut down; with happiness, to approach; and with anxiety, to flee or protect themselves. Once a person takes this action, the motivating emotion starts to disappear. However, the beliefs that helped create the emotions are strengthened. Avoidance, for example, decreases anxiety and increases fear.

Anxious clients often reinforce the motivating powers of anxiety by using it as self-motivation or self-manipulation. They unwittingly use anxiety to motivate themselves to take some action. A person, for example, may imagine failing a class and ending up on skid row if he or she does not finish a project; this scenario creates anxiety, which motivates the person to take action.

CLINICAL IMPLICATIONS

Clients can be taught to switch from a motivation based on feelings to one based on choices. They can use the ACT formula (Emery, 1982) to do this: Accept current reality, Choose what you want, and Take action to get it. This permits clients to move out of the reactive system into the choice system (see Emery & Campbell, 1985). A client accepts the situation as it is, then chooses the experience he or she wants to have, and acts *as if* he or she is having this experience. For example, socially anxious people can accept their feelings and lack of social skills, choose to feel confident at some upcoming event, and act *as if* they are confident when they are in the social situation. They learn that instead of using anxiety as motivation, they can do the task directly.

Future Directions

Where We Are

More understanding about anxiety and the anxiety disorders has been generated during the last fifteen years than was achieved during the entire previous century (Sheehan, 1983). The research findings of the 1980s illustrate the importance of theoretical models and methods that recognize interplay of the many systems that create emotional distress (Chess & Thomas, 1984).

In this chapter we have presented a picture of what is evolving within cognitive-behavioral psychology—the development of a more comprehensive formulation of both normal and abnormal anxiety. This formulation sees anxiety and anxiety states as a complex interplay of biological factors, psychological conditioning, and environmental stress forces (Sheehan, 1983). This emergent perspective is constructive, coalitional, and interactional.

Cognitive-behavioral theorists have accepted the challenge to avoid psychological (e.g., behavioral) reductionism. Instead of conceptualizing anxiety and other emotional distress as a linear and unifactorial process, they have acknowledged the pluralistic, interactional, and multifactorial dynamics of the biopsychological/environmental relationship (process); this in turn broadens understanding of individual psychological development and increases therapeutic potentials (see Marmor, 1983).

Where We Might Go

One exciting direction is further exploration and integration of systems theory; this can be expanded to include not only psychological and biological, but also social, economic, and cultural determinants as well as (Marmor, 1983). Chess and Thomas (1984, 1986) suggest the "goodness-of-fit" model as a framework within which to view the salient dynamics of the organism–environment process in the development of emotions. In their model, congruence between an organism's capacities, motivations, and styles of thinking and behaving versus environmental demands and expectations result in consonance or goodness of fit, whereas excessive stress due to poorness of fit generates emotional distress (problems). Poorness of fit between a person's thoughts, feelings, and actions and environmental demands and expectations can lead to distress in many ways and so requires a multidimensional approach to determine pathogenesis and treatment.

A similar shift towards integration and synthesis is the active movement to bridge the gap between behavioral and psychodynamic theories, specifically between conscious and unconscious determinants of experience and behavior (Mahoney, 1980; Wachtel, 1977; Bowers & Meichenbaum, 1984; Meichenbaum & Gilmore, 1984).

For most cognitive behaviorists the issue is not the existence of unconscious process or deep structure, or the influence of unconscious process on conscious thought. Rather, the cognitive-behavioral concern surrounds the validity of certain psychoanalytic premises regarding unconscious infuences (e.g., that arrested psychosexual development causes unconscious conflict, or that the unconscious is maintained by repression) (Perry

& Laurence, 1984; Meichenbaum & Gilmore, 1984). Cognitive-behavioral theorists believe the psychoanalytic model places too much importance on unconscious processing and too little on the interaction of mental and emotional processing and on social, cultural, and economic determinants.

Hilgard's neodissociation theory (Hilgard, 1979; Perry & Laurence, 1984) is worthy of exploration. Hilgard believes that cognitive functioning is the result of multiple overlapping control systems that are unavailable to consciousness. An example is driving a car while in deep thought or conversation and being unaware of the experience of driving. Hilgard uses his theory to explain certain emotional disorders and to elaborate a viable theory for hypnosis (Perry & Laurence, 1984).

Hilgard's theory may provide a link between cognitive-behavioral theory and more psychodynamic theory that could enrich cognitive-behavioral treatment. For example, the use of hypnosis techniques may prove invaluable in achieving more direct access to deep-structural beliefs (e.g., tacit knowledge), which then could result in more immediate, more thorough, and longer-lasting shifts from the entrenched thinking and behavior that support and perpetuate emotional distress (anxiety).

As we become more sophisticated in understanding emotional distress, the next step will be to translate this understanding into effective intervention.

References

Ahsen, A. (1977). *Psycheye.* New York: Brandon.

American Psychiatric Association. (1968). *Diagnostic and statistical manual of mental disorders* (2nd ed.). Washington, DC: Author.

American Psychiatric Association. (1980). *Diagnostic and statistical manual of mental disorders* (3rd ed.). Washington, DC: Author.

Angyal, A. (1965). *Neurosis and treatment: A holistic theory.* New York: Wiley.

Arnkoff, D. B. (1980). Psychotherapy from the perspective of cognitive theory. In M. J. Mahoney (Ed.), *Psychotherapy process: Current issues and future directions.* New York: Plenum Press.

Bandura, A. (1977). Self-efficacy: Towards a unifying theory of behavior change. *Psychological Review, 84,* 191–215.

Barlow, D. H., & Beck, J. G. (1984). The psychosocial treatment of anxiety disorders: Current status, future directions. In J. B. W. Williams & R. L. Spitzer (Eds.), *Psychotherapy research: Where are we and where should we go?* New York: Guilford Press.

Beck, A. T. (1976). *Cognitive therapy and the emotional disorders.* New York: International Universities Press.

Beck, A. T. (1984). Cognitive therapy, behavior therapy, psychoanalysis, and pharmacotherapy: The cognitive continuum. In J. B. W. Williams & R. L. Spitzer (Eds.), *Psychotherapy research: Where are we and where should we go?* New York: Guilford Press.

Beck, A. T., & Emery, G. (1979). *Cognitive therapy of anxiety and phobic disorders.* Philadelphia: Center for Cognitive Therapy.

Beck, A. T., & Emery, G. (1985). *Anxiety disorders and phobias: A cognitive perspective.* New York: Basic Books.

Beck, A. T., Laude, R., & Bohnert, M. (1974). Ideational components of anxiety neurosis. *Archives of General Psychiatry, 31,* 319–325.

Bedrosian, R. C., & Beck, A. T. (1980). Principles of cognitive therapy. In M. J. Mahoney (Ed.), *Psychotherapy process: Current issues and future directions.* New York: Plenum Press.

Biran, M., & Wilson, G. T. (1981). Treatment of phobic disorders using cognitive and exposure methods: A self-efficacy analysis. *Journal of Consulting and Clinical Psychology, 49,* 886–699.

Bower, G. H. (1981). Mood and memory. *American Psychologist, 36,* 129–48.

Bowers, K. S., & Meichenbaum, D. (Eds.) (1984). *The unconscious reconsidered.* New York: Wiley.

Bowlby, J. (1969). *Attachment and loss* (Vol. 1): *Attachment*. New York: Basic Books.

Bowlby, J. (1973). *Attachment and loss* (Vol. 2): *Separation*. New York: Basic Books.

Carr, D. B., & Sheehan, D. V. (1984a). Evidence that panic disorder has a metabolic cause. In J. C. Ballenger (Ed.), *Biology of agoraphobia*. Washington, DC: American Psychiatric Press, Inc.

Carr, D. B., & Sheehan, D. V. (1984b). Panic anxiety: A new biological model. *Journal of Clinical Psychiatry, 45*, 323–330.

Carrington, P. (1984). *Releasing*. New York: Morrow.

Charney, D. S., Heniger, G. R., & Breier, A. (1984). Noradrenergic function in panic anxiety. *Archives of General Psychiatry, 41*, 751–763.

Chess, S., & Thomas, A. (1984). *Origins and evolution of behavior disorders: From infancy to early adult life.* New York: Brunner/Mazel.

Chess, S., & Thomas, A. (1986). *Temperament in clinical practice*. New York: Guilford Press.

Coleman, R. E. (1981). Cognitive-behavioral treatment of agoraphobia. In G. Emery, S. D. Hollon, & R. C. Bedrosian (Eds.), *New directions in cognitive therapy*. New York: Guilford Press.

Deikman, A. (1982). *The observing self*. Boston: Beacon Press.

Eelen, P. (1982). Conditioning and attribution. In J. Boulougouris (Ed.), *Learning theory approaches to psychiatry*. London: Wiley.

Ellis, A., & Harper, R. A. (1975). *A new guide to rational living*. North Hollywood, CA: Wilshire.

Emmelkamp, P. M. G. (1982). *Phobic and obsessive-compulsive disorders: Theory, research and practice*. New York: Plenum Press.

Emmelkamp, P. M. G., Kuipers, A., & Eggeraat, J. (1978). Cognitive modification versus prolonged exposure *in vivo*: A comparison with agoraphobics. *Behaviour Research and Therapy, 16*, 33–41.

Emmelkamp, P. M. G., & Mersch, P. P. (1982). Cognition and exposure *in vivo* in the treatment of agoraphobia: Short-term and delayed effects. *Cognitive Research and Therapy, 6*, 77–90.

Emery, G. (1981). *A new beginning: How you can change your life through cognitive therapy*. New York: Simon & Schuster.

Emery, G. (1982). *Own your own life: How the new cognitive therapy can make you feel wonderful*. New York: New American Library.

Emery, G., & Campbell, J. (1985). *Rapid relief from emotional distress*. New York: Rawson.

Epstein, S. (1979). The ecological study of emotions in humans. In P. Pliner, K. R. Blankstein, & J. M. Spigel (Eds.), *Perception of emotion in self and others*. New York: Plenum Press.

Field, J. (1981). *A life of one's own*. Los Angeles: J. B. Tarcher.

Fishman, S. M., & Sheehan, D. V. (1985). Anxiety and panic: Their cause and treatment. *Psychology Today, 19*(4), 26–32.

Franks, J. J. (1974). Toward understanding understanding. In W. B. Weimer & D. S. Palermo (Eds.), *Cognition and the symbolic processes*. Hillsdale, NJ: Erlbaum.

Glenberg, A. J. (1983). Anxiety. In E. L. Bassuk, S. C. Schoonover, & A. J. Glenberg (Eds.), *The practitioner's guide to psychoactive drugs* (2nd ed.). New York: Plenum Medical Book.

Goldfried, M. R. (1980). Toward the delineation of therapeutic change principles. *American Psychologist, 35*, 991–999.

Goldfried, M. R., Linehan, M. M., & Smith, S. L. (1978). Reduction of test anxiety through cognitive restructuring. *Journal of Consulting and Clinical Psychology, 46*, 32–39.

Greenberg, L. S., & Safran, J. D. (1984). Integrating affect and cognition: A perspective on the process of therapeutic change. *Cognitive Therapy and Research, 8*, 559–578.

Guidano, V. F., & Liotti, G. (1983). *Cognitive processes and emotional disorders: A structural approach to psychotherapy*. New York: Guilford Press.

Hallam, R. S. (1978). Agoraphobia: A critical review of the concept. *British Journal of Psychiatry, 133*, 314–319.

Hardy, A. B. (1982). Phobic thinking: The cognitive influences on the behavior and effective treatment of the agoraphobic. In R. L. DuPont (Ed.), *Phobia: A comprehensive summary of modern treatments*. New York: Brunner/Mazel.

Hayward, J. W. (1984). *Perceiving ordinary magic*. Boulder, CO: New Science Library.

Hebb, D. O. (1946). On the nature of fear. *Psychological Review, 53*, 259–276.

Hibbert, G. A. (1984). Ideational components of anxiety: Their origin and content. *British Journal of Psychiatry, 144*, 618–624.

Hilgard, E. R. (1979). Divided consciousness in hypnosis: The implications of the hidden observer. In E. Fromm & R. E. Shor (Eds.), *Hypnosis: Developments in research and new perspectives.* New York: Aldine.

Hollon, S. D. (1981). Cognitive-behavioral treatment of drug-induced, pansituational anxiety states. In G. Emery, S. D. Hollon, & R. C. Bedrosian (Eds.), *New directions in cognitive therapy.* New York: Guilford Press.

Hugdahl, K. (1981). The three-systems-model of fear and emotion—A critical examination. *Behaviour Research and Therapy, 19,* 75–85.

Insel, T. R., Ninan, P. T., Aloi, J., Jimerson, D. C., Skolnick, P., & Paul, S. M. (1984). A benzodiazepine receptor-mediated model of anxiety. *Archives of General Psychiatry, 41,* 741–750.

Klein, D. F. (1981). Anxiety reconceptualized. In D. F. Klein & J. Rabkin (Eds.), *Anxiety: New research and changing concepts.* New York: Raven Press.

Lakatos, I. (1974). Falsification and methodology of scientific research programmes. In I. Lakatos & A. Musgrave (Eds.), *Criticism and the growth of knowledge.* London: Cambridge University Press.

Lang, P. J. (1968). Fear reduction and fear behavior: Problems in treating a construct. In J. M. Shlien (Ed.), *Research in psychotherapy* (Vol. 3). Washington, DC: American Psychological Association.

Lang, P. J. (1977). Imagery in therapy: An information processing analysis of fear. *Behavior Therapy, 8,* 862–886.

Lang, P. J. (1979a). A bio-informational theory of emotional imagery. *Psychophysiology, 16,* 495–512.

Lang, P. J. (1979b). Language, image and emotion. In P. Pliner, K. R. Blankstein, & J. M. Spigel (Eds.), *Perception of emotion in self and others.* New York: Plenum Press.

Lang, P. J. (1984). Cognition in emotion: Concept and action. In C. E. Izard, J. Kagan, & R. B. Zajonc (Eds.), *Emotions, cognition, and behavior.* New York: Cambridge University Press.

Lazarus, A. A. (1978). *In the mind's eye.* New York: Rawson.

Lazarus, R. S. (1982). Thoughts on the relations between emotion and cognition. *American Psychologist, 37,* 1019–1024.

Lazarus, R. S. (1984). On the primacy of cognition. *American Psychologist, 39,* 124–129.

Lazarus, R. S., & Folkman, S. (1984). *Stress, appraisal, and coping.* New York: Springer.

Leventhal, H. (1979). A perceptual-motor processing model of emotion. In P. Pliner, K. R. Blankstein, & J. M. Spigel (Eds.), *Perception of emotion in self and others.* New York: Plenum Press.

Leventhal, H. (1980). Towards a comprehensive theory of emotion. In L. Berkowitz (Ed.), *Advances in experimental social psychology* (Vol. 13). New York: Academic Press.

Leventhal, H. (1982). The integration of emotion and cognition: A view from the perceptual motor theory of emotion. In M. S. Clarke & S. T. Fiske (Eds.), *Affect and cognition: The seventeenth annual Carnegie symposium on cognition.* Hillsdale, NJ: Erlbaum.

Leventhal, H. (1984). A perceptual-motor theory of emotion. In L. Berkowitz (Ed.), *Advances in experimental social psychology* (Vol. 17). New York: Academic Press.

Liebowitz, M. R., Fryer, A. J., Gorman, J. M., Dillion, D., Applby, L. L., Levy, G., Anderson, S., Levitt, M., Palij, M., Davies, S. O., & Klein, D. F. (1984). Lactate provocation of panic attacks (Pt. 1): Clinical and behavioral findings. *Archives of General Psychiatry, 41,* 764–770.

Mahoney, M. J. (1980). Psychotherapy and the structure of personal revolutions. In M. J. Mahoney (Ed.), *Psychotherapy process: Current issues and future directions.* New York: Plenum Press.

Marks, I. M. (1969). *Fears and phobias.* London: Heinemann Medical and Academic Press.

Marks, I. M. (1981). *Cure and care of the neuroses: Theory and practice of behavioral psychotherapy.* New York: Wiley.

Marmor, J. (1983). Systems thinking in psychiatry: Some theoretical and clinical implications. *American Journal of Psychiatry, 140,* 833–838.

Marzillier, J. S., Lambert, C., & Kellett, J. (1976). A controlled evaluation of systematic desensitisation and social skills training for socially inadequate psychiatric patients. *Behaviour Research and Therapy, 14,* 225–238.

Mavissakalian, M. (1982). Agoraphobia: The problem of treatment. *Behavior Therapist, 5,* 173–175,

Mavissakalian, M., Michelson, L., Greenwald, D., Kornblith, S., & Greenwald, M. (1983). Cognitive-behavioral treatment of agoraphobia: Paradoxical intention vs. self-statement training. *Behaviour Research and Therapy, 21,* 75–86.

Meichenbaum, D. (1972). Cognitive modification of test anxious college students. *Journal of Consulting and Clinical Psychology, 39,* 370–380.

Meichenbaum, D. (1977). *Cognitive-behavior modification.* New York: Plenum Press.

Meichenbaum, D., & Gilmore, J. B. (1984). The nature of unconscious processes: A cognitive-behavioral perspective. In K. S. Bowers & D. Meichenbaum (Eds.), *The unconscious reconsidered.* New York: Wiley.

Melges, F. T. (1982). *Time and the inner future.* New York: Wiley.

Myklebust, H. R. (1964). *The psychology of deafness* (2nd ed.). New York: Grune & Stratton.

Ost, L. G., Jerremalm, A., & Johansson, J. (1981). Individual response patterns and the effects of different behavioral methods in the treatment of social phobia. *Behaviour Research and Therapy, 19,* 1–16.

Perry, C., & Laurence, J. (1984). Mental processing outside of awareness: The contributions of Freud and Janet. In K. S. Bowers & D. Meichenbaum (Eds.), *The unconscious reconsidered.* New York: Wiley.

Polanyi, M. (1966). *The tacit dimension.* Garden City, NY: Doubleday.

Polanyi, M. (1968). Logic and psychology. *American Psychologist, 23,* 27–43.

Pylyshyn, Z. W. (1973). What the mind's eye tells the mind's brain: A critique of mental imagery. *Psychological Bulletin, 80,* 1–24.

Rachman, S. (1978). Human fears: A three systems analysis. *Scandinavian Journal of Behavior Therapy, 7,* 37–245.

Rachman, S. (1980). Emotional processing. *Behaviour Research and Therapy, 18,* 51–60.

Rachman, S. (1981). The primacy of affect: Some theoretical implications. *Behaviour Research and Therapy, 19,* 279–290.

Rachman, S. (1984). Agoraphobia—A safety-signal perspective. *Behaviour Research and Therapy, 22,* 59–70.

Rachman, S., & Hodgson, R. I. (1974). Synchrony and desynchrony in fear and avoidance. *Behaviour Research and Therapy, 12,* 311–318.

Raimy, V. (1975). *Misunderstanding of the self.* San Francisco: Jossey-Bass.

Rathjen, D. P., Rathjen, E. D., & Hiniker, A. (1978). A cognitive analysis of social performance: Implications for assessment and treatment. In J. P. Foreyt & D. P. Rathjen (Eds.), *Cognitive behavior therapy: Research and application.* New York: Plenum Press.

Redmond, D. E., Jr. (1979). New and old evidence for the involvement of a brain norepinephrine system in anxiety. In W. E. Fann (Ed.), *The phenomenology and treatment of anxiety.* New York: Spectrum Press.

Reiman, E. M., Raichle, M. E., Butler, F. K., Herscovitch, P., & Robins, E. (1984). A focal brain abnormality in panic disorder, a severe form of anxiety. *Nature, 310,* 683–685.

Rosen, S. (1982). *My voice will go with you: The teaching tales of Milton. H. Erickson.* New York: Norton.

Seligman, M. E. P. (1971). Phobias and preparedness. *Behavior Therapy, 2,* 307–320.

Seligman, M., & Hager, J. (1972). *Biological boundaries of learning.* New York: Appleton-Century-Crofts.

Shader, R. I., Goodman, M., & Gever, J. (1982). Panic disorders: Current perspectives. *Journal of Clinical Psychopharmacology, 2,* 2S–10S.

Shaw, P. (1979). A comparison of three behaviour therapies in the treatment of social phobia. *British Journal of Psychiatry, 134,* 620–623.

Sheehan, D. V. (1982). Current perspectives in the treatment of panic and phobic disorders. *Drug Therapy, 12,* 179–193.

Sheehan, D. V. (1983). *The anxiety disease.* New York: Charles Scribner's Sons.

Sheehan, D. V., & Sheehan, K. H. (1982a). The classification of anxiety and hysterical states (Pt. 1): Historical review and empirical delineation. *Journal of Clinical Psychopharmacology, 2,* 235–243.

Sheehan, D. V., & Sheehan, K. H. (1982b). The classification of anxiety and hysterical states (Pt. 2): Toward a more heuristic classification. *Journal of Clinical Psychopharmacology, 2,* 386–393.

Shor, R. (1965). Three dimensions of hypnotic depth. In R. Shor & M. Orne (Eds.), *The nature of hypnosis.* New York: Holt, Rinehart and Winston.

Swartz, G. A., & Tracy, N. L. (Eds.). (1970). *Language-learning system and learning disability.* New York: Simon & Schuster.

Thomas, A., Chess, S., & Birch, H. G. (1968). *Temperament and behavior disorders in children.* New York: New York University Press.

Trower, P., Yardley, K., Bryant, B., & Shaw, P. (1978). The treatment of social failure: A comparison of anxiety-reduction and skills-acquisition procedures on two social problems. *Behavior Modification, 2,* 41–60.

Tversky, A., & Kahneman, D. (1973). Availability: A heuristic for judging frequency and probability. *Cognitive Psychology, 5*, 207–232.

Wachtel, P. L. (1977). *Psychoanalysis and behavior therapy: Toward an integration.* New York: Basic Books.

Waddell, M. T., Barlow, D. H., & O'Brian, G. T. (1984). Cognitive and relaxation treatment for panic disorders: Effects on panic versus "background" anxiety. *Behaviour Research and Therapy, 22*, 393–402.

Weekes, C. (1972). *Peace from nervous suffering.* New York: Hawthorn Books.

Weekes, C. (1978a). *Hope and help for your nerves.* New York: Bantam Books, 1978; New York: Hawthorn Books, 1969; London: Angus & Robertson (under the title *Self help for your nerves*).

Weekes, C. (1978b). Simple, effective treatment of agoraphobia. *American Journal of Psychotherapy, 32*, 357–369.

Weekes, C. (1983, May 7). Luncheon presentation: Fourth national phobia conference. White Plains, NY, Cassette. The Phobia Clinic, White Plains Hospital Medical Center, White Plains, NY 10601.

Weimer, W. B. (1977). A conceptual framework for cognitive psychology: Motor theories of the mind. In R. Shaw & J. D. Bransford (Eds.), *Perceiving, acting, and knowing: Toward an ecological psychology.* Hillsdale, NJ: Erlbaum.

Wheelis, A. (1973). *How people change.* New York: Harper & Row.

Williams, S. L., & Rappaport, A. (1983). Cognitive treatment in the natural environment for agoraphobics. *Behavior Therapy, 2*, 299–314.

Wilson, C. (1986). *The war against sleep.* Newcastle Publishers.

Wilson, G. T. (1980). Toward specifying the "nonspecific" factors in behavior therapy: A social-learning analysis. In M. J. Mahoney (Ed.), *Psychotherapy process: Current issues and future directions.* New York: Plenum Press, 1980.

Wilson, G. T. (1984). Fear reduction methods and the treatment of anxiety disorders. In G. T. Wilson, C. M. Franks, K. D. Brownell, & P. C. Kendall (Eds.), *Annual review of behavior therapy: Theory and practice* (Vol. 9). New York: Guilford Press.

Wise, E. H., & Haynes, S. N. (1983). Cognitive treatment of test anxiety: Rational restructuring versus attentional training. *Cognitive Therapy and Research, 7*, 69–77.

Wolpe, J. (1982). *The practice of behavior therapy* (3rd ed.). New York: Pergamon Press.

Zajonc, R. B. (1980). Feeling and thinking: Preferences need no inferences. *American Psychologist, 35*, 151–175.

Zajonc, R. B. (1984). On the primacy of emotion. *American Psychologist, 39*, 117–123.

Zane, M. D. (1978). Contextual analysis and treatment of phobic behavior as it changes. *American Journal of Psychotherapy, 32*, 338–356.

Zane, M. D. (1982). A method to study and conceptualize changes in phobic behavior. In R. L. DuPont (Ed.), *Phobia: A comprehensive summary of modern treatments.* New York: Brunner/Mazel.

Zane, M. D., & Milt, H. (1984). *Your phobia: Understanding your fears through contextual therapy.* Washington, DC: American Psychiatric Press.

2

Three Theoretical Perspectives on Anxiety: A Comparison of Theory and Outcome

ANDREW A. SWEET, THOMAS R. GILES, AND RENÉE R. YOUNG

The construction of a valid conceptualization of anxiety has been a goal of psychiatric endeavor since the advent of Freud's pioneering work. Consequently, a number of theoretical models of anxiety have been proposed, each with its own set of derivative treatment techniques. The purpose of this chapter is to compare three of the most prominent theoretical formulations of anxiety—the psychoanalytic, behavioral, and cognitive-behavioral approaches—with regard to their distinctions in theory, practice, and empirical support.

We can begin our comparison with the psychoanalytic perspective, particularly Freud's psychic determinism and the central role credited to anxiety in the so-called neuroses. Freud's views underwent several revisions, as did his theories on the role of the dynamic unconscious. Anxiety was first thought to be derived from unemployed libidinal urges, that is, that any interference in the discharge of sexual tensions resulted in anxious feelings and subsequent defensive operations such as repression (Gilliland, 1979). This was radically altered with Freud's 1926 publication of "Inhibitions, Symptoms, and Anxiety," wherein he described "primary anxiety," which could be traced to somatic sources—often to the birth process—as setting the model for "subsequent anxiety," which dealt with the separation from either the mother or another significant object, castration fears, or other crises (perceived or real) in psychosexual development (Freud, 1926/1959).

This second form of anxiety was possible only after ego had differentiated from id. Anxious feelings were thus the province of ego, and from here we enter Freud's familiar tripartite model of realistic, moral, and neurotic anxiety. Freud defined *realistic* anxiety as a response to a real external threat. He believed that this quality of unpleasure was still intimately related to one's early experiences of helplessness, but that it alone could not cause psychological problems. *Moral* anxiety was seen as the factory of shame and guilt feelings resulting from intrapsychic conflicts among the psychic structures, particularly ego versus superego. Finally, *neurotic* anxiety was described and further split into three possible manifestations: (1) as a focused symptom such as a phobic anxiety; (2) as a free-floating, almost aimless sense of unpleasure, an experience caused by multiple and

Andrew A. Sweet. Behavior Therapy Institute of Colorado, Denver, Colorado.

Thomas R. Giles. Eating Disorders Program, Rose Medical Center, Denver, Colorado.

Renée R. Young. Denver University School of Professional Psychology, Denver, Colorado.

unrelated stimuli; or (3) as a full-blown panic attack, neurotic anxiety's most crippling manifestation, which could result in the serious acting out of conflicts and the demand for instant gratification of one's impulses (Fischer, 1970). It is noteworthy that all neurotic forms of anxiety were still believed to result from the failure of the ego's defensive maneuvers to hold down "animal, asocial impulses" (Fischer, 1970, p. 14).

Key to Freud's 1926 reevaluation was the fact that anxiety was no longer construed as leading to defenses such as repression, but the exact opposite was held to be true. That is, when the defenses were inadequate or misused, anxious feelings were said to result.

This classical interpretation of anxiety still holds credence today for many dynamic practitioners, although much has been written theoretically about subsequent derivations (see Compton, 1972). For the psychodynamic theorists, there is an implied intrapsychic balance between the ego's defenses—allowing too much or too little to move into consciousness—and the drives that fuel the psychic complex. "Anxiety . . . [is] . . . a signal . . . response of the ego to the threat of an impending traumatic situation" (Nagera, Colonna, Danskey, First, Gavshon, Holder, Kearney & Radoford, 1970, p. 129). There is the belief that neurotic anxiety is evidence that our mental apparatus is working too hard (Gilman, 1982).

Subsequent psychoanalytic additions and revisions have broadened the possible roots of anxiety to include, among others, (1) a substitute for aggressive drives, (2) a social or superego condemnation, or (3) repressive fears (Compton, 1972). The neo-Freudian theorist Harry Stack Sullivan, whose ideas are currently undergoing a renaissance in psychodynamic circles (Coleman, Butcher, & Carson, 1984), saw anxiety as socially based and derived. Human behavior was conceptualized within an interpersonal context. Therefore, one would inevitably undergo social ridicule and/or condemnation, either real or perceived. For this theorist, "in anxiety the individual flees from his own experience [and therefore] . . . flees from himself." (Fischer, 1970, p. 34).

Ego psychology, another outgrowth of this school, is usually linked with writers such as Edith Jacobsen (1964), Melanie Klein (1969), and Ernst Kris (1975). Here the actual psychodynamics are downplayed in comparison to the various functions and struggles of the ego. Ego's interest in the world, its relations with external objects, and any distortions of these relations are the crucial subject matter. Although the concepts of psychic energy have survived here, more emphasis is given to the intrapsychic conflicts that arise as the result of introjected objects in the person's past that may be providing a model for current psychic, behavior, or affect dysfunctions. From this perspective, anxiety may come about either as a result of the autonomous ego's struggle to differentiate itself or from conflicting introjected morals, values, and symbolic representations. The major difference here is that anxiety is seen as potentially adaptive—a signal that the ego is struggling to identify itself. This is clearly a large step away from an instinct-based model. For these ego theorists, internal conflicts between wishes and fears are central to understanding anxiety (Fischer, 1970; see Compton, 1972, for a more complex description of this theoretical model). There is little basic research on these proposals, and the breadth as well as the complexity of some of the theoretical constructs have posed serious practical problems both for definition and for empirical validation.

The next historically relevant model was behaviorism, derived partly in strong reaction to the mentalistic and disease-based theories of psychoanalysis. Behaviorist roots stretch back in at least two discernible directions—that of Pavlov's work in the early twentieth century, leading to a classical or respondent conditioning model of behavior, and that of E. L. Thorndike and B. F. Skinner slightly later, which lead to the operant or instrumental models of learning.

Although there is clearly no consensus, even now, as to the specific role of classical and operant conditioning models in the etiology and treatment of anxiety (Davey, 1981; Kazdin & Wilson, 1978), behavior therapists have developed a number of paradigms for understanding this phenomenon. Working from a strict experimental position, Mowrer (1939) and Miller (1948) demonstrated that anxiety can be considered to be an internal state learned through classical conditioning. Once established, it would drive and reinforce avoidance behavior.

Two other prominent theorists, Eysenck (1957) and Wolpe (1958), came from a Hullian and Pavlovian background in their early efforts to understand anxiety. They studied both human and infrahuman populations and refined the experimental model for the classical conditioning of a "neurotic reaction." Eysenck (1957) posited a genetic predisposition to the acquisition of such neurotic reactions and combined that with the Pavlovian model to explain acquisition. Wolpe (1958) used his work with the conditioning of experimental neuroses in cats to support the Pavlovian position on the etiology of neurotic anxiety and the importance of reciprocal inhibition in its successful treatment. This reasoning led to the proposition that anxiety could be reduced by the juxtaposition of a relaxation response in human subjects. The outcome, systematic desensitization, is one of the most frequently used methods for the reduction of anxiety responses from a behavioral point of view.

One of the next crucial developments was contributed by Mowrer (1960), who elaborated the two-factor theory of anxiety acquisition and maintenance. In brief, Pavlovian trials were believed to cause the acquisition of conditioned anxiety responses to certain conditioned stimuli. Subsequent avoidance behavior in relation to the conditioned stimuli was believed to lead to, and reinforce, the severity of the conditioned response by removing the opportunity for extinction. Generalization of anxiety responses to salient environmental cues may then occur (see Schwartz, 1978, for an astute exposition of the melding of operant and classical learning paradigms). This two-factor theory has strongly influenced early behavioral treatments for anxiety (Kazdin & Wilson, 1978).

During the 1960s and early 1970s the conditioning models for the etiology and treatment of anxiety disorders prevailed. This was the heyday for studies of the effectiveness of systematic desensitization (Wolpe, 1958). The active mechanism Wolpe believed accounted for the success of this treatment was reciprocal inhibition. The neuronally based learning of an anxiety response could be disinhibited if the subject was experiencing an incompatible emotional response such as relaxation, sexual arousal, or anger. By constructing a hierarchy of increasingly difficult stimuli, the subject could, first imaginally and then actually, approach the fearsome stimuli without experiencing anxiety.

Another example of the influence of conditioning was the work of Cautela (1971) on covert conditioning. Here subjects may be asked to pair fearsome imagery or painful or distasteful images with their symbolic representations of stimuli they want to avoid. By so doing, it was believed, one could acquire a useful anxiety-avoidance response that was not present before. Examples of the uses for this might include the treatment of alcohol abusers or sexual deviancies.

Consistent with this work using simple conditioning models was the use of extinction paradigms. Flooding or implosive therapies were believed to work via this learning principle. During implosion (Levis, 1980; Stampfl & Levis, 1967), for instance, subjects were asked to imagine vividly exaggerated versions of their fears and to allow their anxiety to rise, peak, and extinguish after the neurons fatigued with repeated and unrelenting stimulation. This could be accomplished via imaginal work or with real-life intense exposure to the stimuli.

This work heralded another development, the use of exposure treatments in a more gradual fashion. Marks (1973, 1975, 1981) and colleagues have, since that time, demonstrated the variability in subjects' responses to exposure *in vivo*, and have renounced their belief in any connections between learning principles and exposure treatments. Other behavioral writers have retained a learning paradigm for understanding the effects of exposure therapies (Boyd & Levis, 1983; Mineka, 1979). The basic procedures of these exposure therapies involve having subjects expose themselves gradually and consistently to their fear-provoking situations. This exposure needs to be fairly intense, prolonged, and frequent, and is best practiced often within a short time span.

As we will discuss in a later section, these behavioral treatments had encouraging effects when evaluated with anxiety disorders. The theoretical bases of these techniques, however, have been unable to account for a number of important observations from human and infrahuman studies of fear. This failure may considerably change the application and theoretical conceptualization of modern behavior therapy.

One of the first steps in the revision process occurred with Lang's (e.g., 1968, 1971) reconceptualization of anxiety from a unitary construct—as was assumed with Pavlovian theory—to a tripartite version encompassing cognition, behavior, and physiology. Lang's work on snake phobias and much subsequent work on human fears (e.g., Lick, Sushinsky, & Malow, 1977; Rachman, 1974; Rachman & Hodgson, 1974) indicated that these three response systems often vary in a desynchronous fashion. Some subjects can approach feared objects despite significant levels of subjective anxiety. Others report complete cessation of fear despite robust responses on one or more physiological indicators. Still others report extreme levels of fear without concomitant physiological excitation.

These factors led to treatment considerations encompassing all three response systems. Barlow, Mavissakalian, and Schofield (1980), for example, noted that cessation of behavioral avoidance was unaccompanied by diminution of physiological (heart-rate) response in one agoraphobic subject. This subject later relapsed. Rachman (1977) speculated that variation between subjects' response patterns to fear may indicate variations in etiology. A major implication of these findings is that treatment effectiveness may be augmented by a broad-based assessment of fear response followed by implementation of treatment technique according to which fear-relevant factors are predominant (see Hugdahl, 1981).

Another important finding contributing to the revision of simple conditioning theory is the acquisition of fear responses through vicarious or strictly informational processes (Rachman, 1977). For example, in the history of many phobic cases, there is no evidence of traumatic conditioning trials preceding the onset of the problem. Subjects in several laboratory experiments have acquired anxiety responses to conditioned stimuli by observing other subjects who were subjected to contingent shock (CS) (e.g., Ohman, 1979).

The equipotentiality assumption of conditioning theory—that is, that all conditioned stimuli are equally associable—has also yielded to data indicating that phobias have an uneven distribution across the range of possible CSs (Seligman, 1971). Seligman (1971) explained this finding by proposing that human beings are genetically predisposed to acquire certain fears. Similarly, fears like those observed with agoraphobia are most heavily distributed among young adult women (Mathews, Gelder, & Johnston, 1981). These findings are not entirely consistent with the simple conditioning model (see Rachman, 1977, and deSilva & Rachman, 1981, for additional problems with this paradigm).

Using many of these revisions and refinements, behavioral writers have attempted to account for and treat the many manifestations of clinical anxiety, including so-called free-floating anxiety (Hare & Levis, 1981); agoraphobic syndromes (Goldstein & Chambless, 1978); obsessive–compulsive disorders (Foa & Steketee, 1979); and simple or focused phobic reactions (Emmelkamp, 1979, 1982). Meanwhile, the etiological issues are still being hotly debated (Bellack, Hersen, & Kazdin, 1982; Emmelkamp, 1982; Marks, 1975, 1981; Rachman, 1976; Wolpe, 1982; Eysenck, 1976; Staats, in press). As might be expected, several of these authors advocate a return to the conditioning model and attempt to revise it to account for discrepancies (e.g., Eysenck, 1976). However, a number of other writers, some devoted advocates of conditioning theory in their early work (see Rachman, 1976), now advocate a turn from conditioning theory to theories that emphasize cognition in the etiology and treatment of human fears (see Bandura, 1977). This development may provide both a theoretical and a therapeutic integration of behavior therapy with cognitive behavior therapy. We will discuss this in greater detail later on.

The third and most recently proposed model for the conceptualization of anxiety problems has grown out of the historical learning theory base presented earlier, as well as other social learning theory models. The roots of cognitive-behavior modification (Mahoney, 1974; Mahoney & Arnkoff, 1978) have been linked to Tolman's (1948) cognitive maps, Rotter's (1954) learning of expectancies, and Bandura's (1969) work on vicarious learning processes. Although the scope, bounds, and definition of cognitive-behavior therapy are still in question (Thoresen, 1980; Mahoney & Arnkoff, 1978), proponents share one critical assumption that differs from our previous formulations. All leading theorists (Ellis, 1962; Mahoney, 1974; Meichenbaum, 1977; Beck & Emery, 1985) support the notion that cognitive mediational processes are central to the experience of anxiety and therefore are central to the development of valid approaches to treatment.

The conditioning models are seen as partially useful in studying anxiety, but the cognitive processing of the organism's environment and behavior are central to the cognitive behaviorist's reciprocally determined view of behavior (Agras, Kazdin, & Wilson, 1979, p. 12). The person is seen as "both the agent and the object of environmental influence" (Agras et al., 1979, p. 12). To contrast this with the more radical behavioral positions discussed earlier, behavior of any sort (in this case anxiety) is the sole product of environmental influences. This is viewed both historically, as in the case of classical conditioning, and from a maintenance point of view whereby fear "behavior" is reinforced and develops through generalization processes. The cognitivist does not stop here, however. Organisms are constantly processing and evaluating their environment, so that the interaction of these attributions and conclusions is inextricable from the anxiety response. Thus, within the cognitive-behavioral movement there is commitment to the use of behavioral principles and therapy to promote change (i.e., Beck & Emery, 1985), but more emphasis is placed on the modification of cognitions, beliefs, self-statements, coping responses, and problem-solving strategies (Meichenbaum & Cameron, 1982).

During our attempts to delineate the differences between the cognitive-behavioral approaches and the previously discussed model, we have noted an enormous task in sifting out the "cognitive" from the "behavioral" positions because so many of the foundations have been similar. Perhaps the most useful direction for this chapter would be to understand the historical process that led to the development of cognitive-behavioral approaches as distinct from behavioral conceptions of anxiety.

The arrival of Bandura's (1969) work describing the phenomenon of vicarious learning (without direct reinforcement or conditioning of the organism) is often seen as the major point of divergence for cognitive-behavior modifiers. It was here that the role of attribution, information processing, and thus "cognition" was seen as crucial to understanding anxiety and behavior in general.

As mentioned earlier, the cognitive supporters would later find useful foundations in the works of Kelly (1955) and Ellis (1962) among others. But the crucial difference in the work of Bandura (1969) was that these previous authors did not ascribe to a learning theory model, nor did they come from an experimental psychology background. George Kelly and Albert Ellis broke away from other traditions in clinical psychology to develop their own models. Thus the case has been made by Wilson (1978) that the roots of cognitive-behavioral explanations for psychological phenomena have always been grounded in social-learning theory. As we will see, though, the more recent history finds several divergences from the social learning base.

One of the key contributors to the development of cognitive-behavioral approaches to anxiety was a body of literature that disputed the "simple" conditioning of human beings (Breger & McGaugh, 1965; Brewer, 1974). The major point made here was that an awareness, or some cognitive activity, was necessary for us to understand the human conditioning literature. Mahoney (1974) was one of the first writers to collect much of these data together in supporting his landmark work proposing the cognitive "revolution" in behavior therapy. His work did not really deal with anxiety in itself, but with the whole area of behavior change. In fact, there is little in his book (Mahoney, 1974) dealing directly with anxiety except a review of some of the studies done that supported the usefulness of a cognitive restructuring component in treating analogue anxiety states (test, snake, and speech anxieties).

One of the next relevant developments was Meichenbaum's work (1977) discussing the use of self-instructional training and stress innoculation skills. Anxiety was not dealt with very directly in this book either, but some supportive evidence for adding a self-instructional component to a standard systematic desensitization procedure was offered (Meichenbaum, 1977, pp. 123–124).

The work of both Mahoney and Meichenbaum was presented concurrently with the studies of other writers and researchers who examined the management of anxiety states. Goldfried (1971) and colleagues (Goldfried, Decenteceo, & Weinberg, 1974) presented a theoretical modification to Wolpe's (1958) systematic desensitization model for coping with anxiety. In each case, cognitive coping skills, along with the direct retraining of thought processes through scenes of difficulty for the client, were offered as a way to bolster the effects of this behavioral treatment package. In the same vein, Suinn and his colleagues (Suinn & Richardson, 1971; Suinn, 1975) presented a similar model for Anxiety Management Training with some encouraging supportive data.

In none of the aforementioned works was any cognitive-behavioral theory of anxiety offered, as such. Instead, the idea was presented that a cognitive component of anxiety was evident and that direct cognitive intervention was indicated, which may lead to improvements on the traditional treatment model derived from behavior therapy.

Other cognitive writers have discussed anxiety in general terms. Ellis (1962) and Beck (1976) have both remarked on the future orientation of anxiogenic cognitions and the tendency for the anxiety sufferer to overgeneralize about the meaning of stimuli. Our search of these works did not reveal any broader conceptual view point. Beck and Emery (1985), however, have published a book explicating the cognitive views on anxiety states and treatment. To date, it is the single most comprehensive effort from the cognitive-behavioral school to account for the variety and depth of anxiety as it is seen clinically.

In this book, Beck and Emery (1985) offer the proposition that the cognitive schemas and automatic thoughts that are typical of anxiety states play a crucial role in the development and maintenance of anxiety disorders. Misperceptions about bodily reactions are frequent. Clients with different anxiety disorders are believed to overgeneralize in different ways, which can lead to various manifestations of the problem. These cognitive styles are rehearsed and are very directly related to the way in which these clients see themselves as unable to cope with or to bear what they are experiencing. The book addresses the three types of anxiety previously discussed; phobic, free-floating, and panic. This addition to the literature is a significant step for the cognitive-behavioral theory of anxiety, and supportive empirical evidence is needed to further these clinical propositions. Beck and Emery (1979) have published a manual for interested researchers that is cited in the postscript to their current book (Beck & Emery, 1985).

Finally, one other set of writers have offered a comprehensive theory of anxiety (Guidano & Liotti, 1983). Drawing more divergently on the works of Bowlby (1969, 1973) and Piaget (1926) in developmental theory, as well as some philosophers of science, these writers have constructed a heuristically complex and potentially useful cognitive-developmental model for understanding anxiety disorders. They present what they have discovered clinically to support this theory of the structure of cognitive sets, and the system of cognitions used to protect the underlying cognitive structures. Their book recommends methods and techniques, both cognitive and behavioral, for facilitating changes in the deep cognitive structures of clients suffering from anxiety problems.

The models for a cognitive-behavioral view of anxiety have developed, in some respects, as an outgrowth of behavioral models, but have started to bring in other frameworks to explain the complexity of anxiety responses. These researchers were interested not only in the types of cognitions their subjects were having, but also in their images, fantasies, cognitive avoidance strategies, and overt behavior. The experimental cognitive psychology literature is seen as one potentially useful avenue for this trend (Meichenbaum & Cameron, 1982). Effectiveness of the treatment outcomes is now being measured by the observables that characterize the behavioral literature, as well as by looking at changes in private speech, core cognitive structures, and images. This is proving to be a particularly challenging task (see Nisbett & Wilson, 1977).

In sum, the cognitive behaviorists regard anxiety as an autonomic/behavioral/ cognitive response set that can be directly related to irrational beliefs (Ellis, 1962); faulty or maladaptive cognitions (Beck & Emery, 1985); or central and core cognitions that perpetuate the entire response set (Guidano & Liotti, 1983; McMullin & Giles, 1981). These writers may differentially employ cognitive restructuring techniques and behavioral assignments in their therapy. All these writers would also agree that without deep structural or philosophical changes, lasting improvements will be unlikely. This position is difficult to prove as well as to conceptualize. One example is that Guidano and Liotti (1983) searched through clients' verbal behavior and self-reports to see that "self-schemas" had been revised as the result of therapeutic efforts. A client with agoraphobia not only might be having fewer panic attacks and not avoiding places, but also should be confronting other difficulties in his or her life situations such as marriage, job changes, or becoming independent from parents. These behavioral indices may be used to indicate that the client has experienced "deeper" changes than just symptom relief.

Ellis (1962) might discuss the breadth of philosophical change in relation to existence. He too would regard clients' verbal reports of changes in thinking with a special antenna for places or situations where clients might be protecting their use of an irrational or maladaptive belief. A female client, for instance, may move through her fear of rejection at work but retain maladaptive thought–behavior sequences in relation to rejection from parents or a close friend. A rational-emotive therapist would use a broad-based assessment to determine the degree of shift in personal psychology.

Finally, there is one other observation concerning the interaction between behavioral and cognitive-behavioral models. Recent years have seen a strong shift in the behavioral journals towards the objective study of cognitive processes in anxiety and other emotional states. Concurrently, there has been a move by many cognitive-behaviorists, such as Beck and Ellis, to be seen within the realm of behavior therapy in some fashion. This shift is particularly interesting since both Beck and Ellis were originally trained in the psychodynamic mold and moved away from this model in a more cognitive direction. Now both have placed themselves firmly within the cognitive-behavioral camp, and there is no indication that this will change in the near future. It seems that the methodological rigor of the behaviorists has attracted the cognitive therapists and that the clinically useful and interesting propositions of the cognitive-behaviorists have attracted the behavioral clinicians.

This return to mentalistic models and constructs has naturally caused much debate (Wolpe, 1976a, 1976b; Ledwidge, 1978, 1979; Ross, 1985). Proponents of cognitive-behavioral therapies (Meichenbaum & Cameron, 1982) and others (Beidel & Turner, 1986; Bellack, Hersen, & Kazdin, 1982) have argued that the proverbial cart of cognitive-behavioral treatments may have been put before the horse of a sound theoretical base. This has led some writers to become increasingly divergent in their conceptual development (Mahoney, 1977) while others have called for a careful reexamination of the learning literature and a return to operant and classical paradigms (Wolpe, 1976a; Eysenck, 1982; Elliott, 1982; Flaherty, 1985) and to basic experimental psychology literature (Ross, 1985) in an effort to ground current clinical practices in empirical support. Some leaders in the field have suggested that clinical decisions and progress ought to be clearly guided by the current experimental evidence regardless of technique, theory, or school allegiance (Kazdin & Wilson, 1978; Turner, Calhoun, & Adams, 1981).

Three models for thinking about anxiety have been proposed. Although each has certain distinguishing characteristics, we have seen some blending occurring as we approach the recent past. Perhaps the most useful steps at this point will be (1) to examine more closely the implications of each model by considering some application differences, and (2) to look at the comparative outcome literature in anxiety disorders.

Application

Probably the most useful way to approach this comparison task is to select several key application issues and examine how each of the models treats these. We have selected those deemed critical to a useful comparison: the therapeutic relationship and theorized change pathways ("What changes first?"). These conceptualizations have had a major influence on the treatment techniques characteristic of each school.

The therapeutic relationship is given quite different emphasis by each of these three positions. Psychodynamically oriented psychotherapists would assign the greatest amount of curative power to the relationship factor in treatments. First, a transference relationship would be fostered with the client. It is theorized that all the client's conflicts and emotional difficulties will display themselves within this relationship. Because these theorists believe so strongly in the power of one's early relationships with parental figures, it is assumed that many of the intrapsychic and interpersonal difficulties that arose in one's upbringing will arise again in the therapeutic relationship. At these points they will be "worked through" in more adaptive ways, resolving the conflicts so that anxiety symptoms are lessened. The contemporary ego-analytic thinkers have changed this therapeutic structure. The focus on ego functioning leads clinicians working from this model to build ego strengths directly and to focus on more reality-based perceptions rather than necessarily on historically relevant events or "pure insight" into the role of these events. In both the traditional psychodynamic view and the ego-analytic model, clients' reactions to the therapist and significant others in the present and past environments are the data of immediate concern. Thus the relationship factor is central from these theoretical viewpoints.

Psychodynamic treatment, being based on an explorative, unfolding, and less directive model of intervention, may take several years. The working through of the client's conflicts within this therapy relationship is expected to take time. Clients' defenses, their ego deficits and assets, and the transference process must all be formulated, analyzed, and used in offering interpretations and facilitating insights that will lead to affective and behavioral changes. The termination process is often given extra time because of the crucial role credited to the therapeutic alliance.

The behavioral view of the therapeutic relationship has, by contrast, received very little attention in the literature (see Sweet, 1984). Historically, however, any power believed to exist in the relationship's curative effect was explained from a social learning model. In other words, if in fact clients do find the relationship important, this is held to be so because of the social reinforcement, modeling, and support with which they are provided.

In relation to anxiety disorders in particular, the curative factors are believed to be technique-based, such as exposure *in vivo* or systematic desensitization, rather than resulting from any other relationship factor. There is growing evidence (Sweet, 1984), however, that the quality of the relationship does interact with the variable of technique in being able to predict positive outcomes. This is obviously more true in those cases where the relationship is judged to be good. From the behavioral viewpoint, then, the therapeutic alliance is seen as a *context* for change where the therapist's expertise in helping clients to apply learning principles to their difficulties is regarded as central. The length of treatment is generally regarded as brief; and, since the focus in behavior therapy is on skill acquisition and deconditioning of maladaptive responses, the relationship is only the means to this end, not the focus of the therapy work itself. The process of termination is regarded within a framework of generalizing the new behaviors and responses to the exterior environment. Sessions may be faded over a short time, but, in contrast to the psychodynamicists, little emphasis is placed here.

Cognitive-behavioral clinicians take a slightly different view of their relationship with their clients. Their position might best be described as collaborative (Beck & Emery, 1985). In his review of the cognitive-behavioral movement in 1981, Wilson cited a comment in a paper by Mahoney and Arnkoff (1978, p. 13): ". . . the task of the therapist is that of a diagnostician–educator who assesses the maladaptive cognitive processes and subsequently arranges for learning experiences which will alter cognitions and in turn, the behavior–affect patterns with which they correlate."

This view is only one of the possible positions taken by cognitive-behavioral therapists. For example, Ellis (1962) and Maultsby (1975) have distinctly underplayed the role of the therapeutic relationship and talk more specifically about the role of the therapist as a direct change agent/educator via rational debate, rational behavior homework, and socratic discussion.

Another contrasting position is offered by Guidano and Liotti (1983). They discuss a gentler, slower therapeutic process wherein the therapist at first respects the client's cognitive structures. Gradually, as the process continues, a more challenging position is taken within the context of the relationship, which these writers see as crucial. This model of the relationship could be regarded as closer to the psychodynamic model. Both Guidano and Liotti (1983) and Beck and Emery (1985) have addressed the direct processing of the therapy relationship in sessions as often necessary and useful, saying that this may lead to greater movement in treatment. Neither, however, would claim the central role of this factor in treatment.

In other words, there are many ways in which the cognitive-behavioral writers have addressed this important issue, no one of which has yet captured the majority position in this field. This may well change as an empirical base is formed, a consistent model is elucidated, and the appropriate techniques and factors accounting for change are deduced.

The length of treatment within this model is also quite varied, although estimates have placed it in the same range as the length of behavioral treatment, or as long as 79 sessions on average (Guidano & Liotti, 1983). The amount of treatment time is matched to individual clients and particularly to the range and depth of their dysfunctional belief systems. The collaborative effort continues until both client and therapist deem that it is no longer needed. Termination is processed as it relates to clients' self-attributions for the changes they have made. The focus is on building a sense of self-efficacy, on leniency with one's patterns and life's stressors, and on compounding the newly gained understandings of the client's cognitive processes.

Change Pathways and Techniques

The target for what changes first in the treatment of anxiety disorders varies significantly according to theoretical orientation. Psychodynamic theory is heavily based on the medical model, whereby anxiety disorders are synonomous with disease states of the psyche. Therefore, a first step in the psychodynamic treatment of anxiety involves the detection and *diagnosis* of those underlying disturbances. The diagnostic process involves the use of labels and the description of personality traits and conflicts believed to motivate anxiogenic symptoms.

The assumption of underlying, unconscious motivation provides the basis for the psychodynamic conceptualization of what must change first in the treatment of anxiety disorders. The subjective experience of anxiety, as well as its behavioral manifestations, is considered *symptomatic* of unconscious psychic causes that must be brought to awareness and worked through before any lasting cure can result.

This process can be illustrated with the classical analytic interpretation of agoraphobia. According to this viewpoint, the agoraphobic patient, typically female, suffers from deep dependency needs that are the manifestation of underlying sexual conflicts. The conflicts are typically hypothesized to result from the patient's repressed hostility at not having a penis. This hostility results in powerful urges to exhibit herself in public and thus expose her mother's "crime" (i.e., in not supplying her with a penis). These unconscious urges are deeply disturbing to the patient, who defends against them by becoming unassertive, ingratiating, and severely reclusive (Fenichel, 1945).

Such theorizing makes evident that the principal pathway to change in psychodynamic treatment is in establishing awareness of the underlying conflicts and personality disturbances that cause the symptomatology. Details of the specific manifestations of anxiety and their situational determinants are considered less important. Compared to behavior therapy, psychodynamic therapy is nondirective and interpretive and much more focused on the symbolic nature of patient verbalizations within the confines of the consulting room. The analytic therapist often plays the role of a passive listener, allowing patients to project various aspects of repressed material onto the therapist's "blank screen." This in turn leads to analysis of the transference relationship, free association, dream interpretation, and analytic–interpretive attempts to relate past events to present symptomology. According to theory, this process must lead to conflict awareness and working through *before* lasting change or cure can result.

In contrast to the insight-oriented emphasis of psychodynamic therapy, behavior therapy for anxiety disorders relies more on empirical principles and models of learning.

Following Wolpe's (1958) lead, behavior therapists began to view anxiety disorders not as symptomatic of underlying psychopathology but as maladaptive response habits acquired predominantly through classical conditioning. As a result of this conceptualization, subjective and behavioral aspects of anxiety have become the direct targets of intervention for behavior therapists. Personality constructs and dynamics are not recognized as determinants of behavior. Instead, situational factors are emphasized. Pretreatment assessment is concerned less with diagnosis than with thoughts, feelings, and actions as they occur within a definable stimulus context.

Wolpe (1958) used the principle of reciprocal inhibition to derive a number of treatment interventions for which behavior therapy is recognized—systematic desensitization, assertiveness training, and sex therapy. This in turn spawned many studies that generally found desensitization techniques to be effective procedures in the treatment of anxiety disorders (e.g., Paul, 1966). During this period in the mid- and late 1960s, anxiety reduction via desensitization was usually the primary goal of behavioral intervention. Although anxiety was treated more directly with behavior therapy than with traditional psychotherapy, the latter theoretical positions shared in common the attempt to change internal, subjective processes in order for the behavioral manifestations of anxiety to change subsequently.

The emphasis gradually began to change with the work of Marks and colleagues (e.g., Marks, 1981), who evaluated the effects of different treatment modalities for phobias. Noting that group and individual psychotherapy for these problems was seldom effective, these researchers began to evaluate the effects of systematic desensitization. Several subsequent comparative studies led to the conclusion that desensitization was more effective than traditional treatment for agoraphobia, social phobia, and simple phobia, and often necessitated fewer sessions (Gelder, Marks, & Wolff, 1967). Further studies found desensitization superior to hypnosis (Marks, Gelder, & Edwards, 1968) but just as effective as imaginal flooding in the treatment of agoraphobia (Gelder, Bancroft, Gath, Johnston, Mathews, & Shaw, 1973).

After a number of such studies, investigators became aware that subjects who practiced *in vivo* exposure assignments between desensitization sessions seemed more likely to improve. This discovery provided the impetus for the study of exposure *in vivo* techniques for the treatment of agoraphobia. Although the magnitude of results did not usually exceed that of desensitization in initial studies, therapy time was significantly reduced when exposure techniques were used. This finding led to further evaluation of various treatment parameters that maximized the effectiveness of exposure treatment for anxiety disorders. It also led to the establishment of exposure with response prevention as an effective treatment for bulimia, now considered an anxiety-related disorder (Giles, Young, & Young, 1985), and as the treatment of choice for obsessive–compulsive disorders (the reader is referred to Mathews, Gelder, & Johnston, 1981, for a historical review of this literature).

As a result of studies like those cited here, the primary target of behavioral intervention began to change. Instead of attempting to reduce anxiety in order for phobic behavior to change, more emphasis was given to changing behavior first so that anxiety reduction, presumably through extinction processes, could subsequently occur.

Interestingly, the cognitive-behavioral movement has followed a similar trend.

Early cognitive therapists such as Albert Ellis downplayed traditional learning theory and attributed the cause of all human emotions, including anxiety, to cognition (e.g., Ellis, 1962). Ellis expressed this in terms of an A–B–C model where A was "antecedent event," B was "belief," and C was an emotional or behavioral "consquence." According to this model, antecedents lead to emotional consequences through the intervening action of thought. It is well known, for example, that agoraphobics typically fear a number of antecedents such as crowds, subways, shopping malls, long bridges, and airplane rides. Their emotional consequences include anticipatory fear reactions and severe anxiety once the situations are confronted. The early cognitive theorists, however, were most interested in the agoraphobics' *beliefs* about these situations. Assessment of the cognitive basis of this type of fear might typically reveal the following:

1. I cannot stand to confront my fear.
2. My fear will overwhelm me and cause me to panic.
3. Panic means I will faint or go crazy.
4. Then everyone will laugh at me and think I am strange.
5. It would be awful and catastrophic to be ridiculed. I could not stand it.
6. Everyone must like me.

Initial cognitive-behavioral therapies for such problems focused primarily on verbal/persuasive techniques. A rational-emotive therapist, for example, after assessing the beliefs listed here, might first attempt to convince the client of the irrationality of these beliefs by means of logical and rational argument. The therapist also would be likely to dispute them vigorously during the session. The client would then be advised to facilitate this process between sessions predominantly by means of self-talk—that is, by actively restating or rethinking the reasons for the basic irrationality of his or her beliefs.

As the cognitive-behavioral movement gained increasing acceptance, a number of interesting variations on cognitive techniques were observed in the literature. A. T. Beck's approach, for example, included having the client keep logs of anxiety-provoking thoughts occurring in problematic situations. Clients were advised to write down the specific belief(s), label the logical error involved, and write a counterstatement. Self-disputation by rational counterthinking was also encouraged. The therapist would work collaboratively with the client within each session—through either structural questioning or socratic dialogue—to increase his or her awareness of the illogical nature of the anxiety-related thoughts.

Similarly, therapists using so-called stress inoculation techniques taught clients to prepare for anxiety stressors by means of rational self-talk. Counterstatements were also delineated for use both when the antecedent was being confronted and when the confrontation was terminated. These techniques included not only preparatory statements and rational counters but also instructions for relaxation, deep breathing, coping imagery, and cognitive rehearsal (Meichenbaum, 1977).

Another variant of these procedures is cognitive-restructuring therapy, developed by McMullin and colleagues (e.g., McMullin & Giles, 1981, McMullin, 1986). An intervention representative of this therapy involves the construction of SUDS (subjective units of discomfort scale) hierarchies of antecedent events in fashion similar to that of systematic desensitization. The client is instructed to visualize an anxiety-provoking situation and then vigorously to counter the thoughts that accompany it. Once anxiety is eliminated with this particular visualization, the client is advised to practice the same procedure between sessions both in imagination and *in vivo* until anxiety is significantly overcome. The next item in the hierarchy is then addressed similarly. The available outcome data for this procedure suggest that it may be superior to traditional psychotherapy for anxiety disorders (McMullin, Giles, & Turner, 1982).

The thread of consistency among all these procedures is their reliance on verbal or cognitive counterstatements to modify cognition. This in turn is assumed to ameliorate anxiety and the dysfunctional behavior that may result from it.

As a result of outcome research on *in vivo* exposure and of Bandura's (1977) exposition of self-efficacy theory, the effectiveness of verbal change techniques began to be questioned, and so-called performance-based interventions began gaining favor. Bandura argued that although vicarious or cognitive processes play a significant role in the acquisition of anxiety, the resultant lack of self-efficacy can be modified most effectively by changing behavior. It is noteworthy that many cognitive-behavior therapists, including Ellis (1985, personal communication) and Beck and Emery (1985), currently advocate this approach.

We will review the evidence on the performance assumption in the following section. At this point, however, it is apparent that despite theoretical differences between traditional behavior therapy and cognitive-behavior therapy, both seem to be converging on the use of behavior change techniques as a *first* step toward the modification of affect and cognition. However, an important difference is that cognitive-behavior therapists try to change the cognitive and behavioral components of the anxiety response simultaneously. They propose that anxiety results from the interaction of cognitive and behavior response sets. One example would be the use of exposure to the fearful stimulus and the concurrent use of coping statements like: "This is *only* fear. I won't die. I *can* stand this, and it will eventually abate." We address the empirical status of this approach in the following section.

Comparative Outcome

The efficacy of the three types of treatments discussed earlier has been evaluated by relatively extensive research. The present accumulation of evidence indicates that differences in therapeutic effectiveness and efficiency exist among orientations. Since the question of outcome is of paramount importance to the field, we will next briefly review the status of research according to orientation.

Psychodynamic Psychotherapy

Eysenck (1952) was the first to question whether traditional psychotherapy was more effective than no treatment controls. His review indicated that a curious effect labeled spontaneous remission in untreated control groups equaled the effect on patients of long-term, generally psychoanalytically oriented psychotherapy. The issue of spontaneous recovery led in turn to a long history of outcome evaluations yielding additional findings that have disappointing implications for the field. To summarize these briefly:

1. Dynamic psychotherapy appeared to be more effective than no treatment in some studies, but only equally effective in most.
2. The type of traditional psychotherapy—psychodynamic, psychoanalytic, ego-analytic, or Rogerian—usually did not differentiate outcome.
3. Long-term psychotherapy was no more effective than time-limited (brief) psychotherapy.
4. The type of therapist—male versus female, experienced versus inexperienced, professional versus paraprofessional—did not usually differentiate outcome in the expected direction (for a review of this literature, see Rachman & Wilson, 1980).

These initial findings led to further, more sophisticated outcome research and reviews. A noteworthy example was the study by Sloane, Staples, Cristol, Yorkston, and Whipple (1975), which found dynamic psychotherapy superior to a no-treatment control for a general outpatient population. In a subsequent review, Luborsky, Singer, and Luborsky (1975) concluded that psychotherapy was "effective" but that all psychotherapies, with the possible exception of behavior therapy for simple phobia, were equally effective. Finally, two meta-analytic studies by Smith and Glass (1977) and Andrews and Harvey (1981) indicated that patients treated with psychotherapy did somewhat better than patients receiving no treatment. The Andrews and Harvey paper is somewhat more relevant to this chapter because it focuses more predominantly on anxiety disorders. (Behavior therapy was found significantly more effective than psychotherapy in this paper.)

Rachman and Wilson (1980) exhaustively reviewed and discussed Sloane et al. (1975), Luborsky et al. (1975), Smith and Glass (1977), and the rest of the outcome literature on psychotherapy. Their review uncovered numerous methodological shortcomings in this research. The outcome of traditional psychotherapy was judged as follows (Rachman & Wilson, 1980, p. 93):

> To conclude, there is modest evidence to support the claim that psychotherapy can produce beneficial changes. The negative results still outnumber the positives, and both are exceeded by the number of uninterpretable results. The strength and breadth of the persistent, unquestioned faith in the value of psychotherapy rests on insubstantial foundations.

This conclusion led to the further proposal that outcome researchers ask better questions. Instead of "Is psychotherapy effective?" we should ask "Which interventions are effective with which kinds of problems?" Unfortunately, a number of reviews have indicated that the psychodynamically oriented psychotherapies have yet to be shown more effective than a credible placebo for any of the anxiety disorders (Kazdin & Wilson, 1978; Rachman & Wilson, 1980).

Although the implications of this conclusion are at once significant and discouraging, they are consistent with the "equivalence of therapies" hypothesis proposed by a number of proponents of psychotherapy who are familiar with outcome research (see Giles, 1983a, for review). These experts essentially agree with the conclusion of Luborsky et al. (1975) that the major orientations of psychotherapy, including behavior therapy, are theoretically misguided. In this view, the effectiveness of therapy has nothing to do with techniques in themselves but depends on as yet unelucidated elements common to all therapies (Strupp & Hadley, 1979).

The equivalence of therapies hypothesis has gained wide acceptance in the literature. As Rachman and Wilson (1980) have noted, however, those who support this hypothesis appear to have ignored a number of behavioral outcome studies in their reviews. With a wide range of psychological problems, and perhaps especially with anxiety disorders, behavior therapy and cognitive-behavior therapy appear to be the treatments of choice.

Behavior Therapy and Cognitive-Behavior Therapy

A thorough review of the behavioral and cognitive-behavioral treatment of anxiety disorders would encompass hundreds of studies and thus exceed the scope of this chapter. The primary purpose of this section, therefore, is simply to elucidate the point that differences in outcome between treatments have been documented.

In contrast to dynamic psychotherapy, behavioral and cognitive-behavioral techniques such as flooding, systematic desensitization, exposure *in vivo*, and paradoxical intention have therapeutic effects exceeding those of placebo. This has been demonstrated with single case studies, with studies showing one behavioral technique superior to another or to a credible placebo, and with studies indicating that the effectiveness of a proven intervention such as systematic desensitization or exposure *in vivo* is increased either by varying the application of the intervention or by adding other behavioral or cognitive-behavioral techniques (Giles, 1983b). To illustrate the latter point, the evidence suggests that the effectiveness of exposure *in vivo* for agoraphobia is improved by greater frequency (massing) of exposure sessions (Foa, Jamison, Turner, & Payne, 1980) as well as by long durations of exposure (Stern & Marks, 1973). The addition of paradoxical intention (Ascher, 1981) and spouse-assisted exposure (Barlow, O'Brien, & Last, 1984) also seems to increase the effectiveness of this technique.

Numerous reviews have concluded that such procedures are the treatments of choice for anxiety disorders such as social phobia, obsessive–compulsive disorder, agoraphobia, generalized anxiety disorder, and simple phobia, as well as for anxiety-related disorders such as insomnia and bulimia (e.g., Rachman & Wilson, 1980).

A recent review of the literature added weight to the conclusion that cognitive and behavioral interventions are more effective than traditional psychotherapy. This review listed 53 studies showing significant differences between treatments (Giles, 1983b). Many of these studies were conducted on anxiety disorders. Treatments using either behavioral or cognitive-behavioral techniques were superior to traditional treatments in all 53 studies.

It should be evident from this discussion that the outcome of behavior therapy and cognitive-behavior therapy is comparatively encouraging. However, these therapies are very difficult to distinguish on the basis of outcome alone. Since the resolution of this problem may eventually provide a substantial influence on clinical practice, we next discuss some of the current difficulties in differentiation and their implications for future directions in the field.

The major point of confusion is that the theoretical bases of both behavior therapy and cognitive-behavior therapy have been used to explain the efficacy of techniques derived from both camps (Beidel & Turner, 1986). For example, it is well known that systematic desensitization was derived from Hullian learning concepts that heavily emphasized the role of classical conditioning in both the acquisition and the extinction of maladaptive anxiety responses. Though not denying the effectiveness of systematic desensitization, writers supporting the cognitive position have tended to explain the efficacy of desensitization with terms such as *cognitive restructuring* (Breger & McGaugh, 1965), *expectancy/placebo* (Kazdin & Wilcoxon, 1976), and *self-efficacy* (Bandura, 1977). Similarly, though granting the potential utility of cognitive restructuring procedures, behaviorists explained change mechanisms with such traditional concepts as reciprocal inibition (McMullin & Giles, 1981) and response competition (Staats, 1975).

Although reviews of outcome literature conclude that exposure *in vivo* techniques are preferred for such problems as agoraphobia and obsessive–compulsive disorder, the *explanations* for the efficacy of exposure vary according to orientation. Behaviorists tend to explain it in terms of anxiety inhibition from the extinction of unreinforced conditional stimulus (CS) exposure. Predictably, however, cognitive behaviorists attribute results to core cognitive change (e.g., Bandura, 1977). Similar differences in theory are used to explain the results of paradoxical intention for the treatment of agoraphobia (Michelson & Ascher, 1984). Even the effectiveness of such specifically derived cognitive-behavioral techniques as participant modeling have been attributed to reciprocal inhibition of anxiety due to the presence of a therapist (Wolpe, 1978).

Behavior therapists have included cognitive restructuring and "cognitively based anxiety" within the procedural and conceptual bases of behavior therapy since its inception (Wolpe, 1958). Ironically, too, virtually all the cognitive therapies place great emphasis on using behavior change to modify cognitions (Latimer & Sweet, 1984).

It thus appears that cognitive and behavioral techniques, though clearly the treatments of choice for the various anxiety disorders, provide their efficacy through as yet mysterious channels, which are the subject of much controversy and debate. Future research, therefore, should focus more extensively on testing the theoretical validity of various traditional and cognitive learning concepts that underlie clinical practice. An important step in this direction is the current evaluation of the efficacy of cognitive treatment intervention.

As discussed earlier, the cognitive therapy movement has its basis in the view that beliefs interact with situational factors to cause feelings. This conceptualization has led to the assumption that belief change through cognitive manipulation would cause anxiety responses to diminish. This has led in turn to such techniques as verbal disputes of irrational beliefs (Ellis, 1962); structural questioning and log keeping (Beck & Emery, 1985); and formalized self-dispute interventions based on visualization, cognitive restructuring, and home practice (McMullin & Giles, 1981; McMullin, 1986). Since these ideas are in conflict with the traditional behavioral views of anxiety, they have led to much controversy and debate.

The influence of cognitive factors on the acquisitions of anxiety has been clearly demonstrated (Brewer, 1974; Ohman, 1979). In a series of studies by Ohman and colleagues, however, purely cognitive factors did not seem to effect the extinction of fears in response to clinically relevant stimuli (see Ohman, 1979). For example, after conditioning fear reaction in subjects to slides of snakes and spiders, these experimenters removed the subjects' electrodes and instructed them that no further shock was forthcoming. Surprisingly, these instructions did not diminish fear responses to the slides. These studies and others led Fredrikson (1981, p. 456) to conclude that clinically relevant fear reactions "resist cognitive manipulation once they are acquired."

Fredrikson's conclusion was challenged in a study by Eifert and Schermelleh (1985). After conditioning subjects to slides of snakes, these researchers studied the effects of positive and negative self-statements on extinction. The self-statements significantly infuenced extinction in the expected direction (although subsequent approach behavior was unaffected). The authors concluded that "cognitive restructuring" may indeed evoke emotional responses that can compete with fear.

This controversy is relevant to the efficacy question with purely cognitive restructuring techniques in the treatment of clinical fears. A recent review (Latimer & Sweet, 1984) indicates that such techniques have not augmented the effectiveness of traditional behavior therapy. These authors take the viewpoint that cognitive therapy has been a component of behavior therapy since its inception and represents merely an evolution of technique, placing additional emphasis on cognition. They challenged the field to pay close empirical attention to claims that cognitive techniques significantly advance our efforts to treat various emotional and anxiety disorders. Latimer & Sweet's conclusions have recently been bolstered by an excellent critique of the theoretical bases of cognitive-behavioral therapies (Beidel & Turner, 1986).

A number of empirical evaluations of cognitively based interventions for agoraphobia, social phobia, obsessive–compulsive disorder, and simple phobia have shown disappointing results (e.g., Biran, Augusto, & Wilson, 1981; Biran & Wilson, 1980; Emmelkamp, Kuipers, & Eggeraat, 1978; Emmelkamp & Mersch, 1982; Hayes & Marshall, 1983; and Marks, 1981). In general, these studies indicated that cognitive restructuring per se either did not enhance the effects of *in vivo* exposure or was significantly inferior to a traditional behavioral intervention. Wilson (1982) concluded from such data that interventions using cognitive self-statements alone are clinically inert in the treatment of anxiety disorders and function as placebo treatments alone.

As with the results of the laboratory experiments, however, the results of the cognitive treatment of anxiety disorders are not entirely consistent. Goldfried, Linehan, and Smith (1978), for example, found "rational restructuring" more effective than prolonged exposure in the treatment of test anxiety. Similarly, Moleski and Tosi (1976) found rational-emotive therapy (RET) more effective than desensitization in the treatment of stuttering. Emmelkamp, Mersch, Vissia, and van der Helm (1985) found that cognitive restructuring significantly enhanced the behavioral treatment of social phobia. This latter result is particularly interesting because prior studies of cognitive therapy by Emmelkamp and colleagues showed unimpressive results.

It is possible that continued research will indicate that the "purely" cognitive aspects of problem solving, stress inoculation, RET, and cognitive restructuring are superfluous and ineffective or, perhaps, important with *certain* disorders. This would have a substantial influence on clinical theory and practice (e.g., Latimer & Sweet, 1984). At present, there are enough positive results to indicate that such interventions may prove effective in the treatment of some anxiety disorders and that further research on this subject is required.

Methodological issues are of paramount importance to the proper resolution of this question. Cognitive restructuring techniques should be evaluated in their most sophisticated form (e.g., Beck & Emery, 1985; McMullin & Giles, 1981). Experienced therapists should be used whenever possible, and every attempt should be made to ensure that they adhere to the treatment protocol. Given the results of the Ohman studies, it would also appear necessary that future research in this area give emphasis to clinical (versus analogue) fears.

We favor constructive designs in which cognitive therapy is added to an empirically proven behavioral technique and then compared against this technique alone as well as against a credible placebo. This design tests the assumption that cognitive therapy addresses effectively the components of clinical anxiety states that are missed by behavior therapy. Component designs isolating cognitive restructuring techniques as such from cognitive therapy packages would also be useful for evaluating the practical and theoretical assumptions of cognitive therapies. The reader is referred to Latimer & Sweet (1984) for a further discussion of methodological issues in this area.

Acknowledgment

The authors gratefully acknowledge the assistance and support of Nancy Rainwater, Carolyn Topinka, and Kelly Crumrine in the preparation of this chapter.

References

Agras, W. S., Kazdin, A., & Wilson, G. T. (1979). *Behavior therapy: Toward an applied clinical science.* San Francisco: W. H. Freeman.

Andrews, G., & Harvey, R. (1981). Does psychotherapy benefit neurotic patients? *Archives of General Psychiatry, 38,* 1203–1208.

Ascher, M. (1981). Employing paradoxical intervention in the treatment of agoraphobia. *Behaviour Research and Therapy, 19,* 1–10.

Bandura, A. (1969). *Principles of behavior modification.* New York: Holt, Rinehart & Winston.

Bandura, A. (1977). Self-efficacy: Toward a unifying theory of behavioral change. *Psychological Review, 84,* 191–215.

Barlow, D. Mavissakalian, M., & Schofield, L. (1980). Pattern of desynchrony in agoraphobia: A preliminary report. *Behaviour Research and Therapy, 2,* 307–321.

Barlow, D., O'Brien, G., & Last, C. (1984). Couples treatment of agoraphobia. *Behavior Therapy, 15,* 41–58.

Beck, A. T. (1976). *Cognitive therapy and the emotional disorders.* New York: International Universities Press.

Beck, A. T., & Emery, G. (1979). *Cognitive therapy of anxiety and phobic disorders.* Philadelphia: Center for Cognitive Therapy.

Beck, A. T., & Emery, G. (1985). *Anxiety disorders and phobias: A cognitive perspective.* New York: Basic Books.

Beidel, D. C., and Turner, S. M. (1986). A critique of the theoretical bases of cognitive-behavioral theories and therapy. *Clinical Psychology Review, 6,* 177–197.

Bellack, A., Hersen, M., & Kazdin, A. (1982). *International handbook of behavior modification and therapy.* New York: Plenum.

Biran, M., Augusto, F., & Wilson, G. T. (1981). A comparative analysis of cognitive and behavioral methods in the treatment of scriptophobia. *Behaviour Research and Therapy, 19,* 525–532.

Biran, M., & Wilson, G. T. (1980). Cognitive versus behavioral methods in the treatment of phobic disorders: A self-efficacy analysis. *Journal of Consulting and Clinical Psychology, 49,* 886–899.

Boyd, T. Z., & Levis, D. J. (1983). Exposure is a necessary condition for fear reduction: A reply to DeSilva & Rachman. *Behaviour Research and Therapy, 21,* 143–149.

Bowlby, J. (1969). *Attachment and loss: Vol. 1. Attachment.* New York: Basic Books.

Bowlby, J. (1973). *Attachment and loss: Vol. 2. Separation: Anxiety and anger.* New York: Basic Books.

Breger, C., & McGaugh, J. I. (1965). Critique and reformulation of learning theory approaches to psychotherapy and neurosis. *Psychological Bulletin, 63*, 338–358.

Brewer, W. F. (1974). There is no convincing evidence for operant and classical conditioning in adult humans. In W. B. Weimer & D. S. Palermo (Eds.), *Cognition and the symbolic processes.* Hillsdale, NJ: Erlbaum.

Cautela, J. (1971). Covert conditioning. In A. Jacobs & L. B. Sachs (Eds.), *The psychology of private events.* New York: Academic Press.

Coleman, J. C., Butcher, J. N., & Carson, R. C. (1984). *Abnormal psychology and modern life* (7th ed.). Glenview, IL: Scott, Foresman.

Compton, A. (1972b). A study of psychoanalytic theory of anxiety: 2. Developments of theory of anxiety since 1926. *Journal of the American Psychoanalytic Association, 20*, 341–394.

Davey, G. (1981). Conditioning principles, behaviorism and behavior therapy. In G. Davey (Ed.), *Applications of conditioning theory.* New York: Methuen.

deSilva, P., & Rachman, S. (1981). Is exposure a necessary condition for fear reduction? *Behaviour Research and Therapy, 19*, 227–232.

Eifert, G. H. (1985). Bridging the gap between conditioning theories and cognitive psychology to integrate "traditional" and "cognitive" behavior therapy. *The Cognitive Behaviorist, 7*(1), 2–8.

Eifert, G. H., & Schermelleh, K. (1985). Language conditioning, emotional instruction, and cognitive in conditional responses to fear-relevant and fear-irrelevant stimuli. *Journal of Behavior Therapy and Experimental Psychiatry, 16*, 101–110.

Elliot, C. S. (1982). *The role of semantic conditioning in the cognitive mediation of affect.* Unpublished doctoral dissertation, University of Denver.

Ellis, A. (1962). *Reason and emotion in psychotherapy.* New York: Lyle Stuart.

Ellis, A. (1985). Personal communication. Colorado Springs, CO, Invited address: New developments in rational emotive therapy.

Emmelkamp, P. M. G. (1979). The behavioral study of clinical phobias. In M. Hersen, R. M. Eisler, & P. M. Miller (Eds.), *Progress in behavior modification* (Vol. 8). New York: Academic Press.

Emmelkamp, P. M. G. (1982). Anxiety and fear. In A. S. Bellack, M. Hersen, & A. E. Kazdin (Eds.), *International handbook of behavior modification and therapy.* New York: Plenum.

Emmelkamp, P. M. G., Kuipers, A., & Eggeraat, J. (1978). Cognitive modification versus prolonged exposure *in vivo*: A comparison with agoraphobics as subjects. *Behaviour Research and Therapy, 16*, 33–42.

Emmelkamp, P. M. G., & Mersch, P. (1982). Cognitive and exposure *in vivo* in the treatment of agoraphobia: Short-term and delayed effects. *Cognitive Therapy and Research, 6*, 77–90.

Emmelkamp, P. M. G., Mersch, P. P., Vissia, E., & van der Helm, M. (1985). Social phobia: A comparative evaluation of cognitive and behavioral interventions. *Behaviour Research and Therapy, 23*(3), 365–369.

Eysenck, H. J. (1952). The effects of psychotherapy: An evaluation. *Journal of Consulting Psychology, 16*, 319–324.

Eysenck, H. J. (1957). *The dynamics of anxiety and hysteria.* New York: Praeger.

Eysenck, H. J. (1976). The learning theory model of neurosis—A new approach. *Behaviour Research and Therapy, 14*, 251–267.

Eysenck, H. J. (1982). Neobehavioristic (S–R) theory. In G. T. Wilson & C. M. Franks (Eds.), *Contemporary behavior therapy.* New York: Guilford Press.

Fenichel, O. (1945). *The psychoanalytic theory of neurosis.* New York: Norton.

Fischer, W. F. (1970). *Theories of anxiety.* New York: Harper and Row.

Flaherty, C. E. (1985). *Animal learning and cognition.* New York: Knopf.

Foa, E., Jameson, J., Turner, R., & Payne, L. (1980). Massed versus spaced exposure sessions in the treatment of agoraphobia. *Behaviour Research and Therapy, 18*, 333–338.

Foa, E. B., & Steketee, G. S. (1979). Obsessive–compulsives: Conceptual issues and treatment interventions. In M. Hersen, R. Eisler, & P. M. Miller (Eds.), *Progress in behavior modification* (Vol. 7). New York: Academic Press.

Fredrikson, M. (1981). Orienting and defensive reactions to phobic and conditioned fear stimuli in phobics and normals. *Psychophysiology, 18*, 456–465.

Freud, S. (1959). Inhibitions, symptoms and anxiety. In *Standard edition* (Vol. 20). London: Hogarth. (First published in 1926)

Gelder, M., Bancroft, J., Gath, D., Johnston, D., Mathews, A., & Shaw, P. (1973). Specific and non-specific factors in behavior therapy. *British Journal of Psychiatry, 123,* 445–462.

Gelder, M., Marks, I., & Wolff, H. (1967). Desensitization and psychotherapy in the treatment of phobic states: A controlled inquiry. *British Journal of Psychiatry, 113,* 53–73.

Giles, T. R. (1983a). Probable superiority of behavioral interventions: 1. Traditional comparative outcome. *Journal of Behavior Therapy and Experimental Psychiatry, 14,* 29–31.

Giles, T. R. (1983b). Probable superiority of behavioral interventions: 2. Empirical status of the equivalence of therapies hypothesis. *Journal of Behavior Therapy and Experimental Psychiatry, 14,* 189–196.

Giles, T., Young, R., & Young, D. (1985). Behavioral treatment of severe bulimia. *Behavior Therapy, 16,* 393–405.

Gilliland, R. M. (1979). Anxiety: A psychoanalytic view. In W. E. Fann (Ed.), *Phenomenology and treatment of anxiety.* New York: Spectrum.

Gilman, S. L. (Ed.). (1982). *Introducing psychoanalytic theory.* New York: Brunner/Mazel.

Goldfried, M. (1971). Systematic desensitization as training in self-control. *Journal of Consulting and Clinical Psychology, 37,* 228–234.

Goldfried, M., Decenteceo, E., & Weinberg, L. (1974). Systematic rational restructuring as a self-control technique. *Behavior Therapy, 5,* 247–254.

Goldfried, M., Linehan, M., & Smith, J. (1978). Reduction of test anxiety through cognitive restructuring. *Journal of Consulting and Clinical Psychology, 46,* 32–39.

Goldstein, A. J., & Chambless, D. L. (1978). A reanalysis of agoraphobia. *Behavior Therapy, 9,* 47–59.

Guidano, V. F., & Liotti, G. (1983). *Cognitive processes and emotional disorders: A structural approach to psychotherapy.* New York: Guilford Press.

Hare, N., & Levis, D. J. (1981). Pervasive anxiety: A search for cause and treatment approach. In S. M. Turner, K. S. Calhoun, & H. E. Adams (Eds.), *Handbook of clinical behavior therapy.* New York: Wiley.

Hayes, B., & Marshall, W. L. (1983). *Generalization of treatment effects in training public speakers.* Paper presented at the annual convention of the Association for the Advancement of Behavior Therapy, Los Angeles, CA.

Hugdahl, K. (1981). The three system model of fear and emotion: A critical examination. *Behaviour Research and Therapy, 19,* 75–85.

Jacobsen, E. (1964). *The self and the object world.* New York: International Universities Press.

Kazdin, A. E., & Wilcoxon, L. (1976). Systematic desensitization and nonspecific treatment effects: A methodological evaluation. *Psychological Bulletin, 83,* 729–758.

Kazdin, A. E., & Wilson, G. T. (1978). *Evaluation of behavioral therapy: Issues, evidence and research strategies.* Cambridge, MA: Ballinger.

Kelly, G. A. (1955). *The psychology of personal constructs.* New York: Norton.

Klein, M. (1969). *The psycho-analysis of children* (3rd ed.). New York: Humanities Press.

Kris, E. (1975). *Selected papers of Ernst Kris.* New Haven, CT: Yale University Press.

Lang, P. J. (1968). Fear reduction and fear behavior: Problems in treating a construct. In J. M. Shlien (Ed.), *Research in psychotherapy* (Vol. 3). Washington, DC: American Psychological Association.

Lang, P. J. (1971). The application of psychophysiological methods to the study of psychotherapy and behavior modification. In A. E. Bergin & S. L. Garfield (Eds.), *Handbook of psychotherapy and behavior change.* New York: Wiley.

Latimer, R. P., & Sweet, A. A. (1984). Cognitive versus behavioral procedures in cognitive-behavior therapy: A critical review of the evidence. *Journal of Behavior Therapy and Experimental Psychiatry, 15,* 9–22.

Ledwidge, B. (1978). Cognitive behavior modification: A step in the wrong direction? *Psychological Bulletin, 87,* 353–375.

Ledwidge, B. (1979). Cognitive behavior modification as new ways to change minds: Reply to Mahoney and Kazdin. *Psychological Bulletin, 86,* 1050–1053.

Levis, D. J. (1980). Implementing the technique of implosive therapy. In E. S. Foa & A. Goldstein (Eds.), *Handbook of behavioral interventions.* New York: Wiley.

Lick, J. R., Sushinsky, L. W., & Malow, R. (1977). Specificity of fear survey schedule items and the prediction of avoidance behavior. *Behavior Modification, 1,* 195–203.

Luborsky, L., Singer, B., & Luborsky, L. (1975). Comparative studies of psychotherapies. *Archives of General Psychiatry, 32,* 995–1008.

Mahoney, M. J. (1974). *Cognition and behavior modification*. Cambridge, MA: Ballinger.

Mahoney, M. J. (1977). On the continuing resistance to thoughtful therapy. *Behavior Therapy, 8,* 673–677.

Mahoney, M. J., & Arnkoff, D. (1978). Cognitive and self-control therapies. In S. L. Garfield & A. E. Bergin (Eds.), *Handbook of psychotherapy and behavior change*. New York: Wiley.

Marks, I. M. (1973). Reduction of fears: Toward a unifying theory. *Canadian Psychological Association Journal, 18,* 4–12.

Marks, I. M. (1975). Behavioral treatments of phobic and obsessive–compulsive disorders: A critical appraisal. In M. Hersen, R. M. Eisler, & P. M. Miller (Eds.), *Progress in behavior modification* (Vol. 1). New York: Academic Press.

Marks, I. M. (1981). *Cure and care of neuroses*. New York: Wiley.

Marks, I., Gelder, M., & Edwards, G. (1968). Hypnosis and desensitization for phobias: A controlled prospective trial. *British Journal of Psychiatry, 114,* 1263–1274.

Mathews, A., Gelder, M., & Johnston, D. (1981). *Agoraphobia: Nature and treatment*. New York: Guilford Press.

Maultsby, M. C. (1975). Patients' opinions of the therapeutic relationship in rational behavior psychotherapy. *Psychological Records, 37,* 795–798.

McMullin, R., & Giles, T. (1981). *Cognitive-behavior therapy: A restructuring approach*. New York: Grune and Stratton.

McMullin, R., Giles, T. R., & Turner, R. M. (1982). Cognitive restructuring vs. psychotherapy in the treatment of mental health center outpatients. Paper presented at the Association for the Advancement of Behavior Therapy, New York. (November)

McMullin, R. (1986). *Handbook of cognitive therapy*, New York: W. W. Norton.

Meichenbaum, D. H. (1977). *Cognitive-behavior modification*. New York: Plenum.

Meichenbaum, D. H., & Cameron, R. (1982). Cognitive behavior therapy. In G. T. Wilson & C. M. Franks (Eds.), *Contemporary behavior therapy*. New York: Guilford Press.

Michelson, L., & Ascher, L. M. (1984). Paradoxical intention in the treatment of agoraphobia and other anxiety disorders. *Journal of Behavior Therapy and Experimental Psychiatry, 15,* 215–220.

Miller, N. E. (1948). Studies of fear as an acquirable drive. *Journal of Experimental Psychology, 38,* 89–101.

Mineka, S. (1979). The role of fear in theories of avoidance learning, flooding and extinction. *Psychological Bulletin, 86,* 985–1010.

Moleski, R., & Tosi, D. J. (1976). Comparative psychotherapy: Rational-emotive therapy versus systematic desensitization in the treatment of stuttering. *Journal of Consulting and Clinical Psychology, 44,* 300–311.

Mowrer, O. H. (1939). A stimulus–response analysis of anxiety and its role as a reinforcing event. *Psychological Review, 46,* 553–565.

Mowrer, O. H. (1960). *Learning theory and behavior*. New York: Wiley.

Nagera, H. S., Colonna, A., Danskey, E., First, E., Gavshon, A., Holder, A., Kearney, L., & Radoford, R. (Eds.). (1970). *Basic psychoanalytic conception metapsychology, conflicts, anxiety and other subjects* (Vol. 4). London: George Allen and Unwin.

Nisbett, R. E., & Wilson, T. D. (1977). Telling more than we can know: Verbal reports on mental processes. *Psychological Reviews, 84,* 231–259.

Ohman, A. (1979). Instructional control of autonomic respondents: Fear relevance as a critical factor. In N. Birbaumer & H. Kimmel (Eds.), *Biofeedback and self regulation*. New York: Wiley.

Paul, G. (1966). *Insight vs. desensitization in psychotherapy*. Stanford, CA: Stanford University Press.

Piaget, J. (1926). *La représentation du monde chez l'enfant*. Paris: Presses Universitaires de Frances.

Rachman, S. J. (1974). *The meaning of fear*. Harmondsworth, England: Perquin.

Rachman, S. J. (1976). The passing or two-stage theory of fear and avoidance: Fresh possibilities. *Behaviour Research and Therapy, 4,* 125–131.

Rachman, S. J. (1977). The conditioning theory of fear acquisition: A critical examination. *Behaviour Research and Therapy, 15,* 375–387.

Rachman, S. (1978). Human fears: A three-systems analysis. *Scandinavian Journal of Behavior Therapy, 7,* 237–245.

Rachman, S. J., & Hodgson, R. (1974). 1. Synchrony and desynchrony in fear and avoidance. *Behaviour Research and Therapy, 12,* 311–318.

Rachman, S. H., & Wilson, G. (1980). *The effects of psychotherapy.* New York: Pergamon Press.

Ross, A. O. (1985). To form a more perfect union: It is time to stop standing still. *Behavior Therapy, 16,* 195–204.

Rotter, J. B. (1954). *Social learning and clinical psychology.* New York: Prentice-Hall.

Schwartz, B. (1978). *Psychology of learning and behavior.* New York: Norton.

Seligman, M. (1971). Phobias and preparedness. *Behavior Therapy, 2,* 307–321.

Shapiro, D. (1965). *Neurotic styles.* New York: Basic Books.

Sloane, R. B., Staples, F. R., Cristol, A. H., Yorkston, N. J., & Whipple, K. (1975). *Psychotherapy vs. behavior therapy.* Cambridge, MA: Harvard University Press.

Smith, M., & Glass, G. (1977). Meta-analysis of psychotherapy outcome studies. *American Psychologist, 132,* 752–760.

Staats, A. W. (1975). *Social Behavior.* London: Irwin Dorsey Press.

Staats, A. W. (in press). Paradigmatic behavior therapy: A unified framework of theory, research and practice. In I. M. Evans (Ed.), *Paradigmatic behavior therapy.* New York: Springer.

Stampfl, T. G., & Levis, D. J. (1967). The essentials of inclusive therapy: A learning theory based on psychodynamic behavioral therapy. *Journal of Abnormal Psychology, 72,* 496–503.

Stern, R., & Marks, I. (1973). Brief and prolonged flooding. *Archives of General Psychiatry, 28,* 270–276.

Strupp, H. II., & Hadley, S. W. (1979). Specific versus nonspecific factors in psychotherapy: A controlled study of outcome. *Archives of General Psychiatry, 36,* 1125–1136.

Suinn, R. (1975). Anxiety management training for general anxiety. In R. Suinn & R. Weigel (Eds.), *Innovative therapies: Critical and creative contributions.* New York: Harper and Row.

Suinn, R., & Richardson, F. (1971). Anxiety management training: A nonspecific behavior therapy program for anxiety control. *Behavior Therapy, 2,* 498–510.

Sweet, A. (1984). The therapeutic relationship in behavior therapy. *Clinical Psychology Review, 4,* 253–272.

Thoresen, C. S. (1980). *The behavior therapist.* Monterey, CA: Brooks/Cole.

Tolman, E. C. (1948). Cognitive maps in rats and men. *Psychological Review, 55,* 189–208.

Turner, S. M., Calhoun, K. S., & Adams, H. E. (1981). *Handbook of clinical behavior therapy.* New York: Wiley.

Wilson, G. T. (1978). Cognitive behavior therapy: Paradigm shift or passing phase? In J. P. Foreyt & D. P. Rathjeu (Eds.), *Cognitive behavior therapy: Research and application.* New York: Plenum Press.

Wilson, G. T. (1982). *Cognitive behavior therapy: Contemporary conundra.* Paper presented at the annual convention of the Association for the Advancement of Behavior Therapy, Los Angeles, CA.

Wolpe, J. (1958). *Psychotherapy by reciprocal inhibition.* Stanford, CA: Stanford University Press.

Wolpe, J. (1976a). Behavior therapy and its malcontents: 1. Negation of its bases and psychodynamic fusionism. *Journal of Behavior Therapy and Experimental Psychiatry, 7,* 1–6.

Wolpe, J. (1976b). Behavior therapy and its malcontents: 2. Multimodal eclecticism, cognitive exclusivism and "exposure" empiricism. *Journal of Behavior Therapy and Experimental Psychiatry, 7,* 109–116.

Wolpe, J. (1978). Self-efficacy theory and psychotherapeutic change: A square peg for a round hole. *Advances in Behaviour Research and Therapy, 1,* 231–236.

Wolpe, J. (1982). *The practice of behavior therapy* (3rd ed.). New York: Pergamon Press.

3

Cognitive Assessment of Anxiety Disorders

JEFFREY S. MARTZKE, BARBARA L. ANDERSEN, AND JOHN T. CACIOPPO

Jim, a local electrician and recipient of the Chamber of Commerce's "Businessman of the Year" award, waits anxiously to deliver the customary keynote address at the Chamber's monthly meeting. Although Jim deals skillfully with customers, he will be speaking before a group of peers for the first time since high school. As time passes, Jim's mouth becomes dry, his heart begins to race, and his palms sweat. Jim glances around the audience and imagines that each member in attendance is there to see him falter. He wonders how he ever allowed this to happen. What a fool he is to have agreed to address this gathering! Why didn't he feign an illness or arrange to be "unavailable"? Jim knows each and every member present is a more gifted speaker than he, and imagines their amusement as he envisions himself fumbling through his speech. What if, upon reaching the podium, he finds himself unable to utter a single syllable? He can already hear the snickering and muffled banter of the audience. Worst of all, many businessmen present are his customers, and Jim knows that once he has made a fool of himself he will have lost their respect, not to mention their business.

Cognitive-behavioral conceptualizations of anxiety (e.g., Ellis, 1962; Meichenbaum, 1977) have emphasized the role of dysfunctional cognitions—negative self-statements and evaluations, unrealistic expectations, irrational beliefs—in the development and maintenance of maladaptive emotional reactions. In the preceding vignette, Jim manifested many of the physiological indices of an impending panic attack (such as cardiac acceleration and palmar sweating) and also generated a series of anxiety-related cognitions. Jim maintained irrational beliefs regarding the skill level of his audience and the ramifications of failure. Moreover, he perseverated on a number of task-irrelevant, derogatory self-statements and focused on the most catastrophic outcome (total inability to speak).

The purpose of this chapter is to survey the procedures available for assessing anxiety-related cognitions. The term *cognition* is used here to refer to an individual's thoughts and ideas, in contrast to the term *cognitive process*, which is used to refer to the sequence of elementary information-processing operations and events underlying the elicitation or generation of cognitions. Cognitions, therefore, can be viewed as products and markers of cognitive processes. The assessment procedures described in this chapter focus on the acquisition and categorization of the reportable consequences of people's cognitive processes (e.g., self-statements, beliefs, appraisals, expectations), for the purpose

Jeffrey S. Martzke, Barbara L. Andersen, and John T. Cacioppo. Department of Psychology, University of Iowa, Iowa City, Iowa.

of drawing inferences about the maladaptive cognitive processes underlying anxiety disorders. Not all consequences of cognitive processes are reportable, of course, and this limits the utility of cognitive assessments. Nevertheless, research reviewed in this chapter suggests that procedures exist for monitoring ideation, and that the obtained reports and protocols provide a glimpse of the cognitive components of anxiety-related disorders.

The pervasiveness of the cognitive trend in psychotherapy is evidenced by the increasingly frequent mating of behavioral and cognitive theories—historically pitted against each other in bitter rivalry but now yielding hybrid cognitive-behavioral theories of psychotherapy. For a more detailed discussion of the cognitive trend in behavioral psychology, interested readers are referred to Mahoney (1977). The title of this book bears witness to this trend. The view that cognitive phenomena are inherent to the therapeutic process (Beck, 1970; Goldfried & Davison, 1976), however, has predated the development and validation of procedures designed to assess cognitive content and function. As argued by Kendall and Korgeski (1979), confirmation of a therapeutic process theory is limited by the validity of instruments designed to assess therapeutic change. As a case in point, these authors argue that establishing the efficacy of behavioral treatment necessitated extensive validation of behavioral assessment methodologies. Thus this chapter reviews the efforts of researchers to develop cognitive assessment measures.

Anxious individuals have been characterized by a constellation of overly negative self-statements, excessively high performance standards, selective attention to negative information about themselves, and pathological patterns of attribution for success and failure (Arkowitz, 1977; Glass & Merluzzi, 1981). Given this conceptualization, our ability to test and refine cognitive theories of etiology and process is limited by the reliability and validity of the available cognitive assessment procedures. Hence, in this chapter, we focus on the reliability and validity of cognitive assessment procedures. It is worthwhile noting that, although demonstrations of posttreatment reduction in symptomatology and/or distress are necessary to demonstrate a treatment's value, they are not sufficient to validate purported therapeutic processes. For example, in order to claim that the alteration of cognitions is necessary to reduce anxiety, one must first demonstrate that anxious patients who benefit from cognitive therapy do in fact manifest such changes in thinking from pre- to posttreatment assessments, and that control groups do not.

Second, it is emphasized that despite implied cause–effect relationships between maladaptive cognitions and anxiety, studies that select individuals on some characteristic of interest (e.g., anxiety) and demonstrate group differences on some theoretically relevant dependent measure (e.g., irrational beliefs) are correlational, and cause–effect conclusions are inappropriate. Research in which subjects are randomly assigned to experimental or control groups (e.g., therapy outcome studies) would justify cause–effect conclusions. The number of such studies in the literature is low at present, but it is anticipated that this will be an active area of research in the future.

Evaluative Criteria

Cognitive assessments of anxiety disorders are evaluated here in terms of their reliability (test–retest, interrater, and split-half or internal consistency); validity (predictive, content, and construct); and clinical utility. The criterion employed to evaluate the reliability of the various assessment procedures reviewed depends on the characteristics of the proce-dures. For techniques employing judges' ratings of cognitions (protocol analysis), inter-rater reliability is of particular importance. For assessments based on the assumption that an individual's total score on a self-report scale is the most valid index, measures of the internal consistency of the scale are emphasized. Test–retest indices, on the other hand, are interpreted in a context that acknowledges the situational specificity of many anxiety-provoking circumstances. For instance, although one might expect an anxious individual tested repeatedly under similar conditions to report similar (i.e., reliable) sets of cognitions (e.g., a high frequency of negative self-statements), one need not expect the frequency or pattern of situation-specific cognitions (e.g., "I am terrible thinking on my feet early in the morning") to be consistent across varied testing situations. This is not to say that test–retest reliability is irrelevant or impossible to obtain; it may simply be less appropriate than other measures (e.g., interrater reliability, internal consistency) because of the situational specificity of anxiety-related cognitions.

For most of the assessment techniques discussed, predictive validity can be demon-strated through positive correlations between cognitive indices of anxiety (e.g., a high frequency of irrational beliefs or self-deprecating thoughts) in anticipation of some task or situation and subsequent performance level in the anxiety-producing situation. Content validity is ordinarily established deductively, by randomly selecting a sample of items from the population of interest or, alternatively, through consensual validation. In the latter case, judges rate whether a potential item is representative of the class of items of interest to the researchers. A problem can arise in establishing content validity when no universe of content is entirely agreed on for the factor to be measured (Cronbach & Meehl, 1955). The content validity of scales is generally high, however, if (1) the initial pool of items is derived from spontaneous thought protocols, (2) the resulting pool of items is subjected to independent "representativeness ratings" by judges, and (3) the items consistently rated as most representative are selected for inclusion in the scale.

Finally, construct validity refers to the extent to which a cognitive assessment procedure does, in fact, reflect in a relatively true sense an individual's thoughts and thought process. Construct validation can be demonstrated through a series of tests whose aim is to determine the psychological reality of the variable (i.e., construct). One common method of assessing construct validity, for instance, is the known-groups method. In this validation technique, groups of individuals known to differ on the attribute of interest (e.g., social anxiety) are administered the measure (e.g., thought-listing measure). If the measure accurately gauges the particular attribute of interest, then groups known to differ along this dimension should generate clearly discriminable responses to the measure.

A second common technique uses a multitrait–multimethod matrix (Campbell & Fiske, 1959). Several requirements must be met for this process. First, if the measure of interest is a valid indicator of the construct under study, then predictably high relation-ships should exist with other measures of the construct even when the other measures differ in format (e.g., the verbal protocol, multiple choice, or sentence completion method of assessing cognitions). If the predicted pattern of high intercorrelation is found, then the measure in question is said to have *convergent validity* with other measures of the same construct. Second, measures employing the same assessment method may correlate regardless of the construct under study, since measurement error may be comparable and influential in determining the obtained score. Thus a further criterion of construct validity involves comparing the cognitive measure of interest with measures using the same format (e.g., multiple choice) but indexing discriminable psychological constructs. If the measure in question is only weakly correlated with the theoretically unrelated measures, then the critical measure is said to have *discriminant validity*. Both convergent and discriminant validity are subclasses of the more general notion of construct validity and could be investigated simultaneously using the multitrait–multi-method matrix technique.

In the literature on the cognitive assessment of anxiety disorders, convergent and discriminant validation are frequently employed to examine construct validity even though multitrait–multimethod analyses are relatively uncommon. For example, support for the convergent validity of a cognitive assessment technique (e.g., the Irrational Beliefs Test) is obtained if high correlations with content-similar alternatives (e.g., the Rational Behavior Inventory) and with theoretically related measures (e.g., measures of negative self-statements) or superordinate constructs (e.g., measured heterosocial anxiety) are found. A technique possesses discriminant validity insofar as correlations with measures assessing theoretically similar constructs (e.g., cognitive trait anxiety) exceed correlations with dissimilar psychological constructs measured using a similar assessment format (e.g., a Thurstone attitude scale).

In addition to reliability and validity, the clinical utility of each procedure is important. To be clinically useful, a measure should discriminate anxious clinical samples both from nonanxious normals and from nonanxious clinical samples. There is a paucity of pertinent research testing this model. Wolpe (1969), however, suggested that assertion and anxiety are mutually incompatible processes, such that assertion training by its nature inhibits social anxiety. In a rather stringent test of the hypothesized relationship between assertiveness and anxiety, Fiedler and Beach (1979) found that individuals' questionnaire-based assertiveness scores were significantly correlated with trait anxiety measures for two independent, nonclinical groups of subjects ($r = -.25$ and $-.28$). As expected, assertiveness scores were consistently correlated with heterosocial anxiety and social avoidance scores (e.g., Glass & Arnkoff, 1983). Finally, Schwartz and Gottman (1976) and Lange and Jakubowski (1976) have demonstrated that cognitions play a role in unassertiveness similar to their role in anxiety. Given these findings, research employing unassertive individuals as the target population is considered when assessing the potential clinical utility of various cognitive assessment techniques.

Classification of Assessment Procedures

Procedures for studying anxiety-related cognitions fall into three broad categories: (1) behavioral (performance) measures, (2) measures employing protocol analysis, and (3) structured questionnaires. Briefly, behavioral measures are currently defined as those measures incorporating self or other (e.g., trained judge or confederate) ratings of overt behavior from which deductions may be drawn regarding superordinate cognitive processes. Typically, these measures are employed to assess the individual's skill level or affective state under clearly defined conditions. Behavioral measures can be distinguished from cognitive assessments in that the former rely on overt behavior or self-reports of overt behavior rather than on self-reported thoughts or feelings.

A major set of cognitive assessment techniques—particularly useful when investigators either have no predetermined ideas about what cognitive dimensions are relevant or have only a few untested hunches—is protocol analysis. A protocol analysis can be viewed as a content analysis of self-reported cognitions, with variations occurring in when and how the cognitions are obtained, categorized, and analyzed. The recording of a person's thoughts may, for instance, occur in anticipation of some situation or task, as they occur, or retrospectively (following performance). Some procedures (e.g., think-aloud procedures) are designed to obtain nearly complete thought protocols, whereas others obtain random samples. Finally, some procedures (e.g., videotape reconstruction) provide retrieval cues for retrospective reporting of cognitions, whereas others (e.g., thought listing) do not. Typically, protocol analyses rely on judges' and/or subjects' ratings of content, frequency, and valence factors. There are advantages and disadvantages to each procedure, and we will attempt to identify the type of research question for which each is best suited below.

A second major type of cognitive assessment, the structured questionnaire, relies on an individual's endorsement of thoughts and/or feelings presented by the investigator (e.g., "If I fail this exam, my friends will laugh at me"). Subjects check off (from a predetermined list) those thoughts they had had during some explicit period of time. In addition to noting whether a thought occurred, individuals are often requested to estimate the frequency with which the thought occurred (e.g., "Indicate whether the thought occurred (1) not at all, (2) infrequently, (3) frequently, or (4) almost continuously"). Structured questionnaires simplify the quantification of predetermined dimensions of thought samples, but investigators risk overlooking unspecified yet important and recurrent themes present in a person's thoughts.

We have organized our discussion of cognitive assessment procedures from the broadly applicable protocol analysis methods to the more situation- and content-specific structured questionnaires. Because the items from structured questionnaires are most content-valid when generated from genuine thought samples (i.e., protocols), we first consider protocol analysis. Next we survey structured questionnaires designed to assess the cognitive components of anxiety in specific contexts. Discussion of behavioral measures of skill level and affective state are beyond the scope of this chapter. Interested readers are referred to Eisler (1976), Kent and Foster (1977), Lick and Katkin (1976), or Nay (1977).

Protocol Analyses

Protocol analyses share the assumption that the psychological significance of a person's thoughts and feelings can be examined by content-analyzing a person's reported thoughts, ideas, images, and feelings. Instead of observing people's behavior directly, or asking them to respond to questionnaires, or interviewing them, the investigator obtains protocols from anxious individuals (or from individuals in anxiety-provoking situations) and systematically asks questions of the protocols. As noted earlier, models of underlying processes are then formulated or tested by examining the content of the verbal protocols. In this section we survey five separate procedures for securing and quantifying protocols relevant to the study of anxiety.

The Thought-Listing Technique

Brock (1967) and Greenwald (1968) pioneered a procedure for securing protocols in which individuals list their thoughts and ideas. The majority of studies employing thought-listing techniques score protocols along valence, frequency, and content dimensions, although recent developments in this area include alternative scoring objectives and approaches (e.g., pattern assessment). A detailed discussion of the procedures for administering the thought-listing technique and of the issues surrounding the analysis and interpretation of thought-listing data can be found in Cacioppo and Petty (1981). The current discussion is limited to the utility of the thought-listing technique in studies of the cognitive components of anxiety disorders.

In an illustrative study, men who were either high or low in social anxiety were told they were to engage in a discussion with an unfamiliar woman (Cacioppo, Glass, & Merluzzi, 1979). Subjects were left alone in a room for several minutes and then were asked to list everything about which they had been thinking. Specifically, individuals read the following:

> We are now interested in everything that went through your mind about the upcoming discussion. Please list these thoughts, whether they were about yourself, the situation, and/or others; whether they were positive, neutral, and/or negative. Any case is fine. Ignore spelling, grammar, and punctuation. You will have 2.5 minutes to write. We have deliberately provided more space than we think people will need, to ensure that everyone would have plenty of room. Please be completely honest. Your responses will be anonymous. The next page contains the form we have prepared for your use to record your thoughts and ideas. Simply write down the first thought you had in the first box, the second in the second box, etc. Please put only one idea or thought in a box.

After 2.5 minutes, individuals were instructed to go back and rate their thoughts as favorable toward themselves, unfavorable toward themselves, or neutral (personally irrelevant). Subsequently, subjects rated themselves on semantic differential scales (e.g., good–bad, active–passive).

Subjects were able to follow the thought-listing instructions. Two judges scored the protocols according to the favorableness/unfavorableness of each listed thought relative to the "self," with high interrater reliability ($r = +.95$). Interestingly, analyses revealed that high and low socially anxious men rated their listed thoughts similarly, even though independent judges, who were unaware of the experimental conditions, rated the thoughts listed by high and low socially anxious individuals as being distinctive. Men high in social anxiety were found to generate significantly more negative self-statements and to express more negative self-regard prior to engaging in a discussion with an unfamiliar woman than did men low in social anxiety. The finding that high and low socially anxious individuals rated their self-statements as equally favorable suggests that each group has a unique frame of reference for what constitutes a normal or favorable self-statement. Consistent with this reasoning, previous research has shown that high socially anxious individuals possess more negative expectations regarding social interactions and more negative generalizations about themselves than do low socially anxious individuals (e.g., Clark & Arkowitz, 1975; Smith & Sarason, 1975).

With regard to the cognitive assessment of anxiety, this research highlights the importance of considering the frames of reference employed by the subjects versus those of the judges who are charged with categorizing verbal protocols. When individuals have been randomly assigned to conditions, previous research has revealed few significant differences between subject- and judge-rated thought listings (see Cacioppo & Petty, 1981). When individuals are not randomly assigned to groups, however, as is often the case in studies of anxiety, only the ratings of judges who are blind to the experimental conditions can be assumed to be based on comparable frames of reference across conditions. Whether judge or subject ratings are preferred depends, of course, on the particular research question of interest. As a general rule, however, ratings by independent judges should be included in the analyses of verbal protocols if individuals are not randomly assigned to groups, since these render subject-rated protocols more interpretable.

Although additional empirical work is necessary, the thought-listing procedure has proved informative in research on individuals known to differ in terms of their snake phobia (Huber & Altmaier, 1983), social anxiety (Cacioppo et al., 1979), and in cognitively based outcome studies of social (Malkiewich & Merluzzi, 1980) and test anxiety (Arnkoff, 1980; Bruch, 1978). Most research to date has used simple frequency counts (e.g., the number of negative self-statements), but the organization of thought listings (e.g., profiles, sequence, weightings) is beginning to attract increased attention. For instance, Huber and Altmaier (1983) found weighting the listed thoughts provided a more sensitive measure of differences in the cognitive organization of phobics and nonphobics than did simple frequency counts. Huber and Altmaier obtained thought listings from phobics and nonphobics following behavioral avoidance tasks. Subsequently, individuals were instructed to list the thought they perceived to be the exact opposite of each listed thought. Each bipolar pair of thoughts (thought dimension) was then rated by judges on a 5-point degree-of-threat scale. Subject ratings of salience or intensity of thoughts (from 1 to 3) were multiplied by judged threat ratings to obtain the total threat rating for each thought dimension. Analyses of thought dimensions indicated that phobics and nonphobics did not differ in the type or frequency of original thoughts listed, but that the groups differed in terms of the average total threat rating of the thought dimensions. More specifically, the cognitive systems of phobic individuals tended to be highly restrictive, such that both poles of the thought dimensions possessed high threat salience (an example of such a dimension being, "Snake will bite me" versus "Snake will not bite me")—a finding that may have important implications in the design of cognitive restructuring therapies for phobic individuals.

In sum, the thought-listing technique is useful but limited in several respects. Skepticism has been expressed regarding the ability of individuals to identify the stimuli that elicit cognitive or behavioral responses (cf. Nisbett & Bellows, 1977; Nisbett & Wilson, 1977), and one cannot assume that listed thoughts about causes and processes provide accurate depictions of "real" thoughts. Nevertheless, analyses of an anxious person's thoughts about the source of his or her anxiety may provide useful insights into the actual source, whether or not the person is able to identify it accurately. A second limitation is that the thought-listing technique can be expected to be insensitive to cognitions that are not salient or temporally proximal to the collection of the thought listings. The inability of subjects to recall all of their thoughts may not be problematic if it is the salient cognitions that also are the most important guides for their behavior (cf. Fazio & Zanna, 1981), but this is a difficult hypothesis to test unless more comprehensive cognitive assessment procedures are available. Several protocol procedures have been developed to combat the problem of incomplete recall. One such procedure—termed videotape reconstruction—is discussed next.

Videotape Reconstruction

In the videotape reconstruction procedure, individuals are videotaped while engaged in some target behavior. Subsequently they attempt to reconstruct their thoughts and feelings while reviewing the videotaped behavior. The thoughts and feelings individuals report having experienced are transcribed and content-analyzed in the same manner as described for thought listings. Interrater reliabilities are consistently high in this procedure.

In an illustrative study, Hollandsworth, Glazeski, Kirkland, Jones, and van Norman (1979) employed the videotape reconstruction procedure to compare reported self-statements of low- and high-test-anxious individuals. Women with extreme Test Anxiety Scale scores and average General Anxiety Scale scores (Sarason, 1972) were videotaped while completing a forty-minute mental abilities test. While the women completed the items, physiological measures of skin resistance response rate, heart rate, and respiration rate were obtained. Immediately following task completion, subjects were led to a viewing room where they observed a videotape of their task performance. While watching the videotape, the women were requested to reconstruct the flow of thoughts that had occurred during the testing session. Their self-statements were audiotaped, and the videotape was stopped by the experimenter as each cognition was verbalized. Following the thought reconstruction session, subjects filled out a series of self-report anxiety and arousal questionnaires.

The women's verbalizations were transcribed and subjected to content analysis by two independent judges blind to the research hypotheses. Thoughts and feelings were assigned to one of five classes:

1. On-task (e.g., self-statements focused on test items)
2. Off-task (e.g., self-statements focused on activities occurring prior to or following the task)
3. Positive-evaluation (e.g., self-referent labeling as good, smart, or fast; and task-referent labeling as easy or fun)
4. Negative-evaluation (e.g., self-referent labeling as stupid, slow, or dumb, and task-referent labeling as hard or difficult)
5. Miscellaneous (self-statements not classified within any of these categories and excluded from subsequent analyses).

On-task and positive-evaluation self-statements were considered task-facilitating: off-task and negative-evaluation self-statements were considered task-debilitating.

Results indicated that low- and high-test-anxious women did not differ on physiological or self-report measures of arousal during the testing session. However, low-test-anxious women labeled their arousal as task-facilitating, whereas high-test-anxious women labeled their arousal as task-debilitating. Moreover, the number of reconstructed task-facilitating self-statements was double that of task-debilitating self-statements for the low-test-anxious women, whereas the number of self-statements classified within these categories did not differ for high-test-anxious women. Given these findings, Hollandsworth et al. (1979) argued that treatment of test anxiety should emphasize relabeling of arousal as facilitative and strive to increase and maintain the number of task-facilitating self-statements within test situations rather than instructing subjects in progressive relaxation techniques.

The videotape reconstruction procedure has also proved informative in studies of the cognitive components of social competence (Smye, 1977, cited in Meichenbaum & Butler, 1979; Smye & Wine, 1980). Research by Burgio, Glass, and Merluzzi (1981) and by Chiauzzi and Heimberg (1983), however, raises questions about the sensitivity of this procedure. Burgio et al., for instance, identified women who differed in terms of their level of social anxiety and videotaped the individuals while they engaged in a conversation with a male confederate. Thoughts reported by women after viewing a videotape of their interaction failed to discriminate between the high and low socially anxious groups, even though their responses to a situation-specific self-statement questionnaire (the Social Interaction Self-Statement Test, SISST, to be discussed) did differentiate the groups.

Providing individuals with the retrieval cues inherent to a videotape of their own behavior may lead to more accurate and complete thought recall. Meichenbaum and Butler (1979) have noted, however, that (as with retrospective thought listing) it is impossible to determine the degree to which individuals are recalling rather than constructing the flow of thoughts and feelings reported while they observe themselves on the videotape. Presented with their own oftentimes maladaptive behavior (typically in the presence of an experimenter), individuals may engage in post hoc rationalizations of their behavior. Second, as noted by Burgio et al. (1981), this procedure appears to vary in its sensitivity to group differences across situations. These authors argue that the videotape reconstruction procedure taps many thoughts and ideas that are not specific to important features of anxiety-inducing situations. Nevertheless, the results of Hollandsworth et al. (1979) suggest the videotape reconstruction procedure can be sensitive in assessing the influence of anxiety on problem solving.

In trying to resolve these disparate conclusions, it is interesting to note, that the procedure adopted by Burgio et al. (1981) differs from that adopted by Hollandsworth et al. (1979). Hollandsworth et al. encouraged subjects to verbalize reconstructed thoughts as they were recalled (i.e., concurrent with videotape viewing), whereas Burgio et al. asked subjects to verbalize their thoughts following their viewing of the videotape (i.e., retrospectively). Chiauzzi and Heimberg (1983), who adopted an approach similar to that of Burgio et al., also found the obtained protocols to be similar for high- and low-anxious groups. Differences in the sensitivity of the obtained protocols, therefore, may be attributable to differences in the timing of thought reconstruction relative to videotape presentation. Research comparing retrospective thought-listing to concurrent think-aloud protocols suggests that these procedures do elicit quantitatively and qualitatively different protocols (e.g., Blackwell, Galassi, Galassi, & Watson, 1985). It is still uncertain, therefore, whether it is possible that the lack of sensitivity suggested by the null findings of Burgio et al. and Chiauzzi and Heimberg is attributable to the retrospective nature of their thought reconstruction or to differences in the sensitivity of the videotape reconstruction procedure across situations.

The Think-Aloud Technique

The think-aloud technique is designed for concurrent cognitive assessment. Ericsson and Simon's (1978) review of this technique provides a detailed description of the procedure. Briefly, the subject is asked to verbalize all thoughts and feelings experienced while completing a task, or during a defined time period. In most cases, the individual is performing a task relevant to the researcher's hypothesis (e.g., completing a set of math problems). Reported thoughts and feelings are transcribed and content-analyzed in the same manner as described for thought listing. This procedure is inapropriate for some research topics (e.g., cognitions occurring during heterosocial interactions) and may be further limited in application by its disruptive effects on task performance (Fulkerson, Galassi, & Galassi, 1984). Nonetheless, the think-aloud technique has been used successfully in a number of situations.

Fulkerson et al. (1984) asked college students in the top and bottom third of a classwide distribution of math anxiety scores to think aloud while solving Scholastic Aptitude Test (SAT) math problems. Math anxiety level was unrelated to performance or to the frequency of thoughts, as rated by judges, within 11 categories of cognition. When similar analyses were conducted on the subset of problems for which subjects did not think aloud, cognitive categories concerned with task facilitation (i.e., attention-controlling and self-facilitating cognitions) and inhibition (i.e., irrelevant and self-inhibiting cognitions) were significantly related to performance. These results suggest that think-aloud procedures may impair performance (cf. Ericsson & Simon, 1980). The fact that performance on the subset of "think-aloud questions" correlated only +.44 with performance on non-think-aloud questions further supports this conclusion.

The reactivity of the think-aloud technique may be much less of a problem when used with children who have not yet completely internalized their private speech (Luria, 1961). For example, Fox, Houston, and Pittner (1983) found that high-trait-anxious children reported more thoughts of preoccupation, justification of positive test-taking attitude, and derogation of others during a preexam think-aloud session. Fox et al. argued that the think-aloud technique is particularly useful with children, as their private speech has not been internalized long and they are, therefore, easily trained in the procedure.

One final caveat is warranted regarding the interpretation of think-aloud protocols. It is inappropriate to assume the think-aloud technique elicits verbalizations that are literal expressions of thought. As Meichenbaum and Butler (1979) note, thoughts occur more rapidly than speech, implying that editing is inherent even to the think-aloud approach. Think-aloud protocols are, therefore, best conceived as selective (i.e., nonrandom) samples of thoughts and feelings. Given that cognitive assessment procedures involve obtaining samples of cognitions (as opposed to literal expressions of thought content), concurrent randomized thought-sampling procedures are of interest because they purportedly provide the benefits of concurrent cognitive assessment while minimizing the risk of reactivity.

Other Methods Employing Protocol Analysis

Two alternative approaches for obtaining thought protocols are Hurlburt's (1976) thought-sampling approach and the articulated thoughts during simulated situations (ATSS) technique of Davison, Robins, and Johnson (1983). Briefly, during thought sampling individuals are asked to record what they were thinking just prior to a randomly timed recall cue. The thoughts are rated either immediately or retrospectively (and, in the latter case, by either a judge or the subject) on a series of 5- or 7-point Likert-type scales, 25 of which assess the cognitive, and 17 the affective, nature of the thought. Hurlburt (1980) and Hurlburt, Lech, and Saltman (1984) employed a random tone generator to cue thought recording in both naturalistic and laboratory settings. Preliminary evidence suggested that factor loadings for the cognitive and affective variables were consistent across settings and reliable across time ($p < .01$). Although this method lacks extensive validation and has not been used with anxious subjects, it has potential as an alternative to retrospective thought-listing and think-aloud procedures. The primary advantage of this procedure (in comparison to think-aloud techniques) appears to lie in its ability to provide thought samples across an extended period of time while potentially reducing reactivity. To date, however, the reactivity of this procedure has not been systematically assessed. As with think-aloud techniques, this technique is limited in its situational applicability. Moreover, compared to think-aloud protocols, inferences regarding thought pattern and sequence (Notarius, 1981) drawn from thought sample protocols are limited.

ATSS is a similar procedure developed recently by Davison et al. (1983). In this procedure, the subject pretends that he or she is a participant in a role-played interaction. Subjects verbalize their thoughts during pauses inserted at predetermined intervals throughout the audiotaped session. Judges analyze these recorded verbalizations, allowing for comparisons across role-playing situations and subject groups. Data regarding the validity of the ATSS procedure are mixed. Thoughts reported by college students presented with stressful situations were rated as less rational than thoughts in nonstressful situations. In addition, for highly fearful subjects who also received high scores on the Irrational Beliefs Test (IBT—a self-report measure of beliefs, to be discussed), self-reported anxiety following exposure to personally derogatory conversations was significantly correlated with irrationality scores obtained from ATSS protocols ($r = +.49$, $p < .01$) (Davison, Feldman, & Osborn, 1984). However, irrationality scores based on articulated thoughts were not significantly correlated with IBT or Assertion Inventory scores. This lack of convergence between alternative measures of irrational beliefs raises questions about the validity of the ATSS and underscores the importance of multimethod research. We turn now to a study that compares the thought protocols obtained employing the two most widely used protocol generation techniques, think-aloud and thought-listing.

Multimethod Assessment

We have suggested that multimethod research is necessary to determine the method variance inherent to various cognitive assessment procedures. Recently, Blackwell et al. (1985) compared the thought protocols elicited through think-aloud and thought-listing procedures. Employing a mixed design, Blackwell et al. required math-anxious college students to complete two sets of math problems. For one set, they were asked to think aloud (having received brief training prior to actual data collection); for the other they were asked to list their thoughts, in order of occurrence, immediately following each item. The order of problem set and cognitive assessment procedure was counterbalanced across subjects. Data were obtained on the number of problems solved correctly, the amount of self-reported anxiety, the duration of the data acquisition period for each method, and the frequency of thought protocol cognitions within each of eleven cognitive content categories.

Analysis of the frequency data indicated that think-aloud yielded twice as many thoughts as thought-listing and that the two thought protocols differed on 6 of the 11 content variables. Specifically, thought-listing protocols contained a significantly greater number of thoughts scored as positive problem-solving evaluations and positive self-evaluations. Think-aloud protocols contained a significantly greater number of thoughts scored as review of information, strategic calculations, conclusions, and attention control. Employing proportional cognitive content data (frequency data corrected for total number of responses), significant differences were obtained between procedures for each of the 11 variables. These proportional data mirrored the frequency data, but thought-listing also yielded proportionally more statements categorized as strategic planning, irrelevant, negative self-evaluation, negative problem-solving evaluation, and neutral content. The two procedures differed marginally on the number of problems solved correctly, with fewer questions being answered correctly during the think-aloud phase of the study. Subjects took significantly longer to complete each problem in the thought-listing phase, and they reported a higher level of anxiety following thought-listing than they did following think-aloud—suggesting that thought-listing may have reactive effects as well. Although this research does not resolve the issue of which procedure is "better," it does suggest that the ability of each procedure to assess cognitions may vary according to the type of cognition being assessed.

Blackwell et al. argue that think-aloud techniques may best assess problem-solving cognitions, whereas the thought-listing technique taps proportionally more self-relevant, evaluative cognitions. Moreover, the think-aloud technique appears to provide more of an ongoing record of thoughts than does thought-listing, to be less vulnerable to post hoc rationalization or reconstruction, and to be less dependent on memory. In contrast, they propose, the thought-listing technique is less likely to interfere with task performance and is more easily administered in groups.

Throughout our discussion of protocol analysis procedures, we have noted that various techniques may differ in the cognitive content they best assess, and in the contexts in which they have been demonstrated to be sensitive and nonreactive. Structured questionnaires have been developed to assess anxiety-related cognitions of a specific nature (e.g., beliefs) and, more recently, within unique contexts (e.g., social interaction). We turn now to a consideration of the more content- and situation-specific structured questionnaires.

Structured Questionnaires

Self-report structured questionnaires have been applied primarily in the assessment of anxious individuals' belief systems, self-statements, and expectations (including the assessment of self-efficacy). We have organized our discussion of the development and application of structured questionnaires for research on the process and treatment of anxiety disorders according to the content of the questionnaire's target cognitions.

Assessment of Beliefs

Ellis (1962) proposed that anxiety stems from a set of conscious beliefs that predispose a person to engage in irrational reasoning processes. Although protocol analysis may be employed to assess the frequency of thoughts and feelings indicative of irrational beliefs, several self-report questionnaires have been developed specifically to assess the frequency of maladaptive, irrational beliefs. In contrast to protocol analysis procedures (in which subjects' beliefs are inferred from reported self-statements), belief questionnaires require individuals to estimate the frequency with which previously selected beliefs occurred while they were completing a theoretically relevant task or during a defined period of time. The first scale developed for this purpose was the Irrational Beliefs Test (Jones, 1969).

IRRATIONAL BELIEFS TEST
The Irrational Beliefs Test (IBT) (Jones, 1969) was based on the irrational beliefs identified by Ellis (1962). This self-report inventory requests individuals to estimate on a 5-point scale the degree to which they maintain each of 100 specific beliefs. Ten subscales are used to gauge the irrational beliefs reflecting need for approval, perfectionism, blaming of others, catastrophizing, external attribution of emotions, anxious overconcern, dependency, helplessness, and beliefs that there are perfect solutions to problems. Jones (1969) reported high test–retest reliability (full-scale IBT $r = +.92$, subscale r's ranging from $+.67$ to $+.87$) and internal consistency of subscales (item-to-subscale score coefficients ranging from $+.66$ to $+.80$) for the IBT. Convergent validation was determined by correlating IBT full-scale and subscale scores with summed anxiety symptom checklist scores and anxiety-related Sixteen Personality Factor Questionnaire (16PF) (Cattell, Eber, & Tatsuoka, 1970) subscale scores. The total score on the IBT correlated $+.61$ with the symptom score and had an average correlation of $+.42$ with the six anxiety-related 16PF subscale scores (all correlations reaching significance). Eight IBT

subscales were significantly correlated with summed anxiety scores (multiple-$R = .72$) and anxiety-related 16PF subscales (multiple-R's ranging from .43 to .63).

Additional convergent validity for the IBT was documented by Gormally and colleagues (Gormally, Sipps, Raphael, Edwin, & Varvil-Weld, 1981a) who found IBT scores (combined and subscale) not only predicted heterosocial comfort scores (IBT worry and past influences subscales' $r = -.40$ and $-.42$, respectively), but were also moderately correlated with the Situational Expectancies Inventory (SEI), a measure of subjective risk estimate, to be discussed. (Correlation coefficients were not reported). Smith and Zurawski (1983) administered the IBT and a variety of anxiety measures to a nonclinical sample of college students. The measures employed included the trait form of the State–Trait Anxiety Inventory (Spielberger, Gorsuch, & Lushene, 1970); the Fear of Negative Evaluation Scale (Watson & Friend, 1969); the Test Anxiety Inventory (Spielberger, 1980); and a measure of cognitive and somatic trait anxiety (Schwartz, Davidson, & Coleman, 1978). IBT total scores were correlated with all anxiety scores ($+.38 < r < +.68, p < .001$). However, IBT total scores were also more highly correlated with trait anxiety scores (State–Trait Anxiety Index, or STAI) than with Rational Behavior Inventory scores (an alternative measure of irrational beliefs, to be discussed). On the basis of their results, these investigators postulated that the IBT may be a redundant measure of cognitive anxiety rather than a measure of purported mediating constructs. Alternatively, these results may reflect that the IBT is more sensitive to beliefs related specifically to anxiety than it is to irrational beliefs generally.

The validity of the IBT has been further substantiated through its use as a measure of cognitively based therapy outcome with unassertive (Craighead, 1979); socially anxious (Goldfried & Sobocinski, 1975; Kanter & Goldfried, 1979); and speech-anxious (Trexler & Karst, 1972) individuals, and as a means of identifying group differences with socially anxious clients (Davison et al., 1984; Gormally et al., 1981a; Sutton-Simon & Goldfried, 1979). However, several other outcome studies have failed to obtain posttreatment differences between groups of test-anxious (Casas, 1976) or unassertive (Derry & Stone, 1979) groups, or to differentiate groups of high versus low socially anxious individuals (Burgio et al., 1981).

Finally, the most extensive validation research on the IBT has been conducted by Lohr and associates (Lohr & Bonge, 1981, 1982a, 1982b; Lohr, Bonge, & Jones, 1983; Lohr, Nix, Dunbar, & Mosesso, 1984; Lohr & Rea, 1981). Lohr & Rea (1981) compared test anxiety scores (Personal Report of Public Speaking Anxiety, McCroskey, 1970) of students enrolled in an introductory speech course with concurrently obtained IBT scores. They found that, although in past research therapy designed to change irrational beliefs effectively mediated fear of public speaking (Fremouw & Harmatz, 1975; Fremouw & Zitter, 1978), only one IBT subscale, "demand for approval," was positively correlated with speech anxiety ($r = +.23$), and even this subscale did not differentiate groups of individuals who differed in their level of speech anxiety. Research assessing the relationship between irrational beliefs and assertiveness has obtained inconsistent results (Lohr & Bonge, 1982b; Lohr et al., 1984). In summary, the findings suggest that IBT scores are related to assertiveness, but the percentage of common variance is low.

The data to date indicate that IBT scores are clearly related to social anxiety, whereas their relationship to test anxiety and assertiveness is less clear. The data warrant continued examination of the IBT for anxiety-related research purposes and application with socially anxious clinical populations. Further validation with test-anxious and unassertive individuals is necessary before employing this scale with these clinical populations.

RATIONAL BEHAVIOR INVENTORY

The Rational Behavior Inventory (RBI), developed by Shorkey and Whiteman (1977), is composed of items previously used by Hartman (1971) and Fox and Davies (1971). Two factor analyses yielded a final scale of 37 items that loaded on 11 factors, some consistent with the categories of irrational beliefs identified by Ellis (1962), others reflecting common substrates of several beliefs. Examples of the latter include irrational beliefs that the world should be completely altruistic, that guilt should be assigned for deviance, and that difficult problems should be avoided. Reliabilities (based on college student samples) are +.82 and +.71 for test–retest reliability, and +.73 for split-half reliability. Among college student groups, evidence of the validity of the RBI is provided by significant correlations with 13 of the 14 Personal Orientation Inventory subscales (.23 < $|r|$ < .53) (Shorkey & Reyes, 1978), Rosenberg's Self-Esteem Scale ($r = +.45$), Schulze's dogmatism scale ($r = -.35$), the Srole Anomic Scale ($r = -.35$), and Lane's Authoritarianism Scale ($r = -.16$) (Whiteman, 1979; Whiteman & Shorkey, 1978). Moreover, mental health service providers undergoing brief training in rational–emotive therapy demonstrated a change in RBI scores indicating greater rationality following training (Shorkey & Whiteman, 1977). Finally, Himle, Thyer, and Papsdorf (1982) provided evidence for the convergent validity of the RBI by obtaining significant correlations for a college student sample between RBI scores and measures of state, trait, and test anxiety ($-.31 < r < -.50$, p's < .001).

Smith, Boaz, and Denny (1984) found that irrational beliefs, based on full-scale RBI scores, were correlated with measures of psychological and physical distress (r = +.49 and +.27, respectively; p < .01). These findings were consistent with previous research employing alternative means of assessing irrational beliefs (Knapp, 1979). Smith and Zurawski (1983) assessed the discriminant validity of the RBI, along with the IBT, employing the trait and state anxiety measures described earlier. Unlike the IBT, the RBI was found to have good discriminant validity, correlating higher with the IBT (an alternative measure of irrational beliefs) than any anxiety measure administered to the sample of participating college students. No replication using a clinical sample or measures of other components of emotional distress are yet available, nor has the validity of the RBI been established for specific classes of anxiety disorders (e.g., test anxiety, speech phobia, social anxiety).

As previously discussed, irrational beliefs are the major component of the irrational cognitive philosophies adopted by anxious individuals (Ellis, 1962). Coinciding with this belief system, individuals engage in an internal dialogue, a series of self-statements, regarding recent or impending events and the consequences of alternative (primarily negative) outcomes. It is through this internal dialogue that individuals experience their irrational beliefs (Kendall & Hollon, 1981). Next we consider questionnaires designed to assess these self-statements in anxiety-inducing situations.

Assessment of Self-Statements

Self-statement questionnaires are less specific with respect to the nature of the cognitions they assess (e.g., beliefs, expectations, evaluations) than are irrational belief questionnaires. In lieu of assessing a well-circumscribed set of cognitions, questionnaires may increase their sensitivity by narrowing their context of application (as opposed to their cognitive content of interest). With the exception of the Anxious Self-Statement Inventory, investigators have attempted to increase the sensitivity of their self-statement questionnaires by limiting their context of application.

ASSERTION SELF-STATEMENT TEST

The Assertion Self-Statement Test (ASST), developed by Schwartz and Gottman (1976), has received the greatest research attention among self-statement inventories. This scale was designed to assess the role of self-statements in individuals' ability to complete assertive tasks. Items for the instrument were selected on the basis of consensual validation by college students. Items include "I was concerned that the person would think I was selfish if I refused" (a negative-assertion self-statement) and "I was thinking I am too busy now to say yes" (a positive-assertion self-statement). In Schwartz and Gottman's original study, college students completed the 34-item ASST following participation in a series of role-playing situations. The students were asked to respond to 17 positive and 17 negative self-statements on a 5-point scale indicating how frequently the thought had occurred (from "hardly ever" to "very often").

Schwartz and Gottman found that low-assertive subjects did not differ from their high-assertive peers in knowledge of assertive responses or in ability to behave assertively in a low-threat situation (such as showing a friend how to handle assertive situations). Deficient assertive behavior was manifested by the low-assertive subjects in assertiveness situations in which subjects were personally confronted with an unreasonable request. Analyses of subjects' self-reported self-statements showed that high- and moderate-assertive subjects reported significantly more positive than negative self-statements in these situations, whereas low-assertive subjects did not differ in the number of positive and negative self-statements. In contrast to the "positive cognitive set" characterizing moderate- and high-assertive subjects, low-assertive subjects were "characterized by an 'internal dialogue of conflict' in which positive and negative self-statements compete against each other" (Schwartz & Gottman, 1976, p. 919). These results were replicated by Bruch (1981).

Further research by Bruch, Haase, and Purcell (1984) demonstrated that the ASST has acceptable internal consistency (Cronbach's $\alpha = .78$), but may be best conceptualized as having two independent negative thought factors. Factor analysis suggested that negative self-statements may reflect apprehension over negative interpersonal consequences (e.g., "I was thinking that people will dislike me if I always refuse") or preoccupation with moral standards involving responsibility to others (e.g., "I was thinking that it was better to help others than to be self-centered"). Regression analysis demonstrated, however, that the second negative factor score (reflecting a preoccupation with moral standards) did not contribute significantly to the ability of the ASST to predict assertiveness scores.

Pitcher and Meikle (1980) used a revised form of the ASST to assess differences between high- and low-assertive individuals in positive as well as negative assertion situations. They found that in positive-assertion situations, reported self-statements did not differ between assertiveness groups. In the negative-assertion situation, however, Schwartz and Gottman's findings for assertive refusal situations were replicated.

Heimberg, Chiauzzi, Becker, and Madrazo-Pederson (1983) extended this area of research by administering the ASST to high- and low-assertive college students, psychiatric patients, and normal adults. Although a sample effect was obtained, their results demonstrated that the ASST distinguished low-assertive subjects independent of subject type in a manner consistent with Schwartz and Gottman (1976). This serves as a valuable extension of the "internal dialogue of conflict" hypothesis to socially anxious clinical populations.

Finally, two therapy outcome studies (Craighead, 1979; Derry & Stone, 1979) employed the ASST as a measure of cognitive change. Craighead (1979) reported that instructional self-training resulted in a significant decrease in negative self-statements relative to no treatment and expectancy controls. A similar pattern of results was obtained on Craighead's assertion-specific measure of irrational beliefs, providing evidence for the convergent validity of the ASST. Derry & Stone (1979) also reported posttreatment and follow-up differences between treatment conditions in the number of negative self-statements. Compared with individuals in a behavioral rehearsal alone or behavioral rehearsal and attribution training condition, individuals in the behavioral rehearsal plus cognitive self-statement condition endorsed fewer negative self-statements.

SOCIAL INTERACTION SELF-STATEMENT TEST

Developed by Glass and Merluzzi (Glass, Merluzzi, Biever, & Larsen, 1982), the Social Interaction Self-Statement Test (SISST) is a 30 item scale, presented in a format comparable to the ASST, targeted for the assessment of the cognitive correlates of heterosocial anxiety. The self-statements included were among those generated by a group of pilot subjects in response to ten heterosocial vignettes via the thought-listing procedure. Items generated were first classified as positive, negative, or neutral in valence and subsequently rated by eight judges on an 11-point scale from negative to positive. Based on these judges' ratings, the authors selected the 15 positive (e.g., "What the heck, the worst that can happen is that she won't go for me"; "What do I have to lose? It's worth a try") and 15 negative (e.g., "I hope I don't make a fool of myself"; "I'll probably bomb out, anyway") items with the most extreme ratings. Glass et al. (1982) found that the item-to-total scale correlations ranged from +.45 to +.77 ($p < .001$), and odd versus even item split-half reliabilities were +.73 and +.86 for the positive and negative self-statements, respectively. SISST scores correlated with self-report measures of social anxiety and heterosocial skill (correlations ranging from +.44 to +.77, $p < .001$), and SISST negative self-statement scores were correlated with judge and confederate ratings of skill and anxiety ($.23 < |r| < .32$). Finally, Glass et al. (1982) found that SISST scores discriminated high from low heterosocially anxious men and women. Given these encouraging initial data, research extending validation to clinical samples, employing naturalistic observation of heterosocial interaction to establish predictive validity, and generating and analyzing additional items to yield a more general measure of social anxiety appears justified.

OTHER SELF-STATEMENT QUESTIONNAIRES

Two other self-report questionnaires warrant discussion. The Cognitive Interference Questionnaire (CIQ), a questionnaire designed for use with test-anxious subjects, was developed by Sarason (1978). The CIQ contains 11 self-statements rated on a 5-point frequency-of-occurrence scale, and a 7-point scale on which the degree of "mind wandering" is assessed. The validity of the CIQ has been substantiated through its use as a therapy outcome measure (Kirkland & Hollandsworth, 1980) and as a means of identifying group differences with test-anxious subjects (Hollandsworth et al., 1979; Sarason, 1984; Sarason & Stoops, 1978).

Kendall and Hollon (1980; cited in Kendall & Hollon, 1981) approached the construction of their Anxious Self-Statement Inventory (ASSI) somewhat differently. Employing a known-groups approach, these researchers selected 33 self-statements endorsed significantly more often by subjects in a highly anxious group (based on STAI and Minnesota Multiphasic Personality Inventory [MMPI] anxiety scale scores) than subjects in a moderately anxious group. The 33 items received cross-validation with a second sample of similarly defined criterion groups. Kendall and Hollon (1981) report preliminary findings suggesting that, independent of trait stress level, change scores (from nonstress to preexamination administrations) on the ASSI correlated significantly with changes in state anxiety $(r = +.34)$, but not in depression $(r = +.09)$. Although this measure has not received widespread use, preliminary results suggest that it may be a useful measure of general rather than situation-specific cognitive concomitants of anxiety.

Although self-statement questionnaires show high potential, most inventories require additional validation. With the exception of the ASST, the measures lack validation with clinical samples. Moreover, suprisingly few attempts have been made to compare the self-statement scores obtained employing structured questionnaires to protocol analyses, and few attempts have been made to establish the discriminant validity of many self-statement questionnaires. Finally, performance on self-statement questionnaires may be subject to individuals' post hoc reappraisals of their thoughts. Particularly for cognitively based therapy outcome studies, the potential for demand characteristics appears great. Demonstrations that the number and nature of reported self-statements is independent of social desirability scores, prior to and following cognitively oriented therapy, would further validate the role of self-statement modification in the therapeutic process.

Self-Efficacy Measures

Bandura (1977) argues that behavior change is mediated by a single underlying process—namely, changes in efficacy expectations. Efficacy expectations reflect an individual's expectation that he or she can perform a particular task. Outcome expectations, in contrast, refer to an individual's expectation that specific outcomes will result from a given situation or action. Scales developed to assess efficacy expecations have reflected Bandura's concern that the assessment of efficacy expectations be situation-specific. The instruments are organized in a fashion similar to behavioral avoidance tests such that statements that describe less threatening behaviors ("Look at snake in glass case from a distance") are followed by statements placing an individual in closer proximity to, and ultimately in contact with, the anxiety-inducing situation ("Tolerate snake in lap"). For a brief description of behavioral avoidance tests, see Lang and Lazovik (1963). For each item, subjects indicate whether they feel they could perform the task (an index of efficacy level) and, if so, indicate on a separate scale their confidence (an index of efficacy strength). Confidence scores may range from 0 to 100 (in 10-point increments). Efficacy scales of this nature have been validated through therapy outcome studies with speech-anxious subjects (Jaremko & Walker, 1978, cited in Glass & Merluzzi, 1981) and snake phobics (Bandura & Adams, 1977). Correlational studies have found that scores on efficacy scales are significantly correlated with assertiveness (Lee, 1984a) and snake-approaching behavior in nonphobics (Lee, 1984; $+.66 < r < +.82$, $p < .001$).

Although efficacy scales have been widely used in research designed to examine the relationship between efficacy expectations and subsequent behavior, little emphasis has been placed on determining the psychometric merits of the scales employed. Data suggest the scales possess construct validity; yet questions remain regarding reliability, discriminant validity, and convergent validity.

Initially, Bandura (1977) argued that efficacy expectations played a more central mediating role in behavior change than outcome expectations. More recently, Bandura (1982) has suggested that, in specific situations, interactions between efficacy and outcome expectations will lead to unique affective states. Research on the relationship between efficacy and outcome expectations on subsequent task performance and affective state (Davis & Yates, 1982) supports Bandura's more recent position. In Davis and Yates's study, students manifested depressed affect and performance decrements on an anagram task only when outcome expectations were high and efficacy expectations were low. These results suggest that outcome expectations influence overall affective state.

Researchers assessing the mediating cognitive processes of anxiety have also examined the effect of outcome expectations on affective state. In the next section we examine the reliability, validity, and utility of measures designed to assess anxiety-related outcome expectations.

Outcome Expectancy Measures

In two studies examining the relationship between expectations and anxiety (Lee, 1984a, 1984b), efficacy expectations were better predictors of behavior than outcome expectations; indeed, outcome expectancy measures did not account for a significant portion of variance in behavior over that predicted by efficacy expectations. Nevertheless, greater attention has been paid to the development and validation of outcome than efficacy expectation measures.

SUBJECTIVE PROBABILITY OF CONSEQUENCES INVENTORY

Fiedler and Beach (1978) incorporated the concept of *subjective expected utility* (SEU), a measure of the subjective risk or response cost of certain behaviors, to examine the relationship between outcome expectancies and assertiveness. Bruch et al. (1984) labeled the instrument developed to assess the SEU of a given behavior the Subjective Probability of Consequences Inventory (SPCI). The SPCI is a list of potential positive and negative consequences associated with complying with or refusing a request made by another individual. An example of a positive consequence of refusal is "I will respect myself more"; a negative consequence of refusal is "I will feel guilty." An example of a positive consequence of compliance is "We will become better friends"; a negative consequence of compliance is "I will feel angry and resentful." The SPCI was derived from an original list of potential outcomes that were subsequently subjected to consensual validation by clinical experts to ensure representativeness. SPCI scores are obtained by summing an individual's weighted rating of the cost or benefit assigned to each consequence. Weightings are determined by the probability of occurrence the individual assigns to that consequence.

Fiedler and Beach (1978) presented the SPCI to high-, medium- and low-assertive individuals following each of nine assertion vignettes. Individuals had personally rated the utility of each consequence prior to exposure to the vignettes. For each vignette, subjects were asked to rate the probability of occurrence of each consequence under conditions in which the requests were either complied with or refused. SEU scores were computed for each by multiplying the utility attributed to each consequence by its assigned probability of occurrence. In addition, individuals stated whether they would have refused or complied in each situation (behavioral intent). Results indicated that, although SEU was unrelated to anxiety or assertiveness level, it was highly predictive of behavioral intent, and discriminated high- from low-behavioral-intent groups for peer refusal vignettes.

Bruch et al. (1984) assessed the internal consistency and factor structure of SPCI responses and found the SPCI to be internally consistent (Cronbach's $\alpha = .77$). Responses to the SPCI loaded on four factors defined as negative consequences of refusal, positive consequences of refusal, negative consequences of compliance, and positive consequences of compliance. Bruch et al. (1984) also assessed the assertiveness of their subjects and found the SPCI factor scores accounted for 8% of the total variance in assertiveness scores ($p < .01$).

In summary, modest evidence exists suggesting that SPCI scores are related to assertiveness, particularly in peer refusal situations. The strength of the relationship is not great, however, and further research is necessary to justify inclusion of the SPCI in cognitive assessment batteries for anxiety. It would be particularly worthwhile to assess the predictive validity of the SPCI in light of Fiedler and Beach's (1978) findings. To this end, naturalistic observation is most desirable in assessing assertive behavior, as behavioral intent measures (à la Fiedler & Beach, 1978) may be more susceptible to response bias.

SITUATIONAL EXPECTANCIES INVENTORY

Gormally and associates (Gormally, Sipps, Raphael, Edwin, & Varvil-Weld, 1981a; Gormally, Varvil-Weld, Raphael, & Sipps, 1981b) have developed the Situational Expectancies Inventory (SEI) to assess heterosocial anxiety in males. The SEI employs four social interaction vignettes (e.g., starting a conversation with a female unknown to the respondent while in a cashier's line) described as problematic by heterosocially anxious men who seek treatment (Gormally et al., 1981a). For each vignette, men indicate how they would feel following rejection and acceptance, on a scale from −100 ("horrible") to 100 ("ecstatic"). In addition, men rate the probability of rejection (in 25% increments).

As with the SPCI, SEI risk estimates are computed by multiplying the affective value of rejection by its probability of occurrence. Gormally et al. (1981a) report a test–retest reliability of +.85 and Cronbach's α of .81.

Gormally et al. (1981a) found SEI scores discriminated competent daters from a clinical sample of men in a social skills training program. Moreover, SEI scores were better predictors of heterosocial comfort than were IBT scores ($r = -.51$, $p < .0001$). Moderate correlations between IBT subscale scores and SEI estimates provide evidence for the convergent validity of the SEI. (Correlation coefficients were not reported.) In addition, Gormally et al. (1981b) found that, although both cognitive counseling and skills training resulted in improved dating skills, cognitive counseling led to greater change in SEI scores than did skills training. The attempt to examine the psychometric merits of the SEI prior to employing it as a means of validating cognitive theories of therapeutic process is commendable. Replicability and discriminant validity remain issues, but the SEI appears to hold promise as a measure of outcome expectancies for men. Should future validation studies prove encouraging, development of a similar scale for use with heterosocially anxious women would seem warranted.

GENERALIZED EXPECTANCIES OF OTHERS QUESTIONNAIRE

The final outcome expectancy measure to be discussed is the Generalized Expectancies of Others Questionnaire (GEOQ) developed by Eisler, Frederiksen, and Peterson (1978). Briefly, the GEOQ, which assesses outcome expectancies on a somewhat broader plane, requires that subjects estimate the percentage of time they receive admiration, anger (aggression), fear, understanding, and advantage-taking reactions from others. The items are of the format "How often do you expect they will show fear of you?" ". . . be angry with you?" and so forth. Eisler et al. (1978) found that low-assertive subjects anticipated more frequent favorable reactions from others during social interaction than did high-assertives. To our knowledge, however, this measure has not been employed subsequently.

In summary, structured questionnaires hold the advantage of being (1) quick to administer to large groups; (2) easily scored, quantified, and normed; and (3) helpful in providing retrieval cues for thoughts subjects might erroneously neglect. On the other hand, structured questionnaires have their limitations. The individual must "decide" whether or not his or her unique cognition matches one of the listed cognitions. Novel cognitions (perhaps of low frequency, yet high in subjective impact) often remain unassessed. Furthermore, such questionnaires rarely allow for pattern assessment (the order in which cognitions occur). Finally, structured questionnaires share two additional limitations with measures employing protocol analysis. Specifically, they fail to assess the subjective meaning of reported thoughts, and they may be subject to response bias in reporting.

Conclusion

The recent research attention focused on cognitive assessments of anxiety is encouraging, and a number of assessment procedures with unique strengths and weaknesses now exist. Nevertheless, several general points can be noted.

1. There is a paucity of instances in which cognitive assessments were validated in naturalistic as well as analogue settings (e.g., Galassi, Frierson, & Siegel, 1984). It is difficult, for instance, to recreate all the real-life contingencies of a physics final exam in an analogue experiment employing subjects from an introductory psychology class who receive course credit for their participation in a "psychology experiment." Until naturalistic performance measures are taken, the validity of cognitive assessment procedures for clinical purposes remains uncertain.

2. The validity of self-report measures would be bolstered by demonstrations of independence from social desirability response bias and demand characteristics (Bruch, Juster, & Heisler, 1982; Lohr et al., 1983).

3. The reactivity of cognitive assessment procedures (e.g., thought sampling) has not been determined. As a case in point, evidence exists that, for certain types of tasks, think-aloud procedures may inhibit performance (Fulkerson et al., 1984; Genest & Turk, 1981; Kendall & Hollon, 1981). Research is needed examining the conditions under which specific assessment procedures might influence performance, and how these effects might be quantified or eliminated.

4. With a diversity of cognitive assessment procedures available, mutlitrait–multimethod analyses would provide valuable information regarding the method variance of alternative approaches to assessment (Cone, 1979; Norton, Dinardo, & Barlow, 1983). Few procedures have established validity that justifies exclusion from such analyses. Multitrait–multimethod research would also provide insight into which assessment procedure most effectively indexes specific cognitions under which circumscribed conditions.

In a related vein, the frequent lack of convergence between cognitive therapy outcome measures underscores the utility of multiple outcome measures. These measures, however, need not be limited to cognitive techniques. Although cognitive assessment is important in evaluating cognitive theories of therapeutic change, it is equally important that cognitive indices of improvement be compared to behavioral (e.g., Halford & Foddy, 1982; Malloy, Fairbank, & Keane, 1983) and physiological (Malloy et al., 1983; Schule & Wilsenfeld, 1983) correlates of anxiety. Such research would further validate cognitive assessments in those anxiety-inducing contexts where convergence across measures would be expected.

5. Outcome research comparing cognitively-based therapies (which incorporate thought monitoring) to non–cognitively based therapies (which do not incorporate thought monitoring) cannot discern genuine posttherapeutic changes in cognitive content (and presumably, process) from posttherapeutic changes that may reflect the practice effects of thought monitoring and reporting. Posttreatment cognitive change may, therefore, merely reflect the variable accessability of cognitions—for instance, as might result from the practice effects of therapeutic thought monitoring—rather than actual changes in cognition type or frequency. Outcome studies that compare the effects of cognitively based "therapy" designed solely to increase a subject's awareness of (and, presumably, access to) cognitions versus more traditional cognitively based therapies designed to alter maladaptive cognitions are necessary. This research could discern what portion of therapeutic gain actually reflects alterations in cognition accessibility. The number of such studies is currently low, but, given this issue's importance, we are confident that this will become an active area of research.

References

Arkowitz, H. (1977). Measurement and modification of minimal dating behavior. In M. Hersen, P. Miller, & R. Eisler (Eds.), *Progress in behavior modification* (Vol. 5). New York: Academic Press.

Arnkoff, D. B. (1980). Psychotherapy from the perspective of cognitive theory. In M. Mahoney (Ed.), *Psychotherapy process: Current issues and future directions*. New York: Plenum Press.

Bandura, A. (1977). Self-efficacy: Toward a unifying theory of behavioral change. *Psychological Review, 84*, 191–215.

Bandura, A. (1982). Self-efficacy mechanisms in human agency. *American Psychologist, 37*, 122–147.

Bandura, A., & Adams, N. E. (1977). Analysis of self-efficacy theory of behavioral change. *Cognitive Therapy and Research, 1*, 287–308.

Beck, A. T. (1970). Cognitive therapy: Nature and relation to behavior therapy. *Behavior Therapy, 1*, 184–200.

Blackwell, R. T., Galassi, J. P., Galassi, M. D., & Watson, T. E. (1985). Are all cognitive assessment methods created equal? A comparison of think aloud and thought listing. *Cognitive Therapy and Research, 9*, 399–414.

Brock, T. C. (1967). Communication discrepancy and intent to persuade as determinants of counterarguement production. *Journal of Experimental Social Psychology, 3*, 269–309.

Bruch, M. A. (1978). Type of cognitive modeling, imitation of modeled tactics, and modification of anxiety. *Cognitive Therapy and Research, 2*, 147–164.

Bruch, M. A. (1981). A task analysis of assertive behavior revisited: Replication and extension. *Behavior Therapy, 12*, 217–230.

Bruch, M. A., Haase, R. F., & Purcell, M. I. (1984). Content dimensions of self-statements in assertive situations: A factor analysis of two measures. *Cognitive Therapy and Research, 8*, 173–186.

Bruch, M. A., Juster, H. R., & Heisler, B. D. (1982). Conceptual complexity as a mediator of thought content and negative affect: Implications for cognitive restructuring interventions. *Journal of Counseling Psychology, 29*, 343–353.

Burgio, K. L., Glass, C. R., & Merluzzi, T. V. (1981). The effects of social anxiety and videotape performance feedback on cognitions and self-evaluations. *Behavioral Counseling Quarterly, 1*, 288–301.

Cacioppo, J. T., Glass, C. R., & Merluzzi, T. V. (1979). Self-statements and self-evaluations: A cognitive-response analysis of heterosocial anxiety. *Cognitive Therapy and Research, 3*, 249–262.

Cacioppo, J. T., & Petty, R. E. (1981). The thought-listing technique. In T. V. Merluzzi, C. R. Glass, & M. Genest (Eds.), *Cognitive assessment*. New York: Guilford Press.

Campbell, D., & Fiske, D. (1959). Convergent and discriminant validation by the multitrait–multimethod matrix. *Psychological Bulletin, 56*, 81–105.

Casas, J. M. (1976). A comparison of two mediational self-control techniques for the treatment of speech anxiety. *Dissertation Abstracts International, 36*, 4681B. (University Microfilms No. 76-5701).

Cattell, R. B., Eber, H. W., & Tatsuoka, M. M. (1970). *Handbook for the Sixteen Personality Factor Questionnaire*. Champaign, IL: Institute of Personality and Ability Testing.

Chiauzzi, E., & Heimberg, R. G. (1983). The effects of subjects' level of assertiveness, sex, and legitimacy of request on assertion-relevant cognitions: An analysis by postperformance videotape reconstruction. *Cognitive Therapy and Research, 7*, 555–564.

Clark, J., & Arkowitz, H. (1975). Social anxiety and the self-evaluation of interpersonal performance. *Psychological Reports, 36*, 211–221.

Cone, J. D. (1979). Confounded comparisons in the triple response mode research. *Behavioral Assessment, 1*, 85–95.

Craighead, L. W. (1979). Self-instructional training for assertive-refusal behavior. *Behavior Therapy, 10*, 529–542.

Cronbach, L. J., & Meehl, P. E. (1955). Construct validity in psychological tests. *Psychological Bulletin, 52*, 281–302.

Davis, F. W., & Yates, B. T. (1982). Self-efficacy expectancies versus outcome expectancies as determinants of performance deficits and depressive affect. *Cognitive Therapy and Research, 6*, 23–35.

Davison, G. C., Feldman, P. M., & Osborn, C. E. (1984). Articulated thoughts, irrational beliefs and fear of negative evaluation. *Cognitive Therapy and Research, 8*, 349–362.

Davison, G. C., Robins, C., & Johnson, M. K. (1983). Articulated thoughts during simulated situations: A paradigm for studying cognition in emotion and behavior. *Cognitive Therapy and Research, 7*, 17–40.

Derry, P. A., & Stone, G. L. (1979). Effects of cognitive-adjunct treatments on assertiveness. *Cognitive Therapy and Research, 3*, 213–221.

Eisler, R. M. (1976). The behavioral assessment of social skills. In M. Hersen & A. S. Bellack (Eds.), *Behavioral assessment: A practical handbook.* New York: Pergamon Press.

Eisler, R. M., Frederiksen, L. W., & Peterson, G. L. (1978). The relationship of cognitive variables to the expression of assertiveness. *Behavior Therapy, 9*, 419–427.

Ellis, A. (1962). *Reason and emotion in psychotherapy.* New York: Lyle Stuart.

Ericsson, K, & Simon, H. (1978). *Protocols as data: Effects of verbalizations.* Unpublished manuscript, Carnegie-Mellon University.

Ericcson, K. A., & Simon, H. A. (1980). Verbal reports as data. *Psychological Review, 82*, 215–251.

Fazio, R. H., & Zanna, M. P. (1981). Direct experience and attitude behavior consistency. In L. Berkowitz (Ed.), *Advances in experimental social psychology* (Vol. 14). New York: Academic Press.

Fiedler, D., & Beach, L. R. (1978). On the decision to be assertive. *Journal of Consulting and Clinical Psychology, 46*, 537–546.

Fox, E., & Davies, R. (1971). Test your rationality. *Rational Living, 5*, 23–25.

Fox, J. E., Houston, B. K., & Pittner, M. S. (1983). Trait anxiety and children's cognitive behaviors in an evaluative situation. *Cognitive Therapy and Research, 7*, 149–154.

Fremouw, W. J., & Harmatz, M. G. (1975). A helper model for behavioral treatment of speech anxiety. *Journal of Consulting and Clinical Psychology, 43*, 562–660.

Fremouw, W. J., & Zitter, R. E. (1978). A comparison of skills training and cognitive restructuring relaxation for treatment of speech anxiety. *Behavior Therapy, 9*, 248–259.

Fulkerson, K. E., Galassi, J. P., & Galassi, M. D. (1984). Relation between cognitions and performance in math anxious students: A failure of cognitive theory? *Journal of Counseling Psychology, 34*, 376–382.

Galassi, J. P., Frierson, H. T., Jr., & Siegel, R. G. (1984). Cognitions, test anxiety, and test performance: A closer look. *Journal of Consulting and Clinical Psychology, 52*, 319–320.

Genest, M., & Turk, D. C. (1981). Think-aloud approaches to cognitive assessment. In T. V. Merluzzi, C. R. Glass, & M. Genest (Eds.), *Cognitive assessment.* New York: Guilford Press.

Glass, C. R., & Arnkoff, D. B. (1983). Cognitive set and level of anxiety: Effects on thinking processes in problematic situations. *Cognitive Therapy and Research, 6*, 529–542.

Glass, C. R., & Merluzzi, T. V. (1981). Assessment of social-evaluative anxiety. In T. V. Merluzzi, C. R. Glass, & M. Genest (Eds.), *Cognitive assessment.* New York: Guilford Press.

Glass, C. R., Merluzzi, T. V., Biever, J. L., & Larsen, K. H. (1982). Cognitive assessment of social anxiety: Development and validation of a self-statement questionnaire. *Cognitive Therapy and Research, 6*, 37–55.

Goldfried, M. R., & Davison, G. C. (1976). *Clinical behavior therapy.* New York: Holt.

Goldfried, M. R., & Sobocinski, D. (1975). Effect of irrational beliefs on emotional arousal. *Journal of Consulting and Clinical Psychology, 43*, 504–510.

Gormally, J., Sipps, G., Raphael, R., Edwin, D., & Varvil-Weld, D. (1981a). The relationship between maladaptive cognitions and social anxiety. *Journal of Consulting and Clinical Psychology, 49*, 300–301.

Gormally, J., Varvil-Weld, D., Raphael, R., & Sipps, G. (1981b). Treatment of socially anxious college men using cognitive counseling and skills training. *Journal of Counseling Psychology, 28*, 147–157.

Greenwald, A. G. (1968). Cognitive learning, cognitive response to persuasion, and attitude change. In A. G. Greenwald, T. C. Brock, & T. M. Ostrom (Eds.), *Psychological foundations of attitudes.* New York: Academic Press.

Halford, K., & Foddy, M. (1982). Cognitive and social skills correlates of social anxiety. *British Journal of Clinical Psychology, 21*, 17–28.

Hartman, B. (1971). Sixty revealing questions for 20 minutes. *Rational Living, 5*, 23–25.

Heimberg, R. G., Chiauzzi, E. J., Becker, R. E., & Madrazo-Pederson, R. (1983). Cognitive mediation of assertive behavior: An analysis of the self-statement patterns of college students, psychiatric patients, and normal adults. *Cognitive Therapy and Research, 7*, 455–464.

Himle, D. P., Thyer, B. A., & Papsdorf, J. D. (1982). Relationships between rational beliefs and anxiety. *Cognitive Therapy and Research, 6*, 219–223.

Hollandsworth, J. G., Jr., Glazeski, R. C., Kirkland, K., Jones, G. E., & Van Norman, L. R. (1979). An analysis of the nature and effects of test anxiety: Cognitive, behavioral, and physiological components. *Cognitive Therapy and Research, 3*, 165–180.

Huber, J. W., & Altmaier, E. M. (1983). An investigation of the self-statement systems of phobic and nonphobic individuals. *Cognitive Therapy and Research, 7,* 355–362.

Hurlburt, R. T. (1976). *Self observation and self control.* Unpublished doctoral dissertation, University of South Dakota.

Hurlburt, R. T. (1980). Validation and correlation of thought sampling with retrospective measures. *Cognitive Therapy and Research, 4,* 103–111.

Hurlburt, R. T., Lech, B. C., & Saltman, S. (1984). Random sampling of thought and mood. *Cognitive Therapy and Research, 8,* 263–275.

Jaremko, M. E., & Walker, G. R. (1978). *The content of coping statements in the cognitive restructuring component of stress inoculation.* Unpublished manuscript, University of Richmond.

Jones, R. G. (1969). A factored measure of Ellis' Irrational Belief System (Doctoral dissertation, Texas Technological College, 1968). *Dissertation Abstracts International, 29,* 4379B–4380B.

Kanter, N. J., & Goldfried, M. R. (1979). Relative effectiveness of rational restructuring and self-control desensitization in the reduction of interpersonal anxiety. *Behavior Therapy, 10,* 472–490.

Kendall, P. C., & Hollon, S. D. (Eds.). (1980). *Cognitive-behavioral interventions: Assessment methods.* New York: Academic Press.

Kendall, P. C., & Hollon, S. D. (1981). Assessing self-referent speech: Methods in the measurement of self-statements. In P. C. Kendall & S. D. Hollon (Eds.), *Assessment strategies for cognitive-behavioral interventions.* New York: Academic Press.

Kendall, P. C., & Korgeski, G. P. (1979). Assessment and cognitive-behavioral interventions. *Cognitive Therapy and Research, 3,* 1–22.

Kent, R. N., & Foster, S. L. (1977). Direct observational procedures: Methodological issues in naturalistic settings. In A. R. Ciminero, K. S. Calhoun & H. E. Adams (Eds.), *Handbook of behavioral assessment.* New York: Wiley.

Kirkland, K., & Hollandsworth, J. G., Jr. (1980). Effective test-taking: Skills-acquisition versus anxiety-reduction techniques. *Journal of Consulting and Clinical Psychology, 48,* 431–439.

Knapp, S. (1979). Life events, rationality and emotional disturbance. *Psychological Reports, 45,* 510.

Lang, P. J., & Lazovik, A. D. (1963). Experimental desensitization of a phobia. *Journal of Abnormal and Social Psychology, 66,* 519–525.

Lange, A., & Jakubowski, P. (1976). *Responsible assertive behavior.* Champaign, IL: Research Press.

Lee, C. (1984a). Accuracy of efficacy and outcome expectations in predicting performance in a simulated assertive task. *Cognitive Therapy and Research, 8,* 37–48.

Lee, C. (1984b). Efficacy expectations and outcome expectations as predictors of performance in a snake handling task. *Cognitive Therapy and Research, 8,* 509–516.

Lick, J. R., & Katkin, E. S. (1976). Assessment of anxiety and fear. In M. Hersen & A. S. Bellack (Eds.), *Behavioral assessment: A practical handbook.* New York: Pergamon Press.

Lohr, J. M., & Bonge, D. (1981). On the distinction between illogical and irrational beliefs and their relationship to anxiety. *Psychological Reports, 48,* 191–194.

Lohr, J. M., & Bonge, D. (1982a). The factorial validity of the Irrational Beliefs Test: A psychometric investigation. *Cognitive Therapy and Research, 6,* 225–230.

Lohr, J. M., & Bonge, D. (1982b). Relationships between assertiveness and factorially validated measures of irrational beliefs. *Cognitive Therapy and Research, 6,* 353–356.

Lohr, J. M., Bonge, D., & Jones, C. (1983). Social desirability and endorsement of irrational beliefs. *Psychological Reports, 53,* 395–397.

Lohr, J. M., Nix, J., Dunbar, D., & Mosesso, L. (1984). The relationship of assertive behavior in women and a validated measure of irrational beliefs. *Cognitive Therapy and Research, 8,* 287–297.

Lohr, J. M., & Rea, R. G. (1981). A disconfirmation of the relationship between fear of public speaking and irrational beliefs. *Psychological Reports, 48,* 795–798.

Luria, A. R. (1961). *The role of speech in the regulation of normal and abnormal behavior.* New York: Liveright.

Mahoney, M. J. (1977). Reflections on the cognitive-learning trend in psychotherapy. *American Psychologist, 32,* 5–13.

Malkiewich, L. E., & Merluzzi, T. V. (1980). Rational restructuring vs. desensitization with clients of diverse conceptual level: A test of a client-treatment matching model. *Journal of Counseling Psychology, 27,* 453–461.

Malloy, P. F., Fairbank, J. A., & Keane, T. M. (1983). Validation of a multimethod assessment of posttraumatic stress disorders in Vietnam veterans. *Journal of Consulting and Clinical Psychology, 51*, 488-494.

McCroskey, J. C. (1970). Measures of communication-bound anxiety. *Speech Monographs, 37*, 269-277.

Meichenbaum, D. H. (1977). *Cognitive-behavior modification*. New York: Plenum Press.

Meichenbaum, D. H., & Butler, L. (1979). Cognitive ethology: Assessing the streams of cognition and emotion. In K. Blankstein, P. Pliner, & J. Polivy (Eds.), *Advances in the study of communication and affect: Assessment and modification of emotional behavior* (Vol. 6). New York: Plenum Press.

Nay, W. R. (1977). Analogue measures. In A. R. Ciminero, K. S. Calhoun & H. E. Adams (Eds.), *Handbook of behavioral assessment*. New York: Wiley.

Nisbett, R. E., & Bellows, N. (1977). Verbal reports about causal influences on social judgments: Private access versus public theories. *Journal of Personality and Social Psychology, 35*, 613-624.

Nisbett, R. E., & Wilson, T. P. (1977). Telling more than we can know: Verbal reports on mental processes. *Psychological Review, 84*, 231-259.

Norton, G. R., Dinardo, P. A., & Barlow, D. H. (1983). Predicting phobics' response to therapy: A consideration of subjective, physiological and behavioural measures. *Canadian Psychology, 24*, 50-58.

Notarius, C. I. (1981). Assessing sequential dependency in cognitive performance data. In T. V. Merluzzi, C. R. Glass, and M. Genest (Eds.), *Cognitive assessment*. New York: Guilford Press.

Pitcher, S. W., Meikle, S. (1980). The topography of assertive behavior in positive and negative situations. *Behavior Therapy, 11*, 532-547.

Sarason, I. G. (1972). Experimental approaches to test anxiety: Attention and the uses of information. In C. D. Spielberger (Ed.), *Anxiety: Current trends in theory and research* (Vol. 2). New York: Academic Press.

Sarason, I. G. (1978). The test anxiety scale: Concept and research. In C. D. Spielberger & I. G. Sarason (Eds.), *Stress and anxiety* (Vol. 5). Washington, DC: Hemisphere.

Sarason, I. G. (1984). Stress, anxiety and cognitive interference: Reactions to tests. *Journal of Personality and Social Psychology, 46*, 929-938.

Sarason, I. G., & Stoops, R. (1978). Test anxiety and the passage of time. *Journal of Consulting and Clinical Psychology, 46*, 102-109.

Schule, J. G., & Wiesenfeld, A. R. (1983). Automatic response to self-critical thought. *Cognitive Therapy and Research, 7*, 189-194.

Schwartz, G. E., Davidson, R. J., & Coleman, D. J. (1978). Patterning of cognitive and somatic processes in the self-regulation of anxiety: Effects of meditation versus exercise. *Psychosomatic Medicine, 40*, 321-328.

Schwartz, R. M., & Gottman, J. M. (1976). Toward a task analysis of assertive behavior. *Journal of Consulting and Clinical Psychology, 44*, 910-920.

Shorkey, C., & Reyes, E. (1978). Relationship between self-actualization and rational thinking. *Psychological Reports, 42*, 842.

Shorkey, C., & Whiteman, V. (1977). Development of the Rational Behavior Inventory: Initial validity and reliability. *Educational and Psychological Measurement, 37*, 527-534.

Smith, T. W., Boaz, T. L., & Denny, D. R. (1984). Endorsement of irrational beliefs as a moderator of the effects of stressful life events. *Cognitive Therapy and Research, 8*, 363-370.

Smith, R. E., & Sarason, I. G. (1975). Social anxiety and the evaluation of negative interpersonal feedback. *Journal of Consulting and Clinical Psychology, 43*, 429.

Smith, T. W., & Zurawski, R. M. (1983). Assessment of irrational beliefs: The question of discriminant validity. *Journal of Clinical Psychology, 39*, 976-979.

Smye, M. (1977). *Verbal, cognitive and behavioral correlates of social anxiety*. Unpublished doctoral dissertation, University of Toronto.

Smye, M. D., & Wine, J. D. (1980). A comparison of female and male adolescents' social behavior and cognitions. *Sex Roles, 6*, 213-230.

Spielberger, C. D. (1980). *The Test Anxiety Inventory*. Palo Alto, CA: Consulting Psychologists Press.

Spielberger, C. D., Gorsuch, R., & Lushene, R. (1970). *Manual for the State-Trait Anxiety Inventory*. Palo Alto, CA: Consulting Psychologists Press.

Sutton-Simon, K., & Goldfried, M. R. (1979). Faulty thinking patterns in two types of anxiety. *Cognitive Therapy and Research, 3*, 193-203.

Trexler, L. D., & Karst, T. O. (1972). Rational-emotive therapy, placebo and no-treatment effects on public-speaking anxiety. *Journal of Abnormal Psychology, 79*, 60-67.

Watson, D., & Friend, R. (1969). Measurement of social-evaluative anxiety. *Journal of Consulting and Clinical Psychology, 33,* 448–457.

Whiteman, V. (1979). Development of an Australian version of the Rational Behavior Inventory. *Psychological Reports, 44,* 104–106.

Whiteman, V., & Shorkey, C. (1978). Validation testing of the Rational Behavior Inventory. *Educational and Psychological Measurement, 38,* 1143–1148.

Wolpe, J. (1969). *The practice of behavior therapy.* New York: Pergamon Press.

4

The Future for Cognitive Assessment of Anxiety: Let's Get Specific

PHILIP C. KENDALL AND RICK INGRAM

Despite the relatively short history of cognitive constructs in psychopathology, the variety of cognitive approaches to anxiety is truly remarkable. Various constructs, for example, have emphasized learned helplessness (Lavelle, Metalsky, & Coyne, 1979), internally focused negative attention (Sarason, 1972, 1975), limited depth and breadth of information encoding (Eysenck, 1979), reductions in cognitive capacity to process task-relevant information (Mueller & Thompson, 1984), patterns of anxious self-statements (Cacioppo, Glass, & Merluzzi, 1979; Meichenbaum, 1977), anxious cognitive schemata (Beck, 1976), deficits in storage and retrieval processes (Mueller, 1980), and enhanced processing of socially evaluative information (Smith, Ingram, & Brehm, 1983).

The emergence of such a variety of constructs is a mixed blessing. On the one hand, numerous theoretical ideas engender numerous empirical investigations that contribute to our knowledge of the cognitive corollaries of anxiety. On the other hand, however, such a variety of approaches can ultimately obscure understanding of what are the essential underlying cognitive mechanisms of anxiety. Superficially, for example, it seems eminently reasonable to ask which constructs most accurately model anxiety. As reasonable as this question may sound, however, it is not answerable; extant constructs span a diversity of analytic levels. Although at some point these different constructs may be integrated both theoretically and empirically, for now many of them clearly tap differing levels of conceptual analysis that make direct comparisons of adequacy difficult.

The implications of such a multitude of constructs for the cognitive-behavioral assessment of anxiety are clear. Depending on which construct a particular assessment method taps, empirical results can vary widely and different conclusions can be reached concerning the cognitive contribution to anxiety. It is not possible at present to specify which constructs are the most pertinent to understanding anxiety, but it may be helpful to organize extant constructs so that the conceptual target of anxiety assessment procedures can be specified. Elsewhere we have proposed the utility of a taxonomic system to classify the various elements of cognition (Ingram & Kendall, 1986) and we believe such a system can profitably be applied to the assessment of cognition in anxiety. According to our cognitive taxonomic system, cognition can be divided into its major conceptual elements: (1) cognitive structure, (2) cognitive propositions, (3) cognitive operations, and

Philip C. Kendall. Department of Psychology, Temple University, Philadelphia, Pennsylvania.

Rick Ingram. Department of Psychology, San Diego State University, San Diego, California.

(4) cognitive products. After briefly defining each of these components, we will turn to a discussion of the relevance of these components for the cognitive assessment of anxiety.

Cognitive structure consists of the manner in which information is organized and/or represented internally. *Cognitive propositions* (or content), on the other hand, represent the information that is stored in the cognitive structures. Although definitions vary considerably (Winfrey & Goldfried, 1986), together these two concepts are usually referred to as *schemata*. A schema represents an individual's life experiences stored in a fashion that is cohesive and influential, filtering perceptions and guiding judgments. This structure serves as a mechanism for viewing the self, others, the past, the present, and the future. *Cognitive operations* (or processes) are the processes by which the system operates to input, transform, and output information. Finally, *cognitive products*, as the name implies, are the products of the manipulation of information throughout the system. As such, these are defined as the cognitions that the individual experiences and can typically be made aware of.

Cognitive Schemata

Among researchers interested in cognitive contributions to behavioral functioning, the schema construct has generated an enormous amount of recent interest and enthusiasm. However, the beginnings of the cognitive schema concept date back over half a century (Head, 1920) and have been revived in part by experimental psychologists whose concern with cognition has once again become paramount (e.g., Neisser, 1967). The notion of schemata as structures that guide information processing has also proved conceptually and empirically profitable for social psychologists interested in perception, and has become the cornerstone of the social-cognition domain (e.g., Cantor & Mischel, 1979; Fiske & Linville, 1980; Taylor & Crocker, 1981). Within cognitive-clinical psychology, the overwhelming majority of attention focused on cognitive schemata has been directed toward depressive disorders (Beck, 1967; Ingram, 1984; Kuiper, Derry, & MacDonald, 1982). By contrast, until now much less attention (both theoretically and empirically) has been paid to the cognitive schemata in anxiety.

One exception to the lack of theoretical attention is provided by Beck (1976), who has suggested that the cognitive functioning of anxious individuals is characterized by a schema dominated by propositions of psychological and/or physical danger and harm to the person or to something valued by the person. More recently, Beck and Emery (1985) have employed the concept of *threat* as the anxious person's cognitive focus. Empirically, only limited work has addressed the cognitive schemata operating in anxiety (Merluzzi, Rudy, & Glass, 1981). In one study, for example, Merluzzi, Rudy, and Krejei (1986) used multidimensional scaling techniques to assess the cognitive dimensions employed by low-assertive (socially anxious) individuals in determining the likelihood of their behaving assertively in several different situations. Their results indicated that the key cognitive dimensions focused on by these subjects were the characteristics of the *other* individuals in the situation—specifically, in this case, the status of the other person. From a cognitive-structure standpoint, these results suggest that socially anxious individuals use narrow (unidimensional) schematic representations. In a social situation, socially anxious individuals, who may otherwise have several cognitive content dimensions available, are concerned primarily with the perceived status of the interaction partner. Non–socially anxious individuals may employ a broader range of dimensions in determining how to act in the same social situation. Hence, although socially anxious individuals may possess a number of diverse cognitive schemata, we speculate that propositions particularly relevant to the dimensions of target individuals (such as threat due to status) make up the schema that is activated in a potentially anxiety-arousing situation.

Some indirect support for this speculation was found in a study by Smith et al. (1983). Employing an incidental recall–depth of processing paradigm that presented subjects with information either about themselves or about how other individuals viewed the subject, Smith et al. found that in a socially stressful situation, socially anxious subjects experienced an increase in the recall of information concerning *others' evaluations of themselves*. Conversely, no evidence was found that these individuals displayed an enhanced recall of information relevant to their own evaluations of themselves. These data suggest that socially anxious individuals have cognitive schemata that, when activated, are characterized by a network of propositions reflecting concern over the evaluations of other people and how these people might affect them. This is in contrast to cognitive schemata that process information primarily about the self, as are found in much of the cognitive depression research. It is our view that the particular cognitive schemata that underlie anxiety processes reflect propositions that are concerned with what other people are thinking rather than content that concerns the self as such (see also Mueller & Thompson, 1984).

In a study assessing the specificity of cognitive variables in depression and anxiety, Ingram, Kendall, Smith, Donnell, and Ronan (1986) employed an incidental recall paradigm consisting of depressive, anxious, or nonpsychopathological content stimulus adjectives. Of methodological relevance, subjects were screened using psychometric criteria to constitute groups of anxious (and not depressed), depressed (and not anxious), both anxious and depressed, and neither anxious nor depressed individuals. Procedurally, this allowed for an examination of the specificity of the cognitive phenomena. As would be predicted by a content specificity hypothesis, anxious subjects evidenced an enhanced recall of anxious information, whereas depressed subjects showed greater recall of depressive content adjectives. On the basis of these results, it would appear that the *self*-schema of anxious individuals contains propositions specifically relevant to anxiety (e.g., tense, nervous). The schema *activated* in anxious individuals in potentially anxious or evaluative situations, however, may be more strongly characterized by content concerning *other* individuals and how these others will evaluate or possibly harm the person. Thus, in the Ingram, Kendall, Smith, Donnell, and Ronan (1986) study, the "normal, everyday" anxious self-schema of anxious subjects was tapped. In light of an anxiety-provoking situation, however, as was the case in Smith et al. (1983), where socially anxious subjects were required to speak in front of a group, and with Merluzzi et al. (1986), where anxious subjects were asked to imagine a socially stressful situation, a different schema may have been activated that led subjects *not* to think about themselves in the situation but to focus instead on other people and their evaluations. We propose that the data suggest two anxiety-linked schemata operative in anxiety disorders—one that is self-relevant and contains anxious, questioning content, and an "other" relevant schema that becomes prepotent in potentially stressful situations and that contains propositions relevant to other people and to the evaluations of these other people.

Assessment of Cognitive Schemata

Considerable interest in cognitive schemata is seen in experimental-cognitive, social-cognitive, and cognitive-clinical psychology, and it is both important and timely to turn our attention to the cognitive-behavioral assessment of anxiety-linked schemata. We believe that several interrelated issues are crucial for understanding the contribution of cognitive schemata to anxiety disorders. First, the basic structure and functioning of anxiety schemata are central issues for understanding the cognitive components of anxiety. As we have noted, research evidence from several sources appears to suggest that two schemata may be operative in anxious individuals: (1) a questioning self-schema and (2) a "harmful other" schema. A profitable future direction, we believe, is an examination of these two potential schemata and some steps toward determining their interrelationship. For example, knowledge of the cognitive variables operative in anxiety will be advanced by empirically resolving the issue of which schema (if in fact two distinguishable schemata exist) is active in a given situation and what is its cognitive content. Other basic questions concern the implications of these schemata for typical cognitive functioning in anxiety states. Empirical efforts directed toward answering questions about the sorts of cognitions associated with these schemata, their similarities or differences, the actual behaviors associated with these cognitions, effects on the processing of both internal and external information, and the characteristics of the situations that elicit these schemata are much needed if we are to begin to understand the contributions of cognitive schemata to anxiety.

Schematic Change Processes

One of the most important functions of the assessment process is the determination of change in cognitive variables as a result of therapeutic intervention procedures. From a basic conceptual level, examining the covariance of cognitive variables with improving levels of behavioral and affective functioning affords important information about how those cognitive mechanisms are related to the etiology and course of a given disorder. More important, data on cognitive change factors may also offer insights into the modification and refinement of therapeutic techniques for more effective targeting and alteration of the specific factors crucial to a disorder (Kendall, 1981).

Surgeons, Mechanics, or Carpenters? How to Proceed with the Modification of Schemata?

An important target for future assessment efforts is the manner in which schemata are altered as a result of intervention methods. At present, there are several broad hypotheses concerning the way this may occur in depression (Ingram & Hollon, 1986), and these may be applicable to anxiety. It is conceivable, for example, that the effect of therapeutic processes is the functional amelioration or removal in some manner of the schemata underlying anxiety. Evidence in depression, for instance (Murphy, Simmon, Wetzel, & Lustman, 1984), indicates that effectively treated patients (whether by pharmocological or psychotherapeutic means) show few signs of previous cognitive processes that could be considered indicative of the presence and operation of a depressive schema. Thus therapeutic procedures might functionally eliminate anxious schemata in a manner we might consider analogous to what the medical surgeon does in the case of physical dysfunction. We would therefore label this hypothesis the *cognitive surgeon model* to denote the possibility that the primary change process is in some sense the removal of a troublesome cognitive structure.

Although schematic change hypotheses are rarely specified precisely, and few data exist to suggest how schemata might be changed (Taylor & Crocker, 1981), the underlying assumption among many researchers regarding cognitive change mechanisms appears to be that dysfunctional schemata are not so much eliminated as altered or changed by therapy. Hence, we might call this hypothesis the *cognitive mechanic model*, suggesting that the role of the therapist is to alter or fix the dysfunctional schema in some fashion. Goldfried and Robbins (1983, p. 53) note the possibility that therapy may modify self-schemata by "helping clients to build up new sets of associations about themselves. . . ." Another possibility is that schemata might be altered through their integration with extant and developed schemata that are more functional. Thus, if connections are made between other schemata and the schema underlying anxiety, then this latter schema may be less likely to be activated and, even when activated, may occupy a less dominant position in the cognitive processing of relevant information.

Finally, there is what we will call here the *cognitive carpenter model*. Although a number of researchers have suggested that the change resulting from psychotherapeutic tactics is in the alteration of a schema in some manner, an alternative possibility is that therapy builds new schemata that are functionally incompatible with the anxiety schema. These schemata are procedural rather than declarative schemata (see Nasby & Kihlstrom, 1986) and are characterized by propositions reflecting *how to cope* with anxiety-provoking situations. According to this hypothesis, when a potentially anxiety-arousing situation is encountered, although the anxiety schema will be activated, a coping schema is also activated. This schema would contain propositions that reflect ways to appraise more functionally and then deal effectively with a problem. Relevant schema propositions, for instance, might give rise to questions such as "What is the worst possible thing that could happen to me if I fail this test?" (or "don't make a good impression on this individual," or "can't speak the language in this country"). Such appraisals should decrease the amount of anxious affect the individual experiences while allowing more cognitive capacity actually to focus on the tasks at hand. Thus, in the cognitive carpenter mode, the function of the therapist is to help the individual to build these new schemata that help deal with anxiety situations in an effective way. Although the anxiety schema is not necessarily removed or altered, according to this hypothesis, it becomes less prepotent and hence less functionally troublesome. The individual still experiences some anxiety, but as a coping schema cues the individual to ways to handle this anxiety, it becomes no longer debilitating.

The aforementioned hypotheses are not necessarily mutually exclusive, and it is probable that some combination of these or some other mechanisms may be responsible for the schema-based changes that occur in therapy for anxiety. Nevertheless, these hypotheses can be considered matters of relative emphasis concerning which types of schematic changes might be primarily responsible for improved functioning and reductions in anxiety.

Cognitive Operations

As previously noted, cognitive operations reflect the various procedures by which the components of the system operate. Several cognitive operations have been implicated in anxiety, including—from an information-processing perspective—storage processes, retrieval processes, and limited processing capacity (see Mueller & Thompson, 1984). Perhaps, however, the most extensively developed cognitive operation with regard to anxiety is the notion of anxious self-preoccupation (Sarason, 1975; Wine, 1971). In this context, self-preoccupation reflects an increased level of attention that is directed toward internal factors to the relative exclusion of externally based, task-relevant information. Although the content of this attention may focus on cognitions of doubt and concern with others' evaluation, (Smith et al., 1983), the *process* is one of excessive and detrimental self-focused attention, in much the same manner that self-focused attention is related to depression (Ingram & Smith, 1984). Thus, although there are undoubtedly a number of important operations involved in anxiety, current theory suggests that excessive self-focused attention may be a crucial in the etiology and maintenance of anxiety.

Assessment of Cognitive Operations

Roth and Tucker (1986) note that the nature of self-focused attentional processes can differ depending on the disorder under consideration. In anxiety, they suggest, the cognitions associated with self-focused attention may reflect attempts to gain control over a situation, whereas in depression, self-focused attention is related to a reduction in sensitivity to the external environment. The nature of these potential differences is an important research question. More specifically, comparative research examining the differences in self-focused attention will be important in understanding how this particular cognitive operation contributes to anxiety disorders.

Although they are conceptualized similarly, there may be some important distinctions between self-focused attention and self-preoccupation. Whereas self-focused attention can be viewed as a chronic phenomenon, and hence a "trait" (see Buss, 1980), it is perhaps more typically seen as a state variable that co-varies with a number of situational determinants (e.g., Carver & Scheier, 1981). In contrast, self-preoccupation implies a maladaptive *perseveration* of the self-focused state. Thus one key dimension of internal focusing in anxiety may be the *inflexibility of the process*. Nonanxious individuals, although they enter states of self-focused attention, may be able to shift much more readily out of this state, even if only temporarily, when it is called for by the situation. Such seems to be the case in social-psychological research showing that self-focused attention can have a positive effect on task performance (since the parameters of the task *must* be attended to for adequate performance). Anxious individuals, on the other hand, may have substantially less control over this operation and may continue to focus internally even in situations where external focusing is more adaptive and appropriate. A prime direction for future research is the examination of this flexibility dimension. More generally, future research efforts might profitably be aimed at determining the various parameters of internally directed attention as it relates to anxiety. Although research has shown, for instance, that experimentally increasing self-focused attention impairs the performance of high-test-anxious individuals (Carver, Peterson, Follansbee, & Scheier, 1983), studies examining the naturally occurring incidence and characteristics of self-focused attention among different subgroups of anxiety disorders and in differing situations are needed.

Finally, although some research has examined the cognitive operation of internally directed attention in anxiety, our knowledge of the essential characteristics of anxiety will be furthered by empirical studies of other conceptualizations of such operations. Elsewhere, we have argued that the constructs and empirical methods of an information-processing perspective can benefit cognitive-clinical issues in a variety of ways (Ingram & Kendall, 1986), and we suggest that anxiety theory and research is a prime example in this regard. To date, compared to the extant body of data on anxiety, there are relatively few theoretical and empirical reports concerning information-processing operations (see, for example, Eysenck, 1982; Mueller & Thompson, 1984; Merluzzi et al., 1986). Abundant clinical observation, however, suggests that anxious individuals misinterpret both environmental and internal cues in a manner that arouses, exacerbates, and maintains anxious affect (Beck, 1976). We believe that future research reports that employ information-processing constructs and methodologies (see Ingram & Kendall, 1986) will be an important step in (1) helping to validate empirically the clinical observation of "distorted" processing of information in anxious states and (2) helping to elucidate the cognitive operations that may be at the root of the encoding, storage, and/or retrieval processes that engender dysfunctional information processing and ultimately contribute to anxiety disorders.

Cognitive Products

A final category of cognitive constructs is the idea of *cognitive products*—the conditions, thoughts, ideas, and so on that individuals consciously experience. A number of constructs have specifically dealt with cognitive products (content). Another particularly important concept is the idea of self-talk in anxiety.

Imagine yourself planning a journey that will take you to a South American country for the first time. Imagine also that you will be traveling alone and that you do not speak the native language of the country. A contact person will meet you upon arrival, but much of your time in the foreign land will be spent on your own. As part of this imaginary scenario, you think of the political climate in the country, the extent of poverty said to exist there, and the fact that you are blond and will be readily identified as a *gringa* from the United States. Following this exercise in imagination, reflect on the thoughts that came to your mind as your imagination took you on the journey.

Given the lack of knowledge of the language and the related difficulties, a rational person would likely have a series of questions run through his or her mind. How will I communicate? Will people take advantage of me on prices since I will be an obvious tourist? What if people do not understand my English? These particular sentences may or may not have occurred to each person, but the general theme—asking questions—is likely to have taken place. As the exciting event approaches a certain amount of anxiety occurs; as part of this anxious state, the cognitive activity focuses on addressing the many questions that appear. The "what if" questions that are generated are characteristic of anxious persons.

Change the scenario only slightly so that you, as the main character, are now conversant in the foreign language and are not blond. The self-talk that you experience will be less dominated by questions reflecting anxiety, and more focused on your eager anticipation of the forthcoming journey. Thoughts such as "I want to be sure to visit _____," "I want to find some artisan shops and purchase gifts," or "The weather this time of year will be delightful" no longer represent an anxiety state as much as they do an anticipatory positive affect. The point of this illustration—borne out by some related research—is that the pattern of self-talk associated with anxiety is a series of *automatic questions*.

On the basis of the foregoing analysis, it follows that what may be specific to the self-talk of anxiety disorders is not exact content, but an overabundance of a specific style—asking questions. The key to anxious self-talk may not be necessarily negative or positive, and no specific reference to any one object, event, or person is to be expected. Rather, the feature of the self-talk associated with anxiety is the *automatic questioning* that dominates the internal dialogue. Questions of many types and concerning many issues are apparent. Consistent in its question form, the anxious individual's self-talk places him- or herself in a situation where not only are possibilities recognized, but the resources perceived to be necessary to address these possibilities are absent. The questions are not mere indications of a careful and reflective process but, instead, betray a rapid-fire sense of impending incompetence. Each "what if" carries the message of an inability to handle the forthcoming situation.

Nonanxious individuals whose self-perceptions are not dominated by a sense of incompetence will entertain questions, and some more careful problem solvers will entertain more questions than others. But the automaticity of the questioning and its pervasiveness remain specific to the anxious person. Thus, a continuum could be developed according to the degree to which questions dominate a person's self-talk. The thoughts of anxious individuals would be dominated by questions appearing in an automatic fashion. Careful problem solvers might have more questions than average, but these would appear laced with other thoughts (e.g., alternative solutions) and also at a less automatic pace. A normal rate of questions within the self-dialogue would fall somewhere in the middle, with eager individuals perhaps scoring higher than dullards. Impulsive people would entertain few questions, acting quickly without the benefit of analytic self-talk.

One function of automatic questioning is to maintain uncertainty. The anxious state, in a sense, perpetuates itself. Questions are occurring at a rapid rate, and avoiding the acceptance of reasonable solutions, including avoidance of the attempt to resolve some of the questions, perpetuates the aroused state.

Another distinctive feature of the anxious internal dialogue is the extent to which time and effort are expended on discussing circumstances that are *very unlikely*. A nonanxious person might entertain possibilities, but the bulk of the effort would be realistic and the options would be within reason. Anxiety states have associated with them an excessiveness in the imagined likelihood that otherwise unlikely events will actually take place. Think of the elevator phobic who experiences excessive questioning of the safety of the elevator. Despite documentation of the rarity of malfunction, the mental effort involved here is expanded routinely and with self-perceived justification.

Also associated with anxious automatic questioning is the fact that some measure of hope must be present for the questioning to continue. For one to engage in the intended entertainment of possibilities, one must also have an associated degree of confidence that something may indeed take place to remedy the situation. In the absence of this hope, the internal dialogue turns away from questioning and turns instead toward the general, internal, and negative types of self-talk more characteristic of depression. Depressive self-talk is typically barren of possibilities (e.g., "There is nothing I can do"); definitive (e.g., "I *am* useless"); and devoid of hope (e.g., "There's no use"). It is almost as if the self-talk of the depressive is a closed and inflexible negative answer to the constant querying of the anxious person.

The fact that depressive automatic thinking is characteristically a negative and definitive answer to the automatic questioning of anxious persons does not mean that depression necessarily follows anxiety. It is possible that a depressed person, as hope reemerges, will begin to consider possible solutions and, if emerging into an anxious state, might become burdened by the excessive number of questions that seem to require answers. As depressives are treated and taught to test their assumptions and consider alternative explanations for their self-perceived deficits, the clinician moves gradually, collaborating with the client throughout the data collection process and addressing one question at a time. It is this important aspect of the treatment of depression that might be associated with preventing a client from rushing straight from depression into an anxious state. "O.K., if the world isn't rotten, then what do I do . . . what about this and what about that." Once the depressive's blanket solution—that "all is rotten"—is taken from the client, the therapist must be cautious in introducing only a small number of alternative possibilities at a time.

Correspondingly, just as the emergence from depression may turn on added anxious thoughts, so anxiety states can turn to depression. After repetitious consideration of possibilities, a near constant asking "what if," the person may come to acknowledge that all these possibilities are unlikely and perhaps unreal. As more and more options are eliminated, the hope for a solution is reduced and more depressive mental activities are entertained. As possibilities are in decline, global and negative self-talk can increase.

Assessment of Cognitive Products

An important aspect of cognition in anxiety disorders is the notion of "automatic questioning". That is, the preponderance of cognitive products that occur during an anxiety state take the form of questions ("Is this _____?") as opposed to declarative statements ("This is _____!"), which serve to maintain the uncertainty in any given situation and hence its anxiety-arousing qualities. Clinical experience suggests that this is a sound hypothesis, and empirical data support the proposal. For instance, of the many self-statements generated by subjects instructed to think about a depressing experience and report the thoughts that came to mind, the clear majority were declarative. Moreover, of 100 self-statements included in a systematic evaluation of self-talk in depression, the 30 self-statements that reliably identified criterion groups included 27 declarative sentences (Hollon & Kendall, 1980). In a study of anxious self-talk that employed a similar methodology (Kendall & Hollon, 1985), 15 of the 32 self-statements that reliably identified anxious subjects were questions (e.g., "What am I going to do?" "Can I make it?"). In some cases, anxious subjects' reported self-talk that sounded like a declarative sentence, but was written as a question ("I can't stand it?"). Future research efforts can contribute to understanding the cognitive characteristics of anxiety by further examining the *form* that anxious cognitions take and how this form covaries with anxious affect.

To further illustrate some of the needs facing the assessment of cognitive products in anxiety, it is worthwhile to review work done with the Automatic Thoughts Questionnaire, or ATQ (Hollon & Kendall, 1980). The ATQ is a self-statement inventory presenting subjects with a series of predetermined items and requiring subjects to indicate the frequency with which they have had certain thoughts—an example of the endorsement method of cognitive assessment (Kendall & Hollon, 1981). The scale consists of 30 items that have been found to distinguish depressed from nondepressed college students and samples of clinical cases (Ross & Gottfredson, 1983); that evidence acceptable psychometric features (Dobson & Breiter, 1983); and that show specificity to depressive disorders (Harrell & Ryon, 1983; Hollon, Kendall, & Lumry, 1986). The ATQ has also been employed in studies of the effects of therapy, both process and outcome, and has been found to evidence change (e.g., Simons, Garfield, & Murphy, 1984).

The ATQ is only one example of the endorsement method (see also Kendall & Hollon, 1981), but it is nevertheless a good illustration of the potential merits of the endorsement methodology, for it is clear that a scale that can be studied psychometrically, scored easily, and used in diverse settings with relative ease has merits over other methods that may require greater reliability training for the test scorers and produce a lower ratio of collected to usable data. Efforts to further develop the instrument for the assessment of cognitive functioning specific to anxiety (Kendall & Hollon, 1986) seem worthwhile.

Although there are many issues that future research can address, we believe an important question is determining which kind of valence in self-statement is most predictive of anxiety. That is, anxiety might be linked to either decreases in positive cognition, increases in negative cognition, or some combination (or homeostatic balance) of the two. Kendall (Kendall, 1984; Kendall & Korgeski, 1979) described the idea of "the power of non-negative thinking" to organize the variety of empirical findings that suggest that increases in negative cognition are related to increasing behavioral dysfunction (and decreases in negative thinking related to increased functioning), independent of changes in positive or "nonnegative" cognitions. Since studies that dichotomize total cognition into negative and positive must show shifts in both categories when one changes, an important task for future research efforts is to determine which kind of cognition is in fact crucial to the production, maintainence, and remediation of anxiety states. Additionally, efforts to classify and understand the contribution of "nonvalenced" (neutral) cognition are much needed (e.g., Hays, Kendall, & Barber, 1985). Operational definitions in some studies of self-talk in anxiety appear to define "positive" cognition as anything that is not negative. It seems unlikely, however, that most well-adjusted individuals (save for when they are in a psychological laboratory and are explicitly asked to make evaluative judgments about themselves) experience as many positive self-statements as some investigations assume. It appears more likely that adaptive daily functioning requires individuals to use their cognitive apparatus to produce task-oriented, affectively neutral cognition, and that perhaps dysfunction occurs when cognitive products become excessively affective, regardless of whether the predominant content is negative (e.g., depression) or positive (e.g., mania). Thus studies to evaluate whether cognition is in fact positive or is simply devoid of affective/evaluative content may have important implications for cognitive functioning in anxiety.

Schwartz and Garamoni (1986) have offered an intriguing hypothesis regarding the favorability of cognitions in dysfunctional states. Citing evidence from diverse sources, they suggest that optimal human cognition consists of a homeostatic balance of roughly 62% favorable cognition and 38% negative cognition and, further, that psychological impairment is accompanied by shifts in this balance of cognition. In mild states of impairment, for example, this valence shifts to a more even balance between positive and negative cognition, which they characterize as an "internal state of conflict." When functioning becomes more severely impaired, however, the optimal balance reverses itself to the point where roughly two-thirds of cognition is negative and only a one-third minority is positive, a condition they describe as a "negative dialogue." When adaptive functioning is at its most severely impaired stage, then negative cognition exceeds this two-thirds negative level, and positive cognition is at a correspondingly low level. A variety of studies with dysfunctional populations (e.g., Kendall & Hays, 1986), have offered support for this suggestion.

Finally, *how* the content and valence of self-talk contribute to anxiety states is a crucial issue for future research efforts. Although evidence clearly supports a descriptive association between certain forms, content, and valences in anxiety, there is little empirical evidence to suggest the mechanisms by which these cognitions might affect anxious functioning. Research is also needed that examines the function and meaning of cognitive products in anxiety and empirically relates these variables to the cognitive, affective, and/or behavioral variables that precipitate anxiety disorders.

Anxious Self-Talk and the Treatment of Anxiety

Many inquiries into the role of self-talk in anxiety are at least in part focused on the treatment of an anxiety disorder. Examples of studies that have included some form of cognitive assessment within an anxiety treatment include Kendrick, Craig, Lawson, and Davidson's program for musical-performance anxiety (1982); Kendall, Williams, Pechacek, Graham, Shisslak, and Herzott's (1979) program for the management of stressful medical procedures; and Salovey and Haar's (1983) treatment for writing anxiety.

These studies, as might be expected given the recency of the topical interest, employed varied methods of assessment. In one sense, this detracts from a search for consistency. When consistency does appear, however, despite the use of dissimilar methodologies, one may be witnessing findings that are more compelling than those emerging from exact replications. One theme that does appear to have consistency despite methodological variability is the apparent differential sensitivity to treatment of positive and negative thinking. In several studies where both positive and negative thoughts were assessed, the frequency of positive thinking did not differentiate the groups, nor did it change from pretreatment to posttreatment. In contrast, dysfunctional groups evidenced greater amounts of negative thinking and, consistent with improvement seen on other measures that resulted from treatment, displayed a reduction in negative thinking.

Two reasonable themes have been presented so far: the self-talk of anxious patients is replete with questions, and the beneficial effects of treatment are evident in the reduction of negative thinking. Are these two notions compatible? At first blush, one might be inclined to say no. If the distinctive feature of the cognitive products is the *automatic questioning* aspect of the self-talk, then why does the negative self-talk show the beneficial changes? Other potential incongruities exist as well and might reduce the validity of either or both statements. However, the following analysis ties together both conclusions. The anxious state includes a flood of self-doubts, worries, and perceived challenges from the external and internal environments. Corresponding to this we see the automatic questioning as a distinctive surface feature. During treatment, there are confrontations, exposures, empirical tests, and other analyses of this uncertain thinking; as is often the case, the therapy turns to a consideration of the consequences of the client's uncertainties. The client's automatic question "What will I do if?" often leads to a conclusion such as "But then I'd look foolish." It is the negative consequences of the questioning self-talk that are threatening to the client, and it is this negative thinking that changes during treatment.

Further research is needed to clarify the details of the process of change in the internal dialogue. Our speculations draw on static comparisons of distinct groups and on pre–post changes. Future efforts would be wise to monitor self-talk throughout the course of treatment and analyze for process variations associated with documented outcome.

General Issues in the Cognitive-Behavioral Assessment of Anxiety

The Integration of Cognitive Mechanisms

There are undoubtedly a number of cognitive mechanisms that operate together to produce anxious states. Earlier we mentioned several mechanisms that are promising candidates. Although these and other, yet undetected, mechanisms may be important components, an ultimate understanding of the cognitive basis of anxiety will come from a knowledge of how these mechanisms function together.

Fundamental to the future of cognitive-behavioral assessment of anxiety is the need for theory and research that elucidates the *interaction* of the cognitive mechanisms underlying anxious information processing. On the basis of present conceptions, we propose that a logical sequence of cognitive processing goes as follows: When an individual encounters what might be considered a threatening situation, preattentive factors (Neisser, 1967) trigger the activation of an anxious schema containing proposi-tions or content relevant to how the situation might harm the individual (e.g., Merluzzi et al., 1986). The activated schema may differ from that of normal individuals in being particularly distorted or narrowly unidimensional. Additionally, the anxiety arousal process engenders a flooding of attention internally, creating a state of self-preoccupation (Sarason, 1975; Wine, 1971), which leads to anxious self-talk (Kendall, 1984) in the form of automatic questioning and an impairment in information storage and retrieval processes (Mueller & Thompson, 1984). These processes in turn precipitate inefficient cognitive and behavioral functioning in the particular situation.

Future theoretical and empirical efforts will need to address the relationship that exists among the various cognitive (and other) mechanisms of anxiety. On the basis of such advances, therapy outcome researchers will be able to evaluate the relative efficacy of targeting various points in the sequence. Our initial speculations are that the identifi-cation of the dominant dimension of the client's anxious schema will facilitate therapy and that the removal of negative self-talk (or reduction of excessive questioning) via performance-based procedures will increase competence and coping.

Issues of Specificity

Clearly, the anxious state consists of more than simply cognition. Uneasiness in the stomach, excessive sweating, and muscle tension all illustrate the physiological aspects; verbal dysfluencies, motor twitches, and an uneasy jitteriness are typical of the behav-ioral components. Although we do not argue that these features are unimportant, we suggest that the cognitive features have certain descriptive characteristics that are helpful in differentiating the anxious state from related affective conditions and other maladap-tive behavior patterns.

It has long been recognized that a compelling demonstration that a particular process or variable accounts for a meaningful proportion of variance in a given psycho-pathology requires that the particular process or variable must be (reasonably) unique to that psychopathology. This issue of specificity is particularly relevant in the case of research examining anxiety disorders. Not only are anxiety disorders common relative to other forms of psychopathology (see DSM-III), but anxiety is often correlated with depression and is evident in the "normal" population. Furthermore, when anxiety does reach problematic proportions, it can be considered a dimension that covaries with other neurotic and psychotic disorders. Thus anxiety is a disorder that is sometimes difficult, conceptually and empirically, to disentangle from other disorders.

Since anxiety is so common, a critical issue for future directions in the assessment of anxiety is to establish the specificity (or lack of specificity) of the cognitive processes associated with anxiety disorders. Like any other disorder, anxiety is composed of a number of sources of variance. Presumably, some of the sources are unique to anxiety, whereas others are common to psychological dysfunction in general. An analogy might be helpful here. In any given research paradigm, the partitioning of the sources of variance due to experimental treatments or manipulations is typically represented as

$$\text{Effect} = A + B + AB + E$$

whereas A is the unique variance due to one factor, B is the unique variance due to a second factor, AB is the variance due to an interaction of both factors, and E is the unpredictable error variable due to individual differences. Similarly, the partitioning of the variance that contributes to anxiety might be represented as:

$$\text{Anxiety} = \text{Critical anxious features} + \text{Common psychopathological features} + \text{Individual differences}$$

Here, *critical anxious features* are those that are unique to anxiety and differentiate it from other kinds of psychopathology. An example of potential critical features are the anxious schema that contains propositions specifically relevant to conceptions of fear or harm and the automatic questioning that dominates anxious self-talk. *Common psychopathological* features are those variables that are shared by other disorders (e.g., anxiety and depression)—that is, processes that occur in psychopathology in general. These features differentiate anxiety from normal functioning but not from other kinds of abnormal functioning. A possible candidate for a common psychopathological feature is self-preoccupation, a process that, as we have previously noted, has been conceptually and empirically linked to both anxiety (Sarason, 1975; Wine, 1971; Carver et al., 1983) and depression (Ingram & Smith, 1984; Ingram, Lumry, Cruet, & Seiber, 1986) and may well be associated with other dysfunctional states (e.g., schizophrenia, alcoholism). *Individual differences* represent the error variance in accounting for psychopathology; despite the presence of both critical and common features, any given psychopathology will be expressed in some unique ways depending on the learning history and individual characteristics of the person involved. In addition, since there are several different types of anxiety disorders, this conceptualization could be taken a step further to include features that are critical to particular kinds of anxiety. Thus critical features would compose factors that are common to anxiety disorders (but still different from other kinds of psychopathology), whereas a "specific anxiety disorder" classification would consist of features that differentiate one type of anxiety (e.g., social) from another (e.g., test).

The puzzle is not yet solved, although we can see present advances and possibilities for further understanding of the cognitive side of the anxiety disorders. The call of future research into the anxiety disorders is to recognize and consider the various types of cognitive activities, examine the differential predictiveness of cognitive functioning for the different psychopathologies, and otherwise pay greater attention to the specificity of the symptomatology of disorders.

References

Beck, A. T. (1967). *Depression: Clinical, experimental, and theoretical aspects.* New York: Hoeber.

Beck, A. T. (1976). *Cognitive theory and the emotional disorders.* New York: International University Press.

Beck, A. T., & Emery, G. (1985). *Anxiety and phobias: A cognitive perspective.* New York: Basic Books.

Buss, A. (1980). *Self-consciousness and social anxiety.* San Francisco: Freeman.

Cacioppo, J. T., Glass, C. R., & Merluzzi, T. V. (1979). Self-statements and self-evaluations: A cognitive response analysis of heterosexual anxiety. *Cognitive Therapy and Research*, 3, 249–262.

Cantor, N., & Mischel, W. (1979). Prototypes in person perception. In L. Berkowitz (Ed.), *Advances in experimental social psychology* (Vol. 12). New York: Academic Press.

Carver, C. S., Peterson, L. M., Follansbee, D. J., & Scheier, M. F. (1983). Effects of self-directed attention on performance and persistence among persons high and low in test anxiety. *Cognitive Therapy and Research*, *1*, 333–354.

Carver, C. S., & Scheier, M. F. (1981). *Attention and self-regulation: A control-theory approach to human behavior*. Berlin and New York: Springer-Verlag.

Dobson, K. S., & Breiter, H. J. (1983). Cognitive assessment of depression: Reliability and validity of three measures. *Journal of Abnormal Psychology*, *92*, 107–109.

Eysenck, M. W. (1979). Anxiety, learning, and memory: A reconceptualization. *Journal of Research in Personality*, *13*, 363–385.

Eysenck, M. W. (1982). *Attention and arousal*. New York: Springer-Verlag.

Fiske, S. T., & Linville, P. W. (1980). What does the schema concept buy us? *Personality and Social Psychology Bulletin*, *6*, 543–557.

Goldfried, M. R., & Robbins, C. (1983). Self-schema, cognitive bias, and the processing of therapeutic experiences. In P. C. Kendall (Ed.), *Advances in cognitive-behavioral research and therapy* (Vol. 2). New York: Academic Press.

Harrell, T. H., & Ryon, N. B. (1983). Cognitive-behavioral assessment of depression: Clinical validation fo the Automatic Thoughts Questionnaire. *Journal of Consulting and Clinical Psychology*, *51*, 721–725.

Hays, R., Kendall, P. C., & Barber, C. (1985). *Self-referent speech and psychopathology*. Paper presented at the convention of the Association for Advancement of Behavior Therapy, Houston, TX, November.

Head, H. (1920). *Studies in neurology*. New York and London: Oxford University Press.

Hollon, S. D., & Kendall, P. C. (1980). Cognitive self-statements in depression. Development of an Automatic Thoughts Questionnaire. *Cognitive Therapy and Research*, *4*, 384–395.

Hollon, S. D., Kendall, P. C., & Lumry, A. (1986). The specificity of depressotypic cognitions in clinical depression. *Journal of Abnormal Psychology*, *95*, 52–60.

Ingram, R. E. (1984). Toward an information processing analysis of depression. *Cognitive Therapy and Research*, *8*, 443–478.

Ingram, R. E., & Hollon, S. D. (1986). Cognitive therapy of depression from an information processing perspective. In R. E. Ingram (Ed.), *Information processing approaches to clinical psychology*. New York: Academic Press.

Ingram, R. E., & Kendall, P. C. (1986). Cognitive clinical psychology: Implications of an information processing perspective. In R. E. Ingram (Ed.), *Information processing approaches to clinical psychology*. New York: Academic Press.

Ingram, R. E., Kendall, P. C., Smith, T. W., Donnell, C., & Ronan, K. (1986). *Cognitive specificity in emotional distress*. Manuscript submitted for publication.

Ingram, R. E., Lumry, A., Cruet, D., & Seiber, W. (1986). *Attentional processes in clinical depression*. Manuscript submitted for publication.

Ingram, R. E., & Smith, T. W. (1984). Depression and internal versus external focus of attention. *Cognitive Therapy and Research*, *8*, 139–152.

Kendall, P. C. (1981). Assessment and cognitive-behavioral interventions: Purposes, proposals, and problems. In P. C. Kendall & S. D. Hollon (Eds.), *Assessment strategies for cognitive-behavioral interventions*. New York: Academic Press.

Kendall, P. C. (1984). Behavioral assessment and methodology. In G. T. Wilson, C. M. Franks, K. D. Brownell, & P. C. Kendall (Eds.), *Annual review of behavior therapy: Theory and practice* (Vol. 9). New York: Guilford Press.

Kendall, P. C., & Hays, R. C. (1986). *Self-talk and psychopathology: The balance of positive and negative thinking*. Manuscript submitted for publication, Temple University, Philadelphia.

Kendall, P. C., & Hollon, S. D. (1981). Assessing self-referent speech: Methods in the measurement of self-statements. In P. C. Kendall & S. D. Hollon (Eds.), *Assessment strategies for cognitive-behavioral interventions*. New York: Academic Press.

Kendall, P. C., & Hollon, S. D. (1986). *Development of an anxious self-statements inventory*. Unpublished manuscript in preparation, Temple University, Philadelphia.

Kendall, P. C., & Korgeski, G. P. (1979). Assessment and cognitive-behavioral interventions. *Cognitive Therapy and Research*, *3*, 1–21.

Kendall, P. C., Williams, L., Pechacek, T. F., Graham, L. E., Shisslak, C., & Herzoff, N. (1979). Cognitive-behavioral and patient education interventions in cardiac catheterization procedures: The Palo Alto Medical Psychology Project. *Journal of Consulting and Clinical Psychology, 47,* 49–58.

Kendrick, M. J., Craig, K. D., Lawson, D. M., & Davidson, P. D. (1982). Cognitive and behavioral therapy for musical-performance anxiety. *Journal of Consulting and Clinical Psychology, 50,* 353–362.

Kuiper, N. A., Derry, P. A., & Macdonald, M. R. (1982). Self-reference and person perception in depression. In G. Weary & H. Mirels (Eds.), *Integrations of clinical and social psychology.* New York: Oxford Press.

Lavelle, T. L., Metalsky, G. I., & Coyne, J. C. (1979). Learned helplessness, test anxiety, and acknowledgment of contingencies. *Journal of Abnormal Psychology, 88,* 381–387.

Meichenbaum, D. (1977). *Cognitive-behavior modification: An integrated approach.* New York: Plenum Press.

Merluzzi, T. V., Rudy, T. E., & Glass, C. R. (1981). The information processing paradigm: Implications for clinical science. In T. V. Merluzzi, C. R. Glass, & M. Genest (Eds.), *Cognitive assessment.* New York: Guilford Press.

Merluzzi, T. V., Rudy, T. E., & Krejei, M. (1986). Social skill and anxiety: Information processing perspectives. In R. E. Ingram (Ed.), *Information processing approaches to clinical psychology.* New York: Academic Press.

Mueller, J. H. (1980). Test anxiety and the encoding and retrieval of information. In I. G. Sarason (Ed.), *Test anxiety: Theory, research, and applications.* Hillsdale, NJ: Erlbaum.

Mueller, J. H., & Thompson, W. B. (1984). Test anxiety and distinctiveness of personal information. In H. M. van der Ploeg, R. Schwarzer, & C. D. Spielberger (Eds.), *Advances in test anxiety research* (Vol. 3). Hillsdale, NJ: Erlbaum.

Murphy, G. E., Simons, A. D., Wetzel, R. D., & Lustman, P. J. (1984). Cognitive therapy and pharmacotherapy, singly and together, in the treatment of depression. *Archives of General Psychiatry, 41,* 33–41.

Nasby, W., & Kihlstrom, J. F. (1986). Cognitive assessment of personality and psychopathology. In R. E. Ingram (Ed.), *Information processing approaches to clinical psychology.* New York: Academic Press.

Neisser, V. (1967). *Cognitive psychology.* New York: Appleton-Century-Crofts.

Ross, S. M., & Gottfredson, D. K. (1983). *Cognitive self-statements in depression: Findings across clinical populations.* Paper presented at the meeting of the Association for Advancement of Behavior Therapy, Washington, DC.

Roth, D. L., & Tucker, D. (1986). Neural systems of emotional control on information processing. In R. E. Ingram (Ed.), *Information processing approaches to clinical psychology.* New York: Academic Press.

Salovey, P., & Haar, M. D. (1983). Treating writing anxiety: Cognitive restructuring and writing process training. Paper presented at the Education Research Associates Convention, Montreal.

Sarason, I. G. (1972). Experimental approaches to test anxiety: Attention and the uses of information. In C. D. Spielberger (Ed.), *Anxiety: Current trends in theory and research* (Vol. 2). New York: Academic Press.

Sarason, I. G. (1975). Anxiety and self-preoccupation. In I. G. Sarason & C. D. Spielberger (Eds.), *Stress and anxiety* (Vol. 2). New York: Hemisphere.

Schwartz, R. M., & Garamoni, G. L. (1986). A structural mode of positive and negative states of mind: Asymmetry in the internal dialogue. In P. C. Kendall (Ed.), *Advances in cognitive-behavioral research and therapy* (Vol. 5). New York: Academic Press.

Simons, A. D., Garfield, S. L., & Murphy, G. E. (1984). The process of change in cognitive therapy and pharmacotherapy of depression. *Archives of General Psychiatry, 41,* 45–51.

Smith, T. W., Ingram, R. E., & Brehm, S. S. (1983). Social anxiety, anxious self-preoccupation, and recall of self-relevant information. *Journal of Personality and Social Psychology, 44,* 1276–1283.

Taylor, S. E., & Crocker, J. (1981). Schematic bases of social information processing. In E. T. Higgins, C. P. Herman, & M. P. Zanna (Eds.), *Social cognition: The Ontario symposium on personality and psychology.* Hillsdale, NJ: Erlbaum.

Wine, J. (1971). Test anxiety and direction of attention. *Psychological Bulletin, 76,* 92–104.

Winfrey, L. L., & Goldfried, M. R. (1986). Information processing and the human change process. In R. E. Ingram (Ed.), *Information processing approaches to clinical psychology.* New York: Academic Press.

5

Methodological Issues in Cognitive-Behavioral Treatments of Anxiety Disorders

LARS-GÖRAN ÖST AND LARS JANSSON

The last 20 years have seen intensive development of behavioral and cognitive methods for treating anxiety disorders. Probably no other field in psychiatry has attracted as much interest from behavior therapists. Because of the large number of different treatment methods (Marks, 1981), researchers in this field have encountered numerous methodological issues. A complete discussion of these falls outside the scope of this chapter. We have instead selected some issues that we consider important and that ought to be the subject of future behavioral research on anxiety disorders. These issues concern selection of patients for outcome studies, assessment of outcome for the different disorders, control groups, maintenance of treatment effects and follow-ups, training and supervision of therapists, and process research.

Furthermore, we have taken as a point of departure the experimental group outcome studies of behavioral methods in the different anxiety disorders. These studies are presented in Table 5.1, divided into sections concerning agoraphobia, social phobia, simple phobia, obsessive–compulsive disorder, and generalized anxiety disorder/panic disorder. The criteria for including a study in this table are:

1. The sample consists of clinical patients or community residents (studies on analogue subjects have been excluded).
2. The subjects have been randomly assigned to the conditions used.
3. At least one of these conditions was a behavioral or cognitive treatment.

Regarding simple phobia, all varieties of specific phobias have been included, but animal phobia is excluded because of the difficulty of deciding, for many of these studies, whether an analogue or a clinical sample was used. There is, however, no reason to believe that inclusion of animal phobia studies would have changed the conclusions significantly.

Lars-Göran Öst and Lars Jansson (deceased). Psychiatric Research Center, University of Uppsala, Ulleråker Hospital, Uppsala, Sweden.

TABLE 5.1 Controlled behavioral studies in anxiety disorders

Authors	n	Recruitment/ subjects	Inclusion criteria	Treatment methods	Design	Measures	Results	Percentage improvement	Follow-up
				Agoraphobia					
Gelder & Marks (1966)	20	Inpatients	No	1. Behavior therapy 2. Psychotherapy	Pre-post	A.r. of symptoms A.r. of social adjustment Self-ratings, EPI, CMI	1 = 2	1:30, 2:28	12 mo. (S-R, A)
Yorkston et al. (1968)	12	Inpatients	No	1. Methohexidone + SD 2. Relax. + Saline + SD 3. Relax. + SD 4. Methohexitone	Randomized block	Behavioral test A.r. of phobia Self-rating of fear EPI, BDI, Willoughby	1 = 2 = 3 = 4	No group improved sign.	—
Solyom et al. (1972)	27	Referrals Outpatients	Sparse	1. Aversion relief 2. Pseudoconditioning 3. Habituation	Pre-post	A.r. of phobia depression, anxiety, hysteria, hypochondria FSS-III, IPAT, MMPI	1 = 2 = 3	1:39, 2:21, 3:17	—
Everaerd et al. (1973)	14	Members of a phobia club Outpatients	No	1. Imag. + in vivo flooding 2. Successive approximation	Crossover	Behavioral test A.r. of phobia, etc. Self-rating of phobia FSS-III, MAS, I-E, DI	1 = 2	1:44, 2:60	3 mo. (S-R, A, B)
Gelder et al. (1973)	36	Referrals Outpatients	Elaborated	1. Nonspecific control 2. Desensitization 3. Flooding	Pre-post	Behavioral test A.r. of phobia, etc. Self-rating of phobia FSS, EPI, Mood, Heart rate, SC (Imag.)	2 = 3 > 1 2 = 3 > 1	(only change-scores) 1:19, 2:33, 3:33	6 mo. (S-R, A, B)
Johnston & Gath (1973)	6	Referrals Inpatients	No	1. Diazepam-placebo + flood. 2. Diazepam + flood. 3. No diazepam-placebo + flood. 4. No diazepam + flood.	Crossover	Behavioral test Self-rating ant. anx. sem. diff, mood scale	1 = 2 > 3 = 4	(only change-scores)	—
Lipsedge et al. (1973)	60	Referrals Outpatients	Sparse	1. Methohexitone + SD 2. SD 3. Iproniazide 4. Placebo	Factorial 2 × 3	A.r. of anx., avoid. Self-ratings of anx., avoid.	1 > 2, 3 > 4	(only change-scores)	24 mo. (S-R, A)
Stern & Marks (1973)	16	Referrals Outpatients	No	1. Long flood. + practice 2. Short flood. + practice	Latin square	A.r. of phobia, etc. Self-ratings of phobia Heart-rate, SC (imagery)	1 > 2	1:61, 2:?	—

Study	N	Population	Attention	Conditions	Design	Measures	Outcome	Scores	Follow-up
Emmelkamp (1974)	29	? Outpatients	No	1. Self-observation 2. Flooding + exposure 3. Self-observation + Flood. + Exp. 4. Waiting list control	Pre-post	Behavioral test A.r. of phobia, etc. Self-rating of phobia FSS-III, I-E, SAS, SDS	1 = 2 = 3 > 4	1:39, 2:41, 3:59 4:0	3 mo. (S-R, B)
Emmelkamp & Ultee (1974)	16	? Outpatients	No	1. Successive approximation 2. Self-obs.	Crossover	Behavioral test A.r. of phobia, etc. Self-rating of phobia FSS-III, I-E, SAS, SDS	1 = 2	(only change-scores)	3 mo. (S-R, B)
Hand et al. (1974)	25	Referrals Outpatients	No	1. Exposure, high cohesion 2. Exp, low cohesion	Pre-post	Behavioral test A.r. of phobia, etc. Self-rating of phobia, etc.	1 = 2 1 = 2 1 = 2	1 + 2:75 1:51, 2:48	6 mo. (S-R, A)
Emmelkamp & Emmelkamp-Brenner (1975)	29	? Outpatients	No	1. Video mod. + Ind. self-obs. 2. Video mod. + Group self-obs. 3. Ind. self-obs. 4. Group self-obs.	Factorial 2 × 2	Behavioral test A.r. of phobia, etc. Self-rating of phobia FSS-III, I-E, SAS, SDS	1 = 2 = 3 = 4 1 = 2 = 3 = 4	1-4:33 1-4:44	1 mo. (S-R, B)
Emmelkamp & Wessels (1975)	26	? Outpatients	No	1. Exposure + self-obs. 2. Imag. flooding + self-obs. 3. Flooding/exp. + self-obs.	Pre-post	Behavioral test A.r. of phobia etc. Self-rating of phobia FSS-III, I-E, SAS, SDS	1 = 3 > 2	1:59, 2:43, 3:61	1 mo. (S-R, B)
Ullrich et al. (1975)	24	Referrals Outpatients	No	1. Flooding + alprenolol 2. Flooding + placebo 3. Flooding	Pre-post	A.r. of anxiety, etc. FSS-III	1 > 2 = 3	(only change-scores)	—
Hafner & Marks (1976)	57	Referrals Outpatients	Sparse	1. Group exp. + Waning diazepam 2. Group exp. + Peak diazepam 3. Group exp. + Placebo 4. Ind. exp. + High arousal 5. Ind. exp. + Low arousal	Factorial 2 × 3	Behavioral test A.r. of phobia etc. Self-rating of phobia FSS, MHQ, HDHQ	? 1-3 > 4-5	? 1:69, 2:66, 3:67	6 mo, 12 mo. (S-R, A only)
Mathews et al. (1976)	36	Referrals Outpatients	Several	1. Flood. 8 s. + Exp. 8 s. 2. Flood. + Exp. 16 s. 3. Exposure 16 s.	Pre-post	Behavioral test A.r. of phobia, etc. Self-rating of phobia FSS-III, EPI, 16PF, Mood	1 = 2 = 3 1 = 2 = 3	1-3:45 1-3:32	6 mo. (S-R only)
Hafner & Milton (1977)	23	?	Elaborated	1. Exposure + Propranolol 2. Exposure + Placebo	Pre-post	Self-report: MHQ, HDHQ, H-OQ, FSS	2 > 1	(Only change-scores)	3 mo. (S-R)
Emmelkamp et al. (1978)	21	?	No	1. Cognitive restructuring 2. Exposure in vivo	Crossover	Behavioral test A.r. of phobia, etc. Self-rating of phobia FSS-III, I-E, SAS, SDS	2 > 1	(Only change-scores)	1 mo. (S-R, B only)

(continued)

TABLE 5.1 (Continued)

Agoraphobia (continued)

Authors	n	Recruitment/ subjects	Inclusion criteria	Treatment methods	Design	Measures	Results	Percentage improvement	Follow-up
Tyrer et al. (1978)	15	Referrals Outpatients	Sparse	1. Supraliminal exposure 2. Subliminal exposure 3. Attention control	Pre-post	A.r. of phobia Self-rating of phobia	1 = 2 > 3	1:51, 2:38, 3:3	6 w. (S-R, A)
Zitrin et al. (1978)	46	Advertisements Outpatients	Sparse	1. Behav. ther. + Imipramine 2. Psychother. + Imipramine 3. Behav. ther. + Placebo 4. Imipramine	Pre-post	A.r. of phobia, etc. Self-rating of improvement	1 = 2 = 3	(Only change-scores)	12 mo. (S-R)
Chambless et al. (1979)	27	Advertisements Outpatients	Elaborated	1. Flooding (imagery) 2. Flood. + Methohexitone 3. Attention control	Pre-post	Behavioral test Self-rating of phobia Therapist ratings	1 = 2 = 3 1 > 2 > 3	(no data) (only change-scores)	—
McDonald et al. (1979)	19	Referrals Outpatients	Sparse	1. Self-exposure 2. Discussion control	Pre-post	A.r. of phobia Self-rating, FQ	1 > 2	1:30, 2:11	1 mo. (S-R, A)
Foa, Jameson, Turner & Paynes (1980)	11	Advertisements Outpatients	No	1. Massed + Spaced exposure 2. Spaced + Massed exposure	Crossover	A.r. of anxiety A.r. of avoidance	1 = 2 2 > 1	1:67, 2:52 1:76, 2:48	—
Jannoun et al. (1980)	26	Referrals Outpatients	Several	1. Programmed practice 2. Problem solving	Pre-post	A.r. of phobia, etc. Self-rating of phobia EPI, STAI, FQ	1 > 2	1:49, 2:26	6 mo. (S-R, A)
Jones et al. (1980)	24	Referrals Outpatients	No	1. Group exposure *in vivo* 2. Group disc. + couns. partner 3. Group exp. + couns. partner 4. Wait list control	Pre-post	Behavioral test	3 > 1 = 2 > 4	1:43, 2:44, 3:90, 4:10	3 mo. (B)
Zitrin et al. (1980)	76	Advertisements Outpatients	Several	1. Exposure + imipramine 2. Exposure + placebo	Pre-post	A.r. of phobia etc. Self-rating of phobia MAS, AQ, API	1 > 2	(only change-scores)	13 w. (S-R)
Sinnott et al. (1981)	21	Referrals Outpatients	No	1. Exp. buddy system 2. Exp. no buddy 3. No-treatment control	Pre-post	Behavioral test A.r. of phobia Self-rating, SAS	1 = 2 > 3	1:38, 2:47, 3:-26	3 mo. (S-R, A, B)
Solyom et al. (1981)	40	Referrals Outpatients	No	1. Phenelzine + exposure 2. Phenelzine 3. Placebo + exposure 4. Placebo	Factorial 2 × 2	A.r. of phobia, etc. Self-rating of phobia	1 = 3 > 2 = 4	1:46, 2:13, 3:76, 4:38	2 mo. (S-R)

Study	N	Setting	Diagnosis	Treatments	Design	Measures	Results	Values	Follow-up
Chambless et al. (1982)	21	Advertisements Outpatients	Sparse DSM-III	1. Flood. + Psychotherapy 2. Flood, drug + exp., PT 3. Attn. ctr. + exp., PT	Pre-post	Ther. r. of phobia Self-rating of phobia FSS-III, FPCI	1 = 2 = 3	1:57, 2:36, 3:38	4 mo. (S-R)
Emmelkamp & Mersch (1982)	27	? Outpatients	Sparse	1. Exp. in vivo 2. Cognitive restructuring 3. Combination 1 + 2	Pre-post	Behavioral test A.r. of phobia, etc. Self-rating of phobia FSS-III, I-F, SDS, ASES	1 = 3 > 2	1:44, 2:20, 3:47	1 mo. (S-R, B only)
Emmelkamp et al. (1983)	21	Referrals Outpatients	Sparse	1. Exp. in vivo 2. Assertive training 3. Combination 1 + 2	Pre-post	Behavioral test A.r. of phobia, etc. Self-rating of phobia FSS-III, SDS, ASES; SIG	1 = 3 > 2	1:51, 2:15, 3:55	1 mo. (S-R, B only)
Klein et al. (1983)	45	Advertisements Outpatients	Sparse DSM-III	1. Behav. ther. + imipramine 2. Psychother. + imipramine	Pre-post	A.r. of phobia, etc. Self-rating of phobia	1 = 2	1:47, 2:42	12 mo. (S-R only)
Marks et al. (1983)	45	Referrals Outpatients	Elaborated DSM-III	1. Exp. + imipramine 2. Relax. + imipramine 3. Exp. + placebo 4. Relax. + placebo	Factorial 2 X 2	A.r. of phobia, etc. A.r. of depression Self-rating of phobia FQ, Wakefield, anxiety	1 + 2 = 3 + 4 1 + 3 = 2 + 4	1 + 2:65, 3 + 4:57 1 + 3:67, 2 + 4:56	6 mo. 2 yrs (S-R, A)
Mavissakalian & Michelson (1983)	49	? Outpatients	Elaborated DSM-III	1. Flooding + imipramine 2. Disc. ctr. + imipramine 3. Flooding + placebo 4. Disc. ctr. + placebo	Factorial 2 X 2	Behavioral test A.r. of phobic severity Self-rating, diary, FQ, SRS	1 = 2 = 3 = 4 1 = 2 = 3 > 4	1:95, 2:91, 3:83, 4:85 1:64, 2:71, 3:71, 4:47	—
Mavissakalian, Michelson, & Dealy (1983)	18	? Outpatients	Elaborated DSM-III	1. Imipramine 2. Imipramine + prog. practice	Pre-post	Behavioral test A.r. of phobia, depr. Self-rating of phobia SRS, FQ, SAS, BDI	2 > 1	1:40, 2:100	—
Mavissakalian, Michelson, Greenwald, Kornblith, & Greenwald (1983)	26	? Outpatients	Elaborated DSM-III	1. Self-statement training 2. Paradoxical intention	Pre-post	Behavioral test A.r. of phobic severity Self-rating of phobia FSS-III, FQ, MAS, BDI, SRS	1 = 2 1 = 2	1:100, 2:46 1:8, 2:41	6 mo. (S-R, A, B)
Williams & Rappoport (1983)	20	Advertisements Outpatients	No	1. Exposure in vivo 2. Exp. + Cogn. therapy	Pre-post	Behavioral test Self-rating of phobia FQ, Self-efficacy	1 = 2	1:36, 2:24	3 mo. (S-R, B)
Barlow et al. (1984)	28	Referrals	Elaborated DSM-III	1. Self-exposure + cogn. restruct., with spouse 2. As 1, without spouse	Pre-post	Behavioral test A.r. of phobia Self-rating of phobia Diary, FQ, BDI	1 = 2 1 = 2	(No data) 1:47, 2:34	3 mo. (S-R, B)
Cobb et al. (1984)	19	Referrals Outpatients	Elaborated	1. Self-exposure 2. As 1 + spouse co-ther.	Pre-post	A.r. of phobia FQ, CCEI, MMQ C-CEI, MMQ	? 1 = 2	(No data) 1:43, 2:42	6 mo. (S-R)

(continued)

109

TABLE 5.1 (Continued)

Authors	n	Recruitment/ subjects	Inclusion criteria	Treatment methods	Design	Measures	Results	Percentage improvement	Follow-up
					Agoraphobia				
DeSilva & Rachman (1984)	18	Referrals Outpatients	Sparse	1. Exp.—endurance 2. Exp.—escape/avoidance 3. Wait list control	Pre-post	Behavioral test A.r. of phobia Self-rating of phobia	1 = 2 > 3 1 = 2 > 3	1:54, 2:48, 3:20 1:32, 2:27, 3:0	—
Öst et. al. (1984)	40	Referrals Outpatients	Elaborated DSM-III	1. Phys. react.—AR 2. Phys. react.—exp. 3. Behav. react.—AR 4. Behav. react.—exp.	Factorial 2 × 2	Heart rate Self-rating of anxiety, FSS-III, AQ, AS, API, APQ, BDI, MMQ	1 = 2; 3 = 4	1:70, 2:69, 3:49, 4:55	15 mo. (S-R, B, P)
					Social phobias				
Argyle et. al. (1974)	16	? Outpatients	Sparse	1. SST 2. Psychotherapy	Pre-post	Behavioral test Social situations Q. Minnesota Inv. Soc. Behav. EPI, EPPS	1 = 2	1:24, 2:21	—
Marzillier et. al. (1976)	32	Referrals Outpatients	Elaborated	1. SD 2. SST 3. Wait list control	Pre-post	Behavioral test A.r. most diff. sit. Range of soc. activities Range of soc. contacts Freq. soc. act. & cont. SAD, FNE Adjustment rating scales, PSE, EPI	1 = 2 = 3 1 = 2 = 3 1 > 3; 1 = 2; 2 = 3 1 = 2 > 3	Only change-scores	6 mo. (S-R only)
Hall & Goldberg (1977)	30	Referrals Outpatients	Sparse	1. SD 2. Role playing with feedback	Pre-post	Behavioral test Problem Behavior Checkl. SAD, FNE, SSQ STAI-S Social Strategy Scale	1 = 2 2 > 1	?	3 mo.
Goldfried & Goldfried (1977)	42	Advertisements Outpatients	Several	1. Self-control des. (rel.) 2. Self-control des. (irrel.) 3. Prolonged exp.	Pre-post	Behavioral test Heart rate (rest) Anxiety Differential STAI-S PRCS S-R Inv. of anxiety SAD, FNE	1 = 2 = 3	1:3, 2:19, 3:26	2 mo. (S-R only)

Study	N	Source	Diagnosis	Conditions	Design	Measures	Results (comparison)	Results (numeric)	Follow-up
Trower et. al. (1978)	40	Referrals Outpatients	Several	1. SST—unskilled patients 2. SD—unskilled patients 3. SST—phobic patients 4. SD—phobic patients	Factorial 2 × 2	Behavioral test A.r. of social phobia SSQ-Difficulty SSQ-Frequency A.r. 15 target sit.	3 = 4	3:33, 4:37	Yes. Time not reported.
Kanter & Goldfried (1979)	68	Advertisements Outpatients	Sparse	1. Cogn. restruct. 2. Self-control desens. 3. Combination 1 + 2 4. Wait-list control	Pre–post	Behavioral test STAI-S (T) Anxiety differential SAD FNE S-R Inv. of anxiety Heart rate	1 = 2 = 3 = 4 1 = 3 > 2 = 4 1 = 2 = 3 > 4 1 = 3 > 4, 3 = 4 1 = 2 = 3 > 4 1 = 2 = 3 = 4	1:5, 2:8, 3:13, 4:13 1:23, 2:10, 3:22, 4:4 1:40, 2:26, 3:37, 4:2 1:43, 2:18, 3:32, 4:5	2 mo.
Shaw (1979)	30	Referrals	Several	1. SD 2. Flooding 3. SST	Pre–post	Behavioral test A.r. of social phobia Self-rating of phobia FSS-social items	1 = 2 = 3 1 = 2 = 3	(No data) 1:37, 2:32, 3:33	6 mo.
Falloon et. al. (1981)	16	Referrals Outpatients	Sparse DSM-III	1. Propranolol + SST 2. Placebo + SST	Pre–post	A.r. of difficulty soc. A.r. of frequency soc. Social Anxiety Q. Self-rating of anxiety Self-rating of self-image	1 = 2 1 = 2	1 + 2:37 1 + 2:35	6 mo.
Öst et. al. (1981)	32	Referrals Outpatients	Elaborated DSM-III	1. Phys. react.—applied rel. 2. Phys. react.—SST 3. Behav. react.—AR 4. Behav. react.—SST	Factorial 2 × 2	Behavioral test Heart rate Self-rating of anxiety Five ind. situations SSQ-Difficulty SSQ-Frequency Frequency of social cont. Frequency of social act. FSS-III, APQ-G	1 > 2; 3 = 4 1 = 2; 3 = 4 1 = 2; 4 > 3	1:54, 2:34, 3:38, 4:39 1:7, 2:9, 3:3, 4:0 1:39, 2:34, 3:37, 4:52	
Stravynski et. al. (1982)	29	Referrals Outpatients	Sparse	1. Social skills training 2. SST + cogn. modification	Pre–post	A.r. social targets SAD FNE Wakefield depression Inv. Irrational Beliefs Test	1 = 2	1:51, 2:67	6 mo.

(continued)

TABLE 5.1 (Continued)

Social phobias (continued)

Authors	n	Recruitment/ subjects	Inclusion criteria	Treatment methods	Design	Measures	Results	Percentage improvement	Follow-up
Butler et. al. (1984)	45	Referrals Outpatients	Several DSM-III	1. Exposure + AMT 2. Exposure + Associative t. 3. Wait-list control	Pre-post	A.r. of phobic severity Self-rating ind. hierarchy SAD, FNE FQ-social subscale A.r. of anxiety, depr. STAI, BDI Fear Questionnaire	1 = 2 > 3 1 = 2 > 3 1 > 2 = 3 1 = 2 > 3	1:40, 2:37, 3:8	6 mo.
Jerremalm et. al. (1986)	38	Referrals Outpatients	Elaborated DSM-III	1. Phys. react.—AR 2. Phys. react.—Self-instruct. training 3. Phys. react.—Wait list c. 4. Cogn. react.—AR 5. Cogn. react.—SIT 6. Cogn. react.-Wait list c.	Factorial (2 × 3)	Behavioral test Self-rating of anxiety Heart rate Thought index SSQ-Difficulty FSS-III, APQ, BDI, MMQ	1 = 2 > 3; 4 = 5 > 6 1 = 2 > 3; 5 > 4 = 6 1 = 2 > 3; 4 = 5 > 6	1:54, 2:53, 3:5 4:51, 5:53, 6:5 1:32, 2:53, 3:0 4:29, 5:55, 6:14 1:50, 2:38, 3:2 4:5, 5:7, 6:2	—

Simple phobias

Authors	n	Recruitment/ subjects	Inclusion criteria	Treatment methods	Design	Measures	Results	Percentage improvement	Follow-up
Ritter (1969a)[a]	12	Advertisements Outpatients	Sparse	1. Contact desens. 2. No-contact desens. 3. No-treatment control	Pre-post	FSS-II Behavioral test Self-rating of fear	1 = 2 = 3 1 > 2 = 3 1 > 2 = 3	Only change-scores	—
Ritter (1969b)[a]	15	Advertisements Outpatients	Sparse	1. Contact desens. 2. Demonstration plus participation 3. Live modeling	Pre-post	FSS-II Behavioral test Self-rating of fear	— 1 > 2 > 3 1 = 2 = 3	— 1:37, 2:25, 3:9	—
Leitenberg & Callahan (1973)[a]	18	Advertisements Outpatients	Sparse	1. Reinforced practice 2. Wait-list control	Pre-post	Behavioral test Self-rating of fear	1 > 2 1 > 2	1:72, 2:4 1:32, 2:-3	2 yrs.
Baker et. al. (1973)[a]	30	Advertisements Outpatients	Sparse	1. Ther.-directed desens. 2. Self-directed desens. 3. Wait list control	Pre-post	Acrophobia Q—Anxiety Acrophobia Q—Avoidance Slide discomfort rating FSS-III GSP + 5 inventories	1 = 2 > 3 1 = 2 > 3 1 = 2 > 3 1 = 2 > 3	1:50, 2:65, 3:5 1:62, 2:70, 3:12 1:50, 2:56, 3:3 1:11, 2:14, 3:7	8 mo.

Study	N	Sample	Diagnosis	Treatment conditions	Design	Measures	Results	Effect sizes	Follow-up
Cohen (1977)[a]	70	Self-referrals Outpatients	No	1. Systematic desens. 2. Self-desens.—office 3. Self-desens.—home 4. Wait list control	Pre–post	Acrophobia Q—anxiety; Acrophobia Q—Avoidance; Behavioral test; 4 self-report measures	1,2,3 > 4; 1,2,3 > 4; 1,2,3 = 4	1-3:47, 4:2; 1-3:49, 4:9; 1-3:44, 4:-32	—
Morris & Magrath (1979)[a]	19	Advertisements Outpatients	Sparse	1. Contact des.—warm ther. 2. Contact des.—cold ther. 3. Wait list control	Pre–post	FSS-III; Behavioral test; Self-rating of fear; Fear Situation Q	2 > 1 = 3; 1 = 2 > 3; 1 = 2 = 3	1:68, 2:78, 3:10	—
Bourque & Ladouceur (1980)[a]	50	Advertisements Outpatients	Sparse	1. Participant modeling 2. PM without ther. cont. 3. Modeling + resp. rehearsal 4. Ther.-contr. exposure 5. Client-contr. exposure	Pre–post	Behavioral test; Self-rating of anxiety; Heart rate; Acrophobia Q; Situation Specific Q	1, 2, 3, 4 = 5; 1, 2, 3, 4 = 5; 1, 2, 3, 4 = 5; 1, 2, 3, 4 = 5; 1, 2, 3, 4 = 5	1:75, 2:100, 3:97, 4:100, 5:95	Yes. Time not reported.
Biran & Wilson (1981)[a,c,e]	22	Advertisements Outpatients	Elaborated	1. Guided exposure 2. Cognitive restructuring	Pre–post	Behavioral test; R. of anticipatory fear; R. of performance fear; Level of self-efficacy; Strength of self-efficacy; Situational generalization; HR, SP + 5 self-report Q	1 > 2; 1 = 2; 1 = 2; 1 > 2; 1 > 2; 1 = 2; 1 > 2	1:88, 2:33; 1:74, 2:74; 1:74, 2:68; 1:91, 2:54; 1:83, 2:43	6 mo.
Pendleton & Higgins (1983)[a]	62	Advertisements Outpatients	Sparse	1. Negative practice 2. Systematic desens. 3. Relaxation only 4. Wait list control	Pre–post	Acrophobia Q—Anxiety; Acrophobia Q—Avoidance; Self-rating of fear; Behavioral test; Expectancy Q	1 = 2 > 4; 1 = 2 > 4, 2, 3; 1 = 2 = 3 > 4; 1 = 2 = 3 > 4; 1 = 2 = 3 = 4	Only change-scores	—
Williams et al. (1984)[a,g]	32	Advertisements Outpatients	Several	1. Exposure 2. Guided mastery 3. Wait list control	Pre–post	Level of self-efficacy; Strength of self-efficacy; Anticipatory anx.; Behavioral test; Performance anxiety	2 > 1 > 3; 2 > 1 > 3; 2 > 1 > 3; 2 > 1 = 3; 2 > 1 > 3	1:39, 2:68, 3:8; 1:15, 2:49, 3:-3; 1:35, 2:67, 3:9; 1:6, 2:42, 3:-32	—
Öst, Lindahl, Sterner, & Jerremalm (1984)[b]	18	Advertisements Outpatients	Elaborated DSM-III	1. Exposure in vivo 2. Applied relaxation (AR)	Pre–post	Behavioral test; A.r. of fainting; Self-rating of anxiety; Heart rate, BP; Mutilation Q	1 = 2; 1 = 2; 1 = 2; 1 = 2; 1 > 2	1:55, 2:70; 1:40, 2:79; 1:51, 2:39; 1:62, 2:31	6 mo. (improvements maintained)

(continued)

113

TABLE 5.1 (*Continued*)

Simple phobias (*continued*)

Authors	n	Recruitment/ subjects	Inclusion criteria	Treatment methods	Design	Measures	Results	Percentage improvement	Follow-up
Öst et al. (1982)[c]	34	Advertisements Outpatients	Elaborated DSM-III	1. Behav. react.—exp. 2. Behav. react.—AR. 3. Behav. react.—WLC 4. Phys. react.—exp. 5. Phys. react.—AR 6. Phys. react.—WLC	Factorial (2 × 3)	Behavioral test Heart rate Self-rating of anxiety Claustrophobia S.—Anxiety Claustrophobia S.—Avoid. FSS-III, APQ-G	1 > 2 > 3; 4 = 5 = 6 1 = 2 = 3; 5 > 4 > 6 1 > 2 > 3; 4 = 5 = 6	1:100, 2:61, 3:-37 4:0, 5:0, 6:0 1:59, 2:37, 3:15 4:74, 5:100, 6:8 1:92, 2:60, 3:-1 4:30, 5:79, 6:-11	14 mo.
Shaw & Thoresen (1974)[d]	36	Advertisements Outpatients	Several	1. Modeling (video) 2. Desensitization 3. Placebo control 4. Assessment control	Pre-post	Self-r. fear of dentist Self-r. fear of dental work General fear FSS-100 IPAT anxiety scale	1 = 2 > 3 = 4 1 = 2 > 3 = 4	1:58, 2:57, 3:11 4:-9	3 mo.
Mathews & Rezin (1977)[d]	63	Advertisements Outpatients	Sparse	1. Flood./cop. high aro. 2. Flood.—high aro. 3. Flood./cop. low aro. 4. Flood.—low aro. 5. Relax. control	Factorial (2 × 2)	Dental Anxiety Q. Sem. diff. Behavioral test	1 = 2 = 3 = 4 = 5 1 = 2 = 3 = 4 = 5 ?	?	2 mo.
Wroblewski et al. (1977)[d]	27	Advertisements Outpatients	Sparse	1. Symbolic mod. + relax. 2. Symbolic mod. 3. Attention placebo	Pre-post	Dental Anxiety Scale Behavioral test Self-rating of fear, FSS	1 = 2 = 3 1 > 2 = 3 1 = 2 = 3	?	—
Miller et al. (1978)[d]	21	Referrals Outpatients	Sparse	1. EMG-biofeedback 2. Prog. relaxation 3. Self-relaxation contr.	Pre-post	EMG-level Dental Anxiety Scale STAI-S (T)	1 = 2 > 3 1 = 2 > 3 1 = 2 > 3	1:41, 2:50, 3:-3 1:43, 2:38, 3:18 1:45, 2:37, 3:6	—
Gatchel (1980)[d]	19	Advertisements Outpatients	No	1. Self-control desens. 2. Education/discussion 3. No-treatment control	Pre-post	Dental Anxiety Scale Imagining dental treatment Dental visits	1 > 2 = 3 1 = 2 = 3 1 = 2 > 3	1:31, 2:19, 3:4 1:88, 2:100, 3:33	—
Bernstein & Kleinknecht (1982)[d]	33	Advertisements Outpatients	No	1. Graduated exp. 2. Symbolic modeling 3. Participant modeling 4. Attention-placebo 5. Unaided effort control	Pre-post	Behavioral test Palmar Sweat index Self-rating of pain Dental Fear Survey FSS-II HLCS, EPI, R-SS	1 = 2 = 3 = 4 = 5	?	2 yrs.

Study	N	Source	Diagnosis	Design	Treatments	Outcome measures	Results	Comparison	Follow-up
Gauthier et al. (1985)[d]	15	Advertisements, Outpatients	Sparse	Crossover	1. Flood. + cop. 2. Cop. + flood.	Behavioral test; Self-rating of anxiety; Dental appointments; Self-efficacy	1:84, 2:74; 1:59, 2:49; 1:43, 2:100	1 = 2; 1 = 2; 2 > 1; 1 = 2	4 mo.
Jerremalm et al. (1986)[d]	38	Advertisements, Outpatients	Elaborated DSM-III	Factorial (2 × 2)	1. Cogn. react.—AR 2. Cogn. react.—Self-instructional training 3. Phys. react.—AR 4. Phys. react.—SIT	Behavioral test; Heart rate; Self-rating of anxiety; Thought index; Dental Anxiety Scale; DFS, FSS-III, APQ-S	1:-7, 2:50; 3:73, 4:65; 1:22, 2:37, 3:15, 4:27	1 = 2; 3 = 4; 1 = 2; 3 = 4; 1 = 2; 3 = 4; 1 = 2; 4 > 3; 1 = 2; 3 = 4	12 mo.
Solyom et al. (1973)[f]	40	Referrals, Outpatients	Sparse	Pre-post	1. Aversion relief 2. Systematic desens. 3. Habituation 4. Group psychotherapy	Post-treatm. behavioral test; FSS-III; Flying phobia scale; IPAT Anxiety Scale; Maudsley Personality Inv.	1:45, 2:53, 3:33; 1:52, 2:50, 3:56, 4:11	1 = 2 = 3; 1 = 2 = 3 > 4; 1 = 2 = 3 > 4	8–24 mo. (S-R only)
Denholtz & Mann (1975)[f]	51	Advertisements, Outpatients	Sparse	Pre-post (Modified crossover)	1. Systematic desens. 2. No syst. scene pres. 3. No relaxation 4. Relax. + placebo film	Post-treatment behav. test; Taylor Manifest Anxiety Scale	1:65, 2:15; 3:27, 4:17	1 > 2 = 3 = 4; ?	3.5–5.5 yrs. (interview only)
Howard et al. (1983)[f]	56	Advertisements, Outpatients	Sparse	Pre-post	1. Systematic desens. 2. Implosion 3. Flooding 4. Relaxation 5. Wait list control	Behavioral test; Heart rate; Self-rating of anx.; Attitudes to Flying Q. FSS-III	1:18, 2:20, 3:22; 4:30, 5:-2	1 = 2 = 3 = 4 = 5; 1 = 2 = 3 = 4 = 5; 1 = 2 = 3 = 4 = 5; 1 = 2 = 3 = 4 > 5; 1 = 2 = 3 = 4 > 5	3 mo. (S-R only)

Obsessive–compulsive disorder

Study	N	Source	Diagnosis	Design	Treatments	Outcome measures	Results	Comparison	Follow-up
Stern et al. (1973)	11	Referrals, Outpatients	Sparse	Crossover	1. Thought stopping + 2 2. "Control" thinking + 1	Self-rating of distress; Self-rating of frequency; Evaluation (sem. diff); Danger (sem. diff)	1:28, 2:17	1 > 2; 1 = 2 = 3	—
Marks et al. (1975)	20	Inpatients	Sparse	Pre-post	1. Slow exp. + modeling 2. Rapid exp. 3. Rapid exp. + modeling (All had self-imposed response-prevention)	A.r. of (a) anxiety, (b) avoidance, (c) free-floating anx, (d) panics (e) depr., (f) depers.; EPI; Leyton Obsessional Inv.; Behavior avoidance test	1:59, 2:34, 3:57	1 = 2 = 3; 1 = 2 = 3	2 yrs (S-R, A)

(continued)

115

TABLE 5.1 (*Continued*)

Authors	n	Recruitment/ subjects	Inclusion criteria	Treatment methods	Design	Measures	Results	Percentage improvement	Follow-up
Obsessive–compulsive disorder (*continued*)									
Röper et al. (1975)	10	Referrals	Sparse	1. Passive + participant modeling 2. Control (relaxation) + Participant modeling	Pre-post	Self-rating of (a) fear, (b) obsessions, (c) avoidance; A.r. of a, b, c; Behavioral test; Fear thermometer; Leyton Obsessional Inv.	1 > 2	1:81, 2:100	6 mo.
Hackman & McLean (1975)	10	Outpatients	Sparse	1. Thought stopping + 2 2. Flood./modeling + 1	Crossover	A.r. global severity; P. rating anxiety, avoidance, time, preocc.; Leyton Obs. Inv, EPI	1 = 2	1:35, 2:47	—
Rabavilas et al. (1976)	12	Outpatients	Sparse	1. Short flood. in fant. 2. Long flood. in fant. 3. Short flood. in vivo 4. Long flood. in vivo	Latin-square	(P,T) r. main obsession; A (P,T) r. total obs., anxiety, depression; Leyton Obs. Inv.	1 = 2; 4 > 3	1-4:59	2.8 yrs. (S-R, A)
Boersma et al. (1976)	13	Announcements + referrals Outpatients	No	1. Flood. + RP 2. Gradual exp. + RP 3. Flood. + modeling 4. Gradual exp., RP + mod.	Pre-post	Self-observation of frequency/duration of rituals; A.r.—anxiety; A.r.—avoidance; Leyton Obs. Inv.; SDS	1 = 2 = 3 = 4; 1 = 2 = 3 = 4; 1 = 2 = 3 = 4	1-4:78; 1-4:61; 1-4:64	3 mo. (S-R only)
Emmelkamp & Kraanen (1977)	14	Self-referrals Outpatients	No	1. Therapist-controlled exp. *in vivo* 2. Self-controlled exp. *in vivo*	Pre-post	Self-obs. of rituals; A (P,T) r. (a) anxiety, (b) avoidance; A (T) r. (a) anxious mood, (b) depression; Leyton Obs. Inv.; SDS, Marital Satisf.	1 = 2; 1 = 2; 1 = 2	1 + 2:74; 1 + 2:55; 1 + 2:54	3 mo. (S-R only)
Emmelkamp & Kwee (1977)	5	? Outpatients	Sparse	1. Thought stopping + 2 2. Satiation + 1	Crossover	Self-obs. of obsessions; Self-rating of distress; Leyton Obs. Inv, SDS	1 = 2; 1 = 2	1:15, 2:33; 1 + 2:20	—

Study	N	Source		Conditions	Design	Measures	Outcome	Results	Follow-up
Sookman & Solyom (1977)	33	Referrals Outpatients	Sparse	1. Aversion relief 2. Flood 3. Thought stopping 4. SD + thought stopping	Pre-post	A.r. total obs. symptoms Leyton Obs. Inv. IPAT anxiety scale FSS, EPI	$2 = 4 > 1 = 3$	1:6, 2:53, 3:22, 4:49	—
Kenny et al. (1978)	10	? Outpatients	Sparse	1. Faradic disruption 2. Wait list control	Pre-post	A.r. O-C symptoms A.r. general adjustment Self-rating of O-C sympt. IPAT anxiety scale	$1 > 2$ $1 > 2$	1:59, 2:5 1:67, 2:-40	12 mo.
Rachman et al. (1979) Marks et al. (1980) Mawson et al.	40	Referrals Inpatients	Elaborated	1. Clomipramine + exp. 2. Clomipr. + relaxation 3. Placebo + exp. 4. Placebo + relaxation	2 × 2 factorial	A.r. (a) discomfort, (b) time Comp. Activity Checklist Behavioral Test Wakefield Depr. Scale Hamilton Depr. Scale Free-Floating anxiety	$1 = 2 = 3 = 4$ $1 + 3 > 2 + 4$	1:76, 2:83, 3:60, 4:56	2 yrs.
Emmelkamp & van der Heyden (1980)	6	Referrals Outpatients	Sparse	1. Thought stopping + 2 2. Assertive training + 1	Crossover	Self-monitoring of obs. Self-rating of distress Leyton Obs. Inv. SDS	$1 = 2$ $1 = 2$	1:4, 2:11 1 + 2:38	—
Emmelkamp et al. (1980)	17	Referrals Outpatients	No	1. Exposure + RP 2. 1 + self-instructions	Pre-post	A.r. of anxiety A.r. of avoidance A.r. of anxious mood A.r. of depression Leyton Obs. Inv. SDS	$1 = 2$ $1 > 2$	1 + 2:56 1 + 2:57	6 mo.
Foa, Steketee, & Milby (1980)	8	Referrals In/outpatients	No	1. Exposure + Exp/RP 2. RP + Exp/RP	Pre-post	Self-monitoring of rituals Behavioral test Self-rating of discomfort	$1 = 2$ $1 = 2$ $1 = 2$	1:79, 2:76 1:96, 2:71	—
Foa, Steketee, Turner & Fischer (1980)	15	Self-referrals Outpatients	Sparse	1. Imaginal exposure + Exp/RP 2. Exp/RP	Pre-post	A.r. of severity comp. A.r. of severity obs. A.r. of urges to rit. A.r. of main fear A.r. of avoidance A.r. of overall O-C	$1 = 2$	1:71, 2:69	11 mo.

(continued)

TABLE 5.1 (Continued)

Authors	n	Recruitment/subjects	Inclusion criteria	Treatment methods	Design	Measures	Results	Percentage improvement	Follow-up
Obsessive-compulsive disorder (continued)									
Likierman & Rachman (1982)	12	Outpatients	Sparse	1. Habituation 2. Thought-stopping	Pre-post	Daily diary of obs. Pre- and postsession ass.	1 = 2	(only change-scores)	—
Emmelkamp & De Lange (1983)	12	Referrals Outpatients	Several	1. Self-controlled exp/RP 2. Partner-assisted exp/RP	Pre-post	A.r. of anxiety Maudsley O-C Inv. SDS A.r. anxious mood	2 > 1	1:38, 2:64	6 mo.
Foa et al. (1984)	32	Referrals In-outpatients	Elaborated (DSM-III)	1. Exposure 2. Response Prevention 3. Exp. + RP	Pre-post	Exposure test A.r. of main fear A.r. of avoidance A.r. of obsessions Self-mon. of rituals A.r. of severity of rit. A.r. of urges to rit. Maudsley O-C Inv. Compulsion checklist A.r. of anxious mood, depressed mood, general functioning BDI	3 > 2 > 1 3 > 2 = 1 1 = 2 = 3 3 > 2 = 1	1:51, 2:18, 3:87 1:37, 2:28, 3:62 1:49, 2:45, 3:63 1:25, 2:42, 3:69	12 mo.
Generalized anxiety disorder and panic disorder									
Canter et al. (1975)	28	Referrals in/outpatients	No	1. EMG-fb 2. Progressive relaxation	Pre-post	EMG-activity P rating of improvement T rating of improvement	1 > 2 1 = 2	1:45, 2:21	—
Townsend et al. (1975)	30	Inpatients	Sparse	1. EMG-fb + PR 2. Group psychother.	Pre-post	EMG-level STAI-S STAI-T POMS	1 = 2 1 = 2 1 = 2	1:44, 2:27 1:15, 2:-2 1:11, 2:6	—
Lavallée et al. (1977)	40	Outpatients	Sparse	1. EMG-fb + diazepam 2. EMG-fb + placebo 3. EMG-control + diazepam 4. EMG-control + placebo	2 × 2 factorial	EMG-activity Hamilton Anxiety Scale IPAT-anxiety scale deBonis Trait-State	1 = 2 = 3 > 4 1 = 2 > 3 = 4	1:50, 2:40, 3:35, 4:20 1:48, 2:45, 3:32, 4:28	63 mo. (S-R, A, P)

(continued)

Study	N	Source	Diagnosis	Design	Treatment conditions	Measures	Results	Data	Follow-up
Mathews & Shaw (1977)	10	Referrals	Sparse	Crossover	1. Thought stopping + 2 2. Cogn. desens. + 1	Assessor's rating Self-observation	1 = 2 1 = 2	(no data) 1:30, 2:31	1 mo. (?)
Benson et al. (1978)	32	Outpatients	Sparse	2 × 2 factorial	1. Meditation—high resp. 2. Meditation—low resp. 3. Self-hypnosis—high resp. 4. Self-hypnosis—low resp.	Blood pressure Heart rate Oxygen consumption Hamilton Anxiety Scale Self-rating of anxiety	1 = 3 > 2 = 4 1 = 3 > 2 = 4	1:42, 2:0 3:56, 4:14	—
Lehrer (1978)	20	Referrals Outpatients	Sparse	Pre-post	1. Progressive relaxation 2. Wait list control	Heart rate Skin conductance STAI-S	1 > 2 1 > 2 1 = 2	1:6, 2:-16 1:34, 2:-12 1:26, 2:9	—
Rupert & Holmes (1978)	56	Inpatients	Several	Pre-post	1. Increase HR—ture fb 2. Increase HR—placebo 3. Increase HR—no fb 4. No-treatment control 5. Decrease HR—true fb 6. Decrease HR—placebo 7. Decrease HR—no fb	Heart rate STAI-S STAI-T AACL	1, 2, 3, 5, 6, 7 = 4 1, 2, 3, 5, 6, 7 = 4	?	—
LeBoeuf & Lodge (1980)	26	Outpatients	Several	Pre-post	1. EMG-fb 2. Prog. relax.	EMG-activity Heart rate TMAS STAI-T (S)	1 > 2	1:58, 2:20	3 mo.
Raskin et al. (1980)	31	Announcements	Elaborated (DSM-II)	Pre-post	1. EMG-fb + PR 2. Prog. relax. 3. Transcendental med.	TMAS Current Mood Check-list EMG-activity Self-rating of anxiety	1 = 2 1 = 2 = 3 1 = 2 = 3	1:10, 3:6 1:17, 2:21, 3:31 1:52, 2:31, 3:30	9 mo. (S-R only)
Woodward & Jones (1980)	27	Referrals Outpatients	Sparse	Pre-post	1. Stress-inoculation 2. Self-control desens. 3. Combination 1 + 2 4. Wait list control	Self-rating Anxiety S. Self-obs. of mood FSS-III Behavior rating (?)	1 = 2 = 3 = 4 2 = 3 > 1	1:11, 2:16, 3:19, 4:5 1:-14, 2:28, 3:56	—
Ramm et al. (1981)	12	Outpatients	Sparse	Pre-post	1. AMT with positive self-instruction 2. AMT with negative self-instruction	Five anxiety scales (P) Four target problems (P) Wakefield Depression Q. Fear Q.	1 > 2	1:29, 2:17	3 mo. (S-R)
Jannoun et al. (1982)	26	Outpatients	Sparse	Pre-post	1. AMT 2. Wait list (6 w) + AMT 3. Wait list (8 w) + AMT	Leeds self-rating of anx. STAI-T Hamilton Anxiety Scale	1 > 2 + 3 1 > 2 + 3 1 = 2 + 3	1:35, 2 + 3:-5 1:16, 2 + 3:-1 1 + 2 + 3:39	10 w. (S-R, A)

119

TABLE 5.1 (Continued)

Generalized anxiety disorder and panic disorder (continued)

Authors	n	Recruitment/ subjects	Inclusion criteria	Treatment methods	Design	Measures	Results	Percentage improvement	Follow-up
Taylor et al. (1982)	36	Advertisements	Sparse (DSM-III)	1. Wait list control 2. Relaxation 3. Diazepam + supp. ther. 4. Placebo + supp. ther.	Pre-post	Self-rating of anxiety STAI-S POMS Heart rate	2 > 1, 3, 4	1:-1, 2:17, 3:7, 4:0	—
Lehrer et al. (1983)	61	Advertisements Referrals	Sparse	1. Prog. relax. 2. Meditation 3. Wait list control	Pre-post	Heart rate Skin conductance, EEG EMG (forearm, frontalis) STAI-State IPAT Anxiety inv. SCL-90R	1 = 2 > 3 1 > 2 > 3	1:12, 2:-9, 3:-18 1:35, 2:-9, 3:8	—
Barlow et al. (1984)	20	Outpatients Self-referrals	Several (DSM-III)	1. PR + EMG-fb + CBT 2. Wait list control	Pre-post	EMG-activity Heart rate STAI-S BDI Psychosomatic Symptom S. A.r. of severity	1 > 2 1 > 2 1 > 2	1:27, 2:-5 1:21, 2:-2 1:37, 2:3	3–12 mo. (A only)
Eayrs et al. (1984)	43	Referrals	Several	1. Coping skills tr. 2. Relaxation (tape)	Pre-post	STAI-S STAI-T Symptom checklist Self-rating of severity	1 > 2 1 = 2	1:23, 2:11 1:23, 2:2	6 mo. (S-R)

[a]acrophobia, [b]blood phobia, [c]claustrophobia, [d]dental phobia, [e]darkness phobia, [f]flying phobia, [g]driving phobia.

Key:
Treatment: applied rel. (AR) = applied relaxation; behav. react. = behavioral reactors; behav. ther. = behavior therapy; CBT = cognitive behavior therapy; cogn. react. = cognitive reactors; cogn. restr. = cognitive restructuring; cop. high aro. = coping high arousal; co-ther. = co-therapist; couns. = counseling; des. = desensitization; disc. = discussion; exp. = exposure; fant. = fantasy; fb = feedback; flood. = flooding; high resp. = high responders; HR = heart rate; imag. = imagery; ind. exp. = individual exposure; med. = meditation; mod. = modeling; no syst. scene pres. = no systematic scene presentation; obs. = observation; phys. react. = physiological reactors; PR = progressive relaxation; prog. = programmed; PT = psychotherapy; relax. = relaxation; RP = response prevention; SD = systematic desensitization; self-instruc. = self-instructional training; SST = social skills training; supp. = supportive; ther. cont. = therapist contact; ther.-directed des. = therapist-directed desensitization; tr. = training.

Measures: AACL = Affect Adjective Check List; ant. anx. = anticipatory anxiety; API = Acute Panic Inventory; APQ = Autonomic Perception Questionnaire; AQ = Agoraphobia Questionnaire; a.r. = assessor rating; AS = Agoraphobia Scale; ASES = Adult Self-Expression Scale; avoid. = avoidance; BDI = Beck Depression Inventory; CCEI = Crown-Crisp Experiential Index; CMI = Cornell Medical Index; dent. = dental; depers. = depersonalization; depr. = depression; DFS = Dental Fear Survey; DI = Depression Inventory; EPI = Eysenck Personality Inventory; EPPS = Edwards Personal Preference Scale; FCPI = Fear of Panic's Consequences Index; FNE = Fear of Negative Evaluation; FQ = Fear Questionnaire; FSS-100 = Fear Survey Schedule-100; FSS-III = Fear Survey Schedule-III; GSP = galvanic skin potential; HDHQ = Hostility and Direction of Hostility Questionnaire; HLCS = Health Locus of Control Scale; H-OQ = Hysteroid-Obsessoid Questionnaire; I-E. = internal-external control scale; Inv. Soc. Behav. = Inventory of Social Behavior; IPAT = Intitute of Personality and Ability Testing Anxiety Scale; MAS or TMAS = Taylor Manifest Anxiety Scale; MHQ = Middlesex Hospital Questionnaire; MMPI = Minnesota Multiphasic Personality Inventory; MMQ = Maudsley Marital Questionnaire; P. = patient; POMS = Profile of Mood Scale; PRCS = Personal Report of Confidence as a Speaker; PSE = Present State Evaluation; Q. = questionnaire; R. = rating; R-SS = Repression-Sensitization Scale; SAD = Social Avoidance and Distress Scale; SAS = Self-Rating Anxiety Scale; SC = skin conductance; SCL-90R = Symptom Check List 90 Revised; SDS = Self-Rating Depression Scale; sem. diff. = semantic differential; SP = skin potential; S-R DS or SDS = Self-Rating Depression Scale; S-R Inv. of Anxiety = Self-Report Inventory of Anxiety; SRS = Severity Rating Scale; SSQ = Social Skills Questionnaire; STAI = State Trait Anxiety Inventory; ther. t. = therapist rating

Follow-up: A = assessor rating; B = behavioral test; mo. = months; P = physiological data; S-R = self-report; w. = weeks; yrs. = years

Selection of Patients

The way subjects in psychotherapeutic investigations are recruited is always an important variable in research. Different recruitment methods can produce completely different samples for investigation, and care should always be given to the characteristics of the sample when evaluating a particular research study (Marks, 1981a). Several methods for recruitment are at the researchers' disposal—advertising for patients, accepting referrals from primary-care clinicians or consecutive referrals from hospitals, or taking people from a hospital waiting list.

In anxiety research a large proportion of the studies (from 75 to 93%) have used unsolicited patients, usually recruited by means of referrals. One exception to this is simple phobias, where 78% of the studies used solicited volunteer patients. This could be because simple phobias are perhaps the least clinical of the anxiety disorders. It is remarkable that 35% of the studies on agoraphobia lack information on recruitment methods (see Table 5.2). It is gratifying that such a large proportion of the studies have used unsolicited patients. It seems quite clear that clinical samples have been investigated in these anxiety studies.

What is often lacking, however, is information about how many subjects refused to take part in the investigation or refused a certain treatment. It could be that if one has a large proportion of refusals, the result will be a preselected sample even if appropriate recruitment methods have been used. More data on this are needed in future studies.

INCLUSION CRITERIA

In order for the reader of an experimental study to make a judgment about the efficacy of a certain behavioral method in the treatment of a certain anxiety disorder, it is imperative to know what the included patients are like. Thus the researcher must use specified criteria that the patients have to fulfill in order to be included in the study and others that they must *not* fufill (i.e., that would exclude them). It is clearly not sufficient just to say that "patients suffering from general anxiety" were included.

In Table 5.1 the fourth column describes the inclusion criteria used by each study. More than one-fifth (22%) of the studies used no criteria whatsoever; 46% had very sparse criteria (e.g., a label of the diagnosis and on age range); 14% used several criteria (e.g., a verbal definition of the diagnosis, on age range, and exclusion criteria such as no depression or psychotic symptoms or no psychotropic drugs), and 18% used elaborated criteria, giving the reader a clear picture of the sample of patients. In the last category, criteria from the *Diagnostic and Statistical Manual of Mental Disorders* (DSM-III) (American Psychiatric Association, 1980) were often used if the study was published after 1980. Altogether, only one-third of the reviewed studies used inclusion/exclusion criteria that give the reader a fair chance to evaluate the sample studied. One diagnostic category, however, presents a brighter picture than the others—social phobia, where 58% of the studies used adequate criteria.

When dividing the studies into those published from 1966 to 1979 and those published from 1980 to 1984, respectively, a marked improvement emerged. During the former period there were only 20% and during the latter period 44% that had several or elaborated criteria. Even today, however, half the studies published use criteria that probably result in very heterogenous samples, which in turn makes it difficult to compare the results with those of studies using more stringent criteria.

TABLE 5.2 Recruitment methods and inclusion criteria in the different anxiety disorders

Disorder	No. of studies	Recruitment methods			Inclusion criteria			
		Solicited	Unsolicited	No information	No	Sparse	Several	Elaborated
Agoraphobia	41	7%	93%	35%	41%	27%	7%	25%
Social phobia	12	18%	82%	8%	0	42%	33%	25%
Simple phobia	23	78%	22%	0	13%	61%	9%	17%
Obsessive–compulsive	18	22%	78%	11%	22%	56%	11%	11%
GAD/PD	16	25%	75%	6%	6%	63%	25%	6%
Total	110	28%	72%	16%	23%	45%	14%	18%

Assessment

Since Lang's (1968) classical paper discarding the lump theory of fear, the so-called *three-system model* of anxiety has been generally accepted in behavioral research. It views anxiety as consisting of three loosely coupled components—behavioral (motoric), physiological (autonomic), and subjective (cognitive). In order to obtain as complete as possible a picture of the anxiety disorder under study, it is essential to measure these three components. The most efficient way to do this is to use a behavioral avoidance/approach test *in vivo*, confronting the patient with an object or situation that arouses anxiety. This can most readily be done with phobic and compulsive patients, whereas for patients suffering from generalized anxiety disorder, panic disorder, or posttraumatic stress disorder, some kind of laboratory test is more suitable. This can be in the form of, for example, a stress test, hyperventilation, or slides depicting a traumatic situation, and primarily arouse physiological and subjective or cognitive anxiety reactions. Ideally, samples from the three anxiety components should be measured continuously during the behavioral test or, if this is not possible, immediately at the end of the test.

Behavioral Tests

Another important principle is to administer the behavioral test in as natural a situation as possible in order to increase the validity of the results. This can, of course, impose a number of practical problems, some of them insurmountable. Take simple phobias as an example. For some types of phobias, it is easy to arrange a behavioral test in natural situations—for acrophobia, climbing up a fire escape; for claustrophobia, staying in a small room with the door locked; for flying phobia, taking an airplane. For other types it is much more difficult. A thunderstorm cannot be ordered at a certain time and place for a patient with thunder and lightning phobia: instead, films or slides are used. For blood injury phobia, under some circumstances a visit to a surgical theater can be arranged, but usually a film or videotape must do; for snake phobia, going to the snakes' natural habitat is an uncertain way of confrontation, so an approach test in the laboratory is used instead, even though this hardly represents the situation most frequently avoided by snake phobics.

For social phobia, the problem of a valid behavioral test is also pertinent. As the most interesting facet of the behavioral component in social phobia is not escape/avoidance behavior, but different overt dysfunctional behaviors, video recordings are often necessary to enable trained observers to rate these behaviors reliably. This means that a conversation test with a stranger is very difficult to administer in a natural situation because of the reactivity caused by the video recordings. Thus an analogue situation in a laboratory using confederates as strangers would have to suffice (e.g., Öst, Jerremalm, & Johansson, 1981).

Regarding agoraphobia, it is difficult to think of a behavioral test that is not administered in a natural milieu. The tests that have been used to date are either standardized or individualized. In the former, the patient usually starts at the front door of the hospital and walks away from it into increasingly central parts of the city. Usually the length of the test is determined beforehand (e.g., one mile), and it can be divided into a number of intervals (e.g., 20) of equal length. This has been used by Mavissakalian and Michelson (1983) among others. The advantage of a standardized test is that the performance of each patient can be compared to that of the others. There are, however, some disadvantages. For some agoraphobics, walking downtown is not at the top of their list of agoraphobic situations. Instead, going by bus or subway, standing in line or shopping in a crowded department store may be rated as much more difficult. Another problem is that the direction of the walk might lead toward the patient's house—a safety-signal (Rachman, 1984) for some patients—and further away from home for others. This means that comparability across patients cannot be considered complete even if it usually is higher than for the individualized test. In this task, the patient and experimenter together construct a hierarchy of 10 to 15 situations that should cover all important aspects of the patient's agoraphobic avoidance behavior (Mathews, Gelder, & Johnston, 1981). These situations are constructed in such a way that they all start and end at the patient's home. The test is carried out from the patient's home and he or she chooses the most difficult situation considered possible to perform on the day of the test. If this is performed successfully, the next is tried, and so on until the patient has failed or refused two consecutive situations. This way of administering the test reduces the time involved and the amount of exposure to or training in different phobic situations. The dependent variable obtained from this test is the number (or percentage) of situations completed, which corresponds to the rank number of the last situation performed. The advantage of this test is that it gives a measure of the patient's capability. The disadvantage is the problem of comparability across patients. When using group experimental designs, it would be possible to classify the patients according to the type of top situation their hierarchies contain and to match them accordingly. This, however, has never been done by researchers using the individualized behavioral test. An ideal solution, of course, is to use both types of behavioral test, as has been done by Mavissakalian & Michelson (1983).

For obsessive–compulsive disorders the majority of patients suffering from compulsive rituals can be exposed to a behavioral test divided into discrete steps (e.g., Foa, Steketee, Grayson, Turner, & Latimer, 1984), whereas this is impossible for patients with pure obsessions.

The anxiety reactions displayed by patients diagnosed as generalized anxiety disorder and panic disorder are, by definition (DSM-III; APA, 1980), not elicited by some observable object or situation. This makes it impossible to administer a behavioral test of the kind used in phobias. Instead, one must settle for a laboratory test that can elicit different physiological reactions (e.g., increases in heart rate, electromyography, and skin conductance). This test can use different stressor tasks (e.g., mental arithmetic, imagery of personally stressful scenes, cold pressor test), as used by Barlow et al. (1984); hyperventilation for 2 minutes (Clark & Hemsley, 1982); or injection of lactate or different drugs (Guttmacher, Murphy, & Insel, 1983).

For posttraumatic stress disorder it is obviously impossible to confront the patient *in vivo* with the traumatic situation that started the disorder. However, some kind of symbolic representation in the form of film, slides, audio recording, or the like can be used and the patient's behavioral, physiological, and subjective/cognitive reactions measured (Malloy, Fairbank, & Keane, 1983).

This short review of different behavioral tests that can be used in research on anxiety disorders is far from complete. However, it shows that the literature contains numerous examples of behavioral tests administered in more or less natural situations and with varying validity. An important task for future research in this area is to develop new behavioral tests in as natural situations as possible, and to improve the validity of those already in use.

Measures during a Behavioral Test

Besides different aspects of the patient's overt behavior during the test, physiological and subjective or cognitive reactions can also be assessed. New developments in electronics have given small lightweight cassette recorders (e.g., Medilog and Holter) that the patient can wear around the waist. These permit heart rate, respiration, temperature, skin conductance, and the like to be measured continuously while the patient confronts the anxiety-arousing situation. Furthermore, a subjective rating of overall anxiety (0–8 or 0–10) can be given by the patient at certain intervals or at discrete steps and can also be recorded. The patient may be asked to verbalize negative, catastrophic thoughts as they appear (Williams & Rappoport, 1983), and these can be recorded as well. In some types of behavioral tests (e.g., a conversation or speech test for social phobics) it is too disruptive to have the patient rate the anxiety during the test; in these instances the rating should be done restrospectively immediately after the test has ended.

Other Important Measures in Anxiety Disorders

Various important aspects of anxiety disorders cannot be tapped by a behavioral test, and thus other assessments must be added. Examples are the daily functioning of agoraphobics, the general anxiety level of generalized anxiety disorder (GAD) patients; frequency, intensity, and duration of panic attacks in panic disorder (PD) patients; frequency and intrusiveness of obsessions, urges, and actual rituals in obsessive–compulsive patients; frequency and intrusiveness of recollections and dreams of the traumatic event in posttraumatic stress disorder (PTSD) patients, to name a few. Obviously, then, different types of *self-observation* and recording of these aspects of the disorders are called for in almost all anxiety disorders. Ideally, these should be done before, during, and after the end of treatment, as well as during a period at follow-ups. A well-known example is the daily diary designed by Mathews et al. (1981) and used in some recent studies.

One general problem with self-observation is the difficulty of reliability assessment. If internal events like thoughts and urges are recorded, a reliability assessment is impossible. However, if, for instance, an agoraphobic records outings, time spent out of the home, and so on, part of this can be observed and recorded by a partner and agreement data can be computed.

SELF-REPORT MEASURES

Numerous scales, questionnaires, inventories, and the like have been developed and used in behavioral research on anxiety disorders. These can be classified as specific (e.g., concerning one type of phobia) or general (e.g., Fear Survey Schedule or Fear Questionnaire). A review of these self-report measures would need a chapter of its own, and the reader is referred to recent reviews (e.g., Borkovec, Werts, & Bernstein, 1977; Tasto, 1977) for further details.

The most serious problem with self-report measures is that the patient can influence the data completely and, for various reasons fake better, or worse, than what is really the case. A further complication is that these effects may influence the scores differently before and after treatment. Before treatment the patient may rate his or her reactions as worse than they really are in order to increase the probability of receiving treatment. At the posttreatment assessment, however, the patient may want to please the therapist by rating his or her anxiety as less than it really is. In this way a small, clinically nonsignificant change may be seen as a substantial, clinically significant improvement. How frequently these reactive effects come into play is very difficult to estimate reliably, but the mere possibility of them should caution the researcher from relying on self-report measures exclusively.

INDEPENDENT ASSESSORS

One of the most common methods of assessing different aspects of anxiety disorders is to let a trained, independent assessor interview the patient and rate (often on a 0–8 scale) phobic anxiety, avoidance, generalized anxiety, and panic attacks. The advantage of this method is that various important aspects of the disorder in question can be covered during the interview, and the assessor is not bound by a strict interview scale but can ask any follow-up questions he or she deems necessary. Although the reliability of this method can be assessed, and interrater agreement has been shown to be fairly high, it still suffers from one problem. Basically, the dependent measures that are obtained from this method are still a form of self-rating, albeit filtered through the interviewer. If a patient has decided to deceive the assessor, there is no way that the interview can correct for this and yield an accurate score. Thus the risk of reactive effects that plagues self-rating, self-observation, and self-report measures is also, to an unknown extent, present when an independent assessor is used. Consequently these types of measures should not be used alone.

Associated Problems

It is well known that different anxiety disorders can result in complications of varying difficulty. DSM-III describes depression and excessive use of alcohol or anxiolytic drugs as possible complications for all anxiety disorders. Other reported problems include generalized anxiety, panic attacks, obsessions, compulsions, and depersonalization, as well as disturbances in marital, social, and occupational life. To obtain a broader view of the patients before and after treatment, it is advisable to assess at least some of these associated problems. The most economical, and probably sufficient, way to do this is via self-report scales and/or independent assessor ratings.

Measures Applied in Outcome Research

The different measures applied in the studies reviewed in Table 5.1 have been compiled in Table 5.3, which reveals that the most frequently used assessment strategy was self-

TABLE 5.3 Number of studies using each of various measures in behavioral research on anxiety disorders

| Disorder | n | Behavioral test | | Self-rating of anxiety | Self-observation | Self-report | Independent assessor | Assessment of associated problems |
		Behavior score	Physiological measure					
Agoraphobia	41	23	1	9	2	31	34	33
Social phobia	12	9	3	4	4	12	7	8
Simple phobia	23	17	6	13	0	19	0	7
Obsessive–compulsive	18	5	0	2	8	14	13	14
GAD/PD	16	2	11	7	2	13	7	8
Total n	110	56	21	35	16	89	61	70
%		53	20	33	15	80	55	63

report scales of the disorder in question. They were used in about 80% of the studies, followed by various measures of associated problems 63%, and independent assessor 55%. Behavioral tests were used in 53%, whereas self-rating of anxiety and physiological measures during the behavioral test were applied in only 33% and 20%, respectively. The least common measure was self-observation of anxiety reactions in natural situations (15%).

Assessment according to the three-system model—a behavioral test yielding a measure of overt behavior, autonomic reactions, and subjective anxiety—is very rare. In agoraphobia there is only one study (Öst, Jerremalm, & Jansson, 1984); in social phobia three studies; in simple phobia six studies; and in obsessive–compulsive or GAD/PD there is no study with this type of assessment. Altogether only ten studies (9%) used the type of assessment that would seem the most suitable, providing, of course, that Lang's three-system model of anxiety is accepted.

Looking first at the use of behavioral tests, we find that in agoraphobia only about half the studies have used behavioral tests. These were fairly frequently used (67%) during the first ten years (1966–1975) of research in this area. There was a decline during 1976–1981, when only 31% used them, followed by an upsurge in 1982–1984 (69%). There is no apparant explanation for this fluctuation, but influential researchers' (e.g., Marks's) discontent with the behavioral tests may be one. In social phobics 75% of the studies have used behavioral tests; the only exceptions are three recent studies from England. Thus, except from our own studies (Öst et al., 1981; Jerremalm et al., 1986a), the trend is reversed, with 100% behavioral tests during 1974–1979, and none during 1980–1984. In simple phobias there do not seem to be any fluctuations in the use of behavioral tests, and practical difficulties probably explain the omission of behavioral tests in six studies. In two of these, however (both flying phobia), behavioral testing was used at posttreatment assessment only.

The lack of physiological measures is understandable because of the greater practical difficulties and expenses involved in this type of assessment. Equally difficult to understand is the failure to obtain self-rating data in the behavioral test situation. If a researcher has considered it essential to obtain a behavioral measure from an *in vivo* test, why not also let patients rate their anxiety in that situation, instead of—or in addition to—doing this at a screening interview while imagining how one usually reacts. Of the 56 studies using behavioral tests, only 28 (53%) used self-ratings in that situation, whereas 12 (23%) used physiological measures.

Self-observation of different anxiety reactions in the patients' natural environments has been used surprisingly seldom. The most frequent use is found in obsessive–compulsive disorder (44%) and social phobia (33%), whereas no study in simple phobia and only two each in agoraphobia and GAD/PD used self-observation. The neglect of this type of measure might be explained by a false belief that having the patient observe and record the behavior as it occurs should result in less reliable data than self-rating or assessor rating at a clinical interview before and after treatment. Conversely, it may be argued that self-observation will, if done properly, yield data that are more reliable and less subject to reactive effects than self- or assessor ratings.

Self-rating scales were the most frequently used measure, ranging from 76 to 100% in the studied disorders. There is, however, no reason that this figure should be less than

100% as the research literature today contains reliable self-report scales for all these disorders.

Independent assessor ratings were most frequently used in agoraphobia and obsessive–compulsive disorder, but was completely absent from the simple phobia studies. If GAD/PD is excluded, this corresponds well with disorders showing lack of behavioral testing. Thus it seems that many researchers have substituted assessor ratings for behavioral tests. For instance, in agoraphobia 79% of the studies not using behavioral tests had independent assessor ratings. In social phobia and obsessive–compulsive disorder, this figure was 100%.

Finally, the proportion of studies that had made any kind of assessment of an associated problem or complication of the disorder under study varied from 30 to 80%. These figures clearly need to be improved in future research.

Conclusion

Anxiety disorders are multifaceted and call for multidimensional assessment. *No single* measure today can be considered *the* anxiety measure, one that will give the researcher a complete picture of the disorder in question. Different measures have to be combined in an assessment battery. In our opinion a behavioral test should be given the highest priority, at least in phobias and compulsions. One reason is that behavior scores and physiological data are much less influenced by reactive effects than are the other types of measures. Another reason is that empirical data (Agras & Jacob, 1981) have shown that *in vivo* performance measures have the best ability to discriminate between treatments and to identify change from the beginning to the end of a particular treatment, tested in controlled-outcome studies. Furthermore, it is very important to have a measure of the occurrence of the anxiety disorder in the patient's natural milieu; thus self-observation is necessary. Besides these, a small number of self-report scales concerning the disorder in question and pertinent associated problems should be used. If resources allow, a clinical interview by an independent assessor could be added to assess both primary and associated problems. Despite the very frequent use of independent assessors in current behavioral research, it is our opinion that this can never replace a carefully designed behavioral test in natural situations for most of the anxiety disorders, with their definite behavioral manifestations.

Control Groups

A number of different control groups can be used in behavioral research on anxiety disorders, and a general review is presented by Kazdin (1980). In reviewing the experimental studies compiled in Table 5.1, it is obvious that two basic questions have been addressed. The first is whether the employed therapeutic method has an effect over and above spontaneous improvement across a certain time period. To answer this question, a no-treatment group is included. Rarely, however, is a condition used where the patients never receive treatment (during the time of the study). Most often a variation of the no-treatment group is used—the waiting list control group. The subjects in this condition are told that, because of a lack of therapeutic resources or for some similar reason, they cannot receive treatment immediately but will be treated as soon as the first group of subjects have completed the treatment. The waiting list subjects thus know that they *will* receive treatment at a later stage, whereas no-treatment control subjects know that they *will not* receive treatment within the current research project.

From an ethical point of view the waiting list condition (WLC) is, of course, preferable, but not necessarily from a methodological viewpoint. It is quite possible that subjects in the WLC do very little to activate personal resources to improve when they know that they will be treated anyway, in a number of months. This can result in a degree of improvement that is lower than would be expected. A no-treatment condition, on the other hand, will almost always result in a larger dropout rate—that is, no-shows at the postassessment—than a WLC.

Marks (1984) has suggested an alteration of the WLC that might make it a more stringent comparison. Instead of telling the patients that they will be treated at a later stage, one should tell them that they *might* receive treatment later. The reason for this is that one can never say, at the outset of a treatment study, that the method(s) employed will be effective. If it turns out that the tested method is effective, the patient will of course be offered treatment, but if this is not the case it is not ethical to offer an ineffective treatment to the patient. Furthermore, the patient should be encouraged to use his or her own resources to improve, as for example, self-exposure has been found to be effective for some agoraphobics (e.g., McDonald, Sartory, Grey, Cobb, Stan, & Marks, 1979).

The second basic question addressed is whether it is the treatment method itself or other nonspecific clinical components that are responsible for the changes achieved. To answer this question, a number of supposedly inactive treatments have been designed and compared to the active methods. These are labeled placebo, attention control, nonspecific treatment, minimal treatment, and so on. When using a placebo control group, it is absolutely essential to ascertain that the patients in this condition believe in the treatment they are receiving as much as the patients receiving active treatment do. A simple way of assessing this is by using the credibility scale developed by Borkovec and Nau (1972).

Table 5.4 presents a compilation of the two types of control groups used in the experimental studies summarized in Table 5.1. A total of 44 studies (40%) used some

TABLE 5.4 Outcome of no-treatment and placebo conditions versus the respective active treatments in anxiety disorders

Disorder	No-treatment condition		Placebo condition	
	Worse than active treatment	Equal to active treatment	Worse than active treatment	Equal to active treatment
Agoraphobia	5	0	6	3
Social phobia	3	1	—	—
Simple phobia	9	2	3	6
Obsessive–compulsive	1	0	1	0
GAD/PD	5	2	2	1
Total	23	5	12	10

kind of control group. A no-treatment condition (NTC) or WLC was used in 28 studies, and in 23 of these (82%) the control condition was found to be significantly inferior to the active methods. However, when a nonspecific control group was used, this was inferior to the active treatment in only 55% (12 out of 22) of the studies. It is also noticeable that in the studies on simple phobia, 67% (6 out of 9) of the studies found that the placebo condition was as effective as the compared active treatments, whereas it was inferior in the other anxiety disorders.

The conclusion that can be drawn concerning control groups in behavioral research on anxiety disorders is that continued use of no-treatment or waiting list groups (except for Marks's alteration) does not seem warranted. The probability of a significant change in an anxiety disorder of clinical dignity is fairly low, providing the researcher is studying clinical samples with usual duration of the disorder. On the other hand, a further development of credible placebo conditions that can be used in different types of studies is much desired.

Maintenance and Follow-Up

One of the most important questions in outcome research is whether or not a given treatment produces any long-term effects in a clinical disorder. The way to determine this is by conducting follow-ups of varying lengths to see how stable the changes in target problems are. A total of 36 studies on the main types of phobias and on obsessive–compulsive disorders have included follow-ups of at least 6 months (see Table 5.5). In general, these follow-ups have shown that treatment gains have been maintained over that time period (Jansson & Öst, 1982; Marks, 1981a). However, for generalized anxiety and panic disorders, only 25% of the studies included a 6-month follow-up. In the future, more follow-up studies on the treatment of GAD and PD are absolutely essential.

Today we have some experimental data indicating small correlations between the different response systems in anxiety (Borkovec et al., 1977). These data have led some researchers to propose the use of multivariate assessment to give a more complete picture of changes in target problems (Rachman & Wilson, 1980). Multivariate assessment methods have recently been used more often in assessing changes directly after treatment, but in only a few cases have researchers used multivariate assessment at follow-up. Typically the assessment at follow-up has been made with self-report measures either alone or in combination with assessor ratings of symptoms (see Table 5.5). Very few studies have included any direct behavioral measure, and only three reports have used a complete three-system assessment of the subjective, behavioral, and physiological components of anxiety at a long-term follow-up (Jansson, Jerremalm, & Öst, 1986; Öst, Johansson, & Jerremalm, 1982; Öst, Lindahl, Sterner, & Jerremalm, 1984). Incidentally, these three studies all come from the same research group. Looking at separate articles reporting on long-term results of treatment of agoraphobia, three used only self-report (Emmelkamp & Kuipers, 1979; Hafner, 1976; McPherson, Brougham, & McLaren, 1980); two used self-report and independent assessor (Cohen, Monteiro, & Marks, 1984; Munby & Johnston, 1980); and only one unpublished report used self-report, assessor ratings, and a behavior test (Burns, Thorpe, & Cavallaro, 1983).

In conclusion, it is not at all certain that self-report measures, either alone or

TABLE 5.5 Follow-up assessments in behavioral studies on anxiety disorders

Disorder	n	Percentage including ≥ 6-month follow-up	Measures used at follow-up[a]			
			S-R	S-R+A	S-R+B	S-R+B+P
Agoraphobia	41	32 (13)	38%	54%	0%	8%
Social phobia	12	42 (5)	20%	80%	0%	0%
Simple phobia	23	39 (9)	44%	11%	22%	22%
Obsessive–compulsive	18	50 (9)	11%	89%	0%	0%
GAD/PD	16	25 (4)	50%	50%	0%	0%
Total	110	36 (40)				

[a]S-R = self-report/self-rating, A = independent assessor ratings, B = behavioral test, P = physiological measure.

together with assessor ratings, adequately represent the whole clinical picture at follow-up. We still know little about long-term effects of behavioral treatment on the behavioral and physiological components of anxiety. Given the small correlation between response systems, this is a clear deficit in anxiety research.

Another reason for using three-system assessment at follow-up is that one may study sequences of change in the different response systems over time. The clinically stated opinion that the cognitive and the physiological systems lag behind changes in the behavioral system could perhaps be verified (Leitenberg, 1976; Leitenberg, Agras, Butz, & Wincze, 1971). This was illustrated in one study on 32 agoraphobic patients, where little change was found in the physiological response system directly after treatment. At 7-month and 15-month follow-ups, however, there was a continuing improvement in Δ heart rate, verifying that the physiological component lags behind behavioral changes (Jansson et al., 1986). Another interesting finding in this study was that at the 7-month follow-up, some patients had deteriorated significantly on subjective anxiety ratings and the physiological measure, whereas the behavioral and self-report measures still showed improvement. The deterioration at 7 months gave rise to suggestions for a different maintenance program for some of the patients. If the study had included only self-report measures, this effect would not have been discovered. This study highlights the fine, detailed analyses we can make if three-system assessments are conducted at follow-up.

More data are needed on the pattern of changes in the three response systems over time. It is extremely important that future clinical studies on anxiety treatment include three-system assessment at all assessment points. This would give more credence to the long-term results of behavior therapy.

The traditional view in clinical psychology and psychiatry has been that the treatment effect in itself is maintained until a follow-up point. This view is part of the medical model whereby a given treatment should effect a lasting cure in the patients. The implications of this medical model are not particularly productive. Another view of maintenance is to look for the factors that will lead to sustained improvement and, more precisely; for the factors associated with continued approach behavior after treatment. This is not a new idea in behavior therapy. Several authors have written of a "constructive approach" to behavior therapy, in contrast to an "eliminative" approach (Delprato, 1981; Goldiamond, 1974). A constructive approach asks, "What constructive behaviors can take the place of the problematic behaviors?" Perhaps the treatment of anxiety disorders is effected through one set of procedures (mostly respondent in nature) and maintenance of approach behaviors through a completely different set of factors (mostly operant in nature). The question for the anxiety patients is, therefore, "How can approach behavior be reinforced after formal therapy is over?" Some authors have experimented with buddy groups that meet and carry out exposure practice after treatment (Sinnott, Jones, Scott-Fordham, & Woodward, 1981). Another idea is to educate the couple about exposure principles and instruct the patient's spouse in carrying out reinforcement for approach behavior (McDonald et al., 1979; Barlow et al., 1984). Finally, one could try self-monitoring of approach behaviors and a brief telephone contact once a month to ascertain reinforcement for approach behavior after formal therapy (Jansson, Jerremalm, & Öst, 1984). These different ideas for maintenance programming need a sound empirical basis. Therefore, in the future we need to randomize treated patients into different maintenance programs to study which approach has the best empirical results.

One question is whether we should randomize only successfully treated patients at posttest, or all treated patients. Perhaps the most logical approach would be to randomize maintenance packages among the successfully treated patients only. Otherwise, what would be maintained? Finally, factors associated with sustained improvement could well be the same across different disorders and could even be more or less independent of the original treatment received. Only further research will settle this question. In summary, we need more studies with three-system assessment at each follow-up point and more research on programming maintenance of the treatment gains for anxiety patients.

Training and Supervision of Therapists

The way a psychological treatment is administered is of utmost importance in determining its effects. If the person who administers the treatment is not thoroughly trained in the method, it should be no surprise that the efficacy of the treatment will be limited. Also, if the person who delivers the treatment receives minimal or no supervision on how to apply treatment principles to particular patients, again we should not be surprised if treatment effects are weak. One way of judging research studies, especially studies with unexpected results, is by looking at the experience of the therapists, the amount and type of training, and the amount and type of supervision received.

Table 5.6 presents the proportion of the studies on anxiety that included information on the supervision, training, and clinical experience of the therapists. Table 5.6 shows that information on amount of supervision was provided in only about one-third of the studies on agoraphobia and obsessive–compulsive patients, and to an even lesser degree for the other anxiety disorders. When it comes to information on specific training in therapy methods used in the study and the clinical experience of the therapists, again roughly one-third of the studies included such data (see Table 5.6). The greatest lack of information seems to be in studies on GAD and PD, where no study contained information on supervision and only a very small percentage had data on specific

TABLE 5.6 Information on therapist variables in behavioral studies on anxiety disorders

Disorder	n	Therapist variables		
		Supervision	Training	Clinical experience
Agoraphobia	41	32%	35%	17%
Social phobia	12	13%	47%	40%
Simple phobia	23	17%	31%	31%
Obsessive–compulsive	18	44%	33%	33%
GAD/PD	16	0%	13%	19%
Total	110	25%	32%	26%

training and clinical experience. This is particularly alarming considering the often serious nature of the latter disorders, compared to, for example, specific phobias.

Clearly, information about clinical experience, specific training, and supervision of the therapists is lacking in too many outcome studies on anxiety disorders today. When data of this type are included, they are typically vague and uninformative (e.g., "All therapists were well versed in behavior therapy"). This area definitely needs improvement.

Some treatment methods may be more sensitive to the lack or inadequacy of training and supervision. More cognitively oriented treatments seem to suffer more when the therapists are not adequately trained in the methods under investigation, perhaps because of the complex and intricate nature of the cognitive therapies. The amount of training and supervision is an important variable when relatively easily administered treatments like, for example, exposure *in vivo* are compared to cognitive restructuring. The cognitive treatment could suffer more than exposure from lack of adequate training and supervision. Therefore, some of the negative results for the cognitive treatment could be explained in this way, again underscoring the importance of including such information.

Also, the amount of training in treatment methods and ongoing supervision is perhaps more crucial in certain anxiety disorders than in others. Inadequate training and supervision could be disasterous when treating, for example, generalized anxiety patients, but perhaps not as crucial when treating simple phobias. In the light of this argument, it is even more alarming that information on training and supervision is omitted from nearly all the studies on GAD and PD. Before we can say anything about adequate treatment for these disorders, we badly need methodologically sound research studies on that group.

A related issue is the importance of checking whether the independent variable actually has been varied in a research study. An independent check on how adequately the treatments were delivered is extremely important. This could be done by obtaining video recordings of randomly selected sessions, to be assessed by an authority on a given treatment. This is an important way to ascertain that an adequate trial of a given treatment has been conducted. In some of the studies on anxiety this was done adequately.

Ideally, in future studies on anxiety treatment the following questions should be clearly answered:

1. How many years of clinical experience with behavior or cognitive therapy does the therapist have?
2. What specific training and how much training does the therapist have with the therapeutic methods used?
3. What amount and what type of supervision is provided (e.g., on tape recordings or video, in groups or individually, by whom, etc.)?

This information is essential in determining whether or not a research study is to be considered as an adequate trial of a given treatment.

Process Research

One problem with process research is that research efforts have been devoted to treatment procedures such as client-centered therapy, which has not yet proved its efficacy. It seems logical first to conduct outcome research to establish a given treatment's efficacy for a certain disorder before looking at process factors operating in that treatment (Kazdin, 1980). Process factors should be studied for their relationship to outcome; thus the first requirement is that there be a positive outcome. This could be one reason that process research has not yet produced any clear-cut results. The process research done so far has mostly been done on treatment methods with unknown efficacy (Parloff, Waskow, & Wolfe, 1978).

Behavior therapy for anxiety disorders seems to be a field in which treatment efficacy has been established (Barlow & Beck, 1984; Barlow & Wolfe, 1981; Jansson & Öst, 1982). In theory, behavior therapists have shown some interest in how the therapeutic relationship affects treatment outcome with behavioral change methods (DeVoge & Beck, 1979; Wilson & Evans, 1977). However, little empirical research has been devoted to this question.

It can be concluded from available research on the differences between therapists from different theoretical persuasions that behavior therapists are characterized by more *active behaviors* (guidance, control over session, directive statements) and more *supportive behaviors* (emotional support, empathy) than are therapists from other theoretical standpoints (Brunink & Schroeder, 1979; Cross & Sheehan, 1982; Staples, Sloan, Whipple, Cristol, & Yorkston, 1976).

Process Factors in Anxiety Treatment

The interesting question, however, is whether certain therapeutic behaviors are correlated with enhanced treatment outcome, and some studies have investigated this issue. Morris & Suckerman (1974) found that therapists showing warmth and friendliness were more effective in reducing fear of snakes by using systematic desensitization than were cold, impersonal therapists. The same effect was found in another study of 20 test-anxious patients treated with the same method. In the higher-warmth condition, therapists spoke casually and in an unhurried way, inquired into the patients reactions to treatment, and gave encouragement and support. The outcome was significantly better in the high- than in the low-warmth condition (Ryan & Moses, 1979). However, this result was not replicated in another study on 19 acrophobic patients using contact desensitization as the treatment method. The results were that "warmth" expressed through eye contact, voice intonation, and facial expression made no difference in outcome (Morris & Magrath, 1979). Perhaps "warmth" is more important in systematic desensitization than in other anxiety treatments.

Staples, Sloan, Whipple, Cristol, & Yorkston (1976) studied 29 treatments where the patients received variations of behavior therapy or psychotherapy. Behavior therapists showed significantly higher levels of depth of interpersonal contact, empathy, and self-congruence than did psychotherapists. None of these variables, however, had significant relationship to outcome. The only positive finding in the study was that patients improved more when they perceived higher levels of nonpossessive warmth and accurate empathy in their therapists.

In a retrospective study (Rabavilas, Boulougouris, & Perissaki, 1979) on exposure *in vivo* for 13 phobic and 23 obsessive–compulsive patients, the effects of 26 therapist behaviors were investigated. Depending on the therapeutic effect, the patients were divided into a much improved and an unchanged group. In the much improved group, the patients rated their therapists significantly higher on the following variables: showing more encouragement, explicitness, and challenge; and less tolerant, permissive, and neutral. Emmelkamp and Van der Hout (1983) investigated 13 agoraphobics who had undergone group exposure *in vivo* and found that there was a significant correlation between outcome and therapist characteristics such as empathy, positive regard, and congruity.

In a recent pilot study (Gustavsson, Jansson, Jerremalm, & Öst, 1985) of 12 agoraphobic patients undergoing exposure therapy, a detailed assessment was made by an independent assessor of therapist behaviors during exposure practice. Tape recordings of verbal interactions during the *in vivo* sessions were categorized and rated by the assessor. The results revealed that the more the therapist negotiated with and reminded the patient of the problems' negative consequences, the worse the outcome. No relationship was found for variables such as empathy, encouragement, assurance, praise, or challenge. Furthermore, one outcome study was designed to provide data on the therapeutic effects of praising the client for approach behavior during exposure *in vivo* (Emmelkamp & Ultee, 1974). In this study of 16 agoraphobic patients, it was found that praise from the therapist for approach behavior was not significantly more effective than just giving feedback about approach performance.

It could be concluded from the process research reviewed so far that warmth conveyed through eye contact, voice intonation, and facial expression could influence the outcome of systematic desensitization. For exposure treatment, it appears that explicitness about practice and avoidance of negotiation or permissiveness may lead to better outcome.

Methodological Issues

In looking at the methodological sophistication of these process studies, certain short-comings need to be discussed. One can look at the therapeutic relationship from one of three different perspectives: the patient's, the treating therapist's, or an independent assessor's. If you choose the patient's perspective, you can perhaps administer questionnaires to patients on how they perceived the relationship to their therapist, either directly following each session or after a completed course of therapy. If you choose the therapist's perspective, you might administer questionnaires for the therapist to fill out after each session. The questionnaire could contain information on which behaviors the therapist used during the session and how the session was experienced. Finally, if you choose the independent assessor's viewpoint, you could record therapy sessions and then let the assessor rate, or count, the use of certain behaviors or quality of the therapeutic relationship. There is no reason to believe that these three perspectives will co-vary with one another to any large extent. You could get completely different results depending on which perspective you use in the study. The most reliable perspective is probably the independent assessor's, because an external judge is less influenced by subjective factors than the patient or the therapist and is unaware (if the study is blind) of the results for a particular client. Thus the use of an independent assessor for assessment of real-life therapeutic behaviors seems to be the best design so far for studying process variables in behavior therapy.

Another important point is that different behavioral methods are probably more or less influenced by process factors. Some therapeutic behaviors, for example, could be more optimal in systematic desensitization than in exposure *in vivo*. It makes little sense to talk about facilitative therapist behaviors in "behavior therapy" in general. Rather, it seems more profitable to look for method-specific therapeutic behaviors.

The next logical step in the research on exposure treatments for anxiety disorders might be to study whether certain therapeutic behaviors are more consistently associated with better outcome. These therapeutic behaviors could then be varied in an outcome study, and phobic patients could be randomized to exposure plus certain process factors or exposure without those factors. Treatments including elements of exposure seem to be best, with a sufficiently established efficacy for many anxiety patients (agoraphobics, specific phobics, and obsessive–compulsives) for whom this process strategy seems to be most worthwhile. The other anxiety treatments need first to establish efficacy before turning to process research.

Conclusions

The following conclusions can be drawn regarding the methodological issues discussed in this chapter. First, when selecting which patients to include in a study, the criteria need to be more elaborated than has generally been the case so far. To increase comparability, DSM-III criteria should be used, but these need to be complemented by certain exclusion criteria, such as whether psychotropic drugs were allowed during the time of the study. In assessment, behavioral tests and measurement according to the three-system model should be used whenever possible. Self-observation of anxiety, avoidance, obsessions, rituals, and the like in the patient's natural milieu ought to be used much more frequently than hitherto, and assessment of complications or associated problems should be included in future studies to a larger extent. Placebo conditions with demonstrated credibility also need to be developed and included in future behavioral studies on anxiety disorders. The continued use of a no-treatment or waiting list condition does not seem warranted.

Methods for the maintenance of treatment effects need to be developed and tested experimentally. Follow-up assessments should include the measures originally used before and after treatment. The reduction of assessment battery to include, for example, only self-report measures at follow-up may conceal important changes. It is necessary to use therapists with a suitable training for, and clinical experience in, the treatments studied. If this is not achieved, continuous supervision during the study is essential. Methods for process research need to be developed and used in controlled studies in order to reveal which therapist behaviors are related to good and poor outcomes, respectively.

These conclusions do not mean that we consider the methodological status of behavioral research in anxiety disorders to be deficient. The methodological rigor of behavioral research is unmatched by that of any other therapeutic orientation, but it can and should be further improved and refined in future research.

References

American Psychiatric Association. (1980). *Diagnostic and statistical manual of mental disorders* (3rd. ed.). Washington, DC: Author.

Argyle, M., Bryant, B., & Trower, P. (1974). Social skills training and psychotherapy: A comparative study. *Psychological Medicine. 4*, 435–443.

Baker, B. L., Cohen, D. C., & Saunders, T. J. (1973). Self-directed desensitization for acrophobia. *Behaviour Research and Therapy, 11*, 79–89.

Barlow, D. H., & Beck, G. J. (1984). The psychosocial treatment of anxiety disorders: Current status, future directions. In J. B. Williams & R. L. Spitzer (Eds.), *Psychotherapy research: Where are we and where should we go?* New York: Guilford Press.

Barlow, D. H., Cohen, A. S., Waddel, M. T., Vermilyea, B. B., Klosko, J. J., Blachard, E. B., & DiNardo, P. A. (1984). Panic and generalized anxiety disorders: Nature and treatment. *Behavior Therapy, 15*, 431–449.

Barlow, D. H., O'Brien, G. T., & Last, C. G. (1984). Couples treatment of agoraphobia. *Behavior Therapy, 15*, 41–58.

Barlow, D. H., & Wolfe, B. E. (1981). Behavioral approaches to anxiety disorders: A report on the NIMH–SUNY, Albany, research conference. *Journal of Consulting and Clinical Psychology, 49*, 448–454.

Benson, H., Frankel, F. H., Apfel, R. Daniels, M. D., Schniewind, H. E., Nemiah, J. C., Sifneos, P. E., Crass-weller, K. D., Greenwood, M. M., Kotch, J. B., Arns, P. A., & Rosner, B. (1978). Treatment of anxiety: A comparison of the usefulness of self-hypnosis and a meditational relaxation technique. *Psychotherapy and Psychosomatics, 30*, 229–242.

Bernstein, D. A., & Kleinknecht, R. A. (1982). Multiple approaches to the reduction of dental fear. *Journal of Behavior Therapy and Experimental Psychiatry, 13*, 287–292.

Biran, M., & Wilson, G. T. (1981). Treatment of phobic disorders using cognitive and exposure methods: A self-efficacy analysis. *Journal of Consulting and Clinical Psychology, 49*, 886–899.

Boersma, K., Den Hengst, S., Dekker, J., & Emmelkamp, P. M. G. (1976). Exposure and response prevention in the natural environment: A comparison with obsessive–compulsive patients. *Behaviour Research and Therapy, 14* 19–24.

Borkovec, T. D., & Nau, S. D. (1972). Credibility of analogue therapy rationales. *Journal of Behavior Therapy and Experimental Psychiatry, 3,* 257–260.

Borkovec, T. D., Werts, T. C., & Bernstein, D. A. (1977). Assessment of anxiety. In A. R. Ciminero, K. S. Calhoun, & H. E. Adams (Eds.), *Handbook of behavioral assessment.* New York: Wiley.

Bourque, P., & LaDouceur, R. (1980). An investigation of various performance-based treatments with acrophobics. *Behaviour Research and Therapy, 18,* 161–170.

Brunink, S. A., & Schroeder, H. E. (1979). Verbal therapeutic behavior of expert psychoanalytically oriented, gestalt, and behavior therapists. *Journal of Consulting and Clinical Psychology, 47,* 567–574.

Burns, L. E., Thorpe, G. L., & Cavallaro, A. (1983). Agoraphobia eight years after behavioral treatment: A follow-up study with interview, questionnaire and behavioral data. Paper presented at the World Congress in Behavior Therapy, Washington, DC.

Butler, G., Cullington, A., Munby, M., Amies, P., & Gelder, G. (1984). Exposure and anxiety management in the treatment of social phobia. *Journal of Consulting & Clinical Psychology, 52,* 642–650.

Canter, A., Kondo, C. Y., & Knott, J. R. (1975). A comparison of EMG feedback and progressive muscle relaxation training in anxiety neurosis. *British Journal of Psychiatry, 127,* 470–477.

Chambless, D. L., Foa, E. B., Groves, G. A., & Goldstein, A. J. (1979). Flooding with brevital in the treatment of agoraphobia: Countereffective? *Behaviour Research and Therapy, 17,* 243–251.

Chambless, D. L., Foa, E. B., Groves, G. A., & Goldstein, A. J. (1982). Exposure and communications training in the treatment of agoraphobia. *Behaviour Research and Therapy, 20,* 219–231.

Clark, D. M., & Hemsley, D. R. (1982). The effects of hyperventilation: Individual variability and it's relation to personality. *Journal of Behavior Therapy and Experimental Psychiatry, 13,* 41–47.

Cobb, J. P., Mathews, A. M., Childs-Clarke, A., & Blowers, C. M. (1984). The spouse as co-therapist in the treatment of agoraphobia. *British Journal of Psychiatry, 144,* 282–287.

Cohen, D. C. (1977). Comparison of self-report and overt behavioral procedures for assessing acrophobia. *Behavior Therapy, 8,* 17–23.

Cohen, S. D., Monteiro, W., & Marks, I. M. (1984). Two-year follow-up of agoraphobics after exposure and imipramine. *British Journal of Psychiatry, 144,* 276–281.

Cross, D. G., & Sheehan, P. W. (1982). Secondary therapist variables operating in short-term insight-oriented, and behaviour therapy. *British Journal of Medical Psychology, 55,* 275–284.

Delprato, D. J. (1981). The constructional approach to behavior modification. *Journal of Behavior Therapy and Experimental Psychiatry, 12,* 49–55.

Denholtz, M. S., & Mann, E. T. (1975). An automated audiovisual treatment of phobias administered by non-professionals. *Journal of Behavior Therapy and Experimental Psychiatry, 6,* 111–115.

DeSilva, P., & Rachman, S. (1984). Does escape behavior strengthen agoraphobic avoidance? A preliminary study. *Behaviour Research and Therapy, 22,* 87–91.

DeVoge, J. T., & Beck, S. (1979). The therapist–client relationship in behavior therapy. In M. Hersen, R. M. Eisler, & P. M. Miller (Eds.), *Progress in behavior modification* (Vol. 6). New York: Academic Press.

Eayrs, C. B., Rowan, D., & Harvey, P. G. (1984). Behavioral group training for anxiety management. *Behavioural Psychotherapy, 12,* 117–129.

Emmelkamp, P. M. G., (1974). Self-observation versus flooding in the treatment of agoraphobia. *Behaviour Research and Therapy, 12,* 229–237.

Emmelkamp, P. M. G., & De Lange, I. (1983). Spouse involvement in the treatment of obsessive–compulsive patients. *Behaviour Research and Therapy, 21,* 341–346.

Emmelkamp, P. M. G., & Emmelkamp-Brenner, A. (1975). Effects of historically portrayed modeling and group treatment on self-observation: A comparison with agoraphobics. *Behaviour Research and Therapy, 13,* 135–139.

Emmelkamp, P. M. G., & Kraanen, J. (1977). Therapist-controlled exposure *in vivo* versus self-controlled exposure *in vivo:* A comparison with obsessive–compulsive patients. *Behaviour Research and Therapy, 15,* 491–495.

Emmelkamp, P. M. G., & Kuipers, A. C. M. (1979). Agoraphobia: A follow-up study four years after treatment. *British Journal of Psychiatry, 134,* 352–355.

Emmelkamp, P. M. G., Kuipers, A. C. M., & Eggeraat, J. B. (1978). Cognitive modification versus prolonged exposure *in vivo*: A comparison with agoraphobics as subjects. *Behaviour Research and Therapy, 16*, 33–41.

Emmelkamp, P. M. G., & Kwee, K. G. (1977). Obsessional ruminations: A comparison between thought-stopping and prolonged exposure in imagination. *Behaviour Research and Therapy, 15*, 441–444.

Emmelkamp, P. M. G., & Mersch, P. P. (1982). Cognition and exposure *in vivo* in the treatment of agoraphobia: Short-term and delayed effects. *Cognitive Therapy and Research, 6*, 77–88.

Emmelkamp, P. M. G., & Ultee, K. A. (1974). A comparison of "successive approximation" and "self-observation" in the treatment of agoraphobia. *Behavior Therapy, 5*, 606–613.

Emmelkamp, P. M. G., Van der Helm, M., Van Zanten, B. L., & Plochg, I. (1980). Treatment of obsessive-compulsive patients: The contribution of self-instructional training in the effectiveness of exposure. *Behaviour Research and Therapy, 18*, 61–66.

Emmelkamp, P. M. G., & Van der Heyden, H. (1980). Treatment of harming obsessions. *Behavior Analysis and Modification, 4*, 28–35.

Emmelkamp, P. M .G., & Van der Hout, A. (1983). Failures in treating agoraphobia. In E. B. Foa & P. M. G. Emmelkamp (Eds.), *Failures in behavior therapy*. New York: Wiley.

Emmelkamp, P. M. G., Van der Hout, A., & De Vries, K. (1983). Assertive training for agoraphobics. *Behaviour Research and Therapy, 21*, 63–68.

Emmelkamp, P. M. G., & Wessels, H. (1975). Flooding in imagination versus flooding *in vivo*: A comparison with agoraphobics. *Behaviour Research and Therapy, 13*, 7–15.

Everaerd, W. T. A. M., Rijken, H. M., & Emmelkamp, P. M. G. (1973). A comparison of "flooding" and "successive approximation" in the treatment of agoraphobia. *Behaviour Research and Therapy, 11*, 105–117.

Falloon, I. R. H., Lloyd, G. G., & Harpin, R. E. (1981). The treatment of social phobia: Real-life rehearsal with non-professional therapists. *Journal of Nervous and Mental Diseases, 169*, 180–184.

Foa, E. B., Jameson, J. S., Turner, R. M., & Paynes, L. L. (1980). Massed vs. spaced exposure sessions in the treatment of agoraphobia. *Behaviour Research and Therapy, 18*, 333–338.

Foa, E. B., Steketee, G., & Milby, J. B. (1980). Differential effects of exposure and response prevention in obsessive–compulsive washers. *Journal of Consulting and Clinical Psychology, 48*, 71–79.

Foa, E. B., Steketee, G., Turner, R. M., & Fischer, S. C. (1980). Effects of imaginal exposure to feared disasters in obsessive–compulsive checkers. *Behaviour Research and Therapy, 18*, 449–455.

Foa E. B., Steketee, G., Grayson, J. B. Turner, R. M., & Latimer, P. R. (1984). Deliberate exposure and blocking of obsessive–compulsive rituals: Immediate and long-term effects. *Behavior Therapy, 15*, 450–472.

Gatchel, R. J. (1980). Effectiveness of two procedures for reducing dental fear: Group-administered desensitization and group education and discussion. *Journal of the American Dental Association, 101*, 634–637.

Gauthier, J., Savard, F., Hallé, J.-P., & Dufour, L. (1985). Flooding and coping skills training in the management of dental fear. *Scandinavian Journal of Behaviour Therapy, 14*, 3–15.

Gelder, M. G., Bancroft, J. H. J., Gath, D. H., Johnston, D. W., Mathews, A. M., & Shaw, P. M. (1973). Specific and non-specific factors in behavior therapy. *British Journal of Psychiatry, 123*, 445–462.

Gelder, M. G., & Marks, I. M. (1966). Severe agoraphobia: A controlled prospective trial of behaviour therapy. *British Journal of Psychiatry, 112*, 309–319.

Goldfried, M. R., & Goldfried, A. P. (1977). Importance of hierarchy content in the self-control of anxiety. *Journal of Consulting and Clinical Psychology, 45*, 124–134.

Goldiamond, I. (1974). Toward a constructional approach to social problems. *Behaviorism, 2*, 1–84.

Gustavsson, B., Jansson, L., Jerremalm, A., & Öst, L.-G. (1985). Therapist behaviors during exposure treatment of agoraphobia. *Behavior Modification, 9*, 491–504.

Guttmacher, L. B., Murphy, D. L., & Insel, T. R. (1983). Pharmacological models of anxiety. *Comprehensive Psychiatry, 24*, 312–326.

Hackman, A., & McLean, C. (1975). A comparison of flooding and thought-stopping in the treatment of obsessional neurosis. *Behaviour Research and Therapy, 13*, 263–269.

Hafner, J. B. (1976). Fresh symptom emergence after intensive behavior therapy. *British Journal of Psychiatry, 129*, 378–383.

Hafner, J. B., & Marks, I. M. (1976). Exposure *in vivo* of agoraphobics: Contributions of diazepam, group exposure and anxiety evocation. *Psychological Medicine, 6*, 71–88.

Hafner, J. B., & Milton, F. (1977). The influence of propranolol on the exposure *in vivo* of agoraphobics. *Psychological Medicine, 7*, 418–425.

Hall, R., & Goldberg, D. (1977). The role of social anxiety in social interaction difficulties. *British Journal of Psychiatry, 131*, 610–615.

Hand, I., LaMontagne, Y., & Marks, I. M. (1974). Group exposure (flooding) *in vivo* for agoraphobics. *British Journal of Psychiatry, 124*, 588–602.

Howard, W. A., Murphy, S. M., & Clarke, J. C. (1983). The nature and treatment of fear of flying: A controlled investigation. *Behavior Therapy, 14*, 557–567.

Jannoun, L., Oppenheimer, C., & Gelder, M. (1982). A self-help treatment program for anxiety state patients. *Behavior Therapy, 13*, 103–111.

Jannoun, L., Munby, M., Catalan, J., & Gelder, G. (1980). A home-based treatment program for agoraphobia: Replication and controlled evaluation. *Behavior Therapy, 11*, 249–305.

Jansson, L., Jerremalm, A., & Öst, L.-G. (1984). Maintenance procedures in the behavioral treatment of agoraphobia: A program and some data. *Behavioral Psychotherapy, 12*, 109–116.

Jansson, L., Jerremalm, A., & Öst, L.-G. (1986). Follow-up of agoraphobics treated with exposure *in vivo* or applied relaxation. *British Journal of Psychiatry*, in press.

Jansson, L., & Öst, L.-G. (1982). Behavioral treatments for agoraphobia: An evaluative review. *Clinical Psychology Review, 2*, 311–336.

Jerremalm, A., Jansson, L., & Öst, L.-G. (1986a) Cognitive and physiological reactivity and the effects of different behavioral methods in the treatment of social phobia. *Behaviour Research and Therapy, 24*, 171–180.

Jerremalm, A., Jansson, L., & Öst, L.-G. (1986b). Individual response patterns and the effects of different behavioral methods in the treatment of dental phobia. *Behaviour Research and Therapy, 24*, 587–596.

Johnston, D., & Gath, D. (1973). Arousal levels and attribution effects in diazepam-assisted flooding. *British Journal of Psychiatry, 123*, 463–466.

Jones, R. B., Sinnott, A., & Scott-Fordham, A. (1980). Group *in vivo* exposure augmented by the counseling of significant others in the treatment of agoraphobia. *Behavioural Psychotherapy, 8*, 30–35.

Kanter, N. J., & Goldfried, M. R. (1979). Relative effectiveness of rational restructuring and self-control desensitization in the reduction of interpersonal anxiety. *Behavior Therapy, 10*, 472–490.

Kazdin, A. E. (1980). *Research design in clinical psychology.* New York: Harper and Row.

Kenny, F. T., Mowbray, R. M., & Lalani, S. (1978). Faradic disruption of obsessive ideation in the treatment of obsessive neurosis: A controlled study. *Behavior Therapy, 9*, 209–221.

Klein, D. F., Zitrin, C. M., Woerner, M. G., & Ross, D. C. (1983). Treatment of phobias: 2. Behavior therapy and supportive psychotherapy: Are there any specific ingredients? *Archives of General Psychiatry, 40*, 139–145.

Lang, P. J. (1968). Fear reduction and fear behavior: Problems in treating a construct. In J. M. Shlien (Ed.), *Research in psychotherapy* (Vol 3). Washington, DC: American Psychological Association.

Lavallée, Y. J., LaMontagne, Y., Pinard, G., Annable, L., & Tétreault, L. (1977). Effects of EMG feedback, diazepam and their combination on chronic anxiety. *Journal of Psychosomatic Research, 21*, 65–71.

LeBoeuf, A., & Lodge, J. (1980). A comparison of frontalis EMG feedback training and progressive relaxation in the treatment of chronic anxiety. *British Journal of Psychiatry, 137*, 279–284.

Lehrer, P. M. (1978). Psychophysiological effects of progressive relaxation in anxiety neurotic patients and of progressive relaxation and alpha feedback in nonpatients. *Journal of Consulting and Clinical Psychology, 46*, 389–404.

Lehrer, P. M., Woolfolk, R. L., Rooney, A. J., McCann, B., & Carrington, P. (1983). Progressive relaxation and meditation: A study of psychophysiological and therapeutic differences between two techniques. *Behaviour Research and Therapy, 21*, 651–662.

Leitenberg, H. (1976). Behavioral approaches to treatment of neuroses. In H. Leitenberg (Ed.), *Handbook of behavior modification and behavior therapy.* Englewood Cliffs, NJ: Prentice-Hall.

Leitenberg, H., Agras, W. S., Butz, R., & Wincze, J. P. (1971). Relationship between heart-rate and behavioral change during the treatment of phobias. *Journal of Abnormal Psychology, 78*, 59–68.

Leitenberg, H., & Callahan, E. J. (1973). Reinforced practice and reduction of different kinds of fears in adults and children. *Behaviour Research and Therapy, 11*, 19–30.

Likierman, H., & Rachman, S. J. (1982). Obsessions: An experimental investigation of thought-stopping and habituation training. *Behavioural Psychotherapy, 10*, 324–338.

Lipsedge, M. S., Hajioff, J., Huggins, P., Napier, L., Pearce, J., Pike, D. J., & Rich, M. (1973). The management of severe agoraphobia: A comparison of iproniazid and systematic desensitization. *Psychopharmacologia, 32*, 67–80.

Malloy, P. P., Fairbank, D. L., & Keane, T. M. (1983). Validation of a multimethod assessment of post-traumatic stress disorder in Vietnam veterans. *Journal of Consulting and Clinical Psychology, 51*, 488–494.

Marks, I. M. (1981a). *Cure and care of neuroses.* New York: Wiley.

Marks, I. M. (1981b). Review of behavioral psychotherapy: 1. Obsessive–compulsive disorders. *American Journal of Psychiatry, 138*, 584–592.

Marks, I. M. (1984). Personal communication.

Marks, I. M., Gray, S., Cohen, D., Hill, R., Mawson, D., Ramm, E., & Stern, R. S. (1983). Imipramine and brief therapist-aided exposure in agoraphobics having self-exposure homework. *Archives of General Psychiatry, 40*, 153–162.

Marks, I. M., Hodgson, R., & Rachman, S. J. (1975). Treatment of chronic obsessive–compulsive neurosis by *in vivo* exposure. *British Journal of Psychiatry, 127*, 349–364.

Marks, I. M., Stern, R. S., Mawson, D., Cobb, J., & McDonald, R. (1980). Climipramine and exposure for obsessive–compulsive rituals. *British Journal of Psychiatry, 136*, 1–25.

Marzillier, J. S., Lambert, C., & Kellet, J. (1976). A controlled evaluation of systematic desensitization and social skills training for socially inadequate psychiatric patients. *Behaviour Research and Therapy, 14*, 225–238.

Mathews, A. M., Gelder, M., & Johnston, D. W. (1981). *Agoraphobia: Nature and treatment.* New York: Guilford Press.

Mathews, A. M., Johnston, D. W., Lancashire, M., Munby, M., Shaw, P. M., & Gelder, M. (1976). Imaginal flooding and exposure to real phobic situations: Treatment outcome with agoraphobic patients. *British Journal of Psychiatry, 129*, 362–371.

Mathews, A., & Rezin, V. (1977). Treatment of dental fears by imaginal flooding and rehearsal of coping behaviour. *Behaviour Research and Therapy, 15*, 321–328.

Mathews, A. M., & Shaw, P. (1977). Cognitions related to anxiety: A pilot study of treatment. *Behaviour Research and Therapy, 15*, 503–505.

Mavissakalian, M., & Michelson, L. (1983). Self-directed *in vivo* exposure practice in behavioral and pharmacological treatments of agoraphobia. *Behavior Therapy, 14*, 506–519.

Mavissakalian, M., Michelson, L., & Dealy, R. S. (1983). Pharmacological treatment of agoraphobia: Imipramine versus imipramine with programmed practice. *British Journal of Psychiatry, 143*, 348–355.

Mavissakalian, M., Michelson, L., Greenwald, D., Kornblith, S., & Greenwald, M. (1983). Cognitive-behavioral treatment of agoraphobia: Paradoxical intention vs. self-statement training. *Behaviour Research and Therapy, 21*, 75–86.

Mawson, D., Marks, I. M., & Ramm, E. (1982). Clomipramine and exposure for chronic rituals: 3. Two-year follow-up and further findings. *British Journal of Psychiatry, 140*, 11–18.

McDonald, R., Sartory, G., Grey, S. J., Cobb, J., Stern, R. S., & Marks, I. M. (1979). The effects of self-exposure instructions on agoraphobic outpatients. *Behaviour Research and Therapy, 17*, 83–85.

McPherson, F. M., Brougham, L., & McLaren, S. (1980). Maintenance of improvements in agoraphobic patients treated by behavioral methods—A four-year follow-up. *Behaviour Research and Therapy, 18*, 150–152.

Miller, M. P., Murphy, P. J., & Miller, T. P. (1978). Comparison of electromyographic feedback and progressive relaxation training in treating circumscribed anxiety stress reactions. *Journal of Consulting and Clinical Psychology, 46*, 1291–1298.

Morris, R. J., & Magrath, K. H. (1979). Contribution of therapist warmth to the contact desensitization treatment of acrophobia. *Journal of Consulting and Clinical Psychology, 47*, 786–788.

Morris, R., & Suckerman, K. (1974). Therapist warmth as a factor in automated systematic desensitization. *Journal of Consulting and Clinical Psychology, 42*, 244–250.

Munby, M., & Johnston, D. W. (1980). Agoraphobia: The long-term follow-up of behavioral treatment. *British Journal of Psychiatry, 137*, 418–427.

Öst, L.-G., Jerremalm, A., & Jansson, L. (1984). Individual response patterns and the effects of different behavioral methods in the treatment of agoraphobia. *Behaviour Research and Therapy, 22*, 697–707.

Öst, L.-G., Jerremalm, A., & Johansson, J. (1981). Individual response patterns and the effects of different behavioral methods in the treatment of social phobia. *Behaviour Research and Therapy, 19*, 1–16.

Öst, L.-G., Johansson, J., & Jerremalm, A. (1982). Individual response patterns and the effects of different behavioral methods in the treatment of claustrophobia. *Behaviour Research and Therapy, 20*, 445–460.

Öst, L.-G., Lindahl, I.-L., Sterner, U., & Jerremalm, A. (1984). Exposure *in vivo* vs. applied relaxation in the treatment of blood phobia. *Behaviour Research and Therapy, 22*, 205–216.

Parloff, M. B., Waskow, I. E., & Wolfe, B. E. (1978). Research on therapist variables in relation to process and outcome. In S. L. Garfield & A. E. Bergin (Eds.), *Handbook of psychotherapy and behavior change*. New York: Wiley.

Pendleton, M. G., & Higgins, R. L. (1983). A comparison of negative practice and systematic desensitization in the treatment of acrophobia. *Journal of Behavior Therapy and Experimental Psychiatry, 14*, 317–323.

Rabavilas, A. D., Boulougouris, J. C., & Perissaki, H. (1979). Therapist qualities related to outcome with exposure *in vivo* in neurotic patients. *Journal of Behavior Therapy and Experimental Psychiatry, 10*, 293–294.

Rabavilas, A. D., Boulougouris, J. C., & Stefanis, C. (1976). Duration of flooding sessions in the treatment of obsessive–compulsive patients. *Behaviour Research and Therapy, 14*, 349–355.

Rachman, S. J. (1984). Agoraphobia—A safety-signal perspective. *Behaviour Research and Therapy, 22*, 59–70.

Rachman, S. J., Cobb, J., Grey, S., McDonald, D., Mawson, D., Sartory, G., & Stern, R. S. (1979). The behavioral treatment of obsessional–compulsive disorders, with and without clomipramine. *Behaviour Research and Therapy, 17*, 467–478.

Rachman, S. J., & Wilson, G. T. (1980). *The effects of psychological therapy*. Oxford: Pergamon Press.

Ramm, E., Marks, I. M., Yuksel, S., & Stern, R. S. (1981). Anxiety management training for anxiety states: Positive compared with negative self-statements. *British Journal of Psychiatry, 140*, 367–373.

Raskin, M., Bali, L. R., & Pecke, H. V. (1980). Muscle biofeedback and transcendental meditation. *Archives of General Psychiatry, 37*, 93–97.

Ritter, B. (1969a). Treatment of acrophobia with contact desensitization. *Behaviour Research and Therapy, 7*, 41–45.

Ritter, B. (1969b). The use of contact desensitization, demonstration-plus participation and demonstration-alone in the treatment of acrophobia. *Behaviour Research and Therapy, 7*, 157–164.

Röper, G., Rachman, S. J., & Marks, I. M. (1975). Passive and participant modeling in exposure treatment of obsessive-compulsive neurotics. *Behaviour Research and Therapy, 13*, 271–279.

Rupert, P. A., & Holmes, D. S. (1978). Effects of multiple sessions of true and placebo heart rate biofeedback training on the heart rates and anxiety levels of anxious patients during and following treatment. *Psychophysiology, 15*, 582–590.

Ryan, V. L., & Moses, J. A. (1979). Therapist warmth and status in the systematic desensitization of test anxiety. *Psychotherapy: Theory, research and practice, 16*, 178–184.

Shaw, D. W., & Thoresen, C. E. (1974). Effects of modeling and desensitization in reducing dentist phobia. *Journal of Counseling Psychology, 21*, 415–420.

Shaw, P. M. (1979). A comparison of three behaviour therapies in the treatment of social phobia. *British Journal of Psychiatry, 134*, 620–623.

Sinnott, A., Jones, R. B., Scott-Fordham, A., & Woodward, R. (1981). Augmentation of *in vivo* exposure treatment for agoraphobia by the formation of neighbourhood self-help groups. *Behaviour Research and Therapy, 19*, 339–347.

Solyom, L., McClure, D. J., Heseltine, G. F. D., Ledwidge, B., & Solyom, C. (1972). Variables in the aversion relief therapy of phobias. *Behaviour Therapy, 3*, 21–28.

Solyom, L., Shugar, R., Bryntwick, S., & Solyom, C. (1973). Treatment of fear of flying. *American Journal of Psychiatry, 130*, 423–427.

Solyom, C., Solyom, L., LaPierre, Y., Pecknold, J., & Morton, L. (1981). Phenelzine and exposure in the treatment of phobias. *Biological Psychiatry, 16*, 239–247.

Sookman, D., & Solyom, L. (1977). The effectiveness of four behavior therapies in the treatment of obsessive neurosis. In J. C. Boulougouris & A. D. Rabavilas (Eds.), *The treatment of phobic and obsessive compulsive disorders*. New York: Pergamon Press.

Staples, F. R., Sloane, R. B., Cristol, A. H., Yorkston, N. J., & Whipple, K. (1975). Differences between behavior therapists and psychotherapists. *Archives of General Psychiatry, 32,* 1517–1522.

Staples, F. R., Sloane, R. B., Whipple, K., Cristol, A. H., & Yorkston, N. (1976). Process of outcome in psychotherapy and behavior therapy. *Journal of Consulting and Clinical Psychology, 44,* 340–350.

Stern, R. S., Lipsedge, M. S., & Marks, I. M. (1973). Obsessive ruminations: A controlled trial of thought-stopping technique. *Behaviour Research and Therapy, 11,* 659–662.

Stern, R. S., & Marks, I. M. (1973). Brief and prolonged flooding: A comparison in agoraphobic patients. *Archives of General Psychiatry, 28,* 270–276.

Stravynski, A., Marks, I. M., & Yule, W. (1982). Social skills problems in neurotic outpatients. *Archives of General Psychiatry, 39,* 1378–1385.

Tasto, D. L. (1977). Self-report schedules and inventories. In A. R. Ciminero, K. S. Calhoun, & H. E. Adams (Eds.), *Handbook of behavioral assessment,* New York: Wiley.

Taylor, C. B., Kenigsberg, M. L., & Robinson, J. M. (1982). A controlled comparison of relaxation and diazepam in panic disorder. *Journal of Clinical Psychiatry, 43,* 423–425.

Townsend, R. E., House, J. F., & Addario, D. (1975). A comparison of biofeedback-mediated relaxation and group therapy in the treatment of chronic anxiety. *American Journal of Psychiatry, 132,* 598–601.

Trower, P., Yardley, K., Bryant, B. M., & Shaw, P. (1978). The treatment of social failure. *Behavior Modification, 2,* 41–60.

Tyrer, P., Horn, S., & Lee, I. (1978). Treatment of agoraphobia by subliminal and supraliminal exposure to phobic cine film. *The Lancet, I,* 358–360.

Ullrich, R., DeMuynck, U., Crombach, G., & Peikert, V. (1975). Three flooding procedures in the treatment of agoraphobics. In J. C. Brengelman (Ed.), *Progress in behavior therapy.* Berlin: Springer.

Williams, S. L., Dooseman, G., & Kleifeld, E. (1984). Comparative effectiveness of guided mastery and exposure treatments for intractable phobias. *Journal of Consulting and Clinical Psychology, 52,* 505–518.

Williams, S. L., & Rappoport, A. (1983). Cognitive treatment in the natural environment for agoraphobics. *Behavior Therapy, 14,* 299–313.

Wilson, G. T., & Evans, J. M. (1977). The therapist–client relationship in behavior therapy. In A. S. Gurman & A. M. Razin (Eds.), *Effective psychotherapy. A handbook of research.* New York: Pergamon.

Woodward, R., & Jones, R. B. (1980). Cognitive restructuring treatment: A controlled trial with anxious patients. *Behaviour Research and Therapy, 18,* 401–417.

Wroblewski, P. F., Jacob, T., & Rehm, L. P. (1977). The contribution of relaxation to symbolic modeling in the modification of dental fears. *Behaviour Research and Therapy, 15,* 113–117.

Yorkston, N. J., Sergeant, H. G. S., & Rachman, S. J. (1968). Methohexitone relaxation for desensitising agoraphobic patients. *The Lancet, II,* 651–653.

Zitrin, C. M., Klein, D. F., & Woerner, M. G. (1978). Behavior therapy, supportive psychotherapy, imipramine and phobias. *Archives of General Psychiatry, 35,* 307–316.

Zitrin, C. M., Klein, D. F., & Woerner, M. G. (1980). Treatment of agoraphobia with group exposure *in vivo* and imipramine. *Archives of General Psychiatry, 37,* 63–72.

PART II

CLINICAL APPLICATIONS

6

Childhood Anxiety Disorders

SYLVIA Z. RAMIREZ, THOMAS R. KRATOCHWILL, AND RICHARD J. MORRIS

Assessment and treatment of anxiety disorders in children has increased in recent years. Researchers and practitioners have used a wide range of behavior therapy assessment and treatment techniques to work with both adults and children. In the childhood area, behavior therapy procedures have been affiliated with several different areas or models of the field, including applied behavior analysis, neobehavioristic-mediational stimulus–response (S–R) approaches, social learning theory, and cognitive-behavior modification.

One of the most recent developments in assessment and treatment in the behavior therapy field is cognitive-behavior modification or therapy (Karoly, 1981; Mahoney, 1974; Meichenbaum, 1974, 1977). A major feature of cognitive-behavior therapy procedures is the emphasis placed on cognitive processes or private events as mediators of behavior change in the child client. In this regard, the child's thoughts, feelings, attributions, images, self-statements, and other cognitive factors are considered important and even the major source of the clinical problem.

A number of cognitive-behavior therapy procedures have been incorporated into the general field of behavior modification. These include Ellis's (1962) rational-emotive therapy as well as some of the most recent developments in rational-emotive therapy with children (e.g., Ellis & Bernard, 1983). Cognitive therapy, developed by Beck (e.g., Beck, 1976; Beck & Emery, 1985), and self-instructional training, developed by Meichenbaum and his associates (e.g., Meichenbaum, 1977), now serve as the basis for treatment of a wide range of disorders. Recently behavior therapists have been devoting more attention to the role of cognitions (e.g., self-statements) in anxious and fearful reactions. However, relative to other areas of behavior therapy treatments for childhood anxiety disorders, cognitive procedures have lagged behind.

In this chapter we provide an overview of cognitive-behavioral treatment procedures that have been employed with childhood anxiety disorders. In the first part of the chapter, we present a conceptual framework of anxiety as well as a format for defining cognitive behavior therapy with children. We then provide an overview of some definitional issues in the area of child anxiety disorder. Finally, we provide an overview of some

Sylvia Z. Ramirez and Thomas R. Kratochwill. School Psychology Program, Department of Educational Psychology, The University of Wisconsin—Madison, Madison, Wisconsin.

Richard J. Morris. School Psychology Program, Department of Educational Psychology, The University of Arizona, Tucson, Arizona.

of the cognitive therapy intervention procedures that have been reported in the research literature.

Conceptual Framework of Anxiety

Assessment of children's anxiety disorders typically focuses on three major content areas. A conceptual framework presented by Cone and his associates (Cone, 1978, 1979; Cone & Hawkins, 1977) called the Behavioral Assessment Grid (BAG) provides a useful guideline for conceptualization of anxiety and assessment efforts.

Contents

Three content areas, sometimes referred to as *systems* (Lang, 1968, 1971, 1977) or *channels* (Paul & Bernstein, 1973) can be used to assess anxiety. Rationales for assessing three content areas have been that a comprehensive picture of the client's functioning can be obtained and that treatment focused on these domains of functioning is not necessarily highly correlated with outcome (e.g., Hodgson & Rachman, 1974; Rachman & Hodgson, 1974).

In the *cognitive* system, information from the client obtained through interviews, self-report, self-monitoring, and related assessment strategies is used to validate the existence of anxiety. In the *physiological* channel, measurement of the sympathetic portion of the autonomic nervous system is usually assessed. Measures used to assess this content area have included blood pressure, heart rate, galvanic skin response, temperature, muscular tension, and respiration rate. More than one physiological measure is typically used to define this content area. Third, the *motor* system involves measurement of overt behavior. Some authors divide this area into direct and indirect measures (e.g., Paul & Bernstein, 1973). *Direct measures* refer to the overt behavioral consequences of physical arousal, as when a child trembles in the presence of a particular fear stimulus. *Indirect measures* involve a class of responses that typically include avoidance of the stimulus situation (i.e., actual motor behavior away from a stimulus).

An important issue to consider in assessment using these three contents is the distinction between the mode of measurement and the content area that is being assessed. The three content areas can be measured by different assessment techniques or procedures. For example, a clinician might obtain information on the motor domain through direct observation of a child or through self-report of the child's avoidance of the stimulus situation. It is also evident that some measures cannot be used to assess certain behavioral content areas (i.e., it is impossible to observe cognitions directly).

Methods

The methods used to assess anxiety have been ordered along a continuum of directness representing the extent to which they (1) measure the target response of clinical relevance (i.e., the actual stimulus) and (2) measure the response at the time and place of its natural occurrence (i.e., in the actual presence of the stimulus). In the indirect domain (not to be confused with the indirect and direct dimensions referred to earlier), interview, self-report, and informant ratings, such as checklists and rating scales, can be employed.

These measures are indirect because they are a verbal representation of more clinically relevant activities that occur at some other time and place. In the case of a self-report measure, for example, a client might state that during the past several months he or she has been afraid to go near water and has felt particularly anxious around swimming pools. This form of assessment is useful to validate the existence of possible anxiety but should usually not be the primary data source. The researcher and clinician should supplement self-report assessment with direct measures of behavior to document other manifestations of the problem.

Several measures used in assessing children's anxiety problems are labeled direct because they include assessment of the behavior at the actual time of its natural occurrence. These include self-observation (or monitoring), direct observation by others in either analogue or natural settings, and psychophysiological measures (sometimes considered a subdomain of direct observation).

There are a number of methodological concerns surrounding the assessment of anxiety through the use of a three-mode system. It is beyond the scope of this chapter to provide a detailed review of these issues, but an overview can be found in several sources (e.g., Barrios & Shigetomi, 1985; Cone, 1979; Morris & Kratochwill, 1983; Kratochwill & Morris, 1985).

Definition and Diagnosis

Definition: Fear, Phobia, or Anxiety

As noted in the previous section, anxiety is a multidimensional construct that typically involves motoric, cognitive, and physiological components. In the clinical literature one finds that the terms *fear, phobia,* and *anxiety* have often been used interchangeably. Yet a distinction can be made between fears and phobias, with a phobia regarded as a special fear that has several defining characteristics (Marks, 1969; Miller, Barrett, & Hampe, 1974). A phobia:

1. Is out of proportion to demands of the situation;
2. Cannot be explained or reasoned away;
3. Is beyond voluntary control;
4. Leads to avoidance of the feared situation;
5. Persists over an extended period of time;
6. Is unadaptive;
7. Is not age or stage specific. [Miller et al., 1974, p. 90]

Despite the ambiguity surrounding these criteria, most researchers suggest that fears are distinguished from phobias on the basis of their *persistence, maladaptiveness,* and *magnitude* (e.g., Barrios, Hartmann, & Shigetomi, 1981; Graziano, DeGiovanni, & Garcia, 1979; Marks, 1969; Miller et al., 1974). For example, Graziano et al. (1979, p. 805) noted that "clinical fears" could be defined as those with a duration of over 2 years, or an intensity that is debilitating to the client's routine life-style. Most clinicians would regard an intense fear of short duration (e.g., 3 months) as clinically disturbing enough to warrant intervention.

These guidelines have provided some assistance to researchers and clinicians working in the area of children's fears and phobias, but there remains little agreement on definition (Morris & Kratochwill, 1983; Kratochwill & Morris, 1985). Definitional problems are further complicated by the overlap between terms like *anxiety* and *stress*. Stress in children is said to be "any factor acting internally or externally that makes it difficult to adapt and that induces increased effort on the part of a person to maintain a state of balance within himself and with his external environment" (Humphrey & Humphrey, 1985, p. 4). These authors further acknowledge the interchangeable usage in the professional literature between *stress* and *anxiety* and include fear reduction techniques (e.g., relaxation, systematic desensitization) within the domain of procedures that can be used to treat stress-related problems. This lack of consensus on terminology in the professional literature is especially reflected in diagnostic/classification systems that have been employed in the clinical-psychiatric field.

Diagnosis and Classification

Although diagnostic systems for childhood disorders have become more sophisticated in recent years, the major systems still serve as rough guidelines for classification of childhood anxiety disorders. Research has helped to elucidate the efficacy of various systems, but we still have a long way to go in developing an empirical basis for reliable and valid diagnosis. In the child literature, two major classification systems have been employed, including the clinically derived approaches such as the one developed by the American Psychiatric Association in the *Diagnostic and Statistical Manual of Mental Disorders* (DSM-III) (American Psychiatric Association, 1980), the Group for Advancement of Psychiatry, and the World Health Organization (Rutter, Lebocici, Eisenberg, Sneznevskij, Sadoun, Brooke, & Lin, 1969; Rutter, Shaffer, & Shepherd, 1975; Yule, 1981); and approaches developed from multivariate statistical applications (Achenbach & Edelbrock, 1978; Quay, 1979).

DSM-III

The DSM-III system is the most widely used in psychiatry and psychology. It includes three childhood anxiety disorders: *separation anxiety disorder, avoidant disorder of childhood or adolescence,* and *overanxious disorder.* Overanxious disorder is said to involve generalized anxiety in a variety of situations, whereas the other two types are said to focus on specific situations.

Separation anxiety disorder involves excessive anxiety on separation from a major attachment figure or from home or other familiar surroundings. This disorder is a form of phobia but is not included in the phobic disorder classification because of its unique features and because it is typically associated with childhood. The predominant disturbance of avoidant disorder of childhood or adolescence is a persistent and excessive shrinking from contact with strangers of sufficient severity so as to interfere with social functioning in peer relationships. In addition, there is a clear desire for affection, acceptance, and relationships with family members and other familiar figures that are warm and understanding. Overanxious disorder is characterized by excessive worrying and fearful behavior that is not due to a recent psychological stressor and is not focused on a specific situation or object.

BEHAVIORAL DISORDER INVESTIGATIONS

A number of studies conducted over the past 20 years have identified various dimensions of childhood disturbance (Kazdin, 1985). Most of these studies, conducted with rating scales and checklists, have identified several different childhood disorders, including conduct disorder, immaturity, socialized aggression, and anxiety–withdrawal. Anxiety–withdrawal is characterized by Quay (1979, p. 18) as: "Withdrawal rather than attack, of isolation rather than active enjoyment and of subjectively experienced anxiety and distress rather than apparent freedom from anxiety characterizing conduct disorder." A number of characteristics of the anxiety–withdrawal pattern are commonly identified, including, for example, anxious, fearful, tense, shy, timid, bashful, withdrawn, seclusive, friendless, and even depressed, sad, and disturbed features. Multivariate statistical procedures, such as factor analysis or cluster analysis, are used to identify the disorders (see Achenbach & Edelbrock, 1978; Ross, 1980; Yule, 1981).

CONSIDERATIONS

Both the DSM-III and the classification systems based on behavior disorder studies embrace a construct conceptualization of anxiety. Within this context, both systems have some limitations. In the case of DSM-III, criticism can be leveled because diagnosis rests on impressionistic clinical judgment; diagnosis of individuals is conducted in terms of broadly defined illness (i.e., anxiety disorders); and diagnosis generally neglects social-psychological variables and interpersonal behavior (McLemore & Benjamin, 1979). One of the strongest criticisms of the DSM-III system is its perceived heavy reliance on the medical model or disease conception of illness as applied to deviant behavior (McReynolds, 1979). Some concern has also been expressed over the reliability of the DSM-III system, especially for children. In the case of anxiety-related problems, Werry, Methuen, Fitzpatrick, and Dixon (1983) examined the interjudge reliability of 195 children who had been admitted to an inpatient psychiatric facility in New Zealand. Reliabilities for the subcategories of children's anxiety disorders were as follows: Separation anxiety ($\kappa = .61$, 14.4% of cases), avoidant disorder ($\kappa = .65$, 4.6% of cases), and overanxious disorder ($\kappa = .54$, 4.6% of cases). The researchers also examined the adult-related anxiety diagnoses that were applied to children and found the following reliabilities: simple phobia ($\kappa = .27$, 1.0% of cases) and obsessive–compulsive disorder ($\kappa = .94$, 3.1% of cases).

A number of specific limitations can also be identified in the classification efforts using rating scales and checklists in behavior disorder studies (Morris & Kratochwill, 1983). To begin with, the various dimensions of behavior identified have been based on select samples. A broader sampling of subjects may be necessary to further validate the classification categories derived; when such studies are conducted, they must also take into account a broader range of subject characteristics (such as sex, age, race, and socioeconomic status) (SES) (Achenbach & Edelbrock, 1978). Second, the vast majority of studies that employed checklists and rating scales used these as an indirect assessment of the problem. That is, individuals who completed the scales typically provided the data retrospectively (i.e., after the behavior occurred), rather than at the time the behavior occurred. Within the Cone (1978) conceptualization, such measures would be regarded as "indirect" and would need validation through more direct procedures such as observation in the natural environment. Relatedly, with such assessment it is often unclear whether or not the problem being rated is "perceived" or has actually occurred. Fourth, a number of methodological considerations must be taken into account in the use of checklists and rating scales (McMahon, 1984). For example, such factors as the conditions under which the rating is conducted; the instructions provided the rater; and various psychometric considerations (item content, reliability, method of conducting the factor analysis) must be addressed.

Perhaps the major concern in the diagnosis/classification of anxiety from a behavioral perspective is how the term is defined and used. Traditionally, anxiety has been viewed as a transient emotional behavior, a dispositional trait, or even as a cause or explanation for behavior (Borkovec, Weerts, & Bernstein, 1977). Nietzel and Bernstein (1981), in contrast, advanced a social learning framework for conceptualizing anxiety (pp. 216–219):

1. Anxiety is not a trait or personality characteristic that is internal to the individual.
2. Anxiety can be acquired through different learning mechanisms.
3. Anxiety consists of multiple response components.
4. Anxiety response channels are not highly correlated.

This conceptual framework is useful because the terminology employed in the clinical literature has often been imprecise and not always helpful in understanding how children actually behave. The idea that anxiety consists of multiple response components and that these may not be highly related has important implications for treatment. For example, treatment may need to be focused independently on each response channel. Also, the focus on three response channels may help advance knowledge of what treatments may be effective with different types of response patterns within the anxiety, fear, or phobia construct.

Definition and Conceptual Framework of Cognitive-Behavioral Therapy

Definition: Cognitive-Behavioral Therapy

Before reviewing some of the cognitive therapy procedures and techniques that are used with children experiencing anxiety disorders, it is useful to provide a definitional overview of terms used in the field. Cognitive-behavioral approaches encompass many techniques that despite their differences, share the following assumptions (Kendall & Braswell, 1985, p. 2):

1. Cognitive mediational processes are involved in human learning.
2. Thoughts, feelings, and behaviors are causally interrelated (the program, thus, has a cognitive-affective-behavioral slant).
3. Cognitive activities, such as expectations, self-statements, and attributions, are important in understanding and predicting psychopathology and psychotherapeutic change.

4. Cognitions and behaviors are compatible: (a) cognitive processes can be integrated into behavioral paradigms, and (b) cognitive techniques can be combined with behavioral procedures.
5. The task of the cognitive behavioral therapist is to collaborate with the client to assess distorted or deficient cognitive processes and behaviors and to design new learning experiences to remediate the dysfunctional or deficient cognitions, behaviors, and affective patterns.

Mahoney and Arnkoff (1978) identified three major forms of cognitive behavior therapies: rational psychotherapies, coping-skills therapies, and problem-solving therapies. Albert Ellis's (1962) rational-emotive therapy (RET) is the oldest of the rational psychotherapies. Irrational ideas or self-statements are said to be the fundamental cause of emotional disorder. The task of therapy is to assist the client in recognizing self-defeating irrational ideas and replacing them with more constructive, rational thoughts.

A variation of rational psychotherapy is self-instructional training (SIT) (Meichenbaum, 1976). Meichenbaum (1976) gives less emphasis to the logical analysis of irrational beliefs and argues that the incidence of irrational beliefs per se does not distinguish normal from abnormal populations. Rather, the two groups are said to differ in their coping response to irrational thoughts. The procedure developed by Meichbenbaum (1977) places heavy emphasis on the modeling of cognitive strategies by the therapist and on assisting the child through operant procedures to develop answers to four primary questions: "What is my problem?" "What is my plan?" "Am I using my plan?" and "How did I do?" (Meichenbaum & Goodman, 1971). The child is taught self-instructions to handle each of these aspects of problem resolution and thus learns how to cope with future problems. In this way, self-instructions can be viewed as establishing self-control over one's behavior.

The third variation of rational psychotherapy is Beck's cognitive therapy (Beck, 1976; Beck & Emery, 1985). As with RET and SIT, the ultimate goal is to develop rational adaptive thought patterns. Beck's (1976) cognitive therapy involves the following phases for the client: (1) becoming aware of his or her thoughts, (2) learning to identify inaccurate or distorted thoughts, and (3) replacing inaccurate thoughts with accurate and more objective cognitions. Therapist feedback and reinforcement are important parts of the process.

The second major form of cognitive-behavior therapy identified by Mahoney and Arknoff (1978) is coping-skills therapies. These therapies represent a different use of existing methods and overlap considerably with other approaches such as SIT. Examples include anxiety management training (Suinn & Richardson, 1971), stress inoculation (Meichenbaum, 1973) and modified systematic desensitization (Goldfried, 1971). The critical dimension that characterizes these diverse methods is that of the individual coping with distress producing events.

Problem-solving therapy is the third major form of cognitive-behavior therapy (e.g., D'Zurilla & Goldfried, 1971; Mahoney, 1977). This category also subsumes a heterogeneous collection of principles and procedures that overlap with other cognitive approaches. For example, SIT has a problem-solving focus; however, there are problem-solving interventions that do not emphasize self-instructions but still constitute cognitive-behavioral procedures.

Other terms—*self-control, self-management, self-regulation*—have also been used interchangeably in the clinical literature. Yet some distinctions are useful. Karoly (1981, p. 88) provided the following definition of self-control and self-regulation within the context of the cognitive social learning framework:

> *Self-control* refers to a set of aroused processes (cognitive and instrumental) through which an individual consciously and consistently contributes to changing the likelihood of engaging in a behavior with conflicting temporal contingencies. The behavior in question either may result in immediate reward, but have eventual aversive consequences (as in various addictive disorders) or may involve immediately unpleasant, long-range positive, outcomes. The aroused processes help to facilitate either avoidance (of the short-range positive payoff) or approach (to the short-run negative outcome). Typically, the individual must be motivated to counteract the cues in the immediate environment, which are arranged so as to facilitate the more probable, but maladaptive, patterns of responding (approach to the short-range positive outcomes or avoidance of short-range discomfort or loss).

> *Self-regulation* refers to a set of aroused processes through which an individual consciously and consistently contributes to maintaining the course of goal-directed behavior in the relative absence of external supports or when external supports are of limited utility.

As noted earlier, self-control is a process through which individuals become the primary agents in directing and regulating those aspects of their behavior that lead to preplanned and specific behavioral outcomes and/or consequences (Goldfried & Merbaum, 1973; Kanfer, 1980; Richards & Siegel, 1978). Self-control encompasses numerous intervention methods, each sharing as its common base the recognition of the contribution of cognitive processes to behavior change and the view that individuals can regulate their own behavior.

According to Kanfer (1980), self-control is a special case of self-management with self-control programs using many of the methods of self-management (e.g., self-monitoring and self-instruction). The common element of self-management methods is the role of the therapist as instigator and motivator in helping clients change their behavior.

A Conceptual Framework of Cognitive-Behavioral Therapy

In order to implement cognitive-behavioral strategies with children and to design an effective assessment and treatment program, it is necessary to consider a conceptual model for working with children experiencing fears, phobias, and anxiety disorders. In this regard, Karoly (1981, pp. 89–93) provided a working model for self-management that takes into account the following components:

First, the child's discrimination of rules and situational response requirements is necessary. Any comprehensive assessment of the child who is experiencing problems in this area will need to be assessed for their knowledge of self-management rules, acceptance of content and logic of rules, memory for rules, and ability to recognize the benefit of certain performance standards or codes of conduct.

A second feature of the model involves the child's awareness that his or her non-self-managing behavior has become dissonant with the environmental demands and is problematic in terms of obtaining reinforcing outcomes. Within this context, Karoly suggests assessing the accuracy of the child's awareness of the short-term nature and effects of behavior, the accuracy of the child's awareness of long-term effects of behavior, the child's recognition of the link between short- and long-term outcomes of behavior, the child's recognition of problematic features of short-run or short-term behavioral patterns, and the child's awareness of his or her impact on the behavior of others in the short and long term.

A third component of the model involves motivation or effort and commitment to behavior change. In this regard, the child is assessed along the following dimensions: (1) the child's perception of the value of the self-managed response as compared with the perceived alternatives, (2) the nature of potentially active physiological factors either facilitating or inhibiting the desire to self-manage, (3) the child's willingness to make promises and his or her history of fulfilling them, (4) the stringency or leniency of the child's self-evaluative standards, (5) the child's expectancy of future goal attainment compared with the perceived cost of engaging in self-management, (6) the child's belief in his or her ability to engage successfully in self-management, and (7) the child's habitual mode of attributing responsibility for the accomplishment of tasks relevant to self-management.

The final component of the model involves skills for extended self-management. A variety of skills have been identified as necessary in order for implementation of a self-management program. Such skills as self-observation, self-monitoring, and self-recording; self-evaluation and goal setting; administration of rewards and punishment; self-instructional control of performance; information processing, planning, and problem-solving style; imaginal control of thought and affect, self-perception, and causal attribution; and manipulation of stimulus response, response outcome, and self-efficacy expectations will be necessary.

In the context of this model, the clinician can develop a detailed and comprehensive assessment of the child's ability to manage his or her own performance. The seven questions raised by Karoly (1981, p. 100) can be useful in guiding assessment and eventual intervention with the child. Specifically, the following questions should be considered:

1. Would a self-management treatment model be appropriate?
2. Has the child's overt behavioral disturbance ever been conceptualized within a self-management framework?
3. Would self-management oriented interventions contribute to the maintenance of adaptive learning and/or the prevention of future problems?
4. Is a self-mediated form of intervention warranted on ethical grounds?
5. Is the child invested in changing a high-probability response pattern?
6. Does the assessor have access to the child's performance on a day-to-day basis with significant others or for extended periods of time?
7. Is it possible to identify the primary causes of the child's failure to achieve criterion performance by ruling out knowledge deficiencies, developmental or biological incapacities, motivational insufficiencies, skill deficits, or nonfacilitative environments?

In order to establish an effective cognitive-behavior therapy program, it will be necessary to conduct a very well developed assessment program. A variety of specific assessment devices and procedures can be implemented, including interviews, performance tests, role playing, self-monitoring, rating systems, direct observation, and formal assessment of social and intellectual functioning (Karoly, 1981). Although it is beyond the scope of this chapter to provide a detailed discussion of all assessment techniques that can be employed for anxiety-related problems, the interested reader is referred to several major sources that provide an overview of behavioral and cognitive measures that can be used (e.g., Barrios et al., 1981; Barrios & Shigetomi, 1985; Morris & Kratochwill, 1983).

Treatment Programs

In the treatment of children's anxiety disorders, cognitive self-control procedures focus on helping the child develop specific thinking skills and apply them whenever he or she is confronted with a particular fear- or anxiety-producing stimulus, event, or object. According to Meichenbaum and Genest (1980, p. 403), the self-control approach involves helping the child in the following areas:

1. Become aware of the negative thinking styles that impede performance and that lead to emotional upset and inadequate performance,
2. Generate, in collaboration with the trainer, a set of incompatible, specific self-statements, rules, strategies, and so on, which the trainee can then employ,
3. Learn specific adaptive, cognitive and behavior skills.

In order for the child to participate in cognitive therapy, he or she should be *aware* of the phobia or anxiety to the extent that he or she can identify the various *motoric aspects* of the fear (i.e., what the child does when he or she is afraid); *cognitive components* (i.e., what the child thinks or says to himself or herself when afraid); *physiological* components (i.e., how the body reacts when the child is afraid, and which part(s) of the body is involved); and under which conditions he or she becomes fearful. Second, it demands that the child have the verbal capacity to generate with the therapist a series of incompatible self-statements and rules, which the child can incorporate (at least temporarily) into his or her verbal repertoire. Third, it demands that the child be able to apply these self-statements and rules under those conditions in which he or she experiences anxiety. In addition to these factors, Kanfer (1980, pp. 383–384) outlined the following features that must be taken into account in development of a cognitive self-control treatment program:

1. A behavior analysis, including a description of specific problem behaviors, and of positive and negative reinforcers appropriate for the client's environment that can be enlisted to aid the behavior change process.
2. Observation and self-monitoring of the target behavior.
3. Development of a plan for behavior change. Negotiation of a contract that includes clear specification of the goals to be achieved, the time allowed for the program, and the consequences for achieving it, as well as the methods for producing the behavior change.

4. A brief discussion with the client on the underlying assumptions and rationale of the techniques to be used.
5. Modeling and role play of the desired behaviors.
6. Frequent external verification of progress and of factors that have retarded progress, as well as feedback and reevaluation of the contract.
7. Recording and inspection of qualitative and quantitative data documenting the change. Extension of the desired behavior to many different situations or areas of life.
8. A self-reinforcement program that relies increasingly on the person's self-reactions, is sufficiently varied to avoid satiation, and is effective in changing the target behavior.
9. Execution of new behaviors by the client in his or her natural environment with discussion and correction of the behavior, as needed.
10. Frequent verbalization of the procedural effects, the means by which they are achieved, and situations to which they can be applied in the future.
11. Continuing strong support by the helper for any activity in which the client assumes increasing responsibility for following the program accurately and extending it to other problematic behaviors.
12. Summarizing what has been learned in the change process and preparing the client to transfer the new knowledge and skills to future situations.

It is useful to review a typical cognitive-behavior therapy format for a child experiencing a phobic problem. Richards and Siegel (1978) provide an example of the use of cognitive-behavior therapy in the modification of a child's severe dog phobia. The child was taught Meichenbaum's (1974) self-control technique (self-instruction) as a supplement to other procedures. The self-instructional treatment involved the following five steps:

1. Therapists modeled adaptive self-verbalizations by talking out loud and administering task-relevant instructions to themselves while performing the task (e.g., while petting a dog appropriately, saying, "Relax, take a slow, deep breath; I'm doing fine; this dog is obviously friendly; notice his wagging tail; pet him softly; nothing to worry about").
2. The child performed the task while the therapists instructed her aloud.
3. The child performed the task and instructed herself aloud.
4. The child performed the task and whispered the instructions to herself.
5. The child interacted with dogs while using entirely covert self-instructions.

Steps 2 through 5 also included extensive performance feedback and positive reinforcement to the child.

Supportive Research

Although cognitive-behavior therapy procedures have been used often (e.g., Deffenbacher, 1976; Deffenbacher, Mathis, & Michaels, 1979; Deffenbacher & Michaels, 1980; Denney, 1980; Horan, Layng, & Pursell, 1976; Meichenbaum, 1974; Roberts & Nelson,

1985), only a small number of empirical studies have actually been published on their use in the treatment of childhood anxiety disorders (see Table 6.1).

A distinction is sometimes made between interactive and noninteractive training in self-instructions (cf. Kendall & Braswell, 1985). In the case of noninteractive procedures, training involves the experimenter telling the child what to do or say. In the interactive procedure, the training involves more child–experimenter exchange and can further be subdivided into three categories, as follows.

The first group refers to self-instructions as self-directed verbal commands. Training in this group of studies, though more involved than training provided in the noninteractive studies, is still relatively simple and unelaborated. A second group within the interactive class also employ the self-instructional procedures, but this training is provided within the context of more operant formulations of self-control. In these studies self-instructions are taught as a skill on a par with self-monitoring, self-evaluation, and self-reinforcement. The third and largest group of studies employ a version of training that is designed to imitate more closely the hypothesized processes to Luria's stage theory. This is accomplished by having the trainer first model the desired actions while speaking the self-instructions. The trainer then says the self-instructions with the child as the child carries out the actions. Finally, the child states the self-instructions while accomplishing the task activity (Kendall & Braswell, 1985, pp. 11–12). Several studies have used this interactive self-instructional approach in the treatment of children's fears (e.g., Kanfer, Karoly, & Newman, 1975; Graziano, Mooney, Huber, & Ignasiak, 1979).

In one of the first studies conducted in the self-control area, Kanfer, Karoly, and Newman (1975) compared the effectiveness of two types of verbal controlling responses on the reduction of children's fear of the dark. Forty-five children, 5 to 6 years of age, were selected for the study. Initially, each child could not stay alone in the dark for more than 27 seconds. The children were assigned to one of three research conditions:

1. A *competence* condition, where they heard and rehearsed sentences emphasizing their respective competence and active control in the fear situation—for example, "I am a brave boy (girl). I can take care of myself in the dark."
2. A *stimulus* condition, where they heard and rehearsed sentences emphasizing reducing the aversive qualities of the fear situation—for example, "The dark is a fun place to be. There are many good things in the dark."
3. A *neutral* condition, where they rehearsed sentences related to neutral phrases—for example, "Mary Had a Little Lamb" (Kanfer et al., 1975, p. 253).

Training took place in a well-lighted room, and testing took place in a dark one. Pretest and posttest measures consisted of duration of darkness and terminal light intensity (i.e., degree of illumination children needed to stay in the room).

The results of the study indicated that from the pretest to the first posttest period, the competence and stimulus groups remained in the darkened room significantly longer than the neutral group, and at the second posttest the competence group remained in the room significantly longer than either the stimulus or neutral group, with no significant difference between the stimulus and neutral groups at the second posttest period. On the illumination measure, the competence group was also found to be superior to the other two groups. The authors concluded that training effectiveness was related to the content

TABLE 6.1 Cognitive-behavioral treatment studies of childhood fears, phobias, and anxiety disorders

Study	Subjects	Focus	Outcome measures	Treatment	Results
Ayer (1973)	2 boys and 1 girl (10 years old)	Fear of dental injections	Observations and parent reports	Emotive imagery	No fear of dental injections.
Kanfer, Karoly, & Newman (1975)	45 children (5–6 years old)	Fear of the dark	Time in the dark and an illumination measure	Verbal mediation, competence, stimulus, and neutral conditions	Increased time in the dark for competence and stimulus conditions. Competence condition superior to other conditions on illumination measure.
Craddock, Cotler, & Jason (1978)	58 high school freshmen girls	Speech anxiety	Speech anxiety and behavioral measures	Cognitive rehearsal, systematic desensitization, and control conditions	Cognitive rehearsal most effective on speech anxiety measure. No difference between groups on behavioral measure.
Graziano, Mooney, Huber, & Ignasiak (1979)	5 boys and 2 girls (8–12 years old)	Severe night fears	Parent ratings of training's success and behavioral criteria	Self-instructions with relaxation training, token economy, and praise	Reduced number of fears and fear strength. Improved sleeping patterns.
Graziano & Mooney (1980)	18 boys and 15 girls (6–12 years olds)	Severe night fears	Fear strength questionnaire, fear survey, and parental ratings of nighttime fear behavior	Self-control with relaxation training, token economy, and praise; and a no treatment control	Treatment package more effective than control.
Siegel & Peterson (1980)	42 children (3–5 years old)	Fear of dental treatment	Behavioral Profile Scale, Venham Picture Test, Stanford Preschool Internal-External Scale, and pulse rate	Coping skills, sensory information, and a no treatment condition	No difference between experimental groups. Experimental groups better than control.
Bornstein & Knapp (1981)	12-year-old boy	Multiple phobias	Fear Survey Schedule and behavioral observation measures	"Cognitive" systematic desensitization	Fear-related verbalizations and scores on FSS decreased.

(continued)

TABLE 6.1 (*Continued*)

Study	Subjects	Focus	Outcome measures	Treatment	Results
Fox & Houston (1981)	56 fourth-grade children	Anxiety in evaluative situations	State anxiety measures, behavioral rating of anxiety, performance accuracy measure, and time involved in reciting poem	Self-instruction treatment, "minimal" treatment, and no treatment control	Self-instruction group exhibited *more* signs of behavioral anxiety than other conditions. High trait anxiety group reported *more* state anxiety in self-instruction condition than other conditions.
Leal, Baxter, Martin, & Marx (1981)	30 10th-grade students	Test anxiety	Raven's Standard Progressive Matrices, Anxiety Differential, State–Trait Anxiety Inventory	Cognitive behavior modification, systematic desensitization (SD), and a control condition	Cognitive therapy more effective on self-report measures; SD more effective on performance measures.
Peterson & Shigetomi (1981)	35 girls and 31 boys (2–10 years old)	Medical-related fears	Physiological, observational, and self-report measures	Preoperative information, coping strategies, and modeling, and imagery training	Coping strategies more effective than information or modeling; coping plus modeling more effective than coping or modeling alone.
Kelley (1982)	Learning-disabled children with high test anxiety	Fear, anxiety, and academic performance	Test Anxiety Scale for Children and self-monitoring	Self-directed verbalizations (SCV), Jacobson relaxation and SCV, and Carkhuff counseling control	Reduced fear and anxiety, and improved academic performance for relaxation and SDV. Relaxation and SDV more effective than SDV alone in reducing fear. SDV alone as effective as combined procedures in reducing anxiety and improving academic performance.

Study	N	Fear type	Measure	Treatment/comparison	Results
Mooney (1982)	21 children	Night fears	Parental report and child self-report	Self-control with relaxation training, token economy, and praise; and a waiting control	Less fear for the experimental group than control on parental reports. No difference between groups' self-report assessment and reports of duration of nighttime fear events.
Graziano & Mooney (1982)	34 children	Follow-up of Graziano, DeGiovanni, & Garcia (1979) and Graziano & Mooney (1980) studies	Fear strength questionnaire and telephone contacts	None	Improvements maintained for 31 of 34 children.
Wolfson (1983)	47 children	Aquaphobia	Water avoidance and swimming proficiency	Self-talk with imaginal exposure (ST), self-talk with in vivo exposure (ST/E), attention control with imaginal exposure (AC), attention control with in vivo exposure (AC/E), and no treatment control	ST/E and AC/E greatest gains in reduction of water avoidance. ST and ST/E greatest gains in swimming proficiency.
Rosenfarb & Haynes (1984)	38 children	Fear of the dark	Time in the dark	Self-statements in public and private contexts, modeling in public and private contexts, and control groups	Reduced fear of dark for treatments with self-statements in public context.

of the learned sentences in the respective three groups. The emphasis on the child's competence in dealing with the dark may be the salient component in teaching children to cope with stressful or feared situations.

In a study designed to replicate and extend the Kanfer et al. (1975) investigation, Rosenfarb and Hayes (1984) compared self-statements and modeling in the treatment of children who were afraid of the dark. Unlike the subjects of the Graziano, Mooney, Huber, and Ignasiak (1979) study, the children selected for the experiment may not have been clinically fearful. For example, six children were not included in the study because they showed signs of "intense discomfort and stated that they did not wish to participate in the study" (p. 519). Nevertheless, the same 180-second dark tolerance criterion used in the Kanfer et al. (1975) study was used. Thirty-eight children were assigned to one of six groups: private self-statements treatment, public self-statements treatment, public self-statements control, private modeling treatment, public modeling treatment, or public modeling control.

The results of the study indicated that, when the treatments took place in a public context, the children improved an average of 50 seconds in dark tolerance. In contrast, when the private context was employed, children's dark tolerance decreased an average of 2 seconds. The nonspecific public control group improved an average of 1 second in their dark tolerance.

The major finding of this study was that the treatments were effective only when children were told that the experimenter knew the treatment implemented. Thus the specific nature of the treatments was important, but only when it was public. The study calls into question the mechanisms presumed responsible for the positive effects of disinhibitory modeling and coping self-statements treatments.

In another early study, Graziano, Mooney, Huber, and Ignasiak (1979) used self-control instructions plus relaxation training and pleasant imagery to reduce "severe, clinical level" night fears of long duration in children. Five boys and two girls ranging in age from 8.7 to 12.8 years participated in the study. The children came from six families who were seen for 5 weeks (2 weeks for assessment and 3 weeks for instruction), with the parents and children seen in separate groups. The children were instructed to practice relaxation by imagining a pleasant scene and reciting "brave" self-statements each night with their parents present.

A token economy program was also established whereby the children received tokens for doing their exercises at home and for going to bed and being brave throughout the night. The parents were instructed to initiate the children's exercises at night and to use tokens and praise. The outcome measures included parent ratings of the number of child fears, strength of fears, and behavioral criteria (i.e., 10 consecutive fearless nights).

The results showed that it took from 3 to 19 weeks ($\bar{X} = 8.7$ weeks) for all the children to meet the behavioral criteria. The authors further reported that each child's "fear strength" steadily decreased through posttreatment and the 3-month, 6-month, and 1-year follow-up periods. Also, total number of fears decreased, with only one out of the seven children not completely free of fears at the 1-year follow-up. Finally, both parents and children reported that the program improved the children's fear behavior and sleeping patterns.

Graziano and Mooney (1980) used this treatment program with another set of families having children with "severe, highly disruptive, nighttime fears," comparing the treatment outcome with a matched no-treatment control condition. They found that, in comparison with the control condition, the treatment package was significantly more effective in reducing the strength of fears in the children as well as the frequency and duration of the fearsome events. The children receiving the experimental treatment were also significantly less disruptive, according to parent ratings. Follow-up information via a telephone call also confirmed the effectiveness of the treatment package. At 12 months, for example, only one child in the experimental group did not meet the behavioral criteria discussed here. Follow-up data on the control group were not available, since this group began receiving the treatment package after the experimental group completed their posttest.

Graziano and Mooney (1982) assessed 34 of the 40 families from previous studies (Graziano, Mooney, Huber, & Ignasiak, 1979; Graziano & Mooney, 1980) 2½ to 3 years after treatment. Mailed questionnaires and telephone contacts were used to determine if (1) the significant improvements had been maintained; (2) new, related problems had developed; and (3) generalization of effects had occurred. In a questionnaire similar to one administered previously, parents were asked about the frequency, duration, and intensity of fear episodes and the degree of disruption to the child, siblings, and parents caused by each fear episode. Open-ended questions concerning generalization effects and new problems were also included.

In the treatment studies, 39 of 40 children had significantly reduced or completely overcome their fears. Follow-up assessment showed that of the 34 families located, 31 had maintained their significant improvements. New psychological problems did not characteristically occur following treatment. Generalization effects did not occur for a majority of the children.

Mooney (1982) conducted a study in which electrodermal and subjective responses of 21 severely nighttime-fearful children were compared with 21 non-nighttime-fearful children. Coping responses, demographic information, semantic differential ratings, and parental reports were also compared. Subsequently, the nighttime-fearful children were divided into an experimental group, who received 3 weeks of self-control treatment, and a waiting control group. Responses were compared before treatment and after waiting. The treatment procedure used was the same as that of the Graziano and Mooney (1980) study. Results indicated that after treatment, the experimental group scored lower than the waiting control group on parental reports of nighttime fears. There was no difference between groups on reports of the duration of each nighttime fear event or on children's self-report.

Self-control treatments have also been applied with children experiencing medical- and dental-related fears. Using a variation of the self-control approach, Peterson and Shigetomi (1981) conducted a study with children who were to receive elective tonsillectomies. The 66 children (35 girls and 31 boys), aged 2.5 to 10.5 years ($\overline{X} = 5.47$ years) were assigned to one of four conditions:

1. Preoperative information, where children were invited to a "party" four days before their surgery and informed via a story and a puppet of the "typical hospital stay from admission to discharge"

2. Coping procedures, where children received the preoperative information plus cue-controlled muscle relaxation (using the cue "calm"); distracting mental imagery training (imagining a scene that was "quiet and made them feel happy"); and comforting self-talk (the children, for example, were encouraged to think of the phrase "I will be all better in a little while")
3. Filmed modeling, where the children received the preoperative information plus Melamed and Siegel's (1975) film, *Ethan Has an Operation*
4. Coping plus filmed modeling, where the children were also given a 15-minute hospital tour and spent another 15 to 20 minutes eating ice cream and cookies following the tour.

Six categories of dependent measures were used. The assessment included observational ratings, physiological measures (pulse rate and temperature), and child and parent self-reports.

The results indicated that children receiving the two coping conditions experienced less distress during their hospital stay than did the children in the modeling-only or information-only groups. Furthermore, children receiving the coping plus modeling procedure were more calm and cooperative during invasive procedures than were those in the coping or modeling alone conditions.

In another study, Siegel and Peterson (1980) conducted similar research with children undergoing dental treatment. They compared the coping-skills condition described earlier with a sensory information condition (i.e., children were told what to expect and heard audio tape recordings of the dental equipment) and a no-treatment/ attention condition. The results indicated that there was no significant difference between the coping and sensory information conditions on any of the measures taken during or after restorative treatment, and that both treatment groups fared better on the measures than did the no-treatment control children.

Cognitive procedures have been integrated into other forms of treatment for children's anxiety disorders. For example, one variation of desensitization involves "emotive imagery," a method first used by Lazarus and Abramovitz (1962) to adapt the desensitization procedure to children. Generally the procedure involves the use of anxiety-inhibiting images that arouse feelings of excitement associated with positive experiences. In the procedure a gradual hierarchy is developed. The clinician establishes child hero images, and the child is then asked to close his or her eyes and imagine a sequence of events in which a story is developed about the child's favorite hero. Once the child's emotions are maximally aroused within this story, the lowest item on the hierarchy is presented. The procedure is repeated throughout the systematic desensitization hierarchy until each item is tolerated without distress.

The procedure depends greatly on the child's visual imagery or cognitive skills. Unfortunately, there is little strong empirical research on this topic. For example, Lazarus and Abramovitz (1962) reported some descriptive case studies in which the procedure was used with a dog-phobic 14-year-old, a 10-year old who was afraid of the dark, and an 8-year-old who was afraid of going to school. The procedural steps discussed earlier were implemented, and the authors reported a reduction in the children's fears. In addition, Ayer (1973) reported the use of this visual imagery technique with three children who were afraid of going to the dentist. Specifically, the children were afraid of receiving the anesthetic and were said to have needle phobias. The children were asked to imagine that they were playing with their dogs and the dogs were yelping loudly (minor variations were scheduled with one child). They were then told to keep their eyes closed so they would see none of the dental instruments. This was practiced several times while they imagined the dogs yelping louder and louder. During the dental procedure the children were encouraged by the clinician to intensify the dog's yelping. The anesthetic was then administered in a routine fashion. The author reported that by the third appointment, the children were "visibly relaxed and friendly" (p. 126). More recently, Jackson and King (1981) successfully treated a 5½-year-old boy who was afraid of the dark. A fictional character, Batman, was chosen in a scenario in which the child and Batman joined forces to overcome the fear of the dark. Unfortunately, work in this area has remained at the descriptive case study level, so firm conclusions cannot be drawn from this area of research.

Interestingly, some behavior therapy treatments developed independently of the cognitive therapies have been conceptualized as having a cognitive component or focus. For example, Goldfried (1971) viewed systematic desensitization as training in self-control—that is, an active, cognitively mediated process of learning to cope with anxiety, rather than a passive counterconditioning one. Procedural modifications to increase self-control features with this method include the following:

1. Clients are taught how to relax, how to recognize tension, and how to use relaxation skills to relieve tension.
2. During the tension phase of relaxation exercises, clients focus on feelings of tension and become more sensitive to them. These feelings serve as cues for the application of relaxation.
3. Hierarchies are used that include many different anxiety-arousing themes in order to maximize transfer of the coping skills and increase the variety of situations in which self-control is practiced.
4. At the first experience of tension, clients signal and then continue imagining the scene while actively relaxing away the tension.
5. Clients signal when the anxiety is brought under control and they are once again deeply relaxed. The scene is then cleared, representing a successful trial of coping with tension.
6. Relaxation homework is emphasized, and in vivo application is reinforced and modified in light of the homework assignments.

Bornstein and Knapp (1981) used a modified version of Goldfried's (1971) conceptualization of systematic desensitization in the treatment of a 12-year-old multiphobic boy. Instead of using multithematic hierarchies, three separate hierarchies were constructed in accordance with the fears revealed in the assessment phase. Second, during treatment the child was not provided with instructions to use his developing relaxation skill beyond those areas already completed as a result of training. Aside from these procedural modifications, the treatment followed the guidelines established by Goldfried (1971). Hierarchies ranged from 10 to 15 items, and each item was presented until the scene had been mastered twice. Results indicated that the number of fear-related verbalizations decreased "dramatically" over the course of the treatment. At 1-year follow-up, positive results were maintained. In addition, these improvements were corroborated by results on the Fear Survey Schedule, which revealed "substantial" decreases of scores over time.

In a comparative outcome study, Craddock, Cotler, and Jason (1978) examined the relative effectiveness of cognitive-behavioral rehearsal and systematic desensitization to reduce speech anxiety in 58 high school freshman girls. Initially, 158 freshman girls who had decided not to enroll in a speech course were screened on Paul's (1966) speech-anxiety instrument. The 58 students who were identified as susceptible to speech anxiety were randomly assigned to either systematic desensitization, cognitive rehearsal, or delayed-treatment conditions. In the cognitive condition, subjects were first provided a treatment rationale and the necessary steps relating to preparation and delivery of a speech. During the first treatment session, subjects were also guided in an imaginary exercise to ensure that they would be able to initiate, maintain, and terminate visual images according to instructions.

The remaining treatment sessions consisted of a description of 18 hierarchical steps in preparing and giving a speech as well as three potential coping strategies (e.g., "I handle this step by taking a deep breath and remaining calm"). Each item in the hierarchy was presented for 1 minute. Subjects were requested to imagine themselves using a coping strategy at each step. The researchers found that the cognitive rehearsal group demonstrated a significant reduction in scores on the speech anxiety measure, relative to the control condition. However, on behavioral measures (e.g., stammering, hand tremors) there were no signficant differences among the three groups.

Test anxiety has been treated with cognitive interventions in behavioral research (Barrios & Shigetomi, 1979). Leal, Baxter, Martin, and Marx (1981) selected 30 10th-grade high school students from a population of 122 volunteers on the basis of evidence of test anxiety, coupled with no evidence of general anxiety or study skill deficits. The subjects were assigned ($n = 10$) to either a cognitive modification, systematic desensitization, or waiting-list control group. The cognitive therapy condition was based on previous work by Holroyd (1976) and Meichenbaum (1972). According to the authors (Leal et al., 1981, p. 526):

> Anxiety was explained to the subjects as resulting from their thoughts and self-statements occurring before and during exams. Subjects were told that an awareness of these thoughts and self-statements was necessary so that they could create incompatible responses to anxiety engendering ones. Subjects learned to label emotional arousal, recognize inappropriate responses, and replace self-defeating thoughts and self-statements with more positive alternatives.

The systematic desensitization involved pairing deep-muscle relaxation with presentation of imaginary anxiety-provoking scenes.

The authors used Raven's Standard Progressive Matrices to measure the effects of test anxiety in an analogue test situation and two self-report measures (the Anxiety Differential and the State Trait Anxiety Inventory or STAI). Results of the study indicated that the systematic desensitization treatment was more effective than either the cognitive treatment or control on the performance measure; the cognitive modification treatment was more effective on STAI-S. These results indicate that cognitive-behavior therapy may show its major impact on self-report measures, a finding consistent with other research with older populations (e.g., Holroyd, 1976; Meichenbaum, 1972).

Assessment of children's cognitions during test-taking conditions has been a major focus of research (e.g., Sarason, 1980). In a recent investigation Zatz and Chassin (1985) examined the cognitions of 438 sixth-grade low-, moderate-, and high-test-anxious children under naturalistic test-taking conditions. Children were assessed on several measures: *defensiveness* was measured by the Lie Scale for Children (Sarason, Davidson, Lighthall, Waite, & Ruebush, 1960); *test anxiety* was measured by the Test Anxiety Scale for Children (Sarason et al., 1960); children's *perceptions of their classroom environments* were assessed with the Competition and Teacher Control subscales of the Classroom Environment Scale (Trickett & Moos, 1973); *cognitions during testing* were assessed using a revision of the Children's Cognitive Assessment Questionnaire (Zatz & Chassin, 1983).

The researchers found that high-test-anxious children showed more task-debilitating cognitions during testing. Subjects also had more negative self-evaluations and off-task thoughts and fewer positive self-evaluations. The high-test-anxious children also showed relatively high frequencies of on-task thoughts and coping self-statements. The researchers also examined the role of the classroom environment in the test–anxiety–performance relationship. The performance of high-test-anxious subjects was debilitated only in classrooms where subjects perceived an evaluative threat. Their findings suggested that the poorest person–environment fits are moderately anxious children in low-threat classrooms and high-test-anxious children in low-threat classrooms.

The authors were careful to point out that their data do not support a role for training in on-task or coping statements in the treatment of test-anxious children. On the other hand, the authors noted that improved math performance (in the study) may be associated with an absence of negative thoughts rather than the presence of positive thoughts, a conclusion similar to that reached by Kendall and Hollon (1981).

Fox and Houston (1981) investigated the effectiveness of a cognitive self-statement treatment for reducing anxiety in children in an evaluative situation. The subjects were 56 fourth-grade children who were categorized as either high or low in trait anxiety and then were assigned to self-instructional treatment, so-called minimal treatment, or a no-treatment control group. The evaluative situation involved having children recite memorized material from the state portion of the State–Trait Anxiety Inventory for Children (STAIC) just prior to the subjects' reciting a poem. The other half of the items from the STAIC were administered immediately after subjects recited the poem, with the instruction that the subjects respond to the items according to how they felt while performing in front of a video camera.

Contrary to expectations, the subjects in the self-instruction treatment condition (1) exhibited *more* behavioral anxiety than did subjects in the other two conditions, and (2) hurried through the poem (taking less time to recite it) than did subjects the other two conditions. Self-instruction had no appreciable effect on either performance state anxiety or quality of performance. Additionally, high-trait-anxiety subjects reported more state anxiety while anticipating reciting the poem in self-instruction treatment than in the other two conditions.

The authors speculated on possible reasons for the difference between effects of their study and that of Kanfer et al. (1975), which used a similar approach. First, the self-instructions (especially the more complex ones) may have been distracting to the subjects. Second, in contrast to the self-statements of the Kanfer et al. (1975) study, which were positive, straightforward statements (e.g., "I can take care of myself in the dark"), Fox and Houston (1981) used statements designed to negate negative aspects of the stressful situation (e.g., "Doing this [poem] in front of others won't be so unpleasant"). Although statements that negate negative features of stressful situations have been used in adult treatment programs (cf. Meichenbaum, 1977), Fox and Houston (1981) suggest that they may have a deleterious effect in the treatment of children's fears and anxiety.

Cognitive-behavioral therapies have also been used for treatment of children experiencing learning problems and where anxiety may be a clinical feature. Kelley (1982) assessed the effect of relaxation training and self-directed verbalizations on measures of self-monitored fear, anxiety, and academic performance in learning-disabled children. The subjects were selected from a population of learning-disabled children by pretesting all children on the Test Anxiety Scale for Children (TASC) and selecting those children who scored in the highest 30%. Group 1 was trained in Jacobson relaxation and self-directed verbal commands; group 2 was trained in self-directed commands alone; and group 3 received Carkhuff counseling. Results indicated that Jacobson relaxation and self-directed verbal commands significantly reduced self-monitored fear and TASC anxiety while significantly increasing academic performance. The Jacobson relaxation and self-directed commands combined were more effective in reducing self-monitored fear than were self-directed verbalizations alone. Self-directed commands alone were as effective as the combined procedures in reducing anxiety and increasing academic performance. The study is especially interesting because improvement occurred in academic performance.

In a treatment study of water avoidance of aquaphobic children, Wolfson (1982) compared verbal self-regulation, *in vivo* exposure, and placebo treatments. Forty-seven aquaphobic subjects were assigned to five groups: (1) self-talk with imaginal exposure, (2) self-talk with *in vivo* exposure, (3) attention control with imaginal exposure, (4) attention control with *in vivo* exposure, and (5) no treatment control. Children in the self-talk with *in vivo* exposure and attention control with *in vivo* exposure demonstrated the greatest gains in the reduction of avoidance behavior. Both self-talk with imaginal exposure and self-talk with *in vivo* exposure led to greater gains in swimming proficiency. All treatment groups improved significantly in water approach behavior.

Future Directions

There is still a limited research base on the applications of cognitive behavior therapy to treat children's fears, phobias, and anxiety disorders. Given the paucity and sometimes conflicting nature of research in this area, only cautious statements can be made on the merits of cognitive therapy. We can, however, propose some future directions for research in the area. First, researchers must be careful to delineate the nature and scope of cognitive treatments. In some studies it is not clear what cognitive components were operating or whether these components were occurring across other experimental conditions. One positive direction in future research is to develop standardized treatment manuals for various treatment conditions (Luborsky & DeRubeis, 1984). Such manuals would help to define the therapy, would help ensure appropriate training of clinicians in its delivery and integrity in its administration, and would promote replication of the procedures in subsequent research.

Second, research on cognitive therapies represents a mix of both analogue and clinical fears. For example, Graziano and Mooney (1980) involved children with relatively severe nighttime fears in their study, whereas Kanfer et al. (1975) and Rosenfarb and Hayes (1984) used mildly dark-fearful subjects. We are not criticizing the quality of research with subclinical problems, but we suggest that the generalizability of research to clinical practice may be quite restricted with the current state of analogue research knowledge in the area. To extend knowledge in the area, researchers who have the time and resources should conduct a series of studies beginning with more analogue features and progressing to more clinical disorders.

Replication of research in the cognitive therapy is also needed. Only the Kanfer et al. (1975) study was replicated (i.c., Rosenfarb & Hayes, 1984). The importance of replication is obvious given the interesting findings of the Rosenfarb and Hayes study examining the role of social standard setting in cognitive therapy. The social standard setting influence must also be examined across the many types of cognitive therapies. In future therapeutic research it will be necessary to control for social influence mechanisms. Moreover, it appears that public social criteria for improved performance may operate across a number of cognitive therapies, and it will be useful to control them in clinical research interventions.

Many self-instructional training programs require children to learn a verbal and a motor response simultaneously. Learning two tasks simultaneously may be too difficult for some children, especially young, learning-disabled, and mentally retarded children. For these children, it may be advantageous to establish the motor behavior firmly before introducing the verbal behavior. Systematic research on this issue is needed.

Further research is also needed to evaluate what kinds of self-statements can most effectively be used in treatment programs for children. As was demonstrated in the Fox and Houston (1981) study, simply extrapolating treatment procedures developed with adults to children may not result in the desired effect.

In concert with the three systems for conceptualization of fear or anxiety, it would be very important to include a wider range of outcome measures in future research. Response measures could span the several options that exist within each of the response domains. Moreover, researchers should examine the correspondence or lack of correspondence of these measures as well as the possible differential responsiveness of the measures of different treatments.

Another assessment concern is that cognitions cannot be assessed directly. Typically, verbal and motor responses are assessed and are sometimes taken as a sign of an underlying cognitive process (Roberts & Nelson, 1985). Goldfried and Kent (1972) have identified a number of difficulties with this sign approach. They include the need for inference (from motor to cognitive behavior) that is difficult to validate empirically and the assumption that the underlying process (cognitions) causes generalized responding across situations. Researchers should be aware of these difficulties and should seek solutions to them.

Finally, most of the studies in cognitive therapy have used group comparative outcome methodologies. In the typical study, cognitive therapies are compared to other treatments and/or control conditions. Given the level of knowledge in this area, it is recommended that the efficacy of single treatment components be examined first. This could be accomplished by examining single treatment components in single case designs or by comparing various cognitive treatment components among themselves or to control conditions. The point is that it may be premature for researchers to compare vastly different treatments when the efficacy of specific components remains unknown.

Acknowledgments

This chapter was written while the second author was principal research investigator with the Behavioral and Social Sciences Research Unit of the Waisman Center on Mental Retardation and Human Development at the University of Wisconsin—Madison, which is funded in large part by Grant HD 03352 from the National Institute of Child Health and Human Development.

This chapter was written while Sylvia Z. Ramirez was a predoctoral fellow with the Wisconsin Center for Education Research at the University of Wisconsin—Madison.

References

Achenbach, T. M., & Edelbrock, C. S. (1978). The classification of child psychopathology: A review and analysis of empirical efforts. *Psychological Bulletin, 85,* 1275–1301.

American Psychiatric Association. (1980). *Diagnostic and statistical manual of mental disorders* (3rd ed.). Washington, DC: Author.

Ayer, W. A. (1973). Use of visual imagery in needle phobic children. *Journal of Dentistry for Children,* March–April, 125–217.

Barrios, B. A., Hartmann, D. P., & Shigetomi, C. (1981). Fears and anxieties in children. In E. J. Mash & L. G. Terdal (Eds.), *Behavioral assessment of childhood disorders.* New York: Guilford Press.

Barrios, B. A., & Shigetomi, C. C. (1979). Coping-skills training for the management of anxiety: A critical review. *Behavior Therapy, 10,* 491–522.

Barrios, B. A., & Shigetomi, C. C. (1985). Assessment of children's fears: A critical review. In T. R. Kratochwill (Ed.), *Advances in school psychology* (Vol. 4). Hillsdale, NJ: Erlbaum.

Beck, A. T. (1976). *Cognitive therapy and the emotional disorders.* New York: International Universities Press.

Beck, A. T., & Emery, G. (1985). *Anxiety disorders and phobias.* New York: Basic Books.

Borkovec, T. D., Weerts, T. C., & Bernstein, D. A. (1977). Assessment of anxiety. In A. R. Ciminero, K. A. Calhoun, & H. E. Adams (Eds.), *Handbook of behavioral assessment.* New York: Wiley.

Bornstein, P. H., & Knapp, M. (1981). Self-control desensitization with a multi-phobic boy: A multiple baseline design. *Journal of Behavior Therapy and Experimental Psychiatry, 12,* 281–285.

Cone, J. D. (1978). The behavioral assessment grid (BAG): A conceptual framework and a taxonomy. *Behavior Therapy, 9,* 882–888.

Cone, J. D. (1979). Confounded comparisons in triple response mode assessment research. *Behavioral Assessment, 1,* 85–95.

Cone, J. D., & Hawkins, R. P. (Eds.). (1977). *Behavioral assessment: New directions in clinical psychology.* New York: Brunner-Mazel.

Craddock, C., Cotler, S., & Jason, L. A. (1978). Primary prevention: Immunization of children for speech anxiety. *Cognitive Therapy and Research, 2,* 389–396.

Deffenbacher, J. L. (1976). Relaxation *in vivo* in the treatment of test anxiety. *Journal of Behavior Therapy and Experimental Psychology, 7,* 290–292.

Deffenbacher, J. L., Mathis, H., & Michaels, A. C. (1979). Two self-control procedures in the reduction of targeted and nontargeted anxieties. *Journal of Consulting Psychology, 26,* 120–127.

Deffenbacher, J., & Michaels, A. (1980). Two self-control procedures in the reduction of targeted and nontargeted anxieties—A year later. *Journal of Counseling Psychology, 27,* 9–15.

Denney, D. R. (1980). Self-control approaches to the treatment of test anxiety. In I. G. Sarason (Ed.), *Test anxiety: Theory, research, and application.* Hillsdale, NJ: Erlbaum.

D'Zurilla, T., & Goldfried, M. R. (1971). Problem solving and behavior modification. *Journal of Abnormal Psychology, 78,* 107–126.

Ellis, A. (1962). *Reason and emotion in psychotherapy.* New York: Lyle, Stuart, and Citadel Press.

Ellis, A., & Bernard, M. E. (Eds.) (1983). *Rational-emotive approaches to the problems of childhood.* New York: Plenum Press.

Fox, J. E., & Houston, K. (1981). Efficacy of self-instructional training for reducing children's anxiety in an evaluative situation. *Behavior Research and Therapy, 19,* 509–515.

Goldfried, M. (1971). Systematic desensitization as training in self-control. *Journal of Consulting and Clinical Psychology, 37,* 228–234.

Goldfried, M. R., & Merbaum, M. (1973). A perspective on self-control. In M. R. Goldfried & M. Merbaum (Eds.), *Behavior change through self-control.* New York: Holt, Rinehart and Winston.

Graziano, A. M., DeGiovanni, I. S., & Garcia, K. A. (1979). Behavioral treatments of children's fears: A review. *Psychological Bulletin, 86,* 804–830.

Graziano, A. M., & Mooney, K. C. (1980). Family self-control instruction for children's nighttime fear reduction. *Journal of Consulting and Clinical Psychology, 48,* 206–213.

Graziano, A. M., & Mooney, K. C. (1982). Behavioral treatment of "nightfears" in children: Maintenance of improvement at 2½ to 3 year follow-up. *Journal of Consulting and Clinical Psychology, 50,* 598–599.

Graziano, A. M., Mooney, K. C., Huber, C., & Ignasiak, D. (1979). Self-control instructions for children's fear-reduction. *Journal of Behavior Therapy and Experimental Psychiatry, 10,* 221–227.

Hodgson, R., & Rachman, S. (1974). Desynchrony in measures of fear. *Behavioral Research and Therapy, 12,* 319–326.

Holroyd, K. A. (1976). Cognition and desensitization in the group treatment of test anxiety. *Journal of Consulting and Clinical Psychology, 44,* 991–1001.

Horan, J. J., Layng, F. C., & Pursell, C. H. (1976). Preliminary study on effects of "in vivo" emotive imagery on dental discomfort. *Perceptual and Motor Skills, 42,* 105–106.

Humphrey, J. H., & Humphrey, J. N. (1985). *Controlling stress in children.* Springfield, IL: Charles C Thomas.

Jackson, H. J., & King, N. J. (1981). The emotive imagery treatment of a child's trauma-induced phobia. *Journal of Behavior Therapy and Experimental Psychiatry, 12,* 325–328.

Kanfer, F. H. (1980). Self-management methods. In F. H. Kanfer & A. P. Goldstein (Eds.), *Helping people change* (2nd ed.). New York: Pergamon Press.

Kanfer, F. H., Karoly, P., & Newman, A. (1975). Reduction of children's fear of the dark by confidence-related and situational threat–related verbal cues. *Journal of Consulting and Clinical Psychology, 43,* 251–258.

Karoly, P. (1981). Self-management problems in children. In E. J. Mash & L. G. Terdal (Eds.), *Behavioral assessment of childhood disorders.* New York: Guilford Press.

Kazdin, A. E. (1985). Alternative approaches to the diagnosis of childhood disorders. In P. H. Bornstein & A. E. Kazdin (Eds.), *Handbook of clinical behavior therapy with children.* Homewood, IL: Dorsey Press.

Kelley, M. S. (1982). The effect of relaxation training and self-directed verbalizations on measures of anxiety and learning in learning-disabled children. (United States International University). *Dissertation Abstracts International, 42,* 3806B–3807B.

Kendall, P. C., & Braswell, L. (1985). *Cognitive-behavioral therapy for impulsive children.* New York: Guilford Press.

Kendall, P. C., & Hollon, S. D. (Eds.). (1981). *Assessment strategies for cognitive-behavioral interventions.* New York: Academic Press.

Kratochwill, T. R., & Morris, R. J. (1985). Conceptual and methodological issues in the behavioral assessment and treatment of children's fears and phobias. *School Psychology Review, 14,* 94–107.

Lang, P. J. (1968). Fear reduction and fear behavior. Problems in treating a construct. In J. M. Shlien (Ed.), *Research in psychotherapy* (Vol. 3). Washington, DC: American Psychological Association.

Lang, P. J. (1971). The application of psychophysiological methods to the study of psychotherapy and behavior modification. In A. E. Bergin & S. L. Garfield (Eds.), *Handbook of psychotherapy and behavior change.* New York: Wiley.

Lang, P. J. (1977). Psychophysiological assessments of anxiety and fear. In J. D. Cone & R. P. Hawkins (Eds.), *Behavioral assessment: New directions in clinical psychology.* New York: Brunner/Mazel.

Lazarus, A. A., & Abramovitz, A. (1962). The use of emotive imagery in the treatment of children's phobias. *Journal of Mental Science, 108,* 191–195.

Leal, L. L., Baxter, E. G., Martin, J., & Marx, R. W. (1981). Cognitive modification and systematic desensitization with test anxious high school students. *Journal of Counseling Psychology, 28,* 525–528.

Luborsky, L., & DeRubeis, R. J. (1984). The use of psychotherapy treatment manuals: A small revolution in psychotherapy research style. *Clinical Psychology Review, 4,* 5–140.

Mahoney, M. J. (1974). *Cognition and behavior modification.* Cambridge, MA: Ballinger.

Mahoney, M. J. (1977). Personal science: A cognitive learning therapy. In A. Ellis & R. Grieger (Eds.), *Handbook of rational psychotherapy.* New York: Springer.

Mahoney, M. J., & Arnkoff, D. (1978). Cognitive and self-control therapies. In S. J. Garfield & A. E. Bergin (Eds.), *Handbook of psychotherapy and behavior change* (2nd ed.). New York: Wiley.

Marks, I. M. (1969). *Fears and phobias.* New York: Academic Press.

McLemore, C. W., & Benjamin, L. S. (1979). Whatever happened to interpersonal diagnosis? A psychosocial alternative to DSM-III. *American Psychologist, 34,* 17–34.

McMahon, R. J. (1984). Behavior checklist and rating scales. In T. H. Ollendick & M. Hensen (Eds.), *Child behavioral assessment: Principles and procedures.* New York: Pergamon Press.

McReynolds, W. P. (1979). DSM-III and the future of applied social science. *Professional Psychology, 10,* 123–132.

Meichenbaum, D. H. (1972). Cognitive modification of test anxious college students. *Journal of Consulting and Clinical Psychology, 39,* 370–380.

Meichenbaum, D. (1973). Cognitive factors in behavior modification: Modifying what clients say to themselves. In C. R. Franks & G. T. Wilson (Eds.), *Clinical review of behavior therapy: Theory and practice* (Vol. 1). New York: Brunner/Mazel.

Meichenbaum, D. (1974). *Cognitive behavior modification.* Morristown, NJ: General Learning Press.

Meichenbaum, D. (1976). Toward a cognitive theory of self-control. In G. Schwartz & D. Shapiro (Eds.), *Consciousness and self-regulation: Advances in research.* New York: Plenum Press.

Meichenbaum, D. (1977). *Cognitive behavior modification.* New York: Plenum Press.

Meichenbaum, D., & Genest, M. (1980). Cognitive behavior modification: An integration of cognitive and behavioral methods. In F. H. Kanfer & A. P. Goldstein (Eds.), *Helping people change* (2nd ed.). New York: Pergamon Press.

Meichenbaum, D., & Goodman, J. (1971). Training impulsive children to talk to themselves: A means of developing self-control. *Journal of Abnormal Psychology, 77,* 115–126.

Melamed, B., & Siegel, L. (1975). Reduction of anxiety in children facing hospitalization and surgery by use of filmed modeling. *Journal of Consulting and Clinical Psychology, 43,* 511–521.

Miller, L. C., Barrett, C. L., & Hampe, E. (1974). Phobias in children in a prescientific era. In A. Davids (Ed.), *Child personality and psychopathology: Current topics* (Vol. 1). New York: Wiley.

Mooney, K. C. (1982). *Children's nighttime fears: Behavioral, subjective, and psychophysiological responses.* Unpublished doctoral dissertation, State University of New York at Buffalo.

Morris, R. J., & Kratochwill, T. R. (1983). *Treating children's fears and phobias: A behavioral approach.* Elmsford, NY: Pergamon Press.

Nietzel, M. T., & Bernstein, D. A. (1981). Assessment of anxiety and fear. In M. Hersen & A. S. Bellack (Eds.), *Behavioral assessment: A practical handbook* (2nd ed.). New York: Pergamon.

Paul, G. L. (1966). *Insight vs. desensitization in psychotherapy.* Stanford, CA: Stanford University Press.

Paul, G. L., & Bernstein, D. A. (1973). *Anxiety and clinical problems: Systematic desensitization and related techniques.* Morristown, NJ: General Learning Press.

Peterson, L., & Shigetomi, C. (1981). The use of coping techniques in minimizing anxiety in hospitalized children. *Behavior Therapy, 12,* 1–14.

Quay, H. C. (1979). Classification. In H. C. Quay & J. S. Werry (Eds.), *Psychopathological disorders of childhood* (2nd ed.). New York: Wiley.

Rachman, S., & Hodgson, R. (1974). Synchrony and desynchrony in fear and avoidance. *Behaviour Research and Therapy, 12,* 311–318.

Richards, C. S., & Siegel, L. J. (1978). Behavioral treatment of anxiety states and avoidance behaviors in children. In D. Marholin II (Ed.), *Child behavior therapy.* New York: Gardner Press.

Roberts, R. N., & Nelson, R. O. (1985). Assessment issues and strategies in cognitive behavior therapy with children. In A. Meyers & W. E. Craighead (Eds.), *Cognitive behavior therapy for children*. New York: Plenum Press.

Rosenfarb, I., & Hayes, S. C. (1984). Social standard setting: The Achilles heel of informational accounts of therapeutic change. *Behavior Therapy, 15*, 515–528.

Ross, A. O. (1980). *Psychological disorders of children: A behavioral approach to theory, research and therapy* (2nd ed.). New York: McGraw-Hill.

Rutter, M., Lebocici, S., Eisenberg, L., Sneznevskij, A. V., Sadoun, R., Brooke, E., & Lin, T. Y. (1969). A tri-axial classification of mental disorders in childhood: An international study. *Journal of Child Psychology and Psychiatry, 10*, 41–62.

Rutter, M., Shaffer, D., & Shepherd, M. (1975). *A multi-axial classification of child psychiatric disorders*. Geneva: World Health Organization.

Sarason, S., Davidson, K., Lighthall, F., Waite, R., & Ruebush, B. (1960). *Anxiety in elementary age children*. New York: Wiley.

Siegel, L. J., & Peterson, L. (1980). Stress reduction in young dental patients through coping skills and sensory information. *Journal of Consulting and Clinical Psychology, 48*, 785–787.

Suinn, R. M., & Richardson, F. (1971). Anxiety management training: A nonspecific behavior therapy program for anxiety control. *Behavior Therapy, 2*, 498–510.

Trickett, E. J., & Moos, R. H. (1973). The social environment of junior high and high school classrooms. *Journal of Educational Psychology, 65*, 93–102.

Werry, J. S., Methuen, R. J., Fitzpatrick, J., & Dixon H. (1983). The interrater reliability of DSM-III in children. *Journal of Abnormal Child Psychology, 11*, 341–353.

Wolfson, J. (1983). Self-talk and exposure in the reduction of avoidance in aquaphobic children (Doctoral dissertation, The Louisiana State University and Agricultural and Mechanical College). *Dissertation Abstracts International, 43*, 2721B.

Yule, W. (1981). The epidemiology of child psychopathology. In B. B. Lahey & A. E. Kazdin (Eds.), *Advances in clinical child psychology* (Vol. 4). New York: Plenum.

Zatz, S. L., & Chassin, L. (1983). Cognitions of test anxious children. *Journal of Consulting and Clinical Psychology, 51*, 526–534.

Zatz, S., & Chassin, L. (1985). Cognitions of test-anxious children under naturalistic test-taking conditions. *Journal of Consulting and Clinical Psychology, 53*, 393–401.

7

Simple Phobias

CYNTHIA G. LAST

Simple phobias, often referred to as *specific* phobias, are characterized by four central features: (1) a persistent and irrational fear of an object or situation, (2) a compelling desire to avoid the object or situation, (3) significant distress arising from the disturbance, and (4) recognition by the individual that his or her fear is unreasonable. According to the *Diagnostic and Statistical Manual of Mental Disorders* (DSM-III) (American Psychiatric Association, 1980), the diagnostic category excludes individuals who fear being alone or in public places away from home (*agoraphobia*) and those who fear embarrassment or humiliation in certain social situations (*social phobia*). Thus, simple phobia essentially is a residual category to be employed when agoraphobia and social phobia have been ruled out.

Simple phobias are quite prevalent in the general population, although only a small percentage of victims actually seek treatment for their disorders (Agras, Sylvester, & Oliveau, 1969). Some common types of simple phobias include fear of animals (e.g., snakes, mice, dogs, insects); heights (*acrophobia*); closed spaces (*claustrophobia*); illness or injury; crowds; and storms. The degree of impairment caused by the disorder varies considerably, in large part dependent on how common (or rare) the object or situation is and thus how easily it can be avoided. Cases where the phobic object or situation is prevalent and cannot be avoided may result in considerable impairment. These individuals are most likely to seek treatment for their phobias.

During the past decade, cognitive and cognitive-behavioral interventions have become increasingly popular in the treatment of simple phobias. In this chapter, we first consider the role that cognitions play in specific fears and phobias. This is followed by a discussion of procedures used for assessing cognitions in simple phobias. Next, the various cognitive-behavioral treatment procedures are outlined, and findings from treatment outcome research are reviewed in detail. Finally, future directions for investigation in this area are presented.

The Role of Cognitions

The significance of maladaptive cognitions in the genesis of phobic reactions and maintenance of phobic disorders has been discussed by several cognitive and cognitive-behavioral theorists (Beck, 1976; Ellis, 1962; Meichenbaum, 1977). Specifically, they have proposed that catastrophic or irrational thoughts play a crucial role in mediating

Cynthia G. Last. Department of Psychiatry, University of Pittsburgh School of Medicine, Pittsburgh, Pennsylvania.

maladaptive physiological–emotional and behavioral responses in these, as well as other, disorders.

Within a cognitive-behavioral framework, cognitions are generally viewed both as covert responses to certain stimulus situations and, subsequently, as the stimuli themselves that elicit physiological and behavioral responses. In phobic disorders, specific maladaptive cognitions are thought to elicit fear and anxiety, both prior to (anticipatory anxiety) and during contact with phobic stimuli. Such thoughts generally center on the physiological changes accompanying anxiety, avoidance of or escape from the phobic situation, or anticipation of a catastrophe, and serve to escalate physiological arousal, resulting in avoidance/escape behavior. Thus, maladaptive cognitions are conceptualized as primarily responsible for the maintenance of fear and avoidance patterns that are, in general, characteristic of phobic disorders, including simple phobias.

It is important to note that the proposed role of maladaptive thoughts in the fear process does not necessarily negate the etiological significance of automatic or conditioned fear responses within a learning theory or conditioning model of phobic disorders. Exposure to feared situations may trigger negative self-statements based on prior learning experiences and past memories, which then bring on or increase physiological activity and avoidance/escape behavior (Last & Blanchard, 1982).

Given the hypothesized mediational role of maladaptive thoughts, fear reduction is thought to occur as a consequence of decreasing these self-verbalizations (Beck, 1976; Ellis, 1962; Goldfried & Davison, 1976; Mahoney, 1974; Meichenbaum, 1977). Specifically, decreases in maladaptive cognitions are thought to reduce the physiological component of fear, which in turn eliminates avoidance/escape behavior, since such behavior no longer serves its initial purpose (i.e., avoidance of subjective distress or panic).

Unfortunately, gathering empirical support for this cognitive model of behavior change is difficult. Cognitive treatments of simple phobia usually incorporate some element of actual exposure experience, rendering one unable to evaluate whether cognitive changes or other processes (e.g., exposure and/or habituation) are directly responsible for treatment effects. As Ellis (1979) has pointed out, most cognitive therapies incorporate *in vivo* homework assignments in their treatment program for phobias, since cognitive strategies must be tried out before belief systems and consonant self-verbalizations change. A second problem is that even if future research were to establish that decreases in maladaptive cognitions are characteristic of all successful treatments of phobia, it still would be unclear whether changes in cognitions were causally linked to decreases in fear and avoidance, or whether cognitive changes simply reflected behavior change occurring by other processes (Borkovec, 1978).

In evaluating the role of cognitions in the fear process for simple phobias, several issues warrant attention. First, the production of maladaptive cognitions by simple phobics upon confrontation with their feared situations needs to be established. Second, if such cognitions typically are present, their role in mediating fear needs to be assessed. Finally, the importance of cognitive change to clinical outcome needs to be demonstrated. Although such findings would not illuminate the causal relationship between cognitive and behavior change, such results would lend some support for a role of cognitions in the fear reduction process for this clinical population.

At present, there is some evidence suggesting that catastrophic or negative cognitions are generated by phobics upon confrontation with feared situations, and that this catastrophizing plays a mediational role in eliciting and/or exacerbating fear and panic in clinical populations (Beck, Laude, & Bohnert, 1974; Last & Blanchard, 1982; May, 1977a, 1977b; Rimm, Janda, Lancaster, Nahl, & Dittmar, 1977; Wade, Malloy, & Proctor, 1977). Rimm et al. (1977), using a group of individuals with mild fears of various types, investigated the relationship of cognitions to the maintenance of fearfulness, with primary emphasis on the potential mediating role of catastrophic cognitions. These investigators used an imaginal procedure for eliciting cognitive material during structured interviews, and then categorized thoughts according to type and frequency. In addition, subjects were requested to report the relationship of cognitions to the anxiety response. Although approximately half of the subjects in the study reported catastrophic thoughts during the imagery period, these mildly fearful subjects did not report that catastrophic self-statements mediated fear responses.

In an attempt to evaluate more carefully the potential mediating role of cognitions in fears and phobias, Last and Blanchard (1982) extended the investigation of Rimm et al. (1977) by using subjects with a wide range of intensities of fear—thus including more clinically relevant phobias as well as milder fears—and by employing a more sensitive methodology. Thirty-one subjects participated in a structured interview and imaginal cognitive assessment designed to evaluate the presence and potential mediating role of catastrophic cognitions in eliciting fear responses. When subjects were separated into fearful and phobic groups on the basis of DSM-III criteria, different patterns emerged with respect to cognitive processes. Specifically, whereas phobic individuals generated catastrophic cognitions while imagining being in their feared situations, fearful subjects were significantly less likely to have these types of thoughts. Moreover, the catastrophic thoughts of phobics, as opposed to those of fearful subjects, also were reported to play a crucial role in increasing fearfulness and mediating panic responses. Approximately half of the phobic group reported experiencing an immediate and automatic fear response or fright upon imaginal confrontation with the feared situation or object, which was later subjected to increased and distressing proportions through catastrophic ideation; and the other half reported catastrophizing prior to the first instance of fear and again prior to the point of full-blown panic.

Wade et al. (1977) also have obtained cognitive differences according to intensity of fear. In this investigation, the authors assessed the relationship between imagery content and both fear and avoidance behavior with students who varied greatly in their fear of snakes. During a standard behavioral avoidance test, subjects were asked to rate their fear on a 10-point scale and to verbalize any words or images that were going through their minds. Results showed that reports of aversive imagery were much more frequent for high- than for low-avoidance subjects. In addition, self-report of fear was much higher for subjects who reported negative imagery. Moreover, the authors obtained similar results when subjects imagined themselves in a feared situation, suggesting some comparability between imagined and real situations.

Results of an investigation by Beck et al. (1974), though not conducted with phobics, is of interest since these data also lend support to the mediational role of cognitions in eliciting and exacerbating fear in clinical populations. In this study, the authors hypothesized that catastrophic ideation may be the stimulus that triggers and aggravates anxiety in individuals with generalized or free-floating anxiety. On the basis of structured interviewing of a large number of clients, results indicated that specific catastrophic throughts, primarily related to the theme of psychological or physical danger, precede the onset and exacerbation of anxiety in individuals with acute or chronic anxiety states.

Two psychophysiological studies by May (1977a, 1977b) provide physiological evidence for the role of cognitions in mediating anxiety. In an initial investigation, May (1977a) compared the physiological responses of subjects who were highly fearful of snakes and those who were not fearful to self-generated phobic and nonphobic thoughts. In addition, subjects were asked to form an image of the stimulus after the production of each thought. Results indicated that self-regulated phobic thoughts and images produced greater physiological activity (heart rate and respiration amplitude) than did nonphobic thoughts and images. Moreover, snake-fearful subjects showed greater reactions to phobic thoughts than did nonfearful subjects.

In a second investigation, May (1977b) compared the psychophysiological responses of snake-fearful and nonfearful subjects to phobic and nonphobic stimuli using two modes of presentation—internal (self-generated) and external. In addition to confirming his previous findings, the author found that self-regulated, internally elicited phobic thoughts produced as much or more physiological activity than externally elicited phobic thoughts.

Overall, these investigations suggest that maladaptive cognitions may be an important phenomenon in the genesis and maintenance of fear in clinically significant phobias. Unfortunately, no investigations have been conducted to date that examine whether adaptive cognitive changes accompany phobic improvement during the treatment of simple phobias. Three studies, however, have investigated whether adaptive cognitive changes occur during successful intervention with agoraphobics (Last, Barlow, & O'Brien, 1984a, 1984b; Williams & Rappoport, 1983). Williams and Rappoport (1983) assessed cognitions before and after treating agoraphobics for their driving fears. Subjects received either a strictly behavioral (in vivo exposure) or cognitive-behavioral (in vivo exposure and cognitive therapy) intervention. Results indicated that both treatments were equally effective in reducing fear and avoidance behavior. Increases in coping thoughts, however, occurred for only the cognitively treated clients, whereas significant reductions in fearful thinking were evident for both groups, following treatment.

These findings suggest that decreases in maladaptive thinking accompany clinical improvement, irrespective of the type of treatment administered (behavioral or cognitive-behavioral). However, contrary findings have been reported by Last et al. (1984a). In this case study, the authors repeatedly assessed cognitions throughout the behavioral (in vivo exposure) treatment of an agoraphobic. Although the client markedly improved on behavioral, physiological, and self-report measures of phobia, cognitions appeared to worsen markedly throughout treatment, as evidenced by increases in maladaptive cognitions and, simultaneously, decreases in positive or adaptive thoughts.

In a second investigation, Last et al. (1984b) evaluated the relationship between cognitive change and treatment outcome during behavioral and cognitive-behavioral treatment of agoraphobia using a multiple-baseline design across subjects. Results showed neither treatment to produce clear and consistent changes in cognitions. However, evaluation of the effects of both treatments and cognitions were hampered by several factors: (1) cognitive improvement typically occurring during the baseline phase of the study, (2) marked variability of cognitions often exhibited during the treatment phases, and (3) relatively poor clinical outcome of several subjects. Nevertheless, no lawful relationship between cognitive change and treatment outcome was observed, irrespective of subjects' individual treatment responses.

A fourth study is of interest, though not conducted with phobics. Harris and Johnson (1983) assessed cognitive changes following cognitive-behavioral treatment of test anxiety. Results showed that significant large-magnitude decreases in negative self-statements accompanied successful intervention. In addition, there was some indication that positive self-statements increased following treatment.

Several methodological differences in these four studies may account for the contrary findings. First, cognitions wre assessed more frequently (throughout treatment) by Last et al. (1984a, 1984b). Such repeated assessment was conducted in order to investigate more carefully the process of cognitive change, but may have unexpectedly resulted in increasing the salience of certain thoughts as subjects became more accustomed to attending to thoughts. Thus, changes may have reflected an assessment artifact.

A second consideration is the experimental design used both in the Williams and Rappoport (1983) and Harris and Johnson (1983) studies. The use of a between-groups design and the averaging of data in these investigations precluded analysis of the specific relationship between cognitive changes and individual outcome. It is possible that only a percentage of subjects evinced the pattern of cognitive change suggested by their data, and that results reported by Last and colleagues represent other cases where individuals show cognitive worsening or no improvement during otherwise successful intervention.

Overall, recent findings offer some empirical support for the role of cognitions in the fear process. It appears that catastrophic or maladaptive thoughts are generated by phobics when confronted with feared situations, either imaginally (Last & Blanchard, 1982; Rimm et al., 1977; Wade et al., 1977) or in real life (Last et al., 1984a, 1984b; Wade et al., 1977; Williams & Rappoport, 1983). In addition, phobics' self-report and physiological responses both suggest that such thoughts play a crucial role in increasing and intensifying fearfulness (Last & Blanchard, 1982; May, 1977a, 1977b). Finally, preliminary evidence indicates that reductions in maladaptive thinking may accompany successful intervention with anxiety clients (Harris & Johnson, 1983; Williams & Rappoport, 1983).

Cognitive-Behavioral Treatment

Although numerous cognitive interventions have been developed and used over the years, most of these treatment approaches are based on the theorizing of Ellis (1962), Beck (1976), and Meichenbaum (1977). In addition to underlining the importance of cognitive process, each of these individuals has endorsed specific procedures for altering maladaptive conditions. According to Mahoney and Arnkoff (1978), Ellis's (1962) "rational-emotive therapy," Beck's (1976) "cognitive therapy," and Meichenbaum's "self-instructional training" (1977) may all be subsumed under the category of "cognitive-restructuring," since they all attempt to modify directly specific thoughts and beliefs believed to be mediators of arousal.

According to Ellis (1962), certain core irrational beliefs are conceptualized as being at the root of most emotional disorders. Maladaptive cognitions consonant with these irrational beliefs are seen as responses to real-life experiences and are viewed as leading to emotional distress. The clinical approach to treating emotional disorders, including phobia, generally includes presentation of the rational-emotive therapy rationale (i.e., that irrational thoughts play an important role in subjective distress); monitoring of thought patterns so that clients can become aware of their irrational self-verbalizations and the situations in which they are likely to be elicited; and developing more adaptive thought patterns. In addition, clients are usually assigned *in vivo* homework assignments in order to have practice using these newly acquired cognitions (Ellis, 1979).

A second approach to cognitive restructuring has been discussed by Beck (Beck, 1976; Beck & Emery, 1979). Like Ellis, Beck maintains that certain patterns of irrational cognitions lead to emotional distress and "neurotic" behavior. In the case of phobic and other anxiety disorders, thoughts of danger specifically are targeted for intervention. This is accomplished in a manner somewhat similar to that used in rational-emotive therapy: therapy is aimed at clients discovering maladaptive cognitions, recognizing the consequences of these thought patterns, and substituting more adaptive thoughts for the maladaptive ones already in use. However, whereas Ellis's approach to engendering cognitive change in therapy is one of direct confrontation of the client by the therapist, Beck's approach is less confrontational; the role of the therapist consists primarily of leading the client to discover for him- or herself, through nondirective reflection, that thoughts are inaccurate and maladaptive. As in Ellis's homework assignments, Beck also includes behavioral experience as an important component in changing irrational thought patterns.

Meichenbaum's (1977) self-instructional training, or cognitive-behavioral therapy, stems in large part from the literature on rational-emotive therapy. In this approach, self-verbalization or "self-talk" is viewed as the precipitant for a wide range of emotional and behavioral disorders. In the case of anxiety reactions, the aim of treatment is to have clients become aware of their negative or irrational thought patterns when anticipating or confronting an anxiety-producing situation, and to change these thoughts by substituting more adaptive, coping self-statements. Clients are encouraged to develop their own idiosyncratic coping statements through a skills development approach, and behavioral experience often is incorporated into the treatment package. One noteworthy difference between the approach taken by Ellis and that endorsed by Meichenbaum is that rational-emotive therapy emphasizes the rationality of a thought, whereas self-instructional training places more emphasis on its adaptiveness and constructive alternatives (Mahoney & Arnkoff, 1978).

Although rational-emotive therapy, cognitive therapy, and self-instructional training vary to some extent in the manner in which the procedures are conducted, the effects sought by all three are similar in that they all attempt to have clients generate more adaptive thought patterns.

Several analogue investigations have examined the efficacy of cognitive restructuring techniques alone or in conjunction with behavior therapy in the treatment of fears of small animals (Barrios, Sommervill, Henke, & Merritt, 1981; Denny, Sullivan, & Thiry, 1977; D'Zurilla, Wilson, & Nelson, 1973; Meichenbaum, 1971; Wein, Nelsen, & Odom, 1975) and fears of flying (Girodo & Roehl, 1978). D'Zurilla et al. (1973) compared a cognitive restructuring procedure, which emphasized "perceptual relearning" or relabeling of fear-evoking stimuli, to systematic desensitization in the treatment of individuals with fears of dead and bloody rats. Results showed cognitive restructuring to be superior to systematic desensitization on subjective measures of fear, although neither of these treatments was effective in increasing approach behavior on a standard behavioral task. Wein et al. (1975) also compared cognitive restructuring to systematic desensitization with snake-fearful subjects. Although both treatments produced equal and marked reductions in avoidance behavior, only the cognitive restructuring procedure was successful in decreasing subjective reports of fear.

Denny et al. (1977) investigated the efficacy of using self-verbalization training as an adjunct to participant modeling with spider-fearful subjects. The effects of modeling were compared with and without self-verbalization training. Results showed that self-verbalization training significantly improved outcome on behavioral performance and self-report measures of anxiety.

Barrios et al. (1981) also examined the relative contributions of modeling and cognitive rehearsal. Snake-fearful undergraduates were assigned to one of six treatment conditions: no modeling, modeling only, coping cognitive rehearsal only, distraction cognitive rehearsal only, coping cognitive rehearsal plus modeling, and distraction cognitive rehearsal plus modeling. Although results showed the coping cognitive rehearsal plus modeling treatment to effect the greatest change in fear and avoidance, between-group differences were not statistically significant.

The effect of observing self-verbalizing models has been studied by Meichenbaum (1971) with snake-fearful college students. Subjects were presented with either a mastery model, who demonstrated fearless and mastery behavior only, or with a coping model, who sequentially demonstrated initially fearful behavior and finally mastery behavior. In addition to this manipulation, the model in each of these conditions was instructed either to self-verbalize aloud during the treatment sessions or to remain silent, in order to assess the relative efficacy of behavioral and cognitive modeling versus behavioral modeling alone. Results indicated the observation of coping models to be significantly superior to that of mastery models in reducing fear and avoidance behavior. Moreover, the addition of self-verbalizations to the coping condition significantly improved treatment effectiveness. Thus a coping self-verbalizing model was most effective.

Finally, Girodo and Roehl (1978) compared the efficacy of two different cognitive strategies—coping self-statements and preparatory information training—with undergraduates who reported a fear of flying. Self-ratings of anxiety during actual flights showed that both groups improved, with no differences between the two treatments. There was some indication, however, that coping self-statement training was superior when subjects were confronted with an unexpected missed landing. Further, follow-up revealed greater improvement for subjects who received self-statement training.

Only two studies have been published that have evaluated the efficacy of cognitive or cognitive-behavioral treatments with clinically significant simple phobias (Biran &

Wilson, 1981; Ladouceur, 1983). Biran and Wilson (1981) compared the effectiveness of *in vivo* exposure (participant modeling) and cognitive restructuring using a between-groups design with individuals who had specific fears of either heights, elevators, or darkness. Exposure was found to be superior to purely cognitive intervention on self-report, behavioral, and physiological measures of phobia. Moreover, subjects in the cognitive restructuring group subsequently were offered five sessions of participant modeling, and showed results comparable to those of the original participant modeling group. The authors report that at 6-month follow-up all gains were maintained, with further reductions in the self-report of fear for all participant modeling subjects.

Ladouceur (1983) investigated whether cognitive treatment would increase the effectiveness of participant modeling with dog and cat phobics. In this study, subjects were assigned to one of four treatment conditions: (1) participant modeling alone, (2) participant modeling with simultaneous self-instructional training, (3) participant modeling with self-verbalization ("thinking aloud"), or (4) placebo. In the participant modeling with self-instructional training group, subjects received self-instructional training during participant modeling—that is, while they were actually confronting their feared situations. The authors hypothesized that this treatment would produce the greatest, most rapid, and longest-lasting benefits.

Results indicated that all three participant modeling treatments produced equally rapid and substantial improvements in behavior at posttest, as compared to the placebo group, which showed no change. At 1-month follow-up, however, the combined participant modeling/self-instructional training group showed significantly more phobic behavior than did the other two participant modeling groups. The authors explain these unexpected findings by suggesting that self-instructional training may have distracted attention away from the exposure situations and toward the therapist's guidance, or may have interfered with cognitive processing by creating information overload.

In interpreting findings on the efficacy of cognitive treatment procedures, it is clear that results are discrepant for merely fearful as opposed to truly phobic clients. Whereas the analogue investigations cited earlier tend to support the utility of cognitive restructuring with fearful populations, results from clinical investigations show purely cognitive interventions to be inferior to behavioral treatment (*in vivo* exposure) (Biran & Wilson, 1981), and to be of no additional therapeutic value when combined with behavioral techniques (Ladouceur, 1983). This discrepancy serves to underscore the difficulties often noted in generalizing results obtained from mildly fearful subjects to individuals with clinically significant phobias (Bernstein & Paul, 1971; Garfield, 1978; Last & Blanchard, 1982; Mathews, 1978).

However, in view of the previously established phenomenological importance of cognitions in clinical phobias as opposed to fearful nonphobics, this pattern of results is somewhat surprising (Last & Blanchard, 1982; Rimm et al., 1977). Since individuals with clinically relevant phobias are more likely than mildly fearful individuals to generate catastrophic cognitions and to have these thoughts mediate fear and panic, it would seem reasonable to expect cognitive interventions to be most effective with these subjects.

There are several possible explanations of why cognitive interventions have been shown to be ineffective with clinical phobias. Regardless of the specific cognitive technique used, all cognitive restructuring treatments share the aim of modifying or changing maladaptive cognitions into more productive and adaptive thoughts. However, all the studies reported failed to assess whether specific maladaptive thoughts actually were modified as a result of cognitive treatment. Thus it is unclear whether cognitive restructuring is ineffective because the modification of cognitions is unimportant or irrelevant to therapeutic success or, rather, whether the cognitive restructuring used in these studies was ineffective in achieving the goal of cognitive modification.

Another possible reason for the reported ineffectiveness of cognitive procedures when compared to *in vivo* exposure may be that *in vivo* exposure is at least as effective as cognitive therapy at producing constructive cognitive change. Finally, it is possible that cognitive therapy is relatively ineffective because cognitive modification, though achieved, is unimportant or irrelevant in reducing fear. Rather, extinction of conditioned responses and/or habituation of physiological arousal may be more crucial to successful intervention with phobics, and cognitive changes either reflect behavior change occurring by these processes (Borkovec, 1978) or play a separate, but less important, role in fear reduction.

Assessment of Cognitions

Since the major goal of using cognitive treatments is to modify cognitions, it is somewhat surprising that the vast majority of researchers conducting treatment outcome studies in this area have excluded cognitive measures as major dependent variables in their investigations. Part of the reason for this may be the difficulty inherent in measuring covert events, such as thoughts. In addition, much of the research investigating the relative efficacy of cognitive techniques has been conducted by behaviorally oriented investigators, who may be unfamiliar with available cognitive assessment procedures.

In this section, several types of cognitive assessment techniques are reviewed briefly (for a more detailed review, see Kendall & Hollon, 1981, and Merluzzi, Glass, & Genest, 1981), and systems for categorizing cognitive data are presented. In addition, the reliability, utility, and validity of cognitive measurement and classification are considered.

Several measures have been developed to assess the content and frequency of clients' thoughts. When used with phobics, these cognitive assessment techniques generally are administered during or immediately following contact with phobic stimuli, either imaginally or in real life (*in vivo*). Other, more structured cognitive measures (e.g., self-efficacy measures, attitudinal measures, rating scales) are not considered here, since these measures do not assess the spontaneous occurrence of specific types of thoughts.

One available cognitive assessment technique that is especially simple to administer is the thought-listing procedure (Cacioppo & Petty, 1981). Here, clients are asked to record their thoughts, in written form, on a sheet provided for this purpose. The procedure is administered using a standard time limit, usually 3 minutes. When used with phobics, this technique can be employed immediately following exposure to feared situations by asking subjects to record thoughts they recall having had during the exposure period (Last et al., 1984a, 1984b). The utility of this approach in assessing thoughts prior to contact with phobic stimuli remains to be evaluated, although clinical reports suggest it may be useful in delineating maladaptive cognitions contributing to anticipatory anxiety and avoidance behavior.

An imaginal cognitive assessment procedure has been used by Last and colleagues (Last et al., 1984a; Last & Blanchard, 1982). Phobics are asked to imagine one item of maximum difficulty, selected for each subject on the basis of self-report of fear and avoidance. The same item is imagined at each assessment occasion. Scenes are presented while subjects are comfortably seated in reclining chairs. When clear visualization is reported, subjects are asked to verbalize any thoughts that run through their minds. Verbalizations are usually tape recorded during assessments so that an individual not associated with the study can transcribe the data verbatim.

Genest and Turk (1981) have reviewed "think-aloud" approaches to cognitive assessment. The authors discuss three main types of think-aloud techniques: (1) continuous monologues (in which subjects are asked to report aloud all thoughts as they occur during a given task), (2) thought sampling (in which subjects are interrupted during a given task and asked to report thoughts at those specific times), and (3) event recording or self-monitoring (in which subjects are asked to acknowledge or describe each occurrence of a specific type of thought).

Although the event-recording or self-monitoring approach has been used fairly extensively in clinical practice with phobics, no reports of this technique have appeared in the literature to date. Williams and Rappoport (1983) used a version of the thought-sampling approach in measuring cognitions during the treatment of agoraphobics' driving fears. Cognitions were reported during a behavioral test designed to measure subjects' ability to drive alone. During the test, a beeper sounded every 90 seconds, which activated a tape recorder (attached to a lapel microphone) for a 20-second period. Subjects were instructed to report whatever they were thinking about at the moment the buzzer sounded.

A modified version of the continuous monologue approach has been used by Last et al. (1984a, 1984b). Their *in vivo* cognitive assessment procedure requires phobics to verbalize any thoughts that enter their minds while they are exposed to feared situations. Verbalizations are recorded using a microcassette recorder, carried by the client, which is attached to a lapel microphone.

Unfortunately, few investigations have evaluated the reliability of cognitive assessment procedures. In addition, the validity of these measures has been largely ignored, most probably because of the difficulties involved in validating a self-report measure for which objective criteria are absent. However, using multiple self-report measures of cognitions may provide some basis for concurrent validation of cognitive measures.

Cullen (1968) assessed the test–retest reliability of the thought-listing procedure using normal subjects who responded to messages on two topics. The average test–retest reliability was +.64, which compared favorably with the reliability obtained from several attitude scales also administered.

A more recent examination of the reliability, as well as the validity, of cognitive measures has been conducted with phobic subjects (Last, Barlow, & O'Brien, 1985). Prior to treatment, agoraphobics were assessed repeatedly with an *in vivo* cognitive assessment, imaginal cognitive assessment, and thought-listing procedure for three, five, or seven assessment occasions. Results showed all three measures to have an unstable course across assessment sessions. In addition, some subjects revealed marked cognitive improvement (decreases in maladaptive thoughts and increases in adaptive thoughts) across assessments, suggesting that these measures may be notably "reactive" in some cases. Finally, the congruence between two of the measures—the *in vivo* cognitive assessment and the thought-listing procedure, administered in the same situation—was only modest.

Although these findings cast doubt on the reliability of cognitive assessment techniques, it is unclear whether the observed instability of thoughts across assessments resulted from inaccurate and imprecise measurement or actually reflected genuine fluctuations in cognitions over time and across sessions. Data generated by Last and colleagues indicate that cognitions fluctuate widely, both before and during exposure treatment of agoraphobics (Last et al., 1984b). It is questionable whether stability in cognitions should be expected from phobics during exposure to feared situations.

Another consideration when assessing the reliability of cognitive measures is the selectivity that often occurs when subjects are reporting thoughts. Such selectivity often is observed when using the thought-listing and *in vivo* cognitive assessment procedures. For thought listing, the ability to recall thoughts may vary from session to session, introducing a large degree of error into the data. During *in vivo* cognitive assessments, subjects, though instructed to report all thoughts, generally report a fairly low frequency of cognitions. One obvious reason for this is subjects' discomfort with publicly talking to themselves. In such cases, the use of alternative cognitive assessment techniques may be advisable.

Several systems for classifying cognitive data generated by phobics have appeared during the past few years (Last et al., 1984b; Rimm et al., 1977; Williams & Rappoport, 1983). The content of these categorization schemes and their reported interrater reliability are discussed briefly.

Rimm et al. (1977) proposed a five-category system for classifying negative and neutral self-verbalizations of fearful and phobic subjects. The system was used to classify cognitions reported during an imaginal cognitive assessment. Categories included (1) thoughts suggesting some catastrophic consequence, (2) thoughts connoting avoidance or escape, (3) thoughts indicating an awareness of fear, (4) thoughts objectively describing the situation, and (5) thoughts that could not be readily classified. Approximately 10% of the thoughts reported during the study could not be classified and were included in the fifth category. In addition, interrater agreement using the classification scheme was reported to be 86.5% overall.

Last and Blanchard (1982) used two categories from the Rimm et al. (1977) system—thoughts anticipating negative consequences and thoughts of avoidance or escape—in categorizing the self-verbalizations of fearful and phobic subjects during an imaginal cognitive assessment. Interrater agreement for both categories was 100% in this study.

Last et al. (1984b) expanded the original classification system of Rimm et al. (1977) to include categories for positive as well as negative self-statements. This scheme includes the following categories: (1) thoughts suggesting some anticipated negative event or catastrophic consequence, (2) thoughts suggesting avoidance or escape, (3) thoughts indicating negative affect (awareness or experience of anxiety), (4) thoughts suggesting coping, (5) thoughts indicating approach behavior, (6) thoughts indicating positive affect, (7) thoughts objectively describing the situation (neutral), and (8) thoughts irrelevant to the phobic situation (neutral).

Agreement for type and number of thoughts using this classification system has been reported for two cognitive measures by Last et al. (1984a). Both *in vivo* cognitive assessment and a thought-listing measure were administered repeatedly during the treatment of an agoraphobic. Interrater agreement for type of thoughts reported during the *in vivo* cognitive assessments was 88%, and agreement for number of thoughts was 95% on this measure. On the thought-listing sheets, agreement for both type and number of thoughts was 100%.

In a later study, Last et al. (1985) used three different cognitive assessment techniques—*in vivo* cognitive assessment, imaginal cognitive assessment, and a thought-listing procedure—with agoraphobics as subjects. Interrater agreement was calculated for type and number of thoughts on each measure. Agreement for type of thoughts recorded during *in vivo* cognitive assessments was 96%, and agreement on the number of thoughts was 99%. For the thought-listing procedure, agreement was 91% for type of thoughts and 99% for number of thoughts. For cognitions reported during imaginal cognitive assessments, 89% agreement was obtained for type of thoughts and 98% agreement for number of thoughts.

Williams and Rappoport (1983) developed a categorization system for coding thoughts reported by agoraphobics during a behavioral avoidance test (driving alone). Categories included (1) fearful thoughts, (2) thoughts of bodily states, (3) coping thoughts, (4) diversionary thoughts, and (5) thoughts about driving activities. Both obtained and chance agreement were reported for each type of thought: 93 (8), 90 (6), 62 (0), 85 (2), and 87% (11%) respectively. Obtained agreement was, in all cases, significantly greater than chance agreement rates.

Overall, interrater reliability using cognitive classification schemes is relatively impressive because of the complexity and ambiguity often confronted when coding data of this type. Since agreement generally has been reported as overall agreement, however, difficulties in coding specific categories of thoughts may be obscured. In addition, many investigators have neglected to calculate chance agreement rates and to compare the significance of differences obtained for observed and chance agreement.

Summary and Conclusions

Despite the seeming phenomenological importance of maladaptive cognitions in simple phobias, review of the literature to date does not clearly support the use of cognitive treatments with this population. Although preliminary analogue investigations yielded promising findings, two studies employing clinical phobics as subjects suggest that cognitive techniques are relatively ineffective compared to behavioral treatment when administered alone, and are of no additional therapeutic value when combined with behavioral techniques.

Several possible reasons for this poor showing of cognitive treatments have been reviewed. Although it is plausible that cognitive modification was not actually achieved in treatment outcome studies, failure to measure cognitive change precludes evaluation of this hypothesis. Because preliminary evidence suggests the unreliability of cognitive assessment procedures, however, substantially more research will need to address the development of psychometrically sound cognitive measurement techniques before cognitive change can be evaluated in future investigations.

What directions remain for future research in this area? As mentioned earlier, the development and use of reliable and valid cognitive measures are crucial to evaluation of the efficacy of cognitive treatments. The utility and psychometric properties of more structured cognitive measures (e.g., self-efficacy ratings, attitudinal scales), as well as specific cognitive measures delineated in this chapter, need to be investigated. The use of these measures in future investigations will aid in determining whether, and which, cognitive therapies actually engender constructive cognitive change. Such studies must be conducted before cognitive techniques can be dismissed as ineffective.

Similarly, cognitive measurement also should be used to assess cognitive changes during behavioral, exposure-based treatment of simple phobias. Although exposure treatments clearly are considered the treatment of choice for phobic disorders (Marks, 1978; Mavissakalian & Barlow, 1981), the mechanism of action by which exposure works remains unclear. Systematic testing of alternative hypotheses, including cognitive change, may shed light on this complicated issue and aid in increasing the efficacy of our present treatments for simple phobias.

The potential benefits of alternative cognitive strategies, such as paradoxical intention, warrant attention, especially since preliminary findings with agoraphobics have been quite positive (Mavissakalian, Michelson, Greenwald, Kornblith, & Greenwald, 1983). In addition, the usefulness of cognitive techniques as an adjunct to exposure therapy needs to be explored more carefully. Although empirical findings have not supported the addition of cognitive treatment to standard behavioral treatment, clinical observations suggest that cognitive therapy may aid in prompting clients to "self-expose" between therapy appointments, and to remain exposed to phobic situations for sufficient periods of time. Thus, cognitive therapy may not be of additional therapeutic value to therapist-assisted exposure sessions, but instead may increase the frequency and duration of self-guided exposure, thereby enhancing the overall efficacy of the treatment package.

References

Agras, W. S., Sylvester, D., & Oliveau, D. (1969). The epidemiology of common fear and phobia. *Comprehensive Psychiatry, 10*, 151–156.

American Psychiatric Association. (1980). *Diagnostic and statistical manual of mental disorders* (3rd ed.). Washington, DC: Author.

Barrios, F. X., Somervill, J. W., Henke, K. J., & Merritt, B. R. (1981). Comparison of modeling and cognitive rehearsal in reduction of snake avoidance. *Psychological Reports, 49*, 635–642.

Beck, A. T. (1976). *Cognitive therapy and the emotional disorders.* New York: International University Press.

Beck, A. T., & Emery, G. (1979). *Cognitive therapy of anxiety and phobic disorders.* Philadelphia: Center for Cognitive Therapy.

Beck, A. T., Laude, R., & Bohnert, M. (1974). Ideational components of anxiety neurosis. *Archives of General Psychiatry, 31*, 319–325.

Bernstein, D. A., & Paul, G. L. (1971). Some comments on therapy analogue research with small animal "phobias." *Journal of Behavior Therapy and Experimental Psychiatry, 2*, 225–237.

Biran, M., & Wilson, G. T. (1981). Treatment of phobic disorders using cognitive and exposure methods: A self-efficacy analysis. *Journal of Consulting and Clinical Psychology, 49,* 886–899.

Borkovec, T. D. (1978). Self-efficacy: Cause or reflection of behavioral change? *Advances in Behaviour Research and Therapy, 1,* 163–170.

Cacioppo, J. T., & Petty, R. E. (1981). Inductive techniques for cognitive assessment: The thought listing procedure. In T. V. Merluzzi, C. R. Glass, & M. Genest (Eds.), *Cognitive assessment.* New York: Guilford Press.

Cullen, D. M. (1968). *Attitude measurement by cognitive sampling.* Unpublished doctoral dissertation, Ohio State University, Columbus.

Denny, D. R., Sullivan, B. J., & Thiry, M. R. (1977). Participant modeling and self-verbalization training in the reduction of spider fears. *Journal of Behavior Therapy and Experimental Psychiatry, 8,* 247–253.

D'Zurilla, T. J., Wilson, G. T., & Nelson, R. O. (1973). A preliminary study of the effectiveness of graduated prolonged exposure in the treatment of irrational fears. *Behavior Therapy, 4,* 672–685.

Ellis, A. (1962). *Reason and emotion in psychotherapy.* New York: Stuart.

Ellis, A. (1979). A note on the treatment of agoraphobics with cognitive modification versus prolonged exposure in vivo. *Behavior Research and Therapy, 17,* 162–174.

Garfield, S. L. (1978). Research problems in clinical diagnosis. *Journal of Consulting and Clinical Psychology, 46,* 597–607.

Genest, M., & Turk, D. C. (1981). Think-aloud approaches to cognitive assessment. In T. V. Merluzzi, C. R. Glass, & M. Genest (Eds.), *Cognitive assessment.* New York: Guilford Press.

Girodo, M., & Roehl, J. (1978). Cognitive preparation and coping self-talk: Anxiety management during the stress of flying. *Journal of Consulting and Clinical Psychology, 46,* 978–989.

Goldfried, M. R., & Davidson, G. C. (1976). *Clinical behavior therapy.* New York: Holt.

Harris, G., & Johnson, S. B. (1983) Coping imagery and relaxation instructions in a covert modeling treatment for test anxiety. *Behavior Therapy, 14,* 144–157.

Kendall, P. C., & Hollon, S. D. (Eds.). (1981). *Assessment strategies for cognitive-behavioral interventions.* New York: Academic Press.

Ladouceur, R. (1983). Participant modeling with or without cognitive treatment for phobias. *Journal of Consulting and Clinical Psychology, 51,* 942–944.

Last, C. G., Barlow, D. H., & O'Brien, G. T. (1984a). Cognitive changes during *in vivo* exposure in an agoraphobic. *Behavior Modification, 8,* 93–113.

Last, C. G., Barlow, D. H., & O'Brien, G. T. (1984b). Cognitive changes during behavioral and cognitive-behavioral treatment of agoraphobia. *Behavior Modification, 8,* 181–210.

Last, C. G., Barlow, D. H., & O'Brien, G. T. (1985). Assessing cognitive aspects of anxiety: Stability over time and agreement between several methods. *Behavior Modification, 9,* 72–93.

Last, C. G., & Blanchard, E. B. (1982). Classification of phobics versus fearful nonphobics: Procedural and theoretical issues. *Behavioral Assessment, 4,* 195–210.

Mahoney, M. J. (1974). *Cognition and behavior modification.* Cambridge, MA: Ballinger.

Mahoney, M. J., & Arnkoff, D. (1978). Cognitive and self-control therapies. In S. L. Garfield & A. E. Bergin (Eds.), *Handbook of Psychotherapy and Behavior Change.* New York: Wiley.

Marks, I. M. (1978). Exposure treatments: Clinical applications. In W. S. Agras (Ed.), *Behavior modification: Principles and clinical applications* (2nd ed.). Boston: Little, Brown.

Mathews, A. (1978). Fear reduction research and clinical phobias. *Psychological Bulletin, 85,* 390–404.

Mavissakalian, M., & Barlow, D. H. (Eds.). (1981). *Phobia: Psychological and pharmacological treatment.* New York: Guilford Press.

Mavissakalian, M., Michelson, L., Greenwald, D., Kornblith, S., & Greenwald, M. (1983). Cognitive-behavioral treatment of agoraphobia: Paradoxical intention vs. self-statement training. *Behaviour Research and Therapy, 21,* 75–86.

May, J. R. (1977a). Psychophysiology of self-regulated phobic thoughts. *Behavior Therapy, 8,* 150–159.

May, J. R. (1977b). A psychophysiological study of self and externally regulated phobic thoughts. *Behavior Therapy, 8,* 849–861.

Meichenbaum, D. H. (1971). Examination of model characteristics in reducing avoidance behavior. *Journal of Personality and Social Psychology, 17,* 298–307.

Meichenbaum, D. H. (1977). *Cognitive behavior modification.* New York: Plenum Press.

Merluzzi, T. V., Glass, C. R., & Genest, M. (Eds.). (1981). *Cognitive assessment.* New York: Guilford Press.

Rimm, D. C., Janda, L. H., Lancaster, D. W., Nahl, M., & Dittmar, K. (1977). An exploratory investigation of the origin and maintenance of phobias. *Behavior Research and Therapy, 15,* 231–238.

Wade, T. C., Malloy, T. E., & Proctor, S. (1977). Imaginal correlates of self-reported fear and avoidance behavior. *Behaviour Research and Therapy, 15,* 17–22.

Wein, K. S., Nelson, R. O., & Odom, J. V. (1975). The relative contributions of reattribution and verbal extinction to the effectiveness of cognitive restructuring. *Behavior Therapy, 6,* 459–474.

Williams, S. L., & Rappoport, A. (1983). Cognitive treatment in the natural environment for agoraphobics. *Behavior Therapy, 4,* 299–313.

8

Panic Disorder:
A Hyperventilation Interpretation

RONALD LEY

Pan, the Greek pastoral god of fertility, was depicted as a merry but ugly man with the horns, ears, and legs of a goat, who, when ill tempered, loved to frighten unwary travelers—hence the word *panic*. Whether the fear experienced by the unwary Greek traveler is the same fear experienced by the present-day victims of panic disorder is impossible to know, but chances are that panic attacks have been around for a long time—at least since that moment in the history of civilization when the fight-or-flight response began to lose its adaptive advantage.

Two recently published reviews of panic disorder (Jacob & Rapport, 1984; Stampler, 1982) analyze carefully the diagnostic criteria of panic disorder, summarize research that attempts to identify factors predisposing individuals to panic disorder, discuss the clinical and physiological features of panic disorder, evaluate the efficacy of various treatments, outline current theories of panic disorder, and indicate that the fear-of-fear hypothesis (or a close variant thereof) is their favored explanation of panic disorder. Whereas Jacob and Rapport's paper is broad in scope, Stampler's paper focuses on the development of a theory of panic that integrates the psychophysiological and biochemical features of panic disorder with the clinically observed aspects of the disorder. The primary sources of the features integrated are Arnold (1960), Razran (1961), and Lazarus (1966).

Another recent review of panic disorder (Dittrich, Houts, & Lichstein, 1983) describes the major approaches to the explanation of panic disorder (psychodynamic, psychobiological, and behavioral theories) and evaluates the outcome of the treatments derived from the theories. As for the theories, Dittrich et al. dismiss the psychodynamic theory because the assumption that the panic attack diverts the victim's attention away from unconscious impulses cannot be tested empirically. They also cite conflicting evidence for the mitral valve prolapse theory, criticize chemical induction theories on the grounds that drugs that have nothing to do with specific proposed biochemical mechanisms are successful in treating panic attacks, and claim that support for arousal threshold hypotheses are weak because they are based on patients' retrospective accounts of early childhood experiences.

With respect to treatments, Dittrich et al. dismiss the claims of psychodynamic treatment because the evidence is only anecdotal; fault drug therapies for providing only

Ronald Ley. Department of Educational Psychology and Statistics and Department of Psychology, State University of New York at Albany, Albany, New York.

short-term relief, for not relieving anticipatory anxiety, and for their potential negative side effects; criticize behavioral therapies for not dealing with panic disorder as an entity distinct from agoraphobia, and note that the disorder does not fit the classical conditioning model. Dittrich et al. hold out hope for a cognitive restructuring treatment in which panic sufferers are taught essentially to talk themselves out of having an attack.

Although research interest in panic disorder as an entity independent of agoraphobia is increasing, the bulk of the research that provided the data for the timely reviews cited here came from studies of agoraphobia. The paucity of data from studies on the behavioral treatment of panic disorder is especially frightening. Jacob and Rapport (1984, p. 205) claim that "We have not been able to find a single empirical study in which behavior therapy was applied specifically to the problem of panic."

Although yet another detailed review of the literature relating to the major aspects of panic disorder might be useful, it would not add significantly to what has already been written. Furthermore, space limitations would not permit such a review together with the presentation of a new theory of panic disorder and a review of pertinent literature related to it. At this inchoate stage in the formal investigation of panic disorder, the presentation of some new ideas that generate testable hypotheses should be more valuable than a review of research that has already been reviewed.

The purpose of this chapter is to present a hyperventilation theory of panic disorder and to discuss it in the context of three currently popular explanations of the disorder: the fear-of-fear hypothesis, the lactate acid hypothesis, and psychodynamic theory. Preliminary to the presentation of the theory, the concept of *panic disorder* is analyzed and some principles of respiration germane to hyperventilation are reviewed.

What Is Panic Disorder?

There seems to be general agreement that panic disorder consists of frequent panic attacks (current convention requires a minimum of three attacks during a 3-week period prior to diagnosis), and that panic attacks are marked by the sudden onset of extreme fear, for which there appears to be no cause. For some researchers, such as Goldstein and Chambless (1978), unsignaled sharp outbreaks of very high anxiety are equated with panic attacks.

According to the *Diagnostic and Statistical Manual of Mental Disorders* (DSM-III) (American Psychiatric Association, 1980, p. 230), however, extreme fear is not a sufficient criterion for the determination of panic attacks:

> The panic attacks are manifested by the sudden onset of intense apprehension, fear, or terror, often associated with feelings of impending doom. The most common symptoms experienced during an attack are dyspnea; palpitations; chest pain or discomfort; choking or smothering sensations; dizziness, vertigo, or unsteady feelings; feelings of unreality; paresthesia; hot and cold flashes; sweating; faintness; trembling or shaking; and fear of dying, going crazy, or doing something uncontrolled during the attack. Attacks usually last minutes; more rarely, hours.

Although the DSM-III classification requires that at least four of these "symptoms" (any four) must be reported to have been experienced in order for the attack to be classified as panic, relegating the somatic complaints to symptoms implies that fear is primary and the symptoms (somatic complaints) secondary. The strong inference is that the panic attack begins with the sudden onset of unsignaled fear and that the somatic complaints are the consequence of activation of the autonomic nervous system in response to fear. This analysis seems intuitively sound and has, therefore, become the traditionally accepted explanation for the inferred sequence of events constituting the panic attack.

From this analysis, one can see the seeds of the fear-of-fear explanation of panic disorder—or, more accurately, the "fear-of-experiencing-the-somatic-consequences-of-fear" explanation. That is, the sudden onset of fear of unspecified origin is presumed to produce somatic complaints (responses of the autonomic nervous system), the perception of which increases in turn the intensity of the fear experienced, which increases in turn the intensity of the somatic complaints in an ever-accelerating positive feedback loop. The attack is said to be self-limiting, which, as far as I can determine, means that the attack ends as mysteriously as it begins.

Intuitively sound though this analysis of the panic attack may be, there is no evidence that any four of the "most common symptoms experienced during an attack" are manifestations of autonomic arousal resulting from the sudden onset of unsignaled fear.

In the only study to date that addressed itself to the question of whether panic fear precedes or follows the symptoms listed among the DSM-III criteria, Ley (1985a) found that all the symptoms except for "trembling or shaking" were more frequently reported to have occurred *before* fear was experienced, not after (see Table 8.1). Eight of ten agoraphobes, for whom fear of experiencing a panic attack was an underlying factor, experienced intense dyspnea, and all but one reported that intense palpitations preceded

TABLE 8.1 Intensity of symptoms and sequence of symptoms with respect to experience of fear during the panic attack for 10 agoraphobes

Symptoms	Frequency	Mean intensity[a]	Frequency before fear	Frequency after fear	?
Dyspnea	10	3.6	8	2	0
Palpitations	9	3.7	7	2	0
Chest pain or discomfort	5	2.6	3	1	1
Choking or smothering	7	2.4	5	2	0
Dizziness, vertigo, or unsteady feelings	7	3.1	4	2	1
Feelings of unreality	8	3.5	6	1	1
Paresthesias	4	1.5	1	0	3
Hot or cold flashes	7	3.3	4	1	2
Sweating	8	3.0	5	2	1
Faintness	9	3.0	5	2	2
Trembling or shaking	9	3.9	2	4	3
Sum	83		51	19	13

[a]Rated on a scale of 1 to 5.

fear—that it was, in fact, the sudden, sharp onset of the somatic complaints, for which they could find no cause, that gave rise to their panic fear. In other words, the sudden and unaccountable onset of the sensation of not being able to breathe accompanied by the sensation of a strong and fast-beating heart frightened them.

With little reflection, one can understand readily why such unexplained events should be so frightening. If one cannot breathe, death must be just moments away; if one's heart begins to beat rapidly for no apparent reason, a heart attack and sudden death seem real and highly likely events. The sudden and unexpected onset of somatic events that portend death must be among the most terrifying experiences of one's life, if not the most terrifying.

On the basis of Ley's (1985a) results, it would appear that the panic attack is not simply the sudden and sharp onset of fear of unknown origins. On the contrary, the data suggest that the sudden and sharp onset of fear is in response to the onset of unexpected and unexplainable somatic events (especially dyspnea and heart palpitations) that lead the victim to believe death may be imminent. If this analysis of the panic attack is accurate, then the problem shifts from identifying the cause of fear to identifying the cause of the somatic events.

This analysis of the panic attack episode obviates a fear-of-fear explanation of panic disorder because it would appear that it is neither the anticipation of fear nor the physiological consequences of fear that cause fear. Panic attack victims appear, quite reasonably, to be afraid of experiencing life-threatening somatic events. Furthermore, if the cause of these life-threatening somatic events cannot be determined, panic attack victims may begin to doubt their sanity, thus contributing to the general anxiety produced by a history of attacks and the inability to predict the onset of the next one. On the basis of this analysis, the anomaly is not the panic attack victim who seeks the company of a "safe" person in a "safe" place (i.e., the agoraphobe) but, rather, that brave person who suffers panic attacks and manages to maintain a modicum of independence.

It may be, of course, that there is more than one form of panic attack, or that the means for inducing attacks varies from time to time or from person to person. Certainly common use of the expression *panic attack* by both patients and therapist exceeds the boundaries established by DSM-III.

In order to minimize confusion and maximize clarity, it is recommended that discussions of panic attacks be prefaced by an operational definition of the attack— "panic attack per DSM-III," or "the victim reports experiencing a panic attack," or "an observer reports the victim is experiencing a panic attack," or "sharp changes in a specified pattern of autonomic responses indicate a panic attack," and so on. Besides facilitating communication, this approach might help answer the question of whether there is more than one form of panic attack.

It must be remembered too, that it is a long way from the market to the clinic. The nature of the panic attack, the events that temporally surround the attack, and the events that intervene between the occasion of the attack and the report of the attack may affect the report. In the case of lactate infusion studies or any other experiment designed to elicit fear, it is important to keep in mind that the fear produced in the laboratory may never be exactly the same as, or more intense than, that experienced outside the laboratory. Although the experimental conditions of a laboratory setting may induce some anxiety, the fact that a patient has volunteered for an experiment indicates a considerable level of trust in the experimenter and belief that the experimenter will protect the patient from harm. Therefore, it is doubtful that the experience of *fear* in the laboratory is the same as that outside the laboratory. An example of this can be seen in a statement by a *control* group subject (no history of panic attacks) in a study by Pitts and McClure (1967) in which the subject, who experienced a panic attack following lactate infusion, tells the physician who is monitoring the infusion: ". . . if I didn't know you were doing this to me and that you would not let anything happen to me I would be certain I was dying of a heart attack or something terrible" (p. 1331).

Some Information about Respiration

In order to understand how hyperventilation can be used as the basis for a theory of panic disorder, it is necessary to review a few fundamental principles underlying the physiology, chemistry, and mechanics of respiration. It is commonly understood that respiration provides the means by which oxygen is taken from the air we breathe and delivered to the blood, which carries the oxygen to body tissue where it supports the metabolic process that keeps cells of the tissue alive. No oxygen, no life. And it is generally known that respiration provides the means by which carbon dioxide (CO_2), a by-product of metabolism, is removed from body tissue. The complete story of how this is done is long and complicated (cf. Bouhuys, 1974, 1977; Comroe, 1974; Crofton & Douglas, 1981; Mountcastle, 1968). For present purposes a short and simple explanation will have to do.

Respiration is the only vital function that is partly under direct voluntary control. We can hold our breath for brief periods of time until the level of carbon dioxide in the blood reaches the critical point where voluntary control gives way to the carbon-dioxide-sensitive respiratory reflex center in the medulla. The resulting spinal reflex activates the diaphragm so that it pulls down and out in the lower abdomen while the intercostal muscles expand the rib cage, thus causing a reduction in the air pressure surrounding the lungs. The difference between the air pressure within the thoracic cage and ambient air pressure forces the lungs to expand and fill with air (inhalation). Contraction of the diaphragm and intercostal muscles increases the air pressure surrounding the lungs, causing the lungs to contract and force their gaseous contents (about 7% CO_2) out (exhalation). The expired air reduces the level of CO_2 in the blood and thereby slows down stimulation of the respiratory reflex center. When enough CO_2 has been "blown off," respiration returns to its normal level. Thus the rapid and deep breathing that follows voluntary inhibition of breathing (holding one's breath for a minute or so) is involuntarily regulated by the content of CO_2 in the blood, as is the hyperpnea (rapid and deep breathing) that accompanies vigorous exercise.

Another form of voluntary control of respiration is *overbreathing*—that is, breathing a volume of air that exceeds metabolic demands (hyperventilation). The volume of air breathed per minute (minute volume) is determined by multiplying the volume of air per breath (tidal volume) times the number of breaths per minute (respiration rate). Thus one can hyperventilate by increasing tidal volume (deep breathing) while maintaining a constant respiration rate, or by increasing respiration rate while maintaining a constant tidal volume, or by increasing both tidal volume and respiration rate. Hyperventilation also occurs as part of the pattern of autonomic nervous system responses to emotional arousal—as one of the autonomic changes that constitute the flight-or-fight response.

When the amount of air breathed exceeds metabolic demand (hyperventilation), body tissue does not benefit from surplus oxygen (which cannot be stored), but body tissue suffers indirectly because too much carbon dioxide is being lost. The direct result of this excessive loss of CO_2 is blood alkalosis, an increase in blood pH level beyond 7.45 (the upper limit of the normal range), and a decrease in arterial CO_2 tension (PCO_2). The intensity of the symptoms produced by hyperventilation depends on the degree of hyperventilation: a little doesn't hurt, but a lot could be deadly.

Figure 8.1, which shows the direct relationship between blood alkalosis (pH—a log scale) and arterial tension (PCO_2) was extrapolated from data presented by Arbus,

FIG. 8.1 The relationship between arterial blood tension (PCO_2) and alkalosis (blood pH).

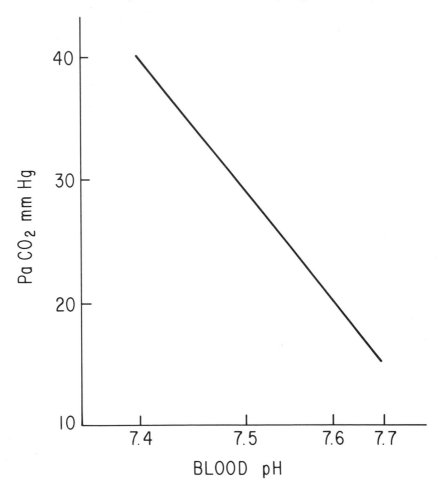

Hebert, Levesque, Etsen, and Schwartz (1969). The secondary effects of hyperventilation are very broad because the decrease in PCO_2 reduces the caliber of the arteries and thereby impedes the flow of blood plasma to body tissue (ischemia), and the increase in blood pH reduces the amount of oxygen that hemoglobin (the transport mechanism in blood plasma that carries oxygen from the alveoli of the lungs to body tissue) can release to body tissue (hypoxia). Thus the heart must pump with greater force and greater frequency in order to compensate for the decrease in arterial tension and increase in alkalosis. When arterial tension drops to a critical point, the sensation of heart palpitations will be experienced.

In addition to a drop in arterial tension, the drop in arterial CO_2 decreases the availability of the stimulus (CO_2) necessary to activate the respiratory reflex center, thereby producing a decrease in respiration rate. In order to compensate for this slowdown, voluntary activation of the diaphragm and intercostal muscles is required. When blood CO_2 is sufficiently low, the sensation of dyspnea (shortness of breath or difficulty breathing) is experienced.

The Hyperventilation Syndrome

Recently, hyperventilation has received considerable attention. Numerous articles have been published on the nature of hyperventilation and on the broad range of its effects (e.g., Engel, Ferris, & Logan, 1947; Fazekas, McHenry, Alman, & Sullivan, 1961; Gliebe & Auerback, 1944; Gotoh, Meyer, & Takagi, 1965; Kerr, Dalton, & Gliebe, 1937; Lum, 1975, 1978–1979, 1981; Magarian, 1982; McKell & Sullivan, 1947; Raichle & Plum, 1972; Waites, 1978; Wheatley, 1975).

Virtually every organ is effected by hyperventilation. The list of symptoms of hyperventilation given in Table 8.2 was obtained from Missri and Alexander (1978). Although the list is not complete, it indicates clearly the broad scope of major processes affected: cardiovascular, neurologic, respiratory, gastrointestinal, musculoskeletal, psychologic. When the list of symptoms reported by Singer (1958) and Lewis (1959) is added to the present list, all the symptoms that are reported to be experienced during panic attacks (see DSM-III classification) are included. Furthermore, every list of symptoms of hyperventilation so far encountered includes the most intense and most frequent symptoms reported to be experienced during panic attacks—palpitations (including tachycar-

TABLE 8.2 Symptoms of hyperventilation

General—Fatigue, weakness, exhaustion

Cardiovascular—Palpitations, tachycardia, precordial pain, Raynaud's phenomenon

Neurologic—Dizziness, lightheadedness, disturbance of consciousness or vision, numbness and tingling of the extremities, tetany (rare)

Respiratory—Shortness of breath, chest pain, dryness of mouth, yawning

Gastrointestinal—Globus hystericus, epigastric pain, aerophagia

Musculoskeletal—Muscle pains and cramps, tremors, stiffness, tetany

Psychologic—Tension, anxiety, insomnia, nightmares

dia), dyspnea (shortness of breath or difficulty breathing), dizziness, and trembling (Barlow, Vermilyea, Blanchard, Vermilyea, DiNardo, & Cerny, 1985; Ley, 1985a).

The variety and intensity of the somatic complaints produced by hyperventilation (i.e., hyperventilatory hypocapnea) depend on a delicate balance between the rate at which carbon dioxide is being blown off and the rate at which it is being produced. Given a constant metabolic rate, increases in the loss of CO_2 through overbreathing are immediately and directly related to increases in pH (alkalosis) and decreases in PCO_2 (arterial tension). Thus, the greater the loss of CO_2, the more intense the somatic complaints. At relatively low levels of hyperventilatory hypocapnea, the somatic effects may go unnoticed; at relatively high levels, the somatic effects may be quite marked but still capable of being tolerated for prolonged periods of time.

Okel and Hurst (1961) required subjects to maintain a very low level of alveolar CO_2 (2% to 2.5%, where the normal level is about 5%) by hyperventilating. The subjects maintained this low level for periods ranging from 171 to 261 minutes. During these periods, blood pH and arterial tension were monitored: pH increased from a mean of 7.41 immediately before hyperventilating to a mean of 7.63 for an average of 217 minutes (3 hours and 37 minutes), and arterial tension (PCO_2) dropped from a mean of 39.67 mm Hg to a mean of 18.67 mm Hg for 217 minutes. Besides demonstrating that a relatively high level of respiratory alkalosis can be tolerated for a prolonged period, the reliability of these data is supported by their close correspondence to the gradient given in Figure 8.1. Parenthetically, Yu, Yim, and Stanfield (1959) found almost identical changes in pH and PCO_2 after 1 to 3 minutes of forceful and rapid breathing in 20 patients diagnosed as suffering from hyperventilation syndrome.

Furthermore, the data of Okel and Hurst support the position that hyperventilatory hypocapnea can exist as a chronic state through faulty voluntary respiratory behavior (breathing too deeply, too rapidly, or both) or faulty involuntary respiratory behavior (e.g., heightened autonomic arousal in response to stress). Although a chronic state of hypocapnea can produce unpleasant symptoms such as lightheadedness and nausea, such symptoms can be tolerated and one can learn to adapt to them. Perhaps the most serious aspect of chronic hyperventilatory hypocapnea is that the sufferer is close to the brink of intense and dramatic somatic complaints.

If in a chronic hyperventilator the resting level of blood pH were high and/or PCO_2 were low, a relatively mild emotionally arousing event that resulted in a brief and sudden sharp rise in rate and/or depth of respiration would be sufficient to raise pH and decrease PCO_2 to such levels that the intensity of the somatic effects could not be tolerated. The curve that describes this relationship is given in Figure 8.2, where the level of pH (a log scale) on the abscissa begins at the normal level of 7.4 and increases to the lethal level of 7.8. The ordinate rising at a pH of 7.8 gives the inversely correlated arterial blood CO_2 tension in millimeters of mercury (mm Hg) spaced at intervals determined by a logarithmic transformation. (See Figure 8.1 for a depiction of the linear relationship.)

The ordinate rising from a pH of 7.4 gives somatic events associated with changes in pH and PCO_2. The threshold of tolerance (pH $= 7.6$, $PCO_2 = 20$) was estimated from the data of Okel and Hurst (1961) and Yu, Yim, and Stanfield (1959). This hypothetical threshold would be expected to vary from person to person and from time to time in the same person as a function of general health and stressfulness of environment. A very low

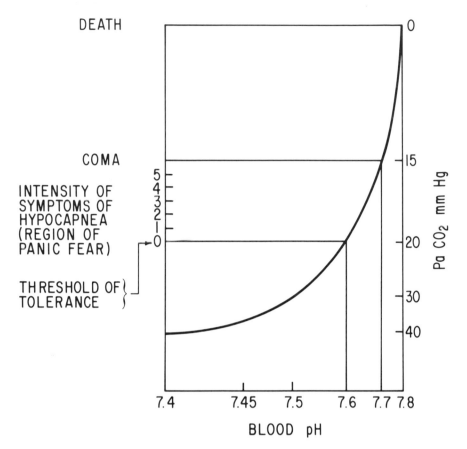

FIG. 8.2 The theoretical curve that describes the relationship between the intensity of symptoms of hypocapnea as a function of blood alkalosis (pH) and arterial blood tension (PCO_2).

threshold would make one susceptible to more intense symptoms of hyperventilatory hypocapnea at lower levels of blood pH or higher levels of PCO_2.

The positively accelerating exponential curve of Figure 8.2 describes the relationship between pH and PCO_2 and allows for the prediction of the intensity of the symptoms of hyperventilatory hypocapnea from either blood pH or PCO_2. Although death is almost certain to occur if pH reaches 7.8, the threshold for coma (pH = 7.7), like the threshold of tolerance (pH = 7.6), may vary from person to person and from time to time within the same person.

A positively accelerating exponential curve seems to provide the appropriate functional relationship between increases in alkalosis and their somatic consequences because changes on the low end of the pH scale (7.4 to 7.6) produce somatic effects that may go unnoticed, whereas changes on the high end (7.6 to 7.8) produce effects that make the difference between life and death. And although Figure 8.2 is not a time function, it is important to note that changes in pH in response to hyperventilating are very rapid. Lewis (1959) reported the case of a hyperventilator who in 10 seconds of overbreathing (17 breaths per minute to 26.7) raised pH from 7.412 to 7.486; in 21 seconds, decreased PCO_2 from 39.3 mm Hg to 26.7 and increased heart rate from 71 beats per minute to 107; and in 84 seconds raised minute–tidal volume of air breathed from 5.7 liters per minute to 43.2. Yu, Yim, and Stanfield (1959, p. 909) reported rapid cardiac changes in a sample of 18 hyperventilators: "The electrocardiographic abnormalities during hyperventilation were reproducible in each patient. They appeared as early as 15 seconds after the beginning of hyperventilation and, in most instances, returned to normal within about one minute after cessation of hyperventilation."

A Hyperventilation Theory of Panic Disorder

The hyperventilation theory of panic disorder to be discussed here was presented in detail in an earlier paper (Ley, 1985b). Therefore, the presentation here will be abbreviated; it will summarize the major features of the theory so that the theory can be contrasted with other current explanations of panic disorder.

The major assumptions of the theory are as follows.

Initiation of Panic Attacks

The theory assumes that the sudden, *unexpected*, and *unexplainable* somatic consequences of hyperventilating (especially the misattribution of heart palpitations and dyspnea) are the cause of the initial fear experienced in panic attacks. It is further assumed that the experience of fear generated by the misattribution of the somatic consequences of hyperventilating activates the autonomic nervous system in preparation for flight or fight. Among the autonomic nervous system responses to threat are an increase in heart rate and respiration rate. The increase in heart rate will increase the intensity of the sensation of palpitations, and the increase in respiration rate will lead to an even greater depletion of CO_2, which in turn will increase pH level (less oxygen will be released from hemoglobin) and decrease arterial tension (less hemoglobin will get to tissue). The effect will be to intensify the symptoms of hyperventilatory hypocapnea very quickly. This positive feedback loop will generate a positively accelerating exponential increase in the intensity of effects until events occur that lead to a diminution in blood pH and increase in PCO_2.

Termination of the Panic Attack

If blood pH were to continue to rise unabated, death would terminate the attack when pH reached 7.8. Short of death, loss of consciousness would terminate the attack by relieving the sufferer from the experience of fear and by reinstating involuntary control of respiration. However, panic attack victims don't die as a consequence of the attacks, and few faint. To account for this, the theory proposes that the drop in arterial CO_2 and drop in arterial tension reduce the supply of CO_2 below the level necessary to stimulate the respiratory reflex center of the medulla, thereby dampening the major source of involuntary respiration. Despite voluntary efforts to activate the weakened diaphragmatic and intercostal muscles (all skeletal muscles will be weakened by the hypoxia and ischemia produced by increased pH and decreased PCO_2), apnea will occur or respiration rate and depth will be decreased dramatically. Although the sensation of dyspnea (the difference between the desire to breathe and the ability to breathe) will be intense, the slowdown of respiration will reduce the amount of CO_2 being blown off and thus allow for the metabolic process to produce the CO_2 necessary to reduce pH so that normal function can resume.

Thus the positive feedback loop that characterizes the initiation of panic attacks is limited by a negative feedback loop that overrides the positive feedback loop when levels of CO_2 in plasma are low and arterial tension is so low that the amount of CO_2 that reaches the respiratory reflex center is insufficient to activate it.

Predisposition to Panic Disorder

The primary predisposition is a tendency to hyperventilate. Garssen, van Veenendaal, and Bloemink (1983) reported that in a group of 12 agoraphobes for whom panic attacks were the main factor underlying their agoraphobic behavior, 11 were diagnosed as hyperventilators and one was questionable. In a similar group of agoraphobes, Ley (1985a) found that the mean respiration rate of 19 breaths per minute was significantly faster than the normal rate of 12 to 14 (Comroe, 1974), thus suggesting hyperventilation.

Anxiety and Stress

If hyperventilation underlies panic disorder, it is important to understand the causes of hyperventilation. As pointed out earlier, hyperventilation is a common autonomic nervous system response to anxiety. In the case of panic disorder, anxiety may be the major contributing factor. Individuals who experience a relatively constant state of anxiety for prolonged periods of time as a consequence of stressful life situations or events are more likely than others to become chronic hyperventilators—for example, soldiers in combat, vulnerable women frightened by the threats of a male-dominated society, workers confronted with unreasonable demands in a hostile workplace, men and women who feel trapped in familial conflicts for which they can see no resolution, or anyone in a stressful environment over which he or she has little or no control.

If such individuals become chronic hyperventilators and thereby live constantly on the brink of debilitating hyperventilatory hypocapnea, any event that leads to a sudden rise in blood pH and fall in PCO_2 would be sufficient to intensify rapidly the symptoms of hypocapnea and thus initiate a panic attack. To the victim or to an onlooker, the event itself (e.g., a startling noise, a heated dispute, a frightening sight, a frightening thought, a nightmare) might appear to be so trivial by comparison with the effect it wrought that it might be dismissed as a causal agent, or the connection might be overlooked, or the victim and/or the onlooker might question the victim's sanity. The victim would appear to be unable to connect responses to causative events. Perhaps this is why the panic attack is often described as "coming out of the blue."

Respiratory Dysfunction

Although a relatively steady state of anxiety generated by a stressful environment is probably the primary cause of chronic hyperventilation, there may be other causes or other factors that interact with anxiety to cause chronic hyperventilation. Since the orifices of the nostrils are considerably smaller than the area of the open mouth or mouth agape (with lips not pursed), and since the nasal passages contain baffles that offer wind resistance (Adams, Boies, & Paparella, 1978), more air can be breathed at a faster rate and with less effort via the mouth than via the nose. Thus the practice of breathing via the mouth rather than via the nose predisposes the breather to chronic hyperventilation and all that this implies.

Although breathing via the mouth may exist simply as a bad habit, it may also be the result of disease (e.g., allergies, sinusitis, rhinitis) or physical obstructions in the nasal passages that impede air flow (e.g., deviated septum, polyps, tumors, septal spurs). In addition to the indirect effects that predispose the mouth breather to chronic hyperventilation, Adams et al. (1978, p. 381) point to some very relevant direct effects: ". . . the diseased nose which is not functioning adequately as a control device of the body can become an etiological factor in various pulmonary and cardiac disorders."

Although organic causes for hyperventilation have been identified (e.g., pain, metabolic acidosis, drug intoxication, hypercapnea, cirrhosis, and central nervous system disorders), they are not of immediate concern to the theory offered here because the connection between these causes and hyperventilation is clear. That is, in the case of organic conditions the resulting hyperventilation is correctly attributed to its cause; the symptoms do not just "come out of the blue."

Other Explanations of Panic Disorder

Fear of Fear

Whereas in ancient Greece the unwary traveler who reported extreme fear of traveling after a frightening experience for which he could give no account was thought to have been visited by the god Pan in one of his ill-tempered moods, the most widely held explanation of panic disorder today appears to be the fear-of-fear hypothesis or some variant thereof (cf. Evans, 1972; Frankl, 1975; Goldstein & Chambless, 1978; Jacob & Rapport, 1984; Malleson, 1959; Stampler, 1982; Weeks, 1977). It is generally understood that the fear-of-fear hypothesis does not literally mean that one is frightened by fear. There may be an element of poetic truth in the phrase made popular by Franklin D. Roosevelt, "The only thing we have to fear is fear itself," but, strictly speaking, one can fear just about anything except fear itself.

Rather, the implication of the fear-of-fear hypothesis is that one can be frightened by the somatic effects of fear. At the time of this writing, the most recent statement that encapsulates the essence of the fear-of-fear hypothesis was found in Jacob and Rapport (1984, p. 205; emphasis in original):

> Internal stimuli may also be involved in producing the panic attacks. . . . Such stimuli in-
> clude palpitations, dizziness, and sensations of choking. The reader will recognize these

sensations as being the *consequences* of anxiety as well. Thus, because the consequences of anxiety can serve as elicitors of anxiety, a vicious "fear of fear" cycle will be established, in which a spiraling increase in fear arousal ultimately results in a full-blown panic attack. . . .

Not to put too fine a point on it, the fear-of-fear hypothesis appears to be circular. That is, the data used in support of the hypothesis are the same evidence that the hypothesis is designed to explain. In the case of panic disorder, the salient feature is the rapid rise in fear. The fear-of-fear hypothesis explains this effect on the basis of the *hypothetical* connection between the somatic consequences of fear and the experience of fear that results from one's conscious awareness of the somatic consequences.

The fact that there are no data to support the hypothesis would not be a serious shortcoming if the hypothesis could be tested. The problem is how to test the basic assumption that fear is augmented by the somatic consequences of itself. The hyperventilation theory of panic disorder, it should be noted, can be put to the test. If hyperventilatory hypocapnea generates the sudden onset of somatic effects that frighten the victim, remediation of the dysfunctional respiration that gives rise to hyperventilation should prevent the somatic effects from occurring or terminate them if they begin. Recent findings lend strong support to this hyperventilation interpretation (i.e., Clark, Salkovskis, & Chalkley, 1985; Salkovskis, Jones, & Clark, 1986; Salkovskis, Warwick, Clark, & Wessels, 1986).

Another problem with the fear-of-fear hypothesis is its inability to account for the initiation of the panic attack. The hypothesis assumes that the attack begins with fear of unspecified origin and escalates to panic. However, results from the single study that addresses this issue (Ley, 1985a) do not support this assumption, but they do support the prediction from the hyperventilation theory that the somatic complaints reported to occur during panic attack episodes *precede* fear.

Regarding the initiation of the panic attack, it is also important to note that means derived from the fear-of-fear hypothesis do not allow for the consistent production of panic attacks in the laboratory. That is, reliable methods for frightening panic attack sufferers into panic attacks have not been demonstrated. There are reports of "spontaneous" panic attacks in the laboratory (e.g., Lader & Mathews, 1970; Cohen, Barlow, & Blanchard, 1985), but the fear-of-fear hypothesis can neither predict nor explain their occurrence. The hyperventilation theory, on the other hand, can explain the "spontaneous" occurrence of the attacks and provide the rationale underlying the means for prediction. Whether in the laboratory or out, whether standing up or lying down (as in the assumed posture of one *instructed* to relax), sufficient overbreathing in patients who suffer panic attacks will produce the symptoms of hyperventilatory hypocapnea, which in turn will lead to reports of experiences that are the same as or similar to those experiences remembered to have occurred during panic attacks (e.g., Garssen, van Veendendaal, & Bloemink, 1983).

Yet another problem with the fear-of-fear hypothesis is the lack of an explanation for the termination of the panic attack. To say that the attacks are self-terminating or that they run their course is, of course, to give no explanation at best, and a misleading one at worst, because the uncritical reader may be led to believe that the question of the termination of the attack has been answered. Furthermore, if fear begets fear, why doesn't every experience of fear lead to a full-blown panic attack in everyone every time fear is experienced? And why are some panic attacks brief whereas others are prolonged?

The explanation for the termination of the panic attack offered by the hyperventilation theory is consistent with principles of biology, chemistry, and physiology. The slowdown in respiration during the height of the panic attack (experienced as dyspnea and sometimes described as a choking sensation) is caused by elevated pH and diminished PCO_2. The effect of this slowdown is a reduction in the loss of CO_2 blown off concurrent with a buildup in the metabolic production of CO_2, thus resulting in a reduction in pH, an increase in PCO_2, and resumption of normal function.

Lactate

Interest in the connection between lactate and anxiety began with the publication of studies reporting that exercise elicited symptoms of anxiety in patients with anxiety neurosis (e.g., Jones & Mellersh, 1946). An explanation for the elicitation of anxiety was suggested by the rapid rise of blood lactic acid with the correlated onset of exercise.

The experimental study of the effects of lactate on anxiety began with Pitts and McClure (1967), who infused, on three separate occasions, either sodium lactate, lactate with calcium, or glucose in saline into the blood of a group of 14 patients whose reported symptoms would qualify them for inclusion in the DSM-III classification of panic disorder. Ten nonpatients served as controls. The results showed clearly that lactate was a potent drug for the production of panic attacks in the patients (those with a history of panic attacks) but not as much so for the controls (no history of panic attacks): Thirteen of the 14 patients suffered an attack from the infusion of lactate, compared with only two of the controls; one of the patients suffered an attack with the infusion of lactate with calcium, whereas none of the controls did; and no one in either group suffered an attack during the glucose-in-saline infusion.

Since the Pitts and McClure study, a number of researchers have reported successful replication of the effect, as well as new findings relevant to the effect (e.g., Appleby, Klein, Sachar, & Levitt, 1981; Fink, Taylor, & Volavka, 1969; Kelly, Mitchell-Heggs, & Sherman, 1971). The effectiveness of lactate infusion in the production of panic attacks in patients with panic disorder has led to considerable speculation on the biochemical basis for this intriguing effect (e.g., Carr & Sheehan, 1984; Lapierre, Knott, & Gray, 1984; Rainey, Frohman, Freedman, Pohl, Ettedgui, & Williams, 1984). The implicit, if not explicit, assumption underlying the speculations seems to be that lactate is a specific probe and that its infusion in blood begins a chain of chemical reactions that ultimately triggers a panic attack. There is reason, however, to question this assumption.

The interaction between lactate infusion and panic attacks makes it clear that patients suffering panic disorder are more *prone* to experience a panic attack following the infusion than are individuals without a history of panic disorder, but the *effects* of lactate infusions are not limited exclusively to victims of panic disorder. Although emphasis has been correctly placed on the large and disproportionate number of patients with panic disorder who respond with panic attacks when infused with sodium lactate, there are also individuals without a history of panic attacks who respond with attacks when infused. These findings might be disregarded as simply a little random "noise" in the data, or they might be accepted as solid data requiring an explanation.

Table 8.3 contains infrequently reported data from the Pitts and McClure (1967) study. The numbers in the columns indicate the number of patients or controls who reported experiencing the symptoms listed in the first column during the three infusion conditions. The bottom line contains the percentages of the total possible number of complaints ($14 \times 21 = 294$, for patients; $10 \times 21 = 210$, for controls) under each of the three infusions.

For the glucose-in-saline infusion, the difference between the patients and the controls (4.4% versus 2.8%) is negligible, and both percentages are so close to zero that one can conclude that the infusion process itself had virtually no effect on either group. For the lactate with calcium infusion, however, 25.5% of the symptoms were reported by the patients and 17.1% for the controls; and for the lactate infusion, 64.6% were reported by the patients and 34.3% for controls. Aside from the actual number of panic attacks reported, the frequency of symptoms increased for both groups compared with the

TABLE 8.3 Symptoms during infusions

Symptom	14 patients with anxiety neurosis			10 normal controls		
	Lactate	Lactate with calcium	Glucose in saline	Lactate	Lactate with calcium	Glucose in saline
Paresthesias	14	3	0	10	1	0
Tremor	14	7	2	5	4	0
"Shakiness"	14	7	2	8	4	0
Dizziness	13	4	0	4	3	0
Palpitations	13	8	2	5	4	2
Giddiness	13	5	0	5	2	0
Cold	11	8	1	3	3	1
Nervousness	11	7	3	6	4	1
Dyspnea	10	4	0	3	2	1
Chest pain	9	2	0	0	1	0
Blurred vision	9	3	0	3	0	0
Nervous chill	9	2	0	1	0	0
Weakness	8	4	1	5	1	1
Lump in throat	7	0	0	1	0	0
Headache	7	5	0	5	4	0
"Smothering"	6	1	0	1	0	0
Sighing	6	2	1	1	2	0
Faintness	5	1	0	2	1	0
Irritability	5	0	1	1	0	0
Nausea	4	2	0	3	0	0
"Choking"	2	0	0	0	0	0
Total symptoms	190	75	13	72	36	6
Percentage of total symptoms	64.6%	25.5%	4.4%	34.3%	17.1%	2.8%

glucose condition, but at a faster rate for the patients than for the controls. That is, in terms of the symptoms reported, lactate produced unpleasant symptoms for both groups, but the patients were sensitive to a greater number of them than were the controls.

Furthermore, a rank-order correlation coefficient between the frequency of complaints for the patients and controls under lactate infusion condition was .70, $p < .01$, a reliable index of the fact that the frequency of the types of symptoms experienced was the same. It would appear that lactate affected the controls in the same pattern as it did the patients, but to a lesser extent. It may be that it simply takes more sodium lactate to induce a panic attack in a person without a history of panic attacks than in a person with such a history. Conversely, smaller dosages of lactate would be uniformly less effective in producing panic attacks, a deduction supported by the findings of Lapierre, Knott, and Gray (1984).

The observation that patients with a history of panic disorder are more likely to report panic attacks when infused with lactate than are individuals without such a history is a correlational fact. That is, given the information that a person suffers panic disorder, probability strongly favors the prediction that this person will respond with a panic attack when infused with lactate. This correlational fact does not, however, tell us whether heightened sensitivity to lactate is the cause of panic attacks or whether the experience of panic attacks is the cause of the heightened sensitivity to lactate. The arguments offered here and elsewhere (Ley, 1986) favor the latter alternative. The hyperventilation theory of panic attacks does not make the assumption that individuals who suffer panic attacks are different from the general population in terms of a unique supersensitivity to lactate. Rather, the theory assumes that the experience of panic attacks is the cause of the heightened sensitivity to lactate or, for that matter, to any agent that produces sensations that are the same as or similar to those associated with the life-threatening events experienced during panic attacks.

The hyperventilation theory of panic disorder can readily incorporate the effects of lactate infusion discussed here. When lactate is infused in blood, it is rapidly converted into bicarbonate, thus increasing pH in proportion to the amount of lactate infused. Furthermore, prolonged hyperventilation will in itself produce lactate (Grosz & Farmer, 1972). A basic assumption of the theory is that the panic attack sufferer either is a chronic hyperventilator, who thus maintains an abnormally high level of blood pH and/or low level of PCO_2, or has a low threshold of tolerance for elevated pH and lowered PCO_2, or both (see Figure 8.2). The increment in pH that results from lactate infusion would bring about a greater number of intense symptoms of hypocapnea (the symptoms that are postulated to initiate the fear experienced in the panic attack) in one who hyperventilates than in one who does not.

Thus sensitivity to lactate could be a function of one's proneness to hyperventilate. The theory suggests that control subjects (subjects with no history of panic disorder) who experienced panic attacks in response to lactate infusion were chronic hyperventilators or individuals who hyperventilated on the occasion of the lactate infusion.

Psychodynamic Theory

Although Freud made the distinction between fear and anxiety (signaled fear versus unsignaled fear), he did not distinguish between panic disorder and extreme anxiety.

From a psychodynamic point of view, the death-throes qualities of the panic attack might be seen as a metaphor for the termination of a life that is excessively stressful, and thus not worth living. Regardless, the same assumptions used to account for anxiety disorders in general (repressed impulses and displacement of unconscious conflict to events in one's life) would apply to panic attacks. And the same treatment (insight into repressed impulses and displaced conflicts through free association and the analysis of dreams) would be prescribed.

The hyperventilation theory of panic disorder makes a clear distinction between panic attacks (episodes of extreme fear in response to intense somatic effects of hyperventilatory hypocapnea) and anxiety. However, the hyperventilation theory makes it equally clear that, as stated earlier, "Individuals who experience a relatively constant state of anxiety for prolonged periods of time as a consequence of stressful life situations or events are more likely than others to become chronic hyperventilators."

The Assessment and Treatment of Panic Disorder

Although it seems quite likely that there is more than one type of panic attack, the assessment and treatment of panic disorder presented here is limited to the hyperventilation-induced variety. From the hyperventilation theory of panic disorder, it follows that the assessment should focus on dysfunctional respiration that might produce the hyperventilation syndrome, and that treatment should be directed toward the correction of faulty respiration for the purpose of preventing the occurrence of the symptoms.

Assessment

The first assessment test for hyperventilation-induced panic attacks requires a modification of the DSM-III classification of panic disorder. This modification would emphasize the central role of dyspnea and/or palpitations among the symptoms presented. An important assumption of the hyperventilation theory of panic disorder is that the extreme fear experienced during the panic attack is the consequence of the patient's belief that he or she is about to die, and that suffocation and/or a heart attack are the chief threats to life. Thus, rather than simply requiring that *any* four of the symptoms listed in the DSM-III classification be presented, this assessment specifies that dyspnea and/or palpitations be among them.

If the first assessment test is positive, the second recommended test is the determination of the order of occurrence of the symptoms with respect to *extreme* fear. If it is clear that the required symptoms (dyspnea and/or palpitations) occurred before *extreme* fear, then hyperventilation is suggested.

The third test recommends the observation of the patient's respiration while relaxed and while stressed. Normal changes in respiratory behavior from relaxed to stressful conditions include an increase in respiration rate (from about 12–14 breaths per minute to 18 or more) and a shift from diaphragmatic breathing to inclusion or dominance of thoracic movement. If, under relaxed conditions, the patient demonstrates a fast rate of respiration (18 or more breaths per minute) or a dominance of thoracic movement, hyperventilation is suggested.

Other behavioral indicators of hyperventilation are dominance of oral over nasal breathing (typically with mouth agape), frequent gasps (sudden fast inhalations), frequent sighs (deep audible inhalations without sudden onset), and frequent yawns.

A fourth test in the assessment of hyperventilation is an investigation of the patient's history of nasal obstructions (e.g., deviated septum) or diseases (e.g., rhinitis or allergies) that interfere with breathing through the nose. Any factors that force the patient to breathe through the mouth, thus facilitating overbreathing, suggest hyperventilation.

A fifth test, the provocation test, requires the patient to breathe deeply and rapidly (about 40 deep breaths per minute) for 1 to 3 minutes. This procedure will provoke hyperventilatory hypocapnea. If the symptoms thus induced are the same as or similar to those experienced during panic attacks, then hyperventilation is suggested. Exact replication of the symptoms experienced during attacks outside the examining room should not be expected, since patients are aware of the fact that they are *voluntarily* inducing the symptoms in the presence of the therapist, not involuntarily experiencing them without help on hand as in the everyday situation. Under test conditions one would not expect the same amount of arousal to be generated as one would in the natural setting, thus contributing to the distinction between the two experiences.

In addition to self-reports and behavioral tests, there are several physiological tests for hyperventilation:

1. The acid test is a chemical analysis of a sample of blood to determine the degree of alkalinity; pH beyond 7.45 suggests hyperventilation.
2. The pressure test measures arterial carbon dioxide tension; PCO_2 below 35 mm Hg suggests hyperventilation.
3. The minute volume test measures the amount of air breathed per minute; minute volumes beyond 10 liters suggest hyperventilation.
4. Gas analysis tests measure a sample of end-tidal air to determine the percentage of CO_2 present; the average proportion of CO_2 is about 7%, smaller proportions suggest hyperventilation.

Treatment

A program of treatment derived from the hyperventilation theory of panic disorder should include the following steps.

INSTRUCTION IN THE PHYSIOLOGY OF RESPIRATION

The patient must be taught the rudiments of respiration because the treatment for dyspnea may appear to be counterintuitive. That is, dyspnea is the sensation experienced when the desire to breathe exceeds the ability to breathe, like the sensation of suffocation experienced when one's "wind has been knocked out." If patients do not understand the rudiments of respiration, they may be unwilling to engage in the treatment for dyspnea—namely, to hold one's breath or to breathe into a paper bag.

Thus instruction in the physiology of respiration should include explanations of how oxygen gets from the lungs to the arteries and to the cells, the acid–base balance and the meaning of pH, the effects of changes in blood pH on the dissociation of oxygen from hemoglobin, the effects of diminished carbon dioxide on arterial tension and its consequent effect on the heart, the mechanics of metabolism, how carbon dioxide is produced, the respiratory reflex center, the function of the diaphragm and intercostal muscles in respiration, voluntary and involuntary control of respiration, and any other topics that will help the patient to understand better the effects of hyperventilation and the means for controlling it (cf. Compernolle, Hoogduin, & Joele, 1979).

INSTRUCTION ON THE EFFECTS OF HYPERVENTILATION

The purpose of this step is to increase the patient's sensitivity to the early symptoms of hyperventilation. Instructions should include an explanation of the distinction between hyperventilation and hyperpnea, a demonstration of how the symptoms of hypocapnea can be induced after a few minutes of rapid and deep breathing, and a description of the earliest somatic and psychological symptoms of hypocapnea.

INSTRUCTION IN BREATHING

If neither nasal obstruction nor disease is indicated, breathing exercises should focus on voluntary control of respiration under both relaxed and stressful conditions. The patient should be given practice in diaphragmatic breathing, breathing through the nose, and exercising voluntary control of the diaphragm and intercostal muscles for the purpose of slowing down respiration rate.

Future Directions

The hyperventilation theory of panic disorder provides both an explanation for the disorder and a logically derived approach to its treatment. The author has tried to make the underlying assumptions of the theory sufficiently explicit so that testable hypotheses can be deduced readily.

Initial research efforts should be addressed to the determination of the efficacy of the treatment—that is, a program of research in which the outcome of the treatment prescribed here is compared with the outcome of other modes of treatment. Although the present treatment calls for a program of remedial breathing, the precise nature of such a program has not been specified. The determination of the most effective program is an empirical question, to be answered by future research.

The effectiveness of such a program, however, will depend to a large extent on our knowledge of the psychophysiology of respiration, a topic that has received relatively little attention. Therefore, more basic research should be directed toward the investigation of the psychophysiology of respiratory phenomena. What are the effects of systematic variations of the parameters of respiration on behavior and experience? What are the psychological factors that affect respiration? And what is the nature of the interactions between respiratory variables and behavior and experience? Despite the fact that respiration is the only vital function over which the organism has partial voluntary control, the psychology of respiration is a neglected area of research.

Another direction for research is the treatment of agoraphobia. To the extent that agoraphobic behavior is motivated by the fear of experiencing panic attacks, the hyperventilation theory and treatment offered here apply to the treatment of agoraphobia. Treatment–outcome strategies apply nicely. For example, Ascher (1981) demonstrated that paradoxical intention plus *in vivo* exposure therapy led to a greater reduction in agoraphobic behavior than did *in vivo* exposure alone. Recently, Bonn, Readhead, and Timmons (1984) reported that agoraphobes treated with breathing retraining plus real-life exposure demonstrated significantly greater long-term improvement on five measures of agoraphobia-related criteria than did agoraphobes treated with real-life exposure alone. These encouraging findings call for more therapy-oriented research.

The future directions for programmatic research pointed to by the hyperventilation theory of panic disorder exceed the few listed here. One last direction, which has very broad implications, will be mentioned. Although the psychology of respiration is no laughing matter, laughing is a matter of respiration. If laughing is truly therapeutic, as tradition and Norman Cousins would have us believe, the determination of the ingredients of laughter that improve health might be made through an analysis of the psychophysiology of respiration. Such a notion tickles the fancy.

Conclusions

The hyperventilation theory maintains that lessons in remedial breathing that lead to control of respiration and thereby prevent overbreathing will provide the necessary prophylaxis for the prevention of panic attacks. The theory does not, however, address itself to the problems of personal and social living that predispose the individual to hyperventilate. These problems can best be dealt with through therapies aimed at resolving the conflicts that underlie the problems, or through those aimed at adjustment to the conditions of life over which one has no control.

References

Adams, G., Boies, L., & Paparella, M. (1978). *Boies' fundamentals of otolaryngology* (5th ed.). Philadelphia: W. B. Saunders.

American Psychiatric Association (1980). *Diagnostic and statistical manual of mental disorders* (3rd ed.). Washington, DC: Author.

Appleby, I., Klein, D., Sachar, E., & Levitt, M. (1981). Biochemical indices of lactate-induced panic: A preliminary report. In D. Klein & J. Rabkin (Eds.), *Anxiety: New research and changing concepts.* New York: Raven Press.

Arbus, G. S., Hebert, L. A., Levesque, P. R., Etsen, B. E., & Schwartz, W. B. (1969). Characterization and clinical application of the "significance band" and acute respiratory alkalosis. *New England Journal of Medicine, 280,* 117-123.

Arnold, M. (1960). *Emotion and personality* (Vols. 1-2). New York: Columbia University Press.

Ascher, L. M. (1981). Employing paradoxical intention in the treatment of agoraphobia. *Behaviour Research and Therapy, 19,* 533-542.

Barlow, D., Vermilyea, J., Blanchard, E., Vermilyea, B., DiNardo, P., & Cerny, J. A. (1985). The phenomenon of panic. *Journal of Abnormal Psychology, 94,* 320-328.

Bonn, J. A., Readhead, C. P. A., & Timmons, B. H. (1984, September 22). Enhanced adaptive behavioural response in agoraphobic patients pretreated with breathing retraining. *The Lancet,* pp. 665-669.

Bouhuys, A. (1974). *Breathing: Physiology, environment, and lung disease.* New York: Grune and Stratton.

Bouhuys, A. (1977). *The physiology of breathing.* New York: Grune and Stratton.

Carr, D., & Sheehan, M. (1984). Panic anxiety: A new biological model. *Journal of Clinical Psychiatry, 45,* 323-330.

Clark, D., Salkovskis, P., & Chalkley, A. (1985). Respiratory control as a treatment for panic attacks. *Journal of Behavior Therapy and Experimental Psychiatry, 16*, 23–30.

Cohen, A. Barlow, D., & Blanchard, E. (1985). The psychophysiology of relaxation-associated panic attacks. *Journal of Abnormal Psychology, 94*, 96–101.

Compernolle, T., Hoogduin, K., & Joele, L. (1979). Diagnosis and treatment of hyperventilation syndrome. *Psychosomatics, 19*, 612–625.

Comroe, J. H. (1974). *Physiology of respiration* (2nd ed.). Chicago: Yearbook Medical Publishers.

Crofton, J., & Douglas, A. (1981). *Respiratory diseases* (3rd ed.). Boston: Blackwell Scientific Publications.

Dittrich, J., Houts, A., & Lichstein, K. (1983). Panic disorder: Assessment and treatment. *Clinical Psychology Review, 3*, 215–225.

Engel, G., Ferris, E., & Logan, M. (1947). Hyperventilation: Analysis of clinical symptomology. *Annals of Internal Medicine, 27*, 683–705.

Evans, I. (1972). A conditioning model of common neurotic pattern—Fear of fear. *Psychotherapy: Theory, Research, and Practice, 9*, 238–241.

Fazekas, J., McHenry, L., Alman, R., & Sullivan, J. (1961). Cerebral hemodynamics during brief hyperventilation. *Archives of Neurology, 4*, 132–138.

Fink, M., Taylor, M., & Volavka, J. (1969). Anxiety precipitated by lactate. *New England Journal of Medicine, 281*, 14–29.

Frankl, V. (1975). Paradoxical intention and deflection. *Psychotherapy: Theory, Research and Practice, 12*, 226–236.

Garssen, B., van Veenendaal, W., & Bloemink, R. (1983). Agoraphobia and the hyperventilation syndrome. *Behaviour Research and Therapy, 21*, 643–649.

Gliebe, P., & Auerback, A. (1944). Sighing and other forms of hyperventilation simulating organic disease. *Journal of Nervous and Mental Disease, 99*, 600–615.

Goldstein, A. J., & Chambless, D. L. (1978). A reanalysis of agoraphobia. *Behavior Therapy, 9*, 47–59.

Gotoh, F., Meyer, J., & Takagi, Y. (1965). Cerebral effects of hyperventilation in man. *Archives of Neurology, 12*, 410–423.

Grosz, H., & Farmer, B. (1972). Pitts and McClure's lactate-anxiety study revisited. *British Journal of Psychiatry, 120*, 415–418.

Jacob, R., & Rapport, M. (1984). Panic disorder. In S. Turner (Ed.), *Behavioral treatment of anxiety disorders.* New York: Plenum Press.

Jones, M., & Mellersh, V. (1946). Comparison of exercise response in anxiety states and normal controls. *Psychosomatic Medicine, 8*, 180–187.

Kelly, D., Mitchell-Heggs, N., & Sherman, D. (1971). Anxiety and the effects of sodium lactate assessed clinically and physiologically. *British Journal of Psychiatry, 119*, 129–141.

Kerr, W., Dalton, J., & Gliebe, P. (1937). Some physical phenomena associated with the anxiety states and their relation to hyperventilation. *Annals of Internal Medicine, 11*, 961–992.

Lader, M., & Mathews, A. (1970). Physiological changes during spontaneous panic attacks. *Journal of Psychosomatic Research, 14*, 377–382.

Lapierre, Y., Knott, V., & Gray, R. (1984). Psychophysiological correlates of sodium lactate. *Psychopharmacology Bulletin, 20*, 50–57.

Lazarus, R. (1966). *Psychological stress and the coping process.* New York: McGraw-Hill.

Lewis, B. I. (1959). Hyperventilation syndrome. *California Medicine, 91*, 121–126.

Ley, R. (1985a). Agoraphobia, the panic attack, and the hyperventilation syndrome. *Behaviour Research and Therapy, 23*, 79–81.

Ley, R. (1985b). Blood, breath, and fears: A hyperventilation theory of panic attacks and agoraphobia. *Clinical Psychology Review, 5*, 271–285.

Ley, R. (1986). *Hyperventilation and lactate infusion in the production of panic attacks.* Paper presented at the Sixth International Symposium on Respiratory Psychophysiology, London.

Lum, L. (1975). Hyperventilation: The tip of the iceberg. *Journal of Psychosomatic Research, 19*, 375–383.

Lum, L. (1978–1979). Respiratory alkalosis and hypocarbia: The role of carbon dioxide in the body economy. *Chest, Heart, and Stroke Journal, 3*, 31–34.

Lum, L. (1981). Hyperventilation and anxiety state. *Journal of the Royal Society of Medicine, 74*, 1–4.

Magarian, G. (1982). Hyperventilation syndromes: Infrequently recognized common expressions of anxiety and stress. *Medicine, 61,* 219–236.

Malleson, N. (1959). Panic and phobia: A possible method of treatment. *The Lancet,* 225–227.

McKell, T., & Sullivan, A. (1947). The hyperventilation syndrome in gastroenterology. *Gastroenterology, 9,* 6–16.

Missri, J., & Alexander, S. (1978). Hyperventilation syndrome: A brief review. *Journal of the American Medical Association, 240,* 2093–2096.

Mountcastle, V. B. (1968). *Medical physiology* (12th ed.) (Vol. 1). St. Louis: C. V. Mosby.

Okel, B., & Hurst, J. (1961). Prolonged hyperventilation in man: Associated electrolyte changes and subjective symptoms. *Archives of Internal Medicine, 108,* 157–162.

Pitts, F., & McClure, J. (1967). Lactate metabolism in anxiety neurosis. *The New England Journal of Medicine, 277,* 1329–1336.

Raichle, M., & Plum, F. (1972). Hyperventilation and cerebral blood flow. *Stroke, 3,* 566–571.

Rainey, J., Frohman, C., Freedman, R., Pohl, R., Ettedgui, E., & Williams, M. (1984). Specificity of lactate infusion as a model of anxiety. *Psychopharmacology Bulletin, 20,* 45–49.

Razran, G. (1961). The observable unconscious and the inferable conscious in current Soviet psychology: Interoceptive conditioning, semantic conditioning, and the orienting reflex. *Psychological Review, 68,* 81–147.

Salkovskis, P., Jones, D., & Clark, D. (1986). Respiratory control in the treatment of panic attacks: Replication and extension with concurrent measures of behaviour and PCO_2. *British Journal of Psychiatry, 148,* 526–532.

Salkovskis, P., Warwick, H., Clark, D., & Wessels, D. (1986). A demonstration of acute hyperventilation during naturally occurring panic attacks. *Behaviour Research and Therapy, 24,* 91–94.

Singer, E. P. (1958). The hyperventilation syndrome in clinical medicine. *New York State Journal of Medicine, 58,* 1494–1500.

Stampler, F. M. (1982). Panic disorder: Description, conceptualization, and implications for treatment. *Clinical Psychology Review, 2,* 469–486.

Waites, T. (1978). Hyperventilation—Chronic and acute. *Archives of Internal Medicine, 138,* 1700–1701.

Weeks, C. (1977). *Simple, effective treatment of agoraphobia.* New York: Hawthorn Books.

Wheatley, C. (1975). Hyperventilation syndrome: A frequent cause of chest pain. *Chest, 69,* 195–199.

Yu, P., Yim, B., & Stanfield, A. (1959). Hyperventilation syndrome. *American Medical Association Archives of Internal Medicine, 103,* 902–913.

9

Cognitive-Behavioral Assessment and Treatment of Agoraphobia

LARRY MICHELSON

Agoraphobia, one of the most chronic and clinically debilitating anxiety disorders, accounts for over half of all anxiety disorders seen for professional treatment (Agras, Sylvester, & Oliveau, 1969). Although descriptive accounts can be traced to ancient Greece, Westphal (1871) first offered the term *agoraphobia* to describe a cluster of symptoms characterized by anxiety while walking unaccompanied through open spaces, anticipatory fear, fear of dying, and social embarrassment. Adding to these clinical accounts, scientific research over the past two decades has greatly advanced our understanding of agoraphobia and related anxiety disorders. Rather than reiterating existing reviews (Brehony & Geller, 1981; Chambless & Goldstein, 1982; Emmelkamp, 1982; Jansson & Öst, 1982; Mathews, Gelder, & Johnson, 1981; Thorpe & Burns, 1983), this contribution will selectively address critical issues in etiology, diagnosis, assessment, and treatment of agoraphobia, integrating cognitive-behavioral perspectives.

Diagnostic and Clinical Dimensions of Agoraphobia

Recent developments in psychiatric diagnostic systems have fostered improved taxonomies for the anxiety disorders in general and agoraphobia in particular. The *Diagnostic and Statistical Manual of Mental Disorders* (DSM-III) (American Psychiatric Association, 1980) has proved to be a useful, albeit imperfect, classification schema. Debate regarding the conceptual and clinical parameters of many DSM-III disorders continues. Although the specific diagnosis of agoraphobia was previously omitted from earlier editions of the manual, DSM-III includes two forms of agoraphobia—with and without panic attacks. Since most agoraphobics experience panic attacks, the utility of the latter condition (without panic) has been questioned. DSM-III defines agoraphobia as

> a marked fear of being alone, or being in public places from which escape might be difficult or help not available in case of sudden incapacitation. Normal activities are increasingly constricted as the fears or avoidance behavior dominate the individual's life. The most common situations avoided involve being in crowds, such as on a busy street or in crowded stores, or being in tunnels, on bridges, on elevators, or on public transportation. Often these

Larry Michelson. University of Pittsburgh School of Medicine, Department of Psychiatry, Western Psychiatric Institute and Clinic, Pittsburgh, Pennsylvania.

individuals insist that a family member or friend accompany them whenever they leave home. [p. 226]

The specific diagnostic criteria include three conditions:

> A. The individual has marked fear of and thus avoids being alone or in public places from which escape might be difficult or help not available in case of sudden incapacitation, e.g., crowds, tunnels, bridges, public transportation.
> B. There is increasing constriction of normal activities until the fears or avoidance behavior dominate the individual's life.
> C. Not due to a major depressive episode, Obsessive Compulsive Disorder, Paranoid Personality Disorder or Schizophrenia. [p. 227]

Although these diagnostic criteria are likely to undergo further refinements (DSM-III-R), the core clinical characteristics of agoraphobia are clearly described. Moreover, the hierarchical exclusion criteria that assign diagnostic priority to affective illness ("not due to a major depressive episode") are also the subject of much controversy, given the depressogenic effects of agoraphobia and findings from recent co-morbidity studies, issues that will be discussed subsequently.

The primary characteristics of agoraphobia include severe *phobic anxiety* and *phobic avoidance* across a variety of feared situations, such as: leaving home alone; driving; using public transportation (buses, trains, taxis, planes, subways); walking around one's neighborhood or a shopping mall; standing in long lines; traveling alone; eating in restaurants; attending concerts, movies, or sporting events; heights, tunnels, bridges, elevators, and escalators; closed or open spaces; and entering situations in which escape might be socially awkward. Many clients report a current or previous episode of being housebound, during which time they were restricted to their homes because of marked phobic anxiety, panic attacks, and anticipatory fear. In severe cases, some individuals even become "roombound," requiring a trusted significant other, most typically their spouse, to accompany them from one room to another, lest panic overwhelm them.

Agoraphobics also relate, though less consistently, that a number of safety signals may reduce the severity, duration, and frequency of panic attacks (Rachman, 1981). For example, being accompanied by a significant other, such as a spouse, child, parent, sibling, or trusted friend, commonly reduces phobic anxiety and avoidance. Similarly, when carefully questioned, clients report a wide variety of defensive maneuvers that they employ as coping strategies. For example, they may routinely engage in what appear to be highly functional shopping forays. However, a more detailed clinical analysis often reveals that these individuals restrict their driving to highly circumscribed routes within a distinct "safety radius," traveling only at certain times to avoid traffic congestion or crowds, and only if they are able to bring their tranquilizers. Hence, what might appear to be only mildly phobic avoidance may, on closer inspection, prove to be highly dysfunctional behavior.

Symptomatology

Although there is a recognizable pattern of phobic anxiety and avoidance, the heterogeneous nature of agoraphobics' fears is also apparent. In a survey of 477 agoraphobics,

Doctor (1982), observed that for many clients particular situations were panic-provoking; yet for other respondents these items were rated as no problem. For example, 43% of the respondents reported driving on freeways as panic-provoking, versus 29% who rated this activity as no problem. Similar differences were evident with regard to airplanes (39% versus 18%), closed-in places (25% versus 17%), heights (23% versus 18%), department stores (20% versus 27%), and crowds (18% versus 15%). These data suggest that there are widely varying patterns in severity among agoraphobics and that the constellation of phobic situations can differ markedly across individuals (Williams, 1985).

Although specific configurations of phobic situations differ across clients, other parameters of the disorder are quite consistent across both North American and European centers. The mean age of onset is approximately 28 years of age and appears to follow a bimodal pattern, with peaks observed at ages 15–20 and 30–40 (Chambless, 1982; Marks, 1970; Mendel & Klein, 1969). The proportion of females to males is approximately 4:1, with women reporting more frequently for treatment. In their analysis of ten agoraphobia studies, Thorpe and Burns (1983) found an average sex breakdown of 80% female/20% male. These findings will be reviewed further in light of the National Institute of Mental Health (NIMH) epidemiology studies. Approximately 70–85% of agoraphobics are married, and the majority are unemployed, although they would prefer to work if their symptoms abated (Chambless, 1982).

Agoraphobics typically present with a chronic history due to the incapacitating nature of the disorder, which directly interferes with their ability to seek treatment. In addition, agoraphobia is often a hidden problem wherein clients are reluctant to seek out treatment lest they be diagnosed as "crazy." In the Agoraphobia Program at the University of Pittsburgh, the average duration of illness for 100 agoraphobics seen for treatment was 11 years. Over 90% had received some form of "treatment," for an average duration of two years, with little or no reported benefit. Parenthetically, it should come as little surprise that many clients with no depressive episodes prior to the onset of their agoraphobia subsequently develop secondary depression as a direct result of the severity and intractability of their symptoms.

Recently, Barlow (1985) used the Anxiety Disorders Interview Schedule (ADIS) to assess anxiety disorder co-morbidity (i.e., the percentage of anxiety disorder cases in which concomitant diagnoses were also designated). Approximately half of the agoraphobia cases assessed received no other DSM-III anxiety disorder diagnosis, with the remaining subjects receiving one (20%), two (27%), or three or more (10%) secondary diagnoses. With regard to the specific secondary diagnosis, 39% of the agoraphobics received a concomitant diagnosis of depression or dysthymia, 12% social phobia, 10% simple phobia, and 2% a personality disorder. In an earlier study, Weissman, Myers, and Harding (1978) conducted a survey in New Haven, Connecticut, and found that over 80% of persons with generalized anxiety disorder, 17% with panic disorder, and 19% with phobic disorders had at least one other anxiety disorder at some time in their life. A relatively frequent (one-third) occurrence of panic disorder was reported among phobics at some point in their life. The authors reported that major depression and anxiety disorders overlapped 7% for generalized anxiety disorder, 2% for panic disorder, and 4% for phobia. These data highlight the importance of assessing agoraphobic clients for the presence of concurrent anxiety and affective disorders.

Epidemiology of Agoraphobia

Recently, the NIMH sponsored a multisite epidemiologic catchment area (ECA) survey of over 3,500 subjects using the Diagnostic Interview Schedule (DIS) to yield DSM-III diagnoses. A special series of epidemiological reports describing the incidence, prevalence, and utilization of mental health services appeared in the *Archives of General Psychiatry*, Vol. 41, October 1984 (cf. Eaton & Kessler, 1984; Myers et al., 1984; Regier et al., 1984, Robins et al., 1984; Shapiro et al., 1984 for complete details). The initial three ECA sites included Baltimore, St. Louis, and New Haven. Although the reader is referred to the original reports for complete findings, a brief summary of the results, as they relate to agoraphobia, is offered herein.

Lifetime prevalence rates of specific psychiatric disorders across the three ECAs revealed that anxiety disorders were the most common psychiatric conditions in Baltimore (25%) and the second most frequently diagnosed conditions in New Haven (10%) and St. Louis (11.1%), with substance abuse being more common in these two ECA sites. With regard to six-month prevalence rates, the most frequent psychiatric disorders among females, irrespective of age, were phobias. Males also exhibited relatively high rates of phobic disorders, with alcohol abuse/dependence being ranked first, followed by phobias as the second most common psychiatric condition (Myers et al., 1984). The rates of agoraphobia, averaged across the three ECA sites, were 1.8% for men and 5.4% for women. As noted by Weissman (1985, p. 282): "The rates of agoraphobia have wider variations between sites (2.7 to 5.8/100) and are considerably higher than the other anxiety diagnoses and than the reports from earlier studies. The rates are two- to four-fold higher in women than men, and twofold higher in less educated persons and non-whites."

Myers et al. (1984) reported that the *lifetime prevalence* and sex distribution rates for agoraphobia, across the three ECA sites averaged together, were 2.7% for males and 8.1% for females. These differences were statistically significant ($p < .01$), indicating that agoraphobia rates were significantly higher for women than for men in all sites (Robins et al., 1984). A number of other interesting findings were reported with regard to race and level of education. Specifically, the lifetime prevalence of agoraphobia was significantly higher among blacks (13.4%) versus nonblacks (7.2%) in Baltimore. Although the other sites did not exhibit differential race patterns of agoraphobia, this finding suggests that intersite differences exist in the incidence and prevalence of agoraphobia (Robins et al., 1984). Differences between college graduates and non–college graduates were also found, with college graduates having an agoraphobia prevalence rate of 2.9% averaged across the three ECA sites, compared to 6.1% for non–college graduates. This difference was statistically significant ($p \le .05$) and suggests decreased risk among college-educated individuals (Robins et al., 1984). Finally, and perhaps most alarming, it was found that the vast majority of respondents with recent DIS diagnoses did not seek out any mental health provider for treatment. Although this was particularly pronounced for persons with cognitive disorders and substance abuse/dependence, subjects with anxiety disorders also exhibited significant underutilization of mental health services (Shapiro et al., 1984). These findings are consistent with the earlier study by Weissman et al. (1978), who found that only a quarter of individuals diagnosed with a current anxiety disorder had received treatment in the past year. Moreover, anxiety disorder sufferers tended toward high use of medical and health facilities for nonpsychiatric symptoms and complaints.

Etiology

Although a complete review of contemporary conceptualizations regarding etiology and maintenance of panic attacks goes beyond the scope of this chapter, a brief summary is offered for clinical and heuristic purposes. Alternative formulations regarding etiology may differ with respect to the relative contribution and interactions of a host of intraindividual and environmental factors. It is generally recognized, however, that a pattern of stressful life events typically precedes the onset of the initial panic attack by three to twelve months. It has been hypothesized that as a result of these life stressors (and possibly deficient coping skills), the individual may experience higher levels of autonomic reactivity and a generalized stress reaction in the form of delayed habituation process, hypervigilance, overreactivity, and a general upward spiraling in state anxiety. It has been reported that agoraphobics exhibit significantly higher autonomic arousal and overreactivity compared to normals, as well as delayed habituation processes (Lader, 1967). These events subsequently place the vulnerable individual at high risk for experiencing an initial panic attack, which often occurs in stimulating environments such as cars, shopping malls, or crowded places.

Once the initial panic attack has occurred, several powerful learning processes are engaged, including classical conditioning, operant conditioning, two-factor operations, cognitive mediation including negative attributions, irrational beliefs, expectancy of harm, and possible learned helplessness progressions. The individual initially escapes the panic situation, although phobic avoidance and panic attacks ensure that the phobic disorder rapidly generalizes to previously safe situations and is maintained over time. Eventually, because of panic attacks, the individual's safety radius may not extend much beyond the security of the home or its immediate vicinity. The continued presence of catastrophic cognitions and negative imagery can mantain the disorder indefinitely, even in the absence of panic attacks (e.g., DSM III—Agoraphobia without Panic Attacks). The mediating role of cognition is evident among housebound agoraphobics who experience so-called spontaneous panic attacks at home in response to phobic ideation and imagery.

The agoraphobics' misattribution of internal psychophysiological events (i.e., changes in heart rate, dizziness, shortness of breath, etc.) results in further negative interoceptive conditioning. This leads to inadvertent phobic conditioning to normal physiological fluctuations in autonomic functioning and results in rapid escalation of relatively innocuous somatic cues such as palmar sweating, which may culminate in a full-blown panic attack. The panic attacks subsequently lead to further interroceptive and environmental phobic conditioning, perpetuating the vicious fear-of-fear cycle (Goldstein & Chambless, 1978). Agoraphobics report fear of losing control, having a heart attack, dying, fainting, or embarrassing themselves in public. Hence they manifest a "fear of fear" (Goldstein & Chambless, 1978) whereby they actively seek to avoid elevated anxiety and panic attacks.

Assessment

Psychiatric Diagnosis of Agoraphobia

DSM-III offers an advancement in the conceptualization and psychiatric diagnosis of anxiety disorders. Psychiatric interviews ranging from an open-ended to a highly structured format have yielded acceptable agreements for the major categories of Axis 1. Several interviews have been developed for epidemiological studies (Diagnostic Interview Schedule [DIS]; Robins, Helger, Croughan, & Ratcliffe, 1981) and differentiation of affective disorders from schizophrenia (Schedule for Affective Disorders and Schizophrenia [SADS]; Endicott & Spitzer, 1978, 1979). These devices, however, do not provide a fine-grained delineation or differential diagnosis of the specific anxiety disorders. For example, the DIS does not include social phobia, generalized anxiety disorder, or posttraumatic stress disorder. Hence, important conceptual, clinical, and methodological issues regarding the specific dimensions of particular anxiety disorders are obscured in studies using these and similar interviews. To remedy this problem, the Anxiety Disorders Interview Schedule (ADIS) was developed and empirically tested at the Center for Stress and Anxiety Disorders in Albany, New York (DiNardo, O'Brien, Barlow, Waddell, & Blanchard, 1983; cf. Barlow, 1985). The ADIS is a structured interview specifically designed to provide differential diagnosis among the various anxiety disorders according to DSM-III criteria. The ADIS also provides detailed clinical information for formulating functional analyses of the phobic parameters of the anxiety disorders. The interview includes screening questions that allow the examiner to ascertain the presence of psychosis, substance abuse, and major affective disorder. In addition, the Hamilton Anxiety Scale and the Hamilton Depression Scale are also included in the schedule to provide greater elaboration of related symptomatology. According to the authors, the average time for administration is approximately 90 minutes. In addition to deriving a primary diagnosis, the examiner also completes information regarding secondary diagnoses that is based on estimates of the relative severity and interference with current functioning due to the client's symptoms. It is also possible to assign two primary diagnoses, in which case severity ratings are completed for both disorders. Hence, in addition to providing a primary diagnosis, the ADIS allows for multiple (i.e., concurrent) diagnoses, which are precluded using the conventional DSM-III hierarchical precepts.

The reliability of the ADIS in diagnosing DSM-III anxiety disorders was originally reported by DiNardo et al. (1983). Two interviewers examined 60 consecutive outpatients and assigned primary and secondary diagnoses based on the ADIS interview. Kappa reliability for the specific diagnostic categories were as follows: agoraphobia with panic attacks = .853; panic disorder = .692; generalized anxiety disorder = .467; social phobia = .771; obsessive–compulsive disorder = .658; major depression = .751; other disorders = .692 (includes bipolar disorder, dysthymic disorder, Axis III, no mental disorder, schizophrenaform disorder, and adjustment disorder).

Recently, Barlow (1985) reported updated kappa coefficients calculated on the first 125 consecutive admissions to their anxiety disorders program. The increased sample size permitted the calculation of kappas on a greater number of cases, with the exception of posttraumatic stress disorder. Kappa coefficients for the specific diagnostic categories, and the respective sample sizes, were as follows: agoraphobia with panic attacks ($n = 41$),

$\kappa = .854$; social phobia ($n = 19$), $\kappa = .905$; simple phobia ($n = 7$), $\kappa = .558$; panic disorder ($n = 17$), $\kappa = .651$; generalized anxiety disorder ($n = 12$), $\kappa = .571$; and obsessive–compulsive disorder ($n = 6$), $\kappa = .825$. It is apparent from these data that agoraphobia, social phobia, and obsessive–compulsive disorders yield high kappa reliability coefficients and can be diagnosed reliably using the ADIS. The lowest reliability coefficient was for simple phobia, which may have been due to difficulty regarding the clinical weighing of primary and secondary disorders among the simple phobics, since almost all of the simple phobics presented with other anxiety disorders (Barlow, 1985). Panic disorder and generalized anxiety disorder may have lower reliabilities because both have limited behavioral referents and because clinicians must therefore rely on clients' self-report of somatic and cognitive symptomatology. DSM-III appears to provide relatively reliable clinical descriptions sufficient to yield replicable diagnoses across raters using the ADIS, with the noted limitations in diagnosing generalized anxiety disorder and simple phobia. Specifically regarding the diagnosis and differential identification of agoraphobia, the ADIS provides a reliable and efficient diagnostic tool, which appears suitable for both clinical and research purposes.

Clinical Interviews

Although identification of specific psychiatric diagnoses is important for clinical, research, and theory-building purposes, the need for and utility of the clinical interview is readily apparent. Clinical interviewing is an essential component in gathering salient information in assessment and treatment planning for agoraphobia. Clinical interviewing has a long, rich history in the field of clinical psychology. Rather than reiterate detailed expositions of the role of clinical interviewing in assessing agoraphobia, the reader is referred to the following sources for informative reviews of the major issues, techniques, and applications of clinical interviews in anxiety disorders in general and agoraphobia in particular. These include Guidano and Liotti (1983), Chambless and Goldstein (1982), Neitzel and Bernstein (1981), and Thorpe and Burns (1983).

Clinician Rating Scales

Clinical rating instruments offer a number of advantages in the assessment of agoraphobia and related symptomatology. Clinical rating forms can be efficient, reliable, and treatment-sensitive strategies for depicting therapeutic change on targeted and generalization areas. Gelder and Marks (1966) developed one of the first standardized rating forms for agoraphobics that measured their psychological symptoms as well as their social adjustment. Evaluators integrate both phobic anxiety and phobic avoidance in assigning overall phobia ratings. The Gelder and Marks form also included general anxiety, depression, depersonalization, and obsessions. Gelder and Marks's (1966) scales were later revised by Watson and Marks (1971), who provided separate evaluations of phobic anxiety and phobic avoidance. Watson and Marks's (1971) version has been widely applied, and its interrater reliability reveals acceptable agreement among clients, clinicians, and independent evaluators (Agras & Jacob, 1981; Emmelkamp, 1979).

Another measure used to derive an overall index of severity is the Global Assessment of Severity Scale (Kelly et al., 1970), a 5-point instrument rated by the clinician in which a score of 1 represents no complaints in normal activity; a score of 2 equals symptoms complained of by the client but not interfering with normal work or social activities; a score of 3 represents symptoms interfering with normal work or social activities in minor ways; a score of 4 indicates normal work or social activities interfered with markedly but not fully prevented or radically changed; and a score of 5 represents normal work or social activities either radically changed or prevented. In research settings, the score is typically determined by a consensus of the primary clinician with the project staff when clients undergo their periodic assessments (cf. Michelson & Mavissakalian, 1983).

Self-Report Measures

Severity

The Self-Rating of Severity Scale (SRS) is a 9-point analogue scale from the Marks and Mathews Fear Questionnaire, which is rated by the client in order to answer the following question, "How would you rate the present state of your phobic symptoms on the scale below?" The scale ranges from 0, representing no phobias present, to 8, representing very severely disturbing and disabling phobias present. The SRS provides a client-rated measure of overall severity and generally correlates highly with the Global Assessment of Severity Scale, completed by the clinician.

Phobia

The Wolpe–Lang Fear Survey Schedule (FSS) (Wolpe & Lang, 1964) has been widely applied to assess the myriad fears of agoraphobics. The FSS provides a reliable and accurate means of identifving numerous phobic stimuli and fear-provoking situations that agoraphobics typically report only after more extensive clinical interviewing. The FSS yields a rapid and valid self-report measure of both the *type* and *severity* of fears and phobias and is sensitive to pre–posttreatment effects. Although the FSS has been employed in numerous studies of phobic populations and provides a means of monitoring the effects of treatment on both targeted and nontargeted phobias, its limitations have also been noted. Bellack and Lombardo (1985, p. 63), observed:

> It is generally more appropriate to use inventory such as the FSS for idiographic rather than nomothetic purposes. Summative, overall scores are statistical abstractions that presumably represent general trends and tendencies. Regardless of the terminology selected, the use of an overall score to predict or summarize behaviors is a trait conception. The use of a trait-descriptive scores should not be expected to predict (relate to) specific response patterns of specific situations. Examination of responses to individual questions or clusters of responses are likely to be much more useful than overall fearfulness scores.

Therefore, although the FSS offers valuable information about the breadth and depth of various fears and phobias, comparisons across subjects with different response patterns may be problematic, particularly when using summary scores.

Marks and Mathews Fear Questionnaire (FQ-T)

The FQ-T is a 25-item self-report instrument developed by Marks and Mathews (1979) to provide a sensitive yet brief device with which to measure pre–post changes among phobics undergoing treatment. The scale was validated on over 1,000 phobic respondents and has good test–retest reliability ($r = .85$). In addition, the concurrent and convergent validity of the FQ-T appears to make it a good candidate for both clinical and research purposes. The scale is sensitive to clinical improvement in that it shows statistically significant differences for agoraphobics undergoing effective treatments. The FQ-T provides a total phobia score as well as subscales including agoraphobia, social anxiety, and blood injury phobia. The FQ-T has been widely endorsed and used by both anxiety disorder researchers and clinicians.

Phobic Anxiety and Avoidance Scale (PAA)

Another popular and clinically sensitive measure is the Phobic Anxiety and Avoidance Scale (PAA). Where possible, it is useful and important to standardize measures across treatment centers. Both in the United States and abroad, the major research centers have each used rating scales for both avoidance behavior and anxiety as originated by Marks and Gelder (1966) and later modified by Watson and Marks (1971). Subjects rate five to ten of their most severe phobic situations on a 9-point rating scale of phobic anxiety and avoidance. The ratings range from 0, representing no anxiety or avoidance, to a maximum score of 8, representing a severe phobic state with continuous phobic anxiety, panic, and invariable phobic avoidance. The scores of these situations are typically averaged to yield a mean clinical measure of phobic anxiety and avoidance.

Self-Report–Mobility Inventory for Agoraphobia (MI)

The MI (Chambless, Caputo, Jasin, Gracely, & Williams, 1985) is a 29-item scale that is rated four times each on a 5-point Likert-type scale. Clients complete items according to how much these situations are avoided, both if the client were alone and if he or she were accompanied. In addition, clients rate how much anxiety or discomfort they would experience if alone or accompanied in these same situations. The MI also provides a panic frequency measure—a report of a number of panic attacks experienced in the past 7 days.

The MI was designed to measure self-reported severity of agoraphobic avoidance and anxiety. The authors note that, unlike other fear questionnaires, the MI allows for a distinction between phobic avoidance and discomfort in situations where the agoraphobic is alone as opposed to accompanied. Since agoraphobics often use significant others to reduce their phobic anxiety or avoidance, it is important to ascertain the situational specificity of the phobic anxiety/avoidance pattern.

Extensive reliability and validity data were collected and reported in the investigation (Chambless et al., 1985). All four subscales were found to be normally distributed, highly internally consistent, and highly reliable over a 31-day pretreatment test interval.

Individual item reliability was also high, with correlations ranging from .48 to .90 (median $r = .76$). Analyses revealed high intercorrelations between the avoidance-alone and discomfort-alone ratings. Therefore, only avoidance-scale ratings were considered in subsequent analyses. The MI demonstrated excellent clinical sensitivity in reflecting pre–post treatment differences and good validity indices. The authors state (p. 40):

> The MI scales offer well-validated assessment measures a broad range of agoraphobic avoidance behavior. This sample of items wider than previous inventories makes the scale more useful for planning behavioral treatment as well as a sensitive measure for research. Moreover, the scale provides an important distinction in measuring avoidance alone and accompanied. This considerable number of agoraphobics are quite mobile when accompanied but severely restricted when on their own.

Finally, as discussed by the authors, many clients seeking treatment report significant situational phobic anxiety with only moderate phobic avoidance. In these cases, data from the present study support the application of the MI to obtain discomfort ratings. Similarly, individual items on the avoidance scales can also be used with confidence with regard to treatment planning.

Anxiety

In addition to assessing clients' phobic anxiety and behavioral avoidance, it is also important to evaluate their level of generalized anxiety to examine its potential mediating effect on therapeutic process and outcome. One of many (Zung Anxiety Scale, Hamilton Anxiety Scale, etc.) anxiety scales used in the assessment of agoraphobia is the Taylor Manifest Anxiety Scale (TMAS) (Taylor, 1953). The scale is used to measure subjects' severity and types of anxiety symptoms. Test–retest reliability over a 3-week period yielded a correlation of .89, which is regarded as psychometrically sound. The scale has good construct, concurrent, and convergent validity. The device has demonstrated good clinical sensitivity as a treatment outcome measure. The TMAS provides specific clinical information regarding clients' level and severity of anxiety-related symptomatology. Therefore, it or a comparable device should be considered in agoraphobia assessment as a method of ascertaining the efficacy of treatment in reducing generalized anxiety symptoms.

Somatic Experiences

The Body Sensations Questionnaire (BSQ) (Chambless, Caputo, Bright, & Gallagher, 1984) is a 17-item scale designed for agoraphobia that includes items assessing sensations associated with autonomic arousal. Agoraphobics report exaggerated fear reactions, often triggered by internal sensations associated with anticipatory or *in vivo* anxiety, resulting in a hypervigilant individual. Chambless and her colleagues developed this self-report questionnaire to identify somatic symptoms that agoraphobics find particularly distressing. Each item is rated on a 5-point scale ranging from not frightened or worried by this sensation (1) to extremely frightened by this sensation (5). The total score is derived by averaging the individual items or events. Typical items from the BSQ include pressure in the chest, numbness in arms and legs, heart palpitations, dizziness, nausea, sweating, disorientation, and confusion. The BSQ was found to be highly internally consistent (Cronbach's α = .87) and stable over a test–retest interval of 31 days (r = .67). Analyses from data for a replication sample revealed, once again, that the scale was internally consistent (α = .88) and moderately reliable (r = .66), for a 6-day interval. The BSQ was found to be clinically-sensitive to treatment effects reflecting significant changes from pre- to posttreatment. In addition, the BSQ discriminated between responses of agoraphobics and those of normal control cohorts.

Panic

Another component of agoraphobia requiring assessment is the presence of panic attacks which are ubiquitous among agoraphobics. Several clinical scales are currently in use, although there are only limited data on their reliability or validity. One scale used at the Agoraphobia Program examines the presence or absence of spontaneous panic attacks during the past week. Spontaneous panic attacks are operationally defined as panic episodes occurring at home without obvious environmental provocation (e.g., family arguments, upsetting phone calls). Several outcome studies reveal the measure reflects treatment outcome differences across conditions. Research is currently under way in North America and Europe to develop reliable and valid measures of panic, which is viewed by some authors as a distinct entity with four or five subtypes, and by other researchers as merely an extreme dimension of the anxiety continuum.

Recently, Michelson (1986a) devised the Daily Symptom Checklist (DSC) to assess the frequency, intensity, duration, predictability, and controllability of clients' anxiety experiences. The DSC includes 30 items divided between cognitive (feelings of losing control) and somatic (difficulty breathing) dimensions. Clients are instructed to record *all* anxiety episodes that they experience as distinct from their baseline (i.e., their normal anxiety state) levels. For each episode, clients check any of the symptoms listed on the form that were manifested. Although cross-center research is now under way to examine the clinical-research utility of the DSC, preliminary reports indicate the checklist is an efficient, reliable, and sensitive device for systematically measuring anxiety elevations (including panic) on a daily basis. Furthermore, the use of both somatic *and* cognitive items provides important treatment planning, process, and outcome information for both clinicians and researchers.

Depression

The presence of clinical depression or dysphoria should be probed for since it is often associated with agoraphobia and to evaluate the impact of treatment on mood. The Beck Depression Inventory (BDI) (Beck, Ward, Mendelsohn, Mock, & Erbaugh, 1961), one of the most widely used instruments to evaluate depression, consists of 21 items containing four alternative statements. The BDI, originally standardized on a sample of 598 psychiatric patients at the Philadelphia General Hospital, has a split-half reliability of .93. The BDI has been found to correlate .61–.66 with ratings of depression made by independent clinicians. In a more recent study, Williams showed that the BDI correlated

.67 with behavioral measures of depression and .82 with the Hamilton Depression Rating Scale. In addition, the BDI has good discriminative validity between anxiety and depression, and is sensitive to treatment effects (Michelson, Mavissakalian, & Marchione, 1985).

General Symptomatology

In addition to examining phobic anxiety avoidance, generalized anxiety, and depression, it is valuable to monitor clients' general symptomatology in both treatment planning and monitoring generalization effects. One of the most reliable and valid general symptomatology scales is the Hopkins Symptom Checklist (HSCL) (Derogatis, Lipman, Rickels, Uhlenhuth, & Coir, 1974). The abbreviated HSCL, often used in agoraphobia research, comprises 58 items, each of which describes a psychiatric symptom. Each item is rated by the subject on a 5-point scale describing the degree to which the subject experienced discomfort from that problem during the past 7 days. Ratings are made on a 5-point scale from 0 (not at all) to 4 (extremely). Five primary symptom scales were derived from the checklist: (1) somatization, (2) obsessive–compulsive, (3) interpersonal sensitivity, (4) depression, and (5) anxiety. In addition, an overall global severity index is scored, which is the total of all ratings. The instrument has been standardized and has yielded internal consistency αs ranging from .77 to .90 and test–retest correlation ranging from .78 to .90. The scale shows good concurrent, convergent, and discriminative validity. In addition, as reported by Derogatis et al. (1974), the scale is responsive to pre–post clinical changes. Overall, the scale's development has followed sound psychometric and clinical principles and has resulted in a useful instrument that can be used as both an outcome and a generalization measure.

Generalization Measures

Several scales have been used by various research centers to examine the generalization effects of treatment to other areas of functioning.

The Locke–Wallace Marital Adjustment Scale (L–W) (Locke & Wallace, 1959) is a 15-item questionnaire developed to measure marital adjustment. The scale consists of a 7-point anchored scale of overall happiness within the marriage, 10 items regarding the couple's agreement or disagreement in areas such as philosophy of life, in-laws, affection, sex, finances, recreation, conventionality, and friends; and 4 multiple-choice general responses, such as "Have you ever wished you had not married?" The reliability coefficient computed by the split-half technique and corrected by Spearman–Brown prophecy formula was reported as .90 (Locke & Wallace, 1959), with a test–retest reliability of .78. The scale has been successfully employed in several investigations to monitor marital adjustment in relation to outcome and maintenance of agoraphobia treatment. Typically, both the client and the spouse complete the scale. The monitoring of marital adjustment has its role in light of studies suggesting that marital satisfaction may play a role in therapeutic outcome and long-term maintenance.

Rotter's (1954) Internal–External Locus of Control (IE) is derived from social learning theory and has been defined as the generalized expectancy of reinforcement contingent on one's own behavior. Locus of control is a construct that attempts to identify self-perceptions and attributions related to personal causality and so might offer insight into clients' differential responsivity to treatment. Despite a voluminous clinical research literature, there are only a few studies examining its utility with agoraphobics. In general, studies have consistently reported positive associations between externality and anxiety (Nelson & Phares, 1971). Archer (1980) found that locus of control, trait anxiety, and situationally bound stimuli interact to result in various patterns of stress response (i.e., psychopathology).

Michelson, Mavissakalian, and Meminger (1983) investigated the prognostic utility of locus of control in the treatment of agoraphobia. Michelson et al. examined locus of control among 50 agoraphobics who participated in a 2 × 2 factorial design study where subjects were randomly assigned to either imipramine plus flooding, imipramine alone, flooding alone, or control condition (programmed practice). Despite marked pre–post improvements, the IE scale was found to be lacking in clinical sensitivity with regard to reflecting these changes. However, the IE scale was found to have utility as a prognostic index of posttreatment levels of functioning, with externality being strongly associated with improvement. Pretreatment internality–externality was a significant predictor of low versus high improvement at the posttreatment phase. Interestingly, the predictive power of the scale was applicable only with subjects rated as being "external" in their locus of control at pretreatment. The results revealed higher rates of improvement among externally oriented subjects, with no differences obtained between internals in regard to their levels of improvement at posttreatment. These results suggest that the IE may lack sensitivity to therapeutic change with respect to reflecting improvements among homogeneous populations of severe agoraphobics. However, the scale does have certain predictive utility for differentiating low from high improvers.

One hypothesis offered to explain these findings is that external subjects may be more receptive to therapeutic influence and persuasion to carry out the principles of *in vivo* exposure, which was the common denominator of all treatment conditions. Conversely, internally oriented subjects may be more independent and self-reliant, to the point that they may be less compliant with therapeutic instructions and directive (i.e., behavioral) treatments. Results from other studies suggest that externals may achieve optimal benefit from a highly structured therapeutic experience, whereas internals benefit more from unstructured clinical strategies. Additional research is needed to delineate the mechanisms by which individual internal–external orientation affects therapeutic response to cognitive-behavioral treatments of agoraphobia.

Temporal Stability of Self-Report Measures in Agoraphobia Assessment

Test–retest reliabilities were performed on some of the preceding measures (cf. Michelson & Mavissakalian, 1983) as part of an ongoing series of investigations supported by the NIMH to the author. Forty subjects meeting DSM-III criteria for agoraphobia completed on two occasions a comprehensive assessment battery. The measures encompassed anxiety, phobia, depression, and general symptomatology dimensions of functioning and consisted of instruments widely employed as outcome measures in agoraphobia research. The test–retest time periods were divided into 4-, 10-, and 16-week intervals to ascertain their temporal stability, an often ignored yet important psychometric parameter that is particularly crucial for clinical outcome studies relying on those scales. As seen in Table 9-1, the agoraphobia assessment instruments were temporally stable over both short and extended time periods.

Overall, the measures exhibited good temporal stability. As expected, the test–retest reliability of the various scales' subscores was generally inferior to that of the total scores. The only exception was the use of the Agoraphobia Subscale of the Fear Questionnaire, which had high reliability across all assessment periods.

In a recent study (Michelson, 1986), the assessment battery's internal consistency was examined using α reliability coefficients on a sample of 160 agoraphobics (DSM-III) with a mean age of 36.9 years, a mean age of onset of 26.6 years, and a mean duration of illness of 10 years. Although additional analyses are currently underway, preliminary psychometric computations reveal good to excellent internal reliability coefficients for many of the measures used in agoraphobia research and clinical practice. The scales, and their α reliability coefficients, were as follows: Fear Survey Schedule = .97; Fear Questionnaire T; FQAG = .64, FQ–Blood Injury = .75, FQ–Social Phobia = .71, FQ Total "A" = .82, FQ Total "B" = .71; Rotter's Locus of Control = .78; Taylor Manifest Anxiety Scale = .91; Beck Depression Inventory = .87; Hopkins Symptom Checklist— Somatization Subscale = .86; Obsessive–Compulsive Subscale = .87; Interpersonal Sensitivity = .85; Depression = .86; Anxiety = .82; and Total Scale = .96. Overall, these data reveal that the various measures used in major phobia centers generally possess good reliability in terms of their internal consistency and temporal stability. Further, all these measures have demonstrated clinical sensitivity to treatment effects—that is, pre- to posttreatment changes across investigations conducted in various centers in the United States, Canada, and Europe.

Behavioral Assessment

Historically, behavioral assessment has played an important role in the expansion of behavioral interventions for anxiety disorders. Three primary behavioral assessment strategies are used in the measurement and treatment of agoraphobia: (1) Standardized Behavioral Avoidance Tests (S-BAT), (2) Idiosyncratic Behavioral Avoidance Tests, and (3) behavioral diaries of self-directed *in vivo* exposure practice. A critique of these behavioral measures vis-à-vis agoraphobia is presented to highlight their major advantages, limitations, and research issues.

STANDARDIZED BEHAVIORAL AVOIDANCE TESTS (S-BAT)

The S-BAT dates back almost two decades to the use of structured walks for anxiety clients, as reported by Agras, Leitenberg, and Barlow (1968). The Agoraphobia Program at the University of Pittsburgh uses a Standardized Behavioral Avoidance Course (S-BAC) as a direct and naturalistic behavioral measure of agoraphobic functioning. The S-BAC is one mile in length and is divided into 20 approximately equal segments, beginning from the front door of the hospital and ending at a crowded urban shopping and business center. Clients are requested to walk the course alone at each assessment.

TABLE 9.1 Temporal stability of agoraphobia outcome measures at 4-, 10-, and 16-week intervals

Measure	Period 1—4 weeks			Period 2—10 weeks			Period 3—16 weeks		
	Test $\bar{X}$	Retest $\bar{X}$	Corr.	Test $\bar{X}$	Retest $\bar{X}$	Corr.	Test $\bar{X}$	Retest $\bar{X}$	Corr.
Self-Rating of Severity	5.5	5.4	.81	5.5	5.2	.91	6.4	5.8	.76
Hopkins Symptom Checklist									
Obsessive–compulsive subscores	17.00	15.69	.60	15.50	15.14	.89	15.00	14.46	.84
Depression subscore	22.38	22.08	.68	21.29	19.86	.77	20.00	19.77	.84
Anxiety subscore	17.69	17.46	.74	15.50	15.21	.69	16.77	15.31	.77
Somatic subscore	24.08	23.31	.76	23.14	23.57	.92	24.00	21.46	.86
Interpersonal subscore	15.85	16.23	.65	14.21	13.07	.78	14.00	13.69	.79
Total score	97.00	94.15	.75	89.64	86.07	.86	89.69	84.69	.84
Fear Survey Schedule									
-Total	146.38	154.54	.82	141.14	132.21	.89	139.62	120.69	.90
Fear Questionnaire									
Agoraphobia subscore	29.46	31.62	.86	29.43	25.93	.86	33.69	31.62	.85
Blood-injury subscore	17.08	19.00	.34	13.14	10.93	.73	14.69	14.15	.86
Social phobia subscore	19.69	21.77	.61	17.50	15.79	.81	16.46	14.08	.84
Total "A"	66.23	72.38	.69	60.07	51.79	.71	64.85	59.85	.90
Total "B"	20.15	19.08	.58	21.36	18.07	.58	19.31	16.54	.90
Taylor Manifest Anxiety Scale (abbreviated form)	19.77	19.92	.90	23.21	19.93	.85	16.69	17.23	.71
Beck Depression Inventory	14.23	13.42	.69	17.64	15.85	.86	13.38	13.62	.84

Source: L. Michelson & M. Mavissakalian, "Temporal Stability of Self-Report Measures in Agoraphobia Research," *Behaviour Research and Therapy*, 21 (1983), 695–698.

Their *in vivo* phobic anxiety and distance traveled away from the front door of the hospital are used as dependent variables. In addition, psychophysiological monitoring and *in vivo* cognitions are also recorded, as described subsequently. Standardized behavioral assessments, such as the S-BAC just described, are used in most agoraphobia clinical research centers.

Advantages of the S-BAC include its provision of a standardized strategy with which to compare clients directly for severity of fears and phobias and to compare scores of *in vivo* anxiety and behavioral avoidance across alternative treatments. The S-BAC also offers a means of direct assessment of fear in psychophysiological and cognitive response systems as well, permitting *in vivo* tripartite monitoring. Since subjects also rate each segment of the S-BAC on a 0–8 SUDS (Subject Units of Discomfort Scale), an index of their subjective *in vivo* anxiety can be used as both a process and an outcome measure.

One of the disadvantages of the S-BAC is that only a single behavior is evaluated— that is, walking a specific course. Hence, subjects with only modest limitations in walking unaccompanied may not find the task sufficiently challenging. Furthermore, questions of "experimental demand effects" with regard to pleasing the experimenter or therapist have been shown to influence mildly fearful individuals (Borkovec, Weertz, & Bernstein, 1977), although there is little empirical evidence that these findings generalize to more severe clinical populations (i.e., agoraphobia). Borkovec (1973a, 1973b) advises the routine use of high demand instructions to minimize potential pre- and posttest demand effect differences as a means of controlling for these nuisance effects.

IDIOSYNCRATIC BEHAVIORAL AVOIDANCE TESTS (I-BAT)

In light of the potential limitations of the S-BAC with regard to generalizability to other realms of functioning, Individualized Behavioral Avoidance Tests (I-BAT) have also been used both in the United States and abroad. Mathews et al. (1981) reported using a 15-item hand-tailored hierarchy of phobic situations that they routinely employ. Clients are requested to attempt each of the idiosyncratic assignments until they reach a point where they can no longer attempt a new item. The scores from the I-BAT generally consist of the number of completed steps. As critiqued by O'Brien and Barlow (1985), however, there are at least two major problems with the scoring method. First, the number of items completed is largely influenced by clients' specific choices of initial items to attempt. Second, the client's behavioral performance provides no information about the *absolute* level of difficulty of the completed phobic tasks.

An Idiosyncratic Behavioral Avoidance Course (I-BAC) was employed in a major outcome study where subjects were requested to complete five idiosyncratic phobic situations identified from their phobic anxiety and avoidance scales (Mavissakalian & Michelson, 1986). The number of situations subjects could enter and remain in for at least 5 minutes was recorded. Subjects also rated their peak level of anxiety during the completed task using the SUDS scale. The I-BAC provided a sensitive measure of both *in vivo* anxiety and idiosyncratic phobic avoidance.

I-BACs have both inherent advantages and corresponding limitations. The obvious advantage is that the assessment can be individually tailored to the specific behavioral deficits and phobic situations for each client. This increases the clinical sensitivity of the overall assessment battery. Unfortunately, since the I-BAC focuses on idiosyncratic situations, comparisons with other subjects, groups, or studies are greatly limited. Hence, I-BACs are generally viewed as more appropriate for within-group comparisons, as in single-case experimental designs, than for between-group experimental outcome studies. In addition, the I-BAC is a time-consuming, relatively expensive, and inefficient assessment strategy when assessing large numbers of clients. Finally, the I-BAC appears to be highly correlated with the S-BAC, raising pragmatic questions as to how much unique variance it contributes to the overall assessment battery.

BEHAVIORAL DIARIES

Self-monitoring of *in vivo* exposure practice, conducted between formal treatment sessions, is a valuable clinical procedure in the treatment of agoraphobia. Many clinicians and most investigators routinely use behavioral diaries to obtain specific data concerning the dimensions and parameters of clients' self-directed exposure (SDE) activities. Behavioral diaries are typically given and collected on a weekly basis. Clients are carefully instructed on how to record all their SDE activities systematically. The diaries generally include the following information: date, time out, time in, whether alone or accompanied, *in vivo* anxiety levels (SUDS), time spent at the destination, and whether the outing was a practice session or just part of the client's normal routine. In addition, subjects' peak anxiety levels can also be assessed. *Practice* is defined as outings undertaken solely for therapeutic purposes. At each clinic visit diaries are reviewed and orally verified. The variables derived from the behavioral diaries can be classified according to the following categories: (1) *frequency* of weekly outings (total and practice outings); (2) *duration* of weekly outings (total time, mean time, practice time alone); and (3) *in vivo anxiety* (SUDS), which includes mean and peak SUDS, both alone and accompanied.

Clinically, behavioral diaries provide a fine-grained delineation of clients' phobic anxiety, phobic avoidance, practice problems, successes, and use of coping skills. The therapist then makes recommendations collaborating with the client to facilitate increased SDE practices. In both clinical and research settings, it is recommended that subjects keep a daily behavioral record of all their SDE outings and practices, recording whether they are alone or accompanied. Their progress should be reviewed weekly with reported gains and improvement reinforced. Clients can then be assigned increasingly difficult phobic tasks and encouraged to proceed with their SDE practices (see the section on programmed practice later).

Although the use of behavioral diaries has increased over the past decade, empirical studies of the utility of self-directed *in vivo* exposure practice in therapeutic outcome for agoraphobics has only recently appeared in the scientific literature. Previous studies such as that by Jannoun, Munby, Catalin, & Gelder (1980), Mathews, Teasdale, Munby, Johnston, & Shaw (1977) have used only relatively few of the many possible diary variables. Recently, Mavissakalian and Michelson (1984) examined the role of self-directed *in vivo* exposure practice in behavioral and pharmacologic treatments of agoraphobia. Forty-nine severe and chronic agoraphobics (DSM-III) were treated with either combined imipramine plus flooding, imipramine alone, or flooding alone; the control condition consisted of programmed practice. Interestingly, none of the behavioral diary measures such as number of outings, number of outings alone, number of practices, or time spent in these activities differentiated treatment groups or discriminated between low and high end state functioning subjects at posttreatment. However, lower levels of anxiety (i.e., SUDS) during *in vivo* outings in general and practice outings in particular appeared to differentiate both effective treatments and highly improved clients. The discrepancy between the behavioral and subjective diary measures, coupled with the significantly greater improvement obtained in the flooding, imipramine, and combined conditions, suggests that therapist-assisted *in vivo* exposure combined with programmed practice enhances the therapeutic benefit derived from an equivalent amount of practice. The differences found on the *in vivo* anxiety measures from the diaries suggest that greater therapeutic effects were derived from the addition of exposure when it was conducted with the therapist, effects that may be mediated through increased habituation of phobic anxiety. Clinically, these results suggest that therapist-assisted *in vivo* exposure might help reduce excessive autonomic arousal and facilitate habituation during self-directed exposure outings. The question of whether imipramine offered similar advantages is highly controversial, particularly in light of recent findings in the same investigation revealing that imipramine-treated subjects experienced psychophysiological increases (i.e., worsening) on many crucial outcome measures. These data support the inclusion of behavioral diaries to provide a more careful delineation of subjects' SDE practices between formal treatment sessions.

In another, independent investigation, Michelson, Mavissakalian, Marchione, Dancu, and Greenwald (1986) examined the role of SDE across cognitive, behavioral, and psychophysiologically based treatments of agoraphobia. Thirty-nine severe and chronic agoraphobics (DSM-III) were randomly assigned to either paradoxical intention (PI), graduated exposure (GE), or progressive deep-muscle relaxation training (RT). Treatment consisted of 12 2-hour, weekly sessions with all subjects receiving programmed practice exposure instructions in addition to their primary treatment. Systematic behavioral diary recordings of all SDE practices, *in vivo* anxiety, duration, and accompaniment were analyzed across and within treatments.

Differential temporal patterns of SDE were revealed across treatments. RT and GE were highly effective, potent, and rapid treatment strategies for fostering SDE practice with regard to complying with treatment instructions and decreasing *in vivo* anxiety. GE appeared to exert significant differential therapeutic effects on SUDS levels, whereas RT exerted more influence on behavioral practice, followed closely by decrements on *in vivo* anxiety measures. Conversely, PI was significantly slower and less potent in its effects with regard to fostering SDE.

Linear regression and discriminant function analyses were conducted to identify which behavioral diary measures were significantly associated with end state functioning at posttreatment. The analyses revealed that SDE variables, particularly subjective anxiety and the behavioral measures, were significantly associated with higher end state functioning at posttreatment. SUDS variables (i.e., *in vivo* anxiety) played a significant role in subsequent therapeutic outcome throughout the entire treatment course. These results highlight the importance of anxiety management training as an important consideration in facilitating both posttreatment and follow-up functioning. It appears to mediate self-directed exposure practices—that is, habituation and overall improvement. In addition, behavioral practice appeared to play an important role as an active component in the context of developing and using self-control coping strategies.

Physiological Assessment

A crucial but infrequently used assessment strategy in agoraphobia treatment and research is the measurement of psychophysiological functioning. In light of the tripartite model of anxiety, and the evidence supporting the effects of psychosocial treatments on physiological processes (Blanchard & Young, 1974), the paucity of physiological assessment in both clinical and research settings is surprising. As observed by Bellack and Lombardo (1985, p. 69),

> Arousal of a sympathetic division of the autonomic nervous system plays a dominant role on most theories of emotion . . . and is widely accepted as a central component of anxiety. For this reason, measurement of physiological arousal is viewed as an integral part of anxiety measurement.

Unlike self-report and behavioral responses, which are under the voluntary control of the subject, physiological measures are relatively immune from potential expectancy bias effects because of the generally involuntary nature of the responses and systems assessed (Bellack & Lombardo, 1985). In addition to being relatively free from demand characteristics and biasing effects, physiological assessments have been regarded as reliable since they are obtained via objective methods that are replicable across various devices. Potential disadvantages with psychophysiological assessment concern the need for expensive equipment and knowledgable technicians, and the reliance on laboratory rather than *in vivo* assessment to ensure reliable and valid evaluations of psychophysiological states.

Although there are relatively few studies examining psychophysiological processes or outcome of agoraphobics undergoing therapy, heart rate has generally been regarded as the most useful index of treatment effects. Heart rate has generally been found to be a reliable and valid index of psychophysiological arousal and anxiety. It is also the most commonly used physiologic measure of fear among clinical researchers in both North America and Europe. Assessment of heart rate also allows for the use of *ambulatory* naturalistic, *in vivo* recordings like those provided by either the Exersentry Monitor or Medilog Recorder, innovative and reliable devices that accurately record *in vivo* heart rate. Conversely, there are few, if any, generally agreed on, reliable, and accurate ambulatory devices that allow for simultaneous assessment of other physiological channels such as galvanic skin responses, electromyography, or respiration. These latter physiological indices are generally restricted to controlled laboratory environments, with a resultant loss of naturalistic *in vivo* responses and diminution of the external validity of the assessment. Extraneous factors including temperature, barometric pressure, and the proximity of radio transmitters can all influence the reliability of the *in vivo* recordings of GSR, EMG, and respiration. The Exersentry and Medilog Systems, however, are not affected by these nuisance variables and offer reliable and valid measures of heart rate outside the laboratory setting.

At the University of Pittsburgh research center, heart rate measures have consistently reflected differential treatment effects that are corroborated with other self-report and independent rater measures. Across several large-scale NIMH investigations, heart rate patterns typically display reductions over the course of treatment. Hence, both within subjects and across experimental groups, heart rate accurately reflects improvement, synchrony, concordance, and outcome status (cf. Michelson & Mavissakalian,

1985; Michelson, Mavissakalian, & Marchione, 1985). Therefore, given the current status of the psychophysiological assessment of phobias, heart rate should be routinely collected in research programs as both a process and an outcome measure.

Two examples of the use of psychophysiological assessment of agoraphobia are presented next. In the first study, Michelson and Mavissakalian (1985) examined the psychophysiological outcome of agoraphobics undergoing behavioral and pharmacologic treatments. As previously noted, 62 severe and chronic agoraphobics participated in the 2×2 factorial study examining the relative and combined efficacy of behavior therapy (prolonged *in vivo* exposure) and pharmacotherapy (imipramine). Tripartite assessments were conducted at pretreatment and at 4 weeks, 8 weeks, 12 weeks, and at 1 month posttreatment. The study revealed significant differential, temporal response and treatment patterns across the *in vivo* psychophysiological measures collected during the S-BAC. Overall, the findings supported the superiority of graduated *in vivo* exposure in effecting more rapid psychophysiological improvements. Conversely, imipramine-treated subjects actually experienced significant increases (i.e., worsening) on many crucial heart rate measures.

Protocol subjects were also compared with normative, nonphobic cohorts at pre- and posttreatment. As expected, agoraphobics evidenced significantly higher rates of physiological reactivity prior to treatment. As treatment progressed, however, there were temporal decreases in these physiological differences between normal and agoraphobic subjects during treatment. By the final assessment phase, treated agoraphobics did not differ significantly from their nonagoraphobic counterparts on any of the psychophysiological measures collected on the S-BAC.

Synchrony–desynchrony and concordance–disconcordance phenomena were also examined and yielded significant findings with regard to both process and outcome status. Another important finding was that "synchronizers" (subjects exhibiting tripartite concordance) exhibited significantly greater behavioral, physiological, and self-report improvement than did subjects identified as "desynchronizers" (i.e., subjects experiencing high levels of disconcordance across the tripartite channels). Moreover, there were significantly greater synchrony rates among exposure subjects, suggesting that this modality facilitated more rapid response symmetry than did pharmacotherapy. There were no additive effects for combining exposure with imipramine with regard to fostering synchrony.

Another study demonstrating the importance of assessing psychophysiological dimensions of agoraphobia is the investigation by Michelson, Mavissakalian, and Marchione (1985), which examined psychophysiological outcomes of agoraphobics undergoing cognitive and behavioral treatments for agoraphobia. This NIMH investigation examined the relative efficacy of paradoxical intention (PI), graduated exposure (GE), and progressive deep-muscle relaxation training (RT) for 39 severe and chronic agoraphobics (DSM-III) who received 12 2-hour weekly sessions. A comprehensive assessment battery was employed including direct measures of behavioral and psychophysiological functioning at pre-, mid-, and posttreatment and at the 3-month follow-up. One of the objectives of the investigation was to examine the relative effectiveness of these alternative treatments and delineate differential response patterns across behavioral, self-report, and psychophysiological domains. A continuous record of heart rate was obtained using the Exersentry (model EX3) heart monitor during the standardized behavioral avoidance course. Heart rate monitoring began with a 5-minute resting (i.e., sitting) baseline followed by a 5-minute walking baseline during which subjects walked at their normal pace with a research assistant within the hospital which is then followed by the S-BAC. Heart rate variables selected for analyses included mean heart rate while sitting (baseline 1), mean heart rate while walking (baseline 2), and mean heart rate for the entire S-BAC. The sitting and walking baselines provided a relative baseline for resting and general activity levels of arousal. The mean heart rate for the entire S-BAC provided an overall index for the physiological effects of the treatments on reducing excessive *in vivo* psychophysiologic phobic arousal.

Significant pre- to posttreatment improvements were observed for GE and RT on the heart rate sitting and walking measure and on the mean heart rate for the S-BAC. Conversely, PI exhibited no pre–posttreatment gains on the heart rate variables and actually evidenced moderate increases in arousal. Interestingly, examining pretreatment to follow-up phases revealed significant improvement for the PI and RT conditions on heart rate sitting and walking measures. The results revealed delayed psychophysiological benefits for PI, indicating that treatment requires greater time for subjects to consolidate and effectively use their newly acquired cognitive coping skills. The data revealed that GE and RT were significantly superior to PI at posttreatment in reducing psychophysiological arousal. By the 3-month follow-up, however, these differences were no longer significant. The enhanced functioning of both the GE and the RT subjects was evident across the major assessment domains. However, RT subjects did experience increases in physiological arousal from the posttreatment to 3-month follow-up. These results suggest that RT may need to be combined with concurrent behavioral strategies such as *in vivo* exposure, to decrease psychophysiological reactivity *in vivo* and facilitate greater levels of end state functioning and long-term maintenance. Hence, the combination of RT or cognitive treatment with exposure might prove to have beneficial synergistic effects.

Both the Michelson and Mavissakalian (1985) and the Michelson, Mavissakalian, and Marchione (1985) studies offer empirical support for monitoring psychophysiological domains, particularly in delineating differential treatment patterns in tripartite functioning. In both investigations the measurement of psychophysiological reactions provided critical data on the efficacy of these modalities in targeting one of the pivotal dimensions of the disorder—psychophysiology. Moreover, to offset potential problems with regard to *response stereotype*, *response specificity*, and *demand characteristics*, the use of multiple physiological measures that are monitored simultaneously would prove to be a significant advance in the psychophysiological assessment of agoraphobia and of anxiety disorders in general. Recognizing the role of individual differences in which response patterns are evoked, modified, or responded to, therapeutic intervention requires the use of multiple, concurrent, psychophysiological assessment. It is likely that technological advances in ambulatory *in vivo* monitoring of additional psychophysiological channels will allow for the concomitant and naturalistic assessment of other psychophysiological parameters as well.

Physiological responses have been effectively used in the classification of blood phobics (Öst, Jerremalm, & Johansson, 1984); social phobics; social anxiety (Beidel &

Turner, 1985); claustrophobics (Öst, Johansson, & Jerremalm, 1982); and agoraphobics (Michelson, 1984b, 1985; Öst et al., 1984). In addition, ambulatory monitoring of clients with panic disorder has been reported by Freedman, Ianni, Ettedgui, and Puthezhath (1985). Twelve subjects with panic disorder and 11 control subjects received 24-hour ambulatory monitoring of heart rate, finger temperature, ambient temperature, and self-rated anxiety. Although no differences were found between groups on tonic levels on any measure, or in their patterns of variation throughout the period, substantial heart rate increases and finger temperature alterations did occur during panic attacks but not during control periods with equally high anxiety ratings. Hence, the application of ambulatory monitoring devices holds much promise in the diagnosis, assessment, and treatment of panic attacks.

Although psychophysiological assessment of agoraphobia is clearly a topical area of research, the application of psychophysiological monitoring raises several concerns. For example, Arena, Blanchard, Andraski, Cotch, and Myers (1983) found only modest reliability coefficients for several psychophysiological measures with 15 college (nonclinical sample) students between the ages of 18 and 23. The authors report examining EMG, heart rate, hand surface temperature, skin resistance level, cephalic vasomotor response, and forearm flexor EMG. This study addressed questions regarding the temporal reliability of these psychophysiological measures. Frontalis EMG appeared to exhibit consistently high reliability coefficients. Hand surface temperature manifested high reliability between sessions repeated within 1 week. Heart rate and forearm flexor EMG indexes were somewhat less consistently reliable. As noted by the authors, however (Arena et al., 1983, p. 458):

> The finding that many of these psychophysiological measures are not highly reliable for normal individuals does not necessarily imply that on a clinical population, there would be similar or even less reliability. Indeed, the postulate of physiological response specificity (Ingle, 1972) would predict that individuals with psychophysiological disorders might quite reliably experience their arousal in one response area.

Hence, further studies are currently underway in several anxiety disorder centers to examine empirically the reliability of physiological measures for the various anxiety disorders.

Cognitive Assessment

The area of cognitive assessment in anxiety disorders has expanded rapidly in both theory and technique (cf. Merluzzi, Glass, & Genest, 1981). In this book, Emery and Tracy (Chapter 1), Martzke et al. (Chapter 3), and Kendall and Ingram (Chapter 4) have cogently reviewed and synthesized the major conceptual, methodological, research, and clinical dimensions of cognitive assessment, particularly as it interfaces with cognitive-behavioral treatments of anxiety disorders. The aim of this section will be to narrow the focus more specifically to cognitive assessment of agoraphobia with regard to current theory and application.

Neisser (1967) described "cognition" as "all the processes by which the sensory input is transformed, reduced, elaborated, stored, recovered and used" (p. 4). Shaw and

Dobson (1981, p. 361) elaborated this definition further by stating that "The cognitive processes include sensation, perception, imagery, attention, recall, memory, problem-solving, and thinking; in short all of the processes generally defined under the rubric of information processing and problem-solving." Furthermore, they note the importance of distinguishing between cognitive content (e.g., self-statements, imagery, expectations) and cognitive processes (e.g., problem-solving, transfer of information from short to long-term memory). *Cognitive content* is typically used to describe clients' self-reports of their ideation, whereas cognitive processes represent heuristic postulates. In the following sections, promising conceptualizations and techniques in cognitive assessment of agoraphobia will be presented, addressing both cognitive content and processes.

Self-Report

The Agoraphobia Cognitions Questionnaire (ACQ) developed by Chambless et al. (1984), comprises fifteen thoughts concerning negative consequences of experiencing anxiety. Each item is rated on a 5-point scale ranging from "the thought never occurs" (1) to "the thought always occurs" (5) when the client is anxious. A total score is computed by averaging responses across the individual items. The reliability and validity of the ACQ were demonstrated in several ways. The ACQ also reflected significant pre–posttreatment changes and was able to differentiate between agoraphobic and normative groups. The ACQ appears to be a promising instrument for the efficient assessment of agoraphobics' cognitions. The external validity of the ACQ, however, will need to be established to ascertain the degree to which it correlates with agoraphobics' actual *in vivo* cognitions.

In Vivo Cognitive Assessment

As noted by Hollon and Kendall (1981a; p. 319),

> In vivo assessment techniques are those procedures designed to directly sample phenomena of interest when and where they actually occur. Such procedures can be clearly discriminative from traditional approaches to assessment that rely on indirect indices (signs) sampled in context other than those in which, and at times other than when, phenomena of interest occur.

In the Agoraphobia Program at the University of Pittsburgh, clients complete an *in vivo* cognitive assessment during their S-BAC. In addition to monitoring their psychophysiological functioning during the S-BAC, clients are also instructed to verbalize their internal dialogue. This yields a direct, continuous recording of cognitions. In our center, subjects receive specific training in verbalizing cognitions consisting of approximately 15 minutes of instruction, modeling, and rehearsal prior to actually undertaking the S-BAC, during which time they dictate continously their thoughts into an unobtrusive recorder. Caccioppo and Petty (1983) offer several methods for teaching individuals how to increase introspection and reported cognitions. We have found it relatively easy to instruct clients in how to verbalize their cognitions to provide an ongoing stream of thought. Subsequently, the cognitions are analyzed in a blind nonsequential order to reduce potential expectancy bias effects. Major categories for cognitive assessments include: (1) *self-defeating thoughts* and *negative statements*, (2) *positive* or *coping thoughts*, and (3) *task-irrelevant* or *neutral thoughts*.

In the Schwartz and Michelson (1986) investigation of states of mind (discussed subsequently) in agoraphobia, it was found that the primary coding categories used were highly reliable. Specifically, negative, self-defeating statements; positive, coping statements; and neutral, task-irrelevant statements yielded interrater reliability coefficients of 95%, 87%, and 90%, respectively. Moreover, the relationship between positive and negative cognitions revealed systematic changes across time for subjects receiving cognitive-behavioral treatments. In addition, subjects exhibiting high end state functioning, high improvement, and high concordance across the tripartite systems displayed significant differential patterns with regard to the ratio of positive to negative cognitions. These findings provide corroborative evidence of the discriminative and concurrent validity of the *in vivo* cognitive assessment.

Recently, Michelson (1986) examined the temporal stability of the *in vivo* cognitive assessment by having 11 agoraphobics (DSM-III) complete the S-BAC on two occasions separated by a 24-hour period. The test–retest reliability for positive cognitions $= .55$, for negative cognitions $= .93$, and for neutral cognitions $= .58$. Interestingly, the *ratio* measure, defined as the ratio of positive cognitions to positive plus negative cognitions, was highly temporally stable, with a test–retest correlation of .85. These findings provide empirical support for the reliability and clinical research utility of using the "ratio" measure in states-of-mind studies (cf. Schwartz & Michelson, 1986). Additional research is underway to examine the temporal stability and reliability of the sequence and structure of the thoughts generated by the *in vivo* cognitive assessment.

In the Michelson et al. (1982) study examining paradoxical intention versus self-statement training, the *in vivo* cognitive assessment revealed several interesting findings. First, there was a clear trend for self-defeating thoughts to decline with both treatments. However, these changes occurred late, between the mid- and posttreatment phases, underscoring the tenacity of faulty cognitions and the longer periods of time required to change them effectively, without a necessarily corresponding increase in positive statements.

On a more sophisticated level, the integration of and balance between positive and negative cognition (states of mind) (cf. Schwartz & Garamoni, 1986; Schwartz & Michelson, in press) provide a refined structural model for interpreting these findings. Most important, perhaps, is that these *in vivo* cognitive assessment procedures portray important treatment differences and outcome patterns supporting their clinical-research utility. The Schwartz and Michelson study (in press) revealed significant differential treatment patterns and therapeutic outcome phenomena that were significantly associated with the relative balance (i.e., ratio) of positive and negative cognitions observed during the *in vivo* assessment prior to treatment, during treatment, and at posttreatment. Therefore, it is highly recommended that both clinicians and researchers consider the use of *in vivo* cognitive assessment as an important, clinically sensitive, and salient tripartite dimension of agoraphobia that should be considered in clinical practice and research.

States-of-Mind Model in Cognitive Assessment

Schwartz and Garamoni (1984, 1986) originated a structural model of positive and negative states of mind drawing on principles of information processing, cybernetic self-regulation, and intrapersonal communication as well as on the less familiar "golden section" hypothesis. The golden section theorem states that "While we construe most events positively, we attempt to create a harmony between positive and negative events such that the latter make a maximal contribution to the whole" (Benjafield & Adams-Webber, 1976, p. 14). The golden section hypothesis is derived from ancient mathematical calculations traced to Pythagoras and supported by contemporary information-processing theory, which posits that there is an optimal balance between positive and negative cognitions that epitomizes adaptive psychological functioning. The golden section can be defined geometrically by the point on a line that divides it into two segments such that the ratio of the smaller to the larger segment is equal to the ratio of the larger segment to the whole. The equality of these ratios is achieved only when the larger segment is equal to .618 and the smaller segment to .382 of the line. Schwartz and Garamoni (1984, in press) note that the golden section has many unique mathematical properties, has been observed in the growth patterns of plants, and has been incorporated into the design of the Parthenon and other buildings because of its aesthetic properties.

The golden section hypothesis, reviewed extensively by Schwartz and Garamoni (1986), proposes five distinct states of mind (SOM) that generate variables depicting various balances between positive and negative cognitions (i.e., $p \div p + n$). The five SOMs include *negative monologue* (NM), *negative dialogue* (ND), *internal dialogue of conflict* (IDC), *positive dialogue* (PD), and *positive monologue* (PM). The two extreme SOMs, PM and NM, are monologic in nature because their extreme SOMs dominate to such an extent that dialectical processes are precluded. Positive dialogue, internal dialogue of conflict, and negative dialogue represent dialogic forms of thought wherein interactions between positive and negative thoughts are substantially represented.

The ratio of positive cognitions to total number of positive plus negative cognitions can be assigned to one of these five states of mind according to set points and ranges developed by Schwartz and Garamoni. The set points for PD, IDC, and ND are fixed at .618, .500, and .382, respectively. The monologic SOMs, (NM and PM) do not have set points and are thus defined in terms of ranges alone. Schwartz and Garamoni note that the set points are based on the idea that self-regulating, cybernetically controlled systems strive to maintain fixed reference values (i.e., homeostasis). Their SOM model hypothesizes that humans monitor their thoughts and feelings in order to maintain a precise balance between positive and negative elements in their internal dialogue. If this monitoring detects significant deviations from the set point, self-regulatory actions are initiated to restore equilibrium. Functional individuals strive to maintain a set point determined by the golden section proportion of .618. Deviations in either direction from this optimal balance represent increased degrees of dysfunction and/or psychopathology.

Schwartz and Garamoni (1984, 1986) have identified 27 empirical studies, including 5 on psychotherapy outcome, that report positive and negative cognition data suitable to evaluate their SOM model. Congruent with their model, functional samples were characterized by PD, mildly dysfunctional samples by IDC, and moderately dysfunctional samples by ND. For example, the obtained mean SOM proportion for functional samples was .630, which does not differ significantly from their hypothesized PD set point of .618. However, the overall mean SOM for dysfunctionals of .455 did differ significantly from the .618 ideal golden section point. For moderate dysfunctionals, the SOM proportion of .374 did not differ from .382, the ND set point. Therefore, these obtained ranges corresponded closely to the theoretical values predicted by their model.

Schwartz and Michelson (in press) state,

> An important application of the SOM model involves the tracking of changes in SOM as a function of psychotherapy. To date, only a few (5) outcome studies have been identified that reported means for positive and negative cognitions which allowed the calculation of SOM proportions. Those studies which included pretreatment assessments revealed that all pre-treatment SOMs fell within the IDC, ND, or NM SOMs. Hence, negative deviations from the positive dialogue are associated with therapy-seeking behavior. At post-treatment, four of the SOMs fell within the PD range whereas two fell in the IDC range, indicating that psycho-therapy typically results in a shift toward more balanced thinking. Moreover, in comparative outcome studies, it was found that the more effective the treatment, the more consistently the post-treatment SOM's fell in the PD range [cf. Schwartz & Garamoni, 1986].

Schwartz and Michelson (in press) noted that although several therapy outcome studies have used cognitive therapy in the agoraphobia literature, most, unfortunately, did not assess positive and negative cognitions, precluding an SOM analysis. In a study conducted by Williams and Rappaport (1983), cognitive measures were included, but methodological problems, including low reliability ratings for the positive coping thoughts ($r = .62$), raised questions about interpreting these data. Treatment outcome studies conducted at the University of Pittsburgh have overcome most of these method-ological problems by using sophisticated talking-aloud *in vivo* cognitive assessment procedures with consistently high reliability for both positive and negative cognitions. A descriptive analysis of one study (Michelson et al., 1982) in terms of SOM, revealed that pretreatment SOM proportions for both paradoxical intention (PI) and self-statement training (SST) groups were in the ND and NM ranges, respectively. The results of these analyses revealed that (Schwartz & Garamoni, 1986, p. 51):

> The PI group progressed from a pretreatment negative dialogue (.384) to an IDC (.500) at post-treatment maintained this IDC (.545) at 1-month follow-up and then peaked at a low level PM (.714) at 6-months follow-up. The average of the three post-treatment measures was .588, which is within the PD range. The SST group progressed from a pretreatment NM (.249) to a PD (.647) at post-treatment, regressed to an IDC (.523) at 1-month follow-up and returned to a PD (.679) at 6-months follow-up. Interestingly, if the positive and negative cognition scores are averaged across the three post-treatment measures, these combined mean result in an SOM proportion of .618, the PD set point to a thousandth.

Hence, the SOM model provides a theoretically and empirically based framework for studying cognitive changes across the course of psychotherapy in general and agoraphobia in particular. The qualitative dimensions of SOMs (e.g., dialogic versus monologic; balanced versus conflicted) provide a rich and descriptive analysis of longitu-dinal changes in cognition and ideational processes throughout the course of therapy and follow-up. Futhermore, examining SOMs across assessment phases yields patterns of change that can illuminate how clients progress cognitively as they gradually develop and integrate new modes of thinking.

In a recent investigation, Schwartz and Michelson (in press) examined the SOMs for 39 severe and chronic agoraphobics (DSM-III) who participated in an NIMH investigation of the effects of relaxation training (RT) versus paradoxical intention (PT) versus graduated exposure (GE), which consisted of 12 weekly treatment sessions conducted by experienced protocol therapists. A tripartite assessment battery was used including measures of behavior, psychophysiology, and cognitions, which were administered at pre-, mid-, and posttreatment and at 3-month follow-up.

Although the overall results from the investigation (cf. Michelson, Mavissakalian, Marchione, 1985) revealed that all treatments achieved significant improvements across tripartite response systems, the GE and RT conditions evinced the greatest potency and stability of treatment effects, as compared to PI. Since all subjects completed *in vivo* cognitive assessments while they were on the S-BAC, it was possible to calculate SOM proportions for all subjects across the four assessment phases. The results of the study provided empirical support for the SOM model and established its utility for studying the process of cognitive change during psychotherapy. As predicted by the model, the sample of moderately disturbed agoraphobics were characterized by an ND (.437) prior to treatment, achieved a PD at midtreatment (.661) and posttreatment (.649), and progressed to a low-level PM at the 3-month follow-up (.702).

Although the analyses revealed significant temporal progressions in SOMs across all treatments, only high endstate functioning, high-improvement, and tripartite-concordance subjects exhibited changes in SOMs characterized by a rapid increase from pre- to midtreatment followed by stabilization of the cognitive trajectories for midtreatment through 3-month follow-up. Conversely, subjects identified as having low endstate functioning, low improvement, or disconcordance manifested smaller and slower increases in SOM.

These findings suggest that the optimal strategy for agoraphobics struggling to overcome their long-standing phobias may be to push their SOM to the maximal extent while still remaining grounded in a dialogic SOM. This may explain the presence of the low-level PM observed at the follow-up. Hence, the optimal trajectory—almost identical for high endstate functioning, high improvement, and concordance—is characterized by rapid increase in SOM at midtreatment and asymptote at the PD–PM boundary.

With regard to between-group differences, a number of interesting conclusions can be drawn. First, despite differences in their foci, both cognitive and behavioral treatments produced significant and meaningful changes in subjects' internal dialogues. These findings are consistent with Bandura's (1977) assertion that cognition may be altered through behavioral interventions. Interestingly, the psychophysiologically based relaxation training manifested the most unstable trajectory, perhaps reflecting decreased opportunities for these subjects to modify their cognitive structures. Finally, the graduated-exposure modality created the opportunity to stimulate and process new information about the dangerousness, predictability, and controllability of these situations (cf. Foa & Kozak, 1986). The trajectory for this group was closer in form to the more cognitively oriented modality, paradoxical intention.

These results support Schwartz and Garamoni's structural (1986) model of positive and negative states of mind and clearly portray the temporal progressions, treatment differences, and outcome status of agoraphobics undergoing cognitive-behavioral treatments. According to Schwartz and Michelson (in press),

> The SOM model represents a structural and information-processing approach to understanding an individual's organization of positive and negative information regarding specific content domains. The basic unit of the SOM model, the self-statement, is clearly a proposition containing either positive or negative information regarding the feared stimulus situation, possible response patterns, or the meanings of these stimulus and response elements. Viewed within this context, the present data suggest that one of the structural principles that explains the organization of fear related information in agoraphobics is the relative balance of positive and negative cognition and affect. Specifically, clinically-defined agoraphobics are characterized by structures that are asymmetrically and negatively-balanced close to the negative dialogue set point of .382. These structures are modified as a function of therapy such that they shift rapidly toward a positive balance defined by borderline PD/PM of about .700. Hence, the present study represents an important attempt at quantitatively delineating the primary organizational principles that underlie the informational structures of agoraphobics and their effective treatment.

Schwartz and Garamoni (1986) state that, "These considerations suggest the need to identify the specific nature of cognitive/affective imbalances in different types of disorders with respect to the relative excess and deficit of positive and negative elements. Such cognitive 'task analyses' (cf. Schwartz & Gottman, 1976) across types of clinical disorders will delineate more precisely unique patterns of cognitive/affective imbalance which have direct implications for the specificity of the cognitive-behavioral interventions." Given the theoretical importance and potential clinical application of the states-of-mind model to anxiety disorders, this area of inquiry will likely receive considerable attention from theoreticians, researchers, and clinicians.

Assessment of Problem-Solving Skills and Attributional Styles in Agoraphobia

Recent cognitive formulations emphasize the potential role of problem-solving skills and attributional processes in the etiology and maintenance of phobic anxiety and avoidance. Deficient problem-solving skills have been reported for a variety of clinical populations, including substance abusers, schizophrenics, and victims of conduct disorders and attention deficit disorders (cf. Platt & Spivack, 1975). However, empirical validation of the presence and nature of problem-solving deficits among agoraphobics has been examined in only one investigation, by Brodbeck and Michelson (1986). The potential theoretical and clinical importance of examining both problem-solving skills and attributional styles of agoraphobics is supported by the cognitive formulations of anxiety disorders. Unfortunately, there is a paucity of psychometrically sound instruments or empirically developed strategies designed specifically for agoraphobics. Because of the relative vacuum of research in this area, there are few available instruments or specific strategies that can be routinely endorsed. Although promising work has been undertaken with regard to the attributional processes and problem-solving deficits for depressed populations (cf., Shaw & Dobson, 1981), parallel developments for agoraphobia have not been as rapid. However, the development of psychometrically sound assessment strategies for the identification of cognitive deficits and the specification of attribution styles for agoraphobics (and other anxiety disorders) is likely to increase significantly over the next decade.

Emmelkamp (1982) proposed that misattribution of physiological arousal, concomitant with deficient problem-solving skills, may contribute to the development of agoraphobia. He argues that external-locus agoraphobics misattribute panic attacks to dangerous, external, situational factors and, subsequently, engage in avoidance behavior rather than attempting to problem-solve for effective methods to cope with stress. Alternatively, Mathews, Gelder, and Johnson (1981) note that prolonged situational stress, coupled with a genetic vulnerability to elevated levels of trait anxiety, can culminate in the initial panic attack. They posit that agoraphobics misattribute physiological arousal to external sources and that avoidance is maintained by recall of aversive events prior to their panic attacks.

Goldstein and Chambless (1978) have emphasized the potential role of interpersonal conflict and misattributional processes in the etiology and maintenance of phobic anxiety and avoidance. They note that a series of stressful life events, particularly those involving interpersonal conflict, often trigger the initial panic attack. Agoraphobics misattribute the initial panic attack as occurring out of the blue, without a precipitating incident, rather than correctly perceiving interpersonal conflict as the source of phobic anxiety. The agoraphobic fails to resolve the interpersonal conflict, and subsequent avoidance is further mediated by catastrophic cognitions and an obsessional focus on anxiety symptoms. Social support systems may then become problematic by reinforcing phobic avoidance and dependence.

Each of these formulations emphasizes that agoraphobics respond differentially to stressful life events or interpersonal interactions. Further, inaccurate attributional processes and ineffective problem-solving strategies may differentiate the agoraphobic from other individuals who merely experience anxiety. However, empirical evidence to support the mediating role of dysfunctional attributional styles and faulty problem-solving skills has been limited.

Studies examining potential differences in attributional style between agoraphobics and normals have been confined to a few reports examining the potential relationship between external locus of control and phobic anxiety. Palmer (1972) found that externality and measures of "total fearfulness" on the Fear Survey Schedule were moderately intercorrelated ($r = .29$) for a sample of male psychiatric patients. Emmelkamp and Cohen-Kettanis (1975) reported that externality and "phobic anxiety" were moderately correlated ($r = .46$) for a group of agoraphobics. Michelson, Mavissakalian, and Meminger (1983) found that the pretreatment assessment of externality was prognostically associated with significantly greater improvement following *in vivo* exposure treatment and/or imipramine. In a recent study, Fisher and Wilson (1985) presented phobic, marital conflict, and neutral videotaped scenes to agoraphobics and normals. Agoraphobics offered internal and global attributions to phobic scenarios in comparison to normals. Both subject groups, however, ascribed internal attributions to the marital conflict scenario. Cumulatively viewed, these studies present equivocal findings that agoraphobia may be associated with externality. Unfortunately, other attributional dimensions and problem-solving capacity remain largely unexplored.

Recently, Brodbeck and Michelson (1986) adapted methodology used in studies of learned helplessness with depressed populations to examine cognitive problem-solving skills and attributional styles of agoraphobics. Twenty-three females with a primary diagnosis of agoraphobia with panic attacks (DSM-III) were compared to a normative control group consisting of 20 normals. Subjects were requested to solve three sets of anagrams, which differed in test difficulty. Subjects also completed an assessment battery that included measures of psychiatric symptomatology, interpersonal problem solving, and general attributional styles. Cognitive problem solving was assessed using anagrams. Interpersonal problem solving was assessed using the Means End Problem-Solving Measure (Platt & Spivak, 1975), which consists of seven interpersonal situations in which a problematic introduction and a successful resolution are presented. The subject's task is to describe the intervening events or relevant means to reach the conclusion. Dependent measures include relevant means, irrelevant means, references to time, and obstacles. The Interpersonal Problem-Solving Assessment Technique (IPSAT) (Nowinsky & Getter, 1977) was used to assess subjects' ability to generate alternative solutions and to select a behaviorally preferred response to 24 problematic situations in two alternative forms. Solutions were scored as effective, avoidant, dependent, inappropriate, or unscorable. The Attributional-Style Questionnaire—Revised (ASQ) (Peterson, Semmel, von Baeyer, Abramson, Metalsky, & Seligman, 1982) assessed positive and negative outcome for affiliative, interpersonal, and achievement situations. A 7-point Likert-scale format was used to elicit *locus of causality, temporal stability, and globality attributions* as well as *perceived likelihood of reoccurrence* and *perceived significance of event.* The original measure developed by Peterson et al. (1982) demonstrated adequate internal consistency and test–retest reliability. A slightly revised version used in the present study included two additional health-related items. Rotter's (1966) Internal–External Locus of Control, the Hopkins Symptom Checklist, the Taylor Manifest Anxiety Scale, and the Beck Depression Inventory (BDI) were also administered.

Analyses revealed that agoraphobics did not differ significantly from normals on cognitive problem-solving measures of anagram performance. Interpersonal problem-solving deficits were, however, exhibited for generating effective alternative solutions and selecting effective behaviorally preferred responses. Moreover, agoraphobics differed from normals on globality attributions, perceived significance, anticipated future outcomes, and performance appraisals toward experimentally induced failure experiences. These results were supportive of Chambless and Goldstein's formulation in which agoraphobics use avoidance strategies in lieu of effective resolution of interpersonal conflicts. Both agoraphobics and normals evidenced a functional style of attributing positive outcomes to internal causes and negative outcomes to a combination of internal and external causes. Hence the results suggest that agoraphobics do not differ from normals on locus of causality and temporal stability attributions.

Despite the moderately depressed nature of the agoraphobic sample (mean BDI score = 17.2), they did not exhibit a depressive attributional style. This raises caution in directly extrapolating the Abramson et al. (1978) reformulated learned helplessness model to other clinical populations. The ASQ results provided preliminary evidence that agoraphobics manifest a dysfunctional attributional style for globality ratings. Agoraphobics attributed positive outcomes to limited-effect causes and negative outcomes to global-effect causes, whereas normals exhibited the opposite pattern. These data corroborate Chambless and Goldstein's position and Beck's formulation that agoraphobics evidence a catastrophic cognitive style that maximizes the impact of negative events and minimizes the impact of positive events. This catastrophic cognitive style might potentially operate as a moderating factor in delaying or inhibiting response initiations to resolve interpersonal conflicts. Finally, with regard to experimental manipulation, it was found that agoraphobics deemphasized their initial success experiences by attributing the cause to limited-effect situations. Conversely, normals emphasized the global effect of positive experiences and minimized the negative effect of failure experiences. Again, agoraphobics emphasized the impact of negative outcomes, whereas normals appear to emphasize the impact of positive ones.

These data reveal that agoraphobics tend to engage in catastrophic appraisals of initial stressful situations and to minimize the impact of positive ones. Normals, on the other hand, appear to exhibit biases that minimize the effect of failure outcomes. Interestingly, agoraphobics also exhibit a greater sensitivity in response to both positive and negative outcomes, rating both as having greater significance to their personal lives. Normals manifest an opposite pattern, deemphasizing the impact of interpersonal events. Agoraphobics manifest differential patterns with regard to anticipated future outcomes. The ASQ revealed that agoraphobics perceive positive outcomes as less likely to reoccur in the future and negative outcomes as significantly more likely to reoccur, with an opposite pattern being observed for normals.

Overall, these findings suggest that agoraphobics perceive limited capability and confidence in their ability to affect change. Agoraphobics exhibit a dysfunctional style that minimizes the impact of positive outcomes and overgeneralizes the effect of negative ones. Agoraphobics also evidence catastrophic cognitions and excessive interpersonal sensitivity. The data are also clinically suggestive for identifying specific dysfunctional attributional patterns that might benefit from therapeutic amelioration. Indeed, reattribution therapies and cognitively based interventions may represent particularly efficacious strategies in remediating these deficits. Finally, research is needed to determine whether attributional styles change as a function of treatment and to examine their mediating role in therapeutic processes.

Concordance–Disconcordance

Concordance–disconcordance refers to the patterns of or association among the tripartite systems-cognition, behavior, and physiology, *within* a particular assessment phase. Another term often confused with concordance is *synchrony*, which refers to the association of the tripartite systems *across* assessment phases. Concordance, as both a process and an outcome phenomenon, is an important area of clinical research in anxiety disorders, as exemplified by the following studies. Michelson and Mavissakalian (1985) assigned 62 severe and chronic agoraphobics in the 2 × 2 factorial design to either imipramine plus programmed practice, imipramine plus prolonged graduated *in vivo* exposure, prolonged *in vivo* exposure alone with programmed practice, or programmed practice alone. Subjects were assessed across the tripartite systems pretreatment and at 4-week, 8-week, 12-week, and 1-month follow-up. They were operationally assigned to categories of concordance versus disconcordance on the basis of their psychophysiological, self-report, and behavioral measures at posttreatment. Analyses revealed that subjects identified as being concordant across the tripartite systems exhibited statistically significant superior outcome compared to their disconcordant counterparts. In addition, differential patterns of concordance were observed among the experimental conditions, with imipramine plus flooding = 50%, imipramine plus programmed practice = 75%, flooding plus programmed practice = 86%, and programmed practice alone = 33%. These results indicate that agoraphobics, identified as exhibiting high levels of physiological, behavioral, and self-report congruency at posttreatment, manifested enhanced therapeutic outcome. Furthermore, the trend for increased concordance among subjects receiving graduated exposure suggests that this modality facilitated more rapid response symmetry. Conversely, the control group (i.e., programmed practice) had rather low concordance rates, indicating that programmed practice, without either therapist-assisted *in vivo* exposure or imipramine, may not be an optimal strategy for maximizing concordance for at least two-thirds of agoraphobics receiving this unitary treatment.

In an independent investigation comparing cognitive and behavioral treatments of agoraphobia, Michelson, Mavissakalian, and Marchione (1985) compared relaxation training (RT) versus paradoxical intention (PI) versus graduated exposure (GE) for agoraphobics. Subjects were identified as being concordant or disconcordant at posttreatment. Discriminant function analyses revealed that the two groups were significantly different at mid- and posttreatment, all in favor of superior clinical functioning among concordant subjects. Moreover, 3-month follow-up analyses revealed significant and superior functioning for subjects identified as having tripartite concordance on other, independent outcome measures. Furthermore, subjects identified as being concordant at posttreatment manifested earlier gains in the therapeutic course and subsequently exhibited superior functioning at the completion of treatment and at the 3-month follow-up. Perhaps most important, 88% of the subjects identified as being concordant met a priori criteria for high endstate functioning, compared to only 12% classified as having low endstate functioning. Conversely, 57% of the discordant subjects were classified as having low endstate functioning, a statistically significant difference ($p \leq .05$). Overall, concordant subjects evidenced significantly greater levels of absolute improvement (82%) compared to disconcordant subjects (50%). Although the treatments themselves were not significantly different with regard to concordance rates (PI = 50%, GE = 64%, and RT = 50%), it is clear that individuals identified as being concordant as posttreatment had significantly superior functioning on major outcome measures both at posttreatment and at the 3-month follow-up. Hence, although the treatments were approximately equal in their ability to affect concordance, the phenomenon of concordance appears to be significantly associated with overall therapeutic gains at both posttreatment and follow-up. In light of the emerging importance of tripartite functioning with regard to both treatment outcome and maintenance, clinicians and researchers should assess concordance as an objective verification that clients have achieved optimal improvement across the tridimensional systems (Michelson, 1984b).

Synchrony–Desynchrony

Whereas concordance concerns the correlation among the tripartite systems *within* an assessment phase, *synchrony* refers to the covariation of the tripartite systems *across* two or more assessment trials, respectively. Synchrony–desynchrony refers to the directional commonality or temporal congruency of the tripartite measures. The recognition that phobic anxiety comprises three response systems has had important theoretical and clinical implications (Lang, 1968, 1977; Rachman & Hodgson, 1974; Hodgson & Rachman, 1974). The exact nature of the relationship between behavioral, physiological, and cognitive response systems of anxiety has eluded both careful definition and programmatic investigation because of the complexity of their interrelations.

Leitenberg, Agras, Butts, and Wincze (1971), in a series of single-case studies, reported both synchronous and desynchronous changes between behavioral and physiological measures in the treatment of simple phobias. Barlow et al. (1980) noted various patterns of synchrony–desynchrony between heart rate and self-reported anxiety, measured during a behavioral avoidance course for three agoraphobics undergoing treatment. Only one subject exhibited synchronous changes between heart rate and subjective anxiety; the other two manifesting desynchrony between these measures.

The short- and long-term implications of desynchrony remain empirically unclear. Theoretical and clinical perspectives posit that individuals who exhibit desynchrony may be hypothesized as being at greater risk for exhibiting relapse or residual clinical impairment. On the other hand, depending on the nature of the treatment and the areas of maximal dysfunction across the tripartite systems, certain desynchronous patterns might be expected as a natural course of specific treatments, perhaps followed subsequently by synchronization.

In the Mavissakalian and Michelson (1982b) study, the patterns of synchrony–desynchrony were examined for a group of 26 agoraphobics who completed a 2×2 factorial study testing the relative and combined efficacy of behavior therapy and pharmacotherapy. One of the aims of the study was to examine the possibility that the tripartite response systems might be affected differentially by the various treatments and that the different response systems may manifest varying rates of improvement. Overall, pretreatment to follow-up comparisons revealed synchronization across behavioral, physiological, and subjective measures. As might be expected, behavioral gains were exhibited earlier in treatment. Heart rate and *in vivo* anxiety did not exhibit improvement commensurate with behavioral changes until much later in the treatment protocol. The heart rate measures appeared to require much longer periods of time in order for the treatment gains to be consolidated. This differential pattern of change fits Hodgson and Rachman's (1974) prediction of a greater tendency for desynchrony to occur in earlier stages of treatment, with a shift to more synchronous patterns in later treatment phases. Interestingly, the combined treatment (imipramine plus flooding) exhibited the highest rate of desynchrony, which might explain the significantly higher relapse rates encountered with combined treatments than with graduated exposure alone (Zitrin et al., 1981). Synchrony–desynchrony may have important short- and long-term implications for long-term maintenance and relapse. Clearly, assessment of tripartite functioning across assessment phases offers an important triangulation of therapeutic improvement in agoraphobia.

Normative Comparisons

Monitoring tripartite channels, investigating both process and outcome phenomena, and longitudinally examining the relative efficacy of various modalities are all important areas of inquiry. Another crucial but often ignored parameter in clinical research concerns the use of *normative cohorts*. As reported by Turner and Michelson (1984b, p. 275),

> Normative (non-phobic) comparisons permit clinical and social evaluations as to the actual efficacy of a particular treatment with regard to restoring subjects to "normal" levels of functioning. The use of normal cohorts should be considered in all outcome research to provide a clinically-salient, social validation of the actual impact of the treatment on both a short- and long-term basis.

An example of the use of normative comparisons is the Michelson and Mavissakalian (1985) study, which examined the psychophysiological outcome of agoraphobics receiving behavioral and pharmacologic treatments. It was found that at pretreatment normal cohorts exhibited significantly lower psychophysiological reactivity than agoraphobics on major heart rate measures. By the 1-month posttreatment assessment, however, treated agoraphobics did not differ significantly from the normative counterparts on any of the heart rate measures collected during the behavioral avoidance test. These findings offer empirical support that the treatments not only yielded statistically significant results but also were highly efficacious in restoring these severe and chronic agoraphobics to normative levels of functioning with regard to autonomic arousal. The use of normative cohorts should be extended to other anxiety disorders as well as to identifying effective treatments and establishing the relative restoration of anxiety subjects to normal levels of behavioral, social, affective, cognitive, and physiological functioning. Continued expansion of the use of normative comparisons for agoraphobia and related anxiety disorders will result in more clinically meaningful, sensitive, and socially valid indices of therapeutic outcome.

Treatment

Graduated Exposure

Graduated exposure (GE) is a generic term employed to describe a complex set of therapeutic procedures used in treating numerous phobic disorders, including agoraphobia. GE entails exposure to anxiety-eliciting stimuli, including objects, situations, or persons to which agoraphobics manifest phobic conditioning. Although there are a number of clinical dimensions of exposure-based techniques that differ widely across specific studies and clinicians, the underlying conceptualization of exposure facilitating habituation and extinction remains evident. Exposure strategies are often misunderstood and mistakenly associated with implosion therapy. The latter implies the use of horrific, frightening, and/or psychodynamic cues to maximize anxiety arousal, which is presumed, by proponents of this approach, to promote rapid extinction. Empirical findings and clinical reports have found such threatening and anxiety-provoking cues to be unnecessary and, in some instances, contratherapeutic. Experimental and applied research literatures regarding the efficacy of exposure techniques argue for increased contact, not emotional arousal, as a crucial element in habituation processes. Within a behavioral paradigm, GE and its many derivations differ across a number of important clinical dimensions. Whether the technique is applied imaginally or *in vivo*, intensively or in a graduated manner, spaced or mass-practiced, therapist- or client directed, individually or in a group format, with or without spouses (or significant others)—these are issues that warrant careful consideration and will be subsequently described.

Imaginal versus In Vivo Exposure

Contemporary findings, culled from diverse studies and research centers, generally suggest that exposure conducted in actual phobic situations (*in vivo*), is generally more efficacious for treating agoraphobia than are visual, auditory, tactile, or similar cues presented imaginally. This may be so because many agoraphobics cannot sustain imagery powerful or detailed enough to allow habituation processes to culminate successfully. Other limitations of imagery-based techniques include the fact that many clients may block their anxiety arousal by minimizing or neutralizing phobic elements of their imagery experiences. This blocking phenomenon can be difficult to monitor and remediate, as the potency, clarity, and duration of exposure in imagery are subject to all the weaknesses of self-report data. Advantages of *in vivo* graduated exposure include direct facilitation of client coping. Confirmation that exposure to real-life situations has occurred is achieved with minimization of escape or avoidance behaviors. Moreover, *in vivo* exposure does not require any imagery training or visualization ability on the part of the client. As noted by Michelson (1985, p. 3):

> It also possesses the inherent advantages of social validity and treatment generalization. First, the phobic targets are selected and practiced in their natural states. Should certain stimuli either prove to be more or less phobic than was originally conceptualized, other more therapeutically relevant phobic targets can be readily substituted. Conversely, when evaluating the efficacy of exposure and imagery, the exact degree of association with corresponding *in vivo* counterparts remains unknown. However, imaginal exposure may be a viable strategy when phobic stimuli cannot be utilized due to its unavailability *in vivo* or being primarily of an imaginal nature (i.e., fear of dying, etc.).

Further research is needed to identify more effective imagery-based treatment strategies, given the potential efficacy and efficiency of this modality.

Pacing of Exposure

Although *in vivo* exposure can be presented with either *rapid* or *gradual* pacing, clinical research supports a graduated approach, whereby clients are exposed to their unique set of phobic situations in a slowly ascending hierarchy. Graduated exposure reduces client dropout, noncompliance, and resistance, while simultaneously facilitating increased self-efficacy. Since the agoraphobic is actively involved in structuring the level of difficulty of each phobic task collaboratively with the therapist, anticipatory anxiety is greatly diminished, along with psychophysiological reactivity during the actual phobic task. In addition, inter- and intrasession habituation is accelerated by reducing excessive and unnecessary emotional-phobic responses.

With respect to the *duration* of sessions, the clinical research literature supports the effectiveness of prolonged *in vivo* exposure in the treatment of agoraphobia. Extended *in vivo* exposure outings maximize habituation effects across the tripartite systems. Sessions lasting between 1½ and 3 hours generally yield greater therapeutic benefits. Another clinical aspect in the implementation of exposure procedures concerns the differential effectiveness of *spaced* versus *massed* treatment sessions. Although long-term outcome results remain equivocal, the short-term benefits reported in recent studies generally favor the use of massed (i.e., frequent and temporally close applications) rather than spaced practice (e.g., once every 2 weeks).

Exposure treatment can entail either therapist or client-directed outings, or both. Overall, research attests to the superior efficacy of therapist-directed exposure, at least initially; this is often viewed as a necessary, though not sufficient, condition in the effective treatment of agoraphobia. During subsequent treatment phases, clients can be encouraged to assume progressively greater responsibility for collaboratively designing and subsequently undertaking their own graduated prolonged *in vivo* exposure sessions, to be carried out between formal treatment sessions. This is typically accomplished with the therapist's instructions, feedback, and encouragement.

In a major outcome study conducted by Mavissakalian and Michelson (1986) examining the relative and combined effectiveness of therapist-assisted *in vivo* exposure, self-directed *in vivo* exposure, imipramine, and placebo, it was found that subjects assigned to *self-directed in vivo* exposure had significantly inferior outcome, with only one-third of these clients being rated as highly improved at posttreatment. Hence, although self-exposure can be an effective and cost-effective strategy for reducing phobic avoidance, the majority of clients appear to require additional *therapist-assisted in vivo* exposure and/or concomitant cognitive-behavioral treatments to enhance the clinical benefits derived solely from self-exposure.

Comparisons of GE using both *individual* and *group* treatment formats reveal no differences in efficacy. In addition, clinicians have noted that group treatment, beyond its obvious efficiency, may offer additional benefits over individual treatment. Specifically, increased support from group cohesion and social reinforcement can facilitate more extensive self-directed exposure, which subsequently facilitates greater overall improvement. Similarly, exposure-based strategies also appear to benefit from the addition of a relative or "significant other" who serves as an adjunct co-therapist to help the client practice prolonged *in vivo* exposure between formal treatment sessions. Although short-term results may not differ markedly, several studies report that those clients with participating spouses or significant others appear to fare better over long-term follow-up, findings that will be discussed in greater detail in the section on marital therapy.

Therapeutic response to graduated *in vivo* exposure procedures is typically reported in the 60–75% range. These figures, however, are actually much closer to 50% if computations also include nonresponders and dropouts. It appears from the clinical research literature that clients who respond favorably to graduated exposure typically begin to manifest noticeable improvements during the first 6 to 10 weeks of treatment, consisting of 1 or 2 weekly 2-hour sessions of GE. Initially favorable responses are likely to continue, with further therapeutic gains if GE is continued. Hence, initial responsivity to GE appears highly associated with subsequent improvement. The converse is not always true, however, in that certain clients who may not obtain a benefit from GE initially may, with the therapist's assistance or the addition of cognitive therapy or relaxation training, subsequently exhibit significant therapeutic progress.

Although research protocols using GE have been reported to last anywhere from a few to numerous sessions, conducted over a 1- to 3-month period, it is not unusual in clinical practice for clients to require more extended treatment to remediate the disorder effectively and remove residual symptoms. To facilitate client improvement and support of significant others, GE strategies should be thoroughly discussed with clients and their relatives, if appropriate. A complete therapeutic rationale of the objectives, procedures, and benefits of the interventions, as well as a discussion of how to cope with transient increases in subjective anxiety while engaged in the self-directed or therapist-assisted *in vivo* exposure outings (Michelson, 1985), is important.

Since unitary GE procedures do not yield significant clinical improvements in approximately 25–40% of the cases treated, it is important that the client's treatment plan include concomitant modalities. Increasing numbers of clinical researchers (cf. DeSilva & Rachman, 1981; Michelson et al., 1985) argue that although exposure may be a necessary means of treating phobic anxiety and phobic avoidance, it is often insufficient by itself.

Exposure is undoubtedly a useful and often *necessary* strategy for the treatment of agoraphobia. Since Marks, Boulougouris, and Marset (1971) demonstrated the superiority of flooding over desensitization, subsequent investigators have confirmed the superiority of exposure strategies over desensitization and flooding in imagination (Emmelkamp & Wessler, 1975; Emmelkamp & Mersh, 1982). Recent treatment outcome reviews (Goldstein & Chambless, 1980; Brehony & Geller, 1981; Jansson & Öst, 1982) indicate that *in vivo* exposure techniques for agoraphobia, compared to purely imaginal exposure, programmed practice or no treatment, are relatively more efficacious strategies. Although these findings are encouraging, there is reason for caution: many outcome studies suffer from design and methodological flaws that thwart treatment comparisons. Varying treatment lengths, quality, intensity, integrity of treatment, diagnostic considerations, absence of multimodal assessments, unproven reliability of measures, lack of adequate descriptions of the treatments, absence of long-term follow-up, and omission of attrition analyses all impede empirical analysis. In addition, most of these studies report statistically significant results based on mean group score changes on subjective scales and rarely using behavioral, cognitive, and/or physiological measures. In addition, few studies systematically report the percentage of clients improved or unimproved, of dropouts, of relapsers, or of clients requiring additional treatment following completion of the study.

Programmed Practice

Programmed practice refers to a variety of therapeutic procedures designed to induce clients' self-directed exposure (SDE) to phobic stimuli. Programmed practice typically uses both bibliotherapeutic and therapist-directed instructions to facilitate the client's SDE practices. Programmed practice relies heavily on self-recording and self-monitoring with regard to the clients' own programmed practice activities between treatment sessions. Clients typically record any occurrence of SDE and associated levels of their subjective anxiety (SUDS) while in actual phobic situations. Additional variables collected and subsequently discussed with the therapist include duration of the outing, distance, purpose, and whether the SDE was carried out as a practice session. These daily records are reviewed with the therapist, and all progress and reported gains are reinforced. Clients are then assigned new phobia tasks and encouraged to proceed with their SDE practice.

Programmed practice makes particular use of the significant other to support the client's practice between found treatment sessions. Partners are instructed, along with clients, in the role of habituation in controverting the disorder and the importance of repeated, prolonged, graduated exposure in reducing phobic anxiety and avoidance. Partners are instructed to allow clients to determine for themselves the level and duration of the phobic experience. However, partners are encouraged to play a supportive role and to encourage clients to remain in the situation until the distress decreases.

Clients are typically encouraged to practice SDE daily, exposing them to a wide variety of target situations typically in several major areas per week. Clients are instructed to remain in each phobic situation until habituation occurs or their level of distress decreases to 3 or below on a scale of 0 to 8 SUDS. It may be necessary for some clients to remain in phobic situations for 1 to 2 hours, particularly during the earlier phases of treatment. Moreover, those clients receiving integrated therapy programs would also use their additional coping strategies (e.g., cognitive therapy, relaxation training) and employ these techniques to attenuate their anxiety. Thanks to the excellent work of Mathews and his colleagues, programmed practice manuals are available for both clients and their significant others. Mathews, Gelder, and Johnson (1981, p. 110) observe:

> Practice in self-exposure is not considered incidental to some other procedures: it forms the core of the treatment . . . this transfer of responsibility for the detailed management of the program to the client and the partner serves a double purpose of reducing the professional time that would otherwise be needed to supervise exposure and of diminishing the client's dependence on continuing contact with the therapist. The involvement of a partner is also seen as a method of increasing social reinforcement for regular practice. In the absence of any clear evidence of differences attributable to alternative types of exposure, graded practice has been adopted as the most acceptable and practical from the clients point of view. However, unlike earlier forms of graded practice, in which anxiety was minimized, a vigorous approach is used in which clients are told to expect and learn to cope with moderate levels of anxiety.

As Mathews et al. further note (p. 111), the major points of programmed practice include:

> 1) From the start, it is made clear that the client rather than the therapist will be responsible for running the treatment program.

2) Whenever possible, a suitable person is recruited to help in the day-to-day running of the program (this is usually the client's spouse but need not be).

3) The client (and the partner) are provided with detailed but simple manuals that outline the nature of agoraphobia, the principles of graded exposure, the methods of coping with anxiety and of encouraging regular practice.

4) The therapist presents himself as an advisor or educator and does not take any active role in exposure practice.

5) The meeting with the therapist is usually in the client's home and takes the form of discussions among the therapist, the client and the partner about the practice program and any problems that have arisen.

6) The time spent with the therapist is limited to about five visits over a month after which the meetings with the therapist are phased out while the client and the partner continue the program.

More extensive descriptions of the home-based treatment method using programmed practice are provided in Mathews et al. (1981); Mathews et al. (1977); and Jannoun et al. (1980). Mathews et al. report that programmed practice can effect many clinical improvements using their efficient strategy of reduced therapeutic contacts and home-based sessions combined with instructions for SDE practice. However, the outcome results from several investigations suggest that these effects are unduly attenuated when programmed practice is used as the *sole* therapeutic modality, and do not yield outcome results comparable to those of more intensive, multimodal approaches that systematically combine programmed practice with cognitive, behavioral, or pharmacologic treatments (cf. Michelson, Mavissakalian, & Marchione, 1985; Mavissakalian & Michelson, 1984). Although programmed practice may be a clinically insufficient treatment in itself, its importance as an adjunctive and complementary component in agoraphobia treatment is readily evident.

Holden, O'Brien, Barlow, Stetson, and Infantino (1983) examined the efficacy of the client-conducted treatment package for agoraphobics using a self-treatment manual evaluated in a multiple-baseline design with six severe female agoraphobics. The results indicated that the self-help manual was not effective. Mavissakalian & Michelson (in press), in an NIMH investigation, examined the relative and combined efficacy of programmed practice with and without imipramine and graduated *in vivo* exposure. The results indicated that GE plus programmed practice and imipramine plus programmed practice were highly and equally effective in treating severe and chronic agoraphobics. However, programmed practice alone yielded an improvement rate of less than one-third of the clients, compared to two-thirds who improved significantly with the other treatments. The results of this study suggest that self-exposure may be a cost-efficient strategy of reducing phobic avoidance for one-third of agoraphobics receiving this treatment but that concomitant treatment with therapist-assisted GE, or tricyclic antidepressants for intractable cases, seems to increase the clinical benefits derived from self-exposure alone. It is noteworthy that two-thirds of the clients receiving programmed practice only did not achieve significant therapeutic benefits, suggesting the need for multimodal, combined, and integrated therapeutic programs that offer and address cognitive mediational processes, psychophysiological functioning, and behavioral dimensions of this complex disorder.

The relatively limited efficacy of programmed practice as the sole treatment becomes apparent with severe and chronic cases of agoraphobia and/or where marital dysfunction, clinical depression, or complex patterns of phobic avoidance and phobic anxiety are present. As an *adjunctive* psychoeducational and self-monitoring component in a multimodal treatment program, however, programmed practice should be regarded as an important, necessary, and efficient means of facilitating overall therapeutic improvement.

Progressive Deep Muscle Relaxation Training (PDMR)

PDMR was developed by Jacobson (1929) and modified by Wolpe (1958) and Bernstein and Borkovec (1973). (The abbreviations PDMR and RT will be used interchangeably to denote various abbreviated Jacobsonian procedures and derivatives.) Jacobson's relaxation training procedures have been found to be effective for insomnia (Nicassio & Bootzin, 1974); asthma (Alexander, 1972); tension headache (Cox, Freundlich, & Meyer, 1974); muscular tension (Miller, Murphy, & Miller, 1978); high blood pressure (Fey & Lindholm, 1978; Parker, Gilbert, & Thoreson, 1978); increased heart rate (Fey & Lindholm, 1978; Paul, 1969a); chronic anxiety (Townshend, House, & Adario, 1975); and phobias (Mathews & Gelder, 1969) (see King, 1980, and Woolfolk & Lehrer, 1984, for more exhaustive reviews).

These citations clearly support the value of PDMR as a useful treatment for a variety of disorders with psychophysiological components. However, there were virtually no controlled outcome studies of PDMR used primarily as a physiological self-control strategy for chronic and severe agoraphobia until quite recently (Michelson et al., 1985). PDMR offers numerous potential benefits as an adjunct to *in vivo* exposure treatment for agoraphobia. The clinical and conceptual rationales for considering PDMR in the treatment of agoraphobia are numerous. First, agoraphobics are reportedly highly prone to spontaneous fluctuations in physiological arousal such as anxiety attacks, which exacerbate further phobic conditioning. A therapeutic procedure that has the effect of lowering physiological arousal may exert a direct impact on the frequency, duration, and severity of anxiety attacks, while also dampening residual levels of autonomic arousal. Agoraphobic symptomatology typically includes marked, persistent, and uncontrolled signs of physical distress antecedent to phobic avoidance. Anxious individuals are highly sensitive to internal experiences of somatic changes (i.e., arousal) and are likely to misinterpret these as anxiety signals (Woolfolk & Lehrer, 1984). Such persons closely attend to these distressing symptoms and their perceived inability to control them (Goldstein & Chambless, 1978). Therefore, an adjunctive treatment that enhances self-control of physiological arousal and somatic reactivity would provide an active coping mechanism in phobic circumstances. The ability to modulate arousal directly promotes habituation and facilitates increased exposure to phobic cues. Decreasing physiological arousal may also enhance tolerance of *in vivo* exposure practices, enabling clients to reduce phobic distress prior to, during, and following exposure, and thereby maximizing habituation processes and minimizing noncompliance and attrition.

Relaxation training may be an important component of *in vivo* exposure as a means of convincing individuals that they may approach the phobic situation without severe risks because their panic attacks may be effectively controlled by the RT coping procedures (Lehrer & Woolfolk, 1984). Given the importance of clinically addressing each of the tripartite dimensions of this complex disorder, relaxation training may represent an effective and viable adjunctive treatment strategy that should facilitate physiological self-control, habituation processes, and increased SDE.

From a conceptual standpoint, PDMR is believed to facilitate emotional processing (Rachman, 1980). Modification of somatic arousal can be viewed as a therapeutic derivative of Lang's (1979) bioinformational theory of emotional processing: behavior, semantic information, or visceral responses may be modified in fear. Given Hugdahl's (1981) and Michelson's (1984b) postulations that different anxiety disorders may "load" differently on Lang's suggested fear components, agoraphobics, with their high levels of physiological arousal, might be ideal subjects for relaxation procedures. There is an exacerbatory cycle in agoraphobia, whereby signs of arousal elicit maladaptive cognitions, which by their catastrophic nature lead to further sympathetic arousal and increased physiological symptoms. Therefore, direct self-modification of psychophysiological arousal represents an option for interrupting this cycle. Even if the affective response is primary, as Zajonc suggests, relaxation may represent an effective means of curtailing the evoked response (Rachman, 1983). Similarly, Silver and Blanchard (1978) view PDMR as a critical variable—a "final common pathway" in the treatment of many anxiety disorders, similar to the notion of "cultivated low arousal" advanced by Stoyva and Budzinski (1974). This is consistent with Goldfried and Trier's (1974) conception of relaxation as an active coping skill.

There has been some controversy regarding the specific action of relaxation training procedures for producing physiological effects, as seen in reviews by Woolfolk and Lehrer (1984), King (1980), and Borkovec and Sides (1979). In large part, methodological issues account for many of the equivocal findings. Lehrer (1978) notes that a number of factors—population differences; variations in dependent measures for assessing anxiety; and variations in procedures employed, duration of training, and conditions of testing—have led to inconsistent findings. There is apparently a "floor effect" that operates in many of the studies using college (i.e., normal) subjects. With little or no PDMR, normal subjects can relax very deeply; therefore, specific effects of PDMR versus comparison treatments are infrequently seen in analogue studies.

Borkovec and Sides (1979), in a cogent review, compared studies demonstrating physiological effects of PDMR with others that did not. These two sets of studies differed significantly on several variables: number of sessions, subject- versus experimenter-controlled sessions, live versus taped administration of training, and normal versus patient samples. Nearly 80% of the studies with actual clinical patients as subjects showed physiological effects for PDMR significantly superior to controls. Borkovec and Sides concluded that there was a strong likelihood of producing significant physiological reductions with PDMR when multisession, subject-controlled sessions, featuring live training, are provided to patients for whom physiological activity constitutes a presenting clinical problem. This is consistent with Lehrer's (1978) finding of physiological effects for anxiety neurotics specific to PDMR, which were not observed in normals.

Öst, Jerremalm, and Johansson (1981) showed specific effects for PDMR in a study involving socially anxious psychiatric patients. Subjects identified as "physiological responders" on the basis of performance on a laboratory role-play assessment, who were treated according to primary symptoms, evinced greater decreases on a combined measure of anxiety and stress. Glasiter (1982) provided additional support for the physiological effects of PDMR in a review of studies employing PDMR with phobic patients with evidence for autonomic effects during sessions, during rest postsessions, and during stress posttraining. PDMR has been employed together with imaginal desensitization in studies reviewed by Jansson and Öst (1984) and Emmelkamp (1982), and that combination has been found to be inferior to *in vivo* exposure. However, one would not expect an effect to be seen for PDMR in the absence of behavioral rationale, instructions for application and programmed practice.

In a recent study by Michelson, Mavissakalian, & Marchione (1985), PDMR, when combined with programmed practice, was found to be a highly effective treatment package for severe and chronic agoraphobics. The results of this study will be presented subsequently in greater detail. However, they corroborate the positive findings reported by other research centers both in the United States and Europe (Öst et al., 1984). Moreover, a recently completed 2-year follow-up of agoraphobics who received PDMR (Öst, personal communication) revealed continued maintenance of clinical improvements achieved at posttreatment.

PDMR versus Pharmacotherapy

Behaviorally based psychophysiological strategies such as PDMR have their biological counterparts in psychiatry in the form of pharmacologic agents that are used to treat agoraphobia via suppression of panic attacks. There are a number of important conceptual and clinical considerations underlying the comparative advantage of PDMR over pharmacotherapy. First, PDMR has been shown to be effective in reducing levels of psychophysiological arousal in anxiety patients. Second, it is an internally based strategy for achieving self-control, which is likely to lead to enhanced self-efficacy and to increase treatment generalization. Third, the value of pharmacotherapy in actually reducing physiological arousal (cf. Michelson & Mavissakalian, 1985) and phobic avoidance and in fostering long-term recovery in agoraphobia remains controversial.

The most effective pharmacological agents, tricyclic antidepressants, (most notably imipramine) lead to some reductions in panic during treatment. However, Telch, Taranon, and Taylor (1983) conducted a review of the literature with regard to the equivocal effects of antidepressants in the treatment of agoraphobia. The authors report that 20% of all agoraphobics in these studies expressed an unwillingness to take the medication. In addition, physical side effects, often mimicking the very symptoms the clients sought to alleviate, were reported as an important reason given for discontinuing the medication, which occurred in approximately 25% of the subjects. In addition to the noxious side effects, subject attrition and dropout rates were problematic. Antidepressant treatments averaged 35–40% dropout rates, well above those for drug-free behavioral treatments. According to Telch et al. (1983):

> A final issue concerning the use of antidepressants in treating agoraphobia is relapse. Phobic relapse is a serious problem commonly reported in the literature. Relapse data from the

previous trials utilizing antidepressant medication with agoraphobics indicated that 27–50% of those patients who initially improved relapsed upon withdrawal of the medication.

The authors concluded that in light of clients' reluctance to receive medication, attrition due to adverse physical side effects, and relapse following cessation of the medication, pharmacotherapy for agoraphobia should be used only with caution in clinical practice. A further limitation of medication is that the majority of agoraphobics are females in their childbearing years, precluding the routine use of these agents because of their potential iatrogenic effects on the developing fetus.

These findings received added support from a recent series of programmatic investigations by Michelson and Mavissakalian (1985) examining behavioral and pharmacologic strategies for agoraphobics. Agoraphobics who received imipramine experienced *increased* psychophysiological reactivity both during and after the treatment program and exhibited *delayed* habituation processes. In addition, subjects receiving imipramine, compared to behavior therapy, experienced significantly *lower* synchrony rates across the major tripartite domains of functioning at posttreatment. In addition, although similar reductions in panic attacks were observed from both behavioral and pharmacologic treatments, there was a significant trend for imipramine subjects to relapse during the 2-year longitudinal follow-up (cf. Mavissakalian & Michelson, 1986). Therefore, nonpharmacological (e.g., PDMR) strategies for reducing visceral arousal, decreasing panic attacks, and decreasing phobic anxiety are likely to improve both short- and long-term outcome. Psychosocial strategies such as PDMR represent viable treatment alternatives and should be the focus of further research as effective, tolerable, and safe psychophysiological treatments for agoraphobia.

Cognitive Features

Agoraphobia has well-known and ubiquitous cognitive features that have generated much theoretical interest and many clinical innovations. Agoraphobics often complain of anxiety-producing thoughts, ideation, and phobic imagery. It is apparent that cognitions often elicit marked levels of subjective distress and physiological arousal (Marks, 1969). Physical symptoms of almost any nature are frequently misconstrued as a prelude to a full-blown panic attack (Goldstein, 1982), and hypervigilence of bodily sensations and negative appraisal of their significance leads to further exacerbation of phobic anxiety and avoidance.

Agoraphobics have also been reported as functioning at high levels of sympathetic nervous system arousal (Marks, 1969; Marks & Lader, 1973; Chambless, 1982). The severity of phobic symptoms also appears to be related to level of physical arousal, which may frequently trigger panic reactions (Goldstein, 1982). The symptoms of physiological arousal are highly disturbing, and, when in distress, clients narrowly focus their awareness on their perceived somatic changes. Perceived lack of control over both cognitions and physiological arousal is a frequent agoraphobic complaint. Catastrophic appraisal of somatic responses quickly results in an escalating spiral of anxiety and fear (e.g., Ascher, 1980; Beck, 1976). Subsequent cognitive appraisal of such avoidant behavior can result in self-perceptions of being "sick," "crazy," or weak; loss of self-esteem; and increased dependence (Brehony & Geller, 1981). A commonly listed complaint among agoraphobics surveyed by Burns and Thorpe (1977) was a feeling of inferiority due to their perceived disability. Likewise, anticipatory anxiety, a major feature of the disorder, is also likely to promote and maintain phobic avoidance. This so-called fear of fear leads clients to adopt a cognitive set in which individuals come to believe they *must* maintain low levels of anxiety at all costs.

Similarly, other cognitive features operating on a deeper (i.e., metacognitive) level than mere catastrophic thoughts include dysfunctional attitudes, perceptions, and beliefs regarding prediction; control; serious threat to physical well-being; ability to deal with danger (Guidano & Liotti, 1983); consequences of anxiety (Beck, 1984; Coleman, 1982); ability to tolerate aloneness (Goldstein, 1982); insistence on immediate and absolute relief and unwillingness to endure distress (Ellis, 1979). Similarly, some researchers report (e.g., Emmelkamp, 1982; Michelson, Mavissakalian, Greenwald, Kornblith, & Greenwald, 1983) that cognitive phenomena may greatly attenuate the effects of exposure treatments. Ideation regarding the need to escape or plans for escape may limit clients' willingness to engage in self-directed practice. Cognitive avoidance (i.e., focusing on rescue factors such as the presence of the therapist or of emergency facilities) during GE may reduce the benefit of exposure treatment. Evaluation after exposure, in the guise of negative self-statements or external attributions, may contribute to future avoidance. Therefore, it is crucial that cognitive mediational factors be fully considered in the treatment of agoraphobia.

Behavioral theories, in attempting to provide a more complete account of anxiety disorders, are increasingly incorporating cognitive and psychophysiological mediational processes as useful explanatory mechanisms and beneficial treatment adjuncts. Recent conceptualizations of anxiety disorders suggest that cognitive interventions aimed at changing negative expectations, inadequate perceptions of safety, cognitive errors, and misattributions may be of significant benefit in ameliorating agoraphobia. The notion that anxiety disorders are construed in terms of tripartite response systems and evidence that these systems change differentially in response to various treatment procedures raises the possibility and the hope that treatments with specific actions may be of particular value if combined, especially given the fact that unitary treatment approaches (exposure) can no longer be presumed to evoke generalized effects across all tripartite systems.

In addition to the theoretical and practical rationales for addressing multiple response systems in agoraphobia, evidence emphasizing the importance of synchronous change warrants the development of more effective procedures. Despite significant clinical advances in exposure research, moderate residual clinical disability is more often the case (Chambless, 1982; Emmelkamp, 1979) than the exception. Clinical models of agoraphobia (Goldstein & Chambless, 1978, 1980) strongly argue in favor of multilevel treatments. According to Goldstein (1982), behavioral treatment aimed only at the conditioned fear and avoidance level is likely to be of limited value. Similarly, certain features of agoraphobia, namely its cognitive and physiological dimensions, may not be sufficiently addressed by treatments based solely on *in vivo* exposure. These issues will now be reviewed along with proposed therapeutic interventions to address them.

Cognitive interventions have only recently been added to the therapists' armamentarium in the treatment of agoraphobia. Despite the recognition of the importance of cognitive mediational processes in the maintenance and effective treatment of agoraphobia, there have only been a few empirical studies of the efficacy of these techniques for agoraphobics. Although there is a voluminous literature consisting largely of methodologically excellent studies of analogue populations that demonstrate the effectiveness of cognitive behavior therapy (CBT) in regard to anxiety management (Barrios & Shigetomi, 1980), there is a paucity of studies examining CBT procedures specifically with agoraphobics.

Anxiety management is an important consideration in the treatment of agoraphobia, although the dramatic aspect of severe phobic avoidance can at first overshadow this aspect and emphasize deficits in behavioral performance. Nevertheless, once clients attempt either self-directed or therapist-directed *in vivo* exposure, the task of therapy shifts naturally to providing clients with positive therapeutic experiences and proper stimulus conditions that will facilitate habituation and extinction. As noted by Rachman (1980), myriad factors influence emotional processing, with cognitive factors being among the most crucial. Catastrophic ideation can result in high levels of emotional distress, which subsequently results in marked psychophysiological arousal to levels prohibiting habituation (Lader & Mathews, 1968). Concerns with security cues an overall avoidant attitude and a tendency to employ noncoping distracting thoughts can virtually block effective exposure–habituation processes.

Many agoraphobics, following years of more severe handicaps, manage to enter several previously avoided phobic situations but pay the price of undue discomfort and phobic anxiety. Another clinical variant are clients who enter phobic situations but employ extensive precautionary measures such as sitting in the back of church, shopping only during off hours, or going out only on "good" days. Clearly, a major component of treatment would seem to be one of cognitive restructuring and anxiety management training.

Cognitive Strategies

CBT modalities have received considerable research attention over the past decade, and have been used to effectively treat phobias, anxiety, depression and other disorders (see review by Miller & Berman, 1983). A number of reviewers, including Kendall and Hollon (1979), Mahoney and Arnkoff (1978), and Rachman and Wilson (1980), have concluded that CBT is significantly superior to untreated controls and is equivalent, and in some cases superior, to other therapies. A recent meta-analytic review of CBT by Miller and Berman (1983) found that clients receiving CBT evidence an average effect size of .83, compared with untreated controls. However, there is no conclusive evidence that CBT is clearly superior to other well-established forms of treatment. This ambiguous standing vis-à-vis other treatments may be an unnecessarily conservative appraisal. Treatment outcome studies in CBT have frequently combined results from cognitive therapy (Beck), cognitive restructuring (Meichenbaum), stress inoculation training, and Ellis's rational-emotive therapy, which have important conceptual and clinical distinctions in presumed loci of effect. Second, many of the reviewed studies featured truncated treatments applied to analogue (nonclinical) populations. Furthermore, many of the outcome studies reviewed treated a broad array of clinical problems, with only a few focusing on agoraphobia.

Barrios and Shigetomi (1980) examined the application of self-statement modification (SSM), in 22 anxiety studies. SSM training procedures were found to be superior to attention-placebo controls. On both self-report and behavioral measures, SSM was superior to other treatment in about 37% of the comparisons and equal in 45% of the comparisons. This review grouped rational restructuring, cognitive restructuring, rational-emotive therapy and stress inoculation training under the SSM rubric. In addition, a number of the reviewed studies include confounding experimental variables such as PDMR as part of their package, and the majority of the studies surveyed pertained to specific fears. Thus, although these results are promising, conclusion must await more definitive outcome investigations that are free of confounds and use clinical populations.

Dushe, Hurt, and Schroeder (1983), in a more focused review of self-statement modification techniques, examined 69 studies and found an average effect size of .74 comparing SSM to no-treatment controls, in contrast to .49 among the non-SMR studies tested in 42 of the studies. Larger effect sizes were noted in studies featuring more intensive cognitive treatments (e.g., cognitive restructuring, behavior rehearsal, and homework) and efficacy was consistently increased with the addition of these components. Complex phobias responded quite well to SSM, yielding average effect sizes of 1.26 (versus no treatment), almost twice the level reported by Smith and Glass (1977), who found effect sizes of .68 aggregating across all forms of treatment and disorders. Overall, these meta-analytic reviews provide empirical support for the efficacy of a variety of CBT strategies for anxiety disorders in general. At present, however, only a handful of studies have specifically examined the effectiveness of CBT for agoraphobia, which will now be reviewed.

Cognitive Treatment of Agoraphobia

Emmelkamp, Kuiper, and Eggeraat (1978) examined cognitive restructuring (entailing Meichenbaum-type self-instructional training) on behavioral and phobic avoidance measures. However, treatment was conducted for only 1 week—far too short a period to result in significant cognitive change, as Emmelkamp (1982) later allowed. Further, therapists in the 1978 study were principally graduate students with unspecified familiarity with cognitive procedures or with the clinical population being treated. In another study, Emmelkamp and Mersh (1982) compared cognitive restructuring, prolonged *in vivo* exposure, and a combination treatment in a between-group design. Cognitive restructuring involved eight 2-hour visits of relabeling cognitions, self-instructional training and emitting more productive self-statements, and insight into unproductive thinking. At posttest, exposure and the combined procedure were clearly superior to cognitive restructuring on phobic anxiety and avoidance measures and on a behavioral measure. At the 1-month follow-up, however, differences between treatments were no longer apparent, as the cognitive group continued to improve while the exposure-alone subjects experienced mild relapse. Thus, in the long run, results for cognitive restructuring equaled, and in some cases exceeded, the effects of exposure.

Recently, Emmelkamp, Brilman, Kuiper, and Mersh (1986) randomly assigned 43 agoraphobics (DSM-III) to either exposure *in vivo*, rational-emotive therapy (RET), or self-instructional training (SIT). Treatment involved six sessions lasting 2½ hours each, conducted over a 3-week period. After a posttest, subjects received no treatment for 1 month and then, following a reassessment, received six 2½-hour sessions of *in vivo* exposure. At midtreatment, all conditions yielded significant improvements on behavioral measures, phobic anxiety, and avoidance scales, the Fear Questionnaire–Agoraphobia Scale (FQ–AG) and the HSCL-90 (Hopkins Symptom Checklist). In addition, the RET group experienced significant improvements on the Irrational Beliefs Test (IBT). Between-group differences revealed that exposure was superior to cognitive treatments, with RET producing greater improvements than SIT on the IBT. During the interim period without treatment, the exposure condition exhibited significant improvement on phobic anxiety and avoidance and the SCL-90, whereas the SIT condition manifested significant gains on the Phobic Avoidance Scale, the FQ–AG, and the IBT, with a borderline (i.e., marginally significant) effect ($p = .06$) reported for the behavioral measure. The RET condition showed no further improvement, with the follow-up data revealing that exposure was superior to the cognitive treatment on phobic anxiety and avoidance. During the second treatment phase, where all subjects received *in vivo* exposure, significant improvements were observed in the RET and on SIT groups on all phobic measures, phobic anxiety, phobic avoidance, and the FQ–AG. Similarly, the exposure–exposure condition also exhibited significant improvements on phobic anxiety FQ–AG, the IBT, and the SCL-90. The RET–exposure condition yielded further gains on the SCL-90.

The only between-group difference was found for the exposure–exposure group, which was superior to the cognitive interventions. With regard to the absolute level of clinical improvement, subjects were assigned to "much improved," "improved," or "failure" categories at mid- and posttreatment. At midtreatment, 10 of the 14 subjects in the exposure condition were rated as much improved or improved ($n = 5$); 11 of the 15 subjects in the RET condition were rated as a failure, and only 1 as much improved. The SIT condition had 1 subject much improved, 7 improved, and 6 rated as failures at midtreatment. At posttreatment none of the subjects in the exposure–exposure condition were rated as failures, with the RET–exposure condition exhibiting the most failures. The exposure–exposure condition had 8 subjects rated as much improved, and 5 as improved. SIT–exposure had 8 subjects rated as much improved, 5 as improved, and 1 as a failure. The RET–exposure condition had 3 subjects who were rated as much improved, 6 who improved, and 4 who were classified as failures.

The authors concluded that exposure was more effective than the cognitive treatments in reducing agoraphobics' anxiety and avoidance. They noted that although both SIT and RET evoked statistically significant improvements on most measures, the clinical improvements achieved were generally less impressive, particularly for RET, where most subjects were rated as failures. However, a number of conceptual, methodological, and interpretive limitations of the study render these conclusions only tentative. First, the fact that exposure subjects continued to improve on anxiety and avoidance measures during the waiting period can be explained by the fact that these subjects received homework assignments (programmed practice) between treatment sessions, whereas other subjects did not. Second, given the highly restricted duration of the cognitive treatment (3 weeks), there was an inadequate opportunity for the subjects to fully learn, integrate, use, and incorporate these cognitive coping strategies in their natural environment during such an attenuated treatment phase. Although subjects may have been able to score higher on the IBT, this may merely reflect an increase in content knowledge, but it does ensure that deeper cognitive structures and schemas have been therapeutically addressed. In addition, one-third of the subjects were on psychotropic medications, thereby precluding a complete analysis of their possible interactive effects with the cognitive and behavioral interventions.

Moreover, Emmelkamp et al. (1986) report that advanced students in clinical psychology served as therapists. Although the therapists received manuals and clinical supervision, there was no objective, independent analysis of treatment integrity, treatment fidelity, or therapist competency. As noted by Strupp (1986) ascertaining therapist expertise is difficult and may be addressed by at least preliminary attention to two major issues: first, the extent to which a clinician adheres to a particular set of technical operations and, second, the level of competence or skill exhibited by the therapist. Strupp states (1986, p. 126):

> A danger is that techniques may show a superficial resemblance to the standard, that is, they may be true to form but not necessarily to the substance of an approach. The principal point here is that the character of the therapeutic influence is only partially and perhaps insufficiently encompassed by the outer form or structure of the therapist communications; and even more important, it is very difficult to study the therapeutic influence merely from the outside (e.g., in terms of "gross outcome"), without reference to the context in which it occurs and in the manner in which the therapist communications are received and processed by the patient.

Similarly, Beck (personal communication, 1986) has noted that it takes several years to train *experienced* clinicians to conduct cognitive therapy faithfully, despite the fact they already have advanced degrees in clinical psychology and have practiced for many years in related areas (e.g., depression, anxiety disorders, etc.). Therefore, it is not unexpected that these student therapists, though more comfortable conducting the *in vivo* exposure, could not provide state-of-the-art cognitive treatment, given their relative inexperience and the complexity of both the treatments and the disorder in question. Hence it will be necessary to replicate these findings in an independent center where cognitive therapy is administered by experienced cognitive therapists whose treatment integrity and fidelity are closely monitored and objectively assessed. Furthermore, these cognitive treatments should be applied over longer periods of time (3–4 months) and there should be a greater opportunity for subjects to learn, integrate, and use their newly acquired cognitive coping skills.

Williams and Rappaport (1983) compared *in vivo* practice alone versus *in vivo* practice combined with "cognitive" techniques with agoraphobics suffering severe driving fear. Cognitive techniques in this case included instruction in selective attention, self-distraction, positive relabeling, and self-instruction. Results of the study were mixed, with the cognitive group performing as well as the exposure group on some measures, better on one, and worse on others. However, these findings must be viewed as tentative in light of a number of clinical and methodological concerns that undermine the validity of the results. For example, all subjects were *prohibited* from actually practicing *in vivo* self-directed exposure between treatment sessions. *In vivo* "cognitive therapy" was said to occupy only 90 minutes of the entire six-session, 11-hour training program, which transpired during only a 2-week period and focused only on driving. The 90-minute "'cognitive" treatment was apparently offered without extensive rationale and involved only 1 or 2 minutes of therapist planning and review of cognitive coping strategies for each driving foray. Nearly 50% of the time, "attention to environment" was endorsed as a "coping strategy"; "self-distraction" was encouraged 20% of the time. It remains unknown which cognitive therapy model such instructions were supposed to represent. Thus it is hardly surprising that no clear advantage emerged from the combined group. It is entirely likely that equivocal effects for cognitive techniques evidenced in this study stem directly from the inadequate treatment administered, lack of systematic instruction *in vivo*, prohibition of independent practice, limited number of sessions, and minimal duration of treatment. Given the attenuated nature of the treatment, it is probable that opportunity for clients to learn, integrate, and effectively apply their cognitive coping skills was severely limited.

Investigators in other phobia research centers have presented more encouraging findings using cognitive procedures with agoraphobics. Ascher (1980) examined the efficacy of paradoxical intention (PI) for several agoraphobics. In a multiple baseline design across two groups of clients, PI was shown to produce significantly greater approach behavior to target locations than did flooding. PI was also found to enhance the exposure intervention significantly.

Michelson et al. (1982) (cf. Mavissakalian, Michelson, Greenwald, Kornblith, & Greenwald, 1983, for expanded discussion) compared PI and self-statement training (SST) with 26 severe and chronic agoraphobics, in which all subjects received 12 weekly 90-minute sessions over a 3-month period, plus instructions for self-directed practice. Both treatments showed clear gains across virtually all measurement domains, in terms of both statistical and clinically significant indices of improvement. In addition, specific temporal effects were observed for the two treatments. Specifically, PI exhibited greater gains during treatment, whereas SST caught up with PI during a 6-month follow-up phase.

Part of the existing difficulty in appraising the potential value of cognitive treatments for agoraphobia so far may stem from differences and variations in the cognitive procedures employed. In Schwartz's (1982) excellent review of cognitive therapies, he notes that cognitions may be viewed as *simple habits* of thought with minimal organization and depth, as *cognitive structures*, plans, or strategies with considerable organization and depth, or as *unconscious cognitions* that are also organized and of great depth. Dushe et al. (1983) indicate that few reviewers of CBT studies have made practical distinctions among cognitive techniques, and draw conclusions as though Ellis's RET, Beck's Cognitive Therapy, and self-statement training are indistinct. Recent work by Hollon and Kriss (1984) suggests that treatments may be more or less metacognitive in nature and that different cognitive behavioral treatments may have different loci of effect. Specifically, differences may exist among cognitive therapies in efficacy for modifying *knowledge structures, cognitive processes*, or *cognitive products*. Some theorists (e.g., Beck, Rush, Shaw, & Emery, 1979; Coleman, 1981; Guidano & Liotti, 1983) suggest that cognitive procedures operating at the level of changing cognitive products (e.g., thoughts or self-statements alone, compared with a focus on larger structures or schemata) are operating at the lowest level and the one least likely to be efficacious in treating complex anxiety disorders like agoraphobia. In this vein, cognitive procedures that are not highly meta-cognitive may be inadequate therapeutic strategies for certain anxiety disorders, such as agoraphobia with its complex metacognitive elements (Beck, 1976; Coleman, 1981; Guidano & Liotti, 1983).

Investigations in which *low*-metacognitive cognitive-behavior modification proce-dures are pitted against exposure (i.e., Biran & Wilson, 1981; Biran, Augusto, & Wilson, 1981, 1983; Williams & Rappaport, 1983) typically find limited benefit associated with the addition of "cognitive coping" strategies as far as endstate performance and anxiety are concerned. Clearly, these findings can be principally regarded as an indictment of the so-called cognitive techniques that were used rather than of the use of cognitive therapy in itself. Furthermore, their attenuated treatments, lack of detailed rationale for clients, prohibition on between-session practice involving cognitive procedures, and so forth, all severely limit any substantive conclusions to be drawn regarding these "low" metacognitive studies.

Another issue concerns the comparison of cognitive and behavioral procedures. Some studies (e.g., Biran et al., 1983) have used cognitive procedures only, versus *in vivo* exposure. However, sophisticated cognitive therapies for phobics typically include behav-ioral components (e.g., Beck, 1984; Beck & Emery, 1979; Coleman, 1982; Ellis, 1979). For example, Emmelkamp et al. (1978) observed a transfer gap, in their cognitive condition, between practicing during the treatment sessions and applying the new form of behavior in real-life situations. These authors suggest that the effect of cognitive restructuring may have been increased further if the cognitive procedure was integrated with exposure. Similarly, Beck's Cognitive Therapy not only offers metacognitive elements in treatment, but also systematically integrates cognitive and behavioral changes via disconfirmatory experiences and cognitive reappraisal (e.g., Beck et al., 1979).

In the Michelson, Mavissakalian, Greenwald, Kornblith, and Greenwald (1983) study, the relative efficacy of two promising cognitive treatments was compared using paradoxical intention and self-statement training. Meichenbaum's SST was selected because it was one of the better recognized approaches and the technique was widely applied with analogue and other phobic populations. The rationale for using PI, as developed by Frankl (1960, 1975), was based on numerous positive clinical and anecdotal reports suggesting it may hold promise as an effective cognitive strategy in the treatment of agoraphobia. Although PI had enjoyed more widespread application to other anxiety-related problems including insomnia (Ascher & Efran, 1978); sexual dysfunction (Ascher & Clifford, 1977); and obsessive–compulsive disorder (Gertz, 1967; Wolpe & Ascher, 1976; Solyom, Garza-Perez, Ledwidge, & Solyom, 1972), there was a vacuum of research regarding its clinical utility with agoraphobics (Ascher, 1980). A recent exception was the study by Ascher (1981) demonstrating that PI induced greater approach behavior in agoraphobics than did graduated exposure *in vivo*. An additional factor behind the choice of these two cognitive strategies was their diametrically opposed instructional sets. Whereas SST was a rational process using cognitive restructuring to reduce self-defeating negative cognitions, PI had an intuitive and experiential quality, trying to engage clients to become as anxious as possible and to employ humor as a coping strategy. Thus, one aim of the study was to examine the differential effects of these two cognitive procedures in the treatment of agoraphobia.

Subjects were asked during each session to describe anxiety-eliciting situations. Typically, difficulties in phobic situations encountered during the previous week were made the focus of the in-session practice for each client. Subjects imagined themselves in anxiety-provoking situations and were instructed to verbalize the appropriate cognitive techniques. For example, subjects in the SST condition imagined they were entering a fearful situation and were learning to *prepare, handle, cope* with, and *reinforce* themselves with appropriate self-statements as instructed and modeled by the therapist. Similarly, subjects in the PI condition imagined they were entering situations with the intention of becoming as anxious and panicky as possible. Therapists encouraged the introduction of humor, which is felt to be an important ingredient in the PI ("I'll show the world that I'm the best fainter anywhere," or "I hope people around here know how to swim because I'm really going to sweat a lot"). In addition, subjects practiced the procedure twice during each session and were encouraged to practice their newly learned cognitive coping strategies regularly between formal treatment sessions.

The results revealed statistically significant pre–post improvements across all domains with both treatments, although a number of superior treatment effects were observed for PI subjects compared to SST subjects. By the 6-month follow-up assessment, however, the groups were approximately equivalent because of the marked improvement in the interim period of the SST subjects. These results were highly encouraging and provided empirical support that cognitive treatments, accompanied by programmed practice instructions to engage in self-directed *in vivo* exposure, can be highly effective for agoraphobia.

Analyses of cognitive changes revealed several interesting results. First, there was a clear trend for self-defeating thoughts to decline with both treatments. The changes, however, occurred relatively late, between the sixth and twelfth weeks of treatment, underscoring the tenacity of faulty cognitions and the extended periods of time required to alter them effectively. Self-defeating thoughts were not necessarily replaced by positive statements. This was particularly the case in the PI group, as PI statements were virtually absent. Indeed, positive statements essentially remained unchanged from the pretreatment levels, although the ratio of positive to negative thoughts evidenced significant improvement. These findings provide support for Schwartz and Garamoni's (1986) theory regarding optimal states of mind, which depicts the ideal ratio of positive to negative thoughts (cf. Schwartz & Michelson, 1986).

In light of the positive findings from this study, a large-scale comparative outcome investigation was undertaken, supported by the National Institute of Mental Health. The primary objective of the study was to examine the differential outcome, process, synchrony, and maintenance effects of PI (representing a cognitive intervention), PDMR (a psychophysiological modality), and GE (a behaviorally focused intervention). In a report based on the first half of the complete sample, Michelson, Mavissakalian, and Marchione (1985) reported on the relative efficacy of these three treatments for 39 severe and chronic agoraphobics (DSM-III). Treatment consisted of 12 2-hour weekly sessions conducted by experienced protocol therapists, whose treatment integrity was objectively monitored. All subjects received an extensive rationale emphasizing self-directed *in vivo* exposure and programmed practice in addition to their primary treatment. A comprehensive assessment battery consisting of clinical ratings of severity, phobia, anxiety, depression, and panic, as well as direct measures of behavioral, psychophysiological, and cognitive response systems was administered at the pretreatment, midtreatment, posttreatment, and 3-month follow-up phases. Because comparative outcome studies simultaneously contrasting behavioral, cognitive, and physiologically based treatments for agoraphobics had not been conducted to date, the study was undertaken to address a number of important conceptual and clinical issues. The overall results revealed statistically significant treatment effects across all conditions, indicating that all modalities were able to yield significant therapeutic improvements for these severe agoraphobics. From pre- to posttreatment, subjects in all conditions exhibited significant improvements across agoraphobia, anxiety, phobia, depression, and behavioral measures.

Overall, the three modalities were relatively and highly effective in effecting significant improvements from pre- to posttreatment and pretreatment to 3-month follow-up assessment. The GE and PDMR conditions, however, evidenced greater *potency* and *stability* of treatment effects than did PI. Interestingly, psychophysiological analyses revealed significant improvements for GE and PDMR treatments from pre- to posttreatment. Conversely, PI subjects experienced increases in physiological reactivity during treatment, not until the 3-month follow-up were they equivalent in their physiological functioning. This finding suggests that PI subjects required additional time to consolidate effectively and use their newly acquired coping skills. It is also important to note that all these psychologically based treatments were relatively effective in treating spontaneous panic attacks, typically regarded as a core feature of agoraphobia. These results attest to the efficacy of these interventions in treating agoraphobia. In addition, subjects' locus-of-control scores were found to have shifted toward greater internality as their assertiveness scores evidenced corresponding increases. These findings suggest that the treatment was able to effect improvements on generalization measures, although they were not directly targeted for therapeutic change.

Several comments are warranted regarding the overall findings. First, although GE was one of the most effective strategies, it also experienced a dropout rate twice that for PI or PDMR. These results suggest that although GE may be a necessary, though not sufficient, condition for the effective treatment of agoraphobia, its combination and possible synergism with relaxation training and/or cognitive therapy merits further study. A multimodal treatment approach would represent a more state-of-the-art treatment of this complex anxiety disorder by simultaneously addressing the three dimensions of the disorder. Treatment integration of this nature is likely to result in improved outcome, synchrony, and maintenance and generalization effects.

Adjunctive Treatment Strategies

PROBLEM-SOLVING

Problem-solving represents a conceptually appealing and clinically salient process that could have important implications in agoraphobia treatment. It has not been subjected to programmatic empirical study, however, and there have been only a few reports examining the utility of problem solving as a treatment for agoraphobia. Jannoun et al. (1980) randomly assigned 28 agoraphobic women to one of two treatments—programmed practice or problem solving. All treatment was carried out in the subjects' homes with the cooperation of their spouses. Assessments were conducted at pretreatment, posttreatment, and 3- and 6-month follow-ups. Programmed practice generally exhibited superiority over problem solving. One therapist, however, obtained unexpectedly large treatment effects, comparable with those of therapists conducting programmed practice. Although the results of the study provided support regarding the importance of self-directed *in vivo* exposure in reducing phobic anxiety and phobic avoidance, the findings also offered suggestive evidence regarding the potential utility of problem solving.

Cullington, Butler, Hibbert, and Gelder (1984), in a replication study designed to test further the efficacy of problem solving without exposure, treated 14 agoraphobic women with problem solving. The problem solving treatment included: (1) conducting all sessions at home, (2) close involvement of the partner in therapy, (3) the use of an instruction manual, (4) a graded approach to exposure, (5) self-monitoring, and (6) homework. Each subject and her partner were instructed to spend an hour a day identifying potentially stressful life problems, discussing alternative ways of resolving these issues, and setting graded targets for problem solving. No advice or directions about *in vivo* exposure were administered. Furthermore, subjects were told that agoraphobia results from undue sensitivity to stress, which can be decreased by resolving problems that contribute to an internal state of anxiety.

The authors report that problem solving was not an effective treatment for agoraphobia. Subjects did not improve significantly either during treatment or at the follow-up. The authors suggest that explanations other than problem solving may have accounted for the initially positive findings from the first study. They note the possibility that the therapist might have encouraged subjects to practice self-directed exposure or might have had an unusually highly motivated group of subjects. Unfortunately, these issues have not yet been resolved. Indeed, in an exchange of letters to the editor, D'Zurilla (1985) raised a number of points suggesting that the problem solving was moderately effective for a number of the subjects in the study. D'Zurilla states (p. 456): The conclusion that problem-solving training is a promising treatment strategy for agoraphobia still stands. It should be noted that the successful results for problem solving were achieved with minimal training of problem-solving skills. With a more intensive training program, the therapist as well as clients' treatment effects might be even greater and more consistent.

Butler and Gelder (1985) responded that the specific problem-solving treatment they used was not efficacious. However, Butler and Gelder did not attempt to generalize their negative findings, leaving the proverbial door open for future research. As noted in their rebuttal (1985, p. 549):

> We do not, however, wish to claim that other versions of problem-solving would produce the same results. Two characteristics of problem-solving treatments may be partly responsible for our results. In the first place, treatment was very brief. Longer treatment may be more effective but also would be more expensive in therapist time. In the second place, exposure of all kinds was excluded in problem-solving so as to clarify the comparison with programmed

practice. It is likely that agoraphobics treated with problem-solving under less restrictive conditions would use some form of exposure as a means of solving their agoraphobic problem. This should increase the effectiveness of problem-solving. . . .

There is at present an inadequate empirical basis regarding the efficacy of problem solving as a treatment for agoraphobia to recommend it as a primary therapeutic strategy. However, the integration of problem-solving training, within a cognitive framework, would be both theoretically well grounded and likely to facilitate clinical improvement and generalization effects. Furthermore, the use of problem solving, not as a self-treatment strategy but as a therapeutic adjunct to exposure, relaxation training, and other behavioral interventions, might prove highly beneficial. The adjunctive use of problem solving could be highly focused with regard to resolving agoraphobia-related problems and increasing exposure practices, thus enhancing treatment outcome.

MARITAL THERAPY

Several authors have emphasized the role of marital discord in the development and maintenance of phobic syndromes (Emmelkamp, 1979; Goldstein & Chambless, 1978). Clinically, there is some evidence that interpersonal conflict plays a mediating role in the development of agoraphobia. Two avenues of research are relevant in this respect: first, reports examining the effects of marital satisfaction on outcome and, second, studies examining whether improvement in phobic functioning was mediated on a short- or a long-term basis by marital adjustment. Hudson (1974) reported that agoraphobics from distressed families exhibited significantly less improvement than subjects from adjusted families. Similarly, Milton and Hafner (1979) observed that prolonged *in vivo* exposure was significantly superior for agoraphobics whose marriages were rated as satisfactory prior to treatment versus those whose marriages were rated as unsatisfactory.

Bland and Hallam (1981) investigated the level of marital satisfaction with regard to subject's responses to prolonged *in vivo* exposure and obtained significant differences between "good" and "bad" marriages with respect to phobic severity. Three-month follow-up analyses indicated that maritally distressed subjects exhibited a significantly greater tendency to relapse compared to subjects in maritally adjusted couples. Interestingly, the improvement was found to be significantly associated with the subject's satisfaction with spouse, rather than the spouse's satisfaction with the subject. These data suggest that although significant differences may not always appear immediately after treatment, maritally distressed agoraphobics may be at greater risk for relapse than are subjects who are maritally well adjusted. It is not surprising that anxiety- and phobic-related problems are significantly maintained by relationship factors. In any reciprocal relationship, where phobic problems exist, they can have a negative impact on marital satisfaction and can exacerbate phobic anxiety and avoidance. For example, over 30 years ago, Webster (1953) examined the records of 75 neurotic outpatients comprising equal numbers of agoraphobics, anxiety neurotics, and conversion hysterics. The author found that agoraphobics reported a disproportionate incidence of marital difficulties. Parenthetically, only those agoraphobics whose husbands participated in the treatment evidenced improvement. Hand and Lamonthagne (1976) found that two-thirds of their agoraphobic subjects were aware of chronic marital problems and that one-third actually experienced acute marital crises after successful treatment of their agoraphobia. Milton and Hafner (1979) found that the 50% of their agoraphobic subjects who were maritally distressed experienced increased symptomatology.

Barlow et al. (1981) reported that marital satisfaction decreased for one-third of the couples successfully treated for the wives' agoraphobia. Treatment consisted of a combination of group sessions with the husband present, graduated exposure, and cognitive restructuring. All subjects, however, had improved at posttreatment. Subjects continued to make progress, raising questions of whether marital satisfaction was a poor prognostic factor for agoraphobia. Bland and Hallam's (1981) study suggests that exposure treatment is effective in the short term and is independent of level of marital stress or dissatisfaction. Marital conflict, however, appears to be associated with higher risk for relapse during follow-up. Chambless and Goldstein (1980) report the use of spouses in their innovative phobia treatment program. However, there are at present limited data regarding the efficacy of their conjoint marital therapy program. Recently, Barlow, O'Brien, and Last (1984) compared 14 agoraphobic women who were treated with cognitive restructuring and self-initiated exposure, with and without their spouses. The authors found substantial advantage with the spouse group when compared to the nonspouse group on measures of agoraphobia. Ratings of social, work, and family functioning also exhibited more rapid improvements among the spouse group, although this comparative advantage had disappeared at posttest. Although it was assumed that the spouse group would exhibit significant advantages with regard to enhancing subject's self-directed *in vivo* exposure outings between treatment sessions, these hypotheses were not confirmed, suggesting that the mechanism of superior clinical efficacy was more complex than merely increasing self-exposure outings. The authors concluded that including husbands in the treatment program provided a substantial clinical advantage, with 12 out of 14 clients responding to treatment. Conversely, women treated without their husbands did not fare as well.

Although additional research needs to be conducted in this area, the use of marital therapy appears to be optimally directed when it is focused specifically on overcoming the client's agoraphobia. As concluded by Cobb, MacDonald, Marks, & Stern, (1980), the treatment of choice for phobias, even when marked marital problems exist, remains behavioral treatment. There is suggestive evidence that the most effective treatment program should begin with behavioral strategies, with marital therapy being used for couples with significant marital adjustment problems (Cobb et al., 1980; Barlow et al., 1984).

Individual Differences, Response Profiles, and Treatment Consonance

In research, and particularly in clinical practice, the role of individual differences has been largely ignored despite theoretical formulations portraying the crucial importance of identifying clients' unique tripartite response patterns (Hugdahl, 1981; Lang, 1977; Rachman, 1978). Empirical studies of the role of individual differences in mediating treatment outcome have only recently been undertaken. Recognizing that anxiety disorders are conceptualized as comprising three loosely interwoven dimensions—cognition, behavior, and physiology—agoraphobics or anxiety subjects in general may manifest any of a variety of possible response profiles. Only rarely, however, have the responses of anxiety subjects been triangulated across the tripartite systems (Rachman, 1978; Rachman & Hodgson, 1974). As discussed by Michelson (1984b, p. 452):

> Inadequate clinical-research attention has been paid to the role of individual differences regarding the tripartite assessment of anxiety disorders. This may be partly due to the theoretical and methodological complexities involved. However, broad conclusions regarding the efficacy of a therapeutic strategy cannot be made on the basis of monitoring only a few response channels. Individual differences which reflect the multideterminant nature of anxiety are expanding our awareness and research focus regarding the need for tridimensional assessment. Reviews of various anxiety disorder treatments attest to the efficacy of many behavioral, physiological and cognitive strategies. However, the application of prescriptive treatments for individuals, based upon their unique anxiety profiles, has not been forthcoming. In light of the complex nature of anxiety disorders, the development of reliable and valid taxonomies, to delineate anxiety profiles across cognitive, physiological, and behavioral dimensions, should yield enhanced treatment outcome. Such efforts would lead directly to more fine-grained functional analyses of all of the anxiety disorders and utilization of prescriptive, and logically more effective, interventions.

Recently, several studies have been reported that examined the role of individual differences and treatment consonance for anxiety disorders. *Consonance* refers to the proposition that subjects with a specific anxiety profile will respond differentially to treatments that focus on remediating that specific deficit. For example, subjects identified as being particularly high on psychophysiological reactivity, with only modest phobic avoidance or minimal cognitive distortions, would be hypothesized as being more responsive to an intervention designed to restore normal levels of psychophysiological functioning, such as PDMR. Conversely, subjects with high levels of cognitive distortions, and only modest psychophsiological reactivity or avoidance, would be predicted to respond more favorably to cognitive therapy. Finally, subjects experiencing marked phobic avoidance, with only mild elevations on the other channels, could be expected to respond more rapidly to behaviorally based (i.e., exposure) treatment.

In reviews of the treatment consonance literature in anxiety disorders (Michelson, 1984b, 1986), a series of studies were examined that revealed marked individual differences and treatment consonance effects. Norton and Johnson (1983) found that meditation-type strategies were most efficacious for "cognitive reactors," whereas relaxation training was more effective for somatically anxious subjects. In a benchmark series of investigations, Öst and his colleagues (1981, 1982, 1984) provided empirical support for the hypothesis that individual differences and treatment consonance have a significant impact on therapeutic outcome. Öst et al. (1981) found that social phobics responded differentially when classified as "behavioral" rather than "physiological" reactors and when receiving behavioral as opposed to psychophysiologically based therapies. When subjects were assigned to a consonant treatment (i.e., behavioral reactors to the behavioral treatment, physiological reactors to the physiological treatment), treatment effects were significantly enhanced.

Öst et al. (1982) replicated these effects for claustrophobics, with behavioral reactors who were assigned to exposure treatment evidencing significantly superior effects at posttreatment compared with those assigned to relaxation training. Conversely, physiological reactors assigned to relaxation training exhibited superior functioning at posttest compared to physiological reactors assigned to exposure treatment. Thus subjects treated with a consonant form of therapy exhibited significantly greater improvement than did subjects receiving a nonconsonant treatment.

In a recent report, Öst et al. (1984) extended their investigations of individual differences and treatment consonance to agoraphobics who were assigned to either behavioral or physiological resonse profile types and randomly assigned to either behaviorally based (i.e., exposure) or physiologically oriented (i.e., relaxation training) treatments. At posttreatment, consonantly treated agoraphobics manifested 80% overall improvement, compared to only a 49% level of high improvement observed among nonconsonantly treated subjects. Behavioral responders receiving exposure exhibited a high end state functioning rate of 75%, compared to only 58% receiving relaxation training. Similarly, physiological reactors receiving relaxation training exhibited a high end state functioning rate of 87.5%, compared to only 37.5% who received exposure, a nonconsonant modality for their response profile.

These studies by Öst et al. support the hypothesis that anxiety subjects exhibit significantly improved outcome when their treatment is specifically matched (i.e., consonant with their response profiles). These findings, culled from independent research centers and across different anxiety disorders, reveal consistently higher rates of improvement and end state functioning for anxiety subjects receiving treatments that are most consonant with their response profiles. Despite the many positive aspects of these studies, however, there were no reports examining the *three* primary response profiles across cognitive-behavioral and physiologically based treatments. In addition, there were no published studies comparing interactions of response typologies across alternative treatments, where the tripartite dismensions were systematically assessed across time.

To address these crucial issues, Michelson (1986) examined treatment consonance and response profiles for agoraphobics undergoing cognitive, behavioral, and physiological treatments (cf. Michelson, Mavissakalian, & Marchione 1985). Subjects were first identified as "cognitive," "behavioral," or "physiological" responders at pretreatment based on detailed a priori operationalized criteria (cf. Michelson, 1986). Once subjects were classified as either behavioral, cognitive, or physiological reactors, they were then grouped according to whether they received a consonant or a nonconsonant treatment. Consonant subjects included behavioral reactors assigned to graduated exposure (GE), cognitive reactors assigned to paradoxical intention (PI), and physiological reactors assigned to relaxation training (RT). Nonconsonant classifications included behavioral reactors assigned to PI or RT, cognitive reactors assigned to RT or GE, and physiological reactors assigned to either PI or GE. Subsequently, individuals who had received a consonant form of treatment were compared with subjects receiving a nonconsonant modality.

As hypothesized, agoraphobics receiving consonant treatments exhibited significantly greater treatment effects and tripartite concordance than did their nonconsonantly treated cohorts. Consonantly treated agoraphobics manifested enhanced levels of end state functioning and short-term maintenance. There was also a pattern of between-group differences observed, which revealed a modest temporal lag, with the majority of differences appearing at the posttreatment and follow-up assessment phases. This suggests that consonance status may operate in a delayed manner, increasing its influence as treatment progresses. Clinically pronounced and significant differences were observed between consonant and nonconsonant subjects on measures of severity, fears, phobias, anxiety, depression, general symptomatology, and psychophysiology. Overall, subjects responded more favorably to treatment when they received therapeutic modalities that were most congruent with their primary response profiles. These differences were observed across the tripartite systems. In sum, these results corroborate findings from studies conducted in independent anxiety disorder centers with claustrophobics, agoraphobics, and social phobics.

As noted by Michelson (1986, p. 22):

> Future research will need to continue to develop reliable and valid response profile taxonomies to delineate specific subtypes across each of the anxiety disorders. Advances in response profiling will directly facilitate the uncovering of various layers of the multidimensional and interactive systems of anxiety disorders. Examination of individual differences, response profiles and treatment consonance may decrease heretofore unexplained treatment outcome variance in comparative outcome studies. Furthermore . . . response profiles may also shift in amplitude and shape over time. There may be as yet unidentified temporal progressions, patterns and developmental stages regarding particular response profiles across the anxiety disorders. Importantly, specific change sequences may be associated with more difficult treatment or potential relapse phenomena. Temporal patterns of response profiles may also shift in response in their personal forces, situational factors, and life events. Thus, careful study of the longitudinal stability of the profiles both within and across anxiety disorders would be valuable.

The tripartite assessment model offers critical advances with regard to the conceptualization, assessment, and treatment of agoraphobia specifically, and anxiety disorders in general. The distinct possibility of designing individually tailored treatments adapted specifically to the unique tripartite profile of each client is on the clinical horizon. Empirical examination of individual differences, and their potential mediating influence on treatment synchrony, concordance, outcome, and maintenance, appears highly promising.

Conclusion

Agoraphobia is a severe, chronic, and debilitating anxiety disorder with relatively high prevalence rates in the general population. Although exposure-based strategies have been regarded as one of the treatments of choice, the *overall* improvement rate does not exceed 50% because of problematic dropout and failure-to-respond rates. Moreover, an increasing number of clinical researchers assert that although exposure may be a necessary means of treating phobic anxiety and avoidance, it is often insufficient by itself. In an attempt to provide a more comprehensive treatment of anxiety disorders, theorists are increasingly incorporating cognitive mediational procedures as useful explanatory mechanisms and treatment strategies. Recent conceptualizations of agoraphobia suggest that cognitive interventions aimed at changing negative expectancies, inadequate perceptions of safety, cognitive errors and distortions, misattributions associated with somatic arousal, and perceptions of control may be beneficial in ameliorating agoraphobia.

Moreover, the notion that anxiety disorders comprise tripartite systems that may respond differentially to various treatment procedures suggests the utility of combining treatments to evoke generalized effects across all domains. Thus it is both theoretically and clinically appealing to address multiple response systems that are likely to yield increased rates of synchrony, concordance, maintenance, and generalization. Indeed, behavioral treatment directed only at conditioned fear and avoidance may be of limited value in that two of the other primary features of agoraphobia—namely, the cognitive and physiological domains of functioning—may not be sufficiently addressed by exposure alone. Contemporary conceptualizations suggest that cognitive procedures operating at the metacognitive level may be the most effective therapeutic strategies for complex anxiety disorders such as agoraphobia.

In addition to examining cognitive mediational strategies, integrating physiological self-control procedures as part of an *in vivo* exposure treatment is both conceptually and clinically sound. Recognizing the marked psychophysiological reactivity and related somatic anxiety arousal of agoraphobics, it is important that effective psychophysiological self-control strategies be developed and combined with *in vivo* exposure strategies. Thus an adjunct to treatment that increases self-control of physiological arousal can provide an active coping strategy during GE practices. This in turn helps clients reduce their phobic arousal and directly promotes habituation, leading to decreased phobic anxiety and avoidance. Moreover, psychosocial approaches for reducing visceral arousal are likely to increase self-control, synchronous improvement and concordance.

Acknowledgments

Preparation of this chapter was supported in part by a grant from the National Institute of Mental Health (MH36299).

References

Abramson, L. Y., Seligman, M. E. P., & Teasdale, J. D. (1978). Learned helplessness in humans: Critique and reformulation. *Journal of Abnormal Psychology, 87,* 32–48.

Agras, S. W., & Jacob, R. J. (1981). Phobia: Nature and measurement. In M. Mavissakalian & D. Barlow (Eds.), *Phobia: Psychological and pharmacologic treatment.* New York: Guilford Press.

Agras, S. W., Leitenberg, H., & Barlow, D. H. (1968). Social reinforcement in the modification of agoraphobia. *Archives of General Psychiatry, 19,* 423–427.

Agras, S., Sylvester, D., & Oliveau, D. (1969). The epidemiology of common fears and phobias. *Comprehensive Psychiatry, 10,* 151–156.

Alexander, A. B. (1972). Systematic relaxation and flow rates in asthmatic children: Relationship to emotional precipitants and anxiety. *Journal of Psychosomatic Research, 16,* 405–410.

American Psychiatric Association. (1980). *Diagnostic and statistical manual of mental disorders* (3rd ed.). Washington, DC: Author.

Archer, R. P. (1980). Generalized expectancies of control, trait anxiety and psychopathology among psychiatric inpatients. *Journal of Consulting and Clinical Psychology, 48,* 736–742.

Arena, J. G., Blanchard, E. B., Andraski, R., Cotch, P. A., & Myers, P. E. (1983). Reliability of psychophysiological assessment. *Behaviour Research and Therapy, 21,* 447–460.

Ascher, L. M. (1980). Paradoxical intention. In A. Goldstein & E. B. Foa (Eds.), *Handbook of behavioral interventions.* New York: Wiley.

Ascher, L. M. (1981). Employing paradoxical intention in the treatment of agoraphobia. *Behaviour Research and Therapy, 19,* 533–542.

Ascher, L. M., & Clifford, R. E. (1977). Behavior considerations in the treatment of sexual dysfunction. In M. Hersen, R. M. Eisler, & P. M. Miller (Eds.), *Progress in behavior modification* (Vol. 3). New York: Academic Press.

Ascher, L. M., & Efran, J. S. (1978). The use of paradoxical intention in a behavioral program for sleep onset insomnia. *Journal of Consulting and Clinical Psychology, 46,* 547–558.

Bandura, A. (1977). Self-efficacy: Toward a unifying theory of behavioral change. *Psychological Review, 84,* 191–215.

Barlow, D. (1985). The dimensions of anxiety disorders. A. H. Tuma & J. D. Maser (Eds.), *Anxiety and the anxiety disorders.* Hillsdale, NJ: Erlbaum.

Barlow, D. H., O'Brien, G. T., & Last, C. G. (1984). Couples' treatment of agoraphobia. *Behavior Therapy, 15,* 41–58.

Barlow, D. H., Mavissakalian, M., & Hay, L. (1981). Couples' treatment of agoraphobia: Changes in marital satisfaction. *Behaviour Research and Therapy, 19,* 245–255.

Barrios, B. A., & Shigatomi, C. (1980). Coping skills training for the management of anxiety: A critical review. *Behavior Therapy, 10,* 491–522.

Beck, A. T. (1976). *Cognitive therapy and the emotional disorders.* New York: International Universities Press.

Beck, A. T. (1984). *Cognitive therapy of agoraphobia.* Unpublished paper.

Beck, A. T., & Emery, G. (1979). *Cognitive therapy of anxiety and phobic disorders.* Philadelphia: Center for Cognitive Therapy.

Beck, A. T., Rush A. J., Shaw, B. F., & Emery, G. (1979). *Cognitive therapy of depression.* New York: Guilford Press.

Beck, A. T., Ward, C. H., Mendelsohn, M., Mock, J., & Erbaugh, J. (1961). An inventory for measuring depression. *Archives of General Psychiatry, 4,* 53–63.

Beidel, D., & Turner, S. (1985). *Empirical subtypes of social anxiety.* Unpublished manuscript, Department of Psychiatry University of Pittsburgh School of Medicine.

Bellack, A. S., & Lombardo, T. W. (1985). Measurement of anxiety. In S. M. Turner (Ed.), *Behavioral theories and treatments of anxiety.* New York: Plenum Press.

Benjafield, J., & Adams-Webber, J. R. (1976). The golden section hypothesis. *British Journal of Psychology, 67,* 11–15.

Bernstein, D. A., & Borkovec, T. D. (1973). *Progressive relaxation training.* Champaign, IL: Research Press.

Biran, M., Augusto, F., & Wilson, G. T. (1981). *In vivo* exposure vs. cognitive restructuring in the treatment of scriptophobia. *Behaviour Research and Therapy, 19,* 525–532.

Biran, M., & Wilson, G. T. (1981a). Cognitive vs. behavioral methods in the treatment of phobic disorders: A self-efficacy analysis. *Journal of Consulting and Clinical Psychology, 49,* 108–125.

Biran, M., & Wilson, G. T. (1981b). Treatment of phobic disorders using cognitive and exposure methods: A self-efficacy analysis. *Journal of Consulting and Clinical Psychology, 49,* 886–889.

Blanchard, E. B., & Young L. D. (1974). Clinical applications of biofeedback training: A review of evidence. *Archives of General Psychiatry, 30,* 573–589.

Bland, K., & Hallam, R. S. (1981). Relationship between response to graded exposure and marital satisfaction in agoraphobics. *Behaviour Research and Therapy, 19,* 335–338.

Borkovec, T. D., & Sides, J. K. (1979). Critical procedural variables related to the physiological effects of progressive relaxation: A review. *Behaviour Research and Therapy, 17,* 119–125.

Borkovec, T. D., Weertz, T. C., & Bernstein, D. A. (1977). Assessment of anxiety. In A. R. Ciminero, K. S. Calhoun, & H. E. Adams (Eds.), *Handbook of behavioral assessment.* New York: Wiley.

Brehony, K. A., & Geller, E. S. (1981). Agoraphobia: Appraisal of research and a proposal from an integrative model. In M. Hersen, P. Miller, & R. Eisler (Eds.), *Progress in behavior modification* (Vol. 12). New York: Academic Press.

Brodbeck, C., & Michelson, L. (1986). Problem-solving skills and attributional styles of agoraphobics. *Cognitive Therapy and Research,* in press.

Burns, L. E., & Thorpe, G. L. (1977). The epidemiology of fears and phobias with particular reference to the rational privacy of agoraphobics. *Journal of International Medical Research, 5,* 1–7.

Butler, G. & Gelder, M. (1985). Problem-solving: Not a treatment for agoraphobia. A reply to D'Zurilla. *Behavior Therapy, 16,* 548–550.

Cacioppo, J. T., & Petty, R. E. (1983). Social psychological procedures for cagnitive response assessments: The thought listing technique. In T. V. Merluzzi, C. R. Glass, & M. Genest (Eds.), *Cognitive asessment.* New York: Guilford Press.

Chambless, D. C. (1982). Characteristics of agoraphobics. In D. L. Chambless & A. J. Goldstein (Eds.) *Agoraphobia: Multiple perspectives on theory of treatment.* New York: Wiley.

Chambless, D. L., Caputo, C., Bright, P., & Gallagher, R. (1984). Assessment of fear of fear in agoraphobics: The *Body Sensations Questionnaire* and the *Agoraphobic Cognitions Questionnaire. Journal of Consulting and Clinical Psychology, 52,* 1090–1097.

Chambless, D. L., Caputo, C., Jasin, S., Gracely, E., & Williams, C. (1985). *The Mobility Inventory for agoraphobia. Behaviour Research and Therapy, 23,* 35–44.

Chambless, D. L., & Goldstein, A. J. (1982). *Agoraphobia: Multiple perspectives on theory and treatment.* New York: Wiley.

Cobb, J. P., MacDonald, R., Marks, I. N., & Stern, R. (1980). Marital versus exposure therapy: Psychological treatments of co-existing marital and phobic–obsessive problems. *European Journal of Behavior Analysis and Modification, 4,* 3–17.

Coleman, R. E. (1981). Cognitive-behavioral treatment of agoraphobia. In G. Emery, S. D. Hollon, & R. C. Bedrosian (Eds.), *New directions in cognitive therapy.* New York: Guilford Press.

Coleman, R. E. (1982). In G. Emery, S. D. Hollon, & R. Bedrosian (Eds.), *New directions in cognitive therapy.* New York: Guilford Press.

Cox, D. J., Freundlich, A., & Meyer, R. G. (1974). Differential effectiveness of electromyograph feedback, verbal relaxation instructions and medication placebo with tension headaches. *Journal of Consulting and Clinical Psychology, 43,* 892–898.

Cullington, A., Butler, G., Hibbert, G., & Gelder, M. (1984). Problem-solving: Not a treatment for agoraphobia. *Behavior Therapy, 15,* 280–286.

Derogatis, L. R., Lipman, R. S., Rickels, K., Uhlenhuth, E. H., & Covi, L. (1974). The Hopkins Symptom Checklist: A self-report symptom inventory. *Behavioral Sciences, 19,* 1–15.

DeSilva, P., & Rachman, S. (1981). Is exposure a necessary condition for fear reduction? *Behaviour Research and Therapy, 19,* 227–232.

DiNardo, P. A., O'Brien, G. T., Barlow, D. H., Waddell, M. T., & Blanchard, E. B. (1983). Reliability of DSM-III anxiety disorder categories using a new structured interview. *Archives of General Psychiatry, 40,* 1070–1074.

Doctor, R. M. (1982). *Major results of a large-scale pretreatment survey of agoraphobics.* Unpublished manuscript, California State University.

Dushe, D. M., Hurt, M. L., & Schroeder, H. (1983). Self-statement modification with adults: A meta-analysis. *Psychological Bulletin, 94,* 408–442.

D'Zurilla, T. J. (1985). Problem-solving: Still a promising treatment strategy for agoraphobia. *Behavior Therapy, 16,* 545–550.

Eaton, W. W., & Kessler, L. G. (Eds.) (1984). *Epidemiologic field methods in psychiatry: the NIMH epidemiologic catchment area program.* New York: Academic Press.

Ellis, A. (1979). A note on the treatment of agoraphobics with cognitive modification with prolonged exposure in vivo. *Behaviour Research and Therapy, 17,* 162–164.

Emmelkamp, P. M. G. (1979). The behavioral study of clinical phobias. In M. Hersen, P. Miller, & R. Eisler (Eds.), *Progress in behavior modification* (Vol. 8). New York: Academic Press.

Emmelkamp, P. M. G. (1982). *Phobic and obsessive–compulsive disorders.* New York: Plenum Press.

Emmelkamp, P. M. G., Brilman, E., Kuiper, H., & Mersh, P. P. (1986). The treatment of agoraphobia: A comparison of self-instructional training, rational motive therapy and exposure in vivo. *Behavior Modification, 10,* 37–53.

Emmelkamp, P. M. G., & Cohen-Kettenis, P. T. (1975). Relationship of locus of control to phobic anxiety and depression. *Psychological Reports, 36,* 390.

Emmelkamp, P. M. G., Kuipers, A. C. M., & Eggeraat, J. B. (1978). Cognitive modification vs. prolonged exposure in vivo: A comparison with agoraphobics as subjects. *Behaviour Research and Therapy, 16,* 33–41.

Emmelkamp, P. M. G., & Mersh, P. P. (1982). Cognition and exposure *in vivo* in the treatment of agoraphobia: Short-term and delayed effects. *Cognitive Research and Therapy, 6,* 72–90

Emmelkamp, P. M. G., & Wessler, H. (1975). Flooding in imagination vs. flooding *in vivo*: A comparison with agoraphobics. *Behaviour Research and Therapy, 13,* 7–15.

Endicott, J., & Spitzer, R. L. (1978). A diagnostic interview: The schedule for affective disorders and schizophrenia. *Archives of General Psychiatry, 35,* 837–844.

Endicott, J., & Spitzer, R. L. (1979). Use of the research diagnostic criteria and the schedule for affective disorders in schizophrenia to study affective disorders. *American Journal of Psychiatry, 136,* 52–56.

Fey, G. S., & Lindholm, E. (1978). Biofeedback and progressive relaxation: Effects on systolic and diastolic blood pressure and heart rate. *Psychophysiology, 15,* 239–247.

Foa, E. B., & Kozak, M. (1986). Emotional processing of fear: Exposure to corrective information. *Psychological Bulletin, 99,* 20–35.

Frankl, V. E. (1960). Paradoxical intention: A logotherapeutic technique. *American Journal of Psychotherapy, 14,* 520–535.

Frankl, V. E. (1975). Paradoxical intention and dereflection. *Psychotherapy: Theory, Research and Practice, 12,* 226–237.

Freedman, R., Ianni, M., Ettedgui, E., & Puthezhath, N. (1985). Ambulatory monitoring of panic disorder. *Archives of General Psychiatry, 42,* 244–248.

Gelder, M. G., & Marks, I. M. (1966). Severe agoraphobia: A controlled prospective trial of behavior therapy. *British Journal of Psychiatry, 112,* 309–319.

Gertz, H. O. (1967). Experience with the logotherapeutic technique of paradoxical intention in the treatment of phobic and obsessive–compulsive patients. *American Journal of Psychiatry, 125,* 548–553.

Glastier, B. (1982). Muscle relaxation training for fear reduction of patients with psychological problems: A review of controlled studies. *Behaviour Research and Therapy, 20,* 493–504.

Goldfried, M. R., and Trier, C. S. (1974). Effectiveness of relaxation as an active coping skill. *Journal of Abnormal Psychology, 83,* 348–355.

Goldstein, A. (1982). Agoraphobia: Treatment, success, treatment failures, and theoretical implications. *Behavior Therapy, 9,* 47–59.

Goldstein, A. J., & Chambless, D. L. (1978). A reanalysis of agoraphobia. *Behavior Therapy, 9,* 47–59.

Goldstein, A. J., & Chambless, D. L. (1980). The treatment of agoraphobia. In A. J. Goldstein & E. G. Foa (Eds.), *Handbook of behavioral interventions.* New York: Wiley.

Guidano, V. F., & Liotti, G. (1983). *Cognitive processes and emotional disorders.* New York: Guilford Press.

Hand, I., & Lamonthagne, Y. (1976). The exacerbation of interpersonal problems after rapid phobia removal. *Psychotherapy: Theory, Research and Practice, 13,* 405–411.

Holden, A., O'Brien, G., Barlow, D., Stetson, D., & Infantino, A. (1983). Self-help manual for agoraphobia: Preliminary report on effectiveness. *Behavior Therapy, 14,* 546–556.

Hollon, S., & Kendall, P. (Eds.). (1981a). *Assessment strategies for cognitive-behavioral interventions.* New York: Academic Press.

Hollon, S., & Kendall, P. (1981b). *In vivo* assessment techniques for cognitive-behavioral processes. In S. Hollon and P. Kendall (Eds.), *Assessment strategies for cognitive-behavioral interventions.* New York: Academic Press.

Hollon, S. D., & Kriss, M. R. (1984). Cognitive factors in clinical research and practice. *Clinical Psychology Review, 4,* 35–76.

Hodgson, R., & Rachman, S. (1974). Desynchrony in measures of fear. *Behaviour Research and Therapy, 12,* 319–326.

Hudson, B. (1974). The families of agoraphobics treated by behavior therapy. *British Journal of Social Work, 4,* 51–59.

Hugdahl, K. (1981). The three-systems model of fear and emotion: A critical examination. *Behaviour Research and Therapy, 19,* 75–85.

Jacobson, E. (1929). *Progressive relaxation: A physiological and clinical investigation of muscular states and their significance in psychology and medical practice.* Chicago: University of Chicago Press.

Jannoun, L., Munby, M., Catalin, J., & Gelder, M. G. (1980). A home-based treatment program for agoraphobia: Replication and controlled evaluation. *Behavior Therapy, 11,* 294–305.

Jansson, L., & Ost, L. (1984). Behavioral treatments for agoraphobia: An evaluative review. *Clinical Psychology Review, 2*, 311–336.

Kelly, D., Guirguis, W., Frommer, E., Mitchell-Heggs, N., & Sargent, W. (1970). Treatment of phobic states with antidepressants: A retrospective study of 246 patients. *British Journal of Psychiatry, 116*, 387–398.

Kendall, P. C., & Hollon, S. D. (Eds.). (1979). *Cognitive-behavioral interventions: Theory, research and practice.* New York: Academic Press.

King, N. J. (1980). The therapeutic utility of abbreviated progressive relaxation: A critical review with implications for clinical practice. In M. Hersen, R. Eisler, & P. Miller (Eds.), *Progress in behavior modification* (Vol. 10). New York: Academic Press.

Lader, M. H. (1967). Palmar skin conductance measures in anxiety and phobic states. *Journal of Psychosomatic Research, 11*, 271–281.

Lader, M. H., & Mathews, A. M. (1968). A physiological model of phobic anxiety and desensitization. *Behaviour Research and Therapy, 6*, 411–421.

Lader, M. H., & Wing, L. P. (1969). Physiological measures in agitated and retarded depressed patients. *Journal of Psychiatric Research, 7*, 189–200.

Lang, P. J. (1968). Fear reduction and fear behavior: Problems in treating a construct. In E. Shlien (Ed.), *Research in Psychotherapy* (Vol. 3). Washington, DC: American Psychological Association.

Lang, P. J. (1977). Imagery in therapy: An information processing analysis of fear. *Behavior Therapy, 8*, 862–886.

Lang, P. J. (1979). A bioinformational theory of emotional imagery. *Psychophysiology, 16*, 495–512.

Lehrer, P. M. (1978). Psychophysiological effects of progressive relaxation in anxiety neurotic patients and of progressive relaxation and alpha feedback in nonpatients. *Journal of Consulting and Clinical Psychology, 46*, 389–404.

Lehrer, P. M., & Woolfolk, R. L. (1984). Are stress reduction techniques interchangeable, or do they have specific effects? A review of the comparative empirical literature. In R. L. Woolfolk & P. M. Lehrer (Eds.), *Principles and practice of stress management.* New York: Guilford Press.

Leitenberg, H., Agras, S., Butts, R., & Wincze, J. (1971). Relationship between heart rate and behavioral change during the treatment of phobias. *Journal of Abnormal Psychology, 78*, 59–68.

Locke, H. J., & Wallace, K. M. (1959). Short-term marital adjustment and prediction tests: Their reliability and validity. *Journal of Marriage and Family Living, 21*, 251–255.

Mahoney, M., & Arnkoff, D. (1978). Cognitive and self-control therapies. In S. Garfield & A. Bergin (Eds.), *Handbook of psychotherapy and behavior change* (Vol. 2). New York: Wiley.

Marks, I. (1969). *Fears and phobias.* New York: Academic Press.

Marks, I. M. (1970). Agoraphobic syndrome (phobic anxiety state). *Archives of General Psychiatry, 23*, 538–553.

Marks, I., Boulougouris, J., & Marset, P. (1971). Flooding versus desensitization in the treatment of phobic patients: A crossover study. *British Journal of Psychiatry, 119*, 353–375.

Marks, I., & Gelder, M. G. (1966). A controlled retrospective study of behaviour therapy in phobic patients. *British Journal of Psychiatry, 111*, 561–573.

Marks, I., & Lader, M. (1973). Anxiety states (anxiety neurosis): A review. *Journal of Nervous and Mental Disease, 56*(1), 3–18.

Marks, I. M., & Mathews, A. M. (1979). Brief standard self-rating for phobic patients. *Behaviour Research and Therapy, 17*, 263–267.

Mathews, A. M. (1978). Fear reduction, research, and clinical phobias. *Psychological Bulletin, 85*, 39–44.

Mathews, A. M., & Gelder, M. G. (1969). Psychophysiological investigations of brief relaxation training. *Journal of Psychosomatic Research, 13*, 1–12.

Mathews, A. M., Gelder, M. G., & Johnson, D. W. (1981). *Agoraphobia: Nature and treatment.* New York: Guilford Press.

Mathews, A. M., Teasdale, J. D., Munby, M., Johnston, D. W., & Shaw, P. M. (1977). A home-based treatment program for agoraphobia. *Behavior Therapy, 8*, 915–924.

Mavissakalian, M., & Michelson, L. (1982a). Agoraphobia: Behavioral and pharmacological treatment ($N = 49$). *Psychopharmacology Bulletin, 18*, (4), 91–103.

Mavissakalian, M., & Michelson, L. (1982b). Psychophysiological patterns of change in the treatment of agoraphobia. *Behaviour Research and Therapy, 20*, 347–356.

Mavissakalian, M., & Michelson, L. (1984). The role of self-directed *in vivo* exposure in behavioral and pharmacological treatments of agoraphobia. *Behavior Therapy, 14,* 506–519.

Mavissakalian, M., & Michelson, L. (in press, a). Agoraphobia: Relative and combined effectiveness of therapist-assisted *in vivo* exposure and imipramine. *Journal of Clinical Psychiatry.*

Mavissakalian, M., & Michelson, L. Agoraphobia: Two-year follow-up of exposure and imipramine treatment. *American Journal of Psychiatry,* (in press, b).

Mavissakalian, M., & Michelson, L. (1986). Agoraphobia: Relative and combined effectiveness of therapist-assisted *in vivo* exposure and imipramine. *Journal of Clinical Psychiatry, 47,* 117–122.

Mavissakalian, M., Michelson, L., Greenwald, D., Kornblith, S., & Greenwald, M. (1983). Cognitive-behavioral treatments of agoraphobia: Short- and long-term efficacy of paradoxical intention vs. self-statement training. *Behaviour Research and Therapy, 21,* 75–86.

Mendel, J. G. C., & Klein, D. F. (1969). Anxiety attacks with subsequent agoraphobia. *Comprehensive Psychiatry, 10,* 190–195.

Merluzzi, T. V., Glass, C. R., & Genest, M. (Eds.). (1981). *Cognitive assessment.* New York: Guilford Press.

Meyers, J. K., Weissman, M. M., Tischler, G. L., Holzer, C. E., Leaf, P. J., Orvaschel, H., Anthony, J., Boyd, J. H., Burke, J. D., Kraemer, M., & Stolzman, R. (1984). Six month prevalence of psychiatric disorders in three communities: 1980–1982. *Archives of General Psychiatry, 41,* 959–967.

Michelson, L. (1984a). Flooding. In A. S. Bellack & M. Hersen (Eds.), *Dictionary of behavior therapy techniques.* New York: Pergamon Press.

Michelson, L. (1984b). The role of individual differences, response profiles and treatment of consonance in anxiety disorders. *Journal of Behavioral Assessment, 6,* 349–368.

Michelson, L. M. (1985). Meta-analysis: Integration, critique and commentary. *Clinical Psychology Review, 5,* 1–2.

Michelson, L. (1986a). *The Daily Symptom Checklist: Psychometric and clinical properties.* Unpublished manuscript. Department of Psychiatry, Western Psychiatric Institute and Clinic, University of Pittsburgh School of Medicine, Pittsburgh, PA.

Michelson, L. (1986b). Treatment consonance and response profiles in agoraphobia: The role of individual differences in Cancelede, behavioral and physiological treatments. *Behaviour Research and Therapy, 24,* 263–275.

Michelson, L., Mannarino, A., Marchione, K., Kazdin, A. E., & Costello, A. (1985). Experimental analysis of expectancy bias in psychotherapy research. *Behaviour Research and Therapy, 23,* 407–414.

Michelson, L., & Mavissakalian, M. (1983). Temporal stability of self-report measures in agoraphobia research. *Behaviour Research and Therapy, 21,* 695–698.

Michelson, L., & Mavissakalian, M. (1985). Psychophysiological outcome of behavioral and pharmacologic treatments of agoraphobia. *Journal of Consulting and Clinical Psychology, 53,* 229–236.

Michelson, L. M., Mavissakalian, M., Greenwald, D., Kornblith, S., & Greenwald, M. (1983). *Cognitive-behavioral treatment of agoraphobia: Paradoxical intention vs. self-statement training.* Paper presented at the Annual Meeting of the Association for Advancement of Behavior Therapy, Los Angeles.

Michelson, L., Mavissakalian, M., & Marchione, K. (1985). Cognitive-behavioral treatments of agoraphobia. Clinical, behavioral, and psychophysiological outcome. *Journal of Consulting and Clinical Psychology, 53,* 913–925.

Michelson, L., Mavissakalian, M., Marchione, K., Dancu, D., & Greenwald, M. (1986). The role of self-directed *in vivo* exposure practice in cognitive, behavioral, and psychophysiological treatments of agoraphobia. *Behavior Therapy, 17,* 91–108.

Michelson, L., Mavissakalian, M., & Meminger, S. (1983). Prognostic utility of locus of control in agoraphobia treatment. *Behaviour Research and Therapy, 21,* 309–313.

Miller, M. P., Murphy, P. J., & Miller, T. P. (1978). Comparison of electromyographic feedback and progressive relaxation. *Journal of Consulting and Clinical Psychology, 46,* 1291–1298.

Miller, R. C., & Berman, J. S. (1983). The efficacy of cognitive behavior therapies: A quantitative review of the research evidence. *Psychological Bulletin, 94,* 39–53.

Milton, F., & Hafner, J. (1979). The outcome of behavior therapy for agoraphobia in relation to marital adjustment. *Archives of General Psychiatry, 36,* 807–811.

Myers, J. K., Weissman, M. M., Tischler, G. L., Holzer, C. E., Leaf, P. J., Orvaschel, H., Anthony, J., Boyd, J. H.,

Burke, J. D., Kraemer, M., & Stoltzman, R. (1984). Six-month prevalence of psychiatric disorders in three communities: 1980 to 1982. *Archives of General Psychiatry, 41,* 959–967.

Neisser, V. (1967). *Cognitive psychology.* New York: Appleton-Century-Cross.

Neitzel, M. T., & Bernstein, D. A. (1981). Assessment of anxiety and fear. In M. Hersen & A. S. Bellack (Eds.), *Behavioral assessment: A practical handbook* (2nd Ed.). New York: Pergamon Press.

Nelson, P. C., & Phares, E. J. (1971). Anxiety, discrepancy between need, value and expectancy: An internal–external control. *Psychological Reports 28,* 663–668.

Nicassio, R., & Bootzin, R. (1974). A comparison of progressive relaxation and autogenic training as treatments for insomnia. *Journal of Abnormal Psychology, 83,* 253–260.

Norton, J. R., & Johnson, W. E. (1983). A comparison of two relaxation procedures for reducing cognitive and somatic anxiety. *Journal of Behavior Therapy and Experimental Pscychiatry, 14,* 209–214.

Nowinsky, J. K., and Getter, H. (1977). *Interpersonal problem-solving assessment techniques scoring manual.* Unpublished manuscript, University of Connecticut.

O'Brien, G. T., & Barlow, D. H. (1984). Agoraphobia. In S. M Turner (Ed.), *Behavioral theory and treatment of anxiety.* New York: Plenum Press.

Öst, L. G. (1985). Coping techniques in the treatment of anxiety disorders: Two controlled case studies. *Behavioral Psychotherapy, 13,* 154–161.

Öst, L. G., Jerremalm, A., & Johansson, J. (1981). Individual response patterns and the effects of different behavior methods in the treatment of social phobia. *Behaviour Research and Therapy, 19,* 1–16.

Öst, L. G., Jerremalm, A., & Johansson, J. (1984). Individual response patterns and the effects of different behavioural methods in the treatment of agoraphobia. *Behaviour Research and Therapy, 22,* 697–707.

Öst, L. G., Johansson, J., & Jerremalm, A. (1982). Individual response patterns and the effects of different behavioural methods in the treatment of claustrophobia. *Behaviour Research and Therapy, 20,* 445–460.

Palmer, R. D. (1972). Relationship of fearfulness to locus of control of reinforced and perceived parental behavior. In R. Rubin, H. Fensterhein, R. Henderson, & L. Almon (Eds.), *Advances in behavior therapy.* (Vol. 3) New York: Academic Press.

Parker, J. C., Gilbert, G. S., & Thoreson, R. W. (1978). Reduction of autonomic arousal in alcoholics: A comparison of relaxation and meditation techniques. *Journal of Clinical and Consulting Psychology, 46,* 879–886.

Paul, G. L. (1969b). Physiological effects of relaxation training and hypnotic suggestion. *Journal of abnormal Psychology, 74,* 425–437.

Peterson, C., Semmel, A., von Baeyer, C., Abramson, L., Metalsky, G. I., & Seligman, M. E. P. (1982). The *Attributional Style Questionnaire. Cognitive Therapy and Research, 6,* 287–300.

Platt, J. J., & Spivack, G. (1975). *Means and problem-solving procedure manual.* Philadelphia: Hahnemann Medical College.

Rachman, S. J. (1978). *Fear and courage.* San Francisco, CA: Freeman.

Rachman, S. (1980). Emotional processing. *Behaviour Research and Therapy, 18,* 51–60.

Rachman, S. (1981). The primary of affect: Some theoretical implications. *Behaviour Research and Therapy, 19,* 279–290.

Rachman, S. (1983). The modification of agoraphobia avoidance behavior: Some fresh possibilities. *Behaviour Research and Therapy, 21* (5), 567–574.

Rachman, S., & Hodgson, R. (1974). Synchrony and desynchrony in fear and avoidance. *Behaviour Research and Therapy, 12,* 311–318.

Rachman, S., & Wilson, G. T. (1980). *The effects of psychological therapy.* Oxford: Pergamon Press.

Regier, D. A., Myers, J. K., Kramer, M., Rolens, L. N., Blazer, D. G., Hough, R. L., Eaton, W. W., & Locke, B. Z. (1984). The NIMH epidemiologic catchment area (ECA) program: Historical context, major objectives and study populations characteristics. *Archives of General Psychiatry, 41,* 934–941.

Robins, L. N., Helger, J. E., Croughan, J., & Ratcliffe, K. (1981). The National Institute of Mental Health *Diagnostic Interview Schedule:* Its history, characteristics and validity. *Archives of General Psychiatry, 38,* 381–389.

Robins, L. N., Helger, J. E., Weissman, M. M., Orvaschel, H., Gruenberg, E., Burke, J. D., Jr., & Regier, D. A.

(1984). Lifetime prevalence of specific psychiatric disorders in three sites. *Archives of General Psychiatry, 38,* 949–958.

Rotter, J. B. (1954). *Social learning and clinical psychology.* Englewood Cliffs, NJ: Prentice-Hall.

Rotter, J. B. (1966). Generalized expectancy for internal vs. external control of reinforcement. *Psychological Monographs, 60*(609), 1–228.

Salzman, L. (1982). Obsessions and agoraphobia. In D. L. Chambless & A. J. Goldstein (Eds.), *Agoraphobia: Multiple perspectives in theory and treatment.* New York: Wiley.

Schwartz, R. M. (1982). Cognitive behavioral modification: A conceptual review. *Clinical Psychology Review, 2,* 267–293.

Schwartz, R. M., & Garamoni, G. L. (1986). A structural model of positive and negative states of mind: Asymmetry in internal dialogue. In P. C. Kendall (Ed.), *Advances in cognitive-behavioral research and therapy* (Vol. 5). New York: Academic Press.

Schwartz, R. M., & Garamoni, G. L. (1984). The internal dialogue and anxiety: Asymmetries between positive and negative coping thoughts. In L. Michelson (Chair), *Cognitive-behavioral assessment and treatment of major anxiety disorders: Current strategies and future perspectives.* Symposium conducted at the meeting of the Association for Advancement of Behavior Therapy, Philadelphia, PA.

Schwartz, R. N., & Garamoni, G. L. (1986). A structural model of positive and negative states of mind: Asymmetry in the internal dialogue. In P. C. Kendall (Ed.), *Advances in cognitive-behavioral research and therapy,* (Vol. 5). New York: Academic Press.

Schwartz, R. N., & Gottman, J. M. (1976). Toward a task analysis of assertive behavior. *Journal of Consulting and Clinical Psychology, 44,* 910–920.

Schwartz, R. N., & Michelson, L. (1986). States of mind model: Cognitive balance in the treatment of agoraphobia. *Journal of Consulting and Clinical Psychology* (in press).

Shapiro, S., Skinner, E. A., Kessler, L. G., Von Korff, M., Germon, P. S., Tischler, G., Leaf, P. J., Benham, L., Colter, C., & Regier, D. A. (1984). Utilization of health and mental health services. *Archives of General Psychiatry, 38,* 971–982.

Shaw, B. F., & Dobson, K. S. (1981). Cognitive assessment of depression. In T. V. Merluzzi, C. R. Glass, & M. Genest (Eds.), *Cognitive assessment.* New York: Guilford Press.

Silver, B. V., & Blanchard, E. B. (1978). Biofeedback and relaxation training in the treatment of psychophysiological disorders: Or are machines really necessary? *Journal of Behavioral Medicine, 1,* 217–239.

Smith, M. L., & Glass, G. (1977). Meta-analysis of psychotherapy outcome studies. *American Psychologist, 32,* 752–760.

Solyom, L., Garza-Perez, J., Ledwidge, B. D., & Solyom, C. (1972). Paradoxical intention in the treatment of obsessive thoughts: A pilot study. *Comprehensive Psychiatry, 13,* 291–297.

Stoyva, J., & Budzinski, T. (1974). Cultivated low arousal: An anti-stress response? In L. V. DiCara (Ed.), *Limbic and autonomic nervous system research.* New York: Plenum Press.

Strupp, H. H. (1986). Psychotherapy, research practice, and public policy. *American Psychologist, 41,* 120–130.

Taylor, J. A. (1953). A personality scale of manifest anxiety. *Journal of Abnormal and Social Psychology, 2,* 285–290.

Telch, M. J., Terarnon, B. H., & Taylor, C. B. (1983). Antidepressant medication in the treatment of agoraphobia: A critical review. *Behaviour Research and Therapy, 21,* 505–517.

Thorpe, G., & Burns, L. (1983). *The agoraphobia syndrome.* Chichester: Wiley.

Townsend, R. Z., House, J. F., & Adario, R. (1975). A comparison of biofeedback mediated relaxation and group therapy in the treatment of chronic anxiety. *American Journal of Psychiatry, 132,* 598–601.

Turner, S., & Michelson, L. (1984a). Anxiety disorders: Current status and emerging concepts in theory, assessment, and research. *Journal of Behavioral Assessment, 6,* 265–279.

Turner, S., & Michelson, L. (1984b). Introductory note: Conceptual and research issues in the anxiety disorders [Special issue]. *Journal of Behavioral Assessment, 6,* 1–2.

Watson, J. P., & Marks, I. M. (1971). Relevant and irrelevant fear in flooding—A crossover study of phobic patients. *Behavior Therapy, 2,* 275–293.

Webster, A. S. (1953). The development of phobias in married women. *Psychological Monographs, 67*(367).

Weissman, M. M. (1985). The epidemiology of anxiety disorders: Rates, risks, and familial patterns. In A. H. Tuma & J. D. Maser (Eds.), *Anxiety and the anxiety disorders* (pp. 275–296). Hillsdale, NJ: Erlbaum.

Weissman, M. M., Myers, J. K., & Harding, P. S. (1978). Psychiatric disorders in a U.S. urban community. *American Journal of Psychiatry, 135,* 459–462.

Weissman, M. M., Tischler, G. L., Holzer, C. E., Leaf, P. J., Orvaschel, H., Anthony, J. D., Boyd, J. H., Burke, J. D., Kramer, M., & Stoltzman, R. (1984). Six-month prevalence of psychiatry disorders in three communities. *Archives of General Psychiatry, 38,* 959–970.

Westphal, C. (1871). Die Agoraphobia: Eine neuropathische erscheinung. *Archiv für Psychiatrie und Nervenkrankheiten, 3,* 138–161.

Williams, S. L. (1984). On the nature and measurement of agoraphobia. In M. Hersen, P. Miller, & R. Eisler (Eds.), *Progress in behavior modification.* New York: Academic Press.

Williams, S. L. (1985). On the nature and measurement of agoraphobia. In M. Hersen, P. Miller, & R. Eisler (Eds.), *Progress in behavior modification.* New York: Academic Press.

Williams, S. L., & Rappaport, J. A. (1983). Cognitive treatment in the natural environment for agoraphobics. *Behavior Therapy, 14,* 299–314.

Wolpe, J. (1958). *Psychotherapy by reciprocal inhibition.* Stanford, CA: Stanford University Press.

Wolpe, J., & Ascher, L. M. (1976). Outflanking "resistance" in a severe obsessional neurosis. In H. J. Eysenck (Ed.), *Case histories in behavior therapy.* London: Routledge, Kegan Paul.

Wolpe, J., & Lang, P. G. (1961). A *Fear Survey Schedule* for use in behavior therapy. *Behavior Research and Therapy, 2,* 27–30.

Zitrin, C. M., Klein, D. F., & Woerner, M. G. (1980a). Combined pharmacological and psychological treatment of phobias. In M. Mavissakalian & D. H. Barlow (Eds.), *Psychological and pharmacological treatment.* New York: Guilford Press.

Zitrin, C. M., Klein, D. F., & Woerner, M. G. (1980b). Treatment of agoraphobia with group exposure *in vivo* and imipramine. *Archives of General Psychiatry, 37,* 63–72.

10

Social Phobia

RICHARD G. HEIMBERG, CYNTHIA S. DODGE, AND ROBERT E. BECKER

Anxiety disorders are increasingly recognized as serious mental health problems. Patients suffering from a variety of anxiety symptoms appear in the offices of psychologists, psychiatrists, and general medical practitioners with ever-increasing frequency. In fact, the results from the first wave of a recent epidemiological survey indicate that phobias (simple, agoraphobic, and social) are the most frequently occurring DSM-III disorders among women and the second most frequent among men (Myers et al., 1984). Thus it appears that the anxiety disorders should be the target of intensive study. Although some anxiety disorders have received this special attention, social phobia remains relatively unstudied (Liebowitz, Gorman, Fyer, & Klein, 1985).

With the publication of the third edition of the *Diagnostic and Statistical Manual of Mental Disorders* (DSM-III) (American Psychiatric Association, 1980), social phobia became a subcategory of the anxiety disorders. The essential feature of social phobia was defined as a persistent, irrational fear of, and compelling desire to avoid situations in which the individual may by exposed to scrutiny by others. Social phobia was first identified by Marks and Gelder (1966) of Great Britain, and the majority of research on the treatment of social phobia has been conducted by European investigators. Although American investigators have extensively studied the phenomenon of anxiety in social interaction, we are just beginning to recognize the severity of social fears and the extent of their disabling impact on the individual. The purpose of this chapter is to summarize what is known about the nature and prevalence of social phobia, to review and evaluate recent psychosocial treatment strategies, and to discuss specific issues related to intervention.

Characteristics of Social Phobia

Everyone can readily identify with the experience of increased anxiety in certain social or performance situations. These situations share the common element of potential social disapproval, as the individual's performance can be readily monitored and evaluated by others. The associated arousal is not a problem for most individuals, however, and some may even report it to be beneficial to their performance. For the social phobic

Richard G. Heimberg and Cynthia S. Dodge. Center for Stress and Anxiety Disorders, Department of Psychology, State Univeristy of New York at Albany, Albany, New York.

Robert E. Becker. Department of Psychiatry, Medical College of Pennsylvania at EPPI, Philadelphia, Pennsylvania.

individual, however, the anxiety experienced is a significant source of distress and is viewed as unreasonable or excessive. Social anxiety may be elicited in a variety of situations, including speaking or performing in public, eating in public, and writing or urinating in the presence of others (American Psychiatric Association, 1980).

Our own research suggests that the fear of conversing, particularly with a member of the opposite sex or with an authority figure, or of asserting oneself are common forms of the disorder. In addition, Amies, Gelder, and Shaw (1983) report that the situation feared most by their sample of social phobics was being introduced to others, followed by meeting people in authority. Anxiety appeared to increase with the degree of formality and the extent to which the person believed he or she was under scrutiny. These data indicate that at least some individuals have a more *generalized* fear of interacting with people rather than the *circumscribed* situational phobia described in DSM-III. This distinction will become more relevant in our discussion of treatment issues.

Marks (1969) presented descriptive and demographic data for a group of 25 social phobics. Symptoms of social fears typically appeared following puberty, and the average age of onset was 19 years. Compared to the other phobias, which affect more women than men, a greater percentage of social phobics are male; Amies et al. (1983) report that their sample was 60% male. They also found that social phobics were more likely to be of single status (i.e., single, divorced, separated, or widowed) and to come from a higher social class than agoraphobics. Our own data on 34 social phobics requesting treatment at the SUNY–Albany Center for Stress and Anxiety Disorders showed 68% as single and 56% as having graduated from college.

The particular somatic symptoms experienced by the social phobic may differ somewhat from those experienced by the agoraphobic. Social phobics were more likely to complain of blushing and muscle twitching, whereas agoraphobics reported more weakness of limbs, difficulty breathing, and dizziness or faintness (Amies et al., 1983). Symptoms typically associated with panic attacks (i.e., heart palpitations, trembling, and sweating) appeared common to both groups. In addition, depressive symptoms have frequently been found to accompany the anxiety disorders and were present in 50% of the Amies et al. sample. In many cases it may actually be the presence of depression that motivates these patients to seek treatment (Munjack & Moss, 1981). With this in mind, it is essential to evaluate the functional relationship between these two symptom clusters for research and clinical purposes. Data will be presented in a later section that suggest that the severity of depressive symptoms influences the outcome of cognitive-behavioral treatment of social phobia.

Another problem that has been associated with anxiety, and with social phobia specifically, is the abuse of alcohol. In a prevalence study, Mullaney and Trippett (1979) reported that one-third of an alcoholic population had disabling agoraphobia or social phobia. They also discovered that the onset of the phobias preceded alcohol problems in a majority of their subjects. Smail, Stockwell, Canter, and Hodgson (1984) attempted to replicate this research and found that 39% of 60 alcoholics had suffered from social phobia during their last typical drinking period. This group also reported evidence for the belief that consuming alcohol will reduce tension, at least as perceived by their sample. In the descriptive data of Amies et al. (1983), 20% of the social phobics were found to consume excessive amounts of alcohol. These data do not define a causal relationship between alcohol abuse and social anxiety, but they do indicate a need to assess for both problems. Social phobics may use alcohol or some other drug to cope with anxiety. If they also seek psychological treatment, the use of alcohol, minor tranquilizers, or beta-adrenergic blockers may affect treatment outcome, and treatment success may be attributed to the substance rather than the client. Alternatively, a social phobic alcoholic may find it difficult to participate in specific forms of treatment for chemical dependency if these treatments carry heavy demands for social interaction or public speaking (e.g., Alcoholics Anonymous) and thereby place themselves at risk for relapse or continued chemical dependency.

Two studies have assessed social phobics' perception of their parents' child-rearing practices and, by implication, the environments in which they were raised. Parker (1979) employed the Parental Bonding Instrument (Parker, Tupling, & Brown, 1979) to measure the dimensions of parental care and overprotection. Forty-one social phobics rated both parents as more overprotective and less caring that the parents of matched controls. These retrospective findings were supported in a survey by Arrindell, Emmelkamp, Monsma, and Brilman (1983) with a sample of 29 social phobics. Thus it appears that social phobics may have grown up in an environment unlikely to support confident and independent social behavior. Although features of childhood environments may be casually related to social phobia, prospective studies are needed to determine the nature of this relationship.

Prevalence of Social Fears and Phobias

Several investigators of social anxiety in nonclinical populations have reported large sample surveys of social fear. For instance, among 223 British college students, 24% of males and 12% of females felt anxious when going out on a date (Bryant & Trower, 1974). Thirty-one percent of the males and 46% of the females reported moderate or worse difficulty at dances and discos. Zimbardo and his associates (e.g., Pilkonis & Zimbardo, 1979) have studied shyness (a close relative of social anxiety) in several cultures. Across the thousands of individuals surveyed, 40% labeled themselves as shy and 80% reported that they had been shy at some point in their lives. In addition, Wallace, Wallechinsky, and Wallace (1977) found speaking before a group to be the most frequent fear in a sample of 3,000 normal adults. These studies demonstrate the frequent occurrence of "uncomfortable" anxiety in evaluative situations, but it is unclear how many of these subjects may have met the diagnostic criteria for social phobia. One key to the severity of social fears is behavioral avoidance. Among college students, social anxiety is inversely related to dating frequency and positively correlated with a desire to avoid (Heimberg, Harrison, Montgomery, Madsen, & Sherfey, 1980).

In their report of the NIMH multisite epidemiological study, Myers et al. (1984) report that the six-month prevalence of social phobia ranged from 0.9% to 1.7% for males and from 1.5% to 2.6% for females. In reviewing clinical samples, Marks (1969) found 8% of the phobic population at Maudsley Hospital to be socially phobic. Social anxiety of clinical proportion is reported to occur in as many as one out of three psychiatric outpatients (Bryant, Trower, Yardley, Urbieta, & Letemendia, 1976) and 7% of inpatients

(Curran, Miller, Zwick, Monti, & Stout, 1980). In a recent series of outpatients seeking treatment at SUNY–Albany's Center for Stress and Anxiety Disorders, 19 of 125 (15.2%) were diagnosed as social phobic, surpassed only by agoraphobics at 32.8% (Barlow, 1985). However, precise estimates of the prevalence of social phobia may be difficult to obtain. Our experience suggests that social phobia may be a more common disorder than suggested by either DSM-III or Myers et al. (1984), but we conjecture that many individuals who would meet the diagnostic criteria for social phobia do not seek treatment. Although they may suffer acute distress, they may not perceive that psychological or psychosocial interventions are relevant to their concerns. Some of these individuals may have adopted an explanation of their problem that may derail their attempts to seek treatment; that is, they may have labeled themselves as *characterologically shy*. Since their problem is defined as characterological ("This is the way I am"), it may also be defined as unchangeable ("This is the way I will always be"). If so, then effort invested in behavior change would appear wasted, and these attributions of causality would function to discourage their seeking treatment. Public education about social phobia and other anxiety disorders may result in more accurate prevalence estimates and also help social phobic individuals obtain treatment.

Components of Social Phobia

Currently, it is common practice to consider fear and emotion from the three systems model, as originally proposed by Lang (1968). This view holds that anxiety cannot be encompassed as a single system, but is represented by cognitive/verbal, physiological, and behavioral components. These different components may or may not co-vary in a given individual, and each idiosyncratic pattern will also vary across time. Although social phobics are not represented by one particular pattern of responding, there are commonalities that may be discussed within each component, suggesting targets for treatment.

Physiological Dimension

Not all social phobics experience panic attacks as defined by DSM-III, but their physiological symptoms may become severe when they are exposed to a phobic stimulus or event. Arousal may be considerable, even when they are only imagining the phobic situation. When a social phobic feels evaluated or scrutinized, the somatic symptoms almost always include tachycardia, sweating, and trembling. At the same time, it has been shown that normals will experience heightened autonomic arousal during stressful public speaking (Dimsdale & Moss, 1980). One might speculate that the phobic's level of autonomic activity somehow becomes more intensified than that of normals, or perhaps that social phobics overattend to these somatic changes (Nichols, 1974). In a study by Johansson and Öst (1982), 34 social phobics were exposed to an anxiety-arousing situation that resulted in significantly increased heart rates. The phobics' self-perceived physiological arousal was highly correlated with their actual heart rate reaction (as measured with a plethysmograph), more so than for claustrophobic patients. These data support the notion that social phobics may be highly sensitive to physiological changes. Focus on internal discomfort and associated fears of embarrassment may often lead to further elevation of symptoms or prolonged anxiety.

Social phobics report that the detection by others of the visible symptoms of physiological arousal is a major motivation for the avoidance of social-evaluative situations. In fact, Amies et al. (1983) report that social phobics experienced more visible signs of physiological arousal (e.g., blushing) than did their agoraphobic sample. In a study by McEwan and Devins (1983), however, highly socially anxious subjects reported significantly more visual signs of anxiety than were actually noticed by their peers. The extent to which this is true may be related to a cognitive style of overattending to the presence of negative cues (both internal and external) in the phobic situation.

Behavioral Dimension

Within the three-systems model, the behavioral component refers to gross motor behavior or actual avoidance of the phobic situation. For the person whose career requires speaking in front of small or large groups, prolonged avoidance may lead to lack of advancement or possible loss of employment. An individual who experiences levels of high anxiety in almost any social interaction is likely to become isolated and depressed as a result of such avoidance. Thus the degree of interference with life can reach a severity that has not been adequately emphasized in the literature. Other social phobics will demonstrate less behavioral avoidance but will suffer through the particular situations with extreme discomfort. In this case, a strong desire to avoid is always present, but a variety of factors will influence the decision to avoid. Although behavioral avoidance may reduce anxiety, the ramifications usually include a barrage of negative self-statements and guilt.

The verbal and nonverbal behaviors displayed by social phobics in their feared situations also require examination. For example, the social skills of the highly socially anxious have been rated as significantly poorer than those of less anxious individuals on global measures (Arkowitz, Lichtenstein, McGovern, & Hines, 1975; Twentyman & McFall, 1975). However, specific differences in the performance of the anxious versus the nonanxious have not been delineated. Although it may be true that skillful individuals talk more and demonstrate more eye contact, simple frequency of these behaviors may not be the crucial variable in social performance (Conger & Farrell, 1981). One interesting dimension of conversation is the timing of responses within the context of the interaction. Fischetti, Curran, and Wessberg (1977) showed that the timing and placement of responses, not their absolute frequency, distinguished socially skilled and nonanxious subjects from their socially unskilled and anxious counterparts. Anxious–unskilled subjects routinely failed to provide social reinforcement at key points in an analogue social interaction task.

The significance of this literature rests on the hypothesis that inadequate social behavior leads to aversive consequences, which in turn produce anxiety and subsequent avoidance. It is also plausible, however, that highly anxious individuals are unable to demonstrate their skills adequately because of preoccupation with their fear. In addition, the anxiety itself may be induced by an overly negative self-evaluative process, whether or not a skills deficit exists (Clark & Arkowitz, 1975).

Cognitive Dimension

The cognitive component of social phobia reflects the individual's subjective perception of the feared event, including anticipatory reactions and post hoc evaluations of performance. A review of the literature by Arkowitz (1977) suggests that patterns of social anxiety and avoidance may be related to: (1) an internal dialogue of debilitating self-statements, (2) overly negative evaluation of social performance, (3) excessively high standards for the evaluation of performance; (4) selective attention and memory for negative information about oneself and one's performance, and (5) a pathological pattern of attribution of the causes of social successes and failures. Evidence is rapidly accumulating that documents the presence of these patterns in socially anxious college students or community volunteers. In this section, we briefly examine the topics of self-statements, negative self-evaluation, and response to interpersonal feedback.

SELF-STATEMENT PATTERNS

Self-statements are typically defined as positive if they appear to facilitate effective performance and negative if they appear to inhibit effective performance. An example of a positive self-statement would be "I'm beginning to feel more at ease," whereas a negative self-statement would be "I hope I don't make a fool of myself" (examples from the Social Interaction Self-Statement Test by Glass, Merluzzi, Biever, & Larsen, 1982). Self-statement patterns of socially anxious persons have been assessed in several studies (Cacioppo, Glass, & Merluzzi, 1979; Glass et al., 1982; Hartman, 1984; Heimberg, Acerra, & Holstein, 1985; Malkiewich & Merluzzi, 1980). Compared to nonanxious subjects, socially anxious persons have reported more negative self-statements (Cacioppo et al., 1979) and fewer positive statements (Heimberg, Acerra, & Holstein, 1985) when anticipating a heterosocial interaction. Negative self-statement scores appear to be particularly sensitive to social anxiety, as they correlate significantly with ratings of social skill and anxiety made by external raters or by persons with whom subjects interacted (Glass et al., 1982). Hartman (1984) reports that the negative self-statements of anxious subjects fall into several categories: (1) thoughts of general social inadequacy, (2) concerns with others' awareness of distress, (3) fear of negative evaluation, and (4) preoccupation with arousal or performance.

Clearly, self-statements bear some relation to the behavior of socially anxious persons, but the design of most studies precludes meaningful conclusions about their causal role. In a recent study by Mandel and Shrauger (1980), male subjects were asked to read and concentrate on a list of self-statements that were either self-enhancing or self-critical, and the extent of their approach to a female peer was unobtrusively assessed. Subjects who received the self-critical statements took longer to initiate conversation and spent less time interacting with the woman than did subjects who received self-enhancing statements. Anxious and nonanxious subjects differed from each other in the same fashion as the self-critical and self-enhancing groups.

NEGATIVE SELF-EVALUATION

Socially anxious individuals almost universally rate themselves poorly. However, these negative evaluations may result from a number of factors. For instance, a person might evaluate his or her actions poorly because they are objectively poor, because he or she is a poor observer, because his or her standards are too stringent, and so forth. Few studies attempt to isolate the causes of this negative self-evaluative style.

In one particularly relevant study (Glasgow & Arkowitz, 1975), males and females were matched for dyadic interactions. High-frequency and low-frequency daters (a classification variable that is related to social anxiety but not identical to it) were then compared on a variety of self-report, behavioral, and rating measures. High- and low-frequency dating males were not distinguishable on a single behavioral measure. Likewise, the women with whom they interacted were unable to tell the difference between them on ratings of either anxiety or social skills. Nevertheless, low-frequency dating males rated themselves significantly more poorly than did high-frequency daters.

Clark and Arkowitz (1975) asked male subjects to participate in two interactions with female confederates. Thereafter, subjects rated their own and others' performances on social skill, anxiety, and the quality of the female's responses to them during the interaction. Undergraduate judges also completed these ratings and served as an index of consensual reality. All subjects were able to match judges' ratings of other persons with reasonable accuracy. When ratings of the skillfullness of their own performance were examined, however, the effects of anxiety became evident. Low-anxious subjects' ratings closely matched judges' ratings. High-anxious subjects gave themselves significantly poorer ratings than they received from the judges. Curran, Wallander, and Fischetti (1980) recently extended this work by investigating differences in self-evaluation among socially anxious individuals who scored either high or low on independently measured social skills. Anxious individuals who were lacking in social skills were accurate in assessing their performance, whereas the skilled but anxious individuals consistently underestimated judges' ratings. Although this study has several methodological problems, it suggests that anxious subjects will consistently view their social performance as inadequate, without consideration of the actual quality of their behavior.

RESPONSE TO INTERPERSONAL FEEDBACK

Two studies have examined the reactions of socially anxious individuals to negative interpersonal feedback. In one of these studies (O'Banion & Arkowitz, 1977), anxious subjects remembered an excess of negative feedback. In the other (Smith & Sarason, 1975), socially anxious subjects showed a variety of reactions to feedback: (1) they perceived the same feedback to be more negative than did low-anxious subjects; (2) they expected to be more likely to receive similar feedback from others; and (3) they expected to have a more adverse emotional reaction to the feedback.

In contrast to the literature on anxious students and volunteers, there is limited empirical research on the cognitive style of social phobic patients. However, Beck and Emery (1979) assert that patients suffering from severe social and performance anxieties endorse a number of beliefs that may lead them to respond to social stimuli in a maladaptive fashion. These include: (1) the belief that others hold a low opinion of them, (2) the belief that approval from others is crucial to a person's well-being, (3) the belief that it is shameful to appear anxious in front of others, and (4) the belief that one's self-esteem or value as a person is determined by one's ability to perform in a competent manner. In addition, Nichols (1974) describes his observations of a sample of 35 severely socially anxious patients and notes several characteristics that are similar to those described earlier: (1) sensitivity to and fearfulness of criticism and disapproval, (2) a tendency to perceive criticism and disapproval that are not actually present, (3) a sense of being less capable than others, (4) rigid concepts of appropriate social behavior, and (5) an increased awareness and fear of scrutiny from others. In addition, his observations speak to the functional relationship between cognitive and physiological events. The patients experienced physiological arousal in response to social stimuli. However, Nichols (1974, p. 304) also describes them as preoccupied with the possibility of becoming further aroused:

> It is an ever-present threat that carries the alarming possibility of attracting attention and causing others to think him odd. In the feared situation, he closely monitors his bodily state watching for "another attack." Detection of the sensations of anxiety may then provoke alarm and a buildup of that response.

To summarize, it seems that social phobic individuals have adopted various beliefs or methods of processing information that direct their attention to their physiological responses, how these responses will affect their behavior, and how others may perceive and negatively evaluate their performance (and apparent nervousness). In the next section, we review cognitive-behavioral models of social anxiety and social phobia that describe the specific cognitive deficits and excesses of these individuals and how they may relate to affect and behavior.

Cognitive-Behavioral Models of Social Anxiety and Phobia

Public Self-Consciousness

Buss (1980) has suggested that socially anxious persons may be high on the dimension of "public self-consciousness." Public self-consciousness is defined as awareness of oneself as a social object. High public self-consciousness suggests that social–evaluative stimuli should be more salient and that the individual may be more reactive to the outcomes of social events. In a study by Fenigstein (1979), women who scored high on a measure of public self-consciousness (Fenigstein, Scheier, & Buss, 1975) were more sensitive and reacted more negatively to interpersonal rejection in a group setting. In a second experiment, public self-awareness (the situational analogue to dispositional self-consciousness) was manipulated by the presence or absence of a small mirror. Female subjects received favorable or unfavorable feedback in the context of an interview. In the high public self-aware (mirror present) condition, subjects reacted more negatively to negative evaluation and more positively to positive evaluation.

Other support is abundant for Buss's position that socially anxious persons are at the extremes of the distribution of dispositional public self-consciousness—that is, that they are preoccupied with how they may come across to others. For instance, in a mulitidimensional scaling task, males sorted situations into categories (Goldfried, Padawer, &

Robins, 1984). Compared to their nonanxious peers, anxious men relied most heavily on the dimension of "chance of being evaluated" in making their judgments about social situations. Nonanxious males relied more on the dimensions of "intimacy" and "academic relevance." In another study (McEwan & Devins, 1983), socially anxious subjects with a history of physiological responsiveness expressed an exaggerated concern that others could detect their physiological arousal. Finally, Smith, Ingram, and Brehm (1983) demonstrated that socially anxious persons are specifically concerned with evaluation by others, but only under conditions of social-evaluative stress.

Self-Presentation

Recently, Schlenker and Leary (1982; Leary, 1983) presented a theoretical analysis of social anxiety that may account for many of the findings outlined here. Social anxiety is defined as anxiety derived from the prospect or presence of personal evaluation in real or imagined social situations. It is said to occur when a person has the goal of creating a particular impression on others and is therefore concerned about their evaluative reactions *and* doubts his or her ability to succeed in creating that impression. If the person is not strongly motivated to create a favorable impression or has no doubt about his or her ability to do so, social anxiety is an unlikely consequence. Given the motivation, however, people may still doubt their ability to create the desired impression. According to Schlenker and Leary (1982, pp. 644–645):

> Although they may want to create a particular impression, they may (a) be uncertain about how to go about doing so (e.g., it may be a novel situation or they may not know what sort of attributes the others are likely to be impressed with); (b) think they will not be able to project the types of images that will produce preferred reactions from others (e.g., they may want to be seen as competent but doubt they will be); (c) think they will not project the quantity of image they seek (e.g., they think they will be seen as slightly competent but want to be seen as extremely competent); or (d) believe that some event will occur that will repudiate their self-presentations, causing them to lose public esteem (e.g., they will fail an upcoming test after having bragged about their ability). In short, despite their desire to create a particular impression, they believe they will not achieve the preferred impression-relevant reaction from others. These conditions should generate social anxiety.

Buss's (1980; Fenigstein et al., 1975) concepts of public self-consciousness and public self-awareness are easily subsumed in Schlenker and Leary's (1982) scheme. Any condition (either dispositional or situational) that serves to focus attention on the self in social situations should also serve to increase the person's motivation for impression management, one of Schlenker and Leary's necessary preconditions for social anxiety. However, heightened public self-awareness or self-consciousness should not increase social anxiety unless the person also doubts his or her ability to accomplish the self-presentational goal (Leary, 1983). In this light, Buss (1980) suggests that public self-consciousness is a necessary but not sufficient condition for social anxiety. Several other factors may also serve to heighten a person's motivation to manage impressions, including the value of the goals a person seeks in social interactions, the evaluative nature of initial encounters, the characteristics of the other persons involved, the importance of the projected image to the person's self-definition, and the size of the audience. Similarly, a person's perception of his or her ability to manage impressions may be influenced by the novelty or ambiguity of social situations, past successes and failures in social situations, perceptions of his or her own physical attractiveness and social skill, and the quality of social performance required to match the person's standards. It is small wonder that judgments about successful self-presentation are often uncertain.

Metacognition

According to Hartman (1983), the socially anxious person engages in too much *self-focused metacognition*. Metacognition refers to self-monitoring of one's own cognitive activity and "involves the direct awareness of one's behavioral intentions and inputs to motor systems and thus allows the person to edit the production of his or her behavior" (Hartman, 1983, p. 440). These executive functions are essential to the fluid integration of social behavior. However, the cognitive, perceptual, physiological, and motor processes that make up social interaction normally occur in semiautomatic fashion. Metacognitive attention is occasionally focused on each of these processes, but only for brief periods. Excessive metacognitive activity—that is, focusing attention on these normally automatic processes—removes or distances the person from the interaction, resulting in social anxiety and impaired performance.

During social interaction, socially anxious persons' attention is deployed in a variety of directions. They may become preoccupied with their physiological arousal and whether it will overwhelm them or become visible to others. They may attempt to observe and evaluate the quality of their social performance, or they may become concerned about the potential for negative evaluation, embarrassment, or other untoward consequences. As they do so, they withdraw their attention from the other person and compromise their ability to be spontaneous participants in the interaction. The self, rather than the environment or the interaction partner, becomes the primary focus of attention.

A person can attend to only so many events or objects at one time, and a focus on oneself interferes with attending to other aspects of the environment. Hartman (1983) suggests that, in any social interaction, the socially anxious individual must attend to three "conversations" rather than one—the conversation with the other person, his or her own internal dialogue, and his or her own metacognitive monologue. Although this formulation is too abstract for direct validation, some recent studies suggest that socially anxious people do experience disrupted attention that may impair social performance. For instance, Kimble and Zehr (1982) introduced a series of experimental assistants to socially anxious and nonanxious women. Anxious women were less able to recall the characteristics of persons to whom they were introduced. Another study (Heimberg, Acerra, & Holstein, 1985) examined the attraction of socially anxious and nonanxious subjects to potential interaction partners. Subjects were led to believe that they would soon interact with a person of the opposite sex who was portrayed as similar or dissimilar to the subject in terms of background, interests, and experiences. As has been repeatedly demonstrated for normal subjects (Byrne, 1971), low socially anxious subjects preferred similar partners over dissimilar ones. However, highly socially anxious subjects failed to show this preference, ranking similar and dissimilar partners equally on an attraction measure. The anxious subjects failed to attend to (or use) important social information in making their judgments of attraction.

Hartman (1983) proposes an integration between his formulation and that of Schlenker and Leary (1982). Schlenker and Leary attribute social anxiety to motivation and doubt about the accomplishment of self-presentational goals. According to Hartman, motivation is increased by the excessive self-focus of socially anxious persons. Doubt is affected by increased awareness of internal states. Physiological arousal and behavioral disruption are mediated by metacognitive self-awareness, and excessive attention to these processes leads to their deterioration. Further observation of this distressed state eventuates in questions about one's self-efficacy, and the necessary conditions for social anxiety suggested by Schlenker and Leary have been met.

Stress-Appraisal

Trower and Turland (1984) present a social learning analysis of social phobia that borrows heavily from Bandura's (1977) self-efficacy theory, Carver's (1979) self-control theory, and the stress-appraisal theory of Lazarus and Opton (1966). Their model distinguishes between two types of expectancies and three types of effects. First, *stimulus–outcome expectancies* are distinguished from *behavior–outcome expectancies*. The former refers to predictions from social cues about likely changes in the environment. The latter refers to predictions that certain actions executed by the individual will result in certain outcomes. Stimulus–outcome expectancies produce effects in the physiological and cognitive domains, whereas behavior–outcome expectancies produce effects in the behavioral domain.

Trower and Turland (1984) further suggest two interdependent systems that interact with the environment. The first is the *appraisal system*, which assesses a given state of environmental affairs. It is the appraisal system that sets up stimulus–outcome expectancies by observing the correlations between social cues and social consequences. Once these expectancies are established, stimulus cues are invested with the ability to elicit anxiety experiences, defined by the authors as autonomic arousal and subjective apprehension. Furthermore, these physiological and cognitive responses, themselves, have stimulus power. Physiological arousal, when detected by the individual, may lead to a redefinition of the situation as more threatening and a negative shift in stimulus–outcome expectancies. As a result, subjective apprehension and anxiety may increase. Similarly, subjective apprehension may lead to increased physiological arousal or a pessimistic revision in stimulus–outcome expectancies.

The second system defined by Trower and Turland is the *coping system*, the person's system for dealing with danger as appraised. On the basis of behavior–outcome expectations (the predicted effects of a specific response and the person's projections of his or her own ability to enact it), the person selects an approach or avoidance response to the social situation. The extremity of the appraised threat affects the person's selection of a coping response and the quality of its execution. As suggested by Carver (1979), this interplay leads to an evaluation of the discrepancy between the standard of behavioral performance required to meet the threat and the person's perception of his or her own skill for dealing with it. A positive judgment (i.e., that skills exceed demands) should lead to direct action—in this case, an approach response. A negative judgment (i.e., that skills are not adequate to the task) should increase the probability of avoidance as a coping strategy. As the size of the discrepancy increases, the probability of an active coping response approaches zero. As we have already seen, socially anxious or social phobic individuals engage in a variety of cognitive responses that should act to increase the discrepancy between *perceived* threat and *perceived* efficacy.

Vulnerability

Beck and Emery (1985) have recently elaborated a cognitive model of phobias and anxiety disorders. Although their model shares many features with the model described by Trower and Turland (1984), their central position in the field of cognitive–behavior therapy suggests that it will be very influential. We will briefly review the central tenets of their theory and then examine its application to social phobia.

A concept that is crucial to Beck and Emery's (1985) model of anxiety, as well as their previous work on depression (Beck, Rush, Shaw, & Emery, 1979), is the *cognitive schema*. Schemas are cognitive structures that are used to label, classify, interpret, evaluate, and assign meanings to objects and events. They help the individual orient to the situation, selectively recall relevant data from memory, and attend to only the most relevant aspects of the ongoing situation. Schemas are the basic structural components of cognitive organization, and they are further organized into coherent groupings labeled *modes*. A mode constitutes a broad section of the cognitive organization and imposes a general bias on the individual that influences the type of set (attitude) that the person selects as he or she moves from one situation to another.

In the anxiety disorders, the individual may be described as functioning in the *vulnerability mode*. Vulnerability is defined by Beck and Emery (1985, p. 67) as "a person's perception of himself as subject to internal or external dangers over which his control is lacking or is insufficient to afford him a sense of safety." When the vulnerability mode is active, incoming information is processed in terms of weaknesses rather than strengths, and the person is more influenced by past events that emphasize his or her flaws than by factors that might predict success. Of course, the individual's sense of vulnerability is maintained by the exclusion or distortion of contradictory data by the predominant cognitive schemas: minimization of personal strengths, magnification of personal weaknesses, selective attention to weaknesses, discounting of the value of past successes, and so on. The similarity of this formulation to Trower and Turland's (1984) stress–appraisal model is evident.

The socially anxious individual may determine his or her degree of vulnerability in evaluative situations by the answers to a series of questions (Beck & Emery, 1985, pp. 147–148):

1. "To what degree is this a *test* of my competence or acceptability? How much do I have to prove myself to me or others?" [Emphasis in original.]
2. "What is my status relative to that of my evaluators?"
3. "How important is it to establish a position of strength about relative power status . . . or a position of acceptability in dealing with social evaluators. . . ?"

4. "What is the attitude of the evaluator? Is he accepting and empathetic or rejecting and aloof? Are his judgments likely to be objective or harsh and punitive?"
5. "To what degree can I count on my skills . . . to carry me through this difficult evaluation?"
6. "What is the likelihood of my being undermined by distracting anxiety or inhibitions?"

In other words, the social phobic is hypervigilant to social threat, is constantly evaluating the severity of potential threat and assessing his or her ability to cope with it. The cognitive distortions described by Beck and Emery (1985), however, keep him or her from coming up with a reasonable estimate of either threat or coping resources.

Beck and Emery (1985) note that the socially anxious individual fears social consequences that, to a very large degree, appear plausible and may indeed be realized. The person who expects to feel uncomfortable on a first date or a job interview or who fears that he or she may have difficulty coming up with something to say when trying to talk to a person he or she finds appealing will occasionally be correct. The social phobic, however, is somewhat unique among victims of anxiety disorders because the fear of these outcomes may actually serve to bring them about. According to the authors, automatic inhibition of speech, thinking, and recall are "primal" responses to anxiety that may distract the person from the social task, provide additional "evidence" for negative self-evaluation, and maintain the primacy of the vulnerability mode.

The theoretical analyses of social anxiety and phobia presented by Beck and Emery, Hartman, Schlenker and Leary, and Trower and Turland, have much in common. Each poses that the person becomes excessively focused on him- or herself. This attentional focus may increase the person's motivation for positive self-presentation but may also cause the person to view the social situation as a threat to his or her domain. Hence, the individual is compelled to keep a watchful eye on all sources of threat and to maintain an ongoing accounting of threats and potential coping responses. This internal focus of attention removes the individual from the social interaction and causes his or her performance to suffer; that is, it brings on the feared event. Oversensitivity to one's own physiological and behavioral responses may further increase the probability that they will be poorly controlled and decrease the person's belief that he or she can perform adequately. Selective attention or emphasis on past or anticipated failures will contribute to a cognitive set that maintains this negative cycle. Although this brief summary does not do justice to any of the models of social anxiety, it emphasizes the potentially important role of cognitive processes in developing and maintaining social phobia. In the next section, we describe the various modes of treatment that have been designed to have an impact on the components of social phobia.

Treatment of Social Phobia

One conclusion of the NIMH–SUNY Albany Conference on Behavior Therapies in Treatment of Anxiety Disorders (Barlow & Wolfe, 1981) was a call for clinical outcome studies on social phobia. Certainly the previous discussion indicates the importance of developing an effective treatment for this disorder; yet little research has been conducted. Since the description of social phobia by Marks and Gelder (1966), investigators in the

United Kingdom have treated many social phobic patients (e.g., Gelder, Bancroft, Gath, Johnston, Matthews, & Shaw, 1973). These patients, however, were typically included in larger samples of mixed phobics, and the results were not typically reported by type of phobia. Homogeneous groups of social phobics have been treated in more recent investigations, but few controlled studies have been conducted to date. These include the evaluations of systematic desensitization, social skills training, imaginal flooding, applied progressive muscle relaxation, exposure, cognitive restructuring procedures, and anxiety management training. The limited number of studies precludes definitive conclusions about treatment effectiveness. We review this literature with an eye toward further study of the treatment of social phobia.

Social Skills Training

Although only a portion of social phobics may be socially inadequate, early studies focused on the evaluation of social skills training for reducing social phobic anxiety. Marzillier, Lambert, and Kellett (1976) compared social skills training to systematic desensitization and a waiting list control condition. Both treatments led to patient improvement, and those who received skills training maintained their level of improvement at the 6-month follow-up. Although these findings appear optimistic, neither treatment produced results statistically superior to the control condition.

Trower, Yardley, Bryant, and Shaw (1978) also evaluated the effectiveness of social skills training and systematic desensitization. Subjects were first classified into social phobic and socially inadequate subgroups (patients characterized perdominantly by anxiety or by an absence of social performance skills), and the effectiveness of the treatments for anxiety reduction and behavior change was examined for each type of patient. Phobic patients reported substantial anxiety reduction with either treatment but showed little change in the quality of their social behavior. As predicted, unskilled patients responded more favorably to skills training and demonstrated positive change on measures of both self-reported anxiety and overt behavior. Shaw (1979) extended this study to include a phobic group treated with imaginal flooding. The flooding approach led to small positive changes that were not significantly different from those produced by the other two treatments.

In a study by Stravynski, Marks, and Yule (1982), 22 "socially dysfunctional" outpatients were treated with either social skills training or social skills plus cognitive modification over 12 1½-hour sessions. Both groups improved significantly and reported increased social interaction with less anxiety, reduced depression, and a reduction in irrational social beliefs. The authors found social skills training to be clinically effective for nonpsychotic outpatients suffering from social anxiety and isolation. We will return to this study in the section on cognitive restructuring techniques.

Falloon, Lloyd, and Harpin (1981) randomly assigned 16 social phobic outpatients to 4 weeks of social skills treatment with propranolol, or SST with placebo. The treatment, conducted by trained undergraduates, consisted of multiple role plays in the clinic, followed by rehearsal in the real situations. Posttest measures of specific fears, generalized social anxiety, self-image, and global tension and anxiety demonstrated significant improvement in both groups. Treatment gains were maintained at the 6-month follow-up. It was concluded that skills training is effective in treating social phobia and can be administered by trained nonprofessionals. We suggest that the repeated behavioral rehearsal is relatively unlike other skills training applications and resembles an exposure-based treatment.

These initial studies were conducted with small groups of subjects and therefore provide a relatively weak test of treatment effectiveness. However, to the extent that social skills training and systematic desensitization are equally useful in reducing social phobic anxiety, the probable mechanism of change should be common to both. In the process of behavioral role playing or visualization of anxiety-provoking scenes, an "exposure effect" may be occurring. That is, anxiety reduction may occur through imaginal or actual exposure to the feared situations rather than by the learning of specific behavioral skills or the counterconditioning of anxiety by reciprocal inhibition. Although studies designed to directly test the mechanism of change in these treatments are sorely needed, this analysis may serve to explain the relatively limited treatment gains realized in these investigations. Both social skills training and systematic desensitization include steps or procedures that might diminish their utility as exposure-based treatments. For instance, the brevity of rehearsals in social skills training and the termination of imagery at the onset of anxiety during desensitization may diminish the patient's ability to become habituated to the phobic stimulus or situation. This rationale, plus the consistent support for exposure treatment of other anxiety disorders (Barlow & Wolfe, 1981), justifies the investigation of prolonged exposure treatment for social phobia. At the same time, if a patient is judged socially inadequate, social skills training is indicated before other interventions are undertaken.

Relaxation Training

Öst, Jerremalm, and Johansson (1981) conducted a creative study in which they attempted to match treatments to subjects' specific patterns of social phobic difficulties. They divided their socially phobic patients into "behavioral reactors" and "physiological reactors," based on heart rate and behavioral measurements taken during a simulated social interaction. Behavioral reactors were those patients who demonstrated inadequate social behavior in the simulation but with relative absence of cardiovascular arousal. Physiological reactors showed the reverse pattern. As predicted, social skills training proved most effective for the behavioral reactors, whereas applied relaxation training was most effective for the physiological reactors. Again, exposure may have been the active ingredient in both treatment conditions. Subjects receiving applied relaxation training were encouraged to use these techniques in natural settings and were given the opportunity to practice their new skills in role-playing situations during treatment sessions.

Interpretation of Öst et al. (1981) is also complicated by concerns about diagnostic classification. It is unclear whether their behavioral reactors are best described as "social phobic" or "socially inadequate." By definition, the behavioral reactors were not physiologically responsive. Their mean pretreatment heart rates during the simulated social interaction ranged from 84.03 to 91.84, compared with 102.55 to 103.31 for the physiological reactors. In our own research, however, the mean heart rate for *all* social phobics, assessed in a similar testing situation, has been 108.2. These two research projects were conducted in different countries, and subjects were selected according to different diagnostic criteria. It is possible that the DSM-III criteria for social phoba, used in our research, led to the selection of individuals most similar to those labeled as "physiological reactors" by Öst and colleagues. If this conjecture proves accurate, it would suggest that applied relaxation training is more effective than social skills training and may be a useful component of treatment for this patient group.

Exposure

Current knowledge proclaims performance-based procedures as the preferred form of treatment for fears and phobias (Barlow & Beck, 1984; Emmelkamp, 1982; Marks, 1981). However, this approach has not been adequately tested with social phobics. Biran, Augusto, and Wilson (1981) compared exposure and cognitive restructuring using a single-case experimental design. Their subjects were three women suffering from "scriptophobia," a variation of social phobia that involves a fear of writing or signing documents in front of others. Following baseline assessment, two subjects received five sessions of cognitive restructuring plus five additional sessions of exposure. The third subject received exposure treatment immediately after the conclusion of the baseline phase. Exposure consisted of *in vivo* performance tasks, which the subjects confronted in a hierarchical fashion. *In vivo* exposure was effective in altering avoidance behavior, but the addition of cognitive restructuring did not increase treatment effectiveness. Interestingly, both patients who received the cognitive intervention judged it to be an important part of their treatment and largely responsible for their successful outcomes.

Butler, Cullington, Munby, Amies, and Gelder (1984) recently compared exposure, exposure plus anxiety management training (a combination of relaxation training, distraction techniques, and rational self-talk), and a waiting list control. Fifteen socially phobic outpatients were assigned to each condition. Patients who received either exposure treatment met weekly with their individual therapist for 7 weeks. At posttest, patients in the two exposure treatments demonstrated significant change, whereas the waiting list group remained unchanged. At the 6-month follow-up, however, the combination of exposure and anxiety management training proved superior to exposure alone. The authors speculate that most patients entered treatment with the knowledge of an anxiety management strategy, but those who received anxiety management training were more likely to employ these techniques effectively. Whether anxiety management has a specific effect of its own or simply facilitates repeated exposure cannot be determined from this research. These two studies provide preliminary support for the use of exposure in the treatment of social phobia. We will return to this issue when describing our own treatment package.

Cognitive Restructuring

Cognitive interventions have become increasingly popular, and recent studies have investigated their effectiveness with anxiety disorders. Unlike the other anxiety disorders, in the social phobic condition, cognitive factors are thought to be central (Emmelkamp, 1982), and common cognitive distortions were outlined in the preceding pages. In addition, cognitive treatments have been shown to be effective in analogue studies of test anxiety, public speaking anxiety, and interpersonal anxiety (Rachman & Wilson, 1980). With socially anxious students, cognitive techniques have produced greater generalization of behavior change across settings than did social skills training (Glass, Gottman, & Shmurak, 1976) and were most preferred by subjects in a study comparing the effectiveness of cognitive intervention, social skills training, and systematic desensitization (Heimberg, Madsen, Montgomery, & McNabb, 1980). Kanter and Goldfried (1979) also reported that a cognitive treatment produced greater self-reported change in the social anxiety of community volunteers than did self-control desensitization.

Despite this positive evidence, few studies have evaluated the effectiveness of cognitive restructuring techniques for appropriately diagnosed social phobic patients. Studies that have been conducted present a mixed view of the efficacy of cognitive restructuring techniques. Although there is room for optimism, evaluations of treatment outcome do not uniformly support the effectiveness of cognitive restructuring for the treatment of social phobia. On the positive side, Stravynski (1983) treated a social phobic patient who responded to anxiety-provoking situations with psychogenic vomiting. Treatment consisted of eight individual sessions of cognitive modification paired with *in vivo* exposure and social skills training. Cognitive modification involved the description of the role of cognitions in the development and maintenance of emotional distress, rational evaluation and modification of problematic thoughts, and discussion with the therapist of changes in thinking patterns. Treatment resulted in total elimination of the vomiting response and reduction of anxiety in four target situations. Gains were maintained at a 1-year follow-up.

Butler et al. (1984) reported that anxiety management training significantly increased the effectiveness of exposure treatment for social phobia. As noted earlier, anxiety management training is a multicomponent package that includes cognitive strategies. "Rational self-talk" was designed to help patients identify and control maladaptive thoughts. Patients pinpointed self-defeating, negative self-statements and rehearsed constructive alternatives. This cognitive restructuring procedure was integrated with daily relaxation practice and the development of individualized distraction techniques. As was the case in Stravynski (1983)'s single-subject report, cognitive restructuring was included in a successful treatment package. The inclusion of other techniques (i.e., relaxation and distraction), however, precludes the assessment of the specific contribution of cognitive restructuring procedures.

Two studies have assessed the specific effectiveness of cognitive restructuring in relation to other treatment procedures. Biran et al. (1981) treated three scriptophobic patients through exposure with or without cognitive restructuring. Exposure, as evaluated in a multiple-baseline-across-subjects design, increased subjects' performance on a behavioral approach test. Cognitive restructuring, modeled on Goldfried's (1979) technique of systematic rational restructuring, failed to produce similar effects, nor did it appear to increase the effectiveness of exposure. Neither treatment was particularly effective in reducing self-reported fear experienced during the behavioral approach test. This finding is difficult to evaluate, however, since no subject reported an average level of fear at baseline that exceeded 4.0 on a 0–10 scale.

Stravynski et al. (1982) compared social skills training alone and social skills training combined with cognitive modification for the treatment of 22 social phobic outpatients. Cognitive modification was based on Ellis's rational-emotive therapy and consumed 30 minutes of the 12 90-minute treatment sessions. In each session, the patient selected a personally distressing situation and analyzed it into its rational-emotive components: the activating event, irrational beliefs, and emotional consequences. The patient then developed disputes for his or her irrational beliefs and a plan for a new course of action. Similar analyses were conducted between sessions. Both groups of patients in this study improved, however, whether or not they received cognitive modification, and cognitive modification did not supplement the effectiveness of social skills training.

The studies by Stravynski et al. (1982) and Biran et al. (1981) provide the most direct examination of cognitive restructuring as a treatment for social phobia. Neither study provides a positive evaluation of its utility, since patients improved equally whether or not they received cognitive restructuring. However, we should not move too quickly to discount the effectiveness of cognitive procedures for social phobia. These studies are flawed in their experimental design and may have administered cognitive procedures in less than maximally effective fashion, thereby contributing to negative outcomes. To document these points, a closer examination of the Stravynski et al. (1982) study is in order.

The study compared social skills training alone to social skills training with cognitive modification administered in individual or group treatment. Each of the 22 patients received one of the active treatments, which precluded the evaluation of placebo or waiting list conditions. However, one of the largest questions about the study involves the description of its subjects. The authors (p. 1379) describe their patients as having "diffuse social phobia (300.23) with avoidant personality disorder (301.82). Many also had a history of adjustment disorder (309.00) with anxiety depression, withdrawal and work inhibition (309.24, 309.23, and 309.83)." These patients appear to be more broadly impaired than is implied by the diagnosis of social phobia. Furthermore, as DSM-III is structured, a diagnosis of social phobia is not made in the presence of avoidant personality disorder. We will return to this complex issue shortly. For now, however, this description implies that the patients treated by Stravynski et al. may be different from those treated in other studies of social phobia (e.g., less socially skilled? less anxious? less distressed about their behavior?). Another difference germane to the evaluation of cognitive restructuring techniques is the representativeness of Stravynski et al.'s subjects on cognitive measures of social anxiety. Two relevant measures, the Social Avoidance and Distress Scale (SADS) and the Fear of Negative Evaluation Scale (FNE) (Watson & Friend, 1969) were administered in the study. Subjects receiving social skills training alone or in combination with cognitive modification achieved pretreatment mean SADS scores of 10.3 (SD = 3.1) and 11.7 (SD = 1.5), respectively. Their respective FNE scores were 12.6 (SD = 5.10) and 13.3 (SD = 3.0). Compare these scores to (1) scores of 16.14 (SD = 6.59) on the SADS and 24.57 (SD = 7.19) on the FNE achieved by subjects in the study by Heimberg, Becker, Goldfinger, and Vermilyea (1985), to be described; (2) scores averaging between 17 and 23 on the SADS and 20–23 on the FNE reported by Butler et al. (1984); and (3) mean scores of 9.11 (SD = 8.01) on the SADS and 15.47 (SD = 8.62) on the FNE in the original normative sample reported by Watson and Friend (1969). Stravynski et al.'s subjects seem rather average on these measures, and the applicability of their findings to more cognitively involved social phobics may be questioned. Similarly, one of Biran et al.'s three subjects achieved a score of only 1 on the SADS.

Negative outcomes for cognitive restructuring in the Stravynski et al. (1982) and Biran et al. (1981) studies may also be related to the methods of administration of cognitive restructuring procedures. In both studies the cognitive procedures were conducted at separate points in time from skills training or exposures, so that each component was self-contained. With this design, the cognitive treatment component must rely on clients' memory of past phobic situations and the thoughts that occurred to them at those times. Clients' recall of cognitions is likely to be incomplete, and the connection between cognition, affect, and behavior difficult to demonstrate. However, integration of the cognitive and behavioral components may aid in understanding this connection by facilitating cognitive awareness. An arrangement of treatment procedures so that cognitive interventions immediately precede and follow exposures or rehearsals should make the problematic cognitions more immediately available for modification, and new cognitive strategies could be promptly incorporated into further exposures or behavioral practice.

The foregoing considerations led to the development and pilot testing of our own multicomponent treatment for social phobia. The program included exposures (within the therapy group, in imagination, and through homework assignments) plus cognitive restructuring (Heimberg, Becker, Goldfinger, & Vermilyea, 1985). Seven social phobic clients, diagnosed according to DSM-III criteria, received the cognitive-behavioral treatment in a small-group format over 14 weekly sessions. The first session was devoted to introductions and communication of treatment rationale; the final session was devoted to generalization of newly acquired skills to problematic situations in the future. During the middle 12 sessions, subjects received 4 3-session cycles of imaginal exposure, exposure to simulated phobic situations in the therapy group paired with systematic cognitive restructuring of patients' thoughts and assumptions as revealed in these simulations, and homework assignments to expose themselves to phobic events in the natural environment. Several self-report questionnaires were administered at pre- and posttreatment and at 3-month and 6-month follow-ups. Each client also participated in a simulation of a personally relevant phobic situation every week for 6 or 10 weeks prior to treatment, throughout treatment, and at each follow-up. This strategy provided a comprehensive assessment of anxiety, since behavioral measures were derived from videotapes of simulations, subjective discomfort ratings were taken every 60 seconds, and heart rate was continuously monitored. Following treatment, these clients demonstrated significant reductions in heart rate, in behavioral signs of anxiety, and in subjective discomfort. These reductions were maintained across the follow-up period for six of the seven patients.

Despite encouraging results, procedural problems in the administration of the treatment package led to the elimination of imaginal exposure. It seemed that the rate of response to imaginal exposure was quite variable. Some clients were also unable to achieve sufficient arousal when visualizing "anxiety-provoking" situations, and others found the stimuli so arousing that they engaged in some cognitive avoidance. Positive response to the total package, however, suggested that imaginal exposure was not a key treatment component. Its deletion left us with what has become our current approach to treatment: exposure to simulated phobic situations in the therapy group, integrated with cognitive restructuring and analysis of the exposure situation, followed by application of new learning and cognitive restructuring in the client's social environment. As we have labeled them, the three components are "performance-based exposure," "cognitive restructuring," and "homework assignments." A study comparing this treatment to a credible group therapy comparison procedure is currently underway. We will now outline this treatment package in more detail.

Cognitive-Behavioral Treatment Procedures

The therapy groups are typically composed of five to seven clients, roughly balanced for sex. This size appears to be optimal for allowing individualized attention and yet a diversity of client background. Weekly sessions are 2 hours long and are conducted by male and female co-therapists, an important ingredient since phobic situations often include interactions with the opposite sex.

Performance-Based Exposure

Social phobics' specific anxiety-eliciting situations are often "available" on an unpredictable or sporadic basis. Thus it may be difficult to develop *in vivo* exposure exercises for them on a regular, therapeutically efficient basis. Whereas an agoraphobic client may venture away from home for a "behavioral walk" at almost any time, the social phobic may confront a feared staff meeting only once each week. Similarly, individuals who fear diverse types of social interactions may have so effectively isolated themselves that they may confront few people with whom to initiate conversations. For these reasons, group therapy was selected as the vehicle for recreating phobic situations. Individualized, personally relevant phobic situations are *simulated* in the group setting, with group members taking on the roles of audience or specific interaction partners (e.g., stranger, boss, professor) as needed.

Preparation for an "exposure simulation" begins with the client's description of his or her phobic situation, including the behavioral characteristics of significant persons in the target environment. The client is questioned about his or her worst fears concerning this situation so that the exposure might incorporate them. For example, a client giving a class presentation might fear negative reactions and verbal disagreement from classmates. Successful presentation in the absence of these reactions may be easily discounted or trivialized by the client. Other group members may then be asked to make specific negative comments or to challenge the target client during the exposure. The idea is to provide the client with an exposure to the feared situation in its totality—the sum of the situation itself and/or the client's dire predictions about what may happen. The goals of exposure include: (1) exposing the client to a realistic dose of his or her own anxiety experience; (2) helping the client to remain in the situation and to continue performing despite the anxiety; (3) eliciting relevant cognitions for use during cognitive restructuring; and (4) as treatment progresses, giving the client the opportunity to rehearse cognitive coping strategies while experiencing anxiety.

Throughout the simulation, emphasis is placed on the physiological and subjective components of anxiety. Clients repeatedly provide anxiety ratings on a 0–100 Subjective Units of Discomfort Scale (SUDS), allowing therapists to assess the effect of the introduction of specific phobic stimuli on clients' anxiety. Clients will often experience moderate initial anxiety, which climbs to a more uncomfortable plateau. Clients are encouraged to continue in the situation until the SUDS ratings begin to come back down, sometimes to below initial levels. One particular situation may be the focus of consecutive exposures until the anxiety response is minimized. Attention is then shifted to variations of this phobic situation or to other areas of concern.

Despite the simulated nature of these exposures, clients have little difficulty becoming involved and often experience the same degree of anxiety and physiological arousal that occurs when they confront naturally occurring phobic events. A portion of their arousal may stem from the nature of the therapeutic environment. Patients are, in fact, being evaluated by the therapists and observed by the other members of the group. Since these are legitimate anxiety-eliciting stimuli for most social phobics, the group sessions may become actual exposure events, and simulations may have a very real therapeutic impact.

Cognitive Restructuring

Cognitive restructuring is fully integrated with performance-based exposures in order to maximize the effectiveness of both procedures. The first two group sessions are devoted to training clients in the concepts of cognitive restructuring. Group members must learn to identify and label cognitive errors or "automatic thoughts" as they occur. Several group exercises and homework assignments have been designed to facilitate this cognitive training, and others have been adopted from the work of colleagues in the field (e.g., Burns, 1980; Sank & Shaffer, 1984). It is crucial that the clients understand their own cognitive style and how the results affect their emotions in order to seriously apply the techniques we recommend.

At the conclusion of any exposure, the client is asked to provide a complete report of the cognitions that occurred to him or her. Once this vivid report is obtained, several procedures may be followed depending on the specific needs of the target client. The techniques most typically employed will cause patients to investigate the meaning of automatic thoughts and examine their logical basis, to examine the standards they set for evaluating their performance, and to question their predictions about how others will react to them in a given situation. A typical approach involves repeated and persistent questioning along the lines of (1) "What does it mean if . . . ?" (2) "What would you have to have done to feel good about . . . ?" and (3) "What is the evidence for . . . ?"

Generally one automatic thought receives attention at a time. The first few automatic thoughts reported by clients are usually quite superficial and tied to the specific situation, but persistent repetition of question (1) may often produce a string of maladaptive thoughts that more and more closely approximate the client's basic or underlying fear. The therapists and the other group members can then help the client to examine the logic of this fear and to create rational responses. Question (2) confronts social phobics' tendency to set unrealistically high standards for evaluating their social performance. The group will assist the client in determining the goal he or she wants to accomplish, the probability of obtaining this goal, and alternative goals that might be considered. In other words, the group will help the client redefine successful performance in a way that is reasonably attainable, and will give the client permission to enjoy that success. Question (3) is addressed through group discussion of the applicability of reported evidence for clients' conclusions and self-evaluations and through the planning and conduct of behavioral experiments. For example, a client who believed that anyone she spoke with would detect her anxiety and consequently reject her asked each of the group members to evaluate her apparent discomfort. All group members recorded their predictions of her anxiety on a SUDS scale prior to the initiation of questioning. The client had predicted SUDS ratings in the 90s, but the other clients viewed her anxiety level in the 20s. This strategy is fashioned after the behavioral experiments described by Beck and Emery (1979).

Over time, as clients gain expertise in analyzing and replacing their automatic thoughts, they are asked to identify probable cognitions and formulate rebuttals imme-diately *before* an exposure. Clients are given the opportunity to design and practice specific coping statements, disputes, and rebuttals and to prepare to use them during the upcoming exposure. Successful performance during the exposure may then be directly attributable to the client's cognitive efforts. Following the simulation, cognitive restruc-turing occurs as described earlier. Additional attention is devoted to analysis of the specific automatic thoughts that were targeted before the exposure and to new automatic thoughts that may have taken the client by surprise. Also, the client is encouraged to look for patterns of response in a variety of phobic situations.

Although each simulation revolves around an individual client, the other group members are included in several ways. Their involvement in the simulation is crucial to helping the target client, and role playing often provides exposure benefit for other clients. In addition, many group members share similar automatic thoughts, allowing cognitive restructuring to benefit more than one client at a time. As the group gains cognitive sophistication, its members become active in helping each other to analyze and modify their automatic thoughts and underlying assumptions.

Homework Assignments

Throughout treatment it is stressed that clients must learn new skills and new ways of viewing anxiety-provoking situations. It is further stressed that these skills must be applied to situations outside the therapy group in order to evaluate their effectiveness. To facilitate this, clients are given specific personalized assignments to carry out between sessions. Clients are asked to initiate specific behaviors or to place themselves in phobic situations for an extended period of time. Before entering feared situations, they are requested to engage in a period of adaptive thinking, to identify likely automatic thoughts, to prepare and rehearse rational rebuttals to these thoughts, and to enter the situation "fully armed for success." Clients conduct a cognitive post mortem after the situation in order to assess their effectiveness in disputing problematic cognitions and to prepare further for later assignments. Finally, clients report the outcome of homework assignments at the next session since the results will influence future exposures and homework.

Treatment Issues

Our multicomponent group therapy and other treatments reviewed here appear promising for the treatment of social phobia, but clinicians and researchers should be aware of potential complications. We will highlight three special problems that may inhibit treatment progress or lead to an increased dropout rate: diagnosis, depression, and severity of social phobic symptoms.

Diagnosis: Social Phobia versus Avoidant Personality Disorder

We have already touched on the potential problems in generalizability of research findings when different methods of classification (e.g., DSM-III versus the *International Classification of Diseases*, 9th edition, or ICD-9) are used. However, even investigators who regularly use DSM-III criteria cannot agree on the distinctions between social phobia and certain personality disorders, most notably avoidant personality.

According to DSM-III, the essential features of avoidant personality disorder are hypersensitivity to potential rejection, humiliation, or shame; an unwillingness to enter into relationships unless given unusually strong guarantees of uncritical acceptance; social withdrawal despite a desire for affection and acceptance; and low self-esteem. To diagnose differentially, DSM-III states that, in social phobias, humiliation is a concern, but that a specific situation, such as public speaking, is avoided, rather than personal relationships. Although DSM-III also states that the two disorders may coexist, a diagnosis of avoidant personality precludes a diagnosis of social phobia.

The confusion in terminology and the overlap of symptoms become most problematic when considering the client who presents with generalized social anxiety and avoidance. Some researchers suggest that clients with multiple social fears should be classified as having an avoidant personality disorder, implying that treatment will be much more difficult, prolonged, or unsuccessful (Greenberg & Stravynski, 1983; Turner, Freund, Strauss-Zerby, & Liebowitz, 1983). Greenberg and Stravynski argue that the avoidant personality desires increased socialization but is likely to need social skills training in addition to anxiety-reducing techniques. We suggest that the distinction between the two groups may be found in whether the person has little desire to confront the phobic event and has adopted avoidance as a comfortable if unfulfilling life-style or whether the person frequently desires to confront avoided situations or does so at great sacrifice. As described, the avoidant personality would appear to be a poor risk for treatments such as our multicomponent group program. However, there is a great need for diagnostic clarification and study of these predictions. Marks and Gelder's original concept of social phobia included both circumscribed and generalized social fears. Common sense dictates that a single phobic concern (e.g., public speaking) would be easier to treat than a generalized fear (e.g., conversing with others). However, it seems premature to label patients with generalized fears as personality disorders when they might also be viewed as experiencing a more severe social phobia or an equally severe phobia of a more common situation. A lack of social skills may negatively influence the treatment process, but this may be assessed as an additional concern, similar to alcohol abuse or moderate depression.

Depression and the Effectiveness of Treatment for Social Phobia

Earlier we mentioned that symptoms of depression often accompany social phobia, suggesting the importance of assessing both anxiety and depression levels. The decision to treat one problem as opposed to the other is made after carefully exploring the functional relationship between anxiety and depression, as well as considering the severity of each. When social anxiety precedes depression, further analysis may reveal that depressive symptoms have progressed from a history of increased avoidance, isolation, and deprivation of social reinforcement. Although it seems intuitive that treatment of the anxiety would result in reduced depression, other factors need to be considered as well.

Recent data from our laboratory indicate that social phobics who score high on the Beck Depression Inventory (BDI) (Beck, Ward, Mendelson, Mock, & Erbaugh, 1961) may be less likely to benefit from cognitive-behavioral group treatment for their anxiety (Klosko, Heimberg, Becker, Dodge, & Kennedy, 1984). Nineteen subjects who received the cognitive-behavioral protocol described earlier were split into high and low depression groups on the basis of their pretreatment BDI scores. After treatment, high-depression subjects reported significantly greater fear of negative evaluation (Watson & Friend, 1969) and greater anxiety on an individualized behavioral avoidance task than did low-depression subjects. Although pretest anxiety measures were similar for the two groups, depressed social phobics were also more likely to drop out of treatment than were nondepressed subjects. Furthermore, dropouts had significantly higher Hamilton (1960) Depression scores at pretest than completers, whereas the pretest Hamilton (1959) Anxiety scores of dropouts did not differ from those of completers. It is possible that depression interferes with the client's motivation, energy, and optimism toward the treatment process. This type of client may require concurrent cognitive-behavioral treatment that targets the depression, or, in some cases, antidepressant medication may be indicated.

Social Phobia and the Therapy Group as a Phobic Stimulus

Our multicomponent treatment seems most ideal when a variety of severity levels are represented among the group members. The social phobic whose anxiety is extreme, however, may be unable to tolerate the anxiety experienced from simply sitting in the group. Often intense anxiety will prevent social phobics from concentrating on (and therefore understanding) the treatment rationale and concepts necessary for the conduct of exposure simulations or cognitive restructuring. Extreme anxiety may similarly inhibit a client's ability to monitor automatic thoughts, and clients may protest that they do not think, they simply get anxious and their hearts beat. During the first few weeks, therapists may need to spend individual time with clients of this type in order to clarify issues and maintain therapeutic motivation. In addition, the group session itself may be targeted as an exposure for the client, with cognitive restructuring aimed at thoughts prior to and during the group. Therapists might periodically ask the client to report on his or her anxiety level and concurrent thoughts during the group.

One could also consider the use of relaxation training, either for the severely anxious client alone or for the entire group. Relaxation skills might then be practiced in exposure simulations in much the same fashion as was described for rational thoughts. The provision of techniques to control arousal level may increase clients' willingness and ability to participate in treatment. As mentioned earlier, the findings of Öst et al. (1981) support the use of relaxation with "physiological reactors."

Conclusions and Future Directions

In this chapter, we have examined many aspects of social phobia and its treatment by behavioral and cognitive-behavioral techniques. Social phobia, the fear of scrutiny and evaluation by others, was first identified by Marks and Gelder (1966) but did not exist as a diagnostic category in the United States until the publication of DSM-III in 1980. As a result, it has received relatively little research attention and has even been referred to as "a neglected anxiety disorder" (Liebowitz et al., 1985, p. 729).

As described in DSM-III, social phobia is relatively rare and, except in extreme cases, not especially incapacitating. However, social phobia appears to be a more common and more severely disabling disorder than originally assumed, and the presence of social phobia may be related to the tendency to abuse alcohol and/or antianxiety medications. In addition, studies like that conducted by Amies et al. (1983) suggest that social phobia is a unique syndrome that may be distinguished from other anxiety disorders, including agoraphobia. These findings underscore the importance of increasing our knowledge and developing effective treatments for social phobia.

Several theories of social anxiety and social phobia have appeared in the last few years. The theories of Beck and Emery; Buss; Hartman, Trower, and Turland; and Schlenker and Leary share many features, including an emphasis on self-focus and concern about one's ability to achieve social goals and fend off social threats. However, they also share a serious liability. Each of these theories relies (in varying degrees) on two sources of data—studies of social anxiety among subclinically anxious college students or volunteers and clinical observations of anxious patients. Little research exists at present on the cognitive functioning of appropriately diagnosed social phobic patients and how they differ from normals or persons with other anxiety disorders or psychiatric diagnoses. The need to conduct research of this nature with patients appears obvious: empirical data on the cognitions, affect, and behavior of social phobic individuals should provide us with information that will validate, disconfirm, or mold our theories. Theories may then help us to develop additional strategies that may increase the effectiveness of available interventions or suggest new ones. Before we can expect ourselves to undertake these research efforts, however, we must have the instruments with which to measure the self-statements, negative evaluations, self-presentational goals, motivations and doubts, metacognitions, stimulus–outcome and behavior–outcome expectancies, and cognitive schema that are proposed to be related to social phobia. Although it is often less "exciting" to do so, we need to invest our efforts in the development of reliable and valid instruments for the cognitive assessment of social phobia.

Several strategies have been employed to treat social phobia. Studies have been reviewed that evaluate the effectiveness of social skills training, applied relaxation training, systematic desensitization, flooding, exposure, and a variety of cognitive restructuring techniques. Most studies suggest that social phobia may be very responsive to treatment and that each of the techniques investigated may produce some degree of improvement in some patients. Unfortunately, the literature on outcome effectiveness is sparse, and it is difficult to draw conclusions about the utility or potential of specific techniques. Cognitive techniques, in particular, require further evaluation.

The first and possibly the most important requirement for future outcome research is simply that there be more of it. It is virtually impossible to make statements about the effectiveness of treatment techniques when a specific technique is represented by only one or two studies. The second requirement is that studies meet high standards of experimental design. Few existing studies of the treatment of social phobia include adequate control procedures. In fact, several between-group studies include no control conditions at all. We are thus constrained from drawing meaningful conclusions about effectiveness or treatment mechanisms from their results.

The evaluation of cognitive restructuring techniques may also depend in large measure on the way in which they are administered. Cognitive techniques are rarely administered in isolation. In fact, they rely heavily on the use of behavioral techniques to gather data about the content of maladaptive cognitions and to provide experiential data with which to evaluate hypotheses and predictions—hence the label cognitive-behavioral. As discussed earlier, cognitive restructuring techniques should produce their greatest effect when thoroughly integrated into a treatment package. Studies that do not administer cognitive techniques in this fashion (Biran et al., 1981; Stravynski et al., 1982) may not represent a valid test. Since these studies are the only ones that have attempted to evaluate the effectiveness of cognitive restructuring in a controlled fashion, its effectiveness for social phobia remains an open question.

Additional research is required in many areas crucial to the understanding and treatment of social phobia. We need to determine:

1. The relative effectiveness of the various treatment strategies
2. The specific components that make the treatments work and the mechanism by which this is accomplished
3. Whether positive changes are maintained over an extended period of time
4. Whether individual differences can predict successful treatment outcome, both in general and for specific techniques
5. Whether cognitive-behavioral techniques may be safely and effectively combined with other treatment approaches, including pharmacologic approaches
6. Whether the distinctions between social phobia and avoidant personality disorder relate to treatment outcome in a meaningful fashion

In this way, we may develop effective treatments for social fears and phobias.

References

American Psychiatric Association. (1980). *Diagnostic and statistical manual of mental disorders* (3rd edition). Washington, DC: Author.
Amies, P. L., Gelder, M. G., & Shaw, P. M. (1983). Social phobia: A comparative clinical study. *British Journal of Psychiatry, 142,* 174–179.

Arkowitz, H. (1977). The measurement and modification of minimal dating behavior. In M. Hersen, R. M. Eisler, & P. M. Miller (Eds.), *Progress in behavior modification* (Vol. 5). New York: Academic Press.

Arkowitz, H., Lichtenstein, K., McGovern, K., & Hines, P. (1975). Behavioral assessment of social competence in males. *Behavior Therapy, 6*, 3–13.

Arrindell, W. A., Emmelkamp. P. M. G., Monsma, A., & Brilman, E. (1983). The role of perceived parental rearing practices in the aetiology of phobic disorders: A controlled study. *British Journal of Psychiatry, 143*, 183–187.

Bandura, A. (1977). *Social learning theory*. Englewood Cliffs, NJ: Prentice-Hall.

Barlow, D. H. (1985). The dimensions of anxiety disorders. In A. H. Tuma & J. D. Maser (Eds.), *Anxiety and the anxiety disorders*. Hillsdale, NJ: Erlbaum.

Barlow, D. H., & Beck J. G. (1984). The psychosocial treatment of anxiety disorders: Current status, future directions. In J. B. W. Williams & R. L. Spitzer (Eds.), *Psychotherapy research: Where are we and where should we go?* New York: Guilford Press.

Barlow, D. H., & Wolfe, B. E. (1981). Behavioral approaches to anxiety disorders: A report on the NIMH–SUNY, Albany, Research Conference. *Journal of Consulting and Clinical Psychology, 49*, 448–454.

Beck, A. T., & Emery, G. (1979). *Cognitive therapy of anxiety and phobic disorders*. Philadelphia: Center for Cognitive Therapy.

Beck, A. T., & Emery, G. (1985). *Anxiety disorders and phobias: A cognitive perspective*. New York: Basic Books.

Beck, A. T., Rush, A. J., Shaw, B. F., & Emery, G. (1979). *Cognitive therapy of depression*. New York: Guilford Press.

Beck A. T., Ward, C. H., Mendelson, M., Mock, J., & Erbaugh, J. (1961). An inventory for measuring depression. *Archives of General Psychiatry, 4*, 561–571.

Biran, M., Augusto, F., & Wilson, G. T. (1981). *In vivo* exposure vs. cognitive restructuring in the treatment of scriptophobia. *Behaviour Research and Therapy, 19*, 525–532.

Bryant, B. M., & Trower, P. E. (1974). Social difficulty in a student sample. *British Journal of Educational Psychology, 44*, 13–21.

Bryant, B., Trower, P., Yardley, K., Urbieta, H., & Letemendia, F. J. J. (1976). A survey of social inadequacy among psychiatric patients. *Psychological Medicine, 6*, 101–112.

Burns, D. D. (1980). *Feeling good: The new mood therapy*. New York: William Morrow.

Buss, A. H. (1980). *Self-consciousness and social anxiety*. San Francisco: Freeman.

Butler, G., Cullington, A., Munby, M., Amies, P., & Gelder, M. (1984). Exposure and anxiety management in the treatment of social phobia. *Journal of Consulting and Clinical Psychology, 52*, 642–650.

Byrne, D. (1971). *The attraction paradigm*. New York: Academic Press.

Cacioppo, J. T., Glass, C. R., & Merluzzi, T. V. (1979). Self-statements and self-evaluations: A cognitive-response model of social anxiety. *Cognitive Therapy and Research, 3*, 249–262.

Carver, C. S. (1979). A cybernetic model of self-attention processes. *Journal of Personality and Social Psychology, 37*, 1251–1281.

Clark, J. V., & Arkowitz, H. (1975). Social anxiety and the self-evaluation of interpersonal performance. *Psychological Reports, 36*, 211–221.

Conger, J. C., & Farrell, A. D. (1981). Behavioral components of heterosocial skills. *Behavior Therapy, 12*, 41–55.

Curran, J. P., Miller, I. W. III, Zwick, W. R., Monti, P. M. & Stout, R. L. (1980). The socially inadequate patient: Incidence rate, demographic and clinical features, and hospital and posthospital functioning. *Journal of Consulting and Clinical Psychology, 48*, 375–382.

Curran, J. P., Wallander, J. L., & Fischetti, M. (1980). The importance of behavioral and cognitive factors in heterosexual–social anxiety. *Journal of Personality, 48*, 285–292.

Dimsdale, J. E., & Moss, J. (1980). Short-term catecholamine response to psychological stress. *Psychosomatic Medicine, 42*, 493–497.

Emmelkamp, P. M. G. (1982). *Phobic and obsessive-compulsive disorders: Theory, research and practice*. New York: Plenum Press.

Falloon, I. R. H., Lloyd, G. G., & Harpin, R. E. (1981). Real-life rehearsal with nonprofessional therapists. *Journal of Nervous and Mental Disease, 169*, 180–184.

Fenigstein, A. (1979). Self-consciousness, self-attention, and social interaction. *Journal of Personality and Social Psychology, 37*, 75–86.

Fenigstein, A., Scheier, M. F., & Buss, A. H. (1975). Public and private self-consciousness: Assessment and theory. *Journal of Consulting and Clinical Psychology, 43*, 522–527.

Fischetti, M., Curran, J. P., & Wessberg, H. W. (1977). Sense of timing. *Behavior Modification, 1*, 179–194.

Gelder, M. G., Bancroft, J. H. J., Gath D. H., Johnston, D. W., Matthews, A. M., & Shaw, P. M. (1973). Specific and nonspecific factors in behaviour therapy. *British Journal of Psychiatry, 123*, 445–462.

Glasgow, R., & Arkowitz, H. (1975). The behavioral assessment of male and female social competence in dyadic heterosocial interactions. *Behavior Therapy, 6*, 488–498.

Glass, C. R., Gottman, J. M., & Schmurak, S. (1976). Response acquisition and self-statement modification approaches to dating-skills training. *Journal of Counseling Psychology, 23*, 520–526.

Glass, C. R., Merluzzi, T. V., Biever, J. L., & Larsen, K. H. (1982). Cognitive assessment of social anxiety: Development and validation of a self-statement questionnaire. *Cognitive Therapy and Research, 6*, 37–55.

Goldfried, M. R. (1979). Anxiety reduction through cognitive-behavioral intervention. In P. C. Kendall & S. D. Hollon (Eds.), *Cognitive-behavioral interventions: Theory, research, and procedures.* New York: Academic Press.

Goldfried, M. R., Padawer, W., & Robins, C. (1984). Social anxiety and the semantic structure of heterosocial interactions. *Journal of Abnormal Psychology, 93*, 87–97.

Greenberg, G., & Stravynski, A. (1983). Social phobia (letter). *British Journal of Psychiatry, 143*, 526.

Hamilton, M. (1959). The assessment of anxiety states by rating. *British Journal of Medical Psychology, 32*, 50–55.

Hamilton, M. (1960). A rating scale for depression. *Journal of Neurology, Neurosurgery, and Psychiatry, 23*, 56–62.

Hartman, L. M. (1983). A metacognitive model of social anxiety: Implications for treatment. *Clinical Psychology Review, 3*, 435–456.

Hartman, L. M. (1984). Cognitive components of social anxiety. *Journal of Clinical Psychology, 40*, 137–139.

Heimberg, R. G., Acerra, M., & Holstein, A. (1985). Partner similarity mediates interpersonal anxiety. *Cognitive Therapy and Research, 9*, 436–445.

Heimberg, R. G., Becker, R. E., Goldfinger, K., & Vermilyea, J. A. (1985). Treatment of social phobia by exposure, cognitive restructuring and homework assignments. *Journal of Nervous and Mental Disease, 173*, 236–245.

Heimberg, R. G., Harrison, D. F., Montgomery, D., Madsen, C. H., & Sherfey, J. A. (1980). Psychometric and behavioral analyses of a social anxiety inventory: The Situation Questionnaire. *Behavioral Assessment, 2*, 403–415.

Heimberg, R. G., Madsen, C. H., Montgomery, D., & McNabb, C. E. (1980). Behavioral treatments for heterosocial problems: Effects on daily self-monitored and roleplayed interactions. *Behavior Modification, 4*, 147–172.

Johansson, J., & Öst, L-G. (1982). Perception of autonomic reactions and actual heart rate in phobic patients. *Journal of Behavioral Assessment, 4*, 133–143.

Kanter, N. J., & Goldfried, M. R. (1979). Relative effectiveness of rational restructuring and self-control desensitization in the reduction of interpersonal anxiety. *Behavior Therapy, 10*, 472–490.

Kimble, C. E., & Zehr, H. D. (1982). Self-consciousness, information load, self-presentation, and memory in a social situation. *Journal of Social Psychology, 118*, 39–46.

Klosko, J. S., Heimberg, R. G., Becker, R. E., Dodge, C. S., & Kennedy, C. R. (1984). *Depression, anxiety, and outcome of treatment for social phobia.* Paper presented at the eighteenth annual meeting of the Association for the Advancement of Behavior Therapy, Philadelphia, November.

Lang, P. J. (1968). Fear reduction and fear behavior: Problems in treating a construct. In J. M. Shlien (Ed.), *Research in psychotherapy* (Vol. 3). Washington, DC: American Psychological Association.

Lazarus, R., & Opton, E. (1966). The study of psychological stress: A summary of theoretical formulations and experimental findings. In C. Spielberger (Ed.), *Anxiety and behavior.* New York: Academic Press.

Leary, M. R. (1983). *Understanding social anxiety: Social, personality, and clinical perspectives.* Beverly Hills, CA: Sage Publications.

Liebowitz, M. R., Gorman, J. M., Fyer, A. J., & Klein, D. F. (1985). Social phobia: Review of a neglected anxiety disorder. *Archives of General Psychiatry, 42*, 729–736.

Malkiewich, L. E., & Merluzzi, T. V. (1980). Rational restructuring versus desenstization with clients of diverse conceptual levels: A test of a client–treatment matching model. *Journal of Counseling Psychology, 27,* 453–461.

Mandel, N. M., & Shrauger, J. S. (1980). The effects of self-evaluative statements on heterosocial approach in shy and nonshy males. *Cognitive Therapy and Research, 4,* 369–381.

Marks, I. M. (1969). *Fears and phobias.* London: Heinemann.

Marks, I. M. (1981). *Cure and care of neuroses.* New York: Wiley.

Marks, I. M., & Gelder, M. C. (1966). Different ages of onset in varieties of phobia. *American Journal of Psychiatry, 123,* 218–221.

Marzillier, J. S., Lambert, C., & Kellett, J. (1976). A controlled evaluation of systematic desensitization and social skills training for socially inadequate psychiatric patients. *Behaviour Research and Therapy, 14,* 225–238.

McEwan, K. L., & Devins, G. M. (1983). Is increased arousal in social anxiety noticed by others? *Journal of Abnormal Psychology, 92,* 417–421.

Mullaney, J. A., & Trippett, C. J. (1979). Alcohol dependence and phobias: Clinical description and relevance. *British Journal of Psychiatry, 135,* 563–573.

Munjack, D. J., & Moss, H. B. (1981). Affective disorder and alcoholism in families of agoraphobics. *Archives of General Psychiatry, 38,* 869–871.

Myers, J. K., Weissman, M. M., Tischler, G. L., Holzer, C. E. III, Leaf, P. J., Orvaschel, H., Anthony, J. C., Boyd, J. H., Burke, J. D., Jr., Kramer, M., & Stoltzman, R. (1984). Six-month prevalence of psychiatric disorders in three communities. *Archives of General Psychiatry, 41,* 959–967.

Nichols, K. A. (1974). Severe social anxiety. *British Journal of Medical Psychology, 74,* 301–306.

O'Banion, K., & Arkowitz, H. (1977). Social anxiety and selective attention for affective information about the self. *Social Behavior and Personality, 5,* 321–328.

Öst, L. G., Jerremalm, A., & Johansson, J. (1981). Individual response patterns and the effects of different behavioral methods in the treatment of social phobia. *Behaviour Research and Therapy, 19,* 1–16.

Parker, G. (1979). Reported parental characteristics of agoraphobics and social phobics. *British Journal of Psychiatry, 135,* 555–560.

Parker, G., Tupling, H., & Brown, L. B. (1979). A parental bonding instrument. *British Journal of Medical Psychology, 52,* 1–11.

Pilkonis, P. A., & Zimbardo, P. G. (1979). The personal and social dynamics of shyness. In C. E. Izard (Ed.), *Emotions in personality and psychopathology.* New York: Plenum.

Rachman, S., & Wilson, G. T. (1980). *The effects of psychological therapy.* Oxford: Pergamon Press.

Sank, L. I., & Shaffer, C. S. (1984). *A therapist's manual for cognitive behavior therapy in groups.* New York: Plenum.

Schlenker, B. R., & Leary, M. R. (1982). Social anxiety and self-presentation: A conceptualization and model. *Psychological Bulletin, 92,* 641–669.

Shaw, P. M. (1979). A comparison of three behaviour therapies in the treatment of social phobias. *British Journal of Psychiatry, 134,* 620–623.

Smail, P., Stockwell, T., Canter, S., & Hodgson, R. (1984). Alcohol dependence and phobic anxiety states: I. A prevalence study. *British Journal of Psychiatry, 144,* 53–57.

Smith, R. E., & Sarason, I. G. (1975). Social anxiety and the evaluation of negative interpersonal feedback. *Journal of Consulting and Clinical Psychology, 43,* 429.

Smith, T. W., Ingram, R. E., & Brehm, S. S. (1983). Social anxiety, anxious self-preoccupation, and recall of self-relevant information. *Journal of Abnormal Psychology, 44,* 1276–1283.

Stravynski, A. (1983). Behavioral treatment of psychogenic vomiting in the context of social phobia. *Journal of Nervous and Mental Disease, 171,* 448–451.

Stravynski, A., Marks, I., & Yule, W.. (1982). Social skills problems in neurotic outpatients: Social skills training with and without cognitive modification. *Archives of General Psychiatry, 39,* 1378–1385.

Trower, P., & Turland, D. (1984). Social phobia. In S. Turner (Ed.), *Behavioral theories and treatment of anxiety.* New York: Plenum Press.

Trower, P., Yardley, K., Bryant, B., & Shaw, P. (1978). The treatment of social failure: A comparison of anxiety-reduction and skills acquisition procedures on two social problems. *Behavior Modification, 2,* 41–60.

Turner, R. M., Freund, B., Strauss-Zerby, S., & Leibowitz, J. (1983). *The effects of DSM-III borderline personality disorder on the outcome of social anxiety symptom reduction.* Unpublished manuscript, Temple University, Philadelphia, PA.

Twentyman, C. T., & McFall, R. M. (1975). Behavioral training of social skills in shy males. *Journal of Consulting and Clinical Psychology, 43,* 384–395.

Wallace, I., Wallechinsky, D., & Wallace, A. (1977). *The people's almanac presents the book of lists.* New York: Morrow.

Watson, D., & Friend, R. (1969). Measurement of social-evaluative anxiety. *Journal of Consulting and Clinical Psychology, 33,* 448–457.

11

Obsessive–Compulsive Disorders

PAUL M. G. EMMELKAMP

Earlier surveys of the prevalence of obsessive–compulsive disorder have given the impression that obsessive–compulsive disorder is a rare condition; its prevalence in the general population has been estimated at .05% (Rüdin, 1953; Woodruff & Pitts, 1964). In the Epidemiologic Catchment Area program, a collaborative effort sponsored by the National Institute of Mental Health (NIMH), the prevalence of 15 specific mental disorders is investigated in large general population samples. Results are available from nearly 10,000 interviews in three metropolitan areas: New Haven, Connecticut; Baltimore, Maryland; and St. Louis, Missouri (Robins, Helzer, Weissman, Orvaschel, Gruenberg, Burke, & Regier, 1984). The lifetime prevalence rate of obsessive–compulsive disorder was approximately 2.5%. Interestingly, the prevalence rate in Baltimore was significantly higher than in St. Louis. Further, the prevalence rate of obsessive–compulsive disorder among women was slightly higher than that for men (3.0 versus 2.0). No differences were found between blacks and others in prevalence rate. In a companion paper (Myers, Weissman, Tischler, Helzer, Leaf, Orvaschel, Anthony, Boyd, Burke, Kramer, & Stoltzman, 1984), the prevalence rates for the 6-month period immediately preceding the interview were reported on the basis of the same community surveys. The mean 6-month prevalence of obsessive–compulsive disorder was found to be 1.6%. The prevalence of obsessive–compulsive disorder was evenly distributed by age. For women, obsessive–compulsive disorder was the fourth most common disorder.

Most obsessive–compulsive disorders start in the early 20s. About 80% of patients report the onset before age 30 (Emmelkamp, 1982a). The form and content of obsessions and compulsions appear to be strikingly similar in Europe (Dowson, 1977; Rachman & Hodgson, 1980; Stern & Cobb, 1978; Zaworka & Hand, 1980); the United States (Welner, Reich, Robins, Fishman, & Van Doren, 1976); Canada (Roy, 1979); and India (Akhtar, Wig, Verma, Pershod, & Verma, 1975).

About 80% of obsessional patients have obsessions as well as compulsions. A minority suffer from obsessions only. Pure rituals without accompanying obsessive thoughts are rare. Usually obsessions precede the rituals, but sometimes the obsessive thoughts follow the performance of rituals, especially with obsessional doubting. The most common obsessional thoughts consist of fears of dirt and contamination. Harming obsessions are reported by about a quarter of the patients.

Factor analyses of obsessional questionnaires revealed several interpretable factors,

Paul M. G. Emmelkamp. Academic Hospital, Department of Clinical Psychology, Groningen, The Netherlands.

which varied from study to study. All studies, however, found two independent factors: *cleaning* and *checking* (Cooper & Kelleher, 1973; Hodgson & Rachman, 1977; Stern & Cobb, 1978; Zaworka & Hand, 1980). Cleaning compulsions are usually associated with fears of contamination. Patients fear that they may become contaminated and therefore clean their house, themselves, and their children. Whenever such a patient touches anything that might be contaminated (such as doorknobs, other people, or food), they have to wash their hands and arms, often for many minutes, or take a bath. With some patients, thoughts alone may provoke washing and cleaning rituals.

Checking rituals may involve checking whether doors and windows are closed, and whether the gas is turned off. Whenever they leave their house, a number of checkers will go back numerous times to see if everything is all right. Checking may also occur in other situations: for example, driving back to see whether an accident has happened, returning to the office to see whether anyone is locked up in a closet, and so forth. Both washing and checking rituals lead to avoidance of situations that are likely to provoke the rituals.

Theoretical Developments

Before discussing the treatment of obsessive–compulsive disorder, the theoretical developments will be discussed that provide the basis for the behavioral and cognitive interventions that are currently used in the treatment of these cases.

Behavioral Formulation

The behavioral formulation of obsessive–compulsive disorder is derived from Mowrer's two-stage theory of fear and avoidance. In Mowrer's view there is a classical conditioning process responsible for the conditioning of fear and an instrumental learning process responsible for the conditioning of the avoidance response. In the training procedure animals receive repeated pairings of a warning signal—for example, tone (CS)—and an aversive stimulus—for example, shock (UCS). After some time the tone will acquire aversive properties and the animal will experience anxiety (CR) on tone presentation when no shock is applied. This phase of the experimental procedure represents the first stage of learning. Anxiety is attached to previously neutral cues through classical conditioning. In the second stage of learning, the animal terminates the tone by making escape responses, thereby reducing the anxiety it experiences. The termination or avoidance of aversive stimuli leads to negative reinforcement (anxiety reduction) thus strengthening the avoidance behavior. The second stage of learning involves operant conditioning. In summary, it is assumed that fear is acquired through a process of classical conditioning and thereafter motivates avoidance behavior.

In the case of obsessive–compulsive disorders, it might be particularly useful to differentiate between active and passive avoidance (Teasdale, 1974). With *passive* avoidance the individual avoids stimuli or situations that might provoke anxiety and discomfort. *Active* avoidance usually refers to the motor component of obsessive–compulsive behavior—for example, checking and cleaning. A clinical example may illustrate the difference between the two types of avoidance. A woman is afraid of being contaminated by objects that may cause cancer. She avoids numerous objects and situations that, in her view, may lead to contamination. In addition she washes and cleans herself many times a day, whenever she fears she has been contaminated. The avoidance of any contamination would be classified as passive avoidance; the washing and cleaning might be described as active avoidance.

As for the classical conditioning component of the two-stage theory, there is little evidence that this type of learning is crucial in the development of obsessive–compulsive behavior (Emmelkamp, 1982a). Typically, ritualistic activities have powerful anxiety-reducing effects in stressful periods. Although patients sometimes give a detailed account of one or more traumatic experiences associated with the development of the obsessive–compulsive behavior, the traumatic situation by itself rarely leads directly to the obsessive–compulsive behavior. Other clinical observations pose further problems for the classical conditioning theory. In a number of obsessional patients, several different obsessions and rituals occur simultaneously. Theoretically, one should find several traumatic episodes to account for the onset of the various obsessions. Thus there is little or no evidence that classical conditioning provides an adequate account of the development of obsessional problems.

More evidence is provided for the second stage of Mowrer's theory. There is clear evidence that the rituals (active avoidance) may serve to reduce anxiety. Rachman and his colleagues studied the provocation of compulsive acts and the effects of performance of the rituals under controlled laboratory conditions. The design of these studies was usually as follows. Obsessive–compulsive behavior was provoked and measurements of subjective anxiety were taken before and after provocation, and after performance of the checking or cleaning ritual. In addition, patients' reactions were tested when the performance of the ritual was interrupted and when it was delayed. Two studies (Hodgson & Rachman, 1972; Röper, Rachman, & Hodgson, 1973) also used psychophysiological assessment (pulse rate variability) during the course of the experiment. The results of these studies can be summarized as follows. With patients whose primary problem was obsessive–compulsive washing arising out of fears of contamination or dirt, contamination led to an increase of subjective anxiety/discomfort, whereas the completion of a washing ritual had the opposite effect. Spontaneous decrease in discomfort occurred when the performance of the hand-washing ritual was postponed for half an hour. The interruption of the ritual produced neither an increase nor a decrease in subjective anxiety/discomfort. (Hodgson & Rachman, 1972; Rachman & Hodgson, 1980). For pulse rate variability, the same trends occurred, but the difference between occasions were not significant (Hodgson & Rachman, 1972).

The results of studies on checkers (Röper, Rachman, & Hodgson, 1973; Röper & Rachman, 1976) are less clear-cut. Here some patients showed an increase rather than a decrease in anxiety/discomfort after performing the ritual. Both Herrnstein's (1969) and Gray's (1975) theories may be better able than Mowrer's theory to explain the rare occasions in a minority of checkers in which performance of rituals had an anxiety-augmenting effect. Herrnstein holds that anxiety reduction in itself is not the reinforcing agent; rather, his theory predicts that subjects should experience less anxiety after the performance of a ritual than they would have experienced if they had not performed the ritual. Take, for example, the patient who must perform a number of stereotyped rituals in order to prevent a new world war. Although the performance of rituals may indeed increase anxiety, it is plausible to assume that this anxiety is less painful than the anxiety and guilt feelings that would arise if nonperformance of the rituals indeed resulted in World War III.

The safety signal theory (Gray, 1975) assumes that it is not anxiety reduction in itself but safety signals that positively reinforce avoidance behavior. This version differs from Mowrer's original theory in that it includes, besides the negative reinforcement (anxiety reduction), the onset of reinforcement of secondary rewarding stimuli (safety signals) as a potential source of reinforcement for avoidance behavior. In sum, patients' performances of rituals usually lead to anxiety reduction. Nevertheless, on some occasions performance of rituals has an anxiety-augmenting effect.

Cognitive Deficits

A substantial number of studies have been reported that investigated cognitive processes of obsessive–compulsive patients. Most of this research has been reviewed elsewhere (Emmelkamp, 1982a), and I will present here only the main findings.

Earlier work in this area focused on the tolerance of ambiguity and rigidity of obsessional patients. Studies that investigated this issue generally support the notion that obsessionals have considerable difficulty in tolerating ambiguity. Studies involving expanded judgment tasks by Beech and his colleagues indicate that obsessionals need to reach decisions more frequently than controls, but, given the opportunity to delay the decision, are inclined to postpone the final decision in order to get more information. The research program of Reed (1977) provides further support for the impairment in decision making as characteristic for obsessive–compulsives.

Person and Foa (1984) investigated whether the concepts of obsessive–compulsives are excessively complex and overspecific or, conversely, whether they are excessively simple. Results of this study suggest that obsessive–compulsives make finer distinctions among items than do nonobsessives, thus supporting the complex-concepts deficit hypothesis. It was further found that this general deficit was more pronounced when obsessional fear items were involved as compared with neutral items.

Carr (1974) stresses the unrealistic threat appraisal as characteristic for obsessive–compulsives. Carr (1974) suggests that obsessionals have an abnormally highly subjective estimate of the probability of an unfavorable outcome in decision making. Results of this study indicate that obsessionals and normals made the same threat appraisal under high-cost conditions. However, under low-cost conditions obsessionals reacted differently from normals, showing responses similar to those under high-cost conditions. A number of events may be perceived by these individuals as unrealistically dangerous, such as the threat of contamination or the consequences of making a wrong decision.

McFall and Wollersheim (1979) formulated a cognitive-behavioral model of obsessive–compulsive disorders in which an attempt was made to integrate the research findings described here. Following Lazarus (1966) they hold that threat is generated by an immediate cognitive "primary appraisal" process whereby individuals estimate the danger of an event relative to their perceived resources to cope with it. Once a primary appraisal of threat has been made, deficits in the secondary appraisal process by understanding the ability to cope with the threat lead to anxiety and obsessive-compulsive behavior. McFall and Wollersheim (1979) hypothesized that a number of unreasonable beliefs are likely to influence the primary appraisal process of the obsessive–compulsive individual. These irrational beliefs include the irrational idea that one should be perfect in order to avoid criticism or disapproval by others and that one is powerful enough to prevent disastrous outcomes by means of rituals.

In the view of McFall and Wollersheim, obsessive–compulsive symptoms reduce uncertainty and anxiety and provide the individual with a sense of control. Obsessionals experience themselves as helpless to cope with threat by more adaptive means "and feel that symptoms are *their best option* for reducing distress" (McFall & Wollersheim, 1979, p. 336; emphasis in original). Beliefs that are associated with the secondary appraisal process include the beliefs that (1) if something is or may be dangerous, one should be terribly upset by it; (2) it is easier and more effective to perform a ritual than it is to confront one's feelings/thoughts directly; and (3) feelings of uncertainty and loss of control are intolerable, they should make one afraid, and something must be done about them.

It is important to note that the primary and secondary appraisal processes are mainly preconscious; it is assumed that these cognitions and beliefs can be elicited relatively easily: "the cognitive model views the source of threat and anxiety not as deeply unconscious primitive drives but rather as unacceptable ideas and feelings much closer to the individual's conscious awareness" (McFall and Wollersheim, 1979, p. 339). Although this cognitive-behavioral formulation of obsessive–compulsives is attractive, it should be noted that research is lacking into the specific irrational beliefs of obsessive–compulsives.

Arousal Deficit

Before reviewing the cognitive behavioral studies into the treatment of obsessive–compulsive disorders, a few comments need to be devoted to the role of arousal in obsessive–compulsive disorder.

Beech and his colleagues (e.g., Beech & Lidell, 1974; Beech & Perigault, 1974) have argued that obsessionals are characterized by an elevated level of physiological arousal. In their view, a pathological state of overarousal is primary in causing indecisiveness: "the obsessional patient's estimate of the probability of making a mistake will deviate from the normal as a function of the abnormality of mood state" (Beech & Lidell, 1974, p. 150). At present, little or no evidence is available that obsessionals are characterized by heightened arousal (Emmelkamp, 1982a). Although there is some evidence (Oberhummer, Sachs, & Stellamoor, 1983) that obsessionals are characterized by a reduced habituation during exposure to a decision-making task in comparison with normal controls, this merely shows that obsessionals have difficulty in making decisions rather than demonstrating a more general arousal disturbance. Thus there is no reason to assign primary importance to pathological arousal as a cause of obsessive–compulsive disorders until new evidence is available. The lack of evidence for the pathological arousal hypothesis is important to note since biological therapies by means of psychopharmaca (e.g., clomipramine) or psychosurgery are partly based on such a notion.

Treatment

The treatment of obsessive–compulsive behavior (rituals) will be reviewed first. The treatment of obsessions unaccompanied by rituals will be discussed in a later section.

Obsessive-Compulsive Behavior

The first attempts to treat obsessive–compulsive behavior by behavior therapy were done by systematic desensitization (Wolpe, 1958). In systematic desensitization the patient is first trained in muscular relaxation and then moves gradually up a hierarchy of anxiety-arousing situations while remaining relaxed at a pace determined by the patient's progress in overcoming the fear. Systematic desensitization has been applied in imagination (e.g., Furst & Cooper, 1970; McGlynn & Linder, 1971; Rackenspreger & Feinberg, 1972; Saper, 1971; Tanner, 1971; Walton & Mather, 1963; Wolpe, 1964; Worsley, 1970). There is, however, little evidence that systematic desensitization is of any value with obsessive–compulsive disorders. Cooper, Gelder, and Marks (1965), in one of the first clinical trials of behavior therapy, compared the results of systematic desensitization with those of supportive psychotherapy and drugs. Of 10 obsessive–compulsives who had been treated by systematic desensitization, only three were found to have improved. The control group actually did slightly better. Beech and Vaughan (1978) reviewed the research in this area and found that the reported success rate of systematic desensitization is slightly over 50%. It is reasonable to assume that the actual success rate is even lower, given the bias in selection of cases for publication by authors and journal editors. The only group study reported in the literature (Cooper et al., 1965) found a success rate of 33%! A closer analysis of the successful cases reveals that the improvement should be attributed to gradual exposure *in vivo* plus self-imposed response prevention, rather than to systematic desensitization in itself.

The use of systematic desensitization as a treatment for obsessive–compulsive behavior was based on the two-stage theory of Mowrer. It was assumed that the urge to ritualize would cease as a result of the anxiety reduction achieved through systematic desensitization. Thus no special emphasis was laid on preventing the rituals from occurring.

Other procedures that have been used with greater or lesser effect include *implosive therapy* (Stampfl & Levis, 1967; Hersen, 1968); *exposure in vivo* procedures with or without response prevention (Fine, 1973; Gentry, 1970; Heyse, 1973; Mills, Agras, Barlow, & Mills, 1973; Petrie & Haans, 1969; Rainey, 1972; Ramsay & Sikkel, 1973; Walton, 1960; a combination of *flooding in imagination and in vivo* (Boulougouris & Bassiakos, 1973; Rachman, Hodgson, & Marzillier, 1970); *aversive therapy* (Le Boeuf, 1974; Solyom, Zamanzadeh, Ledwidge, & Kenny, 1971; Solyom & Kingstone, 1973; Walton, 1960) and *covert sensitization* (Wisocki, 1970). Most of these studies, however, consisted of only one or a few case studies.

Although the theoretical rationales for the various treatment procedures vary greatly, one common element in the treatments seems to be exposure to anxiety-inducing stimuli, either in imagination or *in vivo*. For example, with aversive therapy and covert sensitization patients either must imagine obsessional scenes or are brought directly in contact with stimuli that trigger their rituals. This exposure to the distressing stimuli is followed by the strong aversive stimulus—shock or, in the case of covert sensitization, the imagination of aversive consequence.

EXPOSURE AND RESPONSE PREVENTION

The value of prolonged exposure *in vivo* and response prevention was suggested by uncontrolled studies of Meyer and his colleagues (Meyer, 1966; Meyer & Levy, 1970; Meyer, Levy, & Schnurer, 1974). The essence of their treatment approach, which at that time was called *apotrepic therapy* consisted of response prevention, modeling, and exposure *in vivo*. The treatment involves several stages. After a behavioral analysis, nurses were instructed to prevent the patient from carrying out his or her rituals. Exposure *in vivo* was introduced as soon as the total elimination of rituals under supervision was achieved. The therapist increased the stress by confronting the patient with situations that normally triggered obsessive rituals. During this stage of treatment modeling was employed. With modeling, the therapist first demonstrated what the patient had to do afterward. For example, the therapist touched contaminated objects such as underwear and encouraged the patient to imitate this. When patients could tolerate the most difficult situations, supervision was gradually diminished.

Meyer et al. (1974) reported the results of his program with 15 patients. Most patients showed a marked reduction of compulsive behavior. Since then a number of controlled studies have investigated the components of this therapeutic package, the results of which will be briefly summarized.

1. *Gradual exposure in vivo is as effective as flooding in vivo* (Boersma, Den Hengst, Dekker, & Emmelkamp, 1976; Marks, Hodgson, & Rachman, 1975). Thus it is unnecessary to elicit high anxiety during *in vivo* exposure. Because gradual exposure evokes less tension and is easier for the patient to carry out alone, it is preferable to flooding.

2. *Modeling does not seem to increase treatment effectiveness.* Preliminary data (Hodgson, Rachman, & Marks, 1972) suggested that modeling enhanced the effectiveness of exposure *in vivo*, but subsequent studies found no enhancing effects of modeling (Boersma et al., 1976; Rachman, Marks, & Hodgson, 1973).

3. *Treatment can be administered by the patient in his or her natural environment.* Emmelkamp and Kraanen (1977) contrasted therapist-controlled exposure and self-controlled exposure. Although no significant differences were found between the two conditions, self-controlled exposure was consistently superior to therapist-controlled exposure at 1-month follow-up. Thus, home-based treatment not only is cost-effective but also might result in superior maintenance of treatment-produced change.

4. *Spouse-aided exposure is about as effective as self-controlled exposure.* This issue was investigated by Emmelkamp and De Lange (1983). There was a consistent trend for the partner-assisted group to improve more, but this difference failed to reach statistical significance on most measures. The partner-assisted group improved more at the posttest, but at 1-month follow-up the difference between the two groups disappeared.

5. *Prolonged exposure sessions are superior to shorter ones.* Rabavilas, Boulougouris, Stefanis, and Vaidakis (1977) set out to investigate the optimal duration of exposure

sessions. Prolonged exposure *in vivo* (2 hours) was found to be significantly superior to short exposure segments. Short exposure consisted of 10-minute exposure, followed by 5-minute neutral material, followed by 10-minute exposure, and so on until the 2-hour period had elapsed. Short exposure had a deteriorating effect on the patient's affective state.

6. *Both exposure to distressing stimuli and response prevention of the ritual are essential components.* Although most behavioral programs include response prevention (either therapist-controlled or self-controlled), few studies investigated the contribution of response prevention directly. The first study to investigate this particular issue was reported by Mills, Agras, Barlow, and Mills (1973). Five obsessive–compulsive patients were studies in single-case designs while treatment conditions were systematically varied. Response prevention was found to be more effective than when patients were simply given instructions to stop the rituals. Other series of single-case studies demonstrated again the value of response prevention (Turner, Hersen, Bellack, & Wells, 1979; Turner, Hersen, Bellack, Andrasik, & Capparrell, 1980).

To date, two controlled between-group studies have been reported in the literature. Foa, Steketee, and Milby (1980) assigned eight obsessive–compulsive patients to two treatment conditions: (1) exposure alone followed by exposure and response prevention, and (2) response prevention alone followed by the combined treatment. Altogether, treatment consisted of 20 sessions. Exposure led to more anxiety reduction but less improvement of rituals, whereas the reverse was found for response prevention. When the combined treatment was applied at the second period, the differences between the groups on anxiety and ritualistic behavior disappeared.

In another study (Foa, Steketee, Grayson, Turner, & Latimer, 1984) 32 washers were randomly assigned to one of three treatment groups: (1) exposure *in vivo* only, (2) response prevention only, or (3) a combination of these two procedures. The combined treatment approach was more effective than either procedure on its own. Interestingly, there was some evidence that exposure had a specific effect on anxiety, whereas response prevention was found to affect rituals more. A substantial number of relapses occurred following treatment by a single-component procedure. In sum, both exposure *in vivo* and response prevention appear to be essential elements in the treatment of obsessive–compulsive rituals.

7. *In vivo exposure versus imaginal exposure.* Despite clear evidence that exposure *in vivo* is superior to exposure in imagination with agoraphobics (e.g., Emmelkamp, 1974; Emmelkamp & Wessels, 1975; Stern & Marks, 1973), the relative efficacy of the two exposure modalities with obsessive–compulsives is less well investigated.

The first study that addressed this issue was reported by Rabavilas et al. (1977): actual exposure was superior to exposure in imagination. Foa, Steketee, Turner, & Fisher (1980) assigned 15 checkers randomly to two conditions: (1) exposure *in vivo* (2 hours), and (2) exposure in imagination (90 minutes) followed by exposure *in vivo* (30 minutes). Imaginal exposure did not enhance the effectiveness of exposure *in vivo* at the posttest. More recently, another study of the same research group (Foa, Steketee, & Grayson, 1985) compared *in vivo* exposure and exposure in imagination in 19 checkers. In contrast with the Foa, Steketee, Turner, & Fisher (1980) study, response prevention was not instituted in either group. Although at the posttest the two treatment modalities were equally effective in ameliorating obsessive–compulsive symptoms, there was a tendency for patients treated with *in vivo* exposure to improve further at follow-up. Notably, the studies that found no differences in efficacy of exposure *in vivo* and exposure in imagination involved checkers only. Presumably, exposure in imagination is of more importance to checkers who fear disastrous consequences that cannot be produced in reality than it is for other obsessive–compulsive patients (e.g., washers) with whom actual exposure to distressing stimuli can be easily arranged.

8. *Attention focusing on the feared stimuli may enhance habituation.* Grayson, Foa, and Steketee (1982) compared distraction (playing video games) with attention focusing during exposure *in vivo* sessions. Attention focusing did not differ from distraction with regard to within-session habituation, but it did affect the degree of between-session habituation.

9. *Massed versus spaced exposure.* Emmelkamp, Ruephan, Sanderman, and Van den Heuvell (1987) compared 10 sessions of massed practice with 10 sessions of spaced practice. In the massed practice condition, treatment was conducted four times a week, whereas in the spaced condition sessions were held only twice a week. Results indicated that massed practice was just as effective as spaced pratice. Results are at odds with the results of a study with agoraphobics (Foa, Jameson, Turner, & Payne, 1980), in which the massed practice condition was superior. The authors suggested that this was because massed practice provides less opportunity between treatment sessions for accidental exposure and for the reinforcement of avoidance and escape behavior. However, the results with obsessive–compulsives did not support their findings.

10. *Hospital treatment versus home-based treatment.* Exposure and response prevention have been applied mostly in hospital settings (e.g., Rachman et al., 1973; Mills et al., 1973; Boulougouris & Bassiakos, 1974; Meyer et al., 1974; Röper, Rachman, & Marks, 1975; Foa & Goldstein, 1979), but this does not seem to be essentially since others have treated obsessive–compulsives on an outpatient basis (e.g., Emmelkamp and his colleagues, 1976; 1977; 1980; 1983; 1985a; 1985b; Hoogduin, 1985). To see whether inpatient and outpatient treatment would lead to the same outcome Van der Hout, Emmelkamp, and Kraaykamp (1987) compared inpatient versus outpatient treatment in a quasi-experimental design. No differences were found in the effectiveness of exposure *in vivo* when conducted on a specific behavioral ward in the hospital in comparison with this treatment conducted on an outpatient basis. Given the costs involved, treatment on an outpatient basis is clearly preferable to treatment in the hospital.

11. *Antidepressant drugs (clomipramine) may reduce depressed mood and so enhance compliance.* The only double-blind controlled study comparing the effects of a tricyclic antidepressant (clomipramine) with behavioral treatment (exposure plus response prevention) was conducted at the Maudsley Hospital in London (Marks, Stern, Mawson, Cobb, & McDonald, 1980; Rachman, Cobb, Grey, McDonald, Mawson, Sartory, & Stern, 1979). Results were reported to 2-year follow-up. In a 2 × 2 experimental design, behavioral treatment (exposure versus relaxation) and psychopharmacological treatment (clomipramine versus placebo) were systematically varied. Exposure produced significant lasting improvement in rituals but less change in mood. Clomipramine resulted in significant improvement in rituals and mood, but only in those patients who initially had depressed mood.

12. *The therapist may need to address other targets than the obsessive–compulsive problem.* Clinical observation suggests that obsessive–compulsive patients are often socially anxious and unassertive. In some of these cases the obsessive–compulsive problems might serve the function of avoiding people. Assertiveness training has been applied successfully with a number of cases (e.g., Emmelkamp, 1982b; 1985; Emmelkamp & Van der Heyden, 1980); but controlled studies indicate that obsessive–compulsives may benefit from other approaches than exposure *in vivo* and emphasize the value of a functional analysis (e.g., Queiroz, Motta, Madi, Sossai, & Boren, 1981).

EXPOSURE: PRACTICAL GUIDELINES

The principle of exposure is often easier to state than to carry out in practice. Before starting exposure treatment, it is important for the patient to understand the rationale for the treatment. The patient should understand that the problem is maintained through both passive and active avoidance. The exposure part of the treatment is directed at the patient's passive avoidance. The response prevention part of the treatment deals with the patient's active avoidance.

In the case of an exposure program for cleaning compulsions, treatment usually consists of two elements. First, the patient is exposed to "dirt" or "contaminated" material without being allowed to clean. The exposure to distressing stimuli must last until the patient's anxiety and tension are reduced. A second part of the treatment involves teaching the patient to clean in a nonritualistic way. It is important that both elements are practiced separately. If a patient is first exposed to dirt and immediately afterwards allowed to clean it, the exposure element is of little or no use because the cleaning reduces the fear.

With checkers, it is essential that they themselves feel responsible for their behavior during exposure. For this reason, exposure in the presence of the therapist is often not a genuine exposure, for the patient can easily transfer the responsibility for the action to the therapist. Further, it is important to notice that the nature of the exercises by definition often precludes the repetition of the same exercise during one session. For example, checking the gas can be done only once during an exposure session. If the patient is assigned to do this more often, it is no longer genuine exposure: when the patient carries out the assignment a second time, he is in fact checking whether he has done it right the first time and is thus reassured.

With patients who are compulsively precise, exposure consists of putting all kinds of objects into disarray and changing precise habits. When doubting is the main feature of the obsessional disorder, treatment involves exposure to situations in which the patients must make decisions by themselves and are not allowed to reconsider these decisions. Compulsive buying may be treated by exposure to situations in which patients have ample opportunity to buy but are not allowed to do so. Treatment of compulsive hoarding involves throwing out all kinds of superfluous objects.

Asking for reassurance, a common phenomenon with obsessionals, basically has the same function as rituals. A patient who feels uncertain or afraid may calm down temporarily through reassurance. Looking for reassurance can consist of asking relatives, consulting experts, or looking up items in newspapers and encyclopedias. The response prevention in such cases involves informing relatives of the necessity to stop giving reassurance and instructing the patient to stop asking or looking for reassurance.

These examples of practical applications of exposure and response prevention have been described in more detail elsewhere (Emmelkamp, 1982a).

Cognitive Modification

Cognitions are presumably of paramount importance in mediating overt compulsive behavior. For example, most washing rituals are mediated by unrealistic beliefs about the possibility of contamination, and checking rituals are often provoked by ideas of harm befalling oneself or others. Although exposure *in vivo* does not focus directly on a modification of anxiety-inducing cognitions, treatment leads to cognitive changes with some patients. Similar cognitive changes are found with phobic patients treated by exposure *in vivo*. However, whereas for phobics anxiety reduction during exposure sessions is often sufficient to let them change their unproductive thoughts, this proves to be insufficient for a number of obsessional patients. Obviously, one can hardly expect that a patient who believes that someone unknown to him may die unless he carries out checking rituals will change these irrational beliefs after experiencing anxiety reduction during treatment by exposure *in vivo*.

Emmelkamp, Van de Helm, Van Zanten, and Plochg (1980) investigated whether a modification of cognitions would increase the effectiveness of gradual exposure *in vivo*. Fifteen obsessive–compulsive patients were assigned at random to two conditions: (1) exposure *in vivo* and (2) self-instructional training and exposure *in vivo*. The treatment session in the exposure-only condition consisted of 90-minute gradual exposure *in vivo* in the company of the therapist, preceded by 30-minute relaxation. With self-instructional training and exposure, the first half hour of each session was devoted to self-instructional training: patients were trained to emit more productive self-statements. After a short relaxation period the patients cognitively rehearsed self-instructional ways (including relaxation) of handling anxiety by means of an imagination procedure. Patients had to imagine the situations, which had to be dealt with *in vivo* afterward, to ascertain how anxious they felt, to become conscious of their negative self-statements, and then to replace these by more productive self-statements and relaxation. The self-instructional phase was followed by 90 minutes of gradual exposure *in vivo* to the same situations that were rehearsed. Patients were instructed to use their productive self-statements during the practice *in vivo*.

Self-instructional training did not increase the effectiveness of exposure *in vivo*. If anything, exposure *in vivo* appeared to be superior to the combined approach, although this difference failed to reach statistical significance on most measures. Presumably, time devoted to self-instructional practice during exposure *in vivo* phase has slowed down the tempo at which exposure *in vivo* had been carried out. The meager results are in accord with the results of our studies with agoraphobics (Emmelkamp & Mersch, 1982; Emmelkamp, Kuipers, & Eggeraat, 1978; Emmelkamp, Brilman, Kuipers, & Mersch, 1986). In the present study several patients questioned the usefulness of the self-instructional training, since they did not find that the positive self-statements were helpful during exposure *in vivo*. Despite their attempts to control their anxiety, they became as anxious as before.

More recently Emmelkamp, Visser, and Hoekstra (1987) investigated the value of rationally disputing the irrational beliefs of obsessive–compulsive patients. Sixteen obsessive–compulsive patients were treated by either exposure *in vivo* (self-controlled) or rational therapy along the lines of Ellis. Ellis (1962) uses an A-B-C framework of *rational-emotive therapy*. A refers to an Activating event or experience, B to the person's *Belief* about the activating (A) event, and C to the emotional or behavioral Consequence assumed to result from the *Belief* (B). The crucial elements of treatment involve determining the (irrational) thoughts that mediate the anxiety and discomfort, and to confront and modify them so that undue anxiety is no longer experienced. As previously discussed, there are certain irrational beliefs quite common among obsessionals. In the cognitive therapy condition the therapist challenged such underlying irrational beliefs in a Socratic fashion.

The results of this study indicate that cognitive therapy was almost as effective as exposure *in vivo*. Unfortunately, definite conclusions are precluded, since those exposed *in vivo* in this study did less well than in other studies. Although both cognitive treatment and exposure treatment effected significant and lasting changes in obsessive–compulsive symptoms, the degree of improvement was only moderate in comparison to our earlier studies. Thus the result needs to be replicated before more definitive statements can be made about the value of cognitive therapy with obsessive–compulsive patients.

Long-Term Effectiveness of Behavioral Treatment

Emmelkamp, Hoekstra, and Visser (1985) evaluated the outcome of behavioral treatment approximately 3.5 years after treatment (range 2–6 years). Obsessive–compulsives who had been treated with exposure *in vivo* and (self-imposed) response prevention in various treatment outcome studies at our department participated in this study. Results on anxiety, Depressed Mood (Zung-Self-Rating Depression Scale), and Maudsley Obsessional–Compulsive Inventory revealed that the major changes took place within a remarkably short period—1 month's intensive behavioral treatment. Generally, results after treatment were maintained throughout the follow-up period, but a slight relapse on depressed mood occurred at a 1-month follow-up. However, further improvement occurred between the 1- and 6-month follow-ups, during which period most patients received additional behavioral treatment. It is important to note that no treatment was provided during the period between posttest and 1-month follow-up. No relapse occurred at a follow-up after 3.5 years. This pattern clearly suggests that improvement in depression is related to the behavioral treatment the patients received. At follow-up 24 patients were rated as "much improved," 10 patients as "improved," and 8 patients as "failures."

To establish whether patients' characteristics could be used as predictors for success of behavioral treatment, regression analyses were conducted on several variables, including onset age, initial depression, and initial anxiety. Each of these variables was found to correlate significantly with outcome at posttreatment or 1-year follow-up in Foa, Grayson, Steketee, Doppert, Turner, and Latimer (1983). We were further interested in whether perceived parental characteristics could affect treatment outcome. An inventory was used to assess parental characteristics) (Arrindell, Emmelkamp, Brilman, & Monsma, 1983).

Initial anxiety and depression did predict outcome at posttreatment, but not at follow-up. Interestingly, onset age and parental rejection were not powerful predictors of outcome at posttreatment, but did predict follow-up functioning. Patients whose symptoms had begun at an earlier age maintained their gains better at follow-up than did those whose symptoms had begun later, a finding that corroborates the results of Foa et al. (1983). The contribution of initial anxiety to posttreatment outcome was only marginally significant. Although initial depression proved to be a better predictor of posttreatment outcome than did initial anxiety, there was no relationship with long-term outcome at follow-up. The group that was initially the most depressed improved less on anxiety at the posttest, but this difference disappeared at follow-up, probably because of the continuing treatment that these patients received.

Interestingly, perceived parental rejection, especially by the father, was substantially related to outcome. Obviously, the behavioral treatments that patients received did not deal with these issues. If current results are replicated, it might be worthwhile to investigate the impact of treatments that focus more directly on such feelings of rejection with this subgroup of obsessive–compulsives. The encouraging 3.5-year outcome of rituals in this series was comparable to that in other samples treated similarly by exposure *in vivo* after 2 years (Marks et al., 1975; Mawson, Marks, & Ramm, 1982).

Treatment of Obsessions

Behavioral treatments for obsessions can be grouped into three categories. The first approach involves procedures that focus on a removal of the obsessions (e.g., thought stopping and aversion therapy). The second series of treatments is directed at habituation to the distressing thoughts. Examples of this strategy are prolonged exposure in imagination and satiation training. The third approach does not deal directly with the obsessions but attempts to treat other problems that are presumed to underlie the obsessions—for example, treating obsessional patients through assertiveness training.

Thought Stopping

In thought stopping, patients are requested to imagine one of their obsessions and then to stop the obsessive thought at the therapist's command. Following Wolpe's (1958) introduction to thought stopping, a number of case studies were reported that demonstrated the value of this procedure in reducing unwanted thoughts. With respect to obsessional patients, a number of authors have reported this procedure to have some beneficial effects (Leger, 1978, 1979; Lombardo & Turner, 1979; Samaan, 1975; Stern, 1970; Yamagami, 1971), although others are more negative about the effects achieved (Stern, 1978; Teasdale & Rezin, 1978).

Only four controlled studies have been conducted in which thought stopping was compared with an alternative approach (Emmelkamp & Kwee, 1977; Emmelkamp & Van der Heyden, 1980; Hackman & Mc Lean, 1975; Stern, Lipsedge, & Marks, 1973). The results of thought stopping were variable at best. In none of these studies was thought stopping more effective than control procedures.

Another form of dismissal training is aversion therapy. Several authors claimed that obsessional thoughts can be changed by aversion therapy (Bass, 1973; Kenny, Solyom, & Solyom, 1973; Kushner & Sandler, 1966; Mahoney, 1971) and aversion relief (Solyom & Kingstone, 1973). To date, only one controlled study has investigated the efficacy of aversion therapy with obsessional patients. Kenny, Mowbray, and Lalani (1978) compared faradic disruption of obsessive ideation with no treatment. With faradic disruption, an electric shock was given when patients reproduced an obsessive thought in their minds. It was found that patients treated by faradic disruption showed greater improvement than the waiting list control group. Taking these controlled studies together, dismissal training leads to variable results. Thought stopping has no adequate theoretical basis and its empirical strength is far from convincing.

One problem with the literature involving dismissal training is that no distinction is made between obsessive thoughts that are anxiety-inducing and obsessions that serve to reduce anxiety. Anxiety-inducing obsessions may be accompanied either by rituals to reduce anxiety or by obsessional thoughts that may serve the same function as the rituals. Obsessional patients often engage in "neutralizing" thoughts (anxiety-reducing obsessions) in order to undo the possible harmful effects of their obsessions. For example, one of my obsessive patients had obsessional thoughts of God who cohabitated (anxiety-inducing obsessions), which were immediately followed by neutralizing thoughts, such as: "Not God and not the Holy Ghost." Thinking the neutralizing thought led to temporary relief of the anxiety provoked by the blasphemous thoughts. Treatment here involved exposure to the distressing thoughts, with "response prevention" focused on the neutralizing thoughts. Presumably dismissal training may play an important role in preventing the neutralizing thoughts from occurring so that habituation to the anxiety-inducing obsession can be achieved. However, this issue has not been studied yet.

Habituation Training

Rachman (1976) hypothesized that obsessional ruminations may be regarded as noxious stimuli to which patients have difficulty in habituating. Rachman (1976) suggested "satiation training" as method for treating obsessions. With satiation training, patients are requested to evoke and maintain their obsessions for prolonged periods of up to 15 minutes. The original proposal dealt with the most disturbing obsessions, but in a later publication hierarchical presentation was preferred: "the troublesome obsessions are subjected to habituation training in ascending order as for desensitization" (Rachman & Hodgson, 1980, p. 282). With patients who engage in "neutralizing activities," response prevention instructions are added.

The efficacy of satiation training has not been systematically evaluated with clinical patients. A study by Parkinson and Rachman (1980) suggested that with repeated practice the duration and accompanying discomfort of "normal obsessions" formed to instructions decreased. The clinical value of this study is limited, however, since normal adults rather than obsessional patients participated in this study. Thus their "normal obsessions" were of mild intensity.

About the same time Rachman developed his satiation method, we started to study the effects of prolonged exposure to obsessional material on obsessional patients (Emmelkamp & Kwee, 1977). With this procedure, patients are exposed uninterruptedly to their obsessions for 60 minutes. They are instructed to sit in a relaxed way and to close their eyes. Next, the therapist asks the patients to imagine as vividly as possible the obsessions described by the therapist and not to avoid imagining these scenes in any way. Special attention is given to prevent patients from neutralizing the effects of their obsessional thoughts during exposure sessions. Again and again the obsessions that arouse the most anxiety are described. If the tension aroused by imagining a certain obsession has dropped considerably, this scene is no longer used. The scenes presented by the therapist consist solely of the obsessional material; no attempt is made to increase the feelings of anxiety.

Prolonged exposure differs from satiation training in several respects. First, the therapist guides the imagining of the patient actively in order to prevent covert avoidance and neutralizing. Second, the sessions are prolonged to facilitate habituation occurrence. Third, the most troublesome obsessions are used from the start rather than the scenes being presented in ascending order. It is important to note that no breaks occur during the 60-minute sessions apart from a few seconds after each scene presentation when patients have to rate their level of anxiety.

To establish whether the process of treatment by prolonged exposure in imagination could be interpreted in terms of habituation, we had our patients rate the level of subjective anxiety throughout treatment sessions. As predicted by a habituation model, continuous presentation of obsessional stimuli led to a decrement in response to these stimuli during treatment sessions. After a predicted increase in level of subjective anxiety at the beginning of each session, the ratings show a consistent reduction within sessions (Emmelkamp, 1982a).

Emmelkamp and Kwee (1977) compared the efficacy of prolonged exposure in imagination with that of thought stopping. The subjects were five patients whose major problem was obsessional ruminations but who did not suffer from compulsive rituals. A crossover design was used so that all patients received both treatments. Patients who responded favorably to the treatment usually derived equal benefit from both procedures, suggesting that a common mechanism in both treatments was responsible for the improvement.

The aim of our second study (Emmelkamp & Giesselbach, 1981) was twofold: first, to replicate the therapeutic value of prolonged exposure in imagination with another series of obsessional patients, and, second, to investigate whether the effects of prolonged exposure in imagination are due to habituation to the obsessions or, alternatively, can be accounted for by habituation to fear in general. Once more a crossover design was implemented with six patients with obsessional ruminations unaccompanied by compulsive rituals. With prolonged exposure to irrelevant cues, patients were uninterruptedly exposed to scenes made up of situations that anyone would fear. For each patient, the therapist selected situations that were particularly anxiety-arousing and were unrelated to the patients' obsessions. These scenes involved situations such as being burned to death, being strangled, being devoured by a tiger, dying in an air crash, and the like. Patients had to rate their anxiety after each scene presentation. If a scene ceased to arouse anxiety, the scene was no longer used. The results of this study indicate that relevant exposure resulted in more improvement than irrelevant exposure. Actually, irrelevant exposure even led to a significant deterioration on the distress rating. Taken together, these data indicate that prolonged exposure to the obsessions is a valuable treatment for obsessional ruminations and corroborate the findings of Emmelkamp and Kwee (1977).

In sum, habituation training by means of prolonged exposure in imagination holds promise for the treatment of obsessional ruminations. The therapeutic mechanism by which this procedure achieves its results seems to be exposure to obsessional material instead of exposure to irrelevant fear cues. It should be noted that exposure to obsessional stimuli is a common component of such various treatment procedures for obsessions as thought stopping, aversion therapy, and aversion relief. It is proposed that the effects achieved by these procedures are due to habituation to the obsessional material. It seems worthwhile to investigate further the optimal conditions for such an exposure with obsessional patients.

Alternative Approaches

One important category of obsessions comprises obsessions of harming oneself or others. For example, patients may suffer from obsessions that they might kill or have killed someone or that they might commit suicide. Since we found such patients quite unassertive, we hypothesized that these patients could not handle their aggressive feelings adequately. It was proposed that the harming obsessions were generated by unexpressed aggressive feelings and by the associated feelings of guilt. We wondered whether assertiveness training would lead to a more adequate handling of aggression and hence to a reduction of the harming obsessions.

To test this notion, assertiveness training and thought stopping were compared in a crossover study (Emmelkamp & Van der Heyden, 1980). Subjects were six patients whose major problems were obsessional ruminations concerning harming others or harming themselves.

The results of this study found assertiveness training to be at least as effective as thought stopping. In four of the six cases a considerable decrease in the frequency of obsessions was found after assertiveness training. The results for thought stopping were less positive: in two patients a decrease was found, but with other patients thought stopping even led to an increase in the number of obsessions.

Although no firm conclusions can be drawn on the basis of the results of our studies with pure obsession, because of the small number of subjects involved, it does seem that prolonged exposure in imagination has beneficial effects, whereas the results of thought stopping are more variable. Further, assertiveness training was found to be quite effective in the treatment of harming obsessions. Whether other obsessional patients may also benefit from assertiveness training is a question for further study.

It should be noted that with most obsessional patients treatment (including exposure *in vivo*, marital therapy, and assertiveness training) was continued after the experimental trial was finished. With several patients, prolonged exposure *in vivo* to provoking stimuli was successfully applied. Whether this procedure on its own would have led to a decrease in the frequency of obsessions is unknown and deserves further study. However, this procedure is applicable to a limited category of obsessional patients only—that is, to those patients whose obsessions are triggered by external stimuli.

Concluding Remarks and Future Directions

Research on the behavioral treatment of obsessive–compulsive disorder is falling into place. The effects of exposure *in vivo* and response prevention are now well established for the treatment of compulsive ritualizers. Although recent developments in the treatment of obsessions are promising, there is a great deal to be accomplished by clinical researchers in devising efficient and effective treatment for ruminators. Taking into account the present status of research in this area, there is little reason to recommend one particular approach for the treatment of obsessional ruminations over another. To quote Rachman (1983): "The main obstacle to the successful treatment of obsessions is the absence of robust proven techniques" (p. 53). Rather than treating obsessionals with canned procedures, it would be preferable to carry out a detailed analysis of each case referred for treatment and to devise treatments tailored to patients' individual needs.

One promising area consists of the cognitive approach to the understanding and treatment of obsessional thinking. A cognitive explanation of obsessional–compulsive problems is proposed by Beck (1976) and Salkovskis (1985). In Salkovskis's view, intrusive thoughts are best regarded as cognitive stimuli rather than responses. Beliefs concerning responsibility or blame for harm to self or others are supposed to mediate cognitive responses (negative automatic thoughts) to these cognitive stimuli. Following this model, cognitive therapy of obsessions should focus on the beliefs that mediate the cognitive responses rather than on modifying the intrusive thoughts. This model has yet to be tested, to examine whether such a cognitive approach will make a contribution to the treatment of obsessional patients.

It should be emphasized that it is erroneous to assume that all cognitive therapies are identical. This is underscored in the area of obsessive–compulsives, where self-instructional training did not fare well, whereas rational therapy did seem to produce clinically significant results. This preliminary work appears to suggest that specific irrational beliefs associated with obsessive–compulsive behavior may present a promising area for future studies.

Another area in need of research is the assessment of the cognitive processes of obsessional patients. Currently only very crude measures are available—for example, the Irrational Beliefs Test (Jones, 1968). However, it is questionable whether such a questionnaire is the most appropriate measure to assess the cognitive processes of obsessive–compulsive patients. Themes that are characteristic of the thought content of obsessional patients are absent or underrepresented in this questionnaire. Such themes include the beliefs associated with primary and secondary appraisal processes, as previously discussed. For clinical purposes, other assessment procedures, such as thought listing, may be more useful than questionnaires. One could ask patients at various points each day to list the thoughts that have just run through their mind. In any case, more adequate assessment of the cognitions of obsessive–compulsive patients is essential for a better understanding of these disorders and to permit evaluations of the specific effects of treatments on the thought disorders of these patients.

References

Akhtar, S., Wig, N. H., Verma, V. K., Pershod, D., & Verma, S. K. (1975). A phenomenological analysis of symptoms in obsessive–compulsive neuroses. *British Journal of Psychiatry, 127*, 342–348.

Arrindell, W. A., Emmelkamp, P. M. G., Brilman, E., & Monsma, A. (1983). Psychometric evaluation of an inventory for assessment of parental rearing practices. *Acta Psychiatrica Scandinavia 67*, 163–177.

Bass, B. A. (1973). An unusual behavioral technique for treating obsessive ruminations. *Psychotherapy: Theory, Research and Practice, 10*, 191–193.

Beck, A. T. (1976). *Cognitive therapy and the emotional disorders*. New York: International University Press.

Beech, H. R., & Lidell, A. (1974). Decision-making, mood states and ritualistic behaviour among obsessional patients. In H. R. Beech (Ed.), *Obsessional states*. London: Methuen.

Beech, H. R., & Perigault, J. (1974). Toward a theory of obsessional disorder. In H. R. Beech (Ed.), *Obsessional states*. London: Methuen.

Beech, H. R., & Vaughan, M. (1978). *Behavioural treatment of obsessional states*. New York: Wiley.

Boersma, K., Den Hengst, S., Dekker, J., & Emmelkamp, P. M. G. (1976). Exposure and response prevention in the natural environment: A comparison with obsessive–compulsive patients. *Behaviour Research and Therapy, 14*, 19–24.

Boulougouris, J. C., & Bassiakos, L. (1974). Prolonged flooding in cases with obsessive–compulsive neurosis. *Behaviour Research and Therapy, 11*, 227–231.

Carr, A. T. (1974). Compulsive neurosis: A review of the literature. *Psychological Bulletin, 81*, 311–318.

Cooper, J. E., Gelder, M. G., & Marks, I. M. (1965). Results of behaviour therapy in 77 psychiatric patients. *British Medical Journal, 1*, 1222–1225.

Cooper, J. E., & Kelleher, M. Y. (1973). The Leyton Obsessional Inventory: A principal component analysis on normal subjects. *Psychological Medicine, 3*, 204–208.

Dowson, J. H. (1977). The phenomenology of severe obsessive–compulsive neurosis. *British Journal of Psychiatry, 131*, 75–78.

Ellis, A. (1962). *Reason and emotion in psychotherapy*. New York: Lyle-Stuart.

Emmelkamp, P. M. G. (1974). Self-observation versus flooding in the treatment of agoraphobia. *Behaviour Research and Therapy, 12*, 229–237.

Emmelkamp, P. M. G. (1982a). *Phobic and obsessive–compulsive disorders: Theory, research and practice*. New York: Plenum.

Emmelkamp, P. M. G. (1982b). Recent developments in the behavioral treatment of obsessive–compulsive disorders. In J. Boulougouris (Ed.), *Learning theories approaches in psychiatry*. New York: Wiley.

Emmelkamp, P. M. G. (1985). Compulsive Rituals. In C. Last & M. Hersen (Eds.), *Behaviour therapy case book*. Springer.

Emmelkamp, P. M. G., Brilman, E., Kuiper, H., & Mersch, P. P. (1986). The treatment of agoraphobia: A comparison of self-instructional training, rational emotive therapy and exposure *in vivo*. *Behaviour Modification, 10*, 37–53.

Emmelkamp, P. M. G., & De Lange, I. (1983). Spouse involvement in the treatment of obsessive–compulsive patients. *Behaviour Research and Therapy, 21*, 341–346.

Emmelkamp, P. M. G., & Giesselbach, P. (1981). Treatment of obsessions: Relevant vs. irrelevant exposure. *Behavioural Psychotherapy, 9*, 322–329.

Emmelkamp, P. M. G., Hoekstra, R. J., & Visser, S. (1985). The behavioural treatment of obsessive–compulsive disorder: prediction of outcome at 3.5 years follow-up. In A. Brenner (Ed.), *Psychiatry: The state of the art* (Vol. 4). New York: Plenum.

Emmelkamp, P. M. G., & Kraanen, J. (1977). Therapist controlled exposure *in vivo* versus self-controlled exposure *in vivo*: A comparison with obsessive–compulsive patients. *Behaviour Research and Therapy, 15*, 491–495.

Emmelkamp, P. M. G., Kuipers, A., & Eggeraat, J. (1978). Cognitive modification versus prolonged exposure *in vivo*: A comparison with agoraphobics. *Behaviour Research and Therapy, 16*, 33–41.

Emmelkamp, P. M. G., & Kwee, K. G. (1977). Obsessional ruminations: A comparison between thought-stopping and prolonged exposure in imagination. *Behaviour Research and Therapy, 15*, 441–444.

Emmelkamp, P. M. G., & Mersch, P. P. (1982). Cognition and exposure *in vivo* in the treatment of agoraphobia: Short-term and delayed effects. *Cognitive Research and Therapy, 6*, 77–90.

Emmelkamp, P. M. G., & Rabbie, D. (1981). Psychological treatment of obsessive–compulsive disorders: A follow-up 4 years after treatment. In B. Jansson, C. Perris, & G. Struwe (Eds.), *Biological psychiatry.* Amsterdam: Elsevier.

Emmelkamp, P. M. G., Ruephan, M., Sanderman, R., & Van den Heuvell, C. (1987). Massed vs. spaced exposure in the treatment of obsessive–compulsives.

Emmelkamp, P. M. G., Van de Helm, M., Van Zanten, B., & Plochg, I. (1980). Contributions of self-instructional training to the effectiveness of exposure *in vivo:* A comparison with obsessive–compulsive patients. *Behaviour Research and Therapy, 18,* 61–66.

Emmelkamp, P. M. G., & Van der Heyden, H. (1980). The treatment of harming obsessions. *Behavioural Analysis and Modification, 4,* 28–35.

Emmelkamp, P. M. G., Visser, S., & Hoekstra, R. (1987). Cognitive therapy vs. exposure treatment in the treatment of obsessive–compulsives.

Emmelkamp, P. M. G., & Wessels, H. (1975). Flooding in imagination vs. flooding *in vivo:* A comparison with agoraphobics. *Behaviour Research and Therapy, 13,* 7–16.

Fine, S. (1973). Family therapy and a behavioral approach to childhood obsessive–compulsive neurosis. *Archives of General Psychiatry, 28,* 695–697.

Foa, E. B., & Goldstein, A. (1979). Continuous exposure and complete response prevention in the treatment of obsessive–compulsive neurosis. *Behavior Therapy, 9,* 821–829.

Foa, E. B., Grayson, J. B., Steketee, G., Doppelt, H. G., Turner, R. M., & Latimer, P. R. (1983). Success and failure in the behavioral treatment of obsessive–compulsives. *Journal of Consulting and Clinical Psychology, 51,* 287–297.

Foa, E. B., Jameson, J. S., Turner, R. M., & Payne, L. L. (1980). Massed vs. spaced exposure sessions in the treatment of agoraphobia. *Behaviour Research and Therapy, 18,* 333–338.

Foa, E. B., Steketee, G., & Grayson, J. B. (1985). Imaginal and *in vivo* exposure: A comparison with obsessive–compulsive checkers. *Behavior Therapy, 16,* 292–302.

Foa, E. B., Steketee, G., Grayson, J. B., Turner, R. M., & Latimer, P. R. (1984). Deliberate exposure and blocking of obsessive–compulsive rituals: Immediate and long-term effects. *Behavior Therapy, 15,* 450–472.

Foa, E. B., Steketee, G., & Milby, J. B. (1980). Differential effects of exposure and response prevention in obsessive–compulsive washers. *Journal of Consulting and Clinical Psychology, 48,* 71–79.

Foa, E. B., Steketee, G., Turner, R. M., & Fischer, S. C. (1980). Effects of imaginal exposure to feared disasters in obsessive–compulsive checkers. *Behaviour Research and Therapy, 18,* 449–455.

Furst, J. B., & Cooper, A. (1970). Failure of systematic desensitization in two cases of obsessive–compulsive neurosis marked by fears of insecticide. *Behaviour Research and Therapy, 8,* 203–206.

Gentry, W. D. (1970). *In vivo* desensitization of an obsessive cancer fear. *Journal of Behavior Therapy and Experimental Psychiatry, 1,* 315–318.

Gray, J. A. (1975). *Elements of a two-process theory of learning.* New York: Academic Press.

Grayson, J. B., Foa, E. B., & Steketee, G. (1982). Habituation during exposure treatment: Distraction versus attention-focusing. *Behaviour Research and Therapy, 20,* 323–328.

Hackmann, A., & McLean, C. A. (1975). A comparison of flooding and thought stopping in the treatment of obsessional neurosis. *Behaviour Research and Therapy, 13,* 263–269.

Herrnstein, R. J. (1969). Method and theory in the study of avoidance. *Psychological Review, 76,* 49–69.

Hersen, M. (1968). Treatment of a compulsive and phobic disorder through a total behavior therapy program: A case study. *Psychotherapy: Theory, Research and Practice, 5,* 220–225.

Heyse, H. (1973). Verhaltentherapie bei Zwangneurotiker: Vorläufige Ergebnisse. In J. Brengelman & W. Turner (Eds.), *Verhaltenstherapie.* Berlin: Urban und Scharzenberg.

Hodgson, R. J., & Rachman, S. (1972). The effects of contamination and washing in obsessional patients. *Behaviour Research and Therapy, 10,* 111–117.

Hodgson, R. J., & Rachman, S. (1977). Obsessional–compulsive complaints. *Behaviour Research and Therapy, 15,* 389–395.

Hodgson, R., Rachman, S., & Marks, I. (1972). The treatment of chronic–obsessive–compulsive neurosis: Follow-up and further findings. *Behaviour Research and Therapy, 10,* 181–184.

Hoogduin, W. (1985). *Dwangneurose.* Rotterdam: Academisch Proefschrift.

Jones. R. (1968). *A factored measure of Ellis' irrational beliefs systems with personality and maladjustment correlated.* Unpublished doctoral dissertation, Texas Technological College.

Kenny, F. T., Mowbray, R. M., & Lalani, S. (1978). Faradic disruption of obsessive ideation in the treatment of obsessive neurosis: A controlled study. *Behavior Therapy, 9*, 209–211.

Kenny, F. T., Solyom, C., & Solyom, L. (1973). Faradic disruption of obsessive ideation in the treatment of obsessive neurosis. *Behavior Therapy, 4*, 448–457.

Kushner, M., & Sandler, J. (1966). Aversion therapy and the concept of punishment. *Behaviour Research and Therapy, 4*, 179–186.

Le Boeuf, A. (1974). An automated aversion device in the treatment of a compulsive hand-washing ritual. *Journal of Behavior Therapy and Experimental Psychiatry, 5*, 267–270.

Leger, L. A. (1978). Spurious and actual improvement in the treatment of preoccupying thoughts by thought-stopping. *British Journal of Social and Clinical Psychology, 17*, 373–377.

Leger, L. A. (1979). An outcome measure for thought-stopping examined in three case studies. *Journal of Behavior Therapy and Experimental Psychiatry, 10*, 115–120.

Lombardo, T. W., & Turner, S. M. (1979). Thought-stopping in the control of obsessive ruminations. *Behavior Modification, 3*, 267–272.

Mahoney, M. J. (1971). The self-management of covert behavior: A case-study. *Behavior Therapy, 2*, 575–578.

Marks, I. M., Hodgson, R., & Rachman, S. (1975). Treatment of chronic–obsessive compulsive neurosis by *in vivo* exposure. *British Journal of Psychiatry, 127*, 349–364.

Marks, I. M., Stern, R. S., Mawson, D., Cobb, J., & McDonald, R. (1980). Clomipramine and exposure for obsessive–compulsive rituals: I. *British Journal of Psychiatry, 136*, 1–25.

Mawson, D., Marks, I. M., & Ramm, L. (1982). Clomipramine and exposure for chronic obsessive–compulsive rituals: Two year follow-up and further findings. *British Journal of Psychiatry, 140*, 11–18.

McFall, M. E., & Wollersheim, J. P. (1979). Obsessive–compulsive neurosis: A cognitive-behavioral formulation and approach to treatment. *Cognitive Therapy and Research, 3*, 333–348.

McGlynn, F. D., & Linder, L. A. (1971). The clinical application of analogue desensitization. *Behavior Therapy, 2*, 385–388.

Meyer, V. (1966). Modification of expectations in cases with obsessional rituals. *Behaviour Research and Therapy, 4*, 273–280.

Meyer, V., & Levy, R. (1970). Behavioural treatment of a homosexual with compulsive rituals. *British Journal of Medical Psychology, 43*, 63–67.

Meyer, V., Levy, R., & Schnurer, A. (1974). The behavioural treatment of obsessive–compulsive disorder. In H. R. Beech (Ed.), *Obsessional states*. London: Methuen.

Mills, H. L., Agras, W. S., Barlow, D. H., & Mills, J. R. (1973). Compulsive rituals treated by response prevention. *Archives of General Psychiatry, 28*, 524–530.

Myers, K., Weissman, M., Tischler, L., Holzer, E., Leaf, J., Orvaschel, H., Anthony, C., Boyd, H., Burke, D., Kramer, M., & Stoltzman, R. (1984). Six-month prevalence of psychiatric disorders in three communities: 1980–1982. *Archives of General Psychiatry, 41*, 959–967.

Oberhummer, I., Sachs, G., & Stellamoor, M. (1983). Ein Vergleich psychophysiologischer Reaktionsmuster bei hypochondrischen Patienten und solchen mit Zwangssyndromen. *Zeitschrift für Klinische Psychologie, 12*, 113–125.

Parkinson, L., & Rachman, S. (1980). Are intrusive thoughts subject to habituation? *Behaviour Research and Therapy, 18*, 409–418.

Person, J. P., & Foa, E. B. (1984). Processing of fearful and neutral information by obsessive–compulsives. *Behaviour Research and Therapy, 22*, 259–267.

Petrie, J. F., & Haans, H. H. M. (1960). Enkele recente ervaringen met "behaviour therapy." *Nederlands Tijdschrift voor de Psychologie, 24*, 391–404.

Queiroz, L. O., Motta, M. A., Madi, M., Sossai, D., & Boren, J. (1981). A functional analysis of obsessive–compulsive problems with related therapeutic procedures. *Behaviour Research and Therapy, 19*, 377–388.

Rabavilas, A. D., Boulougouris, J. C., Stefanis, C., & Vaidakis, N. (1977). Psychophysiological accompaniments of threat anticipation in obsessive–compulsive patients. In C. D. Spielberger & I. G. Sarason (Eds.), *Stress and anxiety* (Vol. 4). New York: Wiley.

Rachman, S. (1976). The modification of obsessions: A new formulation. *Behaviour Research and Therapy, 14*, 437–443.

Rachman, S. (1983). Obstacles to the successful treatment of obsessions. In E. B. Foa & P. M. G. Emmelkamp (Eds.), *Failures in behavior therapy*. New York: Wiley.

Rachman, S., Cobb, J., Grey, S., McDonald, B., Mawson, D., Sartory, G., & Stern, R. (1979). The behavioural treatment of obsessional–compulsive disorders with and without clomipramine. *Behaviour Research and Therapy, 17*, 467–478.

Rachman, S., & Hodgson, R. J. (1980). *Obsessions and compulsions*. Englewood Cliffs, NJ: Prentice-Hall.

Rachman, S., Hodgson, R., & Marzillier, J. (1970). Treatment of an obsessional–compulsive disorder by modelling. *Behaviour Research and Therapy, 8*, 385–392.

Rachman, S., Marks, I., & Hodgson, R. (1973). The treatment of obsessive–compulsive neurotics by modelling and flooding *in vivo*. *Behaviour Research and Therapy, 11*, 463–471.

Rackenspreger, W., & Feinberg, A. M. (1972). Treatment of a severe handwashing compulsion by systematic desensitization: A case report. *Journal of Behaviour Therapy and Experimental Psychiatry, 3*, 123–127.

Rainey, C. A. (1972). An obsessive–compulsive neurosis treated by flooding *in vivo*. *Journal of Behavior Therapy and Experimental Psychiatry, 3*, 117–121.

Ramsay, R. W., & Sikkel, R. J. (1973). Behavior therapy and obsessive–compulsive neurosis. In J. Brengelman & W. Turner (Eds.), *Verhaltenstherapie*. Berlin: Urban und Schwarzenberg.

Reed, G. (1977). Obsessional cognition: Performance on two numerical tasks. *British Journal of Psychiatry, 130*, 184–185.

Robins, L. N., Helzer, J. E., Weissman, M. M., Orvaschel, H., Gruenberg, E., Burke, J. D., & Regier, D. A. (1984). Life-time prevalence of specific psychiatric disorders in three sites. *Archives of General Psychiatry, 41*, 949–958.

Röper, G., & Rachman, S. (1976). Obsessional compulsive checking: Experimental replication and development. *Behaviour Research and Therapy, 14*, 25–32.

Röper, G., Rachman, S., & Hodgson, R. (1973). An experiment on obsessional checking. *Behaviour Research and Therapy, 11*, 271–277.

Röper, G., Rachman, S., & Marks, I. M. (1975). Passive and participant modelling in exposure treatment of obsessive–compulsive neurotics. *Behavior Research and Therapy, 13*, 271–279.

Roy, A. (1979). Obsessive–compulsive neurosis: Phenomenology, outcome and a comparison with hysterical neurosis. *Comprehensive Psychiatry, 20*, 528–531.

Rüdin, E. (1953). Ein Beitrag zur Frage der Zwangskrankheit, insobesondere ihre hereditären Beziehungen. *Archiv für Psychiatrie und Nervenkrankheiten, 191*, 14–54.

Salkovskis, P. M. (1985). Obsessional–compulsive problems: A cognitive-behavioural analysis. *Behaviour Research and Therapy, 23*, 571–583.

Samaan, J. (1975). Thought-stopping and flooding in a case of hallucinations, obsessions and homicidal-suicidal behavior. *Journal of Behavior Therapy and Experimental Psychiatry, 6*, 57–65.

Saper, B. (1971). Behavior therapy with clinic patients. *Psychiatric Quarterly, 45*, 204–215.

Solyom, L., & Kingstone, F. (1973). An obsessive neurosis following morning glory seed ingestion treated by aversion relief. *Journal of Behaviour Therapy and Experimental Psychiatry, 4*, 293–295.

Solyom, L., Zamanzadeh, D., Ledwidge, B., & Kenny, F. (1971). Aversive relief treatment of obsessive neurosis. In R. D. Rubin (Ed.), *Advances in behavior therapy*. New York: Academic Press.

Stampfl, T. G., & Levis, D. J. (1967). Essentials of implosive therapy: A learning-theory-based psychodynamic behavioral therapy. *Journal of Abnormal Psychology, 72*, 496–503.

Stern, R. (1970). Treatment of a case of obsessional neurosis using thought-stopping technique. *British Journal of Psychiatry, 117*, 441–442.

Stern, R., & Marks, I. M. (1973). Brief and prolonged flooding: A comparison in agoraphobic patients. *Archives of General Psychiatry, 28*, 270–276.

Stern, R. S. (1978). Obsessive thoughts: The problem of therapy. *British Journal of Psychiatry, 132*, 200–205.

Stern, R. S., & Cobb, J. P. (1978). Phenomenology of obsessive–compulsive neurosis. *British Journal of Psychiatry, 132*, 233–239.

Stern, R. S., Lipsedge, M. S., & Marks, I. M. (1973). Obsessive ruminations: A controlled trial of thought-stopping technique. *Behaviour Research and Therapy, 11*, 659–662.

Tanner, B. A. (1971). A case report on the use of relaxations and systematic desensitization to control multiple compulsive behavior. *Journal of Behavior Therapy and Experimental Psychiatry, 2*, 267–272.

Teasdale, J. D. (1974). Learning models of obsessional–compulsive disorder. In H. R. Beech (Ed.), *Obsessional states*. London: Methuen.

Teasdale, J. D., & Rezin, V. (1978). Effect of thought-stopping on thoughts, mood and corrugator EMG in depressed patients. *Behaviour Research and Therapy, 16*, 97–102.

Turner, S. M., Hersen, M., Bellack, A. S., Andrasik, F., & Capparrell, H. V. (1980). Behavioral and pharmacological treatment of obsessive–compulsive disorders. *Journal of Nervous and Mental Disease, 168*, 651–657.

Turner, S. M., Hersen, M., Bellack, A. S., & Wells, K. C. (1979). Behavioral treatment of obsessive–compulsive neurosis. *Behaviour Research and Therapy, 17*, 79–81.

Van der Hout, M., Emmelkamp, P. M. G., & Kraaykamp, H. (in preparation). Treatment of obsessive compulsives: Hospital based treatment vs. home treatment.

Walton, D. (1960). The relevance of learning theory to the treatment of an obsessive–compulsive state. In H. J. Eysenck (Ed.), *Behaviour therapy and the neurosis*. Oxford: Pergamon Press.

Walton, D., & Mather, M. D. (1963). The application of learning principles to the treatment of obsessive–compulsive states in acute and chronic phases of the illness. *Behaviour Research and Therapy, 1*, 163–174.

Welner, A., Reich, T., Robins, E., Fishman, R., & Van Doren, T. (1976). Obsessive–compulsive neurosis: Record, follow-up, and family studies. I. Inpatient record study. *Comprehensive Psychiatry, 17*, 527–539.

Wisocki, P. A. (1970). Treatment of obsessive–compulsive behaviour by covert sensitization and covert reinforcement: A case report. *Journal of Behavior Therapy and Experimental Psychiatry, 1*, 233–239.

Wolpe, J. (1958). *Psychotherapy and reciprocal inhibition*. Stanford, CA: Stanford University Press.

Wolpe, J. (1964). Behaviour therapy in complex neurotic states. *British Journal of Psychiatry, 110*, 28–34.

Woodruff, R., & Pitts, F. N. (1964). Monozygotic twins with obsessional neurosis. *American Journal of Psychiatry, 120*, 1075–1180.

Worsley, J. L. (1970). The causation and treatment of obsessionality. In L. E. Burns & J. L. Worsley (Eds.), *Behavior therapy in the 1970's*. Bristol, England: John Wright.

Yamagami, T. (1971). Treatment of an obsession by thought-stopping. *Journal of Behavior Therapy and Experimental Psychiatry, 2*, 133–135.

Zaworka, W., & Hand, I. (1980). Phänomenologie (Dimensionalität) der Zwangssymptomatik. *Archiv für Psychiatrie und Nervenkrankheiten, 228*, 257–273.

12

Generalized Anxiety Syndrome

JERRY L. DEFFENBACHER AND RICHARD M. SUINN

The Clinical Nature of the Generalized Anxiety Disorder

Individuals with a generalized anxiety disorder (GAD) experience a chronic, persistent anxiety. The anxiety tends to be moderate in intensity, although it may spike upward at times, and is usually pervasive across time and situations. Because it does not appear to be related to specific situations or external stressors, it has sometimes been labeled "general" or "free-floating." Individuals with GAD experience a kind of chronic cloud of arousal, doom, and apprehension that seems to follow them everywhere, ebbing somewhat from time to time, but never leaving for very long.

Although these descriptions convey a general flavor of what the person experiences, the *Diagnostic and Statistical Manual of Mental Disorders* (DSM-III) (American Psychiatric Association, 1980) criteria for GAD are: (1) significant clinical involvement in at least three of four areas—motor tension, autonomic hyperactivity, apprehensive expectations, and hypervigilance and scanning; (2) presence of anxiety for at least one month; and (3) anxiety that is not a part of another disorder or a reaction to recent life stress.

These characteristics set the GAD off from other anxiety disorders. It differs from adjustment disorders with anxious mood, posttraumatic stress disorders, and phobias in that there is no clear stimulus that elicits anxiety or was associated with its onset. GAD also lacks the clear avoidance and escape behaviors of the phobias. Whereas cognitive, ruminative processes are shared with obsessive–compulsive disorders, thematically organized obsessions or obvious, rigid cognitive and behavioral escape/avoidance behaviors (compulsions) are not present. GAD shares the apparent lack of clear elicitors with panic disorders, but differs in response topography. Panic attacks involve very intense responses for relatively short periods of time, whereas GAD involves chronic, moderate anxiety over time.

Although there are some issues of diagnostic reliability (DiNardo, O'Brien, Barlow, Waddell, & Blanchard, 1983), the GAD characteristics outlined in DSM-III appear to describe a meaningful clinical phenomenon. These DSM-III symptoms can be further elaborated on through reference to three basic response channels from which anxiety disorders are inferred (Deffenbacher & Suinn, 1982; Lang, 1971; Suinn, 1984a): affective–physiological, somatic–behavioral, and cognitive. The patterning across channels will be outlined briefly, along with relevant research on the GAD and high general anxiety. This

Jerry L. Deffenbacher and Richard M. Suinn. Department of Psychology, Colorado State University, Fort Collins, Colorado.

will be done to clarify assessment parameters, provide a working model of the GAD, and link this model and GAD characteristics to cognitive-behavioral interventions.

Affective–Physiological Involvement

Clients with a GAD report significant subjective feelings of anxiety and tension, describing themselves as tense, nervous, and constantly on edge. They experience a chronic sense of apprehension and dread, as if something bad were about to happen, but not of a feeling of panic were it to actually happen. These feelings may be related to certain events but more often are described as not coming clearly from any specific source.

Clients also report heightened autonomic arousal, such as heart pounding, sweating, and a sinking sensation in the stomach. Patterns of autonomic arousal tend to vary uniquely from person to person but are relatively consistent within the individual over time. Within the individual, autonomic arousal waxes and wanes over relatively short periods of time (e.g., up to several hours or even a day or so) but tends to recycle frequently. The arousal may not reach a high intensity but seems to be reelicited repetitively. Additionally, one of the stimuli for recurrent arousal appears to be the proprioceptive cues of arousal itself (Beck, 1972; Evans, 1972). Many experience a kind of fear of fear and react to arousal as a sign of further problems, which triggers a fear of loss of control (Heide & Borkovec, 1984) and more arousal. That is, increased arousal may elicit even greater arousal in a vicious circle until interrupted by some distracting cognitive, behavioral, or environmental event. Heightened arousal may be both a response and a stimulus in the cycles of anxiety experienced in the GAD.

The cycles of arousal may lead to a third aspect of affective–physiological involvement, the presence of anxiety-related psychophysiological disorders. Prolonged, repetitive, unrelieved cycles of anxiety may trigger psychophysiological disorders in vulnerable individuals that appear as tension and migraine headaches, insomnia, fatigue, asthma, ulcerative colitis, and the like (Rimm & Sommervill, 1977). In some cases these disorders may be the presenting problem, and the individual may be relatively unaware of the general anxiety and periods of autonomic arousal that precede them. It may take careful interviewing and self-monitoring to reveal that the individual has both a GAD and a psychophysiological disorder and that the psychophysiological disorder stems from the chronic, unrelieved anxiety of the GAD. Thus the presence of a psychophysiological disorder should prompt the consideration of GAD.

Somatic–Behavioral Involvement

The GAD shows an interesting pattern of somatic–behavioral involvement. On the one hand, motor tension (e.g., shakiness, restlessness, general muscle tension, areas of specific tension such as the neck), and its correlates (e.g., fatigability and inability to relax) are central defining characteristics. They represent effects of heightened arousal on the voluntary musculature and in many ways parallel heightened autonomic arousal. On the other hand, further behavioral involvement tends to be minimal. Individuals with GAD do not show the escape/avoidance behaviors of phobics or the behavioral constriction and stereotypy of compulsive behaviors (Suinn, 1977a). Neither is there the marked behavioral disruption and performance deterioration seen in panic disorders and some phobias. Certainly, individuals with GAD show some avoidance and escape behavior, some ritualistic behavior, and behavioral disruption, but these elements tend to be relatively limited. The major somatic–behavioral involvement appears to be a function of heightened arousal—that is, somatic tension. The autonomic–affective and somatic channels show high arousal, but little of this arousal appears dissipated through constructive coping or even defensive motoric action.

Cognitive Involvement

The cognitive domain shows marked involvement. Considerable portions of attention are devoted to a stream of ruminative, negative self-dialogue and images (Beck, 1972; Beck, Laude, & Bohnert, 1974; Borkovec, 1984; Borkovec, Robinson, Pruzinsky, & DePree, 1983). These cognitive chains seem to tumble along, sometimes eliciting more worry and emotional–physiological arousal and at other times momentarily decreasing worry and arousal. But even when the cognitive chains are interrupted through effective problem solving, successful cognitive avoidance, or environmental distraction, similar cognitive chains start up again some minutes or hours later. These cognitive activities can significantly influence and interfere with cognitive functioning, as shown by distractibility; inability to focus attention and maintain concentration in a sustained way; and interference with memory encoding and decoding, problem solving, and the like (Deffenbacher & Suinn, 1982).

These cognitive processes have several content parameters as well. First, the cognitive content tends to be catastrophic, overgeneralized, and absolutistic in nature (Beck, 1976; Beck et al., 1974; Matthews & Shaw, 1977; Zwemer & Deffenbacher, 1984). Dangers are seen as highly probable, although in reality they are remote and unlikely. Consequences of many events are perceived as terrible and devastating, when they are only somewhat negative. Consequences often imply general negative conditions for the person and/or for long periods of time, when in fact they are time- and situation-limited. Personal standards may be extreme, as the individual demands that events be always under complete, perfect control. Second, the cognitive stream tends to be future-oriented. Individuals with GAD report worrying more about what might happen, events that are hard to predict and control, than about what has happened. Third, although there are a wide variety of individually specific sources of harm to be avoided (Beck et al., 1974), cognitive content appears disproportionately social-evaluative in nature (Borkovec, 1984). That is, these clients are highly sensitive to issues of personal failure, personal perfection, criticism, rejection, embarrassment, and loss of control (Borkovec, 1984; Borkovec et al., 1983; Zwemer & Deffenbacher, 1984). Although fears of personal physical harm appear with some frequency (Beck et al., 1974; Matthews & Shaw, 1977), for many, social–evaluative disasters constitute the major source of preoccupation.

Toward a Tentative Understanding of the GAD

The development and maintenance of the GAD appears to involve several factors. At some point, the combination of stressor characteristics, person variables, and environmental resources leads to the development of a learned anxiety response (Suinn, 1984b; in press, a). Stressor variables such as unpredictable, irreversible, high-intensity events may create a sense of uncontrollability. Dysfunctional ways of appraising the environment and one's coping skills or lack thereof increase susceptibility and reactivity. Additional environmental barriers and lack of social support systems can channel attempts to cope in directions that involve further failure and struggle to try new ways to adjust. With continued failure, the maladaptive anxiety becomes more ingrained and stable.

Learning History

Two different, general histories or processes may be involved in the development of the GAD (Suinn, in press, a). Either or both might be involved for a given client.

One is the development of direct emotional conditioning, where minimal cognitive processing occurs. For example, recent theory and research on information processing have demonstrated that some emotional experiences can be stored without awareness (Hamilton, 1982; Merluzzi, Rudy, & Glass, 1981). Others (e.g., Rachman, 1981; Zajonc, 1980) have also described emotional conditioning independent of the person's awareness of the conditions of learning. Through this history, the individual acquires a vulnerability to emotional–physiological arousal but is unaware of the conditions of its acquisition or prompting (a nonmediated sensitivity to emotional–physiological arousal). Presentation of the initial cues, a subset of them, or similar cues would be expected to elicit all or part of the anxiety response, but the individual would be unaware of the source of the anxiety arousal.

The second history appears to involve more cognitive mediation. Through direct and vicarious conditioning experiences, individuals acquire a certain kind of fear or fear complex. The literature reviewed previously suggests that fears of negative social evaluation, potential physical harm, and loss of control are particularly salient. That is, individuals become particularly sensitive to and fearful of such situations. Their cognitive appraisal of the danger involved in such situations and/or of their coping capacities become distorted. They tend to appraise the danger involved in these situations as much more probable and devastating than it is and/or to evaluate their own coping capacities as much less than they really are. Presentation of external or internal cues relevant to the fear complex would elicit the faulty appraisals and, in turn, the relevant anxiety response components.

Apparent Lack of Cueing

Direct emotional conditioning experiences could account for the apparent lack of environmental prompting. Individuals with such a history are unaware of the stimuli prompting anxiety. Presentation of environmental cues similar to those involved in the initial conditioning would elicit anxiety, but the victims would have no awareness of its source. They would be genuinely mystified about its cause and might spend considerable time ruminating about its source and how to prevent it. They might feel out of control and worry that they were going crazy, which would only increase anxiety. A pervasive sense of worry and dread might develop. Without an appropriate explanation, they might make a variety of misattributions that could further spread anxiety to other situations or personal characteristics.

A second explanation involves a partial extinction process. In the conditioning of anxiety, some stimuli are salient and primary, whereas others are secondary and more ambiguous. It is possible that extinction associated with the primary stimuli could take place without extinction to secondary cues. According to a speculation of Stampfl (1966), these secondary cues still maintain the capacity to elicit anxiety, thereby leading to a "conservation of anxiety" that appears, seemingly at random, whenever these less obvious cues are present. Furthermore, the stimulus pattern during the initial learning may be not only one of cues from the external environment, but also one of cues from internal cognitions, appraisals, feeling states, and the like. Representation of these, of which the individual may have little awareness (Beck, 1976), would also elicit anxiety that appears unstimulated.

The heavily social-evaluative nature of the basic fear complex would also help account for the apparent lack of cueing. As most human behavior is embedded in a social context, cues for possible negative social evaluation constantly surround the individual. Subtle cueing of the fear complex could come from almost anywhere at any time, making the anxiety appear general and unprompted. In a sense, the anxiety *is* general, as the individual is almost always a social creature. If physical harm were a key element in the fear complex, it too could have this general cueing. Physical danger can be found almost anywhere, any time.

Finally, the future orientation of cognitive preoccupation would add to this general cueing element. Even when individuals are not directly involved in a social evaluative or physical harm situation, they can project themselves into such circumstances through imagery and self-talk. These processes, however, are internal and often automatic (Beck, 1976) and are therefore unobservable to outsiders and often to the person, again giving the appearance of lack of cueing.

Response Topography

These characteristics also help explain the response characteristics of the GAD. With pervasive cueing, anxiety would be elicited with a fairly high frequency. Arousal and cognitive response components are free to increase, but overt avoidance behavior is ineffective. Unless the person becomes totally reclusive, there is no where to hide or escape. Since negative evaluation is potentially devastating, however, it must be avoided. Where is the individual to turn? The patient is forced more cognitively toward worry and rumination for solution and avoidance. If he or she can anticipate all possible negative consequences and prevent their occurrence, then safety would be achieved. Generally, anxious individuals believe strongly in the importance of worrying about possible misfortunes and avoiding them at all costs (Zwemer & Deffenbacher, 1984). In worrying, the individual appears to be trying to anticipate and remove all probability of danger. He or she must continually scan the environment for sources of danger and possible solutions or escape routes. The job can never be fully done, however. Since the dangers are too catastrophic, no cognitive rock may be left unturned. Worry must continue and be rechecked. Even though rationally the individual may indicate no connection between unproductive worry and harm prevention, worry is superstitiously reinforced as it seems to prevent even greater harm. The individual feels compelled to worry as if it prevented further bad things from happening—a kind of cognitive compulsion, if you will.

The future orientation adds even more anxiety. Since possibilities are hard to predict and control, the individual is left with an almost endless series of "what if?" questions to ponder. The person must worry more, generating more negative dialogue and images and associated affective–physiological arousal. They cycle continues as the work of worry is never totally done, which accounts for some of the chronic, pervasive, persistent aspects of the GAD.

Worry as a cognitive avoidance process may be partly successful for any of four reasons. First, it may reflect effective problem solving. The individual may think through and develop viable plans for handling a feared situation, thereby relieving anxiety somewhat. As the individual turns to other aspects, however, worry might be less effective and affective–physiological arousal could return, at least for a period of time. Second, at any moment worrying tends to take only a portion of the stimulus situation or its consequences into account. In so doing, it narrows the number of anxiety-eliciting cues, which would result in some decrease in arousal, compared to that elicited by full exposure. The result is partial anxiety reduction. Third, chains of worry may in themselves provide a variety of "safety signals" (Mowrer, 1960; Rachman, 1983); that is, certain worrying activities have been associated with anxiety reduction in the past, so engaging in them brings some reduction of anxiety, at least momentarily. Finally, worry as an attentional process is fragile and interruptible. External events (e.g., the ringing of a phone) or internal events (e.g., an association to a different topic) may distract the individual and lower anxiety. But worry is almost never totally effective. The cueing is pervasive, and worry can never eliminate entirely the probability that negative events will happen—hence the recurrent, chronic nature of GAD.

The partial effectiveness of worry could also account for the moderate intensity of the response. Cognitive avoidance behavior works part of the time. Anxiety starts to rise, but worrying keeps it partially in check. As worry shifts to an uncontrolled aspect, however, anxiety arousal returns. Again, worry might neutralize part of it, and so on. Anxiety would oscillate in a moderate range until some distraction or resolution is available. Since the cueing is pervasive, however, anxiety cycles are likely to be restimulated, accounting for the recurrent, moderate cycles of anxiety.

These characteristics also provide ideal conditions for incubation and lack of extinction (Mowrer, 1960). The individual begins to become aroused for a few seconds or minutes but then begins to worry. If worrying is at least partially successful, arousal reduction will take place to prevent full cognitive and emotional arousal, but without escape such that the fear complex could be extinguished. The core fear is preserved, and worry is strengthened. This would account for the persistence of GAD over time once the disorder becomes established.

Because of the partial success of worry, the individual may also develop a superstitious belief in the importance and effectiveness of worry. Many patients report that worrying seems to keep worse things from happening. They feel they must worry or they will experience even greater anxiety. Their vigilance grows even stronger as they must remain alert for signs of further danger. Hypervigilance thus becomes a natural extension of the superstitious elements of worry. This vigilance only adds more arousal and strain to already stressed autonomic and cognitive systems.

Vigilance can be maintained by an intermittent rate of success, whereby the individual perceives him- or herself as having identified and prevented a negative event and/or perceives him- or herself as being in control. This sense of control can also be maintained in two ways. First, loss of control itself may be a primary or secondary element of the core fear. Cues stemming from a sense of not being in control—that is, not being vigilant and cognitively prepared—could trigger a cycle of arousal and worry, leading to the reinstatement of control. Second, vigilance and worry seem in many cases to prevent the even greater anxiety that the individual fears. Two patients who were treated by the first author exemplify this element. One suffered severe anxiety and depression following a divorce, and the other experienced two panic attacks during international travel. Both indicated that these experiences were so negative that they would never go through them again. Both were exquisitely sensitive to cues of anxiety arousal (and, in one case, depression). Significant portions of their vigilance and worry appeared to be directed toward staying in control and preventng cues of negative affect from escalating.

Although worry as cognitive avoidance appears important in the development and maintenance of GAD response characteristics, other processes may be involved as well. As noted earlier, partial extinction of anxiety can occur. Because of this partial extinction, less anxiety may be elicited by secondary cues, which could account for the moderate intensity of anxiety involved. Additionally, initial learning may have involved more chronic, persistent stressors that did not elicit high anxiety and hence caused only moderate arousal later. With continuous elicitation of anxiety, it might become conditioned to a variety of diverse cues, which would have the capacity to reelicit the lower-intensity anxiety responses in a wide range of situations. Finally, in addition to worry behaviors, clients may employ other coping strategies that are unsuccessful but do temporarily lower anxiety. Research on coping strategies has centered up to now on relationships between coping strategies and general adjustment or depression (Billings, Cronkite, & Moos, 1983; Cohen, 1980; Cohen & Lazarus, 1979; Coyne, Aldwin, & Lazarus, 1981; Folkman & Lazarus, 1984; Lambert, 1981; Lazarus & Folkman, 1984; Moos, 1982; Thompson, 1981). Extending this work, it might be speculated that clients with GAD might show ineffective coping behaviors. For instance, they may use an emotion-focused coping style instead of a problem-solving approach, which may lead to the transient feature of intense arousal.

To summarize this discussion into a tentative schematic, processes involved in the GAD appear to follow those in Figure 12.1. Some external or internal cue stimulates an unmediated sensitivity or an appraisal-mediated fear. Although potentially any unavoidable, uncontrollable fear might be involved in the appraisal-mediated area, social-evaluative fears seem to predominate. Fears of physical harm or uncontrollable emotional arousal also appear in some cases. Anxiety arousal is reflected through heightened physical arousal (anxious affect, autonomic hyperactivity, and motor tension) and negative cognitions (negative self-dialogue, imagery, and worry). Negative cognitions and

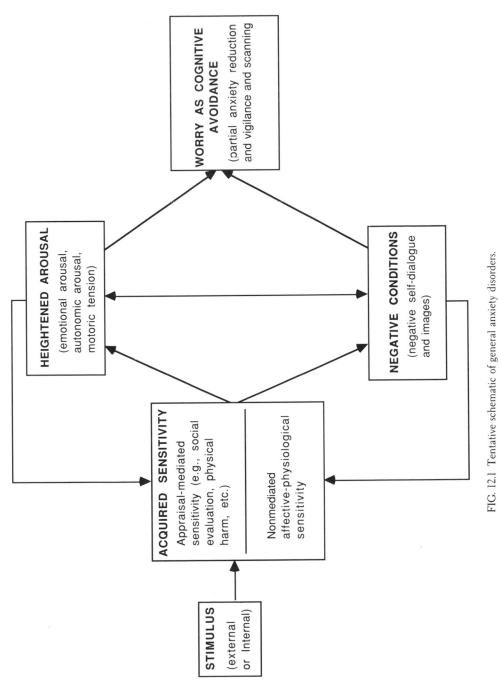

FIG. 12.1 Tentative schematic of general anxiety disorders.

339

arousal can interact and augment each other. For example, heightened arousal can be interpreted as catastrophic and thereby prompt more arousal. Rumination on or imagery of negative, emotionally laden topics can trigger more arousal. Responses in either domain may loop back and further stimulate portions of the basic fear complex. For example, heightened physical arousal or negative cognitions could be seen as "losing control" or "leading to great embarrassment," which could further stimulate social-evaluative fears, leading to greater anxiety. Since feared conditions are pervasive and often future-oriented, behavioral avoidance is impossible. The individual is channeled toward worry as a cognitive avoidance strategy. Worry is partially successful, resulting in a moderating of anxiety. However, worry is not completely successful, resulting in recurrent cycles of anxiety and the development of vigilant scanning for further danger.

Cognitive-Behavioral Treatments of the Generalized Anxiety Disorder

Figure 12.1 and the GAD conceptualization outlined earlier suggest four sites or targets of intervention.

1. Stimuli eliciting the GAD could be reduced or removed (stimulus control). Stimulus control should lower the frequency and magnitude of GAD by reducing its prompting.

2. Fear or fear complexes could be targeted. The full range of cognitive and behavioral interventions theoretically might be brought to bear. Reduction of fear should lower the affective, autonomic, and cognitive aspects, as well as cognitive avoidance processes.

3. Heightened autonomic and affective arousal could be targeted. Control of arousal would significantly alter an important component of GAD directly. Indirectly, control of arousal would break up feedback loops into the fear complex and worry and ruminative processes. Thus control of arousal could reduce a significant element of GAD directly, and indirectly perhaps much of the rest.

4. Negative cognitions and cognitive avoidance could be targeted. Changing cognitive processes would alter directly much of the GAD syndrome. Indirectly, it might alter the basic fear complex and interpretations of affective/physiological arousal.

5. A final strategy would be to target a number of these components simultaneously in a combined intervention approach.

The review of interventions will be organized around these different sites of intervention. Although interventions can be interpreted from many different theoretical perspectives, some traditional conceptualizations will be employed rather than exploring theoretical issues directly. Since few treatment studies have involved DSM-III diagnostic criteria, studies will be reviewed that involve clients who are high on general or trait anxiety, high on worry, or described as generally anxious or "anxiety neurotic." Social-evaluative anxieties will be reviewed in some cases because of the theoretical relevance.

Stimulus-Control Interventions

At first glance, stimulus control would appear to have little relevance. There do not appear to be clear elicitors that could be easily controlled or removed. On the other hand, the GAD might be viewed as a relatively uncontrollable cognitive–emotional–physiological habit disorder. In this view, many environmental circumstances trigger it, and it is therefore under poor stimulus control. Its pervasiveness and impact might be lowered if clients learned to schedule it and bring it under tighter situational control. That is, some relief might be experienced if clients delayed worry and arousal until a given time and/or place.

Borkovec and his colleagues (Borkovec, 1984; Borkovec, Wilkinson, Folensbee, & Lerman, 1983) provide some interesting studies on the stimulus control of worry. Three treatment studies have been completed to date. Subjects are individuals who report that they worry approximately 50% of the day and that worry is a significant problem. Correlational studies (Borkovec, Robinson, Pruzinsky, & DePree, 1983) also showed these subjects to be high on general anxiety and reported tension. In these studies, subjects were exposed to a four-step, stimulus-control package. First, they establish a specific half-hour worry period that takes place at the same time and place daily. Second, they monitor and identify negative, worrisome thoughts and discriminate these from pleasant and task-relevant thoughts. Third, when they identify worries, they postpone worrying until the appointed time and redirect attention to the task or situation at hand. Fourth, when they arrive for the worry period, they worry intensely about concerns and engage in problem solving to eliminate those concerns.

In the first study chronic worriers received the stimulus-control intervention in a 1-hour group session. After 4 weeks, the control group showed no change, whereas the stimulus-control group had significantly reduced the percentage of time spent worrying and the level of unrealistic worry. Stimulus-control subjects spent a lower percentage of time being generally tense, but not significantly lower than controls. The second experiment was parallel to the first, with two changes. First, the stimulus-control condition did not include instructions to problem-solve during worry sessions. Second, two stimulus-control formats were used. In one, subjects wrote down worrying thoughts in a continuous flow. In the other, subjects worried mentally. Both stimulus conditions resulted in significant reductions in percentage of time spent worrying and being generally tense compared to the control group. Written and mental worry conditions did not differ. A third study compared these two stimulus-control procedures to a relaxation placebo. Stimulus-control procedures showed significantly reduced worry compared to the relaxation condition, despite equivalent ratings of credibility and expectancy of improvement. Also, at 6-month follow-up relaxation subjects continued to worry more than those in stimulus-control conditions. In sum, these studies showed that the stimulus control can alter an important GAD component, chronic worry. Chronic worriers were able to lessen their stream of negative rumination and, in some cases, to lower general tension as well.

Although the effectiveness of the stimulus-control package is clear, the mechanisms for its effects are not as clear. In becoming aware of the initiation of worry and terminating it, worriers develop control over worry. This may increase their sense of self-control and self-efficacy and break up superstitious qualities of worry. Alternatively, as they interrupt worry and refocus on the external environment, they may focus in task-relevant ways and engage more effective problem solving skills. With repetitions of stimulus control, cognitive structures may change. For example, a worry that can be effectively delayed is not as bad or as important as the person thought. In turn, worriers may develop a more accepting, less negative view. Also, the intense 30-minute worry periods may lead to extinction. Intense worrying would allow exposure and possible extinction of fears and of the worrying process. Alternatively, although it was not part of the instructions after the first study, the process may lead to improvement in problem solving. This would strengthen cognitive coping and problem-solving skills with which to handle future worrisome events.

CLINICAL CONCLUSION

Stimulus-control procedures effectively reduce chronic worry and might be applied to the GAD. The stimulus-control procedure might be that used by Borkovec and his colleagues. However, it also might contain a concentrated period in which the individual worried and became anxious, but then systematically employed cognitive restructuring, relaxation, problem solving, or other kinds of skills in which he or she had been trained. That is, the initial portions of the instructions might remain the same, but the activities of the 30-minute period might be systematically varied based on the assessment of the client. Another possibility is to alternate skills over worry periods. With some creative thought about stimulus-control procedures, they may be more applicable than initial appearances might suggest.

Behavioral Fear Reduction Interventions

Our conceptualization of the GAD suggests that in some cases a fear complex underlies the disorder. This fear complex commonly involves social–evaluative fear or fear of physical harm. If this fear complex could be elucidated clearly, a variety of behavioral interventions might be applied. Some of the more viable possibilities will be described.

Extinction-based procedures (e.g., flooding and implosion) might be appropriate. Both present clients with the cues for the fear but do not allow cognitive or behavioral avoidance. Anxiety is allowed to rise but is extinguished as clients are not allowed to escape. In flooding, only reality-based cues are presented. This may be done imaginally or through *in vivo* exposure. Implosion involves exposure not only to reality-based stimuli, but also to psychodynamically based elements that are thought to be symbolically involved, such as rejection, sexual, aggressive, or guilt components (Stampfl & Levis, 1967). Presentation of stimuli in implosion, therefore, must rely entirely on imagery so that psychodynamic themes may be included.

Although the extinction approaches have shown considerable success with specific phobias such as claustrophobia (e.g., Öst, Johansson, & Jerremalm, 1982), agoraphobia (e.g., Öst, Jerremalm, & Jansson, 1984), and social phobias (e.g., Öst, Jerremalm, & Johansson, 1981), there has been relatively little application to GAD. Some treatment studies of specific phobias involving implosion or flooding provide indirect evidence of possible change in general anxiety. In these studies measures of general anxiety were included with those for specific phobias. For example, subjects receiving flooding for specific and social fears (Rudenstam & Bedrosian, 1977), test anxiety (Horne & Matson, 1977), and speech anxiety (Weinberger & Engelhart, 1976) showed no reduction of general anxiety. Shoemaker (1976) also found no general anxiety reduction with implosion for anxiety-neurotic patients. In summary, little evidence appears to support the use of these procedures with the GAD.

It could be argued that flooding and implosion have not been properly applied. That would require a clear specification of the fears involved for each patient and the application of flooding and implosion for that fear or fear complex. Such controlled-outcome research with GAD has not been done. These approaches may also suffer from client compliance. They ask clients to experience high levels of anxiety, which may interact with fears of loss of control. On the other hand, these approaches have been successful with individuals who fear high levels of anxiety arousal, such as agoraphobics. Thus the applicability of these procedures and compliance remain open questions.

Modeling-based approaches might also be appropriate. Clients would be exposed to nonanxious, coping behaviors displayed by a model in the presence of the phobic stimuli. Through response facilitation, acquisition, and disinhibition processes (Bandura, 1969; Rosenthal & Bandura, 1978) maladaptive avoidance behaviors would be reduced and adaptive approach behaviors strengthened. Modeling is often delivered in a graduated-approach process, with the therapist providing support and praise to reduce avoidance behavior and encourage continuation. Research suggests that live, graduated, participant modeling is very effective for fear reduction (Rosenthal & Bandura, 1978). There is, however, no known literature applying modeling to GAD.

Reinforced practice (e.g., Leitenberg, Agras, Allen, Butz, & Edwards, 1975) and behavioral rehearsal programs also might be applicable in some cases. Needed skills or approach behaviors could be targeted, rehearsed, and reinforced. Again, no research was found that related these approaches to general anxiety or the GAD.

CLINICAL CONCLUSION

While there is a considerable literature supporting the above procedures with phobias, GAD characteristics may make many of these approaches inapplicable. All require a clear, specification of cues for anxiety arousal. Yet, lack of clarity in cue conditions is one of the defining characteristics of GAD. It may be difficult or impossible for the individual to specify concrete environmental or interpersonal stimuli that elicit anxiety. Without such specification, it is difficult to structure exposure, modeling, or response acquisition interventions. Another limitation may be in the arrangement of modeling or reinforced practice. For example, it may be logistically difficult, to say nothing of the ethics involved, to arrange trials of unpredictable, physical harm. At the present time, it would appear that these approaches are of limited applicability. They should be kept in the therapeutic armamentarium and used where client characteristics suggest their effectiveness, e.g., assertion training for social-evaluative anxiety elements.

Relaxation Interventions

Relaxation interventions target heightened affective and physiological arousal. If effective, they directly reduce affective, autonomic, and somatic-tensional arousal. Indirect effects may be found in the cognitive arena as well (Deffenbacher, Mathis, & Michaels, 1979; Deffenbacher & Parks, 1979; Hutchings, Denney, Basgall, & Houston, 1980); that is, clients may also show reductions in negative cognitions, worry, and vigilant scanning as a result of relaxation. These effects might be due to an increased sense of control and self-efficacy or that as the person applies relaxation and calms affective and physiological arousal, they are better able to employ other cognitive and behavioral coping skills (Zeiss, Lewinshon, & Munoz, 1979).

Of the various relaxation interventions, anxiety management training (AMT) (Suinn, 1976, 1977b) was developed specifically for the treatment of pervasive or general anxiety. AMT acknowledges that GAD clients may not be able to identify the external prompts of anxiety, but that the anxiety response itself has cue or drive properties. With training, clients can become aware of these response-produced cues of anxiety (e.g., tension in the neck and shoulder region) or catastrophic thoughts, and can use them to prompt relaxation coping skills. The application of relaxation coping skills, in turn, reduces the heightened emotional and physiological aspects of anxiety.

AMT is described within a self-control rationale, and the development of relaxation coping skills begins with progressive relaxation training. As clients become proficient in progressive relaxation, they are trained to cue relaxation through the coping skills of breathing-cued relaxation, relaxation imagery, and relaxation without tension (i.e., focusing on and letting tension release without tensing the muscles). Clients learn to discriminate the response-produced cues of anxiety by paying attention to feelings of tension during progressive relaxation, by daily self-monitoring of anxiety reactions, and by focusing on the internal cues of anxiety arousal during therapist-initiated anxiety in the next phase at AMT. As clients develop some control over relaxation, anxiety-arousing scenes are used to elicit arousal and provide practice in discriminating the cues of arousal and applying relaxation. Initially, the therapist heavily structures the retrieval of relaxation. As clients become more proficient in reinitiating relaxation, however, the intensity of anxiety-arousing scenes is increased, and therapist control of relaxation is faded. Increased self-control within sessions is transferred in a graduated manner to real life through homework.

AMT produced general anxiety reduction in college students (Daley, Bloom, Deffenbacher, & Stewart, 1983; Edie, 1972; Hutchings et al., 1980; Nicoletti, 1972). Hutchings et al. (1980) also showed significant reduction of state anxiety and worrisome cognitions in a stressful analogue and maintenance of general anxiety reduction a year later. These studies also showed that AMT could be economically administered in small therapy groups. However, Daley et al. (1983) found large AMT groups to be ineffective, suggesting caution should be exercised in extrapolating results to workshop formats. Berghausen (1977) successfully extended AMT findings to generally anxious community volunteers.

AMT has been applied successfully in medical populations as well. For example, Cragan and Deffenbacher (1984) compared AMT and relaxation as self-control with generally anxious medical outpatients, many of whom would fit GAD criteria. Compared to controls, AMT and relaxation self-control produced general anxiety reduction on a wide variety of indices. Reductions of depression and hostility were also found. No differences were found on resting heart rate or blood pressure indices for AMT, although patients were in the normotensive range on blood pressure. Reductions of general anxiety, hostility, and depression were maintained at 1-month follow-up. Working with stressed gynecological patients, Deffenbacher and Craun (1985) found that AMT reduced general anxiety on a number of indices and ratings of gynecological symptom severity. Three-month and 2-year follow-ups indicated maintenance of general anxiety and gynecological symptom reduction. AMT has been effective with anxiety and stress-related disorders; medical disorders such as dysmenorrhea (Quillen & Denney, 1982); hypertension (Jorgensen, Houston, & Zurawski, 1981), and elements of Type A behavior patterns (Suinn & Bloom, 1978).

AMT has also been successfully applied in patient populations. For example, Jannoun, Munby, Catalan, and Gelder (1980) found that AMT reduced anxiety in agoraphobic patients. Shoemaker (1976) found that AMT lowered general anxiety in anxiety-neurotic clients from a community mental health center, and that these gains were maintained at follow-up. Additionally, general anxiety reduction for AMT was significantly greater than that for implosive therapy. Thus it appears that the effects of AMT on general anxiety reduction found in student, community, and medical populations are also found in psychiatric populations. Across populations, AMT reduced general affective–physiological arousal and, where evaluated, worrisome cognitions, depression, and hostility.

Relaxation as self-control (Deffenbacher & Snyder, 1976) is a procedure similar to AMT. Procedurally, it adds training in other relaxation coping skills (e.g., cue-controlled relaxation) and uses *in vivo* or simulation experiences to induce anxiety arousal and practice of relaxation coping skills. In the study most relevant to the GAD, Cragan and Deffenbacher (1984) found general anxiety reduction across measures for generally anxious medical outpatients. Hostility and depression were reduced as well. Relaxation as self-control subjects also showed a significantly lower resting heart rate than did controls, although there were no differences in blood pressure. All reductions were maintained at 1-month follow-up. As noted previously, relaxation as self-control was as effective as AMT in reducing anxiety, depression, and hostility. Additionally, Öst, Jerremalm, and Johansson (1981) found relaxation as self-control and social skills interventions effective in reducing severe social anxiety in psychiatric outpatients. Relaxation as self-control tended to be more effective on affective–physiological measures, whereas social skills training tended to improve behavioral components more.

Another self-managed relaxation approach is that of self-control desensitization (Goldfried, 1971). In his clinical work, Goldfried found that clients used traditional desensitization as training in relaxation coping skills. He modified desensitization procedures to enhance these self-control aspects. For example, the traditional rationale was replaced with an active, self-control one; monothematic hierarchies with multithematic ones to maximize transfer; and passive counterconditioning procedures with trials in imagining scenes and actively relaxing away tension. Each scene presentation thus represented a trial in coping with tension. Homework emphasized the application of relaxation *in vivo*.

No studies employing self-control desensitization with GAD were found. However, two studies (Kanter & Goldfried, 1979; Shahar & Merbaum, 1981) showed self-control desensitization to be effective in reducing social anxieties, which may be a GAD component. In both, however, there was a trend for systematic rational restructuring, a cognitive procedure, to be more effective.

A number of other applied relaxation programs have been effective with general anxiety. Although procedures differ in small degrees, they tend to contain a number of common elements. Most have self-control rationales, training in progressive relaxation and one or more specific relaxation coping skills, and homework for applying the relaxation to manage anxiety externally. Thus effective applied relaxation procedures not only train clients in relaxation, but also assist them in applying the relaxation to manage anxiety *in vivo*.

In one of the early studies of applied relaxation (Sherman & Plummer, 1973), a complex applied relaxation program lowered general anxiety. A 2-year follow-up (Sherman, 1975) suggested that the self-controlled relaxation skills were continuing to be applied. Similar reductions in general anxiety have been found for other applied relaxation programs, whether applied to generally anxious college students (Borkovec, Grayson, & Cooper, 1978; Lewis, Biglan, & Steinbock, 1978); generally anxious community volunteers (Hillenberg & Collins, 1983; Lehrer, Woolfolk, Rooney, McCann, & Carrington, 1983; Woolfolk, Lehrer, McCann, & Rooney, 1982); anxiety neurotics (Canter, Kondo, & Knott, 1975); or clients meeting DSM-III GAD criteria (Hoelscher, Lichstein, & Rosenthal, 1984). Across these studies, applied relaxation was effective—as effective as other interventions such as meditation and biofeedback. Additionally, two of these studies (Hillenberg & Collins, 1983; Hoelscher, Lichstein, & Rosenthal, 1984) suggested that homework for the practice and application of relaxation enhanced the effect of the applied relaxation program. Perhaps home practice and application of relaxation are important parts of the more effective applied relaxation programs.

Various forms of biofeedback have also been employed with general anxiety. For example, Lehrer (1978) demonstrated that alpha feedback reduced signs of anxiety in anxiety-neurotic patients. Two other studies (Raskin, Johnson, & Rondestveldt, 1973; Townsend, House, & Addario, 1975) applied EMG training to generally anxious individuals, with some success; however, there was limited transfer for Raskin et al. (1973). A prolonged EMG training program proved effective in reducing general anxiety in anxiety neurotics (Canter et al., 1975). Generally, biofeedback procedures have proved no more effective, and in a number of cases less effective, than applied relaxation procedures (Lehrer, 1982). It should be noted, however, that the EMG program of Canter et al. (1975) was somewhat more effective than a relatively simple relaxation program.

CLINICAL CONCLUSION

Relaxation interventions effectively reduce affective–physiological arousal in general anxiety or GAD-like syndromes. Therefore, it seems useful to employ such relaxation-based programs for clients with significant affective, autonomic, and/or somatic–tensional arousal. The most effective programs would appear to include: (1) a self-control rationale that emphasizes the acquisition of active relaxation coping skills; (2) training in the awareness of internal cues of anxiety arousal and the use of these cues to prompt relaxation coping skills; (3) training in basic relaxation and one or more specific relaxation coping skills; (4) training within sessions in the application of relaxation coping skills to reduce tension; and (5) systematic homework for the development and application of relaxation outside therapy. Of the approaches reviewed, AMT and relaxation as self-control are the most comprehensive and flexible. Biofeedback approaches appear to offer little more than the less complicated applied relaxation approaches.

In employing relaxation approaches, therapists should be sensitive to the possibility of relaxation-induced anxiety (Heide & Borkovec, 1983, 1984; Lehrer, 1982)—that is, the tendency for some clients to become anxious during relaxation training. Several explanations have been offered for GAD clients' apparent vulnerability to relaxation-induced anxiety. Some clients may be frightened of the sensations they experience during relaxation. The experience of relaxation may heighten their awareness and attention to anxiety, which the clients fear. Relatedly, some clients may fear losing control during relaxation. For others, attending to internal experiences in general may be aversive. Finally, relaxation may release attention to engage in other worrisome or aversive cognitive activities. Any or all of these factors could lead to an increase in anxiety during relaxation, rather than its lowering.

At least four strategies are relevant to lowering relaxation-induced anxiety. First, clients might be given a kind of paradoxical or counterdemand instruction regarding relaxation. It could be suggested that it may take some time before relaxation comes under their control and that some clients will experience an increase of tension for a period of time. If relaxation-induced anxiety appeared, it could then be explained within this format. A second approach is repeated exposure to relaxation (Heide & Borkovec, 1984). Either frequent approaches, through which clients were exposed gradually to relaxation, or a flooding of relaxation despite anxiety could be employed. With repetition, either approach should increase the client's comfort with relaxation. Third, if relaxation-induced anxiety is experienced with one relaxation technique, training could shift to an alternative, as Heide and Borkovec (1983) found that few subjects prone to relaxation-induced anxiety with one procedure also experienced it with a second. For example, a client who experienced relaxation-induced anxiety with progressive relaxation might be shifted to imagery-based relaxation or biofeedback. Fourth, specific fears involved in relaxation-induced anxiety could be elucidated and treated with an alternative intervention. For example, the fear of loss of control might be flooded or treated with cognitive restructuring. Of these, counterdemand instructions and either repetition of the same relaxation technique or a shift to an alternative technique may be quicker.

Cognitive Interventions

Cognitive interventions directly target negative cognitions and worry. If effective, they lower arousal of negative cognitions and worry as cognitive avoidance. Indirectly, they should decrease vigilant scanning, as it appears to be an extension of the negative cognitions. Also indirectly, they might reduce emotional and physiological arousal by removing many cognitive prompts of physiological and emotional arousal.

Thought stopping (Wolpe, 1973) might interrupt negative cognitive processes. Training in thought stopping typically involves having clients intentionally rehearse undesired thoughts or worries, saying them aloud or engaging in covert rumination. When they are thoroughly immersed in these thoughts, the therapist suddenly shouts, "STOP!" This effectively disrupts the ruminations. Clients are told that, with practice, ruminations can be disrupted in this manner. After this initial demonstration, clients employ this same procedure, shouting, "STOP," and noticing the effects. As clients establish overt control, thought stopping is practiced covertly.

Although this technique has been reported as helpful in some case studies (Wolpe, 1973), Mahoney and Arnkoff (1978) suggested that it has not proved uniquely helpful. One study with general anxiety (Matthews & Shaw, 1977) supported the usefulness of thought stopping with generally anxious patients. It should be noted, however, that thought stopping was embedded in a combined cognitive and relaxation program. At present, it would seem that thought stopping is likely to be ineffective in and of itself, although it may play a role in the treatment of GAD when combined with other cognitive or relaxation coping skills. That is, clients might use thought stopping to interrupt cognitive-physiological chains and then employ new alternative coping responses (Suinn, in press, b). Thought stopping might also be used with stimulus control; clients might initiate a stimulus-control procedure by using thought stopping to interrupt worry—for example, "STOP! I'll just wait until 4:00 P.M. to worry about that."

There are a variety of cognitive restructuring interventions, including rational–emotive therapy (Ellis, 1962); systematic rational restructuring (Goldfried, Decenteceo, & Weinberg, 1974); cognitive modification (Meichenbaum, 1977); and cognitive restructuring (Beck, 1976). They differ somewhat but share a number of common elements. First, clients learn to identify cognitive processes related to anxiety arousal. Second, they identify the dysfunctional, irrational aspects of their thought processes. Third, they are shown ways of altering these negative cognitions and developing new, reality-based counterresponses. Fourth, to some degree within sessions, they practice these new cognitive counterresponses. Fifth, they are given homework to apply these new cognitive responses to manage anxiety *in vivo*.

Cognitive interventions do differ in their method of achieving these goals. For example, rational–emotive therapy tends to involve a more directive confrontation of negative cognitions. Systematic rational restructuring and cognitive modification are less confrontational and focus more on the rehearsal of specific new cognitions. Systematic rational restructuring trains application of the new cognitions in a multithematic anxiety hierarchy, whereas cognitive modification does this while clients imagine a series of steps relative to an anxiety-arousing stimulus—for example, preparing for, confronting, being overwhelmed by, and reinforcing phases. The processes of cognitive restructuring involve more a series of Socratic questions that probe the client's logical processes and then the setting up of *in vivo* experiments that would confirm or disconfirm the client's current cognitions.

Although there is relatively little research on cognitive interventions with GAD, related research on social anxieties, agoraphobia, and general anxiety is promising. For example, rational–emotive therapy (DiLoreto, 1971) and systematic rational restructuring (Kanter & Goldfried, 1979; Shahar & Merbaum, 1981) effectively reduced interpersonal social anxiety. In these studies, cognitive interventions were as effective as other interventions, or more so, and provided a greater generalization to general and other anxieties. Rational–emotive therapy and related interventions (e.g., rational–emotive role reversal and rational–emotive imagery) lowered general anxiety in generally anxious community mental health center clients (Lipsky, Kassinove, & Miller, 1980). Further, rational–emotive therapy tended to be more effective than simple relaxation. Cognitive restructuring was also effective with agoraphobics (Emmelkamp & Mersch, 1982; Mavissakalian, Michelson, Greenwald, Kornblith, & Greenwald, 1983). Interestingly, in both studies initial effects for exposure-based interventions were stronger. By follow-up, however, cognitive restructuring was as effective as the extinction approach and showed some spread of effects that were not noted for the exposure intervention. This suggests the consolidate cognitive skills, which, once consolidated, may be very effective. One study with negative results for generally anxious patients was a cognitive modification intervention (Woodward & Jones, 1980). However, this may have been due to clients' failure to learn to restructure negative cognitions effectively, as the major emphasis appeared to be on rehearsing more adaptive statements. In contrast, a previous study (Mavissakalian et al., 1983) showed that the most important element in cognitive intervention was decreasing the frequency of self-defeating statements, rather than increasing that of positive coping statements.

CLINICAL CONCLUSION

Cognitive restructuring appears effective in reducing the negative cognition and worrisome aspects of general and other anxieties. Therefore, proper consideration should be given to the development of a cognitive restructuring intervention component to deal with the cognitive, worry, and vigilance and scanning elements of the GAD. Components of the most effective program would appear to include the following: (1) systematic self-monitoring of cognitive processes; (2) exploration of the dysfunctional, irrational elements of the negative cognitions; (3) the development of appropriate counterresponses to replace old negative cognitions; (4) rehearsal of these new cognitive counterresponses within and between sessions; and (5) rehearsal of task-relevant approach, and problem-solving cognitive skills. Thought-stopping would appear to add little by itself, although it might be combined with other interventions.

Cognitive restructuring interventions may need to focus on any or all of the following dimensions. First, GAD clients often misestimate event probabilities; that is, unlikely events appear highly likely to them. They may need assistance in accurately estimating event probabilities. Second, they tend to engage in catastrophization—attribution of highly negative, devastating consequences to events. They must develop and apply realistic, mildly negative emotional descriptors. Third, they also think in absolutistic, demanding terms; they insist on approval, perfection, control, and so forth. Demands need to be replaced with more preferential statements. Further, GAD clients often engage in selective abstraction and overgeneralization, whereby they pull out of context realistic negative elements and/or draw far-reaching conclusions about time or personal characteristics. They need assistance in making discriminant statements about events themselves and time. They also may need help in increasing the rate of productive, task-oriented self-instruction and problem-solving strategies. These may help them focus on possible negative events as tasks to be approached and problems to be solved, rather than as catastrophic events.

Combined Interventions

Combined interventions target simultaneously or serially different GAD elements. For example, applied relaxation and assertiveness training might be combined in dealing with an emotionally aroused, unassertive GAD client. On the other hand, stimulus control and cognitive restructuring might be combined for an individual who is highly ruminative and for whom arousal appears to stem from ruminations. Since affective–physiological arousal and cognitive components appear so salient in the GAD, the most probable combined intervention would be some combination of applied relaxation and cognitive interventions.

Stress inoculation (Meichenbaum, 1977) is perhaps the best-known technique that includes both cognitive and relaxation coping skills. In the first phase of stress inoculation, clients learn to conceptualize anxiety in terms of cognitive and emotional–physiological processes. They are also introduced to a sequential breakdown of methods of coping with anxiety, which include preparing for it, confronting or handling normal levels, coping with feeling overwhelmed, and reinforcing oneself for coping. Then clients learn a variety of cognitive and relaxation coping skills. Cognitive skills include not only changing dysfunctional cognitions, but also planning and problem-solving activities such as identifying escape routes and other coping resources. As clients gain skill with these coping responses, stress inoculation provides practice in applying them to reduce anxiety. Cognitive coping skills are rehearsed while clients imagine dealing with various stages of the stressor, and relaxation coping skills are practiced in a kind of self-control desensitization. Homework is used to transfer skills to the external environment.

There is a large research literature that suggests stress inoculation is effective for specific anxieties (Deffenbacher & Suinn, 1982; Meichenbaum, 1977, 1985). Despite the apparent relevance of stress inoculation to GAD, however, the research base is relatively limited. The central difficulty in applying stress inoculation is one that has been encountered with some other behavioral methods. Specifically, stress inoculation requires the identification of specific anxiety-arousing stimuli, presenting a problem in dealing with the GAD. It should be possible to adapt stress inoculation by using specific stressors from the individual's past and training on a number of highly stressful circumstances that apply to many GAD clients. It would also be possible to combine a general cognitive restructuring approach of the therapist's choice with other relaxation-based interventions. For example, a cognitive restructuring approach might be combined with AMT or relaxation as self-control because of the comprehensiveness of these programs and their flexibility. For example, a recent study by Barlow et al. (1984) demonstrated that a program combining relaxation and cognitive methods effectively lowered anxiety in GAD and posttraumatic stress disordered patients.

CLINICAL CONCLUSION

Where assessment indicates that more than one intervention could be appropriate, a combination of interventions should be employed. It may be that a single intervention could eventually prove as effective as the combination. Without a better research base than is currently available, however, the best strategy would be to combine interventions where assessment deemed relevant. In developing combined programs, it is suggested that the general guidelines in the foregoing clinical conclusions sections be employed.

General Treatment Considerations and Future Directions

Like any group, GAD clients pose unique problems for treatment. The rest of this chapter outlines several principles that should facilitate treatment of the generally anxious client. These issues and strategies are thought to be general, cutting across different treatment strategies. Addressing them should clarify the nature of the problem, reduce therapeutic impasses, and improve overall treatment efficiency. The chapter will conclude with some suggestions to facilitate our research on and understanding of GAD.

Assessment

Perhaps more than with a number of other anxiety disorders, assessment of GAD is a continuing, developing process. Over time, the nature of fears, arousal, negative cognitive responses, and worrying emerge. This time seems to be necessary, as the cueing and response characteristics are internal and the client is unaware of them. The therapist should be willing to shift and reformulate his or her conceptualization as the picture becomes clearer.

The emergent aspect of assessment and conceptualization make self-monitoring almost a must. Clients should be encouraged to track and record carefully emotional and physiological arousal, negative self-dialogue and images, and worry and ruminative processes. Clients often resist this kind of self-monitoring at first, but later rate it as very helpful (Matthews & Shaw, 1977). However, they should be encouraged and prompted to continue as it provides a rich source of temporal data that are hard to gather in other ways. Gradually increasing the difficulty of self-monitoring may facilitate client compliance. For example, clients might first track only feelings of affective and physiological arousal. Then, rating the intensity of these feelings could be added. Next, negative self-dialogue and images might be added. Adding complexity to self-monitoring may facilitate compliance without making the task too onerous at any step. Self-monitoring assignments should be reviewed carefully and probed with detailed, concrete questions to facilitate an emerging picture of the unique GAD characteristic for that individual.

Another issue that has received scant attention in the literature is the possibility that anger is involved. Several of our recent studies suggest that general anger and general anxiety may be related. For example, in assessing the effectiveness of cognitive and relaxation interventions for anger reduction, Hazaleus and Deffenbacher (1986) assessed high-anger subjects on trait, state, and self-monitored anger. A general anxiety measure was also included to evaluate generalization effects of treatment. It was noted, however, that the pretreatment mean on general anxiety for men was at the 75th percentile and the 84th for females. This suggested that the high-anger subjects were also generally anxious. A subsequent treatment study (Deffenbacher, Brandon, & Demm, 1985) yielded similar results. A correlational study (Deffenbacher & Demm, 1985) provided further support. A high-anger group with self-identified problems of anger control was compared to a low-anger group without identified problems of anger control. They were assessed on a variety of state, trait, and self-monitored anger measures and an index of general anxiety. A regression analysis predicting anger grouping showed that trait anxiety was the first factor entering the regression equation and that it alone accounted for over 50% of the variance in anger, despite the fact that a large number of other anger measures were entered into the regression equation. Another study (Zwemer & Deffenbacher, 1984) showed that trait anxiety and general anger shared in common a number of irrational beliefs, although blame-proneness differentiated anger, whereas helplessness discriminated trait anxiety. Thus there may be a common cognitive core that contributes to arousal of both general anger and general anxiety. Although these studies have not been done with GAD clients, they suggest that general anger may be related to general anxiety for some clients. In all probability, there are generally anxious clients who do not experience significant problems with anger. Conversely, there may be a number of generally angry individuals with relatively little anxiety. However, this research suggests that general anger may be involved in general anxiety for some individuals and that, therefore, the possibilities should be assessed.

Selection of Treatment Components

Self-monitoring is an important element of any treatment approach selected. Such self-monitoring is important for assessment, as noted earlier, but it also provides the basis for initiating alternative responses. As clients become aware of the affective, physiological, and cognitive aspects of the GAD syndrome, they become able to detect the beginning of an anxiety or worry cycle and to initiate alternative behaviors.

A second element would be to couch the rationale and intervention within a self-control format (Kanfer & Hagerman, 1981). As noted previously, GAD clients often have issues of control. Therefore, describing interventions as promoting client self-control should work with this cognitive bias and reduce issues of therapist control. Procedures can be described as training clients in awareness of the onset of anxiety and in techniques for self-initiating alternative responses with which to reduce or control anxiety. Treatment can be described not as taking control from clients but, rather, as increasing the range and variety of skills with which they can control anxiety.

A third element of treatment design is the importance of practice, both within and between sessions. Within sessions clients should practice new responses to control anxiety. The level of anxiety arousal employed and/or the degree of client control should be increased over sessions so that the clients gain greater control over high anxiety. Practice in the external environment should mirror and follow demonstrated control within the session. That is, clients should be given systematic homework with increasing anxiety arousal in vivo. One example of such homework is that involved in AMT and relaxation as self-control. Clients first apply relaxation coping skills in nonanxious circumstances, then to low levels of anxiety arousal, then to intermediate levels of arousal, and finally to all aspects of anxiety arousal. Regardless of the intervention selected, practice within and between the sessions would seem to increase overall effectiveness (Deffenbacher & Suinn, 1982).

A fourth principle is to target intervention components to response components most salient for a given GAD client (Deffenbacher & Suinn, 1982; Lazarus, 1981; Suinn, 1983, 1984a). This suggestion seems both logical and consistent with some research (e.g., Öst et al., 1981, 1982) with simple and social phobias that shows targeted interventions are more effective, even though the finding is not consistent (e.g., Öst, Lindahl, Sterner, & Jerremalm, 1984). Although currently there is not enough of a research base with the GAD to support or refute this contention, it would seem best to proceed with targeting interventions to response components for which they have the greatest empirical and theoretical effectiveness. The review in the previous section suggests that stimulus control and cognitive restructuring procedures are most applicable to negative cognitions and worry. Applied relaxation approaches would appear most appropriate for affective and physiological arousal. Clients with significant cognitive and arousal components might be treated with a combined approach such as stress inoculation or a combination of cognitive restructuring and applied relaxation. Other behavioral procedures such as modeling, behavioral rehearsal, and extinction-based procedures should be reserved for specific skill deficit problems and/or anxiety elements that are refractory to the other interventions. If anger is identified along with anxiety, then AMT might be appropriate, inasmuch as the training seems equally applicable to both arousal states (Deffenbacher, Brandon, & Demm, 1985; Hart, 1984; Hazaleus & Deffenbacher, 1986).

Realistic, Positive Therapeutic Approach

Client capacity to become aware of and reduce anxiety should be emphasized. It should also be communicated that this will take time and effort. Clients should be told that their anxiety can improve, but only to the extent that they monitor anxiety and practice skills they will be learning. From the start clients should be given a positive therapeutic set, but one that is realistically contingent on their active participation.

Perhaps because of the involvement of social–evaluative fears, individuals with a GAD often are sensitive to and have difficulty in handling failure and setbacks. Efforts, therefore, should be directed toward minimizing therapeutic failures and maximizing success. This can be done, in part, by giving a realistic set regarding the amount of time involved to develop appropriate coping skills. Efforts can be facilitated by making therapeutic steps small and moving clients to the next step when they have demonstrated mastery within sessions. For example, when a client has demonstrated the capacity to reduce anxiety via relaxation or cognitive coping skills within the session, then the application to similar or somewhat less anxiety-arousing circumstances externally may be given.

A parallel issue is some clients' need for instant and dramatic improvement. They seem to have very high expectations for success and become easily discouraged when change is not readily apparent. Again, they should be told from the beginning that progress will be gradual and contingent on mastering certain coping skills. When this explanation is insufficient, other strategies may be useful (Deffenbacher & Suinn, 1982). For example, initial steps of training might target a readily achieved skill, such as relaxation (Suinn, 1980, 1982). Clients might rate their tension level before and after relaxation practice. Reduction of tension within home practice could be noted as a sign of progress. A careful review of self-monitoring assignments may reveal tangible signs of improvement unnoticed by the patient. For example, the client may notice a reduction in the frequency or intensity of anxiety or in anxiety-related psychophysiological disorders such as tension headaches. In reviewing self-monitoring, clients might also be asked to rate how they would have responded in the past. Comparison to their current reactions may reveal an increment in coping capacity otherwise overlooked. Also, with some clients it may be necessary to explore their definitions of success and improvement. Some seem to expect to be able to handle all situations without anxiety and with perfect calm and confidence. A direct discussion of the impracticality of such desirable expectations is relevant. Clients should be given an expectation of coping rather than mastery. That is, they are likely to continue to experience stress and anxiety at different points, but they can learn to manage it and reduce its impact.

Other patients may see GAD characteristics as a kind of personality defect. In turn, they may devalue themselves for having it and see themselves as helpless to make change (Zwemer & Deffenbacher, 1984). Efforts should be made to counteract such views. Instead, anxiety should be described as a natural, learned response stemming from the person's history. Life has taught these clients to be generally tense, but has not taught them how to manage or control it. The emphasis on the learning aspect of generalized anxiety may help decrease personal blaming and helplessness and shift the direction of therapy to learning new, self-managed, coping skills.

Medications

It is not uncommon for GAD clients to be taking minor tranquilizers or antidepressants. Others may be self-medicating with nonprescription drugs, possibly combining them with prescription drugs. The following suggestions are made for dealing with such patients. First, a careful assessment of prescription and nonprescription drug involvement should be made. Clients should monitor medication use on a daily basis, so that the therapist is apprised of current usage. Second, medications should be under close medical supervision. Side effects and possible withdrawal reactions should be monitored carefully, especially if reduction of medication is undertaken. Third, removal or reduction of medication should not be made a precondition for therapy. To do so may remove one of the client's few coping skills. Reduction of medication should follow the development and demonstration of anxiety reduction skills within therapy. Then medication should be withdrawn in gradual steps such that coping capacities without medication are not outstripped. In some cases, a reduction of medication, rather than outright removal, may be a legitimate therapeutic goal.

Maintenance and Termination

Some patients who learn to reduce anxiety find themselves, some months later, experiencing chronic anxiety again. Life events may have resensitized them, but many have failed to continue the skills learned in therapy. Alerting clients to this possibility may be sufficient for some. Continued use of the skills should be described as a lifelong process. That is, life will continue to stress the individual, and anxiety is likely to be experienced to some degree on an ongoing basis. With continued self-monitoring and practice, however, the individual can continue to manage it. Continued self-monitoring and practice tend to make coping easier and more rapid, but not unnecessary.

This orientation toward maintenance and self-control may be helpful but also can be buttressed by termination strategies. Termination should not be considered until the client is showing stable and reliable management of anxiety for a period of time. The therapist may want to maintain contact for some time afterward to support continued consolidation. This might be done by lengthening the interval between later treatment sessions—for example, having sessions every 2 to 3 weeks toward the end of therapy.

Another strategy would be periodic follow-up or booster sessions (e.g., every 3 months) during which progress and self-recording might be reviewed and brief troubleshooting done. An alternative would be continued self-monitoring and application of coping skills, with periodic reports by phone or mail. Clients could also be encouraged to set up periodic self-review of coping efforts. For example, at the first of every month clients might review efforts at managing anxiety and make plans for another month. These strategies are designed to keep clients focused on continued awareness and coping efforts at a time when anxiety may decrease and the need for continued coping efforts may seem less apparent. Long-term maintenance of anxiety reduction appears to result from continued efforts to recognize and manage anxiety.

Future Directions in Understanding and Treating the GAD

The GAD is a relatively common problem complex, but it was only with DSM-III that it was clearly defined and separated from other anxiety disorders. Our knowledge, therefore, is relatively incomplete. Questions abound. For example, is the GAD a relatively uniform phenomenon? Or are there meaningful subgroups with different characteristics and responsiveness to treatment? Is a client marked by salient cognitive, ruminative characteristics similar to the client with heavy autonomic–somatic–affective involvement? What accounts for differences in dominant response characteristics? Are they equally responsive to relaxation interventions? cognitive interventions? medical interventions? Are they equally easy to work with, or do they pose different problems in terms of case management? Research on such questions will shape our understanding of the disorder and sharpen our treatment designs.

Research on treatment effectiveness should include multichannel assessment. This is needed not only for full evaluation of the treatment, but also to assess which GAD components are affected most by the treatment, as some studies (Öst et al., 1981) have suggested that different interventions affect different response components. Assessment in nontargeted domains would increase our understanding of treatment generalization effects. Follow-up assessments are also needed, not only for evaluation of treatment maintenance, but also for a full evaluation of some treatments, as some research has suggested a posttreatment consolidation of effects (e.g., Deffenbacher & Suinn, 1982; Emmelkamp & Mersch, 1982; Mavissakalian et al., 1983), especially for some of the cognitive and relaxation approaches. Without follow-up, the full effects of these treatments would not have been seen and inappropriate conclusions would have been drawn.

Research, whether aimed at treatment or at basic understanding, is much needed. Given the difficulties of collecting large numbers of GAD clients at one time, such research efforts might benefit from a collaborative network of researchers working together (Deffenbacher, 1985), as well as the typical individual research teams. Within this strategy, a group of interested researchers would meet, possibly at conventions such as those of the Association for the Advancement of Behavior Therapy or the American Psychological Association, and outline basic assessment and treatment protocols, designs, and the like. These would then be implemented by a network of collaborating practitioners and centers across the country (e.g., hospital clinics, mental health centers, and university counseling centers). Three protocols here, seven there, six more at another site, and so forth might not be all that useful in themselves but, when collapsed together, could provide an important data base from which to understand the nature and treatment of GAD. Such a strategy, though presenting difficulties in terms of standardization elements and communications, has high external validity in terms of factors such as geography, setting, and therapist. Information from such collaborative field studies, when merged with the findings from specific research teams, could provide a more comprehensive knowledge of the GAD.

References

American Psychiatric Association. (1980). *Diagnostic and statistical manual of mental disorders* (3rd ed.) Washington, DC: Author.

Bandura, A. (1969). *Principles of behavior modification.* New York: Holt, Rinehart and Winston.

Barlow, D., Cohen, A., Waddell, M., Vermilyea, B., Klosko, J., Blanchard, E., & DiNardo, P. (1984). Panic and generalized anxiety disorders: Nature and treatment. *Behavior Therapy, 15,* 431–449.

Beck, A. (1972). Cognition, anxiety, and psychophysiological disorders. In C. Spielberger (Ed.), *Anxiety: Current trends in theory and research* (Vol. 2). New York: Academic Press.

Beck, A. (1976). *Cognitive therapy and the emotional disorders.* New York: International Universities Press.

Beck, A., Laude, R., & Bohnert, M. (1974). Ideational components of anxiety neurosis. *Archives of General Psychiatry, 31,* 319–325.

Berghausen, P. (1977). *Anxiety management training: Need for arousal-cued relaxation.* Unpublished doctoral dissertation, Colorado State University, Fort Collins.

Billings, A., Cronkite, R., & Moos, R. (1983). Social-environmental factors in unipolar depression: Comparisons of depressed patients and nondepressed controls. *Journal of Abnormal Psychology, 92,* 119–133.

Borkovec, T. (1984, September). *Worry: Physiological and cognitive processes.* Paper presented at the 14th Meeting of the European Association for Behavior Therapy, Brussels, Belgium.

Borkovec, T., Grayson, J., & Cooper, K. (1978). Treatment of general tension: Subjective and physiological effects of progressive relaxation. *Journal of Consulting and Clinical Psychology, 46,* 518–528.

Borkovec, T., Robinson, E., Pruzinsky, T., & DePree, J. (1983). Preliminary exploration of worry: Some characteristics and processes. *Behaviour Research and Therapy, 21,* 9–16.

Borkovec, T., Wilkinson, L., Folensbee, R., & Lerman, C. (1983). Stimulus control applications to the treatment of worry. *Behaviour Research and Therapy, 21*(3), 247–251.

Canter, A., Kondo, C., & Knott, S. (1975). A comparison of EMG feedback and progressive relaxation training in anxiety neurosis. *British Journal of Psychiatry, 127,* 470–477.

Cohen, F. (1980). Coping with surgery: Information, psychological preparation, and recovery. In L. W. Poon (Ed.), *Aging in the 1980's: Psychological issues.* Washington, DC: American Psychological Association.

Cohen, F., & Lazarus, R. (1979). Coping with the stresses of illness. In G. Stone, N. Adler, & F. Cohen (Eds.), *Health psychology.* San Francisco: Jossey-Bass.

Coyne, J., Aldwin, C., & Lazarus, R. (1981). Depression and coping in stressful episodes. *Journal of Abnormal Psychology, 90,* 439–447.

Cragan, M., & Deffenbacher, J. (1984). Anxiety management training and relaxation as self-control in the treatment of generalized anxiety in medical outpatients. *Journal of Counseling Psychology, 31,* 123–131.

Daley, P., Bloom, L., Deffenbacher, J., & Stewart, R. (1983). Treatment effectiveness of anxiety management training in small and large group formats. *Journal of Counseling Psychology, 30,* 104–107.

Deffenbacher, J. L. (1985). A cognitive-behavioral response and a modest proposal. *The Counseling Psychologist, 13,* 261–269.

Deffenbacher, J., Brandon, A., & Demm, P. (1985). *Application of anxiety management training to anger reduction.* Unpublished manuscript, Department of Psychology, Colorado State University, Fort Collins.

Deffenbacher, J., & Craun, A. (1985). Anxiety management training with stressed student gynecology patients: A collaborative approach. *Journal of College Student Personnel, 26,* 513–518.

Deffenbacher, J., & Demm, P. (1985). *Correlates of high general anger.* Unpublished manuscript, Department of Psychology, Colorado State University, Fort Collins.

Deffenbacher, J., Mathis, H., & Michaels, A. (1979). Two self-control procedures in the reduction of targeted and nontargeted anxieties. *Journal of Counseling Psychology, 26,* 120–127.

Deffenbacher, J., & Parks, D. (1979). A comparison of traditional and self-control desensitization. *Journal of Counseling Psychology, 26,* 93–97.

Deffenbacher, J., & Snyder, A. (1976). Relaxation as self-control in treatment of test and other anxieties. *Psychological Reports, 39,* 379–385.

Deffenbacher, J., & Suinn, R. (1982). The self-control of anxiety. In P. Karoly & F. Kanfer (Eds.), *Self-management and behavior change: From theory to practice.* New York: Pergamon Press.

DiLoreto, A. (1971). *Comparative psychotherapy: An experimental analysis.* Chicago: Aldine-Atherton.

DiNardo, P., O'Brien, G., Barlow, D., Waddell, M., & Blanchard, E. (1983). Reliability of DSM-III anxiety disorder categories using a new structured interview. *Archives of General Psychiatry, 40,* 1070–1080.

Edie, C. (1972). *Uses of AMT in treating trait anxiety.* Unpublished doctoral dissertation, Colorado State University, Fort Collins.

Ellis, A. (1962). *Reason and emotion in psychotherapy.* New York: Lyle Stuart.

Emmelkamp, P., & Mersch, P. (1982). Cognition and exposure *in vivo* in the treatment of agoraphobia: Short-term and delayed effects. *Cognitive Therapy and Research, 6,* 77–88.

Evans, I. (1972). A conditioning model of a common fear pattern—Fear of fear. *Psychotherapy: Theory, Research and Practice, 9,* 238–241.

Folkman, S., & Lazarus, R. (1984, August). *Intra- and interindividual analysis of coping: Different questions, different answers.* Paper presented at annual meeting of the American Psychological Association, Toronto, Ontario.

Goldfried, M. (1971). Systematic desensitization as training in self-control. *Journal of Consulting and Clinical Psychology, 37,* 228–234.

Goldfried, M., Decenteceo, E., & Weinberg, L. (1974). Systematic rational restructuring as a self-control technique. *Behavior Therapy, 5,* 247–254.

Hamilton, V. (1982). Cognition and stress: An information processing model. In L. Goldberger & S. Breznitz (Eds.), *Handbook of stress; Theoretical and clinical aspects.* New York: Free Press.

Hart, K. (1984). Anxiety management training and anger control for Type A individuals. *Journal of Behavior Therapy and Experimental Psychiatry, 15,* 133–140.

Hazaleus, S., & Deffenbacher, J. (1986). Relaxation and cognitive treatments of anger. *Journal of Consulting and Clinical Psychology, 59,* 222–226.

Heide, F., & Borkovec, T. (1983). Relaxation-induced anxiety: Paradoxical anxiety enhancement due to relaxation training. *Journal of Consulting and Clinical Psychology, 51,* 171–182.

Heide, F., & Borkovec, T. (1984). Relaxation-induced anxiety: Mechanisms and theoretical implications. *Behaviour Research and Therapy, 22,* 1–12.

Hillenberg, J., & Collins, F. (1983). The importance of home practice for progressive relaxation training. *Behaviour Research and Therapy, 21,* 633–642.

Hoelscher, T., Lichstein, K., & Rosenthal, T. (1984). Objective vs. subjective assessment of relaxation compliance among anxious individuals. *Behaviour Research and Therapy, 22,* 187–193.

Horne, A., & Matson, J. (1977). A comparison of modeling, desensitization, flooding, study skills, and control groups for reducing test anxiety. *Behavior Therapy, 8,* 1–8.

Hutchings, D., Denney, D., Basgall, J., & Houston, B. (1980). Anxiety management and applied relaxation in reducing general anxiety. *Behaviour Research and Therapy, 18,* 181–190.

Jannoun, L., Munby, M., Catalan, J., & Gelder, M. (1980). A home-based treatment program for agoraphobia: Replication and controlled evaluation. *Behavior Therapy, 11,* 294–305.

Jorgensen, R., Houston, B., Zurawski, R. (1981). Anxiety management training in the treatment of essential hypertension. *Behaviour Research and Therapy, 19,* 467–474.

Kanfer, F., & Hagerman, S. (1981). The role of self-regulation. In L. Rehm (Ed.), *Behavioral therapy for depression: Present status and future direction.* New York: Academic Press.

Kanter, N., & Goldfried, M. (1979). Relative effectiveness of rational restructuring self-control desensitization in the reduction of interpersonal anxiety. *Behavior Therapy, 10,* 472–490.

Lambert, V. (1981). *Factors affecting psychological well-being in rheumatoid arthritic women.* Unpublished doctoral dissertation, University of California, School of Nursing, Berkeley.

Lang, P. (1971). The application of psychophysiological methods to the study of psychotherapy and behavior change. In A. Bergin & S. Garfield (Eds.), *Handbook of psychotherapy and behavior change.* New York: Wiley.

Lazarus, A. (1981). *The practice of multimodal therapy.* New York: McGraw-Hill.

Lazarus, R., & Folkman, S. (1984). *Stress, appraisal, and coping.* New York: Springer.

Lehrer, P. (1978). Psychophysiological effects of progressive relaxation in anxiety neurotic patients and of progressive relaxation and alpha feedback in nonpatients. *Journal of Consulting and Clinical Psychology, 46,* 389–404.

Lehrer, P. (1982). How to relax and how not to relax: A re-evaluation of the work of Edmund Jacobson: I. *Behaviour Research and Therapy, 20,* 417–428.

Lehrer, P., Woolfolk, R., Rooney, A., McCann, B., & Carrington, P. (1983). Progressive relaxation and meditation: A study of psychophysiological and therapeutic differences between two techniques. *Behaviour Research and Therapy, 21,* 651–662.

Leitenberg, H., Agras, W., Allen, R., Butz, R., & Edwards, J. (1975). Feedback and therapist praise during treatment of phobia. *Journal of Consulting and Clinical Psychology, 43,* 396–404.

Lewis, C., Biglan, A., & Steinbock, E. (1978). Self-administered relaxation training and money deposits in the treatment of recurrent anxiety. *Journal of Consulting and Clinical Psychology, 46,* 1274–1283.

Lipsky, M., Kassinove, H., & Miller, N. (1980). Effects of rational-emotive imagery on the emotional adjustment of community mental health center patients. *Journal of Consulting and Clinical Psychology, 48,* 366–374.

Mahoney, M., & Arnkoff, D. Cognitive and self-control therapies. (1978). In S. Garfield & A. Bergin (Eds.), *Handbook of psychotherapy and behavior change: An empirical analysis* (2nd ed.). New York: Wiley.

Matthews, A., & Shaw, P. (1977). Cognitions related to anxiety: A pilot study of treatment. *Behaviour Therapy and Research, 15,* 503–505.

Mavissakalian, M., Michelson, L., Greenwald, D., Kornblith, S., & Greenwald, M. (1983). Cognitive-behavioral treatment of agoraphobia: Paradoxical intention vs. self-statement training. *Behaviour Research and Therapy, 21,* 75–86.

Meichenbaum, D. (1977). *Cognitive behavior modification: An integrative approach.* New York: Plenum Press.

Meichenbaum, D. (1985). *Stress inoculation training.* New York: Pergamon Press.

Merluzzi, T., Rudy, T., & Glass, C. (1981). The information-processing paradigm: Implications for clinical science. In T. Merluzzi, R. Glass, & M. Genest (Eds.), *Cognitive assessment.* New York: Guilford Press.

Moos, R. (1982). Coping with acute health crises. In T. Millon, C. Green, & R. Meagher (Eds.), *Handbook of clinical health psychology.* New York: Plenum Press.

Mowrer, O. (1960). *Learning theory and behaviour.* New York: Wiley.

Nicoletti, J. (1972). *Anxiety management training.* Unpublished doctoral dissertation, Colorado State University, Fort Collins.

Öst, L., Jerremalm, A., & Jansson, L. (1984). Individual response patterns and the effects of different behavioral methods in the treatment of agoraphobia. *Behaviour Research and Therapy, 22,* 697–707.

Öst, L., Jerremalm, A., & Johansson, J. (1981). Individual response patterns and the effects of different behavioral methods in the treatment of social phobia. *Behaviour Research and Therapy, 19,* 1–16.

Öst, L., Johansson, J., & Jerremalm, A. (1982). Individual response patterns and the effects of different behavioral methods in the treatment of claustrophobia. *Behaviour Research and Therapy, 20,* 445–460.

Öst, L., Lindahl, I., Sterner, U. & Jerremalm, A. (1984). Exposure *in vivo* vs applied relaxation in the treatment of blood phobia. *Behaviour Research and Therapy, 22,* 205–216.

Quillen, M., & Denney, D. (1982). Self-control of dysmenorrheic symptoms through pain management training. *Journal of Behavior Therapy and Experimental Psychiatry, 11,* 229–232.

Rachman, S. (1981). The primacy of affect: Some theoretical implications. *Behaviour Research and Therapy, 19,* 279–290.

Rachman, S. (1983). The modification of agoraphobic avoidance behaviour: Some fresh possibilities. *Behaviour Research and Therapy, 21,* 567–574.

Raskin, M., Johnson, G., & Rondestveldt, J. (1973). Chronic anxiety treated by feedback-induced muscle relaxation. *Archives of General Psychiatry, 28*, 263–267.

Rimm, D., & Sommervill, J. (1977). *Abnormal psychology.* New York: Academic Press.

Rosenthal, T., & Bandura, A. (1978). Psychological modeling: Theory and practice. In S. Garfield & A. Bergin (Eds.), *Handbook of psychotherapy and behavior change: An empirical analysis* (2nd ed.). New York: Wiley.

Rudenstam, K., & Bedrosian, R. (1977). An investigation of the effectiveness of desensitization and flooding with two types of phobia. *Behaviour Research and Therapy, 15*, 23–30.

Shahar, A., & Merbaum, M. (1981). The interaction between subject characteristics and self-control procedures in the treatment of interpersonal anxiety. *Cognitive Therapy and Research, 5* (2), 221–224.

Sherman, A. (1975). Two-year follow-up of training in relaxation as a behavioral self-management skill. *Behavior Therapy, 6*, 419–420.

Sherman, A., & Plummer, I. (1973). Training in relaxation as a behavioral self-management skill: An exploratory investigation. *Behavior Therapy, 4*, 543–550.

Shoemaker, J. (1976). *Treatments of anxiety neurosis.* Unpublished doctoral dissertation, Colorado State University, Fort Collins.

Stampfl, T. (1966). Cited in D. Lewis, Effects of serial CS presentation and other characteristics of the CS on the conditioned avoidance response. *Psychological Reports, 18*, 755–766.

Stampfl, T., & Levis, D. (1967). Essential of implosive therapy: A learning-theory-based psychodynamic behavioral therapy. *Journal of Abnormal Psychology, 72*, 496–503.

Suinn, R. (1976). Anxiety management training to control general anxiety. In J. Krumboltz & C. Thoresen (Eds.), *Counseling methods.* New York: Holt, Rinehart and Winston.

Suinn, R. (1977a). Treatment of phobias. In G. Harris (Ed.), *The group treatment of human problems: A social learning approach.* New York: Grune and Stratton.

Suinn, R. (1977b). *Manual for anxiety management training (AMT).* Fort Collins, CO: Rocky Mountain Behavioral Sciences Institute.

Suinn, R. (1980). Pattern A behaviors and heart disease: Intervention methods. In J. Ferguson & C. Taylor (Eds.), *The comprehensive handbook of behavioral medicine.* New York: Spectrum.

Suinn, R. (1982). Intervention with Type A behaviors: A critical review. *Journal of Consulting and Clinical Psychology, 50*, 933–949.

Suinn, R. (1983). Matching behavior therapy to stress theory: Why the mismatch? *Academic Psychology Bulletin, 5*, 417–434.

Suinn, R. (1984a). Generalized anxiety disorder. In S. Turner (Ed.), *Behavioral theories and treatment of anxiety* (pp. 279–320). New York: Plenum Press.

Suinn, R. (1984b). *Fundamentals of abnormal psychology.* Chicago: Nelson-Hall.

Suinn, R. (in press, a). Stress management by behavioral methods. In J. Nospitz & R. D. Coddington (Eds.), *American Psychiatric Association Task Force on Adjustment Reactions.* Washington, DC: American Psychiatric Association.

Suinn, R. (in press, b). Behavioral approaches to stress management. In M. Asken & J. May (Eds.), *Sport psychology: The psychological health of the athlete.* New York: Spectrum.

Suinn, R., & Bloom, L. (1978). Anxiety management training for Type A persons. *Journal of Behavioral Medicine, 1*, 25–35.

Thompson, S. (1981). Will it hurt less if I can control it? A complex answer to a simple question. *Psychological Bulletin, 90*, 89–101.

Townsend, R., House, J., & Addario, D. (1975). A comparison of biofeedback-mediated relaxation and group therapy in the treatment of chronic anxiety. *American Journal of Psychiatry, 132*, 598–601.

Weinberger, A., & Engelhart, R. (1976). Three group treatments for reduction of speech anxiety among students. *Perceptual Motor Skills, 43*, 1317–1318.

Wolpe, J. (1973). *The practice of behavior therapy* (2nd ed.) New York: Pergamon.

Woolfolk, R., Lehrer, P., McCann, B., & Rooney, A. (1982). Effects of progressive relaxation and meditation on cognitive and somatic manifestations of daily stress. *Behaviour Research and Therapy, 20*, 461–467.

Woodward, R., & Jones, R. (1980). Cognitive restructuring treatment: A controlled trial with anxious patients. *Behaviour Research and Therapy, 18*, 401–407.

Zajonc, R. (1980). Feeling and thinking. *American Psychologist, 35*, 151–175.

Zeiss, A., Lewinsohn, P., & Munoz, R. (1979). Nonspecific improvement effects in depression using interpersonal skills training, pleasant activity schedules, or cognitive training. *Journal of Consulting and Clinical Psychology, 47*, 427–439.

Zwemer, W., & Deffenbacher, J. (1984). Irrational beliefs, anger and anxiety. *Journal of Counseling Psychology, 31*, 391–393.

13

Posttraumatic Stress Disorder

DAVID W. FOY, CLYDE P. DONAHOE, JR., EDWARD M. CARROLL,
JOHANNA GALLERS, AND ROCHELLE RENO

Abstract

Although posttraumatic stress disorder (PTSD) is relatively new as a specific psychiatric diagnosis, reports in professional literature have described predictable intrusive thoughts, sleep disturbance, and avoidance behaviors following trauma exposure for many years. In chronic combat-related PTSD, symptoms of anxiety, disgust, alcohol abuse, suicidal thoughts, hostility, marital distress, depressions, and irritability are likely, along with core PTSD diagnostic symptoms. As yet, no controlled group studies of PTSD treatment have been reported. However, those single-case studies and descriptive reports currently available are reviewed in some detail. Five reports on non-combat-related PTSD and ten combat-related PTSD studies show consistency in the use of reexposure to cues involved in the original trauma to promote trauma processing. A case study demonstrating cognitive-behavioral treatment of combat-related PTSD is described. Future directions for treatment and research on PTSD are discussed, including the role of social support in treatment and suggestions for decreasing treatment dropout rates.

Introduction

The fact that individuals exposed to intense trauma often experience debilitating psychological sequelae has been described in professional literature since early in this century (e.g., Freud, Ferenczi, Abraham, Siminel, & Jones, 1921). Numerous reports document the persistence of severe psychological distress in survivors of concentration camps (Davidson, 1967); World War II combatants (Grinker & Spiegel, 1945); victims of natural disasters (Lindemann, 1944); Hiroshima survivors (Lifton, 1967); and transportation accident victims (Melick, Logue, & Frederick, 1982), with 25% prevalence estimates. However, the inclusion of posttraumatic stress disorder (PTSD) in standard diagnostic nomenclature is a recent event. It has been only 6 years since the 1980 edition of the *Diagnostic and Statistical Manual of Mental Disorders* (DSM-III) (American Psychiatric Association, 1980) listed the predictable social, emotional, and behavioral components of

David W. Foy, Clyde P. Donahoe, Jr., Edward M. Carroll, and Rochelle Reno. Psychology Service, West Los Angeles VA Medical Center, Brentwood Division, and UCLA Medical School, Los Angeles, California.

Johanna Gallers. Psychology Service, West Los Angeles VA Medical Center, Brentwood Division, Los Angeles, California.

PTSD in a new diagnostic category for the disorder (American Psychiatric Association, 1980). The specific diagnostic criteria currently in use are depicted in Table 13-1.

Findings from our own studies (Foy, Sipprelle, Rueger, & Carroll, 1984; Carroll, Rueger, Foy, & Donahoe, 1985) suggest that other specific symptoms that may also be associated with a positive PTSD diagnosis include tension or anxiety, disgust, alcohol abuse, suicidal thoughts, hostility, marital problems, depression, and irritability. These symptoms formed a significant discriminant function in two independent samples of Vietnam combat veterans. The extent to which these findings apply to victims of other types of trauma and to non-help-seeking victims remains to be investigated.

Although PTSD as a specific category is new, the phenomenology of psychological distress following trauma is not. Nevertheless, interest in conducting controlled research on PTSD treatment is only now emerging, perhaps following the recent trend by the popular media toward paying more attention to distress in Vietnam combat veterans. In the absence of a clear treatment of choice, the need for developing more effective methods of treating trauma victims is now firmly established. Despite the fact that no well-controlled group outcome studies have been published yet, a review of the existing case studies and anecdotal reports does provide valuable information about current PTSD treatment efforts. From these modest beginnings will emerge state-of-the-art standards to guide subsequent diagnostic, treatment, and treatment measurement efforts by PTSD researchers and clinicians.

TABLE 13.1 Diagnostic criteria for PTSD

A. Exposure to a significant stressor that would evoke symptoms of distress in almost everyone.
B. Reexperiencing of the trauma through at least one of the following:
    1. recurrent and intrusive memories of the event.
    2. recurrent dreams of the event.
    3. sudden acting or feeling as if the traumatic event were reoccurring because of an association with an environmental or ideational stimulus.
C. Numbing of responsiveness to or reduced involvement with the external world, beginning after the trauma, as shown by at least one of the following:
    1. markedly diminished interest in one or more significant activities.
    2. feeling of detachment or estrangement from others.
    3. constricted affect.
D. At least two of the following symptoms that were not present before the trauma:
    1. hyperalertness or exaggerated startle response.
    2. sleep disturbance.
    3. survivor guilt or guilt about behavior required for survival.
    4. memory impairment or trouble concentrating.
    5. avoidance of activities that arouse recollection of the traumatic event.
    6. intensification of symptoms by exposure to events that symbolize or resemble the traumatic event.
E. Subtypes
    1. PTSD, Acute
        a. symptom onset within six months of trauma.
        b. symptom duration less than six months.
    2. PTSD, Chronic or Delayed. Either of the following, or both:
        a. symptom duration six months or more (chronic).
        b. onset of symptoms at least six months after the trauma (delayed).

Source: From DSM-III (American Psychiatric Association, 1980).

Exposure to life-threatening events and human suffering during war constitutes the most frequent type of trauma associated with the development of PTSD. To date, there is more treatment literature on combat-related PTSD than for all other trauma types combined. Although there may be similarities among types of trauma in the development, course, and treatment of PTSD, the first actual cross-trauma comparison study has yet to be reported. Thus, although the DSM-III definition of an abnormal stressor is generic and makes no distinction between types of trauma, there is currently no empirical basis for such a diagnostic scheme. The literature review in our chapter follows the frequency distribution of PTSD articles currently found. Accordingly, the first section of this chapter is composed of two subsections: (1) treatment reports on PTSD from other than combat trauma; and (2) combat-related PTSD treatment reports. The second section is a controlled case study demonstrating cognitive-behavioral treatment in combat-related PTSD. A discussion of current status and future directions in PTSD treatment constitutes the final section of the chapter.

Treatment of PTSD in Victims of Non-Combat-Related Traumas

Over the past ten years, several authors have described the process of treatment in victims of accidents, natural disasters, and violent crimes. Discussing treatment issues, Dixon (1979) maintained that the therapist's role in helping trauma victims is to elicit memories of the trauma and encourage expression of the painful emotions. The resulting cognitive restoration was described as a means of regaining self-control. Similarly, Horowitz and Kaltreider (1979) presented three primary goals in the treatment of PTSD: (1) helping the individual regain a sense of competence and self-worth; (2) helping the individual continue realistic and adaptive actions; and (3) working through reactions to serious life events. Frederick (1984) suggested that systematic desensitization, flooding, hypnosis, and supportive therapy may be useful in reducing sensitivity to anxiety-provoking stimuli in PTSD. Pynoos & Eth (1984) described the experiences of children after witnessing the homicide of a parent and presented a developmental scheme detailing the kind of responses clinicians are likely to see in such children at each developmental landmark.

Since there are no well-controlled group studies yet available, our literature review is necessarily confined to descriptive reports of PTSD treatment. One such report (Kinzie, Fredrickson, Ben, Flick, & Karls, 1984) dealt with PTSD treatment among survivors of Cambodian concentration camps. DSM-III criteria were used to establish a positive PTSD diagnosis. Thirteen Cambodian refugees, six males and seven females, confined in concentration camps for 2 to 4 years, were treated in psychodynamic therapy. In an attempt to alleviate the observed PTSD symptoms of avoidance, startle reactions, emotional numbness, intrusive thoughts, and nightmares, the refugees were encouraged to talk about their experiences in the camps. However, Kinzie et al. reported that the refugees were reluctant to do so and that discussion of the camp experiences was related to symptom exacerbation. It was suggested that cultural differences may have been responsible for the treatment response difficulties.

Lindy, Green, Grace, and Titchner (1983) recently reported on the treatment of 30 survivors of the Beverly Hills Supper Club fire in Ohio. Short-term psychodynamic psychotherapy was systematically provided in an effort to alleviate PTSD symptoms.

PTSD positive diagnosis was made on the basis of DSM-III criteria. Twenty-two therapists were used to treat the 15 male and 15 female survivors. In conducting therapy over a 6- to 8-week period, the therapists used the following preestablished guidelines:

1. Survivors were instructed to relate all thoughts and feelings about the incident experienced, before, during, and after the fire.
2. Therapists were instructed to link elicited affect back to the trauma.
3. Grief reactions were to be encouraged.
4. Anticipation of something terrible happening in the present was to be interpreted as a fear from the past and not a reality.
5. Guilt and shame were to be interpreted as irrational.
6. Feelings of rage were to be interpreted as feelings of helplessness.

The Psychiatric Evaluation Form, a measure of 19 dimensions of psychological distress, was administered in order to identify psychological disorders other than PTSD. Based on the Psychiatric Evaluation Form results, 9 survivors were diagnosed as having PTSD only, and 21 others as having multiple diagnoses including PTSD. Of the 30 survivors who began the course of treatment, only 10 completed the process and reported symptom reduction. Those individuals diagnosed as "PTSD only" were most likely to complete treatment.

Cienfuegos and Monelli (1983) reported on the treatment of 39 victims or relatives of victims of political repression in Chile by using testimony of their victimization as a therapeutic technique. Although the authors did not use an objective measure of PTSD, symptoms were noted that appeared to support a probable PTSD diagnosis in many of the survivors. Symptoms reported were feelings of helplessness, anxiety, sleep disturbance, memory impairment, fear, social withdrawal, irritability, loss of appetite, and psychosomatic complaints. Descriptions of the repressive activities, along with other historical details, were elicited during the initial therapy session. During the next session, an audiotape was made of the testimony when the individual repeated the story. Following this session, the individual was instructed to write an essay denouncing the violence and injustice suffered. In subsequent sessions, the experiences were discussed in the context of the rest of the individual's life so that the trauma could be integrated. The course of treatment ranged from 3 to 6 weeks in duration. Twelve of the 15 torture cases reportedly experienced a complete diminution of acute symptomatology. Eleven of 15 relatives of executed prisoners achieved symptom control, and 3 of the 5 exiles reported control of symptoms following treatment. Only in the cases of relatives of missing persons was the "testimony" technique found not effective.

In a report of PTSD related to transportation accidents, McCaffrey and Fairbank (1984) presented controlled case studies of two individuals, exposed to this type of trauma, who met DSM-III diagnostic criteria for PTSD. In the first case report, a 31-year-old Army aircraft mechanic who had experienced two separate traumatic events related to his work was treated. In the first incident, he had served as a guard at a helicopter crash site for an extended period while the bodies of crew members whom he knew were recovered and examined. A second incident involved a fatal helicopter crash during a flight on which he had narrowly escaped being a passenger. Shortly after this crash he developed sleep disturbances, nightmares, and guilt; experienced difficulty concentrating; and avoided flying in helicopters. These symptoms subsequently intensified to include severe anxiety surrounding recollections of the traumatic events. The second subject, a 28-year-old woman, presented PTSD symptoms after being involved in four separate automobile accidents within a 4-month period. The patient was injured in one of the accidents, and the car she was driving was demolished in two of the accidents.

During the assessment phase, each subject self-monitored the number and content of nightmares and trauma-related dreams, and gave subjective units of discomfort (SUDS) ratings of anxiety levels at 3-hour intervals during the day. Both subjects participated in a tripartite assessment procedure consisting of psychophysiological, cognitive, and behavioral measures. In the psychophysiological assessment procedure, heart rate and skin resistance level were assessed during the presentation of a video tape consisting of both nontraumatic scenes and scenes related to their particular traumas. Cognitive measures of anxiety were assessed by an 11-point fear thermometer. A behavioral index was obtained by recording whether or not the subject voluntarily terminated the assessment before completion.

The course of treatment consisted of relaxation training, implosive therapy, and self-directed *in vivo* exposure to fearful stimuli. Following two sessions of relaxation training and home practice, subject 1 then had four implosive therapy sessions focusing on his survivor guilt. In four additional sessions, the subject was instructed to visualize a graded series of flying exercises and was encouraged to engage in self-directed *in vivo* exposure to helicopter flying. Subject 2 was presented with a combination of symptom-contingent cues and fear-inducing cues during four implosive therapy sessions. A reduction in anxiety during treatment sessions was reported, but nightmare frequency actually increased. At the end of the fourth session, the patient related her present fears to a past trauma involving her mother. Subsequent implosive therapy sessions focused on her fears and guilt from both the past and present trauma. She was also instructed to engage in *in vivo* driving experiences. Results from those cases showed that administration of a combination of relaxation training, implosive therapy, and *in vivo* exposure was followed by reductions in PTSD symptom intensity in both subjects. Subject 1 returned to active flight status, and subject 2 reported driving without anxiety. Idiosyncratic responses to the tripartite assessment were found. Subject 1 demonstrated a posttreatment reduction primarily in level of physiological arousal to the traumatic stimuli, and subject 2 showed greater decreases in cognitive measures of distress.

In the final case study to be considered, Rychtarik, Silverman, Van Landingham, and Prue (1984), reported on treatment of a 22-year-old female incest victim using implosive therapy. The authors hypothesized that the subject had become conditioned to numerous stimuli present during the incest trauma, which subsequently elicited high levels of arousal. Additionally, stimuli not directly associated with the trauma originally, such as the presence of other older men, elicited high levels of anxiety as a result of stimulus generalization. It was further hypothesized that systematic exposure to the intrusive memories in the absence of avoidance behavior—in her case, the use of alcohol—would reduce symptom intensity and frequency of occurrence. During a 9-day inpatient stay, therapy was administered in 5 sessions conducted over consecutive days. Each implosive therapy session lasted 80 to 90 minutes. Each session was preceded and followed by a 10-minute relaxation period. During the sessions, the subject was exposed through imagery to the scene where her father first forced sexual relations on her. The scene was augmented by having the subject report past and present thoughts and events related to the incident. During each session, a technician in an adjoining room monitored electrodermal activity and signaled increases and decreases in anxiety level to the therapist. Additionally, on each treatment day, the subject was presented with a 5-minute imaginal scene in which she was working side by side with an older man (her stepfather). The scene was preceded and followed by 5 minutes of relaxation. The purpose of this probe scene was to measure treatment-related extinction of generalized arousal to real-life stressors similar to the original trauma. Data collected on autonomic arousal during successive treatment sessions showed a marked reduction in symptom intensity. Upon discharge, there was a sharp decrease in the incidence of incest-related memories, which soon became nonexistent. At 1-year follow-up, the subject continued to report that thoughts of incest were no longer a problem.

In summary, there have been five recent treatment reports in which various psychological methods were used to promote trauma processing in victims from several kinds of natural or man-made disasters. Significantly, each report presents a rationale for reexposing victims to cues involved in the original trauma in order for processing to be accomplished. Several treatment methods representing diverse theoretical frameworks were presented as possible therapeutic strategies for achieving this objective.

Treatment of Combat-Related PTSD

A steadily growing literature on the treatment and management of psychological problems related to service in the Vietnam War has emerged during the last decade. Much of this material consists of discussions of diagnosis and assessment (e.g., Atkinson, Spar, Sheff, White, & Fitzsimmons, 1984; Goodwin, 1980; Keane, Malloy, & Fairbank, 1985); common treatment themes (e.g., Egendorf, 1975); establishing therapeutic alliances (e.g., Haley, 1978; Williams, 1980); and intervention strategies (e.g., Figley, 1978; Horowitz & Solomon, 1975). Although the clinical literature on war-related PTSD is rich in observation and recommended intervention, systematic and controlled treatment outcome data are almost entirely lacking. Egendorf (1982, p. 904) stated in his review of PTSD-related research: "Systematic study in this area has, however, been scant. For example, no major research on clinical outcomes has yet been reported." Unfortunately, we would still have to agree with Egendorf's observation at the time of this writing.

The sizable presence of chronic or cyclical forms of PTSD among Vietnam combat veterans is now well documented (e.g., Foy et al., 1984; Penk, Robinowitz, Roberts, Patterson, Dolan, & Atkins, 1981). However, the *Legacies of Vietnam* (Center for Policy Research, 1981) study suggested that at least some veterans have experienced decreased levels of war-related stress in the years since reentry, possibly as a result of naturally occurring support systems. Thus, a central question for therapy outcome research is whether or not therapeutic interventions can promote clinically significant reductions in subjective distress and psychosocial dysfunction beyond what may occur spontaneously. A more specific concern for therapy outcome research is the identification of clinically effective and cost-effective therapeutic modalities. Additionally, identifying variations in treatment response as a function of individual variables such as race, marital status, and diagnostic complexity is important. Although the existing data base is so sparse as not even to scratch the surface of these issues, there are several descriptive or single case reports that are suggestive of therapeutic modalities worthy of exploration.

Group Therapy

The group therapy format is probably the most frequently used and widely discussed modality in clinical work with Vietnam veterans. Starting with the Vietnam veterans' self-help movement (Shatan, 1973), rap groups have been the primary forum for psychological and social intervention. These groups are multifaceted and may function to reduce stigmatization, promote pride in military service and survival, allow expression of anger and grief, and provide a sense of community (Wilson, 1980). Although clinicians working with Vietnam veterans believe that group therapy assists adjustment and symptom reduction, controlled empirical evaluation of this treatment approach for PTSD is lacking.

Milieu Therapy

Recently, there has been a trend within Veterans Administration (VA) Medical Centers toward the development of specialized inpatient treatment units for Vietnam veterans. These programs typically deemphasize the use of medications in favor of psychosocial interventions. For example, Berman, Price, and Gusman (1982) described a 90-bed inpatient treatment program developed at the VA Medical Center in Palo Alto, California. The unit is open to all Vietnam-era veterans, and group therapy is the primary mode of treatment. Within this modality, each patient reviews his combat and military experiences, is encouraged to take responsibility for his behavior, and receives social support. Psychosocial rehabilitation is also provided to assist in the transition back to the community. An ad hoc program evaluation based on staff ratings for a random sample of 40 program graduates showed that 60% were judged "program successes."

A somewhat different inpatient program at the VA Medical Center in Miami, Florida, has been described by Starkey and Ashlock (1984). Six to eight veterans, each carefully screened for positive PTSD diagnosis, participated in an intensive 3-week program of group therapy, education, psychosocial rehabilitation, and modeling by "successful" veterans. Data collected pre- and posttreatment indicated a reduction in distress and improved clinical profiles on the Minnesota Multiphasic Personality Inventory (MMPI) for veterans who completed the program. Although both programs appear promising, the preliminary analyses were based on small samples and lacked comparison data from control samples.

Hypnosis

Several case reports describe the successful use of hypnotic recall of traumatic events and the accompanying emotional "abreaction" to relieve the distress of "war neuroses." Leahy and Martin (1967) treated a veteran with a 20-year history of anxiety symptoms related to a traumatic incident in which an officer was killed. Treatment consisted of repeated reconstruction of the event with the use of hypnosis, which led to considerable emotional arousal and release. The subject was found to be symptom-free at an 8-month follow-up. Balson and Dempster (1980) describe a treatment procedure used with 15 Vietnam combat veterans suffering from combat stress syndromes. The 8 to 20 treatment sessions consisted of deep hypnotic reconstruction of traumatic events and emotional abreaction. The authors report that short-term success was achieved with all subjects and that symptom removal was maintained at a 6-month follow-up for 12 of the 15 subjects.

Behavior Therapy

It is not surprising that behavioral treatment approaches useful with other anxiety-based disorders have also been used with combat-related PTSD. One of the first case reports based on a behavioral conceptualization of war stress was reported by Little and James (1964). They proposed that exposure to trauma and subsequent symptoms of anxiety and avoidance behavior could be viewed as an incident of one-trial learning. That is, anxiety responses to neutral stimuli were the result of a single conditioned stimulus–unconditioned stimulus (CS–UCS) (traumatic event) pairing. The persistence of the anxiety disorder was attributed to instrumentally learned avoidance responses that were reinforced by decreases in anxiety and sympathetic arousal following the avoidant behavior. The authors report the successful treatment of a "phobic disorder" by means of imaginal exposure to the subject's traumatic war memories.

Both systematic desensitization and flooding procedures have been reported in the case history literature on war-related anxiety problems. Kipper (1977) described a variant of systematic desensitization used in treating anxiety reactions to the Yom Kippur War. Subjects were exposed *in vivo* to traumatic combat stimuli (e.g., bandaged persons, war-related sounds) in a hierarchical order following deep-muscle relaxation. Three clinical cases were presented in which these procedures were used successfully. Follow-up data were not reported.

Keane and Kaloupek (1982) described the use of an imaginal flooding technique that repeatedly exposed the patient to the intrusive thoughts associated with traumatic Vietnam War events. This case study has the virtue of employing a more refined and objective data base than the simple clinical observations used in previous case studies. The authors employed daily self-monitoring (subjective distress, hours of sleep, frequency of nightmares); psychological testing (Spielberger State Anxiety Inventory), and physiological response monitoring (heart rate). These data were collected before and during the course of 19 treatment sessions. The imaginal flooding procedure was followed by a sizable decrease in PTSD symptoms and an increase in adaptive social functioning, both of which were maintained at a 12-month follow-up.

Similarly, a cognitive behavioral approach was described by Miller and Buchbinder (1979) in a single case study with combat trauma. In addition to systematic desensitization, unrealistic beliefs were actively challenged in the manner proposed by Ellis and Harper (1975). Reductions in anxiety, aggression, and insomnia were reported by the authors after 12 weeks of treatment, and maintenance was achieved over a 48-week follow-up.

Drug Therapy

The status of the literature on drug therapy with PTSD is the same as that of psychological forms of intervention; that is, no well-controlled studies have yet been reported. A couple of recent preliminary reports, however, do seem to offer some direction for further clinical trials and controlled research. Kolb, Burris, and Griffiths (1984) reported that two adrenergic blocking agents, propranolol and clonidine, were useful in controlling explosiveness, nightmares, and intrusive thinking. Additionally, benzodiazepines and lithium carbonate have been reported as helpful in reducing PTSD symptom severity (Van der Kolk, 1983).

To summarize, ten published reports were highlighted in the review of combat-related PTSD treatment in order to illustrate the range of treatments that have been used. Although group, milieu, hypnosis, exposure, and drug forms of therapy have been described as separate and distinct, current clinical practice almost surely includes a combination of these modalities. In fact, it is not difficult to find a case in which all the modalities would be useful and synergistic in terms of case management and treatment outcome.

Case History

Mr. K, a 43-year-old Vietnam combat veteran, was the second-oldest child from a working-class family dominated by a harsh father. His mother died of cancer when he was 13 and his father remarried a year later. Although Mr. K did well in school, he dropped out of school at age 17 to join the Navy for 4 years. During his Navy tour he obtained a GED and married the first woman he had ever dated. They produced two children. Following discharge from the Navy he had difficulty finding satisfactory civilian employment and decided to join the Army.

After 6 years in the Army, he was sent to Vietnam as a staff sergeant in charge of a vehicle maintenance team. This tour of duty was punctuated with frequent traumatic combat experiences, including the death of a close friend, his shooting a Vietcong soldier at close range, seeing the death of a truck mate during a convoy attack, finding a burned crew inside a disabled tank, finding the remains of a driver inside a disabled personnel carrier, and witnessing the demolition of a village. The death of his close friend by sniper fire in a "safe" area was particularly traumatic; Mr. K felt personally responsible for their having been in an avoidable dangerous situation.

When he returned from Vietnam his marriage ended in divorce and he began drinking heavily. He received several Army disciplinary actions, usually for going absent without leave. After 3 years, Mr. K volunteered for a second tour in Vietnam, which, in contrast to the first tour, was relatively uneventful.

Following his second Vietnam tour he took a discharge from the Army. During the next 15 years, his life seriously deteriorated. He had two short marriages, lived in five different states, and had a long series of various jobs. He began having Vietnam-related nightmares and flashbacks. His abusive drinking became chronic, resulting in several stints on skid row. In addition to numerous alcohol treatments, there were several psychiatric hospitalizations for depression, anxiety, paranoia, and suicide attempts. Despite his frequent contact with VA mental health programs, neither Mr. K nor his treatment providers identified his Vietnam experiences as a primary source of his problems.

Finally, after another unsuccessful drug-oriented hospitalization, he began psychotherapy with a focus on PTSD, and he agreed to participate in a chronological review of his Vietnam experiences. However, when the review had reached the sixth week of the first tour, with no highly traumatic events having yet been described, his symptoms had increased to such a magnitude that it appeared there was a risk of renewed drinking or suicide. In order to provide more immediate relief, the therapist (Reno) decided to join the first and second authors (Foy and Donahoe) to provide Mr. K with a program of flooding therapy.

Flooding

Mr. K was first given the diagnostic assessment battery described in Table 13.2 and was found to be PTSD-positive on all measures. In particular, he met all the criteria for a DSM-III diagnosis of PTSD, according to the PTSD Diagnostic Scale (Foy et al., 1984). In order to evaluate the efficacy of the treatment, Mr. K was administered the measures described in Table 13.3. All these measures were given pre- and posttreatment; the psychophysiological assessment was also given at 4 and 11 months posttreatment to obtain data on the maintenance of treatment results.

Mr. K was hospitalized 1 week prior to the beginning of treatment. A hierarchy of traumatic events was developed by having Mr. K identify and rank-order his worst experiences from both tours. Six events were identified, with the top rank given to the death of his buddy. The treatment consisted of having Mr. K repetitively recount the events and his thoughts and feelings during the highest scene on his hierarchy. In order to assess change in physiological arousal during treatment, a heart rate finger monitor was attached to one hand. The therapist served as facilitator by asking questions to elicit more detail or to focus greater attention to the subject's thoughts, feelings, and physiological states (e.g., "What was he wearing?" "How did you feel?"). In addition, the therapist promoted cognitive restructuring by the subject for those elements of the scene that evoked self-blame or anger. The subject's causal assumptions about his role in the scene and the tragic outcome were challenged. For example, a step-by-step sequence of events was reconstructed demonstrating that no realistic alternative course of action could have been taken to avoid his buddy's death. The average length of sessions was 1–2 hours, with the traumatic scene being repeated two or three times. Sessions were conducted three times a week for 3 weeks.

The procedure was described to Mr. K prior to the first session. Although he was given a choice, he was encouraged to start with his most traumatic event, the death of his buddy. His anxiety level was extremely high at the initiation of treatment. Following the first session, treatment appeared to be in jeopardy. The subject sobbed repeatedly during each repetition of the "buddy" scene. That evening he stated a desire to leave the hospital and probably would have done so had he not been kept under close surveillance by ward staff and offered all available support. The next day, despite a difficult night

TABLE 13.2 PTSD diagnostic measures

Instrument	Description
Minnesota Multiphasic Personality Inventory	Malloy, Fairbank, and Keane (1983) have found that an MMPI profile of F-28 is characteristic of Vietnam combat veterans with a diagnosis of PTSD.
Combat Exposure Scale (Foy et al., 1984)	This scale operationalizes degree of combat exposure. It has seven items, ranging from no combat involvement to having served three tours of duty.
PTSD Diagnostic Scale (Foy et al., 1984)	This scale uses relevant items from the Problem Checklist and Military History Indexes to assess PTSD on DSM-III criteria. This Problem Checklist has 39 items that assess a range of adjustment problems and psychological symptoms. Fourteen items are characteristic of PTSD according to DSM-III criteria (e.g., nightmares, difficulty falling asleep, vivid unpleasant memories, and excessive jumpiness). Other items are of a more general nature, assessing such problems as excessive eating, sexual problems, and marked self-consciousness.
	Military History Indexes are determined from a structured interview designed to obtain premilitary, military, and postmilitary adjustment history. The Premilitary Adjustment Index covers family stability, relationship with parents, school achievement, disciplinary and legal problems, and social activity. The Military Adjustment Index covers substance use, disciplinary actions, psychiatric contacts, and military honors. The Postmilitary Index covers vocational functioning, legal problems, psychiatric treatment, and current family and interpersonal relationships.
Psychophysiological Assessment (Malloy et al., 1983)	This assessment measures physiological arousal, subjective discomfort, and behavioral avoidance to combat stimuli. In this procedure, the subject views videotaped slide presentations of a family on a trip to a shopping mall ("neutral" scenes), followed by presentations of a Vietnam combat platoon on a patrol ("combat" scenes). The latter scenes become progressively violent. While the patient views the tape, physiological measures are monitored, and after each scene, the patient gives a subjective rating of discomfort related to the scene. The patient is asked to terminate the procedure if he becomes too distressed to continue, giving a measure of behavioral avoidance.

TABLE 13.3 Evaluation measures

Instrument	Description
Psychophysiological assessment	(See Table 13.1 for description.)
Symptom ratings	From an interview, 23 symptom complaints were elicited from the patient. Each symptom was rated daily on a scale from 1 to 10 to assess the severity of the symptom.
Hamilton Depression Scale	This is a standard, commonly used scale to assess degree of depression. It was administered to the patient biweekly one week before and after treatment.
Sleep ratings	The night nurse on duty in the patients' ward monitored how frequently the patient got out of bed each night.
Medication requests	The patient was prescribed Xanax (1 mg. PRN) for anxiety and chloral hydrate (500 mg. PRN) for sleep. From the hospital charts, it was possible to monitor the frequency of medication requests pre- and posttreatment.

during which he experienced nightmares and severe anxiety reactions, he reluctantly consented to continue. By the third session he was experiencing some subjective relief and was a willing participant in treatment from that point on. It is of interest that the first 5 sessions were spent on the first scene. Subsequent scenes were associated with only a minimal level of arousal and were covered much more rapidly—presumably a result of generalization or lower positioning on the hierarchy.

Treatment Results

Flooding was found to be effective in terms of most of the evaluation measures described in Table 13.3. For the psychophysiological assessment, there were changes in physiological arousal, in subjective distress, and in behavioral avoidance of combat stimuli from pre- to posttreatment. More specifically, Figure 13.1 shows that there was a dramatic decrease in heart rate between the beginning and the end of treatment, and that the decrease was maintained at follow-up measures, especially at 11 months. The decrease in respiration rate, shown in Figure 13.1, was less dramatic but was seen both posttreatment and at the 11-month follow-up. It is also of interest to note that there was a decrease in heart rate and respiration in response to "neutral" stimuli as well as to combat stimuli, suggesting, perhaps, that there may have been a decrease in general physiological arousal as well as arousal specific to combat material. Figure 13.1 shows that subjective reports of anxiety or other unpleasant emotions also decreased in intensity after treatment, and this improvement was maintained at the time of follow-up. It was also observed that behavioral avoidance of combat material diminished after the flooding. Mr. K completed exposure to only five combat scenes prior to flooding. After treatment and at both follow-ups, he was able to sustain exposure to all nine combat scenes.

Evaluation results associated with other measures are tabulated in Table 13.4. Only the highest pretreatment mean symptom ratings are presented. It is clear that there were substantial declines in the distress associated with dreams, depression, and guilt. There were also declines, albeit smaller ones, with generalized fear and time spent ruminating about Vietnam. The improvement in depression was echoed by the Hamilton scores, which showed marked decreases during the flooding treatment. Mr. K also requested less medication after flooding. This result is reflected most prominently by the decrease in the frequency of requests for Xanax, an antianxiety drug. It does not appear that the frequency of requests for the drug for sleep (chloral hydrate) changed much, if at all.

Figure 13.2 shows the within-treatment changes in heart rate. This figure clearly illustrates the efficacy and speed with which flooding worked in reducing arousal measured by heart rate. During the first trial there was a huge initial increase in heart rate from 94 beats per minute to 124 beats per minute. By the third trial, this increase had disappeared. By the 16th trial, not only had the arousal spike not reappeared, but the general arousal to Mr. K's most traumatic scene declined well below the baseline level.

Discussion

The treatment results illustrate the effectiveness of flooding for Mr. K. There was considerable improvement noted in reported distress, in physiological arousal, and in

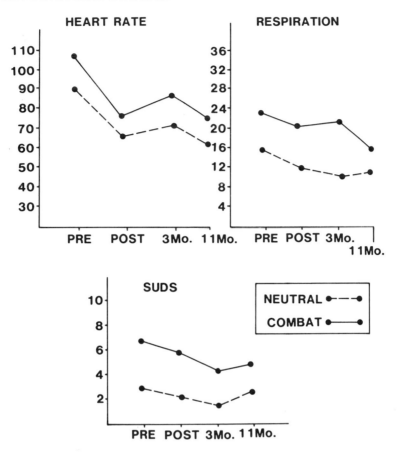

FIG. 13.1 Changes in responses of a combat trauma subject before and after flooding treatment using the psychophysiological assessment method developed by Malloy et al. (1983).

TABLE 13.4 Treatment evaluations (pre- and posttreatment)

	Pretreatment	Posttreatment
Mean symptom ratings		
Vietnam dreams	8.4	2.9
Depression	7.7	4.3
Generalized fear	8.0	7.0
Ruminating about Vietnam	8.7	6.7
Guilt	8.6	4.9
Mean Hamilton scores	27.0	11.5
Mean sleep disturbances/night	1.8	1.2
Medication requests		
Xanax	8	2
Chloral hydrate	4	3

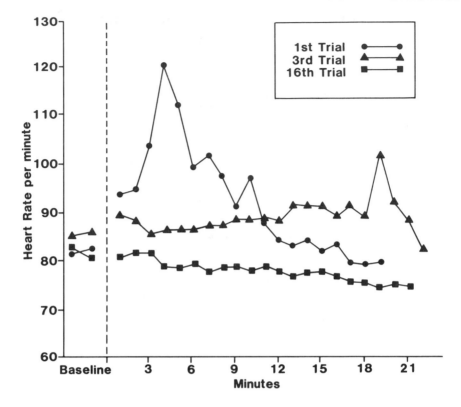

FIG. 13.2 Heart rate response in selected flooding treatment trials with a combat trauma subject.

symptomatology. In the year after flooding, Mr. K has had less frequent and less intense nightmares and flashbacks. For example, for the first time in years, Mr. K is able to get a full night's sleep; when a nightmare does awaken him, he can readily return to sleep. As one might expect, the flooding has been less helpful in treating his alcoholism; he has been hospitalized briefly on two occasions for abusive drinking. He also has continued to work with his therapist in order to improve interpersonal relationships and set realistic vocational goals. It appears that flooding has reduced the acute symptomatology, allowing Mr. K, at last, to begin the process of rebuilding his life that had been so devastated by his responses to his Vietnam experiences.

Current Status and Future Directions in PTSD Treatment

Although there are only the meager beginnings of a PTSD treatment literature, several helpful trends are already apparent.

1. Almost all therapeutic approaches use some sort of review and reprocessing of traumatic events. The review procedures range from the informal discussions of rap

groups to the highly structured, systematic, and repetitive procedures of flooding, implosion, or systematic desensitization. Psychodynamically oriented writers (e.g., Horowitz, 1976; Kardiner & Spiegal, 1947) have also emphasized the importance of ideational recall and emotional working through of traumatic events. The pervasiveness of this theme in the treatment literature strongly suggests that empirical evaluation of trauma-processing techniques needs to be a high priority for future treatment outcome research.

2. A second overarching theme is the significance of social support in establishing therapy rapport and modifying posttraumatic stress responses. In particular, the rap group and milieu therapy formats emphasize both social support and social accountability as necessary elements for change. Accordingly, the role of social support needs to be evaluated by outcome research, both alone and in combination with trauma-processing procedures.

3. The dropout rate for PTSD treatment seems high. Since avoidance and escape behaviors characterize many victims' responses to traumatic cues, it is perhaps understandable that these may again predominate to abort the course of therapy. Our general strategy is to strongly encourage hospitalization during flooding sessions so that a supportive ward environment is assured. If therapy must be rendered on an outpatient basis, a treatment contract can be used to encourage the individual's continuing participation in the full course of therapy. Also important is the involvement of a significant other (spouse, family member, close friend) to provide a social "safety net" during exposure therapy, which may be a period of increased psychological vulnerability for many individuals.

4. With combat-related PTSD in particular, it is becoming increasingly clear that concomitant psychological dysfunction extends well beyond the acute symptoms listed as DSM-III diagnostic criteria. Disruptions in marital, family, and friendship relations have been consistently reported (e.g., Carroll et al., 1985; Roberts et al., 1982). In particular, PTSD seems to interfere with the individual's ability to communicate positively, as in sharing thoughts and feelings and other types of problem solving. In addition, both PTSD victims and their spouses report heightened hostility by the victim and increased fear of aggression by the mate. Although these findings may not be equally applicable across types of trauma, the need for involving the victim's family in education about PTSD, as well as their role in providing support and perhaps participating in communication skills retraining, is underscored.

5. Horowitz (1976) has proposed a cyclical model of PTSD in which control of symptoms follows overcontrol (avoidance) and undercontrol (intrusion) patterns. Different treatment strategies have been suggested to match the two phases: trauma processing for overcontrol, and supportive therapy for undercontrol. Empirical testing of this model could help identify predictable trauma response styles. It may be that some individuals show both elements of avoidance and intrusion, whereas in others, one response style or the other predominates. Appropriate use of such findings could ensure better matching of individuals to treatment type and could reduce the dropout rate.

6. The optimal therapeutic outcome for an individual experiencing PTSD is for the traumatic event to be accepted and integrated in such a way that the individual profits from it. Beneficial consequences could include increased positive motivation for achievement and growth, increased empathy for others experiencing distressing life events,

establishment of life goals to include providing service to other trauma victims, and improved coping attitudes and skills for meeting subsequent life challenges. When a person who has survived a severe trauma is able to acknowledge the experience and share it with others, the potential for beneficial consequences is expanded beyond the indi\v.d- ual himself. In this way, inspiring others becomes possible and serves to enhance and greatly extend the personal growth derived from the PTSD experience. The individual whose treatment was described in the case study specifically asked the authors to use accounts of his experiences to help educate other trauma victims and treatment provid- ers about PTSD. Additionally, he has personally spoken to professional groups about his own perceptions of his combat trauma and the treatment he received.

Trauma processing involves both behavioral and cognitive elements. A first step is repeated reexposure to cues of the original traumatic event so that escape/avoidance responses to trauma cues are controlled. The focus of processing then becomes primarily cognitive as the task of integrating the experience is taken on. The nature of the relationship between the behavioral and cognitive components in terms of contribution to treatment outcome is currently unknown. Future controlled research could be aimed at teasing out independent and interactive effects of these treatment components.

Acknowledgments

Partial support for the preparation of this chapter was provided by Rehabilitation Research and Training Center Grant No. G-009006802 funds to David W. Foy by the National Institute for Handicapped Research. The skilled technical assistance of Kelly Cline is gratefully acknowledged.

References

American Psychiatric Association. (1980). *Diagnostic and statistical manual of mental disorders* (3rd ed.). Washington, DC: Author.
Atkinson, R. M., Sparr, L. F., Sheff, A. G., White, R., & Fitzsimmons, J. T. (1984). Diagnosis of posttraumatic stress disorder in Vietnam veterans: Preliminary findings. *American Journal of Psychiatry, 141* (5), 694– 696.
Balson, P., & Dempster, C. (1980). Treatment of war neuroses from Vietnam. *Comprehensive Psychiatry, 21,* 167–176.
Berman, S., Price, S., & Gusman, F. (1982). An inpatient program for Vietnam combat veterans in a Veterans Administration Hospital. *Hospital and Community Psychiatry, 33,* 919–922.
Carroll, E. M., Rueger, D. B., Foy, D. W., & Donahoe, C. P. (1985). Vietnam combat veterans with posttrau- matic stress disorder: An analysis of marital and cohabitating adjustment. *Journal of Abnormal Psychology, 94,* 329–337.
Cienfuegos, A. J., & Monelli, C. (1983). The testimony of political repression as a therapeutic instrument. *American Journal of Orthopsychiatry, 53*(1), 43–51.
Davidson, S. (1967). A clinical classification of psychiatric disturbances of Holocaust survivors and their treatment. *The Israel Annals of Psychiatry and Related Disciplines, 5,* 96–98.
Dixon, S. (1979). *Working with people in crisis.* St. Louis: Mosley.
Egendorf, A. (1975). Vietnam veterans' rap groups and themes of postwar life. *Journal of Social Issues, 31*(4), 111–124.
Egendorf, A. (1982). The postwar healing of Vietnam veterans: Recent research. *Hospital and Community Psychiatry, 33,* 901–908.

Egendorf, A., Kaduschin, C., Laufer, R., Rothbart, G., and Sloan, L. (1981). *Legacies of Vietnam: Comparative adjustment of veterans and their peers.* New York: Center for Policy Research.

Ellis, A., & Harper, R. A. (1975). *A guide to rational living.* Englewood Cliffs, NJ: Prentice-Hall.

Figley, C. R. (Ed.). (1978). *Stress disorders among Vietnam veterans.* New York: Brunner-Mazel.

Foy, D. W., Sipprelle, R. C., Rueger, D. B., & Carroll, E. M. (1984). Etiology of posttraumatic stress disorder in Vietnam veterans: Analysis of premilitary, military, and combat exposure influences. *Journal of Consulting and Clinical Psychology, 52,* 79–87.

Frederick, C. J. (1984). *Post-traumatic stress reactions of victims of violence and crime: Diagnostic and treatment considerations.* Unpublished manuscript.

Freud, S., Ferenczi, S., Abraham, K., Simmel, E., & Jones, E. (1921). *Psychoanalysis and the war neurosis.* New York: International Psychoanalytic Press.

Goodwin, J. (1980). The etiology of combat-related posttraumatic stress disorder. In T. Williams (Ed.), *Posttraumatic stress disorders of the Vietnam veteran.* Cincinnati, OH: Disabled American Veterans.

Grinker, R. R., & Spiegel, J. P. (1945). *Men under stress.* New York: Blakiston.

Haley, S. (1978). Treatment implications of post-combat stress response syndromes for mental health professionals. In C. Figley (Ed.), *Stress disorders among Vietnam veterans.* New York: Brunner-Mazel.

Horowitz, M. (1976). *Stress response syndromes.* New York: Jason Aronson.

Horowitz, M. J., & Kaltreider, N. (1979). Brief therapy of stress response syndromes. *Psychiatric Clinics of North America, 2,* 365–378.

Horowitz, M., & Solomon, G. (1975). A prediction of delayed stress response syndromes in Vietnam veterans. *Journal of Social Issues, 31*(4), 67–80.

Kardiner, A., & Spiegal, H. (1947). *War stress and neurotic illness.* New York: Harker.

Keane, T. M., & Kaloupek, D. G. (1982). Imaginal flooding in the treatment of a posttraumatic stress disorder. *Journal of Consulting and Clinical Psychology, 50,* 138–140.

Keane, T. M., Malloy, P. F., & Fairbank, J. A. (1985). The empirical development of an MMPI subscale for the assessment of combat-related posttraumatic stress disorder. *Journal of Consulting and Clinical Psychology, 52,* 888–891.

Kinzie, J. D., Fredrickson, R. H., Ben, R., Flick, J., & Karls, W. (1984). Posttraumatic stress disorder among survivors of Cambodian concentration camps. *American Journal of Psychiatry, 141*(5), 645–650.

Kipper, D. A. (1977). Behavior therapy for fears brought on by war experiences. *Journal of Consulting and Clinical Psychology, 45,* 216–221.

Kolb, L. C., Burris, B. C., & Griffiths, S. (1984). Propranolol and clonidine in the treatment of the chronic posttraumatic stress disorders of war. In B. A. Van der Kolk (Ed.), *Post-traumatic stress disorder: Psychological and biological sequelae,* Washington, DC: American Psychiatric Press.

Leahy, M. R., & Martin, I. C. (1967). Successful abreaction after twenty years. *British Journal of Psychiatry, 113,* 383–385.

Lifton, R. J. (1967). *Death in life: The survivors of Hiroshima.* New York: Random House.

Lindemann, E. (1944). Symptomatology and management of acute grief. *American Journal of Psychiatry, 101,* 141–148.

Lindy, J. D., Green, B. L., Grace, M., & Titchner, J. (1983). Psychotherapy with survivors of the Beverly Hills Supper Club fire. *American Journal of Psychotherapy, 37,* 593–610.

Little, J. C., & James, B. (1964). Abreaction of conditioned fear reaction after eighteen years. *Behavioral Research and Therapy, 2,* 59–63.

Malloy, P. F., Fairbank, J. A., & Keane, T. M. (1983). Validation of a multimodal assessment of posttraumatic stress disorders in Vietnam veterans. *Journal of Consulting and Clinical Psychology, 51,* 488–493.

McCaffrey, R., & Fairbank, J. (1984). *Broad spectrum behavioral assessment and treatment of post-traumatic stress disorder related to transportation accidents.* Unpublished manuscript. Portions of the study presented at the annual meeting of the Association for the Advancement of Behavior Therapy, Philadelphia, November.

Melick, M. E., Logue, J. H., & Frederick, C. J. (1982). Stress and disaster. In L. Goldberger & S. Breznitz (Eds.), *Handbook on stress: Theoretical and clinical aspects.* New York: Free Press.

Miller, T. W., & Buchbinder, J. C. (1979). *Clinical effects of cognitive-behavior therapy with a posttraumatic war neurosis Vietnam veteran.* Paper presented at the annual meeting of the Association for Advancement of Behavior Therapy, San Francisco, November.

Penk, W. E., Robinowitz, R., Roberts, W. R., Patterson, E. T., Dolan, M. P., & Atkins, H. G. (1981). Adjustment differences among male substance abusers varying in degree of combat experience in Vietnam. *Journal of Consulting and Clinical Psychology, 49*(3), 426–437.

Pynoos, R. S., & Eth, S. (1984). The child as witness to homicide. *Journal of Social Issues, 40*(2), 87.

Roberts, W. R., Penk, W. E., Gearing, M. L., Robinowitz, R., Dolan, M. P., & Patterson, E. T. (1982). Interpersonal problems of Vietnam combat veterans with symptoms of posttraumatic stress disorder. *Journal of Abnormal Psychology, 91*, 444–450.

Rychtarik, R., Silverman, W., Van Landingham, W., & Prue, D. (1984). Treatment of an incest victim with implosive therapy: A case study. *Behavior Therapy, 15*, 410–420.

Shatan, C. F. (1973). The grief of soldiers: Vietnam combat veterans' self-help movement. *American Journal of Orthopsychiatry, 43*, 640–653.

Starkey, T. W., & Ashlock, L. (1984, December). Inpatient treatment of PTSD: An interim report of the Miami model. VA *Practitioner*, December.

Van der Kolk, B. A. (1983). Psychopharmacological issues in posttraumatic stress disorder. *Hospital and Community Psychiatry, 34*(8), 683–684, 691.

Williams, T. (1980). (Ed.). *Post-traumatic stress disorders of the Vietnam veteran*. Cincinnati, OH: Disabled American Veterans.

Wilson, J. P. (1980). *Towards an understanding of posttraumatic stress disorders among Vietnam veterans*. U.S. Senate testimony on veterans' affairs, Washington, DC, May.

14

Anxiety Disorders in Mentally Retarded People

RICHARD J. McNALLY AND L. MICHAEL ASCHER

This chapter provides a survey of issues related to the joint occurrence of mental retardation and pathological anxiety. Epidemiological, diagnostic, and treatment approaches are reviewed. As a comprehensive chapter has been published on anxiety in mentally retarded people (Ollendick & Ollendick, 1982), we will concentrate on recent developments in this area.

Historical Overview

Societal and professional opinions on the relationship between mental retardation and emotional disorders have varied throughout history (for a review, see Ollendick & Ollendick, 1982). In ancient Greece and Rome, mentally retarded children were not distinguished from those with emotional disorders. Both were scorned, ostracized, and occasionally killed because of the extra burden their care necessitated. The mentally retarded and the emotionally disturbed fared better during the Middle Ages. They were regarded as "holy fools" possessing a special relationship to God and were accordingly treated with kindness. The Reformation, however, brought a change in societal attitudes. Intellectual subnormality and behavioral deviance were viewed as signs of demonic possession. Consequently, these individuals were subject to humiliation and rejection, and were occasionally burned at the stake.

Distinctions between mental retardation and mental illness began to be drawn during the late 18th century. Advances in the biological sciences encouraged the view that mental retardation resulted from organic damage, whereas emotional and behavioral disorders stemmed from environmental causes. Although exceptions to this etiological dichotomy were uncovered, the notion that mental retardation is largely a function of organic damage has survived.

As noted by Ollendick and Ollendick (1982), the demarcation between mental retardation and mental illness led to the belief that mentally retarded people were somehow immune to the emotional problems suffered by intellectually normal people. Although a number of authorities have challenged this belief, and in fact have argued

Richard J. McNally. Department of Psychology, University of Health Sciences/The Chicago Medical School, North Chicago, Illinois.

L. Michael Ascher. Department of Psychiatry, Temple University Medical School, Philadelphia, Pennsylvania.

that mental retardation *increases* the risk for developing psychiatric disorders (e.g., Menolascino, 1965; Phillips, 1967; Rutter, Tizard, Yule, Graham, & Whitmore, 1976), surprisingly little professional attention has been directed toward emotionally disturbed, mentally retarded people (Matson, 1984; Reiss, Levitan, & McNally, 1982). Indeed, most services for the mentally retarded provide educational remediation and vocational habilitation rather than therapy for concomitant emotional problems.

Diagnostic Issues

In accordance with terminology used by the American Association on Mental Deficiency (Grossman, 1977), the current *Diagnostic and Statistical Manual of Mental Disorders* (DSM-III) (American Psychiatric Association, 1980) employs three criteria for diagnosing mental retardation. To be classified as mentally retarded, a person (1) must have deficits in adaptive behavior, (2) must show significantly subaverage general intellectual functioning (IQ < 70) as measured by an individually administered intelligence test, and (3) must exhibit these deficiencies prior to the age of 18. The DSM-III provides IQ guidelines for diagnosing different degrees of mental retardation: mild retardation (50–70), moderate retardation (35–49), severe retardation (20–34), and profound retardation (below 20). IQ scores falling between 71 and 84 are considered indicative of borderline intellectual functioning.

Mentally retarded people make up approximately 2.5% of the general population; approximately 14% are of borderline intelligence. The dramatic behavioral deficits and excesses of the profoundly and severely retarded have attracted considerable attention from educators and behavior modifiers, yet relatively few mentally retarded persons fall in these categories. Indeed, 85% of the mentally retarded fall in the mild range of intellectual impairment (Phillips, 1967). It is this larger group of individuals who are most likely to suffer from emotional disturbances similar to those suffered by intellectually normal people (Jacobson, 1982). In fact, persons with *borderline* mental retardation may be the most vulnerable, yet the most underserved (Reiss, Levitan, & McNally, 1982). They have traditionally been viewed as poor candidates for psychotherapy and have often failed to qualify for psychosocial services because they did not satisfy the criteria for mental retardation. Consequently, it has been unlikely that their psychological problems would have received treatment.

Diagnostic Overshadowing

Although the aforementioned surveys suggest that mentally retarded people are vulnerable to the full range of psychological disorders, psychotherapeutic services have rarely been directed to this population. The relative neglect of mentally retarded, emotionally disturbed persons may be partly due to their falling through a gap in the service delivery system (Reiss, Levitan, & McNally, 1982). It is not uncommon for these individuals to shuttle between mental health centers serving those with psychological problems and developmental centers designed to serve mentally retarded people. Workers at each type of facility believe that it is the responsibility of the other to treat the dual-diagnosed patient. The resultant conflict contributes to the failure of the individual to receive appropriate treatment. A second problem is the emphasis of most professional training programs on education and skills acquisition to the exclusion of components focusing on the treatment of mentally retarded people with emotional problems (Tanguay & Szymanski, 1980). This state of affairs may be partly due to the belief that psychotherapy is an inappropriate treatment for mentally deficient individuals.

Reiss and his associates have addressed a third difficulty that may underlie the relative neglect of emotional disorders in the mentally retarded (Reiss, Levitan, & Szyszko, 1982). They suggest that clinicians may overlook psychiatric disorder in the retarded because the presence of mental retardation diminishes the diagnostic importance of deviant behavior that ordinarily would be considered pathognomonic. Reiss, Levitan, and Szyszko (1982) called this hypothesized phenomenon *diagnostic overshadowing* because "intellectual subnormality is such a salient feature of mental retardation that accompanying emotional disturbances are overshadowed in importance by the presence of intellectual retardation" (p. 567).

Reiss and his colleagues hold that diagnostic overshadowing can occur in two mutually compatible ways. First, because intellectual disability is such a salient characteristic of mentally retarded people, any additional problems (e.g., anxiety, depression) may appear mild in comparison. The diagnostic importance of other emotional problems may be deemphasized or even unnoticed by clinicians. Second, signs of psychiatric disturbance may be viewed as consequences of intellectual deficiency in retarded people. In other words, a concurrent psychiatric disorder may be less likely to be diagnosed as such, but rather attributed to mental deficiency merely because of the salience of the latter.

Although several authors have discussed the possibility of such phenomena (e.g., Chess, 1970; Phillips, 1967; Webster, 1963), experimental evidence for diagnostic overshadowing has appeared only recently. For their first study, Reiss, Levitan, and Szyszko (1982) developed a case description of a man ("Alfred") who was mugged while traveling by bus to his job in a fast-food restaurant, and who subsequently quit his job and refused to ride buses. This hypothetical case was written to suggest a diagnosis of simple phobia, precipitated by a traumatic psychosocial experience. Each of three groups of subjects (registered psychologists) were presented with a slightly different version of the case. One version provided additional data indicative of mental retardation, another indicated the presence of alcoholism, and a third merely described the aforementioned circumstances surrounding the onset of the phobia. Subjects were asked to evaluate Alfred on a series of Likert scales requiring an estimate of the likelihood that Alfred was emotionally disturbed, mentally retarded, alcoholic, psychotic, neurotic, irrational, and tense. The raters were also asked to provide treatment recommendations.

The results provided evidence for diagnostic overshadowing. The terms *neurotic, irrational, emotionally disturbed,* and *psychotic* were rated as significantly less likely to apply in the retardation condition than in either of the other two conditions. Moreover, raters were significantly less likely to diagnose a phobia in either the mental retardation or the alcoholism condition than in the intellectually normal condition. Systematic desensitization was recommended significantly less often in the dual-diagnosis conditions than in the control condition. In accordance with the hypothesis, the presence of mental retardation seemed to diminish the diagnostic significance of the concurrent phobic disorder. The presence of alcoholism also seemed to produce similar, albeit weaker, effects.

These investigators provided a conceptual replication in Experiment II of their paper (Reiss, Levitan, & Szyszko, 1982). They used a 2 (mental retardation versus average intelligence) × 2 (schizophrenia versus avoidant personality disorder) design in which clinical psychologists evaluated one of four case descriptions. Once again, evidence for diagnostic overshadowing was obtained. The same case descriptions were rated as significantly less likely to be instances of schizophrenia, psychosis, an emotional distur- bance, or a personality disorder, and as significantly less likely to need long-term psychotherapy, when the person was also suggested to be retarded as opposed to having average intelligence. These studies indicate that the presence of mental retardation overshadows simple phobia, schizophrenia, and avoidant personality disorder.

Levitan and Reiss (1983) tested the generality of diagnostic overshadowing across disciplines. They used the phobia case description (Reiss, Levitan, & Szyszko, 1982, Experiment I), varied the presence/absence of mental retardation, and presented it to advanced students in clinical psychology and in social work. They found that "Alfred" was rated as less likely to be neurotic, to have an irrational fear, or to require systematic desensitization when he was also described as mentally retarded than when he was not. There were no differences in ratings between the psychology and social work students, thus indicating that previous demonstrations of diagnostic overshadowing were not artifacts peculiar to the discipline of clinical psychology.

Reiss and Szyszko (1983) raised the possibility that diagnostic overshadowing may be due to the relative inexperience many clinicians have in working with mentally retarded patients. To test this hypothesis, they used a 3×2 design in which professional experience with mentally retarded people was crossed with two case description condi- tions. The levels of experience were as follows: psychologists at state developmental disabilities facilities (high-experience group), psychologists at a state mental hospital (moderate-experience group), and clinical psychology graduate students (low-experience group). The two case description conditions provided the same history suggesting schizophrenia but differed in terms of the patient's IQ (60 versus 108). Results indicated that the degree of professional experience was related to diagnostic ratings insofar as the more experienced clinicians detected schizophrenia more often than did their less experienced counterparts. However, the groups did not differ in terms of diagnostic overshadowing. That is, schizophrenia was diagnosed significantly less often when the patient was mentally retarded than when he was intellectually average.

Experimental evidence for diagnostic overshadowing has been reported by investi- gators other than Reiss and his collleagues. Alford and Locke (1984) provided behavioral and nonbehavioral clinical psychologists, who varied in their degree of experience with mentally retarded people, with a brief therapy transcript involving a patient who was either labeled mentally retarded or not. Consistent with previous findings, they found that the presence of the mentally retarded label resulted in significantly less severe ratings of psychopathology. Moreover, the effects of the mentally retarded designation were not affected by orientation or by degree of professional experience. The latter finding replicates the results of Reiss and Szyszko (1983).

Taken together, these studies provide compelling evidence for the existence of diagnostic overshadowing. This phenomenon may contribute to the underdiagnosis of anxiety disorders in the mentally retarded.

Anxiety in Mentally Retarded People

Several writers have postulated that mentally retarded individuals are highly susceptible to anxiety-based problems (e.g., Cochran & Cleland, 1963; Feldhusen & Klausmeier, 1962; Knights, 1963; Malpass, Mark, & Palermo, 1960). Consistent with this assumption, investigators have reported a high prevalence of anxiety and other neurotic symptoms in the mentally retarded. These early studies, of course, did not employ DSM-III criteria and therefore do not permit a precise estimate of the prevalence of the various subtypes of anxiety disorder. They do, however, provide a general sense of the extent of "neurotic anxiety" in this population. Thus Penrose (1938; cited in Ollendick & Ollendick, 1982) found 10.3% of a sample of 1,280 inpatients to be "psychoneurotic." Similarly, Neuer (1974; cited in Ollendick & Ollendick, 1982) classified 13% of a sample of 300 inpatients as "neurotic" as evidenced by restlessness, anxiety, and compulsions. Craft (1959) reported an even higher prevalence (33%) of emotional and personality disturbances in 324 inpatients. Only one patient was diagnosed as obsessive–compulsive, however, and no instances of "anxiety neurosis" were uncovered.

Studies on noninstitutionalized mentally retarded people have reported similar findings. Webster (1963) reported that *all* probands in a study of 159 mentally retarded children ranging in age from 3 to 6 years showed signs of emotional disturbance. As with the aforementioned studies, explicit criteria were not used to diagnose anxiety. Despite the likelihood that psychopathology was overdiagnosed here, Webster's study underscores the fact that mentally retarded individuals are highly susceptible to emotional disturbances.

In a study of mentally retarded adult outpatients in Great Britain, Craft (1960) found that 10.8% were diagnosed as having an "anxiety state." It is unclear whether these patients would be classified today as having a panic disorder or a generalized anxiety disorder. Taken together, the studies by Craft (1959, 1960) suggest that noninstitutionalized mentally retarded people are more at risk for developing an anxiety disorder than are their institutionalized counterparts.

More recently, Phillips and Williams (1975) found that approximately 9% of borderline, mild, and moderately retarded children attending an outpatient clinic met DSM-II (American Psychiatric Association, 1968) criteria for neurosis. Eaton and Menolascino (1982), however, reported only one case of "psychoneurotic anxiety reaction" in a sample of 114 mentally retarded psychiatric outpatients.

A longitudinal study conducted in Great Britain (Richardson, Katz, Koller, McLaren, & Rubinstein, 1979) provides data essentially in agreement with its methodologically inferior predecessors. These investigators followed 222 mentally retarded individuals from birth to 22 years of age. Interviews with probands and parents, observational ratings, and school and hospital records were used as data for assessing psychosocial adjustment. The investigators reported that 26% of the sample exhibited neurotic disorders by early adulthood.

A second approach to the study of anxiety in the mentally retarded has been to compare levels of self-reported anxiety in mentally retarded individuals to age- or IQ-matched controls. These studies have generally found that anxiety in institutionalized individuals is higher than in noninstitutionalized retarded individuals or in their nonretarded peers (Cochran & Cleland, 1963; Feldhusen & Klausmeier, 1962; Malpass, Mark, & Palermo, 1960). Lipman (1960), however, found no difference in self-reported anxiety between retarded and nonretarded individuals of approximately the same age.

Anxiety Disorders in Mentally Retarded People

Ollendick and Ollendick (1982) have reviewed several etiological viewpoints (e.g., cerebral defect, psychodynamic, and experiential, as well as learning) in their comprehensive chapter on anxiety in the mentally retarded. Rather than restate these issues, we will focus on the various anxiety disorders and elucidate the variables that may be implicated in the etiology of each.

Agoraphobia and Panic Disorder

Agoraphobia involves a debilitating fear of being alone and/or of being in public places. The basis of the fear—and subsequent avoidance—is the anticipation that one might become incapacitated with panic and thereby suffer psychological harm (e.g., insanity) or physical harm (e.g., heart attack; American Psychiatric Association, 1980). Current theorizing suggests that unpredictable panic attacks lie at the core of this disorder (Klein, 1981), and that phobic avoidance is a secondary phenomenon involving the desire to avoid places in which panic is likely to occur. Indeed, the current draft of the revised *Diagnostic and Statistical Manual of Mental Disorders* (DSM-IIIR) (American Psychiatric Association, 1985) identifies panic as the core disorder and agoraphobic avoidance as a complication of panic. Thus, according to this proposed revision, patients would be diagnosed as: panic disorder, panic disorder with limited phobic avoidance, or panic disorder with agoraphobia.

There are no data on the prevalence of panic or agoraphobia in the mentally retarded, although Craft's (1960) finding that 10.8% of mentally retarded outpatients suffered from an "anxiety state" suggests that this population is not immune to panic attacks. As mentioned earlier, however, one cannot determine whether Craft's patients had panic or generalized anxiety.

Some treatment studies have used mental retardation as a subject exclusion criterion (e.g., Persson & Nordlund, 1985) thus suggesting that at least some candidates for treatment present with concurrent agoraphobia and mental retardation. But estimates of co-occurrence are impossible without knowledge of how many agoraphobics were excluded for this reason.

In general, although agoraphobics have not been found to differ significantly from the general population in intelligence (Tearnan, Telch, & Keefe, 1984), they often have had low levels of educational achievement (Weissman, 1985). Indeed, as Chambless (1985, p. 309) has stated, "Thus the popular myth among agoraphobic self-help groups in the U.S.A., to the effect that agoraphobia occurs mostly in those who are highly intelligent and imaginative would seem to be just that: a myth." These findings imply that at least some agoraphobics may be functioning in the borderline and mildly retarded range of intelligence.

The paucity of data forces us to speculate about what variables might influence the occurrence of panic and agoraphobia in the mentally retarded. On the one hand, some theoretical perspectives imply that the mentally retarded may be *less* likely than people of normal intelligence to be affected by this condition. For example, theories that posit severe marital distress (e.g., Goldstein & Chambless, 1978) as an important precipitant in the development of agoraphobia imply that fewer mentally retarded individuals should be affected simply because they are less likely to be married than their nonretarded counterparts. On the other hand, a number of writers have argued that "dependent" personalities may be highly likely to develop agoraphobia when confronted with impending or real separation from loved ones (Andrews, 1966). Retarded individuals are, perforce, more dependent on others than are nonretarded people. Such dependency may increase the likelihood of experiencing panic given real or threatened separation from caretakers.

Social Phobia

Social phobias are persistent and irrational fears of being humiliated or embarrassed in public. The socially phobic individual avoids these situations or endures them with great distress (American Psychiatric Association, 1980).

Again, no prevalence data are available on the joint occurrence of social phobia and mental retardation, but there are reasons to believe that mentally retarded people are particularly vulnerable to this disorder. Because of their intellectual limitations, mentally retarded people are likely to experience difficulties in mastering prosocial skills (Rutter et al., 1976). These skill deficits, in turn, may lead to peer rejection, diminished social support, and increased vulnerability for psychopathology, including social phobia.

Consistent with this view, Reiss and Benson (1985) obtained correlations as high as −.76 between depression and degree of social support in mentally retarded patients. These investigators suggested that social deficits that alienate others may ultimately reduce social reinforcement and eventually increase the likelihood of depression. Although the focus of the study by Reiss and Benson (1985) was on depression, it would not be surprising that the same risk factors that increase vulnerability to depression may also influence social anxiety. Indeed, as Wolpe (1979) has noted, many individuals become depressed following prolonged periods of anxiety. Thus a socially unskilled person may experience anxiety following multiple social failures. The consequent deprivation in social reinforcers may, in turn, lead to the depression observed by Reiss and Benson.

If social skills deficits lie at the heart of an increased risk for social anxiety, depression, or both, then direct teaching of these skills would be a reasonable therapeutic intervention. A number of studies have now appeared suggesting that social skills training can be effective with the mentally retarded (for a review, see Robertson, Richardson, & Youngson, 1984). Social skills training has been used to improve functioning in schoolchildren (Kelly, Furman, Phillips, Hathorn, & Wilson, 1979); to increase assertiveness (Bregman, 1984; Gentile & Jenkins, 1980); and to promote adjustment to group home life (Bates, 1980; Matson & Adkins, 1980) and to work (Bornstein, Bach, McFall, Friman, & Lyons, 1980; La Greca, Stone, & Bell, 1983).

In general, these interventions have involved the use of instructions, modeling, role playing, and feedback to construct various social repertoires and have not been directed at the treatment of social phobia in itself. Yet as social skills training appears effective in reducing social fear as well as remediating skills deficits in persons of normal intelligence (e.g., Stravynski, Marks, & Yule, 1982), this approach seems well suited to the treatment of mentally retarded people with social phobia. Indeed, Matson (1981a, 1981b) has demonstrated that these techniques can be adapted to treat mentally handicapped people with social fears. In one study, he treated three moderately retarded preadolescent girls who exhibited severe fears of strangers. More specifically, the patients refused to stand near or talk to adults other than relatives and schoolteachers. The phobia clearly hampered the social functioning of the patients' entire families insofar as the children refused to accompany their parents to the homes of their parents' friends. Participant modeling was used, involving demonstration by the therapist and the patient's mother of appropriate greeting responses, followed by *in vivo* rehearsal of the behaviors. Multiple-baseline analyses conducted across subjects indicated the elimination of the phobia as well as the establishment of prosocial skills.

In a group study, Matson (1981b) randomly assigned 24 mildly and moderately retarded phobics to either participant modeling or to a no-treatment control condition. All patients reported fear and avoidance of public places such as grocery stores. Anecdotal descriptions of typical subjects suggest that they were socially phobic rather than agoraphobic, because their principal concerns involved fear of scrutiny rather than fear of panic and its consequences. Instructions, modeling, role playing, and *in vivo* exposure eliminated phobic behavior, enabling all patients to shop without undue anxiety. Behavioral observation and self-reports were concordant in their agreement on clinical change.

Chiodo and Maddux (1985) applied anxiety management techniques to treat two mildly retarded women who suffered from evaluation anxiety. In the first case, biofeedback and coping self-statements were used with success. The second patient, who feared her vocational supervisor's criticism, was exposed to continual evaluative comments while being successfully taught to generate coping self-statements. The authors noted that the effectiveness of the interventions suggests that "cognitive" procedures may be used with those who are cognitively impaired.

Simple Phobia

A simple phobia involves an irrational fear and a compelling desire to avoid a specific, harmless object or situation. To qualify as a phobia, the fear must produce significant distress, disruption in functioning, or both. Only those phobias not meeting diagnostic criteria for agoraphobia or social phobia are classified as simple (American Psychiatric Association, 1980).

Little systematic work has been done on the prevalence of simple phobias in the mentally retarded, although research has been conducted on fears of unknown severity.

Guarnaccia and Weiss (1974) conducted a factor analysis of the fears of mentally retarded children, as reported by their parents. Four factors were obtained: separation, natural events, injury, and animals. The investigators noted that the findings are similar to those obtained in surveys of children of normal intelligence (e.g., Miller, Barrett, Hampe, & Noble, 1972).

Surveying fears in an institutionalized population, Sternlicht (1979) found that the distribution and types of specific fears in mentally retarded adults were very similar to those for children of the same mental age. Thus nature fears (e.g., storms, the dark) and animal fears were common in mentally retarded adults. In children of normal intelligence, such fears ordinarily dissipate as the child matures (Agras, Chapin, & Oliveau, 1972). As adults rarely *acquire* animal phobias (Marks & Gelder, 1966; McNally & Steketee, 1985), those who are phobic are individuals whose animal fears failed to dissipate during childhood. These findings suggest that mentally retarded people may have an extended—perhaps indefinite—period of vulnerability for developing animal phobias.

Duff, La Rocca, Lizzet, Martin, Pearce, Williams, and Peck (1981) also found that the pattern and intensity of fears in mildly retarded adults was more similar to that of children of the same mental age than to that of their age-matched peers.

Other studies suggest that people of lower intelligence are susceptible to developing specific phobias. In a study conducted in Sweden on the prevalence of dental phobia, Hallstrom and Halling (1984) found that graduates of remedial education programs, and those who repeated grades, represented the largest group of dental phobics (32%). In contrast, those with at least a high school education made up only 8.7% of the phobic sample. These data imply that persons with educational handicaps, and perhaps mental retardation, are overrepresented among dental phobics.

Several case studies have reported successful behavioral interventions with mentally retarded individuals exhibiting simple phobia. Although these reports have conceptualized treatment in various ways (e.g., operant shaping of approach behavior, desensitization of fear), most have included graduated *in vivo* exposure to feared situations. Graduated exposure *in vivo* has been used to eliminate fears of physical examinations (Freeman, Roy, & Hemmick, 1976); mannequins (Waranch, Iwata, Wohl, & Nidiffer, 1981); using the toilet (Luiselli, 1977); escalators (Runyan, Stevens, & Reeves, 1985); heights (Guralnick, 1973); and traveling in cars (Mansdorf, 1976) and in school buses (patient was autistic; Luiselli, 1978).

Two group studies further demonstrate the effectiveness of exposure *in vivo* with this population. Obler and Terwilliger (1970) randomly assigned 30 neurologically impaired children who had either a dog phobia or a bus phobia either to a no-treatment control or to behavior therapy. Approximately one-third of the patients were also mildly mentally retarded. After exposing subjects in the treatment group to pictorial representations of the phobic stimulus, the therapists initiated graduated exposure *in vivo* supplemented with tangible reinforcers delivered contingent on approach behavior. Avoidance behavior significantly diminished in the treatment group, whereas no change was noted in the control. No difference was found in treatment response as a function of IQ, thus underscoring the effectiveness of exposure *in vivo* for mentally retarded, phobic children.

Peck (1977) randomly assigned 20 mildly retarded adults with either a rat or a height phobia to one of five groups: (1) imaginal systematic desensitization, (2) vicarious symbolic desensitization using videotaped fear stimuli, (3) *in vivo* desensitization, (4) attention placebo control, and (5) no treatment control. Although the small number of subjects made statistical significance difficult to obtain, the *in vivo* desensitization group reported the least fear at posttest. Moreover, all four subjects in this group were capable of performing the most difficult hierarchy item following treatment, whereas only one subject per group could do so in the other treatment conditions. *In vivo* desensitization also required the least treatment time.

Obsessive–Compulsive Disorder

Obsessions are recurrent, intrusive, anxiety-inducing thoughts, images, or impulses. Obsessions often pertain to contamination (e.g., "Might I contract venereal disease from touching that toilet seat?"), or to doubt as to whether a certain action was performed (e.g., "Did I lock the door?"). Compulsions are repetitive behaviors and thoughts designed to prevent disasters, to reduce anxiety, or both. Common compulsions are washing one's hands, and repeated checking to ensure that certain actions were performed correctly (American Psychiatric Association, 1980).

Recent epidemiological research using DSM-III criteria has obtained 6-month prevalence rates for obsessive–compulsive disorder as high as 2% of the adult population of the United States (Myers et al., 1984). There are no data on the joint occurrence of mental retardation and obsessive–compulsive disorder. However, several studies have reported that obsessive–compulsives tend to be of above-average intelligence (Rasmussen & Tsuang, 1984). In diagnosing obsessive–compulsive disorder in mentally retarded people, one must be careful to distinguish "compulsive" stereotypic behavior (e.g., hand flapping) from true, anxiety-motivated compulsions (Rachman & Hodgson, 1980, p. 96). The former is common in mentally handicapped individuals—especially those functioning in the severe and profound ranges of retardation—whereas the latter is relatively rare.

Matson (1982) has conducted the only treatment study involving mentally retarded obsessive–compulsives. He used a multiple baseline across behaviors, settings, and patients to treat three mildly retarded adults who ritualistically checked their bodies and their clothes. The patients expressed considerable anxiety about being untidy and disheveled. Matson used a treatment package comprising differential reinforcement of other (nonchecking) behavior, modeling of appropriate on-task behavior, performance feedback, exposure to workshop situations that had triggered checking, and overcorrection as a response prevention technique. This comprehensive approach succeeded in reducing checking as well as subjective reports of anxiety, perhaps because the crucial ingredients of exposure plus response prevention were included (Foa, Steketee, Grayson, Turner, & Latimer, 1984).

Posttraumatic Stress Disorder

Persons exposed to traumatic events outside the range of ordinary experience, such as combat, natural disasters, and rape, may exhibit symptoms of posttraumatic stress disorder (PTSD). Characteristics of PTSD include the reexperiencing of the trauma in the form of intrusive thoughts, flashbacks, and nightmares. Generalized anxiety, depression, exaggerated startle response, and emotional withdrawal from others also commonly occur (American Psychiatric Association, 1980).

Although there exists doubt regarding whether PTSD itself constitutes a valid diagnostic entity (Sierles, Chen, McFarland, & Taylor, 1983), a number of reports suggest the effectiveness of *in vivo* desensitization (Kipper, 1977); imaginal flooding (Keane & Kaloupek, 1982); and implosive therapy (Rychtarik, Silverman, Van Landingham, & Prue, 1984) in the treatment of related fears. Because implosive therapy has been used with a heterogenous group of "emotionally disturbed" mentally retarded individuals with apparently beneficial effects (Silvestri, 1977), this technique may prove useful in treating mentally retarded persons who suffer from PTSD.

Ollendick and Ollendick (1982) suggest that mentally retarded individuals may be particularly susceptible to emotional problems such as PTSD following, for example, the death of a parent. It is questionable, however, whether such a stressor is likely to produce the full range of symptoms (e.g., flashbacks) held to be characteristic of PTSD. On the other hand, limited intelligence may lower the threshold for the elicitation of PTSD symptoms. In any event, there is no reason to believe that mentally retarded individuals are immune to such reactions following stressors such as rape or automobile accidents.

One common potential source of stress for mentally retarded people is involuntary residential relocation. As part of the deinstitutionalization movement, many retarded individuals have been moved from large state facilities to smaller group homes. Although this process is not inevitably stressful—and is, indeed, meant to be therapeutic—a number of authors have reported symptoms characteristic of traumatic stress in some residents (for a review, see Heller, 1984). As prophylactic measures, Heller (1984) recommends involving the resident as much as possible in relocation decisions, preparatory site visits, and the transfer of residents in groups to preserve their friendship networks.

Generalized Anxiety Disorder

This diagnosis requires the presence of persistent, nonphobic, nonpanic anxiety manifested in four areas: (1) motor tension (e.g., inability to relax, trembling); (2) autonomic hyperactivity (e.g., racing heart, sweating hands); (3) apprehensive expectation (e.g., worry, anticipation of harm); and (4) vigilance (e.g., hyperalertness, feeling on edge) (American Psychiatric Association, 1980).

Many early investigators described mentally retarded individuals as pervasively anxious, but lack of precise criteria make these reports difficult to interpret. However, Craft's (1960) observation of "anxiety states" in mentally retarded outpatients suggests the presence of generalized anxiety disorder.

Nonretarded individuals with generalized anxiety are commonly treated with benzodiazepines (Greenblatt, Shader, & Abernethy, 1983), although rarely are these drugs prescribed for mentally retarded persons (Breuning, Davis, & Poling, 1982). Nonretarded anxious people have also been treated successfully with relaxation training (Barlow et al., 1984), a technique showing promise for the mentally retarded as well (Harvey, 1979). Progressive muscle relaxation has been found to help persons functioning as low as in the moderate range of mental retardation (Rickard, Thrasher, & Elkins, 1984). Although subjects in this study were not suffering from generalized anxiety disorder, the fact that they were capable of responding to verbal instructions to relax suggests that this approach is not contraindicated by the presence of intellectual handicap.

Calamari, Geist, and Shahbazian (in press) randomly assigned 32 institutionalized mentally retarded clients to either a multicomponent relaxation treatment or to a control condition. Clients in the treatment group received seven sessions of progressive muscle relaxation training, auditory electromyographic (EMG) biofeedback, modeling, and positive reinforcement; those in the control group listened to relaxing music for seven sessions. The treated clients achieved greater tension reduction than did controls, as evidenced by significant decreases in EMG level and behavioral signs of restlessness. Interestingly, the degree of intellectual impairment was unrelated to success in relaxation training; profoundly retarded clients did as well as mildly retarded ones. These findings suggest that serious intellectual impairment is not a contraindication for biofeedback-assisted relaxation.

Future Directions

When employed with mentally retarded individuals, behavioral methods have primarily targeted disruptive or dangerous responses that impede habilitation programs. This is congruent with the conventional position that the most salient needs of the mentally retarded are those of education and of skills acquisition. This viewpoint, supplemented by other difficulties (e.g., diagnostic overshadowing, deficiencies in professional training), has contributed to the general failure to assess and treat anxiety disorders in this population. The following quote (Costello, 1982, p. 41) exemplifies the prevailing attitude:

> Although the full range of anxiety disorders is seen in the mentally retarded, such diagnoses are commonly not recognized or are managed by nonpsychiatric techniques. The distinction between the concept of anxiety disorder and the rival interpretation of habit disorder is, in any case, a difficult one to make in theory and in practice it is unimportant because behavioral (operant) techniques are usually very effective in the reduction of symptoms. It is important to note that the incidence and intensity of fears and phobias are higher in the mentally retarded than in normal adults and commensurate with those in children of comparable mental age. . . . This finding is especially relevant when discharge from institutional care is attempted. Although psychotherapy has been offered for many years to the mentally retarded . . . supportive therapy and reassurance have the most valuable contribution to make, and so the niceties of differential diagnosis in the anxiety disorders are often not of great practical importance.

In the present review, we have attempted to support an alternative position. Although the relevant literature is scarce, it suggests that anxiety disorders occur in a significant portion of the mentally retarded population. It also suggests that these disorders can be reliably diagnosed and effectively treated. The prevalence of these disorders and the need for treatment have increased in relation to the growing number of retarded individuals who have been affected by the move toward deinstitutionalization and normalization.

The deinstitutionalization movement is based on the hypothesis that habilitation of mentally retarded individuals is enhanced when programs are conducted in community settings—a context that is most stimulating and least restrictive. Certainly the transfer from the institution to the community brings with it many positive changes. Inherent in this environmental shift, however, are components that have the potential to elicit anxiety from mentally retarded people. For example, an individual who has been institutionalized for a significant portion of his or her life has possibly overlearned the routine behavioral patterns necessary to gain maximum reinforcement in this relatively simple setting. In contrast, the community involves much greater complexity, notwithstanding the buffer that may be offered by group homes or community living arrangements. Thus there are a greater number of choices available, with a consequent increase in decisions to be made, as well as many more rules and regulations to which retarded individuals must accommodate. Most important, the social context of the community, composed of a greater percentage of "normal" individuals than is the case for the institution, displays much less patience and tolerance for aberrant behavior.

The resulting anxiety that may be associated with these and other differences encountered by the deinstitutionalized retarded individual will impede his or her ability to benefit from and to thrive in the community (Gollay, Freedman, Wyngaarden, & Kurtz, 1978). To the extent that the amelioration of anxiety disorders can facilitate such adjustment, this area of behavior therapy, largely neglected with the mentally retarded population, should now be fully explored. Appropriate behavioral procedures can be modified to meet the needs of this handicapped group. Fortunately, the evidence reviewed here suggests that techniques such as relaxation, exposure *in vivo*, and social skills training require relatively little modification to be effective with mentally retarded people.

There is no support for the a priori position that anxiety disorders in the deinstitutionalized mentally retarded person should have a low treatment priority, or that there is any behavioral procedure that cannot be modified for use with this population. In fact, with the dearth of relevant data, the converse position rests on stronger ground.

References

Agras, W. S., Chapin, H. N., & Oliveau, D. C. (1972). The natural history of phobia: Course and prognosis. *Archives of General Psychiatry, 26,* 315–317.

Alford, J. D., & Locke, B. J. (1984). Clinical responses to psychopathology of mentally retarded persons. *American Journal of Mental Deficiency, 89,* 195–197.

American Psychiatric Association. (1968). *Diagnostic and statistical manual of mental disorders* (2nd ed.). Washington, DC: Author.

American Psychiatric Association. (1980). *Diagnostic and statistical manual of mental disorders* (3rd ed.). Washington, DC: Author.

American Psychiatric Association. (1985). Anxiety disorders. *DSM-III-R in development.* Washington, DC: Author.

Andrews, J. D. W. (1966). Psychotherapy of phobias. *Psychological Bulletin, 66,* 455–480.

Barlow, D. H., Cohen, A. S., Waddell, M. T., Vermilyea, B. B., Klosko, J. S., Blanchard, E. B., & DiNardo, P. A. (1984). Panic and generalized anxiety disorders: Nature and treatment. *Behavior Therapy, 15,* 431–449.

Bates, P. (1980). The effectiveness of interpersonal skills training on the social skill acquisition of moderately and mildly retarded adults. *Journal of Applied Behavior Analysis, 13,* 237–248.

Bornstein, P. H., Bach, P. J., McFall, M. E., Friman, P. C., & Lyons, P. D. (1980). Application of a social skills training program in the modification of interpersonal deficits among retarded adults: A clinical replication. *Journal of Applied Behavior Analysis, 13,* 171–176.

Bregman, S. (1984). Assertiveness training for mentally retarded adults. *Mental Retardation, 22,* 12–16.

Breuning, S. E., Davis, V. J., & Poling, A. D. (1982). Pharmacotherapy with the mentally retarded: Implications for clinical psychologists. *Clinical Psychology Review, 2,* 79–114.

Calamari, J. E., Geist, C. O., & Shahbazian, M. J. (in press). Evaluation of multiple component relaxation training with developmentally disabled persons. *Applied Research in Mental Retardation.*

Chambless, D. L. (1985). The relationship of severity of agoraphobia to associated psychopathology. *Behaviour Research and Therapy, 23,* 305–310.

Chess, S. (1970). Emotional problems in mentally retarded children. In F. J. Menolascino (Ed.), *Psychiatric approaches to mental retardation.* New York: Basic Books.

Chiodo, J., & Maddux, J. E. (1985). A cognitive and behavioral approach to anxiety management of retarded individuals: Two case studies. *Journal of Child and Adolescent Psychiatry, 2,* 16–20.

Cochran, I. L., & Cleland, C. C. (1963). Manifest anxiety of retardates and normals matched as to academic achievement. *American Journal of Mental Deficiency, 67,* 539–542.

Costello, A. (1982). Assessment and diagnosis of psychopathology. In J. L. Matson & R. P. Barrett (Eds.), *Psychopathology in the mentally retarded.* New York: Grune and Stratton.

Craft, M. (1959). Mental disorder in the defective: A psychiatric survey among inpatients. *American Journal of Mental Deficiency, 63,* 829–834.

Craft, M. (1960). Mental disorder in a series of English out-patient defectives. *American Journal of Mental Deficiency, 64,* 718–724.

Duff, R., La Rocca, J., Lizzet, A., Martin, P., Pearce, L., Williams, M., & Peck, C. (1981). A comparison of the fears of mildly retarded adults with children of their mental age and chronological age matched controls. *Journal of Behavior Therapy and Experimental Psychiatry, 12,* 121–124.

Feldhusen, J. F., & Klausmeier, H. J. (1962). Anxiety, intelligence, and achievement in children of low, average, and high intelligence. *Child Development, 33,* 403–409.

Foa, E. B., Steketee, G., Grayson, J. B., Turner, R. M., & Latimer, P. R. (1984). Deliberate exposure and blocking of obsessive–compulsive rituals: Immediate and long-term effects. *Behavior Therapy, 15,* 450–472.

Freeman, B. J., Roy, R. R., & Hemmick, S. (1976). Extinction of a phobia of physical examination in a seven-year-old mentally retarded boy—A case study. *Behaviour Research and Therapy, 14,* 63–64.

Gentile, C., & Jenkins, J. O. (1980). Assertive training with mildly mentally retarded persons. *Mental Retardation, 18,* 315–317.

Goldstein, A. J., & Chambless, D. L. (1978). A reanalysis of agoraphobia. *Behavior Therapy, 9,* 47–59.

Gollay, E., Freedman, R., Wyngaarden, M., & Kurtz, N. R. (1978). *Coming back: The community experiences of deinstitutionalized mentally retarded people.* Cambridge, MA: Abt Books.

Greenblatt, D. J., Shader, R. I., & Abernethy, D. R. (1983). Current status of benzodiazepines: II. *New England Journal of Medicine, 309,* 410–416.

Grossman, H. J. (Ed.). (1977). *Manual on terminology and classification in mental retardation.* Washington, DC: American Association on Mental Deficiency.

Guarnaccia, V. J., & Weiss, R. L. (1974). Factor structure of fears in the mentally retarded. *Journal of Clinical Psychology, 30,* 540–544.

Guralnick, M. J. (1973). Behavior therapy with an acrophobic mentally retarded young adult. *Journal of Behavior Therapy and Experimental Psychiatry, 4,* 263–265.

Hallstrom, T., & Halling, A. (1984). Prevalence of dentistry phobia and its relation to missing teeth, alveolar bone loss and dental care habits in an urban community sample. *Acta Psychiatrica Scandinavica, 70,* 438–446.

Harvey, J. R. (1979). The potential of relaxation training for the mentally retarded. *Mental Retardation, 17,* 71–76.

Heller, T. (1984). Issues in adjustment of mentally retarded individuals to residential relocation. *International Review of Research in Mental Retardation, 12,* 123–147.

Jacobson, J. W. (1982). Problem behavior and psychiatric impairment within a developmentally disabled population: 1. Behavior frequency. *Applied Research in Mental Retardation, 3,* 121–139.

Keane, T. M., & Kaloupek, D. G. (1982). Imaginal flooding in the treatment of a posttraumatic stress disorder. *Journal of Consulting and Clinical Psychology, 50,* 138–140.

Kelly, J. A., Furman, W., Phillips, J., Hathorn, S., & Wilson, T. (1979). Teaching conversational skills to retarded adolescents. *Child Behavior Therapy, 1,* 85–97.

Kipper, D. A. (1977). Behavior therapy for fears brought on by war experiences. *Journal of Consulting and Clinical Psychology, 45,* 216–221.

Klein, D. F. (1981). Anxiety reconceptualized. In D. F. Klein & J. G. Rabkin (Eds.), *Anxiety: New research and changing concepts.* New York: Raven Press.

Knights, R. M. (1963). Test anxiety and defensiveness in institutionalized and noninstitutionalized normal and retarded children. *Child Development, 34,* 1019–1026.

La Greca, A. M., Stone, W. L., & Bell, C. R. III. (1983). Facilitating the vocational–interpersonal skills of mentally retarded individuals. *American Journal of Mental Deficiency, 88,* 270–278.

Levitan, G. W., & Reiss, S. (1983). Generality of diagnostic overshadowing across disciplines. *Applied Research in Mental Retardation, 4,* 59–64.

Lipman, R. S. (1960). Children's manifest anxiety in retardates and approximately equal MA normals. *American Journal of Mental Deficiency, 64,* 1027–1028.

Luiselli, J. K. (1977). Case report: An attendant-administered contingency management programme for the treatment of a toileting phobia. *Journal of Mental Deficiency Research, 21,* 283–288.

Luiselli, J. K. (1978). Treatment of an autistic child's fear of riding a school bus through exposure and reinforcement. *Journal of Behavior Therapy and Experimental Psychiatry, 9,* 169–172.

Malpass, L. F., Mark, S., & Palermo, D. S. (1960). Responses of retarded children to the Children's Manifest Anxiety Scale. *Journal of Educational Psychology, 51,* 305–308.

Mansdorf, I. J. (1976). Eliminating fear in a mentally retarded adult by behavioral hierarchies and operant techniques. *Journal of Behavior Therapy and Experimental Psychiatry, 7,* 189–190.

Matson, J. L. (1981a). Assessment and treatment of clinical fears in mentally retarded children. *Journal of Applied Behavior Analysis, 14,* 287–294.

Matson, J. L. (1981b). A controlled outcome study of phobias in mentally retarded adults. *Behaviour Research and Therapy, 19,* 101–107.

Matson, J. L. (1982). Treating obsessive–compulsive behavior in mentally retarded adults. *Behavior Modification, 6,* 551–567.

Matson, J. L. (1984). Psychotherapy with persons who are mentally retarded. *Mental Retardation, 22,* 170–175.

Matson, J. L., & Adkins, J. (1980). A self-instructional social skills training program for mentally retarded persons. *Mental Retardation, 18,* 245–248.

Marks, I. M., & Gelder, M. G. (1966). Different ages of onset in varieties of phobia. *American Journal of Psychiatry, 123,* 218–221.

McNally, R. J., & Steketee, G. S. (1985). The etiology and maintenance of severe animal phobias. *Behaviour Research and Therapy, 23,* 431–435.

Menolascino, F. J. (1965). Emotional disturbance and mental retardation. *American Journal of Mental Deficiency, 70,* 248–256.

Miller, L. C., Barrett, C. L., Hampe, E., & Noble, H. (1972). Factor structure of childhood fears. *Journal of Consulting and Clinical Psychology, 39,* 264–268.

Myers, J. K., Weissman, M. M., Tischler, G. L., Holzer, C. E. III, Leaf, P. J., Orvaschel, H., Anthony, J. C., Boyd, J. H., Burke, J. D., Kramer, M., & Stoltzman, R. (1984). Six-month prevalence of psychiatric disorders in three communities: 1980 to 1982. *Archives of General Psychiatry, 41,* 959–967.

Obler, M., & Terwilliger, R. F. (1970). Pilot study on the effectiveness of systematic desensitization with neurologically impaired children with phobic disorders. *Journal of Consulting and Clinical Psychology, 34,* 314–318.

Ollendick, T. H., & Ollendick, D. G. (1982). Anxiety disorders. In J. L. Matson & R. P. Barrett (Eds.), *Psychopathology in the mentally retarded* (pp. 72–119). New York: Grune and Stratton.

Peck, C. L. (1977). Desensitization for the treatment of fear in the high level adult retardate. *Behaviour Research and Therapy, 15,* 137–148.

Persson, G., & Nordlund, C. L. (1985). Agoraphobics and social phobics: Differences in background factors, syndrome profiles and therapeutic response. *Acta Psychiatrica Scandinavica, 71,* 148–159.

Phillips, I. (1967). Psychopathology and mental retardation. *American Journal of Psychiatry, 124,* 29–35.

Phillips, I., & Williams, N. (1975). Psychopathology and mental retardation: A study of 100 mentally retarded children: 1. Psychopathology. *American Journal of Psychiatry, 132,* 1265–1271.

Rachman, S. J., & Hodgson, R. J. (1980). *Obsessions and compulsions.* Englewood Cliffs, NJ: Prentice-Hall.

Rasmussen, S. A., & Tsuang, M. T. (1984). The epidemiology of obsessive–compulsive disorder. *Journal of Clinical Psychiatry, 45,* 450–457.

Reiss, S., & Benson, B. A. (1985). Psychosocial correlates of depression in mentally retarded adults: 1. Minimal social support and stigmatization. *American Journal of Mental Deficiency, 89,* 331–337.

Reiss, S., Levitan, G. W., & McNally, R. J. (1982). Emotionally disturbed mentally retarded people: An underserved population. *American Psychologist, 37,* 361–367.

Reiss, S., Levitan, G. W., & Szyszko, J. (1982). Emotional disturbance and mental retardation: Diagnostic overshadowing. *American Journal of Mental Deficiency, 86,* 567–574.

Reiss, S., & Szyszko, J. (1983). Diagnostic overshadowing and professional experience with mentally retarded persons. *American Journal of Mental Deficiency, 87,* 396–402.

Richardson, S. A., Katz, M., Koller, H., McLaren, J., & Rubinstein, B. (1979). Some characteristics of a population of mentally retarded young adults in a British city: A basis for estimating some service needs. *Journal of Mental Deficiency Research, 23,* 275–285.

Rickard, H. C., Thrasher, K. A., & Elkins, P. D. (1984). Responses of persons who are mentally retarded to four components of relaxation instruction. *Mental Retardation, 22,* 248–252.

Robertson, I., Richardson, A. M., & Youngson, S. C. (1984). Social skills training with mentally handicapped people: A review. *British Journal of Clinical Psychology, 23,* 241–264.

Runyan, M. C., Stevens, D. H., & Reeves, R. (1985). Reduction of avoidance behavior of institutionalized mentally retarded adults through contact desensitization. *American Journal of Mental Deficiency, 90,* 222–225.

Rutter, M., Tizard, J., Yule, W., Graham, P., & Whitemore, K. (1976). Isle of Wight studies, 1964–1974. *Psychological Medicine, 7,* 313–332.

Rychtarik, R. G., Silverman, W. K., Van Landingham, W. P., & Prue, D. M. (1984). Treatment of an incest victim with implosive therapy. *Behavior Therapy, 15,* 410–420.

Sierles, F. S., Chen, J. J., McFarland, R. E., & Taylor, M. A. (1983). Posttraumatic stress disorder and concurrent psychiatric illness: A preliminary report. *American Journal of Psychiatry, 140,* 1177–1179.

Silvestri, R. (1977). Implosive therapy treatment of emotionally disturbed retardates. *Journal of Consulting and Clinical Psychology, 45,* 14–22.

Sternlicht, M. (1979). Fears of institutionalized mentally retarded adults. *Journal of Psychology, 101,* 67–71.

Stravynski, A., Marks, I., & Yule, W. (1982). Social skills problems in neurotic outpatients: Social skills training with and without cognitive modification. *Archives of General Psychiatry, 39,* 1378–1385.

Tanguay, P. E., & Szymanski, L. S. (1980). Training of mental health professionals. In L. S. Szymanski & P. E. Tanguay (Eds.), *Emotional disorders of mentally retarded persons* (pp. 19–28). Baltimore, MD: University Park Press.

Tearnan, B. H., Telch, M. J., & Keefe, P. (1984). Etiology and onset of agoraphobia: A critical review. *Comprehensive Psychiatry, 25,* 51–62.

Waranch, H. R., Iwata, B. A., Wohl, M. K., & Nidiffer, F. D. (1981). Treatment of a retarded adult's mannequin phobia through *in vivo* desensitization and shaping approach responses. *Journal of Behavior Therapy and Experimental Psychiatry, 12,* 359–362.

Webster, T. (1963). Problems of emotional development in young retarded children. *American Journal of Psychiatry, 120,* 37–43.

Weissman, M. M. (1985). The epidemiology of anxiety disorders: Rates, risks, and familial patterns. In A. H. Tuma & J. D. Maser (Eds.), *Anxiety and the anxiety disorders.* Hillsdale, NJ: Erlbaum.

Wolpe, J. (1979). The experimental model and treatment of neurotic depression. *Behaviour Research and Therapy, 17,* 555–565.

15

Anxieties and American Elders: Proposals for Assessment and Treatment

MARIAN L. MacDONALD AND RANDI E. SCHNUR

The fastest-growing age group in the United States today is that population segment denoted as elderly (Gelles & Cornell, 1985; Lorig, Laurin, & Holman, 1984). Twenty-five and a half million Americans (Tolliver, 1983), approximately 11.3% of the U. S. census (VandenBos & Buchanan, 1983), are over the age of 65. By the year 2000, the number of "young old" (persons between 65 and 74 years old) is expected to grow by 23%, and the number of "old old" (persons over age 75) by 60% (Settin, 1982). In short, both the absolute number and the relative proportion of the elderly are increasing; moreover, both trends are expected to continue for some time to come (Fisher, 1986; Patterson et al., 1982).

Like any age group, elders need mental health services. In fact, some gerontologists have suggested that the elderly may well make up a mental health high-risk group (Brody & Kleban, 1983; Cohen, 1977; Ingersol & Silverman, 1978; Morrice, 1976). Studies of the actual level of need for mental health care among elders (viz., Bergman, 1971; Brody & Kleban, 1983; Busse & Pfeiffer, 1969; Butler & Lewis, 1977; Kay, Bergman, Foster, McKeachie, & Roth, 1970; Kramer, Taube, & Redick, 1973; National Center for Health Statistics, 1977; President's Commission on Mental Health, 1978; Redick, Kramer, & Taube, 1973; Redick & Taube, 1980; Roth, 1976; Tolliver, 1983) suggest that approximately 20% of the nation's elders *need*, and around 50% of the nation's elders could benefit from, psychological services.

Given the magnitude of this need, the elderly receive a surprisingly small amount of mental health care (MacDonald, 1983b; Thompson, Gallagher, Nies, & Epstein, 1983). Brody and Kleban (1983) report, on the basis of survey data, that fewer than 20% of those elders who need mental health services ever have their needs met by psychological, psychiatric, or social work professionals. In fact, most psychologists have never worked with a client older than 65 (Dye, 1978; Garfinkle, 1975). Though making up some 11.3% of the country's population, elders account for less than 2% of the caseload among private mental health practitioners (Kucharski, White, & Schratz, 1979), and less than 4% of the caseload in the nation's 472 community mental health center groups (Tolliver, 1983; Waxman, Carner, & Klein, 1984; President's Commission on Mental Health, 1978). Moreover, not only are the elderly receiving less than their fair share of mental health services, but their rate of care per 100,000 individuals is dropping (Patterson et al., 1982).

Marian L. MacDonald and Randi E. Schnur. Department of Psychology, University of Massachusetts at Amherst, Amherst, Massachusetts.

Factors Contributing to the Elderly's Underutilization of, and Underservice by, Mental Health Services

The mismatch between services needed by and services provided to elders is not a problem of recent origin (MacDonald, 1973; Storandt, Siegler, & Elias, 1978). As Cohen and Cooley (1983) point out, the mismatch has been vocally recognized for at least ten years. Nonetheless, very little has been done to rectify it. A host of reasons have been suggested to account for the discrepancy. In light of its persistence, it seems reasonable to suspect that more than one of these reasons are in fact contributing factors. The reasons fall into three categories: those related to elderly consumers, those related to the mental health service delivery system, and those related to mental health practitioners.

With respect to elderly consumers, several characteristics of today's generation of elders might well lead them to underutilize mental health services. Today's elders were born 26 years before the National Institute of Mental Health (NIMH) awarded its first set of clinical training grants, and 45 years before the birth of behavior therapy (Korchin, 1983). In effect, then, today's elders grew up before the field of clinical psychology did; not surprisingly, they are reluctant to define their problems in psychological, as opposed to moral or medical, terms (Lawton, 1978). For example, Waxman, Carner, and Klein (1984) found that even given a relatively severe psychological problem, fewer than 40% of an elderly sample reported a willingness to seek out professional psychological help. Waxman et al. (1984) suggested as one of the reasons for this finding that today's generation of elders hold a highly stigmatized and overly restricted view of "mental illness"—a view that leads them to regard mental health professionals as having little to offer for what they're experiencing.

Kulka and Tamir (1978) also reported data suggesting that part of the reason elders are underserved is that they are reluctant to think of themselves as needing psychological care. Using a survey methodology, they found that a full two-thirds of those elders who *did* define their problems in mental health terms had actually sought, and received, mental health treatment. It seems clear, then, that at least part of the reason elders are receiving insufficient levels of psychological services is that elders themselves do not regard psychological care as one of their needs (Barney & Neukom, 1979; Chafetz, Ochs, Tate, & Niederehe, 1982). Many elders, are genuinely fearful of admitting to having psychological problems, since their stigmatized view of psychopathology leaves them believing that diagnosed psychological problems will lead to prolonged psychiatric hospitalization or institutionalization in a nursing home (Fisher, 1985).

Features of the mental health service delivery system also contribute to the elderly's failure to receive their share of psychological services. There is a supply problem in that there is a critical shortage of mental health professionals trained in gerontology (Birren & Renner, 1981; Santos & VandenBos, 1982). Moreover, there are access problems: most mental health professionals deliver services in their offices (Nietzel, Winett, MacDonald, & Davidson, 1977), although transportation often presents major obstacles for elders, particularly those residing in rural communities or institutional settings or those experiencing some form of chronic physical impairment (MacDonald, 1983b; Redick, 1974; Schmidt, Reinhardt, Kane, & Olsen, 1977; Teeter, Garetz, Miller, & Heiland, 1976; Waxman et al., 1984).

The mental health system also includes financial barriers. Most elders live on a fixed income, with median annual receipts totaling under $5,000 (U.S. Department of Health, Education and Welfare, 1975). Their primary insurance coverage is provided by Medicare, which does not include adequate coverage for psychological treatment (Waxman et al., 1984).

There are also "packaging" barriers: neither mental health clinics nor private practitioners market their services in ways that appeal to today's older generation (Gatz, Smyer, & Lawton, 1980). Most psychological therapies are advertised as "new treatments." Unfortunately, however, today's elders are reluctant to begin using any new type of service, even when such a service is free (Barney & Neukom, 1979).

The system also has entry barriers. Most elders who are experiencing psychological problems first consult physicians rather than mental health practitioners (Lewinsohn & Teri, 1983; Waxman et al., 1984). The physicians they consult, in turn, are far more likely to prescribe medication than to refer their elderly patients for psychological care (Palmore, 1973; Waxman & Carner, 1984). This treatment appears to reflect what Robert Butler, the first director of the National Institute on Aging, termed "professional ageism" (Butler, cited in VandenBos & Buchanan, 1983), since an explanation for the disposition cannot be found in the nature of the problems aging persons present. Older persons have been found to be significantly less likely than are younger ones to be referred by physicians for psychological help, *even given the same behavioral and physical problems* (Kucharski et al., 1979).

A final feature of the system further depresses the level of mental health services that might otherwise be provided to the elderly: "the field of clinical gerontology is woefully lacking in the knowledge base necessary for adequate understanding, assessment, and treatment of older patients" (Lewinsohn & Teri, 1983, p. 2). Storandt (1983, p. 323) suggests that at least part of the cause of this inadequate knowledge base have been quasi-economic factors governing the scientific marketplace: "until very recently there was little demand for knowledge on a topic dealing with a devalued class of people." Another factor, however, has been suggested so often that there must be at least some truth to it: professional ageism on the part of psychologists.

It is unclear whether psychologists' professional ageism is rooted more strongly in American cultural attitudes, which have devalued the role of the elderly ever since the Industrial Revolution (MacDonald, 1973), or in the negative expectations for improvement planted by Freud (1950, pp. 258–259):

> The age of patients has this importance in determining their fitness for psycho-analytic treatment; that, on the one hand, near or above the fifties, the elasticity of mental processes, on which the treatment depends, is as a rule lacking—older people are no longer educable— and, on the other hand, the mass of material to be dealt with would prolong the duration of treatment indefinitely.

Even among behavior therapists, Freud's view has been influential. Clinicians of all theoretical orientations hold pessimistic views regarding the possibility of inducing clinically significant change with elderly clients (MacDonald, 1983b; Pfeiffer, 1980; Waxman et al., 1984). According to Garfield (1978, p. 212):

It has generally been assumed that older people tend to be more rigid and fixed in their ways. Their patterns of behavior have a longer reinforcement history and supposedly their defenses and character structure are more resistant ... and ... they may not learn new skills as readily as younger individuals. Consequently, it could be presumed that they would be less favorable candidates for psychotherapy in terms of their potential for change.

These negative expectations are not inconsequential. Garfinkle (1975) has reported that psychologists actively avoid working with people over age 65. Moreover, Rodin and Langer (1980) have documented how helping professionals, presented with clients having identical behavioral problems and differing only in age, were affected. Age influenced both diagnosis and treatment recommendations, with the elderly more often diagnosed as having underlying organic pathology. Treatment recommendations for this group were more often drug-related and demanded institutionalization, whereas the younger population *presenting the same clinical picture* received recommendations involving less drug therapy and more outpatient care.

Other professional attitudes have been suggested as influential in depressing the levels of services delivered to elders. Kastenbaum (1978) has suggested that psychologists feel reluctant to be associated with elders, on the grounds that they are perceived in general as low-status clients. Goldfarb (1956) has suggested that working with clients known to be in the final stages of development might raise some relatively intense, personal feelings in clinicians. Meerloo (1955) and Grotjahn (1955) both reported that anxiety was often observed in therapists seeing elderly clients. More recently, Karpf (1982) has also noted this anxiety and has suggested that it might result from the therapist's unresolved parental conflicts. MacDonald (1983b), among others (Goldfarb, 1956), has suggested that this anxiety might result from the therapist's direct confrontation with certain difficult realities about life and aging, and life and death. In short, genuinely engaging in therapeutic work with the elderly requires that one come to grips with one's own mortality. As Swenson (1983, p. 329) has so openly expressed it:

> This brings me to the final source of my interest [in aging]: preparing for my own old age. As I have observed the problems that old people have had to cope with, I have asked myself how I would cope with a given problem or how the problem might have been avoided. I study the topic partly to discover more effective ways of helping old people cope with their problems, but also to load my own armamentarium against that inevitable day. For that is one aspect of aging and its problems that makes it different from the other problems psychologists study: We may not all be schizophrenic or neurotic or overweight, but there is only one alternative to old age and most of us try to avoid that alternative.

If professionals' personal anxiety about working with the aging is in fact one of the reasons old people have remained underserved, then two directions, in addition to graduated exposure, should be taken. First, psychologists should recognize that working with elders—as with any population in real need—is a moral imperative (Hall, 1922). Second, psychologists should learn more about what aging really entails.

Facts about Aging

Most people, including psychologists, regard old age as an extraordinarily negative developmental period (Kastenbaum, 1964; MacDonald, 1973; Palmore, 1971; Skinner,

1983). But the facts show that old age is by no means either all or always bad (Birren, 1983).

More than 95% of all people over the age of 65 continue to live successfully in the community (Waxman & Carner, 1984). In fact, more than 70% of all elders own their own housing, free and clear (VandenBos & Buchanan, 1983). Three out of four elders report that the ways they are spending their time are just as interesting as they ever were; fewer than 20% report any problem in finding activities to do (Harris & Associates, 1975). Nearly four-fifths (79%) of all elders report having no major health problems (Harris & Associates, 1981). A full 55% indicate that they feel just as happy as they did when they were younger (Harris & Associates, 1975), and the great majority of elders do *not* report feeling miserable most of the time (Wisocki, 1983).

Only 8% of all elders, compared with 5% of people under 65, report having no close person to talk to (Harris & Associates, 1975). Most older people visit close relatives frequently, socialize regularly with their friends, and participate actively in organized religious and/or volunteer groups (Tyson & MacDonald, 1982). The majority of elders do not report experiencing feelings of anger or irritation (Dean, 1962), and most elders report feeling less concerned than "youngsters" are about financial problems, social appearances, or what other people think (Swenson, 1983). There is some reason to believe, then, that with advancing age many people develop a certain wisdom about how to live successfully. By no means can it be said that becoming older inherently brings a host of changes and differences that are all bad.

Aging does bring with it, however, certain differences and changes. As people age, there are changes in their physical appearance and functioning. Skin wrinkles, dries out, and becomes thinner; surface wounds heal more slowly. Hair thins and grays. In men, especially, there may be baldness. Bones weaken, joints stiffen, and muscles become less efficient (Sinex, 1975).

There are also sensory changes. Reductions in sensitivity to vibratory thresholds have been reported (Kenshalo, 1977). Decrements in visual acuity, light accommodation, and blue–green differentiation have been found as well as an increase in presbyopia (farsightedness) (Hussian, 1981). Interestingly, no changes have been found in olfactory sensitivity (Roves, Cohen, & Shlapack, 1975), although there is apparently a gradual loss of taste buds (Settin, 1982). There is an increase in the auditory threshold and an increase in the incidence of presbycusis, or high-tone loss (Hussian, 1981).

In sum, then, there are age-related normative declines in certain sensory sensitivities and perceptual abilities. Though large enough to be statistically significant, the absolute value of these differences is generally quite small. In fact, age-related reductions in the efficiency of the sensory equipment are so slight among healthy aging people as to be clinically insignificant (Hussian, 1981).

Similarly, on a biochemical level, there do not appear to be any significant, consistent changes in healthy elders' blood (Birren, Butler, Greenhouse, Sokoloff, & Yarrow, 1963). There is a decrease in serum albumin and adrenocorticotropic hormone levels, but the most important differences at this level are the decreases in cerebral blood flow and arterial oxygen saturation (Hussian, 1981), which may result from arteriosclerosis rather than aging per se (Birren et al., 1963).

This latter finding alludes to one of the most prevalent concerns about aging: changes in the anatomy and physiology of the brain. In general, there are age-related reductions in overall brain weight, so that by the age of 75 the brain weighs 8% less than it does at age 30 (Leaf, 1973). Many elders, particularly those correctly diagnosed as having dementia, show evidence of senile plaques in the hippocampus and frontal cortex, neurofibrillary tangles and degeneration, large vacuoles, abnormal microtubules, and the presence of lipofuscin, also known as the "age pigment" (cf. Bondareff, 1977) in the brain (Sinex, 1975). Changes in the neuropil, including loss of dendritic spines, shrinking of dendritic branches, and shrinking in extracellular space, have also been reported (Wisniewski & Terry, 1976). Neuroaxonal dystrophy of the nucleus gracilis is common among elders (Berry, 1975). Additionally, electroencephalogram (EEG) recordings show moderate changes in electrocortical activity with age (Hussian, 1981): generally there is a 1-cycle slowing of the EEG after age 60, with an increase in 7- to 8-cycle activity and a marked decrease in the 11- to 12-cycle range. Alpha activity slows from a baseline of about 10.2 to 10.5 cycles per second in younger samples to a level of 8.0 or 9.0 cycles per second (Birren, 1963; Wang & Busse, 1969). In summary, then, there do appear to be anatomical and physiological brain changes normatively associated with advancing age.

For clinical psychologists, however, what matters is the degree to which these changes significantly affect cognitive functioning. For many years it was generally assumed that cognitive abilities steadily declined over the course of middle and late adulthood (Wechsler, 1958). More recently, however, it has been argued that "the presumed universal decline in adult intelligence is at best a methodological artifact and at worst a popular misunderstanding of the relation between individual development and sociocultural change" (Schaie, 1974, p. 802). The question is not yet settled, but perhaps the most clinically useful summary of the issue is stated as follows (Zarit & Zarit, 1983, p. 38, emphasis added):

> Cognitive impairments, especially decrements of memory and intellect, are one of the most common expectations people have about aging. The aging process is often conceptualized as a gradual downward trajectory, with ever-increasing levels of impairment, until the person is helpless, doddering, and incompetent. This model of aging, however, has not been supported by empirical studies. While there are notable differences in cognitive performance between older and younger persons, the vast majority of individuals over age 65 are able to live independently and to manage their lives in a competent way. Furthermore, estimates of the effects of aging on cognitive performance have been exaggerated by a number of factors, including generational differences and older persons' lack of familiarity with testing procedures. . . . Overall, the cognitive changes that most people experience as they grow older are relatively benign.

Like any demographic group, however, the aging are heterogeneous (Romaniuk, Tilden, & Arling, 1983); for some elders, then, old age is undeniably a period of marked general decline (Birren, 1983, p. 298).

> There are two faces of aging, one optimistic and one pessimistic. . . . The optimistic one revolves about the millions of competent older persons who enjoy a high quality of life. . . . [There is also] the pessimistic face of aging, the large number of poor, unhealthy, and lonely older adults.

The pessimistic face of aging involves primarily that minority of elders—21%, as compared with 8% of those individuals aged 18 to 54—for whom poor health represents a serious problem (Harris & Associates, 1981). There is no natural disease process of aging (MacDonald, 1973), but age does bring with it a reduction in the efficiency of the immunological and autonomic nervous systems (Hussian, 1981). Both changes are of special consequence for health maintenance, since the autonomic nervous system is thought to be responsible for regulating adaptations to both endogenous and exogenous stressors (Frolkis, 1977). With advancing age, then, these reductions leave the body less capable of warding off disease states. Unfortunately, this decreased ability coincides with a period of decreased attention to health maintenance activities (Tyson & MacDonald, 1982), and a shift away from preventive and toward remedial or even no medical care (Birren, 1983; Settin, 1982).

In summary, then, the data about the realities of growing older are by no means generally alarming or negative. It is true that there is a subset of elders, a minority, for whom aging is unpleasant. These individuals typically suffer from poor health, poverty, or both, and doubtless will disproportionately come to the attention of mental health practitioners. For most individuals, however, most of their elderly years are quite positive. The data give no reason to persist in the belief that growing older will necessarily be a negative developmental process, or that working with older people necessarily implies working with people whose limits preclude change, or who are ill or severely disabled, or who are about to die. In fact, life expectancies for people who have survived to old age are surprisingly long (Hayes, with Gladney, 1984). In short, old people are an enormously satisfying, and heterogeneous, group to serve.

Anxiety, Stress, and Coping among Elders

It is important to keep the preceding material in mind when considering how to work with gerontologically related anxiety states. Without this context, professionals are likely to forget that, in general, elders—especially healthy ones—are much more similar to than they are different from younger clients. It follows, then, that elders might, in general, experience the same psychological problems, and respond well to the same psychological treatments, as do younger clients.

It is difficult to establish how much of a problem anxiety is for elders because, as previously noted, persons in this generation of elders are reluctant to seek out help for psychological problems such as anxiety and depression. When elders do seek help for such problems, physicians are the professional group they are most likely to consult (Waxman et al., 1984), although physicians are both unlikely to recognize the presence of anxiety (Brown, 1982; Waxman & Carner, 1984) and, when it is recognized, likely to treat it with masking medications alone (Parry, Balter, Mellinger, Cisin, & Manheimer, 1973; Wasson, Ripeckyj, Lazarus, Kupferer, Barry, & Farce, 1984). To date, in fact, the primary treatment for anxiety in elders has been pharmacotherapy. Perhaps one indication of the extent of anxiety in elders, then, is found in the fact that persons over 60 take antianxiety drugs (benzodiazepines) more frequently than do members of any other age group (Parry et al., 1973).

There is additional reason to believe that anxiety among elders may be a significant problem in both magnitude and impact. Epidemiological data suggest that anxiety may be more common among the elderly than in any other age group (Sallis, Lichstein, Clarkson, Stalgaitis, & Campbell, 1983), occurring with great frequency (Oberleder,

1966), and perhaps more frequently than any other emotional disturbance having an onset in later life (Butler & Lewis, 1977). One recent survey, for example, estimates the proportion of community-dwelling elders experiencing "nervousness, anxiety, or tension" at 17%, with 52% thought to have significant "worries" (Brody & Kleban, 1983). Other estimates are even higher (Janson & Ryder, 1983). Among institutionalized elders, nursing staff rank "anxious mood" as the fourth most frequent behavior problem observed (trailing only depression, pain complaints, and other physical complaints), and as the problem second most deserving of psychological intervention (Haley, 1983).

These figures suggest that the *level* of anxiety among elders is clinically significant. There are data to suggest that the *effects* of anxiety on elders are clinically significant as well. Anxiety and stress have both been implicated as at least contributing factors in a number of other problematic conditions occurring with heightened frequency among elders, including sleep disturbances (Brody & Kleban, 1983); alcohol abuse (Dupree, Broskowski, & Schonfeld, 1984); sexual dysfunctions (Settin, 1982); and decreased responsiveness to psychological interventions for other disturbances (Hoyer, Lopez, & Goldstein, 1983). Perhaps the most important effect of prolonged anxiety in this age group, however, is found in its impact or potential impact on health. Prolonged anxiety and stress have been implicated in the onset of a wide variety of physical disorders (Kahana & Kahana, 1983). Thus anxiety has come to be regarded as at least a significant factor in health (Haupt, Orleans, George, & Brodie, 1979; Preston & Mansfield, 1984), if not a causal factor in illness (Brody & Kleban, 1983; Kiecolt-Glaser et al., 1985). According to Preston and Mansfield (1983, p. 490):

> A large body of research has emerged that has demonstrated a relationship between illness, both chronic and acute, and stressful life events. Many of these researchers believe that stress is a precursor of illness. . . . It follows, then, that maintenance of good health requires stress reduction.

In light of elders' increased physiological susceptibility to disease processes, and in light of the clearly central role continued physical health plays in elders' psychological well-being, stress reduction and effective anxiety management would seem to be of special importance in this population.

Stress, and coping successfully with it, are complex phenomena to understand, particularly with respect to older people. Lazarus and DeLongis (1983) have proposed one of the most comprehensive explanatory models to date. In discussing both sources of stress and types of coping among the elderly, they note that variability in coping, rather than clear central tendencies, is the rule: "Some old people manage poorly, some manage well—this variation exists even among those who are institutionalized" (p. 245).

The major determinant of this variability, according to Lieberman (1975), among others, is the extent of actual deterioration in the elder's life circumstances, including health status. Lazarus and Folkman (1984) argue persuasively, however, that certain individual differences *in addition to* life circumstances play a crucial role in experienced event stressfulness (i.e., coping); furthermore, they contend that the most important individual difference is the set of cognitive appraisals the elder makes of his or her changed life circumstances.

Lazarus and Folkman (1984) suggest that any number of environmental stressors—

loss of a child or spouse, loss of supplementary income or a salary—*can* function as stressors and create anxiety in the aging. Whether such events *do* function as stressors and create anxiety, however, depends to a very large extent on the individual's capabilities at coping (Lazarus & DeLongis, 1983, p. 248):

> People are rarely passive in the face of what happens to them; they seek to change things if they can, and when they cannot, they use cognitive modes of coping by which they may change the meaning of the situation.

It follows, then, that anxiety in the aging is not always negative; it may function as a very adaptive signal that some circumstance or change in circumstances is calling for action or adaptation—that is, is demanding an effective coping response.

Since the writings of Jung (1933, 1953), psychologists have assumed that both coping styles and coping efficiencies change with advancing age (Rosow, 1974). In describing the presumed change, Gutmann (1974) suggested that as people grow older, they move from active mastery to more passive coping and, ultimately, to a regressive reliance on magical modes of coping such as religion. Vaillant (1977) and Pfeiffer (1977) also suggested that there was a change in coping with increasing age, but the change they described was in a *positive* direction. They held that coping becomes *more* realistic and *more* effective with age, with a decreased dependence on immature methods such as projection and acting out, and an increased use of mature ways such as humor, altruism, and suppression. Lazarus and colleagues (Lazarus & DeLongis, 1983; Lazarus & Folkman, 1984) have concluded, however, consistent with data reported by McCrae (1982), that (Lazarus & Folkman, 1984, pp. 172–173):

> Perhaps the best generalization regarding changes in coping over the life span . . . is that as sources of stress in living change with stages of life, coping will change in response. [There is agreement that sources of stress change. But the contention] that coping changes in basic ways, regardless of changes in source of stress, is subject to doubt at the present time. . . . At this stage of knowledge, and without better evidence, it seems best to assume that aging per se brings no changes in coping.

Conceptualizing how best to aid elders in coping with stressors, then, follows the same model proposed for understanding how best to aid adults of any age in coping with stress. Lazarus and DeLongis (1983, p. 250) have found it useful to distinguish between coping directed toward problem solving and coping directed toward the regulation of emotion:

> Problem-focused coping changes the troubled person–environment relationship (i.e., the stressor), whereas emotion-focused coping changes, through realistic or defensive reappraisal, the way an encounter is construed or attended to and therefore the emotional reaction to it. Emotion-focused coping operates through a variety of cognitive acts, such as attentional avoidance, intellectualized detachment, denial, reinterpretation of the past, humor, magical or wishful thinking, and religious faith. If one resolves the trouble through problem-focused efforts, there is no longer any reason to feel threatened; if one engages in emotion-focused coping, the objective situation remains the same, although a more benign emotional reaction is still created.

The relevance of this model for understanding stress reactions in the aging, as a group experiencing an accelerated rate of very real and irreversible losses and therefore as a group experiencing a host of sometimes unchangeable circumstances requiring coping (Hussian, 1981; Kahana & Kahana, 1983; Settin, 1982), is profound. The special relevance of emotion-focused, or cognitive, coping for the aging is underscored by a recent observation. In explaining how problems that older people present differ from problems presented by younger people, Swenson (1983, p. 328) commented that:

> the kinds of problems these [older] people asked about were not the kinds of problems to which I was accustomed. One difference was that very often they were not problems that could be resolved or eliminated. Rather, they were problems to which the person had to learn to adapt.

One final caveat must be included before considering specific methods of assessment and intervention for cases of gerontologically related anxiety. The caveat is a reminder that most elders successfully adapt by themselves to the various major changes they may be experiencing, including widowhood, retirement, relocation, and even serious illness (Gutmann, 1969; Palmore, 1977). It is important to keep this fact in mind when confronted by a troubled elder, and to avoid overintervening by assuming client incompetence where in reality there is only client uncertainty or indecision.

The Assessment Process in Cases of Gerontologically Related Anxiety

It follows from this caveat that a careful assessment is an essential first step in intervention. As is typically the case when working with elders (MacDonald & Eklund, 1985), the assessment must be comprehensive and must take into consideration possible organic, as well as environmental and cognitive, controlling variables when formulating treatment plans. According to Hussian (1981, p. 82):

> Working with the elderly, one begins to marvel at the complexity of the assessment issue. There is no other client population this size which presents more diverse causative possibilities, including those endogenous antecedents of which most psychologists are less than familiar.

As implied by Hussian's (1981) statement, adequate assessment with the aging involves gathering a broader range of information than may ordinarily be the case with younger clients—information concerning behavioral, affective, and cognitive styles characteristic of the person, but also information concerning medical status, cognitive capabilities, and physical/social environmental circumstances (MacDonald & Kerr, 1982). When working with the aging, then, there must be a broadening of the content areas included in the typical assessment. Moreover, because of generational and physiological differences, there must often be a modification of the assessment *process* used to work with the aging as well.

Establishing rapport prior to assessment is essential to gathering accurate information, and doing so often requires adopting a stance different from what works with younger people. Today's generation of elders were raised to be suspicious of psychological professionals. Establishing a trusting relationship requires patience, sensitivity, and a genuine respect for generational differences that are analogous to—and no less profound than—the more typically recognized ethnic and cultural ones.

Two stages are included in assessment. The first is essentially descriptive, whereby an accurate diagnosis is established for the presence of anxiety as the predominant disturbance or reaction (see DSM-III; American Psychiatric Association, 1980). Although this stage is challenging with elders, since the accuracy of this assessment rests largely on the adequacy with which the clinician has established rapport, it is the second stage of assessment that brings the greatest intellectual challenge.

This second stage of assessment may be termed *inferential*. It involves inferring, or hypothesizing, what variables would alter the described condition (i.e., anxiety), if they were changed. One of the great strengths of behavior therapy is that the variables hypothesized to be sufficient for producing anxiety change need not, and in fact usually are not, the same variables that produced the changeworthy state initially (Ullmann & Krasner, 1969). One of the great strengths of behavioral assessment is that, unlike traditional diagnosis, it is considered incomplete without this inferential process, which yields testable hypotheses about where therapy can be directed to effect clinical change.

It is this inferential process that calls for great breadth in working with elders, on two counts. First, clinical problems—more often than is the case with younger people—can emerge because of problems in the person as a psychological being, in the person as a physiological being, or in the setting within which the person must function. Second, far more often than is the case with younger clients, some of the problems causing anxiety will not themselves be changeable. To the extent that the clinician has information about a broad range of variables, compensatory changes potentially effective at counteracting the effects of the unchangeable problem(s) can be identified. For more reasons than one, then, it is wise to gather information over a variety of measurement sources. Whenever possible, these sources should include a battery of self-report tests, direct observations, and consultations with relative or friend informants, as well as the more traditional clinical interview with the elderly client him- or herself. With this age group, under all circumstances, one source of information should always be a medical consultation.

As a starting point, a battery of self-report tests has an obvious advantage. It is capable of generating a tremendous amount of information, about a great many areas, at limited professional cost and under standardized conditions. There can be, however, four major disadvantages to administering lengthy self-report batteries to this population. First, the number of tests currently available is very limited, because few psychometrically acceptable tests have been explicitly designed or extended for use with elderly clients (Crook, 1979). Second, the administration of a large number of tests *can* undermine efforts to establish the sort of trusting alliance essential for gathering accurate information through the clinical interview, and for later being able to use the therapeutic relationship to facilitate change. Third, the current generation of elders are typically unfamiliar with tests and form completion; consequently, they often dislike completing written assessments. Finally, various physiological factors such as visual impairment or decreased resistance to fatigue can make test taking an arduous task, especially for that subset of elders experiencing significant health problems.

Where feasible, however, one or more areas can be profitably assessed, at least adjunctively, using written tests. Among the scales recommended are: the Brief Symptom Inventory (Derogatis, 1977) for evaluating the presence of a variety of disorders and thereby aiding in differential diagnosis; the Morale Scale (Lawton, 1975) or Life Satisfaction Index (Wood, Wylie, & Schaefer, 1969) for evaluating the general sense of well-being; the Life Crisis Inventory (Antonovsky, 1979) for evaluating both the occurrence and the perceived impact of catastrophic life stressors; the Daily Hassles Scale (DeLongis, Coyne, Dakof, Folkman, & Lazarus, 1982) for evaluating the occurrence and impact of common daily irritations and minor stressors; the Health and Daily Living Questionnaire (Moos, Cronkite, Billings, & Finney, 1980; Sidle, Moos, Adams, & Cady, 1969) or the Ways of Coping Checklist (Lazarus & Folkman, 1984) for assessing usual coping styles; and the Social Support Index and Questionnaire (Wilcox, 1981) for assessing the strength of the social network.

Self-report measures were originally developed as efficient substitutes for interviews (MacDonald, 1983a), so one alternative for administering any of these scales in a way that obviates its disadvantages is by embedding its questions in the context of a traditional clinical interview.

The clinical interview remains the most popular and flexible assessment procedure for diagnosing and describing anxiety-related states in elders (Kahana & Kahana, 1983). To be successful, interviews with the elderly must be done with sensitivity—that is, with genuine respect, with a willingness to make adaptations necessitated by any physiological limitations, and with an appreciation for the generational differences characterizing today's elders. Gallagher and Thompson (1983) cite a case study illustrating the importance of this sensitivity. The case involved an 87-year-old male referred for psychosocial evaluation. Two assessment interviews were conducted, one by an inexperienced clinician, who concluded that the client was not experiencing any psychological distress, and one by an experienced clinician, who concluded that the client was suffering from a major depressive episode characterized by intense feelings of guilt and vivid death fantasies (Gallagher & Thompson, 1983, p. 10):

> Why were two distinctly different conclusions drawn? The first interviewer indicated that she viewed Mr. M's severe psychomotor retardation and somatic concerns as general "frailty" due to aging. Also, because he gave vague answers to questions about his feelings, she concluded that there was little evidence of real dysphoria. She attributed Mr. M's lack of communication to his having lived alone for 20 years and assumed that few interpersonal demands had been placed on him during that time. The second interviewer, in contrast, found that Mr. M's hearing loss was a significant factor in the interview process. She asked questions in a loud, deep voice and occasionally wrote them out, to be sure that he understood the question's intent. Mr. M had revealed that he had been unable to hear most of the questions asked in the first interview but felt "too bad" to make an issue of it. He claimed that the first interviewer seemed uninterested in him and provided little direction to assist him in answering difficult questions. In general, he felt frustrated and dissatisfied with that interview, and he appreciated having a second opportunity to express himself more clearly.

Perhaps the greatest strength of interviews with elders is their ability, if sensitively done, to determine not only the occurrence of given events, but also the subjective stressfulness of those events. It is also, perhaps uniquely, possible through an interview to determine perceived relationships between event occurrences and presenting problems. This determination is particularly important when considering optimal points of intervention, and the client him- or herself can be very helpful in avoiding certain inferential pitfalls: "It is often tempting to assume problems that arose subsequent to presumed stressors to be consequences of those stressors, yet this may not be the fact in individual situations" (Kahana & Kahana, 1983, pp. 151–152).

At present, sensitively done interviews are the most effective method for determining subjective evaluations of stressors and temporal relationships between potential stressors and potential stress reactions. As a consequence, particularly when planning intervention strategies, interviews are an indispensable data source. To be optimally informative, however, these interviews often must be conducted differently than is typically the case with younger clients. First, the interviewer must be prepared to keep the interview short, lasting somewhere between 30 and 40 minutes. Older people sometimes tire after spending more than this length of time on a concentrated activity; to prevent fatigue effects, then, it may be necessary to schedule more than one assessment session, over several days.

A second modification that often must be introduced into interviews conducted with older clients is that the interviewer must be patient. Older people tend to have slower reaction times (Settin, 1982) than do younger clients, and to function in a slower general time frame than do younger professionals. Unless interviewers are aware of these differences, they are likely to communicate disinterest or disrespect, as well as to discourage the disclosure of important information, by proceeding at a rate that feels rushed to the elderly interviewee.

A third modification is often required. Many elders suffer from sensory impairments. Under these circumstances, it is important to present questions in a manner compensating for whatever sensory deficiencies there might be—under bright, high-contrast conditions, for example, when talking with persons suffering some visual loss, or in a loud voice with visual aids when interviewing a person with some hearing impairment.

With this particular generation of elders, two additional stylistic interview modifications are also often necessary. Because this generation of elders matured at a time when higher education was not easily available, many of today's elders have limited educational backgrounds. Under these circumstances, it is important to speak in everyday language and not to overinterpret the elder's failure to use or easily understand highly abstract terms. The final, stylistic modification involves the interviewer's stance. This generation of elders were raised to be suspicious of professionals, most especially psychological ones. It is essential to recognize, then, that the interviewer will have to work harder than is ordinarily the case with younger clients to establish trust and rapport. Again, it is important not to overinterpret this cultural difference in levels of initial trust and acceptance.

Comprehensive assessment interviews with the aging should include attention to a broad range of areas, some of them nontraditional. These areas include the following:

1. The interview should begin with an assessment of the presenting problem. Because older people tend to delay seeking treatment for as long as possible (Brody & Kleban, 1983), it is not unusual for presenting problems to be of a long-standing nature. Their extended duration, then, may have resulted in greater symptom severity than is ordinarily observed with similar types of problems in younger people, and may have also resulted in the development of fairly elaborate and perhaps partially effective compensa-

tory mechanisms. All these areas must be assessed when developing a description of the presenting problem and the circumstances under which it is most likely to occur.

2. The behavior throughout the interview should be observed. Physical appearance should be noted with an eye for indirect evidence of financial status (e.g., How new is the clothing?) and health maintenance habits (e.g., How clean are the teeth or dentures? What is the condition of the skin?). Ongoing behavior should be observed to get a rough indication of general physical condition (e.g., Do there appear to be any gross motor or sensory impairments?). And qualities of the verbal exchange should be monitored, allowing a rough assessment of mental status (i.e., cognitive functioning).

3. There should be a discussion of the results of the client's most recent physical examination. Attention should be paid to diagnosed physical illnesses as well as recurring physical complaints. Information should be solicited concerning both prescription and nonprescription ingested medications. A client who has not had a physical examination during the preceding 12 months, or during the previous month if there have been any recent physical changes, should be referred for a full medical examination, including, as a minimum, laboratory work, glucose tolerance tests, and electrolyte assays. Finally, there should be direct inquiry into the client's satisfaction with his or her sexual functioning, which should remain quite pleasurable for any healthy elder.

The importance of obtaining a medical consultation when working with elders cannot be overstated. The reason such a consultation is so important is very straightforward. The aging body is going through biological changes on the cellular level, particularly if disease is present; at the same time, the aging body is less efficient at homeostatic balance (Hussian, 1981). Consequently, the physiological and behavioral symptom of anxiety, which can result from physiological origins in any age group, is more likely to do so with elders, given base rates. Among the biophysical disorders that can cause anxiety are: respiratory alkalosis in hysteria, hypnoxia, and with acetylsalicylic acid; frontal lobe neoplasms; hyperthyroidism and parathyroid deficiencies; Cushing's syndrome; and congestive heart failure (Butler & Lewis, 1977; Hussian, 1981). Moreover, anxiety is a typical concomitant of the onset of any acute physical disorder, and it may remain the only subjectively evident symptom for a significant period of time. Finally, the presence of anxiety may cause physical symptoms that should be adjunctively treated and that, without treatment, would serve to exacerbate the severity of the presenting problem. Hussian (1981) cites as one example of this latter circumstance hypertension resulting from ineffective stress management, which then leads to anxiety in response to the hypertensive condition. In general, then (Hussian, 1981, p. 52):

> the consideration of organic causes is necessary in geriatric psychology. In fact, it is often the case, particularly if suggested in the client's medical history, that such causative factors should be eliminated *first* before proceeding with a nonorganic assessment. Whenever an obvious environmental causative factor is not readily apparent, as in relocation or death of a loved one, internal "organism" variables should be immediately explored. The establishment of endogenous involvement, however, should not preclude the assessment of environmental concomitants or the application of environmental techniques to treatment.

4. The person's current living situation should be evaluated. This evaluation entails assessing the client's usual daily routine, including meal preparation and meal nutri-

tional content, usual sleeping patterns, and usual recreational activities. Financial status and management should also be determined. Physical living situation and household maintenance arrangements should be explored. There should be a deliberate attempt here to assess what might be conceptualized as the physical, social, and personal "demands" of the elder's living environment.

5. The person's social network must be evaluated. Relationships with family members, and the number, type, and quality of contacts with friends, should be explored.

6. The person's reliance on social support services should be determined. Whether the person is currently receiving or has recently received other kinds of therapies (e.g., speech therapy or physical therapy) should be evaluated; with consent, reports from these other professionals describing the nature of the services, and outlining suggestions for effective styles of interaction with the client, should be requested. If the client is involved with social agencies (e.g., the local Home Care or Visiting Nurse association), information should be obtained about the nature and duration of this involvement.

7. There should be an assessment of the person's current level of participation in planned enjoyable activities, including personal (e.g., reading) as well as social (e.g., foster grandparents) ones. The quality—that is, reported enjoyability—of each activity should be directly assessed. This content area is of special importance since involvement in planned activities has been shown repeatedly to be a significant correlate of overall morale in elders (MacDonald, Davidowitz, Gimbel, & Foley, 1982; MacDonald & Settin, 1978).

8. Predominant affects should be directly assessed. Interviewers should inquire about general levels of anxiety, anger, and depression, as well as about general life satisfaction (i.e., morale) and general feelings about the future (i.e., overall hopefulness–hopelessness about things to come).

9. There should be an assessment of recent (i.e., within the past five years) changes in any life area, and a direct assessment of the subjective stressfulness associated with each life change. Consideration should be given to both those changes commonly considered stressful by mental health professionals (e.g., widowhood, physical illness) and other important but somewhat more subtle changes (e.g., relocation of close friends, the effects of inflation). Also, when exploring each individual instance of change, there should be some exploration of the individual's adaptations to each change. This chronicling will provide an index of the individual's range of styles, and preferred styles, of coping.

On the basis of this information, coupled with the information obtained through exploring areas mentioned earlier, the clinician should make a judgment about the closeness of the *person–environment fit* (French, Rodgers, & Cobb, 1974). The concept of the person–environment fit has been tentatively identified as a more powerful predictor of stress reactions than are tallies of stressful life events considered alone (Kahana & Kahana, 1983). In making this assessment, the clinician should remain sensitive to the reality that stress reactions can result either from a single major stressor, or from the cumulative or combined effects of individually inconsequential life events (Rosenthal & Rosenthal, 1983). Finally, in conducting this inquiry, the clinician should remain watchful for any negative side effects from the stress, including especially any negative attempts at adaptation (e.g., alcoholism).

10. Finally, there should be an exploration of the individual's historical development. This exploration should include some understanding of the person's place in his or her family of origin and family of procreation (if applicable), as well as the person's educational, vocational, social, and personal development through young and middle adulthood. Major events over the course of the life span, and adjustments to them, should be placed in chronological context. Finally, any psychiatric history should be explored.

Careful interviews allow two forms of assessment. The first is analogous to the self-report in that clients are asked to collaborate as informants about their own behavior, affect, and cognition. Interviewing also permits a second form of assessment: direct observation of behavior by the clinician.

Direct observation has long been recognized in behavioral assessment as the optimal measurement method for public, circumscribed problems (MacDonald, 1978, 1983a). Where the presenting problem is situationally bound anxiety, then, like that presented in the case of many phobias and compulsions, it is desirable to arrange for direct observation to confirm information obtained through self-report. In any case, there should always be direct observational assessment of the client's cognitive functioning. In most instances it will be apparent from the informal observations routinely included as part of the clinical interview that there is no significant cognitive impairment. In those instances where there is uncertainty, either because of the presence of some cognitive impairment, because of the clinician's unfamiliarity with the presentational styles of this generation of elders, or because of the elder's discomfort at interacting with a psychological professional, it is essential to assess levels of cognitive functioning directly.

Unfortunately, currently available technology for making such an assessment is woefully inadequate. The Wechsler Scale, for all its strengths with younger adult populations, has been severely criticized for its stylistic incompatibility with today's generation of elders (Settin, 1982). Far more frequently used are the Mini-Mental Status Exam (Folstein, Folstein, & McHugh, 1975) and the Mental Status Questionnaire (Kahn, Goldfarb, Pollack, & Peck, 1960). Perhaps the greatest strength of these tests is their ability to help clinicians discriminate between cognitive impairment and depression, a difficult diagnostic discrimination to make on the basis of informal, interview observations alone. Their greatest weakness, however, is nicely stated by Robert Butler (1983; quoted in VandenBos & Buchanan, 1983, p. 305):

> It has always troubled me that psychiatrists have wanted brief mental status examinations. Nothing, in my opinion, is more complex, and appropriately so, than central nervous system functioning. No self-respecting cardiologist, for example, would look for a brief cardiac evaluation for making critical decisions about people's lives. Anything that is as complex as the central nervous system also warrants comprehensive and sophisticated evaluation, even if we do not yet know what that sophisticated assessment methodology should be. Asking somebody to name the President of the United States or to state the day of the week is not very sophisticated or comprehensive. At this point when people fail such a mental status "exam" they are pretty far deteriorated. It does not identify early cases.

There is a final assessment method that it is desirable to include when working with elders. Especially when working with elders who are suffering from some degree of cognitive impairment, it can be enormously useful to gather information from peer, friend, or relative collateral. Kahana and Kahana (1983, p. 151) suggest, in fact, that "at this point, the best determination of stress reactions for clinical purposes is still based on a careful history obtained convergently from both the [elderly] patients and family members."

In all instances, whenever evaluating elders to describe and draw conclusions about an anxiety-related disorder, it is essential to consider multiple sources of information and to attend to contextual factors. It is simple enough to detect the presence of anxiety. What is more complicated is determining whether the anxiety itself should be treated directly, or whether the anxiety is signaling the presence of some as yet unmastered stressor. In the latter case, facilitating effective coping with the stressor or stressors would be the appropriate intervention. In either case, if the anxiety has produced persisting, negative side effects such as alcoholism, insomnia, or hypochondriasis—and if these side effects remain after the anxiety or ineffective coping has been treated successfully—those negative side effects should also be directly addressed.

Although the preceding material has focused on two primary functions of assessment—namely, problem description and problem formulation (i.e., conceptualizations leading to treatment)—it is important to bear in mind that thorough behavioral assessment serves a third function as well. It allows for the monitoring of treatment effectiveness by providing criteria for assessing changes in specific target behaviors as treatment progresses. With elderly clients, both self-monitoring and collateral or observer direct observations can be useful in this regard. Readers interested in additional detail on implementing these methods are referred to the excellent descriptions by Mahoney (1977) on self-monitoring and Hartmann and Wood (1982) on direct assessments by observers.

The Intervention Process in Cases of Gerontologically Related Anxiety

When a careful assessment indicates the presence of maladaptive anxiety in an elder, and when physiological causes for that anxiety have been ruled out, the question becomes how to proceed in treatment. The answer to that question is: carefully, because our knowledge base of how to work well with elders is too limited and restricted to support definitive recommendations at this time (Kahana & Kahana, 1983; Lawton, 1978; Steury & Blank, 1977; Swenson, 1983). Fortunately, however, there is preliminary evidence to support the usefulness of a broad range of behaviorally based interventions (Hussian & Davis, 1985; Pinkston & Linsk, 1984), and this evidence and these interventions will be presented in the concluding pages that follow. One overall generalization is in order, however, at the outset. In the absence of information to the contrary, the most appropriate assumption to make about how to treat elders is that the content of their treatment should be identical to the content that would be used to treat a younger person presenting the same problem under the same circumstances.

Put differently, there is no reason to assume that older people will not respond to the same treatment content known to be effective for younger clients. This point is essential to understand: it is treatment style, not treatment content, that must typically be altered when working with elderly clients. Although readers may clearly recognize in this context that it is incorrect to assume that elders must be treated substantively differently than are younger clients, they should also recognize that, out of context, therapists generally err in assuming that treatments known to be effective with younger populations will not work with elders. For example, when reporting that an insomnia treatment developed for young adults worked equally well with elders, Storandt (1983, p. 326, emphasis added) wrote:

> most [previous] studies of the treatment of insomnia have specifically excluded older clients because the [stimulus control] *treatment was not expected to be effective for this population.*

With older, as with younger, anxious clients, then, the initial treatment decision involves determining whether the anxiety should be treated directly, or whether it should be regarded as reactive—symptomatic of the presence of some other problem that might be a more appropriate target for intervention.

This determination is not always straightforward. It must be made on a case-by-case basis, and it requires comprehensive assessment information about the anxiety's antecedent and consequent cognitive, affective, physiological, and external environmental circumstances, as well as information about the client's general life circumstances, including especially subtle and insidious stressors. Moreover, the accuracy of the determination cannot be known before the fact—that is, before the plan for intervention has confirmed its accuracy by demonstrating treatment effectiveness (MacDonald & Kerr, 1982).

There are, however, some general guidelines that are helpful in making this determination. The clinician should consider treating the anxiety directly when it appears to be situationally bound, and when:

1. The anxiety is of sufficient intensity or duration to cause extreme subjective distress in the absence of objective danger or threat.
2. The anxiety is triggering a physiological reaction resulting in either tissue damage or some other threat to good health.
3. The anxiety is inhibiting the performance of some learned behavior that would be effective in and appropriate to the anxiety-provoking circumstances.
4. The anxiety is instrumental in promoting the maintenance of some maladaptive, perhaps compensatory behavior.

For each of these circumstances, as will be illustrated by examples to follow, several different psychological intervention methods have been used to treat anxiety directly in elders.[1] Across strategies, however, evaluations of treatment effectiveness to date have been largely confined to clinical observations in the context of case reports.

Garfinkel (1979) reported a case describing the direct treatment of an anxiety that was of sufficient intensity to cause great subjective distress in the absence of objective

---

1. The clinician should remember that it may be most appropriate, especially in cases involving tissue damage or other threats to health, to consider psychopharmacological therapies as at least adjunctives, and to make referrals to psychiatric or other medical colleagues for appropriate consultations (Alford, 1983).

danger. The client was a 75-year-old woman in good health. She presented complaints of persistent feelings of tightness in the chest, choking, and a lack of breath. Detailed questioning indicated that these feelings generally occurred together and under situationally bound circumstances—namely, whenever the woman had to "act on her own," especially with strangers. The problems were conceptualized as facets of an anxiety response and were treated using systematic desensitization. The treatment, which extended over several months, was completely successful in eliminating the anxiety.

Linoff and West (1982) reported a case in which anxiety was apparently triggering a distressing physiological reaction, tension headaches. The client was a seriously ill, 89-year-old male nursing home patient, who presented with a 20-year history of headaches. Neurological evaluations for organic etiologies were all negative. During the several months prior to the patient's referral for treatment, his headaches had worsened considerably. At presentation he repeated that his head hurt "all the time."

Treatment involved 19 sessions of relaxation training held over a period of 2 months. Relaxation was first induced by instructions paired with music (i.e., Chopin Nocturnes), and later by music alone. The patient reported that the treatment was completely effective in stopping his headaches; moreover, his self report of effectiveness received corroboration from his medical chart, which indicated that he had requested pain medication for headaches only once during the 6 weeks following treatment.

Hussian (1981) described the direct treatment of an anxiety that was inhibiting the performance of an appropriate behavior. He worked with four nursing home residents (with a mean age of 79) who reported experiencing extreme anxiety at the thought of riding in an elevator. For two of the residents, who were wheelchair-bound, not riding in the elevator meant essentially confining their movements to indoors and, even more so, to one floor of their nursing home residence.

Hussian (1981) instructed the residents in the importance of relaxing when tense and educated them about the safety features of elevators. He also constructed positive self-statements that the residents could use when riding (e.g., "When the doors open, I will confidently go inside and hold onto the rail," and, "If the door sticks, I will not panic. I will press the red button until help arrives"), and instructed them to imagine themselves approaching, entering, and moving in the elevator while rehearsing the positive self-instructions. Finally, Hussian (1981) arranged graduated exposure by accompanying the residents during the elevator rides.

Hussian's (1981) stress inoculation treatment was quite effective. At 2-month follow-up, all four residents were riding in the elevator, several times each day, with minimal self-reported or apparent anxiety.

Bootzin, Engle-Friedman, and Hazelwood (1983) described the direct treatment of an anxiety conceptualized as instrumental in promoting the maintenance of a maladaptive behavior, insomnia. The client was a 65-year-old married man. He complained at presentation primarily of sleep maintenance, rather than sleep onset, problems; his baseline sleep diaries indicated that he typically got less than 4 hours of sleep each night.

Treatment consisted of two components. In the first component, reassuring information about sleep architecture and the benign consequences of sleep deprivation was provided to change the client's cognitive appraisal of his problem. The intent of this component was to reinforce the client's sense of self-efficacy, since "The insomniac's appraisal of the problem may be an important component of its maintenance. Perseverant worry about why one cannot sleep and preoccupation with one's inability to sleep and the consequences of sleeplessness are likely to intensify any existing problems" (Bootzin et al., 1983, p. 99). The second component was progressive relaxation training, which was framed as a coping skill available for use whenever the client needed it, including especially those times when he was experiencing difficulty sleeping.

Before treatment, Bootzin et al.'s (1983) client ("B.") reported sleeping an average of less than 4 hours per night. He was also taking Dalmane and Librium regularly, and self-reported high levels of both anxiety and depression. After 1 month, including four therapy sessions (Bootzin et al., 1983, p. 105):

> B.'s sleep improved substantially. Parallel improvement was observed in his daily ratings of fatigue and functioning during the day. . . . Although B. had been losing weight before treatment, he gained 15 pounds during the treatment and follow-up and was now back to his normal weight. His blood pressure also decreased substantially. He reported that he worried much less about sleep, he infrequently mentioned sleeping difficulties to his friends, and he no longer labeled himself an insomniac. He was particularly pleased with the support he received in withdrawing and staying off of Dalmane.

As these case studies illustrate, relaxation, desensitization, and cognitive strategies have all been reported as effective for directly treating anxiety in elders. At this point, controlled evaluations of these treatments are sorely needed. However, given the carefully documented effectiveness of these treatments with younger populations, and the several case studies demonstrating their effectiveness with elders (see also Chiodo, Walley, & Jenkins, 1983; Dupree, Broskowski, & Schonfeld, 1984; Faloon, 1975; Friedman, 1966; Garrison, 1978; Hussian, 1981; O'Brien, 1978; Sallis et al., 1983; Thyer, 1981; Wander, 1972), it is reasonable now to try these treatments and to expect them to work.

Under some circumstances, peripheral features of the methods must be modified for use with elderly clients. One problem often encountered with standard relaxation training, for example, is that clients may experience arthritic pain when tensing and releasing particular muscle groups.[2] An alternative in this circumstance is to omit tension cycles and instead to instruct the client to focus on and release whatever tension is already present in the affected areas (Bootzin et al., 1983). Another problem sometimes encountered with relaxation training is that sensory impairments may preclude delivering instructions in the standard format. In such cases, alternative methods for conveying instructional content can be effective: Chiodo et al. (1983), for example, describe conducting standard relaxation with written instructions and tactile cues for a hearing-impaired client.

Standard relaxation training may be impossible with persons suffering major physiological impairment such as paralysis. With these individuals, relaxed states may be

---

2. Relaxation training should by no means be avoided in cases involving arthritis, and, in fact, there is some evidence to suggest that it may well be a treatment of choice. Lorig, Laurin, and Holman (1984) demonstrated that relaxation training can produce significant reductions in reported pain among arthritis sufferers; in fact, the National Arthritis Foundation has incorporated relaxation training as a major component in its Arthritis Self-Help course, which is being offered currently in more than 50 cities nationwide.

engendered by arranging circumstances conducive to relaxation. For example, Linoff and West (1982) used suggestions to relax coupled with music when working with a seriously ill, bedridden client; Hussian (1981) taught an elderly woman confined to a wheelchair to relax by repeating soothing self-instructions; and Suinn and Bloom (1978) taught heart patients to relax by visualizing pleasant imagery.

Elders may require modifications in standard desensitization procedures as well. Because of fatigue, shorter than usual (i.e., 20–30 minute) systematic desensitization sessions may be desirable. Furthermore, Lankford and Herman (1978) recommend using shorter imagery scenes and greater scene detail. Friedman (1966) reported success in desensitization by presenting hierarchy items visually, using pictures, for an elderly deaf and mute man. Finally, because *in vivo* or contact desensitization often seems more plausible to this generation of elders than does systematic desensitization (using imaginal stimuli), actual encounters with the anxiety-provoking circumstances should be arranged whenever possible.

Cognitive interventions also seem very plausible to this generation of elders, and it is not at all uncommon to hear an older person say that "What's wrong with me is that I just can't seem to get the right attitude." Unfortunately, despite their promise, cognitive interventions with elders have been evaluated in controlled studies very rarely. There have been case examples reported, however, that, in conjunction with the large literature documenting the effectiveness of cognitive treatments for younger populations, offer support for their value with older clients.

One of the simplest cognitive intervention strategies is education. In some instances, where anxiety is based on misconceptions or misattributions, merely supplying accurate information can be enormously effective. For example, the fear of being a victim of violent crime is the single most pressing concern among elders (Hahn & Miller, 1980), presenting a serious personal problem for some 23% of old people in the United States (Harris & Associates, 1975). This fear often results in severe activity restrictions that are as much of a serious problem as is victimization itself (Dowd, Sisson, & Kern, 1981). However, actual victimization rates among elders are quite low (U.S. Department of Justice, 1979)—lower, in fact, than are rates for any other age group (Janson & Ryder, 1983). Educating elders about the fact that their feeling more at risk of victimization is based on a misconception, and encouraging them to engage in rational self-instructions when away from home, can be sufficient to reduce misinformation-based anxiety.

Education can be equally effective in cases of anxiety based on misattributions (Sparacino, 1978). It is not at all uncommon to encounter an elderly person, sensitized to instances of normal forgetfulness, who is anxious because each instance of forgetfulness is misattributed to the development of Alzheimer-type dementia (Sluss, Gruenberg, Reedman & Rabins, 1983; Zarit, 1982). It is also not uncommon to encounter elders who have become anxious because they have misattributed medication side effects to either mental or physical decline (Hussian, 1981, p. 179):

> A sixty-five-year-old resident of a long-term care facility was referred for rapid onset anxiety and nervousness. On interview, he appeared anxious, showed a short attention span, motor restlessness, and upper extremity tremors. The client was told of the nature of a new medication which he was taking (haliperidol), the frequency of these physical symptoms due

to such medication, and the relationship between these tremors which he had observed and the attribution of physical deterioration which he had made. Then, the relationship between self-labeling and anxiety was discussed. . . . The client stated that he felt better and he returned to his prior level of activity engagement.

A variety of more comprehensive cognitive interventions have also been used to treat anxiety experienced by elders. These strategies include Suinn and Richardson's (1971) anxiety management training (see Garrison, 1978; Sallis et al., 1983); Meichenbaum's (1977) self-instructional training (see Labouvie-Vief & Gonda, 1976); and Meichenbaum's (1985) stress-inoculation training (see Hussian, 1981). Often these methods have been employed when working with elders to enhance the type of coping termed the *regulation of emotion* (Lazarus & DeLongis, 1983), which is the type of coping that must be used with problems that cannot be solved, changed, or compensatorily balanced (see Swenson, 1983). They have also been used, however, when the initial assessment has indicated that the anxiety is reactive.

Problem-solving training (Meichenbaum, 1974) has been especially useful in cases of reactive anxiety; in these instances, the anxiety is regarded as signaling the presence of some other problem, one that is persisting because of a deficiency in problem-solving skills, so that resolving the problem by providing training in problem solving would be the appropriate target for treatment. Problem-solving training has been reported to be effective with both institutionalized and community-dwelling elders (Hussian & Lawrence, 1981; Kahana, 1975; Lorig et al., 1984), and it holds special promise for elders experiencing reactive anxiety, on at least two counts. First, the development of adequate problem-solving skills will not only result in the individual's mastery of the current problematic situation, but will also leave the individual better equipped to master other problematic situations arising in the future. Perhaps more important, however, problem-solving training can serve as a vehicle to enhance the person's efficacy—and outcome—expectations (Bandura, 1977; Langer & Rodin, 1976) at a time in life when the person is likely to feel powerless and fundamentally out of control (Ross, 1983).

The first step in problem solving involves identifying the unsolved problem(s). When exploring potentially problematic areas with elders, two areas, in addition to obviously stressful events (e.g., the onset of a major illness), are especially likely to be identified: deficiencies in current living circumstances, and deficiencies in social support networks.

Current living circumstances may have become problematic because of either a sudden (e.g., marriage of a caretaking daughter) or a gradual (e.g., worsening of an arthritic condition) change. In either case, the appropriate solution involves innovativeness in developing new environments (e.g., living with a friend) or environmental components (e.g., Visiting Nurses, county Home Care workers) that can effectively compensate for the change that has occurred. This approach stands in stark contrast to the options ordinarily encouraged in many types of individual therapies with elders, for it *does not* assume that environments cannot be changed; rather, it actively encourages individuals to find or create new environments that will better suit their needs.

Satisfying social networks have been recognized for some time as essential to the well-being of elders (Caplan, 1974; Henderson, 1977; Kahana & Kahana, 1983). Part of their importance lies in the sheer pleasure that is derived from interacting comfortably with liked people (Quevillon & Lee, 1983). Just as important, however, is the value social support networks have for assisting elders through time of crisis and stress (Gottleib, 1983, p. 281):

> Levels of stress or anxiety may be reduced when supportive peers who were also exposed to a similar stressor on previous occasions signal by their words and affective reactions that the ordeal will pass quickly with benign effects. . . . At a psychological level, feedback from supportive companions that communicates reassurance and affirmation may prevent damage to the parties' self-concepts by conditioning a steadfast sense of self-esteem and personal efficacy. . . . By offsetting pejorative self-attributions about the causes of adversity and about the competencies necessary to control the course and outcome of adversity, supportive companions prevent active coping efforts from being hampered by self-recrimination. Finally, close associates can ameliorate ongoing adjustment strivings by redirecting problem-solving strategies, by providing concrete services and tangible aid, and by intervening in the environment in ways that either prevent exposure to stressors in the first place or enhance the socioemotional provisions that can be marshaled. . . . By shoring up those rational problem-solving activities that eventually lead to mastery and by supplementing the fund of psychosocial assets available in the environment, peer bonds buttress the behavioral dimension of coping.

Social support network deficiencies may be problematic, then, in either of two ways. First, the deficiency may be sufficient to deprive the individual of satisfying social interactions. In such cases the deficiency itself may function as a stressor. In other cases the network deficiency is neither apparent nor consequential until an obvious stressor— one that an adequate social network might well buffer—occurs. In this latter instance, it is especially important for professional helpers to remember to address both the immediate stressor and the social network deficiency during problem-solving training.

When employing problem-solving training with elders—or, in fact, any of the comprehensive cognitive behavior treatment strategies (e.g., anxiety management training, stress-inoculation training, self-instructional training)—it is essential to remain flexible with regard to treatment style. As has been noted, although the substantive content of the intervention should be the same as would be included with younger clients, the process through which that substance is conveyed must very often be changed. As a simple example, in some instances, physical prompts such as index cards with written self-instructions to use *in vivo* can be very useful. As a more complex example, precipitous reports of treatment effectiveness must be recognized as verbalization primarily intended to "please the nice young doctor."

Summary and Recommendations

At present there is not a body of literature evaluating the effectiveness of cognitive interventions for anxiety experienced by elders. I hope that before the end of this decade there will be a substantial literature available, one that not only explores the value of cognitive therapies for elders, but also identifies optimal stylistic parameters to use when intervening.

Even before this literature accumulates, however, clinicians can feel optimistic about using cognitive strategies with older clients, for cognitive therapies have been shown to be effective anxiety treatments for younger populations, and elders have been found to be, in general, more similar to than they are different from younger people.

Working with elders does require certain special sensitivities. With healthy elders, however—who are the large majority of the elderly population—these sensitivities are required not by physiological but, rather, by generational or cultural differences between today's young and today's old.

Surely by the end of this decade, Swenson's (1983) observation that we do not have an adequate knowledge base for asserting with certainty the value of any psychological intervention for any psychological problem experienced by the elderly will no longer be true. In the interim, cognitive strategies appear to be the most promising psychological intervention to try with elders presenting anxiety.

Acknowledgments

The author is grateful to her students—Bob Samuels, Deb Lewis, Tori Eklund, Kim Praderas, Shelley Murphy, and Etiony Aldarondo—for their comments on an earlier draft of this chapter.

References

Alford, G. S. (1983). Pharmacotherapy. In M. Hersen, A. E. Kazdin, & A. S. Bellack (Eds.), *The clinical psychology handbook*. New York: Pergamon.

American Psychiatric Association. (1980). *Diagnostic and statistical manual of mental disorders* (3rd ed.). Washington, DC: Author.

Antonovsky, A. (1979). *Health, stress, and coping: New perspectives on mental and physical well-being*. San Francisco: Jossey-Bass.

Bandura, A. (1977). Self-efficacy: Toward a unifying theory of behavioral change. *Psychological Review, 84*, 191–215.

Barney, J. L., & Neukom, J. E. (1979). Use of arthritis care by the elderly. *Gerontologist, 19*, 548–554.

Bergman, K. (1971). The neuroses of old age. In D. Kay & A. Wolk (Eds.), *Recent developments in psychogeriatrics: A symposium* (British Journal of Psychiatry Special Publication No. 5), 39–50.

Berry, R. G. (1975). Pathology of dementia. In J. G. Howells (Ed.), *Modern perspectives in the psychiatry of old age*. New York: Brunner-Mazel.

Birren, J. E. (1963). Psychophysiological relations. In J. E. Birren, R. N. Butler, S. W. Greenhouse, L. Sokoloff, & M. R. Yarrow (Eds.), *Human aging: A biological and behavioral study*. Washington, DC: U.S. Government Printing Office.

Birren, J. E. (1983). Aging in America: Roles for psychology. *American Psychologist, 38*, 298–299.

Birren, J. E., Butler, R. N., Greenhouse, S. W., Sokoloff, L., & Yarrow, M. R. (1963). *Human aging* (UAPHA No. 986). Washington, DC: U.S. Public Health Service.

Birren, J., & Renner, V. (1981). Concepts and criteria of mental health and aging. *American Journal of Orthopsychiatry, 51*, 242–254.

Bondareff, W. (1977). The neural basis of aging. In J. E. Birren & K. W. Schaie (Eds.), *Handbook of the psychology of aging*. New York: Van Nostrand Reinhold.

Bootzin, R. R., Engle-Friedman, M., & Hazelwood, L. (1983). Insomnia. In P. M. Lewinsohn & L. Teri (Eds.), *Clinical geropsychology: New directions in assessment and treatment*. New York: Pergamon Press.

Brody, E. M., & Kleban, M. H. (1983). Day-to-day mental and physical health symptoms of older people: A report on health logs. *Gerontologist, 23*, 75–85.

Brown, B. (1982). Professionals' perceptions of drug and alcohol abuse among the elderly. *The Gerontologist, 22*, 519–525.

Busse, E. W., & Pfeiffer, E. (1969). Functional psychiatric disorders in old age. In E. W. Busse & E. Pfeiffer (Eds.), *Behavior and adaptation in late life*. Boston: Little, Brown.

Butler, R. N., & Lewis, M. I. (1977). *Aging and mental health* (2nd ed.). St. Louis: Mosby.

Caplan, G. (1974). *Support systems and community mental health*. New York: Behavioral Publications.

Chafetz, P. K., Ochs, C. E., Tate, L. A., & Niederehe, G. (1982). Employment opportunities for geropsychologists. *American Psychologist, 11*, 1221–1227.

Chiodo, J., Walley, P. B., & Jenkins, J. O. (1983). A modified progressive relaxation training program in the rehabilitation of a hearing-imparied client. *International Journal of Behavioral Geriatrics, 2*(1), 43–46.

Cohen, G. (1977). Approach to the geriatric patient. *Medical Clinics of North America, 61*, 855–866.

Cohen, L. D., & Cooley, S. G. (1983). Psychology training programs for direct services and the aging (Status report, 1980). *Professional Psychology, 14*, 431–436.

Crook, T. H. (1979). Psychometric assessment in the elderly. In A. Raskin & L. F. Jarvik (Eds.), *Psychiatric symptoms and cognitive loss in the elderly*. New York: Wiley.

Dean, L. (1962). Aging and decline of affect. *Journal of Gerontology, 17*, 440–446.

DeLongis, A., Coyne, J. C., Dakof, G., Folkman, S., & Lazarus, R. S. (1982). Relationship of daily hassles, uplifts, and major life events to health status. *Health Psychology, 1*, 119–136.

Derogatis, L. (1977). *Brief Symptom Inventory (BSI)*. Baltimore, MD: Johns Hopkins University Press.

Dowd, J. J., Sisson, R. P., & Kern, D. M. (1981). Socialization to violence among the aged. *Journal of Gerontology, 36*, 350–361.

Dupree, L. W., Broskowski, H., & Schonfeld, L. (1984). The gerontology alcohol project: A behavioral treatment program for elderly alcohol abusers. *The Gerontologist, 24*, 510–516.

Dye, C. J. (1978). Psychologists' role in the provision of mental health care for the elderly. *Professional Psychology, 9*, 38–49.

Falloon, I. R. (1975). The therapy of depression: A behavioral approach. *Psychotherapy and Psychosomatics, 25*, 69–75.

Fisher, K. (1985). Survey shows aged hit harder by CMHC cuts. *American Psychological Association Monitor, 16*, 24.

Fisher, K. (1986). Demographics beckon young to maturing field. *American Psychological Association Monitor, 17*, 18–19.

Folstein, M. F., Folstein, S. E., & McHugh, P. R. (1975). "Mini-mental state": A practical method for grading the cognitive state of patients for the clinician. *Journal of Psychiatric Research, 12*, 189–198.

French, J. R. P., Jr., Rodgers, W., & Cobb, S. (1974). Adjustment and person–environment fit. In G. V. Coelho, D. A. Hamburg, & J. E. Adams (Eds.), *Coping and adaptation*. New York: Basic Books.

Freud, S. (1950). On psychotherapy. In *Collected papers* (Vol. 1.) London: Hogarth Press and the Institute of Psychoanalysis.

Friedman, D. (1966). Treatment of a case of dog phobia in a deaf mute by behavior therapy. *Behaviour Research and Therapy, 4*, 141.

Frolkis, V. V. (1977). Aging of the autonomic nervous system. In J. E. Birren & K. W. Schaie (Eds.), *Handbook of the psychology of aging*. New York: Van Nostrand Reinhold.

Gallagher, D., & Thompson, L. W. (1983). Depression. In P. M. Lewinsohn & L. Teri (Eds.), *Clinical geropsychology: New directions in assessment and treatment*. New York: Pergamon Press.

Garfield, S. L. (1978). Research on client variables in psychotherapy. In S. Garfield & A. Bergin (Eds.), *Handbook of psychotherapy and behavior change: An empirical analysis*, (2nd ed.). New York: Wiley.

Garfinkle, P. (1975). The reluctant therapist. *Gerontologist, 15*, 138–141.

Garfinkel, R. (1979). Brief behavior therapy with an elderly patient. *Journal of Geriatric Psychiatry, 12*, 101–109.

Garrison, J. E. (1978). Stress management training for the elderly: A psychoeducational approach. *Journal of the American Geriatrics Society, 26*, 397–403.

Gatz, M., Smyer, M., & Lawton, M. P. (1980). The mental health system and the older adult. In L. W. Poon (Ed.), *Aging in the 1980's*. Washington, DC: American Psychological Association.

Gottlieb, B. H. (1983). Social support as a focus for integrative research in psychology. *American Psychologist, 38*, 278–287.

Gelles, R. J., & Cornell, C. P. (1985). *Intimate violence in families*. Beverly Hills, CA: Sage Publications.

Goldfarb, A. (1956). The rationale for psychotherapy with older persons. *American Journal of Medical Science, 232*, 181–185.

Grotjahn, M. (1955). Analytic psychotherapy with the elderly. *Psychoanalytic Review, 42,* 419–427.

Gutmann, D. (1969). *The country of old men: Cross-national studies in the psychology of later life.* Occasional paper in Gerontology series. Ann Arbor, MI: Institute of Gerontology.

Gutmann, D. L. (1974). The country of old men: Cross-cultural studies in the psychology of later life. In R. L. Levine (Ed.), *Culture and personality: Contemporary readings.* Chicago: Aldine.

Hahn, P. H., & Miller, E. R. (1980). *Project search and inform, Cincinnati–Hamilton County, OH, 1979–80.* Xavier University Graduate Corrections Department, Cincinnati, 1980.

Haley, W. E. (1983). Priorities for behavioral intervention with nursing home residents: Nursing staff's perspective. *International Journal of Behavioral Geriatrics, 1*(4), 47–51.

Hall, G. S. (1922). *Senescence: The last half of life.* New York: Appleton.

Harris, L., & Associates. (1975, 1981). *The myth and reality of aging in America.* Washington, DC: National Council on the Aging.

Hartmann, D. P., & Wood, D. D. (1982). Observational methods. In A. S. Bellack, M. Hersen, & A. E. Kazdin (Eds.), *International handbook of behavior modification and therapy.* New York: Plenum Press.

Haupt, J. L., Orleans, C. S., George, L. K., & Brodie, H. K. (1979). *The importance of mental health services to general health care.* Cambridge, MA: Ballinger.

Hayes, H., with Gladney, M. G. (1984). *Our best years.* Garden City, NY: Doubleday.

Henderson, S. (1977). The social network, support and neurosis. *British Journal of Psychiatry, 131,* 185–191.

Hoyer, W. J., Lopez, M. A., & Goldstein, A. P. (1983). Predicting social skill acquisition and transfer in psychogeriatric inpatients. *International Journal of Behavioral Geriatrics, 1*(1), 43–46.

Hussian, R. A. (1981). *Geriatric psychology: A behavioral perspective.* New York: Van Nostrand Reinhold.

Hussian, R. A., & Davis, R. L. (1985). *Responsive care: Behavioral interventions with elderly persons.* Champaign, IL: Research Press.

Hussian, R. A., & Lawrence, P. S. (1981). Social reinforcement of activity and problem-solving training in the treatment of depressed institutionalized elderly patients. *Cognitive Therapy and Research, 5,* 57–69.

Ingersoll, B., & Silverman, A. (1978). Comparative group psychotherapy for the aged. *Gerontologist, 18,* 201–206.

Janson, P., & Ryder, L. K. (1983). Crime and the elderly: The relationship between risk and fear. *Gerontologist, 23,* 207–212.

Jung, C. G. (1933). *Modern man in search of a soul.* New York: Harcourt, Brace, and World.

Jung, C. G. (1953). *Collected works: VII. Two essays on analytical psychology.* New York: Pantheon.

Kahana, B. (1975). *Competent coping—A psychotherapeutic strategy.* Paper presented at the International Gerontological Association, Jerusalem, Israel, June.

Kahana, B., & Kahana, E. (1983). Stress reactions. In P. M. Lewinsohn & L. Teri (Eds.), *Clinical geropsychology: New directions in assessment and treatment.* New York: Pergamon Press.

Kahn, R. L., Goldfarb, A. I., Pollack, M., & Peck, R. (1960). Brief objective measures for the determination of mental status in the aged. *American Journal of Psychiatry, 117,* 326–328.

Karpf, R. J. (1982). Individual psychotherapy with the elderly. In A. M. Horton (Ed.), *Mental health interventions for the aging.* New York: Praeger.

Kastenbaum, R. (Ed.). (1964). *New thoughts on old age.* New York: Springer.

Kastenbaum, R. (1978). Personality theory, therapeutic approaches, and the elderly client. In M. Storandt, I. Siegler, & M. Elias (Eds.), *The clinical psychology of aging.* New York: Plenum Press.

Kay, D., Bergman, K., Foster, E., McKeachie, A., & Roth, M. (1970). Mental illness and hospital usage in the elderly: A random sample followed up. *Comprehensive Psychiatry, 1,* 26–35.

Kenshalo, D. R. (1977). Age changes in touch, vibration, temperature, kinesthesis, and pain sensitivity. In J. E. Birren & K. W. Schaie (Eds.), *Handbook of the psychology of aging.* New York: Van Nostrand Reinhold.

Kiecolt-Glaser, J. K., Glaser, R., Williger, D., Stout, J., Messick, G., Sheppard, S., Ricker, D., Romisher, S., Briner, W. Bonnell, G., & Donnerberg, R. (1985). Psychological enhancement of immunocompetence in a geriatric population. *Health Psychology, 4,* 25–41.

Korchin, S. J. (1983). The history of clinical psychology: A personal view. In M. Hersen, A. E. Kazdin, & A. S. Bellack (Eds.), *The clinical psychology handbook.* New York: Pergamon Press.

Kramer, M., Taube, C. A., & Redick, R. W. (1973). Patterns of use of psychiatric facilities by the aged: Past, present, and future. In C. Eisdorfer & M. P. Lawton (Eds.), *The psychology of adult development and aging.* Washington, DC: American Psychological Association.

Kucharski, L. T., White, R. M., & Schratz, M. (1979). Age bias referral for psychological assistance, and the private physician. *Journal of Gerontology, 34,* 423–428.

Kulka, R. A., & Tamir, L. (1978). *Patterns of help-seeking and formal support.* Paper presented at the annual meeting of the Gerontological Society, Dallas, Texas, November.

Labouvie-Vief, G., & Gonda, J. N. (1976). Cognitive strategy training and intellectual performance in the elderly. *Journal of Gerontology, 31,* 327–332.

Langer, E., & Rodin, J. (1976). The effects of choice and enhanced personal responsibility: A field experiment in an institutional setting. *Journal of Personality and Social Psychology, 34,* 191–198.

Lankford, D. A., & Herman, S. H. (1978). *Behavioral geriatrics: A critical review.* Paper presented at the first annual NOVA Behavioral Conference on Aging, Port St. Lucie, Florida, May.

Lawton, M. P. (1975). The Philadelphia Geriatric Center Morale Scale: A revision. *Journal of Gerontology, 30,* 85–89.

Lawton, M. P. (1978). Clinical geropsychology: Problems and prospects. In *Master lectures on the psychology of aging.* Washington, DC: American Psychological Association.

Lazarus, R. S., & DeLongis, A. (1983). Psychological stress and coping in aging. *American Psychologist, 38,* 245–254.

Lazarus, R. S., & Folkman, S. (1984). *Stress, appraisal, and coping.* New York: Springer.

Leaf, A. (1973). Getting old. *Scientific American, 229,* 45–52.

Lewinsohn, P. M., & Teri, L. (1983). (Eds.). *Clinical geropsychology: New directions in assessment and treatment.* New York: Pergamon Press.

Lieberman, M. A. (1975). Adaptive processes in late life. In N. Datan & L. H. Ginsberg (Eds.), *Life-span developmental psychology.* New York: Academic Press.

Linoff, M. G., & West, C. M. (1982). Relaxation training systematically combined with music: Treatment of tension headaches in a geriatric patient. *International Journal of Behavioral Geriatrics, 1*(3), 11–16.

Lorig, K., Laurin, J., & Holman, H. R. (1984). Arthritis self-management: A study of the effectiveness of patient education for the elderly. *Gerontologist, 24,* 455–457.

McCrae, R. R. (1982). Age differences in the use of coping mechanisms. *Journal of Gerontology, 37,* 454–460.

MacDonald, M. L. (1973). The forgotten Americans: A sociopsychological analysis of aging and nursing homes. *American Journal of Community Psychology, 1,* 272–294.

MacDonald, M. L. (1978). Measuring assertion: A model and method. *Behavior Therapy, 9,* 889–899.

MacDonald, M. L. (1983a). Assessment of women clients for design of behavioral treatment and outcome evaluation. In E. A. Blechman (Ed.), *Behavior modification with women.* New York: Guilford Press.

MacDonald, M. L. (1983b). Behavioral consultation in geriatric settings. *The Behavior Therapist, 6,* 172–174.

MacDonald, M. L., Davidowitz, J. J., Gimbel, B., & Foley, L. M. (1982). Physical and social environmental reprogramming as treatment for psychogeriatric patients. *International Journal of Behavioral Geriatrics, 1*(1), 15–32.

MacDonald, M. L., & Eklund, V-A. (1985). New perspectives on old age. [Review of *Clinical gerontology,* by P. Lewinsohn & L. Teri (Eds.)]. *Behavioral Assessment, 7,* 102–104.

MacDonald, M. L., & Kerr, B. B. (1982). Behavior therapy with the aging. In A. M. Horton (Ed.), *Mental health interventions for the aging.* New York: Praeger.

MacDonald, M. L., & Settin, J. M. (1978). Reality orientation versus sheltered workshops as treatment for the institutionalized aging. *Journal of Gerontology, 33,* 416–421.

Mahoney, M. J. (1977). Some applied issues in self-monitoring. In J. D. Cone & R. P. Hawkins (Eds.), *Behavioral assessment: New directions in clinical psychology.* New York: Brunner/Mazel.

Meerloo, J. (1955). Psychotherapy with elderly people. *Geriatrics, 10,* 583–587.

Meichenbaum, D. (1974). Self-instructional strategy training: A cognitive prosthesis for the aged. *Human Development, 17,* 273–280.

Meichenbaum, D. (1977). *Cognitive-behavior modification.* New York: Plenum Press.

Meichenbaum, D. (1985). *Stress inoculation training.* New York: Pergamon Press.

Moos, R., Cronkite, R., Billings, A., & Finney, J. (1980). *Health and Daily Living Form Manual.* (Available from authors at Social Ecology Laboratory, Stanford University, and VA Medical Center, Palo Alto, CA 94304.)

Morrice, J. K. W. (1976). *Crisis intervention: Studies in community care.* Oxford: Pergamon Press.

Nietzel, M. T., Winett, R. D., MacDonald, M. L., & Davidson, W. C. II. (1977). *Behavioral approaches to community psychology*. New York: Pergamon Press.

Oberleder, M. (1966). Psychotherapy with the aging: An art of the possible? *Psychotherapy: Theory, Research, and Practice, 3*, 139–142.

O'Brien, J. S. (1978). The behavioral treatment of a thirty-year smallpox obsession and handwashing compulsion. *Journal of Behavior Therapy and Experimental Psychiatry, 9*, 365–368.

Palmore, E. (1971). Attitudes toward aging as shown by humor. *Gerontologist, 11*, 181–186.

Palmore, E. B. (1973). Social factors in mental illness of the aged. In E. W. Busse & E. Pfeiffer (Eds.), *Mental illness in later life*. Washington, DC: American Psychiatric Association.

Palmore, E. (1977). Facts on aging. *Gerontologist, 17*, 315–320.

Parry, H. J., Balter, M. B., Mellinger, G. D., Cisin, I. H., & Manheimer, D. I. (1973). National patterns of psychotherapeutic drug use. *Archives of General Psychiatry, 28*, 769–783.

Patterson, R. L., Dupree, L. W., Eberly, D. A., Jackson, G. M., O'Sullivan, M. J., Penner, L. A., & Kelly, C. D. (1982). *Overcoming deficits of aging: A behavioral approach*. New York: Plenum Press.

Pfeiffer, E. (1977). Psychopathology and social pathology. In J. E. Birren & K. W. Schaie (Eds.), *Handbook of the psychology of aging*. New York: Van Nostrand Reinhold.

Pfeiffer, E. (1980). The psychosocial evaluation of the elderly patient. In E. W. Busse & D. G. Blazer (Eds.), *Handbook of geriatric psychiatry*. New York: Van Nostrand Reinhold.

Pinkston, E. M., & Linsk, N. L. (1984). *Care of the elderly: A family approach*. Elmsford, NY: Pergamon Press.

President's Commission on Mental Health (1978). *Task panel reports* (Vol. III Appendix). Washington, DC: U.S. Government Printing Office.

Preston, D. B., & Mansfield, P. K. (1984). An exploration of stressful life events, illness, and coping among the rural elderly. *Gerontologist, 24*, 490–494.

Quevillon, R. P., & Lee, H-C. (1983). Social involvement as a predictor of subjective well-being among the rural institutionalized aged. *International Journal of Behavioral Geriatrics, 1*(4), 13–19.

Redick, R. W. (1974). *Patterns of use of nursing homes by the aged mentally ill*. Statistical Note 107. Rockville, MD: National Institute of Mental Health.

Redick, R. W., Kramer, M., & Taube, C. A. (1973). Epidemiology of mental illness and utilization of psychiatric facilities among older persons. In E. W. Busse & E. Pfeiffer (Eds.), *Mental illness in later life*. Washington, DC: American Psychiatric Association.

Redick, R. W., & Taube, C. A. (1980). Demography and mental health care of the aged. In J. E. Birren & R. B. Sloane (Eds.), *Handbook of mental health and aging*. Englewood Cliffs, NJ: Prentice-Hall.

Rodin, J., & Langer, E. (1980). Aging labels: The decline of control and the fall of self-esteem. *Journal of Social Issues, 36*, 12–29.

Romaniuk, M., Tilden, E., & Arling, G. (1983). Elderly participants of adult day care: A descriptive profile of behavioral skills and deficits. *International Journal of Behavioral Geriatrics, 2*(1), 19–28.

Rosenthal, T. L., & Rosenthal, R. H. (1983). Stress: Causes, measurement, and management. In K. D. Craig & R. J. McMahon (Eds.), *Advances in clinical behavior therapy*. New York: Brunner/Mazel.

Rosow, I. (1974). *Socialization to old age*. Berkeley: University of California Press.

Ross, H. K. (1983). The neighborhood family: Community mental health for the elderly. *Gerontologist, 23*, 243–247.

Roth, M. (1976). The psychiatric disorders of later life. *Psychiatric Annals, 6*, 417–445.

Roves, C. K., Cohen, R. Y., & Shlapack, W. (1975). Life span stability in olfactory sensitivity. *Developmental Psychology, 11*, 311–318.

Sallis, J. F., Lichstein, K. L., Clarkson, A. D., Stalgaitis, S., & Campbell, M. (1983). Anxiety and depression management for the elderly. *International Journal of Behavioral Geriatrics, 1*(4), 3–12.

Santos, J. F., & VandenBos, R. (1982). *Psychology and the older adult*. Washington, DC: American Psychological Association.

Schaie, K. W. (1974). Translations in gerontology from lab to life. *American Psychologist, 29*, 802–807.

Schmidt, L. J., Reinhardt, A. M., Kane, R. L., & Olsen, D. M. (1977). The mentally ill in nursing homes. *Archives of General Psychiatry, 34*, 687–696.

Settin, J. (1982). *Gerontologic human resources: The role of the paraprofessional*. New York: Human Sciences Press.

Sidle, A., Moos, R. H., Adams, J., & Cady, P. (1969). Development of a coping scale: A preliminary study. *Archives of General Psychiatry, 20,* 226–232.

Sinex, F. M. (1975). The biochemistry of aging. In M. G. Spencer & C. J. Dorr (Eds.), *Understanding aging: A multidisciplinary approach.* New York: Appleton-Century-Crofts.

Skinner, B. F. (1983). Intellectual self-management in old age. *American Psychologist, 38,* 239–244.

Sluss, T. K., Gruenberg, E. M., Reedman, G., & Rabins, P. (1983). Memory changes in community residing men. *International Journal of Behavioral Geriatrics, 2*(1), 39–42.

Sparacino, J. (1978). An attributional approach to psychotherapy with the aged. *Journal of the American Geriatric Society, 26,* 414–417.

Steury, S., & Blank, M. L. (Eds.) (1977). *Readings in psychotherapy with older people.* Rockville, MD: National Institute of Mental Health.

Storandt, M. (1983). Psychology's response to the graying of America. *American Psychologist, 38,* 323–326.

Storandt, M., Siegler, I., & Elias, M. (1978). *The clinical psychology of aging.* New York: Plenum Press.

Suinn, R. M., & Bloom, L. J. (1978). Anxiety management training for pattern A behavior. *Journal of Behavioral Medicine, 1,* 25–35.

Suinn, R. M., & Richardson, F. (1971). Anxiety management training: A nonspecific behavior therapy program for anxiety control. *Behavior Therapy, 2,* 498–510.

Swenson, C. H. (1983). A respectable old age. *American Psychologist, 38,* 327–334.

Teeter, R. B., Garetz, F. K., Miller, W. R., & Heiland, W. F. (1976). Psychiatric disturbances of aged patients in skilled nursing homes. *American Journal of Psychiatry, 133,* 1430–1434.

Thompson, L. W., Gallagher, D., Nies, G., & Epstein, D. (1983). Evaluation of the effectiveness of professionals and nonprofessionals as instructors of "Coping with Depression" classes for elders. *Gerontologist, 23,* 390–396.

Thyer, B. A. (1981). Prolonged in vivo exposure therapy with a 70-year-old woman. *Journal of Behavior Therapy and Experimental Psychiatry, 12,* 69–71.

Tolliver, L-M. (1983). Social and mental health needs of the aged. *American Psychologist, 38,* 316–318.

Tyson, P. A., & MacDonald, M. L. (1982). *Daily activities and home care of community-dwelling elders.* Paper presented at the annual meeting of the Association for Advancement of Behavior Therapy, Los Angeles, November.

Ullmann, L. P., & Krasner, L. (1969). *A psychological approach to abnormal behavior.* Englewood Cliffs, NJ: Prentice-Hall.

United States Department of Health Education and Welfare (1975). *Facts about older Americans* (No. OHD 75-20006 B). Washington, DC: U.S. Government Printing Office.

United States Department of Justice. (1979). *Criminal victimization in the United States, 1977: A national crime survey report.* (No. SD-NCS-N-12). Washington, DC: U.S. Government Printing Office.

Vaillant, G. E. (1977). *Adaptation to life.* Boston: Little, Brown.

VandenBos, G., & Buchanan, J. (1983). Aging, research on aging, and national policy: A conversation with Robert Butler. *American Psychologist, 38,* 300–307.

Wander, Z. W. (1972). Existential depression treated by desensitization of phobias: Strategy and transcript. *Journal of Behavior Therapy and Experimental Psychiatry, 3,* 111–116.

Wang, H. S., & Busse, E. W. (1969). EEG of healthy old persons—A longitudinal study: 1. Dominant background activity and occipital rhythm. *Journal of Gerontology, 24,* 419–426.

Wasson, W., Ripeckyj, A., Lazarus, L. W., Kupferer, S., Barry, S., & Farce, F. (1984). Home evaluation of psychiatrically-impaired elderly: Process and outcome. *Gerontologist, 24,* 238–242.

Waxman, H. M., & Carner, E. A. (1984). Physicians' recognition, diagnosis, and treatment of mental disorders in elderly medical patients. *Gerontologist, 24,* 593–597.

Waxman, H. M., Carner, E. A., & Klein, M. (1984). Underutilization of mental health professionals by community elderly. *Gerontologist, 24,* 23–30.

Wechsler, D. (1958). *The measurement and appraisal of adult intelligence.* Baltimore, MD: Williams and Wilkins.

Wilcox, B. L. (1981). Social support, life stress, and psychological adjustment: A test of the buffering hypothesis. *American Journal of Community Psychology, 9,* 371–386.

Wisniewski, H. M., & Terry, R. D. (1976). Neuropathology of the aging brain. In R. D. Terry & S. Gershon (Eds.), *Aging: III. Neurobiology of aging.* New York: Raven Press.

Wisocki, P. A. (1983). Behavioral approaches to gerontology. In M. Hersen & A. S. Bellack (Eds.), *Progress in behavior modification*. (Vol. 16). New York: Academic Press.

Wood, V., Wylie, M. L., & Schaefer, B. (1969). An analysis of a short self-report measure of life satisfaction: Correlation with rater judgment. *Journal of Gerontology, 24,* 465–469.

Zarit, S. H. (1982). Affective correlates of self-reports about memory of older people. *International Journal of Behavioral Geriatrics, 1*(2), 25–34.

Zarit, S. H., Miller, N. E., & Kahn, R. L. (1978). Brain function, intellectual impairment, and education in the aged. *Journal of the American Geriatrics Society, 26,* 58–67.

Zarit, S. H., & Zarit, J. M. (1983). Cognitive impairment. In P. M. Lewinsohn & L. Teri (Eds.), *Clinical geropsychology: New directions in assessment and treatment.* New York: Pergamon Press.

16

Death-Related Anxiety

ROBERT KASTENBAUM

Is there anything special about "death anxiety"? Should therapy be approached differently when the client's problems touch on death? In attempting to answer these questions, it will be useful to explore the realms of theory, research, and clinical technique, and some of their interconnections.

Death Anxiety: The Research Literature

The academic research literature on death-related topics (sometimes called *thanatology*) is dominated by studies purporting to investigate so-called death anxiety. Actually, the distinction between *fear* and *anxiety* is seldom made clear in these studies, nor is a case made for the distinction between the death anxiety construct and general anxiety. The conceptual status of the death anxiety assessed in most studies is open to question; what is evident, however, is that the respondents are presented with a set of items in which words such as *death*, *dying*, and *dead* appear.

A Typical Study of Death Anxiety

Most studies of death anxiety have most or all of the following characteristics: (1) data obtained by use of a self-report questionnaire; (2) yielding a simple total score; (3) administered to an opportunistic population (usually college students); (4) administered on one occasion; and (5) with results presented in the form of correlations with demographic, self-report or other nonvaried variables; tests of significance may also be reported for possible mean differences between two groups. Absent from most reported studies are: (1) data on the respondents' overall attitude structure or belief system; (2) behavioral measurements or outcomes; (3) theory-based rationale and interpretation; (4) specific implications for behavioral intervention or social policy; and (5) responses from non-Anglo and ethnically diverse populations.

Reviews of the death anxiety literature (Lester, 1967; Kastenbaum & Costa, 1977; Pollak, 1979–1980; Schulz, 1985) have made such criticisms familiar and have not been entirely without effect. The psychometric properties of self-report scales have improved over the years, with the work of Templer and his colleagues (Templer, Ruff, & Franks, 1971; Templer & Ruff, 1971) deserving particular notice. Others have demonstrated that multiple levels of assessment within the same individual are both useful and feasible (e.g.,

Robert Kastenbaum. Adult Development and Aging Program, Arizona State University, Tempe, Arizona.

Feifel & Branscomb, 1973; Rosenheim & Muchnik, 1984–1985). Increased sophistication has also been achieved by some self-report instruments (e.g., Krieger, Epting, & Leitner, 1974; Neimeyer, Epting, & Rigdon, 1983).

Nevertheless, most studies continue in the cookie cutter format noted earlier. The popularity of simplistic death anxiety studies seems to represent a psychological balance between the investigators' own approach–avoidance tendencies toward the subject matter (Kastenbaum, in press). One can appear to be studying death while remaining at a comfortable distance. A typical death anxiety study looks like any other self-report questionnaire project. There is nothing conspicuously "deathy" about the study, and therefore nothing to disturb the researchers. As already noted, the questionnaire is usually adminstered to healthy people in safe situations. Such studies, then, make death a convenient and nonthreatening topic for research by limiting the methodology and, simultaneously, trivializing the problem.

The Findings and Their Interpretation

Despite the limitations inherent in most such death anxiety studies, several findings have emerged with some consistency. These generalizations are noted next, along with brief interpretive considerations.

1. *Adults drawn from physically healthy and nonpsychiatric populations generally have moderate to low scores for death anxiety* (e.g., Lonetto & Templer, 1983; Pandy & Templer, 1972; Stevens, Cooper, & Thomas, 1980; Templer & Ruff, 1971). The problem of interpretation can be illustrated with the most frequently employed instrument, Templer's Death Anxiety Scale (TDAS). This scale yields a potential range of scores from 0 to 15. Normal adult samples almost always score around the statistical midpoint (more often below than above). This finding does provide a basis for identifying individuals and subpopulations whose scores deviate from the norm. Potentially, it also offers an outcome measure, in that reduction of a high score might be viewed as a positive consequence of therapeutic intervention. The paucity of data linking TDAS scores either to behavioral symptomatology or to efficacy of coping however, leaves some key questions unanswered. How, for example, does moderate self-reported death anxiety relate to effectiveness in coping with actual death-related situations? How does a given level of self-reported "death anxiety" relate, if at all, to the individual's tendency to reduce or increase personal risks to survival (such as automobile and occupational safety procedures, heavy smoking, etc.)?

Some clinicians who have worked extensively in this area believe that Americans are very uncomfortable with death-related topics and face serious internal conflicts when called on to act in a death-related situation (e.g., Wahl, 1959; Weisman, 1972). A moderate TDAS score, then, might represent not a relatively comfortable orientation toward death but, rather, an index of denial and other evasive psychological strategies. This means that a therapist who succeeds in reducing an individual's score on the TDAS might have achieved this outcome by strengthening denial mechanisms rather than actually increasing the ability to cope effectively with death-related thoughts, feelings, and situations. Becoming "more normal," in other words, could mean only becoming more normative in fending off potentially death-related disturbances. Furthermore, should an experience in psychotherapy lead to an even greater reduction in the TDAS score, one might have contributed either to exceptional freedom from distress or to exceptional denial, as discussed later.

Very low scores on the TDAS and other scales pose an even more difficult problem of interpretation. Do they represent low anxiety or high denial? None of the scales with which I am familiar yield measures of denial or dissembling, nor have researchers supplemented the scales with independent procedures that might provide such an index. The typical study assesses only "death anxiety," not any of the many other orientations that can be taken toward death, including but not limited to various shades of evasion.

2. *Women tend to have higher TDAS scores than men* (Da Silva & Schork, 1984–1985; Pollak, 1979–1980). Two rather different lines of interpretation must be considered here. The gender difference might represent precisely what it seems to represent: a higher level of death-related perturbation on the part of women. A plausible alternative, however, is that women tend to express their feelings more openly in general. The available data do not allow a definitive choice between these interpretations. In my own clinical experience, the gender difference appears more evident in the open expression of feeling rather than in level of underlying anxiety. I would even propose that men often do not recognize "enough" of their own death-related anxiety, rather than that women express "too much." In any event, clinicians may be well advised to bear in mind the fact that a somewhat higher level of self-reported death anxiety is normative for women and therefore does not necessarily present a signal for therapeutic intervention.

3. *Younger adults tend to report higher levels of death anxiety than do older adults* (e.g., Stricherz & Cunnington, 1981–1982; Tate, 1980). This finding has also emerged from research of a more intensive type than the usual self-report scale (Munnichs, 1968). The available data in this area are not quite as extensive and unanimous as with the generalizations presented earlier. It is clear, however, that measured death anxiety does *not* appear at an elevated level among adults of advanced age, despite their greater actuarial proximity to death.

Of interest to the clinician here is the reminder that subjective concern and objective threat are by no means identical. Studies of time perspective among older adults also indicate that one should not be quick to conclude that a person must be in a state of anxiety or lack a future orientation because of a limited life expectancy (Kastenbaum, 1982; Kulys & Tobin, 1980). Individual differences are large, with some people maintaining a lively interest in the future even if this may be a matter of only months, weeks, or days. Furthermore, the intersection of gender and age could provide helpful cues; for example, somewhat elevated death anxiety in a 20-year-old woman might not be as much of a flag for therapeutic intervention as would the breakthrough of death anxiety in a 60-year-old man.

4. *People suffering from mental or emotional problems are more likely than others to express a higher self-reported death anxiety.* For example, "delta alcoholics" (those unable to abstain) have been found to have higher death anxiety scores to go along with their elevated scores on various measures of general anxiety and depression, and their lower scores on self-esteem (Kumar, Vaidya, & Dwivedi, 1982). The association between

emotional or behavioral disturbance and high death anxiety emerges from intensive clinical research (e.g., Gilliland, 1982), as well as TDAS-type studies (Planansky & Johnston, 1977).

This generalization is consistent with the experience of many clinicians—namely, that a wide variety of subthreshold fears may intrude when the individual's coping strategies fail under pressure. Death-related fears may be especially striking during a psychotic episode, for example, but this does not necessarily mean either that the episode itself was precipitated by such fears or that they must be the primary focus of treatment. Death anxiety can serve as the symbolic expression of a sense of impending catastrophe that in itself poses no direct death threat. One high school student's anxiety attack, for example, marked by hyperventilation, among other symptoms, was accompanied by statements such as "I don't want to die!" Both the high manifest anxiety and the death concern vanished after the student did well on a screening examination important for the professional career his parents were demanding of him. Only by taking all the facts of the situation into account can the clinician judge whether the death-related fears are at the core of the problem or have been recruited by the patient's general sense of helplessness and panic.

Despite numerous studies, the possible relationships among death anxiety, personality structure, and occupation remain unclear. I agree with Rosenheim and Muchnik (1984–1985, p. 21), however, who conclude that "death concern is not limited to certain personality types, certainly not only to 'neurotic' people or those similar to them. Rather, these concerns seem to be present in different forms, or on different levels, in all of us." Involvement in a death-related occupation, however, is not necessarily associated with high scores on a TDAS-type measure. A man who has operated a funeral home for almost half a century gently explained to me why he thinks members of his profession tend to have low death anxiety scores: "We are the ones who ride home from the funeral. I am always the survivor—so far!"

Relatively more sophisticated studies and analyses have made it clear that what has come to be termed "death anxiety" is more usefully regarded as both multidimensional and multilevel (Feifel & Branscomb, 1973; Feifel & Nagy, 1981; Keller, Sherry, & Piotrowski, 1984; Rosenheim & Muchnik, 1984–1985). The total score yielded by the TDAS, for example, comprises self-reported concern for problems as different as fear of cancer and fear of dead bodies, concern about a painful process of dying, and concern about what happens (or does not happen) after death. There may be some justification in continuing to use total scores in establishing population norms for general concern about death. Those who are interested in understanding and helping individuals, however, will require much more specific information regarding idiosyncratic areas of concern. (One of my students, for example, scored in the moderate range on the TDAS, but had a strong fear of cancer because she was a "DES baby." She is not much troubled by most of the areas sampled by the TDAS, but nevertheless is very apprehensive about a possible premature death through cancer. Similarly, other people with scores also in the moderate range may have a particular problem area that would not come to attention on the basis of the total score alone.)

Studies that go beyond the cookie cutter format of self-report instruments have indicated that significant discomfort or perturbation frequently exists at other levels of assessment, such as the psychophysiological or projective. This is the message conveyed by Feifel and Branscomb's (1973) pioneering study that asked the question, "Who is afraid of death?" The answer was: "Everybody!"—but not on the level of direct self-report. LeShan has demonstrated that simple behavioral studies can also reveal a discrepancy between attitude and action. Nurses had a significantly greater latency period in responding to the bedside calls of terminally ill patients—and returned to this pattern of behavior even after they learned of the results and attempted to overcome their discomfort with the dying (LeShan, Bowers, Jackson, Knight, & LeShan, 1964). In a more elaborate clinical study, Breznitz (1983) has clearly shown that verbal disavowal of death-related anxiety can be accompanied by direct indices of psychophysiological distress. At least one form of denial could be operationalized successfully in terms of verbal disavowal in the presence of autonomic arousal.

It is important to remember that findings based on the self-report scales are limited by their dependence on the cross-sectional approach, opportunistic sampling, neglect of minority and ethnic populations, and so on. Most of the superior studies have gone beyond the use of self-report instruments, although such studies are in the minority. Additional problems, but also some interesting challenges for the clinician, will be encountered as we turn now to some of the major theoretical positions.

Conceptual Problems and Choices

The research literature on death anxiety generally includes little attention to theory. Nevertheless, two important theories have been in circulation for some time, each with its cadre of articulate and influential advocates. Little attempt has been made to subject these competing views to systematic research. Despite the difficulties, however, a brief review is appropriate here because both major views do have implications for practice.

From the classical period of psychoanalysis comes the dictum that the human mind is not really capable of comprehending its own demise. From the existential currents that influenced philosophy and psychology in the post–World War II years comes the view that, at root, *all* of our anxieties have their source in the fear of nonbeing. Not every psychoanalyst has agreed with the former position, nor every existentialist with the latter (not to mention the hybrid existential psychoanalyst!). Nevertheless, a battle line was formed soon after World War II between those who saw death anxiety as our most fundamental and characteristically human concern, and those who regarded it as only a secondary transformation of other problems.

We Cannot Fear Death

Freud asserted that manifest concerns about death must have their roots elsewhere (1925a). This conclusion follows from his analysis of both conscious and unconscious thought processes. On the level of everyday awareness, it cannot be death that we fear, because we have never been dead. The concerns that proliferate around "death," then, must represent fears that have derived from experiences we have actually had—and so the familiar examination of childhood insecurities and conflicts is usually the indicated course of action. The unconscious, for its part, does not and cannot believe in its own death. The concepts of negation and finality exist only in the sphere of elaborated reality principle cognition. Unconscious processes (as revealed, for example, by "dream work") are not subject to the constraints of time, space, invariance, and formal logic.

Obviously, Freud's position on this problem will be most persuasive to those who operate within the general psychoanalytic framework. By dismissing Freud's dynamic depth psychology in favor of a cognitive-behavioral approach, one might seem to have dismissed his never-say-die conception as well. There is a facet to Freud's observations, however, that cannot be neglected so easily even by those who reject the overall psychoanalytic approach. There is a philosophical–methodological point so simple that it is often in danger of being overlooked (though not by Freud). This point might be termed the *split-off fallacy*. It can be illustrated most succinctly through a phenomenon that has become familiar in recent years, the near-death experience. Some individuals who are close to death (usually at the scene of an accident or in the operating room) have reported floating above their own inanimate bodies. First brought to general attention through Raymond A. Moody's (1975) collection of reports, the phenomenon has now been verified in a number of competent studies employing a variety of methods (e.g., Greyson & Flynn, 1984; Sabom, 1982). There is no reason to doubt that some people do have an "autoscopic experience." Nevertheless, there is reason to reject claims that these experiences represent a return from the dead. All such reports are provided by an "observing ego," to use psychoanalytic parlance. "I saw *myself* dead" is a self-contradictory statement. In the split-off fallacy, a "dead" self is perceived or constructed by a nondead observing self. In reporting our own deaths, we cannot help but call our own conclusions into doubt (Kastenbaum, 1986).

It is a questionable proposition, then, both methodologically and philosophically, to speak of knowing our own death or deadness. From a Freudian standpoint, whatever it is that we do fear, it is not this unknown and perhaps unknowable state. The therapist has the challenge of identifying and resolving the real cause of distress.

Nevertheless, it would not be fair to include Freud among those who have contributed steadfastly to the denial of death. The experience of World War I prompted one of his most profound essays, *Thoughts for the Times on War and Death*, in which he noted that "We have tried to keep a deadly silence about death" (1925b). For the remainder of his long life, Freud demonstrated an increasing willingness to regard death as a most significant problem—yet it is his earlier formulation, noted earlier, that has proved most influential.

It Is Death We Always Fear

The existential alternative could hardly be more different. The basic proposition here is that at every moment we all live with the threat of nonbeing. What makes the human condition distinctive, in fact, is our ability to recognize both our constant vulnerability and our ultimate fate. A psychology blind to death anxiety would be a very limited psychology indeed.

Kierkegaard (1940), Heidegger (1953), and Sartre (1956) all constructed psychological philosophies in which the problem of death was given salience. Although the term *existential* has been applied to all of these philosophers, they differ greatly in their particular views. For today's clinician, however, other authors may speak more directly. The late Walter Kaufmann (1976, p. 214) proposes that it is the awareness of death that gives life much of its joy and meaning as well as its anxiety:

> Those who have loved with all their heart and mind and might have always thought of death, and those who knew the endless nights of harrowing concern for others might have longed for it.
>
> The life I want is a life I could not endure in eternity. It is a life of love and intensity, suffering and creation, that makes life worth while and death welcome. There is no other life I should prefer. Neither should I like not to die.

The late Ernest Becker (1973) also argued that one can live a fully human life only by acknowledging and coming to terms with death-related anxieties. This is a challenging position for clinicians, who believe that their task is always to reduce anxiety. But according to Becker and some others, our society is altogether too proficient at covering up death-related anxieties. It is important to acknowledge both the objective peril of nonbeing and our own discomfort. Becker further proposes that both depression and schizophrenia represent extreme attempts to control death-related anxiety. The very concept of "mental illness" could be regarded as "a way of talking about those people who burden others with their hyperfears of life and death, their own failed heroics" (Becker, 1973, p. 248).

In Becker's formulation, the "terror of death" is a primary—perhaps *the* primary— motivating force for human behavior, whether as individuals or as a society. Clients who present themselves with such diverse symptoms as fear of traveling and fear of failure really are troubled by the underlying fear of nonbeing. In a traditional Freudian view, then, we would try to get "under" manifest death concern to discover the "real" conflict (such as castration anxiety and its derivatives). Operating within an existential framework, by contrast, we might try to discover the death-driven anxieties that have taken other symptomatic forms.

We Learn to Fear Death

A developmental-learning approach to the origin of death-related concerns has yet to be formulated in detail. Such an approach could build on an already existing research literature on the development of thoughts and attitudes toward death among children and adolescents (Koocher, 1973; Lonetto, 1980), as well as some valuable clinical reports (Wass & Corr, 1984). The quality of work in this area in general is clearly superior to the death anxiety studies already reviewed. Although these studies have their problems, they demonstrate a higher level of craftsmanship and conceptual sophistication. Investigations such as those of Bluebond-Langner (1974) with terminally ill children illustrate what can be learned when one is willing to risk exposure to concrete realities through field research rather than relying on self-report measures.

Without attempting to formulate a comprehensive developmental-learning approach here, it is still possible to suggest several of the major propositions that might be part of such a theory.

1. Death-related concerns develop as part of the general interaction between the individual's level of maturation and his or her distinctive life experiences.

2. Individuals will differ in their priorities of death-related concerns on the basis of this interaction between developmental level and personal experience.

3. Cognitive and behavioral responses to death-related situations are mediated through the particular family and ethnic influences that have been exerted on the individual during early development.

4. These responses never represent "fear" or "anxiety" in a pure form but, rather, include the individual's strategy for coping as well.

5. How the person copes with death-related concerns is best understood within the context of his or her overall strategy for perceiving and dealing with threat.

6. Significant problems in coping with death-related concerns are likely to derive from difficulties with developmental learning as well as with the topic of death per se.

7. Careful attention is required to the "conditions of performance" as well as to the origins of death-related learning. This rule, well established in the general psychology of learning and performance, has been relatively neglected both by the raw empiricism of death anxiety studies and the hard-to-verify abstractions of psychoanalytic and existential positions.

8. Therapeutic intervention is most likely to be successful if it (a) takes into account the client's own cognitive constructs and belief systems, (b) converts generalized apprehension and dysphoria into specific problem situations that can be mastered, and (c) improves the client's competence and confidence in coping with these problems. Furthermore (d) the treatment goal would be established as part of the client–therapist partnership rather than imposed on the client.

The developmental-learning approach can be enriched by insights from the psychoanalytic and existential camps, but perhaps offers a more helpful guide than either to clinical assessment and treatment.

Cognitive-Behavioral Assessment and Treatment

Assessment of Death-Related Concerns

Clients occasionally mention death-related events, thoughts, or concerns spontaneously at first contact. These statements can provide the basis for exploration but should not be assumed to constitute the focal problem brought for treatment. A woman in her early 30s, for example, reported that her stepfather had died a few weeks ago. This statement could have reflected the intensification of her fears concerning her own death. Instead, it became clear that it was the stepfather she had feared—and hated because of a history of sexual abuse. His death was significant to her, but for reasons more closely associated with her relationships with other men. The treatment goal developed by client and therapist focused on increasing her sense of mastery and reducing anxieties experienced when a relationship with a man would become "serious." The client did have concerns about death that could have been taken up in therapy, but this was not the immediate problem to be solved. By contrast, a man in his late 60s explained that he had made an appointment for an initial interview because of pressure from his son and daughter-in-law. "They think I might kill myself. Well, I might." His wife of many years was dying in a particularly painful and depressing way. "I'd kill her, too, if I had the nerve. Death has to be better than this terrible, disgusting dying." In this situation it was obvious that treatment would not even begin unless urgent issues centering around dying and death were addressed. The treatment goal itself took three sessions to establish and was modified by mutual agreement at a later session. The "plan for working out a plan together" seemed to have some therapeutic value of its own.

The absence of any statements pertaining to death appears to be more common in initial interviews. These cases obviously include those in which, in fact, no particular death concern is present. Also included, however, are an unknown number of cases in which the death concern will not surface unless this possibility is explored by the therapist.

The opportunity presents itself conveniently when clients report their symptoms. Beck and Emery (1985) differentiate the cognitive symptoms in anxiety disorders into the realms of sensory–perceptual, thinking difficulties, and conceptual. Symptoms of the first two types can be associated with a wide variety of precipitating problems. Within the conceptual domain, however, there is more likelihood that substantive concerns will be expressed. "Repetitive fearful ideation," for example, may either depict or suggest death concerns. "Fear of physical injury" may be a light disguise for outright fear of death. "Frightening visual images" can point to death-related fears either for oneself or for others. The cognitive-behavioral therapist who has also learned something from psycho-dynamic approaches, for example, may recognize that the client is a person with strong dependency needs and is therefore vulnerable to heightened anxiety when concerned that a protective or nurturant individual may die. It is not always the prospect of one's own death that generates disruptive anxiety.

Another type of symptom configuration may be taken as a marker for possible death-related concerns. (The "possible" must be emphasized, bearing in mind the lack of a one-to-one relationship between symptom and precipitating problem in general.) Among symptoms of anxiety cited by Beck and Emery (1985, pp. 25ff.), attention should be called to the following: inhibition, tonic immobility, blank face, faintness, actual fainting, and rigidity, as well as to most of the specific respiratory symptoms cited— (shortness of breath, pressure on chest, shallow breathing, choking sensation.) The relatively sudden onset of such symptoms has been associated in my experience with a fear of death that chooses a death-mimicking mode of expression. "Scared to death" is another way of putting it.

Two rather different approaches can be used effectively when a configuration of this type is in clear evidence. The decision should be based on the therapist's knowledge and judgment regarding the whole situation; the therapist should not automatically employ one of the alternatives. Judging that it is most important to reduce the anxiety as soon as possible, the therapist could employ a relaxation technique. The prompt (if temporary) reduction of bodily tension can itself be a significant learning experience for the client. A riskier procedure that sometimes might be justified by the situation involves focusing attention on the symptoms and asking the client to describe his or her immediate bodily and mental state in as much detail as possible. Employing this alternative over the years has enabled two clients to verbalize their partial identification with a particular dead person, and a number of others to characterize themselves as "like hardly being alive," "in a shell, dead on the outside," and so on. For unknown reasons, this configuration, in which anxiety is translated into a kind of "deadness," appears to manifest itself in clusters rather than in a steady frequency of cases.

A developmental-learning model can lead to the temptation to lengthen and complicate the assessment procedure because so many variables are relevant and so many interesting questions could be explored. The experienced cognitive-behavioral therapist, however, recognizes that the client should not be placed into a passive, question-answering modality at the hands of a relentless expert if the treatment outcome is to emphasize independence and self-regulation. When the question of possible death-related concern does exist, one can often obtain useful information as part of general assessment procedures that encourage an active role on the part of the client. The following example is of particular interest because the client was not only concerned about death but was, in fact, a terminally ill cancer patient. She had complained about hyperventilation episodes and other symptoms of anxiety. Sobel (1981) was told by the staff that the patient was "denying" and that the symptoms merely expressed her fears of death. He was asked to see the patient in order to break through the (assumed) denial and lead her to accept death (Sobel, 1981, p. 16):

> My strategy as a behaviorist was quite different. After completing a behavioral assessment that included an analysis of current reinforcers for the patient, I asked the patient, (1) what she had observed; (2) what she would like to change; and (3) whether she would like me to help her learn some techniques that she could practice on her own. I had no doubt that the patient was frightened of dying. But more so, the patient felt that the anxiety prevented her from completing certain important life tasks, communicating with loved ones, and maintaining a satisfactory self-image. I described an anxiety-management program, using daily relaxation exercises, imagery of pleasant scenes, and staff reinforcement for anxiety episodes and together practiced the relaxation–meditation exercises. This brief intervention was very successful, despite the fact that we never spoke about death. I did not reinforce a naive denial of her terminal cancer plight, nor did I assume a controlling and mechanistic therapeutic posture. My goal was simply to facilitate self-instruction and primary symptom relief as part of encouraging choice and realistic self-control.

All the examples given here are intended to suggest that good basic assessment in the cognitive-behavioral style provides many opportunities to discover death-related concerns and their significance. Additional questions can be asked and observations made once it has become clear that the client's distress is associated with some facet of dying, death, or grief.

Some Considerations for Therapeutic Intervention

Psychotherapeutic interventions of a cognitive-behavioral type can be effective either as the primary or as a supplementary form of treatment (see the final section). Interestingly, this approach can be consistent with both psychoanalytic and existential orientations. Many existentialists believe that "authentic" life requires recognition of death and the willingness to go forward without guarantees of a "happy ending," much less the prospect of a "happy un-ending." The ability to discuss death and other sources of intense anxiety in therapy and to strengthen one's own coping skills without necessarily believing in a final victory can be seen as an actualization of the existential credo. Similarly, the psychoanalyst's commitment to developing rational mastery is perhaps represented more directly in the cognitive-behavioral therapist's office than on the couch of dreams. Elements of cognitive-behavioral therapy can be seen in some of Freud's own cases—usually those concerned with immediate and practical life problems.

A few specific suggestions might be offered regarding therapy for those with death-related concerns.

1. The end points of each session, important in general, are often especially important because death sensitivity has generalized to terminations and separations in general. One way to deal with the vulnerability and conflict that can arise at the hour's end is to develop a mutually agreed-on outcome goal that includes greater comfort in closing situations.

2. Audiotapes made especially for the client by the therapist and well-selected readings can be useful adjuncts to treatment. Even if the client has relaxed and made progress during the sessions, there may be a subsequent flooding of anxiety that clouds memory and makes him or her again feel helpless. Educational materials suited for the particular client and situation can provide a valuable link between the working sessions and the rest of the client's life.

3. Give particular attention to what *can* be changed in the situation. Terminal illness or the death of a loved one are situations that severely limit the effectuance of therapist and client alike. A high level of anxiety tends to be associated with global perceptions, thereby further interfering with the client's ability to see what remains within the realm of possible control. Cognitive procedures such as guided imagery and exercises in decentering can be especially useful in helping to discover goals that are still approachable by moves the client can still make.

4. Similarly, there is often a strong tendency to become "absorbed" by death situations. For example, the person who is literally grief-stricken may crave reunion with the deceased to such an extent that there is a dedifferentiation in his or her basic perception of self. Under such circumstances, it will be helpful to recognize that the client faces anxiety from two sources—from loss of the loved one, to be sure, but also from his or her own identification with the deceased, which threatens to engulf him or her in death as well. Strengthening the client's sense of self and differentiation from the deceased can be an effective contribution to anxiety reduction.

5. Either the client's anxiety or other aspects of the situation often have isolated him or her from optimal use of personal support systems. A careful exploration of these support systems and their current status is a useful preliminary to subsequent efforts to teach clients how to use these symptoms more effectively. Seriously or terminally ill clients can benefit at times from learning how to reduce the anxiety of family and friends (and thereby preserving significant relationships) without having to play a game of mutual pretense (Glaser & Strauss, 1966).

6. It might save some frustration on the part of the therapist to recognize that even the most effective interventions cannot be expected to overcome or compensate completely and rapidly for significant losses and realistic threats. Therapy does not have to restore losses and protect from all further stress in order to have been useful.

7. Anxiety related to death is not inherently "unadaptive" or "neurotic." As Beck and Emery (1985) and many others have pointed out, anxiety has a valuable signal function in our lives. The individual who is insensitive to the possibility of catastrophic danger is not necessarily at an advantage. Reduction of death anxiety is sometimes but not always an appropriate therapeutic goal. Operating within a society that still has a strong tendency to deny death, the therapist must process exceptional self-knowledge and exercise keen judgment to avoid contributing to the systematic denial and trivialization of death. To put it bluntly, one must always ask, "*Whose* anxiety am I trying to reduce—and why?"

Hospice Care: A New Prospect for the Cognitive-Behavioral Therapist

There is not yet a well-developed clinical science of cognitive-behavioral therapy with death-related problems. Both conceptual clarification and evaluation research of various types are needed. The focus here, however, will be on one emerging area in which there is a largely unmet need for therapeutic interventions.

Virtually unknown in the United States a decade ago, the hospice approach to terminal care is now available through more than 1,200 agencies (Mor, Greer, & Kastenbaum, in press; Zimmerman, 1981). Hospice care differs from the more familiar medical model in several important ways:

1. The focus is on the patient and family as a unit.
2. Care plans center on the particular life-style, preferences, and situation of each patient, as contrasted with a standard protocol.
3. The emphasis is on symptom control, comfort, and quality of life, rather than aggressive treatment and persistent examinations.
4. Support is provided to the natural caregivers and support group so that they, in turn, can continue their relationship with the patient.
5. Planning and delivery of services is done through an interdisciplinary team who strive for continuity of care, whether the patient is at home or in a hospital.

Hospice care is not intended to replace conventional care for all terminally ill patients, but, rather, to exist as an alternative that one can either choose or forego.

Concerns associated with dying and death are obviously central to the hospice situation, whether the patient is hospitalized or receiving care at home. When a hospice system of care is functioning well, it contributes to the amelioration of anxiety. This is accomplished partially through skillful control of pain, nausea, and other symptoms associated directly with the illness. Other important factors include the increased opportunity to remain at home and enjoy a familiar, secure environment; the relatively greater sense of control that family and patient feel because they do, in fact, have more control to exercise than in the traditional care setting; and the more open interpersonal communication network. At home, people generally find it easier to be themselves because they do not have to watch what they say and do in order to please a governing professional staff.

Nevertheless, anxiety and grief are present in the hospice situation as well. Some of the concern is generated by but not directly part of the terminal illness itself. For example, the patient may be a parent who has realistic concerns about the future of spouse and children, or even about an older parent for whom he or she was providing care. Worries about financial matters are not unusual and may at times even take precedence over the prospect of death. Frustration about goals that will never be obtained and projects that will never be completed may be augmented by regrets over missed opportunities and unpleasant episodes with family or friends. In general, concerns of everyday life often are intensified in the pressure cooker of illness and foreshortened life expectancy.

The cognitive-behavioral therapist is seldom on the scene, although there are fortunate exceptions. Most hospice organizations would welcome a therapist's expertise to supplement the input of the standard team: nurse, physician, social worker. The role of counselor has also been mandated for hospices that sign up for federal reimbursement under the existing national demonstration project. This role is sometimes filled by a chaplain with counseling experience who volunteers the service. Hospices are free to select any type of qualified counselor or therapist, and most, I believe, would be very pleased to add an expert in cognitive-behavioral therapy. There are few if any obstacles to providing service on a volunteer basis; many other professionals do the same, notably nurses and social workers (the typical hospice has many more volunteers than paid staff, and this cadre often includes but is not limited to qualified professionals). Reimbursement for behavioral assessment and treatment is not yet part of a well-established pattern. It should be recognized, however, that the formulation of national hospice operational and reimbursement procedures is still in its early phases. A service that proves valuable can become an integral part of the system.

What contributions could a cognitive-behavioral therapist make to hospice care?

1. *Participating in training and supervision of volunteers.* Hospices generally offer high-quality training programs for prospective volunteers who themselves represent an educated, mature, and well-motivated special population. Principles of cognitive-behavioral management would be useful to these volunteers in coping with their own responses to the personal challenge of hospice work, as well as in providing effective care to patients and their families. The cognitive-behavioral therapist could also make a valuable contribution to monitoring and supervision of volunteer performance.

2. *Participating in hospice team planning sessions.* The goals of hospice care are generally congruent with the types of outcome that are sought in cognitive-behavioral therapy. Developing and modifying the care plans for patients and family units is a process that invites the application of principles familiar in the cognitive-behavioral literature.

3. *Providing brief therapy for caregivers.* No matter how strong their personal and/or professional qualifications, those who provide care for the terminally ill person at times may find it difficult to cope with the stresses and conflicts. These caregivers are generally very good learners who can derive significant benefits from brief therapy focused on problems specific to the situation. Restoring the caregiver's sense of balance and feelings of competence can be a very important contribution to the patient's well-being.

4. *Brief, well-focused therapy for the terminally ill patient.* There is no reason to believe that all people require therapy during the course of their final illness. Freedom from physical suffering and the opportunity to interact with people already significant in

their lives is a more universal need, however, and one that hospice care seeks to meet. Nevertheless, there are situations in which the dying person can benefit from appropriate therapeutic intervention. Among the prime advantages of the cognitive-behavioral approach is its relatively equalitarian relationship between client and therapist. Already placed in a position of relative passivity and ineffectuance because of advanced physical disability, the dying person should be spared approaches that reinforce the patient role. Working successfully with the dying person on even one "small" problem can reduce a prevailing sense of frustration and depression.

5. *Participating directly or indirectly in follow-up bereavement contacts.* Hospices generally recognize their responsibility to the surviving family members and engage in some type of follow-up contact. Therapeutic intervention appears indicated in only a minority of cases, and this service can sometimes be provided effectively by volunteers familiar with the family. Grief reactions can be more severe for some survivors, however, threatening both their physical and their mental health. The cognitive-behavioral therapist can provide valuable help either through direct therapeutic interventions or by supervising volunteers and/or hospice staff who already have a relationship with the family.

Some therapists are already active in the conventional health care system, including work with hospitalized patients. It is worth noting that the hospice influence is making itself increasingly felt in traditional settings. Hospital staff members are often among those volunteering for hospice service, and they bring back to their own work some of the knowledge and experiences gained in hospice. Studies attempting to compare hospice with conventional care run the risk of being contaminated by the fact that medical centers are gradually incorporating hospice principles and techniques. The point is that some of the contributions mentioned here can also be made by cognitive-behavioral therapists within traditional health care settings. There appears to be an increasing willingness to consider innovative approaches in care of the terminally ill within conventional settings, and initiative on the part of the cognitive-behavioral therapist might be very well received.

Death-Related Anxiety in a High-Tech Society: A Quick Scan of the Future

Imagine a woman who has lived almost every day of her 60 or so years in a small town clinging to the edges of a mountain. She possesses an intimate knowledge of this small world. It is a highly personalized world made up of face-to-face interactions with people she has always known. It is also a world that we would consider highly ritualized, where lives conform to a pattern that is clear to its inhabitants, if perhaps puzzling to an outsider. The centrality of the church, however, is obvious. Religious observance appears almost casual because it is so thoroughly integrated into community life. This woman is not unusual in her reliance on both the official dogma and ritual of the Catholic church and a powerful overlay of superstition bonded to the core religion through the centuries. She differs in visible ways from women of the same age and national origin who, as native-born Americans, might operate a boutique in Denver, run a nursing home in Baltimore, or take their grandchildren to Disneyland. The invisible differences are even greater. These inward differences will become evident at times, however—which woman will literally faint away in ecstasy when her son comes to visit after an absence of several years? Which woman will spend hours each week at the cemetery and which at the beauty salon?

Consider, now, what barriers to psychotherapeutic intervention would present themselves should the woman of the isolated mountain town develop an anxiety syndrome associated with death. Would the knowledge and skills of a cognitive-behavioral therapist even be relevant? The point here is not to answer this question as such, but to remind ourselves that psychotherapy assumes that both parties share an underlying world view. Client and therapist can differ in many respects, but a core of shared experiences and values would seem to be a necessary condition. Death-related anxiety cannot be assessed and treated apart from its place in the individual's overall cognitive structure and life situation. A therapist who has not climbed the same mountain paths, tended neighboring graves, and observed the same superstitions will be at a disadvantage, to say the least, for years: "We see the world so differently—including the meanings of life and death—that I must hesitate to impose my approach upon hers."

In this little vignette (not entirely hypothetical), the cognitive-behavioral therapist is cast in the role of the modern faced with the challenge of treating someone representing an older life-style. Now comes the real point: the rapid development of a high-tech society has the potential to make a primitive of today's therapist. The mismatch between client and therapist may not be as easy to identify, but for that reason it is even more troublesome. Although innovations have been made in the theory and technique of psychotherapy, practitioners do have a lineage, a tradition that was forged in a world that differs appreciably from today's society—and more so from tomorrow's. Our assumptions—especially those so secure that we are usually unaware of their existence—may become increasingly at variance with those of our clients. No previous culture, for example, raised its children amid the disembodied spirits of the television screen, with its still insufficiently understood impact on our sense of reality. Television, in turn, is rapidly giving way to a variety of other electronic systems, in which the directionality and passage of time can be altered on command (e.g., the video cassette recorder, itself but a fragment of an ongoing technological revolution). The computer is rapidly becoming a "mainframe" of daily life (perhaps filling the void the church has become for many). Life and death begin to take on different meanings when the most intimate companion for some people becomes the computer, and crises can be solved by acquiring new software. "Computerese" already has penetrated our language; its more subtle effects as a model for our lives will soon make themselves known. I have already met people for whom computer systems seem to take precedence over their own personal lives—a "displacement," to use the tempting psychoanalytic phrase.

The preliminary shaping of lives outside our own lives can be discerned in the "high-technification" of society. For centuries society attempted to convey the message that death as well as life was to be interpreted within the context of "God and country." In our mobile, neighbors-are-strangers, latchkey child, post-Vietnam society, these traditional moorings have slipped. Anxiety may remain anxiety and death a continuing source of concern, but the context and even the rules may be changing more rapidly than we realize. An otherwise competent cognitive-behavioral therapist can miss the mark badly by assuming a basic congruence in world view and values with the client. Precisely what role death-related anxiety will play in a high-tech society remains to be seen—but this is possible only if we keep our eyes open.

References

Beck, A. T., & Emery, G. (1985). *Anxiety disorders and phobias.* New York: Basic Books.

Becker, E. (1973). *The denial of death.* New York: Free Press.

Bluebond-Langner, M. (1974). I know, do you? A study of awareness, communication, and coping in terminally ill children. In B. Schoenberg, A. C. Carr, A. H. Kutscher, D. Peretz, & I. Goldberg (Eds.), *Anticipating grief.* New York: Columbia University Press.

Breznitz, S. (1983). Anticipatory stress and denial. In S. Breznitz (Ed.), *The denial of stress.* New York: International Universities Press.

Da Silva, A., & Schork, M. A. (1984–1985). Gender differences in attitudes to death among a group of public health students. *Omega, Journal of Death and Dying, 15,* 77–84.

Feifel, H., & Branscomb, A. B. (1973). Who's afraid of death? *Journal of Abnormal Psychology, 81,* 282–288.

Feifel, H., & Nagy, T. (1981). *Journal of Consulting and Clinical Psychology, 49,* 278–286.

Freud, S. (1925a). The unconscious. In *Collected papers* (Vol. 14). London: Hogarth Press.

Freud, S. (1925b). Thoughts for the times on war and death. In *Collected papers* (Vol. 14). London: Hogarth Press.

Gilliland, J. (1982). *Death anxiety: Relation to subjective state.* Unpublished dissertation, California School of Professional Psychology, Fresno.

Glaser, B. G., & Strauss, A. L. (1966). *Awareness of dying.* Chicago: Aldine.

Greyson, B., & Flynn, C. P. (Eds.). (1984). *The near-death experience.* Springfield, IL: Charles C Thomas.

Heidegger, M. (1953). *Sein und zeit* (7th ed.). Tubingen: Max Niemeyer.

Kastenbaum, R. (1982). Time course and time perspective in later life. In C. Eisdorfer (Ed.), *Annual review of gerontology and geriatrics,* (Vol. 3). New York: Springer.

Kastenbaum, R. (1986). *Death, society, and human experience* (3rd ed.). Columbus, OH: Merrill.

Kastenbaum, R. (in press). Theory, research and application: Some critical issues for thanatology. *Omega, Journal of Death and Dying.*

Kastenbaum, R., & Costa, P. T., Jr. (1977). Psychological perspectives on death. In M. R. Rosenzweig (Ed.), *Annual review of psychology.* Palo Alto, CA: Stanford University Press.

Kaufmann, W. (1976). *Existentialism, religion and death.* New York: New American Library.

Keller, J. W., Sherry, D., & Piotrowski, C. (1984). Perspectives on death: A developmental study. *Journal of Psychology, 116,* 137–142.

Kierkegaard, S. (1940). *The concept of dread.* Princeton, NJ: Princeton University Press.

Koocher, G. (1973). Childhood, death, and cognitive development. *Developmental Psychology, 9,* 369–375.

Krieger, S. R., Epting, F. R., & Leitner, L. M. (1974). Personal constructs, threat, and attitudes toward death. *Omega, Journal of Death and Dying, 5,* 299–310.

Kulys, R., & Tobin, S. S. (1980). Interpreting the lack of future concerns among the elderly. *International Journal of Aging and Human Development, 11,* 111–126.

Kumar, A., Vaidya, A. K., & Dwivedi, C. B. (1982). Death anxiety as a personality dimension of alcoholics and non-alcoholics. *Psychological Reports, 51,* 634.

LeShan, L., Bowers, M., Jackson, E., Knight, J., & LeShan, E. (1964). *Counseling the dying.* New York: Thomas Nelson and Sons.

Lester, D. (1967). Experimental and correlational studies of the fear of death. *Psychological Bulletin, 17,* 26–36.

Lonetto, R. (1980). *Children's conceptions of death.* New York: Springer.

Lonetto, R., & Templer, D. I. (1983). *Death anxiety: The enduring anxiety.* Unpublished manuscript, University of Guelph.

Moody, R. A., Jr. (1975). *Life after life.* Atlanta, GA: Mockingbird Press.

Mor, V., Greer, D., & Kastenbaum, R. (Eds.). (in press). *The hospice experiment: Is it working?* Baltimore, MD: Johns Hopkins University Press.

Munnichs, J. H. A. (1968). *Old age and finitude: A contribution to psychogerontology.* Basel and New York: S. Karger.

Neimeyer, R. A., Epting, F. R., & Rigdon, M. A. (1983). A procedure manual for the Threat Index. *Death Education, 7,* 321–328.

Pandy, R. E., & Templer, D. I. (1972). Use of Death Anxiety Scale in an inter-racial setting. *Omega, Journal of Death and Dying, 3,* 127–130.

Planansky, K., & Johnston, R. (1977). Preoccupation with death in schizophrenic men. *Journal of Diseases of the Nervous System, 38,* 194–197.

Pollak, J. M. (1979–1980). Correlates of death anxiety: A review of empirical studies. *Omega, Journal of Death and Dying, 10,* 97–122.

Rosenheim, E., & Muchnik, B. (1984–1985). Death concerns in differential levels of consciousness as functions of defense strategy and religious belief. *Omega, Journal of Death and Dying, 15,* 15–24.

Sabom, M. B. (1982). *Recollections of death.* New York: Simon and Schuster.

Sartre, J. P. (1956). *Being and nothingness.* New York: Philosophical Library.

Schulz, R. (1985). Thinking about death: Death anxiety research. In S. G. Wilcox & M. Sutton (Eds.), *Understanding death and dying* (3rd ed.). Palo Alto, CA: Mayfield.

Sobel, H. J. (Ed.). (1981). *Behavior therapy in terminal care.* Cambridge, MA: Ballinger.

Stevens, S. J., Cooper, P. E., & Thomas, L. E. (1980). Age norms for Templer's Death Anxiety Scale. *Psychological Reports, 46,* 205–206.

Stricherz, M., & Cunnington, L. (1981–1982). Death concerns of students, employed persons and retired persons. *Omega, Journal of Death and Dying, 12,* 373–380.

Tate, L. A. (1980). *Life satisfaction and death anxiety in aged women.* Doctoral dissertation, California School of Professional Psychology, Fresno.

Templer, D. I., & Ruff, C. F. (1971). Death anxiety scale means, standard deviations, and embeddings. *Psychological Reports, 29,* 173–174.

Templer, D. I., Ruff, C. F., & Franks, C. M. (1971). Death anxiety: Age, sex and parental resemblances in diverse populations. *Developmental Psychology, 4,* 108.

Wahl, C. F. (1959). The fear of death. In H. Feifel (Ed.), *The meaning of death.* New York: McGraw-Hill.

Wass, H., & Corr, C. A. (Eds.). (1984). *Childhood and death.* New York: McGraw-Hill.

Weisman, A. D. (1972). *On death and dying.* New York: Behavioral Publications.

Zimmerman, J. M. (1981). *Hospice: Complete care for the terminally ill.* Baltimore and Munich: Urban and Schwarzenberg.

17

Sexual Dysfunction

JERRY M. FRIEDMAN AND LESLIE CHERNEN

Introduction

Sexual dysfunction can be broadly defined as physiological, cognitive–affective, or behavioral problems that prevent an individual from engaging in or enjoying satisfactory sexual activity, intercourse, or orgasm (Friedman, Weiler, LoPiccolo, & Hogan, 1982). Such difficulties have been commonly found in persons with no other signs of disorder as well as in those suffering from more complex psychological and medical problems. This chapter presents an integrative approach to the description, assessment, and treatment of sexual dysfunction. Our model takes into account the individual's thoughts, feelings, behaviors, physiological functioning, and environmental consequences in the formulation of a broad-based, integrative strategy for treatment.

Historical Roots of Sex Therapy: The Development of a Discipline

Problems of sexual functioning and interventions designed to remediate these problems date back to earliest recorded history. However, sexual problems were not viewed from a theoretical and methodological perspective until the beginning of the 20th century. Under Freud's influence, sexual dysfunctions were viewed as stemming from deep-rooted personality conflicts, specifically as a failure to resolve the Oedipal complex (Freud, 1905/1953). Within this framework, treatment was aimed at the reenactment of Oedipal issues or other unresolved conflicts through the transference relationship. Thus those developmental tasks not completed in childhood could be resolved in a healthy manner. No special adaptation of traditional psychodynamic theory was believed necessary to treat sexual dysfunction, as sexual conflict was viewed as the cause of almost all psychopathology. Treatment of sexual dysfunction was therefore essentially the same as for other forms of psychological difficulty (O'Connor & Stern, 1972).

Criticisms of the psychodynamic approach to sexual dysfunction are numerous. Since analytic theory evolved during a period when knowledge of the basic physiology of sexual responding was virtually nonexistent, a number of Freud's views concerning human sexuality were brought into question by recent biological discoveries (Kinsey, Pomeroy, Martin, & Gebhard, 1953; Masters & Johnson, 1966).

Jerry M. Friedman. Private practice, Stony Brook, New York.

Leslie Chernen. Department of Psychology, University of Massachusetts at Amherst, Amherst, Massachusetts.

Another problem with the analytic approach is its inflexibility. Thus unconscious conflict is seen as the only underlying cause of sexual difficulties and resolution of this conflict as the only cure (Kaplan & Kohl, 1972). But since many people with sexual dysfunctions merely lack knowledge and experience, a nondirective, passive therapeutic approach over months or years may yield little results.

In the late 1950s, interventions based on learning theory were first introduced. This approach propounded the use of short-term direct treatment of sexual dysfunction. Wolpe's (1958) major contribution to the advancement of the discipline was his conceptualization of sexual dysfunction as a conditioned anxiety response to the sexual situation. Thus such dysfunctions were treatable by relaxation procedures and systematic or *in vivo* desensitization (i.e., graduated exposure in imagery or real life). There is a considerable body of literature demonstrating the efficacy of this approach in the treatment of sexual dysfunction in both sexes (Dengrove, 1967; Friedman, 1968; Laughren & Kass, 1975; Obler, 1973). Like the analytic literature, however, most of these studies consist of case reports (Hogan, 1978; Wright, Perrault, & Mathieu, 1977). Without controlled outcome research, the efficacy of these procedures remained controvertible. Other behavioral techniques such as behavior rehearsal, modeling, and assertiveness and communication training have also been used to treat sexual dysfunction (Dengrove, 1967; Lazarus, 1965; Wolpe & Lazarus, 1966). These methods were designed to provide sexually dysfunctional individuals with more appropriate social interaction skills, thereby reducing the concomitant interpersonal social and sexual anxiety.

Several cognitive retraining techniques were developed in the 1960s and subsequently applied to the treatment of sexual dysfunction: These include thought stopping (i.e., a technique for stopping obsessional thoughts concerning sexual performance) (Garfield, McBrearty, & Dichter, 1969); attentional training (i.e., learning to direct attention to physical sensation rather than performance) (Ellis, 1962; Lazarus, 1968); and rational-emotive therapy (including skill training, education, anxiety reduction, and restructuring of irrational thoughts concerning the catastrophic nature of sexual difficulties) (Ellis, 1962, 1971).

Medical and surgical treatments for sexual dysfunction date back to the early 20th century. Hormonal treatments were initially attempted in 1919, and surgical therapies for erectile failure emerged during the 1930s (Gee, 1975). Medical treatments, however, were hampered until recently by limited knowledge of human sexual physiology and an inability to differentiate sexual dysfunctions along the physiological–psychological dimension (LoPiccolo & Friedman, 1985).

In summary, until the end of the 1960s, psychoanalytically oriented therapy was the treatment of choice for sexual dysfunction, although the efficacy of this intervention in treating these disorders had not been demonstrated. Behavioral procedures, though seemingly more effective, had only a minor impact in the sex therapy field. Both the psychoanalytic and behavioral approaches concentrated primarily on treating the individual, and little or no attempt was made to use conjoint therapy (Kaplan, 1979). There was little in the way of medical intervention, as most sexual dysfunctions were viewed as having a psychological diathesis. In addition, few medical or surgical procedures were available.

In the early 1970s Masters and Johnson (1970) made the primary breakthrough in the establishment of sex therapy as a distinctive therapeutic discipline and in the efficacious treatment of sexual dysfunction.

Within the last 16 years, in part because of two major tomes written by Masters and Johnson, *Human Sexual Response* (1966) and *Human Sexual Inadequacy* (1970), sex therapy became distinguished as an independent discipline, separate from individual psychotherapy, marital therapy, or sex education. Masters and Johnson contributed significantly to what is known today about human sexual physiology. In addition, they provided the field with a treatment approach, which, though behavioral in nature, was stated in terminology that was both atheoretical and nonbehavioral. Their focus is on the couple, and their treatment procedure entails brief, time-limited directive therapy aimed at symptom removal rather than uncovering unconscious conflict. The program itself was designed to deal with those causative agents Masters and Johnson viewed as primarily responsible for creating sexual difficulties: performance anxiety, informational and sexual communication deficits, and the assumption of a "spectator" role during sexual activity.

Following the publication of *Human Sexual Inadequacy* (Masters & Johnson, 1970), sex therapy centers sprung up in many places and the basic Masters and Johnson program was accepted by many therapeutic orientations. Helen Kaplan (1974) made the next major breakthrough with her publication of *The New Sex Therapy*. Her major contribution was in the integration of brief sex therapy and psychodynamic theory. Kaplan believes in focusing on current sexual behaviors of the couple until resistance to therapeutic change arises. At this point, she suggests that couple therapy be interrupted and that brief insight-oriented therapy be used with the individual members. Kaplan opened the way for the acceptance of sex therapy by the psychoanalytic community.

Criticism leveled at the sex therapy procedures developed during the 1960s and 1970s have led to an expanding body of research and technology and to modifications by other clinicians designed to remedy perceived shortcomings. The major criticism of the Masters and Johnson (1970) work was that their population was unrepresentative of the majority of people with sexual dysfunction. Couples had to be free of marital problems and severe individual psychopathology in order to be accepted into their program. In addition, since couples had to pay a large fee for a two-week treatment program while residing in St. Louis, they had to be both fairly wealthy and extremely highly motivated. The criticism that Masters and Johnson's inordinately high success rate may have been due to their selectivity has been supported by others who have treated a less selective group (Kaplan & Kohl, 1972). Although the success rate with less selective groups may be lower than that reported by Masters and Johnson (1970), their sex therapy procedures remain the foundation for treatment programs with diverse populations. Currently, sex therapists are treating individuals without sexual partners, the medically ill, the handi-capped, the psychiatrically disturbed, the aged, and the homosexually oriented (Fried-man & Czekala, 1985).

In the last decade, there has also been an amalgamation of diverse forms of therapy, many of them more cognitively oriented, which have contributed both conceptually and therapeutically to the sex therapy discipline. These therapies include cognitive therapy (Ellis, 1962, 1971); family systems therapy (Von Bertalanffy, 1968); communication therapy (Watzlawick, Beavin, & Jackson, 1967); humanistic–existential therapy (Lobitz, LoPiccolo, Lobitz, & Brockway, 1976); and Gestalt therapy (Mosher, 1977, 1979).

Modern sex therapy is thus a blend of cognitive therapy, systems theory, and behavior therapy. This integrative treatment reflects current views concerning the cause and maintenance of sexual difficulties.

The Etiology of Sexual Dysfunctions

The major causative factors in sexual dysfunction have been hypothesized to be: learning history (i.e., the messages about sexuality and sexual behavior that were learned from the family of origin as well as through previous sexual experiences); the relationship between the couple (i.e., the part the presenting problems plays in the couple's interaction and the means by which they communicate); cognitions (i.e., thoughts and attitudes about sexual functioning; and physical factors (i.e., any illness that might interfere with sexual arousal and enjoyment (LoPiccolo & Friedman, 1985). Each of these areas must be explored in order to gain a thorough understanding of the origin and continuance of sexual difficulties.

Learning history had been deemed of major importance in causing sexual dysfunction. Masters and Johnson (1970) proposed that parental prohibitions against masturbation and sex play in childhood, parental opposition concerning adolescent dating and premarital sex, and traumatic or unpleasant childhood or adolescent sexual experiences were the common elements leading to adult sexual dysfunction. Recently, however, it has been observed that many persons in our culture have had similar life history events and supposedly pathogenic upbringings; hence, there must be some mediating variables that lead these factors to have a detrimental effect on the sexual functioning of some individuals and not others.

Cognitive elements appear to play a major role in the development and maintenance of sexual dysfunction. These factors include attitudes, beliefs, and cognitively induced anxiety. Masters and Johnson (1970) contended that performance anxiety or worry about sexual performance, to the extent that it interferes with sexual arousal, is a major causative agent in sexual dysfunction. Albert Ellis (1971) has emphasized the role of unrealistic or irrational expectations in creating sexual difficulties. The tendency of men in this society to have extremely high expectations for their sexual performance and to become very upset if they do not live up to these expectations has a detrimental effect on male sexual functioning. The effects of the women's movement in legitimizing female sexuality has had the side effect of rendering women, as well, more prone to cognitively based performance anxieties.

Relationship factors have been found to play a role in sexual dysfunction. The sexual problem itself, for some couples, may be meeting important psychological needs of each individual. This phenomenon is exhibited when clients "sabotage" therapeutic progress during periods when the sexual dysfunction appears to be improving. Thus a form of reciprocal causality may exist, whereby the couple's sexual dysfunction and their relationship difficulties may each contribute to the other.

Physical disorders are also cited as a causal factor in sexual dysfunction. Several types of physical illness can be instrumental in creating sexual difficulties: (1) illnesses that result in chronic fatigue, pain, or restricted movement; (2) neurological impairments that affect arousal, erection, or ejaculation/orgasm; (3) coronary and diabetic diseases; (4) diseases that interfere with blood flow to the pelvis; and (5) numerous medications and drugs, including antihypertensive and antidepressant medication as well as alcohol, barbiturates, and street drugs.

Each of the etiological factors previously noted may operate in isolation or by a complex interplay of multiple causative agents.

Advances in Assessment of Sexual Dysfunction

The assessment and evaluative process has evolved in a manner parallel to that of advances in conceptualization and treatment of sexual dysfunction. However, some special difficulties affect the sexual dysfunction assessment process that are not found in other disorders. One major problem in this area is the social stigma and embarrassment that affects the truthfulness and completeness of data concerning the individual's sexual functioning. In addition, the complex nature of sexual functioning necessitates a broad range of knowledge on the part of the assessors concerning psychological, physiological, and interpersonal aspects of sexual functioning. The complexity and multifaceted nature of sexual dysfunction increases the difficulty of obtaining a thorough and adequate assessment.

The three major methods of assessing sexual dysfunction are interview, psychometric testing, and medical evaluation. Within these categories there have been significant changes and development allowing for a more holistic understanding of sexual problems.

Interview

The initial interview process has two stages. The first stage is used to determine the nature of the problem and whether or not sex therapy is appropriate. The second stage involves a detailed history taken from each individual in the dysfunctional relationship. Lobitz and Lobitz (1978) described several areas of inquiry: (1) medical history and physical status; (2) demographic data concerning occupation, previous relationships, and length of present relationship; (3) a description of the current sexual interactions of the couple, including both coital and noncoital activity, erection, ejaculation, orgasmic functioning, subjective arousal, and desire; (4) a detailed description of the sexual difficulty itself, including the couple's hypotheses about its cause and any attempts they have made to remediate the problem themselves; (5) a psychosexual history of each partner, including past and present psychological difficulties and the sexual attitudes each partner has learned; (6) the couple's view of the quality of their relationship; and (7) the couple's motivation for therapy and change.

Determination of the cognitive factors (attitudes, beliefs, and cognitions) that may be responsible for the development and maintenance of the sexual dysfunction are an inherent part of the assessment interview. The client's private theories of etiology and perpetuation of his or her sexual difficulties may sometimes be quite accurate, but often they are not. Thus clients' concepts of the cause and maintenance of the problem must be elicited and reframed if necessary to provide them with more accurate information. If the therapist fails to determine these private theories prior to the onset of therapy, the early intervention activities may be incorrectly processed through the client's inaccurate frame of reference. This may lead to future client resistance or misunderstanding of the therapy process.

Clients' expectations and treatment goals must also be explored in the initial interview. Most important in this portion of the history is helping the client to differentiate the concrete from the ideal (e.g., encouraging the client to think in terms of getting his penis to function in a manner that allows him to enjoy sexual intercourse, rather than of becoming a great lover). Unrealistic expectations require early reframing in order to prevent treatment from being judged as a failure by the client as well as the clinician.

The emotional states (i.e., anxiety, fear, guilt, shame, anger, and depression) that are mediated by cognitive factors must also be assessed, as they play a crucial role in the inhibition of sexual feelings and behaviors. Determination of anxieties interfering with autonomic nervous system functioning, possibly including performance demands, fear of failure, memories of parental censure, or threats of unwanted pregnancy, is essential in order to provide early intervention. Assessment of the client's level of depression, if its presence is suspected, is of major import, as depression may affect all phases of the sexual response cycle and must be adequately treated either initially or in conjunction with the sexual dysfunction. Excessive or irrational guilt, as well as feelings or beliefs that sex is "bad" or "dirty," that the body is shameful, or that sexual preferences or object choices are unacceptable may render sexual expression problematic. The clinician must be alert to messages of guilt or shame that may emerge in discussing sex-related concerns (Dailey, 1985).

Such an interview enables the therapist to acquire sufficient information to hypothesize the etiologic and maintaining factors of the dysfunction and to develop an appropriate treatment strategy. It also serves a rapport-building function by demonstrating the therapist's interest and may decrease anxiety by providing a conceptual framework for the problem.

Psychometric Measures

In the past decade psychometric instruments specifically designed for the assessment of sexual functioning have been developed. Prior to that time, projective tests and nonempirically based questionnaires, which lacked reliability and validity, were the only devices available for use in assessing sexual dysfunction (El-Senoussi, 1964).

Three of the best inventories for the assessment of sexual dysfunction among heterosexual clients are:

1. The Sexual Arousal Inventory (Hoon, Hoon, & Wincze, 1976), which is a measure of a woman's arousal in response to various sexual activities
2. The Derogatis Sexual Function Inventory (Derogatis, 1976), which measures an individual's sexual functioning on a nine-dimensional scale
3. The Sexual Interaction Inventory (LoPiccolo & Steger, 1974), which depicts a couple's sexual interaction in terms of the frequency and enjoyment of the specific activity and the level of communication between the partners

These measures provide guidelines for treatment via an identification of arousal deficits, behavior problems, and underlying issues that may affect sexual functioning.

Other psychometric tests, including attitudinal measures and instruments that tap sexual guilt, fear, pleasure, anxiety, sexual orientation, couple compatibility, arousability, and experience, have been developed in the last decade. A pervasive issue for those presenting with sexual concerns is that of body imagery. Although most people are somewhat dissatisfied with their bodies, they must share themselves physically with others in order to express their sexuality. A Body Attitude Scale has been developed to reveal both global and specific attitudes that clients hold toward their bodies (Dailey, 1985). Thus treatment for body imagery discomfort may be provided if deemed necessary. Several other types of attitude questionnaires have been developed to discern negative attitudes toward general sexuality, heterosexuality, homosexuality, masturbation, and sex role flexibility. Attitudes toward any of these issues may be significant in the treatment of sexual concerns. A special issue of the *Journal of Sex and Marital Therapy* (1979, Volume 5, Number 3) provides a review of psychometric test instruments used to assess sexual functioning.

Medical and Physiological Assessment

There have been considerable advances in methods of assessing the physical contributors to sexual dysfunction (Krone, Siroky, & Goldstein, 1983). Genital plethysmography, biochemical laboratory studies, and specialized diagnostic procedures have been used to determine physiological correlates of erectile dysfunction. Additional means of assessing this disorder from a physiological vantage point are the elicitation of spinal reflexes related to the genital area; the measurement of penile blood pressure; and hormonal analyses of testosterone, prolactin, thyroid hormone, luteinizing hormone, and follicle-stimulating hormone levels. More invasive but refined procedures include neurological techniques (i.e., electromyograms of the bulbocavernosus muscle reflex) and radiographic techniques for the visualization of the vascular system. Genital plethysmography, a measure of genital changes caused by genital congestion has been used to assess dysfunction in both sexes. The measurement of nocturnal penile tumescence (i.e., penile erection associated with periods of rapid eye movement, or REM, sleep) is one application of genital plethysmography. This method is used to determine whether normal nighttime erections are occurring, which would then rule out physiological dysfunctions. Vaginal introitus examinations have recently been used with women complaining of painful intercourse to determine whether such previously ignored pathology as hymenal remnants may be present.

The interactive nature of both psychogenic and organic factors in some sexual dysfunctions has only recently been recognized. For example, a man who may occasionally achieve a full erection would have previously been diagnosed as having a psychogenic disorder. However, since some organic problems raise the "threshold" of conditions required for a man to achieve an erection, physiological problems in such a case cannot be ruled out until such potential disorders are fully explored. Thus, even if an individual has clear psychogenic problems, a concomitant organic problem may also be found to coexist (Friedman & Czekala, 1985).

The assessment techniques described here allow for a more highly sophisticated differentiation of various etiological and descriptive factors in sexual dysfunction than was previously possible. Since sexual dysfunction is related to a number of historical, behavioral, relationship, physiological, and personal factors, an evaluation of each of these is necessary for an adequate assessment of sexual dysfunction.

Diagnostic Terminology and Classification

A lack of consensus and precision in the terminology and classification of sexual functions has contributed to confusion and imprecision in this area. For example, the term *frigidity* has been used to describe almost any sexual dysfunction in females, and the term *impotence* has been used to describe lack of sexual interest as well as erectile and ejaculation dysfunction in males. Kaplan (1974) argued for the elimination of the term *impotence* because of its pejorative connotations. Masters and Johnson (1970) described the term *frigidity* as "poor slang" and attempted to outline several male and female dysfunctions to add precision to nosology in this area. Kaplan (1974) classified sexual dysfunctions according to a biphasic delineation of the sexual response cycle that allowed comparative diagnoses for both sexes. This biphasic system distinguished between excitement and orgasmic difficulties. Kaplan (1979) subsequently expanded her system to add disorders of desire as a third phase. The DSM-III classifications of sexual dysfunction is based on Kaplan's system and thus includes diagnoses for inhibited sexual desire (302.71) and inhibited sexual excitement (302.72), as well as three diagnoses for problems of sexual orgasm: inhibited female orgasm (302.73), inhibited male orgasm (302.74), and premature ejaculation (302.75). In addition, there are three other diagnostic categories that do not fall into one of the Kaplan (1979) phases: functional dyspareunia (302.76), functional vaginismus (306.51), and atypical psychosexual dysfunction (302.70) (American Psychiatric Association, 1980).

In an attempt to add more precision to the definitions of sexual dysfunction, Masters and Johnson (1970) and Kaplan, (1974, 1979) have added modifiers to the dysfunction labels just mentioned. Masters and Johnson used modifiers such as *primary* (never) versus *secondary* (sometimes) to further delineate the distinction between dysfunctions. However, the primary/secondary labels were not consistent across dysfunctions. We use *global* versus *situational* to differentiate disorders occurring under all circumstances from those occurring only in particular situations, and *lifetime* versus *nonlifetime* to differentiate those persons whose dysfunction was always present from those who are dysfunctional only temporarily or during a given time period.

The Dysfunctions

Orgasm Phase Dysfunctions

FEMALE ORGASMIC DYSFUNCTION: GLOBAL/LIFELONG
This is a condition in which a woman has never had an orgasm under any circumstances throughout her lifetime (DSM-III diagnosis: inhibited female orgasm).

FEMALE ORGASMIC DYSFUNCTION: SITUATIONAL
This is a condition in which a woman has had the ability to be orgasmic in some situations (e.g., through masturbation) but not in other circumstances. This may or may not be a lifelong pattern (DSM-III diagnosis: inhibited female orgasm).

MALE PREMATURE EJACULATION
There are several currently accepted definitions of premature ejaculation. Since "prematurity" is a relative condition, depending on the partner's desires and responsivity,

diagnosis of this condition is often controvertible. Prematurity has been defined by some sex therapists as ejaculation at a time less than 7 minutes after intromission, unless by choice. Kaplan (1974) defined prematurity as the inability to achieve voluntary control over the ejaculatory reflex. DSM-III defines premature ejaculation as "ejaculation before the individual wishes it, because of recurrent and persistent absence of reasonable voluntary control of ejaculation and orgasm during sexual activity (p. 158)" (DSM-III diagnosis: premature ejaculation).

MALE INHIBITED EJACULATION

This relatively uncommon condition involves an inability to ejaculate even after lengthy stimulation. Most often this condition is situational, limited to intravaginal ejaculation (DSM-III diagnosis: inhibited male orgasm).

Arousal Phase Dysfunctions

FEMALE: DECREASED SUBJECTIVE AND/OR PHYSIOLOGICAL AROUSAL

This is a condition in which there is a reduced physiological response, indicated by lack of lubrication and nipple erection, and/or a loss of subjective arousal (DSM-III diagnosis: inhibited sexual excitement).

MALE: ERECTILE DYSFUNCTION

This condition is diagnosed when a man has difficulty achieving and/or maintaining a sufficiently rigid erection to have intercourse. This condition can be lifelong or not, global or situational (DSM-III diagnosis: inhibited sexual excitement).

Desire Phase Dysfunctions

LOW SEXUAL DESIRE

This condition is difficult to define as, again, it is a relative disorder (depending on partner preferences). In addition, it has no demarcating behavioral or physiological referents, and sexual desire itself is extremely subjective in nature. Additionally, low sexual desire is a multidimensional phenomenon. For example, a person may desire to masturbate but have little urge for partner sex. Another individual may desire sex with his lover but not with his spouse. The DSM-III criteria for a diagnosis of inhibited sexual desire is the persistent and pervasive inhibition of sexual desire. The individual's age, sex, and health; the intensity and frequency of sexual desire; and the context of the individual's life when the diagnosis is made must all be taken into account. This diagnosis should rarely be used unless the lack of desire is distressing to either the individual or the partner. The disorder also must not be caused exclusively by organic factors such as a physical disorder, medication, or another Axis I disorder (American Psychiatric Association, 1980) (DSM-III diagnosis: inhibited sexual desire).

AVERSION TO SEX

This condition is similar to low sexual desire but includes a much stronger negative emotional response to sex, of which the person is cognitively aware. This condition is often conceptualized and treated as a phobia (DSM-III diagnosis: inhibited sexual desire).

Other Dysfunctions

VAGINISMUS

This condition is defined as an involuntary spastic contraction of the pelvic musculature that makes penetration extremely difficult or impossible (DSM-III diagnosis: functional vaginismus).

DYSPAREUNIA

This condition is defined as coital pain (DSM-III diagnosis: functional dyspareunia).

The Incidence of Sexual Dysfunction

It is generally agreed that there is a high incidence of sexual dysfunction in contemporary American marriages. As early as 1929, Davis found that almost one-half of 2,200 married women reported that the were "inadequately prepared for the sexual side of marriage." Rainwater (1966) observed that 14% of middle-class women and 54% of lower-class women were "negative toward sex" or "rejected sexual relations entirely." Lehrman (1971) using Masters and Johnson's (1970) data stated that "one out of every two marriages" was a "sexual disaster area." Kinsey, Pomeroy, Martin, and Gebhard (1953) found that 11% of married women never experienced orgasm in coitus, even after 20 years of marriage. Kinsey, Pomeroy, and Martin (1953) also stated that, from the reports of urologists and endocrinologists, erectile failure and premature ejaculation were widespread difficulties within the general population. Frank, Anderson, and Rubinstein (1978) more recently studied 100 "normal, happily married couples" and found a "surprisingly" high rate of sexual problems (i.e., 40% of the males reported a history of erectile or ejaculatory dysfunction and 63% of the women reported a history of arousal or orgasmic difficulty. Frank et al. (1978) found in addition that 50% of the men and 77% of the women reported difficulties centering around loss of interest in sex or low sexual drive. These high rates of low sex drive continue to be reported in the contemporary literature. Schover and LoPiccolo (1982) found that out of 39 consecutively completed treatment cases at their clinic, 27 (69%) included a diagnosis of low sexual desire in at least one spouse. This included 44% of all male partners seen and 26% of the female partners. Lief (1977) stated that 28% of the patients seen at the Marriage Council of Philadelphia had a primary diagnosis of inhibited sexual desire, including 37% of the women but only 18.7% of the men. Although precise incidence rates of sexual dysfunction in modern life are hard to come by, the foregoing data are representative of the increasingly high frequency of individuals reporting such disorders. The recent societal pressures to be sexually active, the clinical community's increased attention to sexual problems, and the influence of the feminist movement and its focus on women's greater enjoyment of more frequent and varied sexual activity may have all contributed to the heightened reported incidence of sexual dysfunction.

Strategies for Change

Masters and Johnson (1970), in their original treatment program, postulated several common treatment elements for all dysfunctions. Therapy was always conducted conjointly using a male–female co-therapy team. The program consisted of 15 daily sessions, which occurred while the couple resided at the treatment center for a 2-week period. The program initially entailed extensive history taking, followed by a debriefing session in which the therapists proposed possible explanations of the problem's etiology. Homework assignments, consisting of a graded series of sexual tasks, were then introduced. In addition, a ban on intercourse was requested in order to reduce performance anxiety. Further, the discovery and communication of new sensual experiences were fostered through an initial exercise called "sensate focus."

This exercise was used to create a nondemanding experience that would reduce the anxiety to perform, eliminate "spectatoring" by encouraging the couple to focus on their own sexual sensations and feelings, and increase sexual communication by training the couple to provide feedback to each other concerning what felt good to each individual. Stimulation of breasts and genitals was initially proscribed while the couple engaged in a mutual, sensual body massage. Gradually, as the couple became comfortable with the exercise, these body parts were again included. Eventually, intercourse was reintroduced. In addition, therapy focused on education and counseling to eliminate sexual myths and to train more effective verbal and nonverbal communication skills. A male–female sex therapy team was used to facilitate sex-role modeling and communication between the sexes. The graduated exercises, from body massage to intercourse, can be construed as a form of *in vivo* desensitization, although it was not conceptualized as such by Masters and Johnson (1970).

The current treatment program for sexual dysfunction that is based on the procedures originally outlined by Masters and Johnson (1970) also contains elements common to all dysfunctions as well as to particular interventions for each disorder. These procedures include exploration of individual personality processes, relationship restructuring, and prescription of changes in sexual behavior. There has been little research concerning which elements of the total package are of primary importance in fostering change. Thus the experienced clinician, instead of using the same techniques with each case, tends to tailor the sex therapy package to fit individual needs. More or less emphasis is thus placed on various elements of the therapy program, depending on the types of problems that must be addressed.

The therapy program is usually short-term (10 to 20 sessions), and the couple rather than the individual is construed as "owning" the problem. A graduated series of sexual tasks is initiated by the couple in conjunction with a ban on sexual intercourse. These tasks begin with sensate focus exercises.

Several principles currently underlie couple sex therapy and receive varying degrees of emphasis, depending on the particular case. These principles are designed to promote cognitive–affective, behavioral, and psychophysiological change through emphasis on the following:

1. *Mutual responsibility*: The couple is viewed as being mutually responsible for correcting the sexual dysfunction. A distinction between *responsibility* and *blame* is clearly explained to the couple.

2. *Elimination of performance anxiety*: The couple is taught to cease "keeping

score" or to avoid goal-oriented sexual activity aimed at erection, orgasm, or ejaculation. Instead, they are asked to focus on enjoying the pleasant sensations derived from sensual contact. The ban on intercourse and the therapist's permission to engage in other forms of sensual activity promote this therapeutic goal. If anxiety is particularly severe, formal systematic desensitization may be used.

3. *Education*: A common problem of individuals experiencing sexual dysfunction is their lack of knowledge of both basic physiology and effective sexual technique. Accurate knowledge of the sexual response cycle and general principles of more efficacious sexual procedure are imparted to the couple. Verbal discussion, reading materials, and/or educational films are used if necessary.

4. *Attitude change*: Many individuals with sexual dysfunction hold negative attitudes toward sexuality. A variety of methods are used to foster attitude change, including assignment of reading materials using commercially available self-help books that comment positively on sexuality (Heiman, LoPiccolo, & LoPiccolo, 1976; Zilbergeld, 1978); arranging consultation with understanding clergy; recommending sexuality workshops and lectures that impart a more positive sexual value system; and using the therapeutic relationship through rapport building, encouragement, and self-disclosure when appropriate.

5. *Enhancing communication*: Dysfunctional couples often are inhibited about open discussion of sexual issues. In addition, such couples frequently have difficulty clearly communicating sexual likes and dislikes to their partner. Therapy is thus directed toward encouraging communication about preferred techniques and toward disclosing responses to varying forms of stimulation. Such communication may be facilitated by having couples view and discuss movies with sexually explicit content, read sexually explicit literature, share fantasies, guide their partner's hand during sexual activity, and provide each other with verbal and nonverbal feedback during sexual exercises.

6. *Change of destructive sex roles and life-styles*: For many dysfunctional couples, sex may be a low-priority event, and sexual activity may occur only when both partners are mentally and physically fatigued or under time pressure. In other cases, other life influences may be adversely affecting the couple's sex life. Helping couples to become aware of these detrimental influences and to change these patterns can have a dramatic impact on sexual functioning.

7. *Change of disruptive systems and enhancement of the relationship*: Many couples have relationship difficulties in addition to the problem of sexual dysfunction. Major difficulties with communication, problem-solving skills, child management, life-style, and power and control issues may require remediation and may indicate a need for direct restructuring of the marital relationship.

8. *Physical and medical intervention*: The issue of how much of a medical examination is required before initiating a sex therapy program must be addressed at the onset of treatment. A general physical screening, including a routine urologic or gynecologic examination, is usually suggested. Some disorders, however, do not appear to be indicative of physical or medical abnormalities—for example, premature ejaculation. Erectile and desire problems, however, can be caused by a host of diseases and physiological complications thus warranting a very thorough medical evaluation prior to treatment by psychological means.

9. *Change of sexual behavior via teaching of effective sexual technique*: The truly

distinctive element of sex therapy, as compared to other psychotherapeutic approaches, is the therapist's prescribing of a series of specific sexual behaviors. The type of behavioral prescription varies with the dysfunction and will be described in the following section.

Treatment of Specific Disorders

The model described next for treatment of low sexual desire can be thought of as a conceptual framework for all sexual dysfunctions. It borrows extensively from the cognitive-behavioral literature and is illustrative of the manner in which a broad integration of theory and technique from various theoretical orientations can be amalgamated as a treatment paradigm for complex disorders.

Desire Phase Disorders

LOW SEXUAL DESIRE

There are four overlapping components for treating couples with low sexual desire or aversion to sex. These elements, selected from different theoretical orientations, provide a comprehensive and integrative model for treating the disorder within a 15- to 25-session treatment period. The four elements are (1) experiential therapy and sensory awareness, (2) insight, (3) cognitive restructuring, and (4) behavioral assignments.

1. *Experiential therapy and sensory awareness*: It is assumed that sexually related anxieties underlie most cases of low sexual desire, even though many low-desire clients may claim complete neutrality about sex. An attempt is made to allow clients to recognize, using bodily cues, when they are experiencing both positive and negative reactions such as anxiety, fear, satisfaction, and pleasure. Homework and in-session assignments include sensate focus, fantasy training, and body awareness exercises. Emotional responses may be elicited during the session by using encouragement and provocation; by giving permission to be angry, sad, happy, and so forth; and by using Gestalt techniques such as the "empty chair" or imaginal recreation of an earlier trauma.

2. *Insight*: In the insight phase the therapist helps the client understand the causes and maintaining factors of his or her low sexual desire. The rationale for this procedure is that, once an explanation is provided for their behavior, the individual with low sexual desire will feel less anxiety. A number of techniques are used to help the client gain insight into the problem: interpretation, reframing, empathic reflection, response demand, and help in conceptualizing family-of-origin issues within a learning theory approach. During this phase, the higher-desire partner also gains insight into how he or she may be contributing to the maintenance or cause of the problem.

3. *Cognitive restructuring*: The cognitive phase of therapy helps clients identify self-statements that interfere with sexual functioning. Systematic rational restructuring (Goldfried & Davison, 1976), a social-learning adaptation of rational-emotive therapy (Ellis, 1962), is employed during this phase. This procedure teaches clients how hidden irrational or unrealistic beliefs may be mediating their emotions and how changing these unrealistic self-statements can help promote a more realistic reevaluation of specific situations. Individualized coping statements are developed to assist clients in coping

with, rather than avoiding, emotional responses to particular situations. Another technique is the use of the devil's advocate (Goldfried & Davison, 1976), a procedure in which the therapist argues for an irrational belief and the client attempts to convince the therapist that the argument is indeed irrational. A modified transactional analysis framework (Berne, 1964; Steiner, 1974) is used to help clients recognize their own power and also to bridge the gap between feelings and cognitions.

4. *Behavioral interventions*: Behavioral techniques are used to help induce feelings that clients can then process in the experiential sensory awareness exercises. These procedures include sensate focus exercises, behavioral rehearsal, role playing other characters or personality types, and role rehearsal. Assertion training; communication training; the use of caring days (Broderick, Friedman, & Carr, 1981); and problem solving (Goldfried & Davison, 1976) may be used to improve the relationship. Stress reduction procedures, bibliotherapy, the use of films about human sexuality and sexual techniques, and training in initiation and refusal may be included in treatment when necessary. The assignment of fantasy breaks, in which the client is asked to spend several minutes each day consciously having a sexual fantasy, is an example of "priming the pump" to make sex more salient.

The development of effective treatment techniques for low sexual desire lags far behind that for the other sexual dysfunctions because of the complex etiology of the disorder and the repression, denial, relationship discord, and low motivation that are often present. Thus effective treatment of these cases requires an increased integration of techniques and concepts from cognitive-behavioral, Gestalt, psychodynamic, general systems, and other approaches.

Arousal Disorders

LACK OF PHYSIOLOGICAL OR SUBJECTIVE FEMALE AROUSAL

The goal of treatment for this disorder is to enable the woman to respond to sexual stimuli by creating a relaxed, nondemanding, and sensual ambience. Open communication, sensate focus, and allowing the woman to remain in control of the sexual situation are recommended. Focusing on physical sensations and ignoring extraneous thoughts are helpful in increasing subjective arousal. Many of the techniques used in the treatment of inorgasmia can be used to enhance her responsiveness. Issues of intimacy, trust, and feelings of anger or alienation toward the partner must also be explored.

ERECTILE DYSFUNCTION

The treatment of erectile dysfunction focuses on the elimination of performance demands and anxiety and on providing adequate stimulation. The initial sensate focus exercises emphasize sensual, not sexual, pleasure; the prohibition against massaging breasts or genitals eliminates the pressure to perform and, for the male, to have an erection. Many therapists also instruct their clients specifically not to gain an erection. As the couple becomes more comfortable in communicating their preferences and better able to give and receive pleasure in a nonpressured situation, breasts and genitals are eventually added. Intercourse and orgasm continue to be proscribed. After several weeks of intense stimulation without the pressure to achieve an erection or orgasm, the male will usually begin to experience periods of erection during the sensate focus sessions. At this point the "tease technique" (Masters and Johnson, 1970) is introduced. The partner is instructed to cease stimulation of the male's penis should an erection occur and to resume stimulation only after the erection has disappeared. This technique reduces anxiety about losing erections and shows both partners that an erection can be regained if it is lost. The next procedure allows vaginal intromission, but only with the female physically pushing the male's flaccid penis into her vagina while she sits astride his body. The technique, called "stuffing," is often accomplished by the instruction "Do not have an erection." Once the male can no longer avoid having an erection during vaginal containment, slow pelvic thrusting by each partner and, finally, coital ejaculation is also allowed. Throughout this procedure, it is emphasized to the couple that sexual desire and arousal can be present without the male's erection and that both partners can derive a great deal of pleasure from other forms of stimulation.

Orgasmic Disorders

PREMATURE EJACULATION

The major technique used in the treatment of this dysfunction is to stimulate the male until just prior to the point of ejaculatory inevitability. The stimulation is then interrupted until his arousal subsides, at which point stimulation is continued. This procedure is repeated several times before ejaculation is allowed. Two major techniques are used to interrupt sexual stimulation: (1) the pause technique (Semans, 1956), which involves stopping direct stimulation of the penis, and (2) the squeeze technique (Masters & Johnson, 1970), which entails manually squeezing the glans or the base of the penis. This exercise is designed to allow the male to experience a huge amount of stimulation without the occurrence of ejaculation, thus teaching ejaculatory control. Solitary masturbation is initially used to allow the client to concentrate on his own physical sensations without the presence of his partner. Sensate focus exercises usually are prescribed concomitantly at this time. Gradually, ejaculatory control techniques are introduced into couple sessions. When control is gained through manual stimulation, vaginal containment, first without and then including thrusting is reintroduced.

INHIBITED EJACULATION

The treatment for this disorder involves instructing the couple in effective sexually stimulatory exercises in addition to reducing the man's anxiety about sexual performance. The couple is taught ways to provide massive stimulation to the man's penis while the man himself is taught ways to become psychologically aroused and to communicate to his partner the type of stimulation he enjoys. Orgasm triggers such as increasing bodily tension by pointing toes and clenching fists, using Kegel (1952) exercises for genital muscle control, throwing the head back, breathing deeply, rocking rhythmically, and thrusting the pelvis forward are used. Initially the man is taught to ejaculate with self-stimulation. Gradually his partner is introduced into the session and, once he is able to ejaculate in her presence, vaginal containment is introduced at the point of orgasm. The timing of penetration is then slowly moved back until intercourse lasts for some time before ejaculation occurs.

FEMALE PRIMARY ORGASMIC PROBLEMS

Women with primary orgasm problems are treated with a relatively straightforward program developed by Lobitz and LoPiccolo (1972). The steps include:

1. Visual examination of the genitals using a mirror to increase self-knowledge, acceptance, and comfort with her body
2. Exploration of the genital area to determine pleasure-sensitive areas
3. Intense stimulation of these areas using erotic fantasies, explicit literature or photographs, orgasmic "triggers," and role playing of orgasms
4. Introduction of a vibrator if orgasm has not been achieved by the preceding methods
5. Skill training for the partner, involving observing the woman's masturbation, learning to bring her to orgasm in that way, and finally pairing it with coitus.

The use of masturbation for this dysfunction is based on Kinsey, Pomeroy, Martin, and Gebhard's (1953) data, which indicated that the probability of orgasm through masturbation is greater for the average woman than through coitus. Throughout the program the woman is instructed to practice Kegel (1952) exercises, which strengthen the pubococcygeal muscles, which are thought to increase orgasmic potential.

SECONDARY (SITUATIONAL) FEMALE INORGASMIC DYSFUNCTION

The treatment for situational orgasmic dysfunction is not as straightforward as that for primary orgasmic dysfunction, as situational inorgasmia is often entwined with larger interactional patterns of the couple. In some cases, a directed masturbation approach similar to that for primary inorgasmia is effective. If a woman is orgasmic in only one restricted masturbatory pattern, she must learn to expand the stimuli that result in orgasm. This can be accomplished by having her switch positions or stimuli just prior to the point of orgasm. She then gradually learns to initiate these changes at an earlier point of arousal. If a woman is orgasmic alone but not in the presence of a partner, relationship, communication, or attitudinal issues must be explored and treated. Education is also helpful in ensuring that the woman receives adequate sexual stimulation. Many therapists do not consider it a dysfunction if a woman is orgasmic in ways other than intercourse, since there are a large number of women who do not experience coital orgasm. Zeiss, Rosen, and Zeiss (1977) developed a sexual enhancement technique for such women that teaches the association of orgasms brought on by manual clitoral stimulation with arousing thoughts about intercourse. This procedure subsequently entails the woman's use of a dildo during masturbation, the gradual introduction of the male partner into the sessions, and finally intercourse.

Other issues that should be explored with secondary inorgasmia are the adequacy of clitoral stimulation before and after intercourse and the ability of the male partner to delay ejaculation long enough to bring his partner to orgasm.

Other Female Dysfunctions

VAGINISMUS

Vaginismus is treated with the use of a graduated series of dilators to help the woman accept and enjoy vaginal intromission. The woman is initially instructed in relaxation and focus exercises to enhance her arousal. She is subsequently taught Kegel (1952) exercises, with the additional instruction of inserting the dilator during the relaxed phase. The woman gradually increases the size of the dilator used. Couple participation in sensate focus exercises also occurs during this period. The dilator is gradually introduced during the couple session, with the role of insertion eventually being transferred to her partner. Eventually intercourse is introduced, with the woman on top to allow her greater control over penetration and thrusting. Other positions are then gradually introduced.

DYSPAREUNIA

Since the pain associated with dyspareunia may be due to a still undiagnosed medical problem, treatment of this disorder is primarily a matter of pain management. Thus the fear of pain, which often triggers a negative cycle of avoidance, tensions, and subsequently additional pain, is dealt with through anxiety reduction techniques, sensate focus, and the provision of a nondemanding and nonpressured atmosphere where enhanced communication, exploration, and resolution of underlying fears and attitudes may result.

The Issue of Treatment Compliance

Compliance issues may be a major problem in the treatment of sexual dysfunction. Since the adherence to prescribed homework assignments is essential for change in this area, noncompliance—as exemplified by failing to perform homework exercises adequately, or by exceeding the limit of the assignment—can have a major impact on therapeutic progress. It is in the domain of compliance that the cognitive-behavioral therapies play a significant role in sex therapy.

When clients fail to comply with therapeutic activities, it often indicates that the therapist has failed to deal with the client's anxieties about sex or the issue of how the person's sexual problem relates to each partner's individual or relationship dynamic. Thus lack of compliance with prescribed homework assignments does not necessarily indicate a lack of motivation for change but, instead, the individual's fears concerning the restructuring of his or her relationship, or personal changes that might ensue subsequent to enhanced sexual functioning.

Within a cognitive-behavioral framework, there exist both direct and indirect means of alleviating therapeutic noncompliance. The direct approach usually involves three stages. The first step entails the therapist assisting the client in defining the problem and making it amenable to solution. The second step involves promotion of cognitive, emotional, and behavioral change via skills training (e.g., modeling, role playing, imagery rehearsal, and graded *in vivo* exposure) and intervention in the client's self-regulating activity. At this stage, the therapist helps the client in the alteration of self-statements, images, and feelings that interfere with therapeutic progress. This is accomplished through the reduction in the frequency and/or impact of dysfunctional cognitions (i.e., distorted interpretations, unwarranted negative expectations, self-denigrating thoughts, and disruptive feelings such as anxiety and depression). Attempts are also made to enhance adaptive thoughts and feelings (i.e., the use of a problem-solving set that enables the client to view life's difficulties as problems to be solved rather than as emotionally laden threats or provocations to one's well-being) (Meichenbaum, 1985). Finally, clients are trained to modify their cognitive structures or habitual ways of construing the self and the world. They are asked to engage in a series of experiments to determine the validity of their beliefs. In this manner, clients who are handicapped by their misreading of situations, avoidance of opportunities for success, or maladaptive responses can create new experiences for themselves with an ensuing modification in thoughts and feeling (Meichenbaum, 1985). The last stage focuses on the consolidation of changes and on the generalization and maintenance of behavior change and the avoidance of coping with relapses. Thus clients whose sexual dysfunctions are due to relationship or personal issues that are mediated by maladaptive cognitions or emotional responses can be helped to overcome these difficulties and continue to progress in therapy.

The indirect approach for dealing with client noncompliance is the use of paradoxical intention (PI) (Frankl, 1965). Within this approach, clients are assisted in gaining greater control over their lives. The therapist helps them outmaneuver the symptom by requesting that they exaggerate it. An example of the use of this technique is with clients who break the intercourse ban during sensate focus exercises. The therapist can use paradoxical intention techniques by supporting the couple's decision. In addition, they can be told that although they might be unhappy with their current sexual situation, change may be even more threatening. The therapist can show empathy when clients choose not to do exercises that facilitate change and can then allow the couple to write their own assignment. Since clients now have greater control over their own decision making, the fear of change becomes more tolerable and they will usually do what is therapeutically necessary for further progress. Since paradoxical intention can be a potentially risky technique, however, it should primarily be used by experienced clinicians.

Clinical Outcome of Sex Therapy

Masters and Johnson (1970) presented a detailed statistical analysis of the successes and failures in their treatment program. They noted at the outset that their client population was not representative of the population at large, as their clients had higher than average incomes and education, and were all highly motivated. Of the 790 persons treated, 142 were considered treatment failures at the termination of the 2-week program (i.e., an initial failure rate of 12%). A breakdown of failure rates according to type of disorder was as follows: primary impotence—40%; secondary impotence—26%; premature ejaculation—2%; ejaculatory incompetence—18%; total male disorders—17%; primary orgasmic dysfunction—17%; situational orgasmic dysfunction—23%; total female disorders—19%; male and female totals—18% (Belliveau & Richter, 1970). At a 5-year follow-up, an overall success rate remained at 74.5%. This figure, however, did not include 56 clients who were initial treatment failures or 31 clients who were lost to follow-up. Masters and Johnson (1970) reported that treatment failures were most often due to incapacitating anxiety; to client withholding of essential information from the therapist (such as a history of incest, homosexuality, or rape); and/or poor client motivation or errors in judgment by the co-therapy team (Belliveau & Richter, 1970). Kaplan (1974) reported similar outcome data to that of Masters and Johnson (1970). However, she added several additional caveats predictive of therapeutic failure—for example, concomitant psychopathology, excessive vulnerability to stress, depression, alcoholism or drug addiction, a lack of commitment on the part of one partner, or the contingency of such important life decisions as marriage or divorce on the outcome of treatment.

There have been a variety of criticisms of the Masters and Johnson (1970) data and subsequent research in this area. Methodological flaws, according to many investigations, preclude the establishment of definite conclusions concerning the effectiveness of most currently used sex therapy techniques. Hogan's (1978) critique of this literature concerns several issues:

1. The bulk of papers published on the treatment of sexual dysfunctions merely report single case studies or a series of case studies.
2. Confusion remains concerning definition and classification of sexual dysfunctions.
3. Discussions of etiological factors are based on retrospective client self-report, which may be further distorted by the theoretical bias of the investigators.
4. Few studies report objective assessment instruments.

Zilbergeld and Evans (1980) disputed the Masters and Johnson (1970) report of failure rates, rather than success rates. Since failure and nonfailure are not operationally defined, the amount of success achieved by the nonfailure group may be minimal and not comparable to "success" as defined by other investigators. In addition, Zilbergeld and Evans viewed with skepticism the generalization of the Masters and Johnson (1970) findings to a less selective population and the validity of Masters and Johnson's extremely low relapse rates, because of the flexible relapse criteria utilized.

Some investigators, however, have reported results that, though slightly lower than the Masters and Johnson (1970) data, nevertheless depict treatment efficacy. For example, Fuchs, Hack, Abramovici, Timor-Tritsch and Kleinhaus (1975) reported success in 6 out of 9 cases treated for vaginismus in the office and 31 out of 34 cases treated at home, whereas Masters and Johnson (1970) report no failure in all 29 of the vaginismus cases they have treated.

Treatment of premature ejaculation has also been shown to be effective using both the pause and squeeze techniques. Kaplan, Kohl, Pomeroy, Offit, and Hogan (1974) treated 32 couples conjointly using the pause technique, and all who completed the program were cured. Semans (1956) used the pause technique in 8 cases with a 100% success rate. LoPiccolo and Lobitz (1973) treated 6 cases using the squeeze procedure, with a 100% success rate. Mikulas and Lowe (1974) treated 10 cases of premature ejaculation via bibliotherapy in which the squeeze was one component. The mean ejaculation latency for the treatment group increased from 1.8 to 37.2 minutes, while that for the waiting list control group remained at 1.4 minutes. When the clients in the control group were given the bibliotherapy, their mean latency increased to 18.6 minutes. The subject with the least improvement had a latency of 4.5 minutes after treatment.

Heiman and LoPiccolo (1983) treated 69 lower-middle-class couples who were unselected with respect to severity of personal and marital distress. They used standardized instruments to measure change over five time periods: intake, history, posttherapy, and 1-year follow-up. Subjects served as their own controls, and a 15-session weekly treatment was compared with a 15-session daily treatment. Immediate treatment effects showed success in improving sexual and marital satisfaction, as well as specific symptom remission with little decline over the 3-month and 1-year follow-ups. The least improvement occurred for erectile problems and female secondary inorgasmia, as there was some indication of a gradual, nonsignificant decline of overall sexual and marital satisfaction at follow-up. These disorders, however, appeared to show greater maintenance in the weekly as compared to the daily treatment mode, whereas other dysfunctions responded similarly to either treatment regimen.

Because of the lack of controlled research in the area of sexual dysfunctions, the foregoing data are merely suggestive. More controlled outcome studies using standardized assessment techniques, and factorial designs examining client variables, treatment components, and modes of therapy, are necessary in order to provide data that have greater validity and generalizability.

New Treatment Procedures and Future Directions

With the growth of sex therapy and the changing clinical populations, there has been an increased focus on treatment variation and innovation. In the past several years, some promising physically focused treatments have been suggested. Pharmacotherapy, including hormone treatments, has been found useful in the treatment of some sexual dysfunctions. The use of antidepressant medications for mildly to moderately depressed individuals with sexual dysfunction is a case in point. Hormonal treatments of sexual dysfunction are helpful in some situations in which there is a documented endocrine disorder. Hyperprolactinemia, hyperthyroidism, and hypogonadism are all disorders that can be treated by hormonal administration. In instances of erectile failure due to untreatable medical conditions, implantation of penile prosthesis has become more common over the past decade. The implantation of a silicone prosthesis, which results in a permanent tumescent state (Small, Carrion, & Gordon, 1975), or the use of an inflatable penile prosthesis that allows for a change in penile state analogous to tumescence or detumescence (Scott, Bradley, & Timm, 1973) can be used. These implants do not increase sensation or facilitate ejaculation if this is a problem. The importance of sex therapy and counseling to assist such patients and their partners in adjustment to these prosthetic devices has already been suggested (Bullard, Mann, Caplan, & Stoklosa, 1978). Recently success has been reported with an experimental drug, papaverine (Zorgniotti & Lefleur, 1985), a smooth-muscle relaxant that can be injected in the corpus cavernosum. With this treatment, several men with organic erectile failure were able to achieve an erection lasting 10–20 minutes.

The medically ill, the handicapped, and other groups with definite organic dysfunctions are receiving increased attention. There appears to be increased social consciousness concerning the fact that these individuals, despite their physical disabilities, maintain a need for sexual expression. The principles of sex therapy are well suited for this population because of its focus on education, its deemphasis of genital sexuality, and its exploration of other forms of sexual expression. Thus, with adjustments in their behavior, handicapped persons can be helped to find sexual fulfillment. The elderly are another population who would benefit from the sex therapy techniques previously described, as recent studies show the stability of the sexual function throughout the life span (George & Weiler, 1981).

The maturation of sex therapy as a discipline, concomitant with increased accuracy of diagnoses and new treatment procedures, will allow for its applicability to new populations and for the current integration of the discipline into the mainstream of psychotherapeutic treatment.

References

American Psychiatric Association (1980). *Diagnostic and statistical manual of mental disorders* (3rd ed.). Washington, DC: Author.

Belliveau, F. & Richter, L. (1970). *Understanding human sexual inadequacy.* New York: Bantam Books.

Berne, E. (1964). *Games people play.* New York: Grove Press.

Broderick, J., Friedman, J. M., & Carr, E. (1981). Negotiation and contracting. In A. Goldstein, E. Carr, W. Davison, & P. Wehr (Eds.), *In response to aggression.* New York: Pergamon Press.

Bullard, D. G., Mann, J., Caplan, H., & Stoklosa, J. M. (1978). Sex counseling and the penile prosthesis. *Sexuality and Disability, 1,* 184–189.

Dailey, D. M. (1985). Elements of assessment in cases of sexual dysfunction. In D. P. Swiercinsky (Ed.), *Testing adults: A reference guide for special psychodiagnostic assessments.* Kansas City: Test Corporation of America.

Davis, K. B. (1929). *Factors in the sex life of two hundred women.* New York: Harper.

Dengrove, E. (1967). Behavior therapy of the sexual disorders. *Journal of Sex Research, 3,* 49–61.

Derogatis, I. R. (1976). Psychological assessment of sexual disorders. In J. Meyer (Ed.), *Clinical management of sexual disorders.* Baltimore, MD: Williams and Wilkins.

Ellis, A. (1962). *Reason and emotion in psychotherapy.* New York: Lyle Stuart.

Ellis, A. (1971). Rational-emotive treatment of impotence, frigidity and other sexual problems. *Professional Psychology, 2,* 346–349.

El-Senoussi, A. (1964). *The male impotence test.* Los Angeles, CA: Western Psychological Services.

Frank, E., Anderson, C., & Rubinstein, P. (1978). Frequency of sexual dysfunction in "normal" couples. *New England Journal of Medicine, 299,* 111–115.

Frankl, V. E. (1965). The doctor and the soul (2nd ed., R. Winston & C. Winston, Trans.). New York: Knopf.

Freud, S. (1953). Three essays on the theory of sexuality. In *Standard edition* (Vol. 7). (Original work published 1905)

Friedman, D. (1968). The treatment of impotence by Brevital relaxation therapy. *Behaviour Research and Therapy, 6,* 257–261.

Friedman, J. M., & Czekala, J. (1985). Advances in sex therapy techniques. In P. A. Keller & L. G. Ritt (Eds.), *Innovations in clinical practice: A source book* (Vol. 4). Sarasota, FL: Professional Resource Exchange.

Friedman, J. M., Weiler, S. J., LoPiccolo, J., & Hogan, D. R. (1982). Sexual dysfunction and their treatment. In A. S. Bellack, M. Hersen, & A. E. Kazdin (Eds.), *International handbook of behavior modification and therapy.* New York: Plenum Press.

Fuchs, K., Hack, Z., Abramovici, H., Timor-Tritsch, I., & O. Kleinhaus, M. (1975). Vaginismus—The hypnotherapeutic approach. *Journal of Sex Research, 11,* 39–45.

Garfield, Z. H., McBrearty, J. E., & Dichter, M. (1969). A case of impotence successfully treated with desensitization combined with *in vivo* operant training and thoughts substitution. In R. D. Rubin & C. M. Franks (Eds.), *Advances in behavior therapy.* New York: Academic Press.

Gee, W. F. (1975). A history of surgical treatment of impotence. *Urology, 5,* 401–405.

George, L. K., & Weiler, S. J. (1981). Sexuality in middle and later life: The effects of age, education and gender. *Archives of General Psychiatry, 38,* 919–923.

Goldfried, M. R., & Davison, G. C. (1976). *Clinical behavior therapy.* New York: Holt, Rinehart and Winston.

Heiman, J. R., & LoPiccolo, J. (1983). Clinical outcome of sex therapy: Effects of daily vs. weekly treatment. *Archives of General Psychiatry, 40,* 443–449.

Heiman, J., LoPiccolo, L., & LoPiccolo, J. (1976). *Becoming orgasmic: A sexual growth program for women.* Englewood Cliffs, NJ: Prentice-Hall.

Hogan, D. R. (1978). The effectiveness of sex therapy: A review of the literature. In J. LoPiccolo & L. LoPiccolo (Eds.), *Handbook of sex therapy.* New York: Plenum Press.

Hoon, E. F., Hoon, P. W., & Wincze, J. (1976). The SAI: An inventory for the measurement of female sexual arousal. *Archives of Sexual Behavior, 5,* 208–215.

Kaplan, H. (1974). *The new sex therapy.* New York: Brunner/Mazel.

Kaplan, H. S. (1979). *Disorders of sexual desire.* New York: Brunner/Mazel.

Kaplan, H. S., & Kohl, K. (1972). Adverse reactions to rapid treatment of sexual problems. *Psychosomatics, 13,* 3–5.

Kaplan, H. S., Kohl, R. N., Pomeroy, W. B., Offit, A. K., & Hogan, B. (1974). Group treatment of premature ejaculation. *Archives of Sexual Behavior, 3,* 443–452.

Kegel, A. W. (1952). Sexual functions of the pubococcygeal muscle. *Western Journal of Obstetrics and Gynecology, 60,* 521.

Kinsey, A. C., Pomeroy, W. B., & Martin, C. E. (1952). *Sexual behavior in the human male.* Philadelphia: W. B. Saunders.

Kinsey, A. C., Pomeroy, W. B., Martin, C. W., & Gebhard, P. H. (1953). *Sexual behavior in the human female.* Philadelphia: W. B. Saunders.

Krone, R. J., Siroky, M. B., & Goldstein, I. (Eds.). (1983). *Male sexual dysfunction.* Boston: Little, Brown.

Laughren, J. P., & Kass, D. J. (1975). Desensitization of sexual dysfunction: The present status. In A. S. Gurman & D. G. Rice (Eds.), *Couples in conflict: New directions in marital therapy.* New York: Jason Aronson.

Lazarus, A. A. (1965). The treatment of a sexually inadequate man. In L. Ullman & L. Krasner (Eds.), *Case studies in behavior modification.* New York: Holt, Rinehart and Winston.

Lazarus, A. A. (1968). Behavior therapy in groups. In G. M. Gazda (Ed.), *Basic approaches to group psychotherapy and group counselling.* Springfield, IL: Charles C Thomas.

Lehrman, V. (1971). *Masters and Johnson explained.* Chicago: Playboy Press.

Lief, H. I. (1977). Inhibited sexual desire. *Medical aspects of human sexuality, 11*(7), 94–95.

Lobitz, W. C., & Lobitz, G. K. (1978). Clinical assessment in the treatment of sexual dysfunction. In J. LoPiccolo & L. LoPiccolo (Eds.), *Handbook of sex therapy.* New York: Plenum Press.

Lobitz, W. C., & LoPiccolo, J. (1972). New methods in the behavioral treatment of sexual dysfunction. *Journal of Behavior Therapy and Experimental Psychiatry, 3*(4), 265–271.

Lobitz, W. C., LoPiccolo, J., Lobitz, G., & Brockway, J. (1976). A closer look at "simplistic" behavior therapy for sexual dysfunction: Two case studies. In H. J. Eysenck (Ed.), *Case studies in behavior therapy.* London: Routledge and Kegan Paul.

LoPiccolo, J., & Friedman, J. M. (1985). *Sex therapy: An integrative model.* In S. J. Lynn & J. P. Gurshe (Eds.), *Contemporary psychotherapies: Models and methods.* Columbus, OH: Bell and Howell.

LoPiccolo, J., & Hogan, D. (1979). Multidimensional behavioral treatment of sexual dysfunction. In O. Pomerlieu & J. P. Brady (Eds.), *Behavioral medicine.* Baltimore, MD: Williams and Wilkins.

LoPiccolo, J., & Lobitz, W. C. (1973). Behavior therapy of sexual dysfunction. In L. A. Hamerlynck, L. C. Handy, & E. J. Mash (Eds.), *Behavior change: Methodology, concepts, and practice.* Champaign, IL: Research Press.

LoPiccolo, J., & Steger, J. C. (1974). The sexual interaction inventory: A new instrument for assessment of sexual dysfunction. *Archives of Sexual Behavior, 3,* 585–595.

Masters, W. H., & Johnson, V. E. (1966). *Human sexual response.* Boston: Little, Brown.

Masters, W. H., & Johnson, V. E. (1970). *Human sexual inadequacy.* Boston: Little, Brown.

Meichenbaum, D. (1985). Cognitive-behavior therapies. In S. J. Lynn & J. P. Garshe (Ed.), *Contemporary psychotherapies: Models and methods.* Columbus, OH: Charles E. Merrill.

Mosher, D. L. (1977). The gestalt awareness expression cycle as a model for sex therapy. *Journal of Sex and Marital Therapy, 3,* 229–242.

Mosher, D. (1979). The gestalt experiment in sex therapy. *Journal of Sex and Marital Therapy, 5*(2), 117–133.

Mikuals, W. C., & Lowe, J. C. (1974). *Self-control of premature ejaculation.* Paper presented at the Rocky Mountain Psychological Association, Denver.

Obler, M. (1973). Systematic desensitization in sexual disorders. *Journal of Behavior Therapy and Experimental Psychiatry, 4,* 93–101.

O'Connor, J. F., & Stern, L. (1972). Results of treatment in functional sexual disorders. *New York State Journal of Medicine, 72,* 15.

Rainwater, L. (1966). Some aspects of lower class sexual behavior. *Journal of Social Issues, 22*(2), 96–109.

Reynolds, B. S. (1977). Psychological treatment models and outcome results for erectile dysfunction: A critical review. *Psychological Bulletin, 84,* 1218–1238.

Scott, F. B., Bradley, W. E., & Timm, G. (1973). Management of erectile impotence. *Urology, 2,* 80–82.

Schover, L. R., & LoPiccolo, J. (1982). Treatment effectiveness for dysfunctions of sexual desire. *Journal of Sex and Marital Therapy, 8*(3), 179–197.

Semans, J. H. (1956). Premature ejaculation: A new approach. *Southern Medical Journal, 49,* 355–357.

Small, M. P., Carrion, H. M., & Gordon, J. A. (1975). Small–Carrion penile prosthesis. *Urology, 5,* 479–486.

Steiner, C. M. (1974). *Scripts people live.* New York: Grove Press.

Von Bertalanffy, L. (1968). *General systems theory: Foundations, developments, applications.* New York: Braziller.

Watzlawick, P., Beaven, J. H., & Jackson, D. D. (1967). *Pragmatics of human communications: A study of interactional patterns, pathologies, and paradoxes.* New York: Norton.

Wolpe, J. (1958). *Psychotherapy by reciprocal inhibition.* Stanford, CA: Stanford University Press.

Wolpe, J., & Lazarus, A. A. (1966). *Behavior therapy techinques.* New York: Pergamon Press.

Wright, S., Perrault, R., & Mathieu, M. (1977). Treatment of sexual dysfunction: A review. *Archives of General Psychiatry, 34,* 881–890.

Zeiss, A. M., Rosen, G. M., & Zeiss, R. A. (1977). Orgasm during intercourse: A treatment strategy for women. *Journal of Consulting and Clinical Psychology, 45*(5), 891–895.

Zilbergeld, B. (1978). *Male sexuality: A guide to sexual fulfillment.* Boston: Little, Brown.

Zilbergeld, B., & Evans, M. (1980 August). The inadequacy of Masters and Johnson. *Psychology Today,* pp. 28–43.

Zorgniotti, A. W., & Lefleur, R. S. (1985). Auto-injection of the corpus cavernosum with a vaso-active drug combination for vasculogenic impotence. *Journal of Urology, 133*(1), 39–41.

18

Migraine and Tension Headaches

MEREDITH STEELE McCARRAN AND FRANK ANDRASIK

Of all the bodily sources of chronic pain, headaches seem the most easily related to psychogenic causes. We speak anecdotally of "a pain in the neck" and "my aching head," and comment on what a "headache" certain difficult tasks must be. People use body language to express such psychological states as anxiety, stress, depression, and worry by holding or touching their heads. Despite the intuitively close association between psychological states and head pain, the cognitive-behavioral assessment and treatment of recurrent headache pain has perhaps only just reached its adolescence.

The first psychologically oriented headache treatment studies began to appear in the literature only some 15 years ago (e.g., Budzynski, Stoyva, & Adler, 1970; Sargent, Green, & Walters, 1972). The lateness of this date may seem surprising at first, given that the importance of psychological factors in headaches has been recognized at least since Wolff published his pioneering studies of headache in 1937. In fact, medical researchers had been actively engaged in addressing the problems of headache classification, etiology, and treatment for many years, particularly in the case of migraine.

Just as the search for physiological explanations for headache pain dominated the medical literature, it also permeated the awakening psychological literature in the form of biofeedback studies. The emergence of more psychological, or cognitive, explanations for headache etiology, maintenance, and treatment are younger still (Holroyd, Andrasik, & Westbrook, 1977), and at present coexist in an uneasy flux with the physiological explanations (Holroyd, et al., 1984). Stimulated both by the early successes of biofeedback treatment and by the failure to find consistent physiological correlates to those successes, the scope and the number of cognitive-behavioral studies of headache have increased dramatically. As with any adolescent, this area of research has shown growth from a period of scattered, global efforts to an increasing refinement of technique and clarification of issues both important and unimportant; there remains, however, much room for growth. This chapter will examine the psychological assessment and treatment of headache, the emerging role of cognitive factors as necessary and possibly vital components of headache treatment success, and the aspects of cognitive-behavioral approaches to headache that require further research and clarification.

Meredith Steele McCarran. Department of Psychology, State University of New York at Albany, Albany, New York.

Frank Andrasik. Pain Therapy Centers, Greenville General Hospital, Greenville, South Carolina.

Variations of Headache Activity

Fifteen separate types of headache have been identified by the Ad Hoc Committee on the Classification of Headache, a panel of distinguished medical experts gathered in 1962. Of these 15 types, the first 3—migraine, muscle-contraction, and combined headaches—represent by far the most prevalent complaints. For example, 94% of the patients seeking treatment at a headache clinic received the diagnosis of tension and/or migraine headache (Lance, Curran, & Anthony, 1965). In the general population, survey data indicated that 50–70% of all people experience headache at some time (Andrasik, Holroyd, & Abel, 1979; Kashiwagi, McClure, & Wetzel, 1972), and that 40% of these headaches are muscle contraction or tension headaches. Estimates of prevalence for migraineurs have ranged from 2.7% to 18.8% of the population (Leviton, 1978).

Recurrent headache, usually thought to be a problem of adulthood, also occurs in childhood, before the age of 5 in perhaps as many as 25% of headache sufferers (Selby & Lance, 1960). A gradual increase in headache incidence is found as children get older, and the evidence indicates that youthful sufferers do not "grow out of it." For example, Bille (1981) reported a 23-year follow-up of individuals who suffered from migraine headaches as children; the majority (60%) continued to experience headaches in adulthood. Interestingly, although slightly more than half the headache sufferers under the age of 10 are male (Prensky, 1976; Silanpaa, 1983), by adulthood, approximately 76% of tension and migraine sufferers are female (Bille, 1962).

Muscle contraction or tension headaches are characterized by pain and stiffness in the neck area, as well as a bandlike pain or ache bilaterally or around the head. Onset is typically insidious, and resolution is usually slow, but the peak pain levels reportedly are rarely sharp or intense; rather, the pain remains steady and dull. Many individuals experience tension headache symptoms on a daily or near-daily basis. The pain is attributed to sustained muscle contractions and the resultant stimulation of pain receptors in the contracted muscles and in compressed intramuscular arterioles (Haynes, 1980). The Ad Hoc Committee (1962, p. 162) clearly states that this sustained muscular contraction results "as part of the individual's reaction to life stresses."

Migraine headaches, though typically less frequent than tension headaches, characteristically provide the sufferer with an intense, throbbing, painful experience. Frequently only one side of the head is involved, and pain is often located behind the eye or in the region of the temple. Onset is sudden, and typical duration varies from an hour to several days. Accompanying symptoms include anorexia, pallor, and fatigue, and, less often, nausea, vomiting, dizziness, sensitivity to light or sound, and paresthesias. "Classic" migraine occurs in approximately 10% of cases; these people experience neurological prodromes such as visual lines, spots, or stars, or ringing in the ears, prior to the onset of the headache. People who experience "common" migraines lack the prodromes but otherwise exhibit headache symptoms similar to those of classic migraine. The presence or absence of prodromes has not been found to be a factor influencing success is psychological treatment.

A two-stage vascular process hypothetically underlies migraine headache. Initially, presumably as a reaction to stress, cranial vasoconstriction occurs, both internally and externally. An overreactive vasodilation follows, and, as the cranial vessels overexpand

and fill with blood, the migraineur experiences a pounding or throbbing pain. A number of biochemical events coincide with the vascular reactivity, probably contributing to both the physiological changes and the subjective experience of pain (Kudrow, 1982).

Persons suffering from combined headache exhibit significant symptoms of both tension and migraine types, usually coexisting in each attack. As many as one third of all headache sufferers experience combined headache, which has led to the proposal that discrete headache variants may be an artifact. Bakal (1982) and Raskin and Appenzeller (1980), noting that no definitive laboratory tests exist that distinguish headache types, and that persons with headaches frequently report varying levels of severity and location of pain, propose a "severity model" for conceptualizing headache. In this model, a continuum of vascular involvement accounts for the differences in symptom presentation; tension headache is simply a less severe form of headache than is migraine. Though appealing for its parsimony, the severity model of conceptualizing headaches has yet to be supported in controlled research. Further, factor analytic studies of adult headache symptoms have resulted in two stable syndromes that tend to support the separate migraine and tension headache categories (Arena, Blanchard, Andrasik, & Dudek, 1982; Kroner, 1983).

An important dimension included in the severity model, however, is the proposed role of cognitive and affective events in the etiology and maintenance of headache. The phenomenon of pain, in general, is a complex sensory experience, entailing considerably more than simple physiological changes. Studies by Melzack (1973) and by Rachman and Philips (1975) demonstrate that sensory intensity, affectivity, and evaluative components contribute interactively to the overall pain experience. Social learning influences the subjective experience of pain, contributing to the frequently noted phenomenon of highly individualized responses to reportedly similar levels of pain.

A Cognitive-Behavioral Model of Headache

There is almost universal agreement among headache investigators that psychological factors play an instrumental role in the pathogenesis and amelioration of headache. In 1948, Wolff (1948, p. 431) stated that appropriate treatment for headache must "help the individual understand the basis of his tension, the factors in his life that aggravate it, and to aid him in resolving his conflicts." Dalessio (1972, p. 414) supported that position in a primarily medical review of the disorder, stating the need for "procedures that relieve anxiety and induce relaxation by improving the attitudes, habits, and life situation of the patient." The interplay of somatic and psychological factors quickly becomes evident as the practitioner interviews the typical headache patient, for the most commonly reported antecedent of headache is stress. For example, Leviton, Slack, Masek, Bana, and Graham (1984) found that "an especially hard day," "worrying a lot," and "unexpected excitement or pressure" were the most commonly acknowledged contributors of headache. The psychological status of the individual clearly plays a role in the precipitation of headache.

Cognitive approaches to headache pain acknowledge the role of psychological factors as integral, not peripheral, to reports of head pain. In a cognitive-behavioral model of headache, the headache-prone individual responds to environmental stressors with negative cognitions, which in turn increase the perceived threat. As the body responds to the perceived threat, physiological changes occur in the muscular, vascular, and neurochemical systems. The resultant pain may also be responded to with feelings of helplessness and with negative cognitions, which in turn exacerbate the pain experience.

The key difference between the cognitive-behavioral model and the traditional model for headaches is that in the former, physiological arousal per se is not the problem but, rather, how the individual maladaptively construes events and his or her own stress reactions (Meichenbaum, 1975). Thus "challenging but controllable tasks are likely to induce effort without distress," as Frankenhaeuser (1980, p. 207) observed in studies of individual biochemical responsiveness to stressful tasks, whereas appraisal of tasks as uncontrollable and aversive induces heightened physiological arousal. Lazarus (1984) and Beck (1976) also argue that preexisting faulty cognitive sets may predispose persons to respond to stressors maladaptively, thereby more frequently and effectively locking them in to the stress–negative appraisal–pain cycle. In the cognitive-behavioral conceptualization of headache, therapeutic interventions that address the psychological correlates and antecedents of headache provide the most effective prevention of and amelioration of headache.

Traditionally, anxiety and stress have been the psychological co-factors presumed to contribute most predominantly to both tension and migraine headaches (Friedman, Von Storch, & Merritt, 1954). For example, Henryk-Gutt and Rees (1973) found that 54% of migraine attacks recorded over a 2-month period by 50 classical migraineurs coincided with reports of anxiety, overwork, anger, resentment, emotional strain, or relief from strain. Data from a group of headache sufferers and their controls, however, found no differences in the level of recently experienced life stresses (Andrasik, Blanchard, Arena, Teders, Teevan, & Rodichok, 1982).

Preliminary data on childhood headache sufferers, in whom excessive life stresses might be hypothesized to be precursors to the headache experience, also found equivalent levels of life stresses to the control children. Thus, although headache patients and non–headache sufferers retrospectively report the same level of stress, the headache patients find that their stress seems to lead to subsequent head pain. The headache sufferers' cognitive reaction to stress may prove to be a source of the differing physiological reaction; research needs to be done to address this question. As will be seen, training in coping with cognitive stress certainly reduces reported headache symptoms.

Anxiety as a source of recurrent headache pain also has proved to be a consistently identified psychological mediator of the pain experience (Barber, 1959; Bihldorff, King, & Parnes, 1971; Ziegler, Rhodes, & Hassanein, 1978); yet its specific role in headache has proved problematic to determine. Migraineurs and tension headache sufferers often report themselves to be anxious, but results of the few controlled studies conducted have been equivocal. Price and Blackwell (1980) found that female migraineurs scored significantly higher than controls on the Taylor Manifest Anxiety Scale and the Spielberger Trait Anxiety Inventory, scored higher on the Lie Scale of the Eysenck Personality Inventory, but rated a highly stressful film as significantly less unpleasant than did the controls. The authors speculate that migraineurs, though able to recognize and report feelings of anxiety in themselves, tend to minimize negative aspects of external stimuli.

Another controlled effort to determine an anxiety–headache linkage was that recently conducted by Garvey (1985). He compared the headache activity of 20 patients with diagnosable anxiety disorders to that of 49 controls who worked in various capacities at a medical center. There was no significant difference in headache rate between the groups, although those anxiety-disordered patients who experienced headaches tended to have them more frequently. The studies of both stress and anxiety in the etiology of headache suffer from being retrospective, and from the impossibility of determining whether the headaches precede or result from the reported anxiety or stress. A person suffering the debilitating effects of a headache, in search of a cause for such pain, may easily conclude that "I must have had a hard day" or "I must be worried." Such ex post facto reasoning could lead to the conclusion that anxiety or stress produces headache symptoms. Longitudinal studies examining anxiety, stress, and head pain, and their concordance in time, might resolve this issue.

A psychological variable that also may interact with headache is depression. The most common somatic complaint of patients presenting for depression is headache (Diamond, 1983), and chronic headache sufferers frequently present with depressive symptoms as well. Again, the problem of determining primacy occurs; an assessment task for the practitioner is to determine whether the patient is depressed from living with recurrent pain, or whether depressive symptomatology led to vulnerability for headache. Preliminary evidence suggests that elevated scores on measures of depression are prognostic of poor response to behavioral treatment of headache (Banchard, Andrasik, Neff, Jurish, & O'Keefe, 1981). On the other hand, Cox and Thomas (1981) and Gerber, Miltner, Birbaumer, and Lutzenberger (1983) have found that with successful reduction in head pain, depressive symptomatology also decreases. This adds evidence to the argument that at least some recurrent headache sufferers evince depressive symptoms secondary to their recurrent pain.

Assessment Issues

The multidimensional nature of headache pain becomes especially salient in the area of assessment, both of headache pain and of the headache sufferer. From a cognitive-behavioral perspective, experiential, psychological, environmental, and physiological elements make up the important components of the headache complaint. The diagnosis of headache type, though useful in treatment planning, provides a necessary but only preliminary step in headache assessment. It should be remembered that the Ad Hoc Committee on the Classification of Headaches listed 15 types of headache. Although the great majority of headache patients present with migraine, muscle tension headache, or a combination of the two, those few exceptions may have headaches of organic etiology such as brain tumor or seizure disorder. In addition, uncontrolled use of analgesics (Kudrow, 1982) or ergotomines (Ala-Hurula, Myllyla, & Hokkanen, 1982) by the headache sufferer may lead to incidents of "rebound headache," which can compromise treatment outcome.

Age of onset and number of years of headache problems can be variables reciprocally influencing treatment, possibly due to concomitant factors associated with recurrent pain, such as depression and negative expectational set. As noted earlier, depression in the patient may hinder responsiveness to behavioral treatments (Blanchard et al., 1981). Bakal and Kaganov (1979) argue that one consequence of recurrent headache pain is that the physiological processes involved become increasingly independent of the original precipitants, until the former become autonomous and serve to maintain headache symptoms independent of environmental influences.

Because a cognitive-behavioral model of headache emphasizes the role of the psychological antecedents and consequences, as well as the frequency, duration, and intensity of the headache, post hoc reporting of headache activity has been found to be inadequate for research purposes. Following initial assessment of headache type and psychological variables, most researchers have used some written record of current headache activity, such as the headache diary (Budzynski, Stoyva, Adler, & Mullaney, 1973). The headache diary provides quantifiable information useful in planning and, if necessary, tailoring treatment for the individual. A typical diary procedure involves requesting the patient to self-monitor and record frequency of headache, duration of the headache, intensity of pain along a predetermined scale, and amount and type of medication taken. From a cognitive-behavioral standpoint, more detailed methods of diary recording are necessary to include the dimensions of affectivity and cognition about pain. Items contained in the McGill Pain Questionnaire (Melzack, 1975) and in the visual analogue procedure of Price, McGrath, Rafii, and Buckingham (1983) address these aspects of pain and could be adapted to headache recordings. A scoring procedure that takes into account the cognitive and affective components of pain as well as the sensory components may help to resolve the frequently discrepant reactions of different patients to similar levels of sensory pain.

Cognitive-Behavioral Interventions for Headache

Biofeedback, the treatment that precipitated psychologists' interest in headache prophylaxis, still predominates in the literature for both tension and migraine headaches. Following closely in both time of appearance and subsequent popularity was relaxation training. Both treatments will be briefly reviewed here because of their current popularity and because aspects of them are incorporated in most cognitive-behavioral treatments. Biofeedback is superficially appealing for its apparently parsimonious mechanism of action: target a headache-related physiological mechanism for change, and the headache itself will change. For tension headache, psychologists have concentrated on feedback for electromyographic (EMG) changes in the muscles of the forehead and neck. Two separate physiological mechanisms have been targeted for extensive study in biofeedback treatment for migraine headache, peripheral hand temperature via thermal biofeedback, and cephalic blood flow via temporal vasoconstriction biofeedback.

Clinical Interventions for Migraine Headache

Thermal biofeedback, the most commonly reported nonpharmacological treatment for migraine headache, arose from a fortuitous laboratory discovery that a migraineur's hands showed a consistent slight drop in temperature when she experienced headaches.

The developers of the procedure, Sargent, Green, and Walters (1972), trained migraineurs to raise their hand temperature through biofeedback and reported a significant drop in headache activity. The mechanism of action presumably involved shunting of bloodflow from the cranium to the hands, thereby counteracting the cephalic vasodilation phase of the migraine. To facilitate the warming of patients' hands, Sargent, Green and Walters (1972, 1973) recommended combining thermal biofeedback with the aspects of autogenic training involving self-instruction of feelings of warmth and heaviness to promote relaxation (Schultz & Luthe, 1969). Thus cognitive and relaxation mediators were incorporated early into this presumably physiological procedure in order to enhance treatment outcome; the resultant methodology did not permit evaluation of the separate contributions of each component.

Although the effectiveness of thermal biofeedback as a treatment for migraine headache and its superiority to placebos have been well documented, the effectiveness of separate process mechanisms underlying the treatment's success remains undetermined. Unfortunately, studies comparing hand warming to hand cooling have resulted in similar positive treatment outcomes (Kewman & Roberts, 1980; Largen, Matthew, Dobbins, & Claghorn, 1981). Another study found that self-hypnosis, thermal biofeedback, or a plausible placebo (alpha wave feedback) provided equally effective headache relief (Andreychuk & Skriver, 1975). The vascular explanation for the effectiveness of biofeedback in the treatment of migraine headache appears less demonstrable when such varied, and indeed opposing, physiological processes produce similar improvements in migraineurs.

Cognitive approaches to headache pain have emphasized preventive measures rather than palliative functions. General theories of adaptive coping (Bandura, 1977; Lazarus, 1966) note that cognitive factors contribute to the appraisal of threat; Beck and Emery (1985) posit that cognitive misinterpretations in anxious individuals of benign physical symptoms lead to catastrophizing and debilitating exacerbations of these symptoms. One's cognitive approach to and interpretation of life events and physical symptoms mediate a subsequent pain experience; hence, if the cognitive pattern of responses can be changed, the ensuing pain experience may be altered or eliminated. Turk and Genest (1979) suggest that "anything that comes from a machine will produce transient effects unless we also address treatment to life situations and to psychological variables" (p. 301). The implications of these cognitive approaches are that cognitive-behavioral components are of primary importance in the generation of the pain experience, and should prove to be of primary importance in the long-term amelioration of that pain.

One of the first studies to examine the role of cognitive-behavioral variables in a migraine population (Mitchell & White, 1977) employed a sequential dismantling strategy. Attempting to identify the reactive components of a complete behavioral package for migraine headaches, the researchers had all 12 subjects first self-record all migraine headache activity, then taught 9 of these subsequently to monitor stressful events. Still later, 6 of the subjects were taught self-controlled relaxation skills; finally, 3 of these latter subjects were taught cognitive coping skills. All subjects received treatment for the same length of time by the same therapists; only the number of components presented differed. Mitchell and White found that self-recording of headaches and self-monitoring of stressful events provided no substantial reduction in headache activity, but that significant reductions occurred as specific control skills and coping techniques were acquired. Those subjects who had received all four components of treatment—hence the largest range of coping skills—improved the most (mean headache reduction of 83% versus 55%, 4%, respectively) and maintained these improvements at the 3-month follow-up.

One of the advantages of the Mitchell and White study was its coeffectiveness. Treatment was conducted in groups, and the majority of training in procedures was placed on tapes for home use. Compare this expensive equipment, specialized training for the therapist, and individualized approach typical of biofeedback treatment for migraine headache. A separate attempt to examine the effectiveness of self-directed treatment, conducted by Kohlenberg and Cahn (1981), minimized therapist contact even further by restricting contacts to the telephone or to mail. Fifty-one migraineurs were matched for headache frequency and then randomly assigned to receive either a Control book, containing information about headaches, the Treatment book, which explained the physiological and emotional migraine, relaxation procedures, and specific cognitive coping techniques be used on a day-to-day basis. In addition, a liquid crystal finger temperature band and an explanation of the relationship of changing hand temperature to headache activity was included. Both books produced equally favorable confidence ratings by their users, but the group receiving the Treatment book showed a statistically greater reduction in migraine frequency, intensity, and duration—a difference that had increased by 3-month follow-up. The inclusion of biofeedback and relaxation procedures with the cognitive procedures, however, limits the conclusions that can be drawn about the relative effectiveness of the cognitive components in this study.

Separating cognitive components from existing multicomponent treatment packages has not proved easy for investigators of migraine treatment. Lake, Rainey, and Papsdorf (1979), for example, assigned 24 patients to one of four conditions: (1) self-monitoring control, (2) frontalis EMG biofeedback, (3) hand temperature feedback, or (4) temperature feedback plus rational-emotive therapy (RET) (Ellis, 1962). All biofeedback procedures included the use of relaxation exercises and autogenic thoughts; the RET component was appended to three of the biofeedback sessions as a 40-minute extension for those subjects in the thermal biofeedback plus RET group.

At the end of treatment all four groups had slightly reduced headache activity, but there were no significant differences between the groups. It should be noted, however, that all the treatments were presented in very attenuated form; biofeedback occurred in eight sessions over 4 weeks, and RET, as mentioned, was presented in a total of 2 hours over three sessions at the end of biofeedback. The authors note that two subjects had even that amount of RET training curtailed because of "pressures of time." In addition, Lake et al. presented a unique form of bidirectional training for both thermal and EMG biofeedback, instead of unidirectional hand warming or muscle relaxation, and made no mention of presenting any rationale for their procedures to the subjects. One should not find it surprising, then, that migraineurs with a mean headache history of 13.8 years made only slight progress in changing either physiological or psychological responses in such a brief treatment time with little or no rationale for the treatment techniques provided.

Huber and Huber (1979) also looked at the contribution of RET training by combining it with autogenic training for 6 long-term migraine patients. Although the cognitive components of this treatment again were not examined separately, the study is unique in its exclusive use of patients who had been unsuccessfully treated pharmacologically as well as by relaxation biofeedback prior to entering the study. The combination of autogenic and RET training conducted over 12 weeks reduced headache duration by 60% from baseline levels, and continued to have significant lasting effects 13 months posttreatment. Here, although the effects of RET cannot be individually analyzed, enough time has been allotted for the subjects to incorporate and rehearse the psychological treatments, resulting in marked treatment success.

Other investigators have concentrated on comparing cognitive stress coping techniques with vasoconstriction biofeedback (Friar & Beatty, 1976). The latter treatment was developed as a more direct method of controlling the excessive dilation of the temporal artery presumed to be integral to the migraine experience. Knapp and Florin (1981) tested the relative effectiveness of vasoconstriction biofeedback training, cognitive stress coping training, and two serially varied combinations of these treatment modalities. Because the authors also wished to clarify psychological variables involved in headache maintenance and improvement, they repeatedly probed with mood indicators, psychosomatic symptom inventories, and evaluations of stressful situations. Treatment for the 20 migraineurs consisted of ten 60-minute sessions of biofeedback, cognitive stress coping training, or a combination of five sessions of each. All groups showed significant reductions in headache activity at the end of treatment, with no significant differences between groups in either headache activity or vasoconstriction ability. Because each group consisted of an n of 4, power to detect differences would be quite low; yet only the cognitively trained groups demonstrated significantly less depression, less irritability, and more positive self-evaluation at posttest.

At a 1-year follow-up of these subjects (Knapp, 1982), improvements in voluntary control of vasoconstriction had disappeared, but improvements in headache activity were maintained for all treatment groups. Differences in the psychological variables of depression, irritability, and positive self-evaluation had also disappeared at follow-up, as the biofeedback group had made gains over that period of time to match the levels previously attained by the cognitive training groups. Because of the disappearance of factors originally presumed to be active in causing improvements in headache activity, and since all treatments had proved equivalent at producing and maintaining these improvements, Knapp speculated, on the basis of the verbal reports of his subjects, that increases in perceived self-efficacy in managing migraine and its triggering factors might underlie the results.

In a very similarly constructed study using 25 migraineurs, Gerhards, Rojahn, Boxan, Gnade, Petrik, and Florin (1983) compared cognitive stress coping therapy ($n = 13$) to vasoconstriction biofeedback ($n = 12$) and again found equivalent headache improvement for both techniques at the end of 10 sessions of training. In this study, the effects on the psychological variables were not more pronounced in the cognitive therapy group than in the biofeedback group. Again, cognitive variables effectively mediated migraine attacks, as efficiently as did biofeedback.

In summary of the studies examining cognitive-behavioral treatment of migraine headache, we have found that this approach to treatment provides headache relief equivalent to that of both thermal and vasoconstriction biofeedback. Maintenance of improvements also appears to be excellent. In one study (Huber & Huber, 1979), cognitive approaches successfully ameliorated the headache pain of biofeedback failures. Since cognitive-behavioral techniques are more widely available, are less costly, require less specialized training for the therapist, and seem to provide lasting improvements in migraine headaches, one could argue that their initial equivalence of effects to biofeedback actually represents a strong argument in favor of cognitive approaches to migraine.

Clinical Interventions for Tension Headache

Biofeedback for tension headache sufferers has concentrated on the reduction of tension in the trapezius muscle of the neck and the frontalis muscle of the forehead. This approach stems from early findings that tension headache patients show twice the level of frontalis activity seen in control groups, and that these patients show increments in muscle tension during headache periods (Budzynski et al., 1973). EMG biofeedback from these muscle groups typically provides the patient with a variable tone or click, or readings from a meter, which provide constant feedback about the level of tension in that particular muscle group.

Although the research indicates that EMG biofeedback provides an average clinical improvement of 60% in tension headache sufferers (Blanchard, Andrasik, Ahles, Teders, & O'Keefe, 1980), the factors responsible for this improvement may not be the presumed physiological response changes. Process analyses have found treatment effectiveness to be independent of direction of change for the EMG levels (Andrasik & Holroyd, 1980; Holroyd & Penzien, 1983; Holroyd et al., 1984). Further, Budzynski et al.'s (1973) findings of increased frontalis EMG levels for tension headache patients have not been supported; in some cases tension headache sufferers have been shown to have normal or even below normal resting levels of frontalis muscle activity, and correlations between EMG levels and pain intensity during headache periods have been weak at best (Philips, 1978). In addition, the muscle tension levels of migraine patients often exceed those of tension patients (Andrasik, Blanchard, Arena, Saunders, & Barron, 1982).

Therefore, as mentioned earlier, although the control of physiological processes has not received support as the crucial factor in the efficacy of biofeedback or relaxation treatments for headache, nevertheless, these treatments have been shown to be effective in a significantly large portion of sufferers. At this date, physiological change mechanisms cannot be ruled out as a factor in the improvements found, but the lack of empirical support for them is noteworthy.

Just such criticisms have led other researchers (Bakal, 1982; Holroyd & Andrasik, 1982a; Turk, Meichenbaum, & Berman, 1979) to suggest that cognitive factors such as expectation, motivation, coping, and perceived success play a more than incidental role in the reduction of headache. An examination of the procedures used in both biofeedback and relaxation training reveals that, in all cases, cognitive components are integral to the treatment protocol. Patients do not simply get "hooked up" and told to change the respective physiological responses in the desired direction; instructions regarding specific methods of cognitively affecting bodily responses are carefully delineated. In recognition of the role this nonspecific factor may play in treatment success, cognitive stress coping has arisen as a third alternative psychological explanation and treatment for headache.

Two single-subject studies represent the first efforts by psychologists to examine the role of cognitive variables in determining and controlling the perception of tension headache pain (Mitchell & White, 1976; Reeves, 1976). Reeves obtained baseline recordings of headache activity and EMG levels in a young female referred for chronic tension headache. Three phases of treatment were then instituted: the first involved having the subject identify "headache situations"; the second taught the subject cognitive coping skills in a modified stress inoculation procedure (Meichenbaum, Turk, & Burstein, 1975); and the third phase involved EMG–biofeedback training. The subject showed a 33% reduction in headache activity once she had been instructed to alter her cognitive appraisal and negative self-statements in stressful situations. Interestingly, these reductions were not accompanied by decreases in frontalis EMG until after she had begun EMG biofeedback training, when both her headache frequency and her EMG readings showed reductions. A 6-month follow-up showed maintenance of gains with no symptom substitutions.

Mitchell and White (1976) obtained similar results with a single chronic tension headache sufferer, but without including EMG biofeedback at all. Following a 6-week baseline period, the subject was trained to identify antecedent stressful situations and to practice relaxation responses, followed by training in self-change procedures including thought stopping, projected rehearsal, and covert and overt assertion training. By the end of 14 weeks of training, the subject's headache activity had reduced to zero, a level that maintained at both the 3- and 6-month follow-ups.

The first group design to compare the effectiveness of cognitive procedures for tension headache with EMG–biofeedback procedures was conducted by Holroyd, Andrasik, and Westbrook (1977). Chronic tension headache sufferers were assigned to a cognitive stress coping group, an EMG–biofeedback group, or a waiting list control group. Following eight biweekly individual sessions of training, the cognitive stress coping group showed a marked reduction in headache activity, whereas the EMG–biofeedback group showed considerably more modest improvement. Examination of individual data revealed that whereas all of the cognitive stress coping group reported substantial decreases in headache activity posttreatment, responses in the EMG–biofeedback group reflected wide variability, with improvement ranging from 14% to 91%. Reductions in frontalis muscle tension were not found to be significantly related to headache improvement.

The Holroyd et al. study demonstrated not only that cognitive procedures induce improvements in headache complaints, but also that nonspecific variables may easily play a role in the reduction of headache activity. That some members of the EMG–biofeedback group showed substantial reductions in headache activity despite uncorrelated EMG levels reflects the influence of variables not controlled for in either the classic biofeedback studies or the preceding cognitive coping studies. A 2-year follow-up (Holroyd & Andrasik, 1982b) of these subjects revealed that the stress coping group reported continued use of the coping strategies they had been taught, and that they were still highly significantly improved. About one-half of the biofeedback group had maintained headache improvements, but the rest reported minimal or no improvement, and some had even sought further medical treatment. The long-term maintenance of treatment gains following cognitive stress coping training indicates that this procedure encompasses potent and lasting effects in the treatment of tension headache.

In an effort to elucidate some of the specific factors active in successful cognitive-behavioral treatment of tension headaches, Holroyd and Andrasik (1978) conducted a group design consisting of four groups of approximately 10 subjects each. One group was taught cognitive stress coping techniques similar to those used in the Holroyd et al. (1977) study; the second group received the same training with the addition of muscle relaxation training; the third group focused on headache discussion in a group format; and the fourth group consisted of a symptom-monitoring control. The discussion group provided a controlled, credible therapeutic environment without providing specific interventions for the members. Both cognitive treatment groups and the headache discussion group showed significant reductions in headache activity, while the symptom-monitoring group remained unchanged. Also, Holroyd and Andrasik again found that EMG levels remained unrelated to headache improvement.

Interviews conducted posttreatment in this study revealed that all of the cognitive self-control subjects used cognitive coping strategies learned in treatment, and that all but one of the headache discussion group members had devised their own coping techniques, which were often quite similar to those taught to the cognitive self-control groups. Significantly, the one individual from the headache discussion group who did not devise his own coping techniques showed only minimal improvement in headache activity. Holroyd and Andrasik speculated that although the different groups received different causal explanations for their symptoms, all groups were taught that mastery of symptoms was possible. Again, it should be noted that sensitization to precipitating stressors for tension headache, though probably necessary for symptom improvement, is not sufficient to cause such improvement; the active element in the preceding studies appears to lie in the acquisition and use of active coping strategies (Meichenbaum, 1975).

Further support for the specificity of action of active coping strategies in the treatment of tension headaches was garnered in the group treatment study of Figueroa (1982). Comparing cognitive stress coping training to traditional psychotherapy and self-monitoring, Figueroa divided 15 subjects into three groups, two of which received active group therapy for seven 90-minute sessions. The behavioral group received training in recognizing stressful situations, recognizing their own tension responses, and developing skills to deal more effectively with both of the former as well as to deal with pain. The psychotherapy group discussed headaches and possible underlying conflicts that individuals were experiencing, whereas the self-monitoring group simply completed their headache diaries and mailed these to the clinic weekly. Only the behavioral group showed significant decreases in frequency of headache, severity of headache, amount of medication taken, and disability of pain; no significant changes over time occurred for those in either the psychotherapy group or the self-monitoring group.

Bakal, Demjen, and Kaganov (1981) also reported substantial support for a treatment based approximately on Meichenbaum's cognitive theory of self-control in a group of 45 headache patients. Mean headache duration and intensity both decreased by approximately 50% posttreatment, and had reduced slightly further at a 6-month follow-up of 20 subjects. The data from this study are difficult to interpret, however, as the authors used a group of subjects diagnosed as suffering from muscle contraction, migraine, or combined muscle contraction–migraine headaches. Although Bakal, Demjen, and Kaganov report that differences in response to treatment did not reach statistical significance among the groups, this does not tell us anything about clinical differences in responsiveness. They did note that persons with continuous or near-continuous headache pain (more typically associated with muscle contraction headaches) failed to experience relief from the cognitive treatment.

Steger and Harper (1980) pursued a slightly different approach to tension headaches by comparing EMG biofeedback treatment incorporating cognitive-behavioral components to general relaxation practice. Steger and Harper sought to determine whether the most cost-effective procedure of home-based relaxation training alone could suffice as treatment for tension headaches. Twenty adult tension headache sufferers were divided into 2 groups. The first received EMG biofeedback training, which incorporated individualized specific cognitive stress coping techniques; the second received prerecorded cassette tapes of relaxation exercises, which they were instructed to use twice a day at home. Although only the relaxation group demonstrated significant reductions in frontalis EMG levels posttreatment, only the biofeedback group demonstrated improvement in headache intensity and frequency. The authors speculated that the focus on specific stress coping techniques formed the active component of successful treatment in this study. The results of the study, however, were confounded by differences in therapist contact and in individualization of treatment, precluding strong conclusions.

Using a within-subjects design, Anderson, Lawrence, and Olson (1981) sought to compare the efficacy of relaxation training to cognitive stress coping training, and each individual component to a combined form of treatment. Each of 14 college student tension headache sufferers, following a baseline recording phase, received three sessions of either coping or relaxation training, followed by both treatments combined, or they received six sessions of either coping, relaxation, or coping plus relaxation. The study is remarkable for the success achieved; all subjects showed zero levels of headache activity posttreatment, and no significant differences were noted between coping and relaxation training. A slight additive effect for the combined procedures accrued. One potential explanation for the lack of difference between the cognitive coping and the relaxation procedures lies in the fact that the experimenters specifically taught the relaxation subjects to use autogenic phrases when experiencing incipient headache activity; in short, they encouraged a cognitive coping response.

A third study comparing the effects of cognitive coping training to relaxation procedures eliminated the autogenic phrases and instead employed EMG feedback-assisted relaxation (Kremsdorf, Kochanowicz, & Costell, 1981). In two single-subject experiments, they varied the order of presentation of cognitive skills training, EMG biofeedback, and a combination of the two. Although EMG biofeedback influenced frontalis muscle activity, cognitive coping appeared primarily responsible for the therapeutic gains. Improvement in headache activity did not begin until cognitive training was begun; the addition of biofeedback training did not seem to have an additive effect, but instead allowed improvements to be maintained. The authors note, however, that biofeedback should not be discarded as a technique but, rather, should be used as an adjunct to cognitive strategies, since the technology gives easily interpreted "hard" measures of success to the headache sufferer.

Finally, arguing that tension headache consists of both psychological and physiological components, and therefore should respond best to a treatment that addressed both components, Bell, Abramowitz, Folkins, Spensley, and Hutchinson (1983) reported on a comparison of biofeedback, brief eclectic psychotherapy, and a combination of the two in the treatment of 31 tension headache sufferers. The 12-session EMG–biofeedback procedure they used clearly contained strong elements of cognitive stress-coping training as well as relaxation training. The psychotherapy condition consisted of six 1-hour sessions focused generally on identifying dynamic issues such as unmet dependency needs, hostile impulses, and tendencies toward somatization and denial, and briefly on identifying stressors and developing coping strategies.

The authors found that all three groups had improved on measures of headache activity, with the biofeedback-only group showing the best results, and that the two groups incorporating biofeedback training showed greater gains in reducing psychological disturbance than did the group receiving psychotherapy alone. Bell et al. attributed these results to "the powerful placebo effects of biofeedback" and argued that the psychotherapy had been conducted over far too brief a time to be maximally effective. They conceded that the similarity of results for the three groups may have depended on factors common to all three, which were the elements of cognitive coping training.

Glimpses of Specific Cognitive Processes

How to separate out the effective elements of cognitive coping from the effective elements of EMG biofeedback? A well-controlled and comprehensive examination of specific and nonspecific effects of EMG–biofeedback on tension headache was that conducted by Andrasik and Holroyd (1980). Thirty-nine tension headache sufferers received one of four treatments: (1) EMG feedback for decreases in frontalis muscle tension; (2) false EMG feedback indicating muscle tension reduction, when in fact it remained the same; (3) false EMG feedback indicating muscle tension reduction, when in fact it increased; and (4) a headache-monitoring control. Therapist contact, home practice, and treatment credibility were all equalized. The results proved most interesting; regardless of whether the subjects learned to increase, decrease, or maintain their frontalis EMG levels, subjects in the three active treatments showed large-scale reductions in headache activity, and these improvements were maintained at a 6-week follow-up. Andrasik and Holroyd conclude that "it may be less crucial that headache sufferers learn to directly modify EMG activity than it is that they learn to monitor the insidious onset of headache symptoms and engage in some sort of coping response" (p. 584).

A 3-year follow-up of 72% of the subjects in the foregoing experiment (Andrasik & Holroyd, 1983) found that all biofeedback subjects retained high levels of headache improvement, and that no differences existed among the three biofeedback groups. Whether or not the subjects had been trained to lower, raise, or maintain frontalis EMG levels remained unrelated to long-term maintenance, whereas the headache-monitoring control group demonstrated slight increases in headache activity from baseline over the 3-year follow-up period.

The most careful examination to date of the change mechanisms underlying improvements in tension headache was a recent study by Holroyd, Penzien, Hursey, Tobin, Rogers, Holm, Marcille, Hall, and Chila (1984). Forty-three tension headache sufferers received EMG–biofeedback and were informed that the display reflected decreasing EMG levels. In fact, however, the display for half the subjects reflected EMG increases, which were displayed as decreases. Within these two groups, subjects were informed that the visual displays of their performance reflected above-average success (high-success group) or below-average success (moderate-success group). Subjects in the high-success groups, whether increasing or decreasing their EMG levels, rated themselves as more successful at learning biofeedback skills and showed substantially more improvement in headache activity than did subjects in the moderate-success groups. Actual changes in EMG activity were uncorrelated with outcome. Holroyd et al. argue convincingly that cognitive changes mediated by performance accomplishments form the active component of headache modulation. The authors posit that high-success subjects are induced to view their headaches as having an internal locus of control, and that they themselves can be self-efficacious in influencing their headaches; tests for self-efficacy and locus of control administered to the subjects supported these conclusions.

Taken as a whole, the studies of cognitive-behavioral approaches to tension headache indicate that the results have been equivalent to or better than improvements achieved through EMG–biofeedback. The consistent lack of correlation in the relationship of EMG levels to headache improvements provides convincing evidence against the hypothesis underlying EMG biofeedback treatment for tension headache. The successes originally ascribed to that approach now seem possibly to be due to the cognitive changes induced by specific stress coping techniques or by the performance successes experienced in the biofeedback situation. Nevertheless, several questions remain about what constitute the active elements of the cognitive-based treatments.

Summary and Conclusions

The cognitive-behavioral approaches described by the several researchers here derived from such varied sources as Ellis, Meichenbaum, Beck, and Lazarus. No one approach appeared markedly more potent than the others. Factors in common to all the cognitive-behavioral treatments for tension headaches were:

1. The subjects learn to identify and monitor sources of stress and anxiety.
2. The subjects learn to identify the role their thoughts play in their reactions to stressors.
3. The subjects learn specific coping strategies.

Many of the researchers used stress-monitoring alone as a treatment condition and found it to be ineffectual in changing headache activity. On the other hand, the role of learning specific stress coping strategies appeared central to success in several studies (Holroyd & Andrasik, 1978; Kremsdorf et al., 1981; Figueroa, 1982).

The positive results achieved by members of discussion-only groups, however, as in Holroyd and Andrasik (1978), or by eclectic psychotherapy groups, as in Bell et al. (1983), provide contradictory evidence to the need for stress coping training. In each of these cases, the subjects received no specific suggestions for alterations in cognitions or behaviors; yet the subjects improved comparably to those who had received such suggestions. Interestingly, these subjects reported using stress coping techniques of their own devising, which points to the possibility that nonspecific effects from exposure to a group of people experiencing similar stressful bodily reactions may prove to be therapeutically adequate.

Given the effectiveness of cognitive-behavioral approaches to headache treatment, research is needed to clarify which components represent the necessary and sufficient elements of success. The three-stage model elucidated here readily lends itself to experimental analysis. Dismantling strategies in group designs and single-subject research may help reveal whether, for example, specific stress coping strategies should be included in treatments for headache, or whether subjects need only to be directed toward developing self-generated coping strategies. Individual differences may play a key role in this and other aspects of successful treatment approaches. For example, many of the treatment successes in biofeedback and in nondirective approaches, on interview, reported developing their own idiosyncratic coping mechanisms as a result of exposure to explanations of the antecedents of headache.

Better, more comprehensive assessment procedures are necessary for better determination of cognitive patterns in headache-prone individuals. Fitting the intervention to the subject may promote still higher rates of treatment success. Perhaps persons with high initial abilities to recognize stressors and their own cognitive reactions to them would prove to be good candidates for cognitive interventions, whereas persons with low recognition of cognitive mediation of their headaches would be good candidates for cognitive treatment coupled with biofeedback, wherein they receive frequent external, hard measures of progress. On the other hand, persons who become reliably tense prior to headache activity might benefit from the addition of relaxation exercises to their cognitive-behavioral training.

Progress in cognitive-behavioral interventions for headaches ultimately holds ramifications for the general public health. With the determination of key elements for treatment, and the honing of technique into an efficient package, home-based cassette programs and self-help manuals could inexpensively and rapidly relieve the public of a common, debilitating complaint. Teaching children the techniques of positive cognitive coping might not only prevent the later development of problem headaches, but also provide them with a useful skill for dealing with the vicissitudes of life.

Clearly, at this point it is fair to conclude that cognitive variables play a role in the mediation of both migraine and tension headaches. Furthermore, treatments based on cognitive-behavioral formulations provide stable, long-lasting improvements for headache sufferers, probably due to the emphasis on acquisition of a life skill rather than a specific technique. Given the mixed and often puzzlingly contradictory results of traditional physiological biofeedback treatments for headache, cognitive-behavioral interventions appear to offer a pragmatic and promising approach to the treatment of headache.

Acknowledgments

Preparation of this chapter was supported by Research Career Development Award 1 K01 NS00818 and Grant 1 R01 NS16891, both from the National Institute of Neurological Communicative Disorders and Stroke and awarded to Frank Andrasik.

References

Ad Hoc Committee on Classification of Headache. (1962). Classification of headache. *Journal of the American Medical Association, 179,* 717–718.

Ala-Hurula, V., Myllyla, V., & Hokkanen, E. (1982). Ergotomine abuse: Results of ergotomine discontinuation, with special reference to the plasma concentration. *Cephalalgia, 2,* 189–195.

Anderson, N. B., Lawrence, P. S., & Olson, T. W. (1981). Within-subject analysis of autogenic training and cognitive coping training in the treatment of tension headache pain. *Journal of Behavior Therapy and Experimental Psychiatry, 12,* 219–223.

Andrasik, F., Blanchard, E. B., Arena, J. G., Saunders, N. L., & Barron, K. D. (1982). Psychophysiology of recurrent headache: Methodological issues and new empirical findings. *Behavior Therapy, 13,* 407–429.

Andrasik, F., Blanchard, E. B., Arena, J. G., Teders, S. J., Teevan, R. C., & Rodichok, L. D. (1982). Psychological functioning in headache sufferers. *Psychosomatic Medicine, 44,* 171–182.

Andrasik, F., & Holroyd, K. A. (1980). A test of specific and nonspecific effects in the biofeedback treatment of tension headache. *Journal of Consulting and Clinical Psychology, 48,* 575–586.

Andrasik, F., & Holroyd, K. A. (1983). Specific and nonspecific effects in the biofeedback treatment of tension headache: 3-year follow-up. *Journal of Consulting and Clinical Psychology, 51,* 634–636.

Andrasik, F., Holroyd, K. A., & Abel, T. (1979). Prevalence of headache within a college student population: A preliminary analysis. *Headache, 19,* 384–387.

Andreychuk, T., & Skriver, C. (1975). Hypnosis and biofeedback in the treatment of migraine headache. *International Journal of Clinical and Experimental Hypnosis, 23,* 172–183.

Arena, J. G., Blanchard, E. B., Andrasik, F., & Dudek, B. (1982). The headache symptom questionnaire: Discriminant classificatory ability and headache syndromes suggested by a factor analysis. *Journal of Behavioral Assessment, 4,* 55–69.

Bakal, D. A. (1982). *The psychobiology of chronic headache.* New York: Springer.

Bakal, D. A., Demjen, S., & Kaganov, J. A. (1981). Cognitive behavioral treatment of chronic headache. *Headache, 21,* 81–86.

Bakal, D. A., & Kaganov, J. A. (1979). Symptom characteristics of chronic and nonchronic headache sufferers. *Headache, 19,* 285–289.

Bandura, A. (1977). Self-efficacy: Toward a unifying theory of behavioral change. *Psychological Review, 84,* 191–215.

Barber, T. X. (1959). Toward a theory of pain: Relief of chronic pain by prefrontal leucotomy, opiates, placebos, and hypnosis. *Psychological Bulletin, 56,* 430–460.

Beck, A. T. (1976). *Cognitive therapy and the emotional disorders.* New York: International Universities Press.

Beck, A. T., & Emery, G. (1985). *Anxiety disorders and phobias: A cognitive perspective.* New York: Basic Books.

Bell, N. W., Abramowitz, S. I., Folkins, C. H., Spensley, J., & Hutchinson, G. L. (1983). Biofeedback, brief psychotherapy and tension headache. *Headache, 23,* 162–173.

Bihldorff, J. P., King, S. H., Parnes, L. R., (1971). Psychological factors in headache. *Headache, 11,* 117–127.

Bille, B. (1962). Migraine in school children. *Acta Paediatrica Scandinavica, 51,* 1–151.

Bille, B. (1981). Migraine in childhood and its prognosis. *Cephalalgia, 1,* 71–75.

Blanchard, E. B., Andrasik, F., Neff, D. F., Jurish, S. E., & O'Keefe, D. M. (1981). Social validation of the headache diary. *Behavior Therapy, 12,* 711–715.

Blanchard, E. B., Andrasik, F., Ahles, T. A., Teders, S. J., & O'Keefe, D. (1980). Migraine and tension headache: A meta-analytic review. *Behavior Therapy, 11,* 613–631.

Budzynski, T. H., Stoyva, J. M., & Adler, C. S. (1970). Feedback-induced muscle relaxation: Application to tension headache. *Journal of Behavior Therapy and Experimental Psychiatry, 1,* 205–211.

Budzynski, T. H., Stoyva, J. M., Adler, C. S., & Mullaney, D. J. (1973). EMG biofeedback and tension headache: A controlled outcome study. *Psychosomatic Medicine, 35,* 484–496.

Cox, D., & Thomas, D. (1981). Relationship between headaches and depression. *Headache, 21,* 261–263.

Dalessio, D. J. (Ed.). (1972). *Wolff's headache and other head pain* (3rd ed.). New York: Oxford University Press.

Diamond, S. (1983). Depression and headache. *Headache, 17,* 173–180.

Ellis, A. (1962). *Reason and emotion in psychotherapy.* New York: Lyle Stuart.

Figueroa, J. L. (1982). Group treatment of chronic tension headaches: A comparative treatment study. *Behavior Modification, 6,* 229–239.

Frankenhaeuser, M. (1980). Psychobiological aspects of life stress. In S. Levine & H. Ursin (Eds.), *Coping and health*. New York: Plenum Press.

Friar, L. R., & Beatty, J. (1976). Migraine: Management by trained control of vasoconstriction. *Journal of Consulting and Clinical Psychology, 44*, 46–53.

Friedman, A. P., Von Storch, T. J. C., & Merritt, H. H. (1954). Migraine and tension headaches: A clinical study of 2,000 cases. *Neurology, 4*, 773–788.

Garvey, M. J. (1985). Occurrence of headaches in anxiety disordered patients. *Headache, 25*, 101–103.

Gerber, W. D., Miltner, W., Birbaumer, N., & Lutzenberger, W. (1983). Cephalic vasomotor feedback therapy: A controlled study of migraineurs and normals. In K. A. Holroyd, B. Schlote, & H. Zenz (Eds.), *Perspectives in research on headache* (pp. 171–182). Lewiston, NY: C. J. Hogrefe.

Gerhards, F., Rojahn, J., Boxan, K., Gnade, C., Petrik, M., & Florin I. (1983). Biofeedback versus cognitive stress-coping therapy in migraine headache patients. In K. A. Holroyd, B. A. Schlote, & H. Zenz (Eds.), *Perspectives in research on headache* (pp. 147–162). Lewiston, NY: C. J. Hogrefe.

Haynes, S. N. (1980). Muscle contraction headache: A psychophysiological perspective of etiology and treatment. In S. N. Haynes & L. R. Gannon (Eds.), *Psychosomatic disorders: A psychophysiological approach to etiology and treatment*. New York: Gardner.

Henryk-Gutt, R., & Rees, W. L. (1973). Psychological aspects of migraine. *Journal of Psychosomatic Research, 17*, 141–153.

Holroyd, K. A., & Andrasik, F. (1978). Coping and the self-control of chronic tension headache. *Journal of Consulting and Clinical Psychology, 46*, 1036–1045.

Holroyd, K. A., & Andrasik, F. (1982a). A cognitive-behavioral approach to recurrent tension and migraine headache. In P. C. Kendall (Ed.), *Advances in cognitive-behavioral research and therapy* (pp. 275–320). New York: Academic Press.

Holroyd, K. A., & Andrasik, F. (1982b). Do the effects of cognitive therapy endure? A two-year follow-up of tension headache sufferers treated with cognitive therapy or biofeedback. *Cognitive Therapy and Research, 6*, 325–334.

Holroyd, K. A., Andrasik, F., & Westbrook, T. (1977). Cognitive control of tension headache. *Cognitive Therapy and Research, 1*, 121–133.

Holroyd, K. A., & Penzien, D. B. (1983). EMG biofeedback and tension headache: Therapeutic mechanisms. In K. A. Holroyd, B. A. Schlote, & H. Zenz (Eds.), *Perspectives in research on headache* (pp. 147–162). Lewiston, N.Y.: C. J. Hogrefe.

Holroyd, K. A., Penzien, D. B., Hursey, K. G., Tobin, D. L., Rogers, L., Holm, J. E., Marcille, P. J., Hall, J. R., & Chila, A. G. (1984). Change mechanisms in EMG biofeedback underlying improvements in tension headaches. *Journal of Consulting and Clinical Psychology, 52*, 1039–1053.

Huber, H. P., & Huber, D. (1979). Autogenic training and rational-emotive therapy for long-term migraine patients—An explorative study of a therapy. *Behaviour Analysis and Modification, 3*, 169–177.

Kashiwagi, T., McClure, J. N., & Wetzel, J. D. (1972). Headache and psychiatric disorders. *Diseases of the Nervous System, 33*, 659–663.

Kewman, D., & Roberts, A. H. (1980). Skin temperature biofeedback and migraine headache: A double-blind study. *Biofeedback and Self-Regulation, 5*, 327–345.

Knapp, T. W. (1982). Treating migraine by training in temporal artery vasoconstriction and/or cognitive behavioral coping: A one-year follow-up. *Journal of Psychosomatic Research, 26*, 551–557.

Knapp, T. W., & Florin, I. (1981). The treatment of migraine headache by training in vasoconstriction of the temporal artery and a cognitive stress-coping training. *Behaviour Analysis and Modification, 4*, 267–274.

Kohlenberg, R. J., & Cahn, T. (1981). Self-help treatment for migraine headaches: A controlled outcome study. *Headache, 21*, 196–200.

Kremsdorf, R. B., Kochanowicz, N. A., & Costell, S. (1981). Cognitive skills training versus EMG biofeedback in the treatment of tension headache. *Biofeedback and Self-Regulation, 6*, 93–102.

Kroner, B. (1983). The empirical validity of clinical headache classification. In K. A. Holroyd, B. Schlote, & H. Zenz (Eds.), *Perspectives in research on headache*. Lewiston, NY: C. J. Hogrefe.

Kudrow, L. (1982). Paradoxical effects of frequent analgesic use. *Advances in Neurology, 33*, 335–341.

Lake, A., Rainey, J., & Papsdorf, J. D. (1979). Biofeedback and rational-emotive therapy in the management of migraine headache. *Journal of Applied Behavioral Analysis, 12*, 127–140.

Lance, J. W., Curran, D. A., & Anthony, M. (1965). Investigations into the mechanism and treatment of chronic headache. *Medical Journal of Australia, 2,* 904–914.

Largen, J. W., Matthew, R. J., Dobbins, K., & Claghorn, J. L. (1981). Specific and nonspecific effects of skin temperature control in migraine management. *Headache, 21,* 36–44.

Lazarus, R. S. (1966). *Psychological stress and the coping process.* New York: McGraw-Hill.

Lazarus, R. S. (1984). On the primacy of cognition. *American Psychologist, 39,* 124–129.

Leviton, A. (1978). Epidemiology of headache. In V. S. Schoenberg (Ed.), *Advances in neurology.* New York: Raven Press.

Leviton, A., Slack. W. V., Masek, B., Bana, D., & Graham, J. R. (1984). A computerized behavioral assessment for children with headaches. *Headache, 24,* 182–185.

Meichenbaum, D. H. (1975). Toward a cognitive theory of self-control. In G. Schwartz & D. Shapiro (Eds.), *Consciousness and self-regulation: Advances in research* (Vol. 1). New York: Plenum Press.

Meichenbaum, D. H., Turk, D., & Burstein, S. (1975). The nature of coping with stress. In I. Sarason & C. Spielberger (Eds.), *Stress and Anxiety* (Vol. 2). Washington, DC: Hemisphere.

Melzack, R. (1973). *The puzzle of pain.* New York: Penguin.

Melzack, R. (1975). The McGill pain questionnaire: Major properties and scoring methods. *Pain, 7,* 277–299.

Mitchell, K. R., & White, R. G. (1976). Self-management of tension headache: A case study. *Journal of Behavior Therapy and Experimental Psychiatry, 7,* 387–389.

Mitchell, K. R., & White, R. G. (1977). Behavioral self-management: An application to the problem of migraine headaches. *Behavior Therapy, 8,* 213–221.

Phillips, C. (1978). Tension headache: Theoretical problems. *Behaviour Research and Therapy, 16,* 249–261.

Prensky, A. L. (1976). Migraine and migrainous variants in pediatric patients. *Pediatric Clinics of North America, 23,* 461–471.

Price, D. D., McGrath, P. A., Rafii, A., & Buckingham, B. (1983). The validation of visual analogue scale as ratio scale measures for chronic and experimental pain. *Pain, 17,* 45–56.

Price, K. P., & Blackwell, S. (1980). Trait levels of anxiety and psychological responses to stress in migraineurs and normal controls. *Journal of Clinical Psychology, 36,* 658–660.

Rachman, S., & Philips, C. (1975). *Psychology and medicine.* London: Temple Smith.

Raskin, N. H., & Appenzeller, O. (1980). *Headache.* Philadelphia: W. B. Saunders.

Reeves, J. L. (1976). EMG-biofeedback reduction of tension headache: A cognitive skills-training approach. *Biofeedback and Self-Regulation, 1,* 217–225.

Sargent, J. D., Green, E. E., & Walters, E. D. (1972). The use of autogenic training in a pilot study of migraine and tension headaches. *Headache, 12,* 120–124.

Sargent, J. D., Green, E. E., & Walters, E. D. (1973). Preliminary report on the use of autogenic feedback training in the treatment of migraine and tension headaches. *Psychosomatic Medicine, 35,* 129–135.

Schultz, J. H., & Luthe, W. (1969). *Autogenic training* (Vol. 1). New York: Grune and Stratton.

Selby, G., & Lance, J. W. (1960). Observations on 500 cases of migraine and allied vascular headache. *Journal of Neurology, Neurosurgery, and Psychiatry, 23,* 23–32.

Sillanpaa, M. (1983). Changes in the prevalence of migraine and other headaches during the first seven school years. *Headache, 23,* 15–19.

Steger, J. C., & Harper, R. G. (1980). Comprehensive biofeedback versus self-monitored relaxation in the treatment of tension headache. *Headache, 20,* 137–142.

Turk, D. C., & Genest, M. (1979). Regulation of pain: The application of cognitive and behavioral techniques for prevention and remediation. In P. C. Kendall & S. D. Hollon (Eds.), *Cognitive behavioral interventions: Theory, research and practice.* New York: Academic Press.

Turk, D. C., Meichenbaum, D. H., & Berman, W. H. (1979). Application of biofeedback for the regulation of pain: A critical review. *Psychological Bulletin, 86,* 1322–1338.

Wolff, H. G. (1937). Personality features and reactions of subjects with migraine. *Archives of Neurology and Psychiatry, 37,* 895–921.

Wolff, H. G. (1948). *Headache and other head pain.* New York: Oxford University Press.

Ziegler, D. K., Rhodes, R. J., & Hassanein, R. S. (1978). Association of psychological measurements of anxiety and depression with headache history in a nonclinic population. *Research Clinical Studies in Headache, 6,* 123–135.

19

Eating Disorders

FRANCIS C. HARRIS AND CAROLYN F. PHELPS

Richard Morton (1694) first described anorexia nervosa in two patients suffering from "nervous consumption." He differentiated this disorder from somatic illnesses such as tuberculosis, noting that a psychological disturbance probably was responsible for the emaciation. Nearly two centuries later, Gull (1868) reiterated the psychological nature of the disorder then known as *hysteric apepsia*. Later, he would give anorexia nervosa its name, describing pathognomonic signs as a "morbid mental state" and a "perversion of the ego." During the next 40 years, case histories of "typical" patients periodically appeared in the medical literature (Garfinkel & Garner, 1982). For example, Albutt described one patient as

> A young woman thus afflicted, her clothes scarcely hanging together on her anatomy, her pulse slow and slack, her temperature two degrees below normal mean, her bowels closed, her hair like that of a corpse dry and lusterless, her face and limbs ashy and cold, her hollow eyes the only vivid thing about her. . . . This wan creature whose daily food might lie on a crown piece, will be busy yet on what funds God only knows. (cited in Garfinkel & Garner, 1982, p. 14)

Much of the eating disorders literature is still characterized by detailed clinical descriptions and case histories recounting the success of a very wide range of interventions. Unfortunately, very few controlled treatment outcome investigations of anorexia and bulimia have been conducted. The rather sparse data suggest that various behavioral interventions have been successful in promoting short-term changes in weight and eating behavior under controlled conditions. However, those investigations with follow-up periods greater than 9 months rarely report maintenance of treatment gains.

This chapter will review the extant literature regarding: (1) the definition and incidence of anorexia and bulimia, (2) instruments and strategies useful in the assessment of anorexia nervosa and bulimia, and (3) behavioral and cognitive-behavioral treatment of eating disorders.

Francis C. Harris. Department of Psychiatry, Western Psychiatric Institute and Clinic, University of Pittsburgh School of Medicine, Pittsburgh, Pennsylvania.

Carolyn F. Phelps. Department of Psychology, University of Pittsburgh, Pittsburgh, Pennsylvania.

Definition and Incidence of Anorexia Nervosa

DSM-III (American Psychiatric Association, 1980) describes anorexia nervosa as a psychopathological syndrome with the following diagnostic criteria:

a. Loss of 25% of original body weight (from a normal weight)
b. Distorted body image
c. Intense fear of becoming obese
d. Refusal to maintain a normal body weight
e. No known physical illness that could account for the disorder. [p. 67]

Anorexia occurs predominantly in females (85–95%), with 12 to 18 years of age being a particular high-risk period. Although onset of the disorder is usually in adolescence, many have noted its occurrence in patients over 25 years of age (Garfinkel, 1974; Garfinkel & Garner, 1982; Hsu, 1983). The term *anorexia* appears to be a misnomer, as loss of appetite frequently is absent from the clinical picture, (Hsu, 1983). Instead, it is more common for patients to *deny* that they experience hunger than to experience an actual loss of appetite like that exhibited by some depressed patients. Therefore, research diagnostic criteria (RDC) (Feighner, Robins, Guze, Woodruff, Winokur, & Munoz, 1972) requiring onset prior to age 25 and a loss of appetite may be too stringent, resulting in the exclusion from investigations of many anorectic patients (Rollins & Piazza, 1978). Psychological and physical concomitants of the disorder have been described previously (Bemis, 1978; Bruch, 1973; Crisp, Hsu, Harding, & Hartshorn, 1980; Morgan & Russell, 1975). The anorectic patient has been characterized as withdrawn, isolated, introverted, stubborn, selfish, perfectionistic, and manipulative. Additionally, anorectics often deny the existence of any problems, particularly those involving food or weight. These patients also exhibit a number of sterotypical behavior patterns, such as avoidance of public eating, idiosyncratic and monotonous diets, preoccupation with food and weight, binging, vomiting, laxative abuse, hyperactivity, lying, and stealing. Furthermore, there appears to be strong evidence for two subtypes of anorectics: *restricting-anorectics*, who control weight by food refusal and exercise, and *bulimic-anorectics*, whose weight loss is a function of vomiting and/or laxative abuse (Beumont, 1977; Beumont, George, & Smart, 1976; Casper, Eckert, Halmi, Goldberg, & Davis, 1980; Garfinkel & Garner, 1982). Clinical and psychosocial variables also have distinguished the two groups such that bulimic-anorectics were perceived as more disturbed than restricting-anorectics (Beumont, 1977; Beumont et al., 1976; Casper et al., 1980). Thus it may be important to consider potential difference *among* anorectics when evaluating treatment outcome studies.

It appears that the prevalence of anorexia nervosa has increased over the past ten years, although precise statistics are not available. Epidemiological reports have been fraught with methodological problems such as inconsistent diagnostic criteria and inadequate archival records. Recent data, however, generally are supportive of an increasing prevalence of anorexia, with a sharp rise noted in the number of cases reported over the last decade (Duddle, 1973; Jones, Fox, Babigan & Hutton, 1980). Unfortunately, it is not clear to what extent this increase merely reflects an increase in public and professional awareness of the disorder. Despite these methodological problems, conservative estimates suggest 1 in every 250 females develops the disorder (American Psychiatric Association, 1980; Crisp, Palmer, & Kalucy, 1976).

Definition and Incidence of Bulima

Dietary chaos syndrome (Palmer, 1979), binge-purge syndrome (Hawkins, Fremuow, & Clement, 1984) bulimarexia (Boskind-White & White, 1983), bulimia nervosa (Russell, 1979), and bulimia (American Psychiatric Association, 1980) all have been used to describe an eating pattern in which binge eating is alternated with behaviors that minimize the likelihood of weight gain (typically, self-induced vomiting, fasting, and/or laxative and diurectic abuse). DSM-III (American Psychiatric Association, 1980, pp. 70–71) outlines the principal features of bulimia as:

1. Recurrent episodes of binge eating (rapid consumption of a large amount of food in a discrete period of time, usually less than two hours).
2. At least three of the following:
   a. Consumption of high caloric, easily ingested food during a binge.
   b. Inconspicuous eating during a binge
   c. Termination of such eating episodes by abdominal pain, sleep, social interruption, or self-induced vomitng
   d. Repeated attempts to lose weight by severely restrictive diets, self-induced vomiting, or use of cathartics or diuretics
   e. Frequent weight fluctuations greater than ten pounds due to alternating binges and fasts
3. Awareness that the eating pattern is abnormal and fear of not being able to stop eating voluntarily
4. Depressed mood and self-deprecating thoughts following eating binges
5. The bulimic episodes are not due to Anorexia Nervosa or any known physical disorder

Thus, according to DSM-III, bulimics may be but are *not nescessarily* overweight, and *they may or may not use vomiting* as a weight control mechanism. Terms such as *bulimarexia* and *bulimia nervosa* have been used by some writers to denote the presence of bulimia in normal-weight females, many of whom have had a history of anorexia (Boskind-White & White, 1983; Hamilton, Gelwick, & Meade, 1984; Russell, 1979). Contrary to the DSM-III definition of bulimia, these investigators implicitly distinguish between overweight binge eaters and normal-weight binge–purgers. They also include in one group both patients with and without a history of anorexia nervosa. It is possible, however, that a prior history of anorexia among bulimics may be significant in terms of etiology, response to treatment, and course of the disorder. Since no two labels describe an identical disorder, it is difficult to compare the results of treatment outcome studies. Hamilton and his colleagues (Hamilton et al., 1984) have suggested the adoption of DSM-III criteria for research purposes since they provide the most encompassing definition. However, the DSM-III definition may be too broad, as it would include several different groups of people such as overweight binge eaters who do not purge, normal-weight binge eaters who do not purge, overweight binge–purgers, and normal-weight binge–purgers. Inclusion of patients with several different patterns is problematic in that potential differences are obscured among those individuals who would be diagnosed as bulimic according to these criteria. For example, it would be useful to examine whether obese binge eaters who do not purge differ significantly from normal-weight binge eaters who do purge.

Bulimics have been described as affectively overreactive, impulsive, anxious, histrionic, significantly depressed, and more sexually and socially sophisticated than their anorectic counterparts. In addition, bulimics appear to exhibit more suicidal ideation and more alcohol and drug dependency than do anorectics (Beumont, 1977; Beumont et al., 1976; Casper et al., 1980; Crisp et al., 1980; Garfinkel & Garner, 1982; Hamilton et al., 1984; Russell, 1979).

Like anorexia, bulimia occurs predominantly in females. Onset appears to be somewhat later, however, as data suggest 16- to 24-year-old women are at the greatest risk (Bruch, 1973; Hamilton et al., 1984). Three recent epidemiological studies have estimated the prevalence of bulimia at 8–13% (Fairburn & Cooper, 1982; Halmi, Falk, & Schwartz, 1982; Hamilton et al., 1984). Fairburn and Cooper's (1982) sample consisted of 669 subjects responding to a questionnaire in a women's magazine. The other two studies (Halmi et al., 1982; Hamilton et al., 1984) used college student populations, who by virtue of their age are at greater risk for the development of the disorder. Nonetheless, Hamilton and his collegues (1984) suggest that even a more conservative prevalence estimate of 1–2% for "DSM-III bulimia" in a college student population is "alarmingly high" (p. 18).

Assessment of Eating Disorders

Several instruments have been developed to assess eating attitudes and eating behaviors in anorectic and bulimic patients. These instruments have been used as aids in differential diagnoses and as treatment outcome measures. Instruments in which reliability and validity have been demonstrated include the Eating Attitudes Test (EAT) (Garner & Garfinkel, 1979), the Eating Disorder Inventory (EDI) (Garner, Olmstead, & Polivy, 1983), the Binge Scale (BS) (Hawkins & Clement, 1980), and the Bulimia Test (BULIT) (Smith & Thelen, 1984).

Eating Attitudes Test (EAT)

The Eating Attitudes Test (EAT) (Garner & Garfinkel, 1979) is a 40-item, forced-choice, self-report inventory that quantifies features commonly associated with eating-disordered patients. Each item is answered on a six-point Likert scale ranging from "always" to "never." Possible total EAT scores range from 0 to 120, with higher scores positively related to a more severe eating disturbance (Garfinkel & Garner, 1982). Results from two validation studies using anorectic and normal control subjects indicated that the EAT has high internal consistency (Cronbach's alpha = .79 for an anorectic sample and .94 for a combined sample of anorectic and normal subjects). Correlations between EAT scores and group membership were high ($r = .87$), demonstrating adequate discriminant validity (Garfinkel & Garner, 1982; Garner & Garfinkel, 1979). Although the EAT is also frequently used for the assessment of bulimic patients, no formal reliability and validity information for bulimics is available.

Eating Disorder Inventory (EDI)

The Eating Disorder Inventory (EDI) (Garner et al., 1983) is a 64-item forced-choice, self-report, multiscale inventory designed to assess the psychological and behavioral aspects of anorexia and bulimia. It follows a format identical to that of the EAT, with each item answered on a 6-point Likert scale ranging from "always" to "never." The EDI comprises eight subscales measuring (1) drive for thinness, (2) bulimia, (3) body dissatisfaction, (4) ineffectiveness, (5) perfectionism, (6) interpersonal distrust, (7) interoceptive awareness, and (8) maturation fears.

Results from a study of anorectic ($n = 113$) and normal control women ($n = 577$) indicated that the EDI appears to have adequate internal consistency as all subscales had coefficients greater than .80. Validity was established in a variety of ways. First, adequate agreement was demonstrated between anorectic patients' self-report profiles and clinicians' ratings of symptoms associated with each of the eight subscales ($r = .43$–$.68$, $p \leq .001$). Validity for specific subscales was established by demonstrating that comparison groups (bulimic-anorectics, restricting-anorectics, bulimics, obese and formerly obese subjects, and recovered anorectics) scored in the expected directions on specific subscales. For example, bulimic-anorectics ($n = 65$) scored significantly higher than restricting anorectics ($n = 48$) on the "bulimia" and "body dissatisfaction" subscales ($p < .01$) Additionally, bulimics scored similarly to bulimic-anorectics on the "drive for thinness," bulimia," and "body dissatisfaction" subscales. Interestingly, bulimics could not be distinguished from bulimic-anorectics. No significant differences were found between recovered anorectics ($n = 17$) and normal control subjects on any subscale. Recovered anorectics also scored significantly ($p \leq .001$) lower than the anorectic sample on all the scales. Finally, the relationships between specific subscale scores and a variety of instruments (e.g., EAT, BDI, Locus of Control, etc.) was assessed. For instance, there was a significant, positive relationship between the "drive for thinness" subscale and the EAT restraint scale (Herman & Polivy, 1975). Although the authors maintain the EDI was developed to assess psychological correlates of both anorexia *and* bulimia, important aspects of bulimia, such as impulsivity and mood lability, were omitted. Thus, prior to concluding it is useful in assessing psychological and behavioral aspects of bulimia, further validation of the EDI using a bulimic sample is necessary.

Binge Scale (BS)

The Binge Scale (BS) (Hawkins & Clement, 1980) is a forced-choice, self-report inventory that quantifies features commonly associated with bulimia. Examples of items include:

How often do you binge eat?
a. Seldom
b. Once or twice a month
c. Once a week
d. Almost every day

Which of the following best describes your eating behavior when binge-eating?
a. I eat more slowly than usual
b. I eat about the same I usually do
c. I eat very rapidly.

Possible total BS scores range from 0 to 24 with a mean score of 5.63 for normal-weight college women. Results from a pilot study of normal and overweight undergraduate women ($n = 391$) indicated the BS appears to have adequate internal consistency (Cronbach's alpha $= .68$). Additionally, there appears to be a positive relationship between the BS and the EAT (Hawkins & Clement, 1984; Phelps, 1984). Based on this relationship and the assumption that vomiting is a pathognomonic sign of bulimia, Hawkins and Clement (1984) recommend the presence of self-induced vomiting and an EAT total score greater than 30 as criteria for the psychometric identification of bulimia. However, these criteria may be too restrictive in excluding those who use laxatives or fast following a binge. For inclusion of these two groups, we suggest that the classification of "bulimia" should be based on the mean total BS score for normal-weight women. Specifically, "bulimia" would be defined by a total BS scale score greater than or equal to 14 (i.e., 2 standard deviations above the mean).

Bulimia Test (BULIT)

The Bulimia Test (BULIT) (Smith & Thelen, 1984) is a 36-item, forced-choice, self-report questionnaire that assesses specific characteristics of bulimia. It was designed to differentiate bulimics from those with other eating disorders, and bulimics from those with no eating disorder. Possible total BULIT scores range from 30 to 150, with scores greater than or equal to 102 indicative of bulimia. Results from a preliminary investigation suggest the BULIT has adequate test–retest reliability ($r = .87$) over a 2-month period. Concurrent validity, evaluated by correlating total BULIT scores with group membership based on judgments from clinical interviews, also was demonstrated ($r = .54, p \leq .0001$). Items regarding weight and menstrual regularity were the "best items" for differentiating bulimic-anorectics from individuals who exhibited only bulimia (Smith & Thelen, 1984).

Clinical Interview

In addition to these instruments, a thorough clinical interview should be undertaken to provide information regarding the patient's presenting problem and the patient's psychosocial functioning. Guidelines for the assessment of eating-disordered patients have been recounted elsewhere (Garfinkel & Garner, 1982; Harris, Hsu, & Phelps, 1983). All stress the importance of obtaining a detailed history of the disorder, which would include information regarding:

1. Binging and dieting behavior (type and quantity of food consumed, where eaten, time of day eaten, feelings associated with eating)
2. Vomiting (onset, frequency, method)
3. Laxative and/or diuretic use
4. Exercise
5. Frequency with which the patient weighs herself
6. Weight history (lowest, highest, fluctuations, current, and patient's perception of her ideal weight)
7. Thoughts regarding eating and weight

8. Events preceding food refusal/binge–purge episodes
9. Attempts to alter the eating disorder (self-help and help from others)
10. Medical status
11. Special relationships with family members and peers
12. Activities
13. Academic performance
14. Drug and alcohol use
15. Motivation to change

Assessment of Eating Disorder Correlates

A primary characteristic of behavioral assessment is to provide information for treatment planning. Such an assessment program must be both broad-based and exhaustive (Craighead, Kazdin, & Mahoney, 1981). Thus the evaluation of core features of eating disorders, though necessary, is not sufficient, particularly since changes in symptomatic behavior do not necessarily result in a corresponding improvement in other areas of functioning (e.g., dysphoria, interpersonal competence). Unfortunately, typical assessment procedures used with anorectic and bulimic patients have not been designed to evaluate correlates that may be crucial in determining treatment outcome, success of relapse prevention efforts, and generalization of treatment effects. What is needed, then, is a more comprehensive approach to the assessment of eating-disordered patients.

DEPRESSION

Eating disorder and affective disorder patients share many features, such as dysphoria, abnormal cortisol functioning, appetite and sleep disturbances, and an increased incidence of family history of depression. Primarily because of this shared symptomatology, some investigators have posited that anorexia and bulimia are merely variants of affective disorders (Cantwell, Sturzenberger, Burroughs, Salkin, & Green, 1977; Hudson, Laffer, & Pope, 1982). Although information regarding this hypothesis has been inconsistent, it is clear that many "depressive features" do improve with weight restoration and/or the return of normal eating patterns, and that depression is present in some anorectic or bulimic patients. Thus assessment of depression appears to be one useful measure of treatment outcome. The Beck Depression Inventory (BDI) (Beck, Ward, Mendelson, Mock, & Erbaugh, 1961) is an efficient and valid method of evaluating depression and has been used to assess pre- and posttreatment change.

INTERPERSONAL COMPETENCE

Despite the paucity of systematically collected information regarding psychosocial functioning in eating-disordered patients, there appear to exist behavioral correlates of anorexia and bulimia that fall under the rubric of psychosocial competence. In fact, diverse approaches (biological, family systems, psychodynamic, behavioral) to the conceptualization and treatment of eating disorders all indicate that (1) food refusal and binge eating are related to interpersonal stress and (2) eating-disordered patients often use food refusal and binge eating when an appropriate interpersonal response would be more effective in solving the problematic situation. The use of problem-solving training in the treatment of eating-disordered patients has been recommended by several authors (Fairburn, 1981, 1985; Garner & Bemis, 1982, 1984; Harris et al., 1983; Harris & Phelps, 1985).

In an effort to approach systematically the assessment of interpersonal problem-solving skills in eating-disordered patients, we recently developed a method of assessing interpersonal problem-solving ability in anorectic and bulimic patients. The Diet–Phelps Interpersonal Problem Solving Inventory (Diet–PIPSI) is a 28-item instrument consisting of problematic interpersonal situations that typically are encountered by eating-disordered patients. For each item, the respondent is instructed to (1) list all the possible solutions *anyone* could employ to solve the problem, (2) select the responses *she* would actually do, and (3) indicate which solution *best* solves the problem, regardless of what she actually might do. Having subjects respond to these three questions provides information about the type of problem-solving deficit they may exhibit. However, since preliminary data suggest the deficit is in response implementation, total Diet–PIPSI scores are based on the subject's response to "What would you do?" Two sample items follow:

> Item 19: You go to a party with your best friend. When you get there, you feel very nervous because you do not know very many people. To make matters worse, your friend leaves you and starts flirting with other guys. You feel like you do not fit in. You also are angry with your friend for deserting you.

> Item 22: You feel as if your mother criticizes you a lot. Although you wouldn't mind constructive criticism, she always seems to complain about your appearance. Today she tells you, "You weigh too much."

Responses are rated on a 5-point scale ranging from least effective (1) to most effective (5). The possible range of total Diet–PIPSI scores is 28–140.

The instrument was constructed and evaluated according to the behavior-analytic model presented by Goldfried and D'Zurilla (1969). Specifically, a situational analysis of potentially stressful situations was conducted. Next, a pool was formed of possible responses to each situation. Each possible response was evaluated by experts in terms of its likely effectiveness in solving the problem. A scoring manual was then developed, based on the expert judges' ratings. Based on responses from 118 non-eating-disordered subjects, the Diet–PIPSI appears to have adequate internal consistency (Cronbach's $\alpha = .77$). Stringent agreement percentage calculations demonstrated high inter-observer agreement (range $= 79\%$–87%; $\bar{X} = 83.35\%$). Results from a preliminary investigation of bulimics ($n = 15$) and normal control subjects ($n = 15$) demonstrated that the Diet–PIPSI also possesses concurrent and discriminant validity. Specificially, the Diet–PIPSI was negatively correlated with the EAT and the Binge Scale, suggesting that poor problem solvers were more likely to binge–purge in response to stressful situations than were good problem solvers. The fact that 93% of the bulimics were identified accurately on the basis of their Diet–PIPSI scores certainly supports the hypothesis that bulimics exhibit poor interpersonal problem-solving skills. Additionally, a comparison of bulimic and nonbulimic subjects' responses to the Diet–PIPSI suggested that skill deficits may be specific to *implementing* effective solutions rather than generating or identifying the "best" solution.

Behavioral Treatments

A negative reinforcement paradigm has been employed by behavioral clinicians to explain the development and maintenance of anorexia nervosa *and* bulimia (Harris et al., 1983; Harris & Phelps, 1985; Leitenberg, Gross, Peterson, & Rosen, 1984; Rosen & Leitenberg, 1982). Subjective feelings of anxiety are experienced in response to the fear of weight gain brought on by urges to eat. Food refusal and purging become negatively reinforced by decreasing the possibility of gaining weight and consequently decreasing subjective feelings of anxiety. Food refusal and/or purging responses subsequently are employed to reduce anxiety arising from *other* sources (e.g., interpersonal conflict). Additionally, eating- or weight-related responses such as frequent weighing, food refusal, and vomiting may be positively reinforced when the patient is rewarded for losing weight or "being ill" (Harris et al., 1983; Harris & Phelps, 1985).

Anorexia Nervosa

Operant conditioning, systematic desensitization, and social skills training have been used often in the treatment of anorexia nervosa. Low body weight, maladaptive eating behavior, fear of becoming obese, and social skills deficits all have been designated as target behaviors in behavioral treatment investigations.

Operant conditioning procedures have been aimed at rapid weight restoration through environmental manipulation. Thirty-two investigations used appropriate eating behavior ($n = 7$) or weight gain ($n = 25$) as the criterion for positive reinforcement (Agras & Werne, 1978; Azzerad & Stafford, 1969; Bachrach, Erwin, & Mohr, 1965; Bhanji & Thompson, 1974; Bianco, 1972; Blinder, Freeman, & Stunkard, 1970; Blue, 1979; Brady & Rieger, 1972; Eckert, Goldberg, Halmi, Casper, & Davis, 1979; Elkin, Hersen, Eisler, & Williams, 1973; Fichter & Kessler, 1980; Garfinkel, Kline, & Stancer, 1973; Garfinkel, Moldofsky, & Garner, 1977; Geller, 1975; Halmi, Powers, & Cunningham, 1975; Hauserman & Lavin, 1977; Kehrer, 1977; Leitenberg, Agras, & Thompson, 1968; Lobb & Schaefer, 1972; McGlynn, 1980; Neumann & Gaoni, 1975; Parker, Blazer, & Wyrick, 1977; Pertschuk, 1977; Pertschuk, Edwards, & Pomerleau, 1978; Poole & Sanson, 1978; Rosen, 1980; Rosman, Minuchin, Liebman, & Baker, 1976; Stumphauser, 1969; Vandereyeken & Pieters, 1978; Werry & Bull, 1975; Wulliemier, 1978).

Typically, a patient would be allotted social or material privileges such as visitors, time out of her bedroom, or access to television based on her daily weight or food consumption. With the exception of two studies (Eckert et al., 1979; Wulliemier, 1978), single-subject strategies have been employed. Unfortunately, only 5 of the 32 investigations used appropriate control procedures such that treatment effects appeared to be the result of the behavioral intervention (Eckert et al., 1979; Garfinkel et al., 1977; Pertschuck, 1977; Vandereyeken & Pieters, 1978; Wulliemier, 1978). Additionally, treatment almost always occurred in an inpatient setting, where manipulation of the environment was achieved easily. Thus it was not surprising that all the investigations reported rapid, *short-term* weight gain. Unfortunately, very little attention was paid to the assessment of posthospital adaptive functioning. Follow-up adjustment frequently consisted of unsubstantiated reports from the patient or relatives. The 14 studies that attempted to assess psychosocial competence did not define competence adequately. Furthermore, in 9 of these investigations *no* improvement or a *deterioration* in adaptive functioning, was reported (Agras & Werne, 1978; Blinder et al., 1970; Brady & Rieger, 1972; Fichter & Kessler, 1980; Garfinkel et al., 1977; Halmi et al., 1975; Pertschuck, 1977; Rosman et al., 1976). These results led several investigators (Bianco, 1972; Blinder et al., 1970; Garfinkel et al., 1977; Geller, 1975; Hauserman & Lavin, 1977) to conclude that operant conditioning techniques are effective in the short-term restoration of weight, but may *not* affect other important aspects of the disorder such as effective interpersonal behavior.

Systematic desensitization has been employed in 4 studies in an attempt to alter the anorectic's fear of weight gain (Hallsten, 1965; Lang, 1965; Ollendick, 1979; Schnurer, Rubin, & Roy, 1973). According to these investigators, the patient's weight phobia is the primary maintaining factor of the disorder. Desensitization hierarchies all consisted of anxiety-producing situations associated with weight gain or eating. Their specific content varied and included travel away from home; being the center of attention (Lang, 1965); eating at home (Hallsten, 1965); changes in appearance associated with weight gain (Ollendick, 1979; Schnurer et al., 1973); food (Schnurer et al., 1973); and criticism (Lang, 1965; Ollendick, 1979). Similar to the operant conditioning programs, systematic desensitization generally was effective in short-term weight restoration. However, more durable effects were noted by Ollendick (1979) who combined cognitive restructuring with the desensitization treatment. His results suggest that a cognitive-behavioral approach may be more effective than behavioral strategies alone in the treatment of anorexia. Unfortunately, none of the investigations examined psychosocial adjustment before or after treatment.

The presence of social isolation and social anxiety exhibited by many patients *after* the attainment of a normal weight led Pillay and Crisp (1981) to hypothesize that interpersonal competence might be an important variable in predicting treatment outcome. To examine the role of psychosocial competence in anorexia nervosa, they developed and evaluated a social skills training program. Program evaluation consisted of assessing two anorectic groups: those receiving social skills training plus the "established therapy program" and an attention placebo group who received only the established treatment. Differences between groups at posttreatment indicated social skills training was associated with a more rapid decrease in general anxiety, depression, and fear of negative evaluation than was the "established" therapy program.

However, two important results emerged at the follow-up assessment one year later. First, posttreatment differences between the groups were negligible at follow-up. Second, the attention placebo group appeared to experience less difficulty and a greater frequency of social interaction than did the social skills group. Pillay and Crisp (1981) concluded that social skills training was less effective than the standard treatment in promoting change in terms of both weight and psychosocial functioning. However, the inadequacy of the social skills program itself may account for these results. Specifically, social skills training consisted of tasks such as responding to a word association test and responding to contrived interpersonal situations. Therefore, it is possible that their program did not teach the necessary social skills that would result in increased interpersonal effectiveness. A more appropriate social skills program would: (1) delineate the specific stressful situations or problematic responses that have some relationship to the patient's maladaptive eating behavior and (2) use behavioral role rehearsal to teach alternative, effective interpersonal responses.

Bulimia

Three recent investigations report the application of behavior therapy in the treatment of bulimia (Leitenberg et al., 1984; Linden, 1980; Rosen & Leitenberg, 1982). In a single case report, Linden (1980) described a multifaceted intervention that included response delay, stimulus control, and assertiveness training. During the treatment proper, binge–purging was reduced from 6 times per week to once per week. Follow-up checks at 3 and 6 months indicated the patient's eating behavior continued to improve. Unfortunately, psychosocial adjustment was not assessed. Moreover, it is unclear which component, if any, accounted for the reduction in bulimic behavior.

Rosen and Leitenberg (1982) employed an exposure plus response prevention program in the treatment of bulimia. This program first was applied in the treatment of one bulimic patient. Specifically, the patient was instructed to eat preselected food from three categories (large meal, junk food, snacks) until she experienced a strong urge to vomit. There were six exposure sessions for each category. Sessions involving large meals and junk food were conducted in local restaurants. Instead of vomiting, the patient was instructed to focus on the level of her anxiety. Response prevention continued until the urge to vomit subsided. No instructions to avoid binging or vomiting at home were given during the supervised exposure sessions. During this phase of treatment, the longest consecutive period without vomiting was 2 days. In the next phase, the patient was instructed to decrease vomiting gradually during the following week. Self-report data indicated that binging and vomiting had ceased by day 44. Only one binge–purge episode was noted at a 10-month follow-up assessment. Improvement in self-esteem and a decrease in mood lability also were reported by the patient.

In a second investigation, similar results were obtained with five bulimic patients (Leitenberg et al., 1984). Additionally, self-report assessments of eating attitudes, depression, and self-esteem revealed improvement on all three variables at posttreatment. Despite favorable outcomes in both studies, neither employed follow-up periods of sufficient duration.

Cognitive-Behavioral Treatments

Cognitive-behavioral approaches conceptualize eating disorders as the direct result of the patient's beliefs, attitudes, and assumptions regarding the meaning of weight (Garner & Bemis, 1982, 1984). In contrast to behavioral models, *cognitive* variables are posited as the mediators maintaining the disorder. This conceptualization is based on clinical observations that distorted thinking and belief systems often persist in eating-disordered patients, despite the amelioration of aberrant eating patterns (Fairburn, 1985; Garner & Bemis, 1982).

Anorexia Nervosa

Cognitive variables have been suggested as the bases for models of the disorder's etiology and treatment (Garner & Bemis, 1982, 1984). Specifically, these variables include cognitive processes (selective attention and cognitive distortion) involved in positive and negative self-reinforcement; cognitive features of self-concept deficits; and cognitions typical of anorectics (e.g., "I will be happier if I lose weight," "If I eat one cookie, I will gain weight.") Garner and Bemis (1984) invoke "cognitive self-reinforcement" as a primary mediator of anorectic behavior. They contend that rigorous dieting and other attempts to maintain a low body weight result in increased feelings of mastery, self-control, and personal competence, which in turn reinforce the anorectic behavior. Additionally, constructs such as cognitive schemas are used to explain how anorectics filter, distort, retain, and recall information that is consistent with their belief systems and behavior.

Although some aspects of a cognitive-behavioral intervention are similar to other approaches, modification of belief structures is assumed necessary for successful treatment outcome (Garner & Bemis, 1982, 1984). Consequently, the primary purpose of assessment is to delineate the patient's attitudes regarding her weight and self-worth, performance-related values, beliefs surrounding her own development, errors in formal reasoning, and general cognitive style. Adapting procedures from a number of cognitive theorists, Garner and Bemis (1982, 1984) recommend strategies that focus on correcting maladaptive cognitions, cognitive processes, and cognitive structures. These authors have described an anorectic cognitive style characterized by dichotomous reasoning, overgeneralization, magnification, personalization, selective abstraction, and superstitious thinking.

Guidano and Liotti (1983) also contend that the anorectic's behavior is governed by two of Ellis's irrational beliefs: the dire need to be loved and the unbearability of disappointment. The treatment proposed by Garner and Bemis (1982, 1984) is a five-step model in which patients are instructed to self-monitor "thinking," pinpoint the relationship between cognitions and maladaptive behaviors, examine the validity of their beliefs, substitute more adaptive interpretations of incoming information, and modify their underlying assumptions. This process is accomplished through the use of specific interventions designed particularly for anorectics. Procedures modified from Ellis's rational-emotive therapy and Beck's cognitive therapy of depression include:

1. Particulation of beliefs
2. Perspective taking
3. Decatastrophizing
4. Restructuring internal imperatives (i.e., challenging a patient's "I should . . ." and "I must . . ." self-statements)
5. Reattributions of self-perceptions regarding weight
6. Behaviorally testing the validity of beliefs
7. Thought stopping/thought substitution

Additionally, behavioral rehearsal and reinforcement of adaptive, competent behavior (e.g., assertiveness, autonomous decision making, engagement in pleasant events) are recommended.

The role of cognitive processes as causal agents in the development and maintenance of anorexia nervosa remains an empirical question. The concept of self-reinforcement, much less "cognitive" self-reinforcement, is controversial (Gross, 1984). Furthermore, the measurement of cognitive processes and structures is fraught with methodological problems. Nonetheless, the proposed intervention does emphasize the importance of examining variables other than weight or eating behavior in the treatment of anorexia. Anecdotal accounts suggest that this cognitive-behavioral approach is effective in the treatment of anorectic patients (Garfinkel & Garner, 1982; Garner & Bemis, 1982, 1984). However, the superiority of cognitive-behavioral interventions over other treatments remains undemonstrated.

Bulimia

Three investigations have described the implementation of cognitive-behavioral strategies in the treatment of bulimia (Boskind-Lodahl & White, 1978; Fairburn, 1981; Long & Cordle, 1982). Using a group therapy format, Boskind-Lodahl and White (1978) emphasized the importance of focusing on situations that elicit binge eating. The purpose of treatment was to develop a repertoire of alternative responses to these situations through assertiveness training, self-exploration, and the group therapy process (Boskind-Lodahl & White, 1978). The group met for 11 weekly 2-hour sessions. Results from a preliminary investigation indicated that 8 of the 12 bulimic participants reported the persistence of binge eating at posttreatment and at the 1-year follow-up. The authors suggested that an increase in the patient's interpersonal interactions may have accounted for the results (Boskind-Lodahl & White, 1978). That is, evidence regarding bulimics' psychosocial competence suggests that an increase in the frequency of interpersonal interactions may result in a concomitant increase in *stressful* interpersonal interactions, which could be antecedents of binge–purge episodes.

Long and Cordle (1982) described the treatment of two bulimic patients using a similar intervention. The treatment plan included behavioral self-control procedures, nutritional education, cognitive restructuring, and resocialization. Specifically, resocialization consisted of encouragement to increase interpersonal interactions and assertiveness training. Results indicated both patients exhibited improved eating patterns and improved social interactions at posttreatment and at a 1-year follow-up assessment.

Fairburn (1981) described an intervention for bulimic patients that included behavioral self-control procedures, dietary education, cognitive restructuring and problem-solving training. According to Fairburn (1982), the patient relies on binge eating as a means to alleviate distress. The use of binge eating as a problem-solving response not only perpetuates the disorder, but also creates additional problems for the patient. Therefore, the purpose of problem-solving training is to enable the patient to respond more effectively when confronted with a problematic situation. Although a systematic evaluation of this intervention has not been conducted, preliminary data indicate 9 of the 11 bulimic patients who participated reported decreases in the number of binge–purge episodes. Twelve-month follow-up data on 6 of these patients revealed that 2 continued to improve and were no longer bulimic. Four patients reported infrequent binge–purging (i.e., once in 3 months).

Recently Fairburn (1985) hypothesized dysfunctional beliefs, values, and cognitions as the primary maintaining variables in bulimia. In contrast to Garner and Bemis (1982, 1984), Fairburn did not imply that these factors operate as causal agents in the development of the disorder, nor did he attempt to outline superordinate processes and structures (i.e., cognitive self-reinforcement, cognitive schemas). Fairburn's treatment is presented in three phases.

Phase 1 consists of eight appointments scheduled over 4 weeks, in which the focus is on behavioral control of weight and the modification of eating patterns. Specific interventions include establishment of a target weight range, self-monitoring of eating patterns, education regarding the physical consequences of bulimia, nutritional and dietary reeducation, stimulus-control procedures to reduce the liklihood of binge–purge episodes, generation of alternative behaviors to bulimia, and examining the functions bulimia serves such as tension reduction and social withdrawal.

Phase 2 is more cognitively oriented and comprises eight weekly sessions. Problem-solving training and identification and modification of dysfunctional cognitions characterize this stage. Problem solving consists of problem definition, generation of alternative responses, evaluation of each potential solution, selection of a solution, response implementation, and evaluation of the effectiveness of the problem-solving process.

Finally, phase 3, consisting of three sessions spaced at 2-week intervals, emphasizes the maintenance of treatment gains and the troubleshooting of potential problems through a relapse prevention plan. Although preliminary data and clinical descriptions of positive outcomes suggest that Fairburn's treatment package may be an effective treatment for bulimia, he cautions that formal empirical evaluations are necessary prior to concluding its superiority over other approaches.

Summary and Future Directions

Anorexia nervosa and bulimia appear to be two distinct eating disorders whose incidences have been increasing over the past 20 years. Behavioral investigations have implemented operant conditioning procedures, systematic desensitization, social skills training, and response prevention in the treatment of these disorders. Although all appear to be successful in short-term improvements of weight and/or eating behavior, maintenance and generalization of treatment effects and success of relapse prevention have been elusive. In contrast, cognitive-behavioral strategies have focused on altering variables such as irrational beliefs, dysfunctional thoughts, and problem-solving skills. Although anecdotal accounts and case reports suggest cognitive-behavioral interventions are effective in the treatment of eating disorders, their superiority over other methods awaits empirical verification. It is suggested that a comprehensive assessment of eating-disordered patients should include evaluations of both the primary features and the interpersonal correlates of the disorders. Such an evaluation would provide information relevant to treatment planning and the evaluation of treatment outcome evaluation.

Finally, to some people a chapter on eating disorders might seem out of place in a book on anxiety disorders. This is primarily because anorexia and bulimia have been viewed as either unique forms of psychopathology or, less frequently, as subtypes of affective disorders. These conceptualizations have typically led to the application of methods previously developed and refined for the assessment and treatment of obesity and depression. Although these strategies have been somewhat successful, they have not dealt adequately with what many clinicians and researchers consider to be the core feature of anorexia and bulimia—that is, the "fear of weight gain." More recent (Harris et al., 1983; Ollendick, 1979; Rosen, 1980; Rosen & Leitenberg, 1982) conceptualizations of eating disorders have taken into account the anxiety reduction functions of fasting and/or purging. It is our hope that such conceptualizations will lead to the development of tripartite taxonomic models of anorexia and bulimia. Such models, focusing on the interaction of subjective experiences, motor behaviors, and physiological responses, likely would provide important information about the selection and development of individualized cognitive-behavioral treatment strategies. Specifically, such a point of view would promote the integration of strategies such as interpersonal problem-solving training, stress management training, and a variety of behavioral techniques in providing multimodal—and hence more effective—treatment. This book is testimony to the contribution of such models to the understanding and treatment of other anxiety disorders.

References

Agras, S., & Werne, J. (1978). Behavior therapy in anorexia nervosa, a data-based approach to the question. In J. P. Brady & H. K. H. Brodie (Eds.), *Controversy in psychiatry*. Philadelphia: Saunders.

American Psychiatric Association. (1980). *Diagnostic and statistical manual of mental disorders* (3rd ed.). Washington, DC: Author.

Azzerad, J., & Stafford, R. L. (1969). Restoration of eating behavior in anorexia nervosa through operant conditioning and environmental manipulation. *Behaviour Research and Therapy, 7*, 165–171.

Bachrach, A. J., Erwin, W. S., & Mohr, J. P. (1965). The control of eating behavior in an anorectic by operant conditioning techniques. In L. P. Ullmann & L. Krasner (Eds.), *Case studies in behavior modification*. New York: Holt, Rinehart and Winston.

Beck, A. T., Ward, C. H., Mendelson, M., Mock, J., & Erbaugh, J. (1961). An inventory for measuring depression. *Archives of General Psychiatry, 4*, 561–571.

Bemis, K. M. (1978). Current approaches to the etiology and treatment of anorexia nervosa. *Psychological Bulletin, 85*(3), 593–617.

Beumont, P. J. V. (1977). Former categorization of patients with anorexia nervosa. *Australian and New Zealand Journal of Psychiatry, 11*, 223–226.

Beumont, P. J. V., George, G. C. W., & Smart, D. E. (1976). "Dieters" and "vomiters and purgers" in anorexia nervosa. *Psychological Medicine, 6*, 617–622.

Bhanji, S., & Thompson, J. (1974). Operant conditioning in the treatment of anorexia nervosa: A review and retrospective study of eleven cases. *British Journal of Psychiatry, 124*, 166–172.

Bianco, F. J. (1972). Rapid treatment of two cases of anorexia nervosa. *Journal of Behavior Therapy and Experimental Psychiatry, 3*, 223–224.

Blinder, B. J., Freeman, D. M. A., & Stunkard, A. J. (1970). Behavior therapy of anorexia nervosa: Effectiveness of activity as a reinforcer of weight gain. *American Journal of Psychiatry, 126*(8), 72–82.

Blue, R. (1979). Use of punishment in the treatment of anorexia nervosa. *Psychological Reports, 44*, 743–746.

Boskind-Lodahl, M., & White, W. C., Jr. (1978). The definition and treatment of bulimarexia in college women—A pilot study. *Journal of the American College Health Association, 27*, 84–97.

Boskind-White, M., & White, W. C., Jr. (1983). *Bulimarexia*. New York: Norton.

Brady, J. P., & Rieger, W. (1972). Behavioral treatment of anorexia nervosa. In T. Thompson & W. S. Dockens III (Eds.), *Proceedings of the International Symposium on Behavior Modification*. New York: Appleton-Century-Crofts.

Bruch, H. (1973). *Eating disorders: Obesity, anorexia nervosa and the person within*. New York: Basic Books.

Cantwell, D. P., Sturzenberger, S., Burroughs, J., Salkin, B., & Green, J. K. (1977). Anorexia nervosa: An affective disorder? *Archives of General Psychiatry, 34,* 1087–1093.

Casper, R. C., Eckert, E. D., Halmi, K. A., Goldberg, S. C., & Davis, J. M. (1980). Bulimia: Its incidence and clinical importance in patients with anorexia nervosa. *Archives of General Psychiatry, 37,* 1030–1034.

Craighead, W. E., Kazdin, A. E., & Mahoney, M. J. (1981). *Behavior modification: Principles, issues, and applications*. Boston: Houghton Mifflin.

Crisp, A. H., Hsu, L. K. G., Harding, J., & Hartshorn, J. (1980). Clinical features of anorexia nervosa. *Journal of Psychosomatic Research, 24,* 179–191.

Crisp, A. H., Palmer, R. L., & Kalucy, R. S. (1976). How common is anorexia nervosa? A prevalence study. *British Journal of Psychiatry, 128,* 542–554.

Duddle, M. (1973). An increase of anorexia nervosa in a university population. *British Journal of Psychiatry, 123,* 711.

Eckert, E. D., Goldberg, S. C., Halmi, K. A., Casper, R. C., & Davis, J. M. (1979). Behavior therapy in anorexia nervosa. *British Journal of Psychiatry, 134,* 55–59.

Elkin, T. E., Hersen, M., Eisler, R. M., & Williams, J. G. (1973). Modification of caloric intake in anorexia nervosa: An experimental analysis. *Psychological Reports, 32,* 75–78.

Fairburn, C. G. (1981). A cognitive-behavioral approach to the treatment of bulimia. *Psychological Medicine, 11,* 707–711.

Fairburn, C. G. (1982). Binge-eating and its management. *British Journal of Psychiatry, 141,* 631–633.

Fairburn, C. G. (1985). Cognitive-behavioral treatment for bulimia. In D. M. Garner & P. E. Garfinkel (Eds.), *Handbook of psychotherapy for anorexia nervosa and bulimia*. New York: Guilford Press.

Fairburn, C. G., & Cooper, P. J. (1982). Self-induced vomiting and bulimia nervosa: An undetected problem. *British Medical Journal, 284,* 1153–1155.

Feighner, J. P., Robins, E., Guze, S. B., Woodruff, R. A., Jr., Winokur, G., & Munoz, R. (1972). Diagnostic criteria for use in psychiatric research. *Archives of General Psychiatry, 26,* 57–63.

Fichter, M. M., & Kessler, W. (1980). Behavioral treatment of an anorectic male: Experimental analysis of generalization. *Behavioral Analysis of Medicine, 4,* 152–168.

Garfinkel, P. E. (1974). Perception of hunger and satiety in anorexia nervosa. *Psychological Medicine, 4,* 309–315.

Garfinkel, P. E., & Garner, D. M. (1982). *Anorexia nervosa: A multidimensional perspective*. New York: Brunner-Mazel.

Garfinkel, P. E., Kline, S. A., & Stancer, H. C. (1973). Treatment of anorexia nervosa using operant conditioning techniques. *Journal of Nervous and Mental Disease, 157*(6), 428–433.

Garfinkel, P. E., Moldofsky, H., & Garner, D. M. (1977). The outcome of anorexia nervosa: Significance of clinical features, body image, and behavior modification. In R. A. Vigersky (Ed.), *Anorexia nervosa*. New York: Raven Press.

Garner, D. M., & Bemis, K. (1982). A cognitive-behavioral approach to anorexia nervosa. *Cognitive Therapy and Research, 6*(2), 123–150.

Garner, D. M., & Bemis, K. M. (1984). Cognitive therapy for anorexia nervosa. In D. M. Garner & P. E. Garfinkel (Eds.), *Handbook of psychotherapy for anorexia nervosa and bulimia*. New York: Guilford Press.

Garner, D. M., & Garfinkel, P. E. (1979). The eating attitudes test: An index of the symptoms of anorexia nervosa. *Psychological Medicine, 9,* 273–279.

Garner, D. M., Olmstead, M. P., & Polivy, J. (1983). Development and validation of a multidimensional eating disorder inventory for anorexia nervosa and bulimia. *International Journal of Eating Disorders, 2,* 15–34.

Geller, J. L. (1975). Treatment of anorexia nervosa by the integration of behavior therapy and psychotherapy. *Psychotherapy and Psychosomatics, 26,* 167–177.

Goldfried, M. R., & D'Zurilla, T. J. (1969). A behavioral-analytic model for assessing competence. In C. D. Spielberger (Ed.), *Current topics in clinical and community psychology* (Vol. 1). New York: Academic Press.

Gross, A. M. (1984). Self-directed behavior change in children: Is it self-directed? *Behavior Therapy, 15,* 501–514.

Gull, W. W. (1868). The address in Medicare delivered before the Annual Meeting of the BMA at Oxford. *Lancet, 2*, 171.

Guidano, V. F., & Liotti, G. (1983). *Cognitive processes and emotional disorders: A structural approach to psychotherapy*. New York: Guilford Press.

Hallsten, E. A. (1965). Adolescent anorexia treated by desensitization. *Behaviour Research and Therapy, 3*, 87–91.

Halmi, K. A., Falk, J. R., & Schwartz, E. (1982). Binge eating and vomiting: A survey of a college population. *Psychological Medicine, 11*, 697–706.

Halmi, K. A., Powers, P., & Cunningham, S. (1975). Treatment of anorexia nervosa with behavioral modification. *Archives of General Psychiatry, 32*, 93–96.

Hamilton, M. K., Gelwick, B. P., & Meade, C. J. (1984). The definition and prevalence of bulimia. In R. C. Hawkins, W. J. Fremouw, & P. F. Clement (Eds.), *The binge–purge syndrome*. New York: Springer.

Harris, F. C., Hsu, L. K. G., & Phelps, C. F. (1983). Problems in adolescence. Assessment and treatment of bulimia nervosa. In M. Hersen (Ed.), *Outpatient behavior therapy: A clinical guide*. New York: Grune and Stratton.

Harris, F. C., & Phelps, C. F. (1985). Anorexia nervosa. In M. Hersen & A. S. Bellack (Eds.), *Handbook of clinical behavior therapy with adults*. New York: Plenum Press.

Hauserman, N., & Lavin, P. (1977). Post-hospitalization continuation treatment of anorexia nervosa. *Journal of Behavior Therapy and Experimental Psychiatry, 8*, 309–313.

Hawkins, R. C., & Clement, P. F. (1980). Development and construct validation of a self-report measure of binge-eating tendencies. *Addictive Behaviors, 5*, 219–226.

Hawkins, R. C., & Clement, P. F. (1984). Binge eating. Measurement problems and a conceptual model. In R. C. Hawkins, W. J. Fremouw, & P. F. Clement (Eds.), *The binge–purge syndrome*. New York: Springer.

Hawkins, R. C., Fremouw, W. J., & Clement, P. F. (1984). *The binge–purge syndrome: Diagnosis, treatment, and research*. New York: Springer.

Herman, C. P., & Polivy, J. (1975). Anxiety, restraint, and eating behavior. *Journal of Abnormal Behavior, 84*, 666–672.

Hsu, L. K. G. (1983). The etiology of anorexia nervosa. *Psychological Medicine, 13*(2), 231–238.

Hudson, J. I., Laffer, P. S., & Pope, H. G., Jr. (1982). Bulimia related to affective disorder by family history and response to the dexamethasone suppression test. *American Journal of Psychiatry, 139*(5), 685–687.

Jones, D. F., Fox, M. M., Babigan, H. M., & Hutton, H. E. (1980). Epidemiology of anorexia nervosa in Monroe County, New York: 1960–1976. *Psychosomatic Medicine, 42*, 551–568.

Kehrer, H. E. (1977). Behandlung der anorexia nervosa mit verhaltenstherapie. *Medicinische Klinik, 70*, 427–432.

Lang, P. J. (1965). Behavior therapy with a case of anorexia nervosa. In L. P. Ullmann & L. Krasner (Eds.), *Case studies in behavior modification*. New York: Holt, Rinehart and Winston.

Leitenberg, H., Agras, W. S., & Thompson, L. E. (1968). Sequential analysis of the effect of selective positive reinforcement in modifying anorexia nervosa. *Behaviour Research and Therapy, 6*, 211–218.

Leitenberg, H., Gross, J., Peterson, J., & Rosen, J. C. (1984). Analyses of an anxiety model and the process of change during exposure plus response prevention treatment of bulimia nervosa. *Behavior Therapy, 15*, 3–20.

Linden, W. (1980). Multi-component behavior therapy in a case of compulsive binge-eating followed by vomiting. *Journal of Behavior Therapy and Experimental Psychiatry, 11*, 297–300.

Lobb, L. G., & Schaefer, H. H. (1972). Successful treatment of anorexia nervosa through isolation. *Psychological Reports, 30*, 245–246.

Long, C. G., & Cordle, C. J. (1982). Psychological treatment of binge-eating and self-induced vomiting. *British Journal of Medical Psychology, 55*, 139–145.

McGlynn, F. D. (1980). Successful treatment of anorexia nervosa with self-monitoring and long-distance praise. *Journal of Behavior Therapy and Experimental Psychiatry, 11*, 283–286.

Morgan, H. G., & Russell, G. F. M. (1975). Values of family background and clinical features as predictors of long term outcome in anorexia nervosa: Four year follow-up of 41 patients. *Psychological Medicine, 5*, 355–371.

Morton, R. (1694). *Phthisiologica: Or a treatise of consumptions*. London: S. Smith & B. Walford.

Neumann, M., & Gaoni, B. (1975). Preferred food as the reinforcing agent in a case of anorexia nervosa. *Journal of Behavior Therapy and Experimental Psychiatry, 6,* 331–333.

Ollendick, T. H. (1979). Behavioral treatment of anorexia nervosa: A five year study. *Behavior Modification,* 3(1), 124–135.

Palmer, R. L. (1979). The dietary chaos syndrome: A useful new term? *British Journal of Medical Psychology, 52,* 187–190.

Parker, J. B., Jr., Blazer, D., & Wyrick, L. (1977). Anorexia nervosa: A combined therapeutic approach. *South Medical Journal, 70,* 448–452.

Pertschuk, M. J. (1977). Behavior therapy: Extended follow-up. In R. A. Vigersky (Ed.), *Anorexia nervosa.* New York: Raven Press.

Pertschuk, M. J., Edwards, N., & Pomerleau, O. F. (1978). A multiple-baseline approach to behavioral intervention in anorexia nervosa. *Behavior Therapy, 9,* 368–376.

Phelps, C. F. (1984). *Assessment of interpersonal competence in an eating disordered population: Development and evaluation of an instrument.* Unpublished master's thesis, University of Pittsburgh, Pittsburgh, PA.

Pillay, M., & Crisp, A. H. (1981). The impact of social skills training within an established inpatient treatment program for anorexia nervosa. *British Journal of Psychiatry, 139,* 533–539.

Poole, A. D., & Sanson, R. W. (1978). A behavioral program for the management of anorexia nervosa. *Australian and New England Journal of Psychiatry, 12,* 49–53.

Rollins, N., & Piazza, E. (1978). Diagnosis of anorexia nervosa: A critical reappraisal. *Journal of the American Academy of Child Psychiatry, 17,* 126–137.

Rosen, J. C., & Leitenberg, H. (1982). Bulimia nervosa: Treatment with exposure and response prevention. *Behavior Therapy, 13,* 117–124.

Rosman, B. L., Minuchin, S., Liebman, R., & Baker, L. (1976). Input and outcome of family therapy in anorexia nervosa. In J. L. Claghorn (Ed.), *Successful Psychotherapy.* New York: Brunner/Mazel.

Russell, G. F. M. (1979). Bulimia nervosa: An ominous variant of anorexia nervosa. *Psychological Medicine, 9,* 429–448.

Schnurer, A. T., Rubin, R. R., & Roy, A. (1973). Systematic desensitization of anorexia nervosa as a weight phobia. *Journal of Behavior Therapy and Experimental Psychiatry, 4,* 149–153.

Smith, M. C., & Thelen, M. H. (1984). Development and validation of a test for bulimia. *Journal of Consulting and Clinical Psychology, 52*(5), 863–872.

Stumphauser, J. S. (1969). Application of reinforcement contingencies with a 23 year old anorectic patient. *Psychological Reports, 24,* 109–110.

Vandereyeken, W., & Pieters, G. (1978). Short-term weight restoration in anorexia nervosa through operant conditioning. *Scandinavian Journal of Behavior Therapy, 7*(4), 221–236.

Werry, K. S., & Bull, D. (1975). Anorexia nervosa: A case study using behavior therapy. *Journal of the American Academy of Child Psychiatry, 14,* 567–568.

Wulliemier, F. (1978). Anorexia nervosa: Gauging treatment effectiveness. *Psychosomatics, 19,* 497–499.

20

Anxiety Associated with Chemotherapy and Other Noxious Medical Procedures

CAROL I. DIENER AND WILLIAM H. REDD

In recent years medicine has made numerous discoveries resulting in more effective treatment for cancer. The National Cancer Institute estimates that, of nearly one million new cases of cancer diagnosed in 1985, approximately half the patients will survive for 5 years or longer. Although for oncologists and professionals working in cancer research this 5-year survival rate represents real progress in the war against cancer, lay people still view the diagnosis of cancer as a death sentence. Indeed, the word *cancer* has the power to instill dread and fear in most of us (Illich, 1976). In a comprehensive study of cancer patients receiving treatment at major cancer centers, Derogatis et al. (1983) found that nearly one-half (47%) of cancer patients have emotional reactions severe enough to warrant DSM-III psychiatric diagnoses. The most frequent reaction to learning of the diagnosis involves an adjustment disorder, with depression as the primary feature.

Anger, depression, and anxiety are the most well documented psychological consequences of cancer (Freidenbergs, Gordon, Hibbard, & Diller, 1980; Plumb & Holland, 1977; Schain, 1976) and recent research has shown the efficacy of psychosocial interventions such as education and supportive counseling (Gordon, Freidenbergs, Diller, Hibbard, Wolf, Levine, Lipkins, Ezrach, & Lucido, 1980). This has resulted in increased appreciation of the importance of including psychologists and social workers on oncology treatment teams (Budman & Wertlieb, 1979; Kellerman 1980; Morgan, Kremer, & Gaylor, 1979).

During the last four years a large and rapidly expanding literature on the psychosocial aspects of cancer and its treatment has emerged (see, e.g., Andrykowski, & Redd, in press; Burish & Lyles, 1981, 1983; Goldberg & Tull, 1983; Meyerowitz, Heinrich, & Schag, 1983; Redd & Hendler, 1983). This literature shows an increasing recognition that cancer and its treatment often have a significant impact on almost all aspects of the patient's life.

In addition to providing support and education for the social and emotional impact of cancer, psychological interventions can be useful as adjunctive therapy for some physical components of cancer as well. For example, the increase in cancer survival rates

Carol I. Diener. Department of Psychology, University of Illinois, Urbana, Illinois.

William H. Redd. Departments of Neurology and Pediatrics, Memorial Sloan-Kettering Cancer Center, New York, New York.

is mainly due to more aggressive medical interventions, particularly chemotherapy and radiation. However, this improvement in survival rate carries with it a high price—severe side effects. Chemotherapy can be accompanied by a number of noxious side effects including loss of hair, fatigue, severe nausea and vomiting, and sterility. Because of the severity of these side effects, some patients choose to terminate recommended treatment rather than to continue to undergo the treatment side effects (Seigel & Longo, 1981). Thus effective interventions to reduce or eliminate these side effects becomes an important goal. Several theoretical models have been proposed for the role of anxiety in heightening these side effects as well as in contributing to anticipatory nausea, noncompliance with medical treatment, and even reduced effectiveness of treatment (cf. Averill, 1973; Meyerowitz, Sparks & Spears, 1979; Nerenz, Leventhal, & Love, 1982; Thompson, 1981).

Behavioral interventions have proved very effective in the treatment of side effects. This chapter focuses on the treatment of anxiety and distress associated with chemotherapy and other noxious medical procedures. Several behavioral intervention programs are described, and issues relating to the treatment of both adult and pediatric oncology patients are addressed. The purpose is to review current research and consider future directions.

Development of Anticipatory Reactions

An examination of the physical and psychological conditions associated with the diagnosis and treatment of cancer reveals numerous factors and environmental contingencies that might facilitate the development of behavioral problems. In many cases such problems begin as naturally occurring responses to treatment and the social isolation associated with it. With continued treatment and repeated hospitalizations, these behavioral symptoms can acquire a life of their own; that is, they can occur independently of the factors that initially prompted them. Depending on the age and physical condition of the patient, these problems range from extreme anxiety reactions to medical procedures to regressive acting-out.

For some patients the side effects of cancer chemotherapy can cause more anxiety and distress than the disease itself. These side effects may even be responsible for many patients' decision to terminate treatment prematurely (Lazslo, 1983). During the long course of repeated chemotherapy infusions, approximately 40% of patients become sensitized to the chemotherapeutic agents and develop phobiclike aversions. This phenomenon results in increasing anxiety, stress, and pretreatment nausea, which may begin several days before each scheduled treatment. Specific environmental cues (the hospital, a particular smell, even a freeway exit sign) can trigger a bout of nausea at any time. These anticipatory side effects are conceptualized by researchers in the area as the result of classical, respondent conditioning (Andrykowski, Redd, & Hatfield, 1985; Redd & Andrykowski, 1982). According to this formulation, the infusion of cytotoxic drugs functions as an unconditioned stimulus, producing nausea and vomiting as the unconditioned response. Environmental stimuli repeatedly associated with the treatment (e.g., the sound of the doctor's voice, a particular smell) acquire the ability to elicit nausea and vomiting. In other words, these associated cues become conditioned stimuli and elicit nausea and vomiting even though chemotherapeutic agents are not present. This learning is automatic and not within the patient's control.

The development of anticipatory side effects to chemotherapy is gradual, usually first appearing after the fourth or fifth course of treatment and escalating in severity during subsequent courses. Patients beginning chemotherapy are typically apprehensive; most have heard stories about the horrors of "chemo" (a term now well known to many lay people). Interestingly, most patients find the first infusion much easier than they expected. Except with the most toxic protocols, patients typically experience only mild posttreatment nausea and vomiting following their first infusion. As the course of treatment continues, however, with weekly or twice monthly infusions, patients begin to notice side effects. With subsequent infusions, these side effects generally become more severe. Patients are at first confused and wonder why they feel uneasy as they prepare for treatment. They often report that the odors of the waiting room are especially unpleasant and that familiar foods and activities make them nauseated. Each month the problems become worse. For some patients, a call from the clinic nurse or the mere thought of treatment makes them nauseated. Unfortunately, patients do not understand why they are reacting in what seems, to them, a bizarre manner. Many patients think that their reactions represent some neurotic problem.

In addition to anticipatory nausea and anxiety, many patients experience insomnia and other anxiety-mediated problems days and nights before each clinic visit. Patients often report being preoccupied by thoughts of chemotherapy and find themselves thinking about upcoming events in terms of their proximity to treatment (Redd, in press, b). One cancer patient reported being in a favorite restaurant 30 miles from the treatment center where he received his chemotherapy. A nurse from the oncology unit walked in, and the patient began to feel nauseated as soon as he saw her. As he ate his meal he became more nauseated, until finally he went to the restroom and vomited. Another individual reported becoming nauseated when she drove past the hospital where she had received her chemotherapy 10 years earlier. A 30-year-old Hodgkins survivor reported an incident that occurred when he was sailing on the river along-side the hospital where he had been treated as a young adolescent. He said that as soon as he noticed the entrance to the chemotherapy clinics, he felt nauseated and began vomiting.

Although research has failed to identify a personality type or set of attitudes that characterize the patient who is most likely to experience anticipatory reactions, there does appear to be a strong association between the appearance of anticipatory side effects and patient anxiety. First, patients who are characteristically anxious and are preoccupied by worry (i.e., who have high trait anxiety) are most likely to develop anticipatory side effects (Andrykowski, Redd, & Hatfield, 1985; Nerenz et al., 1982). Such patients (i.e., those with high trait anxiety) are also more likely to experience chemotherapy infusions as unpleasant and depressing (van Komen & Redd, 1985). Moreover, patients who report feeling highly anxious during initial treatment are most likely to experience aniticipatory nausea and vomiting during subsequent treatments. The physical setting in which treatments are administered also appears to affect the development of aversion reactions. Finally, a strong association has been observed between the severity, duration, and frequency of posttreatment nausea and vomiting and the development of pretreatment reactions. Those patients who report posttreatment nausea and vomiting that are either longer, more frequent, or more severe than the typical reaction are more likely to develop anticipatory side effects (Andrykowski et al., 1985; Fetting et al., 1983; Ingle, Burish, & Wallston, 1984; Morrow, 1982; Wilcox, Fetting, Nettesheim, & Abeloff, 1982). Two correlates follow from this relationship. First, patients receiving highly emetic drugs are at great risk for developing anticipatory reactions. For example, patients treated with cisplatin are at great risk, since cisplatin is the chemotherapy drug that currently produces the most severe posttreatment side effects. Second, for patients on the same drug protocol, those patients who have more severe reactions to chemotherapy are more likely to develop anticipatory side effects. It is also important to emphasize that there have been no instances reported in the literature in which a patient developed anticipatory nausea and/or vomiting without first experiencing severe posttreatment side effects (Andrykowski, Redd, & Hatfield, 1985). Thus it appears that the presence of any factor that increases the emeticity of a protocol increases the likelihood that patients will experience nonpharmacologic side effects. Perhaps because of theoretical biases of investigators or folk wisdom (ignorance), initial research on the development of anticipatory reactions to chemotherapy focused on the role of personality factors. Coping style (Altmaier, Ross, & Moore, 1982); psychopathology (Chang, 1981); and other personality variables have been proposed as causal factors. None of these personality/psychopathology hypotheses, however, have been supported by empirical results, and most investigators in the area have shifted their attention to the study of factors related to respondent conditioning. Indeed, at present, all the data collected on the development and control of anticipatory side effects of chemotherapy are consistent with a respondent conditioning interpretation of symptom development (Andrykowski et al., 1985).

Because of the large number of factors influencing the development of anticipatory reactions and the complexity of their interaction(s), it is not possible to specify the exact prevalence of such aversions. It is clear, however, that anticipatory side effects do affect a considerable number of patients and reported prevalence has ranged from 25% to 65%. A conservative estimate would be that at least 33% of chemotherapy patients eventually acquire aversions to their treatment (Redd & Andrykowski, 1982; Nicholas, 1982).

Control of Anticipatory Reactions

In response to the failure of antiemetic drugs to control anticipatory nausea/vomiting and the research on the role of respondent conditioning in the development of these side effects, researchers have investigated the application of behavioral methods of control. Four procedures have been studied: (1) passive relaxation (hypnosis) used with guided imagery, (2) progressive muscle relaxation training with imagery, (3) EMG–biofeedback, and (4) systematic desensitization. Each of these procedures has been studied by independent groups of investigators using different research designs. Since no direct comparison of the four procedures has been conducted, the following discussion focuses on each procedure separately.

Passive Relaxation

A major focus of initial research on anticipatory nausea control was the use of hypnosis in conjunction with pleasant, relaxing imagery. A number of clinical reports (Dash, 1980; Dempster, Balson, & Whalen, 1976; LaBaw, Holton, Tewell, & Eccles, 1975; Olness, 1981) have consistently found that the use of hypnosis, in conjuction with pleasant, relaxing imagery, is effective in reducing both pre- and postchemotherapy nausea/vomiting and patient distress/anxiety.

Taking the research a step further, Redd, Andresen, and Minagawa (1982) reported a study in which female cancer patients participated in a clinical intervention. Their initial study involved an individual-analysis, multiple-basline design. All of the women had been treated without success with antiemetic drugs for prechemotherapy vomiting. Patients were first taught a simple hypnosislike relaxation technique (passive relaxation) in the therapist's office. The patient was instructed to fixate on a point on a wall or to close her eyes; the therapist then systematically directed the patient to focus her attention on various muscle groups (e.g., arms, legs, neck, back, or lower torso). Feelings of relaxation and comfort were emphasized. Once the patient was still and relaxed, the therapist described several pleasant images (e.g., a quiet beach on a warm day, a grassy field in springtime). These scenes were individualized, and the therapist described relevant colors, scents, textures, and sounds of the setting. Following two training sessions, the therapist directed the patient through these procedures before and during regular chemotherapy treatments. When the therapist assisted, anticipatory vomiting was eliminated in all patients. Patients also reported clinically significant reductions in nausea. However, anticipatory nausea and vomiting reappeared when patients underwent chemotherapy without the use of the relaxation/imagery technique. Anticipatory side effects were subsequently reeliminated when the procedures were reintroduced in later sessions.

Zeltzer and her associates (Zeltzer, Kellerman, Ellenberg, & Dash, 1983; Zeltzer, LeBaron, & Zeltzer, 1982; Zeltzer, Zeltzer, & LeBaron, 1982) used similar procedures to reduce postchemotherapy nausea and vomiting in adolescents. Eight patients received training sessions using an eye fixation technique and guided imagery. After instruction in the use of the techniques, posttreatment nausea and vomiting were reduced in frequency and intensity, but not in duration.

Progressive Muscle Relaxation Training with Imagery

Burish and his colleagues (Burish & Lyles, 1979, 1981; Lyles, Burish, Krozely, & Oldham, 1982) have conducted a series of studies assessing the effectiveness of progressive muscle relaxation training (Bernstein & Borkovec, 1973) used with imagery to control anticipatory side effects. Adult patients with anticipatory nausea were studied across 5 to 10 consecutive chemotherapy treatments divided into baseline, treatment, and follow-up phases. Measures of pulse rate, blood pressure, anxiety, and depression were obtained during chemotherapy infusions, as well as nurses' observations of vomiting. After no-treatment baseline conditions, the therapist directed patients in progressive muscle relaxation and guided imagery both before and during chemotherapy injections. During the follow-up phase the therapist was withdrawn and patients were instructed to use the relaxation and imagery intervention on their own before and during chemotherapy. In their group comparison research, no-treatment and therapist-contact control groups were added to better assess the contribution of nonspecific factors.

Results have been consistent across their research. Therapist-directed progressive muscle relaxation with guided imagery resulted in reductions in pulse rate and blood pressure, as well as in self-reported anxiety and nausea. Patients in control conditions did not have these reductions. Follow-up results have been less impressive, however. When the therapist was no longer present, patients in the treatment groups did not display as large a reduction in nausea and physiological arousal.

EMG–Biofeedback

Multiple-muscle-site EMG–biofeedback in conjunction with relaxation training and imagery has been used in one case study by Burish and his colleagues (Burish, Shartner, & Lyles, 1981). The intervention strategy closely followed those of Burish's previous research cited earlier. Biofeedback was used to augment the relaxation training during drug infusions. Once the patient could effectively reduce her physiological arousal (as measured by EMG) and maintain that quiet state, relaxing images were presented during drug infusions. As in their earlier studies, the patient's distress and nausea were reduced.

Systematic Desensitization

Another technique that has been used to control anticipatory nausea and vomiting is systematic desensitization (Morrow & Morrell, 1982). This procedure involves three general steps. First, the patient is instructed in the use of a relaxation technique, usually progressive muscle relaxation training. Second, the patient and therapist construct a hierarchy of stimuli relevant to the feared situation, ranging from the least to the most anxiety-provoking. Third, the patient practices relaxation training while visualizing the increasingly aversive scenes within the hierarchy. In their initial study of the use of systematic desensitization, Morrow and Morrell (1982) randomly assigned 60 cancer patients to one of three conditions: (1) systematic desensitization, in which patients were taught an abbreviated form of progressive muscle relaxation training and, while relaxed, were asked to imagine chemotherapy-related stimuli (e.g., seeing the drugs, feeling the needle stick); (2) supportive counseling intended to control for therapist attention, expectancy effects, and other nonspecific factors; and (3) a no-treatment control. Patients were asked to rate the frequency, severity, and duration of their prechemotherapy nausea and vomiting during two baseline and two follow-up chemotherapy treatments. Between chemotherapy treatments, patients assigned to treatment groups received two sessions of either the systematic desensitization or individual counseling. The results showed that during the two follow-up chemotherapy treatments, desensitized patients reported significantly less severe anticipatory nausea and vomiting. They also experienced significantly shorter duration of anticipatory nausea than did patients in the other two conditions (who did not differ significantly from each other).

The consistency of the positive results obtained in the group of studies just reviewed is remarkable: clinically significant reductions in anticipatory nausea and vomiting were achieved despite wide variations in type of cancer, stage of the disease, and chemotherapy protocol. From these results it is clear that behavioral techniques have a place as an adjunctive treatment in the care of many chemotherapy patients.

Fear of Medical Procedures in Children

In addition to developing aversion to chemotherapy, another major problem for cancer patients is the fear of painful procedures and routine injections. These fear responses can become so debilitating that some patients report being overwhelmed by anxiety and preoccupied by dread for 2 or 3 days before each scheduled treatment (Redd & Hendler, 1983). This preoccupation can result in additional time off from work, decreased productivity, and a general reduction in the quality of life. Techniques to reduce fear and anxiety associated with painful medical procedures can greatly improve the patients' quality of life.

Research in this area has been focused on pediatric patients because the likelihood of severe fear being developed is particularly high. For example, a child with leukemia must undergo repeated bone marrow aspirations and lumbar punctures as well as routine monitoring and chemotherapy infusions. A child who actively resists these procedures may render treatment extremely difficult. Since pain- and anxiety-controlling medications are generally ineffective in these instances and often have unwanted side effects, nurses and parents are called on to restrain the child physically while the necessary treatment is administered. Although this type of intervention is necessary, it increases the stressfulness of the situation for the pediatric patient.

Although the use of relaxation training, systematic desensitization, and positive reinforcement programs to reduce anxiety and phobic reactions to dental and medical treatment is well documented (cf. Klorman, Hilpert, Michael, LeGana, & Sveen, 1980; McNamara, 1979; Melamed & Siegel, 1980), the application of these procedures to pediatric cancer treatment is not extensive. The published research to date includes evaluations of the use of behavioral treatment "packages" (Jay & Elliot, 1983; Katz, Kellerman, & Siegel, 1980; Kellerman, 1980; Kellerman, Zeltzer, Ellenberg, & Dash, 1983) and case reports (Dash, 1980; LaBaw, Holton, Tewell, & Eccles, 1975).

Behavioral interventions to alleviate distress during painful medical procedures and encourage compliance with treatment/rehabilitation generally involve a combination of positive motivation, emotive imagery, and hypnosis. As was pointed out earlier, recommendations for their application in pediatric oncology are drawn from a number of sources outside pediatric medicine, the primary ones being childhood early education and child clinical psychology. Specific applications in pediatric oncology are relatively new and preliminary in scope.

Positive Motivation

Perhaps the most widely used behavioral intervention method with children is positive motivation. Such programs can be used to encourage patient compliance as well as to motivate the patient to practice the technique that will help control pain and distress. In our work at Memorial Sloan-Kettering, we often give points exchangeable for special treats and privileges to motivate young patients to cooperate with unpleasant treatment procedures. One example is a 6-year-old boy who kicked and cried during routine mouth care; he was so disruptive that three nurses were required to complete the daily procedure. A simple contingency system was initiated: if he did not kick or hit the nurses during mouth care and was generally cooperative, his mother would read him a favorite story. If he actively resisted, two more nurses would be called and he would miss the storybook time with his mother. After 3 days of behavioral intervention his resistance to mouth care was no longer a problem: he was cooperative and proud of his accomplishment. Similar positive incentive programs have been used with pediatric patients to increase compliance with radiation treatment (i.e., special privileges given for holding still) and routine blood tests.

Emotive Imagery

Another technique is "emotive imagery" (cf. Lazarus & Abramovitz, 1962); it involves telling the child a story designed to distract him or her from the pain associated with treatment. Similar to distraction techniques and hypnosis, it takes advantage of the child's openness to fantasy. The therapist begins working with the child in the office, away from the medical treatment area. After establishing rapport with the child, the therapist determines the child's favorite storybook hero and the things the child likes to do. The therapist then tells the child a series of stories involving the child and his or her hero. Each subsequent story brings the child closer to the feared setting, while the hero helps the child master the situation. This procedure resembles systematic desensitization used with adults. The rationale is that if strong anxiety-inhibiting emotive images are elicited in the context of feared stimuli, the anxiety reaction to those stimuli will be reduced. By being told a story that involves favorite storybook heroes interacting with the phobic stimulus, the child comes to associate these stimuli with positive feelings of self-assertion, pride, and affection. As the therapist relates the story, the feared stimuli are introduced in a hierarchical fashion, from least to most distressing.

The following narrative shows how emotive imagery can be used to reduce a young child's fear of needles. In such cases the patient is usually referred because his or her level of agitation and resistance has increased with repeated treatments. The therapist begins by asking the patient to describe what treatment was like and to try to explain what frightened him or her. Although many young patients find it difficult to identify the problem, they often state that they wish it weren't so scary and that they could be braver. The therapist then explains that she wants to teach the child how to get his or her mind off the needle and how to learn to keep calm. She also explains to the patient that she will be telling a story and that the child can help by filling in missing parts. She then asks the patient to close his or her eyes, and she might begin:

> David, you know about Batman and Robin, right? You know that they have special powers and can help children do lots of things. They can help us be strong and brave and they can even help reduce pain. Let me tell you one way they do this. On one of their trips to a faraway planet they found a special invisible glove. It was in a box with other treasures from long ago. Beside the glove was a note. It told them about the glove's special powers. The glove would

protect them whenever they wore it. To test it out, Batman put it on and was able to lift the Batmobile with one hand. One day Robin was going to the doctor and asked Batman if he could use it. Batman knew how much Robin hated going to the doctor's: he doesn't like getting shots. So Batman gave it to Robin and Robin wore it proudly. As Robin got ready to go into the doctor's office, he felt scared, but remembered that he had the magic invisible glove for protection. He went into the office for his shot, put out his arm, and—to his great surprise—he didn't feel a thing. It was magic. Robin was so happy. Would you like to try on the glove? Oh, good. Hold out your hand and let me help you put it on. How does it feel? Does it fit? Pull it up high, all the way to your shoulder. Good. Let's go into the treatment room and try on the glove there. It will be fun, okay? Good. . . .

If the child displays any anxiety, the therapist slows down the story and approaches the fear object (task) less directly. Throughout the intervention the therapist is careful to be sensitive to the child's emotional reaction and is ready to pace the story according to the child's needs.

Diener (1984) reported a case of a 4-year-old boy with leukemia who was afraid of needles. At the time of referral his level of noncompliance was high. When his name was called in the waiting room and the nurse announced that it was time for his chemotherapy, the young patient would hide behind a chair and begin kicking when anyone came near. His father would have to carry him to the treatment room. In other situations the child was quite pleasant and was well liked. His disruptive behavior in the waiting room was indeed atypical. During a series of sessions conducted in the therapist's office, the patient learned to use imaginary gloves to make treatment easier. Before each infusion the parents guided the patient in putting on the gloves. As the patient's mother stated: "It was amazing. David put on the magic glove and went through chemotherapy without any problem." His mother also recounted an interesting incident. One day David and his parents were waiting to see the doctor when they noticed that another child was crying and fighting, obviously afraid of the treatment he was about to receive. David leaned over to his mother and whispered: "Mom, should I lend him my magic glove? Of course, he'll have to give it back so I can use it later." It is important to point out that such desensitization is best used with fears that are irrational and not directly linked to aversive treatment (e.g., fears of the dark, or of being alone). In the case of fears of procedures that actually cause significant pain (e.g., bone marrow aspiration), one would not expect emotive imagery used alone to be consistently effective. The problem is that, after the child was desensitized, he or she would again experience the pain and aversive stimulation caused by the procedure, and the fear would return. That is, the child would be reconditioned. Rather than relying solely on desensitization, one would be advised to use relaxation and distraction techniques. Rather than trying to remove the fear and later having it reestablished, the therapist should block the patient's perception of the pain during the actual treatment. Such a strategy would help reduce the subjective aversiveness of treatment as well as fostering the reduction of anticipatory anxiety.

Hypnosis

As should be clear from the preceding discussion, emotive imagery is similar to hypnosis. Although the use of hypnosis to relieve acute pain has a long history, many clinicians and most lay people do not understand it. In fact, many fear it. This is unfortunate, as research has demonstrated the effectiveness of hypnosis with individual pediatric patients (Hilgard & LeBaron, 1984). Hypnosis involves a relatively simple dissociation process in which the patient learns to focus his or her attention on stimuli, images, and/or thoughts that are unrelated to the source of pain. Hilgard and LeBaron (1984) have coined the term "imaginative involvement" to refer to the process by which the individual becomes "hypnotized." They maintain that this process involves the individual's becoming cognitively engaged in a task such that other (i.e., "external") stimuli are blocked or reduced in intensity. This dissociation is common in everyday life: reading a book and being unaware of the noise around you, playing tennis with a cut finger and not noticing the pain and blood until the match is over. In clinical settings hypnosis involves a therapist's gaining the patient's cooperation and then directing the patient's attention to images that are distinct from those associated with the treatment setting. The aim is to distract the patient. Although all individuals are capable of this type of cognitive dissociation, some individuals are more skilled than others, and various scales of hypnotizability have been developed to assess this skill. The essential characteristic appears to be an ability to engage in fantasy; individuals who score high on scaling hypnotizability also report being able to become deeply involved in reading, dreams, and the aesthetic appreciation of nature. Research has shown that children as a group are more hypnotizable than adults (Hilgard & LeBaron, 1984). They appear to be less reality-bound and easily become absorbed in fantasy.

Comprehensive Behavior Modification

As was stated earlier, Jay, Elliott, Ozolins, and Olson (1982) have devised a comprehensive behavioral intervention for children undergoing painful cancer treatment. This package integrates techniques outlined earlier and pain/anxiety reduction procedures devised for pediatric dental patients. This multifaceted program is offered in order to ensure that the intervention is maximally flexible so as to meet the special needs of the child. With an individual patient, emphasis can be placed on certain components, or the components can be adjusted to permit better tailoring of the intervention to the child's individual needs. Treatment components include: (1) breathing exercises, (2) reinforcement, (3) imagery, (4) behavioral rehearsal, and (5) filmed modeling. Although a large-scale evaluation of the package has not been conducted, preliminary individual cases confirmed the utility of comprehensive behavioral intervention.

In order to help reduce anxiety and to facilitate attentional distraction, deep breathing exercises are taught during training sessions and then carried out during scheduled treatments. The child might first be asked to imagine blowing up a plastic bubble, taking deep breaths and then slowly letting the air out. The therapist might explicitly pace the child's breathing by counting and squeezing his hand in rhythm with slow breathing. If the child shows signs of "losing it," the therapist might say to the child: "Keep it up. Slow, easy, soft breathing. You can do it. Slow . . . , easy . . . , one . . . two . . . , slow . . . , three . . . ," and so forth. In many ways the therapist functions as a coach, using all of his or her clinical skill. It is especially important that the therapist be sensitive to subtle signs of mounting anxiety in the child and, at the same time, able to engage the child and maintain the child's attention.

Before each treatment the child and the therapist decide on a toy or prize that the child will "work for." Jay and her colleagues give patients trophies for doing well. To obtain the trophy, the child's job is to lie still and do the breathing exercise. The criterion for winning is not mastery of the procedure without crying or getting upset; rather, all that is required is cooperation and using the skills that have been taught.

To help distract the child's attention, Jay and her colleagues use emotive imagery during training sessions as well as during scheduled medical procedures. To teach the child how to cooperate and reduce anxiety about the unknown, the patient is taken through all phases of the procedure during training sessions. During these practice sessions the child assumes each role, playing doctor, nurse, and patient.

Jay and her associates have made two films to help train the patient in the completion of bone marrow aspiration. In these films a child of approximately the same age narrates scenes showing him going through the procedure. The patient describes his fears and concerns as the nurse prepares him for the aspiration. The patient also explains how he copes. The child's description is realistic; he readily admits that he is afraid and that it isn't easy. In accounts of the behavioral intervention, Jay has stressed that the film is based on a coping, rather than a mastery, model. That is, the film facilitates the child's identification with the model. Although the child depicted in the film is successful and cooperates without resistance, his fear is acknowledged and his hardiness is reinforced.

Broader Clinical Issues

In anxiety-producing situations young children often look to their parents for emotional support and for making sense of the situation (Redd, in press, a). Research (Bloom, 1975, 1977) suggests that a complex feedback loop exists between the child and the parent. If the parent is calm and relaxed, the child is more likely to believe the situation is safe. If the parent is clearly anxious, the child's own fears are increased. Parental tone of voice, posture, and eye gaze are subtle but powerful cues for the child during stressful events. Jay and her colleagues (Jay, Ozolins, Elliot, & Caldwell, 1983) have found that parental presence during invasive procedures can increase a child's agitation.

To the extent that parents can become actively involved in reducing their child's pain and distress, one would expect the anxiety spiral to lessen. To treat a pediatric oncology patient who was noncompliant during routine medical procedures, Diener and Ambuel (1985) trained the parents. Serving as behavioral interventionists, the parents learned to direct their child in self-hypnosis and relaxation. The parents were also encouraged to distract their child during infusions by playing checkers and reading aloud. The goal is to reduce both child and parental distress by teaching the parent(s) how to carry out the behavioral techniques.

The picture is even more complex when the patient is an adolescent. Adolescence has been viewed by many as a particularly stressful period of life (Clapp, 1976; Easson, 1970). The diagnosis of cancer and the subsequent treatment may make the normal developmental tasks of adolescence more difficult (Easson, 1970; Erikson, 1959). At the time when they should be exerting greater autonomy and mastery over their own lives, adolescent cancer patients often find themselves becoming more dependent on parents and medical staff (Slavin, 1981). This unavoidable regression results in a concern with loss of control and feelings of helplessness (Kellerman & Katz 1977; Zeltzer, 1980; Zeltzer,

LeBaron, & Zeltzer, 1982). For this reason it is important that the adolescent patient be actively involved in the behavioral intervention. Such a strategy should help ameliorate distress and increase the patient's sense of control and self-worth.

Anxiety in Adults

Although research in behavioral oncology with adults has focused almost exclusively on the control of chemotherapy side effects, considerable clinical effort has been directed toward other anxiety disorders in adult cancer patients. The use of desensitization to treat severe anxiety reactions in adults is clearly shown in a case study report by Redd (1980). The patient was a 53-year-old woman whose anxiety reaction to ingesting food prevented her rehabilitation following gastrointestinal surgery. The patient initially sought medical treatment because she felt weak and was unable to retain solid foods. She first noticed unusual throat sensations when she ate and would vomit approximately 10 minutes after each meal. Initial medical evaluation indicated a mass in her esophagus and upper part of her stomach. The patient was successfully treated with radiation to reduce the tumor and was symptom-free. She led a fairly normal life until 5 months later, when the original symptom (regurgitating solid foods) reappeared and laboratory tests revealed the recurrence of the tumor. Although surgery to remove the tumor was successful, she continued to complain of discomfort associated with swallowing. Although the oncologist had repeatedly assured the patient that all laboratory reports showed no tumor obstruction and the presence of a total functional digestive system, she insisted that the discomfort experienced while swallowing food was caused by her cancer. Despite her efforts to retain food, she could not inhibit gagging and regurgitating following consumption of solid foods.

During the first four intervention sessions, the patient quickly learned progressive muscle relaxation (Bernstein & Borkovec, 1973) and at the beginning of the third session reported that she had successfully tried the exercises on her own. During each subsequent session the patient was directed through the exercises and then was given small amounts of selected foods. Nursing staff were instructed to give her her daily meals as usual and to provide positive feedback if she ate anything on her plate. They were not to pressure or coax her to eat, and if she did not eat they were to ignore the entire issue. Since before the program began the nursing staff had devoted great efforts to coaxing her and getting her any food she wanted, it was felt that her refusal to eat might be, in part, an attention-getting device. For that reason the intervention program included extinction of her resistant behavior and social reinforcement of eating.

Nineteen days after the program had been implemented, the patient's condition was stable and hyperalimentation was discontinued. She was able to retain all foods and was discharged as an outpatient. Although she maintained her weight and had no difficulty retaining solid foods, she continued to complain of the throat sensation. Her fear that the sensation meant tumor recurrence slowly extinguished, however, and, at her 6- and 12-month follow-up appointments, she stated that she no longer believed a tumor was causing her discomfort.

In both the case study just outlined and the interventions with children and adolescents, a combination of *in vivo* desensitization and reinforcement of effective coping was used to reduce behavioral distress. Although the complexity of the interventions precluded the identification of the exact mechanism(s) of control, it is clear that such behavioral intervention can facilitate the administration of prescribed medical regimens and permit successful rehabilitation.

Clinical Issues

Behavioral interventions remain an interpersonal event between clinician and patient, and the development of rapport and trust cannot be underestimated. Because of the brief nature of many of the behavioral interventions discussed, it is desirable to develop this trust quickly. One area that we have found important in this arena is the labeling of various techniques. We initially called our passive relaxation with imagery technique "hypnosis." This label, however, had negative connotations for many patients. As discussed by Redd, Rosenberger, and Hendler (1982), some patients feel that if the nausea can be controlled through hypnosis, the nausea must be psychological in origin, not the result of toxic drugs. These patients then assume they are emotionally or mentally weak and should be able to "tough it out" or gain psychological control over the nausea on their own. Additionally, some patients fear hypnosis because of its treatment in popular literature and entertainment as a method of mind control. Those patients who have ever observed hypnosis have typically witnessed hypnotic subjects behaving in an embarrassing manner (one patient asked if he would act like a chicken). These portrayals have led patients to refuse to participate in our treatment procedure and to opt instead to continue to suffer from the side effects of chemotherapy or even to refuse continued drug treatment.

For many patients the loss of personal autonomy and the feelings of helplessness regarding the disease are psychologically debilitating. This loss of personal control is emphasized by the use of the term *hypnosis.* In a study by Hendler and Redd (1985) 100 patients were interviewed to assess their beliefs about hypnosis and relaxation as well as their willingness to try a behavioral procedure. Patients were randomly assigned to groups receiving identical descriptions of a behavioral intervention labeled either "hypnosis," "relaxation," or "passive relaxation with guided imagery." The results of this study indicated that patients believed hypnosis involved an unconscious, powerful state resulting in a loss of control. They were significantly less likely to be willing to try the technique than were patients in the other two label conditions. This was true independently of the patients' degree of nausea, vomiting, and pain due to chemotherapy treatments. Thus it is clear that the very name of the intervention is an important component in whether or not patients will cooperate with and benefit from behavioral adjunctive treatment.

Behavioral interventions have been shown effective in reducing the fear and anxiety associated with chemotherapy and other noxious medical procedures, as well as eliminating anticipatory nausea and vomiting. However, there is still much work to be done to make these interventions more widely available and cost-effective. Both patient and staff education programs are necessary to demystify the interventions and to describe their effectiveness. This educational effort can also address the common misconception that the patient who needs behavioral interventions is "weak" or, worse yet, "crazy." Accurate understanding of the respondent conditioning that causes anticipatory nausea by both staff and patients will help dispel these false beliefs.

The use of nonpsychology personnel such as oncology nurses, hospital-based social workers, and family members as primary therapists to make the interventions more widely available and cost-effective needs further exploration. The chemotherapy nurse would seem a logical choice for teaching the relaxation techniques described earlier in this chapter to reduce both the fear and pain associated with the treatments and the anticipatory nausea. One might speculate that the nurse's role in providing this welcomed relief for the oncology patient might contribute to less professional burnout and staff turnover on chemotherapy units.

The involvement of family members in the adjunctive treatment of the pediatric patient can reap benefits for both the patients and the family members. As discussed in the section on pediatric interventions, this involvement is a fruitful area for future research. It is clear at this point that behavioral interventions have multiple possibilities that have only begun to be explored.

Future Directions

During the relatively brief history of behavior therapy (since the mid-1960s), anxiety management has been of primary interest. From systematic desensitization and progressive muscle relaxation to biofeedback and cognitive therapies to reduce stress, behavioral clinicians have sought to understand and control both acute and chronic anxiety. This interest has even increased with the advent of behavioral medicine. In the case of cancer, the highly aggressive and invasive treatment regimens are nearly always associated with significant pain and anxiety. Patients often report that since their diagnosis their lives are dominated by worry and dread. Indeed, some patients find the treatment worse than the disease itself.

For these reasons the first area of study in behavioral oncology has been the reduction of patient distress. This work has involved the application of both operant (i.e., positive reinforcement of compliance and effective coping and self-control procedures), and respondent (i.e., passive and active relaxation, hypnosis, and desensitization) procedures. They have also been systematically integrated in comprehensive behavioral programs to control children's distress. These applications have introduced both theoretical and clinical issues that are likely to dominate research in the field and affect the focus of behavioral medicine in the future.

The first issue concerns the mechanisms underlying behavioral control of anxiety, pain and somatic symptoms associated with invasive procedures. Does it simply involve physiological relaxation, or is cognitive distraction the controlling mechansim? All the techniques that have been used to control patient distress have involved a combination of anxiety control and distraction techniques. Programs using relaxation training, hypnosis, and biofeedback have all involved the use of imagery in conjunction with relaxation. In all cases the imagery is designed to engage the patient in thoughts *unrelated* to the treatment being administered. In our ongoing research we are investigating distraction techniques that do not involve relaxation. In this work children play video games during chemotherapy infusions. Preliminary results strongly suggest that such cognitive distraction is effective. What is more, physiological measures (i.e., heart rate and blood pressure) indicate that arousal may actually increase when patients are engaged in video game playing; yet their subjective experience is that of relaxation and absence of pain and/or nausea. Indeed, effective behavioral symptom control may be possible in the absence of physiological relaxation. Garcia (1985, personal communication) has argued that the primary beneficial effect of relaxation exercises in controlling pain and distress control may be distraction. If our research findings continue to be replicated, we might well conclude that the introduction of active distraction tasks during painful or anxiety-provoking procedures may be more cost-effective and easier to implement than traditional relaxation training. Our preliminary results indicate that this is particularly true with children. Anxiety control during invasive medical procedures may require active coping rather than desensitization. Indeed, as was suggested earlier, when the threat is real and the anxiety is a natural response to aversive stimulation, desensitization may be fruitless. The desensitized patient may simply be resensitized during subsequent treatments.

Another area of behavioral medicine that will be increasingly important in the future, as behavioral medicine gains wider acceptance in medicine, is its integration with other methods. Rather than behavioral intervention being the exclusive domain of the psychologist, it appears that nurses and other direct care personnel are eager to learn how to implement behavioral programs. Indeed, attendance at professional workshops is heavy and often dominated by those in nursing and rehabilitation. The broadening domain may also include parents and other family members.

The future of behavioral medicine to control anxiety and distress in medical patients is wide. Behavioral intervention methods offer techniques whose effectiveness can be demonstrated in concrete terms. It is our experience that medical personnel and the patients they treat are open to behavioral intervention. In fact, they welcome it.

References

Altmaier, E. M., Ross, W. E., & Moore, K. (1982). A pilot investigation of the psychologic function of patients with anticipatory vomiting. *Cancer, 49*, 201–204.

Andrykowski, M. A., & Redd, W. H. (in press). Life-threatening disease: Biopsychosocial dimensions of cancer care. In R. L. Morrison & A. S. Bellack (Eds.), *Medical factors and psychological disorders: A handbook for psychologists*. New York: Plenum Press.

Andrykowski, M. A., Redd, W. H., & Hatfield, A. K. (1985). The development of anticipatory nausea: A prospective analysis. *Journal of Consulting Clinical Psychology, 53*, 447–454.

Averill, J. R. (1973). Personal control over aversive stimuli and its relationship to stress. *Psychological Bulletin, 80*, 286–303.

Bernstein, D. A., & Borkovec, T. D. (1973). *Progressive relaxation training: A manual for the helping professions*, Champaign, IL: Research Press.

Bloom, K. (1975). Social elicitation of infant social behavior. *Journal of Experimental Child Psychology, 20*, 51–58.

Bloom. K. (1977). Patterning of infant vocal behavior. *Journal of Experimental Child Psychology, 23*, 367–377.

Burish, T. G., & Lyles, J. N. (1979). Effectiveness of relaxation training in reducing the aversiveness of chemotherapy in the treatment of cancer. *Behavior Therapy and Experimental Psychiatry, 10*, 357–361.

Burish, T. G., & Lyles, J. N. (1981). Effectiveness of relaxation training in reducing adverse reactions to cancer chemotherapy. *Journal of Behavioral Medicine, 4*, 65–78.

Burish, T. G., & Lyles, J. N. (1983). Coping with the adverse effects of cancer treatments. In T. G. Burish & J. N. Lyles (Eds.), *Coping with chronic disease: Research and applications*. New York: Academic Press.

Burish, T. G., Shartner, C. D., & Lyles, J. N. (1981). Effectiveness of multiple muscle-site EMG biofeedback and relaxation training in reducing the aversiveness of cancer chemotherapy. *Biofeedback and Self-Regulation, 6*, 523–535.

Chang, J. C. (1981). Nausea and vomiting in cancer patients: An expression of psychological mechanisms. *Psychosomatic, 22*, 707–709.

Clapp, M. J. (1976). Psychosocial reactions of children with cancer. *Nursing Clinics of North America, 11*, 73–82.

Dash, J. (1980). Hypnosis for symptom amelioration. In J. Kellerman (Ed.), *Psychological aspects of childhood cancer*. Springfield, IL: Charles C Thomas.

Dempster, C. R., Balson, P., & Whalen, B. T. (1976). Supportive hypnotherapy during the radical treatment of malignancies. *International Journal of Clinical and Experimental Hypnosis, 24*, 1–9.

Derogatis, L. R., Morrow, G. R., Fetting, J., Penman, D., Piasetsky, S., Schmale, A. M., Henrichs, M., & Carnicke, C. L., Jr. (1983). The prevalence of psychiatric disorders among cancer patients. *Journal of the American Medical Association, 249*, 751–757.

Diener, C. I. (1984). *Controlling the behavioral side effects of cancer treatment*. Urbana, IL: Norman Baxley and Associates.

Diener, C. I., & Ambuel, B. (1985). *Developmental and familial considerations in behavioral interventions in pediatric oncology*. Unpublished manuscript, University of Illinois, Urbana.

Easson, W. M. (1970). *The dying child*. Springfield, IL: Charles C Thomas.

Erikson, E. (1959). Identity and the life cycle. *Psychological Issues*, Monograph 1. New York: International Universities Press.

Fetting, J. H., Wilcox, P. M., Iwata, B. A., Criswell, E. L., Bosmajian, L. S., & Sheidler, V. R. (1983). Anticipatory nausea and vomiting in an ambulatory oncology population. *Cancer Treatment Reports, 67*, 1093–1098.

Freidenbergs, I., Gordon, W. A., Hibbard, M., & Diller, L. (1980). Assessment and treatment of psychosocial problems of the cancer patient: A case study. *Cancer Nursing, 3*, 111–119.

Goldberg, R., & Tull, R. M. (1983). *The psychosocial dimensions of cancer*. New York: Free Press.

Gordon, W. A., Freidenbergs, I., Diller, L., Hibbard, M., Wolf, C., Levine, L., Lipkins, R., Ezrachi, O., & Lucido, D. (1980). Efficacy of psychosocial intervention with cancer patients. *Journal of Consulting and Clinical Psychology, 48*, 743–759.

Hendler, C. S., & Redd, W. (1986). *Fear of hypnosis: The role of labeling the patients' acceptance of behavioral interventions*. Behavior Therapy, 17, 2–13.

Hilgard, J. R., & LeBaron, S. (1984). *Hypnotherapy of pain in children with cancer*. Los Altos, CA: William Kaufman.

Illich, I. (1976). *Medical nemesis*. New York: Random House.

Ingle, R. J., Burish, T. G., & Wallston, K. A. (1984). Conditionability of cancer chemotherapy patients. *Oncology Nursing Forum, 11*, 97–102.

Jay, S. M., & Elliott, C. H. (1983). Psychological intervention for pain in pediatric cancer patients. In G. B. Humphrey, L. P. Dehner, G. B. Grindley, & R. T. Acton (Eds.), *Pediatric oncology* (Vol. 3). Boston: Martinus Neijhoff.

Jay, S. M., Elliott, C. H., Ozolins, M., & Olson, R. A. (1982). *Behavioral management of children's distress during painful medical procedures*. Paper presented at the American Psychological Association Convention, Washington, DC.

Jay, S. M., Ozolins, M., Elliot, C. H., & Caldwell, S. (1983). Assessment of children's distress during painful medical procedures. *Health Psychology, 2*, 133–147.

Katz, E. R., Kellerman, J., & Siegel, S. E. (1980). Behavioral distress in children with cancer undergoing medical procedures: Developmental considerations. *Journal of Consulting and Clinical Psychology, 43*, 356–365.

Kellerman, J. (1980). Comprehensive psychosocial care of the child with cancer: Description of a program. In J. Kellerman (Ed.), *Psychological aspects of childhood cancer*. Springfield, IL: Charles C Thomas.

Kellerman, J., & Katz, E. R. (1977). The adolescent with cancer: Theoretical, clinical and research issues. *Journal of Pediatric Psychology, 2,* 127–131.

Kellerman, J., Zeltzer, L., Ellenberg, L., & Dash, J. (1983). Adolescents with cancer: Hypnosis for the reduction of the acute pain and anxiety associated with medical procedures. *Journal of Adolescent Health Care, 4,* 85–90.

Klorman, R., Hilpert, P. L., Michael, R., LeGana, C., & Sveen, O. B. (1980). Effects of coping and mastery modeling on experienced and inexperienced pedodontic patients' disruptiveness. *Behavior Therapy, 11*(2), 156–168.

LaBaw, W., Holton, C., Tewell, K., & Eccles, D. (1975). The use of self-hypnosis by children with cancer. *American Journal of Clinical Hypnosis, 17,* 233–238.

Lazarus, A. A., & Abramovitz, A. (1962). The use of "emotive imagery" in the treatment of children's phobias. *Journal of Mental Science, 108,* 191–195.

Lazslo, J. (1983). *Antiemetics and cancer chemotherapy.* Baltimore, MD: Williams and Wilkins.

Lyles, J. N., Burish, T. G., Krozely, M. G., & Oldham, R. K. (1982). Efficacy of relaxation training and guided imagery in reducing the aversiveness of cancer chemotherapy. *Journal of Consulting and Clinical Psychology, 50,* 509–524.

McNamara, J. (Ed.). (1979). *Behavioral approaches to medicine.* New York: Plenum Press.

Melamed, B. G., & Siegel, L. J. (1980). *Behavioral Medicine.* New York: Springer.

Meyerowitz, B. E., Sparks, F. C., & Spears, I. N. (1979). Adjuvant chemotherapy for breast carcinoma: Psychosocial implication. *Cancer, 43,* 1613–1616.

Morrow, G. R. (1982). Prevalence and correlates of anticipatory nausea and vomiting in chemotherapy patients. *Journal of the National Cancer Institute, 68,* 484–488.

Morrow, G. R., & Morrell, B. S. (1982). Behavioral treatment for the anticipatory nausea and vomiting induced by cancer chemotherapy. *New England Journal of Medicine, 307,* 1476–1480.

Nerenz, D. R., Leventhal, H., & Love, R. (1982). Factors contributing to emotional distress during cancer chemotherapy. *Cancer, 50,* 1020–1027.

Nicholas, D. R. (1982). Prevalence of anticipatory nausea and emesis in cancer chemotherapy patients. *Journal of Behavioral Medicine, 5,* 461–463.

Olness, K. (1981). Imagery (self-hypnosis) as adjunct therapy in childhood cancer: Clinical experience with 25 patients. *American Journal of Pediatric Hematology/Oncology, 3,* 313–321.

Plumb, M. M., & Holland, J. (1977). Comparative studies of psychological function in patients with advanced cases of self-reported depressive symptoms. *Journal of Psychosomatic Medicine, 39,* 264–276.

Redd, W. H. (1980). *In vivo* desensitization in the treatment of chronic emesis following gastrointestinal surgery. *Behavior Therapy, 11,* 421–427.

Redd, W. H. (in press, a). *Behavioral intervention to reduce child distress.* Memorial Sloan-Kettering Cancer Center Psychology/Oncology Handbook.

Redd, W. H. (in press, b). Common physical problems and their nonpharmacologic management: Nausea and vomiting with chemotherapy. *Memorial Sloan-Kettering Handbook in Psychosocial Oncology.*

Redd, W. H., Andresen, G. V., & Minagawa, R. Y. (1982). Hypnotic control of anticipatory emesis in patients receiving cancer chemotherapy. *Journal of Consulting and Clinical Psychology, 50,* 14–19.

Redd, W. H., & Andrykowski, M. A. (1982). Behavioral intervention in cancer treatment: Controlling aversion reactions to chemotherapy. *Journal of Consulting and Clinical Psychology, 50,* 1018–1029.

Redd, W. H., & Hendler, C. S. (1983). Behavioral medicine in comprehensive cancer treatment. *Journal of Psychosocial Oncology, 1*(2), 3–17.

Redd, W. H., Rosenberger, P. H., & Hendler, C. S. (1982). Controlling chemotherapy side effects. *American Journal of Clinical Hypnosis, 25,* 161–172.

Schain, W. (1976). Psychosocial issues in counseling and mastectomy patients. *The Counseling Psychologist, 6,* 45–49.

Seigel, L. J., & Longo, D. L. (1981). The control of chemotherapy-induced emesis. *Annals of Internal Medicine, 95,* 352–359.

Slavin, L. A. (1981). Evolving psychosocial issues in the treatment of childhood cancer: A review. In G. P. Koocher & J. E. O'Malley (Eds.), *The Damocles syndrome: Psychosocial consequences of surviving childhood cancer.* New York: McGraw-Hill.

Thompson, S. C. (1981). Will it hurt less if I can control it? A complex answer to a simple question. *Psychological Bulletin, 90*, 89–101.

van Komen, R. W., & Redd, W. H. (1985). Personality factors associated with the development of anticipatory nausea/vomiting in patients receiving cancer chemotherapy. *Health Psychology, 4*, 189–202.

Wilcox, P. M., Fetting, J. H., Nettesheim, K. M., & Abeloff, M. D. (1982). Anticipatory vomiting in women receiving Cyclophosphamide, Methotrexate, and 5-FU (CMF) adjuvant chemotherapy for breast carcinoma. *Cancer Treatment Reports, 66*, 1601–1604.

Zeltzer, L. (1980). The adolescent with cancer. In J. Kellerman (Ed.), *Psychological aspects of childhood cancer.* Springfield, IL: Charles C Thomas.

Zeltzer, L., Kellerman, J., Ellenberg, L., & Dash, J. (1983). Hypnosis for reduction of vomiting associated with chemotherapy and disease in adolescents with cancer. *Journal of Adolescent Health Care, 4*, 77–84.

Zeltzer, L., LeBaron, S., & Zeltzer, P. (1982). Children on chemotherapy: Reduction of nausea and vomiting with behavioral intervention. *Clinical Research, 30*, 138A.

Zeltzer, L., Zeltzer, P. M., & LeBaron, S. (1982). Cancer in adolescents. In M. S. Smith (Ed.), *Chronic disorders in adolescence.* Acton, MA: PSG Publishing Company.

21

Essential Hypertension: A Methodological Review

ROBERT A. DiTOMASSO

Hypertension (elevated arterial blood pressure) is a major chronic life-threatening disorder in our society (Herd & Weiss, 1984). In the classic *Harrison's Principles of Internal Medicine*, Williams and Braunwald (1983) have noted: "An elevated arterial pressure is probably the most important public health problem in developed countries—being common, asymptomatic, readily detectable, usually easily treatable, and often leading to lethal complications if left untreated" (p. 1475). In view of its potential consequences, the early detection and treatment of hypertension is a major health care concern today. Little wonder, then, that the assessment and management of this disorder have been the focus of scores of investigations in medicine and clinical health psychology.

Definition

According to the most recent report by the Joint National Committee on Detection, Evaluation, and Treatment of High Blood Pressure (U.S. Department of Health and Human Services, 1984), hypertension is defined as blood pressure exceeding 140/90 mm Hg. The diagnosis of hypertension is not confirmed unless, however, one of two conditions is met: either (1) the mean of two or more diastolic readings on at least two subsequent visits must equal or exceed 90 mm Hg, *or* (2) the mean of multiple systolic readings on two or more subsequent visits must consistently exceed 140 mm Hg (U.S. Department of Health and Human Services, 1984).

Classification

The scheme for categorizing hypertension is based on diastolic or systolic blood pressure levels within specified ranges (U.S. Department of Health and Human Services, 1984). Based on diastolic readings, there are three categories: mild hypertension (90–104 mm Hg), moderate hypertension (104–114 mm Hg), and severe hypertension (115 mm Hg or higher). Based on systolic pressure and when the diastolic reading is below 90 mm Hg, there are two categories: borderline isolated systolic hypertension (140–159 mm Hg) and isolated systolic hypertension (160 mm Hg and higher).

Robert A. DiTomasso. West Jersey Health System Family Practice Residency Program, Tatem-Brown Family Practice Center, Voorhees, New Jersey.

Etiology

Hypertension is classified as either primary or secondary in nature. At present, the etiology of primary, idiopathic, or essential hypertension, which makes up 90–95% of the cases, remains unknown. Secondary hypertension may result from a number of causes, including renal disease (renal hypertension), endocrine problems (e.g., primary aldosteronism), arotic coarctation (narrowing), and adrenal tumor (Shaprio & Goldstein, 1982; Williams & Braunwald, 1983).

Incidence

Seer (1979) has proposed that the incidence of hypertension in our society is at epidemic proportions, with estimates ranging from 10% to 30% of the adult population being affected. Similarly, McMahon (1984) reported that between 15% and 25% of adults surveyed suffer from hypertension. Prevalence estimates are dependent on the demographic characteristics of the population studied, as well as the basic criteria used to define the condition. For example, in a white suburban population, whereas one in five people would have blood pressure exceeding 160/95, more than two in five people would have blood pressures greater than 140/90 (Williams & Braunwald, 1983).

Risks of Hypertension

There are clearly documented risks for mortality and morbidity associated with hypertension. Patients suffering from moderate and severe hypertension exhibit an increased morbidity and mortality from several diseases, most especially the cardiovascular diseases. Based on the Framingham study (Kannel, 1976), hypertension was found to be predictive of myocardial infarction, congestive heart failure, and stroke, as well as damage to the kidneys, eyes, and other organs. Of critical import, risks for mortality and morbidity increase in direct proportion to increases in blood pressure. Moreover, systolic and diastolic blood pressure appear to be of equal importance.

Treatment

The major aim of treatment for hypertension is simply to reduce patient risks for mortality and morbidity. A variety of treatment methods are available today, including: pharmacotherapy; cognitive behavior therapy (relaxation training, biofeedback, stress management); weight reduction; sodium restriction; moderation in alcohol and caffeine consumption; physical exercise; and drug compliance (Shapiro & Goldstein, 1982; U.S. Department of Health and Human Services, 1984). During the past 25 years pharmacotherapy has been clearly demonstrated as an efficacious treatment for mild, moderate, and severe hypertension. In reports published in the late 1960s by the Veterans Administration Cooperative Study Group on Antihypertensive Agents (1967, 1970), pharmacotherapy reduced cardiovascular mortality and morbidity in both moderate and severe hypertensives. Similarly, the positive benefits of antihypertensive drugs have been demonstrated in mild hypertensives. In a recent meta-analysis of 51 outcome studies with mildly hypertensive patients (Andrews, MacMahon, Austin, & Byrne, 1982), drug therapy was clearly superior to nondrug treatments. Drug therapy demonstrated an average effect size of 2.9, which was maintained at the end of a 27-week interval from treatment to assessment. Despite the documented effectiveness of pharmacotherapy, the search for nonpharmacological alternatives and adjunctive treatments (Shapiro & Goldstein, 1982; Seer, 1979) was initiated for a variety of reasons. First, because pharmacotherapy is not effective in all patients, adjunctive therapy must be considered. Second, patient nonadherence, particularly among hypertensives, is well documented. Third, antihypertensive drugs are associated with aversive side effects. Bulpitt and Dollery (1973) administered a side effects questionnaire to 477 patients in a hypertension clinic who reported one or more of a variety of symptoms including sleepiness, limb weakness, nocturnal awakening to urinate, postural hypotension, impotence, ejaculatory failure, and increased defecation. Also, in a recent issue of *The Medical Letter* (1983) antihypertensive agents were noted as probably interfering with sexual functioning more than any other class of drugs. Fourth, some patients simply prefer not to take medication. Finally, in view of some recent evidence suggesting that hydrochlorothiazide and other diuretics may place patients at increased risk for cardiac abnormalities (e.g., multifocal premature ventricular contractions, and sudden death), Wadden and Stunkard (1982) have urged caution and emphasized the benefits of behavioral interventions. In light of recent interest in the behavioral treatment of essential hypertension, numerous investigators in the area of behavioral medicine have attempted to evaluate empirically the efficacies of various treatments.

In this chapter, then, the clinical outcome research on the cognitive-behavioral treatment of essential hypertension will be critically analyzed and reviewed, and future directions for research in this area will be considered. The term *cognitive-behavioral treatment* will be restricted to relaxation therapy, biofeedback training, and stress management training. Particular emphasis will be given to the methodological characteristics of these studies by highlighting their strengths and limitations. The relative efficacies of these treatments will thus be considered within the parameters on internal and external validity set by the research studies aimed at evaluating clinical significance.

The present methodological analysis will be organized according to a variety of carefully selected criteria as outlined in Table 21.1. For each study an entry was made in order to determine the specific characteristics of the study with respect to treatment conditions, sample demographics, diagnostic verification, concurrent pharmacotherapy and whether it was stabilized, the blood pressure assessment process, the research design and measurement paradigm, treatment delivery, and follow-up. These specific criteria were carefully chosen in order to pinpoint the exact methodological strengths and shortcomings evidenced in this body of literature. The value of such an approach is to extract the meaning of a large number of studies within the limits set by the methodological character or rigor of the studies making up an area—in this case, the treatment of hypertension. The identification of trends within this area clearly serves the function of identifying recommendations for refining subsequent investigations.

Clinical researchers often face seemingly insurmountable tasks (DiTomasso & McDermott, 1981) and consequently must make decisions in the design and implementation of investigations that in many instances compromise the integrity of a study. Many real and practical problems in applied research necessitate a justifiable departure from what would be considered methodologically ideal. With these points in mind the view of Mahoney (1978) that the perfect experiment is inconceivable, and would be impossible to conduct even if it were conceivable, is well taken. The categorization of the outcome studies within each subsequent section is based on the type of design of the study, ranging from anecdotal reports and case studies at the lower end of the continuum of rigor to the controlled between-groups outcome studies at the higher end, a scheme previously described by Blanchard (1979).

Relaxation Therapies

Single-Subject Experiments

In probably the earliest single-subject experimental evaluation of relaxation for hypertension, Brady, Luborsky, and Kron (1974) studied the effects of metronome-conditioned relaxation (MCR) on diastolic blood pressure (DBP) in four essential hypertensives. The design was an ABA for two subjects and an ABAB for the other two subjects. Details related to the treatment regarding delivery, monitoring, and experimenter were ambiguous. Mean DBP reductions during treatment phase 1 were 2.8, 0, 5.9, and 4.8. For those two subjects who received a second treatment phase, mean reductions comparing baseline 1 to treatment phase 2 were 11.0/9.5 mm Hg.

In a study with a simpler design, Beinman, Graham, and Ciminero (1978a) evaluated the effects of relaxation training in two male hypertensives. Patient 1 was a 35-year-old male with a 3-year history of elevated blood pressure who had previously been on four different antihypertensives; patient 2, a 27-year-old male with a 5-year history who refused medication. Each patient was treated with self-control relaxation training, a modified self-control technique for tension reduction. Patients were instructed to practice at home twice a day until differential relaxation was introduced. During the phase of differential relaxation, each patient was assisted in focusing on internal and external anxiety cues, which were to be used as cues for relaxation. Average blood pressure reductions were 14.9/15.9 and 17.5/9.4 mm Hg for patients 1 and 2, respectively. Follow-up measures were gathered at 1, 2, and 6 months follow-up for patient 1 and at 1 and 2 months for patient 2. Blood pressures were maintained in the normotensive range for each patient at his respective follow-up level.

In a follow-up of a patient, Beinman, Graham, and Ciminero (1978b) studied the effect of treatment generalization in the 35-year-old patient just discussed. Despite blood pressure reductions in the psychology clinic and natural environment, this patient continued to exhibit elevated blood pressure in the medical setting. The patient received five sessions of self-control systematic desensitization. Data were collected by a trained research assistant, who was kept blind to the purpose of the study. At posttreatment, the patient exhibited reduced blood pressure in the medical setting, paralleled by reductions on psychophysiological measures. Prior to the initiation of desensitization, the patient never experienced a blood pressure in the normotensive range in the medical setting.

TABLE 21.1 Outcome characteristics of studies on the cognitive-behavioral treatment of essential hypertension

Study	Conditions	N	Age	Sex	Dx	Meds	Meds stable	BP assessment	Design	Outcome
Relaxation therapy: Single-subject experiments										
Brady et al. (1974)	MCR	4	33.2	4M	Y	N Except 1 S	Y	Same technician; self-recorded	ABA; ABAB	1. DBP: B1 > A1; B2 > A2 2. DBP: A1 − B1 = −2.8, −5.9, −4.8 A1 − B2 = 11.0, 9.5 A2 − B2 = −13.5, −9.5
Benman et al. (1978a)	SCRT	2	35 and 27	2M	Y	N	—	*In vivo*; in session	AB With F-up	S1: Avg. S/D Change = −14.9/−15.9; at follow-up, normotensive at 1, 2, and 6 months S2: Avg. S/D change = −17.5/−9.4; at follow-up, normotensive at 1, 2 mo.
Benman et al. (1978b)	SD	1	35	1M	Y	N	—	?	ABAC	1. BP Reduction to normotensive range 2. Anxiety reduction
Agras et al. (1980)	PMR	5	62	4M, 1F	Y	N	—	Infrasonde recorder; independent readers; calibrated	ABA	1. Avg. S/D change = −7.3/−5.1 2. Generalized BP lowering beyond therapy
Martin & Epstein (1980)	R	2	28; 24	2F	?	1Y; 1N	?	*In vivo*; in session	MBD-SS	S1: Control over DBP S2: Control over SBP 2. At follow-up; improvement to normo-tensive
Controlled between-groups outcome: Relaxation versus no-treatment control										
Stone & DeLeo (1976)	1. PSR 2. C	19	1. 28 2. 28	17M, 2F	Y	N	—	Independent blind observer	CBGOS; NR	1. PSR post > PSR pre 2. PSR SBP/DBP > C SBP/DBP; avg. change supine = −13.4/−10.1 and up = −13.9/−10.1 3. PSR post DBH > PSR pre DBH 4. PSR DBH > C DBH 5. BP and DBH changes correlated supine (r = .54) and upright (r = .62)
Southam et al. (1982)	1. RT 2. NTC	42	50.7	28M, 14F	Y	Y (67%)	N	Automated; blind independent readers	CBGOS; R; S	1. RT avg. SBP/DBP clinic change = −11.7/−12.6; NTC, −3.6/−2.5 RT avg. SBP/DBP work site change = −7.8/−4.6; NTC, −0.1/+1.7 2. RT SBP/DBP clinic > NTC SBP/DBP; RT SBP/DBP work site > NTC SBP/DBP 3. At follow-up, RT DBP > NTC DBP; RT avg. change = −6.0/−12.1 & NTC Avg. change = +1.3/−2.2

Study	Treatments	N	Age	Gender				BP measurement	Design	Results
Pender (1984)	1. PMR 2. C	44	1. 54.4 2. 55.6	1. 11M, 11F 2. 9M, 13F	Y	1. Y, 7SS 2. Y, 13SS	Y	Mercury sphygmomanometer; Gulf & Western, calibrated	CBGOS; M	1. PMR avg. change = −8.0 2. Base to follow-up: PMR sig. Lower SBP/DBP
Deabler et al. (1973)	1. C 2. R+HYP-ND 3. R+HYP-D	21	45.7 (23–65)	?	?	Y, 12SS	?	Automated; compared to manual	CBGOS; R	1. R+HYP-ND: during hyp avg. SBP decline of 17%; C = No change R+HYP-D: during R avg. SBP decline = 9 to 15%; during HYP, 16% 2. R+HYP-ND: during R avg. DBP decline = 15.5%; during HYP, 19.5% R+HYP-D: during R avg. DBP decline = 3–10%; during HYP, 14% C: no change
Relaxation versus placebo										
Brauer et al. (1979)	1. PMR-Th 2. PMR-Audio 3. NIP	29	1. 54.9 2. 59.2 3. 57.8	1. 8M, 2F 2. 8M, 1F 3. 9M, 1F	Y	Y	N	Blind experienced nurses	CBGOS; R	1. At post and follow-up avg. SBP/DBP change: PMR-Th = −11.0/−6.1, −17.8/−9.7 PMR-Audio = −5.3/−1.0, +.7/−4.3 NIP = 8.8/−4.5, −1.6/−1.1 Between: at post, PMR-Th = PMR-Audio = NIP At follow-up, on SBP PMR-Th > PMR-audio = NIP; on DBP, PMR-Th = Audio = NIP 2. PMR-Th post DBP > PMR-Th pre DBP PMR-Th follow-up SBP/DBP > PMR-Th pre SBP/DBP
Bali (1979)	1. PMR 2. BSP	18	1. 37.3 2. 37.3	18M	Y	N	—	Mercury manometer	CBGOS; M+R	1. PMR avg. sig. SBP/DBP change = −12/−9 and anxiety reduction 2. Replication when controls treated 3. At follow-up, results maintained 4. BSP: no sig. effect
Cottier et al. (1984)	1. PMR 2. PC	26	1. 34.1 2. 35.8	1. 12M, 5F 2. 5M, 2F	Y	N	—	Automated	CBGOS	1. Home BP: PMR > PC; avg. PMR BP change = −3 and PC = −2 2. Clinic BP: PMR = PC 3. Plasma epinephrine PMR > PC 4. O_2 consumption: PMR post > PMR pre

(*continued*)

TABLE 21.1 (Continued)

Study	Conditions	N	Age	Sex	Dx	Meds	Meds stable	BP assessment	Design	Outcome
				Relaxation versus relaxation						
Nath & Rinehart (1979)	1. PMR-I 2. PMR-G	15	26–52	1. 4M, 5F 2. 2M, 4F	Y	Y	Y	Aneroid sphygmomanometer	BGOS; NR	1. PMR-I = PMR-C 2. PMR post SBP > PMR pre SBP 3. PMR avg. SBP/DBP change = −8.73/−5.0 4. PMR postsession SBP/DBP > PMR pre
Agras et al. (1982)	1. RT-IE 2. RT-DE	30	1. 55.1 2. 52.7	1. 5M, 10F 2. 4M, 11F	Y	Y	Y	Blind instructor	CBGOS; R; CR	1. RT-IE avg. SBP/DBP pre-post change = −17.0/−7.1; RT-DE = −2.4/−6.3 RT-IE SBP > RT-DE SBP, RT-IE DBP = RT-DE DBP 2. Three-session avg: RT-IE avg. SBP/DBP change = −7.0/−2.4; RT-DE = −2.4/−96 RT-IE SBP > RT-DE SBP, RT-IE DBP = RT-DE DBP
Wadden (1983)	1. PMR-I 2. PMR-C	31	21–65	1. 7M, 9F 2. 8M, 7F	Y	Y	Y	Trained nurses; interobserver reliability; responsible for same patients	BGOS	1. PMR-C > PMR-I on relaxation compliance 2. PMR-I = PMR-C 3. PMR avg. SBP/DBP pre-post change = −6.4/−5.2 4. Higher BP correlated with larger SBP/DBP reductions 5. Generalization from clinic to home 6. Negative correlation between BP decline and type-A measures
Wadden (1984)	RT-SA RT-C CT-C	48	21–65	1. 7M, 9F 2. 8M, 7F 3. 6M, 3F	Y	Y, 32SS	Y	Trained nurses; interobserver reliability, responsible for some patients	CBGOS-S-R	1. RT-SA = RT-C = CT-C 2. Avg. SBP/DBP pre-post change = −6.9/−5.2 3. Avg. SBP post follow-up change sustained; avg. DBP post follow-up sig. change = −2.2 4. Sig. reduction in post anxiety and depression 5. Initial SBP and DBP significant predicted post, 1-, and 5-mo. follow-up and 1-mo. follow-up respectively

Relaxation versus biofeedback

Study	Conditions	N	Age	Sex				Measurement	Classification	Results
Goldstein, Shaprio, & Thananopavaran (1984)	1. R 2. R+EMG 3. R-ND 4. SMC	58	1. 53.9 2. 52.2 3. 53.2 4. 52.8	1. 10M, 3F 2. 11M, 3F 3. 13M, 4F 4. 12M, 2F	Y	Y, 4ISS	Y	Automated; calibrated; in session; *in vivo*	CBGOS; M	1. On morn. SBP/DBP R = R + EMG > SMC R-ND > SMC. 2. On eve. SBP R + EMG > SMC & R-ND; on eve. DBP, R & R + EMG > SMC. 3. Avg. SBP/DBP changes: R = −8.6/−4.0; R+EMG = −7.6/−4.7 R-ND = −3.8/−3.7 SMC = +3.2/+.4
Shoemaker & Tasto (1975)	1. MR 2. BPBF-N 3. WLC	15	?	?	N	?	?	Automated	CBGOS; R	1. Avg. SBP/DBP changes: MR = −6.8/−7.6, BPBF-N = 6/−1.2, WLC = 1.6/1.2. 2. Pre–post analysis: on SBP, no sig. change; on DBP, MR and BPBF-N, sig. change
Walsh et al. (1977)	1. APWV-BF 2. PR	24	24–69	1. 15M, 9F 2. 9M, 7F	?	Y, 50%	?	Automated	CBGOS; M+R	1. DBP during sessions; APWV-BF > PR. 2. SBP/DBP reductions over sessions phase 1: APWV-BF = PR. 3. Avg. DBP pre–post change: PR + meds. = −1.7, APWV-BF + no meds. = −4.83 APWV-BF + meds. = −2.4, PR + No meds. = .83
Goebel et al. (1980)	1. RO 2. R+EMG 3. BPBF 4. R+BPBF 5. TA	130	29–65	?	Y (almost all)	Phase 1, 2, 3 N, Y, N		Automated	CBGOS; R	1. Overall avg. BP change = −6.9/−4.4. 2. Sig. SBP/DBP decreases in each treatment group: controls, no charge. 3. No sig. between-group differences
Cohen & Sedlacek (1983)	1. EMG+TB+SRP 2. BRR 3. WLC	30	1. 47.4 2. 48.2 3. 37.8	1. 4M, 6F 2. 5M, 5F 3. 4M, 6F	Y but 3	Y		Recorded by therapists, patient, blind nurse	CBGOS; R	1. EMG+TB+SRP > BRR and WLC on field independence. 2. Avg. SBP/DBP base to post: EMG+TB+SRP = −13.0/−12.0; BRR returned to base; WLC, no change. 3. Sig. correlation between DBP change and embedded figures and picture completion

(continued)

527

TABLE 21.1 (*Continued*)

Study	Conditions	N	Age	Sex	Dx	Meds	Meds stable	BP assessment	Design	Outcome
Relaxation versus biofeedback (*continued*)										
Sedlacek et al. (1983)	1. BRR 2. EMG+T-BF 3. C	30	?	?	Y	Y, except 3	?	Self-recorded	CBGOS; R	1. Avg. SBP/DBP pre-post change: EMG+T-BF = −14/−12; avg. SBP/DBP pre follow-up change: EMG+T-BF = −8/−10 2. At follow-up, BP changes not significant 3. At follow-up SBP/DBP changes = +5/+1 4. Med. change: EMG + T-BF: 30% decreased by 50%
Case et al. (1980)	1. HYP-H 2. HYP-N 3. N HYP-H 4. N HYP-N	15	42.6	12M, 13F	?	N	—	Automated	CBGOS	1. Avg. % change: during HYP induction in hypertensive = +5.7/+4.4 & in normotensives = +3.6/+6.1; during self-hypnosis in BH = +7.2/+7.6
Friedman & Taub (1977)	1. HYP 2. BF 3. HYP + BF 4. MOC	48	1) 48.2 2) 47.1 3) 47.2 4) 48.3	8M, 2F 11M, 2F 10M, 3F 9M, 2F	Y	Y	Y	Automated	CBGOS; R	1. Avg. DBP pre-post changes; HYP = −8.2, MOC = −2.9, BF = −4.3, HYP + BF = −2.8, HYP > MOC & HYP + BF 2. Avg. DBP follow-up: HYP = −8.0, MOC = −2.8, HYP + BF = −4.0, HYP > MOC & HYP & BF
Yoga and meditation: Single-group outcome										
Datey et al. (1969)	Shav	47	46	37M, 10F	?	Y, almost all	Y	Regular intervals	SGOS	1. Avg. BP pre-post change: Non-med pts = −26.9 2. Avg. BP pre-post change: controlled med pts follow meds = −35; Med pts following meds + Shav = −37

Study	Groups	N	Age	Sex				Measurement	Code	Results
Sundar et al. (1984)	1. Shav 2. Shav+Med	25	1. 36.3 2. 45.4	1. 19M, 1F 2. 4M, 1F	Y	Y group 2	Y	Independent observer	TGOS	3. Avg. BP pre-post change: Uncontrolled med patients following meds = −27.2; med. patients following meds + Shav = −37.2 4. Med. reduction by 33%: in pts. adequately controlled = 13 of 22; in patients not adequately controlled = 6 of 15
Benson et al. (1974)	TM	22	43.1	1M, 12F	N	N	—	Random zero sphygmomanometer	SGOS	1. Avg. SBP/DBP pre-post change = −7.0/−3.8 2. TM post > TM pre
Blackwell et al. (1976)	TM	7	46.3	6M, 1F	Y	Y	Y	Clinic, work or home; trained nurses, fixed time	SGOS	1. Avg. SBP/DBP pre-post change: at home = −7.48/−6.09, in clinic = −4.16/−1.61 2. Avg. SBP/DBP pre follow-up change: at home = −12.98/−7.23, in clinic = −2.56/−4.03
Pollack et al. (1977)	TM	20	40.5	10M, 10F	Y	N except 9 pts	?	Mercury sphygmomanometer	SGOS	1. Avg. SBP change within 1st mo: TM = 8.9 2. Avg. SBP change during final 3 mo: no different from control value
Controlled between-groups outcome										
Seer & Raeburne (1980)	1. TM 2. Plac 3. WLC	41	43.2	23M, 18F	Y	N	—	Blind observer; random zero sphygmomanometer; fixed time; never preceded practice	CBGOS; R; CR	1. TM = Plac > WLC TM and Plac: Modest DBP Declines 2. At follow-up: TM and Plac sustained 3. Responders; higher initial BP

(continued)

TABLE 21.1 (Continued)

Study	Conditions	N	Age	Sex	Dx	Meds	Meds stable	BP assessment	Design	Outcome
					Biofeedback: Multiple-case studies					
Ford et al. (1983)	1. QRT-EMG and T-BF	15	?	?	Y	?	?	?	MCS	1. At follow-up: 5 of 15 (33%) in mod. improved, much improved, or recovered
Green & Green (1983)	TBF	12	44.2	4M, 8F	Y	Y except 5SS	?	?	MCS	1. Avg. SBP/DBP pre-post change = −7.18/−6.72 2. Avg. SBP/DBP pre follow-up change = −8.8/−16.6 3. Avg. med. index decreased to 0 for 6 patients at follow-up 4. Replicated with 55 E.H on meds; 85% med.-free
Lido & Arnold (1983)	BF-EMG and/or TBF+R	12	?	?	?	?	?	?	MCS	1. Follow-up: of 12 patients, 11 reported improvement; most recent SBP/DBP reported readings in normotensive range
					Single-group outcome					
Patel (1973)	Y and BF	20	57.35	11M, 9F	Y	Y except 1S	N	Clinical sphygmomanometer	SGOS	1. Avg. SBP/DBP pre-post change = −26/−16 2. Avg. med. requirement change = −41% 3. Subjective improvement reported
Patel (1976)	R+TM+BF	14	58.5	5M, 9F	?	Y except 1S	Y	Experienced nurse; random zero sphygmomanometer	SGOS	1. Avg. SBP/DBP pre-post change = −22.6/−13.4 2. Avg. serum cholesterol change = −24.5 mg/100 ml
Kleinman et al. (1977)	SBP-BF	8	49.3 (26–63)	8M	Y	N	—	Manual; automated self-recorded	SGOS	1. Avg. SBP/DBP pre-post change = −6.0/−8.0 SBP-BF post SBP = SBP-BF pre SBP SBP-BF post DBP > SBP-BF pre DBP 2. Avg. SBP/DBP pre-post session change: control session: −.5/−1.6 BF sessions = −4.4/−4.1 Avg. SBP declines during SBP-BF > control Avg. DBP declines during SBP-BF = control 3. At follow-up (n = 3), BP change maintained 4 mo.

Single-subject experiments — Controlled between-groups outcome: Biofeedback versus no-treatment control

Study	Conditions	N	Age (range)	Sex		Medication	BP measurement	Design	Results
Leigh (1978)	BF	17	40.5	?	?	Y, 7SS	?	SGOS	1. Avg. BP pre-post change = −6.8
Harrison et al (1979)	R+BF	22	42.3 (26–64)	14M, 8F	?	Y	Standard cuff method	SGOS	1. Avg. SBP/DBP pre-post change not significant
Single-subject experiments									
Benson et al. (1971)	BF	7	47.9 (30–54)	5M, 2F	Y	Y, except 1S	Automated	A-B (replicated)	1. Avg. SBP base TRT change = −16.5 individual S change = −3.5, −33.8, −29.2, −16.5, −16.1, −9, −17.3
Blanchard et al. (1975)	BF (visual)	4	39.25 (25–50)	3M, 1F	?	N except 2SS on diazepam	Automated	ABAB	1. Avg. SBP change: from A_1 to B_1 = −26.4, from B_1 to A_2 = +9.0; from A_2 to B_2 = −13.7; from B_2 to follow-up = +5.5
Kristt & Engel (1975)	SBP-BF	5 hospitalized patients	58.8 (46–70)	1M, 4F	Y	Y	Constant cuff method	ABA	1. Avg. SBP/DBP pre-post change = −18.2/−7.5
Controlled between-groups outcome: Biofeedback versus no-treatment control									
Elder et al (1973)	1. DBP-BF 2. DBP-BF+VR 3. C	18	23–59	18M	?	N, many Ss on CNS depressants	Automated; reliability checked	CBGOS; R	1. Avg. SBP/DBP pre to follow-up: −14.8/−12.1 2. On SBP DBP-BF = DBP-BF+VR = C on post and follow-up 3. On DBP post DBP-BF+VR > DBP-BF and C
Hager & Surwit (1978)	BP-BF TM+R (control)	30	?	15M, 15F	Y	Y	Automated	CBGOS; R	1. BP-BF = TM+R (control) Avg. within-session SBP/DBP change: −4.1/−1.6; BP-BF = TM+R
Frankel et al. (1978)	1. DBP-BF+FEMG-BF+AT+PR 2. BPBF-N 3. NTC	22	28–63	12M, 10F	Y	N, except 7Ss	Blind nurse	CBGOS; S + R	1. DBP-BF + FEMG-BF + AT + PR; Avg. pre-post change: supine = 0/−1.0, standing = +1/0. Avg. SBP/DBP pre-post change: DBP-BF + FEMG-BF + AT + PR = −3.2; BP-BF-N = −5/−2. 2. $r = 0$ between MMPI, EPI, ZMAC, JAS, BSS, and outcome
Blanchard et al. (1979)	1. BP-BF 2. EMG-BF 3. AP	33	39.5 (23–56)	16M, 17F	Y	Y, 15Ss	Automated	CBGOS; M + R	1. Avg. SBP/DBP pre-post change: BP-BF = −8.1/−1.4, EMG-BF = +1.4/−1.3, AP = −9.5/−1.3 2. On SBP, BP-BF post > BP-BF pre; AP post > AP pre 3. BP-BF = EMG-BF = AP

(continued)

TABLE 21.1 (Continued)

Study	Conditions	N	Age	Sex	Dx	Meds	Meds stable	BP assessment	Design	Outcome
										Controlled between-groups outcome: Biofeedback versus no-treatment control (continued)
McGrady et al. (1981)	1. EMC-BF + R 2. C	43	1. 55 2. 42	1. 7M, 15F 2. 5M, 11F	Y	Y, 19M group 1 12 in group 2	Y	Standard mercury sphygmomanometer; automated; calibrated	CBGOS	1. On SBP, DBP, EMG (forehead), urinary cortisol, plasma aldosterone: EMG-BF + R > C 2. 10 mm Hg or more change in SBP or DBP: EMG-BF+R =68%, C = 19%
Hafner (1982)	1. TM 2. TM+BF 3. NTC	14	48.9	8M, 6F	Y	Y, except 2Ss	Y	Automated	CBGOS; R	1. TM = TM+BF = NTC; between-occasions effect sig. 2. Avg. SBP/DBP pre-post change: TM = −14/−13.3; TM + BF = −21.6/−15/1; Avg. SBP/DBP post follow-up change: TM = +1.9/−5; TM + BF = +.8/+.4, NTC = −8.6/−2
Patel & North (1975)	1. Y+R+BF 2. C	40	1. 57.4 2. 57.2	1. 9M, 11F 2. 9M, 11F	?	1. Y19 2. Y18	Y	Fixed time; standard procedure	CBGOS; M	1. Avg. SBP/DBP pre-post change: Y+R+BF = −20.4/−14.2; C = −.5/−2.1 2. Avg. % drug requirement change: Y+R+BF = −41.9%, C = 0% 3. On follow-up, BP change maintained 4. Total avg. % drug requirement change: at 6 mo., Y+R+BF = −40.2%; at 3 mo., C = +5.5%
Patel (1975b)	1. R+M+BF (GSR, EMG, EEG)	32	58.5 (34–75)	21M, 11F	?	1. Y, 14SS 2. Y, 15SS	?	Trained nurse; mercury sphygmomanometer	CBGOS; R	1. On exercise test: R+M+BF post > R+M+BF pre on SBP/DBP, C post = C pre on SBP/DBP. On cold pressure test, results identical. 2. On exercise and cold pressor tests, R+M+BF > C on SBP/DBP maximum rise and recovery time except SBP rise on exercise test.

(continued)

Study	Conditions	N	Age	Sex				Measurement	Design	Results
Patel (1975c)	1. Y+R+BF 2. C	32	1. 59.3 2. 58	1. 5M, 11F 2. 6M, 10F	?	Y except 2Ss in group 1 in control	?	Independent observer, mercury sphygmomanometer	CBGOS; R	1. On exercise test, Y+R+BF post > Y+R+BF pre & C post = C pre on max. SBP rise, SBP recovery time, max. DBP rise & DBP recovery time. On exercise, Y+R+BF > C on SBP recovery time, max. DBP rise, DBP recovery time. 2. On cold pressor test, Y+R+BF post > Y+R+BF pre and C post =C pre on Max SBP rise, SBP recovery time, max. DBP rise, DBP recovery time. On cold pressure, Y+R+BF >C on max SBP rise, SBP recovery time, max. DBP rise, DBP recovery time
Patel & Carruthers (1977)	1. M+R+BF 2. C	22	1. 54.3 2. 43.5 3. 40.7 4. 42.9	8M, 14F; 7M, 11F; 6M, 12F; 6M, 12F	?	Y 12SS	?	Random zero sphygmomanometer	CBGOS; NR	1. Avg. SBP/DBP pre-post change: M+R+BF = -18.6/ -11.2 Sig. reduction in pulse rate, cholesterol, and triglyceride 2. On SBP, DBP, and serum cholesterol, M+R+BF > C
Patel et al. (1981)	1. BF (R+SM) 2. C	204	35-64	123M, 81F	Y	N	—	Trained nurse; random zero sphygmomanometer	CBGOS; R	1. Avg. SBP/DBP pre-8 wk. change: BF(R+SM) = -13.8/-7.2, C = -4.0/-1.4 Avg. SBP/DBP pre-8 mo. change: BF(R+SM) = -15.3/-6.8; C = -6.1/-63 2. % of Ss with BP > 140/90 at 8 wk: BF(R+SM) = 19.6% SBP, 10.6% DBP C = 8.2% SBP, 3.6% DBP % of SS with BP 140/90 at 9 mo: BF (R+SM) = 22.4% SBP, 11.5% DBP; C =11.4% SBP, 2.7% DBP
Biofeedback versus placebo										
Patel & North (1975)	1. Y+BF 2. AP	37	1. 58.5 2. 58.4	1. 6M, 11F 2. 7M, 10F	Y	Y, almost all	Y	Nurse; random zero sphygmomanometer	CBGOS; R	1. Avg. SBP/DBP pre-post change: Y+BF = -26.1/-15.2, AP = -8.9/-4.2 2. Y+BF post > Y+BF pre AP post > AP pre 3. Results replicated with AP SS treated: Avg. SBP/DBP pre-post change = -28.1/-15.0

TABLE 21.1 (Continued)

Study	Conditions	N	Age	Sex	Dx	Meds	Meds stable	BP assessment	Design	Outcome
	Biofeedback versus biofeedback									
Surwit et al (1978)	1. SBP and HR-BF 2. EMG-BF 3. M	24	?	1. 6M, 2F 2. 6M, 2F 3. 7M, 1F	Y	Y, 50%	Y	Automated; experimenter in adjoining room	CBGOS; M	1. On SBP, combined groups avg. presession-postsession change = −3.4 2. At 6 wk. follow-up, SBP+HR-BF =EMG-BF =M Avg. SBP change = −6/−3 3. At 1-yr. follow-up, avg. SBP/DBP +3/ +3 greater than at 6 wks. follow-up
Glasgow et al. (1982)	1. SMC 2. SBP-BF 3. R 4. SB-BF+R 5. R+SBP-BF	53	?	?	?	N, except 7Ss	—	Self-recorded; health professional also	CBGOS; M	1. SBP-BF and R: yield immediate BP lowering 2. On SBP, SBP-BF = R; on DBP, R > SBP-BF 3. SBP-BF+R > SBP-BF & R 4. SBP-BF: slightly greater long-term effects than R
Engel et al. (1983)	1. R+SBP-BF 2. SBP-BF+R 3. R+R+SBP-BF 4. SBP-BF+SBP-BF+R 5. SM+R+SBP-BF	60	46.1	43M, 17F	?	N except 27Ss	?	?	BGOS	1. SBP-BF+R: showed greater likelihood of being taken off diuretic 2. At 6 mo. follow-up, BP follow-up > BP baseline after last intervention
Elder & Eustis (1975)	DBP-BF-D DBP-BF-M	22	50.23 (23–80)	14M, 8F	N	Y, 20Ss	Y	Automated	TGOS	1. On SBP and DBP, DBP-BF-M post > DBP-BF-M pre; DBP-BF-D post > DBP-BF-D 2. DBP-BF-M > DBP-BF-D
	Stress management: Single-group outcome									
Kallinke et al. (1982)	SM (PMR)	48	38.3 (18–57)	48M	Y	Y, 48% of Ss	Y	Automated; in lab; self-recorded also	SCOS	1. Avg. SBP/DBP pre-post change for individually treated Ss = −19/−10; gains maintained at 12 mo. 2. Avg. SBP/DBP pre-post change for group treated Ss = −14/−10 3. Combined Avg. SBP/DBP pre-post change = −17/−10

534

Controlled between-groups outcome: Stress management versus control

Study	Treatments	N	Age	Sex				Measure	Design	Results
Ewart et al. (1984)	1. CT 2. AO(DT)	20	1. 57.1 2. 58.7	1. 3M, 7F 2. 4M, 6F	Y	Y	Y	Random zero sphygmomanometer	CBGOS; R	1. CT post > CT pre on hostility and combativeness 2. Avg. SBP/DBP change in reactivity during problem solving: CT = −8.8/−3.0 AO(DT) = −3.5/−0.7; SBP declines sig. 3. Avg. pre and post SBP/DBP: AOCDT = 154.9/92.7 to 149.6/91.9; CT = 156.8/96.8 to 145.6/92.2; no change on post to follow-up for both groups
Charlesworth et al. (1984)	1. SM 2. C	54	?	32M, 8F	Y	Y, 83% of Ss	?	Self-recorded; upon arising, after work, before bed	CBCOS; R	1. Avg. SBP/DBP pre-post change: SM = −6.1/−2.9, C = no change 2. Avg. SBP/DBP pre-post change: C group after treatment = −3.8/−2.6 3. SM increased health behavior 4. Frequency of practice and amount of BP change during relaxation sig. correlation with BP reduction after program
Jorgensen et al. (1981)	1. AMT 2. WLC	18	1. 54.4 2. 54.3	?	Y	Y except 1	?	Automated	CBGOS; R	1. On SBP/DBP AMT post > AMT pre 2. On stress test on SBP WLC > AMT 3. On recovery, on SBP/DBP AMT > WLC 4. AMT Ss maintained reductions at follow-up

Stress management versus placebo

Study	Treatments	N	Age	Sex				Measure	Design	Results
Drazen et al. (1982)	RET+ASRT AMT HEC (AC)	22	40.3 (22–63)	16M, 6F	N	?	?	Nurse	CBCOS; R	1. At post and follow-up RET+ASRT = AMT = HEC(AP) 2. Avg. SBP/DBP pre-post change: RET + ASRT = −21.3/−11.5 AMT = −10.8/−6.6 3. Avg. SBP/DBP pre follow-up change: RET + ARST = −16.3/−8.3 AMT = −12.9/−11.6 4. Gains maintained from post to follow-up.

(continued)

TABLE 21.1 (Continued)

Study	Conditions	N	Age	Sex	Dx	Meds	Meds stable	BP assessment	Design	Outcome
					Stress management versus placebo (continued)					
Crowther (1983)	1. SM + RI 2. RI 3. AP	34	47.3 51.9 48.3	1. 6M, 6F 2. 4M, 8F 3. 3M, 7F	?	Y	N	Sphygmomanometer	CBCOS; M + R; CR	1. On SBP and DBP at post and follow-up, SM+RI = RI > AP 2. Avg. SBP/DBP pre-post change: SM + RI −20.8/−11.3; RI = −23.4/−15.6 Avg. SBP/DBP pre follow-up change: SM + RI = −17.5/−8.6; RI = −15.7/−14.1
				Controlled between-groups outcome: Behavior therapy versus pharmacotherapy						
Taylor et al. (1977)	1. Med 2. P + Med 3. R + Med	40	?	7M, 4F 8M, 2F 8M, 2F	Y	Y	Y	Independent observer; separate setting and time; blind nurse	CBCOS; R	1. Avg. SBP/DBP pre-post and pre-follow-up change: Med. = −1.1/−3; −6.8/−1.5 P+Med = −2.8/−1.8; −4.0/−3.5 R+Med. = −13.6/−4.9; −12.0/−6.2 2. On SBP only R+Med > Med 3. On SBP & DBP, P+Med = Med 4. On SBP only R+Med > P+Med 5. Follow-up: R+Med maintained
Luborsky et al. (1980)	1. Meds. 2. AT 3. Meds. + AT	15	47 54 66	9M, 6F	Y	Y except group 2	Y	Same physician	CBCOS; R	1. Avg. SBP/DBP pre-post change: Med = −29.8/ −24.8 AT = −7.0/−10.4 2. On SBP/DBP, Med > AT, Med > Med + AT
Luborsky et al. (1982)	1. MED 2. MCR 3. MCME 4. BF	51	38 (20–55)	?	?	Y except group 2, 3, and 4	?	Random zero sphygmomanometer	CBCOS; R	1. Avg. SBP/DBP pre-post change standing and lying: Med = −18.8/−10.3; −13.5/−7.2 MCR = −6.3/−5.4; −6.9/−2.4 MCME = −4.7/−3.0; −.4/−1.4 BF = −6.5/−5.5; −2.6/−43 2. On SBP Med > MCR > BF = MCME

536

3. % patients > 10 mm BP decrease
   Med = 70%
   MCF = 31%
   MCME = 18%
   BF = 36%
4. On compliance, Med > MCR
5. Benefits maintained at 1- and 3-mo. follow-up

Note: Y = yes; N = no; ? = ambiguous, or not mentioned; M = male; F = female; BP = blood pressure; SBP = systolic blood pressure; DBP = diastolic blood pressure; post = posttest; pretest.

For relaxation therapy studies: APWV-BF = arterial pulse wave velocity biofeedback; BF = biofeedback; BPBF = blood pressure biofeedback; BPBF-N = blood pressure biofeedback—noncontinuous; BRR = Benson's relaxation response; BSP = brief supportive psychotherapy control; C = control; CT-C = cognitive therapy—couples; EMG+TB+SRP = EMG + thermal biofeedback + self-regulation procedures; Hyp = hypnosis; HYP-H = hypnotizable hypertensives; HYP-N = hypnotizable normotensives; MCR = metronome-conditioned relaxation; MOC = measurement-only control; MR = muscle relaxation; N HYP-H = nonhypnotizable hypertensives; N HYP-N = nonhypnotizable normotensives; NIP = nonspecific individual psychotherapy; NTC = no-treatment control; PC = placebo control; PMR = progressive muscle relaxation; PMR-Audio = tape-conducted progressive muscle relaxation; PMR-C = progressive muscle relaxation—couples; PMR-G = progressive muscle relaxation—group; PMR-I = progressive muscle relaxation—individual; PMR-Th = therapist-conducted progressive muscle relaxation; PR = progressive relaxation; PSR = psychologic relaxation; R = relaxation; R+EMG = relaxation + EMG biofeedback; R+Hyp-D = relaxation + hypnosis—drugs; R+Hyp-ND = relaxation + hypnosis—no drugs; R-ND = relaxation without drugs; RO = relaxation only; RT = relaxation training; RT-C = relaxation therapy—couples; RT-DE = relaxation—delayed blood pressure lowering expectation; RT-IE = relaxation—immediate blood pressure lowering expectation; RT-SA = relaxation therapy—subject alone; SCRT = self-control relaxation; SD = systematic desensitization; SMC = self-monitoring control; TA = transactional analysis; WLC = waiting list control.

For yoga and meditation studies: Plac = placebo; Shav = shavasana; Shav + med = shavasana; Shav + med = shavasana + medication; TM = transcendental meditation.

For biofeedback studies: AP = attention placebo; BF-EMG &/or TBF + R = EMG and/or thermal biofeedback + relaxation; BF/(R+SM) = biofeedback (relaxation + stress management); BPBF-N = blood pressure biofeedback—noncontinuous; DBP-BF = diastolic blood pressure biofeedback; DBP-BF-D = diastolic blood pressure biofeedback distributed; DBP-BF-M = diastolic blood pressure biofeedback massed; DBP-BF + FEMG-BF + AT + PR = diastolic blood pressure biofeedback + frontalis EMG biofeedback + autogenic training + progressive relaxation; DBP-BF + VR = diastolic blood pressure biofeedback + verbal reinforcement; M = meditation; NTC = no-treatment control; QRT-EMG & T-BF = quieting response training—EMG + thermal biofeedback; R+M+BF = relaxation + meditation + biofeedback; R+TM+BF = relaxation + transcendental meditation + biofeedback; SBP-BF = systolic blood pressure—biofeedback; SBP+HR-BF = systolic blood pressure + heart rate biofeedback; SMC = self-monitoring blood pressure control; TBF = thermal biofeedback; Y & BF = yoga and biofeedback; Y+R+BF = yoga + relaxation + biofeedback.

For stress management studies: AMT = anxiety management training; Ao(DT) = assessment only (delayed treatment); HEC = hypertension education counseling (attention control); RET-ASRT = rational-emotive therapy + assertiveness training; SM(PMR) = stress management including progressive muscle relaxation; SM+RI = stress management + relaxation imagery.

For behavioral versus pharmacotherapy: AT = autogenic training; MCME = metronome-conditioned mild exercise (placebo); Med = medication; P+Med = placebo + medication; R+Med = relaxation + medication.

Designs and methodology: CBGOS = controlled between-group outcome study; CR = credibility ratings; M = matched; MBD-SS = multiple-baseline design across subjects; MCS = multiple case studies; M+R = matching plus randomization; NR = nonrandomized; R̄ = randomized; S̄ = stratified; S̄GOS = single-group outcome study; TGOS = two-group outcome study.

537

Following desensitization, the patient's blood pressure readings were normotensive except for one diastolic reading. Of course, the results of this study can be generalized only to a setting in which desensitization is preceded by progressive relaxation training.

In this small *n* study, Agras, Taylor, Kraemer, Allen, and Schneider (1980) tested whether relaxation training yields effects on blood pressure over a 24-hour period, as opposed to being limited to periods of actual practice. Five patients who were considered poorly controlled essential hypertensives were studied in the hospital environment. Each patient was admitted to the hospital for 7 days and had to have the diagnosis verified by his or her physician. Average blood pressure on admission was 167.2/93.2 mm Hg. In this single-subject reversal design (ABA), blood pressure was assessed by a member of the nursing staff. Tracings were read and recorded independently by two observers. Also, the blood pressure recorder was calibrated against a mercury manometer prior to each patient's admission and was also checked twice during each admission. Blood pressure was measured every quarter-hour from 7 A.M. to 3 P.M. and every half-hour from 3 P.M. to 12 A.M. Thereafter, measurements were obtained every 2 hours. The initial 18 hours of recording were considered as adaptation. Each subject was treated with progressive muscle relaxation by an experienced therapist who met with each patient at 9 A.M., 1 P.M., and 6 P.M. each day for 3 days. Patients were also placed on a controlled salt diet to achieve a slightly positive sodium balance to counteract the potential blood pressure lowering effect of the hospital diet. Daily activity of the patient was controlled by restricting the patient to the ward except for 1 hour each evening and by prohibiting the patient from sleeping during the day or early evening. Regarding outcome, SBP and DBP were observed to drop in 33 of 45 and 34 of 45 sessions, respectively. Over the course of 9 therapy sessions, the average reductions in blood pressure were 7.3/5.1 mm Hg, with the greatest effects evident by the fifth session. The authors concluded that relaxation produced immediate effects. An analysis of the time it took blood pressure to return to pretreatment levels showed that the effects of relaxation extended beyond the treatment sessions. Finally, there was a significant decline of blood pressure on treatment days subsequent to the 9 A.M. and 1 P.M. sessions, as well as an effect observed during sleep. The greatest generalization occurred at night, as SBP and DBP were lowered at night during the treatment phase relative to the control phases. Of course, the findings of this study are limited in generalizability to inpatients.

Martin and Epstein (1980) assessed the situational specificity of relaxation. Employing a multiple-baseline design across subjects and settings, these authors treated two nonobese adult females who were recently diagnosed as hypertensive. Subject 1 was a 28-year-old black female with a 1-year duration of hypertension who was being treated with antihypertensive agents. Subject 2 was a 24-year-old female with a 6-month history of hypertension who was never on medication. Blood pressure measures were obtained prior to and subsequent to each session in the lab, as well as *in vivo* three times daily. Lab measures were taken by the senior author with a mercury column sphygmomanometer; *in vivo* measures, by the subjects using an aneroid-meter sphygmomanometer. The first author employed a dual stethoscope and trained each subject to measure her own pressure following several sessions at which time baseline measures were obtained in the lab. Between every 2 and 4 weeks, five consecutive reliability measures were obtained and independently documented. This study was conducted in four phases: baseline, relaxation training in lab, relaxation practice *in vivo*, and maintenance (home self-monitoring with active and passive relaxation). Implementation of relaxation was associated with decreases in diastolic blood pressure for subject 1 in the lab and at home and for subject 2 in the lab. Home diastolic pressure for subject 2 had decreased across the baseline period and continued this trend during treatment. During maintenance, subject 1 became noncompliant and independently discontinued her medication as well as the relaxation and monitoring. After beginning compliance, her diastolic blood pressures were within normal limits by 6-month follow-up. For subject 2, who complied with instructions, maintenance and follow-up data revealed a continued decline and maintenance of diastolic blood pressure within the normal range. In terms of systolic pressure there was a decreasing trend observed during lab baseline sessions for subject 1, with associated declines following implementation of treatment on home measures of subject 1 and on lab and home measures for subject 2. Increases, declines, and final increase in systolic pressure for subject 1 mirrored the self-reports of noncompliance, compliance, and noncompliance described earlier. In overview the size of blood pressure reduction was from 10 to 12 mm Hg. One of the major limitations of the study, however, was the lack of more objective measures of relaxation in the lab and at home.

In overview, in the single-subject experiments and barring other limitations, the controlling effects of relaxation were demonstrated in medicated and unmedicated subjects. Certainly, the simplest AB design as found in Beinman et al. (1978a, 1978b) is subject to a variety of confounding factors and yields only tentative conclusions. Stronger support is found in the ABA and ABAB studies (Agras et al., 1980; Brady et al., 1974), and especially in the latter case, where the effects of the treatment were demonstrated twice. However, generalization to the clinical setting with the ABAB design is limited by the sequential confounding of earlier phases and multiple treatment interference (Hersen & Barlow, 1976). Finally, the multiple-baseline approach (Martin & Epstein, 1980) tends to be weaker than the reversal designs.

Controlled Between-Groups Outcome Studies

In the next series of studies, a relaxation treatment was compared to a no-treatment control, placebo, both, another form of relaxation, and biofeedback.

RELAXATION VERSUS NO-TREATMENT CONTROL

In a nonrandomized between-groups outcome study, Stone and DeLeo (1976) compared psychological relaxation with a control condition in a group of nonmedicated patients from a hospital population. Urinary sodium excretion was measured to rule out dietary salt restriction as an alternative hypothesis for change. Propsective subjects received an extensive medical evaluation, including a complete history and physical exam, several blood pressure determinations, and measurements of plasma dopamine beta hydroxylase (DBH) and plasma renin activity. Blood pressure measurements were obtained by a blind independent observer. All the patients maintained an unrestricted dietary sodium intake. Relaxation treatment (Buddhist meditation) was delivered by one of the authors, who instructed subjects to practice the technique twice daily. Controls were seen for blood pressure determination once a month over a 6-month observation period. Analysis by *t* tests revealed that following 6 months of relaxation, supine and upright blood pressures were significantly less than baseline. Also, the relaxation group had significantly lower DBP compared to the controls. These changes were also reflected in reduced DBH activity and a significant decline of plasma renin activity. These two findings indicate that blood pressure reduction was associated with a decline in peripheral adrenergic activity, with a change in the renin angiotensin system.

In asking whether the effects of relaxation training generalize to the patient's natural environment (work), Southam, Agras, Taylor, and Kraemer (1982) randomly assigned 42 patients from a work site and community to relaxation training or a no-treatment control. Two out of three of the subjects were prescribed medication. Although no attempt was made to stabilize medication during the course of the study, medication changes were judged at the end of the study by three physicians who were unaware of the subjects' group status. Blood pressure was measured by an automatic blood pressure recorder and a semiautomatic ambulatory blood pressure recorder and were read independently by two individuals who were kept blind to subject group status. Also, subjects completed a questionnaire assessing changes in life-style habits. Treatment subjects received eight 30-minute individual sessions of progressive muscle relaxation at weekly intervals, with instructions to practice brief relaxation exercises during the work day. The findings revealed significant differences between the treatment and control groups on SBP and DBP at the clinic as well as the work site. Average in-clinic changes for the relaxation group and the control groups were $-11.7/-12.6$ and $-3.61/-2.5$ mm Hg, respectively. In the work setting, average change in the treatment group was $-7.8/-4.6$, whereas in the control group mean change was $-0.1/+1.7$ mm Hg. Alternative causes for change, such as weight change, medication change, activity, medication, and health habits, were ruled out. However, one of the control subjects began transcendental meditation (TM), while another began deep-breathing relaxation-related training. A comparison of baseline to follow-up at 6 months on in-clinic measures showed a mean change of $-6.0/-12.1$ for the treatment group and $+1.3/-2.2$ for controls. Although no significant differences were observed between the two groups on SBP, the DBP difference was significant. It would have been beneficial to ascertain the time between relaxation practice and blood pressure measurement at the work site in order to rule out the influence of this variable.

In another controlled outcome study (Pender, 1984) patients from a hypertension monitoring program who were currently on a salt-restricted diet were studied. A group of 30 subjects were selected, as well as an additional 30 who were matched on diagnosis, sex, age, number of medications, and SBP. A total of 22 individuals from each group agreed to participate. Seven subjects in the treatment group and 13 in the control group were on antihypertensive medication and exhibited a high level of compliance. All participants were told that if they received a new medication or if their dosage was altered during the study, then their data would not be used. They were also instructed to maintain their level of activity and diet. The PMR group received 3 sessions of 90 minutes duration on a once-a-week basis, with instructions to practice once a day and to monitor their practice. Subjects were also given 18 autogenic phrases to repeat during relaxation. The control subjects received health counseling (attention), blood pressure and weight monitoring, diet education, discussion of compliance, and educational material. The effects of relaxation training were corroborated by statistically significant reductions in muscle tension and an increase in digital temperature. On the average SBP was reduced by 8 mm Hg in the treatment group relative to the controls, which was statistically significant at follow-up. Average SBP/DBP reduction in the treatment subjects were $-9/-7$ mm Hg, compared to $-1/-1$ mm Hg in the controls. The treatment group also showed a significant decline in DBP, while the controls did not. On DBP, however, there was no significant differences between the groups. None of the subjects reported great changes in exercise or diet, and sodium intake was similar for both groups.

Deabler, Fidel, Dillenkoffer, and Elder (1973) evaluated a combination of relaxation plus hypnosis in medicated and unmedicated subjects and compared these conditions to a control condition. Of a total of 21 patients, 12 were not on medication and 6 subjects each were randomly assigned to a relaxation plus hypnosis–no drug group and a control group. The remaining 9 subjects made up a relaxation plus hypnosis–drug group. Each subject was a patient who had a diagnosis of essential hypertension and no organic pathology. There was no indication of whether medication was stabilized in the drug groups. Subjects treated with relaxation and hypnosis received progressive muscle relaxation followed by hypnosis. These subjects were also instructed to practice on the evenings of the days of sessions, especially after leaving the hospital. The control subjects had initial readings obtained and then returned seven times for readings to be gathered. Significant reductions on SBP and DBP were obtained in both treatment groups, while the controls evidenced no significant change.

RELAXATION VERSUS PLACEBO

Brauer, Horlick, Nelson, Farquhar, and Agras (1979) compared the relative efficacy of progressive deep-muscle relaxation (therapist-conducted), progressive deep-muscle relaxation (audiotape home use), and a nospecific psychotherapy control. Of 35 patients recruited from a VA outpatient clinic, 4 decided not to participate prior to therapy, and 2 dropped out in an early phase of treatment. All subjects were receiving concurrent drug therapy. However, no guidelines were set regarding the stabilization of medical or pharmacological treatment during the course of the study. Subjects were matched with regard to mean blood pressure and then randomly assigned to groups. Blood pressures were obtained and recorded in a standardized manner by one of two experienced nurses who were kept blind to group status. Pre and post blood samples were also obtained to determine the activity level of DBH, an enzyme providing an indication of sympathetic activity. Treatment was provided by a behavioral psychiatrist, a senior faculty cardiologist, and a second-year medical student, who were distributed across treatment conditions. As a further control, clinic physicians and staff members who were responsible for medical care of the patients were kept blind to the treatment groups to which patients had been assigned. Likewise, all treatment sessions were made at a time and place that was separate from the patient's medical clinic visits. Frequency of clinic attendance, time spent with and attention from the therapists, and amount of homework were controlled. In the therapist-conducted relaxation condition, subjects received individual training in deep-muscle relaxation and were asked to practice for 20 minutes each day with a relaxation tape. In the tape-recorded instruction condition, subjects were trained in relaxation with minimal therapist contact, and subjects received tapes containing relaxation lessons. Forms were mailed directly to the therapist by the subjects, who would answer questions via phone. In the nonspecific therapy condition, subjects received nondirective counseling about stress and tension. Several interesting findings emerged. First, at posttreatment no significant between-group differences were observed on systolic or diastolic pressure. However, at 6-month follow-up the therapist-conducted relaxation group showed a decrease in systolic blood pressure relative to the other groups, whereas no significant between-group differences were found on diastolic pressure. Second, within-group analyses revealed a significant reduction in diastolic pressure, with no change on the systolic measure for the therapist-conducted relaxation group. At 6-month follow-up, however, significant systolic and diastolic reductions were found for this condition. For the remaining conditions no significant changes were found at the end of treatment or at follow-up. Third, an analysis of the pharmacological treatment of subjects within groups was conducted through chart review by a physician unaware of the subjects' group status. At 6-month follow-up the number of subjects who had increases or decreases in medication dosage was similar across groups. The authors analyzed the results by therapists and found that for one therapist the pattern of results differed from those for the other, with improvement in the nonspecific patients and no change in the relaxation condition. Excluding this therapist's data from the analysis revealed a significant diastolic change favoring the therapist-conducted group at post-treatment. Within-group reanalysis showed significant changes on systolic and diastolic pressure for this condition at the end of treatment. Of course, this analysis is post hoc in nature and must be viewed with caution. Finally, no significant change in DBH activity was observed between the three groups from pre- to posttreatment.

Bali (1979) compared progressive muscle relaxation and a brief supportive psycho-therapy control condition. Eighteen males who had previously been diagnosed as essential hypertensive, had been placed on medication (2–4 years previously), and had subsequently discontinued their medication because of ineffectiveness or side effects served as subjects. After obtaining permission from their physicians, all subjects received a thorough physical examination to confirm the diagnosis and rule out other illnesses. Nine pairs of subjects matched on age, blood pressure, weight, and anxiety were randomly assigned to groups. Relaxation subjects received training in Jacobsonian relaxation and were also instructed to practice at least once a day for 20 minutes and for a few minutes every hour. Control subjects received brief supportive psychotherapy focusing on their hypertension and were asked to rest in bed for 20 minutes at least once a day, as well as to explore an object (e.g., a plant) for a few minutes every hour. The findings revealed significant reductions in blood pressure averaging 12 mm Hg systolic and 9 mm Hg diastolic in the treatment group only. Significant reductions in anxiety were also observed in this group as measured by the Taylor Manifest Anxiety Scale. Although the groups were similar in effectiveness expectations, the control subjects practiced significantly less than the treated subjects during a 3-month period. It is possible that differences in compliance might have accounted for the results, although Bali discounted this possibility as highly unlikely. Of even further importance, the observed effects of relaxation were replicated when the control subjects were treated. Finally, decreases in blood pressure and anxiety were sustained at the 12-month follow-up period.

Cottier, Shapiro, and Julius (1984) assessed the efficacy of progressive muscle relaxation with mild hypertensives. These patients were either untreated or were receiving no more than two antihypertensive drugs, the latter group being weaned off medication over the course of 6 weeks. Subjects were then informed that at some point they would receive an active drug or a placebo. In actuality both groups were given a placebo until the completion of the study at week 22. Patients were also asked to maintain their typical diet and level of physical activity during this trial. Each subject was trained to obtain blood pressure measurements to the criteria of three successive agreements between the patient and an instructor. During two 14-day periods (weeks 4 to 6 and 20 to 22), patients obtained their own blood pressures twice a day at home (morning and evening) at the same time following 2 minutes of rest. Also, each patient's blood pressure gauge was calibrated against a mercury manometer prior to each 14-day period. Oxygen consumption and anxiety measures (State Trait Anxiety Inventory) were also obtained.

Subjects were randomly assigned to progressive muscle relaxation or a control condition. Relaxation subjects were treated individually and were asked to practice twice a day at home with a tape. Control subjects were seen for the same number of visits. The senior author served as therapist and was unaware of the subjects' blood pressure or hormonal status.

The findings revealed an 82% compliance rate with self-reported daily relaxation practice. No significant differences emerged between the treatment and control groups on office blood pressure at posttreatment. Descriptively, over the course of the trial, office blood pressure decreased in both groups from weeks 0 to 6, followed by a further decrease with the administration of the placebo in both groups up to week 14. Subsequently, blood pressure in the controls started to increase; relaxation-treated subjects maintained the decrease. As noted earlier, however, the average clinic blood pressures at posttreatment were not different. In contrast, on pretreatment and posttreatment comparisons of home blood pressures, moderate increases in blood pressures were observed in most of the control subjects, while some of the treated subjects demonstrated substantial reductions. At posttreatment for treated subjects, mean home blood pressure change was −3 mm Hg; for controls, mean home blood pressure change was +2 mm Hg. Interestingly, 5 of the 17 subjects practicing relaxation achieved home blood pressures below 135/85. Also, plasma epinephrine decreased in relaxation subjects and increased in controls, a statistically significant difference. Finally, further analysis of treated subjects revealed that responders were characterized by elevated heart rate, norepinephrine levels, and anxiety levels.

RELAXATION VERSUS RELAXATION

Nath and Rinehart (1979) compared individually and group-administered progressive muscle relaxation. Twenty essential hypertensives in whom the diagnosis was verified ranging in age from 26 to 52 years were assigned in a nonrandom manner to 2 groups. These groups had a disproportionate number of males and females, and of the initial 20 subjects 5 were dropped because of failure to attend sessions or medication changes. Mortality effects exist here in the sense that the less motivated and difficult patients were dropped from the study. All subjects except for two were taking antihypertensive medication, which was stabilized throughout the study. All subjects received four treatment sessions held at the same time each day to reduce variations in blood pressure through-out the day. Data were analyzed by separate ANOVAs where MANOVA would have been more appropriate to reduce Type I error. Individually and group-administered relaxation were equally effective, with mean decreases before and after teaching sessions ranging from 3.6 to 8.7 mm Hg systolic and 2.8 to 8.3 mm Hg diastolic. Moreover, significant decreases were observed on SBP within teaching sessions and from the beginning to the end of the program. Significant decreases in DBP, however, occurred only within teaching sessions.

Agras, Horne, and Taylor (1982) studied the role of expectation in evaluating the efficacy of relaxation training. Thirty essential hypertensives who were under medical care and most of whom were on medication were randomly assigned to groups: relaxa-tion training–immediate blood pressure lowering expectation (RTIE) or relaxation train-ing–delayed blood pressure lowering expectation (RTDE). The RTIE group was in-formed that treatment would yield immediate effects, which would be sustained and enhanced with practice; the RTDE group, that the effects of therapy would be delayed over the course of treatment, that they might show a minimal increase, but that it would decrease with practice. Subjects were tested to ensure that the expectancy was believed, and this was confirmed by two blind independent observers who showed 100% agree-ment. Relaxation was delivered by an instructor who was blind to subject condition and was completed in 1 day (three sessions). Blood pressures were measured by the blind instructor with a standard sphygmomanometer. Subjects were assessed for treatment credibility and perceived relaxation and showed no significant differences between conditions. The findings indicated that the effects of relaxation can be mediated by cognitive processes. Subjects given the immediate expectation showed significantly greater reduction in SBP than did the delayed expectancy subjects (−17 mm Hg versus −2.4 mm Hg). Similar findings were found when average change over three sessions in SBP was compared for the two groups. No significant differences in DBP were observed.

Wadden (1983) compared individually administered relaxation training with cou-ples-administered training. Thirty-one essential hypertensives, all of whom had spouses or other family members who were willing to attend treatment sessions, participated in the program. All subjects were referred by their physicians, were previously diagnosed as hypertensive for at least 6 months, had no other physical problems, and were randomly assigned to groups following stratification according to type and number of medications. Two trained female nursing students who exhibited acceptable levels of interobserver reliability collected BP measurements. Each nurse used the same BP measurement instruments throughout the course of the study and saw the same subjects each session. An additional trained student collected home BP measurements (generalization data). Subjects received eight weekly sessions of relaxation training, which included progressive muscle relaxation, passive relaxation, visual imagery, and home practice. They were also informed never to practice relaxation at least 3 hours prior to each session. Treatment was delivered by two advanced clinical psychology students, who were distributed across conditions.

Several interesting findings emerged from this study. First, those subjects in the couples-relaxation condition exhibited significantly better compliance with relaxation practice than did individually treated subjects. Second, significant SBP and DBP pretest–

posttest reductions averaging 6.4 mm Hg and 5.2 mm Hg, respectively, were observed. Between posttest and follow-up no further decrease was observed on SBP; DBP, however, decreased by 2.3 mm Hg. No significant differences between groups emerged. Third, although medication was stabilized during treatment and at 1-month follow-up, at 5-month follow-up medication was eliminated in 4 subjects on the individually administered condition, all of whom were on diuretics. Two subjects in the other condition were begun on diuretics, and an additional subject was placed on a beta blocker. A reanalysis of the 5-month follow-up data after eliminating all medication change subjects revealed no between-groups differences on SBP or DBP reductions. No differences were observed between drug-treated and non-drug-treated subjects at any assessment period. Fourth, similar blood pressure reductions were found in the clinic ($-5.4/-4.8$) and in the home ($-4.8/-3.3$). Fifth, initial systolic blood pressure was positively correlated with systolic change at posttreatment and 1-month follow-up; initial diastolic blood pressure was significantly correlated with diastolic change at 1-month follow-up. Finally, significant negative relationships were observed between blood pressure reduction and two Type A scales of the Jenkins Activity Survey.

Methodologically, the lack of a control group places limitations on this study. Moreover, in the analysis of blood pressure ANCOVA (analysis of convariance) with repeated measures was used, whereas a comparable MANCOVA (multivariate analysis of covariance) would have been preferable. Mortality effects may also be operating, since only 29 of 31 subjects attended follow-up. In addition, treatment generalization was assessed by selecting and studying subjects who lived close to the clinic. No analysis was conducted in comparing these to the remaining subjects who did not live near the clinic.

In a later study, Wadden (1984) sought to determine the potent elements of relaxation therapy by contrasting its effects with a minimal treatment condition. Essential hypertensives ($N = 48$) who were referred by their physicians for behavioral treatment and who had a spouse or significant other willing to attend treatment participated. Of the total sample 32 were being concurrently treated with drugs and had their medication stabilized for a 90-day period prior to the study. Following stratification with respect to the use of antihypertensives, subjects were randomly assigned to groups. Two nurses who obtained all blood pressure measurements were trained until a high level of interobserver reliability was attained. They used the same manometer and stethoscope, were responsible for the same subjects throughout the study, and were blind to the experimental hypotheses. Following a 3-week baseline period, subjects received either subject-alone relaxation, couples relaxation therapy, or couples cognitive therapy. Subjects were instructed not to practice their therapy for a minimum of at least 3 hours preceding the session. Treatment was delivered by two experienced male graduate students who treated subjects in all three conditions on the basis of a detailed manual. Expectancy and treatment credibility were also assessed. The subject-alone relaxation group received training in the relaxation response, progressive muscle relaxation, passive muscle relaxation, and visual imagery. The couples group was identical except that these subjects attended all sessions with spouses. In the couples cognitive therapy group subjects received a training program in rational-emotive therapy and assertion training. There were no significant differences between groups on ratings of treatment effectiveness or credibility. Overall mean declines from pretest–posttest were 6.9/5.2 mm Hg. On

SBP there was no further decline during follow-up, with a significant change maintained at 5-month follow-up. On DBP there was a further significant decline by 2.2 mm Hg between posttest and 1-month follow-up. No significant between-groups differences on SBP or DBP were observed. With respect to medication use, at 5-month follow-up diuretics were stopped in 4 subjects in the subject-alone condition. In the couples relaxation group 2 were begun on diuretics and 1 subject was started on beta blockers. Initial SBP significantly correlated with SBP decline at posttest, 1-month, and 5-month follow-up; initial DBP, with DBP decline at 1-month follow-up only. Reductions by groups were as follows: subject alone (6.2/4.9 mm Hg), couples relaxation (6.6/5.4 mm Hg), couples cognitive (8.5/5.4 mm Hg).

RELAXATION VERSUS BIOFEEDBACK

In an investigation by Goldstein, Shapiro, and Thananopavaran (1984), an extensive screening procedure resulted in the selection of patients diagnosed as suffering from essential hypertension. These authors excluded obese and alcoholic patients and those receiving drugs (other than antihypertensives), as well as those in psychotherapy. Of 108 subjects selected for participation prior to baseline, patient mortality was found at various phases of the study for a variety of reasons. Further mortality was evidenced in each condition, totaling 14 patients. Of the 58 subjects who eventually initiated partici- pation, 17 discontinued medication because of side effects or ineffectiveness of drug therapy 6 months prior. During initial visits to the lab prebaseline assessments were obtained on three separate days during a 2-week period with a mercury sphygmoma- nometer after sitting quietly for 10 minutes. Patients also received instruction in the use of an electronic sphygmomanometer for measuring daily blood pressure at home under standardized conditions. On each occasion that the patient returned to the lab—always at the same time of day—their use of the home pressure monitoring device was checked. The device itself was also checked against a mercury sphygmomanometer during each visit to the lab. Patients obtained self-measurements in the morning and evening on a daily basis and mailed this information back to the lab twice a week. Also included was information regarding medication use, food intake, alcohol consumption, stressors, and life-style changes. Subjects also completed a variety of self-report measures including the State Trait Anxiety Inventory–Trait Form, the Jenkins Activity Survey, the Recent Life Change Questionnaire, and the Hostility and Direction of Hostility Questionnaire. Following the completion of baseline measures, medicated patients were assigned to the following conditions: relaxation ($n = 13$), relaxation plus biofeedback ($n = 14$), or self- monitoring ($n = 14$). These groups were similar regarding age, sex, race, and average lab baseline blood pressure. An attempt was made to equate these groups for type of antihypertensive medication. Unmedicated subjects were assigned to a relaxation/ nondrug group ($n = 17$). When this group was greater than 50% filled, patients were selected from a waiting list to ensure its similarity with the other three groups. Patients in the relaxation condition were exposed to the following: a progressive muscle relaxation– like procedure (without muscle tensing), pleasant relaxing imagery, a 20-minute audio- tape of the procedure for daily home use, and encouragement to practice relaxation exercises when in stressful situations. The relaxation/nondrug subjects were treated in an identical fashion except, of course, for the absence of medication. In the relaxation/

biofeedback group treatment was identical to the other relaxation condition for the first two sessions. Subsequently, they received EMG biofeedback of frontalis muscle (shaping) as the patient was taken through the standard relaxation procedure. The self-monitoring group simply monitored their pressure, with emphasis on lowering it through awareness. From baseline to end of treatment all three treatment groups differed significantly from controls on SBP and DBP morning measures. On evening SBP measures, relaxation/ biofeedback differed significantly from self-monitoring and relaxation/nondrug. Relaxation and relaxation/biofeedback were equally effective. On DBP measures, relaxation and relaxation/biofeedback differed significantly from the control group. Relaxation without drugs did not reduce blood pressure as much as the other two relaxation conditions. Despite blood pressure reductions in the laboratory over the treatment course, the four groups did not differ significantly. Regarding variables related to success in treatment, patients with the highest blood pressures were most successful. Likewise, the only significant correlation was negative ($r = -.34$) and was that between change in SBP and the Recent Life Changes Questionnaire. Regarding drug compliance, which was checked daily, it was comparable across groups. On follow-up at one year, decreasing trends were observed for all groups, with the relaxation groups exhibiting the largest decreases. One patient in the relaxation group and 2 in the relaxation/biofeedback group had medications reduced, whereas 3 in the latter group were off medication altogether.

Shoemaker and Tasto (1975) compared muscle relaxation, noncontinuous blood pressure biofeedback, and a waiting list control condition in a randomized controlled group outcome study. Fifteen volunteers responded to a request sent to all faculty and other employees of a university asking for those suffering from essential, not secondary, hypertension. The diagnosis was apparently not confirmed. Moreover, there were no data regarding concurrent medication. In assessing outcome, the first 5 measures were eliminated to account for habituation. Comparisons were made on the basis of a premeasure consisting of the lowest recorded DBP reading obtained during three different premeasurement days. Thus, mean reductions observed are statistically conservative. Mean systolic/diastolic changes for the three groups were as follows: relaxation ($-6.8/$ -7.6 mm Hg), biofeedback ($0.6/-1.2$ mm Hg), and control ($1.6/1.2$ mm Hg). On pretest–posttest analysis no significant SBP differences were observed, whereas the relaxation and biofeedback conditions showed significant reductions in DBP. Finally, relaxation showed a decrease in blood pressure across sessions and within sessions.

Walsh, Dale, and Anderson (1977) evaluated biofeedback pulse wave velocity and progressive relaxation. Pulse wave velocity, which equals pulse transit time between the heart's right ventricular actions and the finger's pulse, divided into the arterial distance between the two pulse points, is highly correlated with SBP. This study was conducted in two phases. In phase 1, 24 essential hypertensives participated, but no information about recruitment procedures or independent verification of diagnosis was mentioned. Subjects were age-matched and randomly assigned to groups. Approximately one-half of these subjects were taking medication (tranquilizers, muscle relaxants, or diuretics). Of the original group of subjects, 16 entered phase 2.

During phase 1, subjects were treated once a week for 5 weeks. Biofeedback subjects received auditory and visual feedback signals of pulse transit time, which varied with pulse wave velocity. Subjects were also given verbal feedback in mm Hg for SBP and

DBP before and after each session but were not told to engage in any home practice. Progressive-relaxation subjects listened to a relaxation tape and were instructed to practice this technique once daily at home. In phase 2, subjects received five 90-minute-long sessions of a combination of biofeedback plus relaxation and instructions to practice relaxation daily. Subjects were not instructed to continue practicing relaxation during the follow-up stage. The findings indicated that within sessions biofeedback was significantly better than relaxation in lowering DBP. Across sessions in phase 1, however, biofeedback and relaxation were equally effective in reducing SBP and DBP. Those subjects receiving medication fared better with biofeedback in decreasing DBP; with relaxation, the opposite was true. During the second phase the combination of relaxation plus biofeedback had a negative impact on subjects' abilities to reduce blood pressure. Since those subjects who remained for phase 2 had higher blood pressures, selective attrition may have accounted for this finding. A comparison of mean blood pressures from pretreatment to the end of phase 2 revealed mean decreases of 12/9 mm Hg. Although the biofeedback group showed larger reductions than the relaxation group on SBP at 3-month follow-up, this difference faded at the 1-year follow-up.

In a preliminary report of 4 completed years of a 6-year study, Goebel, Viol, Lorenz, and Clemente (1980) studied a large sample (N = 130) and obtained long-term baselines and follow-ups in examining the effects of relaxation and biofeedback. All subjects were patients of a renal and hypertension clinic and had been screened for a verified history of essential hypertension. The majority of patients were taking one or more antihypertensive medications. Subjects were randomly assigned to groups: relaxation only (RO), relaxation plus EMG biofeedback (REMG), blood pressure biofeedback only (BPBF), relaxation plus biofeedback (R+BPBF), and transactional analysis (TA—attention placebo control). The latter group received equal time and attention but none of the active components of the other conditions. This study was conducted in three phases. In phase 1 (stabilization), patients were seen once a week for medication adjusted for a period lasting between 6 and 26 weeks. In phase 2 (learning and fading), subjects were seen for 6 weeks twice a week and for 6 weeks on a once-a-week basis, during which medications were stabilized. In phase 3 (transfer and follow-up), subjects were seen once a week for 6 weeks, during which medications were adjusted, with further follow-up once a month for 6 months and 1 year later. Blood pressure measurements were automated by a device that was checked frequently for accuracy. In the RO group patients listened to relaxation tapes comprising modified Jacobsonian and imagery techniques, which were used at home for practice twice daily. The REMG group listened to relaxation tapes and received EMG biofeedback training from the forehead. The third group (BPBF) received blood pressure biofeedback from one of two devices. In the R+BPBF group subjects listened to relaxation tapes and received feedback from one of two devices. In all treatment groups finger temperature was monitored for half of the subjects and skin potential for the other half, as measures of relaxation without feedback. The control group discussed a book and listened to a series of tapes at home on human relations. Selected results of this investigation will be discussed. Data from the main study were analyzed by a series of t tests and showed that on before and after measures the control group blood pressure was unchanged. The overall mean declines for the four experimental groups were signficant and equaled 6.9/4.4 mm Hg. A multivariate analysis of variance would have been preferred and would have reduced likelihood of probability pyramiding. Also, 34 of the 38 patients decreased SBP, and 35 of the 38 decreased DBP. Considerable variability in declines on systolic (0.7 to 30 mm Hg) and diastolic (3 to 19 mm Hg) pressures were shown. No significant differences between treatment were found, leading to the tentative conclusion that relaxation and biofeedback are equally effective. The authors were awaiting the remainder of the data before drawing definitive conclusions. Although the experimental groups were significantly different from the attention placebo condition, the absence of credibility ratings leaves an important question unanswered.

Cohen and Sedlacek (1983) compared a biofeedback/self-regulation package and Benson's relaxation response with a waiting list control condition on blood pressure and attentional measures. Volunteers ($N = 30$) who were referred by private or clinic physicians were randomly assigned to groups. Blood pressures were recorded with a sphygmomanometer and stethoscope by the therapist before and after each session, on a once-a-day basis, by the patients at a regular time, and by a blind nurse once every 2 weeks. All but 3 of the subjects were being treated with antihypertensives, which were stabilized during the course of the study. Participants were also instructed to maintain current dietary habits. Biofeedback self-regulation subjects received 20 sessions comprising EMG for 4 weeks; thermal biofeedback for 4 weeks; and either EMG, thermal, or no feedback for the remaining weeks. Treatment also included cognitive components such as imagery and autogenic phrases, and subjects were encouraged to practice at home twice a day for 15–20 minutes. Relaxation treatment subjects were seen once a week for 5 weeks and then again 5 weeks later. These patients learned Benson's relaxation response and were also asked to practice at home. The control subjects who were told that they would receive treatment at a later time were asked to keep blood pressure records. Subjects were measured on dependence/independence instruments—(Embedded Figures Test (EFT), Block Design (BD), and Picture Completion (PC); attention deployment—Digit Span (DS); and capacity to sustain attention—Absorption Scale (AS). The biofeedback group not only revealed a significant increase in field independence (EFT and BD) relative to the other two groups, but they decreased DBP significantly at posttest. While the mean change for this group was $-13.0/-12.90$ mm Hg, the relaxation group returned to baseline on blood pressure while the controls remained unchanged. There were significant correlations between DBP changes and the EFT scales ($r = .54$) and Picture Completion ($r = .32$). As the authors admitted, the biofeedback group did receive more therapist contact and more sessions of treatment, as well as a variety of self-regulation strategies. They concluded that despite whether they learned to control autonomic functions, the value of biofeedback may be that it helps patients to facilitate selection and discrimination of sensory cues.

Sedlacek, Cohen, and Boxhill (1983) (abstract) compared the relaxation response to EMG plus thermal biofeedback and a control condition. All but three subjects were being treated with antihypertensives. Patients self-recorded blood pressure with a sphygmomanometer. Relaxation patients, biofeedback, and controls received 9, 24, and 5 sessions, respectively. An advanced doctoral candidate in psychology and a psychiatrist, the first and second authors, served as therapists and followed a standard protocol. The psychology student treated 90% of the biofeedback patients. The findings supported the superiority of biofeedback, which produced significant decreases in SBP and DBP, with average declines of $-14/-12$ mm Hg. At 4-month follow-up the results were still significant, although there was a small increase in SBP and DBP. Relaxation and control subjects showed no significant changes. In terms of medication, 30% of the biofeedback-treated patients had their medication cut in half. The clear superiority of biofeedback, however, might be explained by the fact that biofeedback patients received three times as many sessions (therapist contact) as the relaxation subjects.

In sum, on the basis of four studies comparing relaxation therapy to an untreated control condition, there is evidence that relaxation therapy is superior on both clinical and *in vivo* measures to mere monitoring of blood pressure. On the basis of three studies comparing relaxation to a placebo control exclusively, however, the findings are less conclusive. Relaxation would appear to be superior to a nonspecific attention control under certain quasi-treatment circumstances and even then on only certain aspects of blood pressure and in certain measurement settings, as described previously. Moreover, in those studies contrasting various formats for delivering relaxation therapy (alone versus couples; individual versus group), the observed effects on blood pressure appear to be equivalent. In addition, the specific instructions (cognitive expectancy) given to patients may in turn produce differential outcomes. Finally, in three of the six studies comparing relaxation with biofeedback, relaxation was as effective as biofeedback, whereas in the remaining three studies biofeedback was superior to relaxation. In two of these latter studies (Cohen & Sedlacek, 1983; Sedlacek et al., 1983), the biofeedback patients clearly received more treatment per se in the form of therapist contact, attention, and number of sessions. These procedural differences may account for the discrepant findings across the studies. On the other hand, these biofeedback treatment protocols more accurately reflect what is done in clinical practice, which in turn is indirectly related to the training to criterion issue to be discussed later. The real question here is whether relaxation would be as effective as biofeedback with a more intense delivery of the relaxation treatment in these studies.

HYPNOSIS

Case, Fogel, and Pollack (1980) evaluated the immediate and long-term effects of hypnosis in mild essential hypertensives. None of the subjects were receiving medication for at least one month prior to the initiation of the study. Four groups were compared: hypnotizable hypertensives, hypnotizable normotensives, nonhypnotizable hypertensives, and nonhypnotizable normotensives. Subjects received self-hypnosis training and were instructed to practice 6–10 times a day for a 1–2 minutes. A comparison of hypnotizable hypertensives and normotensives revealed small but significant increases in SBP and DBP in both groups during self-hypnosis. This effect decreased, however, over the course of 10–15 minutes. At 4-month follow-up the effects of self-hypnosis were found to vary. For example, whereas blood pressure was unchanged in 7 patients and rose in 3, in 5 blood pressure declined. Patients were divided into three groups on the basis of response: pressor responders (maximum increase in BP of 25%), depressor responders (maximum BP decline of at least 7%), and nonresponders. Subjectively, most patients reported improvement in mood, behavior, and well-being regardless of blood pressure change. Despite the apparent subjective improvement experienced by the subjects, the immediate effect of hypnosis appears to be pressor. The long-term effect is unimpressive. Even in depressor responders, one could not justifiably conclude that self-hypnosis was responsible for the observed change. An overall average change across all patients calculated by the present author equaled −4.9/+15 mm Hg.

Friedman and Taub (1977) compared hypnosis with biofeedback, hypnosis plus biofeedback, and a measurement-only control condition. The total sample comprised unmedicated and medicated patients, the latter being stabilized on drugs. Automated blood pressure measurements were obtained with a London Pressurometer. Reliability checks were gathered throughout the study by preceding and following each series of automated readings with two manually obtained measurements with a standard sphygmomanometer. However, baseline pressure was established on a very limited sample of 10 readings taken in one session. Subsequently, subjects were assessed on a well-known and standardized measure of hypnotic susceptibility. High hypnotically susceptible subjects were randomly assigned to a hypnosis-only (HYP) condition or a hypnosis plus biofeedback (HYP+BF) condition; low- and high-susceptible subjects were randomly assigned to a biofeedback-only group (BF) or a measurement-only control (MOC) condition. HYP and HYP+BF subjects were also trained in autohypnosis and instructed to employ it as well as placing themselves in a relaxed position twice a day for 3-minute periods. BF and MOC subjects were requested to perform the same exercise but without hypnosis. At 1-month follow-up only 1 subject was lost from the MOC group. Mean reductions in DBPs across groups ranged from a low of 2.8 mm Hg and 2.9 mm Hg in the HYP+BF and MOC conditions to a high of 8.2 mm Hg in the HYP group. The HYP group was significantly more improved than the MOC and HYP+BF conditions, whereas the BF group (mean reductions of 4.3 mm Hg) was not significantly different from any of the other groups. Only the BF and HYP groups showed significant within-group changes from baseline to the 1-month follow-up. For the BF group only, however, the seventh session and 1-week follow-up measures differed significantly from the baseline. In the HYP group, all the measurement periods differed significantly. Analysis for the 1-month follow-up data revealed that the HYP group once again differed significantly from the MOC and HYP+BF groups. The BF group was not significantly different from any of the other groups. In response to the possible criticism that the findings could in part be a function of high hypnotic susceptibility, the BF and MOC groups were categorized into low- and high-susceptible subjects. In both instances, and contrary to this hypothesis, low-susceptible subjects showed greater blood pressure reductions.

In sum, the findings in the area of hypnosis are equivocal. Whereas hypnosis was associated with a pressor response in one instance, in another instance it was helpful in reducing blood pressure. Further research aimed at evaluating the effects of hypnosis is therefore warranted.

Methodological Analysis

In reviewing the conclusions based on the research in this section, the findings must be considered with the following methodological points in mind. Of the 24 studies reviewed so far, approximately 79% made attempts to verify or confirm the diagnosis of essential hypertension. Although in about 13 or 54% of these studies subjects were concurrently being treated with antihypertensive medication, in 10 or 76% of these studies medication was clearly stabilized throughout the trial. Regarding assessment of blood pressure, a variety of controls to reduce measurement bias were incorporated. Six investigators automated the measurement process (Case et al., 1980; Cottier et al., 1984; Deabler et al., 1973; Friedman & Taub, 1977; Goldstein et al., 1984; Shoemaker Tasto, 1975; Southam et al., 1982), and four others ensured that the individuals collecting the measurements were kept blind (Agras et al., 1980; Agras et al., 1982; Cohen & Sedlacek, 1983; Stone & DeLeo, 1976). Still others maintained controls such as employing the same technician through-out with the same subjects (Brady et al., 1974; Wadden, 1983, 1984); calibrating instruments (Agras et al., 1980; Pender, 1984); and checking for accuracy (Goebel et al., 1980; Goldstein et al., 1984; Wadden, 1983). With respect to follow-up measures, in 14 or 58% of the studies such measures were obtained and ranged from 1 week and 1 month in 1 study to 1 year in 4 studies. In the remaining 6 studies follow-ups were gathered within the 4- to 6-month range. Despite what appear to be some generally sound methodological characteristics, however, there are some consistent problems with respect to the treatment delivery process. In only 4 studies was a blind therapist used. Moreover, in only three of the 24 studies was treatment monitored in some manner to ensure a standardized presentation. For example, Wadden (1983, 1984) employed a standardized and detailed treatment manual. Finally, in only 14 or 58% of these studies were the characteristics of the therapist specified.

Transcendental Meditation (TM) and Yoga

The impact of TM and other yogalike treatments on blood pressure was examined in a small number of investigations.

Single-Group Outcome Studies

In an uncontrolled single-group outcome study, Datey, Deshmukh, Dalvi, and Vinekar (1969) studied the impact of Shavasan, a yogic relaxation exercise, in 47 hypertensives (32 essential, 12 renal, and 3 arteriosclerotic). The majority of the patients were on drug therapy; those not on drugs were first given a placebo for at least 30 days before treatment. During treatment the drug requirement of the patients was stabilized. All subjects attended a cardiac center on a daily basis to learn the yoga exercise and were subsequently advised to come weekly to have their blood pressure measured. The exercise proper lasted for 30 minutes, with most subjects acquiring it within 3 weeks. Details regarding the treatment and its delivery were ambiguous. Nonetheless, following Shavasan the typical nonmedicated subject exhibited a blood pressure decline of 26.9 mm Hg. For those controlled with drugs, the average decrease was −37 mm Hg after treatment. Finally, for those not adequately controlled with drugs, the average decline after Shavasan was −37.2 mm Hg. In each of these latter instances, however, it must be noted that the average decline from drug therapy was −35 mm Hg in the first instance and −27.2 in the second instance. Although treatment was associated with improvement most of the reduction was associated with medication. In these groups, however, 13 out of 22 and 6 out of 15 reduced their drug intake by at least 35%.

In a later study Sundar, Agrawal, Singh, Bhattacharya, Udupa, and Vaish (1984) compared shavasana (Shavasan) with shavasana plus drug therapy. Twenty-five essential hypertensives received 6–8 weeks of weekly pretherapy blood pressure checks by an independent observer. In medicated subjects drug therapy was stabilized. Subjects were instructed to practice at least twice a day for half a year. Specifications regarding the delivery of treatment were lacking. However, follow-ups ranging from 6 months to 3 years were obtained. Average SBP/DBP reductions for the shavasana and shavasana plus medication groups were 14.0/12.3 and 31.2/18.8 mm Hg, respectively. At follow-up, compliers with practice maintained their improvement, but noncompliers showed significant increases in blood pressure.

Benson, Rosner, Marzetta, and Klemchuk (1974) studied 22 unmedicated borderline essential hypertensives. There was no independent diagnostic verification. Blood pressure was measured by a random zero sphygmomanometer, which allowed for bias-free measurement observations. Although treatment was not monitored, a questionnaire was used to assess the frequency of meditation practice. Significant pretest–posttest changes of −7.0/−3.8 mm Hg were observed.

Blackwell, Hanenson, Bloomfield, Magenheim, Gartside, Nidich, Robinson, and Zigler (1976) assessed the effects of TM with seven essential hypertensives. A university campus paper ad yielded 13 volunteers, all of whom received a physical exam and were currently on medication. Both patients and their private physicians agreed to the stabilization of medication, which was verified at each visit to the clinic. Baseline data were collected over a 10-week period. Blood pressure was measured at work or home and at the clinic by a trained nurse following a rest period of 15 minutes. Subjects were taught to obtain blood pressures *in vivo* four times a day at regular time intervals. The reliability of subject measurements was confirmed. All subjects were taught TM during weekly sessions over the course of 12 weeks, and subjects practiced twice daily. Comparing baseline to week 9 to 12 of meditation, average home and clinic blood pressure changes were −7.48/−6.09 and −4.16/−1.61, respectively. At 6-month follow-up home and clinic measures were −12.98/−7.23 and −2.56/−4.03 mm Hg, respectively. Based on a number of *t* tests, 6 of 7 subjects revealed significant home blood pressure reductions on SBP; 5 of 7, significant DBP reductions. On clinic blood pressures 4 subjects showed significant reductions on SBP and DBP. At 6-month follow-up 3 subjects showed significant SBP and DBP reductions at home, while 5 subjects showed clinic reductions. Since the number of statistical comparisons by *t* tests equaled 50, the conclusions must be viewed with caution. This issue seriously raises the potential for chance findings here.

In this uncontrolled single-group study (Pollack, Weber, Case, & Laragh, 1977), 20 previously diagnosed patients were treated. Nine of the subjects were concurrently treated with antihypertensives, but there was no indication of whether medication was stabilized. Blood pressures were measured by a standard mercury sphygmomanometer with measurements gathered at least 1 hour after the end of meditation. Control measures were defined as the average of several measurements obtained during a 3-month period prior to the initiation of the study. All patients were sent to the International Meditation Center, where they were taught by three qualified teachers. SBP decreased significantly by an average of 8.9 mm Hg during the first month of meditation and was significant at the end of months 2 and 3. During the final 3 months of the study, however, SBP did not differ significantly from the baseline value. DBP did not change significantly at any time during the course of the study. Meditation was associated with a significant decrease in pulse rate during the first month. Pulse rate also decreased during months 2 and 4 but was not significantly better than the control value during the rest of the investigation. Plasma renin activity did not change at all during the course of the study. Fourteen of the patients, however, did report positive feelings of well-being, whereas those who wished to discontinue reported anxiety, depression, and insufficient time for meditation practice.

Controlled Between-Groups Outcome Studies

TM VERSUS WAITING LIST CONTROL AND PLACEBO

Seer and Raeburn (1980) compared TM, a placebo (with no mantra), and a waiting list control in unmedicated hypertensives. All blood pressure assessments were gathered by a medical psychologist who was unaware of the subjects' group status. Bias-free blood pressure measures were obtained by means of a random zero sphygmomanometer. To control for diurnal variations, a specific time was established for each subject and adhered to throughout the course of the study. Measurements were never preceded by meditation or practice. Subjects also completed a variety of psychological inventories and were randomly assigned to one of three groups. Treatment subjects were seen for 25 weekly sessions by the senior author, who was kept blind to assessment data. In the TM condition subjects were required to sit quietly twice daily for 20 minutes and to repeat a mantra. The label TM was never used with the subjects. The treatment itself was developed from information provided by an experienced TM instructor. In the placebo group the training was closely modeled after the TM treatment except that subjects were not instructed in the use of a mantra. Rather, subjects were taught to allow thoughts, images, and emotions to come to mind and fade away. The waiting list control group received the same type and frequency of assessment sessions but otherwise received no instructions. No significant differences in credibility between the treatment and placebo groups were observed. The findings revealed no significant differences on SBP. On DBP the TM and placebo group revealed a significant decline but did not differ from each other. At follow-up, the TM and placebo groups maintained their changes.

In overview, except for Seer and Raeburn (1980), the studies reviewed in this section are uncontrolled single-group or between-group comparisons and, as such, suffer from a variety of threats to internal validity such as history, maturation, testing, instrumentation, and regression. The findings must be carefully viewed with these points in mind. With respect to shavasana, the available studies yielded relatively large blood pressure reductions in unmedicated patients, and a small additive effect in medicated patients. Regarding TM, the observed changes were, relatively speaking, of a smaller magnitude and within the modest range. Because of the methodological inadequacies in the studies, however, the findings are inconclusive. The only well-controlled study in this area (Seer & Raeburn, 1980) showed that TM was equal to a placebo condition, both of which produced modest reductions in blood pressure that were maintained at follow-up. In this study a variety of controls were incorporated, including blind BP assessment, a fixed measurement period across days, and treatment credibility assessment. These results would imply that TM may be no better than nonspecific attention.

Methodological Analysis

In general, from a methodological standpoint the studies reviewed in this section have a number of both strengths and shortcomings. In 75% of the studies the diagnosis was confirmed. Also, in the four studies in which subjects received medication (Datey et al., 1969; Sundar et al., 1984; Blackwell et al., 1976; Pollack et al., 1977), there were clear attempts in three cases to stabilize the medication. Regarding problem areas, in only three studies (Benson et al., 1974; Seer & Raeburn, 1980; Sundar et al., 1984) was an attempt made to eliminate bias in the BP assessment process. In terms of follow-up, in only three studies were such measures obtained. Finally, with respect to the delivery of treatment, in only one instance was a blind therapist–experimenter employed. In none of these studies was there clear evidence of treatment monitoring, and in only two instances (Pollack et al., 1977; Seer & Raeburn, 1980) were the therapists identified. Even here, however, the specific characteristics of the therapists were not clarified.

Biofeedback

Various forms and combinations of biofeedback have been tested and applied in the treatment of essential hypertension. Typically, these treatments have included EMG feedback, temperature feedback, blood pressure feedback, yoga plus biofeedback, and the like. In this section the outcome literature in this area will be examined.

Multiple-Case Studies

EMG AND THERMAL BIOFEEDBACK

Ford, Stroebel, Strong, and Szarek (1983) reported the results of Quieting Response Training, which incorporated EMG and thermal biofeedback, for a variety of psychosomatic disorders. In this multiple case study the results of treating 340 patients are described. The discussion in the present context will be limited, however, to 15 essential hypertensives who were treated. Besides the clearly uncontrolled nature of this study, there is an obvious lack of information about important and relevant variables. Percentage decreases in diastolic blood pressure were categorized as follows: no improvement (0–9%), slight (10–14%), moderate (15–19%), and much—that is, DBP in normal range for 1 year with no medication or recovered (20–24%). Follow-up results for hypertensives revealed that only 33% of the patients fell within the moderately improved or recovered categories. In accounting for these findings, the authors suggest that noncompliance with daily home practice was apparent based on their clinical observations.

In another study, Green and Green (1983) described the results of thermal biofeedback (autogenic vasodilation in the legs) with 12 patients. In this uncontrolled multiple case study patients had an established diagnosis of essential hypertension, and all but 5 were on medication. Details regarding possible stabilization of medication and blood pressure assessment were unclear. Patients received an average number of 27.5 sessions, with a range from 13 to 34. Three patients were still in treatment at the time of the report. The overall observed mean change in blood pressure was −7.8/−6.72 mm Hg. The medication index dropped at follow-up to zero for 6 of the 7 subjects on drugs, and the remaining subjects eventually decreased medication use to zero. The authors claim that for 55 additional patients treated, similar findings were obtained, with 87.5% of them free of medication. Although these findings are quite impressive, these results are based on case studies where a variety of variables with respect to internal validity threats could account for the results (e.g., change in sodium intake). Regarding external validity, the authors claimed that their patients were selected for training by referring physicians and, as such, might not be representative of the general population of drug-treated hypertensives.

In a retrospective review of 58 cases, Lido and Arnold (1983) considered whether training to criterion level in EMG and thermal biofeedback therapies was associated with long-term improvement for a variety of diagnostic groups. They hoped to shed some light on the issue of whether merely presenting biofeedback treatment for a designated number of sessions, without addressing whether learning to criterion has been achieved, is a valid test of therapy. In this study, patients who had previously received biofeedback-assisted relaxation therapy were analyzed. Criteria for inclusion in this follow-up study were having one of six major diagnoses including essential hypertension, participation in a minimum of four therapy sessions, and termination of therapy for more than half a year.

Patients had been exposed to a variety of relaxation approaches with an emphasis on *in vivo* practice. A part of each session was also devoted to EMG and digital thermal biofeedback training. The therapist and patients were unaware of any given criterion levels of training at that time. Rather, EMG and thermal biofeedback criterion levels of 1.1 microvolts or less and 95° Farenheit, respectively, were chosen after the conclusion of the basic follow-up study. These criteria were selected simply on the basis of their demonstrated success from other clinical researchers.

Patient self-ratings of improvement as obtained by a survey questionnaire (73% return rate) 1 to 5 years posttherapy were collected by a research technician, not by the therapist. A comparison of respondents and nonrespondents on a number of variables (age, number of sessions, biofeedback training levels, compliance, home practice, medication reduction, length of time posttherapy, and level of improvement during therapy) revealed no differences. In general, collapsing across all diagnostic groups and comparing rated improvement across those who achieved the training criterion versus those who did not provided support for the importance of training to criterion. Significantly, greater improvement rates were found for those patients achieving the established EMG or skin temperature levels. With hypertensives, 11 of 12 reported improvement, and most recent blood pressures reported by these patients were in the normotensive range. However, this study has a number of limitations. First, level of criterion was not experimentally manipulated in this study, which precludes cause–effect conclusions. Second, the characteristics of the overall sample were described as opposed to the characteristics of patients in each diagnostic group. Third, a number of important questions regarding diagnostic verification, blood pressure measurement, and medication usage were left unanswered. Fourth, the findings are based on patient self-report. As a partial control for this problem, there was a 92% agreement between patient reports and an independent rater who reviewed patients' symptom diaries, self-reports, and therapist's notes. This independent rater showed 100% agreement with a second independent rater.

In summary, despite the generally encouraging findings reported in the foregoing case studies, the limitations of the case study method apply here (Kazdin, 1980). Because of alternate explanations and other sources of bias, these findings are inconclusive and tentative at best.

Single-Group Outcome Studies

YOGA, RELAXATION, OR MEDITATION PLUS BIOFEEDBACK

Patel (1973) studied a combination of yoga and biofeedback in 20 hypertensives, 19 of whom were well controlled on medication. This sample included 14 essential hypertensives, 2 renal hypertensives, 1 intracranial hypertensive, and 3 women who developed essential hypertension following a toxemic pregnancy. Blood pressure was measured with an ordinary clinical sphygmomanometer, which the author checked against other manometers used in the practice. However, no reliability data are reported. Another limitation is that the majority of the recordings were made by the investigator. Even though these recordings were often checked by a nurse or another physician, reliability data were again not reported. To determine percentage reduction in medication associated with the treatment program, medication dosage was adjusted during the course of this trial. Previous attempts to reduce medication had resulted in increased blood pressure. Subjects were treated individually for 36 sessions, and subjective improvement was evidenced by the favorable comments made by some of the patients. Mean reduction in systolic/diastolic blood pressure (160 to 134)/(102 to 86) was 26/16 mm Hg, despite a 41% decrease in medication required. An individual case analysis of these data revealed the following: stopped medication ($n = 35$), reduced medication intake by 33–60% ($n = 7$), no change in medication with improved blood pressure ($n = 4$), and no change in blood pressure ($n = 4$).

Patel (1976) evaluated the effects of relaxation and meditation reinforced by biofeedback on blood pressure and serum cholesterol. In a group of 14 hypertensives who had previously served as controls in an earlier study (Patel & North, 1975), life-style habits were closely monitored during the course of treatment. All subjects except one were on antihypertensive drug therapy, which was stabilized. After six weeks of therapy and practice, mean reduction was 22.6/13.4 mm Hg. Average reduction in serum cholesterol was 24.5 mg/100 ml. Despite the encouraging results, the findings are extremely limited by the absence of a control group.

Kleinman, Goldman, Snow, and Korol (1977) attempted to account for subject variability in response to biofeedback training with respect to stress level. Eight male unmedicated essential hypertensives who exhibited minimum blood pressure of 140/95 mm Hg on at least 3 measurements participated. During the first few weeks of the study (control period), the patients had three to five blood pressures measured once a week. Subsequent to the first control session, each patient was taught to measure his own blood pressure and to record it 5 times daily at home and work. At completion of the control period, systolic blood pressure biofeedback was begun and continued for 9 weekly sessions. Although follow-up data were gathered 4 months posttreatment, data were available on only 3 of the original patients.

Average blood pressure reductions from the beginning of the three control sessions to the end of the last two treatment sessions were −6/−8 mm Hg. The observed systolic change was not significant; the diastolic, significant. Average changes during control and feedback sessions were −.5/−1.6 mm Hg and −4.4/−4.1 mm Hg within sessions, with a similar pattern of significance. Follow-up measures taken outside the lab revealed maintenance of reduction at 4 months, although only three patients participated. A comparison of control blood pressure for those subjects who remained to the rest of the group revealed that they were quite comparable. Nonetheless, mortality remains an issue here. Finally, although high-stress patients had significantly higher blood pressures during the control period, the magnitude of change during the training sessions was similar regardless of stress level.

In another uncontrolled study, Leigh (1978) described the results obtained with biofeedback in his laboratory. The lack of specification of variables and procedures clearly limits this study. Ten borderline hypertensives who received four biofeedback sessions subsequent to three baseline sessions showed an average decline of 6.8 mm Hg ranging from a low of 0 to a high of 34.6 mm Hg. Subsequently, in an effort to determine whether biofeedback could be potentiated by drug therapy, an additional 6 subjects were studied. Four of the subjects received placebo, hydralazine, and librium in separate trials while simultaneously receiving biofeedback during lowered blood pressure. None of the drugs was particularly helpful in potentiating the effect of biofeedback. However, whenever a subject's systolic pressure was reduced after taking a capsule (regardless of what it was), the individual seemed to be able to lower SBP to a far greater degree during the subsequent nonmedication session. Average changes during drug and post sessions for hydralazine, placebo, and librium were −1.5, −4.78, −5 and −5.3, 12, 7, respectively. In view of the limitations of this study, these results are far from definitive.

In a preliminary report Harrison and Rao (1979) examined the effects of relaxation and biofeedback in 22 black hypertensives. Participants were physician-referred or self-referred, the latter group receiving a physical exam to rule out other disease processes. The sample was limited to motivated individuals with a strong desire to take responsibility for their health. The treatment program proper comprised an eight-step process incorporating the following: biofeedback, progressive relaxation, autogenic training, respiration, attitudes toward relaxation, mental imagery, guided relaxation imagery, and imagery for health. Auditory biofeedback was incorporated into all sessions. Also, instructions were presented on audiotape to ensure standardization. Subjects were asked to practice for a minimum of 20 minutes a day at home. Subsequent to the training program, subjects were given a test designed to assess relaxation level during relax instructions and the performance of two mental tasks. At the completion of the program, subjects were invited to become involved in a weekly group relaxation class incorporating discussions on stress and relaxation. Despite observed differences between initial and final systolic and diastolic readings as well as during the test, no significant differences were observed.

In reviewing the findings from these single-group outcome studies, a yoga and relaxation biofeedback combination and blood pressure biofeedback were associated with moderately large blood pressure reductions in some instances. Nonetheless, the nature of the research design employed in these studies—the preexperimental one-group pretest–posttest design—is rather weak (Campbell & Stanley, 1963). These studies are jeopardized by a variety of internal and external validity threats and must be viewed with caution.

Single-Subject Experiments

BIOFEEDBACK

Benson, Shapiro, Tursky, and Schwartz (1971) evaluated the efficacy of biofeedback in seven moderate to severe hypertensive patients, one of whom was suffering from renal artery stenosis. Six of the seven patients were concurrently on medication, which was stabilized. In this single-subject AB design, subjects received from 5 to 16 baseline sessions. The last 5 sessions for each subject were used to calculate a median SBP. Average number of treatment sessions was 21.7 (range 8–34). Treatment was continued until no reduction in blood pressure occurred in 5 sessions. During the baseline phase and treatment, median SBP declined from 164.9 mm Hg (139.6–213.3) to 148.4 mm Hg (131.7–179.5). Individual changes in SBP varied from an increase of 0.9 mm Hg in the renal artery stenosis patient to a decline of 33.8 mm Hg. Five of the seven patients exhibited declines ranging from 16.1 mm Hg to 33.8 mm Hg.

Blanchard, Young, and Haynes (1975) evaluated an open-loop feedback device using a closed-circuit television monitor in four patients with elevated blood pressure. In this ABAB design, subjects were provided with feedback of SBP on a minute-by-minute schedule. Subjects were also asked to attempt to reduce their blood pressure by using the feedback on the monitor. Of four subjects treated, two were psychiatric inpatients receiving 5 mg of Valium, which was stabilized throughout the study. Subjects were asked not to alter their pattern of respiration or muscle tension level and were observed to confirm this. Interrecorder and intrarecorder reliabilities of the polygraph readings were assessed. Introduction of feedback was associated with a decline in systolic blood pressure ranging from 9 to 55 mm Hg. Return to baseline led to increases in blood pressure in all subjects ranging from 1.0 mm Hg to 16 mm Hg. Reintroduction of feedback, which was limited to two of the subjects, led to additional declines over those evidenced during the previous treatment phase by 4.3 and 6.0 mm Hg. Follow-up of these two subjects revealed relative maintenance of these gains. Despite the relatively controlled nature of this study, the investigators admitted to several potentially limiting factors. First, instructions to lower blood pressure were restricted to the feedback phase. It is likely that subjects maintained differential expectations across phases. Second, subjects may have relaxed themselves during the feedback phase. This threat may be even more likely as subjects viewed more stimulating material during the control phases. Finally, length of follow-up, which was reported for only two of the subjects, was quite short and restricted only to the lab.

Kristt and Engel (1975) studied whether five hypertensives could learn to control their blood pressure through operant conditioning and sustain changes over a 3-month follow-up in laboratory and home settings. These patients had the diagnosis of essential hypertension repeatedly verified during their 10-year association with the clinic. Prospective subjects had to agree both to comply with the study protocol and to be hospitalized for 3 weeks during the training period. To control the novelty associated with seeing a new physician, all the subjects were seen by the senior author for a period of at least half a year before referral to the study. The study was conducted in three phases. Phase 1 comprised a 7-week pretraining assessment period during which patients were taught to self-monitor home blood pressures at home. Subjects mailed these self-monitored charts to the investigators on a daily basis. At the end of pretraining these patients who had been receiving between one and three antihypertensive medications were stabilized on lower doses as a means of compensating for being hospitalized. During phase 2 patients received visual SBP biofeedback on a beat-by-beat basis, including a digital readout indicating points for successful performance, with the criterion being made progressively more difficult (shaping). During weeks 1, 2, and 3 of this phase, subjects learned to lower, raise, and alternately lower and raise SBP, respectively, for 14 sessions each week. They were never instructed in how to raise or lower blood pressure but were simply told to develop their own technique. Each training session included a number of baseline trials to stabilize SBP so that training could be initiated. During the end of this phase subjects were trained in a blood pressure–lowering maneuver and instructed to practice it between 4 and 30 times daily. During training all patients exhibited control over SBP. Concomitant changes in heart rate, breathing rate, muscle tension, and EEG activity were absent, implying that relaxation was not responsible for the observed changes. During follow-up sessions in the lab at 1 and 3 months, the ability of the subjects to sustain SBP control was evident. Pre- and posttreatment blood pressures at home showed average reductions of 18.2/7.5 mm Hg, with significant SBP reductions in 4 patients and significant DBP reductions in 2 patients. The average amount of SBP lowering achieved by subjects through practice was 15.8 mm Hg based on home recordings mailed to the investigators.

In sum, in the preceding single-subject studies the controlling effects of biofeedback were demonstrated. Although in one of these studies an AB design was employed (Benson et al., 1971), the effect was demonstrated in six of seven subjects. The remaining studies employed ABAB (Blanchard et al., 1975) and ABA designs (Kristt & Engel, 1975), both of which clearly supported biofeedback.

Controlled Between-Groups Outcome Studies

BLOOD PRESSURE BIOFEEDBACK VERSUS CONTROL

There are 16 studies included in this section. The first 5 dealt with blood pressure biofeedback. Elder, Ruiz, Deabler, and Dillenkoffer (1973) compared two methods of DBP conditioning and a control condition (no feedback) in 18 male hospitalized hypertensives. Many of the patients were being treated with central nervous system (CNS) depressants (e.g., diazepam); however, there was no mention of whether medication dosage was stabilized. All patients had received bed rest and a sodium-free diet for a period of at least 3 days prior to participating in the study. An automated indirect method of measuring blood pressure was employed, and reliability checks between the automatic and standard methods were obtained. Subjects were randomly assigned to one of three groups: DBP biofeedback (shaping), DBP biofeedback (shaping) plus contingent verbal reinforcement, and a no-feedback control condition. Subjects received 8 consecutive morning and afternoon sessions during which treatment subjects were told to lower blood pressure any way they could, with a light signal indicating success. Controls received the same instructions except for the meaning of the light. These subjects were asked to relax, clear their minds, and attend to lowering their blood pressure. After the eighth session, each patient was asked to come back for a follow-up exam in 1 week. Of the total number of subjects, 9 remained for an additional week, of whom 8 returned for follow-up. Of the 9 patients who were discharged prior to follow-up, only 3 returned for follow-up. Of course, the follow-up period was of an extremely short duration.

On SBP there was an absence of significant change from the first to the last treatment session. However, the biofeedback plus verbal reinforcement group did exhibit a trend for SBP to decrease over trials. Analysis of follow-up scores on this measure also failed to yield significant differences. On the diastolic measure, DBP biofeedback plus verbal reinforcement was significantly better than the other two groups over the course of third-to-last session. Also, the biofeedback-only group was significantly better than the control group over the last two sessions. The combined treatment exhibited an effect earlier than biofeedback alone. The results demonstrated that diastolic pressure was reduced by as much as 25% over a 4-day period and persisted for a week follow-up. The latter point, however, must be considered carefully, as only 11 of the 18 subjects returned for follow-up. No comparison of completers versus noncompleters was made. Of the available subjects, mean reductions from pretest to follow-up were −14.8/−12.1 mm Hg.

In view of the criticism about the length and cost of biofeedback treatment, Hager and Surwit (1978) tested an inexpensive apparatus and home training approach. Thirty essential hypertensives who were either on a constant dose of antihypertensive medication or not on medication at all volunteered. Subjects were loaned an automated readout sphygmomanometer, trained in a standardized measurement technique, and then asked to practice the technique for 1 week with opportunity for correction of procedural mistakes. Subjects were randomly assigned to groups and trained in either Benson's meditation–relaxation condition (control) or in the use of a cuff plus counter device as a means of SBP biofeedback. They were asked to obtain pressures and practice twice a day for 5 days a week over a 4-week period, for a total of 40 training sessions. Data were recorded and mailed to the investigators by the subjects. In view of reliance on the subjects for assessment, the absence of reliability data is a clear limitation. The effects of numerous demographic variables on blood pressure change were ruled out. These variables were also equally distributed across conditions. Collapsing across groups pretreatment–posttreatment pressure changes revealed significant systolic and diastolic reductions on the morning and afternoon sessions. The mean reductions on systolic and diastolic measures were −4.1 mm Hg and −1.6 mm Hg, respectively. An analysis of prepractice levels showed no significant systolic change over 4 weeks but did reveal a significant effect on diastolic presure. However, there were no group differences in pressure level changes over the course of 4 weeks. Neither treatment yielded clinically significant reductions. However, the observed reductions were from a mean pressure of 130/83, considerably lower than the mean office pressure of 146/95, which was a criterion for participation, and lower than their lab pressures of 143/91. In explaining the findings, the authors argue that the patients were habituated to home and work settings such that their pressure dropped, thereby creating a floor effect as subjects attempted to lower blood pressure after habituation. Failure to find differences between groups may be accounted for in part by the fact that many subjects reported difficulty in relaxing while using the feedback, whereas others found the technique too complex and had difficulty following instructions. Finally, only 17 of 30 subjects completed the program.

Frankel, Patel, Horowitz, Friedewald, and Gaardner (1978) compared a multicomponent treatment package (DBP and frontalis EMG feedback, autogenic training, progressive relaxation) to noncontingent blood pressure feedback (sham) and a no-treatment control condition (weekly blood pressure checks). Twenty-two subjects in whom a comprehensive hypertension evaluation was conducted were selected. Seven subjects were continued on a previous level of diuretics, and the remainder were unmedicated. Prior to random assignment based on stratification of drug use, subjects received a 6- to 8-week period of blood pressure determinations requiring DBP readings between 90 and 105 mm Hg. Active and sham treatment subjects were treated for 20 sessions (16 weeks). Active treatment subjects were asked to practice EMG feedback and autogenic training and relaxation (audiocassette) on a regular schedule at home. Untreated subjects received 16 weekly blood pressure measurements only. Following the 16-week period, the control groups (7 sham, 3 untreated) received the active protocol. Treatment was conducted by the senior authors, who mutually monitored treatment delivery. Blood pressure measurements were gathered in the lab by a nurse who was blind to subject condition and in the clinic by an independent observer. For the total number of treated subjects (including crossover subjects), no significant change occurred over the course of the 4-month program. Average changes in the treatment group were minimal: $0/-1$ mm Hg (supine) and $+1/0$ mm Hg (standing). Mean blood pressures in the lab also showed no significant change during treatment. Mean declines observed during the last 6 sessions were quite comparable between active (3/2 mm Hg) and sham treatment (5/2 mm Hg). Encouraging results were found for only one subject.

Blanchard, Miller, Abel, Haynes, and Wicker (1979) compared blood pressure biofeedback, EMG biofeedback, and an attention placebo control condition. Subjects were offered monetary payments as a motivator for participation. Of 33 who agreed to participate, 28 completed, with the 5 dropouts distributed across the conditions. A consulting physician performed a standardized medical workup to establish the diagnosis. There was no other contact between the physicians and the subjects. An automatic blood pressure recording system was employed to reduce potential measurement bias. Subjects were matched on average systolic baseline blood pressure and then randomly assigned to groups. Subjects in the blood pressure biofeedback condition received feedback on a closed circuit monitor and were instructed to use the feedback data to assist them in determining a mental strategy to help lower their blood pressure. They were also told to practice relaxation and to try lowering blood pressure at home. Those subjects in the EMG biofeedback condition were informed that the pitch of a tone varied with level of muscle tension in their forehead. They were instructed to use the signal to relax and that relaxation would lower their blood pressure. Subjects in the attention placebo (relaxation) group were told to relax as deeply as possible and that this would help to lower blood pressure. They were also asked to practice at home on a once-a-day basis. Eight follow-up sessions were spread over a 4-month period during which subjects did not receive feedback but were asked to attempt to continue lowering their blood pressure. They were also reminded to continue practicing on a daily basis. In describing the results the authors noted (p. 105):

Overall, it appears that the slight benefits the BP feedback group received from treatment were maintained up to four months after the treatment ended. For the relaxation group, however, there was a tendency for the BP's to return over the four months to pretreatment levels. The BP's of the EMG feedback group never dropped and remained at the elevated levels during follow-up.

On generalization measures obtained in a physician's office, only the relaxation group showed significant reductions on systolic pressure. The authors concluded that none of the treatments was a success.

YOGA, MEDITATION, OR RELAXATION PLUS BIOFEEDBACK

In the next series of studies the combined effects of biofeedback and relaxationlike procedures such as yoga, meditation, and relaxation were evaluated. McGrady, Yonker, Tan, Fine, and Woerner (1981) studied the extent to which biofeedback-assisted relaxation would reduce blood pressure, forehead EMG levels, and several biochemical parameters (e.g., renin activity). Patients ($N = 43$) suffering from essential hypertension were selected. During year 1 of the study, 13 subjects participated; during year 2, the remaining 30. In this pretest–posttest control group design, subjects were randomly assigned to one of two conditions: biofeedback-assisted relaxation or control (blood pressure measurement). The majority of subjects were taking antihypertensive medication and were asked not to alter medication or diet during the study proper. Nevertheless, three of five subjects were dropped because of changes in medication dosage. During the first year measurements were obtained with a mercury sphygmomanometer; during year 2, with an automated device (calibrated weekly against the mercury device). Despite the possibility of measurement bias by the experimenter for subjects treated during year 1, comparative data across the two procedures were not calculated. Treatment subjects received 16 sessions of biofeedback-assisted relaxation comprising EMG forehead feedback. These subjects were taught autogenic-type relaxation and instructed to practice twice a day for 15 minutes. Control subjects had blood pressure measurements taken on a weekly basis. Significant reductions from pretest to posttest were observed in the treatment group on SBP, DBP, EMG levels, urinary cortisol, and plasma aldosterone. Average blood pressure decreases in the treatment group were 11/6 mm Hg. The control group showed no significant changes. An analysis of individual subjects revealed the superiority of the treatment over the control group on blood pressure reductions and EMG levels. A major limitation of this study is the absence of follow-up data.

Hafner (1982) compared meditation and meditation plus biofeedback with a no-treatment control condition. Of 21 patients with a verified diagnosis of essential hypertension, 19 were referred for failure to respond to medication. Fourteen subjects were fully treated. Blood pressure measurement was automated, thereby minimizing experimenter bias. Subjects also completed a variety of self-report questionnaires measuring hostility, assertiveness, anxiety, depression, and extent of meditation practice. Subjects were randomly assigned to conditions. Medication was stabilized at pretreatment. A repeated measures MANOVA revealed a significant occasions effect (pre–post–3-month follow-up) for systolic and diastolic blood pressure. No differences between groups were observed. Basically, both treatments were associated with significant declines in systolic and diastolic blood pressure, which were maintained at 3-month follow-up. The hypothesis that adding biofeedback-aided relaxation to meditation would increase blood pressure reductions was not supported. In addition, as the authors noted, "The overall reduction in blood pressure was not significantly greater in either treatment group than that shown by control group" (p. 313).

As a further extension of Patel (1973), in this investigation (Patel, 1975a) 20 essential hypertensives were treated by yogic relaxation reinforced by biofeedback and compared with 20 sex- and age-matched hypertensive controls. All but 3 of the 40 subjects were on antihypertensive drug therapy, which was not stabilized during treatment per se. Rather, dose was adjusted to maintain blood pressure within a "satisfactory" range. Despite this limitation, however, the investigator kept the following variables constant across conditions: appointment time, history-taking procedure, investigators, number of attendances, duration of sessions, and the blood pressure measurement procedure. Prior to the initiation of drug therapy, the average systolic and diastolic blood pressures were 201.5/121.8 mm Hg in the treatment group and 197.0/115.0 mm Hg in the controls. Subsequent to drug therapy the average pretreatment systolic and diastolic blood pressures were 159.1/100.1 mm Hg in the treated subjects and 163.1/99.1 in the control subjects. Treatment subjects received half-hour sessions of relaxation three times a week for 3 months; controls were asked to rest on a couch for this period of time. During follow-up, although no formal training was administered, only the treatment subjects were asked to practice relaxation and meditation. The findings revealed an average decline of 20.4 mm Hg in SBP and 14.2 mm Hg in DBP for the treated subjects. The controls evidenced an average decline of 0.5 mm Hg systolic and 2.1 mm Hg diastolic. Although the average treatment subject drug dosage requirement declined 41.9% (range 33–100%) during this period, the drug regimen for the controls remained unchanged. Average end-of-trial blood pressure for the relaxation subjects was 138.7/85.9 mm Hg. Average end-of-trial arrival blood pressure at follow-up was 144.6/86.0 mm Hg, which at 12-month follow-up was 144.4/86.7 mm Hg. In contrast, similar measures for control subjects revealed average blood pressures of 162.6/97.0, 167.7/97.1, and 163.6/98.1 mm Hg, respectively.

Patel (1975c) reported a preliminary investigation designed to test whether yoga and biofeedback could prevent the rises in blood pressure precipitated by daily life stresses. A total of 32 patients, the majority of whom were on antihypertensive medication, were randomly assigned to a yoga and biofeedback treatment or a control group. No information was provided about patient sampling, diagnostic confirmation, or whether medication was stabilized. Baseline blood pressures were gathered following a 20-minute rest while lying down. All patients were administered two stress tests, including an exercise test (climbing a 9-inch step 25 times) and a cold pressor test (patient informed a minute before the left hand was placed in 4° Centigrade water for 80 seconds). Blood pressure was taken before and after the tests and every 5 minutes until blood pressure reached the original baseline or until 40 minutes had elapsed. During the next 6 weeks the treatment group received relaxation and meditation training reinforced by biofeedback for 12 sessions. Control subjects attended the same number of sessions and were asked to relax on their own. Four measures were analyzed: maximum systolic rise in mm Hg, systolic recovery time in minutes, maximum diastolic rise in mm Hg, and diastolic recovery time in minutes. On the exercise test and cold pressor test, pretest–posttest comparisons were significant on all measures within the treatment group. The control group showed no significant changes. In terms of between-group comparisons, treated subjects performed significantly better on all measures except maximum systolic rise following the exercise test. Despite the encouraging findings, it must be noted that several statistical comparisons (*t* tests) were made that could increase the probability of a Type 1 error. A more efficient method would have been MANOVA. Likewise, even though someone independent of the investigator gathered data, the accuracy of the measures obtained with the sphygmomanometer could be questioned and were at best only approximate. Finally, the findings might be limited to those subjects taking antihypertensive medication.

In another outcome study Patel (1975b) examined whether relaxation and meditation reinforced by biofeedback could change the pressor response to stress in hypertensive patients. Thirty-two hypertensive patients, 29 of whom were taking antihypertensive medication, were randomly assigned to a treatment and control group. The number of subjects on medication in each group was distributed as evenly as possible. All blood pressure assessments were obtained by a trained nurse, but no apparent reliability check was performed on her data. Also, there was no indication of whether the nurse was blind to subject status. Blood pressure baselines were obtained after 20 minutes of rest in the supine position. Subjects were also exposed to an exercise test and a cold pressor where the subject was alerted 60 seconds before immersing the left hand in 4°C water.

During the 6-week pretest–posttest period, all patients attended the clinic twice a week. Treatment subjects received 30 minutes of relaxation–meditation training reinforced by biofeedback (regarding galvanic skin resistance or GSR, EMG, and alpha waves). They were also instructed to practice relaxation and meditation for 20-minute periods daily, to monitor their tension and relaxation, and to use environmental stimuli as signals to perform relaxation. On each outcome measure, the maximum rise in mm Hg and recovery time on systolic and diastolic blood pressures were evaluated. The findings revealed that on both measures significant pretest–posttest differences were obtained on systolic and diastolic pressure in the treatment group, whereas control group changes were not significant. Between-group comparisons revealed that the treatment group was significantly better than the control group on systolic and diastolic blood pressure for maximum rise and recovery time, except for the systolic rise after the exercise test. Despite the less extreme response of the treatment subjects, the findings are open to criticism. From a statistical standpoint, multiple tests were performed, thereby increasing the likelihood of probability pyramiding. Also, as Patel (1975b) admitted, a continuous automatic measure of blood pressure would have been preferred, since circulatory adjustment begins as soon as an event is over. Finally, the majority of subjects were being concurrently treated with medication, which may have changed their responses thereby limiting generalizability to unmedicated subjects.

Patel and Carruthers (1977) evaluated a treatment package comprising educational and motivational components as well as relaxation and meditation reinforced by biofeedback (GSR and EMG). Four groups were compared: 22 hypertensives, 18 normotensives, 18 smokers, and 18 untreated normotensive controls. Twelve of the hypertensive subjects were on a constant dose of drug therapy; 10 were untreated. Significant mean pretest–posttest reductions of a magnitude of 18.6/11.2 mm Hg were observed. Significant reductions in pulse rate, cholesterol, and triglycerides with no concomitant change in body weight were observed in the hypertensive group. In comparison to controls, the treated hypertensives showed significant reductions in systolic blood pressure, diastolic blood pressure, and serum cholesterol.

Patel, Marmot, and Terry (1981) conducted a randomized controlled trial of biofeedback-aided behavioral methods. A total of 204 employees exhibiting two or more coronary risk factors agreed to serve as subjects. Blood pressure measurements were obtained by a trained nurse who used a random zero sphygmomanometer. To reduce measurement bias, all blood pressure measurements (excluding those for first 25 subjects in each group) were conducted by the same nurse. All observers underwent special training. Plasma renin activity and plasma aldosterone concentrations were analyzed for a subsample of 54 subjects by blind radioimmunoassay. Subjects were randomly assigned to biofeedback and a control group. Both groups received health education literature regarding the modification of dietary fats and smoking. The treatment group received training in breathing exercises, deep-muscle relaxation, meditation, galvanic–skin resistance feedback, and a stress education program. The results demonstrated a significant decline in SBP and DBP at 8 weeks posttreatment and at 8-month follow-up. Significant reductions in plasma renin activity and plasma aldosterone were observed between the treatment and control group at posttreatment but not at follow-up. Data were analyzed by t tests as opposed to multivariate procedures. Also, nonspecific effects and therapist contact are threats operating here. The authors did, however, rule out dietary change as a potential threat to validity.

Patel and North (1975) compared yoga and biofeedback with an attention placebo control condition. Of 43 known hypertensives, 37 agreed to participate and were randomly assigned to conditions. During the first phase of treatment subjects met in a group and received a broad-based educational intervention. During phase 2, subjects were treated individually and were taught relaxation breathing exercises followed by transcendental meditation, during which subjects received biofeedback (Relaxameter–GSR90 and EMG). Subjects were encouraged to practice twice daily and were provided with a visual cue (a red disc attached to their watch) to remind them to practice. Control subjects attended the same number of sessions for the same length of time as the treated subjects. However, during this time they were asked to relax on a couch. They were neither given specific instructions to relax nor connected to any biofeedback device. Statistical comparisons revealed a reduction of 26.1/15.2 mm Hg in the treatment group compared to a reduction of 8.9/4.2 mm Hg in the controls. Although between-group differences were highly significant, control subjects exhibited significant reductions in both SBP and DBP. When the control subjects were administered the same treatment package, they showed changes similar to those found in previously treated subjects. The previously treated subjects showed very little change in blood pressure during this period. In overview, although the authors incorporated several controls, two subjects changed their medication during the trial. Also, since credibility ratings were not obtained for each treatment, the question remains whether the treatment itself was viewed as more credible than simply lying on a couch. A more effective comparison control would have incorporated a pseudofeedback component.

Surwit, Shapiro, and Good (1978) compared the relative efficacies of SBP and heart rate biofeedback, EMG biofeedback, and meditation in essential hypertensives. Subjects had to have the permission of their own physician, who was asked to provide a medical history. Fifty percent of the subjects were taking antihypertensive or psychotropic medications. Subjects were matched (age, sex, medication usage, systolic or diastolic elevation, and lability of hypertension) and assigned to groups. They were instructed to maintain current dosages of medication and dietary habits and to inform the investigator otherwise. Feedback group subjects were instructed to employ a mental strategy that would provide correct feedback. Relaxation subjects were instructed in meditation (Benson's relaxation response). Treatments were delivered by two female experimenters who ran the same subjects throughout the study and were equally distributed across groups. All subjects were instructed to practice blood pressure lowering strategies between sessions and to monitor this practice. No significant changes in practice compliance or medication were reported over the course of the study. A number of interesting findings emerged. First, there were variations in blood pressure under differing conditions of measurement. Blood pressures were found to be highest during physician exams and lowest during baseline sessions and initial training sessions. Second, a significant effect for trials within sessions was observed with average reductions of 3.4 mm Hg. Third, an analysis of first and last trials across baseline, training, and follow-up revealed that within-session declines during baseline exceeded those during treatment. Fourth, labile patients were more variable and occasionally experienced larger reductions over trials and sessions than nonlabile patients. Fifth, a comparable analysis of medicated subjects showed that slightly greater reductions in SBP occurred across trials. Finally, there were no significant differences between groups at 6-week follow-up, with average reductions of 6/3 mm Hg. However, at 1-year follow-up only 50% of the patients returned. Average pressure was about 3/3 mm Hg greater than at 6-week follow-up and at the initial training sessions.

In the second in a series of reports, Glasgow, Gaardner, and Engel (1982) contrasted SBP biofeedback (F), relaxation (R), relaxation with a blood pressure feedback, and a self-monitoring control condition (C). Seven of the 53 subjects studies were on medication. Subjects were matched and assigned to groups. During the first 3-month treatment phase subjects received control procedures, biofeedback, or relaxation. During the second 3-month treatment phase subjects either continued with their original treatment or switched to the alternative treatment. The findings revealed that biofeedback and relaxation each produced immediate blood pressure lowering effects. Biofeedback and relaxation were equally effective in reducing SBP, but relaxation reduced DBP more. The combined treatment biofeedback plus relaxation was superior to either treatment. Finally, biofeedback yielded slightly better long-term effects than did relaxation.

Engel, Glasgow, and Gaardner (1983) reported a follow-up study, the third in a series aimed at evaluating SBP biofeedback and relaxation, each alone and in combination. Those subjects who had not received both active treatments previously were given the opportunity to receive the alternative therapy. Control subjects were offered both treatments. The five groups were as follows: RF, FR, RRF, FFR, and CCRF. For patients on diuretic therapy, those who had maintained diastolic blood pressure below 90 mm Hg for the last 30 days of treatment during daily self-monitoring and weekly professional monitoring were instructed to discontinue drug therapy. Follow-up was initiated after completion of all treatments or during a 3-month monitoring period for previously medicated subjects. There were four follow-up assessment periods, at 1, 2, 3, and 6 months. An analysis of patient mortality revealed no significant differences between noncompleters and completers on age and blood pressure. However, an analysis of subjects who refused further treatment ($n = 16$) and who refused to enter follow-up ($n = 14$) indicated motivational differences (e.g., unwillingness to adhere to self-monitoring). The results must be viewed with these points in mind. For 13 patients who were discontinued on drug therapy, daily monitoring for 3 months following the baseline protocol showed that they maintained the declines associated with treatment to justify continued nonmedication. A comparison of these patients with those who continued on diuretic therapy revealed that they were similar on age, stature, and prebaseline and baseline blood pressures. Statistical analysis supported the fact that the incidence of patients taken off medication in the different groups receiving biofeedback first was significantly greater than for those receiving relaxation first. An analysis of the 6-month follow-up data clearly supported the fact that blood pressure reductions were significantly below baseline for at least 6 months subsequent to the completion of the last treatment, with the time between baseline and completion of follow-up varying from 12 months (FR and RF) to 15 months (FFR and RRF) to 18 months (CCRF).

Elder and Eustis (1975) conducted a study of instrumental blood pressure conditioning comprising massed versus distributed diastolic biofeedback. Subjects were assigned to one of two groups, which differed in the rate at which conditioning sessions were conducted. The first 19 subjects were placed in the spaced practice group; the last 4, in the massed practice group. Comparison of systolic and diastolic blood pressures of the first and second half of the sessions revealed significant decreases in both the spaced and massed groups. Statistical comparisons supported the superiority of the massed over the spaced condition in three of four analyses. Follow-up data on the distributed practice group were obtained 1 month after the final training session. At this time SBP showed a return toward the basal level, while DBP remained at those levels observed during the last conditioning session. An individual analysis of subjects' responses revealed that very few of the subjects were able to reduce their blood pressure by as much as 20%. The authors argued that since most of the subjects in this study were on antihypertensive agents, these drugs may have interfered with autonomic learning by direct or indirect interference with neural transmission. Second, the absence of a verifying medical exam may have resulted in the inclusion of subjects suffering from secondary hypertension, the latter setting a limit on the learning of subjects. To account for the superiority of massed over distributed practice, the authors relied on the principle of retroactive interference.

In sum, the preceding review warrants several conclusions about the effects of biofeedback on blood pressure.

1. On the basis of case study data, thermal biofeedback appears to be associated with improvement.
2. Training to criterion on EMG and thermal biofeedback for essential hypertension seems to be clinically important. However, further experimental research is necessary to fully address this issue.

3. Based on uncontrolled single group studies, moderately large blood pressure reductions were associated with combinations of biofeedback, yoga, and meditation.
4. On the basis of single-subject studies, biofeedback does appear to have a controlling effect on blood pressure.
5. Based on controlled between-group studies, in seven instances biofeedback combined with a relaxationlike procedure was better than a control condition, and in three instances biofeedback equaled the control conditions.
6. Although biofeedback and relaxation appear to be equally effective, the combination appears to be better than either treatment alone.
7. Presenting biofeedback in a massed fashion is somewhat superior to a distributed presentation.

Methodological Analysis

The foregoing conclusions must be viewed carefully in terms of several methodological considerations. In only 56% of the studies was the diagnosis verified. In 63% of the studies subjects were concurrently treated with antihypertensives; however, in only 11 of 17 or 65% of the cases was medication sustained at a constant dose. Furthermore, in only 3.7% of the investigations was a blind experimenter control employed, and in only 11.1% of the studies was treatment delivery monitored in some fashion. Likewise, in only 18.5% of the cases was the therapist identified and described. Follow-up data, however, were obtained in 60% of these studies. With respect to blood pressure measurements, in 14 of the 27 studies attempts were made to eliminate bias by automating the procedure or employing a random zero sphygmomanometer.

Stress Management

The effect of stress management training on blood pressure was evaluated in six studies. These treatment packages often incorporated one or more of a variety of procedures including cognitive therapy, imagery, and relaxation. In general, the use of cognitively oriented interventions is a distinguishing characteristic of these treatments, which are specifically designed to restructure patients' thinking and perceptions of patients about environmental stressors.

Single-Group Outcome Studies

In a study by Kallinke, Kulick, and Heim (1982) a stress management program focusing on a behavior analysis of factors related to blood pressure variability in patients was evaluated. Approximately half of the sample ($n = 48$) were being treated with stabilized antihypertensive medication. Subjects in this study consisted of 26 consecutive individually treated cases and 22 subjects treated in a group format. Measurements for the individual cases obtained 3 weeks before treatment and 3 weeks posttreatment revealed a significant mean reduction of $-19/-10$ mm Hg. Follow-up at 12 months revealed that gains were maintained. In the group-treated subjects, a significant average reduction of −14/−10 mm Hg was observed. No significant differences between individually and group-treated subjects were observed. Combining all subjects, the average blood pressure reductions were −17/−10 mm Hg. Also, no significant differences between drug- and non-drug-treated subjects were found. The uncontrolled nature of this study leaves numerous threats to internal validity unattended.

Controlled Between-Groups Outcome Studies

STRESS MANAGEMENT VERSUS NO-TREATMENT CONTROL

Ewart, Taylor, Kraemer, and Agras (1984) assessed the effects of a marital communication training program on blood pressure reactivity. Criteria for inclusion in this study were: diagnostic confirmation; physician agreement to stabilize medication; blood pressure greater than or equal to 140/90 mm Hg on at least one of three successive visits; the existence of spouse/partner conflict; and evidence of SBP reactivity exceeding 5 mm Hg during discussion of a relationship issue relative to a baseline conversation. Treatment subjects received nine 90-minute sessions of communication training (e.g., managing conflict) and were compared to an assessment-only (delayed training) condition. Each therapist followed a detailed treatment manual and was supervised to ensure appropriate application of the treatment. A comparison of trained and untrained subjects revealed that treated couples exhibited less hostility and combativeness after treatment. During a problem-solving task, treated and control subjects exhibited a mean decline in reactivity of 8.8/3.0 mm Hg and 3.5/0.7 mm Hg, respectively. Both systolic declines were significant, whereas diastolic reactivity was essentially unchanged. Finally, in both conditions comparisons revealed significant declines in SBP and DBP from pretest to posttest with no change from posttest to a 4-month follow-up. Both groups exhibited comparable reductions. To explain these findings, Ewart et al. relied on information from a post-experimental questionnaire. The control group reported twice as many visits to their physicians during this period as compared to the treated subjects. Also, whereas only one treatment subject reported an increase in medication, five control subjects had their dosage increased. Consequently, the changes observed in the control group could possibly be attributed to their overall more frequent use of health care services (increased medical attention) as well as medication dosage adjustments.

Charlesworth, Williams, and Baer (1984) evaluated and replicated a group work site stress management program in subjects recruited from a screening program in a corporation with a white-collar population. Diagnosis was verified either by documentation from their present physician or if average blood pressure exceeded 140/90 mm Hg based on three separate clinic measurements. The majority of subjects were being treated with medication, although there was no indication of whether it was stabilized. Blood pressure was self-recorded by a standard procedure after awakening, following return home from work, and before bedtime. The accuracy of subject self-recordings was checked twice during the study by use of a binaural stethoscope. Of course, the reactivity of the measurement process itself may have improved reliability during those checks, which might not reflect reliability at other times. The stress management program consisted of four groups of eight subjects each and included progressive differential relaxation, cue conditioning, autogenic training, stress hierarchy, visual and symbolic imagery, modified systematic desensitization, cognitive restructuring, and assertiveness training. The control group simply comprised an extended baseline delayed-treatment condition. Subject attrition was evident in both groups, but completers and noncompleters were similar on numerous dimensions. Significant improvements on pretest–posttest measures for the treatment group ($-6.1/-2.9$ mm Hg) were found. The controls did not change. When the controls were treated, however, they also exhibited significant SBP/DBP declines averaging $-3.8/-2.6$ mm Hg. Frequency of practice was positively correlated with blood pressure reduction. A 3-year follow-up on 18 of the 40 participants revealed significant reductions averaging $-7.4/-5.3$ mm Hg.

Jorgensen, Houston, and Zurawski (1981) compared anxiety management training (AMT) and a delayed treatment control condition in 18 outpatients. With the exception of 1 subject, all were receiving antihypertensive medication. Each session was trichotomized: baseline, mild stressful task, and recovery. Subjects were randomly assigned to groups. AMT included 40 minutes of taped instruction in progressive muscle relaxation and rehearsal in using this coping response for stress elicited in the therapy setting. Control subjects remained in a delayed treatment condition. Treatment was delivered by two advanced clinical psychology trainees who treated half of the subjects in each condition. To standardize treatment presentation, each therapist used a detailed manual and had received previous experience in treating two pilot subjects. During the mild stressful task, a lab assistant who was blind to treatment condition administered the Stroop Test. During posttest and follow-up, treatment subjects were not instructed to use their coping skills when blood pressure was being measured. On resting pressures AMT significantly decreased SBP and DBP from pretest to posttest. Unexpectedly, on a mildly stressful task, AMT subjects showed significantly less improvement on SBP than controls, and no difference on DBP. During the recovery period, however, the AMT group showed significantly lower SBP and DBP than did controls. AMT subjects maintained these reductions at follow-up.

STRESS MANAGEMENT VERSUS PLACEBO

In two studies comparisons with a placebo condition were made. Drazen, Nevid, Pace, and O'Brien (1982) compared a rational-emotive therapy/assertiveness training treatment package (RET/AT) and anxiety management training with an attention control condition (hypertension education counseling). Subjects, recruited from a blood pressure screening program, were not on medication. Blood pressures were recorded by the company's nurse, and no mention of measurement reliability was made. Treatments were delivered in groups and scheduled during 10 lunch periods. An advanced graduate student with several years experience in behavioral techniques served as the therapist. ANCOVA on posttest and follow-up blood pressures with pretreatment blood pressure as the covariate revealed no significant group differences. However, an analysis of within-group change from pretreatment to posttreatment demonstrated significant declines in SBP and DBP for the RET/AT group, while the AMT group showed only significant DBP reduction. A similar analysis in the attention control group was not significant. Pretest to follow-up analyses revealed identical patterns of results, although there was a nonsignificant trend for reduced DBP in the control group. An analysis of posttreatment to follow-up change indicated that treatment gains were maintained. Despite the observed within-group changes, the lack of between-group differences precludes a definitive conclusion that the effects of the treatments were more than merely a function of therapist attention and routine blood pressure monitoring.

Crowther (1983) compared a combination of a stress management package (based on the work of Richard Suinn and Donald Meichenbaum) plus relaxation imagery to relaxation alone and an attention placebo control condition. The first 39 volunteers who met criteria for eligibility were selected for participation; of these, 34 completed the study. Subjects were matched on several variables, including age, sex, systolic and diastolic blood pressure, duration of illness, and length of time treated with medication, and then were randomly assigned to groups. The stress management group received eight 60-minute sessions of the following: relaxation imagery training, instructions to practice daily at home, and stress management training emphasizing relaxation and positive self-statement coping strategies. Relaxation imagery subjects received eight 45-minute individualized relaxation imagery training sessions and instructions in daily home practice. Control group subjects received eight weekly 15-minute blood pressure checks and were told that such monitoring increases compliance with medical treatment. They were also encouraged to comply with medical treatment. Although this treatment as described does not appear to be an attention placebo group in the typical sense, comparisons of treatment credibility (expected effectiveness ratings) were comparable across conditions. Despite this control, these subjects did in fact receive less attention than subjects in the other conditions with respect to the actual duration of sessions. Blood pressure reliability checks were obtained randomly by an independent observer on two occasions for each subject. This procedure is a useful control for assessing experimenter bias in blood pressure measurement as long as the experimenter is kept blind to which measurements are being checked. Finally, as a measure of treatment generalization, those subjects with home blood pressure devices were instructed to gather data at home, while those without such equipment were asked to report pressures obtained by their physician or nurse. The control group exhibited no significant differences between systolic pressures from pretreatment throughout follow-ups. The stress management group exhibited significantly higher pretreatment systolic pressures than did those observed at the end of treatment and at 1-month and 3-month follow-up, but no different from those obtained during the first session of treatment. The systolic pressures at 1 month for this group were significantly higher than those at posttreatment, whereas the first treatment session pressures were significantly greater than those at posttreatment and 3-month follow-up but not different from those at 1-month follow-up. For the relaxation imagery group, pretreatment systolic measures were significantly greater than those at posttreatment, 1-month and 3-month follow-up; the latter three measures did not differ significantly from each other. At posttreatment the systolic measurements of the stress management and relaxation imagery groups were significantly lower than those of the control group but did not differ from each other.

Identical comparisons for diastolic pressures yielded no significant changes for control subjects. For the stress management and relaxation imagery group, pretreatment diastolic pressures significantly exceeded those at posttreatment, 1-month and 3-month follow-ups but were not different from those at first treatment sessions. For both treatment groups, the first treatment diastolic pressures were significantly greater than those found at posttreatment and 3-month follow-up, but not those at 1-month follow-up. Finally, the diastolic pressures of each treatment group were significantly better than those of the control group at posttreatment and 3-month follow-up, but not significantly different from each other. At 1-month follow-up, only the diastolic pressures of the relaxation imagery group were significantly better than those of the control group. In an analysis of maintenance of treatment gains, there were no significant differences observed between the 3- and 6-month follow-up on both measures for subjects in the three conditions.

The percentage of subjects attaining normal blood pressures at designated points in the stress management, relaxation imagery alone, and control conditions, respectively, were: posttreatment (66.7%, 83.3%, 10%); 1-month follow-up (50%, 58.3%, 20%); 3-month follow-up (58.3%, 58.3%, 0%); and 6-month follow-up (54.5%, 45.4%, 0%). A significantly larger number of subjects in each treatment group achieved this normotensive criterion at posttreatment and 3-month follow-up compared to the control group. Similar data for medication changes also supported the helpfulness of the treatments. Finally, on generalization measures there were no significant differences between experimental and generalization systolic and diastolic pressures. In overview, the decreases were 20.8/11.3 for the stress management group and 23.4/15.6 for the relaxation imagery group at posttreatment. At 6-month follow-up, comparable changes were 17.5/8.2 and 15.7/14.1, respectively.

In reviewing the findings from the available stress management studies, several conclusions emerge. Based on the single group outcome study (Kallinke et al., 1982), moderately large reductions were found. However, the design of the study precludes definitive conclusions. The controlled studies indicate that stress management is superior to an untreated control condition in lowering blood pressure reactivity and resting blood pressures and maintaining these changes on follow-up. Whether this treatment is superior to a placebo condition, however, is unsupported in one study and supported in another. Further research addressing this question is needed.

Methodological Analysis

A methodological analysis of the studies in this section reveals several interesting findings. First, in 67% of the studies the diagnosis of essential hypertension was confirmed. In 83% of the cases concurrent drug treatment was evident, although in only two of the studies was medication clearly stabilized. With respect to the treatment delivery process, in only one of the six studies was a blind therapist used, and in only two of six cases was an attempt made to monitor treatment delivery. On a more positive note, the therapists were clearly identified in two-thirds of these studies, and in all of the studies follow-ups were gathered at intervals ranging from 6 weeks to 3 years. Finally, the blood pressure measurement process was automated in two instances, while in one case a random zero device was employed.

Behavioral Treatment versus Medication

In this final section the comparative effects of psychological therapy and medication are reviewed. The relative efficacy of the behavioral treatments and the medical standard of care is a necessary comparison to determine whether behavioral therapy is a viable treatment alternative as opposed to simply being an adjunctive treatment.

Controlled Between-Groups Outcome Studies

Taylor, Farquhar, Nelson, and Agras (1977) recruited 40 subjects from a cardiovascular risk factor and hypertension clinic. Nine subjects were dropped as a result of missed appointments, implying that they were less motivated for treatment. All subjects were receiving medical therapy. All referring physicians were blind to treatment conditions and were told not to ask information about the treatment being received by a patient. Likewise, patients were asked not to reveal their treatment to their physician. The circumstances surrounding blood pressure measurement were also carefully controlled. Blood pressure was measured independently in time and place from the study by a nurse who was blind to subject status. Medical treatment involved a standardized algorithm for raising and lowering medication. The relaxation plus medical treatment subjects were trained in relaxation and were instructed to practice it and apply it. The placebo plus medical treatment subjects were with the therapist for an equal amount of time but were asked instead to discover an alternative method for dealing with tension. Although the authors reported that the placebo therapy was viewed as genuine and useful, standard credibility ratings were not obtained. Pretest–posttest differences for the medical treatment only group, the medical treatment plus placebo group, and the relaxation plus medical treatment group were as follows: $-1.1/0.3$ mm Hg, $-2.8/-1.8$ mm Hg, and $-13.6/-4.9$ mm Hg. On SBP relaxation plus medical treatment was significantly better than medication only, whereas on DBP this difference only approached significance. Also, the medication plus placebo and medication-only group were not different on SBP or DBP. The relaxation plus medication group and medication plus placebo differed significantly on SBP, while DBP approached significance. On follow-up, for the relaxation plus medication group the blood pressure reductions were maintained, while for the remaining groups there was a tendency toward improvement. There were no significant differences between groups at follow-up. Finally, there were no significant differences between groups on medication changes.

Luborsky, Ancona, Masoni, Scolari, and Longoni (1980) evaluated the effects of pharmacotherapy, autogenic training, and a combined treatment. In this study 15 essential hypertensives ranging in age from 31 to 74 years were assigned to three conditions to achieve a balance in terms of severity of hypertension, mean arterial blood pressure, lability of blood pressure, and degree of diastolic pressure. Those subjects receiving drug therapy were treated with diuretics or diuretics plus an antisympathetic. Drug therapy was maintained throughout the course of treatment. From pretreatment to posttreatment only the drug therapy group showed significant change. This group was clearly superior to the other conditions. Surprisingly, the combined treatment group was not significantly better than either treatment. This finding could have been influenced by a number of methodological factors. First, regardless of an attempt at random assignment to groups, the authors pointed out that the combined group comprised subjects who were significantly older. In addition, initial blood pressures for the combined groups were significantly higher than for the other conditions. Despite evidence indicating a correlation between initial blood pressure level and degree of improvement, Luborsky et al. found the absence of a correlation within each group. In fact, the drug therapy group, which showed the most improvement, demonstrated the lowest initial blood pressures. Finally, despite the observed differences between groups, individual analysis of subject responses revealed that relaxation is a useful alternative for some patients.

Luborsky, Crits-Cristoph, Brady, Kron, Weiss, Cohen, and Levy (1982) compared pharmacological and behavioral treatments in 51 mild to moderate essential hypertensives. Thirty-seven percent of the patients reduced their blood pressure below the lower limit merely as a function of habituation and were excluded from participation. At the initiation of baseline, none of the patients were taking antihypertensives. Those who had been on antihypertensives (diuretics) had their medication discontinued with their physician's permission for at least 3 days prior to the start of baseline. Following the baseline period subjects were randomly assigned to groups, with the restriction that groups were comparable on mean baseline blood pressure. Treatment was delivered in an initial 6-week phase followed by a 6-week crossover phase. All patients were instructed to maintain a low-salt diet and received a standard procedure designed to promote adherence. Blood pressure assessments were obtained by the same trained technician, who used a random-zero sphygmomanometer to reduce potential experimenter bias. Also, during one session of each treatment each patient had blood pressure taken with the random zero device as well as other casual measurements, which showed high correlations.

The four treatment conditions were as follows: antihypertensive medication (MED), metronome-conditioned relaxation (MCR), metronome-conditioned mild exercise (MCME—placebo), and systolic pressure biofeedback (BF). In the MED condition each patient was prescribed an individually tailored medication regimen of one or more diuretics. The MCR subjects received metronome-conditioned relaxation, which was monitored to ensure proper adherence by the patient to the treatment protocol. In the MCME condition, subjects listened to a tape instructing patients in a series of active exercises with a simultaneous metronome beat at 130 beats per minute. Both the patient and the technician were provided with the expectation that this treatment could be helpful in lowering blood pressure. In the biofeedback group subjects received three 60-minute sessions per week over a 5-week time period. The comparability of this condition to other conditions in terms of the number and distribution of sessions was compromised with the intent of optimizing effects with respect to massed practice in biofeedback. The findings showed that the medicated subjects had the most improvement and exhibited a significantly greater decline than the other three conditions on standing systolic measures and than either the MCME group or the BF group on lying-down systolic measures. Although the MCR and BF groups differed more than the placebo, this difference was not significant. With respect to the percentage of patients within conditions who exhibited more than a 10 mm Hg decline in pressure, once again the MED condition was superior by showing a rate approximately twice as great as MCR and BF and four times as great as the placebo. Also, in the MCR and BF groups, those with elevations on the Jenkins Activity Survey benefited more, and those with greater baseline life changes and stress benefited less.

In overview, medication is clearly superior to relaxation, relaxationlike treatments, and biofeedback. Although combining relaxation with medication was superior to medication alone, medication was superior to medication plus autogenic training in another instance. Moreover, medication combined with relaxation was better than medication plus placebo, whereas medication alone was better than a psychologic placebo only. One problem in the interpretation of these latter findings is the absence of credibility ratings across the treatments, which precludes definitive conclusions. In short, one could not argue that the treatments were perceived as equally believable by the subjects, which could account in part for the results.

Methodological Analysis

A methodological review of studies on this area reveals that in two of three cases the diagnosis was confirmed. Also, all studies included a condition in which subjects were on medication, and in two of these three studies medication was clearly stabilized. In only one of three studies were blind experimenters used and treatments monitored. In no instance was the therapist clearly identified. In all instances, however, some attempt was made to control the assessment process. Finally, follow-ups ranging from 1 to 6 months were evident.

Major Conclusions

On the basis of the data obtained from the preceding studies on the cognitive-behavioral treatment of hypertension, the mean outcomes for systolic and diastolic blood pressures were computed, where possible, for each treatment across studies. As shown in Table 21.2, when available, means were calculated for relevant studies and categorized as a function of the type of research design used to evaluate the treatment, ranging from case studies to controlled studies. In reviewing the overall means for each treatment, the cognitive-behavioral treatments clearly exceed the control condition. The average changes for relaxation and biofeedback are quite comparable, whereas for yoga and meditation the mean changes are somewhat larger. As noted previously, however, the bulk of the meditation studies were uncontrolled. In fact, in the one instance where a controlled study was conducted, the results were somewhat comparable to relaxation and biofeedback. The multicomponent package including TM, relaxation, or yoga reinforced by biofeedback yielded greater changes than the unimodal behavioral treatments but was similar to the stress management treatment. As noted previously, the stress management packages usually incorporated multiple treatments. Finally, each behavioral treatment exceeded the placebo treatments, which in turn was better than the self-monitoring control. Combining the results across all cognitive behavioral treatments yielded a mean decline of 11.7/8.2 mm Hg. A similar calculation for the controlled between-groups studies demonstrated a more modest decline of 9.4/6.9 mm Hg. These conclusions must

TABLE 21.2 Mean decline in systolic and diastolic blood pressures (in mm Hg) across studies

				Treatments			
Design	Relaxation	Biofeedback	Yoga and meditation	Yoga, meditation, or relaxation plus biofeedback	Stress management	Control	Placebo
Case studies	—	7.2/6.7	—	—	—	—	—
Single-group outcome	—	5.6/5.5	12.5/11.7	24.3/14.7	17.0/10.0	—	—
Single-subject experiments	11.8/9.7	16.1/7.5	—	—	—	—	—
Controlled between-groups outcome studies	8.2/5.2	6.1/5.1	4.8/8.0	14.3/9.1	13.6/7.0	—	—
Overall	8.7/6.7	8.3/5.5	11.2/11.0	16.3/10.2	14.2/7.6	1.9/.8	6.3/4.8

be viewed with some caution, as statistical analyses were not conducted in comparing the treatments. The data in this section are based on only those studies from which mean values were available. Furthermore, the blood pressure changes must be interpreted in view of the methodological limitations of the studies within each section as outlined in detail earlier. Finally, in the 40 studies in which follow-up data were collected, there is evidence to support the view that the observed changes were maintained. Length of follow-up measures ranged from 1 week to 5 years with an average of 8.6 months.

Future Directions

In view of the methodological analyses presented in previous sections, there are a number of implications for future research in this area.

First, the need for independent diagnostic verification of essential hypertension in subjects is crucial. Second, when subjects are concurrently treated with medication, stabilization of the dosage and verification of it are necessary. Likewise, controlling for variables such as weight change, changes in sodium intake, and exercise, which may also alter blood pressure, are necessary in order to eliminate these factors as alternative hypotheses for change. Third, the use of an independent blind therapist–experimenter is important for eliminating experimenter bias effects. Fourth, the explicit characteristics of therapists should be clarified to permit appropriate generalizations. Fifth, the need to monitor the delivery of treatments to ensure standardized and appropriate presentation of therapy is sorely needed. Sixth, regarding the assessment of blood pressure, the duration of baseline measures should be extended for as long as possible given the natural variability of blood pressure and the potential for habituation effects to be confused with therapy effects. On a related note, the need to continue to eliminate bias in the use of the measurement process itself is clear. Seventh, the need for long-term follow-up is clearly the true test of the potency of a treatment for essential hypertension. Finally, in the majority of the studies reviewed the lack of multivariate analysis is clearly evident. Multivariate analysis is one sure-bet approach for reducing the probability of type one errors in future studies.

Future clinical research comparing multicomponent treatment packages for essential hypertension would be especially useful in view of their demonstrated efficacy in some other areas. Although it is clear that cognitive-behavioral treatments are effective in reducing blood pressure in essential hypertensives, the magnitude of these changes would continue to justify their use as adjunctive treatments. One of the additional benefits of cognitive-behavioral treatments may be the resultant reductions in medication dosage. Moreover, these treatments may be particularly useful in treating borderline hypertensives before the need for medication becomes necessary. Finally, research aimed at identifying predictors of outcome as well as homogeneous subgroups of hypertensives may allow for the development of specific therapy packages for specific types of patients.

References

Agras, W. S., Horne, M., & Taylor, C. B. (1982). Expectation and blood pressure lowering effects of relaxation. *Psychosomatic Medicine, 44,* 389–395.

Agras, W. S., Taylor, B., Kraemer, H. C., Allen, R. A., & Schneider, J. A. (1980). Relaxation training: Twenty-four-hour blood pressure reductions. *Archives of General Psychiatry, 37,* 859–863.

Andrews, G., MacMahon, S. W., Austin, A., & Byrne, D. G. (1982). Hypertension: Comparison of drug and non-drug treatments. *British Medical Journal, 284,* 1523–1526.

Bali, L. R. (1979). Long-term effect of relaxation on blood pressure and anxiety levels of essential hypertensive males: A controlled study. *Psychosomatic Medicine, 41,* 637–646.

Beinman, I., Graham, L. E., & Ciminero, A. R. (1978a). Self-control progressive relaxation training as an alternative nonpharmacological treatment for essential hypertension. *Behaviour Research and Therapy, 16,* 371–375.

Beinman, I., Graham, L. E., & Ciminero, A. R. (1978b). Setting generality of blood pressure reduction and the psychological treatment of reactive hypertension. *Journal of Behavioral Medicine, 4*(1), 445–453.

Benson, H., Rosner, B. A., Marzetta, B. R., & Klemchuck, H. M. (1974). Decreased blood pressure in subjects who practiced meditation. *Journal of Chronic Diseases, 27,* 163–169.

Benson, H., Shapiro, D., Tursky, B., & Schwartz, G. E. (1971). Decreased systolic blood pressure through operant conditioning techniques. *Science, 173,* 740–742.

Blackwell, B., Hanenson, I., Bloomfield, S., Magenheim, H., Gartside, P., Nidich, S., Robinson, A., & Zigler, R. (1976). Transcendental meditation in hypertension: Individual response patterns. *Lancet, 1,* 223–226.

Blanchard, E. B. (1979). Biofeedback and the modification of cardiovascular dysfunction. In R. J. Gatchel & K. P. Price (Eds.), *Clinical applications of biofeedback: Appraisal and status.* New York: Pergamon Press.

Blanchard, E. B., Miller, S. T., Abel, G. G., Haynes, M., & Wicker, R. (1979). Evaluation of biofeedback in the treatment of essential hypertension. *Journal of Applied Behavior Analysis, 12,* 99–109.

Blanchard, E. B., Young, L. D., & Haynes, M. R. (1975). A simple feedback system for the treatment of elevated blood pressure. *Behavior Therapy, 6,* 241–245.

Brady, J. P., Luborsky, L., & Kron, R. E. (1974). Blood pressure reduction in patients with essential hypertension through metronome-conditioned relaxation. *Behavior Therapy, 5,* 203–209.

Brauer, A. P., Horlick, L., Nelson, E., Farquhar, J. W., & Agras, W. S. (1979). Relaxation therapy for essential hypertension. *Journal of Behavioral Medicine, 2,* 21–29.

Bulpitt, C. J. & Dollery, C. T. (1973). Side effects of hypotensive agents evaluated by a self-administered questionnaire. *British Medical Journal, 3,* 485–490.

Campbell, D. T., & Stanley, J. C. (1963). *Experimental and quasi-experimental designs for research.* Chicago: Rand-McNally.

Case, D. B., Fogel, D. H., & Pollack, A. A. (1980). Intrahypnotic and long-term effects of self-hypnosis on blood pressure in mild hypertension. *International Journal of Clinical and Experimental Hypnosis, 28*(1), 27–38.

Charlesworth, E. A., Williams, B. J., & Baer, P. E. (1984). Stress management at the worksite for hypertension: Compliance, cost-benefit, health care and hypertension-related variables. *Psychosomatic Medicine, 46*(5), 387–397.

Cohen, J., & Sedlacek, K. (1983). Attention and autonomic self-regulation. *Psychosomatic Medicine, 45*(3), 243–257.

Cottier, C., Shapiro, K., & Julius, B. (1984). Treatment of mild hypertension with progressive muscle relaxation: Predictive value of indexes of sympathetic tone, *Archives of Internal Medicine, 144*(10), 1954–1958.

Crowther, J. H. (1983). Stress management training and relaxation imagery in the treatment of essential hypertension. *Journal of Behavioral Medicine, 6*(2), 169–187

Datey, K. K., Deshmukh, S. N., Dalvi, C. P., & Vinekar, S. L. (1969). Shavasan: A yogic exercise in the management of hypertension. *Angiology, 20,* 325–333.

Deabler, H. L., Fidel, E., Dillenkoffer, R. L., Elder, S. T. (1973). The use of relaxation and hypnosis in lowering high blood pressure. *American Journal of Clinical Hypnosis, 16,* 75–83.

DiTomasso, R. A., & McDermott, P. A. (1981). Dilemma of the untreated control group in applied research; A suggested solution. *Psychological Reports, 49,* 823–828.

Drazen, M., Nevid, J. S., Pace, N., & O'Brien, R. M. (1982). Worksite-based behavioral treatment of mild hypertension. *Journal of Occupational Medicine, 24*(7), 511–514.

Drugs that cause sexual dysfunction. (1983). *Medical Letter, 25*(64), 73–76.

Elder, S. T., & Eustis, N. K. (1975). Instrumental blood pressure conditioning in outpatient hypertensives. *Behaviour Research and Therapy, 13*, 185–188.

Elder, S. T., Ruiz, Z. R., Deabler, H. L., & Dillenkoffer, R. L. (1973). Instrumental conditioning of diastolic blood pressure in essential hypertensive patients. *Journal of Applied Behavior Analysis, 6*, 377–382.

Engel, B. T., Glasgow, M. S., & Gaardner, K. R. (1983). Behavioral treatment of high blood pressure: 3. Follow-up results and treatment recommendations. *Psychosomatic Medicine, 45*, 23–30.

Ewart, C. K., Taylor, C. B., Kraemer, H. C., & Agras, W. S. (1984). Reducing blood pressure reactivity during interpersonal conflict: Effects of marital communication training. *Behavior Therapy, 15*, 473–484.

Ford, M. R., Stroebel, C. F., Strong, P., & Szarek, B. L. (1983). Quieting response training: Long-term evaluation of a clinical biofeedback practice. *Biofeedback and Self-Regulation, 8*(2), 265–278.

Frankel, B. L., Patel, D. J., Horowitz, D., Friedwald, W. T., & Gaardner, K. R. (1978). Treatment of hypertension with biofeedback and relaxation techniques. *Psychosomatic Medicine, 40*, 276–293.

Friedman, H., & Taub, H. A. (1977). A six-month follow-up of the use of hypnosis and biofeedback procedures in essential hypertension. *International Journal of Clinical and Experimental Hypnosis, 25*(4), 335–347.

Glasgow, M. S., Gaardner, K. R., & Engel, B. T. (1982). Behavioral treatment of high blood pressure: 2. Acute and sustained effects of relaxation and systolic blood pressure biofeedback. *Psychosomatic Medicine, 44*, 155–170.

Goebel, M., Viol, G. W., Lorenz, G. J., & Clemente, J. (1980). Relaxation and biofeedback in essential hypertension: A preliminary report of a six-year project. *American Journal of Clinical Biofeedback, 3*, 20–29.

Goldstein, J. B., Shapiro, D., & Thananopavaran, C. (1984). Home relaxation techniques for essential hypertension. *Psychosomatic Medicine, 46*(5), 398–414.

Green, E. E., & Green, A. M. (1983). General and specific applications of thermal biofeedback. In J. V. Basmajian (Ed.), *Biofeedback: Principles and practice for clinicians*. Baltimore, MD: Williams and Wilkins.

Hafner, R. J. (1982). Psychological treatment of essential hypertension: A controlled comparison of meditation and meditation plus biofeedback. *Biofeedback and Self-Regulation, 7*(3), 305–316.

Hager, J. L., & Surwit, R. S. (1978). Hypertension self-control with a portable feedback unit or relaxation. *Psychophysiology, 14*, 97–98.

Harrison, D. D., & Rao, M. S. (1979). Biofeedback and relaxation in blacks with hypertension: A preliminary study. *Journal of the National Medical Association, 71*(12), 1223–1227.

Herd, J. A., & Weiss, S. M. (1984). Overview of hypertension: Its treatment and prevention. In J. D. Matarazzo, S. M. Weiss, J. A. Herd, N. E. Miller, & S. M. Weiss (Eds.), *Behavioral health*. New York: Wiley.

Hersen, M., & Barlow, D. (1976). *Single case experimental designs*. New York: Pergamon Press.

Jorgensen, R. S., Houston, B. K., & Zurawski, R. M. (1981). Anxiety management training in the treatment of essential hypertension. *Behaviour Research and Therapy, 19*, 467–474.

Kallinke, D., Kulick, B., & Heim, P. (1982). Behaviour analysis and treatment of essential hypertensives. *Journal of Psychosomatic Research, 26*(5), 541–549.

Kannel, W. B. (1976). Some lessons in cardiovascular epidemiology from Framingham. *American Journal of Cardiology, 37*(2), 269–282.

Kazdin, A. E. (1980). *Research design in clinical psychology*. New York: Harper and Row.

Kleinman, K. M., Goldman, H., Snow, M. Y., & Korol, B. (1977). Relationship between essential hypertension and cognitive functioning: II. Effects of biofeedback training generalized to non-laboratory environment. *Psychophysiology, 14*(2), 192–197.

Kristt, D. A., & Engel, B. T. (1975). Learned control of blood pressure in patients with high blood pressure. *Circulation, 51*, 370–378.

Leigh, H. (1978). Self-control, biofeedback, and change in psychosomatic approach. *Psychotherapy and Psychosomatics, 30*(2), 130–136.

Lido, L. M., & Arnold, G. E. (1983). Does training to criterion influence improvement? A follow-up study of EMG and thermal biofeedback. *Journal of Behavioral Medicine, 6*(4), 397–404.

Luborsky, L., Ancona, L., Masoni, A., Scolari, G., & Longoni, A. (1980–1981). Behavioral versus pharmacological treatments for essential hypertension: A pilot study. *International Journal of Psychiatry in Medicine, 1980, 10*, 33–40.

Luborsky, L., Crits-Christoph, P., Brady, J. P., Kron, R. E., Weiss, T., Cohen, M., & Levy, L. (1982). Behavioral versus pharmacological treatments for essential hypertension—A needed comparison, *Psychosomatic Medicine, 44,* 203–213.

Mahoney, M. J. (1978). Experimental methods and outcome evaluation. *Journal of Consulting and Clinical Psychology, 46*(4), 660–673.

Martin, J. E., & Epstein, L. H. (1980). Evaluating the situational specificity of relaxation in mild essential hypertension. *Perceptual and Motor Skills, 5*(2), 667–674.

McGrady, A. V., Yonker, R., Tan, S., Fine, T. H., & Woerner, M. (1981). The effect of biofeedback-assisted relaxation training on blood pressure and selected biochemical parameters in patients with essential hypertension. *Biofeedback and Self-Regulation, 6*(3), 343–353.

McMahon, F. G. (1984). *Management of essential hypertension.* New York: Futuria.

Nath, C., & Rinehart, J. (1979). Effects of individual and group relaxation therapy on blood pressure in essential hypertensives. *Research in Nursing and Health, 2*(3), 119–126.

Patel, C. H. (1973). Yoga and biofeedback in the management of hypertension. *Lancet, 2,* 1053–1055.

Patel, C. H. (1975a). Twelve-month follow-up of yoga and biofeedback in the management of hypertension. *Lancet, 1,* 62–64. (a)

Patel, C. H. (1975b). Yoga and biofeedback in the management of hypertension. *Journal of Psychosomatic Research, 19*(5–6), 355–360.

Patel, C. H. Yoga and biofeedback in the management of "stress" in hypertensive patients. *Clinical Science and Molecular Medicine,* 1975, 48, 171–174, Supplement (b), (c)

Patel, C. H. (1976). Reduction of serum cholesterol and blood pressure in hypertensive patients by behavior modification. *Journal of the Royal College of General Practitioners, 26,* 211–215.

Patel, C. H., & Carruthers, M. (1977). Coronary risk factor reduction through biofeedback-aided relaxation and meditation. *Journal of the Royal College of General Practitioners, 27,* 401–405.

Patel, C. H., Marmot, M. S., & Terry D. J. (1981). Controlled trial of biofeedback-aided behavioral methods in reducing mild hypertension. *British Medical Journal (Clinical Research), 20,* 2005–2008.

Patel, C. H., & North, W. R. (1975). Randomized controlled trial of yoga and biofeedback in the management of hypertension. *Lancet, 2,* 62–64.

Pender, N. J. (1984). Physiologic response of clients with essential hypertension to progressive muscle relaxation training. *Research in Nursing and Health, 3,* 197–203.

Pollack, A. D., Weber, M. A., Case, D. B., & Laragh, J. H. (1977). Limitations of transcendental meditation in the treatment of hypertension. *Lancet,* January 8, 71–73.

Sedlacek, K., Cohen, J., & Boxhill, C. (1983). Comparison between biofeedback and relaxation response in the treatment of hypertension. *Psychosomatic Medicine, 45*(3).

Seer, P. (1979). Psychological control of essential hypertension: A review of the literature and methodological critique. *Psychological Bulletin, 86,* 1015–1035.

Seer, P., & Raeburn, J. M. (1980). Meditation training and essential hypertension: A methodological study. *Journal of Behavioral Medicine, 3*(11), 59–71.

Shapiro, D., & Goldstein, I. B. (1982). Behavioral perspectives on hypertension. *Journal of Consulting and Clinical Psychology, 50,* 841–858.

Shoemaker, J. E., & Tasto, D. L. (1975). The effects of muscle relaxation on the blood pressure of essential hypertensives. *Behaviour Research and Therapy, 13,* 29–41.

Southam, M. A., Agras, W. S., Taylor, C. B., & Kraemer, H. C. (1982). Relaxation training: Blood pressure lowering during the working day. *Archives of General Psychiatry, 39,* 715–717.

Stone, R. A., & DeLeo, J. (1976). Psychotherapeutic control of hypertension. *New England Journal of Medicine, 294,* 80–84.

Sundar, S., Agrawal, S. K., Singh, V. P., Bhattacharya, S. K., Udupa, K. N., & Vaish, S. K. (1984). Role of yoga in management of essential hypertension. *Acta Cardiologica* (Brussels), 39(3), 203–208.

Surwit, R. S., Shapiro, D., & Good, M. I. (1978). Comparison of cardiovascular biofeedback, neuromuscular biofeedback, and meditation in the treatment of borderline essential hypertension. *Journal of Consulting and Clinical Psychology, 46,* 252–263.

Taylor, C. B., Farquhar, J. W., Nelson, E., & Agras, W. S. (1977). Relaxation therapy and high blood pressure. *Archives of General Psychiatry, 34,* 339–342.

U.S. Department of Health and Human Services. (1984, September). *The 1984 report of the Joint National Committee on Detection, Evaluation, and Treatment of High Blood Pressure.* NIH Publication No. 84-1088.

Veterans Administration Cooperative Study Group on Antihypertensive Agents. Effects of treatment on morbidity in hypertension. I. Results in patients with diastolic blood pressure averaging 115 through 129 mm Hg. *Journal of the American Medical Association,* 1967, 202, 1028–1034.

Verterans Administration Cooperative Study Group on Antihypertensive Agents. Effects of treatment on morbidity in hypertension: II. Results in patients with diastolic blood pressure averaging 90 through 114 mm Hg. *Journal of the American Medical Association,* 1970, 213, 1143–1152.

Wadden, T. A. Predicting treatment response to relaxation therapy for essential hypertension. *Journal of Nervous and Mental Disease,* 1983, 171(11), 683–689..

Wadden, T. A. Relaxation therapy for essential hypertension: Specific or nonspecific effects. *Journal of Psychosomatic Research,* 1984 28(1), 53-61.

Wadden, T. A. & Stunkard, A. J. Possible dangers in the pharmacological treatment of mild essential hypertension (letter). *New England Journal of Medicine,* 1982, 307, 1523-1524.

Walsh, P., Dale, A., & Anderson, D. E. Comparison of biofeedback pulse wave velocity and progressive relaxation on essential hypertensives. *Perceptual and Motor Skills,* 1977 44(pt. 1), 839–843.

Williams, G. H., & Braunwald, E. (1983). Hypertensive vascular disease. In R. G. Petersdorf, R. D. Adams, E. Braunwald, K. J. Issellacher, J. B. Martin, & J. D. Wilson (Eds.), *Harrison's principles of internal medicine* (10th Ed.). New York: McGraw-Hill.

22

Programming Treatment Generalization

MICHAEL A. GREENWALD

Maintenance and generalization of positive therapeutic outcomes are principal consider-ations in behavior therapy, which are ideally addressed throughout all phases of treat-ment, from initial assessment onward. This chapter will review issues and stategies useful in promoting maintenance and generalization in the behavioral treatment of anxiety disorders. *Generalization* will be defined, following Olson and Dowd (1984), as the occurrence of thoughts, behaviors, or strategies learned in the therapeutic environment, under different, extratherapeutic circumstances. *Maintenance* may be seen as a special case of generalization, pertaining to the durability of treatment gains post-termination.

A number of general issues merit consideration for the therapist attempting to promote generalization and maintenance. These include: adequacy and scope of assess-ment, client understanding, involvement in and collaboration with treatment, intensity and comprehensiveness of treatment, evaluation of treatment impact, and generalization programming and relapse prevention. Various issues will be addressed here according to treatment phase. Before turning to these matters, however, a brief discussion of general cognitive factors influencing impact and durability of treatment will be undertaken.

Cognitive Factors Influencing Impact and Durability of Treatment

Meichenbaum (1976, 1977) notes that in promoting generalization and maintenance, it is essential that clients acknowledge that they have made meaningful changes and attribute these to self rather than therapist or environmental influences. Thus an important therapeutic task is not only the promulgation of new or appropriate behavior, but also attention to the manner in which it is perceived and organized. Performance-based procedures are often highly effective in changing feelings of self-efficacy (Goldfried & Robins, 1983). But cognitive changes do not necessarily follow changes in behavior (Beck, Rush, Shaw, & Emery, 1979).

Recent work in social cognition and experimental cognitive psychology offers intriguing theoretical perspectives and practical recommendations (some familiar, some new) for consideration by clinicians seeking to maximize treatment effect and duration. The interested reader is encouraged to examine excellent discussions by Goldfried and Robins (1983), Hollon and Kriss (1984), and Turk and Speers (1983). Turk and Speers suggest that practitioners would do well to go beyond conscious cognitive *content* and

Michael A. Greenwald. Department of Psychology in Education, University of Pittsburgh, Pittsburgh, Pennsyl-vania.

consider cognitive *processes* that structure perception (and mediate incoming stimuli) and cognitive *structures* (schemata) that constitute enduring aspects of cognitive organizations.

The construct *schema* may be particularly useful in understanding clients' perceptions, expectations, and evaluations of their own behavior and social and environmental circumstances, especially with respect to how self-efficacy information is processed (Goldfried & Robins, 1983). Schemata are templates that individuals impose on the world, consisting in general of domains of organized information and affects: ideas about some stimulus domain, category attributes, prototypic exemplars of the stimulus domain, and specification of the relationships of attributes of the stimulus domain. Thus, as Turk and Speers suggest, the stimulus domain called "dog" features necessary characteristics for category membership (mammalian carnivore of given general description); a range of attributes (hair length, size, temperament, range of colors); exemplars (e.g., Lassie, Rin Tin Tin); and an affective valence related to the dog concept (e.g., affection–fear, love–hate). Schemata serve useful organizing functions; however, they may also impair effective functioning by creating biases in how information is perceived, classified, or stored or the manner in which information is selectively or inaccurately retrieved (Goldfried & Robins, 1983).

One important type of schemata is the *self-schema*, representing the organized set of knowledge, attributes, and beliefs about one's self derived from previous experience. As Turk and Speers suggest, apart from confirmatory biases inherent in the operation of schemata and in cognitive processing, an important source of confirmation of *self-schemata* is produced by an individual's behavior. Individuals affirm and strengthen self-schemata by placing themselves in circumstances that reflect self-attributes; they act in ways that create a context that supports given aspects of self. Thus self-schemata may be influenced by changes in one's behavior; in addition, individuals may constrain their behavior so as to affirm a particular view of self. As most astute clinicians recognize, change in behavior does not automatically lead to change in self-schemata.

There is growing evidence to the effect that self-schemata influence input of information about the self: one tends to ignore information contradictory to one's view of oneself. In addition, self schemata can influence retrieval of information about the self and may make one more resistant to counter-schematic information. Schemata may bias in self-serving and self-disparaging ways, Thus, socially anxious individuals recall more negative information and interpret negative feedback more unfavorably than do non-socially anxious individuals (O'Banion & Arkowitz, 1977); they are more likely to attribute social failure to self and less likely to take credit for successes, and they expect higher levels of negative feedback than controls (Sutton-Simon & Goldfried, 1983). Finally, they may avoid circumstances where view of self as socially anxious is likely to be disconfirmed. Clinically, a socially anxious individual may fail to be changed by apparently successful performance and may avoid situations that would tend to disconfirm this view.

A variety of cognitive processes are responsible for transforming new information and modifying schemata in the process of making meaning of one's environment. There are said to be *active* and *automatic* modes of cognitive-processing, the former requiring considerable attention and implemented where the individual is confronted with novel stimuli or where habitual modes of responding are inadequate. This mode is reflective and has metacognitive aspects: the individual is conscious of his or her cognitive activity and its regulation. The latter mode of information processing is automatic, routine, and vulnerable to stereotypic response. Thus promoting active cognitive processing is likely to be of clinical value under certain circumstances.

Efficient information processing relies upon the use of processing "short cuts" or heuristics. Although these are often useful in generating evidence for making inferences and solving problems, are pervasive in human thinking, and provide accurate guides for action in many circumstances, these heuristics may leave individuals vulnerable to a variety of biases. For example, people are believed to employ an "availability" heuristic when they estimate the frequency or probability of certain events: judgments are made on the basis of how easily or rapidly similar instances of the event are remembered, rather than on the base rates of the event. Thus an agoraphobic client may estimate the likelihood of a panic attack in a supermarket as highly likely, based on recall of a single frightening incident, rather than with respect to countless shopping experiences in the same market without incident. Any of a number of factors, according to Hollon and Kriss (1984), might influence the retrieval of a given circumstance from memory, including vividness, concreteness, importance or meaning, and affective state of the individual at the time of recall, among others. The "representativeness" heuristic (Tversky & Kahneman, 1974) involves making judgments regarding the degree to which a given stimulus or set of evidence matches the essential features of some schema—for example, how likely is it that a given outcome could be explained by a particular set of antecedents. The third heuristic, "anchoring with adjustment" describes the failure of individuals to adjust beliefs in the face of disconfirming evidence.

Biases in judgment formation may lead to bias in maintaining a judgment; continued preoccupation with an outcome or schema may increase its availability and perceived likelihood, so that occurrences appear more likely than they are in fact (Turk & Speers, 1983). Other cognitive biases, including illusory causation, egocentric bias (tendency to see outcomes as contingent on one's behavior, even in situations where such perceptions are minimally supported), self-serving bias (crediting oneself for achievement and exculpating oneself for undesired outcomes), attribution errors (such as attributing outcomes to personal disposition where environmental circumstances are more likely influences), and others (see Nisbett & Ross, 1980; Turk & Speers, 1983) are likely to constrain an individual's actions in initiating and maintaining change efforts.

The authors cited appear to agree that the major implication of cognitive and social cognitive theory and research is that beliefs, once adopted and organized into cognitive structures, are quite difficult to change. Presumably, universal processes make it unlikely that individuals will by themselves act in such a way as to be involved in "corrective experiences," nor will they benefit from such experiences should they occur. Since change *does* occur, existing beliefs may change or be changed via pathways suggested by Ross (1977): through the force of evidence, by replacing an existing explanatory system with a whole new system (e.g. via passionate persuasion), or by providing insight into processes that govern thinking and belief maintenance. The last approach is consistent with the emphasis on active client meaning-making and evaluation that typifies therapeutic approaches that are highly metacognitive in nature. Therapist activities that anticipate, interrupt, or directly modify automatic cognitive processes are more likely to promote benefit from corrective experiences and pervasive change at the self-schema level. Specific treatment elements and procedures directed at cognitive objectives will be detailed next.

Strategies for Offsetting Biasing

Hollon and Kriss (1984) suggest a number of metacognitive elements to be employed in treatment to offset biasing influences of existing knowledge structures and information-processing heuristics, based on their review of the social cognition literature and clinical experience. These are briefly described here and elaborated on where appropriate.

Systematic Self-Monitoring

Since evidence exists to suggest people are more often theory-driven than data-driven when monitoring events, training in systematic self-monitoring skills is a major treatment activity for offsetting biased observation and information retrieval. More descriptive, immediate, and structured systems are said to be freer from bias than unstructured, inferential, or delayed methods for recording data. A behavioral record (which may include thoughts, feelings, description of numerical self-reported units of distress, and so on) serves an important function as a stable archive for hypothesis testing. Progress between visits may be reviewed with respect to this archive to:

- Demonstrate the operation of cognitive biasing (e.g., describe how the week "seemed" and then compare this verbal account with the record of how, specifically, it went)
- Identify instances of successful actions or coping (which might otherwise be ignored)
- Test hypotheses or beliefs regarding ability to change, to make progress in treatment (e.g., "Last week I could only remain in the supermarket for 10 minutes; this week I could stay for 20") or
- Test beliefs about the nature of the disorder (how long anxiety episodes last, actual degree of functional impairment on any occasion)

Client predictions regarding ability to function, ability to tolerate distress, and so forth may be recorded a priori and their accuracy evaluated postpractice via diary review. Finally, the act of self-recording *in vivo* may even have the effect of permitting a different cognitive orientation (e.g., active versus automatic processing, observer versus participant perspective) as is seen in Beck and Emery's (1979) uses of recording and counting anxious cognitions as a means of distancing oneself from anxious responding.

Promoting a Cognitive Set Sensitive and Disfavorable to Biasing

Teach about biasing as part of the treatment rationale. Encourage a multiple observation mode: since individuals appear vulnerable to drawing inappropriate inferences regarding causality on the basis of single instances or cues, forewarn clients about this tendency and encourage them to suspend conclusions until multiple trials have been observed. Hollon and Kriss (1984) note that when subjects in cognitive biasing experiments were asked to suspend judgments in this way, their inferences were more nearly normative and consistent with a "scientific" approach to causality. A formal and systematic review of written records of assigned practice is an excellent setting for detecting and challenging this error and fostering a multiple observation "set."

Since individuals commonly misrecall earlier predictions that have been subsequently disconfirmed, appear to be less subjectively "surprised" by new information then they "ought" to be, and minimize performance accomplishments by noting that they "knew all along that they could do it" (sadly, an attitude often not generalized to tasks yet to be attempted), Hollon and Kriss suggest formal prediction generation and recording as a "debiasing" technique. Client predictions are elicited, amplified, and recorded in detail *prior* to involvement in specific activities or events. Clients are asked to specify in advance their level of expected accomplishment or impairment, the occurrence of specific negative or positive outcomes, the estimated numerical value of feeling, and so on. As may be seen, this permits a test of whether this biasing phenomenon applies to a given client, permits a test of the predictive value of anticipatory fear or catastrophic expectation, identifies specific biasing tendencies, and undermines the confidence clients might have in their dysfunctional expectations.

Encourage Perspective Change

Biased or arbitrary perspectives may be challenged by encouraging clients to access or construct alternate knowledge sets. Goldfried and Robins (1983) suggest inviting clients to shift from viewing situations from a subjective to an objective perspective, as a means of influencing the availability and salience of information about events. Hollon and Kriss (1984) note that this is only one of a variety of useful perspective-changing procedures. Individuals are routinely able to provide different sets of inferences for "people in general" versus themselves; and, in the case of depressed clients, these authors report that individuals can often generate detailed, reasonable, and effective plans for action when asked "What would you have done before you got depressed?" when only moments before they appeared unable to formulate any coherent plan for themselves. This may represent failure to activate relevant knowledge structures.

This tactic may be employed with any number of variants. Clients may be invited to generate what they might do if not anxious; what a (presumably competent) friend might do, say, or think about a given situation; what the therapist might do; and so on. Therefore, recognition that although they, of course, are too anxious to think of what to do, they can be asked to imagine what another individual who is perceived as effective might do, and this is likely to help them access relevant information. Subsequently, direct tests of the hypothesis that one can be too anxious to cope can be conducted. (Links to other procedures, such as covert rehearsal, at this point, may be obvious: one might ask the individual, after imagining their effective model perform, next to imagine acting/ feeling/thinking as that model, and fading to imaginal coping by self, or identifying (and removing) attitudinal or behavioral barriers that might prevent the client from coping.)

People tend to fail to take social role constraints into account when drawing interpersonal inferences, both in and out of therapy. They may be advised of this bias, the aforementioned authors suggest: Do you remember how sure of themselves your parents seemed and how unsure you now feel as a parent? Parents, teachers, therapists, and certain others seem wise in part because of their social role. Privately, from a person-to-person perspective, they are no longer "larger than life." Clients might be invited to secure the opinion or private perspective of others perceived as powerful. Often this bias appears in therapy when clients make invidious comparisons between themselves and the therapist. These authors suggest that this bias may be weakened by arranging for clients to participate actively in problem solving and applying skills to themselves throughout treatment, by structuring discussion so as to shape clients toward taking the lead in cognitive appraisal, list making, generating solutions, and the like. Then, when clients do invoke comparisons with therapists or others, there is recourse to evidence of client capability, which undercuts powerful helper versus weak or helpless patient inferences.

The tendency for individuals to assume that others share their perceptions and opinions may lead clients to underestimate the role their own idiosyncratic ideas and beliefs play in forming subsequent feelings and behavior. Hollon and Kriss (1984) suggest that encouraging clients to poll others unobtrusively about their views might be useful in attenuating this tendency. Thus socially anxious individuals who are convinced that others would be hostile or critical if their discomfort were apparent might poll credible others about their possible reactions, disguising the fact that this is a personal concern. They might frame it as a concern of a friend, or perhaps of a character in a movie or soap opera. Shifting to an alternative knowledge set might also be useful in this example: Would the *client* be angry or critical if a *stranger* appeared anxious while speaking to a group?

Clients often compare their distorted *subjective* view of their deficiencies in ability to function with an "objective" view of someone else's ability to function. Goldfried and Robins (1983) suggest that therapists structure evaluative discussion of this nature so as to encourage clients to notice the disparity between their subjective and objective view of their behavior. When a client describes an idealized other (who is capable, and so forth) the therapist elicits examples of that person's behavior until he or she can draw attention to a vivid behavioral example in which the client demonstrates similarity to the other.

Aid Retrieval of Success Experiences

Another debiasing procedure advocated by Goldfried and Robins (1983) involves actively helping clients identify their successes. A natural orientation for clients whose histories contain many experiences of failure is to minimize current perceptions and past recollections of success experiences. Anticipating this tendency during rationale, and careful cognitive review of self-monitoring data and homework (see the section on "Making Homework Matter",)—in other words, active structuring for deliberate retrieval of success experiences, over a period of time—is helpful in offsetting this bias.

Predict Attributional Response

Individuals have a tendency to attribute novel or unexpected outcomes (e.g., absence of anxiety in a circumstance that formerly elicited it) to external or chance factors (it was a good day, my spouse was with me). Goldfried and Robins (1983) suggest that it may be useful to inform clients in advance what they might expect if they engage in a given course of action. This may include teaching about "attributional set," predicting the kind of attributions the client is likely to make, and inviting him or her to take an objective as opposed to a participant view of their actions. Again, perspective change may be helpful: what a camera would see and what an unbiased observer would conclude about what, specifically, *they* did and its relationship to the outcome.

Preempt Confirmatory Bias

Distorted memory retrieval and faulty information search strategies represent cognitive and behavioral means by which confirmatory bias operates, according to Hollon and Kriss (1984). Alert to this tendency, therapists may wish to be active in helping clients recognize inconsistent events, actions, and feelings, and to sort through their experience for differences from or exceptions to their beliefs. The self-monitoring record is one tool that can be used for this purpose. Another is training in principles of proof by disconfir- mation, via covert imaginal rehearsal and role play, including role reversal. An important therapeutic tactic involves asking clients to demonstrate a priori how, specifically, they might discover information that might confirm or disconfirm an existing belief. Biased methods for obtaining data are thereby elicited and noted in advance, and more appropriate methods can be substituted.

In assigning weights to data, individuals appear overly influenced by concrete sensory data, according to Nisbett and Ross (1980). There are many rules for not being overinfluenced by secondhand data ("Don't believe everything you read," "Seeing is believing"), but, curiously, we seem to have inadequate protection from overinfluence by concrete sensory data. People engage in an almost ritualistic offering of anecdotes, single- case histories ("I heard about a woman who died of fright, swallowed her tongue, etc.") in response to statistical or abstract arguments. Concrete information, even if correctly perceived, can still generate incorrect inferences. Nisbett and Ross (1980) urge the development of prescriptive homilies that offer challenge to such statements, including, "Yes, that's interesting, but what does it prove?" Individuals may be advised about the vividness error (and its likely underlying availability heuristic), and drilled in cognitive error recognition (e.g., fact versus feeling, filtering, magnification, and the like; see Beck, 1976; Beck & Emery, 1979; Burns, 1980).

The major implication from the foregoing is the importance of ongoing and active attention to client information-processing in treatment. Clients cannot be expected to notice successes and accord them value in the same manner as their therapists do. It is necessary to direct client attention to changes and structure client evaluation throughout treatment.

Assessment Phase

Adequacy and Scope of Assessment

Among the most likely causes of treatment failure, including failures of generalization and maintenance, is incomplete or faulty analysis of client problems (Foa & Emmel- kamp, 1983). This error has several forms: misdiagnosis and resultant misapplication of a less effective or ineffective psychological procedure for a more effective procedure; attribution of psychological cause to organic disorder and consequent mismanagement; and failure to conduct an accurate functional behavior analysis, which often results in failure to deal with environmental influences or social circumstances moderating client behavior. Since a number of excellent references exist that address biological (e.g., Bockar, 1981) and functional behavior analysis (Hersen & Bellack, 1976), and as this topic is addressed earlier in this book, it will not be examined in detail here. Instead, selected aspects of initial analysis that bear on generalization and maintenance will be briefly noted, including attention to tripartite functioning and client orientation to treatment.

Assessment of Tripartite Functioning

Interest in the three-component analysis of fear (Lang, 1968, 1977) continues to grow, and a number of writers (Hugdahl, 1981, Rachman, 1983; Deffenbacher, & Suinn, 1982) suggest that treatment tactics should be selected on the basis of an analysis of an individual's anxiety profile. Inquiry concerning the client's affective–physiological responding might be directed toward eliciting subjective feelings of anxiety and tension, heightened autonomic arousal, and increases in anxiety-related psychophysiological disorders. Cognitive evaluation might include a determination of arousal-related defects in learning and memory; cognitive performance deterioration; presence of stereotypic, inflexible approaches to problem-solving; spectator role; and attentional difficulty (e.g., preoccupation with worrisome rumination, catastrophic ideation or imagery, overconcern with autonomic arousal). As people are often unaware of internal processes or external phenomena that relate to anxious arousal, *in vivo*, imaginal, or self-monitoring assessment formats may be helpful. Finally, behavioral responses including muscle tension, performance deterioration, rigidity, stereotypy, compulsivity, behavioral constriction, avoidance, or escape might be noted (Deffenbacher & Suinn, 1982).

Prescriptive treatment based on a tripartite assessment has received increasing endorsement in recent years, although as Wilson (1984) notes, current evidence does not favor the straightforward assumption of matching treatment form to the manner of problem expression. Nonetheless, it seems prudent to monitor change across response domains throughout treatment of anxiety disorder (Brehony & Geller, 1984; Jansson & Öst, 1982) as phobic behavior, physiology and cognition may change *independently* (Barlow, Mavissakalian, & Schofield, 1980; Rachman & Hodgson, 1974). There is some preliminary evidence that synchrony (increased co-variation among response systems over time) during treatment leads to significantly greater outcome at posttreatment and follow-up (Michelson & Mavissakalian, 1985; Michelson, Mavissakalian, & Marchione, 1985). Promoting synchrony throughout treatment by monitoring response systems and providing additional specific treatment elements as appropriate may lead to more extensive and durable treatment effects. Since anxiety disorders commonly have significant cognitive components (e.g., Beck, 1976), the cognitive response domain should be monitored throughout therapy and directly modified where necessary.

Assessing Pattern of Anxiety Response

Related to tripartite assessment and functional behavior analysis in anxiety disorder is Beck's (1982) recommendation that clinicians and researchers be aware that the effects of stress can be described in two major categories, *activation* and *demobilization*, which have implications for management. The first category relates to sympathetic nervous system arousal and involves diffuse anxiety, tension, "charged-up" feelings, and seeming preparation for aggressive action. Its associated cognitive pattern contains the imperative "something must be done." This reaction is often addressed via cognitive antidotes implying "*nothing* must be done," and activation responds frequently to systematic programs of relaxation, diversion, and pharmacological sedation, which damps sympathetic response.

A second syndrome involves *demobilization* (generalized weakness, drop in blood pressure) and activation of gastrointestinal and urinary systems, and is often seen in conditions of chronic fatigue, exhaustion, fainting or weak spells, and the like. This symptom set apparently results from parasympathetic system stimulation or involvement. This syndrome does not respond as uniformly to interventions such as relaxation or sedation; in fact, these may exacerbate it. Graduated activities, even exercise, are often useful behavioral treatment elements, as are pharmacological energizers such as tricyclic antidepressants or anticholinergic drugs, which block parasympathetic activity. As cognitive structure associated with this response commonly involves a sense of being trapped, blocked, defeated, or deprived, an often appropriate cognitive intervention is to help clients take action, via graded tasks, and reevaluate their perceptions of inefficacy.

Client Orientation toward Treatment

MOTIVATION

Marshall and Gauthier (1983) remind us that although it is often stressed that client positive motivation to change is crucial to successful treatment outcome, one should be careful in attributing failure to a lack of motivation, as this may divert attention from the need to change what the therapist is doing. Careful inquiry during assessment may cast light on client issues that relate to motivation. Rather than think in terms of motivation as though it were a psychic force operating along a continuum from low to high, it may be helpful to recall Lewin's "force field analysis" (1936) as a means of appreciating the variety of influences affecting a client's ability to proceed. Ambivalent motivation is more likely the rule than the exception, as clients are often, in effect, asking the therapist to help them accomplish what they would otherwise avoid, and which, in some cases, powerful reinforcement contingencies or skill deficits support. Motivation to change may be confounded with cognitive–affective factors (to be discussed), including beliefs concerning capacity to change; perceived implications (personal and social) of change; misinformation about the disorder; perceived inability to tolerate treatment; experiences in previous treatment; expectations; therapist behavior, length, pace, intensity, or nature of treatment; beliefs regarding the need for active collaboration and practice; and other cognitive processes. Certain of these factors may be classed as expectations, others as attitudes and beliefs facilitative or obstructive of treatment, still others as limitations in knowledge base or constraints due to cognitive processes and performance deficits. Reinforcement contingencies in the social or marital environment may also masquerade as motivational issues.

Therefore, it is often useful to inquire in detail about the perceived personal and social significance about the problem, client "theories" concerning why they think they have this problem, results of previous formal (psychotherapeutic) and informal (personal) attempts to change, and the perceived implications of change and nonchange ("failure" or "success" in treatment). It is said that every cloud has a silver lining—are there any possible positive benefits associated with the status quo? Why change? How might they react, if by some magic, the problem were resolved tomorrow? What implications would such change have on their life? Finally, what might the client be prepared to do to participate in bringing about change and for how long?

ATTITUDE TOWARD TREATMENT

In discussing failure in obsessive–compulsive disorder, Foa, Steketee, Grayson, and Doppett (1983) note that attitude toward treatment exerts an impact on refusal, dropout, premature termination, and ultimate gain in treatment. Some patients enter treatment as a result of family pressure rather than a strong personal investment in behavior change. Others experience considerable distress, yet enter treatment reluctantly and engage themselves in treatment in a limited fashion, in response to fear concerning the potential distress they believe they may be expected to undergo. This may relate to dysfunctional conceptions about ability to tolerate distress, limited expectations regarding the utility of treatment, unfortunate or disturbing experiences with prior therapists, or the plausibility of the proposed intervention. It is useful to probe for this information during assessment.

CONCEPTION OF DISORDER

At the outset it is often helpful to have clients describe what they know about their disorder, why they believe they have this particular problem, and any suspicions they might have about the "true" nature of their difficulties. Patients may hold specific beliefs regarding their disorder (e.g., the necessity of avoiding high levels of arousal lest they provoke physical or mental collapse) that would lead to limited engagement in treatment. Discussion of patients' ideas about their disorder allows the therapist to examine their knowledge for inaccuracies, which may be addressed during the rationale, but, more important, helps the clinician appreciate the climate of ideas, beliefs, information, and fantasies that may constrain clients' actions during treatment. Where clients have strong reservations regarding physiological versus psychological conceptions of the disorder, additional medical workups may be indicated and carried out. This communicates open-mindedness and models flexibility and willingness to test out various theories about a given set of circumstances.

PATIENT EXPECTATIONS

Closely related to motivation are client expectations regarding change. What is the relative amount of improvement that the client seeks, and within what interval? Guidano and Liotti (1983) suggest that obsessive–compulsive clients should be led to expect moderate gains in treatment, lest their cognitive style in the light of equivocal progress in early treatment lead to loss of morale and disengagement. In general, helping patients align their expectations concerning typical rates of change, common hurdles in treatment, and the like seems a useful strategy in treating anxiety disorder.

Since expectations may in part be the direct result of previous experience, it may be useful to ascertain client reactions to previous treatment, previous therapist behavior, and results of informal attempts to change. With regard to the former, what did the previous therapist do or not do that was especially helpful or unhelpful? What did the patient expect of the previous therapy or therapist activity? Were the expectations met? Regarding personal attempts at problem resolution: What, specifically, did the client attempt, for how long, and with what effect? Were there specific barriers to sustaining or implementing efforts? Finally, what are the patient's expectations for the current therapy and therapist?

PATIENT ASSETS

Has the client had life experiences in which he or she persisted at a difficult task and achieved a measure of success (e.g., a musical instrument, craft, athletic activity)? Nested within accounts of successful achievement are often patterns or recipes for sustained, goal-directed activity in the face of difficult obstacles. Does the patient present with particular capabilities, assets, or resources that might be used in treatment, such as organizational skills, ability to employ imagery, capacity for analytic thinking?

Preparing Clients for Treatment: Client Understanding, Involvement, and Collaboration with Treatment

Meichenbaum (1984), in surveying the literatures in operant conditioning, developmental research on metacognition, and cognitive behavior modification, suggests that investigators concerned with the generalizability and durability of treatment effects offer similar suggestions for enhancing the likelihood that these will be obtained. Specifically (p. 9), there is a need to ensure that the client:

(1) understands the reasons why he or she is being seen and that he or she has a problem;
(2) collaborates in the selection of the skills to be worked upon;
(3) appreciates how the skills to be worked on in the clinic will be helpful in changing behavior in the criterion situation;
(4) considers when and how he or she will practice such skills in other situations; and
(5) anticipates and reacts constructively to possible negative consequences.

Thus client preparation, understanding, and carefully supervised involvement are important factors to consider when promoting generalized improvement.

Collaborative Relationship

The importance of establishing a collaborative relationship cannot be overstated. Foa et al. (1983) note that exposure treatments require a good patient–therapist working relationship, defined as a combination of warmth, support, empathy, firmness, and insistence. They report a study conducted by Rabavilas, Boulougouris, and Perissaki (1979) of phobic and obsessive–compulsive patients treated with exposure, which found that patients who rated therapists as respectful, understanding, interested, encouraging, challenging, and explicit improved more. Gratification of dependency needs, permissiveness, and tolerance were negatively related to outcome. For maximum benefit during flooding treatment, therapists and patients need to be involved in a collaborative relationship to permit "engaged exposure" (no distraction, moderate levels of arousal, and vivid presentation of cues—according to Rachman, 1980). In this instance, the client is being asked to abandon typical anxiety-relieving measures such as distraction, avoidance, use of alcohol or drugs, or extensive "safety rituals," principally on the advice of the therapist. Thus the level of trust patients have for their therapist is likely to be a major factor in enabling them to engage in highly distressing activities and to tolerate high levels of anxiety. Collaboration, support, and trust are also crucial for maximizing client disclosure, necessary for eliciting and addressing cognitive barriers to generalization and maintenance and for setting a therapeutic pace acceptable to the client (e.g., developing appropriate exposure or programmed practice steps). Without a good working relationship, the therapist may not be able to uncover covert cognitive and *in situ* avoidance. For example, some agoraphobic clients may appear quite capable of functioning during therapist and self-directed exposure; however, this apparent capacity for independent functioning may be instead moderated by the fact that a safety person is within telephone contact at all times, or the client may be carrying hidden safety measures (e.g., a tranquilizer hidden in a tissue for "emergency" use). Clients rarely volunteer such information but may be likely to disclose it if prompted by a trusted therapist.

The therapeutic relationship, however, is only one aspect of client preparation. A second is a credible rationale for understanding the problem and the proposed course of intervention. Emmelkamp and Van Der Hout (1983) found that among early terminators and nonacceptors of treatment for agoraphobia were individuals whose treatment expectations were discongruent with those of therapists, who held beliefs that "one must overcome fears on your own" and who held fearful expectations about what treatment would involve (e.g., insufferable distress). Early visits encourage and reinforce disclosure about concerns, expectations, and questions regarding treatment. These reveal dimensions to be addressed during the rationale.

Rationale

Prior to treatment, an extensive rationale is offered to the client which details information about the client's disorder and its development, variables that influence its exacerbation, and measures which seem to afford relief from a general standpoint and from the client's own historical standpoint (using examples from the client's history where appropriate). Proposed intervention strategies are presented in a manner that is logical and consistent with the client's understanding of the disorder, and steps of training and typical obstacles or barriers in mastering and applying procedures are anticipated and described. The rationale is more than an informational lecture. It is an occasion for structuring expectancies and feelings about the relationship with the therapist, the nature of the work to be undertaken, and the respective responsibilities of each participant, as well as an opportunity to identify and correct misinformation.

One aspect of the rationale involves orientation to commonly experienced obstacles in treatment, for example, that individuals sometimes experience increases in anxiety during initial stages of exposure treatments, experience ambivalence toward homework tasks (even those mutually identified and agreed on), and experience ups and downs (uneven course, setbacks) in making treatment progress—even periods of boredom or inclinations to avoid practice assignments or drop out of treatment. The precise orientation information offered will vary with disorder, treatment procedures employed, and client disposition. In general, judicious preparation for and prediction of client response is likely to increase therapist credibility, patient disclosure, and capacity for problem resolution, should issues occur. For example, agoraphobic clients are often informed, as part of the rationale for exposure treatment, that they may experience transient increases in anxiety during the initial treatment stages, simply because they will be putting themselves in contact with circumstances that in the past have been highly upsetting and that they now thoroughly avoid. Therefore, although therapy will be paced so that they will not be exposed to any more distress than they can safely tolerate, they are likely to experience higher levels of anticipatory fear, increased arousal, and consequent fatigue after practice. This is normal and typically diminishes over time. Individuals are likely to have mixed feelings about practice (graded self-exposure as assigned homework) in both early and later treatment stages; they may find it difficult to make time to do the homework and hence may put off assignments until late in the week (thus maximizing anticipatory fear). These common feelings and reactions, to be overcome as part of the therapy process, should be both predicted and discussed when they arise. The role of anticipatory fear is also described: since anticipatory fear is usually the last fear of the disorder to subside, and since it is a frequent cause of behavioral avoidance, clients are informed that it is necessary to expect and "push through" anticipatory fear in order to do the programmed practice likely to be helpful in overcoming the disorder. This example, though highly truncated, illustrates the use of rationale as an opportunity to predict likely reactions in the normal treatment course, and to address these issues.

Other issues that may be commonly anticipated are reservations about the "real" cause of anxiety (some hidden medical problem?), the implications of "setbacks," and client beliefs that anxiety must diminish before exposure should be permitted (e.g., only practicing on "good" days). Providing information regarding course, outcome, and cognitive issues throughout therapy, as will be seen in the active treatment phase and later sections, will help to minimize premature disengagement or demoralization during treatment. Rachman and Hodgson (1980) and Marshall and Gauthier (1983) suggest intensive client preparation before exposure treatments are conducted, including: (1) providing clients with an overall perspective promoting optimism regarding change; (2) detailed program description with logical, theoretical, and empirical bases for the procedure to be used, including therapist's experience with the technique; and (3) induction of appropriate demands for change.

A third aspect of client preparation for treatment is the establishment of a contract in which the activities and expectations for both client and therapist are specified well enough that both are prepared to proceed. This need not be written but should be described in sufficient detail that both parties have a working understanding of what is to occur in treatment and what will be required (e.g., self-monitoring, homework assignments, etc.).

Handouts or assigned reading materials (e.g., Beck and Emery, 1979; Matthews, Gelder, & Johnston, 1981) pertinent to the disorder, the nature of treatment, or the treatment course may be beneficial treatment adjuncts. It is helpful, before dispensing such materials, to ascertain client response to outside readings. If readings are compatible with the client's wishes or inclinations, the purpose of the assigned materials should be clearly explained, including the use to be made of them. Content should be integrated into treatment discussions.

Self-Monitoring

An important aspect of training involves the implementation of systematic self-observation. A simple log can provide details of problem situations, increase awareness, and develop a base of relatively unbiased information regarding client progress and training and application efforts. As noted in the section on offsetting biasing, this data base can be used to help alleviate client concerns about progress, promote objective analysis, and help clients appreciate performance accomplishments.

Active Treatment Phase

Training Considerations

MASTERING RELEVANT SKILLS

A primary aim in cognitive-behavioral treatment of anxiety disorders is to prepare the client to function more effectively and with increasing independence in nontherapy situations. Therefore, active collaboration in mastering relevant skills, applying these skills in a variety of settings, evaluating progress, and surmounting specific barriers connected with applying coping skills in these settings are ongoing tasks for the generalization-minded therapist. Generalization-mindedness is seen by many (Baer, Wolf, & Risley, 1968; Olson & Dowd, 1984; Stokes & Baer, 1977) as an essential therapeutic pursuit. This orientation might be incorporated into rationale and stressed throughout training or treatment.

It is essential that clients be well trained in a given coping skill—for example, anxiety management training (Suinn & Richardson, 1977); stress inoculation training (Meichenbaum, 1976); relaxation as self-control (Deffenbacher, 1981); or application of cognitive procedures (Beck & Emery, 1979)—if it is to be of any significant value in managing distress. Most writers recognize the importance of modeling, coaching with feedback, and using drills and homework in aiding skill development. "Overtraining" is recommended by Baer (1981), Miller (1984), and others.

Deffenbacher and Suinn (1982) suggest that coping skills be developed and rehearsed within the session to ensure that they are reliably learned so that the client becomes familiar with the procedures and experiences successful application. As training progresses, clients should be purposefully exposed to anxiety arousal within the session, to become aware of internal cues and to practice application and trouble shooting within a controlled setting. Of course, this should be graded by client capabilities.

In intermediate stages of treatment aimed at self-control of anxiety symptoms, clients may be asked to elicit arousal in session by vividly imagining phobic scenes, dismissing the image, and applying coping skills to symptoms of anxiety. They may be asked to bring on symptoms such as rapid heart rate or lightheadedness through exercise or exertion and to practice applying coping procedures (e.g., diaphragmatic breathing, relaxation) to help alleviate these. Eventually, they may be encouraged to independently seek out anxiety-eliciting situations in which to apply coping skills. These measures should be paced to client proficiency in applying the skills and should take health factors into account. Meichenbaum (1977) trains clients to apply behavioral and cognitive skills gradually, first to stressful but not phobic situations, and subsequently to increasingly anxiety-eliciting circumstances.

BEHAVIORAL CONSIDERATIONS AFFECTING MASTERY AND GENERALIZATION

Baer (1981) suggests that behavior changes that fail to generalize sometimes need only better teaching. A common mistake of teachers is the use of limited numbers of examples, or failure to train to the point of behavioral fluency (higher rate of performance, high accuracy of performance, fast latency of performance in situation, and strong response). Thus the therapist should *test* for fluency of coping skill and adjust training accordingly.

Stokes and Baer (1977), in a thorough review of applied behavior analysis techniques aimed at assessing and programming generalization, emphasize that therapists need to program generalization actively, rather than passively expect it as an outcome of training. The authors identify a variety of techniques valuable in achieving these ends.

Sequential modification involves the use of specific procedures aimed at accomplishing the desired changes in every context in which generalization is desired, across all identified responses, settings, and conditions. Thus systematic attention should be given to having clients applying coping skills in the external environment: first demonstrating competence within the therapy session; then, externally, beginning with nonthreatening situations; then moving on to mildly, moderately, and highly stressful situations (Deffenbacher & Suinn, 1982).

With highly anxious clients, it may be necessary to elicit anxiety and practice application of coping procedures within the session, fading to practice in therapist's office with minimal therapist prompting, extended to practicing in an adjacent office and then to graded homework assignments in increasingly challenging settings. The therapist may assist practice at home with telephone contact scheduled during or after practice. *In vivo* practice with therapist accompaniment can be a useful aid to overcoming barriers to implementation and promoting generalization. Moreover, therapists can assure that clients can (and will) apply procedures properly. In any case, systematic sequential modification requires active identification of and practice within *each* context in which the client expects to function adequately as a result of treatment. In the case of agoraphobia, for example, exhaustive treatment and generalization of treatment effects require careful scrutiny for residual pockets of avoidance: clients will occasionally suggest that such activities as using public transportation, driving on the turnpike, and so on are not activities they typically do or might be interested in. If these are in fact residual areas of avoidance, their mastery is important lest treatment effects be unnecessarily circumscribed.

INTRODUCTION TO NATURAL MAINTAINING CONTINGENCIES

A number of writers have supported Stokes and Baer's contention that a highly dependable generalization programming mechanism consists of transferring control from the therapist to stable, naturally operating contingencies in the environment that can be trusted to operate in the client's environment (Olson & Dowd, 1984). It may be helpful to consider not only who or what in the natural environment might be maintaining problem behaviors, but also what environmental resources are available to support generalization and maintenance. Thus programmed practice assignments may be constructed with attention to their reinforcing value—for example, planning an outing to a setting, currently avoided, which in the past was highly reinforcing, such as a shopping trip downtown, visits with acquaintances long unseen, and the like.

Perhaps the most important consideration in the behavioral programming of generalization, according to Baer (1981) and Stokes and Baer (1977), is aiming for a natural community of reinforcement that will support behavior change *posttreatment*. Natural reinforcement contingencies "not only support already made behavior changes that fit them: they elaborate, extend, polish, refine and perfect those changes and maintain them . . ." (Baer, 1981, p. 15). Baer suggests that a good rule is *not* to make any deliberate behavior changes that will *not* meet natural communities of reinforcement: breaking this rule commits one to maintain and extend the behavior change by oneself indefinitely. Thus an astute therapist is highly sensitive to possible natural reinforcing activities and social circumstances, and is willing to use these in generalizing and maintaining change.

It may be helpful to encourage an improved agoraphobic patient, for example, to become associated with a natural community of reinforcement consistent with premorbid interests, which supported independent behavior, continued exposure to a variety of circumstances (previously phobic) and which was incompatible with avoidance behavior or self-mandated tightly controlled levels of arousal. This would involve identifying past (or encouraging new) hobbies, interests, or activities, including work, where previously avoided settings or levels of physical arousal might be routinely experienced. Once beyond fears of contamination, rekindling an interest in gardening, camping, refinishing furniture, and so on might be useful in establishing natural communities of reinforcement for continued exposure for a patient seen for obsessive–compulsive disorder (contamination rituals). Of course, the cognitive significance of such activities would need to be carefully evaluated during the latter stages of treatment, and implementation would require collaboration and timing. But patients are more likely to resume previously rewarding activities in which exposure is subsumed than to remain on an indefinite schedule of self-exposure to phobic stimuli. This theme will be referred to again in the section on maintenance as life-style change.

TRAIN SUFFICIENT EXEMPLARS

One of the most valuable areas of generalization programming, according to Stokes and Baer, is the training of sufficient exemplars (ideal models) of stimulus conditions or responses. In other words, the patient is trained to perform the desired behavior in a number of effective ways, perhaps even by different trainers and in a variety of diverse settings and in the presence of a wide range of persons. In a cognitive intervention this implies drill aimed at producing a broad array of effective coping responses (e.g., drill on a wide variety of adaptive thinking responses to previously upsetting cognitions) in as many settings as possible. In an exposure treatment, this means practice in diverse problem situations of a given class (e.g., many different supermarkets of different size, location, etc.), in the company of different persons, under a variety of environmental and personal conditions (weather, crowding, fatigue, level of arousal, etc.).

TRAIN LOOSELY

A simple technique associated with generalization suggests teaching be conducted with relatively little control over the stimuli presented and correct responses allowed, so as to maximize the sampling of relevant dimensions for transfer to other situations and other forms of the behavior (Stokes & Baer, 1977). What this suggests is that careful management of psychoeducational techniques to "a precisely repetitive handful of stimuli or formats, may, in fact, correspondingly restrict generalization" (p. 358). Although the authors allow that such a consideration lacks extensive empirical validation, there are implications for practice. It may be desirable to train flexibly, balancing individual adaptation of procedures with concerns for fidelity, effectiveness, and consistency in application. Whatever one is teaching, a number of presentations, settings, social environments, variations in content, and reinforcement strategies should be involved.

PROGRAM COMMON STIMULI

Generalization may be enhanced by having sufficient stimuli common to both training and generalization settings. This may take several forms. One way to program common stimuli is to choose salient stimuli that have an already established eliciting function for other important client behaviors (e.g., returning to the same shopping mall where the client has already coped successfully in the company of a trusted companion). Training in the neutral situation, where feasible, or adjusting the training situation so that it is as similar to the criterion situation as can be arranged, is another application of this principle. A recent survey by Krantz, Hill, Foster-Rawlings, and Zeeve (1984) indicates that 84% of cognitive behavior therapists endorsed training *in vivo*, but less than half commonly employ the procedure, presumably because of infeasibility. Clinicians might consider approximating *in vivo* practice by employing features of office surroundings that offer stimuli salient to client problem situations, as a means of increasing use of this procedure.

Another application of programming common stimuli is the use of cues in both training and application—using imagery, key words or phrases, or breathing sequences in relaxation training, and maxims or slogans in training cognitive procedures (e.g., "Am I confusing a feeling with a fact?").

TRAIN TO GENERALIZE

Involve clients in the collaborative effort of identifying contexts where skills need to be employed, and in troubleshooting problems in application. Teach clients the need to program generalization and test for its occurrence. As training progresses, maintenance and generalization may be promoted by teaching general strategies, according to Bedrosian and Beck (1980). Training to generalize is one aspect of an increasingly metacognitive orientation during treatment that helps individuals become more able to understand, verbalize, and employ steps in the coping process.

Making Homework Work

COMPLIANCE

Shelton and Levy (1981) hold that since noncompliance with therapeutic regimen is commonplace, therapists might anticipate it, understand possible causes, and take active steps to reduce its occurrence. The importance of a collaborative relationship and an understanding of treatment rationale and the basis for a given task have already been noted. Lazarus and Fay (1984) emphasize that clients are more likely to follow assignments where the value and rationale are appreciated and where assignments are perceived as relevant and are not too difficult, time-consuming, or threatening.

Shelton and Levy propose that clients may be noncompliant with homework as a result of skill or knowledge deficits, interfering cognitions or beliefs, or environmental variables (e.g., insufficient stimulus cues for practice, or reinforcement contingencies disfavorable to practice). They provide a detailed discussion of measures for enhancing compliance with homework, including:

1. Using detailed, written instructions
2. Providing direct skill training (where applicable) to ensure that the client has the capacity to enact the prescribed behavior
3. Providing reinforcement by therapist or significant other (especially of approximations versus successful task outcome)
4. Moving from small tasks to larger, more complex tasks
5. Helping clients to use cues to carry out homework at the appropriate time and place
6. Getting public commitment to comply
7. Utilizing written contracts
8. Maximizing motivation and expectations, and examining beliefs about the task a priori, including preparation for potential problems
9. Employing cognitive rehearsal
10. Anticipating and reducing possible negative effects of compliance
11. Tailoring assignments to fit within client's daily activities
12. Monitoring compliance via various sources
13. Employing paradoxical strategies where necessary

Client understanding should be tested *before* clients leave the session, so that the therapist is assured that they know their assignments and exactly when and where the assignments will take place. Following rationale, review, and description of assignments, it is sometimes helpful to model or have clients enact the behavior. Some clinicians suggest that homework not be assigned until a patient completes a form of the assignment in session (see the discussion later of in-session fading). This not only permits observation of the skill but also provides an opportunity for coaching and encouragement as appropriate.

It may be useful to probe for each and every influence that might prevent a given assignment from being attempted or completed. This can be presented as a way of making the assignment fail-safe and of identifying solutions to obstacles in advance. One should not end a session with a vague (or even an enthusiastic) promise to *try* an assignment. It is better to adjust tasks until one is identified that the client *will* do.

Finally, compliance with homework must be made to matter. If clients are to engage in extratherapeutic work, it must be made important in the therapy by therapist attention and encouragement for compliance, and concern for noncompliance. Deffenbacher (1981) notes that a common problem in treatment is that therapists often, by excusing lack of compliance or paying little attention to homework, do not take seriously their own injunctions about the importance of homework. Setting the initial portion of the visit aside for homework and diary review and *nonpunitively* probing for barriers to task completion (e.g., lack of understanding, difficulty of practice step, etc.) may lead to the proper regard for homework and effective problem solving regarding compliance.

CREATING THE PROPER COGNITIVE SET FOR HOMEWORK

Clients may enter treatment demoralized by previous independent attempts to change their behavior or disgusted by their apparent failure of will power to bring about reductions in anxiety. Thus they may be pessimistic about homework assignments, preoccupied with the need to perform successfully, or concerned with failure and its implications (which may include incurability, therapist disapproval, etc.)

Therefore, apart from behavioral considerations (e.g., designing homework assignments maximally likely to be accomplished—see also the discussion of behavioral considerations for homework) an appropriate cognitive perspective might be promoted that takes into account general (typical) and specific (idiosyncratic) concerns about homework. Homework is framed as *the* major active method for obtaining information crucial to developing increasingly effective coping responses. Any information that can be obtained (even information detailing the nature of avoidance of homework) is likely to be useful, leading to a more complete understanding of the client's difficulties and development of better tailored methods to approach and master them. The therapist's explicit assumption is that the individual is doing the best he or she can with the resources (cognitive/behavioral) currently available. Therefore, what is important is how assignments can be structured so that the client can help gather information and make approximations to effective coping. Barriers and obstacles to coping are expected, even welcomed as opportunities for learning problem solving, troubleshooting skills, and—as the client becomes more competent—opportunities for mastering his or her difficulties. Many anxious clients are likely to view success or failure on a given task as of grave import, as an index of internal limitation (in the case of nonsuccess), and linked to self-condemnation. Common concerns may be described, and, where appropriate, additional rationale, Socratic questioning, or reference to personal history for examples of mastering other difficult tasks may be employed. Specific concerns leading to reluctance to complete a particular assignment, including previous failure to apply a given procedure with consistency or success, may also be addressed at the outset.

Since homework is likely to prove difficult at points and will be met with varying levels of motivation and avoidance, these common reactions are introduced for discussion and identified as normal obstacles individuals encounter in the process of change. Orienting clients to life experiences in which they have successfully applied sustained effort in learning a skill and applying it to challenging situations may be helpful.

BEHAVIORAL CONSIDERATIONS FOR HOMEWORK

It almost goes without saying that to expect anxious clients to attempt anxiety-eliciting tasks requires careful attention to the magnitude of the tasks. In treating severely agoraphobic clients, we typically start with the client's present functioning, and, as a rule of thumb, and especially in early treatment, set the smallest possible objective, one that is almost certain to be attained. Such "baby steps" are presented as the most effective way clients can be assured of success and increasing confidence. Carver and Scheier (1982) note that helping clients focus on small steps is likely to promote favorable expectancy and continued effort, as compared with the paralysis individuals may experience when confronted with a large-scale undertaking. Setting large goals early in treatment is disadvantageous in two ways other than likely noncompliance: if clients are successful, they may be prone to be discouraged at the large amount of effort and subsequent exhaustion deriving from completing the assignment; on the other hand, should they be unable to complete the task, their feelings of helplessness and pessimism regarding future efforts are likely to increase. Thus it may be valuable to pay careful attention to the construction of assignments, even where clients are eager or confident, in order that tasks be fail-safe. As treatment progresses, pacing task difficulty, client capability, and expectations is of continuing importance.

Occasionally, clients misconstrue assignments. Deffenbacher (1981) notes that clients being trained in relaxation occasionally failed to practice at home since they were not anxious at the time (as they were not experiencing distress, they believed they had no need to practice). Probing for client understanding of the assignment and its rationale may be valuable in minimizing this sort of misunderstanding.

Pitfalls in Training

THERAPIST PERSISTENCE

In a discussion of flooding failure, Marshall and Gauthier (1983) suggest that therapists, as well as clients, should be prepared to be persistent. They must be prepared to continue flooding until anxiety abates, despite moderate levels of client distress. Careful assessment of client readiness and capacity to tolerate distress, a combination of support and firmness, and willingness to modify procedures so that clients are likely to succeed in habituation are important considerations. Finally, attention must be paid to the duration of flooding sessions (longer is usually better), the need for clients to experience diminution of anxiety before the sessions end, and spacing of exposure visits. In severe obsessive–compulsive disorder, treated by flooding and response prevention, more frequent, closely spaced visits may be of value.

EXTREME NONCOMPLIANCE WITH *IN VIVO* EXPOSURE

Rachman and Hodgson (1980) discuss treatment failure in obsessive–compulsive disorder with respect to client failure to adhere to exposure or response prevention treatment components. They suggest the following possible tactics for increasing compliance:

1. Drugs to reduce anxiety or depression that might be interfering with treatment
2. Intensive preparation for treatment

3. Graduated approach
4. Use of modeling to improve compliance (e.g., therapist modeling)
5. Strictly enforced, externally imposed response prevention (e.g., inpatient treatment).

Some of these suggestions apply equally to severe phobia—intensive preparation, modeling, very graduated approach, and pharmacological assistance—although the latter should be weaned as soon as practicable. If therapists are willing to fractionate practice steps sufficiently, including using imaginal desensitization as an approximation, they are likely to help even highly avoidant individuals make gradual approaches to feared stimuli. Occasionally, reasonable concerns need to be identified and addressed: one man was unwilling to participate in *in vivo* flooding in part because of a history of fecal incontinence when anxious. Medication for bowel control removed one barrier to exposure.

Finally, not all clients are good candidates for given behavioral procedures. In example, Mavissakalian, Michelson, Greenwald, Kornblith, and Greenwald (1983) found that although paradoxical intervention was an effective treatment element for agoraphobic clients, some simply would not get the hang of the procedure despite extensive rationale, supervised practice, and systematic and graded homework assignments.

COVERT AVOIDANCE OF TREATMENT

Foa and Emmelkamp (1983) have noted that obsessive–compulsive clients may be compliant with treatment but avoidant of feared stimuli not expressly assigned, as if they were compliant with the letter but not the spirit of the task. Performance of secret rituals, such as refraining from handwashing but covertly using a hand lotion to cleanse symbolically, is another example of avoidance that may operate out of view of the therapist. This may represent a halfhearted commitment to change, among other things.

In agoraphobia, Emmelkamp (1982) has noted covert avoidance, in which individuals engage in exposure but mediate the exposure experience with cognitive focus on availability of hospitals, knowledge of friends' houses in the area, and so forth. This may minimize treatment impact. Occasionally, apparent improvement in agoraphobics is inflated with multiple secret daily support calls to a safety person. Flooding experiences and homework assignments may be cognitively limited in threat (and, arguably, in impact and generalizability) by the client's knowledge that a safety person is likely to be at a particular location during practice.

TREATMENT COMPREHENSIVENESS AND SCOPE

Ellis (1983), in discussing failures in rational-emotive therapy, suggests that therapists are often not persistent enough with difficult cases, and fail to provide treatment of sufficient breadth and depth. For example, therapists may focus on multiple symptoms superficially as opposed to dealing with one effectively, address obvious symptoms to the exclusion of more subtle difficulties, or overemphasize cognitions while underemphasizing events and experiences. Therapists may fail by providing insufficient remediation of dysfunctional thinking.

Lazarus (1981) notes that when maintenance is short-lived, sometimes it becomes apparent that too few problem areas have been covered. Brehony and Geller (1984) and Foa and Emmelkamp (1983) note that marital treatment, assertion training, and other treatments for secondary symptoms of anxiety disorder are often indicated. In general, Lazarus's (1984) general dictum that comprehensive treatment probably offers the best protection against relapse merits consideration.

Rachman's (1980) discussion of "emotional processing" offers a number of measures a therapist might employ to determine whether treatment is complete, apart from direct client report of improvement. As is being suggested, direct client report as a measure of gain is subject to bias and may be influenced by cognitive issues, such as the belief that one cannot benefit from further treatment, that avoided settings are really not that important, or that treatment is too much work. These and other beliefs (see next section) may limit treatment.

COGNITIVE ISSUES DURING TREATMENT

Cognitive issues during treatment may influence client involvement, morale, and even premature termination in anxiety disorder. Although these may be examined for in assessment and common psychological hurdles may be anticipated and discussed during rationale, they may nonetheless emerge during treatment and play a role in treatment course and outcome. Therapists might expect motivation to change during treatment. For example, agoraphobic clients who have been severely impaired (e.g., housebound) may find their commitment to change slowing down when their distress has been alleviated and they can function relatively well within a safety radius. This may be mediated by a number of underlying cognitive concerns. Therefore, it is useful to inquire about reactions to treatment and perceived implications of change, and to monitor mood and associated thoughts. Homework or programmed practice logs are useful indicators of cognitive undercurrents, where clients do not bring up this material spontaneously. Noncompliance with practice or overly conservative practice may indicate a plateau in which the client is overconcerned with the return of anxiety ("I'm feeling somewhat better—why press my luck?" "I've got to be careful or I might have a breakdown"). Occasionally, popular advice columns or television or newspaper accounts of new medication treatments may induce pessimism about whether behavioral treatment is effective or appropriate.

Coleman (1981) notes several cognitive pitfalls that occur in the face of initial success. One involves response to variations in anxiety level during treatment. If clients experience little anxiety entering a situation initially, they may (mistakenly) believe it won't again be experienced at a similar or higher level. Should strong anxiety reappear in the situation, or in the case where repeated exposure seems to have made a given situation anxiety-free, patients may become discouraged and self-pitying.

Sometimes clients compare themselves with others believed to be suffering from the same condition who appear to have made faster progress, or compare their rate of progress to their own timetable for change and concern themselves with "I should be better by now" or "Why is this taking so long?" Alternately, while experiencing a period of slow progress, some clients experience pessimism, boredom, or sadness: "Why do I have to continue to practice? Why can't I just be like everybody else?"

Marlatt and Gordon (1985) note that beliefs about the course or outcome of treatment may play a significant role in determining *actual* outcome. If people believe that a lapse (e.g., a setback) indicates failure of treatment or the result of overwhelming endogenous disease, they may be more likely to cease efforts to change and resign themselves to the deteriorating course predicted by their beliefs of disease.

These issues must be addressed as they occur, wherever they cannot be anticipated. Careful cognitive monitoring and evaluation of expectancies, behavior, overall treatment experience, and gains throughout may minimize these somewhat (see the next section, on client evaluation of treatment impact) but more specific cognitive restructuring of upsetting ideation, employing cognitive therapy procedures, may be in order (Beck, 1976; Beck & Emery, 1979; Beck et al., 1979).

Client Evaluation of Treatment Impact

Olson and Dowd (1984) hypothesize that behavioral strategies may be more effective in producing initial behavioral accomplishments and cognitive strategies more important in maintaining and consolidating change. Clinical experience and recent work in social cognition and experimental psychology suggest that an amalgam of the two holds maximum promise for achieving pervasive and durable change.

Performance-based procedures are often effective in changing feelings of self-efficacy (Goldfried & Robins, 1983). But cognitive changes *do not necessarily* follow changes in behavior (Beck et al., 1979). As Beck and colleagues have shown, it is often essential for therapists to help clients put behavioral accomplishments into perspective. An important therapeutic task, according to Meichenbaum (1976, 1977) and Olson and Dowd (1984), is to help clients attend to novel or improved behavior (and to *notice* changes as they occur) and attribute accomplishments to their own efforts, rather than to therapist or environmental supports. Wilson (1984) suggests that this can be aided in part by encouraging clients to analyze and understand how they brought about change (see more detailed discussion in the section on maintenance and relapse prevention).

Several levels of client cognitive appraisal are ideally addressed during treatment; these are believed to relate to generalized and durable improvement in functioning:

1. Awareness of success experiences, including gains in mastery of self-control skills as well as perception of improved coping in problematical situations
2. Attributions regarding change (i.e., promoting internal–stable beliefs concerning ability to manage distress)
3. Reactions to difficult tasks, including failure experiences
4. Attributions about self

As treatment progresses, therapists should take an active role in monitoring and structuring clients' evaluation of their experience, and provide useful contexts for noticing change, attributing source of gains, and evaluating performance. This therapeutic posture is sensitive to cognitive biasing tendencies, dysfunctional attributional styles, and idiosyncratic self-limiting or pejorative aspects of self-schema, and corrects these where possible during treatment.

Homework review or debriefing after flooding or other procedures is the principal occasion for assessing cognitive impact of treatment. Therapists wary of client tendencies to overlook or discount successful experiences, to focus self-evaluation on vivid negative experiences, to misattribute success to external causes and difficulty to internal flaws, will take steps to probe for and correct these. Specific probe questions (to be discussed) might be routinely employed to examine client appraisal of behavior, question attributions regarding performance, and challenge subjective perjorative views (see Beck, 1976; Beck & Emery, 1979; Hollon & Kriss, 1984). Where appropriate, reframing tactics (Bandler & Grinder, 1982; Piaget & Binkley, 1981; Watzlawick, Weakland, & Fisch, 1974) may be employed to structure client evaluation in order that a positive construction of behavior may be recognized. It is our contention that careful cognitive review and structure extends the impact and meaning of homework, and is likely to enhance further change efforts as well as change at the self-schema level, thereby increasing durability and generalized effect of treatment.

Cognitive review of therapy experience is a major component of cognitive therapy (Beck et al., 1979; Beck & Emery, 1979; Raimy, 1975) and is the major method for changing misconceptions and dysfunctional thoughts, beliefs, and schemata. Aspects of cognitive evaluation based on Beck's work and the earlier mentioned methods for alleviating cognitive biasing will be described in detail in this section.

MAKING HOMEWORK MATTER: HOMEWORK AND PRACTICE REVIEW

A series of probe questions aimed at client evaluation of experience seek to maximize positive construction of activities. Since clients minimize or ignore performance accomplishments, they may be asked to review their self-monitoring record from the perspective of identifying *any* discernible positive differences, no matter how small. Clients may, for example, in describing a given practice situation, be insensitive to differences, focusing on the fact that they are still anxious. Directing attention to the level of subjective distress may help them begin to make meaningful distinctions that imply incremental gain.

They may be asked, following Goldfried and Robins (1983), to compare current observations (level of distress; duration of anxiety episode; severity and frequency of disturbing thoughts, feelings, behaviors; level of performance accomplishment) with those of another point in time. Thus: "It's true that you were anxious. But how anxious were you last week when you were in the same situation?" The same principle applies to mastery of coping skill: clients are likely to sort their experience for signs of no difference, and therapists must gently help them discover evidence favoring differences in their data.

For the most part, homework review can proceed rapidly, with attention to new steps, differences between past performance and present performance, encouragement, and test for agreement regarding evaluation. Comparison questions are, obviously, employed to favor detection of meaningful (in the sense of therapeutically useful) differences. Variations include: "Is this a new step?" "When was the last time you were in a supermarket by yourself?" "You were a 6 [on a 10-point scale of self-rated anxiety] while driving through the tunnel. How anxious would you have predicted you might be? Would you have even *attempted* the drive last month?" Almost any client record is likely to contain material which may be positively construed. Since clients are likely to think the worst, therapists must be prepared to help clients see sensible alternative constructions where they reasonably exist, and limit the extent of negative implication. Clearly, therapists must test for this with follow-up questions. Otherwise, they may get clients to acknowledge gains but find that their perspective shifts to rate of change, other people, and so forth.

For example, clients may minimize current accomplishments with respect to what is yet to be accomplished ("Big deal, so I drove to the store. I want to drive to Canada!") or diminish their progress by comparison with others ("Any 4-year-old can do that! How many adults have panic attacks in their own backyard?"). Again, reference to performance compared with the past performance may be employed. However, the therapist needs to be sensitive to implication, and can probe for this by asking, "What does the fact of your not being able to go further than your backyard this week mean to you or about you?" This may elicit beliefs concerning hopelessness or concern about pace or appropriateness of treatment, and these may be addressed by rationale, Socratic questioning regarding all-or-nothing thinking (e.g., Beck et al., 1979), recourse to self-monitoring records, or perspective change ("How would you feel about *my* first trip to the store in 5 years if you were my therapist and I was your patient?"). Occasionally, cognitive review may need to be somewhat more than a cursory review, in order to align expectation, evaluation, and behavior.

As important as retrieval and acknowledgment of success experiences in treatment is minimization of residue from nonsuccess experiences (notice that the term *failure* is not used as it has a pervasive implication). Clients are likely to employ anxiety as a sole criterion for success in coping, and need to be alerted (during rationale) and reminded (during treatment) to take notice of the fact of exposure itself as novel behavior. Increases in tolerance, expansion of safety radius, increases in activity, and the like also constitute gains.

Clients may be alerted to the purpose of homework review, the existence of biasing and negative evaluation, and the need for objective appraisal. Thus the therapist avoids a cheerleader role, and the two can actively and collaboratively examine the record for instances of successful actions that might otherwise be ignored, unnecessarily gloomy depiction of progress or performance, or self-derogation.

Another aspect of homework review is probing for attributions concerning performance. Clients may be asked to account for cause of successful coping ("What do you feel was responsible for you to ——?" "I was able to travel because it was a good day") and challenged to generate alternative constructions or to notice the limitations of their attributional style: success experiences are due to caprice, whereas failure is due to internal defect. Agoraphobic clients, for example, are likely to attribute normal fluctuations in anxiety that accompany treatment as a sign of incipient relapse. The presence of increased distress is likely to be seen as a setback. Apart from general information given about setbacks in rationale, clients should be encouraged to view situations where he or she experiences distress as single situations ("How would you have viewed getting somewhat nervous in your car before you had this problem?") and asked to help generate and test hypotheses to explain increased anxiety other than exacerbation. It may be necessary to model appropriate alternative attributions early in treatment.

ELICITATION OF COGNITIVE ASPECTS OF AVOIDANCE

Individual diaries or records may occasionally show performance plateaus that are secondary to covert avoidance or self-imposed expectations or self-generated rules for practice (e.g., "I must not experience any exposure to contamination," "I must not have any level of anxiety"). Therefore, variations in practice, noncompliance with homework, and overly conservative goal setting might be addressed for their implications, and beliefs associated with these challenged with appropriate cognitive procedures, such as disproof by behavioral experiment (Beck & Emery, 1979). Where individuals are stalled, *in vivo* cognitive therapy (Sacco, 1981) might be considered.

Sometimes, clients entertain beliefs about capacity to function that are moderated by superstition or magical thinking ("I can go anywhere as long as I know I can call my husband if I need him"). This information is not typically volunteered, although periodic probes for any routine precautions a client is still taking may elicit these. Included are rituals to help one feel safer during practice, carrying medication (just in case), taking along excessive sums of money, and the like. These should be addressed as previously suggested; otherwise, attributions for capacity to function will be likely to remain external to self.

COGNITIVE EVALUATION OF CHANGES OVER THE COURSE OF TREATMENT

Homework, coping skill practice and exposure experiences may be reviewed individually, to examine what meaning individuals make of these. In addition to making sense of performance on a given occasion, individuals also draw implications about their progress overall. As suggested earlier, clients may be prepared during rationale for common psychological hurdles in treatment, and typical treatment course. Nonetheless, their overall reaction to treatment might be solicited from time to time in treatment, in order that underlying assumptions or beliefs might be addressed as necessary.

BELIEFS REGARDING THE SELF

Closely related to perceptions of progress in general, treatment credibility, and overall gains are beliefs concerning the self, especially with respect to the disorder. Careful attention to client language may give indirect evidence of change in self-view. More directly, do clients continue to refer to their difficulty with a diagnostic label, as if it were an internally located disorder? or as a handicapping (implication: permanent) condition? Late in treatment, clients may be asked if they still have the disorder. If so, what are the implications of having this condition or symptoms of this condition? Again, these themes and their hidden constraints may be examined with cognitive procedures. Clients may be invited to participate in determining whether they are diagnosable under current criteria if they continue to believe they are still ill. In addition, scrutiny of the meaning or implications of regarding oneself as a latent anxiety disorder case may be productive.

Homework is typically assigned to test assumptions or beliefs about anxiety and weaken catastrophic thoughts and unnecessary cognitive constraints on action. This leads to the final aspect of cognitive evaluation, view of self in the future. In regarding course and outcome of treatment together, and emphasizing a coping orientation toward future life problems, it is helpful to examine for fears and implications concerning onset and recurrence—what it means to have had this difficulty in the first place ("I am a fragile creature"), and identification of real differences between the individual who presented for treatment x weeks ago, and the individual currently taking an increasingly long view of themself and their capacities. As a result of gains, mastery of coping skills, careful review of performance and shifting of treatment responsibility during therapy, it is likely that the individual will experience an increased sense of self-efficacy. A formal inventory of assets and capabilities is likely to highlight this or indicate the need for further work.

Latter Treatment Phase: Maintenance and Relapse Prevention

Earlier sections have been directed toward therapeutic activities that minimize client distress, promote development of new behavior and improved information processing, apply these learnings to problem situations, and incorporate these changes into clients' view of self and/or behavior in ways compatible with increased self-efficacy. This section describes suggestions and activities aimed at maintenance and preventing relapse. Jansson, Jerremalm, and Öst (1984) observe that whereas many writers on behavioral treatment urge that maintenance be programmed into treatment, little empirical research detailing how this is to be done in anxiety disorder is currently available. Thus recommendations for programming maintenance are limited to suggestions based on current practice and clinical experience. A recent survey of cognitive behavior therapy researchers and clinicians (Krantz et al., 1984) asked respondants to endorse frequency of use, perceived effectiveness, and applicability of strategies culled from the behavioral literature. Strategies included:

- Promote internal attributions of change.
- Train general strategies.
- Identify barriers to maintenance.
- Transfer directiveness from therapist to client.
- Discuss needs for continuing change efforts.
- Plan for high-risk situations.
- Fade frequency of sessions.
- Work on a variety of targets.
- Involve client in planning transfer and maintenance.
- Plan for recovery from setback.
- Discuss application (of skills) to untreated situations.
- Schedule booster contacts.
- Change environment to support new behaviors.
- Address problems for others stemming from client gains.
- Enlist significant others to help maintain gains.
- Practice beyond criterion (overlearning).
- Train in natural settings.

The foregoing are grouped by frequency of reported use from "often" to "rarely" used. Of the eleven often-used strategies, cognitive-behavioral emphases on collaboration, training in general strategies, and development of problem-solving skills can be seen.

The balance of this section will describe issues and strategies associated with maintenance.

Consolidation of Treatment Gains

A number of writers (Bedrosian & Beck, 1980; Meichenbaum, 1977; Olson & Dowd, 1984) encourage that treatment emphasize the client's ability to understand and verbalize steps in the therapeutic process, as a means of consolidating and extending therapeutic gains. Jansson et al. (1984) for example, advocate reviewing treatment goals, rationale, course, outcome, and principles for continued exposure with agoraphobic patients.

ORIENTATION TO MAINTENANCE AND RELAPSE PREVENTION:
ESTABLISHING AN APPROPRIATE "SET" FOR FUTURE COPING

Individuals should be oriented, during initial treatment and as they experience recovery, to their role in maintaining and extending gains and responding to relapse. Education about relapse serves two purposes, according to Miller (1984): it provides the patient with realistic expectations about future course, and encourages the patient to realize that they are not made "all better" at the end of treatment. They will instead probably need to cope with their difficulties for some time. Future events may require that they retrace their steps and relearn skills which have been disused. Thus a rationale underscoring the importance of preparing for maintenance and future coping sets off the final phase of treatment.

Cognitive issues regarding expectations of "cure" may need to be probed, including the seeming unfairness of having to take responsibility for continued gains. Foa and Emmelkamp (1983) has described treatment failure in obsessive–compulsive patients who were prepared to make a short-term commitment to comply with the demands of brief treatment, but who had reservations about long-term commitment to maintenance. It may be useful to elicit attitudes and beliefs regarding need for continued practice, perceived level of improvement, ability to cope, and implications of possible future occurrence of symptoms, and to provide cognitive remediation where necessary. Metaphors and examples of common posttreatment course may be useful in promoting a coping orientation (Marlatt & Gordon, 1985).

REVIEW

Review of content of treatment may be helpful in demonstrating mastery of content and principles of treatment. Miller (1984), Lazarus and Fay (1984), and Jansson, Jerremalm, and Öst (1984) suggest summarizing treatment rationale, course, and outcome of treatment. The latter authors constructed a list of instructions with agoraphobic clients detailing specific action to be taken in case of setback. Deffenbacher and Suinn (1982) developed plans with clients for reinstituting coping skills following a period of disuse. Quizzes or procedures that encourage active client demonstration of knowledge may be more valuable than lecture. Clients, as part of the review process, may even be invited to construct a survival kit consisting of written outline of treatment, training steps, and records of their mastery of a particular self-control skill (so they might trace their steps, should they need to take their skill out of mothballs in the future), including a motivational tape or a letter to oneself, predicting the need to take action, prescribing in detail useful action that might be taken, and offering encouragement. In essence, these activities require that clients analyze and demonstrate their understanding of how they have changed.

TRAINING IN PROBLEM SOLVING

As treatment progresses, clients are increasingly led to assume greater responsibility in problem solving, with role reversal and modeling by the therapist, in reference to problems in learning and employing self-control skills. Training in general problem solving (e.g., Goldfried & Davison, 1976) may be a useful treatment element.

RELAPSE PRACTICE

Related to problem solving is client capacity to problem-solve difficult problem scenarios. Late in treatment, problem-solving proficiency can be probed with a series of "what if" questions that encourage clients to "think the unthinkable" and actively plan how they might cope with relapse situations. Marlatt and Parks (1982) employ relapse fantasies with problem drinkers to determine likely precipitants, the manner in which problem circumstances are construed, and anticipated likely reactions.

A range of possible relapse situations can be generated and carefully examined for both implications (cognitive impact) and actions (behavioral and problem-solving capacities). Questions can be framed to elicit how clients might characterize a given set of circumstances and what specific action they might take. For example, agoraphobic clients might be asked to consider returning to a once-phobic situation (one "mastered" during treatment) and experiencing high levels of anxiety:

1. What might this mean to you or about you? (attribution probe)
2. How would you size up the situation? (problem-definition probe)
3. What action might you take? (coping resource probe; e.g., exposure versus no plan)
4. How might you proceed if the action you took did not alleviate the problem? (backup or troubleshooting strategies versus none)
5. Suppose that action had no effect? (problem-solving probe)
6. What would it mean to you to have had fear again in this situation? (implication probe)

Kendall (1984) encourages clinicians to model and practice ways to interpret a relapse and strategies for improving next time. Rehearsal via vivid projected imagery or "emotional fire drills" (Lazarus & Fay, 1984) is another variation for orienting clients toward future coping.

TESTING COGNITIVE-BEHAVIORAL ORIENTATION TO ANXIETY

In the final stages of treatment, individuals should be encouraged, initially under therapist supervision, to become increasingly and independently involved in exposure to remaining anxiety-related circumstances. Likewise, ability to distinguish between symptoms of normal arousal and "phobic" anxiety, and tolerance for these, may be tested via anxiety-eliciting imagery, arousal elicitation (such as exercise or overbreathing), involvement in activities that were formerly avoided (e.g., watching frightening films) and the like. Individuals who are not able to distinguish between illness and normal levels of distress and arousal, or who continue to avoid these, are not yet candidates for termination.

LIFE-STYLE CHANGE

Marlatt and Gordon (1985) and colleagues (Marlatt & Gordon, 1980; Marlatt & Parks, 1982) offer excellent suggestions for assessing and planning changes in life-style, as an important element in maintaining gains and preventing relapse. It may be necessary to actively program circumstances that will support and encourage gains and modify and reduce interpersonal, marital, or vocational stressors as a means of increasing chances for durable change. Some individuals will be making a transition from highly avoidant or ritualized circumstances, to relatively uncontrolled and unstructured ones. Now that clients are free of anxiety, how shall they choose to spend their time? Systematic life-style planning and modification may minimize the impact of "apparently irrelevant decisions" influencing a return to habitual patterns of avoidance and stressful life situations.

Changes in Therapy Structure

INCREASING PATIENT RESPONSIBILITY

During latter sessions, this is seen by a number of writers to be of value in promoting independent client function. Miller (1984), for example, recommends moving from an active, directive role to a consultant role. Patients are encouraged (as they are ready) to develop and monitor agenda items in sessions.

INCREASING METACOGNITIVE ORIENTATION

As clients are led to take increasingly active roles in problem analysis and planning, they become more oriented to an active, problem-solving mode. Session focus in latter sessions is less on coping with specific situations and more oriented toward general issues. Therapists may enhance this orientation by shifting responsibility for cognitive review of self-monitoring information to clients, thus promoting linkages between self-monitoring, self-evaluation, and self-instruction.

Treatment in the latter stages may become highly metacognitive in another respect. Guidano and Liotti (1983) suggest that cognitive therapy for emotional disorders should, in the latter stages, emphasize developmental review. In other words, the therapeutic dyad examines the life circumstances that led to the development of assumptions and beliefs about the self that served as the infrastructure for dysfunctional ideation associated with distress.

Fading therapist contact, scheduling follow-up visits, employing booster sessions as needed, and using similar forms of tapering may also be useful maintenance elements. Spacing of sessions may be increased, and contact with client or significant other by telephone or mail may be employed as means for monitoring progress posttreatment. Posttreatment contact should include some form of assessment and should be sensitive to client reluctance to indicate continued limitation. Where a significant other has been involved in treatment, their report concerning a client's follow-up status can be very helpful in evaluating whether gains have been maintained and encouraging booster contacts if indicated.

Summary and Conclusions

A variety of procedures and suggestions have been described that are believed to be of value in promoting maintenance and generalization of treatment gains in cognitive-behavioral interventions with anxiety disorders. In general, these involve providing comprehensive assessment and treatment, ensuring to the greatest extent possible that treatment experiences are cognitively integrated by clients and taking active steps to promote transfer of skills to extratherapeutic settings during and after treatment.

In early treatment stages, thorough behavioral and cognitive assessment, including three-systems functioning, pattern of anxiety response, and client orientation to treatment may help ensure a good fit between client expectations and perceptions, clinical presentation, and treatment procedures. Preparation for treatment, by means of integrating assessment information, description of procedures, and details of potential treatment course into a sensible rationale, is likely to maximize client understanding, involvement, and collaboration. Attention to client orientation to treatment may permit greater impact of treatment, as well as increasing potential client effort, persistence, willingness to disclose reactions or reservations concerning treatment procedures, and willingness to continue in treatment for long enough to thoroughly ameliorate hidden avoidance, challenge limiting assumptions about the self, transfer skills into increasingly challenging circumstances, and prepare for future problems.

Throughout treatment, it is suggested that considerable therapist effort should be directed toward both the behavioral competence clients have in applying coping skills and the meaning clients are making of their therapy experience and their ability to function in increasingly challenging settings. Careful attention to systematically structured assignments, paced to client readiness and ability to tolerate increasing anxiety and engineered for maximal chances for success, is an important component of comprehensive treatment. Just as important is anticipation of common hurdles in treatment and guided review of cognitive response to treatment. Intensive treatment is the major foundation for generalization and maintenance of behavior change.

In later treatment stages, it is suggested that gains be formally consolidated via clients' shift in role from trainee to problem solver, increasing client activity and responsibility for setting treatment goals, involvement in problem-solving practice and demonstration of knowledge of rationale and treatment steps. Clients are oriented toward future application of skills and life-style changes that minimize precipitating stressors and that imply continued practice of self-control skills.

Future research needs to be directed toward identifying optimal generalization and maintenance strategies in the behavioral treatment of anxiety. At this point it is difficult to appreciate which recommendations are essential and which are clinically sensible but unnecessary. For example, to what extent do such measures as booster sessions, involving significant others, or adjunctive treatments such as assertion training of marital therapy affect course and outcome? Recent research has addressed client profiling and consequent treatment matching as a possibly fruitful approach for promoting synchrony, thereby leading to more pervasive and durable treatment effects. More needs to be known about the value of tailored inventions and the importance of promoting synchrony among response systems during treatment. Likewise, the value of medication and its impact on course, outcome, durability, and generalized effect of treatment needs to be better understood. How might medication be optimally sequenced with other treatment elements, or what stage might it be reduced in favor of increased emphasis on self-control skills? The utility of Guidano and Liotti's (1983) suggestions for developmental review for maintenance and generalization has yet to be established, as is benefits resulting from life-style modification. Finally, our current conceptions of cognitive factors affecting course and outcome need to be refined and upgraded in the light of new findings in experimental cognitive psychology. Ross (1985) suggests we need to examine critically the utility and scientific status of recent contributions from cognitive psychology.

Conclusion

This chapter has emphasized the importance of assessment, client preparation, and carefully orchestrated cognitive and behavioral monitoring and structuring in the treatment of anxiety disorder. It is argued that intensive and thorough interventions, which probe for their impact throughout, hold great promise for promoting behavioral change and allied changes in self-efficacy, which presage and permit durable change. Although treatment technology has passed the "train and hope" stage of sophistication, an empirically developed technology for maintenance and generalization is still in its infancy. Future progress is likely to benefit most from a marriage of clinical innovation and cognitive and behavioral science.

References

Baer, D. M. (1981). *How to plan for generalization*. Lawrence, KS: H & H Enterprises.

Baer, D. M., Wolf, M., & Risley, T. (1968). Some current dimensions of applied behavior analysis. *Journal of Applied Behavior Analysis, 1*, 91–97.

Bandler, R., & Grinder, J. (1982). *Reframing*. Moab, UT: Real People Press.

Barlow, D. H., Mavissakalian, M., & Schofield, L. D. (1980). Patterns of desynchrony in agoraphobia: A preliminary report. *Behaviour Research and Therapy, 18*, 441–448.

Beck, A. T. (1976). *Cognitive therapy and the emotional disorders*. New York: New American Library.

Beck, A. T. (1982). Differing patterns of stress and anxiety reactions. *Cognitive Behavior Therapy Newsletter, 4*(2), 2–4.

Beck, A. T., & Emery, G. (1979). *Cognitive therapy of anxiety and phobic disorders*. Unpublished manual, Center for Cognitive Therapy, Philadelphia, PA.

Beck, A. T., Rush, A. J., Shaw, B. F., & Emery, G. (1979). *Cognitive therapy of depression*. New York: Guilford Press.

Bedrosian, R. C., & Beck, A. T. (1980). Principles of cognitive therapy. In M. Mahoney (Ed.), *Psychotherapy process*. New York: Plenum Press.

Bockar, J. A. (1981). *Primer for the psychotherapist* (2nd ed.). New York: Spectrum Publications.

Brehony, K. A., & Geller, E. S. (1984). Agoraphobia: Appraisal of research and a proposal for an integrative model. In M. Hersen, P. Miller, & R. Eisler (Eds.), *Progress in behavior modification* (Vol. 12). New York: Academic Press.

Burns, D. D. (1980). *Feeling good*. New York: William Morrow.

Carver, C. S., & Scheier, M. F. (1982). An information-processing perspective on self-management. In P. Karoly & F. H. Kanfer (Eds.), *Self-management and behavior change: From therapy to practice*. New York: Pergamon Press.

Coleman, R. E. (1981). Cognitive-behavioral treatment of agoraphobia. In G. Emery, S. D. Hollon, & R. C. Bedrosian (Eds.), *New directions in cognitive therapy*. New York: Guilford Press.

Deffenbacher, J. L. (1981). Anxiety. In J. L. Shelton & R. L. Leroy (Eds.), *Behavioral assignments and treatment compliance: A handbook of clinical strategies*. Champaign, IL: Research Press.

Deffenbacher, J. L., & Suinn, R. M. (1982). The self-control of anxiety. In P. Karoly & F. H. Kanfer (Eds.), *Self-management and behavior change: From theory to practice*. New York: Pergamon Press.

Ellis, A. (1983). Failure in rational emotive therapy. In E. B. Foa & P. M. G. Emmelkamp (Eds.), *Failures in behavior therapy*. New York: Wiley.

Emmelkamp, P. M. G. (1982). *Phobic and obsessive–compulsive disorders*. New York: Plenum Press.

Foa, E. B., & Emmelkamp, P. M. G. (Eds.). (1983). *Failures in behavior therapy.* New York: Wiley.

Foa, E. B., Steketee, G., Grayson, J. B., & Doppett, H. G. (1983). Treatment of obsessive–compulsives: When do we fail? In E. B. Foa & P. M. G. Emmelkamp (Eds.), *Failures in behavior therapy.* New York: Wiley.

Goldfried, M. R., & Davison, G. C. (1976). *Clinical behavior therapy.* New York: Holt, Rinehart and Winston.

Goldfried, M. R., & Robins, C. (1983). Self-schema, cognitive bias, and the processing of therapeutic experiences. In P. C. Kendall (Ed.), *Advances in cognitive-behavioral research and therapy* (Vol. 2). New York: Academic Press.

Guidano, V. F., & Liotti, G. (1983). *Cognitive processes and emotional disorders: A structural approach to psychotherapy.* New York: Guilford Press.

Heide, F. J., & Berkovec, T. D. (1984). Relaxation-induced anxiety: Mechanisms and theoretical implications. *Behavior Research Therapy, 22*(1), 1–12.

Hersen, M., & Bellack, A. S. (1976). *Behavioral assessment: A practical handbook.* New York: Pergamon Press.

Hollon, S. D., & Kriss, M. R. (1984). Cognitive factors in clinical research and practice. *Clinical Psychology Review, 4,* 35–76.

Hugdahl, K. (1981). The three-systems model of fear and emotion: A critical examination. *Behaviour Research and Therapy, 19,* 75–85.

Jansson, L., Jerremalm, A., & Öst, L. (1984). Maintenance precedents in the behavioral treatment of agoraphobia: A program and some data. *Behavioral Psychotherapy, 12,* 1–7.

Jansson, L., & Öst, L. (1982). Behavioral treatments for agoraphobia: An evaluative review. *Clinical Psychology Review, 2,* 311–336.

Kendall, P. C. (1984). On miracles, magic and good tricks: Toward generalization in cognitive-behavior self-control therapy with children. *The Cognitive Behaviorist, 6*(1), 4–7.

Krantz, S. E., Hill, R. D., Foster-Rawlings, S., & Zeeve, C. (1984). Therapist's use of and perceptions of strategies for maintenance and generalization. *The Cognitive Behaviorist, 6*(1), 19–22.

Lang, P. J. (1968). Fear reduction and fear behavior: Problems in treating a construct. In E. Shlien (Ed.), *Research in psychotherapy* (Vol. 3). Washington, DC: American Psychological Association.

Lang, P. J. (1977). Physiological assessment of anxiety and fear. In J. D. Cohen & R. P. Hawkins (Eds.), *Behavioral assessment: New directions in clinical psychology.* New York: Brunner/Mazel.

Lang, P. J. (1979). A bioinformational theory of emotional imagery. *Psychophysiology, 16,* 495–512.

Lazarus, A. A. (1981). *The practice of multimodal therapy.* New York: McGraw Hill.

Lazarus, A. A., & Fay, A. (1984). Some strategies for promoting generalization and maintenance. *The Cognitive Therapist, 6*(1), 7–9.

Lewin, K. (1936). *Principles of topological psychology.* New York: McGraw-Hill.

Marlatt, A., & Gordon, S. G. (1980). Determinants of relapse: Implications for the maintenance of behavior change. In P. O. Davison & S. M. Davison (Eds.), *Behavioral medicine: Changing health lifestyles.* New York: Brunner-Mazel.

Marlatt, G. A., & Gordon, S. G. (1985). *Relapse prevention.* New York: Guilford Press.

Marlatt, G. A., & Parks, G. A. (1982). Self-management of addictive behaviors. In P. E. Karoly & F. H. Kanfer, *Self-management and behavior change.* New York: Pergamon Press.

Marshall, W. L., & Gauthier, J. (1983). Failures in flooding. In E. B. Foa & P. M. G. Emmelkamp (Eds.), *Failures in behavior therapy.* New York: Wiley.

Matthews, A. M., Gelder, M. G., & Johnston, D. W. (1981). *Agoraphobia: Nature and treatment.* New York: Guilford Press.

Mavissakalian, M., Michelson, L., Greenwald, D., Kornblith, S., & Greenwald, M. (1983). Cognitive-behavioral treatment of agoraphobia: paradoxical intention vs. self-statement training. *Behaviour Research and Therapy, 21,* 75–86.

Meichenbaum, D. (1976). Cognitive-behavioral management of anxiety, anger, and pain. In P. Davidson (Ed.), *The behavioral management of anxiety, depression, and pain.* New York: Brunner/Mazel.

Meichenbaum, D. (1977). *Cognitive-behavior modification: An integrative approach.* New York: Plenum Press.

Meichenbaum, D. (1984). Fostering generalization: A cognitive-behavioral approach. *The Cognitive Behaviorist, 6,* 9–10.

Michelson, L., & Mavissakalian, M. (1985). Psychophysiological outcome of behavioral and pharmacological treatments of agoraphobia. *Journal of Consulting and Clinical Psychology, 53*(2), 229–236.

Michelson, L., Mavissakalian, M., & Marchione, K. (1985). Cognitive and behavioral treatments of agoraphobia:

Clinical, cognitive, behavioral and psychophysiological effects. *Journal of Consulting and Clinical Psychology, 53*(6), 913–925.

Miller, I. W. (1984). Strategies for maintenance of treatment gains for depressed patients. *The Cognitive Behaviorist, 6*(1), 10–13.

Nisbett, R. E., & Ross, L. (1980). *Human inference: Strategies and shortcomings of social judgment.* Englewood Cliffs, NJ: Prentice-Hall.

Olson, D. H., & Dowd, E. T. (1984). Generalization and maintenance of therapeutic changes. *The Cognitive Behaviorist, 6,* 13–19.

Piaget, G. W., & Binkley, B. (1981). *Overcoming your barriers: A guide to personal programming.* New York: Irvington Publishers.

Rabavilas, A. D., Boulougouris, J. C., & Perissaki, C. (1979). Therapist qualities related to outcome with exposure *in vivo* in neurotic patients. *Journal of Behavior Therapy and Experimental Psychiatry, 10,* 293–294.

Rachman, S. (1980). Emotional processing. *Behaviour Research and Therapy, 18,* 51–60.

Rachman, S. (1983). The modification of agoraphobic avoidance behavior: Some fresh possibilities. *Behaviour Research and Therapy, 21*(5), 567–574.

Rachman, S., & Hodgson, R. (1974). Synchrony and desynchrony in fear and avoidance. *Behaviour Research and Therapy, 12,* 311–318.

Rachman, S., & Hodgson, R. (1980). *Obsessions and compulsions.* Englewood Cliffs, NJ: Prentice-Hall.

Raimy, V. (1975). *Misunderstandings of the self.* San Francisco: Jossey-Bass.

Ross, A. O. (1985). To form a more perfect union: It is time to stop standing still. *Behavior Therapy, 16,* 195–204.

Sacco, W. P. (1981). Cognitive therapy *in vivo.* In G. Emery, S. D. Hollon, & R. C. Bedrosian (Eds.), *New directions in cognitive therapy.* New York: Guilford Press.

Shelton, J. L., & Levy, R. L. (1981). *Behavioral assignments and treatment compliance: A handbook of clinical strategies.* Champaign, IL: Research Press.

Stokes, T. F., & Baer, D. M. (1977). An implicit technology of generalization. *Journal of Applied Behavior Analysis, 10,* 345–367.

Sutton-Simmon, K., & Goldfried, M. R. (1983). Cognitive processes in social anxiety. In M. R. Goldfried & C. Robins (Eds.), *Self-schema, cognitive bias, and the processing of therapeutic experiences.* New York: Academic Press.

Turk, D. C., & Speers, M. A. (1983). Cognitive schemata and cognitive processes in cognitive-behavioral interventions: Going beyond the information given. In P. C. Kendall (Ed.), *Advances in cognitive-behavioral research and therapy.* New York: Academic Press.

Tversky, A., & Kahneman, D. (1974). Judgment under uncertainty. *Science, 185,* 1124–1131.

Watzlawick, P., Weakland, C., & Fisch, R. (1974). *Change: Principles and problem formation and public resolution.* New York: Norton.

Wilson, G. T. (1984). Fear reduction methods and the treatment of anxiety disorders. In C. M. Franks, G. T. Wilson, P. C. Kendall, & K. D. Brownell (Eds.), *Annual review of behavior therapy.* New York: Guilford Press.

Index